The **Rough Guide** to

The Czech and Slovak Republics

written and researched by

Rob Humphreys

with additional contributions from

Sław~~mir Adamczak~~

D1304729

NEW YORK • LONDON • DELHI

www.roughguides.com

Contents

◄◄ Kratochvile ◄ Telč

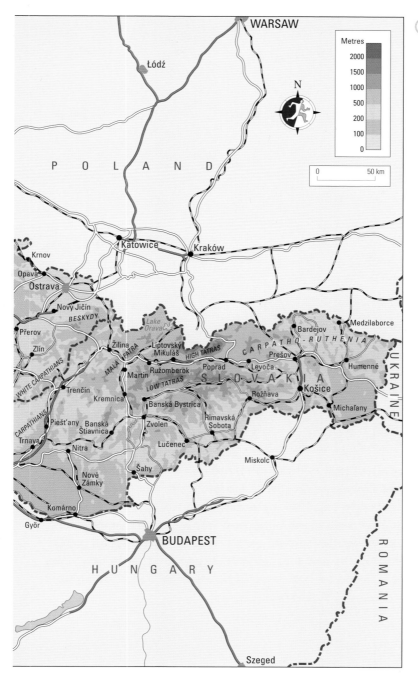

Metres
2000
1500
1000
500
200
100
0

N

0   50 km

WARSAW

Łódź

P O L A N D

Krnov

Opava

Ostrava

Katowice

Kraków

Nový Jičín

BESKYDY

Přerov

Zlín

Žilina

MALÁ FATRA

Lake Orava

Liptovský Mikuláš

HIGH TATRAS

CARPATHO-RUTHENIA

Bardejov

Medzilaborce

Prešov

Humenné

WHITE CARPATHIANS

Martin

Ružomberok

LOW TATRAS

Poprad

Levoča

S L O V A K I A

Košice

UKRAINE

Trenčín

Kremnica

Banská Bystrica

Rožňava

Michaľany

CARPATHIANS

Piešťany

Banská Štiavnica

Zvolen

Rimavská Sobota

Trnava

Nitra

Lučenec

Miskolc

Nové Zámky

Šahy

Komárno

Győr

BUDAPEST

H U N G A R Y

ROMANIA

Szeged

5

Introduction to

The Czech and Slovak Republics

The only thing I know about Slovakia is what I learned first-hand from your foreign minister, who came to Texas.

George W. Bush replying to a Slovak journalist.
Bush had, in fact, met the leader of Slovenia.

The complexities of central European politics can be baffling to outsiders. In fact, even those who knew their Slovaks from their Slovenes were surprised when, on New Year's Day 1993, after seventy years of (sometimes turbulent) cohabitation, the Czechs and Slovaks went their separate ways and Czechoslovakia ceased to exist. To the outsider, at least, it had looked like a match made in heaven. Yet just three years after the Velvet Revolution – when true to their pacifist past, the Czechs and Slovaks had shrugged off forty-one years of Communist rule without so much as a shot being fired – came the Velvet Divorce.

In the following decade, the two republics continued to grow apart, economically and politically, only to find themselves reunited within the **European Union**, when they both joined in 2004. Despite the general apathy towards politics, accession to the European Union was a cause for

6

major celebrations. At last, the Czechs and Slovaks felt they'd returned to the fold, and shed their old Eastern Bloc identity. As it happens, apart from the obligatory high-rise suburbs, the major cities fail to conform to most people's idea of former Eastern Europe. Luxury hotels have sprouted up all over Prague and Bratislava, and all the major cities buzz with a cultural and commercial diversity unknown of fifteen years ago.

Out in the countryside, life can sometimes seem more reminiscent of the early twentieth century than the twenty-first. Instead of posters exhorting the country's citizens to fulfil the next five-year plan, there are now billboards advertising mobile phones, investment portfolios and cars, but otherwise little appears to have changed. That said, the political and economic upheaval in both republics has been bewildering for those who lived through the Communist era, and along with the new-found freedom have come the usual suspects: multinationals, mafia and all the vices that plague the western world. Few Czechs or Slovaks would want to turn the clock right back,

Fact file

The Czech and Slovak Republics are landlocked countries in the geographical **centre of Europe**, roughly equidistant from the Baltic and Adriatic seas. The highest **mountains** are Sněžka (1602m) in the Czech Republic, and Gerlachovsky štít (2655m) in Slovakia.

The **population** of the Czech Republic is 10.2 million, of whom roughly ninety-five percent are Czech, with significant Romany, Slovak, Polish and German minorities. Slovakia's population is 5.38 million, of whom eighty-five are Slovak, with over half a million Hungarians and an estimated quarter of a million Romanies.

Forty percent of the Czech Republic's **trade** is with Germany and eight percent with Slovakia. Twenty-seven percent of Slovakia's trade is with Germany and sixteen percent with the Czech Republic.

but when the Czech Communists receive twenty percent of the vote, and the most popular Slovak politician is a nationalist who inveighs against the EU and NATO, it's clear that not everybody's happy with the changes.

Most Czechs and Slovaks, however, simply shrug their shoulders at the problems, since neither nation has ever felt in full control of its historical destiny.

▲ Folk festival, South Moravia

▲ Church of sv Mikuláš, Malá Strana, Prague

When **Czechoslovakia** was founded in 1918, it was always a marriage of convenience: the Czechs reasoned that the Slovaks would help dilute the number of ethnic Germans in the new country; the Slovaks needed to escape the unwanted attentions of the Hungarians, who were keen to reform Greater Hungary. The Nazis broke up the marriage in 1938 by forcing the Slovaks into a Faustian pact; ten years later, any thoughts of divorce were thrown out of the window as the country disappeared behind the Iron Curtain; and in 1968, Warsaw Pact tanks trampled on the country's dreams of "socialism with a human face". The 1989 **Velvet Revolution** only took place because the Soviet leader Gorbachev allowed it to. Even the break-up of the country was cooked up by the intransigent leaders of the two main political parties, and went ahead without a popular referendum.

In contrast to the political upheavals that have plagued the region, the Czech and Slovak Republics have suffered very little physical damage over the last few centuries. Gothic castles and Baroque chateaux have been preserved in abundance, town after town in Bohemia and Moravia has retained its old medieval quarter, and even the wooden architecture of Slovakia has survived beyond all expectations. Geographically speaking, the two republics are the

Walking and hiking

The Czechs and Slovaks are keen walkers, and both countries are crisscrossed with a dense, easily followed, 48,000-kilometre network of way-marked, colour-coded paths ranging from a gentle stroll to a serious hike, leaving no excuse not to get into the countryside and take some exercise. All 1:50,000 hiking maps show the trails and each path has regular signposts, with distances and approximate walking times. To make sure you don't lose your way there's even a colour-coded marker or *značka* every 100m or so, maintained annually by teams of local volunteers.

most diverse of all the former Eastern Bloc states. Together they span the full range of central European cultures, from the old German towns of the west to the Hungarian and Rusyn villages in East Slovakia. In physical terms, too, there's enormous variety: Bohemia's rolling hills, lush and relentless, couldn't be more different from the flat Danube basin, or the granite alpine peaks of the High Tatras, the beech forests of the far east, or the coal basins of the Moravian north.

Where to go

Before the fall of Communism, a staggering ninety percent of foreign tourists visiting Czechoslovakia never strayed from the environs of the Czech capital, **Prague**. While that no longer holds true, Prague is still the main focus of most people's trips to the Czech Republic, certainly English-speaking tourists. Of course, much of the attention heaped on Prague is perfectly justified. It is one of the most remarkable cities in Europe, having emerged virtually unscathed from two world wars. Baroque palaces and churches shout out from the cobbles, Gothic pinnacles spike the skyline, and Art Nouveau and functionalist edifices line the boulevards.

The rest of the Czech Republic divides neatly into two: Bohemia to the west and Moravia to the east. Prague is the perfect launching pad from which to explore the rolling hills and forests of Bohemia, at

Trains

The most relaxing way to travel round the Czech and Slovak Republics is by train. The system, bequeathed by the Habsburgs in 1918, is one of the most dense in Europe, and has changed little since those days, with less than ten percent of lines allowing train speeds of over

120kph. In addition, many are wonderfully scenic, such as the single-track one that winds its way through the Šumava, or the Slovak line that follows the Hron valley and includes a 360-degree switchback. Heritage railways are beginning to emerge, too, with several old forest railways now running steam train excursions on summer weekends.

▲ Train running through the Tatras

their most unspoilt in South Bohemia, whose capital is **České Budějovice**, a grid-plan medieval city and home to the original Budweiser beer. The real gem of the region is **Český Krumlov**, arguably the most stunning medieval town in the country, beautifully preserved in a narrow U-bend of the River Vltava. To the west, **Plzeň** produces the most famous of all Czech beers, Pilsener Urquell, the original golden nectar from which all other lagers derive. Meanwhile, along the German border, a triangle of relaxing **spa towns** – Karlovy Vary, Mariánské Lázně and Františkovy Lázně – retain an air of their halcyon days in the last years of the Habsburg Empire. Pine-covered mountains form Bohemia's natural borders, and the weird **sandstone rock "cities"** of the České Švýcarsko and Český ráj and Krkonoše, in the north and east of the region, make for some of the most memorable landscapes.

Moravia, the eastern province of the Czech Republic, is every bit as beautiful as Bohemia, though the crowds here thin out significantly. The largest city, **Brno**, has its own peculiar pleasures – not least its interwar functionalist architecture – and gives access to the popular Moravian karst region, or **Moravský kras**, plus a host of other nearby castles and chateaux. The southern borders of Moravia comprise the country's main wine region, while in the uplands that form the border with Bohemia are two of the most perfectly preserved medieval towns in the entire country, **Telč** and **Slavonice**. To the north, **Olomouc** is perhaps Moravia's most charming city, more immediately appealing than Brno, and just a short step away from the region's highest mountains, the **Jeseníky** in Moravian Silesia, and the **Beskydy**, renowned for their folk architecture.

Although the Slovak capital, **Bratislava**, can't compare with Prague, it does have its virtues, not least its compact old town and its position on one of Europe's great rivers, the Danube. The flat plain of the Danube basin is of little visual interest, but there are two historic towns that make worthwhile day-trips from the capital: **Trnava**, Slovakia's most important ecclesiastical town, and **Nitra**, the spiritual centre of Slovak Catholicism.

In the central mountain regions, well-preserved medieval mining towns like **Banská Štiavnica** and **Kremnica** still smack of their German origins. Other towns, like those in the Váh valley, are mainly of interest as bases for exploring the chief attractions of the region, the **mountains** of the Malá Fatra, Low Tatras, and – tallest and most spectacular of the lot – the **High Tatras**. These jagged granite peaks are Slovakia's most popular tourist destination, and justifiably so. Within easy reach, however, is the **Spiš region**, the country's architectural high point. The area is dotted with intriguing medieval towns, like **Levoča**, originally built by German settlers, now preserved almost untouched since the sixteenth century. And just a step away is the **Slovenský raj**, a thickly wooded region of verdant ravines and rocky outcrops.

▲ Staré mesto, Bratislava

Further east still is **Prešov** the cultural centre of the Rusyn minority who inhabit the villages to the north and east. Here, you'll find an extraordinary wealth of **wooden churches**. Finally, **Košice**, Slovakia's second largest city, boasts Europe's easternmost Gothic cathedral and has a strongly Hungarian ambience. It's also a good launch pad for exploring the Slovak karst region or **Slovenský kras**, and the beech forests of the Vihorlat region by the Ukrainian border.

When to go

In general, the climate is continental, with short, fairly hot summers and chilly winters. **Spring** can be a good time to visit, as the days tend to warm quickly, with consistently pleasant, mild weather for most of May. This is also the blossom season, when the fruit trees that line so many Czech and Slovak roads are in full flower. **Autumn** is also recommended, with clear and settled weather often lasting for days on end in September and October.

With both countries heavily forested, this is also a great time to appreciate the changing colours of the foliage.

Winter can be a good time to come to Prague: the city looks beautiful under snow and there are fewer tourists to compete with. Other parts of the country have little to offer during winter (aside from skiing), and most sights stay firmly closed between November and March. **Summer** is, of course, still the season that sees the largest number of tourists descend on the two countries. Certainly, temperatures are at their highest, with the occa-

▲ Karlštejn

Wooden churches

The Czech and Slovak Republics boast an amazing number of **wooden churches**. While timber-framed houses have, on the whole, been super-seded by bricks and mortar, wooden churches have survived in many villages. The densest cluster is to be found in the Rusyn villages in the far east of Slovakia, and most, though by no means all, are Greek-Catholic.

Elsewhere in Slovakia, vast Lutheran churches survive from the days when Protestants were forbidden to build their churches in stone. One or two survive in Bohemia, but for Czech wooden churches, you need to head into Moravia, to the Wallachian region of the Beskydy hills, where there's a varied collection of Roman Catholic wooden churches.

▲ Wooden church, Lukov

sional heat wave pushing readings well above 30°C. While that can be advantageous if you fancy swimming in a lake or river, it's not fun in Prague, which is also at its most crowded in July and August.

Average temperatures (°C)

	Jan	Feb	Mar	Apr	May	June	July	Aug	Sept	Oct	Nov	Dec
Prague												
Av temp (°C)	-1	0	4	9	14	17	19	18	14	9	4	0
Brno												
Av temp (°C)	-2	-1	3	8	13	16	18	17	14	8	3	-1
Bratislava												
Av temp (°C)	-1	0	5	10	15	18	20	19	16	10	4	0
Banká Štiavnica												
Av temp (°C)	-3	-2	2	7	12	15	18	17	13	8	2	-1
Košice												
Av temp (°C)	-3	-2	3	9	14	17	19	18	14	9	3	-1

Note that these are **average daily temperatures**. At midday in summer, Bratislava can be blisteringly hot. Equally, in most mountainous regions it can get extremely cold and wet at any time of the year.

things not to miss

It's not possible to see everything that the Czech and Slovak republics have to offer in one trip – and we don't suggest you try. What follows is a subjective selection of the two countries' highlights, from historical castles and striking Renaissance architecture to handsome mountain ranges – all arranged in colour-coded categories to help you find the very best things to see, do and experience. All entries have a page reference to take you straight into the guide, where you can find out more.

01 Spišský hrad Page **560** • This sprawling medieval castle is quite simply the most stunning hilltop ruin in Slovakia.

02 Budvar Beer Page 209 •
Taste the original Budweiser beer in the former medieval butchers' stalls of the Masné kramy in České Budějovice.

03 Jindřichův Hradec, zámek Page 201 •
This chateau's forbidding exterior gives no hint of the exuberant interior executed by Italian architects in the sixteenth century.

05 Terezín Page 278 •
This Habsburg-era military fortress was transformed into a "model" Jewish ghetto by the Nazis, though in reality it was simply a transit camp en route to Auschwitz.

04 České Švýcarsko (Bohemian Switzerland)
Page 287 • Switzerland it may not be, but this forested border region features outlandish sandstone outcrops and boat trips down the River Kamenice.

06 **Český ráj** Page **305** • Natural playground within easy reach of Prague, with densely wooded hills, sandstone rock "cities" and a smattering of ruined castles.

07 **Raft trips in the Pieniny**
Page **554** • Ride a log raft down the River Dunajec, which forms the border between Slovakia and Poland.

08 **Levoča** Page **556** • Attractive walled medieval town, originally settled by Saxons, whose church is packed full of the finest Gothic altarpieces in Slovakia.

09 **Litomyšl** Page **341** • This pint-sized Bohemian town, which is the birthplace of Bedřich Smetana, is home to a very handsome Renaissance chateau and the weird and wonderful Portmoneum, designed by self-taught artist Josef Váchal.

10 **Rožnov pod Radhoštěm** Page **437** • Moravian town that's home to the largest and most impressive open-air folk museum in either republic.

11
Plzeň brewery
Page **238** • World-famous brewery, where, in 1842, the world's first lager, Pilsner Urquell, was produced.

12 Mariánské Lazně Page
245 • Elegant fin-de-siècle Bohemian spa town set in verdant wooded hills – and once a firm favourite with European royalty.

13 Třeboňsko
Page **201** • South Bohemian flatlands with the pretty walled town of Třeboň at its heart, surrounded by medieval carp ponds.

14 **Banská Štiavnica** Page **508** Well-preserved former silver and gold-mining town, settled by German miners in medieval times, and beautifully situated on terraced slopes.

15 **Veletržní palác, Prague** Page **141** The finest modern art museum in the Czech Republic, and a functionalist masterpiece in its own right.

16 **Španělská synagoga** Page **121** • Prague's most ornate synagogue houses a fascinating exhibition on the fate of the city's Jewish population since 1848.

17 **Žďár nad Sazavou, Zelená Hora** Page **392** • Star-shaped Gothic–Baroque pilgrimage church by Giovanni Santini, dedicated to the martyr St John of Nepomuk.

18 Moravský kras Page 368 •

Moravia's karst region, just outside Brno, replete with cave systems featuring superb stalactites and stalagmites and an underground river.

19 Karlovy Vary

Page **257** • Grandiose late nineteenth-century spa town lying in a steep valley, and home to the Czech Republic's premier film festival.

20
Slovenský raj Page **561** •
Scramble up the ravines of the pine-forested Slovenský raj, with the aid of chains and ladders.

21
Český Krumlov
Page **212**
Medieval town of steep cobbled streets, picturesquely situated in a tight U-bend of the River Vltava.

22
Obecní dům Page **131** •
Prague's Art Nouveau jewel from 1911, housing a café, several restaurants, an exhibition space and a concert hall.

24 **High Tatras** Page **537** • The jagged, granite peaks of the High Tatras, which rise up dramatically from the Poprad plain, are the most spectacular mountains in Slovakia.

23 **Slavonice** Page **387** • Slavonice's tiny old town sports more pictorial sgraffito facades than any other town in either republic.

25 **Vlkolínec** Page **530** • UNESCO-listed, hillside Slovak village, lined with pristinely preserved timber-built cottages.

26 **Prague Castle** Page **84** • Landmark castle that's home to the cathedral, royal palace, several museums and galleries, and the president.

27 **Pernštejn** Page **371** • Highly atmospheric hilltop Gothic castle with dizzying sheer walls and spectacular views across the wooded hills.

28 **Telč** Page **386** • Telč's vast, arcaded main square is one long parade of perfectly preserved sixteenth-century facades and gables, culminating in a handsome Renaissance chateau.

29 **Bardejov** Page **574** • Walled medieval town, originally built by Saxon colonists, now home to Slovakia's finest collection of icons.

Basics

Basics

Getting there

Unless you're coming from a neighbouring European country, the quickest and easiest way to get to either the Czech or Slovak republic is by plane. There are direct flights from just about every European capital to Prague, and even some now to Bratislava. There are also one or two non-stop flights from North America to Prague or Vienna, though you'll get a much wider choice – and often lower fares – if you fly via London or another more popular European gateway.

Airfares depend primarily on availability, but they also vary with **season**, with the highest fares charged from Easter to October, and around Christmas and New Year. Fares will ordinarily be cheaper during the rest of the year, which is considered low season, though some airlines also have a shoulder season – typically April to mid-June and mid-September to October – and a correspondingly shorter high season. Note also that flying on weekends usually adds to the round-trip fare; price ranges quoted below assume midweek travel.

Another option, if you're travelling from Britain or elsewhere in Europe, is to go by **train**, **bus** or **car**, though these usually take considerably longer than a plane and may not work out that much cheaper. For more details, see p.29.

Booking flights online

Many airlines and discount travel websites offer you the opportunity to book your tickets online, cutting out the costs of agents and middlemen, and often giving you a discount at the same time. Good deals can often be found through discount or auction sites, as well as through the airlines' own websites.

Online booking agents and general travel sites

Ⓦ **www.cheapflights.co.uk** (in UK & Ireland), Ⓦ **www.cheapflights.com** (in US), Ⓦ **www.cheapflights.ca** (in Canada), Ⓦ **www.cheapflights.com.au** (in Australia). Flight deals, travel agents, plus links to other travel sites.
Ⓦ **www.cheaptickets.com** Discount flight specialists (US only).
Ⓦ **www.ebookers.com** Efficient, easy to use flight finder, with competitive fares.
Ⓦ **www.etn.nl/discount** A hub of consolidator and discount agent links, maintained by the non-profit European Travel Network.
Ⓦ **www.expedia.co.uk** (in UK), Ⓦ **www.expedia.com** (in US), Ⓦ **www.expedia.ca** (in Canada). Discount airfares, all-airline search engine and daily deals.
Ⓦ **www.flyaow.com** "Airlines of the Web" – online air travel info and reservations.
Ⓦ **www.gaytravel.com** US gay travel agent, offering accommodation, cruises, tours and more.
Ⓦ **www.hotwire.com** Bookings from the US only. Last-minute savings of up to forty percent on regular published fares. Travellers must be at least eighteen and there are no refunds, transfers or changes allowed. Log-in required.
Ⓦ **www.kelkoo.co.uk** Useful UK-only price-comparison site, checking several sources of low-cost flights (and other goods & services) according to specific criteria.
Ⓦ **www.lastminute.com** (in UK), Ⓦ **www.lastminute.com.au** (in Australia), Ⓦ **www.lastminute.co.nz** (in New Zealand), Ⓦ **www.site59.com** (in US). Good last-minute holiday package and flight-only deals.
Ⓦ **www.opodo.co.uk** Popular and reliable source of low UK airfares. Owned by, and run in conjunction with, nine major European airlines.
Ⓦ **www.orbitz.com** Comprehensive web travel source, with the usual flight, car rental and hotel deals but also great follow-up customer service.
Ⓦ **www.priceline.co.uk** (in UK), Ⓦ **www.priceline.com** (in US). Name-your-own-price website that has deals at around forty percent off standard fares.
Ⓦ **www.skyauction.com** Bookings from the US only. Auctions tickets and travel packages to destinations worldwide.
Ⓦ **www.travelocity.co.uk** (in UK), Ⓦ **www.travelocity.com** (in US), Ⓦ **www.travelocity.ca**

(in Canada), ⓦ www.zuji.com.au (in Australia). Destination guides, hot fares and great deals for car rental, accommodation and lodging.

ⓦ www.travelshop.com.au Australian site offering discounted flights, packages, insurance, and online bookings. Also on ☎ 1800/108 108.

ⓦ travel.yahoo.com Incorporates some Rough Guides material in its coverage of destination countries and cities across the world, with information about places to eat and sleep.

From Britain and Ireland

The most competitive airfares are with the no-frills **budget airlines**. At the time of going to press, easyJet was offering return fares to Prague or Bratislava for as little as £50–70, from a selection of British airports, while British Midland's budget arm, bmibaby, was offering similar fares to Prague from, among others, Gatwick and Manchester. Others are slowly joining the field, and no doubt more will follow: SkyEurope currently fly to Prague, Bratislava and Košice from London Stansted and Manchester, while Jet2.com fly to Prague from Leeds/Bradford and Belfast, EUjet from Kent, and Ryanair fly London Stansted to Brno. Note, however, that the cheaper tickets need to be booked well in advance – if you don't book early, the price can skyrocket. Most cheap tickets are either non-refundable or only partially refundable, and non-exchangeable.

British Airways (BA) and Czech Airlines (ČSA) both have a wider choice of flight times from London to Prague; BA flies from **Heathrow** and **Gatwick**, while ČSA flies from all three major London airports, plus **Birmingham**, **Edinburgh** and **Manchester**. Austrian Airlines and BA all have a wide choice of flight times from London Heathrow to Vienna. The national airlines have been forced to become competitive, so if you book well enough in advance you'll find return fares from as low as £70. ČSA also operates a regular non-stop service from **Dublin** and **Cork** to Prague, starting at €125 return from Dublin and €250 from Cork.

Finding the best deal involves ringing round, or checking the websites of a few of the discount specialist agents (see opposite), and comparing prices, routes and timings. Students under 32 and anyone under 26 should enquire about discounts on sched-uled flights, or contact the likes of STA Travel (see opposite). Note, however, that in peak season, discount flights are often booked up weeks in advance. If this is the case, it might be worth considering flying to a neighbouring European city such as Linz, Budapest, Wroclaw and Kraków, all of which are only a couple of hours' train ride from the border.

Airlines

Austrian Airlines UK ☎ 0870/124 2625; Ireland ☎ 1-800/509142, ⓦ www.aua.com.
bmibaby UK ☎ 0870/264 2229; Ireland ☎ 1890/340 122; ⓦ www.bmibaby.com.
British Airways UK ☎ 0845/773 3377, Ireland ☎ 1800/626 747, ⓦ www.britishairways.com.
Czech Airlines (ČSA) UK ☎ 0870/4443 747; Ireland ☎ 818/200 014; ⓦ www.csa.cz.
easyJet UK ☎ 0871/750 0100, ⓦ www.easyjet.com.
EUjet UK ☎ 0870/414 1414, ⓦ www.eujet.com.
Jet2.com UK ☎ 0871/226 1737, ⓦ www.jet2.com.
Ryanair UK ☎ 0871/246 000, Ireland ☎ 0818/30 30 30, ⓦ www.ryanair.com.
SkyEurope UK ☎ 020/7365 0365, ⓦ www.skyeurope.com.

Specialist agents and operators in Britain

Bridgewater Travel ☎ 0161/703 3003, ⓦ www.bridgewater-travel.co.uk. Accommodation and package deals.
ČEDOK ☎ 020/7580 3778, ⓦ www.cedok.co.uk. Former state-owned tourist board offering flights, accommodation and package deals.
CIE Tours International Ireland ☎ 01/703 1888, ⓦ www.cietours.ie. General flight and tour agent.
Czech & Slovak Tourist Centre ☎ 020/7794 3263, ⓦ www.czech-slovak-tourist.co.uk. Accommodation, bus tickets, flights and tourist information.
Czech Birding ⓦ www.czechbirding.com. Regular bird-watching tours of the Czech Republic.
Czech Travel ☎ 01376/560592, ⓦ www.czechtravel.freeuk.com. Rooms and flats for rent in Prague and Bohemia, plus flights.
Czechbook Agency UK ☎ 01503/240629, ⓦ www.czechbook.fsnet.co.uk. Self-catering flats, B&Bs and pensions in the Czech and Slovak republics.
Explore Worldwide ☎ 01252/760 000, ⓦ www.exploreworldwide.com. Tailor-made trips to Prague and walking in the Tatras.
Hotel Connect ☎ 0845/230 8888, ⓦ www.hotelconnect.co.uk. Accommodation in Prague and Bratislava.

Interhome UK ☎020/8891 1294, www.interhome
.co.uk. Over four hundred self-catering houses,
cottages and apartments throughout the Czech and
Slovak republics.

Joe Walsh Tours Ireland ☎01/676 0991, ⓦwww
.joewalshtours.ie. Long-established general budget
fares and holiday agent.

Martin Randall Travel UK ☎020/8742 3355,
ⓦwww.martinrandall.com. Small-group cultural
tours led by experts on art, archeology and music.

North South Travel UK ☎01245/608 291,
ⓦwww.northsouthtravel.co.uk. Friendly, competitive
travel agency, offering discounted fares worldwide –
profits are used to support projects in the developing
world, especially the promotion of sustainable tourism.

Ramblers Holidays ☎01707/331133, ⓦwww
.ramblersholidays.co.uk. Long-established and
reputable walking-holiday specialist offering organized
trips to Prague.

Slovak Wildlife Society ☎020/8451 7555,
ⓦwww.slovakwildlife.org. Holidays seeking out
wolves, bears and eagles in Slovakia – proceeds go to
conservation work.

STA Travel UK ☎0870/1600 599, ⓦwww
.statravel.co.uk. Worldwide specialists in low-cost
flights and tours for students and under-26s, though
other customers welcome.

Trailfinders UK ☎020/7938 3939, ⓦwww
.trailfinders.com; Republic of Ireland ☎01/677
7888, ⓦwww.trailfinders.ie. One of the best-
informed and most efficient agents for independent
travellers.

USIT Northern Ireland ☎028/9032 7111, ⓦwww
.usitnow.com; Republic of Ireland ☎0818/200 020,
ⓦwww.usit.ie. Specialists in student, youth and
independent travel – flights, trains, study tours, TEFL,
visas and more.

By train

Travelling **by train** is a pleasantly old-fashioned and extremely leisurely way to reach
either of the two republics. You can travel
from London to Prague or Bratislava (via
Vienna) overnight in around twenty hours by
train. The fares, however, barely compete
with standard scheduled airline tickets.

The routes

There are several possible routes from London to Prague. The most direct, and often
cheapest route, is **via Brussels and Frankfurt**, with a change in both. From Frankfurt,
there's an overnight service to both Prague
and Vienna, arriving early the following morn-

ing. Travelling **via Paris** tends to be a bit
more expensive, but offers a direct overnight
service to Vienna (for Prague you still have to
change trains at Frankfurt). If you're heading
straight for Bratislava, you must make your
way from Vienna's Westbahnhof, to the Süd-
bahnhof and catch a train to Bratislava.

Although you can simply crash out on the
seats on the overnight service to Prague
or Vienna, it makes sense to book a **couchette** (if it's not already included in your
ticket), which costs around £15 one-way in a
six-berth compartment, rising to £25 in a
three-berth compartment. Couchettes are
mixed-sex and allow little privacy; for a bit
more comfort, you can book a bed in a sin-
gle-sex two-berth **sleeper** for around £50
for a two-berth compartment. You should be
able to book your couchette or sleeper when
you buy your ticket, but if you have any
problems, contact German Railways (Deutsche Bahn) – see p.30. However you decide
to sleep, if you're heading for Prague, you'll
probably be woken up in the early hours
of the morning when the train crosses the
Czech border.

Tickets and passes

Fares for continental rail travel are much
more flexible than they used to be, so it's
worth shopping around for the best deal,
rather than taking the first offer you get.
The standard price for a return ticket from
London–Prague tends to start at around
£200, but if you look out for special offers
on ⓦwww.europeanrail.com and elsewhere,
you can usually bring the price down considerably; tickets are usually valid for two
months and allow as many stopovers as you
want on the specified route. If you're travelling with one or more companions, you may
be eligible for a further discount.

Those **under 26** can often purchase discounted tickets from the rail agents listed on
p.30, thus saving up to 25 percent on the
return fare. Travellers **over 60** can also get
similar discounts between, but not within,
European countries by purchasing a **Rail
Plus** card at a cost of £12. However, before
you can buy this card, you must already
possess a Senior Rail Card (£18); both are
valid for a year. Rail Plus is available from Rail
Europe's London office at 178 Piccadilly.

Apart from Rail Europe's Piccadilly office, virtually the only way **to buy** an international train ticket at the moment is via a travel agent or over the phone or Internet with one of the rail agents listed below. However, while Eurostar can book your ticket from any station in the UK, they can only book your onward travel to selected European (mostly French) destinations; conversely, Rail Europe and the other national rail agents can only book your journey from London onwards – for travel within the UK, contact National Rail. Independent rail agents can book you from anywhere in the UK to anywhere in Europe.

If you're planning to visit the Czech and Slovak republics as part of a more extensive trip around Europe, it may be worth purchasing an **InterRail pass** (@www.interrail. com), which gives you unlimited rail travel within certain countries; you must, however, have been resident in Europe for at least six months. InterRail tickets are currently zonal: to travel to the Czech and Slovak republics and back, you'll need at least a three-zone pass, starting at £295 for a month for those under 26, and £415 for those aged 26 and over. Passes are not valid in the UK, though you're entitled to discounts in Britain and on Eurostar and cross-Channel ferries. Either way, though, you're only really going to make the cost worthwhile if you do a lot of travelling.

North Americans, **Australians** and **New Zealanders** who don't qualify for the Inter-Rail pass can obtain a **Eurail** pass (@www .railpass.com), which comes in various forms, and must be bought before leaving home. For more information, and to reserve tickets, contact: Rail Europe in North America (US ☎1-877/257-2887, Canada ☎1-800/361-RAIL, @www.raileurope.com) and CIT World Travel (☎02/9267 1255 or 03/9650 5510, @www .cittravel.com.au) or Rail Plus (@railplus .raileurope.com) in Australia.

Rail contacts

@www.seat61.com The world's finest train website, full of incredibly useful tips and links.
European Rail ☎020/7387 0444, @www. europeanrail.com. Rail specialists that consistently offer competitive prices on international rail tickets from anywhere in the UK.

Eurostar ☎08705/186 186, @www.eurostar.com. Latest fares and youth discounts (plus online booking) on the London–Paris and London–Brussels Eurostar service, and competitive add-on fares from the rest of the UK.
German Railways (Deutsche Bahn) UK ☎0870/243 5363, @www.bahn.de. Competitive discounted fares for any journey from London across Europe, with very reasonable prices for those journeys that pass through Germany.
International Rail UK ☎0870/751 5000, @www .international-rail.com. Offers Eurostar, all European passes and tickets, international sleepers, ferry crossings and more.
National Rail UK ☎0845/748 4950, @www .nationalrail.co.uk. First stop for details of all train travel within the UK – fares, passes, train times and delays due to engineering works.
Rail Europe UK ☎08705/848 848, @www .raileurope.co.uk. SNCF-owned information and ticket agent for all European passes and journeys from London.
Trainseurope UK ☎0900/195 0101, @www .trainseurope.co.uk. Agent specializing in organizing discounted international rail travel.

By bus

One of the cheapest ways to get to the Czech Republic and Slovakia is **by bus**. There are direct services from London's Victoria Station more or less daily throughout the year. The most popular destination is Prague, but several bus companies offer direct services to Plzeň, Jihlava, Brno, Olomouc, Ostrava and Bratislava. For Bratislava, it may be more convenient to go to Vienna, and change buses there. The journey is bearable (just about), but only really worth it if you absolutely can't find the extra cash for a budget flight. Prices between companies vary very slightly so it's worth ringing round to find the best deal; a return ticket to Prague can cost as little as £60. Addresses and telephone numbers for all current operators are given opposite.

Another option worth considering if you're heading for other parts of Europe as well as the Czech and Slovak republics is a **Euro-lines pass**. The pass, which covers all the major cities in Europe (including Prague and Vienna, but not Bratislava), is valid for either fifteen days (low season mid-Sept to May: £129 under 26/£149 26 & over; high season June to mid-Sept: £165 under 26/£195 26

& over), thirty days (low season: £169/£209; high season: £235/£290) or sixty days (low season: £211/£265; high season: £259/£333).

From May to October **Busabout** offers a hop-on, hop-off bus service, which calls in at Prague, plus numerous other cities in western Europe including Vienna, but, again, not Bratislava. The **Unlimited Pass** allows unlimited travel from two weeks (£219 under 26/£239 26 & over) to six months (£729/£819); the **Flexipass** gives you anything from eight days' travel (£249/£279) to twenty days' travel (£519/£579), which can be spread over the season. The buses travel along pre-determined circular routes in one direction only, so for instance you can only travel from Prague to Vienna and not vice versa.

Bus contacts

Busabout ☎ 020/7950 1661, ⓦ www.busabout .com. European bus passes.

Capital Express ☎ 020/7243 0488, ⓦ www .capitalexpress.cz. Regular services via Eurotunnel from London to Prague, Brno, Plzen, Ostrava and Olomouc.

Eurolines UK ☎ 08705/808 808, ⓦ www.eurolines .co.uk; Republic of Ireland ☎ 01/836 6111, ⓦ www .eurolines.ie. Tickets can also be purchased from any National Express or Bus Éireann agent.

Kingscourt Express ☎ 020/8673 7500, ⓦ www .kce.cz. Czech-based bus company running regular services from London to Prague, Brno, Jihlava and Plzen.

By car

With two or more passengers, **driving** to the Czech and Slovak republics can work out relatively inexpensive. However, it is not the most relaxing option, unless you enjoy pounding along the motorway systems of Europe for the best part of a day and a night.

The **Eurotunnel** service through the Channel Tunnel doesn't significantly affect total travel times, though it does of course speed up the cross-Channel section of the journey. Eurotunnel operates a 24-hour service carrying cars, motorcycles, buses and their passengers to Calais. At peak times, services run every fifteen minutes, with the journey lasting 35 minutes. Off-peak fares hover between £200 and £300

return (passengers included), though special offers do appear from time to time.

The alternative cross-Channel options for most travellers are the conventional **catamaran ferry** links between Dover and Calais, Ostend or Zeebrugge. Fares vary enormously with the time of year, month and even day that you travel, and the size of your car. If you book in advance, the cheapest off-peak summer fare on the Dover–Calais run, for example, can be as little as £170 return per carload. Journey times are usually around ninety minutes. If you're travelling from north of London, however, it might be worth taking one of the longer ferry journeys from Rosyth, Newcastle or Harwich. To find out the cheapest fares across the channel, check out ⓦ www.ferrysmart.co.uk.

Once you've made it onto the continent, you've got some **1000km of driving** ahead of you. Theoretically, you could make it in twelve hours solid, but realistically it will take you longer. The most direct route from Calais or Ostend is via Brussels, Liège (Luik), Cologne (Köln), Frankfurt, Würzburg and Nuremberg (Nürnberg), entering the country at the **Waidhaus–Rozvadov** border crossing. If you're heading straight for Slovakia, continue along the autobahn from Nuremberg (Nürnberg) in a southeasterly direction via Regensburg, Passau, Linz and Vienna, entering Slovakia at the Berg–Bratislava border crossing. Motorways in Belgium and Germany are free, but to travel on any motorways within Austria, the Czech Republic or Slovakia, you'll need to buy the relevant **tax disc** in each of those countries, available from all border crossings and most post offices and petrol stations.

If you're travelling by car, you'll need proof of ownership, or a letter from the owner giving you permission to drive the car. A British or other EU driving licence is fine; all other drivers are advised to purchase an International Driving Permit (IDP). You also need a red warning triangle in case you break down, a first-aid kit (both these are compulsory in the Czech and Slovak republics), and a "Green Card" for third party insurance cover at the very least. An even better idea is to sign up with one of the national motoring organizations, who offer continental breakdown assistance and, in extreme circumstances, will get you and your vehicle brought back home if necessary.

Cross-channel contacts

DFDS Seaways ☎ 08705/333 000, ✆ www .dfdsseaways.co.uk. Newcastle to Amsterdam.
Eurotunnel ☎ 0870/535 3535, ✆ www .eurotunnel.com. Folkstone–Calais through the tunnel.
Hoverspeed ☎ 0870/240 8070, ✆ www .hoverspeed.co.uk. Dover to Calais and Ostend.
Norfolk Line ☎ 0870/870 1020, ✆ www .norfolkline.com. Dover to Dunkirk.
P&O Stena Line ☎ 0870/600 0600, ✆ www.posl .com. Dover to Calais and Zeebrugge.
Sea France ☎ 0870/571 1711, ✆ www.seafrance .com. Dover to Calais
Stena Line ☎ 08704/00 67 98, ✆ www.stenaline .co.uk. Harwich to the Hook of Holland.
Superfast Ferries ☎ 0870/234 0870, ✆ www .superfast.com. Rosyth near Edinburgh to Zeebrugge.

From the USA and Canada

Czech Airlines (ČSA) is the only airline to offer non-stop flights from North America to the Czech Republic. Its most frequent service is to Prague from **New York**'s JFK airport, followed by **Montréal**, with only a couple of flights a week departing from **Toronto**. Flying time from New York to Prague is about eight and a half hours; Montréal to Prague is around ten hours. ČSA occasionally code-shares with Delta, which means through-ticketing, good connections and often competitive prices can be had from other US cities such as Chicago, LA, San Francisco and Washington. Otherwise, the cheapest flights are usually via London or one of the other major European gateways.

Fares depend very much on the flexibility of the ticket and on availability. Tickets tend to be comparatively expensive if you buy directly from the national airlines, with an economy class New York–Prague or Vienna return costing between $1000 and $1200, and a Montréal–Prague return rarely going below C$1000. By contrast, agents and consolidators regularly offer New York–Prague or Vienna return fares of between $600 and $800, and Toronto–Prague return fares of around C$1000. Note that the cheaper fares usually mean that the ticket is non-exchangeable and non-refundable.

You'll get a much wider choice of flights and ticket prices if you opt for the **one- and two-stop flights** offered by the major carriers (a selection of which are listed below) allowing you to depart from any number of North American gateways via one of the major European cities. Another option is to fly into Berlin, Leipzig or Vienna, all of which are around five hours by train from Prague. If Prague is part of a longer European trip, you'll also want to check out details of the **Eurail** pass (see p.30).

Airlines

Air Canada ☎ 1-888/247-2262, ✆ www .aircanada.ca.
Air France US ☎ 1-800/237-2747; Canada ☎ 1-800/667-2747; ✆ www.airfrance.com.
American Airlines ☎ 1-800/433-7300, ✆ www .aa.com.
Austrian Airlines ☎ 1-800/843-0002, ✆ www .aua.com.
British Airways ☎ 1-800/AIRWAYS, ✆ www .ba.com.
Czech Airlines (ČSA) US ☎ 800/223-2365 or ☎ 212/765-6545; Canada ☎ 416/363-3174; ✆ www.czechairlines.com.
Delta Air Lines ☎ 1-800/241-4141, ✆ www .delta.com.
Lufthansa US ☎ 1-800/645-3880; Canada ☎ 1-800/563-5954; ✆ www.lufthansa.com.
Swiss ☎ 1-877/FLY-SWISS, ✆ www.swiss.com.
United Airlines ☎ 1-800/538-2929, ✆ www .united.com.

Discount agents and tour operators

Airtech ☎ 212/219-7000, ✆ www.airtech.com. Standby seat broker; also deals in consolidator fares and courier flights.
Backroads ☎ 1-800/GO-ACTIVE, ✆ www .backroads.com. Cycling, walking and multisport trips to the Czech Republic and Austria.
Blue Danube Tours ☎ 1-800/268 4155 or 416/362 5000, ✆ www.bluedanubeholidays.com. Extensive range of city breaks and tours operating out of Toronto.
Czech Active Tours ☎ 269-327-0619, ✆ www . czechactivetours.com. Guided walks for small groups and customized tours in the Czech Republic.
Czech & Slovak Heritage Tours ☎ 1-888-427-8687, ✆ www.czechheritage.com. Coach tours in the Czech and Slovak republics.
Czech Walking.com ☎ 1-866-443-8687, ✆ www.czechwalking.com. Walking and cycling tours in the Czech and Slovak republics.

Elderhostel ☎1-877/426 8056, ⓦwww
.elderhostel.org. Specialists in educational and
activity holidays for those aged 55 and over
(companions may be younger). They offer educational
trips to the Czech and Slovak republics.
General Tours ☎1-800/221-2216, ⓦwww
.generaltours.com. City breaks to Prague and tours
of Bohemia.
**International Gay and Lesbian Travel
Association** ☎1-800/448 8550 or 954/776 2626,
ⓦwww.iglta.com. The IGLTA provides lists of gay-
owned or gay-friendly travel agents, accommodation
and other organizations.
Isram World ☎1-800/223-7460, ⓦwww.isram
.com. City breaks and multi-city Czech packages.
Kolotour ☎1-800/524-7099, ⓦwww.kolotour
.com. Five- to ten-day cycling tours through the Czech
Republic.
REI Adventures ☎1-800/622-2236, ⓦwww.rei
.com/travel. Cycling and hiking tours from Prague to
Vienna or Budapest.
Romantic Czech Tours ☎206/517-4495,
ⓦwww.romanticczechtours.com. Customized
walking, biking and sightseeing tour operator
specializing in the Czech and Slovak republics.
STA Travel US ☎1-800/329-9537, Canada ☎1-
888/427-5639, ⓦwww.statravel.com. Worldwide
specialists in independent travel; also student IDs,
travel insurance, car rental, rail passes, and more.
Summit International Travel ☎1-800/527-
8664, ⓦwww.summittours.com. Highly regarded
specialists in the area. Walking, bicycling and car
packages of the Czech Republic, plus customized
tours.
TFI Tours ☎1-800/745-8000 or 212/736-1140,
ⓦwww.lowestairprice.com. Well-established
consolidator with a wide variety of global fares; less
competitive on the US domestic market.
Travel Cuts US ☎1-800/592-CUTS, Canada ☎1-
888/246-9762, ⓦwww.travelcuts.com. Popular,
long-established student-travel organization, with
worldwide offers.

From Australia and New Zealand

Flight time from Australia and New Zealand
to Prague or Vienna is over twenty hours,
and can be longer depending on routes,
with those flights touching down in Southeast Asia the quickest and cheapest on
average. To reach Prague, you'll have to
change planes in one of the main European
gateways. Given the length of the journey
involved, you might be better off including a
night's stopover in your itinerary, and indeed

some airlines include one in the price of the
flight.

The cheapest direct scheduled flights to
European gateways are usually to be found
on one of the Asian airlines. Average return
fares (including taxes) from eastern gateways to London are A$1500–2000 in low
season, A$2000–2500 in high season (fares
from Perth or Darwin cost around A$200
less). You'll then need to add A$100–200
onto all these for the connecting flight to
Vienna. Return fares from Auckland to London range between NZ$2000 and NZ$2500
depending on the season, route and carrier.

Airlines in Australia and New Zealand

Aeroflot Australia ☎02/9262 2233, ⓦwww
.aeroflot.com.au.
Alitalia Australia ☎02/9244 2445, New Zealand
☎09/308 3357, ⓦwww.alitalia.com.
American Airlines Australia ☎1300/130 757,
New Zealand ☎0800/887 997, ⓦwww.aa.com.
British Airways Australia ☎1300/767 177, New
Zealand ☎0800/274 847 or 09/356 8690, ⓦwww
.britishairways.com.
Czech Airlines (ČSA) Australia ☎02/92 47 77 06,
ⓦwww.csa.cz/en.
Delta Australia ☎02/9251 3211, New Zealand
☎09/379 3370, ⓦwww.delta.com.
Garuda Indonesia Australia ☎1300/365 330
or 02/9334 9944, New Zealand ☎09/366 1862,
ⓦwww.garuda-indonesia.com.
KLM Australia ☎1300/303 747, New Zealand
☎09/309 1782, ⓦwww.klm.com.
Lauda Air Australia ☎02/9251 6155; New Zealand
☎09/522 5948; ⓦwww.laudaair.com.
Lufthansa Australia ☎1300/655 727, New
Zealand ☎0800/945 220, ⓦwww.lufthansa.com.
Malaysia Airlines Australia ☎13 26 27, New
Zealand ☎0800/777 747, ⓦwww
.malaysia-airlines.com.
Qantas Australia ☎13 13 13, New Zealand
☎0800/808 767 or 09/357 8900, ⓦwww.qantas
.com.
Singapore Airlines Australia ☎13 10 11, New
Zealand ☎0800/808 909, ⓦwww.singaporeair
.com.
Sri Lankan Airlines Australia ☎02/9244 2234,
New Zealand ☎09/308 3353, ⓦwww.srilankan
.aero.
Thai Airways Australia ☎1300/651 960, New
Zealand ☎09/377 3886, ⓦwww.thaiair.com.
Virgin Atlantic Airways Australia ☎02/9244
2747, ⓦwww.virgin-atlantic.com.

Travel agents and tour operators in Australia and New Zealand

Australians Studying Abroad ☏3/9822 6899, ⓦwww.asatravinfo.com.au. Cultural, historical and political package tours of Prague and Bohemia.

Flight Centres Australia ☏13 31 33, ⓦwww .flightcentre.com.au; New Zealand ☏0800 243 544, ⓦwww.flightcentre.co.nz. Rock-bottom fares worldwide.

Gateway Travel Australia ☏02/9745 3333, ⓦwww.russian-gateway.com.au. Packages to the Czech and Slovak republics.

OTC Australia ☏1300/855 118, ⓦwww.otctravel .com.au. Deals on flights, hotels and holidays.

Silke's Travel Australia ☏02/8347 2000, ⓦwww .silkes.com.au. Gay and lesbian specialist travel agent.

STA Travel Australia ☏1300/733 035, New Zealand ☏0508/782 872, ⓦwww.statravel.com. Worldwide specialists in low-cost flights, overlands and holiday deals. Good discounts for students and under-26s.

Student Uni Travel Australia ☏02/9232 8444, ⓦwww.sut.com.au; New Zealand ☏09/379 4224, ⓦwww.sut.co.nz. Great deals for students.

Trailfinders Australia ☏02/9247 7666, ⓦwww .trailfinders.com.au. One of the best-informed and most efficient agents for independent travellers.

travel.com.au and **travel.co.nz** Australia ☏1300/130 482 or 02/9249 5444, ⓦwww.travel .com.au; New Zealand ☏0800/468 332, ⓦwww .travel.co.nz. Comprehensive online travel company, with discounted fares.

Red tape and visas

Citizens of the US, Canada, Australia, New Zealand and the EU need only a full passport to enter the Czech Republic or Slovakia, though the passport itself must be valid for at least six months beyond your return date. UK citizens can stay up to 180 days; all other EU and US citizens, Canadians, Australians and New Zealanders can stay up to ninety days. All visitors must register with the police within three days of arrival (if you're staying in a campsite, hostel, pension or hotel, this will be done for you). Entry requirements do change, so if in doubt, check with your nearest embassy or consulate before you leave, or look on the Czech and Slovak foreign ministry websites ⓦwww.mfa.cz or ⓦwww .foreign.gov.sk.

If you do need a visa, note that they are no longer issued at border stations, but must be obtained in advance from a Czech embassy or consulate. If you wish to extend your visa or your stay, you need to go to the Foreigners' Police headquarters in Prague or Bratislava (addresses are given in the directories of those cities).

For an updated list of Czech and Slovak embassies and consulates abroad, go to ⓦwww.mfa.cz. Foreign embassies and consulates in Prague are listed on p.160; those in Bratislava are listed on p.474.

Czech embassies and consulates

Australia 169 Military Rd, Dover Heights, Sydney, NSW 2030 ☏02/9371 8877, ⓦwww.mzv .cz/sydney.

Austria Penzingerstrasse 11–13, 1140 Vienna ☏0222/894 2125, ⓦwww.mzv.cz/vienna.

Canada 541 Cooper St, Ottawa, Ontario K2P 0G2 ☏613/562-3875, ⓦwww.mzv.cz/ottawa.

Germany Wilhelmstrasse 44, 10117 Berlin ☏030/226 380, ⓦwww.mzv.cz/berlin.

Ireland 57 Northumberland Rd, Ballsbridge, Dublin 4 ☏01/668 1135, ⓦwww.mzv.cz/dublin.

New Zealand 48 Hair St, Wainuiomata, Wellington ☏44/939 1610.

South Africa 2 Fleetwood Ave, Claremont 7708, Cape Town ☎021/797 9835, ⊛www.mzv .cz/capetown.
UK 26 Kensington Palace Gdns, London W8 4QY ☎020/7243 1115, ⊛www.mzv.cz/london.
USA 3900 Spring of Freedom St, NW, Washington DC 20008 ☎202/274-9100, ⊛www.mzv .cz/washington.

Slovak embassies and consulates

Australia 47 Culgoa Circuit, O' Malley, Canberra ACT 2606 ☎06/290 1516, ⊛www .slovakemb-aust.org.
Austria Armbrustergasse 24,1190 Vienna ☎01/318 905-5214.

Canada 50 Rideau Terrace, Ottawa, Ontario K1M 2A1 ☎613/749 4442, ⊛www.ottawa.mfa.sk.
Germany Pariser Strasse 44, 107 07 Berlin ☎030/88926, ⊛www.berlin.mfa.sk.
Ireland 20 Clyde Rd, Ballsbridge, Dublin 4 ☎01/660 0012.
New Zealand Level 10, PriceWaterhouseCoopers Centre, 188 Quay Street, Auckland ☎09/366 5111.
South Africa 930 Arcadia St, Arcadia, Pretoria ☎012/342 2051.
UK 25 Kensington Palace Gardens, London W8 4QY ☎020/7313 6470, ⊛www.slovakembssy.co.uk.
USA 3523 International Court NW, Washington DC 20008 ☎202/237 1054, ⊛www.slovakemabssy-us .org.

 # Insurance and health

Even though EU health care privileges apply in both republics, you'd do well to take out an insurance policy before travelling to cover against theft, loss and illness or injury. Before paying for a new policy, however, it's worth checking whether you are already covered: some all-risks home insurance policies may cover your possessions when overseas, and many private medical schemes include cover when abroad. In Canada, provincial health plans usually provide partial cover for medical mishaps overseas, while holders of official student/ teacher/youth cards in Canada and the US are entitled to meagre accident coverage and hospital in-patient benefits. Students will often find that their student health coverage extends during the vacations and for one term beyond the date of last enrolment.

After checking out the possibilities above, you might want to contact a specialist travel insurance company, or consider the travel insurance deal we offer (see box overleaf). A typical travel insurance policy usually provides cover for the loss of baggage, tickets and – up to a certain limit – cash or cheques, as well as cancellation or curtailment of your journey. Many policies can be chopped and changed to exclude coverage you don't need – for example, sickness and accident benefits can often be excluded or included at will. If you do take medical coverage, ascertain whether benefits will be paid as treatment proceeds or only after you return home, and if there is a 24-hour medical emergency number. When securing baggage cover, make sure that the per-article limit – typically under £500/$750 and sometimes as little as £250/$400– will cover your most valuable possession. If you need to make a claim, you should keep receipts for medicines and medical treatment, and in the event you have anything stolen, you must obtain an official statement from the police (see p.41).

Rough Guides travel insurance

Rough Guides has teamed up with Columbus Direct to offer you **travel insurance** that can be tailored to suit your needs.

Readers can choose from many different travel insurance products, including a low-cost **backpacker** option for long stays; a **short-break** option for city getaways; a typical **holiday** package option; and many others. There are also annual **multi-trip** policies for those who travel regularly, with variable levels of cover available. Different **sports** and **activities** (trekking, skiing, etc) can be covered if required on most policies.

Rough Guides travel insurance is available to the residents of 36 different countries with different language options to choose from via our website – ⓦwww .roughguidesinsurance.com – where you can also purchase the insurance.

Alternatively, UK residents should call ☏0800 083 9507; US citizens should call ☏1-800 749-4922; Australians should call ☏1 300 669 999. All other nationalities should call +44 870 890 2843.

Health matters

No inoculations are required for the Czech and Slovak republics, and on a short visit you're unlikely to fall victim to anything worse than an upset stomach.

With the Czech and Slovak republics both within the EU, EU citizens receive free emergency **hospital treatment** on production of a European Health Insurance Card (EHIC), valid for five years, which will replace the E111 in 2006. Nationals of other countries should check whether their government has a reciprocal health agreement with the Czech or Slovak republics, or whether they are covered by their personal medical insurance.

If you should fall ill, it's easiest to go to a **pharmacy** (*lékárna* in Czech, *lekáreň* in Slovak). Pharmacists are willing to give advice (though language may be a problem) and able to dispense many drugs available only on prescription in other Western countries. They usually keep normal business hours, but at least one in each major town will be open 24 hours for minor problems. If it's an emergency, dial ☏155 for an ambulance and you'll be taken to the nearest hospital (*nemocnice/ nemocnica*).

Health issues

One of the most common problems visitors encounter are **ticks**, tiny little parasites no bigger than a pin head, which bury themselves into your skin. If you're anywhere near woodland below 1200m, there's a possibility you may encounter them. Removing ticks by dabbing them with alcohol, butter or oil is now discouraged; the medically favoured way of extracting them is to pull them out carefully with small tweezers. There is a very slight risk of picking up some very nasty diseases from ticks such as encephalitis. Symptoms for the latter are initially flu-like, and if they persist, you should see a doctor immediately.

Health websites

ⓦ**http://health.yahoo.com** Information on specific diseases and conditions, drugs and herbal remedies, as well as advice from health experts.
ⓦ**www.fitfortravel.scot.nhs.uk** Scottish NHS website carrying information about travel-related diseases and how to avoid them.
ⓦ**www.istm.org** The website of the International Society for Travel Medicine, with a full list of clinics specializing in international travel health.
ⓦ**www.tripprep.com** Travel Health Online provides an online-only comprehensive database of necessary vaccinations for most countries, as well as destination and medical service provider information.

Costs, money and banks

In general terms, the Czech and Slovak republics are incredibly cheap for Westerners, with the exception of accommodation, which is comparable with many EU countries. That said, price differentiation across the countries are now quite marked: costs in the centre of Prague (and, to a lesser extent, Bratislava) creep ever upwards, while in some parts of the countryside, they remain much more static.

Most of your daily allowance will go on accommodation, with even the cheapest places charging around £10/$18 a night. All other basic costs, like food, drink and transport, remain very cheap indeed. To put things in perspective, however, it's worth bearing in mind that the average monthly salary for Czechs is around 17,000Kč (£375/$700), and less than that for Slovaks.

Currency

The Czech and Slovak republics use separate currencies, both known as the **crown**. The Czech crown is fully convertible, so it's possible to buy some currency and bring it with you; the Slovak crown is not fully convertible, which theoretically means you can't buy any currency until you arrive in the country. For the most up-to-date exchange rates, consult the useful currency converter websites ⓦwww.oanda.com or ⓦwww.xe.com/ucc.

The currency in the Czech Republic is the **Czech crown** or *koruna česká* (abbreviated to Kč or CZK), which is divided into one hundred relatively worthless hellers or *haliře* (abbreviated to h). At the time of going to press there were around 45Kč to the pound sterling, 30Kč to the euro and around 25Kč to the US dollar. Notes come in 20Kč, 50Kč, 100Kč, 200Kč, 500Kč, 1000Kč and 2000Kč (less frequently 5000Kč) denominations; coins as 1Kč, 2Kč, 5Kč, 10Kč, 20Kč and 50Kč, plus 10h, 20h and 50h.

The currency in Slovakia is the **Slovak crown** or *Slovenská koruna* (abbreviated to Sk), which is divided into 100 heller or *halér* (abbreviated to h). At the time of going to press there were around 55Sk to the pound sterling, 40Sk to the euro and around 30Sk to the US dollar. Notes come in 20Sk, 50Sk, 100Sk, 200Sk, 500Sk and 1000Sk (less frequently 5000Sk) denominations; coins as 1Sk, 2Sk, 5Sk and 10Sk, plus 10h, 20h, 50h.

Travellers' cheques, credit and debit cards

Although they are the traditional way to carry funds, **travellers' cheques** are no longer the cheapest nor the most convenient option – bank cards are better, see below – although they do offer safety against loss or theft. The usual fee for buying travellers' cheques is one or two percent, though this fee may be waived if you buy the cheques through a bank where you have an account. Be sure to keep the purchase agreement and a record of the cheques' serial numbers safe and separate from the cheques themselves. In the event that cheques are lost or stolen, the issuing company will expect you to report the loss forthwith to their nearest office; most companies claim to replace lost or stolen cheques within 24 hours.

Credit cards are a very convenient way of carrying your funds, and can be used either in ATMs or over the counter. Mastercard, Visa and American Express are

The euro

Despite the numerous prices quoted in euros all over Prague, the Czechs have not adopted the euro yet. That said, a few of the places that quote euro prices will accept euros, usually at a pretty fair rate (€1 for around 30Kč).

Business hours

Business hours in both republics are generally Monday to Friday 9am to 5pm, though most supermarkets and tourist shops work longer hours. Smaller shops usually close for lunch for an hour sometime between noon and 2pm. Those shops that open on Saturday are generally shut by noon or 1pm, and very few open on Sunday. The majority of pubs and restaurants outside the big cities tend to close between 10pm and 11pm, with food often unavailable after 9pm.

accepted just about everywhere. Remember that all cash advances are treated as loans, with interest accruing daily from the date of withdrawal; there may be a transaction fee on top of this. However, you may be able to make withdrawals from **ATMs** in Prague using your **debit card**, which is not liable to interest payments, and the flat transaction fee is usually quite small – your bank will be able to advise on this. Make sure you have a personal identification number (PIN) that's designed to work overseas.

Changing money

Most Czech and Slovak **banks** will be prepared to change travellers' cheques and give cash advances on credit cards – look for the window marked *směnárna/ zmenáreň*. Commissions at banks are fairly reasonable (generally under three percent), but the queues and the bureaucracy can mean a long wait. Quicker, but more of a rip-off in terms of either commission or exchange rate, are the exchange outlets which exist in the bigger towns and cities.

Banking hours are usually Monday to Friday 8am to 5pm, often with a break at lunchtime. Outside of these times, you may find the odd bank open, but otherwise you'll have to rely on exchange outlets and international hotels.

Wiring money

Having money **wired** from home using one

of the companies listed below is never convenient or cheap, and should be considered a last resort. It's also possible to have money wired directly from a bank in your home country to a bank in the Czech Republic or Slovakia, although this is somewhat less reliable because it involves two separate institutions. If you go this route, your home bank will need the address of the branch bank where you want to pick up the money and the address and telex number of the Prague head office, which will act as the clearing house; money wired this way normally takes two working days to arrive, and costs around £25/$40/CA$54/AU$52/NZ$59 per transaction. If you're in really dire straits, get in touch with your consulate in Prague or Bratislava, who will usually let you make one phone call home free of charge, and will – in worst cases only – repatriate you, but will never, under any circumstances, lend you money.

Money-wiring companies

Travelers Express Moneygram US ☎1-800/444-3010, Canada ☎1-800/933-3278, UK, Ireland and New Zealand ☎00800/6663 9472, Australia ☎11800/6663 9472, ⊛www .moneygram.com.

Western Union US and Canada ☎1-800/CALL-CASH, Australia ☎1800/501 500, New Zealand ☎0800/005 253, UK ☎0800/833 833, Republic of Ireland ☎66/947 5603, ⊛www.westernunion .com (customers in the US and Canada can send money online).

Information, websites and maps

The Czechs and Slovaks maintain only a handful of tourist offices abroad, where you can get hold of pamphlets and brochures. However, the Czechs have a network of Czech Centres, which promote Czech art and culture and with lots of Czech and Slovak websites now available online in English, it should be easy enough to glean some useful information about either republic before you set out.

Czech tourist offices

Once in the Czech Republic, you'll find most large towns and cities now have a **tourist office**, usually known as an *informační centrum*, specifically designed to assist visitors. Most will hand out (or sell for a small fee) basic maps and pamphlets on local sights. They may also be able to assist with finding accommodation, but don't rely on this. Hours vary and are detailed in the text. In those places where there is no information centre, your best bet is probably to try the reception at the nearest large hotel. In Prague itself, simply go to one of the branches of the **PIS** (*Pražská informační služba*), whose staff can book accommodation and theatre and concert tickets, and answer most questions.

Czech Centres abroad

Austria Herrengasse 17, 1010 Vienna ☎ 01/535 2360, ⊛ www.czechcentres.cz/vienna.
Belgium 150 ave A. Buyllan, 1050 Brussels ☎ 02/641 8944, ⊛ www.czechcentres.cz/brussel.
Canada 401 Bay St, Suite 1510, Toronto, Ontario M5H 2Y4, ☎ 416/363-9928, ⊛ www.czechtourism .com

Czech tourist offices abroad

Canada 401 Bay Street, Suite #1510, Toronto, Ontario M5H 2Y4 ☎ 416-363-9928, ⊛ www.czechtourism.com.
Ireland ☎ 0353/1283 6068, ⊛ www .czechtourism.com.
UK ☎ 020/7631 0427, ⊛ www .czechtourism.com.
USA 1109 Madison Ave NY10028 ☎ 212-288-0830, ⊛ www .czechtourism.com.

Germany Friedrichstrasse 206, 10969 Berlin ☎ 030/208 2592, ⊛ www. www.czechcentres .cz/berlin.
Slovakia Hviezdoslavovo nám 8, 814 99 Bratislava ☎ 02/5920 3305, ⊛ www.czechcentres .cz/Bratislava.
UK 95 Great Portland St, London W1 5RA ☎ 020/7291 9920, ⊛ www. www.czechcentres .cz/london.
USA 1109 Madison Ave, New York, NY 10028 ☎ 212/288-0830, ⊛ www. www.czechcentres .cz/newyork.

Useful websites

Czech language ⊛ www.bohemica.com. Czech language and culture – especially language. You can learn it online and there are lots of links to Czech sites. ⊛ www.locallingo.com. Download phrases and learn Czech online.
Ex-pats ⊛ www.expats.cz. Good online resource for anyone staying in Prague: visitor info, news, listings and message boards galore.
Fleet Sheet ⊛ www.fsfinalword.cz. Daily one-page digest of the day's Czech news sent as a free email.
General Czech information ⊛ www.czechsite .com, ⊛ www.myczechrepublic.com. Both these sites have useful background information, up-to-date news and tourist links on the Czech Republic.
General Slovak information ⊛ www.slovakia .com. Useful, up-to-date, basic information on Slovak history, politics and culture.
High Tatras ⊛ www.tatry.sk. Excellent guide to the High Tatras, with plenty of info, travel and accommodation details, and particularly good for walkers, climbers and skiers.
Maps ⊛ www.mapy.cz. This site will provide you with a thumbnail map to help you find any hotel, restaurant, pub, shop or street in Prague (and elsewhere in the Czech Republic). ⊛ www .supernavigator.sk does the same in Slovakia.
News ⊛ www.ctk-online.cz and ⊛ www.tasr.sk.

Weekly news in English from the Czech News Agency (CTK) and the Slovak News Agency (TASR).

Prague Post ⓦ www.praguepost.cz. A very useful site, not just for getting the latest news, but also for finding out what's on in Prague over the coming week, and for general tourist information.

Radio Prague ⓦ www.radio.cz/english. An informative site well worth visiting, with updated news and weather as audio or text.

Radio Slovakia International ⓦ www.rsi.sk. News, culture and sports snippets, general info about the country, extensive archives and of course, you can listen online.

Romanies ⓦ www.romnews.com. Website of RomNews Society, with loads of news about Romanies all over Europe and lots of links.

Slovak Spectator ⓦ www.slovakspectator.sk. Online version of the Bratislava-based English-language weekly, with news, sport, weather and listings.

Slovak Tourist Board ⓦ www.sacr.sk. The official Slovak Tourist Board website with basic, but useful information on the country.

Welcome to the Czech Republic ⓦ www.czech .cz. Basic information on the country in English, and on the worldwide network of Czech Centres, run by the Czech Foreign Ministry.

Slovak tourist offices

The **BIS** (*Bratislavská informačná služba*) in Bratislava is a tourist office specifically set up to give information to foreign visitors, selling maps, booking accommodation and helping with general enquiries. Most large towns and cities in Slovakia have their own tourist office, or centre for *informácie*, many of them affiliated to AiCES (*Asociácia informačných centier*; ⓦ www.aices.sk). Otherwise, your best bet for local information and help with

Slovak tourist offices abroad

Czech & Slovak Tourist Centre 16 Frognal Parade, Finchley Road, London NW3 5HG ☎ 020/7794 3263, ⓦ www.czech-slovak-tourist.co.uk. In Britain, the Slovak embassy points callers in the direction of this friendly North London travel agent.

Slovak Information Center 406 East 67th St, New York, NY 10021 ☎ 212-737 3971. This New York centre is the nearest you'll get to a national tourist office in the US.

accommodation is probably the reception of the nearest hotel.

Maps

There are lots of good **maps** available now in the Czech and Slovak republics; most tourist offices will sell maps and all bookshops usually have a comprehensive selection. Geodézie (ⓦ www.geodezie.cz) in the Czech Republic, and VKÚ (ⓦ www .vku.sk), the military mapmakers, in Slovakia, produce an excellent range of road maps, with the 1:200,000 version probably the best general car touring atlas; and the incredibly detailed 1:100,000 version good for cyclists.

SHOCart (ⓦ www.shocart.cz), along with several other competitors, do a series of 1:50,000 walking maps, which cover the whole of the Czech Republic, marking all the colour-coded paths which crisscross the countryside. In Slovakia, the 1:50,000 series is produced by VKÚ; again, it covers the whole country, and in the more popular walking areas there's usually a 1:25,000 version. Local town plans (*plán města* or *mapa mesta*), showing bus, tram and trolleybus routes, should be available from most bookshops and some hotels.

Map outlets

UK and Ireland

National Map Centre Ireland 34 Aungier St, Dublin ☎ 01/476 0471, ⓦ www.mapcentre.ie.
Stanfords 12–14 Long Acre, WC2E 9LP ☎ 020/7836 1321, ⓦ www.stanfords.co.uk. Other branches in Manchester & Bristol.

USA and Canada

Longitude Books 115 W 30th St #1206, New York, NY 10001 ☎ 1-800/342-2164, ⓦ www .longitudebooks.com.
World of Maps 1235 Wellington St, Ottawa, ON, K1Y 3A3 ☎ 1-800/214-8524 or 613/724-6776, ⓦ www.worldofmaps.com.

Australia and New Zealand

Map World 371 Pitt St, Sydney ☎ 02/9261 3601, ⓦ www.mapworld.net.au. Branches in Perth, Canberra and Brisbane.
Map World (New Zealand) 173 Gloucester St,

Addresses and town names

The street name is always written before the number in **addresses**. The word for street (*ulice/ulica*) is either abbreviated to *ul.* or simply missed out altogether – Celetná ulice, for instance, is commonly known as Celetná. Other terms often abbreviated are *náměstí/námestie* (square), *třída/trieda* (avenue), and *nábřeží/nábrežie* (embankment), which become *nám., tř./tr.* and *nábř./nábr.* respectively.

House numbers can be confusing, too. Most places have two numbers: one in red, which is the house registration number, introduced by the Habsburgs in the 1770s, and one in blue or black, which is the conventional house number. In some addresses, both numbers will be written down, the house number first, separated by a forward slash.

Bear in mind when using a Czech or Slovak **index** that "Ch" is considered a separate letter and comes after H in the alphabet. Similarly, "Č", "Ď", "Ĺ", "Ř", "Š" and "Ž" are all listed separately, immediately after their non-accented cousins.

Many towns and villages in the Czech and Slovak republics were once (or still are) inhabited by **German** (or **Hungarian**) minorities. In these places we have given the German (or Hungarian) name in brackets after the Czech or Slovak, for example Mariánské Lázně (Marienbad).

Christchurch ☏ 0800/627 967, ⊛ www.mapworld .co.nz.

Mapland 372 Little Bourke St, Melbourne ☏ 03/9670 4383, ⊛ www.mapland.com.au.

Crime and personal safety

Both republics have relatively low crime rates, and as a tourist, you're unlikely to have to have any dealings with the national police: *Policie* (in Czech) or *Polícia* (in Slovak). The only time you may be asked to provide some form of identification is if stopped whilst driving.

The national **police** force, who wear navy blue, grey and white in the Czech Republic, and khaki-green with red lapels in Slovakia, are under the control of their respective ministries of interior. However, if you do need the police – and above all if you're reporting a serious crime – you should always go to the municipal police, run by the local authorities and known as *Městská policie* (in Czech) and *Mestská polícia* (in Slovak); their uniforms differ from region to region, though black is a popular choice.

In addition, there are various **private police** forces, who also dress in black – hence their nickname *Černí šerifové* (Black Sheriffs) – employed mostly by hotels and banks. They are allowed to carry guns, but have no powers of arrest, and you are not legally obliged to show them your ID.

Avoiding trouble

Almost all the problems encountered by tourists in the Czech and Slovak republics are to do with **petty crime** rather than more serious physical confrontations. Theft from cars and hotel rooms is commonplace, but Prague is also currently one of the worst cities in Europe for pickpockets. Sensible precautions include making photocopies of your passport, leaving passport and tickets in the hotel safe and noting down travellers'

Emergencies

Ambulance	☎155
Police	☎158
Fire	☎150

cheque and credit card numbers. If you have a car, don't leave anything in view when you park it, and take the cassette/radio with you if you can. Vehicles are rarely stolen, but luggage and valuables left in cars do make a tempting target and rental cars are easy to spot.

In theory, you're supposed to carry some form of **identification** at all times, and the police can stop you in the street and demand it. In practice, they're rarely bothered if you're clearly a foreigner (unless you're driving). In

any case, the police tend to confine themselves to "socially acceptable" activities like traffic control and harassing Romanies.

What to do if you're robbed

If you are unlucky enough to have something stolen, you will need to go to the police to report it, not least because your insurance company will require a police report. It's unlikely that there'll be anyone there who speaks English, and even less likely that your belongings will be retrieved but, at the very least, you should get a statement detailing what you've lost for your insurance claim. Try the phrase *byl jsem oloupen* (pronounced something like "bill sem ollow-pen") or (if you're a woman) *byla jsem oloupena* – "I have been robbed".

Travellers with disabilities

Under the Communists very little attention was paid to the needs of the disabled. With both countries now in the EU, attitudes are changing rapidly – all new buildings now provide disabled access – but there's a long way to go, and the chronic shortage of funds in both countries makes matters worse.

Transport is a major problem, since buses and all except the newest trams and trains are virtually impossible for wheelchairs, though some Prague metro and train stations now have facilities for the disabled. The prevalence of cobbles, and general lack of ramps, make life hard even on the streets.

At the time of writing, none of the **car rental** companies could offer vehicles with hand controls in either republic. If you're driving to central Europe, most cross-Channel ferries now have adequate facilities, as does British Airways for those who are flying.

The Czechs have produced a guide to the country's **accessible accommodation** and attractions called *Wheeling the Czech Republic*, available from tourist offices and from the Centrum paraple, Ovčárská

471, Malešice, Prague 10 (☎274 771 478, ⓦwww.paraple.cz).

For a list of wheelchair-friendly hotels, restaurants, metro stations in Prague, order the **guidebook** *Accessible Prague/Přístupná Praha* from the Prague Wheelchair Association (*Pražská organizace vozíčkářů*), Benediktská 6, Staré Město (☎224 827 210, ⓦwww.pov.cz). The association can organize an airport pick-up if you contact them well in advance, and can help with transporting wheelchairs.

Contacts for travellers with disabilities

UK and Ireland

Access Travel 6 The Hillock, Astley, Lancashire M29 7GW ☎01942/888 844, ⓦwww

.access-travel.co.uk. Small tour operator that can arrange flights, transfer and accommodation.
Holiday Care 2nd floor, Imperial Building, Victoria Rd, Horley, Surrey RH6 7PZ ℡0845/124 9971 or ℡0208/760 0072, ⓦwww.holidaycare.org.uk. Information on all aspects of travel.
Irish Wheelchair Association Blackheath Drive, Clontarf, Dublin 3 ℡01/818 6400, ⓦwww.iwa.ie. National voluntary organization working with people with disabilities with related services for holidaymakers.
RADAR (Royal Association for Disability and Rehabilitation) 12 City Forum, 250 City Rd, London EC1V 8AF ℡020/7250 3222, minicom ℡020/7250 4119, ⓦwww.radar.org.uk. A good source of advice on holidays and travel abroad.

USA and Canada

Access-Able ⓦwww.access-able.com. Online resource for travellers with disabilities.
Directions Unlimited 123 Green Lane, Bedford Hills, NY 10507 ℡1-800/533-5343 or 914/241-1700. Tour operator specializing in custom tours for people with disabilities.
Mobility International USA 451 Broadway, Eugene, OR 97401 ℡541/343-1284, ⓦwww

.miusa.org. Information and referral services, access guides, tours and exchange programmes. Annual membership $35 (includes quarterly newsletter).
Society for the Advancement of Travelers with Handicaps (SATH) 347 Fifth Ave, New York, NY 10016 ℡212/447-7284, ⓦwww.sath.org. Non-profit educational organization that has actively represented travellers with disabilities since 1976.
Wheels Up! ℡1-888/389-4335, ⓦwww.wheelsup.com. Provides discounted airfare, tour and cruise prices for disabled travellers; also publishes a free monthly newsletter and has a comprehensive website.

Australia and New Zealand

ACROD (Australian Council for Rehabilitation of the Disabled) PO Box 60, Curtin ACT 2605 ℡02/6282 4333 (also TTY), ⓦwww.acrod.org.au. Provides lists of travel agencies and tour operators for people with disabilities.
Disabled Persons Assembly 4/173–175 Victoria St, Wellington, New Zealand ℡04/801 9100 (also TTY), ⓦwww.dpa.org.nz. Resource centre with lists of travel agencies and tour operators for people with disabilities.

Directory

Bottles Neither republic is quite yet a fully paid-up member of the throwaway culture, and many drinks still come in bottles with a deposit that can be reclaimed at the supermarket. Otherwise, there are bottle banks scattered around most towns and cities.
Children The attitude to kids is generally very positive in both republics. That said, you'll see few babies out in the open, unless snuggled up in their prams, and almost no children in pubs, cafés or even most restaurants. Children are generally expected to be unreasonably well behaved and respectful to their elders, and many of the older generation may frown at over-boisterous behaviour. Kids under six go free on public transport; six- to fourteen-year-olds pay half-fare. Dis-

posable nappies are becoming more widely available, but convenience food for babies is still fairly thin on the ground.
Electricity This is the standard continental 220 volts AC. Most European appliances should work as long as you have an adaptor for continental-style two-pin round plugs. North Americans will need this plus a transformer.
Gay men and lesbians Homosexuality is legal in both republics, with the age of consent at fifteen (in the Czech Republic) and sixteen (in Slovakia), whatever your sexuality. That said, on the whole attitudes remain very conservative.
Laundry Self-service laundrettes don't exist, except in Prague, though you can get clothes beautifully service-washed or

dry-cleaned for a very reasonable price at a *čistírna* as long as you've got a few days to spare.

Left luggage Most bus and train stations have lockers and/or a 24-hour left-luggage office.

Lost property Most train stations have lost property offices – look for the sign *ztráty a nálezy*. If you've lost your passport, then get in touch with your embassy (see p.160).

Smoking Like most continental Europeans, the Czechs and Slovaks are keen smokers, and you'll find very few no-smoking areas in cafés, pubs or restaurants, though there is no smoking on the public transport system. If you're a smoker and need a light, say *máte oheň?* Matches are *zápalky*.

Tampons Tampons (*tampóny*) and sanitary towels (*dámské vložky*) are cheap and easy to get hold of in department stores and supermarkets.

Time The Czech and Slovak republics are generally one hour ahead of Britain and six hours ahead of EST, with the clocks going forward in spring and back again some time in autumn – the exact date changes from year to year. Generally speaking, Czechs and Slovaks use the 24-hour clock.

Tipping is normal practice in cafés, bars, restaurants and taxis, though this is usually done by simply rounding up the total. For example, if the waiter tots up the bill and asks you for 74 crowns, you should hand him a 100-crown note and say "take 80 crowns".

Toilets Apart from the automatic ones in the big cities, toilets (*záchody, toalety* or *WC*) are few and far between. In some, you still have to buy toilet paper (by the sheet) from the attendant, whom you will also have to pay as you enter. Standards of hygiene can be low. Gentlemen should head for *muži* or *páni*; ladies should head for *ženy* or *dámy*. In dire straits you should make use of conveniences in restaurants and pubs, as most Czechs and Slovaks do.

Guide

Guide

The Czech Republic

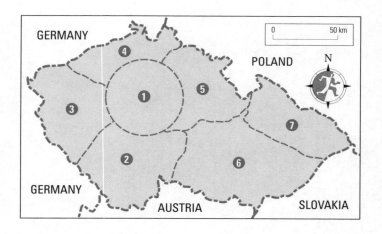

Basics

With the official break-up of Czechoslovakia on January 1, 1993, the Czech Republic became one of Europe's newest nations, with a population of just over ten million. Compared to their former Slovak compatriots, the Czechs have had comparatively few problems in gaining recognition on the international stage, entering NATO and the EU with ease. In playwright Václav Havel, the Czechs had a president many people had actually heard of; the capital city – Prague – has been one of the most popular tourist destinations of the last decade; and they have had, for much of that time, a stable government widely praised at home and abroad for the speed and efficacy of its economic reforms.

Getting around

The most relaxing way of travelling around the Czech Republic is by **train**. The system, bequeathed by the Habsburgs in 1918, is one of the most dense in Europe, and has changed little since those days, with only a small percentage of the tracks allowing train speeds of over 120kph. Though often wonderfully scenic, it's also extremely slow, so if you're in a hurry, buses are nearly always faster. Bus and train timetables can be found in the "Travel details" section at the end of each chapter.

Trains

The country's state-run train system, Czech Railways, **České dráhy** or **ČD** (⊛ www .cdrail.cz), remains the country's largest employer, largely due to overemployment, and runs at a huge loss. The constant threats to close down up to a third of the railway system – which cast a shadow over much of the last decade – look more likely than ever to become a reality. In the meantime, enjoy the system while you can.

There are two main **types of train** (*vlak*): *rychlík* (R) or *spěšný* (Sp) trains are the faster ones which stop only at major towns, while *osobní* (or *zastavkový*) trains stop at just about every station, averaging as little as 30kph. Fast trains are further divided into SuperCity (SC), which are first class only, EuroCity (EC) or InterCity (IC), for which you need to pay a supplement, and Expres (Ex).

Tickets and fares

Once you've worked out when your train leaves (for which, see overleaf), the best thing to do when buying a **ticket** (*lístek*) is to write down all the relevant information (date/time/ destination) on a piece of paper and hand it to the ticket clerk. This avoids any linguistic misunderstandings – rectifying any mistakes involves a lengthy bureaucratic process and costs you ten percent of the ticket price.

If you want a return ticket (*zpáteční*) or you're travelling on a *rychlík* train, you must say so, though the former is rarely cheaper than buying two singles. Overall, fares, which are calculated by the kilometre, remain remarkably low; a second-class single from Prague to Brno still only costs around £5/$8.50. First-class carriages (*první třída*) exist only on fast trains; tickets are fifty percent more expensive, but should guarantee you a seat on a busy train. There are half-price **discount fares** for children under 16, and you can take two children under 6 for free (providing they don't take up more than one seat). There are even some "crèche carriages" on the slower trains – marked with a "D" on the timetable – where those with children under 10 have priority over seats.

For all international services (and any other trains marked with an "R" on the timetable), you can buy a **seat reservation** (*místenka*). It's advisable to get one if you're travelling at the weekend on one of the main routes and want to be sure of a seat. The *místenka* costs very little, but you must get it at least an hour before your train leaves, and either after or at the same time as you purchase your ticket.

Information and timetables

With very few English-speakers employed on the railways, it can be difficult getting **train information**. The larger stations have a simple airport-style arrivals and departures board, which includes information on delays under the heading *zpoždění*. Many stations have poster-style displays of arrivals (*příjezd*) and departures (*odjezd*), the former on white paper, the latter on yellow, with fast trains printed in red.

All but the smallest stations also have a comprehensive display of timings and route information on rollers. These **timetables** may seem daunting at first, but with a little practice they should become decipherable. First find the route you need to take on the diagrammatic map and make a note of the number printed beside it; then follow the timetable rollers through until you come to the appropriate number. Some of the more common Czech notes at the side of the timetable are *jezdí jen v...* (only running on...), or *nejezdí v* or *nechodí v...* (not running on...), followed by a date or a symbol: a cross or an "N" for a Sunday, a big "S" for a Saturday, two crossed hammers for a weekday, "A" for a Friday and so on. Small stations may simply have a board with a list of departures under the title *směr* (direction) followed by a town. A platform, or *nástupiště*, is usually divided into two *kolej* on either side.

Buses

Buses (*autobusy*) go almost everywhere, and from town to town they're often faster than the train. Bear in mind, though, timetables tend to be designed around the needs of commuters, and tend to fizzle out at the weekend.

In many towns and villages, the **bus station** (*autobusové nádraží*) is adjacent to the train station, though you may be able to pick up the bus from the centre of town. The bigger terminals, like Prague's Florenc, are run with train-like efficiency, with airport-style departure boards and numerous platforms. Often you can book your ticket in advance, and it's essential to do so if you're travelling at the weekend or early in the morning on one of the main routes. For most minor routes, simply buy your

Bus timetable symbols

X or crossed hammers – only on weekdays
S – Saturday only
N – Sunday only
b – Monday to Saturday
a – Saturday, Sunday and holidays only
P – Monday only
V – Friday only
c – schooldays only
g – daily except Saturday
d – Monday to Thursday
y – Tuesday to Friday

ticket from the driver. Large items of luggage (*zavazadlo*) go in the boot, and you'll have to pay the driver a few crowns for the privilege. Minor bus stops are marked with a rusty metal sign saying *zastávka*. If you want to get off, ask *já chci vystoupit?*; "the next stop" is *příští zastávka*.

Bus **timetables** (ⓦ www.vlak-bus.cz) are even more difficult to figure out than train ones, as there are no maps at any of the stations. In the detailed timetables, each service is listed separately, so you may have to scour several timetables before you discover when the next bus is. A better bet is to look at the departures and arrivals board. Make sure you check on which day the service runs, since many run only on Mondays, Fridays or at the weekend (see the section on trains for the key phrases).

City transport

City transport is generally excellent, with buses (*autobus*), trolleybuses (*trolejbus*) and sometimes also trams (*tramvaj*) running from dawn until around midnight in most major towns (and all night in Prague and Brno). Ticket prices vary from place to place (generally around 10Kč for an adult; reduced rates for those aged 6–14; under-6s travel free), but are universally cheap. In Prague and Brno, various passes are available (see the relevant city accounts).

With a few exceptions, you must buy your ticket (*lístek* or *jízdenka*) before getting on board. Tickets, which are standard for all types of transport, are available from newsagents, tobacconists and the yellow machines at major stops, and are validated in the punching machines once you're on board. There are no conductors, only plain-clothes inspectors (*revizoři*), who make spot checks and will issue an on-the-spot fine of 400Kč.

Taxis are cheap and plentiful. Beware, however, that tourists are seen as easy prey by some taxi drivers, especially in Prague. The best advice is to have your hotel or pension call you one, rather than pick one up on the street or at the taxi ranks.

Driving

Czech **car** ownership is on the rise, but traffic outside the big cities is still pretty light. Road conditions are generally not bad, though the motorway system is very limited. The only place where you might encounter difficulties is in the bigger cities and towns, where the lane system is confusing, tramlines hazardous and parking a nightmare. You have to be 18 or over to drive in the Czech Republic, and if you want to travel on long-distance motorways within the Czech Republic, you'll need a **motorway tax disc** or *dálniční známka*, which currently costs around 100Kč for ten days, 200Kč for a month, and is available from all border crossings and most post offices and petrol stations.

If you're bringing your own car, you'll need proof of ownership, or a letter from the owner giving you permission to drive the car. A British or other EU **driving licence** is fine; all other drivers are advised to purchase an International Driving Licence. You also need a red warning triangle in case you break down, a national identification sticker and a

first-aid kit (these are all compulsory in the Czech Republic), and a "Green Card" for third party insurance cover at the very least. An even better idea is to sign up with one of the national motoring organizations, who offer continental breakdown assistance and, in extreme circumstances, will get you and your vehicle brought back home if necessary.

Rules of the road

Rules and regulations on Czech roads are pretty stringent, with on-the-spot fines regularly handed out, up to a maximum of 5000Kč. The basic rules are driving on the right (introduced by the Nazis in 1939); compulsory wearing of seatbelts; headlights on at all times (Nov–March); no under 12s in the front seat, hands-free mobiles only and no alcohol at all in your blood when you're driving. Theoretically, Czechs are supposed to give way to pedestrians at zebra crossings, but few do. However, Czechs do give way to pedestrians crossing at traffic lights when turning right or left. You must also give way to trams, and, if there's no safety island at a tram stop, you must stop immediately and allow passengers to get on and off. As in other continental countries, a yellow diamond sign means you have right of way, a black line through it means you don't; it's important to clock this sign before you reach the junction since the road markings at junctions rarely make priorities very clear. A blank sign in a red circle means "no entry" except to those vehicles stated underneath (in Czech).

Vehicle crime is not unknown so don't leave anything visible or valuable in the car. Restric-

Traffic signs

Průjezd zakázán	closed to all vehicles
Dálkov provoz	by-pass
Objížďka	diversion
Nemocnice	hospital
Choďte vlevo	pedestrians must walk on the left
Zákaz zastavení	no stopping
Rozsviť světla	switch your lights on
Bez poplatku	free of charge
Úsek častých nechod	area where accidents often occurs
Nebezpečí smyku	slippery road
Při sněhu a náledí cesta uzavřena	road closed due to snow or ice
Pozor dětí	watch out for children

Rental agencies

Abroad

Avis Australia ☎13 63 33 or 02/9353 9000, ⓦwww.avis.com.au; Canada ☎1-800/272-5871, ⓦwww.avis.com; Ireland ☎021/428 1111, ⓦwww.avis.ie; New Zealand ☎09/526 2847 or 0800/655 111, ⓦwww.avis.co.nz; UK☎0870/606 0100, ⓦwww.avis.co.uk; US ☎1-800/230-4898.

Budget Australia ☎1300/362 848, ⓦwww.budget.com.au; Canada ☎1-800/472-3325, ⓦwww.budget.com; Ireland ☎09/0662 7711, ⓦwww.budget.ie; New Zealand ☎09/976 2222 or ☎0800/652-227, ⓦwww.budget.co.nz; UK ☎01442/276 266, ⓦwww.budget.co.uk; US ☎1-800/527-0700.

Europcar Australia ☎1300/131 390, ⓦwww.deltaeuropcar.com.au; Canada & US ☎1-877/940 6900, ⓦwww.europcar.com; Ireland ☎01/614 2888, ⓦwww.europcar.ie; UK ☎0870/607 5000, ⓦwww.europcar.co.uk.

Hertz Australia ☎13 30 39 or 03/9698 2555, ⓦwww.hertz.com.au; Canada ☎1-800/263-0600, ⓦwww.hertz.com; Ireland ☎01/676 7476, ⓦwww.hertz.ie; New Zealand ☎0800/654 321, ⓦwww.hertz.co.nz; UK ☎0870/844 8844, ⓦwww.hertz.co.uk; US ☎1-800/654-3131.

Holiday Autos Australia ☎1300/554 432, ⓦwww.holidayautos.com.au; Ireland ☎01/872 9366, ⓦwww.holidayautos.ie; New Zealand ☎0800/144 040, ⓦwww.holidayautos.co.nz; UK ☎0870/400 0099, ⓦwww.holidayautos.co.uk.

National Australia ☎13 10 45, ⓦwww.nationalcar.com.au; New Zealand ☎0800/800 115 or ☎03/366-5574, ⓦwww.nationalcar.co.nz; UK ☎0870/400 0099, ⓦwww.nationalcar.com; US ☎1-800/962-7070, ⓦwww.nationalcar.com.

Thrifty Australia ☎1300/367 227, ⓦwww.thrifty.com.au; Ireland ☎1800/515 800, ⓦwww.thrifty.ie; New Zealand ☎09/309 0111, ⓦwww.thrifty.co.nz; UK ☎01494/751 600, ⓦwww.thrifty.co.uk; US and Canada ☎1-800/847-4389, ⓦwww.thrifty.com.

In Prague

Continental Rent a Car Revoluční 24, Nové Město ☎222 314 228, ⓦwww.dvorak-rentacar.cz.

Czechocar Prague airport and the Kongresové centrum 5 května 65, Nusle ☎261 222 079, ⓦwww.czechocar.cz.

---

tions on **parking** are commonplace in Czech towns, with pay-and-display meters the easiest system to decipher; more complicated are the voucher schemes, which require you to buy a voucher from a newsagent, tourist office or bookshop. Illegally parked cars will either be clamped or towed away – if this happens, phone ☎158 to find out the worst.

Speed limits are 130kph on motorways (and if you travel any faster you will be fined), 90kph on other roads and 50kph in all cities, towns and villages – you need to remember these, as there are few signs to remind you. In addition, there's a special speed limit of 30kph for level crossings (you'll soon realize why if you try ignoring it). Many level crossings have no barriers, simply a sign saying *pozor* and a series of lights: a single flashing light means that the line is live; two red flashing lights mean there's a train coming.

Fuel and car rental

Petrol (*benzín*) comes as *natural* (unleaded 95 octane), *super plus* (unleaded 98 octane), *special* (leaded 91 octane) and *nafta* (diesel); LPG or *plyn* is also available from some petrol stations. The price of petrol is cheaper than in much of Western Europe, currently costing around 25Kč a litre (£0.50/$0.80). If you have car trouble, dial ☎1230 at the nearest phone and wait for assistance. For peace of mind it might be worth taking out an insurance policy which will pay for any on-the-spot repairs and, if necessary, ship you and your passengers home free of charge.

Car rental is easy to arrange, with all the major companies operating out of Prague airport, with offices downtown and some in Brno. If you book in advance with a multinational you're looking at around £50/$90 per day for a small car, £180/$330 a week. You'll

Useful hiking terms

cesta/stezka/pěšina	road/path/trail
bouda	mountain refuge
hranice	border
jeskyně	cave
lanovka/lánova draha	chairlift/cable car
les	wood
lyžařský vlek	ski lift
pramen	spring
rozhled/vyhlídka	viewpoint
skála	rock
údolí	valley
vodopad	waterfall

get a much cheaper deal, however, if you go for a Škoda and book your car through a local agent once you've arrived in the country; prices can be as low as £10–20/$18–35 a day, though the reliability of the cars and the service that you receive can be variable. To drive a car in the Czech Republic, you need to be 18, but in order to rent a car, you'll need to be at least 21, have a clean licence, and have been driving for at least a year.

Cycling and hiking

Cycling is now a popular leisure activity in the Czech Republic, and the rolling countryside, though hard work on the legs, is rewarding. Facilities for bike rental are improving, especially in the more touristy areas, and the increasing number of bike shops makes repairs possible and spare parts slightly easier to obtain. To take your bike (*kolo*) on the train, you must buy a separate ticket before taking it down to the freight section of the station, where, after filling in the mountains of paperwork, your bike should be smoothly sent on to its destination.

Hiking is a very popular pastime with young and old alike, the most enthusiastic indulging in an activity curiously known as going *na trampu*; dressing up in quasi-military gear, camping in the wilds, playing guitar and singing songs round the campfire. There is a dense network of paths that covers the whole countryside – sometimes reaching even within the city boundaries of Prague. All the trails are colour-coded with clear markers every 200m or so and signs indicating roughly how long it'll take you to reach your destination.

Many of the walks are fairly easy-going, but it can be wet and muddy underfoot even in summer, so sturdy boots are a good idea, particularly if you venture into the mountains proper. There are no hiking guides in English, but it's easy enough to get hold of 1:50,000 maps which cover the whole country and detail all the marked paths in the area (see p.40).

Planes and boats

Domestic **flights**, run by ČSA and a variety of other carriers, link Prague with Brno and Ostrava, and there are regular international flights to the Slovak cities of Bratislava, Poprad and Košice. Though not exactly cheap, particularly when compared with the train or bus, they can prove useful if time is short and you want to get to eastern Slovakia quickly, reducing the travel time from Prague to Košice to two hours from twelve, for example. If you do decide to fly, make sure you book well in advance as demand is high, and flights to places like Poprad in the High Tatras are booked solid in the high season. Further details can be obtained from ČSA offices or agents in most large towns.

The opportunity for travelling by **boat** (*lod*) is pretty limited in the Czech Republic, but there are a few services worth mentioning. From Prague, boats sail all the way upriver to Orlík, with a change of vessel at each of the dams on the way, and downriver to Mělník, where the Vltava flows into the Labe (Elbe). There's also a summer service on Lake Lipno in South Bohemia, and down the River Labe between Děčín and Hřensko (see box on p.189 for more information on boat trips).

Accommodation

Accommodation is likely to be by far the largest chunk of your daily expenditure, unless you're camping. Overall, standards in pensions, hotels and hostels have improved enormously. Only in Prague, and, to a lesser extent, in Brno, is it difficult to find reasonably-priced accommodation. For a rundown on the price codes used in this book, see the inside front cover.

If you're going to Prague anytime from Easter to September or over the Christmas and New Year period, it's as well to arrange accommodation before you arrive. There are inexpensive accommodation specialists who can arrange this for you (see p.28 for a list of current operators), plus websites like ⓦ www.czechhotels.cz and ⓦ www.camp .cz for campsites. Another alternative is to use the listings in the guide to ring or email a hotel and book yourself in.

Hotels, pensions and private rooms

On the whole, the country has come a long way from the bad old days when foreign visitors were shepherded into high-rise monstrosities and charged three times as much as locals for services that were uniformly bad. That said, old Communist hotel dinosaurs live on, some places still charge more for the foreigners and "service with a snarl" is still occasionally encountered.

All **hotels** operate a star system, though it's self-regulatory and therefore none too reliable. Prices vary wildly and, unsurprisingly, tend to be much higher in areas that receive the most tourists. The vast majority of rooms now have en-suite bathrooms and TVs, with continental breakfast either included in the price or offered as an optional extra, and you'll find a restaurant and/or bar in almost every hotel.

Most guesthouses bill themselves as **pensions**. Again, prices and standards can vary widely, and a well-run pension can often be cheaper, friendlier and better equipped than many hotels. **Private rooms**, too, are a case of pot luck. You can be sure that they will be clean and tidy, but in what proximity you'll be to your hosts is difficult to predict. You might be sharing bathroom, cooking facilities, etc, with the family – Czech hospitality can be somewhat overwhelming, although meals other than breakfast are not generally included in the price. In some parts of the countryside you'll see plenty of signs saying either *ubytování* or *pokoje* ("accommodation" and "rooms" in Czech) or, more frequently, *Zimmer Frei* ("rooms available" in German). In some towns and cities, you may be able to book rooms through the local tourist office (details are listed throughout the *Guide*).

Hostels and student rooms

A smattering of **hostels** are now affiliated to Hostelling International (ⓦ www.iyhf.org), but these are few and far between, vary wildly in size and quality, and are often in obscure, out-of-the-way places. For more details, get hold of a copy of Hostelling International's hostel booklet, published annually. There are, of course, lots of other unofficial hostels – especially in Prague – where you can pay very little and usually get very little in return, beyond a place to lay your sleeping bag.

A more reliable alternative to hostels in the big university towns is **student accommodation** – known as *kolej* – which is let out cheap to travellers from June to August. Though often heavily booked up in advance by groups, they'll try their best to squeeze you in. Addresses can change from year to year, so to find out the most recent, go to the local tourist office.

Other dormitories, which go by the catch-all term of *ubytovna*, can be anything from sports halls to dorms used to house immigrant workers or workers on vacation. They are uniformly cheap and basic with few facilities beyond a bunk bed, toilet and cold shower, though they may remain unconvinced that a foreign tourist should demean themselves by staying there.

Camping and other options

Campsites (*autokemping*) are plentiful all over the Czech Republic. Some are huge affairs, with shops, swimming pools, draught beer and so on; others, known often as *tábořiště*, are just a simple stretch of grass with ad hoc toilets and a little running water. In the majority of sites, facilities are just about adequate, but don't get your expectations up too high. Many sites feature chalets (*chaty* or *bungolovy*), which vary in size and facilities from rabbit hutches to mini villas; prices start at around £10/$14 for two people.

Very few campsites are open all year round, most opening in May and closing in September. Even though prices are inflated for foreigners, costs are still reasonable; two people plus car and tent weigh in at around

£5–8/$9–14. Campfires, though officially banned, are tolerated at many campsites, and the guitar-playing barbecues can go on until well into the night.

Mountain huts

In the mountains of the Krkonoše, there are a fair number of **mountain huts** (*bouda* or *chata*) scattered about the hillsides. Some are just like hotels and charge similar prices, but the more isolated ones are simple wooden shelters costing around £5/$9 per person, with minimal facilities. A few are accessible by road, and most are only a few miles from civilization. Ideally, these should be booked in advance through the various accommodation agencies in the nearest settlements. The more isolated ones work on a first-come, first-served basis, but if you turn up before 6pm, you're unlikely to be turned away.

Communications

The Czech postal system is pretty efficient, the phone system slightly less so. Nevertheless, the phone system has improved enormously and has undergone a radical overhaul, with all numbers within the country

now made up of nine digits. Czechs are also keen web-users and access to the Internet is possible in most towns and cities across the country.

Post

Most **post offices** (*pošta*) are open from 8am to 5pm Monday to Friday, and Saturdays until noon. They're pretty baffling institutions with separate windows for just about every service. Look out for the right sign to avoid queueing unnecessarily: *známky* (stamps), *dopisy* (letters) or *balky* (parcels).

Outbound mail is reasonably reliable, with letters or postcards taking around four to five working days to reach Britain, a week to reach North America. You can buy stamps from newsagents, tobacconists and some kiosks, as well as at the post offices. Postal charges at the time of going to print were 9Kč for postcards within Europe and 12Kč to North America (check ⓦwww.cpost.cz for the latest and see p.632 for a list of countries in Czech).

Poste restante (pronounced as five syllables in Czech) services are available in major towns, but remember to write Pošta 1 (the main office), followed by the name of the town. Get the sender to write their name and address on the back so that mail can at least be returned if something goes wrong.

Useful telephone numbers

Czech telephone numbers
In 2002, all Czech regional prefixes became an integral part of telephone numbers, and all numbers are now nine digits. For some places, such as Prague, this simply means that the first digit of all phone numbers is now 2, as opposed to the old prefix of 02. However, in other places, the initial digits bear no relation to the old prefix; for example in Plzeň, all numbers now begin with 37, instead of 019 (the old regional prefix). It is necessary to dial all nine digits even when calling from within the town, city or region.

Phoning the Czech Republic from abroad
From Britain & Ireland: ☏00 + 420 (Czech Republic) + number.
From the USA & Canada: ☏011 420 (Czech Republic) + number.
From Australia & New Zealand: ☏0011 420 (Czech Republic) + number.

Phoning abroad from the Czech Republic
To the UK: ☏0044 + area code minus zero + number.
To the Republic of Ireland: ☏00353 + area code minus zero + number.
To the USA & Canada: ☏001 + area code + number.
To Australia: ☏0061 + area code minus zero + number.
To New Zealand: ☏0064 + area code minus zero + number.

Phones

All **public phones** have instructions in English, and if you press the appropriate button the language on the digital read-out will change to English. The **dialling tone** is a short followed by a long pulse; the **ringing tone** is long and regular; **engaged** is short and rapid (not to be confused with the connecting tone which is very short and rapid). The standard Czech response is *prosím*; the word for "extension" is *linka*. If you have any problems, ring ☎1181 to get through to international information.

You can make **international calls** from all phones, though rates are expensive. The majority of public phones take only **phone cards** (*telefonní karty*), currently available in 50, 100 and 150 units from post offices, tobacconists and some shops (prices vary). Alternatively, you can buy **pre-paid phone cards**, which will give you much longer call time any from any public or private phone; simply phone the toll-free access number and then punch in the PIN given on the card. In **coin-operated phones**, you need to insert a minimum of 3Kč to make a local call, 5Kč for long distance – if you stock up with enough coins, it is perfectly possible to make an international phone call.

You can also make phone calls from the local **telephone exchanges** situated in Prague, Brno and a few other cities. Write down the town and number you want, leave a deposit of around 200Kč and wait for your name to be called out. Keep a close watch on the time unless you've unlimited funds. Calls from a telephone exchange cost slightly less, but avoid making any calls from hotels, where the surcharge is usually outrageous.

As well as the aforementioned pre-paid phone cards, you can also get a **telephone charge card** from your phone company back home. In the **US and Canada**, AT&T, MCI, Sprint, Canada Direct and other North American long-distance companies all enable their customers to make credit-card calls while overseas, billed to your home number. Call your company's customer service line to find out if they provide service from the Czech Republic, and if so, what the toll-free access code is.

In the **UK and Ireland**, British Telecom (☎0800/345 144, ⊛www.payphones

.bt.com/2001/phone_cards/chargecard) will issue free to all its customers the BT Charge Card, which can be used in 116 countries; AT&T (dial ☎0800/890 011, then 888/641-6123 when you hear the AT&T prompt to be transferred to the Florida Call Centre, free 24hr) has the Global Calling Card; while NTL (☎0500/100 505) issues its own Global Calling Card, which can be used in more than sixty countries abroad, though the fees cannot be charged to a normal phone bill.

To call **Australia and New Zealand** from overseas, telephone charge cards such as Telstra Telecard or Optus Calling Card in Australia, and Telecom NZ's Calling Card can be used to make calls abroad, which are charged back to a domestic account or credit card. Apply to Telstra (☎1800/038 000), Optus (☎1300/300 937), or Telecom NZ (☎04/801 9000).

Mobile phones

If you want to use your **mobile** in the Czech Republic, you'll need to check with your phone provider whether it will work abroad, and what the call charges are. Unless you have a tri-band phone, it is unlikely that a mobile bought for use in the US will work in Europe. By contrast most mobiles in Australia and New Zealand use GSM, which works well in Europe.

In the UK, you usually have to inform your phone provider before going abroad to get international access switched on. You may get charged extra for this depending on your existing package. You are also likely to be charged extra for incoming calls when abroad, as the people calling you will be paying the usual rate. If you want to retrieve messages while you're away, you'll have to ask your provider for a new access code, as your home one is unlikely to work abroad. Most UK mobiles use GSM too.

For further information about using your phone abroad, check out ⊛www.telecomsadvice.org.uk/features/using_your_mobile_abroad

Email

One of the best (and cheapest) ways to keep in touch while travelling is to sign up for a **free Internet email address** – if you haven't already done so – that can be accessed from anywhere, for example Yahoo! (⊛mail.yahoo.com) or Hotmail (⊛www.hotmail.com). Once you've set up your account, you'll be able to pick up and send mail from any Internet café, web kiosk or hostel or hotel with Internet access.

You can get online at various cafés and bars in large Czech cities, though there aren't that many specialist cybercafés. The easiest way to find out how to get online is to ask the local tourist office. For details of how to plug your laptop in when abroad, plus information on country codes around the world, and electrical systems in different countries, check out the useful website ⊛www.kropla.com.

Media

In Prague and Brno, it's possible to get day-old copies of most of the broadsheet **English papers**, though one that you can buy on the day of issue is the European edition of *The Guardian*, printed in Frankfurt (it arrives on the streets of Prague and Brno around mid-morning). Similarly, the *International Herald Tribune* is widely available the same day, and contains a useful distilled English version of the *Frankfurter Allgemeine Zeitung*. Other papers tend to be a day or so old.

The Prague Post (⊛www.praguepost.com) is an **English-language weekly** aimed at the expat community, but good for visitors, too; it's a quality paper with strong business coverage and a useful pull-out Prague listings section. In the **magazine** market, you'll find the best coverage of contemporary Czech politics in English in *The New Presence/Nová přítomnost*, a bilingual current affairs magazine, directly inspired by the Masaryk-funded *Přítomnost*, which was one of the leading periodicals of the First Republic.

It's a sign of the times that the majority of **Czech newspapers** are German-owned. The only Czech-owned paper is the left-wing *Právo*, formerly the official mouthpiece of the Communist Party (when it was known as *Rudé právo* or "Red Justice"). Its chief competitor is *Mladá fronta dnes*, former mouthpiece of the Communist youth movement, now a very popular centre-right daily. *Lidové noviny* (the best-known *samizdat* or underground publication under the Com-

munists and the equivalent of *The Times* under the First Republic) is now a much less respected right-wing daily, while the orange-coloured *Hospodáské noviny* is the Czech equivalent of the *Financial Times* or *Wall Street Journal*. The country's most popular tabloid is *Blesk*, a sensationalist tabloid with lurid colour pictures, naked women and reactionary politics. If all you want, however, is yesterday's (or, more often than not, the day before yesterday's) international sports results, pick up a copy of the daily *Sport*.

Česká televize's two state-owned **TV channels**, ČT1 and ČT2, have both been eclipsed as far as ratings go by the runaway success of the commercial channel, Nova. The latter features lots of American sitcoms dubbed into Czech, plenty of game shows, striptease weather and comprehensive coverage of Czech football. Prima, the other commercial channel, has yet to make any significant inroads into Nova's audience monopoly. ČT2 is your best bet for foreign films with subtitles; it also shows news in English from the BBC on Monday to Friday at 8am, and on Saturday and Sunday at 7am.

On the **radio**, the BBC World Service (⊛www.bbc.co.uk/worldservice) now broadcasts loud and clear on 101.1FM, mostly in English, with occasional bits of Czech programming. The state-run Český rozhlas has four stations: ČR1 Radiožurnál (94.6FM), which is mainly current affairs; ČR2 (91.3FM), which features more magazine-style programming; Regina (92.6FM), which features news and pop music; and ČR3 Vltava (105FM), which plays classical music. The president broadcasts his presidential Sunday evening chat on ČR1; an English-language news summary goes out Monday to Friday at 5.30pm. The three top commercial channels are Evropa 2 (88.2FM), Radio Bonton (99.7FM) and Kiss 98 FM (98FM), which dish out bland Euro-pop. More interesting is Radio 1 (91.9FM), which plays a wide range of indie rock.

Eating and drinking

The good news is that you can **eat and drink** very cheaply in the Czech Republic: the food is filling and the beer flows freely.

The bad news is that the kindest thing you can say about Czech food is that it is hearty. Forty years of culinary isolation under the Communists introduced few innovations to Czech cuisine, with its predilection for pork, gravy, dumplings and pickled cabbage. Fresh vegetables (other than potatoes) remain a rare sight on traditional Czech menus, and salads are still waiting for their day.

That said, the choice of **places to eat** has improved enormously over the last decade. In Prague, at least, you could spend a whole week eating out and never go near a dumpling, should you so wish. Czechs themselves are very keen on pizzas, and there are now some very good pizzerias in the larger towns and cities – there are even some passably authentic ethnic restaurants ranging from Japanese and Lebanese to Balkan and French in Prague, and, to a lesser extent, Brno.

For a comprehensive **glossary of Czech food and drink** terms, see the language section on p.632.

Breakfast, snacks and bufets

Despite the fact that breakfast cereal consumption is on the rise in the Czech Republic, Czechs generally have little time for **breakfast** (snídaně) as such. Many get up so early in the morning (often around 5 or 6am) that they don't have time to start the day with anything more than a quick cup of coffee or tea. Most hotels will serve the "continental" basics of tea, coffee, rolls and cold cheese and meat. Bear in mind, though, that if you get up much past 10am, you'll have missed it and may as well join the country's working population for lunch.

Pastries (pečivo) are available from most bakeries (pekařství), but rarely in bars and cafés, so you'll probably have to eat them on the go. The traditional pastry (koláč) is more like sweet bread; dry and fairly dense with only a little flavouring in the form of hazelnuts (oříškový), poppy-seed jam (makový), prune jam (povidlový) or a kind of sour-sweet curd cheese (tvarohový).

With breakfast, Czechs tend to have white rolls, which come in two basic varieties: rohlík, a plain finger roll, and houska, a rougher, tastier round bun. Czech **bread** (chléb) is some of the tastiest around when fresh. The standard loaf is domácí or šumava, a dense mixture of wheat and rye, which you can buy whole, in halves (půl) or quarters (čtvrtina). Český chléb is a mixture of rye, wheat and whey, with distinctive slashes across the top; kmínový chléb is the same loaf packed full of caraway seeds. Moskva remains popular, despite the name – a moist, heavy, sour-dough loaf that lasts for days. Fresh milk (mléko) is available in most supermarkets either plnotučné (full fat) or nízkotučné (semi-skimmed). Look out, too, for kefir, deliciously thick sourmilk, or acido-filní mléko, its slightly thinner counterpart.

The ubiquitous street **takeaway** is the hot dog or párek, a dubious-looking frankfurter (traditionally two – párek means a pair), dipped in mustard and served with a white roll (v rohlíku). A greasier option is bramborák, a thin potato pancake with little flecks of bacon or salami in it. In Prague, felafal or kebabs (known as gyros) form another popular takeaway choice, usually with pitta bread and salad.

The country's slowly dwindling number of stand-up **bufets** or jídelna often open from as early as 6am and offer everything from light snacks to full meals. A cross between a British greasy spoon and an American diner, they're usually self-service (samoobsluha) and non-smoking, and occasionally have rudimentary seats. The cheapest of the wide range of meat sausages on offer is sekaná, bits of old meat and bread squashed together to form a meat loaf – for connoisseurs only. Guláš (goulash) is popular, though it may bear little relation to the original of that name – usually Szegedinský (pork with sauerkraut) after the Hungarian town. Less substantial fare boils down to chlebíčky – artistically presented open sandwiches with differing combinations of gherkins, cheese, salami, ham and aspic – and mountains of mayonnaise-based salad (salát), bought by weight (200g is a medium-sized portion).

Like the Austrians who once ruled over them, the Czechs have a grotesquely sweet tooth, and the coffee-and-cake hit is part of the daily ritual. The **cukrárna** is the place to go for cake-eating. There are two main types of cake: dort, like the German Tort, consist of a series of custard cream, chocolate and sponge layers, while *řez* are lighter square cakes, usually containing a bit of fruit. A *věneček*, filled with "cream", is the nearest you'll get to an eclair; a *větrník* is simply a larger version with a bit of fresh cream added; and a *kobliha* is a doughnut. One speciality to look out for is a *rakvička*, which literally means "little coffin", an extended piece of sugar like a meringue, with cream, moulded vaguely into the shape of a coffin. Whatever the season, Czechs have to have their daily fix of ice cream (*zmrzlina*), available in soft form from machines or scooped, either dispensed from little window kiosks in the sides of buildings, or dished out from within a *cukrárna*.

As for **fast food**, pizza places abound, though they can vary from vague approximations to quality imitations. Other staple Czech fast-food snacks include *hranolky* (chips/French fries) or *krokety* (croquettes) served with tartare sauce (*tartarská omačka*). Czech crisps (*chips*) have struggled to compete with foreign imports, but a few new brands are holding their own. Finally, it should also be noted that *McDonald's* now has a prime slice of real estate in almost every major Czech city.

Eating out

The division between cafés, bars, pubs and restaurants is pretty blurred. **Restaurants** (*restaurace* in Czech) are primarily there to serve you food, but some will also have a bar area where you can simply have a drink. Others style themselves as *vinárna* or **wine-bars**, though they, too, often serve food. Equally, while many **cafés** (*kavárna* in Czech) realize most of their customers only want a drink and maybe a slice of cake, many serve up cheap, hot snacks and even full meals. Czech **pubs** (*pivnice*, *hostinec* or *hospoda* in Czech) are on the whole the cheapest places to eat, and almost exclusively serve standard Czech food. Cheaper still is the local stand-up *bufet*, usually a self-service café serving basic, hot Czech meals.

Czech menus

Away from the big hotels, the **menu** (*jídelní lístek*), which should be displayed outside, is often in Czech only, and deciphering it without a grounding in the language can be quite

a feat. Just bear in mind that, on the whole, the right-hand column lists the prices, while the far left column gives you the estimated weight of every dish in grams; if what you get weighs more or less, the price will alter accordingly (this applies in particular to fish).

Most menus start with the **soups** (*polévky*), one of the region's culinary strong points and mainly served at lunchtimes. Posher restaurants will have a serious selection of **starters** (*předkrmy*), such as *uzený jazyk* (smoked tongue), *tresčí játra* (cod's liver) or perhaps *kaviárové vejce* (a hard-boiled egg with caviar on top). *Šunková rolka* is another favourite, consisting of ham topped with whipped cream and horseradish. You're more likely, though, to find yourself skipping the starters, which are usually little more than a selection of cold meats.

Main courses tend to be divided into several separate sections. *Hotová jídla* (ready-made meals), which should arrive swiftly, and *jídla na objednávku* or *minutky* (meals made to order), for which you'll have to wait. In either case, dishes are overwhelmingly based on **meat** (*maso*), usually pork, sometimes beef. The Czechs are experts on these meats, and although the quality could often be better, the variety of sauces and preparative techniques is usually good. The difficulty lies in decoding names such as *klašterny tajemství* ("mystery of the monastery") or even a common dish like *Moravský vrabec* (literally "Moravian sparrow", but actually just roast pork).

Fish (*ryby*) is generally listed separately, or along with chicken (*drůbez*) and other fowl like duck (*kachna*). River trout (*pstruh*) and carp (*kapr*) – the traditional dish at Christmas – are the cheapest and most widely available fish, and, although their freshness may be questionable, they are usually served, grilled or roasted, in delicious buttery sauces or breadcrumbs.

Side dishes (*přílohy*), most commonly served with fish and fowl, generally consist of potatoes (*brambory*), though with meat dishes you'll more often be served **dumplings** (*knedlíky*), one of the mainstays of Bohemian cooking. The term itself is misleading for English-speakers, since they resemble nothing like the English dumpling – more like a heavy white bread. *Houskové knedlíky* are

Vegetarians

Czech meat consumption has dropped dramatically since 1989, but it remains one of the highest in the world. It's hardly suprisingly then that **vegetarianism** is still a minority sport. Needless to say, you're better off in Prague than anywhere else in the country. For a start, places which cater mostly for expats usually have one or two veggie options, and there are plenty of pizzerias.

Even in traditional Czech places, most menus have a section called *bezmasa* (literally "without meat") – don't take this too literally, though, for it simply means the main ingredient is not dead animal; dishes like *omeleta se šunkou* (ham omelette) can appear under these headings, so always check first. The staple of Czech vegetarianism is *smažený syr*, a slab of melted cheese, deep-fried in breadcrumbs and served with tartar sauce (*tartarská omačka*) – beware, though, as it's sometimes served *se šunkou* (with ham). Other types of cheese can also be deep fried, as can other vegetables: *smažené žampiony* (mushrooms) and *smaženy květák* (cauliflower). Emergency veggie standbys which most Czech pubs will knock up for you without too much fuss include *knedlíky s vejci* (dumplings and scrambled egg) or *omeleta s hráskem* (pea omelette).

Veggie phrases to remember are *"jsem vegeterián/vegeteriánka. Máte nejaké bezmasa?"* (I'm a vegetarian. Is there anything without meat?); for emphasis, you could add *"nejím maso nebo ryby"* (I don't eat meat or fish).

---

made from flour and come in large slices (four or five to a dish), while *bramborové knedlíky* are smaller and made from potato and flour. Occasionally, you may be treated to *ovocné knedlíky* (fruit dumplings), the king of *knedlíky* and usually served with melted butter and soured cream as a sweet main course.

Fresh **salads** rarely rise above the ubiquitous *obloha*, usually a bit of tomato, cucumber and lettuce, or cabbage (*zeli*), often swimming in a slightly sweet, watery dressing. *Šopský* salads, made with a feta-like cheese, are a pale imitation of Greek salads (without olives), but are generally fresher and more substantial than most other salads on offer.

With the exception of *palačinky* (pancakes) filled with chocolate or fruit and cream, **desserts** (*moučníky*), where they exist at all, can be pretty unexciting.

Drinking

Traditional Czech **pubs** are smoky, male-dominated places, where 99 percent of the customers are drinking copious quantities of Czech beer by the half-litre. If you want a more mixed environment, you're better off heading for a wine cellar or café, where you'll get a better selection of wine and spirits, but probably only bottled beer.

Coffee and tea

Coffee (*káva*) is drunk black and is usually available in espresso (*presso*) form: small, black and strong, though by no means as diminutive as in Italy. Occasionally, you may still come across the original pre-1989 Czech coffee, called somewhat hopefully *turecká* (Turkish) – it's really just hot water poured over coffee grains. Downmarket *bufets* sell *ledová káva*, a weak, cold black coffee, while at the other end of the scale *Viděňská káva* (Viennese coffee) is a favourite with the older generation, served with a dollop of whipped cream. Another rather rich option is a mix with advocaat, *Alžírská káva*.

Tea (*čaj*) is drunk weak and without milk, although you'll usually be given a glass of boiling water and a tea bag so you can do your own thing – for milk, say *"s mlékem"*. If you want really good tea, you should look out for a *čajovna*, one of the country's growing number of tea-houses: calm, no-smoking cafés that take their tea drinking very seriously.

Beer

Alcohol consumption among Czechs has always been high, and in the decade following the events of 1968 it doubled, as a whole generation found solace in drinking, mostly beer (*pivo*). The Czechs have been top of the world league table of beer consumption for some time now, though it's a problem that seldom spills out onto the streets; violence in pubs is uncommon and you won't see that many drunks in public.

Czech beer ranks among the best in the world and the country remains the true home of most of the lager drunk around the world today. It was in the Bohemian city of Plzeň (Pilsen) that the first **bottom-fermented** beer was introduced in 1842, after complaints from the citizens about the quality of the top-fermented predecessor. The new brewing style quickly spread to Germany, and is now blamed for the bland rubbish served up in the English-speaking world as lager or Pils.

The distinctive flavour of Czech beer comes from the famous hand-picked Bohemian **hops** known as Žatec (Saaz) Red, the Moravian **barley**, and the soft local water; it should then be served with a high content of absorbed carbon dioxide – hence the thick, creamy head. Under the Communists, brewing methods in the Czech Republic remained stuck in the old ways, but the 1990s saw many breweries opt for modernization: pasteurization, de-oxidization, rapid maturation and carbon dioxide injections – all of which mean less taste, more fizz. Nowadays, it's actually quite hard to find a pub that serves Czech beer the way it should be – your best bet is to opt for the local beer and, if possible, head for the brewery tap.

Beer is served by the half-litre; if you want anything smaller, you must specifically ask for a *malé pivo* (0.3 litres). The average jar is medium strength, usually about 1050 specific gravity or 4.2 percent alcohol. Somewhat confusingly, the Czechs class their beers using the **Balling scale**, which measures the original gravity, calculated according to the amount of malt and dissolved sugar present before fermentation. The most common varieties are 10° (*desítka*), which is generally slightly weaker than 12° (*dvanáctka*). Light beer (*světlé*) is the norm, but many pubs also serve a slightly sweeter dark variety (*černé*) – or, if you prefer, you can have a mixture of the two (*řezané*).

Wine and spirits

Czech **wine** (*víno*) will never win over as many people as has Czech beer, but since the import of French and German vines in the fourteenth century, it has produced a modest selection of medium-quality wines. The main wine region is South Moravia, though a little is produced around the town of Mělník (see p.163). Suffice to say that most domestic wine is pretty drinkable – Frankovka is a perfectly respectable, though slightly sweet, red; Veltlínské zelené a good, dry white – and rarely much more than 60Kč a bottle in shops, while the best stuff can only be had from the private wine cellars (*sklepy*), hundreds of which still exist out in the regions. A Czech speciality to look out for is *burčák*, a very young, fizzy, sweet, misty wine of varying (and often very strong) alcoholic content, which appears on the streets in the vine harvest season for three weeks in September.

All the usual **spirits** are on sale and known by their generic names, with rum and vodka dominating the market. The home production of brandies is a national pastime, which results in some almost terminally strong liquors. The most renowned of the lot is *slivovice*, a

---

Czech etiquette

It's common practice to **share a table** with other eaters or drinkers; *je tu volno?* ("Is this seat free?") is the standard question. Waiter-service is the norm, even in pubs, so sit tight and a beer should come your way. You may have to ask to see the **menu** (*jídelní lístek*) in pubs and some cafés to indicate that you wish to eat. When food arrives for your neighbours, it's common courtesy to wish them bon appetit (*dobrou chuť*). When you want to leave, simply say *zaplatím, prosím* (literally "I'll pay, please"), and your **tab** will be totted up. A modest form of **tipping** exists in all establishments, generally done by rounding up the bill to the nearest few crowns, though beware that the waiters haven't already done this for you. On leaving, bid your neighbours farewell (*na shledanou*).

plum brandy originally from the border hills between Moravia and Slovakia. You'll probably also come across *borovička*, a popular Slovak firewater, made from pine trees; *myslivec* is a rough brandy with a firm following. There's also a fair selection of intoxicating herbal concoctions: *fernet* is a dark-brown bitter drink, known as *bavorák* (Bavarian beer) when it's mixed with tonic, while *becherovka* is a supposedly healthy herbal spirit made to a secret recipe from the Bohemian spa town of Karlovy Vary, with a very unusual, almost medicinal taste; it can also be mixed with tonic, when it's known as *beton*.

Although illegal in some parts of Europe **absinthe** has enjoyed something of a renaissance in the Czech Republic. The preferred poison of Parisian painters and poets in the nineteenth century, absinthe is a nasty green spirit made from fermented wormwood – it even gets a biblical mention in Revelation: "and the name of the star is called Wormwood: and the third part of the waters became wormwood; and many men died of the waters, because they were made bitter". St John wasn't wrong: at 170 degrees proof, it's dangerous stuff and virtually undrinkable neat. To make it vaguely palatable, you need to set light to an absinthe-soaked spoonful of sugar, and then mix the caramelized mess with the absinthe.

There's not much to say about Czech **soft drinks**, with the exception of the high-energy drink Semtex, a can of which will amuse friends back home. Last of all, if you're looking for a decent **mineral water** (*minerální voda*), ask for the ubiquitous Mattoni, a mild and not too fizzy option.

Castles, churches and museums

The Czech Republic boasts well over a thousand castles, many of which have been converted for modern use, while others have been returned to their former owners. The country's churches and monasteries are similarly blighted by years of structural neglect and, more recently, by art thefts; most now lock their doors outside worshipping hours. Museums and galleries, by contrast, thrived under the Communists, filled to the gunwales with dull propaganda. Many have bitten the dust, others have changed out of all recognition, but most are now much more interesting to visit.

Castles and guided tours

Czech castles divide into two categories: a **hrad** is a defensive castle, usually medieval in origin and character, while a **zámek** is more of a chateau, built for comfort rather than for military purposes. The basic **opening hours** for both are the same: Tuesday to Sunday 9am to noon, then 1 to 4pm or later. From the end of October to the beginning of April, most castles are closed. In April and October, opening hours are often restricted to weekends and holidays only.

Whatever the time of year, if you want to see the interior of the building, nine times out of ten you'll be compelled to go on a **guided tour** (*průvodce*) that usually lasts for an hour. More and more places are now offering a choice of tours, of varying length, and some places insist on a minimum number of people before they begin a tour. Since most tours are in Czech (occasionally German) ask for an *anglický text*, an often unintentionally hilarious English resumé of the castle's history. You may also be asked to wear special furry overshoes (*papučky*), which protect and polish the floors at the same time. Tours almost invariably set off on the hour, and the last one leaves an hour before the lunchtime break (in other words, 11am) and an hour before the final closing time. Entrance charges are still comparatively low, rarely exceeding 100Kč – only the exceptions are quoted in the text – and students and children usually get in for half-price.

Churches, monasteries and synagogues

Getting into **churches** can present something of a problem. While a few important churches operate in much the same way as museums, charging an entry fee, particularly for their crypts or cloisters, hundreds of more minor Baroque churches that litter the countryside – a legacy of the Counter-Reformation – are usually kept locked due to the enormous number of art thefts that have taken place. For the most part, you can peek inside through the railings of the porch, but the only time you can guarantee the church is fully open is just before and after services in the early morning (around 7 or 8am) and/or evening (around 6 or 7pm); times are posted outside the main doors. Otherwise, it's worth asking around for the local *kněz* (priest) or *kaplan*, who's usually only too happy to oblige with the key (*klíč*).

In the Czech Lands, widespread agnosticism and the punitive policies of the last regime (self-confessed believers were not allowed to join the Party or take up teaching posts) have left many churches in a terrible state of disrepair. A similar fate has befallen the country's **monasteries** (*klášter*), many of which were closed down by the Emperor Joseph II in the late eighteenth century, while the remainder fell prey to the Communists. Nowadays, the buildings have become schools, factories and prisons, or been returned to their former orders, but a few remain as museums, which keep similar opening hours to the country's castles.

The country's once considerable Jewish population has been whittled down to an official figure of around 2000, over half of whom live in Prague, one of only a handful of places where regular worship still takes place. A few **synagogues** and graveyards have been saved from neglect, and some are well worth visiting, such as those in Plzeň, Děčín, Kolín, Mikulov, Boskovice and Třebíč.

Museums and galleries

Czech **museums** have tended to be stronger on quantity than quality, with exclusively Czech labelling designed to baffle any passing foreigner. This is changing slowly as tourism becomes more important, and many places do have at least an *anglický text* on offer. There are two main types of museum outside Prague: a *krajské*, *okresní* or *oblastní muzeum* (district museum) traces the local history through arts, crafts and old photos, while a *městské muzeum* (town museum) is more provincial still, with stuffed animals and displays of mushrooms the only diversion. Occasionally you'll come across a real gem, but many of the local museums are far from riveting, and school groups are often the only visitors.

The big cities boast the best **art galleries** (*galerie umění*), though even the collections of Prague's Národní galerie (National Gallery)

pale in comparison with those of most major Western European and North American cities. For a start, many of the country's best artists – like Kupka and Mucha – worked abroad for much of their careers, and the majority of their works now grace the galleries of Paris and New York. However, previously unshown work from the 1950s and 60s has now found its way onto gallery walls, alongside exhibitions of up-and-coming contemporary artists.

Opening hours for museums and galleries tend to be from 9 or 10am to 4pm or later, usually without a break at lunch. Most stay open all year round and some switch from a Tuesday–Sunday summer routine to Monday–Friday during the winter. Full opening hours are detailed in the guide. Ticket prices are still negligible outside Prague, and students usually go for half-price.

Public holidays, festivals and entertainment

There are remarkably few large-scale national **festivals**. Aside from the usual religious-oriented celebrations, most annual shindigs are arts-, music- and sports-based events, confined to a particular town or city. In addition, there are also folkloric events in the nether regions, the Strážnice folk festival in Moravia being by far the most famous.

Public holidays

National holidays (*Státní svátek*) were always a potential source of contention under the Communists, and they remain controversial even today. May Day, once a nationwide compulsory march under dull Commie slogans, remains a public holiday, though only the skinheads, anarchists and die-hard Stalinists take to the streets nowadays. Of the other *slavné májové dny* (Glorious May Days), as they used to be known, May 5, the beginning of the 1945 Prague Uprising, has been binned, and VE Day is now celebrated along with the Western Allies on May 8, and not on May 9, as it was under the Communists, and still is

Public holidays

B

January 1 New Year's Day (*Nový rok*)
March/April Easter Monday (*Velikonoční pondělí*)
May 1 May Day (*Svátek práce*)
May 8 VE Day (*Den osvobození*)
July 5 Introduction of Christianity (*Den slovanských věrozvěstů Cyrila a Metoděje*)
July 6 Death of Jan Hus (*Den upálení mistra Jana Husa*)
September 28 Czech State Day (*Den české státnosti*)
October 28 Foundation of the Republic (*Den vzniku samostatného československého státu*)
November 17 Battle for Freedom and Democracy Day (*Den boje za svobodu a demokracii*)
December 24 Christmas Eve (*Štědrý den*)
December 25 Christmas Day (*Vánoce*)
December 26 Saint Stephen's Day (*Den sv Štěpana*)

in Russia. September 28, the feast day of the country's patron saint, St Wenceslas, is now Czech State Day. Strangely, however, October 28, the day on which the First Republic was founded in 1918, is still celebrated, despite being a "Czechoslovak" holiday (and, for a while, Communist Nationalisation Day).

Festivals and annual events

At **Easter** (*Velikonoce*), the age-old sexist ritual persists of whipping girls' behinds and calves with braided birch twigs tied with ribbons (*pomlázky*) – objects you'll see being furiously bought and sold from markets in the run-up to Easter Sunday. To prevent such a fate, the girls are supposed to offer the boys a coloured Easter egg and pour a bucket of cold water over them. What may once have been an innocent bucolic spring frolic has now become another excuse for Czech men to harass any woman who dares to venture onto the street during this period.

Two ancient rituals which herald the end of winter continue in some parts of the country. The "**Slaughter of the Pig**", known as *zabíjačka*, takes place in rural parts towards the end of January, traditionally a time when all other winter provisions are exhausted. Every single bit of the animal is prepared as food for the feast that accompanies the event. Halloween comes early to the Czech Republic on April 30, when the "**Burning of the Witches**" (*pálení čarodějnic*) takes place. It's an old pagan ritual, during which huge bonfires are lit across the country and old brooms are thrown

out and burned to ward off evil spirits.

As in the rest of the Christian world, **Christmas** (*Vánoce*) is a time for over-consumption and family gatherings, and is therefore a fairly private occasion. At the beginning of December, **Christmas markets** selling gifts, food and mulled wine (*svarák*) spring up in the main squares of the country's larger cities and towns. On December 4, the feast day of **St Barbara**, cherry-tree branches are bought as decorations, the aim being to get them to blossom before Christmas. On the evening of **December 5**, numerous trios, dressed up as St Nicholas (*svatý Mikuláš*), an angel and a devil, tour round the neighbourhoods, the angel handing out sweets and fruit to children who've been good, while the devil dishes out coal and potatoes to those who've been naughty. The Czech St Nicholas has white hair and a beard, and dresses not in red but in a white priest's outfit with a bishop's mitre.

With a week or so to go, large barrels are set up in the streets from which huge quantities of live *kapr* (carp), the traditional Christmas dish, are sold. **Christmas Eve** (*Štědrý večer*) is traditionally a day of fasting, broken only when the evening star appears, signalling the beginning of the Christmas feast of carp, potato salad, schnitzel and sweet breads. Only after the meal are the children allowed to open their presents, which miraculously appear beneath the tree thanks not to Santa Claus but to *Ježíšek* (Baby Jesus).

Birthdays are much less important in the Czech Republic than in English-speaking countries. Even their Czech equivalent, saints' **name days**, which fall on the same day each year, are a fading tradition. Saints' days for popular names like Jan or Anna were once practically national celebrations since everyone was bound to know at least one person with those names.

The arts

Theatre (*divadlo*) has always had a special place in Czech culture, one which the events of 1989 only strengthened. Not only did the country end up with a playwright as president, but it was the capital's theatres that served as information centres during those first few crucial weeks.

In Prague, tourists are also a lucrative source of income and there are several English-language theatre companies now based there, but outside of Prague there's obviously precious little in English. Ticket prices

Festivals diary

April
Late April to early May Brno: International Trade Fair.
Late April to early May Šumperk: home-grown Jazz Festival.

May
Early May Prague: Czech-Moravian soccer cup final at the Strahov stadium.
May 12 to June 2 Prague Spring International Music Festival.
Mid-May Olomouc: Flower Festival.
Mid-May Zlín: International Children's Film Festival.
Late May Vlčnov: Folk Festival.
Late May Prague: Puppet Festival.
Late May to early June Ostrava: Janáček International Music Festival.

June
June Olomouc: Spring Music Festival.
Mid-June Český Krumlov: Five-Petalled Rose Festival.
Mid-June Litomyšl: National Opera Festival.
Mid-June Mariánské Lázně: International Festival of Mime.
Mid-June Pelhřimov: Festival of Records and Curious Performances.
Late June to early July Strážnice: International Folk Festival.

July
July Karlovy Vary: International Film Festival.
Early July Chrudim: Puppet Festival.
Late July Uherské Hradiště: Czech/Slovak Film Festival.
Late July/early Aug Telč: International Folk Festival.

August
Early Aug Valtice: Baroque Music Festival.
Mid-Aug Domažlice: Chodové Folk Festival.
Late Aug Brno: International Grand Prix motorcycling event.
Late Aug Strakonice: Biennial International Bagpipers' Festival.

September
Early Sept Kroměříž: Chamber Music Festival.
Early Sept Žatec: Hop (and beer) Festival.
Mid-Sept Tábor: Setkání Festival.
Late Sept to early Oct Brno: International Music Festival.
Late Sept to early Oct Teplice: Beethoven Music Festival.

October
Early Oct Pardubice: Velká Pardubická steeplechase.
Early Oct Plzeň: Beer Festival.

are low, and the venue and the event itself are often interesting enough to sustain you – older-generation Czechs go as much for the interval promenade as for the show itself. There's less of a linguistic problem with **opera**, of course, and **concerts**, with Dvořák, Janáček and Smetana's works in particular all regularly performed.

With numerous permanent **puppet theatres** (*loutkové divadlo*) across the country, Czech puppetry is still very popular. Sadly, few traditional marionette or puppet-only theatres survive; the rest have introduced live actors into their repertoire, making the shows less accessible if you don't speak the language. However, this trend has produced innovative and highly professional companies like Hradec Králové's Drak (❀ www .draktheatre.cz), which has toured extensively throughout Europe and now only occasionally uses puppets in its shows.

The **cinema** (*kino*) remains a cheap and popular form of entertainment in the Czech Republic. Hollywood blockbusters form a large part of the weekly fare, but the Czech film industry continues to produce a handful of decent films each year. The majority of films are usually shown in their original language with subtitles (*titulky*) rather than dubbing (*dabing*). The month's film listings are usually fly-posted up around town or outside each cinema. Film titles are nearly always translated into Czech, so you'll need to have your wits about you to identify films such as *Prci, prci, prcičky 2* as *American Pie 2*.

Sport

For a small nation, the Czechs have a pretty good record when it comes to sporting triumphs: over the last two decades, they have consistently produced world-class tennis players, a strong national football team and several of the world's top ice hockey players. The two **sports** which pull in the biggest crowds, by far, are football and ice hockey. Getting tickets to watch a particular sport is easy (and cheap) enough on the day – only really big matches sell out. Participating in sports activities is also getting easier, though the Czechs are fairly lacklustre about the health kick.

Football

The Czech national **football** or soccer (*fotbal*) team have enjoyed mixed fortunes since splitting from the Slovaks in 1993, making the final of Euro 1996 and the semi finals of Euro 2004, but failing to qualify for the 1998 and 2002 World Cups. As with most former Eastern Bloc countries, the best home-grown players have, almost without exception, chosen to seek fame and fortune abroad since the 1990s. As a result, domestic teams usually struggle in European competitions.

The most consistent team in the *Česko-moravského liga* (❀ www.fotbal.cz) is Sparta Praha, though 2002 saw Slovan Liberec emerge as the league champions for the first time ever, followed by Baník Ostrava two years later. The season runs from August to November and March to May, and matches are usually held on Saturdays. Tickets for domestic games are around 100Kč and four-figure crowds remain the norm, but for the moment, however, the best thing about Czech football is the beer.

Ice hockey

Ice hockey (*lední hokej*) runs soccer a close second as the nation's most popular sport. It's not unusual to see kids playing their own form of the game in the street, rather than kicking a football around. As with soccer, the fall of Communism prompted an exodus by the country's best players who left to seek fame and fortune in North America's National Hockey League (NHL), most notably Jaromír Jágr. Having won Olympic gold in 1998, and three World Championships on the trot from 1999–2001, the Czech national team continue to rank among the world's top five hockey nations (❀ www.iihf.com).

Unlike in soccer, there are several teams usually in close contention for the *Extraliga* title. Games are fast and physical, cold but compelling, and can take anything up to three hours. They are held in the local *zimní stadión* (winter stadium), usually on Saturday afternoons. The season starts at the end of September and culminates in the annual World Championships, when the fortunes of the national side are subject to close scrutiny, especially if pitched against the Slovaks or the Russians.

1

Prague and around

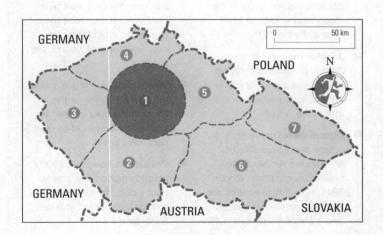

GERMANY

GERMANY

POLAND

AUSTRIA

SLOVAKIA

N

0   50 km

1
2
3
4
5
6
7

CHAPTER ONE · # Highlights

* **Pražský hrad** Perched high above the city, and the seat of power for over a millennium, Prague Castle is home to the cathedral, the royal palace, several museums and art galleries, and the president. See p.84

* **Malá Strana terraced gardens** Ornamental Baroque gardens hidden away in the steep backstreets of Malá Strana. See p.101

* **Josefov** Prague's former Jewish ghetto is still home to six synagogues and an atmospheric medieval cemetery. See p.116

* **Obecní dům** The most ornate and accessible of all Prague's Art Nouveau masterpieces, completed in 1911, now houses cafés, restaurants, exhibition spaces and a concert hall. See p.131

* **Staroměstské náměstí (Old Town Square)** Prague's busy showpiece square, dominated by the Art Nouveau Hus Monument and best known for its astronomical clock. See p.109

* **Karlův most (Charles Bridge)** The city's wonderful medieval stone bridge peppered with Baroque statuary, has been the main link between the two banks of the river for over five hundred years. See p.105

* **Veletržní palác** Prague's vast modern art gallery is the finest in the country and an architectural sight in its own right. See p.141

* **Prague tea-houses** A 1990s reaction against the smoky, boozy pub, tea-houses provide the perfect chill-out zone. See p.151

△ Obecní dům

Prague and around

With some six hundred years of architecture virtually untouched by natural disaster or war, few other cities in Europe, look as good as **Prague**. Straddling the winding River Vltava, with a steep wooded hill to one side, the city retains much of its medieval layout, the street facades remain smothered in a rich mantle of Baroque, and the historical core has successfully escaped the vanities and excesses of postwar redevelopment. During the decades of Soviet-imposed isolation, very few westerners visited Prague. However, since the 1990s, all that has changed: the city is now one of the most popular city breaks in Europe, and the streets around the main sights are jam-packed with tourists for much of the year.

Prague is surprisingly compact, its city centre divided into two unequal halves by the **River Vltava**. The steeply inclined left bank is dominated by the castle district of **Hradčany**, which contains the most obvious sights – the castle or Hrad itself, the city's cathedral, and the old royal palace and gardens – as well as a host of museums and galleries. Squeezed between the castle hill and the river are the picturesque Baroque palaces and houses of the **Malá Strana** (Little Quarter) – around 150 acres of twisting cobbled streets and secret walled gardens – home to the Czech parliament and most of the city's embassies, and dominated by the green dome and tower of the church of sv Mikuláš.

The city's twisting matrix of streets is at its most confusing in the original medieval hub of the city, **Staré Město** – (Old Town) – on the right bank of the Vltava. The Karlův most, (Charles Bridge), its main link with the opposite bank, is easily the city's most popular historical monument, and the best place from which to view Prague Castle. Staré Město's other great showpiece is its main square, Staroměstské náměstí, where you can view Prague's famous astronomical clock. Enclosed within the boundaries of Staré Město is the former Jewish quarter, or **Josefov**. The ghetto walls and slums have long since gone and the whole area was remodelled at the end of the nineteenth century, but six synagogues, a medieval cemetery and a town hall survive as powerful reminders of a community that has existed here for over a millennium.

South and east of the old town is the large sprawling district of **Nové Město**, whose main arteries make up the city's commercial and business centre. The nexus of Nové Město is Wenceslas Square (Václavské náměstí), focus of the political upheavals of the modern-day republic. Further afield lie various **suburbs**, most of which were developed only in the last hundred years or so. The single exception is **Vyšehrad**, one of the original fortress settlements of the newly arrived Slavs in the last millennium, now the final resting place of leading Czech artists of the modern age, including the composers Smetana and Dvořák.

If Prague's city centre is a revelation, the city's outer suburbs, where most of the population live, are more typical of eastern Europe: seemingly half-built, high-rise housing estates, known locally as *paneláky*, swimming in a sea of mud. However, once you're clear of the city limits, the traditional, provincial feel of **Bohemia** (Čechy) immediately makes itself felt. Many Praguers own a *chata* (country cottage) somewhere in these rural backwaters, and every weekend the roads are jammed with weekenders. Few places are more than an hour from the centre by public transport, making an easy day-trip for visitors.

The most popular destinations for foreign day-trippers are the castles of **Karlštejn** and **Konopiště**, both of which suffer from a daily swarm of coach parties. You're better rewarded by heading north, away from the hills and the crowds, to the chateaux of **Nelahozeves**, in the village of Dvořák's birth, and nearby **Veltrusy**, or to the wine town of **Mělník**. The wooded hills around **Křivoklát** in the northeast or **Kokořín** in the southwest, both around 40km from Prague, are also good places to lose the crowds. Even further afield is the undisputed gem of the region, the medieval silver-mining town of **Kutná Hora**, 60km east of Prague, with a glorious Gothic cathedral.

Prague (Praha)

The Czechs have a legend for every occasion, and the founding of **PRAGUE** is no exception. Sometime in the seventh or eighth century AD, the Czech prince Krok (aka Pace) moved his people south from the plains of the River Labe (Elbe) to the rocky knoll that is now Vyšehrad (literally "high castle"). His youngest daughter, **Libuše**, who was to become the country's first and last female leader, was endowed with the gift of prophecy. Falling into a trance one day, she pronounced that they should build a city "whose glory will touch the stars", at the point in the forest where they would find an old man constructing the threshold of his house. He was duly discovered on the Hradčany hill overlooking the Vltava, and the city was named **Praha**, meaning "threshold". Subsequently, Libuše was compelled to take a husband and again fell into a trance, this time pronouncing that they should follow her horse to a ploughman, whose descendants would rule over them. Sure enough, a man called **Přemysl** (meaning "ploughman") was discovered and became the mythical founder of the Přemyslid dynasty, which ruled Bohemia until the fourteenth century.

So much for the legend. Historically, Hradčany and not Vyšehrad appears to have been the site of the first Slav settlement. The Vltava was relatively shallow at this point, and it probably seemed a safer bet than the plains of the Labe. Under the Přemyslids the city prospered, benefiting from its position on the central European trade routes. Merchants from all over Europe came to settle here, and in 1234 the first of Prague's historic towns, the **Staré Město**, was founded to accommodate them. In 1257, King Otakar II founded the **Malá Strana** on the slopes of the castle as a separate quarter for Prague's German merchants. When the Přemyslid dynasty died out in 1306, the crown was handed over by the Czech nobles to the Luxembourgs, and it was under **Charles IV** (1346–78) that Prague enjoyed its **first golden age**. In just thirty years, Charles transformed Prague into one of the most important cities in fourteenth-century Europe, establishing institutions and buildings that survive today – the Charles University, St Vitus Cathedral, the Charles Bridge, a host of monasteries and churches – and founding an entire new town, **Nové Město**, to accommodate the influx of students and clergy.

Surprisingly enough, it was under a Habsburg, **Rudolf II** (1576–1612), that the city enjoyed its **second golden age**, inviting artists, scientists (and quacks) from all over Europe, and filling the castle galleries with the finest art. However, following the defeat of the Protestants at the 1620 **Battle of Bílá hora** (White Mountain) on the outskirts of the city, came the period the Czechs refer to as the **dark ages**, when the full force of the Counter-Reformation was brought to bear on the city's people. Paradoxically, though, the spurt of **Baroque rebuilding** during this period lent Prague its most striking architectural aspect, and the majority of the city's impressive palaces date from this period.

The next two centuries saw Prague's importance gradually whittled away within the Habsburg Empire. Two things dragged it out of the doldrums: the first was the **industrial revolution** of the mid-nineteenth century, which brought large numbers of Czechs in from the countryside to work in the factories; and the second was the contemporaneous **Czech national revival** or *národní obrození*, which gave Prague a number of symbolic monuments, such as its

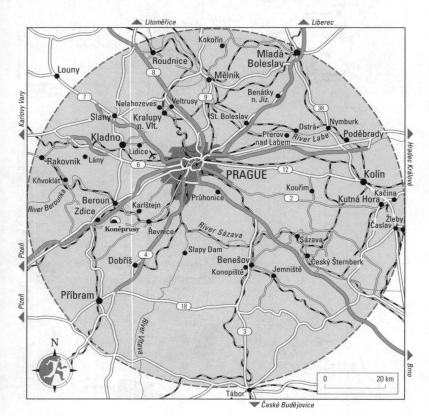

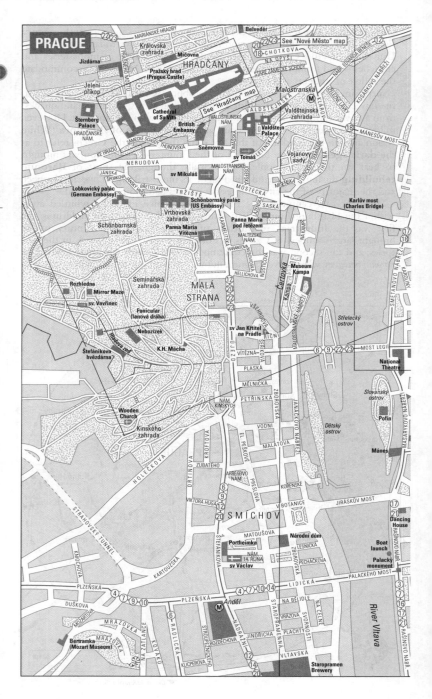

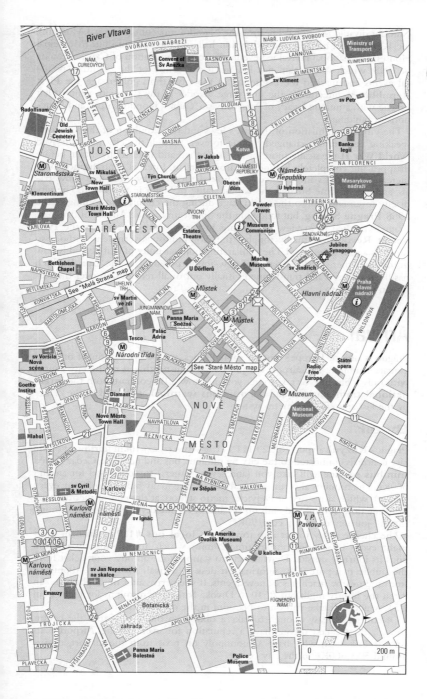

Národní divadlo (National Theatre), the Národní muzeum (National Museum), the Rudolfinum concert and exhibition hall and the Obecní dům (Municipal House). The national revival led eventually to the foundation of Czechoslovakia in 1918, which once again put Prague at the centre of the country's political events and marked the beginning of the city's third golden age, the **First Republic**. Architecturally, the first three decades of the twentieth century left Prague with a unique legacy of Art Nouveau, Cubist, Rondo-Cubist and Functionalist buildings.

The virtual annihilation of the city's Jews and the expulsion of the German-speaking community changed Prague forever, though the city itself survived **World War II** physically more or less unscathed and industrially intact, before disappearing completely behind the Iron Curtain. Internal centralization only increased the city's importance – it hosted the country's macabre show trials, and at one time boasted the largest statue of Stalin in the world. The city briefly re-emerged onto the world stage during the cultural blossoming of the **1968 Prague Spring**, but following the Soviet invasion in August of that year, Prague vanished from view once more. Just over twenty years later, the **1989 Velvet Revolution** finally toppled the Communist government without so much as a shot being fired. The exhilarating popular unity of that period is now history, but there is still a sense of new-found potential in the capital, which has been restored and transformed visually out of all recognition over the past fifteen years or so.

Arrival

Prague is one of Europe's smaller capital cities, with a population of one and a quarter million. The airport lies just over 10km northwest of the city centre, with only a bus link or taxi to get you into town. By contrast, both the **international train stations** and the main **bus terminal** are linked to the centre by the fast and efficient metro system.

By air

Prague's **Ruzyně** airport (☏220 111 111, ⓦ www.csl.cz) 10km northwest of the city centre, is connected to the city by minibus, bus and taxi. The Čedaz shared **minibus service** will take you (and several others) to your hotel for around 360Kč. The minibus also runs a scheduled service (daily 5.30am–9.30pm; every 30min), which stops first at Dejvická metro station, at the end of metro line A (journey time 20min) and ends up at náměstí Republiky (journey time 30min); the full journey currently costs 90Kč.

The cheapest way to get into town is on **local bus #119** (daily 5am–midnight; every 15–20min; journey time 20min), which stops frequently and also ends its journey outside Dejvická metro station. You can buy your ticket from the public transport (DP) information desk in arrivals (daily 7am–10pm), or from the nearby machines or newsagents. If you arrive after midnight, you can catch the hourly night bus #510 to Divoká Šárka, the terminus for night tram #51, which will take you on to Národní in the centre of town.

Of course, it's easy enough to take a **taxi** from the airport into the centre, though Prague taxi drivers have a reputation for overcharging. Airport Cars (☏220 113 892), who have a monopoly on taxis from the airport, charge around 500–600Kč to the city centre.

By train and bus

International trains arrive either at the old Art–Nouveau **Praha hlavní nádraží**, on the edge of Nové Město and Vinohrady, or at **Praha–Holešovice**, which lies in an industrial suburb north of the city centre. At both stations you'll find exchange outlets (and a branch of the PIS tourist office at Hlavní nádraží), as well as a 24-hour left-luggage office (*úschovna zavazadel*) and accommodation agencies (see p.80). Both stations are on metro lines, and Hlavní nádraží is only a five-minute walk from Václavské náměstí (Wenceslas Square). If you arrive late at night, there's even a hostel in Hlavní nádraží itself (see p.83).

Domestic trains usually wind up at Hlavní nádraží or the central **Masarykovo nádraží** on Hybernská, a couple of blocks east of náměstí Republiky. Slower trains and various provincial services arrive at a variety of obscure suburban stations: trains from the southwest pull into **Praha–Smíchov** (metro Smíchovské nádraží); trains from the east arrive at **Praha–Vysočany** (metro Českomoravská); trains from the west at **Praha–Dejvice** (metro Hradčanská); and trains from the south very occasionally rumble into **Praha–Vršovice** (tram #6 or #24 to Václavské náměstí).

Prague's main **bus** terminal is **Praha–Florenc** (metro Florenc), on the eastern edge of Nové Město, where virtually all long-distance international and domestic services terminate. It's a confusing (and ugly) place to end up, but it has a left-luggage office upstairs (daily 5am–11pm) and you can make a quick exit to the adjacent metro station. **Busabout buses** (see p.31) currently arrive at *Top Hotel* (bus #115 from metro Chodov), but check the website for the latest.

Information

Once in Prague, the main tourist office is the **Prague Information Service** or **PIS** (Pražská informační služba), whose main branch is at Na příkopě 20, Nové Město (April–Oct Mon–Fri 9am–7pm, Sat & Sun 9am–5pm; Nov–March Mon–Fri 9am–6pm, Sat & Sun 9am–3pm; Ⓦwww.prague-info.cz). There are additional PIS offices in the main train station, Praha hlavní nádraží, and within the Staroměstská radnice on Staroměstské náměstí (same hours), plus a summer-only office in the Malá Strana bridge tower on the Charles Bridge. PIS staff speak English, but their helpfulness varies enormously; however, they can usually answer most enquiries, organize accommodation, and sell maps, guides and theatre tickets.

PIS also distributes and sells some useful **listings** publications, including *Culture in Prague/Česká kultura* (Ⓦwww.ceskakultura.cz), a monthly English-language booklet listing the major events, concerts and exhibitions, *Přehled*, a more comprehensive monthly listings magazine (in Czech only) and the weekly **English-language paper**, *Prague Post* (Ⓦwww.praguepost.com), which carries selective listings on the latest exhibitions, shows, gigs and events around the capital.

The PIS should be able to furnish you with a quick free reference **map** of central Prague, but to locate a specific street, or find your way round the suburbs, you'll need a detailed city map (*plán města*). Kartografie Praha produces the cheapest and most comprehensive ones: the 1:20,000 map (available in both booklet and fold-out form), which covers the city centre as well as many of the suburbs, has a full street index and marks the metro, tram and bus routes. Maps are available from PIS offices, street kiosks, most bookshops (*knihkupectví*) and some hotels.

City transport

The centre of Prague, where most of the city's sights are concentrated, is reasonably small and best explored on foot. At some point, however, in order to cross the city quickly or reach some of the more widely dispersed attractions, you'll need to use the city's cheap and efficient **public transport** system, known as *dopravní podnik* (ⓦwww.dp-praha.cz), comprising the metro and a network of trams and buses. To get a clearer picture, it's good to invest in a city map (see p.75), which marks all the tram, bus and metro lines.

Tickets and passes

Prague's **transport system** used to have a simple ticketing system – not any more. Most Praguers simply buy monthly passes, and to avoid having to understand the complexities of the single ticket system, you too are best off buying a travel pass (for more on which, see below). To get free maps (as well as tickets and passes), head for the **information offices** of the public transport system (*dopravní podnik* or DP; ⓦwww.dp-praha.cz), at the airport (daily 7am–7pm), Nádraží Holešovice (Mon–Fri 7am–6pm), Můstek and Muzeum metro stations (daily 7am–9pm), and the Černý Most and Anděl metro stations (Mon–Fri 7am–6pm).

You can buy a **travel pass** (*časová jízdenka*) for 24 hours (*na 24 hodin*; 100Kč), three days (*na 3 dny;* 200Kč), seven days (*na 7 dní*; 250Kč) or fifteen days (*na 15 dní*; 280Kč); no photos or ID are needed, though you must write your name and date of birth on the reverse of the ticket, and punch it to validate when you first use it. Most Praguers buy a monthly (*měsíční*; 420Kč), quarterly (*čtvrtletní*; 1150Kč) or yearly (*roční*; 3800Kč) pass, for which you need ID and a passport-sized photo. All the passes are available from DP outlets, and the 24-hour pass is also available from ticket machines.

Probably the single most daunting aspect of buying a ticket is having to use the **ticket machines**, found inside all metro stations and at some bus and tram stops. Despite the multitude of buttons on the machines, for a single **ticket** (*lístek* or *jízdenka*) in the two central zones (*2 pásma*), there are just two basic choices. The 8Kč version (*zlevněná*) allows you to travel for up to fifteen minutes on the trams or buses, or up to four stops on the metro; it's known as a *nepřestupní jízdenka* (no change ticket), although you can in fact change metro lines (but not buses or trams). The 12Kč version (*plnocenná*) is valid for one hour at **peak times** (Mon–Fri 5am–8pm) – or an hour and a half off-peak – during which you may change trams, buses or metro lines as many times as you like, hence its name, *přestupní jízdenka* (changing ticket). Half-price tickets are available for children aged 6–14; under-6s travel free.

If you're buying a ticket from one of the machines, you must press the appropriate button – press it once for one ticket, twice for two and so on – followed

Prague addresses, house signs and numbers

In order to help locate **addresses** more easily, we have used the names of the city districts as they appear on street signs, for example Hradčany, Staré Město, etc. Prague's **postal districts**, which also appear on street signs, are too large to be of much help in orientation, since the city centre lies almost entirely within Prague 1.

In the older districts, many houses have retained their original medieval **house signs**, a system that is still used today, though predominantly by pubs, restaurants and wine bars, for example *U zeleného hroznu* (The Green Grape). In the 1770s, the Habsburgs, in their rationalizing fashion, introduced a numerical system, with each house in the city entered onto a register according to a strict chronology. Later, the conventional system of progressive **street numbering** was introduced; so don't be surprised if seventeenth-century pubs like *U medvídků* (The Little Bears) have, in addition to a house sign, two numbers, in this case 345 and 7; when written down the numbers are separated by a forward slash; on the building, the former Habsburg number appears on a red background, the latter modern number on blue.

by the enter (*výdej*) button, after which you put your money in. The machines do give change, but if you don't have enough coins, you may find the person on duty in the metro office by the barriers can give you change or sell you a ticket. Tickets can also be bought, en masse, and rather more easily, from a tobacconist (*tabák*), street kiosk, newsagent, PIS office or any place that displays the yellow DP sticker. When you enter the metro, or board a tram or bus, you must validate your ticket by placing it in one of the electronic machines to hand.

There's nothing to stop people from freeloading on the system of course, since there are no barriers. However, plain-clothes **inspectors** (*revizoři*) make spot checks and will issue an on-the-spot fine of 400Kč (800Kč if you don't cough up immediately) to anyone caught without a valid ticket or pass; controllers should show you their ID (a small metal disc), and give you a receipt (*paragon*).

The metro

Prague's futuristic, Soviet-built **metro** is fast, smooth and ultra-clean, running daily from 5am to midnight with trains every two minutes during peak hours, slowing down to every four to ten minutes by late in the evening. Its three lines (with a fourth planned) intersect at various points in the city centre and the route plans are easy to follow. The stations are fairly discreetly marked above ground with the metro logo, in green (line A), yellow (line B) or red (line C). The constant bleeping at metro entrances is to enable blind people to locate the escalators, which are a free-for-all, with no fast lane. Once inside the metro, it's worth knowing that *výstup* means exit and *přestup* will lead you to one of the connecting lines at an interchange. The digital clock at the end of the platform tells you what time it is and how long it was since the last train.

Trams and buses

The electric **tram** (*tramvaj*) system, in operation since 1891, negotiates Prague's hills and cobbles with remarkable dexterity. After the metro, trams are the fastest and most efficient way of getting around, running every five to eight minutes at peak times, and every five to fifteen minutes at other times – check the timetables posted at every stop (*zastávka*), which list the departure times from that specific stop.

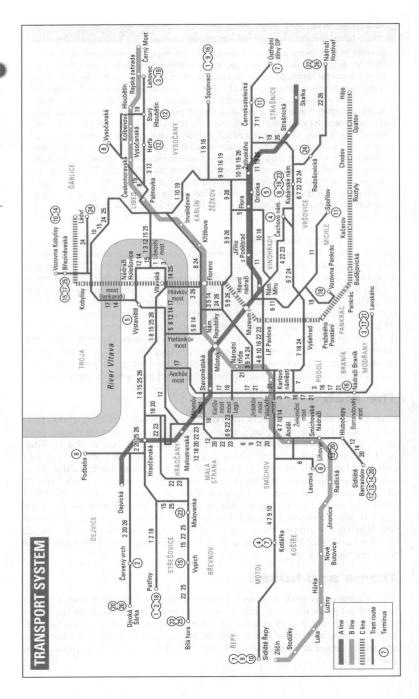

Tram #22, which runs from Vinohrady to Hradčany via the centre of town and Malá Strana, is a good way to get to grips with the lie of the land, and a cheap way of sightseeing, though you should beware of pickpockets. From Easter to October, interwar **tram #91** runs from Výstaviště to náměstí Republiky via Malá Strana (Sat & Sun hourly 1–7pm) and back again; the ride takes forty minutes and costs 15Kč. **Night trams** (*noční tramvaje*; #51–58) run roughly every thirty to forty minutes from around midnight to 4.30am; the routes are different from the daytime ones, though at some point all night trams pass along Lazarská in Nové Město.

Unless you're intent on staying in the more obscure suburbs, you'll rarely need to use Prague's **buses** (*autobusy*), which, for the most part, keep well out of the centre of town; they operate similar (though generally less frequent) hours to the trams, and route numbers are given in the text where appropriate. **Night buses** (*noční autobusy*) run just once an hour between midnight and 5am from náměstí Republiky.

Taxis, cars and bikes

Taxis come in all shapes and sizes, and, theoretically at least, are extremely cheap. However, if they think they can get away with it, many Prague taxi drivers will attempt to overcharge; the worst offenders, needless to say, hang out at the taxi ranks closest to the tourist sights. Officially, the initial fare on the meter should be around 30Kč plus 22Kč per kilometre within Prague. The best advice is to hail a cab or have your hotel or pension call you one, rather than pick one up at the taxi ranks. Two cab companies with fairly good reputations are: Profitaxi ☏261 314 151; AAA ☏233 113 311.

You really don't need a **car** in Prague, since much of the city centre is pedestrianized and the public transport system is so cheap and efficient. The city authorities, quite rightly, make it very awkward for drivers to enter the city centre, and finding a parking space is also extremely difficult. Much of the centre is pay-and-display (Mon–Sat only); illegally parked cars will either be clamped or towed away – if this happens, phone ☏158 to find out the worst. A sensible option is to park near one of the metro stations out of the centre, several of which have park-and-ride schemes: try Hradčanská, Opatov or Skalka.

Cycling is seen as more of a leisure activity in the Czech Republic, rather than a means of transport. Prague has a handful of brave cycle couriers but the combination of cobbled streets, tram lines and sulphurous air is enough to put most people off. Facilities for **bike rental** are still not that widespread, but if

---

Boats on the Vltava

In the summer months there's a regular **boat service** on the River Vltava run by the PPS (*Pražská paroplavební společnost*; ☏224 930 017, ⓦwww.paroplavba.cz) from just south of Jiráskův most on Rašínovo nábřeží (see map on p.124). In the summer three or four boats a day run to Troja (see p.146) in the northern suburbs (June–Aug daily; April, Sept & Oct Sat & Sun only; 150Kč return). There are also very infrequent services north to Mělník (see p.163) and south to Slapy via Zbraslav.

In addition, the PPS also offers **boat trips** around Prague (mid-March to Oct daily; 150–250Kč) on board a 1930s paddlesteamer. Another option is to hop aboard the much smaller boats run by Prague-Venice (☏603 819 947, ⓦwww.prague-venice .cz), which depart for a half-hour meander over to the Čertovka by Kampa island (270Kč). The boats depart from the north side of the Charles Bridge on the Staré Město bank.

you're determined to give cycling a go, head for City Bike, Královdorská 5, Staré Město ☎776 180 284; they also organize group rides through Prague.

Accommodation

Accommodation is twice as expensive in Prague as anywhere else in the country, and is still likely to be by far the largest chunk of your daily expenditure, with most half-decent hotels happily charging 5000Kč and upwards for a double room. The problem is that there's a chronic shortage of decent, inexpensive to middle-range places in Prague. At the bottom end of the scale, there are plenty of hostel beds for around 400Kč per person.

Prague is pretty busy for much of the year, and as such doesn't have much of a **low season** (Nov–March excluding New Year) – February and November are probably the quietest months. If you're going to visit anytime from Easter to September, or over the Christmas and New Year period, you need to book well in advance either directly with the hotels or through one of the specialist agencies listed on p.28. Prices are at their highest over the public holidays, but drop by as much as a third in the low season, and sometimes come down a bit in July and August when business custom is low.

If you arrive in Prague without having booked a room, there are several **accommodation agencies** you can turn to (see below), most of which will book you into either a hotel or pension, and some of which can also help you find a hostel bed or a private room in an apartment. Before agreeing to part with any money, be sure you know exactly where you're staying and check about transport to the centre – some places can be a long way out of town.

Accommodation agencies

AVE ☎251 551 011, ⌨www.avetravel.cz; hours vary but the airport desk is open daily 7am–10pm. AVE is the largest agency in Prague, with offices at the airport, both international train stations, and several points throughout the city, and is therefore an excellent last-minute fall-back. They offer rooms in a selection of hotels, pensions and hostels, plus a few private rooms.

Mary's Travel Services Italská 31, Vinohrady ☎222 254 007, ⌨www.marys.cz; metro Náměstí Míru; daily 9am–7pm. Good-value agency that will book hotels, pensions and private rooms in Prague, and a few other locations in the Czech Republic.

Pragotur Za Poříčskou bránou 7, Karlín ☎221 714 130, ⌨www.prague-info.cz. The main office is situated just across the road from Florenc bus station, but they also operate through the various PIS tourist offices (see p.75). They can book anything from hotels to hostels, but they specialize in private rooms.

Prague Accommodations ☎608 228 999, ⌨www.pragueaccommodations.com. Good choice of self-catering apartments spread across the old town, bookable online.

Hotels and pensions

Prague now boasts a huge variety of **hotels** and **pensions**, from big multinational chain hotels to places with real character in the old town. The vast majority of rooms have en-suite bathrooms and TVs, with continental breakfast either included in the price or offered as an optional extra. There's no hard and fast rule as to what constitutes a hotel and what a pension – though if you come across a "residence", then there's likely to be some kind of self-catering facility – and it's certainly not reflected in the price. Standards overall still vary somewhat unpredictably, and service with a snarl, a hangover from Communist days, and sheer incompetence, can still be encountered here and there.

With plenty of centrally located hotels, there's really no need to stay out in the suburbs unless you're on a tight budget. The quietest central areas to stay in are on the left bank in Malá Strana and Hradčany, though there's more choice, and more nightlife, in Staré Město and Nové Město. Rather than trekking around any of the places listed below on the off chance that they will have vacancies, you're better off making a reservation in advance by email or phone before you leave for Prague, or using one of the agencies listed opposite.

Hradčany and Malá Strana

Dientzenhofer Nosticova 2 ☎257 316 830, ⓦwww.dientzenhofer.cz. Birthplace of its namesake, and a very popular pension due to the fact that it's one of the few reasonably priced places (anywhere in Prague) to have wheelchair access. **7**

Dům U velké boty (The Big Shoe) Vlašská 30 ☎257 532 088, ⓦwww.dumuvelkeboty.cz. The sheer anonymity of this pension, in a lovely old building in the quiet backstreets, is one of its main draws. Run by a very friendly couple, who speak good English, it has a series of characterful, tastefully modernized rooms, some with en-suite, some without. Breakfast is extra, but worth it. **7**

Dům U zlatého koně (The Golden Horse House) Úvoz 8 ☎257532 700, ⓦwww.goldhorse.cz. Small, plain, clean, en-suite rooms at bargain prices in a perfect location on the way up to the Hrad. Breakfast is an extra 100Kč. **4**

Nosticova Nosticova 1 ☎257 312 513, ⓦwww .nosticova.com. A Baroque house with ten beautifully restored apartments replete with antique furnishings, sumptuous bathrooms and small kitchens, on a peaceful square not far from the Charles Bridge. **9**

Prague Room Nerudova 10 ☎257 532 921, ⓦwww.pragueroom.com. This is without doubt Malá Strana's most amazing bargain: a variety of well-furnished rooms, some with fab views, others with self-catering facilities. **2**

U Karlova mostu Na Kampě 15 ☎257 531 430, ⓦwww.archibald.cz. Situated on a lovely tree-lined square, just off the Charles Bridge, the rooms in this former brewery have real character, despite the modern fittings. **9**

U kříže (The Cross) Újezd 20 ☎257 313 272, ⓦwww.ukrize.com. Modern hotel on a busy street in the south of Malá Strana; cheap considering the location, just make sure you don't get a room overlooking the tram tracks. **6**

U žluté boty (The Yellow Boot) Jánský vršek 11 ☎257 532 269, ⓦwww.zlutabota.cz. Hidden away in a lovely old backstreet, this Baroque hotel has real character: the odd original ceiling, exposed beams, and in one room, a ceramic stove and authentic wood-panelling. **8**

Staré Město

Avalon-Tara Havelská 15 ☎224 228 083,ⓦwww .prague-hotel.ws; metro Můstek. Perfect location right over the market on Havelská, with seven very small, plainly furnished but clean rooms, with or without en-suite facilities. **6**

Betlém Club Betlémské náměstí 9 ☎222 221 574, ⓦwww.betlemclub.cz; metro Národní třída. Small rooms, but acceptable decor, plus a Gothic cellar for breakfast, and a perfect location on a quiet square at the heart of the old town – service can be flaky, so book ahead and make sure you get confirmation. **7**

Černá liška (The Black Fox) Mikulášská 2 ☎224 232 250, ⓦwww.cernaliska.cz; metro Staroměstská. Well-appointed rooms, all with lovely wooden floors, some with incredible views onto Old Town Square, quieter ones at the back. **9**

Cloister Inn Konviktská 14 ☎224 211 020, ⓦwww. cloister-inn.com; metro Národní třída. Pleasant, well-equipped hotel housed in a nunnery in one of the backstreets; the rooms are basic, but the location is good. There are even cheaper rooms in the *Pension Unitas*, in the same building (see below). **8**

Expres Skořepka 5 ☎224 211 801, ⓦwww .hotel-expres.com; metro Národní třída. Friendly little hotel with few pretensions: cheap and cheerful fittings, low prices and an excellent location right in the centre of Staré Město. **6**

Josef Rybná 20 ☎221 700 111, ⓦwww.hoteljosef .com. This designer hotel exudes modern professionalism, the lobby is a symphony in off-white efficiency and the rooms continue the crisply maintained minimalist theme. **9**

U medvídků (The Little Bears) Na Perštýně 7 ☎224 211 916, ⓦwww.umedvidku.cz; metro Národní třída. The rooms above this famous Prague pub are plainly furnished, quiet considering the locale, and therefore something of an Old Town bargain; booking ahead essential. **7**

Unitas Bartolomějská 9 ☎224 211 020, ⓦwww .unitas.cz; metro Národní třída. Set in a Franciscan nunnery, the *Unitas* offers both simple twins and bargain dorm beds in its "Art Prison Hostel", converted secret-police prison cells (Havel stayed in P6). No smoking or drinking, but unbelievably cheap. **3**

Nové Město

Alcron Štepánska 40 ☎ 222 820 000, ⓦ www
.radisson.com; metro Muzeum/Můstek. Giant
1930s luxury hotel, just off Wenceslas Square, that
has been superbly restored to its former Art Deco
glory by the Radisson SAS chain. Double rooms
here start at around 9000Kč and are without doubt
the most luxurious and tasteful you'll find in Nové
Město. ❾

Grand Hotel Evropa Václavské nám. 25 ☎ 224
215 387, ⓦ www.evropahotel.cz; metro Muzeum.
Potentially the most beautiful hotel in Prague, built
in the 1900s and sumptuously decorated in Art
Nouveau style. Yet despite its prime location and
its incredible decor, this place is run like an old
Communist hotel – a blast from the past in every
sense. The rooms are furnished in repro Louis XIV,
and there are some cheaper ones without en-suite
facilities. ❽

Imperial Na poříčí 15 ☎ 222 316 012, ⓦ www
.hotelimperial.cz; metro náměstí Republiky. The
café on the ground floor is a 1914 period piece;
the vast hotel/hostel above it is much more basic
– clean, simply furnished doubles, triples and
quads with shared facilities only. ❹

Jerome House V jirchářích 13 ☎ 224 911 011,
ⓦ www.jerome.cz; metro Národní třída. Discreetly
tucked away in a nice, quiet area just south of
Národní, the *Jerome* offers plain, clean, bright
rooms with upbeat, modern design, plus the odd
original feature. ❼

Salvator Truhlářská 10 ☎ 222 312 234, ⓦ www
.salvator.cz; metro náměstí Republiky. Very good
location for the price, just a minute's walk from
nám. Republiky, with small but clean rooms (the
cheaper ones without en-suite facilities), and a
sports bar on the ground floor; advance booking
advisable. ❹

Further afield

Alpin Velehradská 25, Žižkov ☎ 222 723 551,
ⓦ www.alpin.cz; metro Jiřího z Poděbrad. Clean,
bare, bargain rooms on the edge of Vinohrady and
Žižkov. ❶

City Belgická 10, Vinohrady ☎ 222 521 606,
ⓦ www.hotelcity.cz; metro náměstí Míru. Quiet
Vinohrady locale with cheap, clean rooms, some
en-suite doubles and family suites, all within walking distance of the top of Wenceslas Square. ❹

Crowne Plaza Koulova 15, Dejvice ☎ 224 393
111, ⓦ www.crowneplaza.cz; tram #8 from metro
Dejvická to Podbaba terminus. Prague's classic
1950s Stalinist wedding-cake hotel, with its dour
socialist realist friezes and large helpings of marble, is now run by Austrians. ❽

Triška Vinohradská 105 ☎ 222 727 313, ⓦ www
.hotel-triska.cz; metro Jiřího z Poděbrad. Large
turn-of-the-twentieth-century hotel with comfortable rooms; they've made an effort with the interior
decor, the service is good and it's close to the
metro. ❺

Hostels

There are a fair few **hostels** in Prague which cater for the large number of
backpackers who hit the city all year round – and these are supplemented
further by a whole host of more transient, high-season-only hostels. Prices in
hostels range from 200Kč to 600Kč for a bed, usually in a dormitory. A few
operate curfews – it's worth asking before you commit yourself – and, although
many rent out blankets and sheets, it's as well to bring your own sleeping bag.
Note that some of the accommodation agencies in Prague also deal with hostels; see p.80 for details.

Some Prague hostels give discounts to HI (Hostelling International; ⓦ www
.hihostels.com), and a few can be booked via the HI's online booking service,
including the centrally located **Traveller's Hostels**, whose chain of hostels are
particularly popular with US students. Their main booking office is at Dlouhá
33, Staré Město (☎ 224 826 662, ⓦ www.travellers.cz), where there is also a
hostel (see opposite); dorm beds go for 350Kč and upwards per person.

Prague's university, the Karolinum, rents out over a thousand very basic **student rooms** from June to mid-September, starting at around 200Kč for a bed.
Go to the central booking office at Voršilská 1, Nové Město (Mon–Fri only;
☎ 224 933 825; metro Národní třída).

Apple Královodvorská 16, Staré Město ☎ 222 231 050, ⓦ www.applehostel.cz; Náměstí Republiky. Everything from en-suite doubles to twelve-bed dorms in this clean and friendly old town hostel right on Náměstí Republiky. Doubles from 650Kč, dorm beds from 370Kč; breakfast included.

Clown and Bard Bořivojova 102, Žižkov ☎ 222 716 453, ⓦ www.crownandbard.com; tram #5, #9 or #26 from metro Hlavní nádraží to Husinecká stop. Žižkov hostel that's so laid-back it's horizontal, and not a place to go if you don't like partying. Nevertheless, it's clean, undeniably cheap, stages events and has laundry facilities. Doubles from 900Kč, dorm beds from 250Kč.

Hostel Týn Týnská 19, Staré Město ☎ 224 808 333, ⓦ www.hosteltyn.web2001.cz; metro Náměstí Republiky. The most centrally located hostel, just metres from Old Town Square. Doubles from 1200Kč, six-bed dorms 400Kč.

Klub Habitat Na Zderaze 10, Nové Mesto ☎ 224 921 706, ⓦ www.hotelline.cz; metro Karlovo náměstí. One of the best hostels in Prague, offering a discount to HI members. Book ahead. Doubles from 1000Kc, dorm beds from 400Kc.

Sir Toby's Hostel Dělnická 24, Holešovice ☎ 283 870 635, ⓦ www.sirtobys.com; tram #1, #5, #25 or #26 from metro Vltavská. Out in Holešovice, but Sir Toby's is among the most welcoming and efficiently run hostels in the city and the centre is only a tram ride away. Dorm beds from 340Kč, doubles from 1200Kč.

Traveller's Hostel Dlouhá 33, Staré Město ☎ 224 826 662, ⓦ www.travellers.cz; metro Náměstí Republiky. Very centrally located partying hostel and booking office above the Roxy nightclub – if there's not enough room here, they'll find you a dorm bed somewhere for around 400Kč. Doubles from 1250Kč.

Vesta Wilsonova 8, Nové Město ☎ 224 617 118, ⓦ www.ckvesta.cz; metro Hlavní nádraží. A good last resort if you arrive in the main train station (Praha hlavní nádraží) late at night, this hostel is in the station itself; functional doubles from 600Kč, and you can ask for sole occupancy.

Campsites

Prague abounds in **campsites** – there's a whole rash of them in Troja (see p.146) – and most are relatively easy to get to on public transport. Facilities, on the whole, are rudimentary and poorly maintained, but the prices reflect this, starting at around 300Kč for a tent and two people.

Džbán SK Aritma, Nad lávkou 5, Vokovice ⓦ www .camp.cz/dzban; tram #20 or #26 from metro Dejvická to Nad Džbánem stop, 15min from tram stop and 4km west of the centre, near the Šárka valley. Large field with tent pitches, bungalows, shop, restaurant, tennis courts, lake swimming and gym. Open all year.

Herzog Trojská 161, Troja ☎ 283 850 472, ⓦ www .campherzog.cz; bus #112 from metro Nádraží Holešovice. Good location, one of several along the road to Troja chateau, situated in someone's large back garden, April–Oct.

Kotva U ledáren 55, Braník ☎ 244 461 712, ⓦ www.kotvacamp.cz; tram #3, #16, #17 or #21 from Karlovo náměstí metro to Nádraží Braník stop. The oldest, and nicest, site, with a riverside location twenty minutes by tram south of the city. Open April–Oct.

Sokol Troja Trojská 171a, Troja ☎ 233 542 908, ⓦ www.camp-sokol-troja.cz; bus #112 from metro Nádraží Holešovice. Well-organized site along the road to the Troja chateau and zoo; kitchen, laundry and restaurant on site. Open all year.

Hradčany

HRADČANY is wholly dominated by the city's omnipresent landmark, **Prague Castle**, or Pražský hrad, the vast hilltop complex that looks out over the city centre from the west bank of the River Vltava. Site of a Slav settlement in the seventh or eighth century AD, there's been a castle here since at least the late ninth century, and since then whoever has had control of the Hrad has exercized authority over the Czech Lands. It continues to serve as the seat of the president, though the public are free to wander round from the early hours until late at night, since the castle is also home to several museums and galleries.

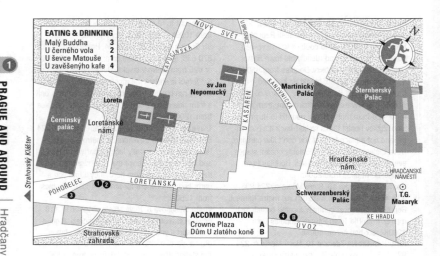

The rest of the castle district, or Hradčany, has always been a mere appendage, its inhabitants serving and working for their masters in the Hrad. Even now, despite the odd restaurant or *pivnice* (pub) in amongst the palaces (and even in the Hrad itself), there's very little real life here beyond the stream of tourists who trek through the castle and the civil servants who work either for the president or the government, whose departmental tentacles spread right across Hradčany and down into neighbouring Malá Strana. All of this makes it a very peaceful and attractive area in which to take a stroll, and lose the crowds who crawl all over the Hrad.

Stretched out along a high spur above the River Vltava, Hradčany shows a suitable disdain for the public transport system. There's a choice of **approaches** from Malá Strana, all of which involve at least some walking. From Malostranská metro station, most people take the steep short cut up the Staré zámecké schody, which brings you into the castle from its rear end. A better approach is up the stately Zámecké schody, where you can stop and admire the view, before entering the castle via the main gates. From April to October, you might also consider coming up through Malá Strana's wonderful terraced gardens, which are connected to the castle gardens (see p.101). The alternative to all this climbing is to take tram #22 or #23 from Malostranská metro, which tackles the hairpin bends of Chotkova with ease, and deposits you either outside the Královská zahrada (Royal Gardens) to the north of the Hrad, or, if you prefer, outside the gates of the Strahovský klášter (monastery), at the far western edge of Hradčany.

Pražský hrad (Prague Castle)

Viewed from the Charles Bridge, **Pražský hrad** (known to the Czechs simply as the Hrad), stands aloof from the rest of the city, protected, not by bastions and castellated towers, but by a rather austere palatial facade – an "immense unbroken sheer blank wall", as Hilaire Belloc described it – above which rises the great Gothic mass of St Vitus Cathedral. It's the picture-postcard image of Prague, and is spectacularly lit-up at night, though for the Czechs the castle has been an object of disdain as much as admiration, its alternating fortunes mirroring the shifts in

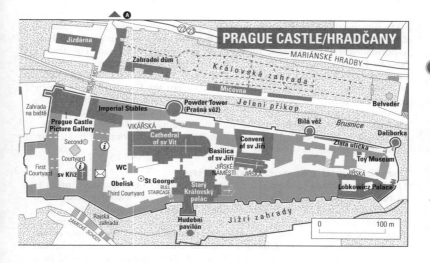

the nation's history. The golden age of Charles IV and Rudolf II and the dark ages of the later Habsburgs, interwar democracy and Stalinist terror – all have emanated from the Hrad. When the first posters appeared in December 1989 demanding "HAVEL NA HRAD" ("Havel to the Castle"), they weren't asking for his reincarceration. Havel's occupancy of the Hrad was the sign that the reins of government had finally been wrested from the Communist regime.

Visiting the castle

Pražský hrad (ⓦwww.hrad.cz) is open daily April–October 5am–midnight, November–March 6am–11pm; sights within the castle (unless otherwise stated) are open daily April–October 9am–5pm, November–March 9am–4pm.

You can wander freely through most of the streets, courtyards and gardens of the castle and watch the changing of the guard without a ticket. There are two main types of multi-entry **ticket** available for the sights within the castle: **Route A** (350Kč), which gives you entry to most of the sights within the castle apart from the art galleries: the choir, crypt and tower of the cathedral, the Old Royal Palace, the Basilica of sv Jiří, the Prašná věž (Powder Tower), and the Zlatá ulička; and **Route B** (220Kč), which only covers the cathedral, the Old Royal Palace and the Zlatá ulička. Tickets are available from the main information centre in the third courtyard, opposite the cathedral, where you can also hire an audioguide (in English) for another 200Kč for two hours.

The art collections of the Jiřský klášter and the Obrazárna Pražského hradu, the toys at the Muzeum hraček, the museum in the Lobkovický palác, and the exhibitions held in Císařská konírna and Jízdárna, all have different opening hours and separate admission charges.

Within the castle precincts there are several cafés and restaurants, which are not quite as extortionate as you might expect from their location. If you simply want a quick cup of coffee and a place to write some postcards, head for the *Café Poet*, which has tables outside in the shade and is hidden away in the peaceful and little-visited Zahrada na baště.

The site has been successively built on since the Přemyslid princes erected the first castle here in the ninth century, but two **architects** in particular bear responsibility for the present outward appearance of the Hrad. The first is **Nicolo Pacassi**, court architect to Empress Maria Theresa, whose austere restorations went hand in hand with the deliberate run-down of the Hrad until it was little more than an administrative barracks. For the Czechs, his grey-green eighteenth-century cover-up, which hides a variety of much older buildings, is unforgivable. Less apparent, though no less controversial, is the hand of **Josip Plečnik**, the Slovene architect who was commissioned by T.G. Masaryk, president of the newly founded Czechoslovak Republic, to restore and modernize the castle in his highly distinctive style in the 1920s.

The first and second courtyards

The **first courtyard** (první nádvoří), which opens on to Hradčanské náměstí, is guarded by Ignaz Platzer's blood-curdling *Battling Titans* – two gargantuan figures, one on each of the gate piers, wielding club and dagger and about to inflict fatal blows on their respective victims. Below them stand a couple of impassive presidential sentries, sporting blue uniforms that deliberately recall those of the First Republic. The hourly **Changing of the Guard** is a fairly subdued affair, but every day at noon there's a much more elaborate parade, accompanied by a brass ensemble which appears at the first-floor windows to play a gentle, slightly comical, modern fanfare.

To reach the **second courtyard** (druhé nádvoří), you must pass through the early Baroque Matyášova brána (Matthias Gate), originally a freestanding triumphal arch in the middle of the long since defunct moat, now set into one of Pacassi's blank walls. Grand stairways on either side lead to the presidential apartments in the south wing, and to the **Španělský sál** (Spanish Hall) and the **Rudolfova galerie** (Rudolf Gallery) in the north wing – two of the most stunning rooms in the entire complex. Sadly, both are generally out of bounds, though concerts are occasionally held in the Španělský sál.

Surrounded by monotonous Pacassi plasterwork, the courtyard itself is really just a through-route to the cathedral. The most visible intrusion is Anselmo Lurago's **chapel of sv Kříž**, which cowers in one corner. Its richly painted interior, dating mostly from the mid-nineteenth century, used to house the cathedral treasury, a macabre selection of medieval reliquaries. In the north wing of the courtyard are the former **Císařská konírna** (Imperial Stables), which still boast their original, magnificent Renaissance vaulting dating from the reign of Rudolf II, and are now used to house temporary exhibitions (Tues–Sun 10am–6pm).

Obrazárna Pražského hradu (Prague Castle Picture Gallery)

The remnants of the imperial collection, begun by the Habsburg Emperor Rudolf II, are housed in the **Obrazárna Pražského hradu** (daily 10am–6pm), opposite the old imperial stables. The surviving collection is definitely patchy, but it does contain one or two masterpieces that are well worth seeing, and visiting the gallery is a great way to escape the castle crowds. One of the collection's finest paintings is **Rubens**' richly coloured *Assembly of the Gods at Olympus*, featuring a typically voluptuous Venus and a slightly fazed Jupiter. The illusionist triple portrait of Rudolf (when viewed from the left), and his Habsburg predecessors (when viewed from the right), by Paulus Roy, is typical of the sort of tricksy work that appealed to the emperor. Even more famous is the surrealist portrait of Rudolf by Giuseppe Arcimboldo, portraying him as a collage of fruit, with his eyes as cherries, cheeks as apples and hair as grapes. Elsewhere, there's an early, very beautiful *Young Woman at her Toilet* by **Titian**, and a superbly observed *Portrait of a Musician* by one of his pupils, Bordone. **Veronese**'s best offering is his portrait of his friend Jakob König, a German art dealer in Venice, who worked for, among others, Rudolf II. Look out, too, for **Tintoretto**'s *Flagellation of Christ*, a late work in which the artist makes very effective and dramatic use of light.

St Vitus Cathedral

St Vitus Cathedral (chram sv Víta) is squeezed so tightly into the third court-yard that it's difficult to get an overall impression of this chaotic Gothic edifice. Its asymmetrical appearance is the product of a long and chequered history, for although the foundation stone was laid in 1344, the cathedral was not completed until 1929 – exactly 1000 years after the death of Bohemia's most famous patron saint, Wenceslas.

The inspiration for the medieval cathedral came from Emperor Charles IV, who, while still only heir to the throne, had not only wangled an independent archbishopric for Prague, but had also managed to gather together the relics of Saint Vitus. Inspired by the cathedral at Narbonne, Charles commissioned the Frenchman **Matthias of Arras** to start work on a similar structure. Matthias died eight years into the job in 1352, with the cathedral barely started, so Charles summoned **Peter Parler**, a precocious 23-year-old from a family of great German masons, to continue the work, but the cathedral got no further than the construction of the choir and the south transept before his death in 1399.

Little significant work was carried out during the next four centuries, and the half-built cathedral became a symbol of the Czechs' frustrated aspirations of nationhood. Not until the Czech national revival (*národní obrození*) of the nineteenth century did building begin again in earnest, with the foundation, in 1859, of the **Union for the Completion of the Cathedral**. A succession of architects, including Josef Mocker and Kamil Hilbert, oversaw the completion of the entire west end, and with the help of countless other Czech artists and sculptors, the building was transformed into a treasure-house of Czech art. The cathedral was finally given an official opening ceremony in 1929, though in fact work continued right up to and beyond World War II.

The sooty Prague air has made it hard now to differentiate between the two building periods. Close inspection, however, reveals that the **western facade**, including the twin spires, sports the rigorous if unimaginative work of the neo-Gothic restorers (their besuited portraits can be found below the rose window), while the **eastern section** – best viewed from the Belvedér – shows the building's authentic Gothic roots. The south door (see Zlatá brána, p.89) is also pure Parler. Oddly then, it's above the south door that the cathedral's tallest steeple reveals the most conspicuous stylistic join: Pacassi's Baroque topping resting absurdly on a Renaissance parapet of light stone, which is itself glued onto the blackened body of the original Gothic tower.

The nave

The cathedral is the country's largest, and once inside, it's difficult not to be impressed by the sheer height of the **nave**. This is the newest part of the building, and, consequently, is decorated mostly with twentieth-century furnishings. The most arresting of these is the cathedral's modern **stained-glass** windows, which on sunny days send shafts of rainbow light into the nave. The effect is stunning, though entirely out of keeping with Parler's original concept, which was to have almost exclusively clear-glass windows. The most unusual windows are those by František Kysela, which look as though they have been shattered into hundreds of tiny pieces, a technique used to greatest effect in the rose window over the west door with its kaleidoscopic *Creation of the World* (1921). In keeping with its secular nature, two of the works from the time of the First Republic were paid for by financial institutions: the *Cyril and Methodius* window, in the third chapel in the north wall, was commissioned from Art Nouveau artist Alfons Mucha by the Banka Slavie; while on the opposite side of the nave, the window on the theme *Those Who Sow in Tears Shall Reap in Joy* was sponsored by a Prague insurance company.

Of the cathedral's 22 side chapels, the grand **Chapel of sv Václav**, by the south door, is easily the main attraction. Although officially dedicated to St Vitus, spiritually the cathedral belongs as much to the Přemyslid prince, Václav (Wenceslas, of Good King fame; see box below), the country's patron saint, who was killed by his pagan brother, Boleslav the Cruel. Ten years later, in 939, Boleslav repented, converted, and apparently transferred his brother's remains to this very spot. Charles, who was keen to promote the cult of Wenceslas in order to cement his own Luxembourgeois dynasty's rather tenuous claim to the Bohemian throne, had Peter Parler build the present chapel on top of the original grave; the lion's head **door-ring** set into the north door is said to be the one to which Václav clung before being killed. The chapel's rich, almost Byzantine decoration is like the inside of a jewel casket: the gilded walls are inlaid with semi-precious Bohemian stones, set around ethereal fourteenth-century frescoes of the Passion; meanwhile the tragedy of Wenceslas unfolds above the cornice in the later paintings of the Litoměřice school.

Though a dazzling testament to the golden age of Charles IV's reign, it's not just the chapel's artistic merit which draws visitors. A door in the south wall gives access to a staircase leading to the coronation chamber (closed to the public) which houses the **Bohemian crown jewels**, including the gold crown of Saint Wenceslas, studded with some of the largest sapphires in the world. Closed to the public since 1867, the door is secured by seven different locks, the keys kept by seven different people, starting with the president himself – like the

Good King Wenceslas

As it turns out, there's very little substance to the story related in the nineteenth-century Christmas carol, *Good King Wenceslas looked out*, by J.M. Neale, itself a reworking of the medieval carol *Tempus adest floridum*. For a start, **Václav** was only a duke and never a king (though he did become a saint); he wasn't even that "good", except in comparison with the rest of his family; the St Agnes fountain, by which "yonder peasant dwelt", wasn't built until the thirteenth century; and he was killed a full three months before the Feast of Stephen (Boxing Day) – the traditional day for giving to the poor, hence the narrative of the carol.

Born in 907, Václav inherited his title at the tender age of thirteen. His Christian grandmother, Ludmilla, was appointed regent in preference to Drahomíra, his pagan mother, who had Ludmilla murdered in a fit of jealousy the following year. On coming of age in 925, Václav became duke in his own right and took a vow of celibacy, intent on promoting Christianity throughout the dukedom. Even so, the local Christians didn't take to him, and when he began making conciliatory overtures to the neighbouring Germans, they persuaded his pagan younger brother, Boleslav the Cruel, to do away with him. On September 20, 929, Václav was stabbed to death by Boleslav at the entrance to a church just outside Prague.

seven seals of the holy scroll from Revelation. Replicas of the crown jewels can be seen in the Lobkovický palác (see p.92).

The chancel and crypt

Having sated yourself on the Chapel of sv Václav, buy a ticket from the nearby box office and head off to the north choir aisle – the only place where you can currently enter the **chancel**. Slap bang in the middle of the ambulatory, close to the Saxon Chapel, is the perfect Baroque answer to the medieval Chapel of sv Václav, the **Tomb of St John of Nepomuk**, plonked here in 1736. It's a work of grotesque excess, designed by Johann Bernhard Fischer von Erlach's son, Johann Michael, and sculpted in solid silver with free-flying angels holding up the heavy drapery of the baldachin. Where Charles sought to promote Wenceslas as the nation's preferred saint, the Jesuits, with Habsburg backing, replaced him with another Czech martyr, John of Nepomuk (Jan Nepomucký), who had been arrested, tortured, and then thrown – bound and gagged – off the Charles Bridge in 1393 on the orders of Václav IV, allegedly for refusing to divulge the secrets of the queen's confession. A cluster of stars was said to have appeared over the spot where he drowned, hence the halo of stars on every subsequent portrayal of the saint.

The Jesuits, in their efforts to get him canonized, exhumed his corpse and produced what they claimed to be his tongue – alive and licking, so to speak (it was in fact his very dead brain). In 1729, he duly became a saint, and, on the lid of the tomb, back-to-back with the martyr himself, a cherub points to his severed tongue, sadly no longer the "real" thing. The more prosaic reason for John of Nepomuk's death was simply that he was caught up in a dispute between the archbishop and the king over the appointment of the abbot of Kladruby, and backed the wrong side. John was tortured on the rack along with two other priests, who were then made to sign a document denying that they had been maltreated; John, however, died before he could sign, and his dead body was secretly dumped in the river. The Vatican finally admitted this in 1961, some 232 years after his canonization.

Before you leave the chancel, check out the sixteenth-century marble **Imperial Mausoleum**, situated in the centre of the choir, and surrounded by a fine Renaissance grille, on which numerous cherubs are irreverently larking about. It was commissioned by Rudolf II and contains the remains of his grandfather Ferdinand I, his Polish grandmother Queen Anne, and his father Maximilian II, the first Habsburgs to wear the Bohemian crown. Rudolf himself rests beneath them, in one of the two pewter coffins in the somewhat cramped **Royal Crypt** (Královská hrobka). Rudolf's coffin (at the back, in the centre) features yet more cherubs, brandishing quills, while the one to the right contains the remains of Maria Amelia, daughter of the Empress Maria Theresa. A good number of other Czech kings and queens are buried here, too, reinterred last century in incongruously modern 1930s sarcophagi, among them the Hussite King George of Poděbrady, Charles IV and, sharing a single sarcophagus, all four of his wives. The exit from the crypt brings you out in the centre of the nave.

In the summer months (April–Oct daily 9am–4.15pm), you can get a great view over the castle and the city from the cathedral's **Hlavná věž** (Great Tower), the entrance to which is in the south aisle – be warned, there are around three hundred steps before you reach the top. Be sure, too, to check out Parler's **Zlatá brána** (Golden Gate), over the doorway to the south transept, which is decorated with a remarkable fourteenth-century mosaic of the *Last Judgement*, recently restored to something like its original, rich colouring.

Starý královský palác (Old Royal Palace)

Across the courtyard from the Zlatá brána, the **Starý královský palác** (Old Royal Palace) was home to the princes and kings of Bohemia from the eleventh to the sixteenth centuries. It's a sandwich of royal apartments, built one on top of the other by successive generations, but left largely unfurnished and unused for the last three hundred years. The original Romanesque palace of Soběslav I now forms the cellars of the present building, above which Charles IV built his own Gothic chambers; these days you enter at the third and top floor, built at the end of the fifteenth century.

Immediately past the antechamber is the bare expanse of the massive **Vladislavský sál** (Vladislav Hall), the work of Benedikt Ried, the German mason appointed by Vladislav Jagiello as his court architect. It displays some remarkable, sweeping rib-vaulting which forms floral patterns on the ceiling, the petals reaching almost to the floor. It was here that the early Bohemian kings were elected, and since 1918 every president from Masaryk to Havel has been sworn into office in the hall. In medieval times, the hall was also used for banquets and jousting tournaments, which explains the ramp-like **Riders' Staircase** in the north wing (now the exit). At the far end of the hall, to the right, there's an outdoor **viewing platform**, from which you can enjoy a magnificent view of Prague (at its best in the late afternoon).

From a staircase in the southwest corner of the hall, you can gain access to the Ludvík Wing. The rooms themselves are pretty uninspiring, but the furthest one, the **Bohemian Chancellery**, was the scene of Prague's **second defenestration** (see p.132 for details of the first). After almost two centuries of uneasy coexistence between Catholics and Protestants, matters came to a head over the succession to the throne of the Habsburg Archduke Ferdinand, a notoriously intolerant Catholic. On May 23, 1618, a posse of more than one hundred Protestant nobles, led by Count Thurn, marched to the chancellery for a showdown with Jaroslav Bořita z Martinic and Vilém Slavata, the two Catholic governors appointed by Ferdinand. After a "stormy discussion", the two councillors (and their personal secretary, Filip Fabricius) were thrown out of the window. As a contemporary historian recounted: "No mercy was granted them and they were both thrown dressed in their cloaks with their rapiers and decoration head-first out of the western window into a moat beneath the palace. They loudly screamed *ach, ach, oweh!* and attempted to hold on to the narrow window-ledge, but Thurn beat their knuckles with the hilt of his sword until they were both obliged to let go." There's some controversy about the exact window from which they were ejected, although it's generally agreed that they survived to tell the tale, landing in a medieval dungheap below, and – so the story goes – precipitating the Thirty Years' War.

Back down in the Vladislavský sál, there are more rooms to explore through the doorways on either side of the Riders' Staircase, but you're better off heading down the ramp to the **Gothic and Romanesque chambers** of the palace. Although equally bare, they contain an interesting exhibition on the development of the castle through the centuries, plus copies of the busts by Peter Parler's workshop, including the architect's remarkable self-portrait; the originals are hidden from view in the triforium of the cathedral.

The Basilica and Convent of sv Jiří

The only exit from the Old Royal Palace is via the Riders' Staircase, which deposits you in Jiřské náměstí. Don't be fooled by the russet red Baroque facade of the **Basilica of sv Jiří** (St George) which dominates the square; inside is Prague's most beautiful Romanesque building, meticulously scrubbed clean and restored to re-create something like the honey-coloured stone basilica that replaced the original tenth-century church in 1173. The double staircase to the chancel is a remarkably harmonious late-Baroque addition and now provides a perfect stage for chamber music concerts. The choir vault contains a rare early thirteenth-century painting of the New Jerusalem from Revelation – not to be confused with the very patchy sixteenth-century painting on the apse – while to the right of the chancel, only partially visible, are sixteenth-century frescoes of the **burial chapel of sv Ludmila**, grandmother of St Wenceslas, who was strangled by her own daughter-in-law in 921 (see box on p.88), thus becoming Bohemia's first Christian martyr and saint. There's a replica of the recumbent Ludmilla, which you can inspect at close quarters, in the south aisle.

Rudolfine and Baroque art collection

Next door is Bohemia's first monastery, the **Jiřský klášter** (St George's Convent) founded in 973 by Mlada, sister of the Přemyslid prince Boleslav the Pious, who became its first abbess. Closed down and turned into a barracks by Joseph II in 1782, it now houses the Národní galerie's **Rudolfine and Baroque art collection** (Rudolfinské a barokní umění). To be honest, this is a collection of only limited interest to the non-specialist. The art collection begins upstairs with a brief taste of the overtly sensual and erotic **Mannerist paintings** that prevailed during the reign of Rudolf II, including Bartolomeus Spranger's colourfully erotic works, Hans von Aachen's sexually charged *Suicide of Lucretia* and Josef Heintz's riotous orgy in his *Last Judgement*.

The rest of the gallery is given over to a vast collection of Czech **Baroque art**, as pursued by the likes of Bohemia's Karel Škréta and Petr Brandl, whose paintings and sculptures fill chapels and churches across the Czech Lands. Perhaps the most compelling reason to wade through the gallery is to admire the vigorous, gesticulating sculptures of Matthias Bernhard Braun, and, to a lesser extent, Ferdinand Maximilian Brokof.

Zlatá ulička and the castle towers

Around the corner from the convent is **Zlatá ulička** (Golden Lane), a seemingly blind alley of miniature sixteenth-century cottages in dolly-mixture colours, built for the 24 members of Rudolf II's castle guard. The lane takes its name from the goldsmiths who followed (and modified the buildings) a century later. By the nineteenth century, it had become a kind of palace slum, attracting artists and craftsmen, its two most famous inhabitants being Jaroslav Seifert, the Nobel prize-winning Czech poet, and Franz Kafka, who came here in the evenings in the winter of 1916 to write short stories. Finally, in 1951, the Communists kicked out the remaining residents and turned most of the houses into souvenir shops for tourists.

At no. 24, you can climb a flight of stairs to the **Obranná chodba** (defence corridor), which is lined with wooden shields, suits of armour and period costumes. The **Bílá věž** (White Tower), at the western end of the corridor, was the city's main prison from Rudolf's reign onwards. In the opposite direction, the corridor leads to **Daliborka**, the castle tower dedicated to its first prisoner, the young Czech noble Dalibor, accused of supporting a peasants' revolt at the beginning of the fifteenth century, who was finally executed in 1498. According to Prague legend, he learnt to play the violin while imprisoned here, and his playing could be heard all over the castle – a tale that provided material for Smetana's opera, *Dalibor*.

To get inside the castle's other tower, the **Prašná věž** (Powder Tower) or Mihulka, which once served as the workshop of gunsmith and bell-founder

Tomáš Jaroš, you'll have to backtrack to Vikářská, the street which runs along the north side of the cathedral. The Powder Tower's name comes from the lamprey (*mihule*), an eel-like fish supposedly bred here for royal consumption, though it's actually more noteworthy as the place where Rudolf's team of alchemists was put to work trying to discover the philosopher's stone. Despite its colourful history, the exhibition currently on display within the tower is dull, with just a pair of furry slippers and hat belonging to Ferdinand I to get excited about.

Muzeum hraček (Toy Museum) and the Lobkovický palác

If you continue east down Jiřská, which runs parallel with Zlatá ulička, you'll come to the courtyard of the former Purkrabství (Burgrave's House) on the left, which hides a café, exhibition space and **Muzeum hraček** daily 9.30am–5.30pm). With brief, Czech-only captions and unimaginative displays, this is a disappointing venture, which fails to live up to its potential. The succession of glass cabinets contains an impressive array of toy cars, robots and even Barbie dolls, but there are too few buttons for younger kids to press, and unless you're really lost for something to do, you could happily skip the whole enterprise.

The hotchpotch historical collection in the **Lobkovický palác** (Tues–Sun 9am–5pm; Ⓦwww.nm.cz), on the opposite side of Jiřská, is marginally more rewarding, despite the ropey English text provided. The exhibition actually begins on the top floor, but by no means all the objects on display deserve attention. The prize exhibits are replicas of the Bohemian crown jewels, an interesting sixteenth-century carving of *The Last Supper*, originally an altarpiece from the Bethlehem Chapel, and the sword (and invoice) of the famous Prague executioner Jan Mydlář, who could lop a man's head off with just one chop, as he demonstrated on 24 Protestant Czechs in 1621 (see p.110).

The Castle Gardens

For recuperation and a superlative view over the rest of Prague, head for the **Jižní zahrady** (South Gardens), accessible via Plečnik's copper-canopied Bull Staircase on the south side of the third courtyard. Alternatively, make a short detour beyond the castle walls from the second courtyard, by crossing the **Prašný most** (Powder Bridge), erected in the sixteenth century to connect the newly established royal gardens with the Hrad. Beyond the bridge, opposite Jean-Baptiste Mathey's plain French Baroque Jízdárna (Riding School), now an art gallery, is the entrance to the Royal Gardens or **Královská zahrada** (April–Oct daily 10am–6pm), founded by Emperor Ferdinand I on the site of a former vineyard. Today, this is one of the best-kept gardens in the capital, with fully functioning fountains and immaculately cropped lawns. Consequently, it's a very popular spot, though more a place for admiring the azaleas and almond trees than lounging around on the grass. It was here that tulips brought from Turkey were first acclimatized to Europe before being exported to the Netherlands, and every spring there's an impressive, disciplined crop.

Built into the gardens' south terrace is Rudolf's distinctive Renaissance ballgame court, known as the **Míčovna** (occasionally open to the public for concerts and exhibitions) and tattooed with sgraffito. At the far end of the gardens is Prague's most celebrated Renaissance legacy, the **Belvedér**, a delicately arcaded summerhouse topped by an inverted copper ship's hull, built by Ferdinand I for his wife, Anne. Unlike the gardens, the Belvedér is open most of the year and is now used for exhibitions of contemporary artists. At the centre of the palace's miniature formal garden is the **Zpívající fontána** (Singing Fountain), built shortly after the palace and so named from the musical sound of the drops of water falling in the metal bowls below. From the garden terrace you can enjoy an unrivalled view of the castle's finest treasure – the cathedral.

Chotkovy sady and the Bílkova vila

Adjacent to the Belvedér is the **Chotkovy sady**, Prague's first public park, founded in 1833. You can enjoy an unrivalled view of the bridges and islands of the Vltava from its south wall, or check out the elaborate, grotto-like memorial to the nineteenth-century Romantic poet **Julius Zeyer**, from whose blackened rocks emerge life-sized, marble characters from his works.

Across the road from the park and hidden behind its overgrown garden, the **Bílkova vila** (mid-May to mid-Oct Tues–Sun 10am–6pm; mid-Oct to mid-May Sat & Sun 10am–5pm), at Mieckiewiczova 1, honours one of the most unusual Czech sculptors, František Bílek (1872–1941). Born in Chýnov (see p.198), in a part of South Bohemia steeped in Hussite tradition, Bílek lived a monkish life, spending years in spiritual contemplation, reading the works of Hus and other Czech reformers. The villa was built in 1911 to Bílek's own design, intended as both a "cathedral of art" and the family home. At first sight, it appears a strangely mute red-brick building, out of keeping with the extravagant Symbolist style of Bílek's sculptures: from the outside, only the front porch, supported by giant sheaves of corn, and the sculptural group, the fleeing Comenius and his followers, in the garden, give a clue as to what lies within.

Inside, the brickwork gives way to bare stone walls lined with Bílek's religious sculptures, giving the impression that you've walked into a chapel rather than an artist's studio: "a workshop and temple", in Bílek's own words. In addition to his sculptural and relief work in wood and stone, often wildly expressive and anguished, there are also ceramics, graphics and a few mementoes of Bílek's life. His work is little known outside his native country, but his contemporary admirers included Franz Kafka, Julius Zeyer and Otakar Březina, whose poems and novels provided the inspiration for much of Bílek's art. Bílek's living quarters have also now been restored and opened to the public, with much of the original wooden furniture, designed and carved by Bílek himself, still in place: check out the dressing table for his wife, shaped like some giant church lectern, and the wardrobe decorated with a border of hearts, a penis, a nose, an ear and an eye, plus the sun, stars and moon.

From Hradčanské náměstí to Strahovský klášter

The monumental scale and appearance of the rest of Hradčany, outside the castle, is a direct result of the **great fire of 1541**, which swept up from Malá Strana and wiped out most of the old dwelling places belonging to the serfs, tradesmen, clergy and masons who had settled here in the Middle Ages. With the Turks at the gates of Vienna, the Habsburg nobility were more inclined to pursue their major building projects in Prague instead, and, following the Battle of Bílá hora in 1620, the palaces of the exiled (or executed) Protestant nobility were up for grabs too. The newly ensconced Catholic aristocrats were keen to spend some of their expropriated wealth, and over the next two centuries they turned Hradčany into a grand architectural showpiece. As the Turkish threat subsided, the political focus of the empire gradually shifted back to Vienna and the building spree stopped. For the last two hundred years, Hradčany has been frozen in time, and, two world wars on, its buildings have survived better than those of any other central European capital.

Hradčanské náměstí

Hradčanské náměstí fans out from the castle gates, surrounded by the over-sized palaces of the old Catholic nobility. For the most part, it's a tranquil space that's overlooked by the tour groups marching through, intent on the Hrad. The one spot everyone heads for is the ramparts in the southeastern corner, by the top of the Zámecké schody, which allow an unrivalled view over the red rooftops of Malá Strana, past the famous green dome and tower of the church of sv Mikuláš and beyond, to the spires of Staré Město.

Until the great fire of 1541, the square was the hub of Hradčany, lined with medieval shops and stalls but with no real market as such. After the fire, the developers moved in; the powerful Lobkowicz family replaced seven houses on the south side of the square with the over-the-top sgraffitoed pile at no. 2, now known as the **Schwarzenberský palác** after its last aristocratic owners (the present-day count, Karl, is one of the republic's leading capitalists). The palace now houses the **Vojenské historické muzeum** (Museum of Military History). Predictably enough, it was the Nazis who founded the museum, though the Czechs themselves have a long history of manufacturing top-class weaponry for world powers (Semtex is probably their best-known export), so it's no coincidence that one of the two Czech words to have made it into the English language is pistol (from *pišťale*, a Hussite weapon) – the other is *robot*, in case you're wondering. The museum was undergoing renovation at the time of writing, but is due to reopen in 2006.

Šternberský palác – the Old European art collection

A passage down the side of the Arcibiskupský palác leads to the early eight-eenth-century **Šternberský palác** (Tues–Sun 10am–6pm Ⓦ www.ngprague .cz), which houses the Národní galerie's **old European art collection**, mostly ranging from the fourteenth to the eighteenth century, but excluding works by Czech artists of the period (you'll find them in the Jiřský klášter in the Hrad). It would be fair to say that the collection is relatively modest, in comparison with those of other major European capitals, though the handful of masterpieces makes a visit here worthwhile.

The **first floor** kicks off with Florentine religious art, most notably a series of exquisite miniature triptychs by Bernardo Daddi, plus several gilded polyptychs by the Venetian artist Antonio Vivarini. Moving swiftly into the gallery's large Flemish contingent, it's worth checking out Dieric Bouts' *Lamentation*, a com-plex composition crowded with figures in medieval garb, and the bizarre *Well of Life*, painted around 1500 by an unknown artist. The latter features a squatting Christ depicted as a Gothic fountain issuing forth blood, which angels in turn serve in goblets to passing punters. One of the most eye-catching works is Jan Gossaert's *St Luke Drawing the Virgin*, an exercise in architectural geometry and perspective which used to hang in the cathedral. The section ends with a series of canvases by the least famous members of the Brueghel family; before you head upstairs, though, don't miss the side rooms containing Orthodox icons from Venice and the Balkans to Russia.

The **second floor** contains one of the most prized paintings in the whole collection, the *Feast of the Rosary* by Albrecht Dürer, depicting, among oth-ers, the Virgin Mary, the Pope, the Holy Roman Emperor, and even a self-portrait of Dürer himself (top right). This was one of Rudolf's most prized acquisitions (he was an avid Dürer fan), transported on foot across the Alps to Prague (he didn't trust wheeled transport with such a precious object). There are other outstanding works here, too: two richly coloured Bronzino portraits, a Rembrandt, a Canaletto of the Thames, a whole series by the

Saxon master, Lucas Cranach, and a mesmerizing *Praying Christ* by El Greco. Rubens' colossal *Murder of St Thomas* is difficult to miss, with its pink-but-tocked cherubs hovering over the bloody scene. Nearby, in the hugely expanded (and uneven in quality) Dutch section, there's a wonderful portrait of an arrogant young gun named Jasper by Frans Hals. A few of the rooms in the gallery have preserved their original decor, the best of which is the Chinoiserie of the čínský kabinet.

From Nový Svět to Loretánské náměstí

At the other end of Hradčanské náměstí, Kanovnická heads off towards the northwest corner of Hradčany. Nestling in this shallow dip, **Nový Svět** (meaning "New World", though not Dvořák's) provides a glimpse of life on a totally different scale from Hradčanské náměstí. Similar in many ways to the Zlatá ulička in the Hrad, this cluster of brightly coloured cottages, which curls around the corner into Černínská, is all that's left of Hradčany's medieval slums, painted up and sanitized in the eighteenth and nineteenth centuries. Despite having all the same ingredients for mass tourist appeal as Zlatá ulička, it remains remarkably undisturbed, save for a few swish wine bars, and Gambra, a surrealist art gallery at Černínská 5 (Wed–Sun noon–6pm), which sells works by, among others, the renowned Czech animator, **Jan Švankmajer**, and his wife Eva, who live nearby.

Up the hill from Nový Svět, Loretánské náměstí is dominated by the phenomenal 135-metre-long facade of the **Černínský palác** (Černín Palace), decorated with thirty Palladian half-pillars and supported by a swathe of diamond-pointed rustication. For all its grandeur, it's a miserable, brutal building, whose construction nearly bankrupted future generations of Černíns, who were forced to sell the palace in 1851 to the Austrian state. Since the First Republic, the palace has housed the Foreign Ministry, and during the war it housed the Nazi bureaucracy and the German State Minister for Bohemia and Moravia, Karl Hermann Frank. On March 10, 1948, it was the scene of Prague's third – and most widely mourned – defenestration. Only days after the Communist coup, **Jan Masaryk**, only son of the founder of Czechoslovakia and the last non-Communist in the cabinet, plunged 45 feet to his death from a top-floor bathroom window. Whether it was suicide (he had been suffering from bouts of depression, partly induced by the country's political path) or murder will probably never be satisfactorily resolved, but for most people Masaryk's death cast a dark shadow over the newly established regime.

The facade of the **Loreta** (Tues–Sun 9am–12.15pm & 1–4.30pm), immediately opposite the Černínský palác, was built by the Dientzenhofers, a Bavarian family of architects, in the early part of the eighteenth century, and is the perfect antidote to the Černíns' humourless monster. It's all hot flourishes and twirls, topped by a tower which lights up like a Chinese lantern at night, and by day clanks out the hymn *We Greet Thee a Thousand Times* on its 27 Dutch bells (it does special performances of other tunes from time to time, too).

The facade and the cloisters are, in fact, just the outer casing for the focus of the complex, the **Santa Casa**, founded in 1626 and smothered in a mantle of stucco depicting the building's miraculous transportation from the Holy Land. Legend has it that the Santa Casa (Mary's home in Nazareth), under threat from the heathen Turks, was transported by a host of angels to a small laurel grove (*lauretum* in Latin, hence Loreta) in northern Italy. News of the miracle spread across the Catholic lands, prompting a spate of copycat shrines. During the Counter-Reformation, the cult was actively encouraged in an attempt to broaden the popular appeal of Catholicism. The Prague Loreta is one of fifty to be built in the Czech Lands, each of the shrines following an identical design, with pride of place given to a limewood statue of the *Black Madonna and Child*, encased in silver.

Behind the Santa Casa, the Dientzenhofers built the much larger **Church of Narození Páně** (Church of the Nativity), which is like a mini-version of sv Mikuláš, down in Malá Strana. The Santa Casa's serious financial backing is evident in the **treasury** on the first floor of the west wing, much ransacked over the years but still stuffed full of gold. The light fittings are a Communist period piece, but most folk come here to gawp at the master exhibit, an outrageous Viennese silver monstrance designed by Fischer von Erlach in 1699, and studded with diamonds taken from the wedding dress of Countess Kolovrat, who had made the Loreta sole heir to her fortune.

Strahovský klášter (Strahov Monastery)

Continuing westwards from Loretánské náměstí, Pohořelec, an arcaded street-cum-square, leads to the chunky remnants of the zigzag eighteenth-century fortifications that mark the edge of the old city, as defined by Charles IV back in the fourteenth century. Close by, to the left, is the **Strahovský klášter** (Ⓦ www.strahovmonastery.cz), founded in 1140 by the Premonstratensian order. Having managed to evade Joseph II's 1783 dissolution of the monasteries, it continued to function until shortly after the Communists took power, when, along with all other religious establishments, it was closed down and most of its inmates thrown into prison; following the events of 1989, the monks have returned.

It's the monastery's two ornate **libraries** (daily 9am–noon & 1–5pm; 70Kč), though, that are the real reason for visiting Strahov; the entrance for both is to the right as you enter the outer courtyard. The first library you come to is the later and larger of the two, the **Filosofický sál** (Philosophical Hall), built in some haste in the 1780s in order to accommodate the books and bookcases from Louka, a Premonstratensian monastery in Moravia that failed to escape Joseph's decree. The walnut bookcases are so tall they touch the library's lofty ceiling, which is busily decorated with frescoes by the Viennese painter Franz Maulbertsch on the theme of the search for truth. Don't, whatever you do, miss the collection of curios exhibited in the glass cabinets outside the library, which features shells, turtles, crabs, lobsters, dried-up sea monsters, butterflies, beetles, plastic fruit and moths. There's even a pair of whales' penises set amidst a narwhal horn, several harpoons and a model ship. The other main room is the low-ceilinged **Teologický sál** (Theological Hall), studded with ancient globes, its wedding-cake stucco framing frescoes on a similar theme, executed by one of the monks seventy years earlier. Outside the hall, the library's oldest book, the ninth-century gem-studded Strahov Gospel, is displayed – look out, too, for the cabinet of books documenting Czech trees, each of which has the bark of the tree on its spine.

If you leave the monastery through the narrow doorway in the eastern wall, you enter the gardens and orchards of the **Strahovská zahrada**, from where you can see the whole city in perspective. The gardens form part of a wooded hill known as Petřín, and the path to the right contours round to the Stations of the Cross that lead up to the miniature Eiffel Tower known as the Rozhledna. Alternatively, you can catch tram #22 or #23 from outside Strahov's main entrance to Malostranská metro or the centre of town.

Malá Strana

MALÁ STRANA, Prague's picturesque Little Quarter, sits below the castle and is, in many ways, the city's most entrancing area. Its peaceful, often hilly, cobbled backstreets have changed very little since Mozart walked them during his frequent visits to Prague between 1787 and 1791. Despite the quarter's miniscule size – it takes up a mere 600 square metres of land squeezed in between the river and Hradčany – it's easy enough to lose the crowds, many of whom never stray from the well-trodden route that links the Charles Bridge with the castle. Its streets conceal a whole host of quiet terraced gardens, as well as the wooded Petřín hill, which together provide the perfect inner-city escape in the summer months. The Church of sv Mikuláš, by far the finest Baroque church in Prague, and the Kampa Museum, with its unrivalled collection of works by František Kupka, are the two major sights.

Malostranské náměstí

The main focus of Malá Strana has always been the sloping, cobbled **Malostranské náměstí**, which is dominated and divided into two by the church of sv Mikuláš (see below). Trams and cars hurtle across it, regularly dodged by a procession of people – some heading up the hill to the Hrad, others pausing for coffee and cakes at the numerous bars and restaurants hidden in the square's arcades and Gothic vaults.

Towering above the square, and the whole of Malá Strana, is the church of **sv Mikuláš** or St Nicholas (daily 9am–4pm), easily the most magnificent Baroque building in the city, and one of the last great structures to be built on the left bank, begun in 1702. For Christoph Dientzenhofer, a German immigrant from a dynasty of Bavarian architects, this was his most prestigious commission and is, without doubt, his finest work. For the Jesuits, who were already ensconced in the adjoining college, it was their most ambitious project yet in Bohemia, and the ultimate symbol of their stranglehold on the country. When Christoph

Mozart in Prague

Mozart made the first of several visits to Prague with his wife Constanze in 1787, staying with his friend and patron Count Thun in what is now the British Embassy (Thunovská 14). A year earlier, his opera *The Marriage of Figaro*, which had failed to please the opera snobs in Vienna, had been given a rapturous reception at Prague's Nostitz Theater (now the Stavovské divadlo; see p.96); and on his arrival in 1787, Mozart was already flavour of the month, as he wrote in his diary: "Here they talk about nothing but Figaro. Nothing is played, sung or whistled but Figaro. Nothing, nothing but Figaro. Certainly a great honour for me!" Encouraged by this, he chose to premiere his next opera, *Don Giovanni*, later that year, in Prague rather than Vienna. He arrived with an incomplete score in hand, and wrote the overture at the Dušeks' Bertramka villa in Smíchov (now the Mozart Museum; see p.147), dedicating it to the "good people of Prague". Apart from a brief sojourn whilst on a concert tour, Mozart's fourth and final visit to Prague took place in 1791, the year of his death. The climax of the stay was the premiere of Mozart's final opera, *La Clemenza di Tito*, commissioned for the coronation of Leopold II as King of Bohemia (and completed whilst on the coach from Vienna to Prague). The opera didn't go down quite as well as previous ones – the empress is alleged to have shouted "German hogwash" from her box. Nevertheless, four thousand people turned out for the funereal memorial service, held in Malá Strana's church of sv Mikuláš to the strains of Mozart's *Requiem Mass*.

died in 1722, it was left to his son Kilian Ignaz Dientzenhofer, along with Kilian's son-in-law, Anselmo Lurago, to finish the project, which they did with a masterful flourish, adding the giant green dome and tower – now among the most characteristic landmarks on Prague's left bank. Sadly for the Jesuits, they were able to enjoy the finished product for just twenty years, before they were banished from the Habsburg Empire in 1773.

△ Palace Gardens

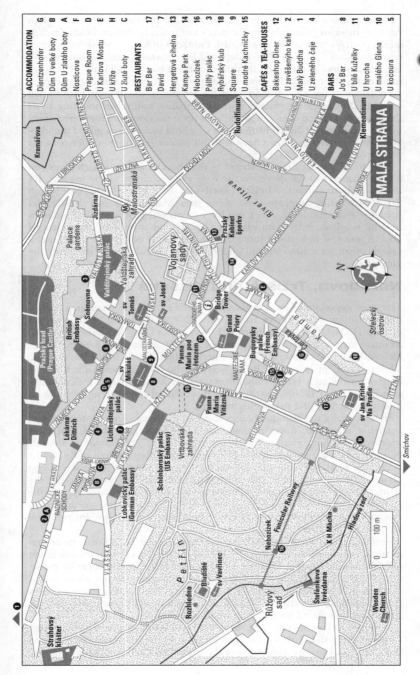

ACCOMMODATION

Dientzenhofer	G
Dům U velké boty	B
Dům U zlatého boty	A
Nosticova	F
Prague Room	D
U Karlova Mostu	E
U kříže	H
U žluté boty	C

RESTAURANTS

Bar Bar	17
David	7
Hergetová cihelna	13
Kampa Park	14
Nebozízek	16
Pálffy palác	3
Rybářský klub	18
Square	9
U modré Kachničky	15

CAFÉS & TEA-HOUSES

Bakeshop Diner	12
U zavěšenýho kafe	2
Malý Buddha	1
U zeleného čaje	4

BARS

Jo's Bar	8
U bílé Kuželky	11
U hrocha	6
U malého Glena	10
U kocoura	5

MALÁ STRANA

Smíchov

Nothing about the relatively plain west facade prepares you for the High Baroque **interior**, dominated by the nave's vast fresco, by Johann Lukas Kracker, which portrays some of the more fanciful miraculous feats of St Nicholas. Apart from his role as Santa Claus, he is depicted here rescuing sailors in distress, saving women from prostitution by throwing them bags of gold, and reprieving from death three unjustly condemned men. Even given the overwhelming proportions of the nave, the dome at the far end of the church, built by the younger Dientzenhofer, remains impressive, thanks, more than anything, to its sheer height. Leering over you as you gaze up at the dome are four terrifyingly oversized and stern Church Fathers, one of whom brandishes a gilded thunderbolt, while another garottes a devil with his crozier, leaving no doubt as to the gravity of the Jesuit message.

Exhibitions are occasionally staged in the church's gallery, which gives you a great chance to look down on the nave and get closer to the frescoes. It's also possible to climb the **belfry** (April–Oct daily 10am–6pm; Nov–March Sat & Sun 10am–5pm), for fine views over Malá Strana and the Charles Bridge. Before you leave, check out the exceptional Rococo pulpit wrought in pink scagliola, busy with cherubs, a pieta and topped by an archangel on the point of beheading some unfortunate. And don't miss the church's superb organ, its white case and gilded musical cherubs nicely offsetting the grey pipes.

Nerudova, Tržiště and Vlašská

The most important of the various streets leading up to the Hrad from Malostranské náměstí is **Nerudova**, named after the Czech journalist and writer Jan Neruda (1834–91), who was born at U dvou sluncŭ (The Two Suns), at no. 47, an inn at the top of the street. His tales of Malá Strana immortalized bohemian life on Prague's left bank, though he's perhaps best known in the West via the Chilean Nobel prize-winner, Pablo Neruda, who took his pen-name from the lesser-known Czech. Historically, this was the city's main quarter for craftsmen, artisans and artists, though the shops and restaurants that line Nerudova now are mostly predictably and shamelessly touristy.

Architecturally, the Baroque houses that line the steep climb up to the Hrad are fairly restrained, many retaining their medieval barn doors, and most adorned with their own peculiar house signs (see p.77). Halfway up the hill, Nerudova halts at a crossroads where it meets the cobbled hairpin of Ke Hradu, which the royal coronation procession used to ascend; continuing west along **Úvoz** (The Cutting) takes you to the Strahovský klášter (see p.96). On the south side of Úvoz, the houses come to an end, and a view opens up over the picturesque jumble of Malá Strana's red-tiled roofs, while to the north, narrow stairways squeeze between the towering buildings of Hradčany, emerging on the path to the Loreta.

Running (very) roughly parallel to Nerudova – and linked to it by several picturesque side streets and steps – is **Tržiště**, which sets off from the south side of Malostranské náměstí. Halfway up on the left is the **Schönbornský palác**, now the US Embassy. The entrance, and the renowned gardens, are nowadays watched over by closed-circuit TV and twitchy Czech policemen – a far cry from the dilapidated palace in which Kafka rented an apartment in March 1917, and where he suffered his first bout of tuberculosis.

As Tržiště swings to the right, bear left up **Vlašská**, home to yet another **Lobkovický palác**, now the German Embassy. In the summer of 1989, several thousand East Germans climbed over the garden wall and entered the embassy compound to demand West German citizenship, which had been every German's right since partition. The neighbouring streets were soon jam-packed with abandoned Trabants, as the beautiful palace gardens became a muddy home to the refugees. Finally, the Czechoslovak government gave in and organized special trains to take the East Germans over the federal border, cheered on their way by thousands of Praguers, and thus prompted the exodus that eventually brought the Berlin Wall down.

Valdštejnský palác and around

To the north of Malostranské náměstí, up Tomášská, lies the **Valdštejnský palác**, which takes up the whole of the eastern side of **Valdštejnské náměstí** and Valdštejnská. As early as 1621, Albrecht von Waldstein started to build a palace which would reflect his status as commander of the Imperial Catholic armies of the Thirty Years' War. By buying, confiscating, and then destroying 26 houses, three gardens and a brick factory, he succeeded in ripping apart a densely populated area of Malá Strana to make way for one of the first, largest and, quite frankly, most undistinguished Baroque palaces in the city – at least from the outside.

The Czech upper house, or **Senát**, is now housed in the palace, and can be visited on a guided tour at weekends (Sat & Sun 10am–4pm). The former stables are also accessible to the public, as they contain the **Pedagogické muzeum** (Tues–Sat 10am–12.30pm & 1–4.30pm; Ⓦwww.pmjak.cz). This is a small and old-fashioned exhibition on Czech education and, in particular, the influential teachings of Jan Amos Komenský (1592–1670) – often anglicized to John Comenius – who was forced to leave his homeland after the victory of Waldstein's Catholic armies, eventually settling in Protestant England. To get to the exhibition, go through the main gateway and continue straight across the first courtyard; the museum is on your right.

If you've no interest in pedagogical matters, the palace's formal gardens, the **Valdštejnská zahrada** (April–Oct daily 10am–6pm) – accessible from the palace's main entrance, from the piazza outside Malostranská metro and also from a doorway in the palace walls along Letenská – are a good place to take a breather from the city streets. The focus of the gardens is the gigantic Italianate *sala terrena*, a monumental loggia decorated with frescoes of the Trojan Wars, which stands at the end of an avenue of sculptures by Adriaen de Vries. The originals, which were intended to form a fountain, were taken off as booty by the Swedes in 1648 and now adorn the royal gardens in Drottningholm. In addition, there are a number of peacocks, a carp pond, a massive semicircular grotto, with mysterious doors set into it, and an old menagerie that's now home to a mini-parliament of eagle owls.

One of the chief joys of Malá Strana is its steeply terraced **palácové zahrady** (palace gardens; April–Oct daily 10am–6pm), hidden away behind the Baroque palaces on Valdštejnská, on the slopes below the castle. There are five small, interlinking gardens in total, dotted with little pavilions, terraces of vines, and commanding superb views over Prague. If you're approaching from below, you can enter either via the Ledeburská zahrada on Valdštejnské náměstí, or the Kolowratská zahrada on Valdštejnská which connect. You can also exit or enter via the easternmost garden, the Malá Fürstenberská zahrada, which connects with the Jižní Zahrady (see p.92) beneath the Hrad itself.

Another option is to seek out the **Vojanovy sady** (daily: April–Sept 8am–7pm; Oct–March 8am–5pm), securely concealed behind a ring of high walls off U lužického semináře. Originally a monastic garden belonging to the

Carmelites, it's now an informal public park, with sleeping babies, weeping willows, and lots of grass on which to lounge about; outdoor art exhibitions and occasional concerts also take place here.

Southern Malá Strana

Karmelitská is the busy cobbled street that runs south from Malostranské náměstí along the base of Petřín towards the suburb of Smíchov, becoming Újezd at roughly its halfway point. Between here and the River Vltava are some of Malá Strana's most picturesque and secluded streets. The island of **Kampa**, in particular, makes up one of the most peaceful stretches of riverfront in Prague and the modern art collection on display in the **Museum Kampa** is definitely worth a visit.

Before you set off to explore this part of town, however, you should pop through the doorway at no. 25, on the corner of Karmelitská and Tržiště, to see one of the most elusive of Malá Strana's many Baroque gardens, the **Vrtbovská zahrada** (April–Oct daily 10am–6pm), founded on the site of the former vineyards of the **Vrtbovský palác**. Laid out on Tuscan-style terraces, dotted with ornamental urns and statues of the gods by Matthias Bernhard Braun, the gardens twist their way up the lower slopes of Petřín Hill to an observation terrace, from where there's a spectacular rooftop perspective on the city.

Maltézské náměstí and around

From the trams and traffic of Karmelitská, it's a relief to cut across to the calm restraint of **Maltézské náměstí**, one of a number of delightful little squares between here and the river. It takes its name from the Order of the Knights of St John of Jerusalem (better known by their later title, the Maltese Knights), who in 1160 founded the nearby church of **Panna Maria pod řetězem** (Saint Mary below-the-chain), so called because it was the knights' job to guard the Judith Bridge. The original Romanesque church was pulled down by the knights themselves in the fourteenth century, but only the chancel and towers were successfully rebuilt by the time of the Hussite Wars. The two bulky Gothic towers are still standing and the apse is now thoroughly Baroque, but the nave remains unfinished and open to the elements.

The Knights have reclaimed (and restored) the church and the adjacent Grand Priory, which backs onto **Velkopřevorské náměstí**, another pretty little square to the south, which echoes to the sound of music from the nearby Prague conservatoire. Following the violent death of John Lennon in 1980, Prague's youth established an ad hoc shrine smothered in graffiti tributes to the ex-Beatle along the Grand Priory's garden wall. On the opposite side of the square from the priory, sitting pretty in pink behind a row of chestnut trees, is the Rococo **Buquoyský palác**, built for a French family and appropriately enough now the French Embassy.

Kampa

Heading for **Kampa**, the largest of the Vltava's islands, with its cafés, old mills and serene riverside park, is the perfect way to escape the crowds on the Charles Bridge, from which it can be accessed easily via a staircase. The island is separated from the left bank by Prague's "Little Venice", a thin strip of water called **Čertovka** (Devil's Stream), which used to power several mill-wheels until the last one ceased to function in 1936. In contrast to the rest of the left bank, the fire of 1541 had a positive effect on Kampa, since the flotsam from the blaze effectively stabilized the island's shifting shoreline. Nevertheless, Kampa was still subject to frequent flooding right up until the Vltava was dammed in the 1950s.

For much of its history, the island was the city's main wash house, and it wasn't until the sixteenth and seventeenth centuries that the Nostitz family, who owned Kampa, began to develop the northern half of the island; the southern half was left untouched and is today laid out as a public park, with riverside views across to Staré Město. To the north, the oval main square, **Na Kampě**, once a pottery market, is studded with slender acacia trees and cut through by the Charles Bridge.

Housed in an old riverside water mill, the **Museum Kampa** (daily 10am–6pm; Ⓦ www.museumkampa.cz) is dedicated to the private art collection of Jan and Meda Mládek. As well as temporary exhibitions, this stylish modern gallery also exhibits the best of the Mládeks' collection, including a whole series of works by the Czech artist František Kupka, seen by many as the father of abstract art. These range from early Expressionist watercolours to transitional pastels like *Fauvist Chair* from 1910, and more abstract works, such as the seminal oil paintings, *Cathedral* and *Study for Fugue in Two Colours* from around 1912. The gallery also displays a good selection of Cubist and later interwar works by the sculptor Otto Gutfreund and a few collages by postwar surrealist Jiří Kolář.

Panna Maria Vítězná

Halfway down busy Karmelitská is the rather plain church of **Panna Maria Vítězná** (Mon–Sat 9.30am–5.30pm, Sun 1–5pm; Ⓦ www.pragjesu.com), which was begun in early Baroque style by German Lutherans in 1611, and later handed over to the Carmelites after the Battle of Bílá hora. The main reason for coming here is to see the **Pražské Jezulátko** or *Bambino di Praga*, a high-kitsch wax effigy of the infant Jesus as a precocious three-year-old, enthroned in a glass case illuminated with strip lights, donated by one of the Lobkowicz family's Spanish brides in 1628. Attributed with miraculous powers, the *pražské Jezulátko* became an object of international pilgrimage equal in stature to the Santa Casa in Loreta, similarly inspiring a whole series of replicas. It continues to attract visitors (as the multilingual prayer cards attest) and boasts a vast personal wardrobe of expensive swaddling clothes – approaching a hundred separate outfits at the last count – regularly changed by the Carmelite nuns. If you're keen to see some of the infant's outfits, there's a small museum, up the spiral staircase in the south aisle. Here, you get to see his lacy camisoles, as well as a selection of his velvet and satin overgarments sent from all over the world. There are also chalices, monstrances and a Rococo crown studded with diamonds and pearls to admire.

Petřín

The scaled-down version of the Eiffel Tower is the most obvious landmark on the wooded hill of **Petřín**, the largest green space in the city centre. The tower is just one of the exhibits built for the 1891 Prague Exhibition, whose modest legacy includes the **funicular railway** (*lanová dráha*; every 10–15min; daily 9.15am–8.45pm), which climbs up from a station just off Újezd. As the carriages pass each other at the halfway station of Nebozízek, you can get out and soak in the view from the restaurant of the same name. At the top of the hill, it's possible to trace the southernmost perimeter wall of the old city – popularly known as the **Hladová zed'** (Hunger Wall) – as it creeps eastwards back down to Újezd, and northwestwards to the Strahovský klášter. Instigated in the 1460s by Charles IV, it was much lauded at the time (and later by the Communists) as a great public work which provided employment for the burgeoning ranks of the city's destitute (hence its name); in fact, much of the wall's construction was paid for by the expropriation of Jewish property.

Follow the wall southeast and you come to the aromatic **Růžový sad** (Rose Garden), whose colour-coordinated rose beds are laid out in front of Petřín's observatory, the **Štefánikova hvězdárna** (times vary; Ⓦwww.observatory .cz), run by star-gazing enthusiasts. The small astronomical exhibition inside is hardly worth bothering with, but if it's a clear night, a quick peek through the observatory's two powerful telescopes is a treat. Follow the wall northwest and you'll come to Palliardi's twin-towered church of **sv Vavřinec** (St Lawrence), from which derives the German name for Petřín – Laurenziberg.

Opposite the church is a series of buildings from the 1891 Exhibition, starting with the diminutive **Rozhledna** (daily: April–Oct 10am–7pm; Nov–March 10am–5pm), an octagonal interpretation – though a mere fifth of the size – of the Eiffel Tower which shocked Paris in 1889, and a tribute to the city's strong cultural and political links with Paris at the time; the view from the public gallery is terrific in fine weather. The next building along is the **Bludiště** (daily: April–Oct 10am–7pm; Nov–March 10am–5pm), a mini neo-Gothic castle complete with mock drawbridge. The first section of the interior features a **mirror maze**, followed by an action-packed, life-sized diorama of the Prague students' and Jews' victory over the Swedes on the Charles Bridge in 1648. The humour of the convex and concave mirrors that lie beyond the diorama is so simple, it has both adults and kids giggling away. From the tower and maze, the path with the Stations of the Cross will eventually lead you to the perimeter wall of the Strahovský klášter (see p.96), giving great views over Petřín's palatial orchards and the sea of red tiles below.

Staré Město

STARÉ MĚSTO, literally the Old Town, is Prague's most central, vital ingredient. Most of the capital's busiest markets, shops, restaurants and pubs are in this area, and during the day a gaggle of shoppers and tourists fills its complex and utterly confusing web of narrow streets. The district is bounded on one side by the river, on the other by the arc of Národní, Na příkopě and Revoluční, and at its heart is **Staroměstské náměstí**, Prague's showpiece main square, easily the most magnificent in central Europe.

Merchants and craftsmen began settling in what is now Staré Město as early as the tenth century, and in the mid-thirteenth century it was granted town status, with jurisdiction over its own affairs. The fire of 1541, which ripped through the quarters on the other side of the river, never reached Staré Město, though the 1689 conflagration made up for it. Nevertheless, the victorious Catholic nobles built fewer large palaces here than on the left bank, leaving the medieval street plan intact with the exception of the Klementinum (the Jesuits' powerhouse) and the Jewish quarter, Josefov, which was largely reconstructed in the late nineteenth century (see p.116). Like so much of Prague, however, Staré Město is still, on the surface, overwhelmingly Baroque, built literally on top of its Gothic predecessor to guard against the floods which plagued the town.

In their explorations of Staré Město, most people unknowingly retrace the **králová cesta**, the traditional route of the coronation procession from the medieval gateway, the Prašná brána (see p.131), to the Hrad. Established by the Přemyslids, the route was followed, with a few minor variations, by every king until the Emperor Ferdinand IV in 1836, the last of the Habsburgs to bother having himself crowned in Prague. It's also the most direct route from the Charles Bridge to Prague's main square, Staroměstské náměstí, and therefore a natural choice. However, many of the real treasures of Staré Město lie away from the *králová cesta*, so if you want to escape the crowds, it's worth heading off into the quarter's silent, twisted matrix of streets, then simply following your nose – for details of specific sights to the south of Karlova, see p.114.

Karlův most (Charles Bridge)

The **Karlův most**, or Charles Bridge – which for over four hundred years was the only link between the two halves of Prague – is by far the city's most familiar monument. It's an impressive piece of medieval engineering, aligned slightly askew between two mighty Gothic gateways, but its fame is due almost entirely to the magnificent, mostly Baroque statues, additions to the original structure, that punctuate its length. Individually, only a few of the works are outstanding, but taken collectively, set against the backdrop of the Hrad, the effect is breathtaking.

The bridge was begun in 1357 to replace an earlier structure that was swept away in 1342 by one of the Vltava's frequent floods. Charles IV commissioned his young German court architect, Peter Parler, to carry out the work, which was finally completed in the early fifteenth century. For the first four hundred years it was known simply as the Prague or Stone Bridge – only in 1870 was it officially named after its patron. Since 1950, the bridge has been closed to vehicles, and is now one of the most popular places to hang out, day and night: the crush of sightseers never abates during the day, when the niches created by the bridge-piers are occupied by souvenir hawkers and buskers, but at night things calm down a bit, and the views are, if anything, even more spectacular.

A bronze **crucifix** has stood on the bridge since its construction, but its gold-leaf Hebrew inscription, "Holy, Holy, Holy Lord", from the Book of Isaiah, was added in 1696, paid for by a Prague Jew who was ordered to do so by the city court, having been found guilty of blasphemy before the cross. Somewhat incredibly, the local Jewish community recently succeeded in persuading the local council to erect a plaque below the statue, explaining that the charges were drummed up and the inscription designed to humiliate Prague's Jews. The first of the sculptures wasn't added until 1683, when a bronze statue of **St John of Nepomuk** appeared as part of the Jesuits' persistent campaign to have him canonized (see p.89); this later inspired hundreds of copies, which adorn bridges throughout central Europe. On the base, there's a bronze relief depicting his martyrdom, the figure of John now extremely worn through years of being touched for good luck. The statue was such a propaganda success with the Catholic Church authorities that another 21 were added between 1706 and 1714. These included works by Prague's leading Baroque sculptors, including Matthias Bernhard Braun and Ferdinand Maximilian Brokof; the remaining piers (and a few swept away in the 1890 flood) were filled in with unimaginative nineteenth-century sculptures. The originals, mostly crafted in sandstone, have weathered badly over the years and have now been replaced by copies and put into storage in the Lapidárium (see p.146).

The bridge towers, at each end of the bridge, can be climbed for a bird's eye view of the masses pouring across. The **Malostranská mostecká věž** (April–Oct daily 10am–6pm) is made up of two unequal towers, connected by a castellated arch, which forms the entrance to the bridge. The smaller, stumpy tower was once part of the original Judith Bridge (named after the wife of Vladislav I, who built the twelfth-century original); the taller tower is

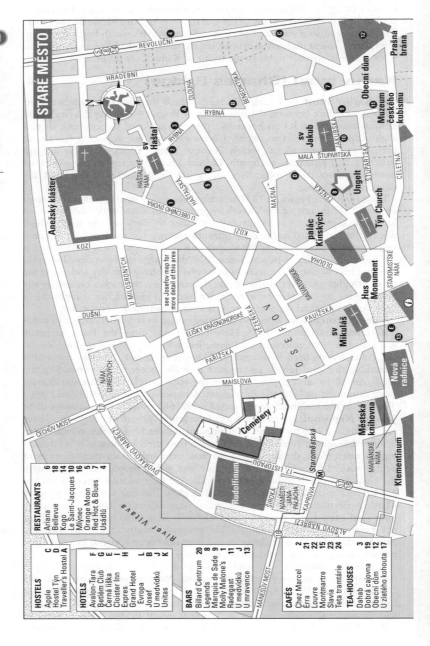

STARÉ MĚSTO

HOSTELS

Apple	C
Hostel Týn	D
Traveller's Hostel	A

HOTELS

Avalon-Tara	F
Betlém Club	G
Černá liška	E
Cloister Inn	I
Expres	H
Grand Hotel	
Evropa	L
Josef	B
U medvídků	J
Unitas	K

RESTAURANTS

Ariana	6
Bellevue	18
Kogo	14
La Saint-Jacques	10
Mlýnec	16
Orange Moon	5
Red Hot & Blues	7
Usadlů	4

BARS

Billard Centrum	20
Legends	8
Marquis de Sade	9
Molly Malone's	1
Radegast	11
U medvídků	J
U mravence	13

CAFÉS

Chez Marcel	2
Erra	21
Louvre	22
Montmartre	15
Slavia	23
Teta tramtária	24

TEA-HOUSES

Dahab	3
Dobrá čajovna	19
Obecní dům	12
U zlatého kohouta	17

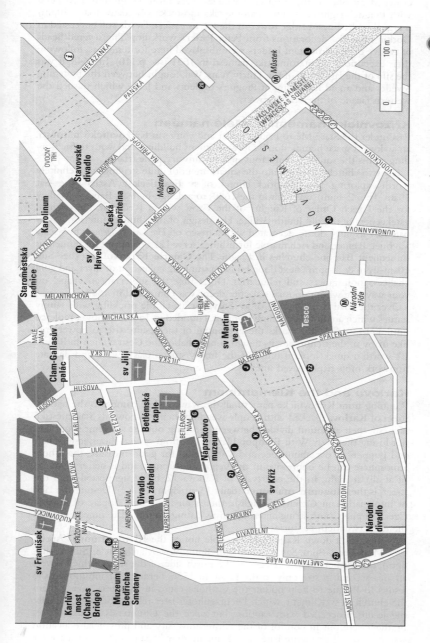

crowned by one of the pinnacled wedge-spires more commonly associated with Prague's right bank. The Staroměstská mostecká věž (daily 10am–10pm) is arguably the finest bridge tower of the lot, its eastern facade still encrusted in Gothic cake-like decorations from Peter Parler's workshop. The severed heads of twelve of the Protestant leaders were displayed here for ten years, following their executions on Staroměstské náměstí in 1621 (see p.110). In 1648, it was the site of the last battle of the Thirty Years' War, fought between the besieging Swedes and an ad hoc army of Prague's students and Jews, which trashed the western facade of the bridge tower.

Křižovnické náměstí to Malé náměstí

Pass under the Staré Město bridge tower and you're in **Křižovnické náměstí**, an awkward space hemmed in by its constituent buildings and, with traffic hurtling across the square, a dangerous spot for unwary pedestrians.

The two churches facing onto the square are both quite striking and definitely worth exploring. The half-brick church of **sv František z Assisi** (Tues–Sat 10am–1pm 2–6pm) was built in the 1680s to a design by Jean-Baptiste Mathey for the Czech Order of Knights of the Cross with a Red Star, the original gatekeepers of the old Judith Bridge. The design of the church's interior, dominated by its huge dome, decorated with a fresco of *The Last Judgement* by Václav Vavřinec Reiner, and rich marble furnishings, served as a blueprint for numerous subsequent Baroque churches in Prague. The **Galerie Křižovníků** (Tues–Sun 10am–1pm & 2–5pm), next door, houses a stunning collection of silver and gold chalices, monstrances and reliquaries. Don't miss the subterranean chapel on your way out, whose unusual stalactite decor was completed in 1683.

Over the road is the church of **sv Salvátor**, its facade prickling with saintly statues which are lit up enticingly at night. Founded in 1593, but not completed until 1714, sv Salvátor marks the beginning of the Jesuits' rise to power and, like many of their churches, its design copies that of the Gesù church in Rome. It's worth a quick look, if only for the frothy stucco plasterwork and delicate ironwork in its triple-naved interior.

Karlova and the Klementinum

Running from Křižovnické náměstí all the way to Malé náměstí is the narrow street of **Karlova**, packed with people wending their way towards Staroměstské náměstí, their attention divided between checking out the souvenir shops and not losing their way. With Europop blaring out from several shops, jesters' hats and puppets in overabundance and a strip club for good measure, the whole atmosphere can be oppressive in the height of summer, and is better savoured (if at all) at night. In the courtyard of Karlova 12, badly signposted from the street, is the **Muzeum marionet** (daily 11am–8pm; 100Kč). Despite the lack of information in Czech or English, there's an impressive display of historic Czech puppets, both string and rod, mostly dating from the late nineteenth and the early twentieth centuries.

As they stroll down Karlova, few people notice the **Klementinum** (April–Oct Mon–Fri 2–8pm, Sat & Sun 10am–8pm; Nov–March Sat & Sun 10am–8pm), the former Jesuit College on the north side of the street, which covers an area second in size only to the Hrad. In 1556, Ferdinand I summoned the Jesuits to Prague to help bolster the Catholic cause in Bohemia, giving them the church of sv Kliment, which Dientzenhofer later rebuilt for them. Initially, the Jesuits proceeded with caution, but once the Counter-Reformation set in, they were put in control of the entire university and provincial education system. From their secure base at sv Kliment, they began to establish space for a great Catholic seat of learning in the city by buying up the surrounding land, demolishing more than thirty old town houses, and, over the next two hundred years, gradually building themselves a palatial headquarters. In 1773, soon after the Klementinum was completed, the Jesuits were turfed out of the country and the building handed over to the university authorities.

Nowadays, the Klementinum houses the National Library's collection of over five million volumes, but much of the original building has been left intact. The **entrance**, inconspicuously placed just past the church of sv Kliment, on Karlova, lets you into a series of rather plain courtyards. The entrance to the **Zrcadlová kaple** (Mirrored Chapel) is immediately to the left after passing through the archway on the far side of the first courtyard; its interior of fake marble, gilded stucco and mirror panels boasts fine acoustics but is only open for concerts. Nearby is the visitors' entrance, where thirty-minute guided tours (in English) set off for the Klementinum's two most easily accessible attractions. The most spectacular sight is the **Barokní sál** (Baroque Library), a long room lined with leather tomes, whose ceiling is decorated by one continuous illusionistic fresco praising secular wisdom, and whose wrought-iron gallery balustrade is held up by wooden barley-sugar columns. Upstairs, at roughly the centre of the Klementinum complex, is the Jesuits' **Astronomická věž** (Astronomical Tower), from which you can enjoy a superb view over the centre of Prague.

Malé náměstí

After a couple more shops, boutiques, hole-in-the-wall bars and a final twist in Karlova, you emerge onto **Malé náměstí**, a square originally settled by French merchants in the twelfth century. The square was also home to the first apothecary in Prague, opened by a Florentine in 1353, and the tradition is continued today by the pharmacy **U zlaté koruny** (The Golden Crown) at no. 13, which boasts chandeliers and a restored Baroque interior. The square's best-known building, though, is the russet-red, neo-Renaissance **Rott Haus**, originally an ironmonger's shop founded by V.J. Rott in 1840, whose facade is smothered in agricultural scenes and motifs inspired by the Czech artist Mikuláš Aleš. At the centre of the square is a (non-functioning) fountain from 1560, which retains its beautiful, original wrought-iron canopy.

Staroměstské náměstí

East of Malé náměstí is **Staroměstské náměstí** (Old Town Square), easily the most spectacular square in Prague, and the traditional heart of the city. Most of the brightly coloured houses look solidly eighteenth-century, but their Baroque facades hide considerably older buildings. From the eleventh century onwards, this was the city's main marketplace, known simply as Velké náměstí (Great Square), to which all roads in Bohemia led, and where merchants from all over Europe gathered. When the five towns that made up Prague were united in 1784, it was the Old Town Square's town hall that was made the seat of the new city council, and for the next two hundred years the square was the scene of the country's most violent demonstrations and battles. Nowadays, it's busy with tourists all year round: in summer, cafés spread out their tables, in winter there's a Christmas market, and all year round tourists pour in to watch the town hall's astronomical clock chime, to sit on the steps of the Hus Monument, and to drink in this historic showpiece.

The most recent arrival in the square is the colossal **Jan Hus Monument**, a turbulent sea of blackened bodies – the oppressed to the right, the defiant to the left – out of which rises the majestic moral authority of Hus himself (for more on whom, see p.116), gazing to the horizon. For the sculptor Ladislav Šaloun, a maverick who received no formal training, the monument was his life's work. Commissioned in 1900 when the Art Nouveau style Viennese Secession was at its peak, but strangely old-fashioned by the time it was completed in 1915, it would be difficult to claim that it blends in with its Baroque surroundings, yet this has never mattered to the Czechs, for whom its significance goes far beyond aesthetic merit. The Austrians refused to hold an official unveiling; in protest, on July 6, 1915, the 500th anniversary of the death of Hus, Praguers smothered the monument in flowers. Since then it has been a powerful symbol of Czech nationalism: in March 1939, it was draped in swastikas by the invading Nazis, and in August 1968, it was shrouded in funereal black by Praguers, protesting at the Soviet invasion. The inscription along the base is a quote from the will of Comenius, one of Hus's later followers, and includes Hus's most famous dictum, *Pravda vítězí* (Truth Prevails), which has been the motto of just about every Czech revolution since then.

Staroměstská radnice

It wasn't until the reign of King John of Luxembourg (1310–46) that Staré Město was allowed to build its own town hall, the **Staroměstská radnice**. Short of funds, the citizens decided against an entirely new structure, buying a corner house on the square instead and simply adding an extra floor; later on, they added the east wing, with its graceful Gothic oriel and obligatory wedge-tower. Gradually, over the centuries, the neighbouring merchants' houses to the west were incorporated into the building, so that now it stretches all the way across to the richly sgraffitoed **Dům U minuty**, which juts out into the square.

On May 8, 1945, on the final day of the Prague Uprising, the Nazis still held on to Staroměstské náměstí, and in a last desperate act set fire to the town hall – one of the few buildings to be irrevocably damaged in the old town in World War II. The tower was rebuilt immediately, but only a crumbling fragment remains of the neo-Gothic **east wing**, which once stretched almost as far as the church of sv Mikuláš. Set into the paving nearby are 27 **white crosses** commemorating the Protestant leaders who were condemned to death on the orders of the emperor Ferdinand II, following the Battle of Bílá hora. They were publicly executed in the square on June 21, 1621: twenty-four enjoyed the nobleman's privilege and had their heads lopped off; the three remaining commoners were hung, drawn and quartered.

Today, the town hall's most popular feature is its *orloj* or **Astronomical Clock** – on the hour (daily 8am–8pm), a crowd of tourists gathers in front of the tower to watch a mechanical dumbshow by the clock's assorted figures. The Apostles shuffle past the top two windows, bowing to the audience, while perched on pinnacles below are the four threats to the city as perceived by the medieval mind: Death carrying his hourglass and tolling his bell, the Jew with his moneybags (since 1945 minus his stereotypical beard), Vanity admiring his reflection, and a turbaned Turk shaking his head. Beneath the moving figures, four characters representing Philosophy, Religion, Astronomy and History stand motionless throughout the performance. Finally, a cockerel pops out and flaps its wings to signal that the show's over; the clock then chimes the hour.

The powder-pink facade on the south side of the town hall now forms the **entrance** to the whole complex. The town hall is a popular place to get married, but casual visitors can also get to see the inside. Temporary exhibitions are held on the ground floor, and you can climb the **tower** (40Kč) for a panoramic sweep across Prague's spires; tickets are available from the third floor. On the fourth floor, there's a vast **model** of contemporary Prague, made over the course of twenty years out of cardboard and plexiglass. Despite being steeped in history, there's not much of interest here, apart from a few decorated ceilings with chunky beams and a couple of Renaissance portals. More atmospheric are the town hall's Romano-Gothic cellars, and the Gothic **chapel**, designed by Peter Parler, which has patches of medieval wall painting, and wonderful grimacing corbels at the foot of the ribbed vaulting.Visitors also get to see the clock's **Apostles** close up – and if you're there just before the clock strikes the hour, you can watch them going out on parade; the figures all had to be re-carved by a local puppeteer after the war.

The church of sv Mikuláš and palác Kinských

The destruction of the east wing of the town hall in 1945 rudely exposed Kilian Ignaz Dientzenhofer's church of **sv Mikuláš** (Mon noon–4pm, Tues–Sat 10am–4pm, Sun noon–3pm), built for the Benedictines in just three years between 1732 and 1735. The south front is decidedly luscious – Braun's blackened statuary pop up at every cornice – promising an interior to surpass even its sister church of sv Mikuláš in Malá Strana, which Dientzenhofer built with his father immediately afterwards (see p.97). Inside, however, it's a much smaller space, theatrically organized into a series of interlocking curves. It's also rather plainly furnished, partly because it was closed down by Joseph II and turned into a storehouse, and partly because it's now owned by the very "low", modern, Czechoslovak Hussite Church. Instead, your eyes are drawn sharply upwards to the impressive stuccowork, the wrought-iron galleries and the trompe l'oeil frescoes on the dome.

The largest secular building on the square is the Rococo **palác Kinských** (Tues–Sun 10am–6pm; ⓦ www.ngprague.cz), designed by Kilian Ignaz Dientzenhofer and built by his son-in-law Anselmo Lurago. In the nineteenth century it became a German *Gymnasium*, which was attended by, among others, Franz Kafka (whose father ran a haberdashery shop on the ground floor). The palace is perhaps most notorious, however, as the venue for the fateful speech by the Communist prime minister, Klement Gottwald, who walked out on to the grey stone balcony one snowy February morning in 1948, flanked by his Party henchmen, to address the thousands of enthusiastic supporters who packed the square below. It was the beginning of *Vítězná února* (Victorious February), the bloodless coup which brought the Communists to power and sealed the fate of the country for the next 41 years.The upper floor now hosts top-flight exhibitions of graphic art put on by the Národní galerie.

The Týn church and Ungelt

Staré Město's most impressive Gothic structure, the mighty **Týn church** (Chrám Matky boží před Týnem; Mon–Fri 9am–1pm; ⓦ www.tynska.farnost.cz), whose two irregular towers, bristling with baubles, spires and pinnacles, rise like giant antennae above the arcaded houses which otherwise obscure its facade, is a far more imposing building than sv Mikuláš. Like the nearby Hus monument, the Týn church, begun in the fourteenth century, is a source of Czech national pride. In an act of defiance, George of Poděbrady, the last Czech and the only Hussite King of Bohemia, adorned the high stone gable with a statue of himself and a giant gilded *kalich* (chalice), the mascot of all Hussite sects.The church remained a hotbed of Hussitism until the Protestants' crushing defeat at the Battle of Bílá hora, after which the chalice was melted down to provide the newly ensconced statue of theVirgin Mary with a golden halo, sceptre and crown.

Despite being one of the main landmarks of Staré Město, it's well-nigh impossible to appreciate the church from anything but a considerable distance, since it's boxed in by the houses around it, some of which are actually built right against the walls. The church's **interior** has recently been restored and the rather appealing gloom of the place has been swept away. Instead, the lofty, narrow nave is now bright white, and punctuated at ground level by black and gold Baroque altarpieces. The pillar on the right of the chancel steps contains the red marble **tomb of Tycho Brahe**, the famous Danish astronomer, who arrived in Prague wearing a silver and gold false nose, having lost his own in a duel in Rostock. Court astronomer to Rudolf II for just two years, Brahe laid much of the groundwork for Johannes Kepler's later discoveries – Kepler getting his chance of employment when Brahe died of a burst bladder in 1601 after joining Petr Vok in one of his notorious binges.

Behind the Týn church lies the **Týn** courtyard, better known by its German name, **Ungelt** (meaning "No Money", a pseudonym used to deter marauding invaders), which, as the trading base of German merchants, was one of the first settlements on the Vltava. A hospice, church and hostel were built for the use of the merchants, and by the fourteenth century the area had become an extremely successful international marketplace; soon afterwards the traders moved up to the Hrad, and the court was transformed into a palace. The whole complex has since been restored, and the Dominicans have reclaimed one section, while the rest houses various shops, restaurants, and a luxury hotel.

Dům U zlatého prstenů

Back on Týnská, you'll come to the handsome Gothic town house of **Dům U zlatého prstenů** (House of the Golden Ring; Tues–Sun 10am–6pm; ⓦwww.citygalleryprague.cz), now used by the City of Prague Gallery to show some of its twentieth-century Czech art. If you're not heading out to the modern art museum in the Veletržní palác (see p.141), then this is a good taster. The permanent collection is spread out over three floors, and arranged thematically rather than chronologically, while the cellar provides space for installations by up-and-coming contemporary artists; there's also a nice café across the courtyard.

On the first floor, symbolism looms large, with *Destitute Land*, Max Švabinský's none-too-subtle view of life under the Habsburg yoke, and a smattering of works by two of Bohemia's best-loved eccentrics, Josef Váchal and František Bílek. There's a decent selection of dour 1920s paintings, too, typified by *Slagheaps in the Evening II* by Jan Zrzavý, plus the usual Czech Surrealist suspects, Josef Síma, Toyen and Jiří Štyrský. More refreshing is the sight of Eduard Stavinoha's cartoon-like *Striking Demonstrators 24.2.1948*, an ideological painting from 1948 that appears almost like Pop Art. Antonín Slavíček's easy-on-the-eye Impressionist views of Prague kick off proceedings on the second floor, along with works by Cubist Emil Filla, and abstract artist Mikuláš Medek. Also on this floor, there's the chance to see a lot of 1980s works that don't often see the light of day nowadays, such as Michael Rittstein's political allegory *Slumber beneath a Large Hand*. Highlights on the third floor include an excellent collection of mad collages by Jiří Kolář, abstract Vorticist works by Zdeněk Sýkora, and studies for kinetic-light sculptures by Zdeněk Pešánek.

From Celetná to Anežský klášter

Celetná, whose name comes from the bakers who used to bake a particular type of small loaf (*calty*) here in the Middle Ages, leads east from Staroměstské náměstí direct to the Prašná brána, one of the original gateways of the old town. It's one of the oldest streets in Prague, lying along the former trade route from the old town market square, as well as on the *králová cesta*. Its buildings were smartly refaced in the Baroque period, and their pastel shades are now crisply maintained. Most of Celetná's shops veer towards the chic end of the Czech market, making it a popular place for a bit of window-shopping. Dive down one of the covered passages to the left and into the backstreets, however, and you'll soon lose the crowds, and eventually end up at the atmospheric ruins of Anežský klášter, now home to the Národní galerie's Gothic Czech art collection.

Two-thirds of the way along Celetná, at the junction with Ovocný trh, is the **Dům U černé Matky boží** (House at the Black Madonna), built as a department store in 1911–12 by Josef Gočár and one of the best examples of Czech Cubist architecture in Prague (see p.136 for more). Appropriately enough, the building now houses a small but excellent **Muzeum českého kubismu** (Museum of Czech Cubism; Tues–Sun 10am–6pm; ⓦ www.ngprague.cz). There's a little bit of everything, from sofas and sideboards by Gočár himself to paintings by Emil Filla and Josef Čapek, plus some wonderful sculptures by Otto Gutfreund. If the above has only whetted your appetite, there are more Czech Cubist exhibits in the Veletržní palác (see p.141), and more Cubist buildings in Vyšehrad (see p.136), models of which are displayed in the museum.

Celetná ends at the fourteenth-century Prašná brána (see p.131), beyond which is náměstí Republiky, at which point, strictly speaking, you've left Staré Město behind. Back in the old town, head north from Celetná into the backstreets which conceal the Franciscan church of **sv Jakub** or St James (Mon–Sat 9.30am–noon & 2–4pm, Sun 2–4pm), with its distinctive bubbling, stucco portal on Malá štupartská. The church's massive Gothic proportions – it has the longest nave in Prague after the cathedral – make it a favourite venue for organ recitals, Mozart masses and other concerts. After the great fire of 1689, Prague's Baroque artists remodelled the entire interior, adding huge pilasters, a series of colourful frescoes and over twenty side altars. The most famous of these is the tomb of the Count of Mitrovice, in the northern aisle, designed by Fischer von Erlach and Prague's own Maximilian Brokof.

Anežský klášter

Further north through the backstreets, the **Anežský klášter** (Convent of St Agnes), Prague's oldest surviving Gothic building, stands within a stone's throw of the river as it loops around to the east. It was founded in 1233 as a Franciscan convent for the Order of the Poor Clares, and takes its name from Agnes (Anežka), youngest daughter of Přemysl Otakar I, who left her life of regal privilege to become the convent's first abbess. Agnes herself was beatified in 1874 to try to combat the spread of Hussitism amongst the Czechs, and was officially canonized on November 12, 1989, just four days before the Velvet Revolution.

The convent itself was closed down in 1782 and fell into rack and ruin. It was squatted for most of the next century, and although saved from demolition by the Czech nationalist lobby, its restoration only took place in the 1980s. The convent now houses the Národní galerie's **medieval art collection** (Tues–Sun 10am–6pm; ⓦ www.ngprague.cz), in particular the Gothic art, which first flourished here under the patronage of Charles IV.

The exhibition is arranged chronologically, starting with a remarkable silver-gilt casket from 1360 used to house the skull of St Ludmilla. The nine panels from the altarpiece of the Cistercian monastery at Vyšší Brod in South Bohemia, from around 1350, are among the finest in central Europe: the *Annunciation* panel is particularly rich iconographically. The real gems of the collection, however, are the six panels by **Master Theodoric**, who painted over one hundred such paintings for Charles IV's castle chapel at Karlštejn (see p.178). These larger-than-life half-length portraits of saints, church fathers and so on, are full of intense expression and rich colours, their depictions spilling onto the embossed frames.

The three late fourteenth-century panels by the **Master of Třeboň** show an even greater variety of balance and depth, and the increasing influence of Flemish paintings of the period. Since the quality of the works in the gallery's largest room is pretty uneven, it's worth moving fairly swiftly on to the smaller rooms beyond, where you'll find woodcuts by Cranach the Elder, Dürer and the lesser-known Hans Burgkmair – the seven-headed beast in Dürer's *Apocalypse* cycle is particularly Harry Potter. Finally, don't miss the superb sixteenth-century wood sculptures, including an incredibly detailed scene, *Christ the Saviour and the Last Judgement*, in which Death's entrails are in the process of being devoured by a frog.

Southern Staré Město

The southern half of Staré Město is bounded by the *králová cesta* (the coronation route) to the north, and the curve of Národní and Na příkopě, which follow the course of the old fortifications, to the south. There are no showpiece squares like Staroměstské náměstí here, but the complex web of narrow lanes and hidden passageways, many of which have changed little since medieval times, makes this an intriguing quarter to explore, and one where it's easy to lose the worst of the crowds (and yourself).

From Ovocný trh to Uhelný trh

South of Celetná lies **Ovocný trh**, site of the old fruit market, its cobbles fanning out towards the back of the lime-green and white **Stavovské divadlo** (Estates Theatre). Built in the early 1780s by Count Nostitz (after whom the theatre was originally named) for the entertainment of Prague's large and powerful German community, the theatre is one of the finest Neoclassical buildings in Prague, reflecting the enormous self-confidence of its patrons. The Stavovské divadlo has a place in Czech history too, for it was here that the Czech national anthem, *Kde domov můj* (Where is My Home), was first performed, as part of the comic opera *Fidlovačka*, by J.K. Tyl. It is also something of a mecca for Mozart fans, since it was here, rather than in the hostile climate of Vienna, that the composer chose to premiere both *Don Giovanni* and *La Clemenza di Tito*. This is, in fact, one of the few opera houses in Europe which remains intact from Mozart's time, though it underwent major refurbishment during the nineteenth century – it was here that Miloš Forman filmed the concert scenes for his Oscar-laden *Amadeus*.

On the north side of the Stavovské divadlo is the home base of the **Karolinum** or Charles University, named after its founder Charles IV, who established it in 1348 as the first university in this part of Europe. To begin with, the university had no fixed abode; it wasn't until 1383 that Václav IV bought the present site. All that's left of the original fourteenth-century building is the Gothic oriel window which emerges from the south wall; the rest was trashed by the Nazis in 1945. The new main entrance is a modern red-brick curtain wall building by Jaroslav Fragner, set back from the street and inscribed with the original Latin name *Universitas Karolina*. Only a couple of small departments and the chancellor's office and administration are now housed here, with the rest spread over the length and breadth of the city. The heavily restored Gothic vaults, on the ground floor of the south wing, are now used as a contemporary art gallery (daily 10am–6pm).

The junction of Melantrichova and Rytířská is always teeming with people pouring out of Staroměstské náměstí and heading for Wenceslas Square. Clearly visible from Melantrichova is Prague's last surviving **open-air market** – once a German market, which stretched all the way from Ovocný trh to Uhelný trh. Traditionally a flower and vegetable market, it runs the full length of the arcaded Havelská, and sells everything from celery to CDs, with plenty of souvenirs and wooden toys in between. The market runs west into **Uhelný trh**, which gets its name from the *uhlí* (coal) that was sold here in medieval times. Nowadays, however, it's Prague's red-light district – particularly Perlová and Na Perštýně – and although you'll see little evidence during the day, it can get busy at night, as a result of which the local authorities are constantly trying to move the trade elsewhere.

Wax Museum Prague (Muzeum voskových figurín)

The entrance fee may be steep for many Czechs, yet the **Wax Museum Prague** (daily 9am–8pm; 250Kč; Ⓦ www.waxmuseumprague.cz), at Melantrichova 5, is aimed primarily at a domestic audience. For anyone familiar with London's Madame Tussaud's, the formula is predictable enough, but unless your grasp of Czech history, past and present, is pretty good, many of the wax tableaux will remain slightly baffling. The most popular section with the locals is the podium of commie stooges ranging from Lenin to the Czechs' home-grown Stalinist, Klement Gottwald, followed by today's generation of Czech politicians dressed in bad suits, sat amidst naff office furniture.

Sv Martin ve zdi and Bartolomějská

South of Uhelný trh, down Martinská, the street miraculously opens out to make room for the twelfth-century church of **sv Martin ve zdi** (St Martin-in-the-Walls), originally built to serve the Czech community of the village of sv Martin, until it found itself on the wrong side of the Gothic fortifications. It's still essentially a Romanesque structure, adapted to suit Gothic tastes a century later; it was, however, closed down in 1784 by Joseph II and turned into a warehouse, shops and flats. The city bought the church in 1904 and thoroughly restored it, adding the creamy neo-Renaissance tower, and eventually handing it over to the Czech Brethren. For them, it has a special significance as the place where communion "in both kinds" (ie bread and wine), one of the fundamental demands of the Hussites, was first administered to the whole congregation, in 1414. To be honest, there's very little to see inside, which is just as well as it's only open for concerts nowadays.

Around the corner from sv Martin ve zdi is the gloomy, lifeless street of **Bartolomějská**, dominated by a tall, grim-looking building on its south side, which served as the main interrogation centre of the universally detested **Communist secret police**, the *Statní bezpečnost*, or *StB*. The building is now back in the hands of the Franciscan nuns who occupied the place prior to 1948, and its former police cells now serve as rooms for a small *pension* – it's even possible to stay in Havel's old cell (see p.81).

Betlémské náměstí

After leaving the dark shadows of Bartolomějská, the brighter aspect of **Betlémské náměstí** comes as a welcome relief. The square is named after the **Betlémská kaple** (Tues–Sun: April–Oct 10am–6.30pm; Nov–March 10am–5.30pm), whose high wooden gables face on to the square. The chapel was founded in 1391 by religious reformists, who, denied the right to build a church, proceeded instead to build the largest chapel in Bohemia, with a total capacity of three thousand. Sermons were delivered not in the customary Latin, but in the language of the masses – Czech. From 1402 to 1413, **Jan Hus** preached here (see box on p.224), regularly pulling in more than enough commoners to fill the chapel. Hus was eventually excommunicated for his outspokenness, found guilty of heresy and burnt at the stake at the Council of Constance in 1415.

The chapel continued to attract reformists from all over Europe for another two centuries until it was handed over to the Jesuits. The chapel was demolished following the expulsion of the Jesuits in 1773, and only three outer walls now remain from the medieval building, with patches of their original biblical decoration. The rest is a scrupulous reconstruction by Jaroslav Fragner, using the original plans and a fair amount of imaginative guesswork. The initial reconstruction work was carried out after the war by the Communists, who were keen to portray Hus as a Czech nationalist and social critic as much as a religious reformer.

At the western end of the square stands the **Náprstkovo muzeum** (Tues–Sun 9am–5.30pm; Ⓦ www.aconet.cz/npm), whose founder, Czech nationalist Vojta Náprstek, was inspired by the great Victorian museums of London while in exile following the 1848 revolution. Despite the fact that the museum could clearly do with an injection of cash, it still manages to put on some excellent temporary ethnographic exhibitions on the ground floor, and does a useful job of promoting tolerance of different cultures. The permanent collection of Náprstek's American, Australasian and Oceanic collections occupies the top two floors. Náprstek's technological exhibits now form part of the collections of the Národné technické muzeum (see p.141).

Muzeum Bedřicha Smetany

A few blocks west, in a gaily decorated neo-Renaissance building on the riverfront, is the **Muzeum Bedřicha Smetany** (daily except Tues 10am–noon & 12.30–5pm). Bedřich Smetana (1824–84) was without doubt the most nationalistic of all the great Czech composers, taking an active part in the 1848 revolution and the later national revival movement. He enjoyed his greatest success as a composer with *The Bartered Bride*, which marked the birth of Czech opera. However, he was forced to give up conducting in 1874 with the onset of deafness, and eventually died of syphilis in a mental asylum. Sadly, the museum fails to capture much of the spirit of the man, though you get to see his spectacles, and the garnet jewellery of his first wife. Still, the views across to the castle are good, and you get to wave a laser baton around in order to listen to his music.

Josefov

It is crowded with horses; traversed by narrow streets not remarkable for cleanliness, and has altogether an uninviting aspect. Your sanitary reformer would here find a strong case of overcrowding.

Walter White, "A July Holiday in Saxony, Bohemia and Silesia" (1857)

Less than half a century after Walter White's comments, all that was left of the former ghetto of **JOSEFOV** were six synagogues, the town hall and the medieval cemetery. At the end of the nineteenth century, a period of great economic growth for the Habsburg Empire, it was decided that Prague should be turned into a beautiful bourgeois city, modelled on Paris. The key to this transformation was the *asanace* or "sanitization" of the ghetto, a process, begun in 1893, which reduced the notorious malodorous backstreets and alleyways of Josefov

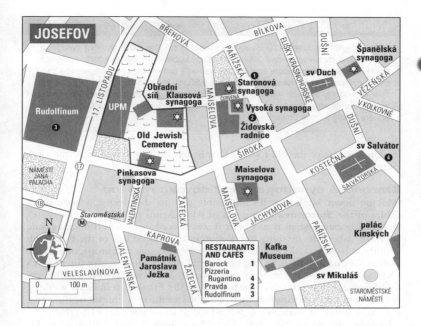

to rubble and replaced them with block after block of luxurious five-storey mansions. The Jews, the poor, the Gypsies and the prostitutes were cleared out so that the area could become a desirable residential quarter, rich in Art Nouveau buildings festooned with decorative murals, doorways and sculpturing. This building frenzy marked the beginning of the end for a community which had existed in Prague for almost a millennium.

In any other European city occupied by the Nazis in World War II, what little was left of the old ghetto would have been demolished. But although Prague's Jews were transported to the new ghetto in Terezín and eventually Auschwitz, the Prague ghetto itself was preserved by Hitler himself in order to provide a site for his planned "Exotic Museum of an Extinct Race". By this grotesque twist of fate, Jewish artefacts from all over central Europe were gathered here, and now make up one of the richest collections of Judaica in Europe, and one of the most fascinating sights in Prague.

The former ghetto

Geographically, Josefov lies to the northwest of Staroměstské náměstí, between the church of sv Mikuláš and the River Vltava. The warren-like street plan of Josefov disappeared during the sanitization, and through the heart of the old ghetto runs the ultimate bourgeois avenue, **Pařížská**, a riot of turn-of-the-twentieth-century sculpturing, spikes and turrets, home to swanky boutiques and cafés. If Josefov can still be said to have a main street, though, it is really the parallel street of **Maiselova**, named after the community's sixteenth-century leader. The sheer volume of tourists – over a million a year – that visit Josefov has brought with it the inevitable rash of souvenir stalls flogging dubious "Jewish" souvenirs, and the whole area is now something of a tourist trap. Yet

117

Visiting Josefov

All the "sights" of Josefov (🌐 www.jewishmuseum.cz), bar the Staronová synagoga, are covered by an all-in-one 300Kč ticket, available from the quarter's numerous ticket offices. Opening hours vary but are basically daily except Saturday April–October 9am–6pm and November–March 9am–4.30pm. In order to try and regulate the flow of visitors, at peak times a timed entry system comes into operation, giving you around twenty minutes at each sight, though don't worry too much if you don't adhere rigidly to your timetable.

to skip this part of the old town is to miss out on an entire slice of the city's cultural history.

Staronová synagoga and Židovská radnice

Walking down Maiselova, it's impossible to miss the steep sawtooth brick gables of the **Staronová synagoga** or Altneuschul (Old-New Synagogue), so called because when it was built it was indeed very new, though as time went on, it became anything but. Begun in the second half of the thirteenth century, it is, in fact, the oldest functioning synagogue in Europe, one of the earliest Gothic buildings in Prague and still the religious centre for Prague's Orthodox Jews. Since Jews were prevented by law from becoming architects, the synagogue was probably constructed by the Franciscan builders working on the convent of sv Anežka. Its five-ribbed vaulting is unique in Bohemia; the extra, purely decorative rib was added to avoid any hint of a cross.

To enter the synagogue (April–Oct Mon–Thurs & Sun 9.30am–6pm, Fri 9.30am–5pm; Nov–March Mon–Thurs & Sun 9.30am–5pm, Fri 9.30am–2pm; 200Kč), you must buy a separate ticket from the ticket office opposite the synagogue's entrance on Červená (or from one of the other ticket offices in Josefov). Men are asked to cover their heads out of respect – paper *kippahs* are available at the ticket office, though a handkerchief will do. To get to the **main hall**, you must pass through one of the two low vestibules from which women are allowed to watch the proceedings. Above the entrance is an elaborate tympanum covered in the twisting branches of a vine tree, its twelve bunches of grapes representing the tribes of Israel. The low glow from the chandeliers is the only light in the hall, which is mostly taken up with the elaborate wrought-iron cage enclosing the *bimah* in the centre. In 1357, Charles IV allowed the Jews to fly their own municipal standard, a moth-eaten remnant of which is still on show. The other flag – a tattered red banner – was a gift to the community from Emperor Ferdinand III for helping fend off the Swedes in 1648. On the west wall is a glass cabinet, shaped like Moses' two tablets of stone and filled with tiny personalized light bulbs, which are paid for by grieving relatives or friends and light up on the anniversary of the person's death (there's even one for Kafka).

Just south of the synagogue is the **Židovská radnice** (Jewish Town Hall), one of the few such buildings to survive the Holocaust. Founded and funded by Maisel in the sixteenth century, it was later rebuilt as the creamy-pink Baroque house you see now, housing an overpriced kosher restaurant. The belfry, permission for which was granted by Ferdinand III, has a clock on each of its four sides, plus a Hebrew one stuck on the north gable which, like the Hebrew script, goes "backwards".

Pinkasova synagoga

Jutting out at an angle on the south side of the Old Jewish Cemetery (see p.120), with its entrance on Široká, the **Pinkasova synagoga** was built in the

1530s for the powerful Pinkas family, and has undergone countless restorations over the centuries. In 1958, the synagogue was transformed into a chilling memorial to the 77,297 Czech Jews killed during the Holocaust. Of all the sights of the Jewish quarter, the Holocaust memorial is perhaps the most moving, with every bit of wall space taken up with the carved stone list of victims, stating simply their names, dates of birth and dates of transportation to the camps. It is the longest epitaph in the world, yet it represents only the merest

Prague's Jews

Jews probably arrived in Prague as early as the tenth century and, initially at least, are thought to have settled on both sides of the river. In 1096, at the time of the first crusade, the earliest recorded **pogrom** took place, which may have hastened the formation of a much more closely knit "Jewish town" within Staré Město during the twelfth century. However, it wasn't until much later that Jews were actually herded into a **walled ghetto** (and several centuries before the word "ghetto" was actually first coined in Venice), sealed off from the rest of the town and subject to a curfew. From the beginning, though, they were subject to laws restricting their choice of profession to usury and the rag trade; in addition, some form of visible identification, a cap or badge (notably the Star of David), remained a more or less constant feature of Jewish life until the Enlightenment.

During the **1389 pogrom**, 3000 Jews were massacred over Easter, some while sheltering in the Old-New Synagogue – an event commemorated every year thereafter on Yom Kippur. By contrast, the reign of Rudolf II (1576–1612) was a time of economic and cultural prosperity for the Prague Jewish community. The Jewish mayor, **Mordecai Maisel**, Rudolf's minister of finance, became one of the richest men in Bohemia and the success symbol of a generation. This was the "golden age" of the ghetto: the time of **Rabbi Löw**, the severe and conservative chief rabbi of Prague, who is now best known as the legendary creator of the Jewish "golem" (a precursor of Frankenstein's monster).

It was the enlightened **Emperor Joseph II** (1780–90) who did most to lift the restrictions on Jews. His 1781 Toleration Edict ended the dress codes, opened up education to all non-Catholics, and removed the gates from the ghetto. The community paid him homage in the following century by officially naming the ghetto Josefov, or Josefstadt. It was not until the **1848 revolution**, however, that Jews were granted equal status as citizens and permitted to settle outside the ghetto. Gradually, the more prosperous Jewish families began to move to other districts of Prague, leaving behind only the poorest Jews and strictly Orthodox families, who were rapidly joined by the underprivileged ranks of Prague society: Gypsies, beggars, prostitutes and alcoholics. By 1890, only twenty percent of Josefov's population was Jewish, yet it was still the most densely populated area in Prague.

After the **Nazi occupation** of Prague on March 15, 1939, the city's Jews were subject to an increasingly harsh set of regulations, which saw them again barred from most professions, placed under curfew, and compelled once more to wear the yellow Star of David. In November 1941, the first transport of Prague Jews set off for the new ghetto in Terezín, 60km northwest of Prague. Of the estimated 55,000 Jews in Prague at the time of the Nazi invasion, over 36,000 died in the camps. Many survivors emigrated to Israel and the USA. Of the 8000 who registered as Jewish in the Prague census of 1947, a significant number joined the Communist Party, only to find themselves victims of Stalinist anti-Semitic wrath during the 1950s.

It's difficult to calculate exactly how many Jews now live in Prague – around a thousand were officially registered as such prior to 1989 – though their numbers have undoubtedly been bolstered by a new generation of Czech Jews who have rediscovered their roots, and by the new influx of Jewish Americans and Israelis.

fraction of those who died in the Nazi ghettos and concentration camps. All that remains of the synagogue's original decor is the ornate *bimah* surrounded by a beautiful wrought-iron grille, supported by barley-sugar columns. Upstairs in a room beside the women's gallery, there's now a harrowing exhibition of naive drawings by children from the Jewish ghetto in Terezín (see p.278), most of whom later perished in the camps.

Starý židovský hřbitov (Old Jewish Cemetery)

At the heart of Josefov is the **Starý židovský hřbitov** (Old Jewish Cemetery), called *beit hayyim* in Hebrew, meaning House of Life. Established in the fifteenth century, it was in use until 1787, by which time there were an estimated 100,000 buried here, one on top of the other, as many as twelve layers deep. The enormous number of visitors has meant that the graves themselves have been roped off to protect them, and a one-way system introduced: you enter from the Pinkasova synagoga, on Široká, and leave by the Klausová synagoga (see opposite). The oldest grave, dating from 1439, belongs to the poet Avigdor Karo, who lived to tell the tale of the 1389 pogrom. Get there before the crowds – a difficult task at most times of the year – and you'll find the cemetery a poignant reminder of the ghetto, its inhabitants subjected to inhuman overcrowding even in death. The rest of Prague recedes beyond the sombre ash trees and cramped perimeter walls, the haphazard headstones and Hebrew inscriptions casting a powerful spell.

△ Starý židovský hřbitov

Obřadní síň and the other synagogues

Immediately on your left as you leave the cemetery is the **Obřadní síň**, a lugubrious neo-Renaissance house built in 1906 as a ceremonial hall by the Jewish Burial Society. Appropriately enough, it's now devoted to an exhibition on Jewish traditions of burial and death, good to peruse before you head off into the cemetery.

Close to the entrance to the cemetery is the **Klausová synagoga**, a late-seventeenth-century building, founded in the 1690s by Mordecai Maisel on the site of several medieval prayer halls (*klausen*), in what was then a notorious red-light district of Josefov. The ornate Baroque interior contains a rich display of religious objects from embroidered *kippah* to *Kiddush* cups, and explains the very basics of Jewish religious practice.

Founded and paid for entirely by Mordecai Maisel, the neo-Gothic **Maiselova synagoga**, set back from the neighbouring houses on Maiselova, was, in its day, one of the most ornate synagogues in Josefov. Nowadays, its bare white-washed turn-of-the-twentieth-century interior houses an exhibition on the history of the Czech Jewish community up until the 1781 Toleration Edict, its glass cabinets filled with gold and silverwork, *hanukkah* candlesticks, *torah* scrolls and other religious artefacts.

East of Pařížská, up Široká, stands the **Španělská synagoga** (Spanish Synagogue), built in 1868. By far the most ornate synagogue in Josefov, every available surface of its stunning, gilded Moorish interior is smothered with a profusion of floral motifs and geometric patterns, in vibrant reds, greens and blues, which are repeated in the synagogue's huge stained-glass windows. The interior houses an interesting exhibition on the history of Prague's Jews, from the time of the 1848 emancipation. Lovely, slender, painted cast-iron columns hold up the women's gallery, where the displays include a fascinating set of photos depicting the old ghetto at the time of its demolition. There's a section on Prague's German-Jewish writers, including Kafka, and information on the planned Nazi museum and the Holocaust. In the **zimní synagoga** (winter synagogue) on the first floor, there's an exhibition of silver religious artefacts, a fraction of the 6000 pieces collected here, initially for Prague's Jewish Museum, founded in 1906, and later under the Nazis.

Around náměstí Jana Palacha

As Kaprova and Široká emerge from Josefov, they meet at **náměstí Jana Palacha**, previously called náměstí Krasnoarmejců (Red Army Square) and embellished with a flower bed in the shape of a red star, in memory of the Soviet dead who were temporarily buried here in May 1945. It was probably this, as much as the fact that the building on the east side of the square is the Faculty of Philosophy where Palach (see p.127) was a student, that prompted the authorities to make the first of the post-Communist street-name changes here in 1989 (there's a bust of Palach on the corner of the building). By a happy coincidence, the road which intersects the square from the north is called 17 listopadu (17 November), originally commemorating the day in 1939 when the Nazis closed down all Czech institutions of higher education, but now equally good for the 1989 march (see p.129).

The north side of the square is taken up by the **Rudolfinum** or Dům umělců (House of Artists), designed by Josef Zítek and Josef Schulz. One of the proud civic buildings of the nineteenth-century national revival, it was originally built to house an art gallery, museum and concert hall for the Czech-speaking community. In 1918, however, it became the seat of the new Czechoslovak

On Kafka's trail

Franz Kafka was born on July 3, 1883, above the *Batalion* Schnapps bar on the corner of Maiselova and Kaprova (the original building has long since been torn down, but a gaunt-looking modern bust now commemorates the site). He spent most of his life in and around Josefov. His father was an upwardly mobile small businessman from a Czech-Jewish family of kosher butchers (Kafka himself was a vegetarian), his mother from a wealthy German-Jewish family of merchants. The family owned a haberdashery shop, located at various premises on or near Staroměstské náměstí. In 1889, they moved out of Josefov and lived for the next seven years in the beautiful Renaissance Dům U minuty, next door to the Staroměstská radnice, during which time Kafka attended the *Volksschule* on Masná (now a Czech primary school), followed by a spell at an exceptionally strict German *Gymnasium*, located on the third floor of the palác Kinských.

At eighteen, he began a law degree at the German half of the Karolinum, which was where he met his lifelong friend and posthumous biographer and editor, Max Brod. Kafka spent most of his working life as an accident insurance clerk, until he was forced to retire through ill health in 1922. Illness plagued him throughout his life and he spent many months as a patient at the innumerable spas in *Mitteleuropa*. He was engaged three times, twice to the same woman, but never married, finally leaving home at the age of 31 for bachelor digs on the corner of Dlouhá and Masná, where he wrote the bulk of his most famous work, *The Trial*. He died of tuberculosis at the age of 40 in a sanatorium just outside Vienna, on June 3, 1924, and is buried in the Nový židovský hřbitov in Žižkov (see p.139).

Nowadays, thanks to his popularity with Western tourists, Kafka has become an extremely marketable commodity, with his image plastered across T-shirts, mugs and postcards all over the city centre. A ludicrous statue of Kafka riding on the shoulders of the golem has recently been erected outside the Spanish Synagogue and now provides photo opportunities for tourists. The best place to head for, though, is the small **museum** (Tues–Sat 10am–6pm), on the site of Kafka's birthplace next door to the church of sv Mikuláš, which retells Kafka's life simply but effectively with pictures and quotes (in Czech, German and English).

parliament, only returning to its original artistic purpose in 1946. It's now one of the capital's main exhibition and concert venues, and home to the **Czech Philharmonic**, with a wonderfully grand café on the first floor.

UPM – the Decorative Arts Museum

A short way down 17 listopadu from the square is the **UPM**, or Umělecko-průmyslové muzeum (Tues–Sun 10am–6pm; ⓦ www.upm.cz), installed in another of Schulz's worthy nineteenth-century creations, richly decorated in mosaics, stained glass and sculptures. Literally translated, this is a "Museum of Decorative Arts", though the translation hardly does justice to what is one of the most fascinating museums in the capital. The museum's consistently excellent temporary exhibitions are staged on the ground floor, with the permanent collections on the floor above. Audioguides to the collections are available, at no extra cost, though they're by no means essential, as there's lots of information and labelling in English.

The displays start with the **Votive Hall** (Votivní sál), which is ornately decorated with trompe l'oeil wall hangings, lunette paintings and a bewhiskered bust of Emperor Franz-Josef I. Next door is the **Story of a Fibre**, which displays textile exhibits, ranging from a sixteenth-century Brussels tapestry of Samson bringing down the temple to some 1930s curtains by the Surrealist artist Toyen. The room is dominated by a double-decker costume display: above, there are richly embroidered religious vestments from the fifteenth to eighteenth centuries; below, fashionable attire from the eighteenth century to contemporary catwalk concoctions.

More rooms are planned to open on this side of the Votive Hall, but at the time of going to press, you have to backtrack to reach the **Arts of Fire**, home to the museum's impressive glass, ceramic and pottery displays, ranging from eighteenth-century Meissen figures to Art Nouveau vases by Bohemian glassmakers such as Lötz. To catch the best examples of Cubist works on display, head for the room's Gočár-designed Cubist bookcase, and look out, too, for Jan Zrzavy's three-piece glass mosaic from the 1930s.

The **Print and Images** room is devoted mainly to Czech photography, and includes numerous prints from the art form's interwar heyday, including several of František Drtikol's remarkable 1920s geometric nudes, Jaromír Funke's superb still-lifes and Josef Sudek's contemplative studio shots. Finally, in the **Treasury**, there's a kind of modern-day *Kunstkammer* or cabinet of curiosities: everything from ivory *objets d'art* and seventeenth-century Italian *pietro dure* or hardstone mosaics, to miniature silver furniture and a goblet made from rhino horn.

Nové Město

NOVÉ MĚSTO is the city's main commercial and business district, housing most of its big hotels, cinemas, nightclubs, fast-food outlets and department stores. Architecturally, it comes over as big, bourgeois and predominantly late nineteenth century, yet Nové Město was actually founded way back in 1348 by Emperor Charles IV as an entirely new town – three times as big as Staré Město – intended to link the southern fortress of Vyšehrad with Staré Město to the north. Large market squares, wide streets, and a level of town planning far ahead of its time were employed to transform Prague into the new capital city of the Holy Roman Empire. However, this quickly became the city's poorest quarter after Josefov, renowned as a hotbed of Hussitism and radicalism throughout the centuries. In the second half of the nineteenth century, the authorities set about a campaign of slum clearance similar to that inflicted on the Jewish quarter; only the churches and a few important historical buildings were left standing, though Charles' street layout survived pretty much intact. The leading architects of the day began to line the wide boulevards with ostentatious examples of their work, which were eagerly snapped up by the new class of status-conscious businessmen – a process that continued well into the last century, making Nové Město the most architecturally varied part of Prague.

The obvious starting point, and probably the only place in Prague most visitors can put a name to, is Wenceslas Square, known to the Czechs as **Václavské náměstí**, hub of the modern city and somewhere you'll find yourself passing through again and again. The two principal, partially pedestrianized, streets which lead off it are **Národní třída** and **Na příkopě**, which together form the *zlatý kříž* (golden cross), Prague's commercial axis and for over a century the most expensive slice of real estate in the capital. The *zlatý kříž*, and the surrounding streets, also contain some of Prague's finest late-nineteenth-century, Art Nouveau and twentieth-century architecture. The rest of Nové Město, which spreads out northeast and southwest of the square, is much less explored and, for the most part, still heavily residential; unusually for Prague, using the tram and metro systems to get around here will save some unnecessary legwork.

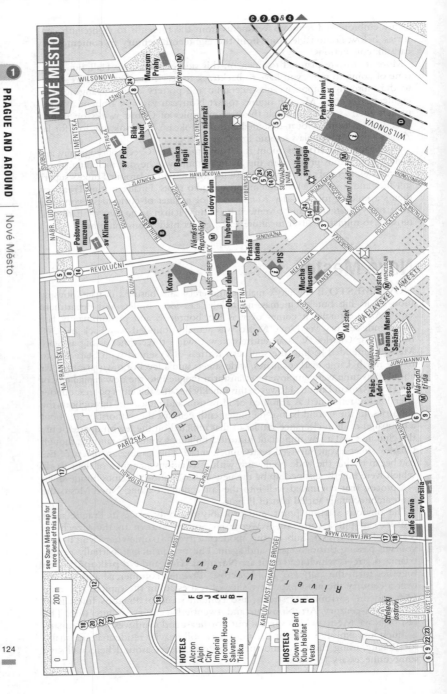

NOVÉ MĚSTO

HOTELS
Alcron F
Alpin G
City J
Imperial A
Jerome House E
Salvator B
Triška I

HOSTELS
Clown and Bard C
Klub Habitat H
Vesta D

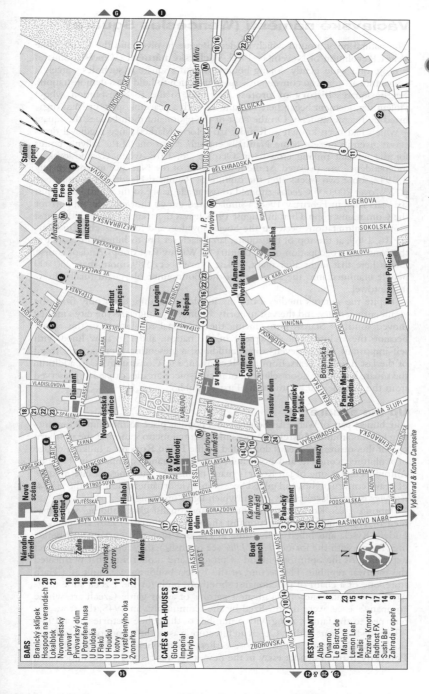

Václavské náměstí (Wenceslas Square)

The natural pivot around which modern Prague revolves, and the focus of the Velvet Revolution of November 1989, **Václavské náměstí** (Wenceslas Square) is more of a wide, gently sloping boulevard than a square as such. It's scarcely conventional – or even convenient – space in which to hold mass demonstrations, yet the square's **history of protest** goes back to the 1848 revolution, whose violent denouement began here on June 12 with a peaceful open-air Mass organized by Prague students. On the crest of the nationalist disturbances, the square – which had been known as Koňský trh (Horse Market) since medieval times – was given its present name. Naturally enough, it was one of the rallying points for the jubilant milling crowds on October 28, 1918, when Czechoslovakia's independence was declared. At the lowest point of the Nazi occupation, on July 3, 1942, some two weeks after the capture of Reinhard Heydrich's assassins (see p.133), over 200,000 Czechs gathered to swear allegiance to the Third Reich. Just six years later, in February 1948, a similar-sized crowd showed their support for the Communist coup. Then in August 1968, it was the scene of some of the most violent confrontations between the Soviet invaders and local Czechs. On January 16, 1969, at the top of the square, Jan Palach set fire to himself in protest at the continuing occupation of the country by Warsaw Pact troops. And, of course, it was here that night after night, in late November 1989, more than 250,000 people crammed into the square, until the Communist old guard finally threw in the towel.

Despite the square's medieval origins, its oldest building dates only from the eighteenth century, and the vast majority are much younger. As the city's money moved south of Staré Město during the industrial revolution, so the square became the architectural showpiece of the nation, and it is now lined with self-important six- or seven-storey buildings, representing every artistic trend of the last hundred years, from neo-Renaissance to Constructivist. In addition, the square has a very good selection of period-piece arcades or *pasáže*, preserved from the commercial boom of the First Republic.

Up the square

The busiest part of Wenceslas Square and a popular place to meet up before hitting town is around **Můstek**, the city's most central metro station, at the northern end of the square. The area is dominated by the **Palác Koruna**, a hulking wedge of sculptured concrete and gold, built for an insurance company in 1914 by Antonín Pfeiffer, one of Jan Kotěra's many pupils. The building is a rare mixture of heavy constructivism and gilded Secession-style ornamentation, but the *pièce de résistance* is the palace's pearly crown which lights up at night.

Opposite Palác Koruna is a recent neo-functionalist glass building, accompanied by two much older functionalist shops from the late 1920s, designed by Ludvík Kysela and billed at the time as Prague's first glass curtain-wall buildings. Along with the former *Hotel Juliš* (see opposite), they represent the perfect expression of the optimistic mood of progress and modernism that permeated the interwar republic. The second of the Kysela buildings was built as a **Baťa** store, one of a chain of functionalist shoeshops built for the Czech shoe magnate, Tomáš Baťa, one of the greatest patrons of avant-garde Czech art, whose company's assets were nationalized by the Communists in 1948; the store was returned to the family, along with a number of their shoe factories, after 1989.

Twenty-five years earlier, Czech architecture was in the throes of its own version of Art Nouveau, one of whose earliest practitioners was Jan Kotěra. The **Peterkův dům**, a slender essay in the new style, was his first work, undertaken at the age of 28. Kotěra, a pupil of the great architect of the Viennese Secession, Otto Wagner, eventually moved on to a much more brutal constructivism. Another supreme example of Czech functionalism, a few doors further up at no. 22, is the **Hotel Juliš**, designed by Pavel Janák, who had already made his name as one of the leading lights of the short-lived Czech Cubist (and later Rondo-Cubist) movement (see p.136).

Further up on the same side of the square is the **Melantrich** publishing house, whose first floor is occupied by the offices of the Socialist Party newspaper, *Svobodné slovo* (The Free Word). For forty years the Socialist Party was a loyal puppet of the Communist government, but on the second night of the demonstrations in November 1989, the newspaper handed over its well-placed balcony to the opposition speakers of the Občanské fórum (Civic Forum). Melantrich House faces two of the most ornate buildings on the entire square, the Art Nouveau **Grand Hotel Evropa** and its slim neighbour, the *Hotel Meran*, both built in 1903–5. They represent everything the Czech modern movement stood against, chiefly, ornament for ornament's sake, not that this has in any way dented their renown. The *Evropa*, in particular, has kept many of its sumptuous original fittings intact, though at the time of writing, the whole place was at a particularly low ebb in terms of service and popularity.

The Wenceslas Monument and the Národní muzeum

A statue of St Wenceslas (sv Václav) has stood at the top of the square since 1680, but the present **Wenceslas Monument**, by the father of Czech sculpture, Josef Václav Myslbek, was only unveiled in 1912. It's worthy and heroic but pretty unexciting, with the Czech patron saint sitting resolutely astride his mighty steed, surrounded by smaller-scale representations of four other Bohemian saints – his grandmother Ludmilla, Procopius, Adalbert and Agnes – added in the 1920s. In 1918, 1948, 1968, and again in 1989, the monument was used as a national political noticeboard, festooned with posters, flags and slogans and, even now, it remains the city's favourite soapbox venue.

A few metres below the statue, on January 16, 1969, a 21-year-old student, **Jan Palach**, set himself alight in protest against the continuing occupation of his country by the Soviets. The spot is marked by a simple memorial to the *obětem komunismu* (the victims of Communism), adorned with flowers and photos of Palach and Jan Zajíc, another student who followed suit a month or so later.

Dominating the top, southern end of Wenceslas Square sits the broad, brooding hulk of the **Národní muzeum** (daily: May–Sept 10am–6pm; Oct–April 9am–5pm; Ⓦ www.nm.cz), built by Josef Schulz and deliberately modelled on the great European museums of Paris and Vienna. Along with the Národní divadlo (see p.130), this is one of the great landmarks of the nineteenth-century Czech national revival, sporting a monumental gilt-framed glass cupola, worthy clumps of sculptural decoration and narrative frescoes from Czech history.

The museum is old-fashioned and underfunded, but it's worth taking at least a quick look at the ornate marble entrance hall and the splendid monumental staircase leading to the **Pantheon** of Czech notables at the top. Arranged under the glass-domed hall are 48 busts and statues of distinguished bewhiskered Czech men (plus a couple of token women and Czechophile Slovaks), including the universally adored T.G. Masaryk, the country's founding president, whose statue was removed by the Communists from every other public place. The rest of the museum is dowdy and badly labelled, though those with children might like to head upstairs for the fossils and stuffed animals. The museum's temporary exhibitions, displayed on the ground floor, can be very good indeed, so it's always worth checking to see what's on.

Wilsonova

At the southern end of Wenceslas Square is some of the worst blight that Communist planners inflicted on Prague – above all, the six-lane highway that now separates Nové Město from the residential suburb of Vinohrady to the east and south and effectively cuts off the National Museum from Wenceslas Square. Previously known as Vitězného února (Victorious February Street) after the Communist coup, the road was renamed **Wilsonova** in honour of US President Woodrow Wilson (a personal friend of the Masaryk family), who effectively gave the country its independence from Austria-Hungary in 1918 by backing the proposal for a separate Czechoslovak state.

The former **Prague Stock Exchange**, alongside the Národní muzeum, only completed in the 1930s but rendered entirely redundant by the 1948 coup, was another victim of postwar reconstruction. The architect Karel Prager was given the task of designing a new "socialist" **Federal Assembly** building on the same site, without destroying the old bourse. He opted for a supremely unappealing, bronze-tinted, plate-glass structure, supported by concrete stilts and sitting uncomfortably on top of its diminutive predecessor. Since the break-up of the country, the building has lost its *raison d'être* once more, and now provides a home for, among other things, Radio Free Europe's headquarters.

Next to the old parliament building, the grandiose **Státní opera** (State Opera; ⓦ www.opera.cz), built by the Viennese duo Helmer and Fellner, looks stunted and deeply affronted by the traffic which now tears past its front entrance. It was opened in 1888 as the Neues Deutsches Theater, shortly after the Czechs had built their own National Theatre on the waterfront. Always second fiddle to the Stavovské divadlo, though equally ornate inside, it was one of the last great building projects of Prague's once all-powerful German minority. The velvet and gold interior is still as fresh as it was when the Bohemian-born composer Gustav Mahler brought the traffic to a standstill, conducting the premiere of his *Seventh Symphony*.

The last building on this deafening freeway is **Praha hlavní nádraží**, Prague's main railway station. One of the final glories of the dying empire, it was designed by Josef Fanta and officially opened in 1909 as the Franz-Josefs Bahnhof. Arriving in the subterranean modern section, it's easy to miss the station's surviving Art Nouveau parts. The original entrance on Wilsonova still exudes imperial confidence, with its wrought-iron canopy and naked figurines clinging to the sides of the towers. You can sit and admire the main foyer from the *Fantová kavárna* (daily 6am–11pm); it's also worth heading north from the foyer to take a peek at the ceramic pillars in the former station restaurant.

Národní and Na příkopě

Národní and **Na příkopě** trace the course of the old moat, which was finally filled in 1760. Their boomerang curve marks the border between Staré Město and Nové Město (strictly speaking, the dividing line runs down the middle of both the streets). Ranged around here is a variety of stylish edifices, including some of the city's most flamboyant Art Nouveau buildings.

Jungmannovo náměstí and around

Heading west from Můstek, before you hit Národní třída proper, you must pass through **Jungmannovo náměstí**, which takes its name from Josef Jungmann (1772–1847), a prolific writer, translator and leading light of the Czech national revival, whose pensive, seated statue was erected here in 1878. This small, ill-proportioned square boasts one of Prague's most endearing architectural curiosities, Emil Králíček and Matěj Blecha's unique **Cubist streetlamp** (and seat) from 1912, which is currently crumbling away beyond the Jungmann statue in the far eastern corner of the square.

On the south side stands the square's most imposing building, the chunky, vigorously sculptured **Palác Adria**. It was designed in the early 1920s by Pavel Janák and Josef Zasche, with sculptural extras by Otto Gutfreund and a central *Seafaring* group by Jan Štursa. Janák was a pioneering figure in the short-lived, prewar Czech Cubist movement; after the war, he and Josef Gočár attempted to create a national style of architecture appropriate for the newly founded republic. The style was dubbed Rondo-Cubism— semi circular motifs are a recurrent theme – though the Palác Adria owes as much to the Italian Renaissance as it does to the new national style.

Originally constructed for the Italian insurance company Reunione Adriatica di Sicurità – hence its current name – the building's *pasáž* still retains its wonderful original portal featuring sculptures by Bohumil Kafka, depicting the twelve signs of the zodiac. The theatre in the basement of the building was once a studio for the multimedia **Laterna magika** (Magic Lantern) company. In 1989, it became the underground nerve centre of the Velvet Revolution, when Civic Forum found temporary shelter here shortly after their inaugural meeting on the Sunday following the November 17 demonstration. Against a stage backdrop for Dürenmatt's *Minotaurus*, the Forum thrashed out tactics in the dressing rooms and gave daily press conferences in the auditorium during the crucial fortnight before the Communists relinquished power.

Through the unpromising courtyard back near the Jungmann statue, you can gain access to the church of **Panna Maria Sněžná** (St Mary-of-the-Snows). Once one of the great landmarks of Wenceslas Square, towering over the backs of the old two-storey houses that lined the square, it's now barely visible from any of the surrounding streets. Charles IV, who founded the church, envisaged a vast coronation church on a scale comparable with St Vitus Cathedral, on which work had just begun. Unfortunately, the money ran out shortly after completion of the chancel; the result is curious – a church that is short in length, but equal to the cathedral in height. The hundred-foot-high vaulting – which collapsed on the Franciscans who inherited the half-completed building in the seventeenth century – is awesome, as is the gold and black Baroque altar which touches the ceiling. To get an idea of the intended scale of the finished structure, take a stroll through the **Františkanská zahrada**, to the south of the church, which links up with one of the arcades off Wenceslas Square.

The Masakr – November 1989

On the night of Friday, November 17, 1989, a 50,000-strong, officially sanctioned student demo, organized by the students' union, SSM (League of Young Socialists), worked its way down Národní with the intention of reaching Wenceslas Square. Halfway down the street they were confronted by the *bílé přílby* (white helmets) and *červené barety* (red berets) of the hated riot police. For what must have seemed like hours, there was a stalemate as the students sat down and refused to disperse, some of them handing out flowers to the police. Suddenly, without any warning, the police attacked, and what became known as the **masakr** (massacre) began. No one was actually killed, though it wasn't for want of trying by the police. Under the arches of Národní 16, there's a small symbolic bronze relief of eight hands reaching out for help, a permanent shrine in memory of the hundreds who were hospitalized in the violence.

Národní třída

The eastern end of **Národní** is taken up with shops, galleries and clubs, which begin to peter out as you near the river. Three-quarters of the way down on the north side is an eye-catching duo of Art Nouveau buildings designed by Osvald Polívka in 1907–8. The first, at no. 7, was built for the **pojišťovna Praha** (Prague Savings Bank), hence the beautiful mosaic lettering above the windows, advertising *život* (life insurance) and *kapital* (loans), as well as help with your *důchod* (pension) and *věno* (dowry). Next door, the slightly more ostentatious **Topičův dům**, built for a publishing house, provides the perfect accompaniment, with a similarly ornate wrought-iron and glass canopy.

At the western end of Národní, overlooking the Vltava, is the gold-crested **Národní divadlo** (National Theatre), proud symbol of the Czech nation. Refused money by the Habsburg state, Czechs of all classes dug deep into their pockets to raise funds for the venture themselves. The foundation stones were laid in 1868 and in June 1881, the theatre opened with a premiere of Smetana's opera *Libuše*. In August of the same year, fire ripped through the building, destroying everything except the outer walls. Within two years the whole thing was rebuilt – even the emperor contributed this time – opening once more to the strains of *Libuše*. The grand portal on the north side of the theatre is embellished with suitably triumphant allegorical figures, and inside, every square inch is taken up with paintings and sculptures by leading artists of the Czech national revival.

Standing behind and in dramatic contrast to the National Theatre is its state-of-the-art extension, the modern glass box of the **Nová scéna** (New Stage), designed by Karel Prager, the leading architect of the Communist era, and completed in 1983. It's one of those buildings most Praguers love to hate – it has been memorably described as looking like "frozen piss" – though compared to much of Prague's Communist-era architecture, it's not that bad.

The **Café Slavia**, opposite the theatre, has been a favourite haunt of the city's writers, dissidents and artists (and, inevitably, actors) since the days of the First Republic. The Czech avant-garde movement, *Devětsil*, led by Karel Teige, used to hold its meetings here in the 1920s; the meetings are recorded for posterity by another of its members, the Nobel prize-winner Jaroslav Seifert, in his *Slavia Poems*. The café has been carelessly modernized since those Arcadian days, but it still has a great riverside view and Viktor Oliva's *Absinthe Drinker* canvas on the wall.

Na příkopě

Heading northeast from Můstek metro station, at the bottom end of Wenceslas Square, you can join the crush of bodies ambling down **Na příkopě** (literally "on the moat"). The big multinational franchises have staked their claim on this stretch of Prague, with the **Pasáž Myslbek**, fronted by Marks & Spencer, one of the few contemporary works of architecture in central Prague. The street has, of course, been an architectural showcase for more than a century and was once lined on both sides with grandiose Habsburg-era buildings; the Art Nouveau **U Dörflerů**, at no. 7, from 1905, with its gilded floral curlicues, is one of the few survivors along this stretch.

There are another couple of interesting buildings at nos. 18 and 20, designed by Polívka over a twenty-year period for the **Zemská banka** and connected by a kind of Bridge of Sighs suspended over Nekázanka. The style veers between 1890s neo-Renaissance and later Art Nouveau elements, such as Jan Preisler's gilded mosaics and Ladislav Šaloun's attic sculptures. It's worth nipping upstairs to the main banking hall of what is now the **Živnostenka**

UPOZORNĚNÍ: ZAPLACENÉ VSTUPNÉ A SERVISNÍ POPLATKY SE NEVRACÍ, VSTUPENKA SE NEVYMĚŇUJE.
V případě zrušení akce je třeba uplatnit nárok na vrácení vstupného v místě, kde byla vstupenka zakoupena. V takovém případě bude se vstupným servisní poplatek označený na přední straně jako S.P.1. Servisní poplatek označený jako S.P. se nevrací. Náhrada zvláštních nákladů (např. hotel, jízdní výlohy) se neposkytuje. Vstupné je včetně DPH v zákonné sazbě 235/2004 Sb. o DPH ve znění pozdějších předpisů. Nevystavuje vstupenku vysokým teplotám vlivům a chránit ji před světlem a PVC. Padělání vstupenky je trestné. V případě poškození, zničení, ztráty nebo krádeže nebude vstupenka nahrazena novou a nebude poskytnuta její plná kompenzace. Zákaz vnášení zbraní, skleněných nádob, plechovek, PET lahví, alkoholických nápojů, toxických a jiných omamných látek, audio-video zařízení včetně fotoaparátů. Zákaz fotografování a pořizování audio-video záznamu v průběhu akce. U vstupu může být prováděna bezpečnostní kontrola. Pořadatelská služba může provádět osobní prohlídky. Diváci, kteří přijdou po zahájení akce, budou usazeni podle pokynů pořadatele. Změna programu a termínu vyhrazena. Majitel této vstupenky uděluje souhlas s tím, že fotografie, filmy nebo videozáznamy s jeho osobou smějí být pořízeny a užity, a to bez peněžité náhrady.

IMPORTANT: NO REFUNDS SHALL BE MADE FOR THE ENTRANCE FEE AND THE SERVICE FEES PAID AND THE TICKET SHALL NOT BE EXCHANGED.
In case of cancellation of the event the entrance fee will be refunded only at the location where the ticket was purchased. In such case, the service fee marked on the front side as S.P.1 will be refunded along with the entrance fee. The service fee marked as S.P. will not be refunded. Special expenses (e. g. hotel, travel expenses) will not be refunded. The entrance fee includes the effective amount of VAT pursuant to Act 235/2004 Coll. (VAT Act) as amended. Do not expose the ticket to high temperatures and keep it away from light and PVC. Forgery of the ticket is a punishable offence. In case of damage, destruction, loss or theft the ticket will not be replaced with a new one and no other compensation will be provided. Bringing weapons, glass vessels, cans, polyethylene bottles, alcoholic drinks, toxic or other narcotic substances or audiovisual equipment incl. photo cameras is prohibited. Taking photographs and making audiovisual recordings during the event is prohibited. A security check may be performed by the entrance. A body search may be performed by the organizer. Participants arriving after the beginning of the event will be seated according to the instructions of the organizer. The programme, date and time are subject to change. The owner of these tickets gives his/her consent that photographs, movies or video recordings with him/herself might be made and used without any financial compensation.

www.ticketpro.cz   call centre: +420 296 333 333   E: ticket@ticketpro.cz

PRAŽSKÉ JARO 2006

Generální partner ČESKÁ SPOŘITELNA, a.s.

SLOVENSKÁ FILHARMONIE

Vladimír Válek – dirigent

Boris Berezovskij – klavír

středa 31.květen 2006 od 20:00 hodin

Obecní dům

4618.0740.8415.6911

ZONA • ZONE
Přízemí
SEKCE • SECTION

Vlevo
RADA • ROW

33
MÍSTO • SEAT

12

VSTUPNÉ **275,00 Kč** (250,00 + 0,00 + 25,0

CENA (VSTUPNÉ + S.P1 + S.P2)

HILT-07 HILTON

4618.0740.8415.6911

banka, at no. 20, to appreciate the financial might of Czech capital in the last decades of the Austro-Hungarian Empire. Yet more financial institutions, this time from the dour 1930s, line the far end of Na příkopě, as it opens up into náměstí Republiky, including the state's palatial **Národní banka** (National Bank).

Mucha Museum

Dedicated to probably the most famous of all Czech artists in the West, the **Mucha Museum** (daily 10am–6pm; 120Kč; Ⓦ www.mucha.cz), housed in the Kaunicky palác on Panská, southwest of Senovážné náměstí, has proved very popular indeed. **Alfons Mucha** (1860–1939) made his name in fin-de-siècle Paris, where he shot to fame after designing the Art Nouveau poster *Gismonda* for the actress Sarah Bernhardt. "Le Style Mucha" became all the rage, but the artist himself came to despise this "commercial" period of his work, and in 1910, he moved back to his homeland and threw himself into the national cause, designing patriotic stamps, banknotes and posters for the new republic.

The whole of Mucha's career is covered in the permanent exhibition, and there's a good selection of informal photos, taken by the artist himself, of his models, and Paul Gauguin (with whom he shared a studio) playing the harmonium with his trousers down. The only work not represented here is his massive *Slav Epic*, but the excellent video (in English) covers the decade of his life he devoted to this cycle of nationalist paintings. In the end, Mucha paid for his Czech nationalism with his life; dragged in for questioning by the Gestapo after the 1939 Nazi invasion, he died shortly after being released.

Náměstí Republiky

The oldest structure on **náměstí Republiky** is the **Prašná brána** (Powder Tower; April–Oct daily 10am–6pm), one of the eight medieval gate-towers that once guarded Staré Město. The present tower was begun by Vladislav Jagiello in 1475, shortly after he had moved into the royal court, which was situated next door at the time. A small historical exhibition inside traces the tower's architectural metamorphosis up to its present remodelling by the nineteenth-century restorer Josef Mocker. Most people, though, ignore the displays and climb straight up for the modest view from the top.

Attached to the tower, and built on the ruins of the old royal court, the **Obecní dům** (Municipal House) is by far the city's most exciting Art Nouveau building, one of the few places that still manages to conjure up the atmosphere of Prague's fin-de-siècle café society. Conceived as a cultural centre for the Czech community, it's probably the finest architectural achievement of the Czech national revival. Designed by Osvald Polívka and Antonín Balšánek, it is extravagantly decorated inside and out with the help of almost every artist connected with the Czech Secession. From the lifts to the cloakrooms, just about all the furnishings remain as they were when the building was completed in 1911, and every square inch of the interior and exterior has recently been lovingly renovated.

The simplest way of soaking up the interior – peppered with mosaics and pendulous brass chandeliers – is to have a drink in the cavernous café, or a meal in the equally spacious *Francouská restaurace* or the *Plzeňská restaurace* in the basement. For a more detailed inspection of the building's spectacular interior (which includes paintings by Alfons Mucha, Jan Preisler and Max Švabinský, among others), you can sign up for one of the regular **guided tours** (150Kč); tickets are available from the new information and ticket centre (daily 10am–6pm; Ⓦ www.obecni-dum.cz) on the ground floor, beyond the main foyer. Several rooms on the second floor are given over to temporary art exhibitions, while the building's **Smetanova síň**, Prague's largest concert hall, stages numerous concerts, including the opening salvo of the Pražské jaro (Prague Spring Festival) – traditionally a rendition of Smetana's *Má vlast* (My Country) – which takes place in the presence of the president.

Around Karlovo náměstí

The streets south of Národní and Wenceslas Square still run along the medieval lines of Charles IV's town plan, though they're now lined with grand nineteenth- and twentieth-century buildings. Of the many roads which head down towards Karlovo náměstí, **Vodičkova** is probably the most impressive, running southwest for half a kilometre from Wenceslas Square. You can catch several trams (#3, #14 or #24) along this route, though there is a handful of buildings worth checking out on the way. The first, **U Nováků**, is impossible to miss, thanks to Jan Preisler's mosaic of bucolic frolicking (its actual subject, *Trade and Industry*, is confined to the edges of the picture) and Polívka's curvilinear window frames and delicate, ivy-like ironwork – look out for the frog-prince holding up a window sill. Originally built for the Novák department store in the early 1900s, for the last sixty years it has been a cabaret hall, restaurant and café all rolled into one, and the original fittings have long since been destroyed.

Halfway down the street stands the imposing neo-Renaissance **Minerva** girls' school, covered in bright-red sgraffito. Founded in 1866, it was the first such institution in Prague and later became notorious for the antics of its pupils, the Minervans – most famously Milená Jesenská, romantically linked with, among others, Franz Kafka – who shocked bourgeois Czech society with their experimentations with fashion, drugs and sexual freedom.

Karlovo náměstí

Vodičkova eventually curves left into Prague's biggest square, **Karlovo náměstí**, created by Charles IV as Nové Město's cattle market (Dobytčí trh). Unfortunately, its once impressive proportions are no longer so easy to appreciate, obscured by a tree-planted public garden and cut in two by the busy thoroughfare of Ječná. The Gothic **Novoměstská radnice** or New Town Hall, at the northern end of the square, sports three steep, triangular gables embellished with intricate blind tracery. It was built, like the one on Staroměstské náměstí, during the reign of King John of Luxembourg, though it has survived rather better, and is now one of the finest Gothic buildings in the city. It was here that Prague's **first defenestration** took place on July 30, 1419, when the radical Hussite preacher Jan Želivský and his penniless religious followers stormed the building, mobbed the councillors and burghers, and threw twelve or thirteen of them out of the town hall windows onto the pikes of the Hussite mob below. Václav IV, on hearing the news, suffered a stroke and died just two weeks later. So began the long and bloody Hussite Wars. Nowadays, you can only visit the town hall if it's staging one of its temporary exhibitions (May–Sept Tues–Sun 10am–6pm).

Following the defeat of Protestantism two centuries later, the Jesuits demolished half the east side of the square to build their college and the accompanying church of **sv Ignác** (St Ignatius), begun in 1665. The statue of St Ignatius, which sits above the tympanum surrounded by a sunburst, caused controversy at the time, as until then only the Holy Trinity had been depicted in such a way. The church, modelled, like so many Jesuit churches, on the Gesù in Rome, is quite remarkable inside, a salmon-pink and white confection, with lots of frothy stuccowork and an exuberant powder-pink pulpit dripping with gold drapery, cherubs and saints.

The assassination of Reinhard Heydrich

The assassination of Reinhard Heydrich in 1942 was the only attempt the Allies ever made on the life of a leading Nazi. It's an incident which the Allies have always billed as a great success in the otherwise rather dismal seven-year history of the Czech resistance. But, as with all acts of brave resistance during the war, there was a price to be paid. Given that the reprisals meted out on the Czech population were entirely predictable, it remains a controversial, if not suicidal, decision to have made.

The target, **Reinhard Tristan Eugen Heydrich**, was a talented and upwardly mobile anti-Semite (despite rumours that he was partly Jewish himself), a great organizer and a skilful concert violinist. He was a late recruit to the Nazi Party, signing up in 1931 after his dismissal from the German Navy for dishonourable conduct towards a woman. However, he swiftly rose through the ranks of the SS to become second in command to Himmler and, in the autumn of 1941, *Reichsprotektor* of the puppet state of *Böhmen und Mähren* – effectively, the most powerful man in the Czech Lands. Although his rule began with brutality, it soon settled into the tried-and-tested policy which Heydrich liked to call *Peitsche und Zucker* (literally, "whip and sugar").

On the morning of May 27, 1942, as Heydrich was being driven by his personal bodyguard, *Oberscharführer* Klein, in his open-top Mercedes from his house north of Prague to his office in Hradčany, three Czechoslovak agents (parachuted in from England) were taking up positions in the northern suburb of Libeň. The first agent, Valčik, gave the signal as the car pulled into Kirchmayer Boulevard (now V Holešovičkách). Another agent, a Slovak called Gabčík, pulled out a gun and tried to shoot. The gun jammed, at which Heydrich, rather than driving out of the situation, ordered Klein to stop the car and attempted to shoot back. At this point, the third agent, Kubiš, threw a bomb at the car. The blast injured Kubiš and Heydrich, who immediately leapt out and began firing at Kubiš. Kubiš, with blood pouring down his face, jumped on his bicycle and fled downhill. Gabčík meanwhile pulled out a second gun and exchanged shots with Heydrich, until the latter collapsed from his wounds. Gabčík fled into a butcher's, shot Klein – who was in hot pursuit – in the legs and escaped down the backstreets.

Meanwhile back at the Mercedes, a baker's van was flagged down by a passer-by, but the driver refused to get involved. Eventually, a small truck carrying floor polish was commandeered and Heydrich was taken to the Bulovka hospital. Heydrich died eight days later from the fragments of horsehair and wire from the car seat which had infected his spleen, and was given full Nazi honours at his Prague funeral; the cortège passed down Wenceslas Square, in front of a crowd of thousands. As the home resistance had forewarned, revenge was quick to follow. The day after Heydrich's funeral service in Berlin, the village of **Lidice** (see p.182) was burnt to the ground and its male inhabitants murdered; two weeks later, the men and women of the village of **Ležáky** (see p.341) suffered a similar fate.

The plan to assassinate Heydrich had been formulated in the early months of 1942 by the Czechoslovak government-in-exile in London, without consultation with the Czech Communist leadership in Moscow, and despite fierce opposition from the resistance within Czechoslovakia. Since it was clear that the reprisals would be horrific, the only logical explanation for the plan is that this was precisely the aim of the government-in-exile's operation – to forge a solid wedge of resentment between the Germans and Czechs. In this respect, if in no other, the operation was ultimately successful.

Cathedral of sv Cyril and Metoděj (Heydrich Martyrs' Monument)

West off Karlovo náměstí, down Resslova, the noisy extension of Ječná, is the Orthodox cathedral of **sv Cyril and Metoděj** (Tues–Sun 10am–5pm), originally constructed for the Roman Catholics by Bayer and Dientzenhofer in the eighteenth century, but since the 1930s the main base of the Orthodox church in the Czech Republic. Amid all the traffic, it's extremely difficult to imagine the scene here on June 18, 1942, when seven of the Czechoslovak secret agents involved in the most dramatic assassination of World War II (see box on p.133) were besieged in the church by over seven-hundred members of the Waffen SS. Acting on a tip-off by one of the Czech resistance who turned himself in, the Nazis surrounded the building just after 4am and fought a pitched battle for over six hours, trying explosives, flooding and any other method they could think of to drive the men out of their stronghold in the crypt. Eventually, all seven agents committed suicide rather than give themselves up. There's a plaque at street level on the south wall commemorating those who died, and an exhibition on the whole affair in the crypt itself, which has been left pretty much as it was; the entrance is underneath the church steps on Na Zderaze.

The islands and the embankments

Magnificent turn-of-the-twentieth-century mansions line the Vltava's right bank, almost without interruption, for some two kilometres from the Charles Bridge south to the rocky outcrop of Vyšehrad. It's a long walk, even just along the length of **Masarykovo** and **Rašínovo nábřeží**, though there's no need to do the whole lot in one go; you can hop on a tram (#17 or #21) at various points, drop down from the embankments to the waterfront itself, or escape to one of the two islands connected to them, Střelecký ostrov and Slovanský ostrov, better known as Žofín.

The islands

Access to either of the two islands in the central section of the Vltava is from close to the Národní divadlo. The first, **Střelecký ostrov**, or Shooters' Island, is where the army held their shooting practice, on and off, from the fifteenth until the nineteenth century. Closer to the left bank and accessible via the most Legií (Legion's Bridge), it became a favourite spot for a Sunday promenade and is still popular, especially in summer. The first Sokol sports festival took place here in 1882, while the first May Day demonstrations were held here in 1890.

The second island, **Slovanský ostrov**, more commonly known as **Žofín** (after the island's concert hall, itself named after Sophie, the domineering mother of the Emperor Franz-Josef I), came about as a result of the natural silting of the river in the eighteenth century. By the late nineteenth century it had become one of the city's foremost pleasure gardens, where, as the composer Berlioz remarked, "bad musicians shamelessly make abominable music in the open air and immodest young males and females indulge in brazen dancing, while idlers and wasters . . . lounge about smoking foul tobacco and drinking beer." On a good day, things seem pretty much unchanged from those heady times; concerts, balls, and other social gatherings take place here, and there are rowing boats for hire from May to September.

Along the embankment

Most of the buildings along the waterfront are private apartments and therefore inaccessible. One exception to this, and architecturally atypical of this part of Prague, is the striking white functionalist mass of the **Mánes** art gallery (Tues–Sun 10am–6pm), halfway down Masarykovo nábřeží. Designed in open-plan style by Otakar Novotný in 1930, it spans the narrow channel between Slovanský ostrov and the waterfront, close to the onion-domed Šítek water tower. The gallery is named after Josef Mánes, a traditional nineteenth-century landscape painter and Czech nationalist, and stages contemporary art exhibitions. Clearly visible from Mánes is the **Tančící dům** (Dancing House), also known as "Fred and Ginger" after the shape of the building's two towers, which look vaguely like a couple ballroom dancing. It was designed in the 1990s by the Canadian-born Frank O. Gehry and the Yugoslav-born Vlado Milunič, and stands next door to the block of flats where Havel lived before becoming president (when he wasn't in prison).

Further along the embankment, at **Palackého náměstí**, the buildings retreat for a moment to reveal an Art Nouveau sculpture to rival Šaloun's monument in Staroměstské náměstí (see p.109): the **Monument to František Palacký**, the great nineteenth-century Czech historian, politician and nationalist, by Stanislav Sucharda. Like the Hus Monument, which was unveiled three years later, this mammoth project – fifteen years in the making – had missed its moment by the time it was completed in 1912, and found universal disfavour. The critics have mellowed over the years, and nowadays it's appreciated for what it is – an energetic and inspirational piece of work. Ethereal bronze bodies, representing the world of the imagination, shoot out at all angles, contrasting sharply with the plain stone mass of the plinth and, below, the giant, grimly determined, seated figure of Palacký himself, representing the real world.

Vyšehradská and Ke Karlovu

Behind Palackého náměstí, off **Vyšehradská**, the intertwined concrete spires of the **Emauzy** monastery are an unusual modern addition to the Prague skyline. The monastery was one of the few important historical buildings to be damaged in the last war, in this case by a stray Anglo-American bomb. The cloisters contain some extremely valuable Gothic frescoes, but since the return of the monks from their forty-year exile, access has become unpredictable. Heading south from here, Vyšehradská descends to a junction, where you'll find the entrance to the **Botanická zahrada** (daily 9am–6pm), the university's botanic gardens laid out in 1897 on a series of terraces up the other side of the hill. Though far from spectacular, the garden is one of the few patches of green in this part of town, and the 1930s greenhouses (*skleníky*) have recently been restored to their former glory.

On the far side of the gardens, Apolinářská runs along the south wall and past a grimly Gothic red-brick maternity hospital with steep, stepped gables, before joining up with **Ke Karlovu**. Head north up here and right into Na bojišti, where you'll find **U kalicha** (ⓦ www.ukalicha.cz), the pub immortalized in the opening passages of the consistently popular comic novel *The Good Soldier Švejk*, by Jaroslav Hašek. In the story, on the eve of the Great War, Švejk (Schweik to the Germans) walks into *U kalicha*, where a plain-clothes officer of the Austrian constabulary is sitting drinking and, after a brief conversation, finds himself arrested in connection with the assassination of Archduke Ferdinand. Whatever the pub may have been like in Hašek's day (and even then, it wasn't his local), it's now unashamedly orientated towards reaping in the euros, and about the only authentic thing you'll find inside – albeit at a price – is the beer.

Further north along Ke Karlovu, set back from the road behind wrought-iron gates, is a more rewarding place of pilgrimage, the russet-coloured **Vila Amerika** (Tues–Sun 10am–5pm), now a museum devoted to the Czech composer **Antonín Dvořák** (1841–1904), who lived for a time on nearby Žitná. Even if you've no interest in Dvořák, the house itself is a delight, built as a Baroque summer palace around 1720 and one of Kilian Ignaz Dientzenhofer's most successful secular works. Easily the most famous of all Czech composers, Dvořák, for many years, had to play second fiddle to Smetana in the orchestra at the Národní divadlo, where Smetana was the conductor. In his forties, Dvořák received an honorary degree from Cambridge before leaving for the "New World", and his gown is one of the very few items of memorabilia to have found its way into the museum's collection, along with the programme of a concert given at London's Guildhall in 1891. However, the tasteful period rooms echoing with the composer's music and the tiny garden dotted with Baroque sculptures compensate for what the display cabinets may lack.

Vyšehrad

At the southern tip of Nové Město, around 3km south of the city centre, the rocky red-brick fortress of **VYŠEHRAD** (Ⓦ www.praha-vysehrad.cz) – literally High Castle – has more myths attached to it per square inch than any other place in Bohemia. According to Czech legend, this is the place where the Slav tribes first settled in Prague, where the "wise and tireless chieftain" Krok built a castle, and whence his youngest daughter Libuše went on to found Praha itself (see p.70). Alas, the archeological evidence doesn't bear this claim out, but it's clear that Vratislav II (1061–92), the first Bohemian ruler to bear the title "king", built a royal palace here, to get away from his younger brother who was lording it in the Hrad. Within half a century the royals had moved back to Hradčany and into a new palace, and from then on Vyšehrad began to lose its political significance.

Czech Cubism in Vyšehrad

Even if you harbour only a passing interest in modern architecture, it's worth seeking out the cluster of **Cubist villas** below the fortress in Vyšehrad. Whereas Czech Art Nouveau was heavily influenced by the Viennese Secession, it was Paris rather than the imperial capital that provided the stimulus for the short-lived but extremely productive Czech Cubist movement. In 1911, the Skupina výtvarných umělců or SVU (Group of Fine Artists) was founded in Prague and quickly became the movement's organizing force. **Pavel Janák** was the SVU's chief theorist, **Josef Gočár** its most illustrious exponent, but **Josef Chochol** was the most successful practitioner of the style in Prague.

Cubism is associated mostly with painting, and the unique contribution of its Czech offshoot was to apply the theory to furniture (some of which is now on permanent display at the Muzeum českého kubismu, see p.113) and **architecture**. In Vyšehrad alone, Chochol completed three buildings, close to one another below the fortress, using prismatic shapes and angular lines to produce the sharp geometric contrasts of light and dark shadows characteristic of Cubist painting.

The most impressive example of Czech Cubist architecture, brilliantly exploiting its angular location, is Chochol's apartment block **nájemný obytný dům** at Neklanova 30; begun in 1913 for František Hodek, and now housing a restaurant on the ground floor. Further along Neklanova, at no. 2, there's Antonín Belada's Cubist street facade, and around the corner is the largest project of the lot – Chochol's **Kovařovicova vila**, which backs onto Libušina. From the front, on Rašínovo nábřeží, it's possible to appreciate the clever, slightly askew layout of the garden, designed right down to its zigzag garden railings. Further along the embankment is Chochol's largest commission, the **rodinný trojdům**, a large building complex with a heavy mansard roof, a central "Baroque" gable with a pedimental frieze, and room enough for three families.

Keen to associate himself with the early Přemyslids, Emperor Charles IV had a system of walls built to link Vyšehrad to the newly founded Nové Město, and decreed that the *králová cesta* (coronation route) begin from here. These fortifications were destroyed by the Hussites in 1420, but over the next two hundred years the hill was settled again, until the Habsburgs turfed everyone out in the mid-seventeenth century and rebuilt the place as a fortified barracks, only to tear it down in 1866 to create a public park. By the time the Czech national revival movement became interested in Vyšehrad, only the red-brick fortifications were left as a reminder of its former strategic importance; they rediscovered its history and its legends, and gradually transformed it into a symbol of Czech nationhood. Today, Vyšehrad is a perfect place from which to escape the human congestion of the city and watch the evening sun set behind the Hrad.

The fortress

There are several **approaches to the fortress**: if you've come by tram #3, #7, #16, #17 or #21, which trundle along the waterfront to Výtoň stop, you can either wind your way up Vratislavova and enter through the Cihelná brána, or take the steep stairway from Rašínovo nábřeží that leads up through the trees to a small side entrance in the west wall. Alternatively, from Vyšehrad metro station, walk west past the ugly Kongresové centrum Praha, and enter through the twin gateways, between which there's an **information centre** (daily: April–Oct 9.30am–6pm; Nov–March 9.30am–5pm).

However you come, head for the blackened sandstone church of **sv Petr and Pavel**, rebuilt in the 1880s by Josef Mocker in neo-Gothic style (with further, even more ruthless additions in the 1900s) on the site of an eleventh-century basilica. The twin open-work spires are now the fortress's most familiar landmark, and if luck is on your side, you should be able to view the church's polychrome interior, though opening times can be a bit erratic (daily except Tues 9am–noon & 1–5pm).

Vyšehradský hřbitov (Vyšehrad Cemetery)

One of the first initiatives of the national revival movement was to establish the **Vyšehradský hřbitov** (daily: March, April & Oct 8am–6pm; May–Sept 8am–7pm; Nov–Feb 9am–4pm), which spreads out to the north and east of the church. It's a measure of the part that artists and intellectuals played in the foundation of the nation, and the regard in which they are still held, that the most prestigious graveyard in the city is given over to them: no soldiers, no politicians, not even the Communists managed to muscle their way in here (except on artistic merit).

To the uninitiated only a handful of figures are well-known, but for the Czechs the place is alive with great names (there is a useful plan of the most notable graves at the entrance nearest the church). Ladislav Šaloun's grave for **Dvořák**, situated under the arches, is one of the more showy ones, with a mosaic inscription, studded with gold stones, glistening behind wrought-iron railings. **Smetana**, who died twenty years earlier, is buried in comparatively modest surroundings near the Slavín monument. The Prague Spring Festival begins on the anniversary of his death (May 12) with a procession from his grave to the Obecní dům.

The grave of the Romantic poet **Karel Hynek Mácha** was the assembly point for the 50,000-strong demonstration on November 17, 1989, which triggered the Velvet Revolution. This was organized to commemorate the 50th anniversary of the Nazi closure of all Czech higher education institutions in 1939.

The focus of the cemetery, though, is the **Slavín monument**, a bulky stele, covered in commemorative plaques and topped by a sarcophagus and a statue representing Genius. It's the communal resting place of over fifty Czech artists, including the painter Alfons Mucha, the sculptors Josef Václav Myslbek and Ladislav Šaloun, the architect Josef Gočár and the opera singer Ema Destinnová (see p.204).

The rest of the fortress

The next best thing to do after a stroll around the cemetery is to head off and explore the **Kasematy** or dungeons (daily: April–Oct 9.30am–6pm; Nov–March 9.30am–5pm), which you enter via the Cihelná brána. After a short guided tour of a section of the underground passageways underneath the ramparts, you enter a vast storage hall, which shelters several of the original statues from the Charles Bridge, and, when the lights are switched off, reveals a camera obscura image of a tree.

The rest of the deserted fortress makes for a pleasant afternoon stroll; you can walk almost the entire length of the ramparts, which give some superb views out across the city. The heavily restored **rotunda of sv Martin** – one of a number of Romanesque rotundas scattered across Prague – is the sole survivor of the medieval fortress, built by Vratislav II in the eleventh century; it's only open for services. Time is probably better spent lounging on the grass to the south of the church, where you'll come across the gargantuan legendary statues by Myslbek that used to grace the city's Palackého most.

The suburbs

By the end of his reign in 1378, Charles IV had laid out his city on such a grand scale that it wasn't until the industrial revolution hit Bohemia in the mid-nineteenth century that the first **suburbs** began to sprout up around its boundaries. A few were rigidly planned, with public parks and grid street plans; most grew with less grace, trailing their tenements across the hills and swallowing up existing villages on the way. Most still retain a distinctive individual identity, and are free from the crowds in the centre, all of which makes them worth checking out on even a short visit to the city.

Vinohrady

Southeast of Nové Město is the predominantly late-nineteenth-century suburb of **VINOHRADY**, Prague's most resolutely bourgeois suburb up until World War II. In one of its two main squares, **náměstí Jiřího z Poděbrad** (metro Jiřího z Poděbrad), stands Prague's most celebrated modern church, **Nejsvětější Srdce Páně** (Most Sacred Heart of Our Lord), built in 1928 by Josip Plečník, the Slovene architect responsible for much of the remodelling of the Hrad. It's a marvellously eclectic and individualistic work, employing a sophisticated potpourri of architectural styles: a Neoclassical pediment and a great slab of a tower with a giant transparent face in imitation of a Gothic rose window. Plečník also had a sharp eye for detail; look out for the little gold crosses set into the brickwork both inside and out, and for the celestial orbs of light suspended above the heads of the congregation.

Žižkov

Though they share much the same architectural heritage, **ŽIŽKOV**, unlike Vinohrady, is a traditionally working-class area, and was a Communist Party stronghold even before the war, earning it the nickname Red Žižkov. Its peeling turn-of-the-twentieth-century tenements are home to a large proportion of Prague's Romany community, and it boasts more pubs per head than any other district in Prague. The main reason for venturing into Žižkov is to visit the ancient landmark of Žižkov hill, the city's main Olšany cemeteries, at the eastern end of Vyšehradská, and the aforementioned pubs.

Žižkov TV tower

At over 100m in height, the Televizní vysílač or **Žižkov TV tower** (daily 10am–11.30pm; 150Kč; ⓦ www.tower.cz) is the tallest building in Prague – and the most unpopular. Close up, it's an intimidating futuristic piece of architecture, made all the more disturbing by the addition of several statues of giant babies crawling up the sides, courtesy of artist David Černý. Begun in the 1970s in a desperate bid to jam West German television transmission, the tower only become fully operational in the 1990s. In the course of its construction, however, the Communists saw fit to demolish part of a nearby Jewish cemetery that had served the community between 1787 and 1891; a small section survives to the northwest of the tower. From the fifth-floor café or the viewing platform on the eighth floor, you can enjoy a spectacular view across Prague. To get to the tower, take the metro to Jiřího z Poděbrad and walk northeast a couple of blocks – it's difficult to miss.

The cemeteries

Approaching from the west, the first and the largest of the **Olšanské hřbitovy** (Olšany cemeteries; metro Flora) – each of which is bigger than the entire Jewish quarter – was originally created for the victims of the great plague epidemic of 1680. The perimeter walls are lined with glass cabinets, stacked like shoeboxes, containing funereal urns and mementoes, while the graves themselves are a mixed bag of artistic achievement, reflecting funereal fashions of the day as much as the character of the deceased. The cemetery's two most famous incumbents are an ill-fitting couple: Klement Gottwald, the country's first Communist president, whose ashes were removed from the mausoleum on Žižkov hill after 1989 and reinterred here; and the martyr Jan Palach, the philosophy student who set himself alight in protest at the continuing Soviet occupation in January 1969.

Immediately east of Olšany is the **Nový židovský hřbitov** or New Jewish Cemetery (April–Sept Mon–Thus & Sun 9am–5pm, Fri 9am–1pm; Oct–March Mon–Thus & Sun 9am–4pm, Fri 9am–1pm), founded in the 1890s when the one by the Žižkov TV tower was full. It's a melancholy spot, particularly in the east of the cemetery, where large, empty allotments wait in vain to be filled by the generation who perished in the Holocaust. In fact, the community is now so small that it's unlikely the graveyard will ever be full. Most people come here to visit **Franz Kafka**'s grave, 400m east along the south wall and signposted from the entrance (for more on Kafka, see p.122). He is buried, along with his mother and father (both of whom outlived him), beneath a plain headstone; the plaque below commemorates his three sisters who died in the camps.

Žižkov hill

Žižkov hill (also known as Vítkov) is the thin green wedge of land that separates Žižkov from Karlín, a grid-plan industrial district to the north. From its westernmost point, which juts out almost to the edge of Nové Město, is probably the definitive panoramic view over the city centre. It was here, on July 14, 1420, that the Hussites enjoyed their first and finest victory at the **Battle of Vítkov**, under the inspired leadership of the one-eyed general, Jan Žižka (hence the name of the district). Ludicrously outnumbered by more than ten to one, Žižka and his fanatically motivated troops thoroughly trounced Emperor Sigismund and his papal forces.

Despite its overblown totalitarian aesthetics, the giant concrete **Žižkov monument** (Ⓦwww.pamatnik-vitkov.cz) which graces the crest of the hill was actually built between the wars as a memorial to the Czechoslovak Legion who fought against the Habsburgs – the gargantuan equestrian statue of the mace-wielding Žižka, which fronts the monument, is reputedly the world's largest. The building was later used by the Nazis as an arsenal, and eventually became a Communist hacks' mausoleum. In 1990, however, the bodies were cremated and quietly reinterred in Olšany, and at present there's an ongoing legal battle over what should happen next with the monument.

To get to the monument, take the metro to Florenc, walk under the railway lines and then up the steep lane U památníku. On the right as you climb the hill is the **Armádní muzeum** (Tues–Sun 10am–6pm; Ⓦwww.militarymuseum .cz), guarded by a handful of unmanned tanks, howitzers and armoured vehicles. Before 1989, this museum was a glorification of the Warsaw Pact, pure and simple; its recent overhaul has produced a much more evenly balanced account of both world wars, particularly in its treatment of the previously controversial subjects of the Czechoslovak Legion, the Heydrich assassination (see p.133) and the Prague Uprising.

Holešovice and Bubeneč

The late-nineteenth-century districts of **HOLEŠOVICE** and **BUBENEČ**, tucked into a huge U-bend in the Vltava, have little in the way of magnificent architecture, but they make up for it with two sizeable areas of green: to the south, **Letná**, where Prague's largest gatherings occur; and to the north, the **Stromovka park**, bordering the Výstaviště funfair and international trade fair

The Stalin monument

Letná's – indeed Prague's – most famous monument is one which no longer exists. The **Stalin monument**, the largest in the world, was once visible from almost every part of the city: a thirty-metre-high granite sculpture portraying a procession of people being led to communism by the Pied Piper figure of Stalin, popularly dubbed *tlačenice* (the crush) because of its resemblance to a Communist-era bread queue. Designed by Jiří Štursa and Otakar Švec, it took 600 workers 500 days to erect the 14,200-ton monster. Švec, the sculptor, committed suicide shortly before it was unveiled, as his wife had done three years previously, leaving all his money to a school for blind children, since they at least would not have to see his creation. It was eventually revealed to the cheering masses on May 1, 1955 – the first and last popular celebration to take place at the monument. Within a year, Khrushchev had denounced his predecessor and, after pressure from Moscow, the monument was blown to smithereens by a series of explosions spread over a fortnight in 1962. All that remains above ground is the statue's vast concrete platform and steps, on the southern edge of the Letná plain, now graced with David Černý's symbolic giant red **metronome** (which is lit up at night); it's also a favourite spot for skateboarders and another good viewpoint.

grounds. In addition, Holešovice boasts a couple of excellent museums: the city's **Národní technické muzeum**, which shows off the Czechs' past scientific and industrial achievements, and the **Veletržní palác**, Prague's impressive modern art museum.

Letná

A high plateau hovering above the city, across the river to the north of Staré Město, the flat green expanse of **Letná** was the traditional assembly point for invading and besieging armies. It was laid out as a public park in the mid-nineteenth century, but its main post-1948 function was as the site of the May Day parades. For these, thousands of citizens were dragooned into marching past the south side of the city's main football ground, the Sparta stadium, where the old Communist cronies would take the salute from a giant red podium. The post-Communist Party parades still take place here, but are a shadow of their former selves.

Národní technické muzeum (National Technical Museum)

Despite its dull title, the **Národní technické muzeum** (Tues–Fri 9am–5pm, Sat & Sun 10am–6pm; Ⓦ www.ntm.cz) on Kostelní is a surprisingly interesting museum. Its showpiece hangar-like main hall contains an impressive gallery of motorbikes, Czech and foreign, and a wonderful collection of old planes, trains and automobiles, from Czechoslovakia's industrial heyday between the wars, when the country's Škoda cars and Tatra soft-top stretch limos were really something to brag about. The oldest car in the collection is Laurin & Klement's 1898 *Präsident*, more of a motorized carriage than a car; the museum also boasts the world's oldest Bugatti. Upstairs, there are interactive displays (a rarity in a Czech museum) tracing the development of early photography, and a collection of some of Kepler's and Tycho Brahe's astrological instruments. Below ground, guided tours are offered of a mock-up of a coal mine (11am, 1pm & 3pm).

Veletržní palác

Situated at the corner of Dukelských hrdinů and Veletržní, some distance from the nearest metro station, the **Veletržní palác** (Tues–Sun 10am–6pm; 250Kč; Ⓦ www.ngprague.cz), or Trade Fair Palace, gets nothing like the number of visitors it should. For not only does the building house the Národní galerie's excellent nineteenth- and twentieth-century Czech and international art collection, it is also an architectural sight in itself. A seven-storey building constructed in 1928 by Oldřich Tyl and Josef Fuchs, it is Prague's ultimate functionalist masterpiece, not so much from the outside, but inside, where its gleaming white vastness is suitably awesome.

The main exhibition hall is used for its original purpose, trade fairs, with the Národní galerie confined to the north wing. Nevertheless, the gallery is both big and bewildering, and virtually impossible to view in its entirety – you can even pay a reduced fee to visit just part of the collection: 100Kč for one floor; 150Kč for two and so on; or 250Kč for the whole gallery (audioguides in English are included in the price). Special exhibitions occupy the ground and fifth floors, while the permanent collection occupies the first to fourth floors – the popular French art collection can be found on the third floor. The account below takes a chronological approach, beginning on the fourth floor, with nineteenth-century art.

To reach the Veletržní palác by public transport, catch tram #5 or #14 from náměstí Republiky, tram #12 from Malostranská metro, tram #17 from Staroměstská metro, or tram #12 or #17 from Nádraží Holešovice to Veletržní stop. If you need a bite to eat, the pub, *U houbaře* (The Mushroom), opposite the museum at Dukelských hrdinů 30, is a good bet.

Nineteenth-century art

The **nineteenth-century art** collection kicks off with a series of bronze sculptures from the second half of the century by **Josef Václav Myslbek**, the father of Czech sculpture. The painting collection, however, begins earlier in the century with Antonín Machek's well-crafted portraits of the Czech bourgeoisie, and his 32 naive scenes depicting Bohemian rulers from Krok to Ferdinand IV. Close by are Ludvík Kohl's fantasy paintings: the one of Vienna's Stephansdom shows the cathedral with two complete towers (instead of one); his imaginary completion of Prague's St Vitus Cathedral was eventually fulfilled more or less to the letter by nineteenth-century architects.

In this exhaustive survey of Czech nineteenth-century painting, the influential **Mánes family** have several sections to themselves. Antonín Mánes succeeded in getting the Czech countryside to look like Italy, and thus gave birth to Romantic Czech landscape painting. Three of his offspring took up the brush: Quido specialized in idealized peasant genre pictures; Amálie obeyed her father's wishes and restricted herself to a little gentle landscape painting; Josef was the most successful of the trio, much in demand as a portrait artist, and one of the leading exponents of patriotically uplifting depictions of national events (he himself took part in the 1848 disturbances in Prague).

The next few sections can be taken at a steady trot, though make sure you check out the eye-catching paintings of Yugoslavia by **Jaroslav Čermák**, a man who lived life to the full, was decorated for his bravery by the Montenegran prince Nicholas I, and died of a heart attack at the age of just 48. **Mikuláš Aleš**, whose designs can be seen in the sgraffito on many of the city's nineteenth-century buildings, is under-represented, though you can admire his wonderfully decorative depiction of the historical meeting between George of Poděbrady and Matthias Corvinus.

Prize for most striking portrait goes to Václav Brožík's *Lady with a Greyhound*, possibly a portrayal of his wife, the daughter of a wealthy Parisian art dealer. **Antonín Chittussi**'s Corot-esque landscapes proved very popular in the Parisian salons of the 1880s; beyond hang several misty, moody streetscapes by Jakub Schikaneder (one of whose ancestors was Mozart's librettist).

Several wood sculptures by **František Bílek** offer a taste of his anguished style, but for a more comprehensive insight into his art, you should visit the Bílkova vila (see p.93). **Jan Preisler**'s mosaics and murals, which can be found on Art Nouveau buildings all over Prague, tend to be ethereal and slightly detached, whereas his oil paintings, like the cycle of *Black Lake* paintings displayed here, are more typically melancholic, and reveal the influence of the Norwegian painter Edvard Munch (see below). The most successful Czech exponent of moody post-Impressionism was **Antonín Slavíček**, whose depictions of Prague remain perennially popular.

The fourth floor collection ends in the foyer area, known rather wonderfully as the respirium, where sculptures by **Stanislav Sucharda** and **Jan Štursa**, two of the most important Czech Art Nouveau artists, predominate. On the balcony, there's a mixed bag of applied art from architectural drawings and models to lino patterning and wrought-ironwork. Architects whose work is featured include **Jan Kotěra**, Balšánek, Polívka and Oldřich, and there are several iridescent Lötz vases from Klašterský Mlýn to admire.

Czech Art 1900–1930

On entering the **1900 to 1930 Czech art** collection, on the third floor, visitors are confronted by **Otakar Švec**'s life-sized *Motorcyclist*, a great three-dimensional depiction of the optimistic speed of the modern age.

These are followed by a whole series of works by **František Kupka**, who was Czech by birth, but lived and worked in Paris from 1895. In international terms, Kupka is by far the most important Czech painter of the last century, having secured his place in the history of art by being (possibly) the first artist in the western world to exhibit abstract paintings. His seminal *Fugue in Two Colours* (*Amorpha*), one of two abstract paintings Kupka exhibited at the Salon d'Automne in 1912, is displayed here, along with some earlier, pre-abstract paintings.

The Edvard Munch retrospective exhibited in Prague in 1905 prompted the formation in 1907 of the first Czech modern art movement, Osma (The Eight), one of whose leading members was **Emil Filla**, whose *Ace of Hearts* and *Reader of Dostoyevsky* – in which the subject appears to have fallen asleep, though, in fact, he's mind-blown – are both firmly within the Expressionist genre. However, it wasn't long before several of the Osma group were beginning to experiment with Cubism. Filla eventually adopted the style wholesale, helping found the Cubist SVU in 1911. **Bohumil Kubišta**, a member of Osma, refused to follow suit, instead pursuing his own unique blend of Cubo-Expressionism, typified by the wonderful self-portrait, *The Smoker*, and by the distinctly Fauvist *Players*.

To round out the Czech Cubist picture, there's furniture and ceramics (and even a Cubist chandelier) by Gočár, Janák and Chochol, as well as sculptures by **Otto Gutfreund**, a member of SVU, whose works range from the Cubo-Expressionist *Anxiety* (1911–12) to the more purely Cubist *Bust* (1913–14). After World War I, during which he joined the Foreign Legion but was interned for three years for insubordination, Gutfreund switched to depicting everyday folk in technicolour, in a style that prefigures Socialist Realism, examples of which can be seen a little further on in the gallery. His life was cut short in 1927, when he drowned while swimming in the Vltava.

Josef Čapek, brother of the playwright, Karel, is another Czech clearly influenced by Cubism, as seen in works such as *Accordion Player*, but like Kubišta, Čapek found Filla's doctrinaire approach difficult to take, and he left SVU in 1912. Another artist who stands apart from the crowd is **Jan Zrzavý**, who joined SVU, but during a long career pursued his own peculiarly individual style typified by paintings such as his 1909 self-portrait, in which he appears Chinese, and *Valley of Sorrow*, his own personal favourite, painted while still a student, and depicting a magical, imaginary and very stylized world.

French Art Collection

At this point, on the third floor, signs begin to appear tempting you on to the ever popular **French art** collection, which features anyone of note who hovered around Paris in the fifty years from 1880 onwards. There are few masterpieces here, but it's all high-quality stuff, most of it either purchased for the gallery in 1923, or bequeathed by art dealer Vincenc Kramář in 1960.

The collection kicks off with several works by **Auguste Rodin**, particularly appropriate given the ecstatic reception that greeted the Prague exhibition of his work in 1902. Rodin's sculptures are surrounded by works from the advance guard of Impressionism: Courbet, Delacroix, Corot, Sisley and early Monet and Pissarro. Among the other works here, there's a characteristically sunny, Provençal *Green Wheat* by **Vincent van Gogh**, and *Moulin Rouge* by Toulouse-Lautrec, with Oscar Wilde looking on. Beyond, the loose brushwork, cool turquoise and emerald colours of **Auguste Renoir**'s *Lovers* are typical of the period of so-called High Impressionism. *Bonjour Monsieur Gauguin* is a tongue-in-cheek tribute to Courbet's painting of a similar name, with **Paul Gauguin** donning a suitably bohemian beret and overcoat. Also on display is the only known self-portrait by **Henri Rousseau**, at once both confident and comical, the artist depicting himself, palette in hand, against a boat decked with bunting and the recently erected Eiffel Tower.

There's also a surprisingly good collection of works by **Pablo Picasso**, including several paintings and sculptures from his transitional period (1907–08), and lots of examples from the heights of his Cubist period in the 1910s; his *Landscape with Bridge* from 1909 uses precisely the kind of prisms and geometric blocks of shading that influenced the Czech Cubist architects. In addition, there's a couple of late paintings by Paul Cézanne, a classic *pointilliste* canvas by Georges Seurat and Cubist works by Braque. *Joaquine* painted by **Henri Matisse** in 1910–11 is a first-rate portrait, in which both Fauvist and Oriental influences are evident. Look out too for Marc Chagall's *The Circus*, a typically mad work from 1927, and a rare painting by Le Corbusier himself, which clearly shows the influence of Fernand Léger, one of whose works hangs close by.

Czech Art 1930–2000

On the second floor, the section covering **Czech art from 1930 to 2000** gives a pretty good introduction to the country's artistic peaks and troughs. To be honest, though, there's too much stuff here – paintings, sculptures and installations – to take in at one go. Below are one or two highlights.

First off, there's a wild kinetic-light sculpture by **Zdeněk Pešánek**, a world pioneer in the use of neon in art, who created a stir at the 1937 Paris Expo with a neon fountain. Devětsil, founded back in 1920, was the driving force of the Czech avant-garde between the wars, and is represented here by the movement's two leading artists: **Toyen** (Marie Čermínová) and her lifelong companion **Jindřich Štyrský**, whose abstract works – they dubbed them "Artificialism" – reveal the couple's interest in the French Surrealists.

Avant-garde photography featured strongly in Devětsil's portfolio, and there are several fine abstract works on display. One Czech artist who enthusiastically embraced Surrealism was **Josef Šíma**, who settled permanently in Paris in the 1920s; several of his trademark floating torsoes and cosmic eggs can be seen here.

Fans of Communist kitsch should make their way to the excellent **Socialist Realism** section, heralded by Karel Pokorný's monumental *Fraternisation* sculpture, in which a Czechoslovak soldier is engaging in a "kiss of death" with a Soviet comrade. Among the paintings on display are works with wildly optimistic titles such as *We Produce More, We Live Better*, and Eduard Stavinoha's cartoon-like *Listening to the Speech of Klement Gottwald, Feb 21, 1948*. Note, too, the model of Otakar Švec's now demolished Stalin statue, which once dominated central Prague (see p.140).

In the 1960s, **performance art** (umění akce) was big in Czechoslovakia, and it, too, has its own section. Inevitably, it's difficult to recapture the original impact of some of the "happenings": the paltry "remnants of an installation" by Zdeněk Beran look a bit forlorn. Other photographs, such as those of Zorka Ságlová's *Laying out Nappies near Sudoměř*, give you a fair idea of what you missed. Eva Kmentová's *Footprints* betray their ephemeral intentions by being reproduced in a gallery: her plastercasts were originally exhibited for one day only in 1970 before being signed and given away.

The gallery owns several works by **Jiří Kolář** – pronounced "collage" – who, coincidentally, specializes in collages of random words and reproductions of other people's paintings. The rest of the contemporary Czech art collection is interesting enough, if taken at a canter. Ivan Kafka's phallic *Potent Impotency* installation should raise a smile, and there's the occasional overtly political work such as *Great Dialogue* by Karel Nepraš, in which two red figures lambast each other at close quarters with loudspeakers.

Foreign Art

The most recent addition to the gallery's permanent display is the bluntly entitled **Foreign Art** exhibition on the first floor. There are one or two gems here, beginning with **Gustav Klimt**'s mischievous *Virgins*, a mass of naked bodies and tangled limbs painted over in psychedelic colours, plus one of the square landscapes he used to like painting during his summer holidays in the Salzkammergut.

Egon Schiele's mother came from the South Bohemian town of Český Krumlov, the subject of a tiny, gloomy, autumnal canvas, *Dead City*. The gallery also owns one of Schiele's most popular female portraits, wrongly entitled *The Artist's Wife*, an unusually graceful and gentle watercolour of a seated woman in green top and black leggings. In contrast, *Pregnant Woman and Death* is a morbidly bleak painting, in which Schiele depicts himself as both the monk of death and the life-giving mother.

Perhaps the most influential foreign artist on show is **Edvard Munch**, whose two canvases hardly do justice to the considerable effect he had on a generation of Czech artists after his celebrated 1905 Prague exhibition. Look out for **Oskar Kokoschka**'s typically vigorous landscapes, dating from his brief stay in Prague in the 1930s, when the political temperature got too hot in Austria.

It's at this point that you get to see one of **Joan Miró**'s characteristically abstract Surrealist works called simply *Composition*. The floor ends with a few works by Fluxus, Vienna's very own, extremely violent 1960s performance art group, and a photo of one of Hermann Nitsch's bloody happenings.

Výstaviště and Stromovka

Five minutes' walk north up Dukelských hrdinů takes you right to the front gates of the **Výstaviště** (Tues–Fri 2–9pm; free; Sat & Sun 10am–9pm), a motley assortment of buildings, originally created for the 1891 Prague Exhibition, that have served as the city's main trade fair arena and funfair ever since. The Communist Party held its rubber-stamp congresses in the flamboyant stained-glass and wrought-iron **Průmyslový palác**, at the centre of the complex, from 1948 until the late 1970s, and more recently several brand new permanent structures were built for the 1991 Prague Exhibition, including a circular theatre, Divadlo Spirála, and Divadlo Globe, a reconstruction of Shakespeare's Globe Theatre in London, used for summer-only productions of the bard's plays in English and Czech.

The grounds are at their busiest on summer weekends, when hordes of Prague families descend on the place to down hot dogs, drink beer and listen to traditional brass-band music. Apart from the annual fairs and lavish special exhibitions, there are a few permanent attractions, such as the city's **Planetárium** (Mon–Fri 8.30am–noon & 1–8pm, Sat & Sun 9.30am–noon & 1–8pm; Ⓦ www.planetarium.cz), which has static displays and shows videos, but doesn't have telescopes (for which you need to go to the Štefánikova hvězdárna – see p.104); the **Maroldovo panorama** (Tues–Fri 2–5pm, Sat & Sun 11am–5pm), a giant diorama of the 1434 Battle of Lipany (see p.595); and the **Lunapark**, a run-down funfair and playground for kids. In the long summer evenings, there's also an open-air **cinema** (*letní kino*), and regular performances by the **Křižíkova fontána** (Ⓦwww.krizikovafontana.cz), dancing fountains devised for the 1891 Exhibition by the Czech inventor František Křižík, which perform a music and light show to packed audiences; for the current schedule, ask at the tourist office, or check the listings magazines or the website Ⓦwww .krizikovafontana.cz. Lastly, to the right as you enter the fairgrounds, there's the excellent and much overlooked **Lapidárium** (Tues–Fri noon–6pm, Sat & Sun 10am–6pm; Ⓦwww.nm.cz), official depository for the city's monumental sculptures that have been under threat from demolition or the weather in the last century or so.

To the west is the *královská obora* or royal enclosure, more commonly known as **Stromovka**. Originally a game park for the noble occupants of the Hrad, it's now Prague's largest and leafiest public park. From here, you can wander northwards to Troja and the city's zoo (see below), following a path that leads under the railway, over the canal, and on to the Císařský ostrov (Emperor's Island) – and from there to the right bank of the Vltava. Bus #112, which runs hourly, will take you back to metro Nádraží Holešovice.

Troja

Though still well within the municipal boundaries, the suburb of **TROJA**, across the river to the north of Holešovice and Bubeneč, has a distinctly provincial air. Its most celebrated sight is Prague's only genuine chateau, the late-seventeenth-century **Trojský zámek** (April–Sept Tues–Sun 10am–6pm; Nov–March Sat & Sun 10am–5pm; bus #112 from metro Nádraží Holešovice), perfectly situated against a hilly backdrop of vines. Despite a recent renovation and rusty red repaint, its plain early Baroque facade is no match for the action-packed, blackened figures of giants and titans who battle it out on the chateau's monumental balustrades. To visit the **interior**, you'll have to join one of the guided tours. The star exhibits are the gushing frescoes depicting the victories of the Habsburg Emperor Leopold I (who reigned from 1657 to 1705) over the Turks, which cover every inch of the walls and ceilings of the grand hall; ask for the *anglický text* when you enter. You also get to wander through the chateau's pristine trend-setting French-style formal **gardens**, the first of their kind in Bohemia.

On the other side of U trojského zámku, which runs along the west wall of the chateau, is the city's capacious but underfunded **zoo** (daily: March 9am–5pm; April, May, Sept & Oct 9am–6pm; June–Aug 9am–7pm; Nov–Feb 9am–4pm; Ⓦwww.zoopraha.cz), founded in 1931 on the site of one of Troja's numerous hillside vineyards, its trying its best to upgrade its animal enclosures. All the usual animals are on show here – including elephants, hippos, giraffes, zebras, big cats and bears – and kids, at least, will have few problems enjoying themselves. In the summer, you can take a chairlift (*lanová dráha*) from the duck pond to the top of the hill, where the prize exhibits – a rare breed of miniature horse known as Przewalski – hang out.

Another reason for coming out to Troja is to visit the city's newly renovated **botanická zahrada** (daily: April 9am–6pm; May–Sept 9am–7pm; Oct 9am–5pm; Nov–March 9am–4pm; Ⓦwww.botanicka.cz), hidden in the woods to the north of the zámek. The botanic gardens feature a vineyard, a Japanese garden, several glasshouses and great views over Prague. Hidden in the woods a little higher up the hill, there's also a spectacular, new, curvaceous greenhouse, **Fata Morgana** (Tues–Sun only), with butterflies flitting about amidst the desert and tropical plants.

Dejvice to Smíchov

Spread across the hills to the northwest of the city centre are the leafy garden suburbs of **Dejvice** and **Střešovice**, peppered with fashionable villas built between the wars for the upwardly mobile Prague bourgeoisie and commanding magnificent views across the north of the city.

In Střešovice, you'll find Prague's local transport museum, **Muzeum MHD** (April to mid-Nov Sat & Sun 9am–5pm; 20Kč; ⓦ www.dp-praha.cz), at Patočkova 4 – to get there take tram #1, #2, #15, #18, #25 or the historic tram #91 to Vozovna Střešovice. Housed in a 1909 tram shed, the majority of its exhibits are red-and-cream municipal trams from the last century, though there are one or two buses and trolleybuses too and an exhibition covering everything from horse-drawn trams to the Soviet-built metro.

Müllerova vila

The most famous Střešovice villa, the **Müllerova vila** (April–Oct Tues, Thurs, Sat & Sun 9am, 11am, 1, 3 & 5pm; 300Kč; 100Kč more for an English guide; ☏ 224 312 012, ⓦ www.mullerovavila.cz) at Nad hradním vodojemem 14, is open to the public. Designed by the Brno-born architect, Adolf Loos – regarded by many as one of the founders of modern architecture – and completed in 1930, it's a typically uncompromising box, wiped smooth with concrete rendering. However, Loos' most famous architectural concept, the Raumplan, or open-plan design, is apparent in the living room, which is overlooked by the dining room on the mezzanine level, and, even higher up, by the boudoir, itself a Raumplan in miniature. The house is also decorated throughout in the rich materials and minimal furnishings that were Loos' hallmark: green and white Cipolino marble columns, with an inset aquarium in the living room and mahogany panelling for the dining room ceiling. To visit the house, you must phone in advance as each guided tour is limited to seven people; to reach the house, take tram #1 or #18 from metro Hradčanská, four stops to Ořechovka.

Hvězda

A couple of kilometres southwest of Dejvice, trams #1, #2 and #18 terminate close to the hunting park of **Hvězda** (Tues–Sun: April & Oct 10am–5pm; May–Sept 10am–6pm), one of Prague's most beautiful and peaceful parks. Wide, green avenues of trees radiate from a bizarre star-shaped building (*hvězda* means "star" in Czech) designed by the Archduke Ferdinand of Tyrol for his wife in 1555. It houses a small exhibition on the **Battle of Bílá hora** (White Mountain), the first battle of the Thirty Years' War, which took place in 1620 a short distance southwest of Hvězda. However, it's the building itself – decorated with delicate stuccowork and frescoes – that's the greatest attraction; it makes a perfect setting for the chamber music concerts occasionally staged here.

Bertramka (Mozart Museum)

In the hills above the late-nineteenth-century suburb of **Smíchov** is Prague's Mozart Museum, known as the **Bertramka** (daily: April–Oct 9.30am–6pm; Nov–March 9.30am–5pm, ⓦ www.bertramka.cz), where, so the story goes, the composer put the finishing touches to his *Don Giovanni* overture, the night before the premiere at the Stavovské divadlo (see p.114). As long ago as 1838, the villa was turned into a shrine to Mozart, though very little survives of the house he knew, thanks to a fire on New Year's Day 1871 – not that this has deterred generations of Mozart-lovers from flocking here. These days, what the museum lacks in memorabilia, it makes up for with its Rococo ambience, lovely garden and regular Mozart recitals. To get to Bertramka, take the metro to Anděl, walk a couple of blocks west or go one stop on a tram up Plzeňská, then turn left up Mozartova.

Zbraslav

One of Prague's more intriguing museums is situated in the little-visited village of **ZBRASLAV**, 10km south of the city centre, though within the municipal boundaries. Přemyslid King Otakar II built a hunting lodge here, which was later turned into a Cistercian monastery – more recently, the buildings used to house the National Gallery's modern Czech sculptures, a few of which still pepper the grounds. Now, however, **Zámek Zbraslav** (Tues–Sun 10am–6pm; Ⓦwww.ngprague.cz) shelters the gallery's remarkably extensive Asian art collection.

The collection starts downstairs with Japanese art ranging from late-nineteenth-century lacquerwork lunchboxes and exquisite landscapes of birds and flowers on silk, to seventeenth-century travelling altarpieces and cracked glaze porcelain. Upstairs, there's a vast array of Chinese exhibits from Neolithic axes and ancient funerary art to Ming vases, dishes and even roof tiles. Highlights include an incredibly naturalistic eleventh-century wooden statue of one of the Buddha's aged disciples, a large standing gilded and lacquered Burmese Buddha, and an erotic Yab-Yum, a central icon of Tantric Buddhism.

Appropriately enough, the museum has a tea-house (*čajovna*) in the cloisters, and plenty of grass outside, on which to picnic. To reach the gallery, take bus #129, #241, #243, #255, #314 or #360 from metro Smíchovské nádraží or the local train from Smíchovské nádraží to Praha-Zbraslav – there's even the occasional PPS boat (see p.79).

Eating and drinking

While traditional Czech food still predominates in the city's pubs, the choice of places where you can eat is vast compared with the rest of the country. You can spend a whole week eating out and never go near a dumpling, should you so wish. Like most Czechs, Praguers are very keen on pizzas, and there is now a vast range of restaurants serving up everything from sushi to Afghan cuisine, some at prices aimed more at the passing tourist trade and the expat community than your average Czech. So while it's fun to sample authentic Czech food, and experience Czech eating habits, many visitors are happy to pay a bit more for food that is tastier and more imaginative, albeit not always very Czech.

Not surprisingly, the places in the main tourist areas along Mostecká and Karlova, on either side of the Charles Bridge, and on Staroměstské náměstí and Wenceslas Square, tend to be overpriced, relying on their geographical position, rather than the quality of their food, to bring in custom. Venture instead into the backstreets, such as those north of Celetná, south of Karlova, or south of Národní, and you're more likely to find better service, better value and perhaps even better food.

Snacks and fast food

Czechs are beginning to get into **sandwiches**, and the best city-wide chain is *Paneria* (Ⓦwww.paneria.cz), which specializes in providing sandwiches, toasted panini and pastries for Prague's hungry office workers; there are branches at

Kaprova 3 and Maiselova 4 (both metro Staroměstská) and elsewhere in the city. Expat favourites include the self-service breakfast, **bagel** and soup outfit, *Bohemia Bagel*, Újezd 16 (Ⓦwww.bohemiabagel.cz; tram #6, #9, #12, #20, #22 or #23, stop Újezd) and Masná 2 (metro Staroměstská), both of which have an Internet café attached. More varied and upmarket sandwiches, wraps, bread and cakes can be had from *Bakeshop Praha*, V Kolkovně 2 (metro Náměstí Republiky), which has a few eat-in bar stools. Another bakery worth heading for is *Albio*, Truhlářská 18 (metro Náměstí Republiky), an organic **bakery** and health food shop rolled into one.

Obviously the usual multinational burger chains have their outlets splattered all over Prague. For something more uniquely Czech, head for *Havelská Koruna*, Havelská 21 (metro Můstek), an authentic no-frills, self-service *jídelna* serving **Czech comfort food** classics such as *sekaná*, goulash and *zelí*, all for under 50Kč (you pay at the exit). For some authentic but cheap Indian **veggie** canteen food, look no further than *Beas Týnská* 19 (Ⓦwww.beas-dhaba.cz; metro Malostranská/Náměstí Republiky). Local veggies head for the multinational health food café *Country Life*, Melantrichova 15 and Jungmannova 1 (closed Sat; metro Můstek). Other quick-bite options include *Dahab Yalla*, Dlouhá 33, which serves felafel and other **Middle Eastern** snacks (metro Náměstí Republiky), as does *Anis,* at Jungmannova 21 (metro Národní třída).

Cafés

At the beginning of the twentieth century, Prague boasted a café society to rival that of Vienna or Paris. A handful of these classic Habsburg-era haunts have survived, or been resurrected, and should definitely be sampled. The cafés listed below are a mixed bunch. The majority serve just coffee and cakes, and more often than not, alcohol; others also serve up cheap and filling (though rarely gourmet) meals.

Malá Strana

Bakeshop Diner Lázeňská 16; tram #12, #20, #22 or #23 one stop from metro Malostranská. Stylish modern diner decked out in light wood and political/avant-garde posters. Breakfasts, sandwiches, melts and salads. Daily 7am–10pm.

U zavěšeného kafe Úvoz 6; tram #12, #20, #22 or #23 from metro Malostranská to Malostranské náměstí. A pleasant smoky cross-over café/pub, serving cheap beer and traditional Czech food in a handy spot on the way up or down from the Hrad. A "hanging coffee" is one that has been paid for by the haves for the have-nots who drop in. Daily 11am–midnight.

Staré Město

Chez Marcel Hašťalská 12 Ⓦwww.chezmoi.cz; metro Náměstí Republiky. Effortlessly chic French café-bistro. A good place to grab a coffee or a *tarte tatin*, read a French mag or eat some moderately priced bistro-style food. Mon–Sat 8am–1am, Sun 9am–1am.

Érra Konviktská 11; metro Národní třída. Vaulted cellar café in the backstreets off Betlémské

náměstí that's popular with a fashionable mixed straight/gay crowd. Tasty salads and snacks on offer too. Daily 11am–midnight.

Montmartre Řetězová 7; metro Staroměstská. Surprisingly small, barrel-vaulted café that was once a famous First Republic dance and cabaret venue, frequented by the likes of Werfel, Jesenská and Hašek. Mon–Fri 9am–11pm, Sat & Sun noon–11pm.

Grand Café Orient Ovocný trh 19; metro Náměstí Republiky. Superb reconstruction of a famous Cubist café from 1911 on the first floor of the Cubist museum. Cakes, pancakes and coffee. Daily 9am–9pm.

Nové Město

Globe Pštrossova 6 Ⓦwww.globebookstore .cz; metro Národní třída/Karlovo náměstí. Large, buzzing café, at the back of the English-language bookstore of the same name, that's a serious expat hangout, but enjoyable nevertheless; live music Fri & Sat eve. Daily 10am–midnight.

Imperial Na poříčí 15 Ⓦwww.hotelimperial.cz; metro Náměstí Republiky. An endearingly shabby yet grand Habsburg-era *Kaffeehaus* which has retained its original, over-the-top ceramic tiled decor. The locals clearly approve of its unpretentious air, too, and the free doughnuts go down a treat. Mon–Thurs 9am–midnight, Fri & Sat 9am–1am, Sun 9am–11pm.

Louvre Národní 20 Ⓦ www.kavarny.cz/louvre; metro Národní třída. Turn-of-the-twentieth-century café, closed down in 1948, but now back in business and a very popular refuelling spot for Prague's shoppers. Dodgy colour scheme, but high ceiling, mirrors, daily papers, lots of cakes, a billiard hall and window seats overlooking Národní. Mon–Fri 8am–11.30pm, Sat & Sun 9am–11.30pm.

Obecní dům náměstí Republiky 5 Ⓦ www .obecni-dum.cz. The vast *kavárna*, with its famous fountain, is in the more restrained south hall of this huge Art Nouveau complex, and has recently been glitteringly restored – an absolute aesthetic treat. Daily 7.30am–11pm.

Slavia Národní 1; metro Národní třída. Famous 1920s riverside café that has a special place in the city's cultural and political history (see p.130). Despite losing much of its former character and all of its clientele, it still pulls in a mixed crowd from shoppers and tourists to older folk and the pre- and post-theatre mob. Daily 9am–11pm.

Teta tramtárie Jungmannova 28 Ⓦ www .tetatramtarie.cz; metro Můstek. At the front, it's a funky, smoky café; at the back it's a *cukrárna* and a giant children's play area; upstairs there's a kids' bookshop and theatre venue. Daily 7.30am–10pm.

Velryba (The Whale) Opatovická 24; metro Národní třída. One of the most determinedly cool, student cafés in Prague. Smoky, loud and serving cheap Czech food (plus several veggie options) and a wide range of malt whiskies. Daily 11am–midnight.

Restaurants and wine bars

The influx of tourists has, of course, pushed the prices in some restaurants out of the reach of many Czechs, who tend more than ever to stick to pubs when eating out. However, even in the city's top restaurants, you can't guarantee faultless food and service, so keep an open mind. Service is gradually becoming more sophisticated, though surly staff are still no rarity, nor are unscrupulous waiters who exercise dubious arithmetics when totting up the bill. Beware of extras in the pricier restaurants, where you will be charged for everything you touch, including the almonds you thought were courtesy of the house.

Hradčany

U ševce Matouše (The Cobbler Matouš) Loretánské náměstí 4 ☎ 220 514 536; tram #22 or #23 from metro Malostranská to Pohořelec stop. Large steak and chips, for around 300Kč, is the speciality of this former cobbler's, which is one of the few half-decent places to eat in the castle district. Bottled beer only. Daily 11am–4pm & 6pm–11pm.

Malá Strana

Bar Bar Všehrdova 17 ☎ 257 312 246. Unpretentious cellar restaurant with big cheap salads, savoury (mostly veggie) pancake dishes and sweet crêpes/*palačinky* on offer. Daily noon–2am; food stops at midnight.

David Tržiště 21 ☎ 257 533 109, Ⓦ www .restaurant-david.cz. Formal, small, family-run restaurant that specializes in doing classic Bohemian cuisine full justice; main dishes go for around 500Kč. Daily 11.30am–11pm.

Hergetová cihelna Cihelná 2b ☎ 257 535 534, Ⓦ www.kampagroup.com. Slick, smart restaurant, run by the *Kampa Park* family, specializing in tasty pizzas cooked in a wood-fired oven for around

250Kč. The riverside summer terrace overlooks Charles Bridge. Daily 11.30am–1am.

Kampa Park Na Kampě 8b ☎ 296 826 102, Ⓦ www.kampagroup.com. Pink house exquisitely located right by the Vltava on Kampa Island with a superb fish and seafood menu, with main dishes around 750Kč, top-class service and tables outside in summer. Daily 11.30am–1am.

Nebozízek (Little Auger) Petřínské sady 411 ☎ 257 515 329, Ⓦ www.nebozizek.cz. Situated at the halfway stop on the Petřín funicular. The view is superb, there's an oodoor terrace and a traditional Czech menu heavy with game dishes for 300–400Kč. Daily 11am–11pm.

Pállfy palác Valdštejnská 14 ☎ 257 530 522, Ⓦ www.palffy.cz. Grand candle-lit room on the first floor of the conservatoire, and a wonderful outdoor terrace from which you can survey the red rooftops of Malá Strana; the international menu, with main courses for 500Kč and upwards, doesn't always live up to the setting. Daily 11am–11pm.

Rybářský klub U sovových mlýnů 1 ☎ 257 534 200; tram #12, #20, #22 or #23 from metro Malostranská to Hellichova stop. Freshwater fish – carp, catfish, eel,

Prague's tea-houses

Prague's **tea-houses** are a post-Communist phenomenon, though they have their historical roots in the First Republic. Partly a reaction to the smoke-filled, alcohol-driven atmosphere of the ubiquitous Czech pub, and partly a reaction against the multinational, fast-food culture that has now arrived in Prague, tea-houses tend to be non-smoking, slightly hippified places to enjoy a quiet cuppa and chill out. The tea-drinking is taken very seriously and there's usually a staggering array of leaves on offer, some commanding pretty high prices.

Dahab Dlouhá 33, Staré Město Ⓦ www.dahab.cz; metro Náměstí Republiky. The mother of all Prague tea-houses, a vast Bedouin tent of a place serving tasty Middle Eastern snacks, couscous and hookahs to a background of funky world music. Daily noon–1am.

Dobrá čajovna Václavské náměstí 14, Nové Město Ⓦ www.cajovna.com; metro Můstek/Muzeum. Mellow, rarefied tea-house, with an astonishing variety of teas (and a few Middle Eastern snacks) served by waiters who slip by silently in their sandals. Branch at Boršov 2, off Karoliny Světlé, Staré Město; metro Staroměstská. Mon–Fri 10am–9.30pm, Sun 3–9.30pm.

Malý Buddha Úvoz 46, Malá Strana; tram #12, #20, #22 or #23 one stop from metro Malostranská. Typical Prague tea-house decor, with a Buddhist altar in one corner and (mainly) vegetarian Vietnamese snacks on the menu. A very useful haven just down from the Hrad. Tues–Sun 1–10.30pm.

U zeleného čaje (The Green Tea) Nerudova 19, Malá Strana; tram #12, #22 or #23 one stop from from metro Malostranská. A great little stopoff for a pot of tea or a veggie snack en route to or from the Hrad; the only problem is getting a place at one of the four tables. Daily 11am–10pm.

U zlatého kohouta Michalská 3, Staré Město; metro Můstek. Hidden away in a courtyard off Michalská, this is another secretive, relaxing *čajovna* worth knowing about, located in the heart of Staré Město. Mon–Fri 10am–9.30pm, Sat & Sun 2–9.30pm.

---

pike and others – simply prepared for under 250Kč, at this unpretentious riverside restaurant, situated in the park on Kampa Island. Daily noon–11pm.

Square Malostranské náměstí 5 ☏ 296 826 104, Ⓦ www.kampagroup.com. One famous turn-of-the-twentieth-century café has changed beyond all recognition – it's now a very smart bar and restaurant, which serves an imaginative and well-executed international menu: pasta dishes, salads and main courses for 200–300Kč. Daily 8am–1am.

U modré kachničky Nebovidská 6 ☏ 257 320 308, Ⓦ www.umodrekachnicky.cz. Intimate little restaurant, decorated with murals and antiques. Offers a mouth-watering selection of dishes, including many Czech favourites – such as roast duck with pears – given the gourmet treatment. Main dishes for under 500Kč. Branch at Michalská 16 ☏ 224 213 418; metro Národní třída. Daily 11.30am–11.30pm.

Staré Město and Josefov

Ariana Rámová 6 ☏ 222 323 438, Ⓦ www.sweb .cz/kabulrest; metro Náměstí Republiky. Welcom-

ing Afghan restaurant (formerly known as *Kabul*) serving up inexpensive, authentic spicy food a stone's throw from the Old Town Square. Daily 11am–11pm.

Barock Pařížská 24 ☏ 223 329 221; metro Staroměstská. Trendy, candle-lit café-restaurant bathed in russet with framed photos of supermodels on the walls, and wannabes at the bar. The breakfasts are top-notch and the main dishes from the East are all good and under 500Kč. Mon–Fri 8.30am–1am, Sat 10am–2am, Sun 10am–1am.

Bellevue Smetanovo nábřeží 18 ☏ 222 221 443, Ⓦ www.pfd.cz; metro Národní třída. The view of Charles Bridge and the Hrad is outstanding and they serve imaginative Czech-centred cuisine – hardly surprising then that main courses are 650–850Kč and you need to book ahead to eat here. Mon–Sat noon–3pm & 5.30–11pm, Sun 11am–3pm & 7–11pm.

Kogo Havelská 27 ☏ 224 214 543, metro Můstek. Divided into two intimate spaces by a passageway with a small courtyard out back, this place offers decent pasta, pizza and salads for under 350Kč, served by courteous and efficient waiters. Branch at Na příkopě 22 ⓣ221 451 259; metro Náměstí Republiky. Daily 11am–11pm.

Le Saint-Jacques Jakubská 4 ⓣ222 322 685, ⓦwww.saint-jacques.cz; metro Náměstí Republiky. Excellent French brasserie cuisine on offer here in the heart of the so-called "French quarter", with main dishes 400–600Kč and tasteful live music nightly. Mon–Fri noon–3pm & 6pm–midnight, Sat & Sun 6pm–midnight.

Mlýnec Novotného lávka 9 ⓣ221 082 208, ⓦwww.pfd.cz; metro Staroměstská. Michelin-approved international cuisine and a fabulous terrace overlooking the Charles Bridge and the Castle – expect to pay 500–600Kč upwards for your main dish. Daily noon–3pm & 5–11pm.

Orange Moon Rámová 5 T222 325 119 ⓦwww .orangemoon.cz. Popular Burmese restaurant that cooks up spicy curries for under 200Kč, washed down with Czech beer. Daily 11.30am–11.30pm.

Pizzeria Rugantino Dušní 4 ⓣ222 318 172; metro Staroměstská. This pizzeria, just off Dlouhá, is the genuine article: an oak-fired oven, gargantuan thin bases, numerous toppings to choose from, and Bernard on tap. Mon–Sat 11am–11pm, Sun 5–11pm.

Pravda Pařížská 17 ⓣ222 326 203; metro Staroměstská. Trendy restaurant on Prague's premier chic street, pulling in fashionable customers. Service is attentive and the excellent menu ranges from Cajun to Vietnamese, with main dishes starting at around 350Kč. Daily noon–1am.

Red Hot & Blues Jakubská 12 ⓣ222 314 639; metro Náměstí Republiky. Laid-back joint deep in the heart of expat territory serving chilli-hot Tex-Mex – *burritos*, *étouffées* and Creole food – to the sound of jazz and blues. Daily 9am–11.30pm

Nové Město

Albio Truhlářská 18–20 ⓣ222 325 414, ⓦwww .albio.cz; metro Náměstí Republiky. Prague's most sophisticated vegetarian restaurant serves a whole range of healthy dishes from wholewheat pasta and noodles to filled baguettes and (be warned) fish. Daily 11am–10pm.

Dynamo Pštrossova 29 ⓣ224 932 020; metro Národní třída. Eye-catching retro 1960s designer decor, competent fish, chicken, steak and pasta dishes for around 300Kč and an incredible single malt whisky selection make this place a popular, trendy little spot. Daily 11.30am–midnight.

Le Bistrot de Marlène Plavecká 4 ⓣ224 921 853, ⓦwww.bistrotdemarlene.cz; metro Karlovo náměstí. Excellent French cuisine in a stylish, formal restaurant with exceptional service, in the

backstreets near Vyšehrad. Main dishes for around 600Kč. Mon–Fri noon–2.30pm & 7–10.30pm, Sat 7–10.30pm.

Lemon Leaf Na Zderaze 14 ⓣ224 919 056, ⓦwww.lemon.cz; metro Karlovo náměstí. Attractive, popular Thai restaurant, with hot and spicy meat and fish curries going for around 200Kč. Mon–Thurs 11am–11pm, Fri 11am–12.30am, Sat 12.30pm–12.30am, Sun 12.30pm–11pm.

Pizzeria Kmotra (Godmother) V jirchářích 12 ⓣ224 934 100, ⓦwww.kmotra.cz; metro Národní třída. This inexpensive, sweaty, basement pizza place is one of Prague's most popular, and justifiably so – if possible book a table in advance. Branch at Jindriicha Plachty 27, Smíchov; metro Anděl. Daily 11am–midnight.

U sádlů (The Lard) Klimentská 2 ⓣ224 813 874, ⓦwww.usadlu.cz; metro náměstí Republiky. Deliberately over-the-top themed medieval banqueting hall serving inexpensive hearty fare and lashings of frothing ale. Branch at Balbínova 22, Vinohrady; metro Muzeum/Náměstí Míru. Daily 11am–11.30pm.

Zahrada v opeře Legerova 75 ⓣ224 239 685, ⓦwww.zahradavopere.cz; metro Muzeum. Striking modern interior and beautifully presented food from around the world at democratic prices (main dishes for around 300Kč). The entrance is around the back of the Radio Free Europe building. Daily 11.30am–1am.

Further afield

La Crêperie Janovského 4, Holešovice ⓣ220 878 040, ⓦwww.lacreperie.cz; tram #1, #5, #8, #12, #14, #17, #25 or #26. Stylish, inexpensive, French-run crêperie serving sweet and savoury pancakes, French liqueurs and even the rare Nová Paka beer. Mon–Sat noon–11pm, Sun 11am–10pm.

Mailsi Lipanská 1, Žižkov ⓣ222 717 783; metro Jiřího z Poděbrad. Prague's only Pakistani restaurant is a friendly unpretentious place that's great for a comfort curry for around 300Kč, as hot as you can handle. Daily noon–3pm & 6–11pm.

Sushi Bar Zborovská 49, Smíchov ⓣ290 001 517, ⓦwww.sushi.cz; tram #6, #9, #12, #20, #22 or #23 to Újezd stop. Minimalist sushi bar in the part of Smíchov just south of Malá Strana. The sushi and sashimi set dishes are delicious, but beware of mounting bills as dishes cost 300–600Kč. Daily noon–10pm.

Radost FX Café Bělehradská 120 Vinohrady; metro I. P. Pavlova. Without doubt the best choice of vegetarian dishes in town (okay, so there's not much competition), plus funky music, drawing in a large expat posse, particularly for the Sunday brunch. Daily 11.30am–4am.

Pubs and bars

In the last fifteen years the Prague **pub** scene has diversified enormously, with the establishment of expat American-style bars, "Irish" pubs and smarter, designer places that attract a more mixed crowd of young professionals. Nevertheless, there are still plenty of traditional Czech *pivnice* left: smoky, male-dominated places, primarily designed for drinking copious quantities of Czech beer. Food, where served, is almost always of the traditional Czech variety – cheap and filling, but ultimately it could shorten your life by a couple of years.

Hradčany

U černého vola (The Black Ox) Loretánské náměstí 1; tram #22 or #23 from metro Malostranská to Pohořelec stop. Great traditional Prague pub doing a brisk business providing the popular light beer Velkopopovický kozel in huge quantities to thirsty local workers, plus a few basic pub snacks. Daily 10am–10pm.

Malá Strana

Jo's Bar Malostranské náměstí 7; metro Malostranská. A narrow bar in Malá Strana that was the original American expat/backpacker hangout. It no longer has quite the same vitality but it's still a good place to hook up with other travellers. Downstairs is *Jo's Garáž*. Daily 11am–2am.

U bílé kuželky (The White Bowling Pin) Míšeňská 12; metro Malostranská. Not a bad pub considering its touristy location right by the Charles Bridge. Reasonably priced Pilsner Urquell, Czech pub food and the occasional accordionist. Daily 11am–11pm.

U hrocha (The Hippo) Thunovská 10; metro Malostranská. A genuine smoky, Czech local in the heart of Malá Strana – difficult to believe but true. Cheap grub and well-served beer. Daily noon–11.30pm.

U kocoura (The Cat) Nerudova 2. One of the few famous old pubs left on Nerudova, serving Budvar, plus the obvious Czech stomach-fillers. Daily 11am–11pm.

U malého Glena Karmelitská 23 Ⓦwww.malyglen .cz; metro Malostranská. Smart-looking pub/jazz bar that attracts a fair mixture of Czechs and expats thanks to its better-than-average food and live music in the basement. Daily 8.30am–2am.

Staré Město

Legends Týn (Ungelt) Ⓦwww.legends.cz; metro náměstí Republiky. Heaving, loud, full-blown expat bar in the Týn courtyard, which shows the big TV sports events and has disco theme nights. Mon–Wed & Sun 11am–1am, Thurs–Sat 11am–3am.

Marquis de Sade Templová 8; metro Náměstí Republiky. Great space: huge high ceiling, big comfy sofas, and a leery, mostly expat crowd. Crap beer and limited snacks, but a good place to start the evening or end it. Daily 2pm–2am.

Molly Malone's U Obecního dvora 4 Ⓦwww .mollymalones.cz; metro Staroměstská. Best of Prague's Irish pubs with real Irish staff (who speak very little Czech), an open fire, draught Kilkenny and Guinness, and decent Irish-themed food. Mon–Thurs & Sun 11am–1am, Fri & Sat 11am–2am.

Radegast Templová 2; metro náměstí Republiky. Typically old-style smoky, boozy *pivnice* divided into booths, serving its namesake plus decent Czech food. Attracts Czechs and expats. Daily 11am–12.30pm.

U medvídků (The Little Bears) Na Perštýně 7 Ⓦwww.umedvidku.cz; metro Národní třída. A Prague beer hall going back to the thirteenth century and still much as it ever was (make sure you turn right when you enter, and avoid the new bar to the left). The Budvar comes thick and fast, and the food is pub standard. Mon–Sat 11.30am–11pm, Sun 11.30am–10pm.

U mravence (The Ant) U radnice 20; metro Staroměstská. Incredibly, given the top tourist location, this is an alright Czech pub, serving typical Czech pub food at reasonable prices. Daily 11am–midnight.

Nové Město

Billard Centrum V cípu 1 Ⓦwww.billardcentrum. cz; metro Můstek. Den of table football, table tennis, bowling, snooker and pool with Černá hora beer to quench your thirst. Daily 11am–2am.

Branický sklípek Vodičkova 26; metro Můstek. Convenient downtown pub decked out like a pine furniture showroom, serving typical Czech fare, and jugs of Prague's Braník beer. The rough and ready Branická formanka next door opens and closes earlier. Mon–Fri 9am–11pm, Sat & Sun 11am–11pm.

Novoměstský pivovar Vodičkova 20 Ⓦwww .npivovar.cz; metro Národní třída. Micro-brewery which serves its own well-tapped misty 11-degree home brew, plus Czech food, in a series of bright, sprawling modern beer halls. Mon–Sat 11.30am–10.30pm, Sun noon–10pm.

Pivovarský dům Corner of Lipová/Ječná; metro Karlovo náměstí. Busy micro-brewery dominated by its big shiny copper vats, serving excellent light, mixed and dark unfiltered beer (plus banana, coffee and wheat varieties), and all the standard Czech pub dishes (including *pivný sýr*). Daily 11am–11.30pm.

U Fleků Křemencova 11 ⓦ www.ufleku.cz; metro Karlovo náměstí. Famous medieval *pivnice* where the unique dark 13° beer, Flek, has been exclusively brewed and consumed since 1499. Seats over 500 German tourists at a go, serves short measures (0.4l), slaps an extra charge on for the music and still you have to queue. This is a tourist trap and the only reason to visit is to sample the beer, which you're best off doing during the day. Daily 9am–11pm.

U kotvy (The Anchor) Spalená 11; metro Národní třída. All-night spot that's perfect for a last Stáropramen and a slice of pizza before you attempt to work out how to catch a night tram home. Daily 24hr.

U Potrefená husa (The Wounded Goose) Jiráskovo náměstí 1; metro Karlovo náměstí. Very popular Czech chain of smart, convivial brick cellar pubs that attracts a mix of young and middle-aged professionals; Staropramen and very decent pub food on offer. Daily 11.30am–1am.

Further afield

Hospoda na verandách Nádražní 90, Smíchov; metro Anděl. The new official Staropramen brewery tap, and therefore the place to taste Prague's most popular beer. Daily 11am–11pm.

Letenský zámeček Letenské sady, Holešovice ⓦ www.letenskyzamecek.cz; tram #1 or #25 from metro Vltavská to Letenské náměstí stop. Convenient beer garden opposite the Národní technické muzeum serving Velkopopovický kozel, and slightly upgraded Czech pub food, including some veg-

gie options, in the *Ullman* restaurant inside. Daily 11am–11.30pm.

Lokalblok náměstí 14 října 10, Smíchov ⓦ www .lokalblok.cz; metro Anděl. Groovy new modernist bar on the ground floor with a climbing wall in the basement. Daily 11am–midnight, Sat & Sun noon–10pm.

U buldoka (The Bulldog) Preslova 1, Smíchov ⓦ www.ubuldoka.cz; metro Anděl. Great, off-beat Smíchov pub serving Gambrinus and classic Czech pub food, with occasional DJ nights in the psychedelic cellar. Mon–Fri 11am–midnight, Sat & Sun noon–midnight.

U houbaře (The Mushroom) Dukelských hrdinů 30; tram #5 from metro Náměstí Republiky to Veletržní stop. Comfortable, perfectly normal pub serving Pilsner Urquell and pub food, perfectly placed directly opposite the Veletržní palác (Museum of Modert Art). Daily 11am–midnight

U Houdků Bořivojova 110; tram #5 or #26 from metro Náměstí Republiky to Husinecká stop. Friendly pub in the heart of Žižkov with a beer garden, Velkopopvický kozel and cheap Czech food. Daily 10am–11pm.

U vystřeleného oka (The Shot-Out Eye) U božích bojovníků 3, Žižkov; metro Florenc. Big, loud, smoky, heavy-drinking pub just south of Žižkov Hill, off Husitská, with (unusually) good music playing and lashings of Měštan beer, plus absinthe chasers. Mon–Sat 3.30pm–1am.

Zvonařka (The Bell) Šafaříkova 1 ⓦ www.zvonarka .cz; tram #6 or #11 from metro I. P. Pavlova to Nuselské schody stop. The slick, futuristic interior hosts DJs at the weekend, while the terrace has great views over the Nuselské schody and Botič valley. Mon–Sat 11am–2am, Sun 11am–midnight.

Entertainment and the arts

For many Praguers, **entertainment** is confined to an evening's drinking in one of the city's beer-swilling *pivnice*. But if you're looking for a bit more action, there's plenty to keep you from night-time frustration. To find out **what's on**, check the **listings** sections in *Prague Post* (ⓦ www.praguepost.com), or the Czech listings monthly *Culture in Prague/Česká kultura* (ⓦ www.ceskakultura.cz), and keep your eyes peeled for flyers and posters. To buy **tickets** in advance, try one of the agencies such as Ticketpro, which has branches all over the city, with outlets in the Staroměstská radnice (Old Town Hall), Staroměstské náměstí, Staré Město (Mon–Fri 9am–6pm, Sat & Sun 9am–5pm; ⓦ www.ticketpro.cz), plus at Rytířská 31, Staré Město and in the Lucerna pasáž, Štěpánská 61, Nové Město.

Clubs and live venues

While most Praguers go to bed pretty early, a dedicated minority, including many of the city's expats and tourists, stay up until the wee small hours. To service this crowd, Prague has a good selection of late-night pubs and bars (see above) and a handful of half-decent **clubs**. Local DJs, and the odd international one, perform at most of these, and there are a few good one-off raves throughout the year (a case of scouring the fly posters around), but many clubs double as **live music venues**. As well as indigenous live acts, spanning the entire range of musical tastes from Czech reggae to thrash, a surprising array of world music bands find their way to Prague, along with a few big names from the USA and UK.

Rock, pop and dance music

Major Western **bands** often include Prague in their European tours and, to be sure of a full house, many offer tickets at below their usual price in the West. There are gigs by Czech bands almost every night in the city's clubs and discos – a selection of the better venues is listed below, though you should always check in the local listings before setting out.

Abaton Na Košince 8, Libeň ☎602 324 434, ⓦwww.fanonline.cz/abaton; metro Palmovka. Large cavernous factory venue in the suburbs that hosts some of the city's best raves and gigs.

Akropolis Kubelíkova 27, Žižkov ☎296 330 911, ⓦwww.palacakropolis.cz; tram #5, #9 or #26 to Lipanská stop. Two live venue spaces and a whole complex of bars in scruffy Žižkov, this place is the nerve centre of the city's alternative and world music scene and puts on the most eclectic programme of gigs in Prague. Live venue doors open 7pm.

Futurum Zborovská 7, Smíchov ☎257 328 571, ⓦwww.musicbar.cz; metro Anděl. Impressive, high-tech club which hosts Czech bands and DJs playing anything from retro nights to house. Daily 8pm–3am.

Karlovy lázně Smetanovo nábřeží 198, Staré Město ☎222 220 502, ⓦwww.karlovylazne.cz; metro Staroměstská. Mega, high-tech club on four floors of an old bathhouse by the Charles Bridge; techno on the top floor, progressively more retro as you descend to the Internet café on the ground floor. Daily until 5am.

Lucerna music bar Vodičkova 36, Nové Město ☎224 217 108, ⓦwww.musicbar.cz; metro Můstek. Not to be confused with the big venue of the same name, this is an unsophisticated, sweaty cellar bar in the Lucerna pasáž that hosts all sorts of gigs as well as themed discos. Daily 8pm–3am.

Mecca U Průhonu 3, Holešovice ☎283 870 522, ⓦwww.mecca.cz; tram #5, #12 or #15 from metro Nádraží Holešovice to U Průhonu stop. Despite being out in Prague 7, this converted factory is one of the best, and most popular, clubs in Prague. Café/restaurant daily 11am–11pm; club Fri & Sat until 6am.

Radost FX Bělehradská 120, Vinohrady ☎224 254 776, ⓦwww.radostfx.cz; metro I. P. Pavlova. Still the slickest (and longest-running) all-round dance club venue in Prague, attracting the usual mix of clubbers and despots; good veggie café upstairs (see p.152). Daily until 4am.

Roxy Dlouhá 33, Staré Město ☎224 826 296, ⓦwww.roxy.cz; metro náměstí Republiky. The centrally located Roxy is a great little venue: a laid-back rambling old theatre with an interesting programme of events from arty films and exhibitions to exceptional live acts and house DJ nights. Daily from 7pm.

Sedm vlků (Seven Wolves) Vlkova 33, Žižkov ⓦwww.sedmvlku.cz; tram #5 or #26 from metro náměstí Republiky to Husinecká stop. Club-bar with cellar and resident DJs who make the most of the impressive sound system. Mon–Sat 6pm–3am.

Jazz

Prague has a surprisingly long indigenous jazz tradition, and is home to a handful of good jazz clubs. With little money to attract acts from abroad, the artists are almost exclusively Czech and tend to do virtually the entire round of venues each month. The one exception to all this is *AghaRTA*, which attracts a few big names each year. More often than not, it's a good idea to book a table at the jazz clubs listed below – this is particularly true of *AghaRTA* and *Reduta*.

AghaRTA Jazz Centrum Krakovská 5, Nové Město ☎222 211 275, ⓦwww.agharta.cz; metro Muzeum. Probably the best jazz club in Prague, with a good mix of Czechs and foreigners and a consistently good programme of gigs; situated in a side street off the top end of Wenceslas Square. Mon–Fri 5pm–midnight, Sat & Sun 7pm–midnight.

Jazz Club Železná U průhonu 3, Holešovice ☏283 870 522, ⓦwww.mecca.cz; metro Vltavská. For the moment, *Železná* has moved out to the club *Mecca* where it now stages its mixed bag of jazz, jam, dance and world music sessions. Gigs start at 8pm.

Reduta Národní 20, Nové Město ☏224 933 487, ⓦwww.redutajazzclub.cz; metro Národní třída. Prague's best-known jazz club – Bill Clinton played his sax here in front of Havel – and its most unreconstructed. Gigs daily from 9pm; box office open from 5pm.

U malého Glena Karmelitská 23, Malá Strana ☏257 531 717, ⓦwww.malyglen.cz; tram #12 or #22 one stop from metro Malostranská. Tiny downstairs stage worth checking out for its eclectic mix of Latin jazz, be-bop and blues. Daily until 2am.

U staré paní (The Old Woman) Michalská 9, Staré Město ☏224 228 090, ⓦwww.ustarepani.cz; metro Můstek. Decent old town jazz restaurant that really gets going when the live contemporary jazz kicks in from 9pm onwards. Daily 7pm–2am.

Ungelt Jazz & Blues Club Týn 2, Staré Město ☏224 895 748, ⓦwww.jazzblues.cz; metro Náměstí Republiky. Relative newcomer to the Prague jazz scene, *Ungelt* is a good cellar venue, puts on a good selection of jazz, blues and funk and understandably pulls in lots of tourists. Daily 7pm–2am.

Gay and lesbian Prague

Prague has a small, but burgeoning **gay and lesbian scene**, with its spiritual heart in leafy Vinohrady and neighbouring Žižkov. On the web, you can find out lots of up-to-date listings from ⓦgayguide.net/europe/czech/prague. Once in Prague, get hold of the bi-monthly gay magazine *Amigo*, which has a shop at Příčná 7, Nové Město ☏222 233 250, ⓦwww.amigo.cz, open Tuesday to Saturday. You'll also find useful flyers at the places listed below. At many clubs, you'll be given a drinks ticket, which you must keep hold of or be liable to a hefty minimum charge.

"A" Klub Milíčova 25, Žižkov ☏222 781 623; tram #5, #9 or #26 to Lipanská stop. The city's premier lesbian bar with women-only Friday nights. It's small but stylish and definitely worth checking out. Daily 7pm–6am.

Arco Voroněžská 24, Vinohrady ☏271 740 734, ⓦwww.arco-guesthouse.cz; tram #4, #22 or #23 from metro Náměstí Míru to Krymská stop. Gay Internet café and guesthouse. Mon–Fri 8am–1am, Sat & Sun 9am–1am.

Babylonia Martinská 6, Staré Město ☏224 232 304 ⓦwww.amigo.cz/babylonia; metro Národní třída. Prague's most centrally located gay sauna, with steam baths, pools and massage on offer. Daily 2pm–3am.

Friends Bartolomějská 11, Staré Město ☏221 236 772, ⓦwww.friends-prague.cz; metro Národní třída. Friendly, laid-back mixed gay/lesbian cellar bar in the centre of the old town. Daily 4pm–3am.

Gejzee...r Vinohradská 40, Vinohrady ☏222 516 036, ⓦwww.gejzeer.cz; metro Náměstí Míru. Prague's largest and most popular gay club with dance floor, DJs and the inevitable darkroom. Thurs 8pm–4am, Fri & Sat 9pm–5am.

Termix Třebízského 4a, Vinohrady ☏222 710 462, ⓦwww.club-termix.cz; metro Jiřího z Poděbrad. Prague's latest gay/lesbian club is a stylish place, with lots of dancing, as well as chill-out and dark rooms. Daily 8pm–5am.

The arts

Alongside the city's numerous cafés, pubs and clubs, there's a rich **cultural life** in Prague. Music is everywhere, especially in the summer, when the streets, churches, palaces, opera houses, concert halls and even the gardens are filled with the strains of classical music. Mozart had strong links with the city, and of course the Czechs themselves produced four top-drawer classical composers. In addition, Prague boasts three opera houses, three excellent orchestras and a couple of festivals that attract top-class international artists. Even if you don't understand Czech, there are theatre performances worth catching – Prague has a strong tradition of mime, "black light theatre" (visual trickery created by "invisible" actors dressed all in black), and puppetry, and many cinemas show films in their original language, with some even showing Czech films with English subtitles.

You can obtain **tickets** from the box office (*pokladna*) of the venue concerned, but you might find it easier to go to one of the city's numerous **ticket agencies** – it will cost you more, but might save you a lot of hassle. Ticketpro has branches all over the city. Ticket **prices**, with a few notable exceptions, are still good value, starting at just 250Kč. Lastly, don't despair if everything is officially sold out (*vyprodáno*), as standby tickets are often available at the venue's box office on the night, an hour before the start of the performance, and, if all else fails, there are usually touts outside.

By far the biggest annual event is the Pražské jaro (Prague Spring), the country's most prestigious **international music festival**, which traditionally begins on May 12, the anniversary of Smetana's death. The main venues are listed on below, but keep an eye out for concerts in the city's churches and palaces, gardens and courtyards; note that evening performances tend to start fairly early, either at 5 or 7pm.

Main opera houses and concert halls

Národní divadlo (National Theatre) Národní 2, Nové Město ☎224 901 448, ⊛www.narodni-divadlo .cz; metro Národní třída. Prague's grandest nineteenth-century theatre is the living embodiment of the Czech national revival movement, and continues to put on a wide variety of mostly, though by no means exclusively, Czech plays, plus the odd opera and ballet. Worth visiting for the decor alone. Box office daily 10am–6pm. Closed July & Aug.

Obecní dům – Smetanova síň náměstí Republiky 5, Nové Město ☎222 002 105 ⊛www.obecni-dum .cz; metro Náměstí Republiky. Fantastically ornate and recently renovated Art Nouveau concert hall which usually kicks off the Prague Spring festival, and is home to the excellent Prague Symphony Orchestra. Box office Mon–Fri 10am–6pm.

Rudolfinum Alšovo nábřeží 12, Staré Město ☎224 893 352, ⊛www.rudolfinum.cz; metro Staroměstská. A truly stunning Neo-Renaissance concert hall from the late-nineteenth century, that's home base for the Czech Philharmonic (⊛www.ceskafilharmonie.cz). The Dvořákova síň is the large hall; the Sukova síň is the chamber concert hall. Box office Mon–Fri 10am–6pm, plus 1hr before performance.

Státní opera Praha (Prague State Opera) Wilsonova 4, Nové Město ☎224 227 266, ⊛www .opera.cz; metro Muzeum. A sumptuous nineteenth-century opera house, built by the city's German community, which once attracted star conductors such as Mahler and Zemlinsky. Now it's the number two venue for opera, with a repertoire that tends to focus on Italian pieces. Box office Mon–Fri 10am–5.30pm, Sat & Sun 10am–noon & 1–5.30pm, plus 1hr before performance. Closed mid-July to mid-Aug.

Stavovské divadlo (Estates Theatre) Ovocný trh 1, Staré Město ☎224 215 001, ⊛www.narodni-divadlo .cz; metro Můstek. Prague's oldest opera house, which witnessed the premiere of Mozart's *Don Giovanni*, puts on a mixture of opera, ballet and straight theatre (with simultaneous headphone translation available). Box office daily 10am–6pm, plus 30min before performance. Closed mid-July to mid-Aug.

Theatres

Černé divadlo Jiřího Srnce Reduta, Národní 20, Nové Město ☎222 933 487, ⊛www.redutajazzclub .cz; metro Národní třída. One of the founders of Laterna magika, Jiří Srnec puts on black light shows that are a cut above the competition, at various venues around Prague. Box office daily 11am–9.30pm.

Divadlo Archa Na poříčí 26, Nové Město ☎221 716 333, ⊛www.archatheatre.cz; metro Florenc. By far the most exciting, innovative venue in Prague, with two very versatile spaces, plus an art gallery and a café. The programming includes music, dance and theatre with an emphasis on the avant-garde – English subtitles or translation often available. Box office Mon–Fri 10am–6pm, plus 2hr before performance.

Divadlo Image Pařížská 4, Staré Město ☎222 329 191, ⊛www.imagetheatre.cz; metro Staroměstská. One of the more innovative and entertaining of Prague's ubiquitous black theatre venues. Box office daily 9am–8pm.

Divadlo minor Vodičkova 6, Nové Město ☎222 232 530, ⊛www.minor.cz; metro Karlovov náměstí. The former state puppet theatre puts on children's shows most days, plus adult shows on occasional evenings – sometimes with English subtitles. Box office Mon–Fri 9am–1.30pm & 2.30–8pm, Sat & Sun 11am–8pm.

Divadlo Spejbla a Hurvínka Dejvická 38, Dejvice ☏ 224 316 784, ⊛ www.spejbl-hurvinek.cz; metro Dejvická/Hradčanská. Features the indomitable puppet duo Spejbl and Hurvínek, created by Josef Skupa earlier this century and still going strong at one of the few puppets-only theatres in the country. Box office Tues, Thurs & Fri 10am–2pm & 3–6pm, Wed 10am–2pm & 3–7pm, Sat & Sun 1–5pm.

Duncan Centre Branická 41, Braník ☏ 244 461 342, ⊛ www.duncanct.cz; tram #3, #16, #17 or #21, stop Přístaviště. Occasional dance performances by resident and visiting artists at this theatre based in a school for contemporary dance in the southern suburb of Braník.

Laterna magika (Magic Lantern) Nová scéna, Národní 4, Nové Město ☏ 224 931 482, ⊛ www .laterna.cz; metro Národní třída. The National Theatre's Nová scéna, one of Prague's most modern and versatile stages, is the main base for Laterna magika, founders of multimedia and "black light" theatre way back in 1958. Their slick productions continue effortlessly to pull in crowds of tourists. Box office Mon–Sat 10am–8pm.

Národní divadlo marionet Žatecká 1, Staré Město ☏ 222 324 565, ⊛ www.riseloutek.cz; metro Staroměstská. This company's rather dull marionette version of Mozart's *Don Giovanni* (⊛ www .Mozart.cz) has proved extremely popular, but they also put on more interesting kids' shows at the weekends. Box office daily 10am–8pm.

Ponec Husitská 24a, Žižkov ☏ 224 817 886, ⊛ www.divadloponec.cz. Former cinema, now innovative dance venue and centre for the annual Tanec Praha dance festival in June/July. Box office 2hr before performance.

Švandovo divadlo Štefánikova 57, Staré Město ☏ 234 651 111, ⊛ www.svandovodivadlo.cz; metro Anděl. Pioneering, exciting and experimental, Švandovo is a new addition to the Prague theatre scene. Productions are in Czech (some with English subtitles), but there are gigs too. Box office Mon–Sat 2pm–7am.

Cinemas

Aero Biskupcova 31, Žižkov ☏ 271 771 349, ⊛ www.kinoaero.cz; tram #9, #10, #16 or #19, stop Biskupcova. Crumbling art-house cinema that shows rolling mini-festivals, retrospectives and independent movies.

Evald Národní 28, Nové Město ☏ 221 105 225, ⊛ www.cinemart.cz; metro Národní třída. Prague's most centrally located art-house cinema, shows a discerning selection of new releases interspersed with plenty of classics.

Lucerna Vodičkova 36, Nové Město ☏ 224 216 972; metro Můstek. Without doubt the most ornate commercial cinema in Prague, decked out in Moorish style by Havel's grandfather, in the pasáž the family once owned.

MAT Studio Karlovo náměstí 19, Nové Město ☏ 224 915 765, ⊛ www.mat.cz; metro Karlovo náměstí. Tiny café and cinema popular with the film crowd, with an eclectic programme of shorts, documentaries and Czech films with English subtitles. Entrance is on Odborů.

Ponrepo – Bio Konvikt Bartolomějská 11, Staré Město ☏ 224 237 233; metro Národní třída. Really old classics from the black-and-white era, dug out from the National Film Archives. Membership cards (150kč) can only be bought Mon–Fri 2–5pm, and you need to bring a photo.

Shopping, sports and activities

The passing tourist can find bargains in goods like glass, ceramics and wooden toys. Czechs also continue to produce cassettes, LPs, books and, of course, smoked meats and alcohol at a fraction of Western prices. The backstreets of Malá Strana and Staré Mesto are good for finding interesting little **shops**, or follow Praguers to Nové Mesto and the covered shopping malls in and around Wenceslas square. The two **sports** which draw in the biggest crowds are soccer and ice hockey, and getting a ticket is easy (and cheap) enough on the day – only really big matches sell out.

Shopping

There's a superb **English-language bookstore**, Anagram, Týn 4, Nové Město (Mon–Sat 10am–8pm, Sun 10am–7pm; ⊛ www.anagram.cz; metro náměstí Republiky), which has lots of books on Czech politics and culture, plus a small secondhand section. The Globe, Pštrossova 6 (Daily 10am–midnight; ⊛ www

.globebookstore.cz; metro Národní třída/Karlovo náměstí), is an expat book-store par excellence – both a social centre and superbly well-stocked store, with an adjacent café and friendly staff. You can get most foreign **newspapers and magazines** at the kiosks at the bottom of Wenceslas Square, outside metro Můstek.

Prague has two main **department stores**; Kotva, nám. Republiky 8, Nové Město; and Tesco, Národní 26, Nové Město. If it's food, flowers or wooden toys that take your fancy, visit Havelská, Staré Město (Mon–Fri 8am–6pm, Sat & Sun 9am–6pm; metro Můstek), the only open-air fruit and veg **market** in central Prague.

For **records and music,** head to Bontonland, Palác Koruna, Václavské nám. 1 (Mon–Fri 9am–7pm, Sat 9am–1pm; Ⓦ www.bontonland.cz; metro Můstek). This is Prague's biggest record store, in the *pasáž* at the bottom of Wenceslas Square, with rock, folk, jazz and classical, and headphones for previews to boot. There's a classical branch at Jungmannova 20 in Nové Město.

Sports and activities

Prague's (and the Czech Republic's) most successful **football** (soccer) club is Sparta Praha (Ⓦ www.sparta.cz), who play at a stadium by the Letná plain (five minutes' walk from, or one tram stop east of, metro Hradčanská). The city's second most successful team, Slavia Praha (Ⓦ www.slavia.cz) are having their stadium redeveloped and currently play at the Stadion Evžena Rozičk-ého, Zátopkova, behind the massive Strahov stadium (bus #143, #149, #176 or #217). Sparta Praha (Ⓦ www.hcsparta.cz) is Prague's top **ice hockey** team; their *zimní stadión* (winter stadium) is at Za elektrárnou (metro Nádraží Hole-šovice), next door to the Výstaviště exhibition grounds in Holešovice. Prague's only other first-division team are Slavia Praha (Ⓦ www.hc-slavia.cz), who won the league for the first time ever in 2003 and play at Eden on Vladivostocká in Vršovice (tram #22 or #23 from metro Náměstí Míru or tram #6, #19, stop Kubánské náměstí).

For a refreshing **swim**, head for Divoká Šárka, Vokovice (May to mid-Sept daily 9am–7pm; tram #20 or #26 from metro Dejvická to the Divoká Šárka terminus). Idyllically located in a craggy valley to the northwest of Prague, with two small outdoor pools filled with cold but fresh and clean water, it's great for a full, hot day out. Food and drink and plenty of shade available, too. The most famous of Prague's outdoor pools is Podolí Plavecký, stadion Podolská 74 (Mon–Fri 6am–9.45pm, Sat & Sun 8am–7.45pm; Ⓣ 241 433 952; Ⓦ www.pspodoli.cz; Podolí, tram #3, #17 or #21, stop Kublov), set against a sheltered craggy backdrop, with a children's wading pool and water slide, grass and draught beer.

Listings

Airlines Austrian Airlines Ⓣ 220 114 324, Ⓦ www. aua.com; bmibaby Ⓣ 224 810 180, Ⓦ www .bmibaby.com; British Airways Ⓣ 222 114 444, Ⓦ www.britishairways.com; Czech Airlines (ČSA) Ⓣ 220 104 310, Ⓦ www.csa.cz; Delta Ⓣ 224 946 733, Ⓦ www.delta.com; easyJet Ⓣ 296 333 333, Ⓦ www. easyjet.com; KLM Ⓣ 233 090 933, Ⓦ www.klm.com.

Cultural centres American Information Center Tržiště 15, Malá Strana Ⓣ 257 530 640, Ⓦ www

.usembassy.cz; metro Malostranská. By appoint-ment Mon–Thurs 1–4pm. Austrian Cultural Institute (Rakouský kulturní fórum), Jungmannovo náměstí 18, Nové Město Ⓣ 221 181 777, Ⓦ www .aussenministerium.at/pragkf; metro Můstek. Gal-lery Mon–Fri 10am–5pm. British Council (Britská rada), Bredovský dvůr, Politických vězňů 13, Nové Město Ⓣ 221 991 160, Ⓦ www.britishcouncil .cz; metro Můstek/Muzeum. Mon–Fri 9am–5pm. Goethe Institut, Masarykovo nábřeží 32, Nové

Moving On

If you're catching a **train out of Prague**, don't leave buying your ticket until the last minute, as the queues can be long and slow and make sure you check from which station your train is departing. You can buy international train tickets (*mezinárodní jízdenky*) at either Praha hlavní nádraží or Praha-Holešovice. For **buses to destinations around Prague**, you may need to head out to one of the more obscure bus terminals, all of which are easy enough to reach by metro. To find out which one you want, ask at any of the PIS offices in town or check the comprehensive (and extremely complicated) timetables at Praha-Florenc: *stání* is the bus stand; *odjezd* is the departure time.

Město ☎221 962 111, ⊕www.goethe.de; metro Národní třída. Mon–Fri 9am–6pm. Hungarian Cultural Centre (Madarské kulturní středisko), Rytířská 25–27, Staré Město ☎224 222 424 ⊕www .magyarintezet.hu/praga; metro Můstek. Mon–Thurs 10am–7pm, Fri 10am–2pm. Institut Français (Francouzský institut), Štěpánská 35, Nové Město ☎221 401 011, ⊕www.ifp.cz; metro Muzeum. Café: Mon & Fri 8.30am–7pm, Tues–Thurs 8.30am–7.30pm. Slovenský institut Jilská 16, Staré Město ☎224 948 135 ⊕www.slovakemb.cz; metro Národní třída. Mon, Wed & Fri 10am–1pm, Tues & Thurs 1–4pm.

Dentist Václavské náměstí 33, Nové Město ☎224 228 984, ⊕www.edcdental.cz.

Embassies and consulates Australia, Klimentská 10, Nové Město ☎296 578 350, ⊕www.embassy .gov.au/cz; metro Náměstí Republiky. Britain, Thunovská 14, Malá Strana ☎257 402 111, ⊕www .britain.cz; metro Malostranská. Canada, Muchova 6 ☎272 101 800, ⊕www.Canada.cz; metro Hradčanská; Germany, Vlašská 19, Malá Strana ☎257 113 111, ⊕www.german-embassy.cz; metro Malostranská. Ireland, Tržiště 13 ☎257 530 061; metro Malostranská. New Zealand, Dykova 19 ☎222 514 672; metro Jiřího z Poděbrad. Poland, Valdštejnská 8, Malá Strana ☎257 530 388, ⊕www.polamb.cz; metro Malostranská. Slovakia, Pod hradbami 1, Dejvice ☎233 113 051; metro Dejvická. Ukraine, Charlese de Gaulla 20, Dejvice ☎224 226 157; metro Dejvická. USA, Tržiště 15, Malá Strana ☎257 530 663, ⊕www.usembassy .cz; metro Malostranská.

Exchange offices 24hr service at 28 října 13,

Nové Město; metro Můstek.

Hospitals For an English-speaking doctor, you should go to the private Nemocnice na Homolce, Roentgenova 2, Motol ☎257 271 111; bus #167 from metro Anděl. If it's an emergency, dial ☎155 for an ambulance and you'll be taken to the nearest hospital.

Laundrettes Laundry Kings, Dejvická 16, Dejvice (Mon–Fri 6am–10pm, Sat & Sun 8am–10pm; ☎233 343 743, ⊕www.laundry.czweb.org; metro Hradčanská); Laundryland, Na příkopě 12, Nové Město and many other branches (Mon–Fri 9am– 8pm, Sat 9am–7pm & Sun 11am–7pm; ☎777 333 466, ⊕www.laundryland.cz; metro Můstek); and Prague Laundromat, Korunní 14, Vinohrady (daily 8am–8pm; ☎222 510 180, ⊕www.volny.cz /laundromat; metro Náměstí Míru.

Left luggage Prague's main bus and train stations have lockers which have instructions in English. The train stations also have 24hr left luggage offices.

Lost property The main train stations have lost property offices – look for the sign *ztráty a nálezy* – and there's a central municipal one at Karoliny Světlé 5, Staré Město. If you've lost your passport, then get in touch with your embassy (see above).

Pharmacies 24hr chemists at Palackého 5, Nové Město (☎224 946 982); metro Můstek).

Police If you wish to extend your visa or your stay, you need to go to the Cizinecká policie (Foreigners' Police), Olšanská 2, Žižkov and Sdružení 1, Pankrác. In an emergency dial ☎158.

Post office 24hr office/poste restante at Jindřišská 14, Nové Město.

Central Bohemia

Few capital cities can boast such extensive unspoilt tracts of woodland so near at hand as Prague. Once you leave the half-built high-rise estates of the outer suburbs behind, the softly rolling hills and somnolent villages of central **Bohemia** (Čechy) take over.

To the north, several chateaux grace the banks of the Vltava, including that of the wine-producing town of **Mělník**, on the Labe (Elbe) plain. Beyond Mělník lie the wooded gorges of the **Kokořínsko** region, too far for a day-trip unless you've your own transport, but perfect for a weekend in the country. One of the most obvious day-trip destinations is to the east of Prague: **Kutná Hora**, a medieval silver-mining town with one of the most beautiful Gothic cathedrals in the country and a macabre gallery of bones in the suburb of **Sedlec**.

Further south, there are a couple of chateaux worth visiting along the **Sázava valley**; while nearby, two more, **Průhonice** and **Konopiště**, are set in exceptionally beautiful and expansive grounds – with a car, you could take in several in a day. Southwest of Prague, a similar mix of woods and rolling hills surrounds the popular castle of **Karlštejn**, a gem of Gothic architecture, dramatically situated above the River Berounka. There are numerous possibilities for walking in the region around Karlštejn and, further upstream, in the forests of **Křivoklátsko**. West of Prague, near Kladno, there are two places of pilgrimage: **Lány** is the resting place of the founder of the modern Czechoslovak state and summer residence of the president; and **Lidice**, razed to the ground by the SS, recalls the horror of Nazi occupation.

Transport throughout Bohemia is fairly straightforward, thanks to a comprehensive network of railway lines and regional bus services, though connections can be less than smooth and journeys slow. However, if you're planning to see a few places outside Prague, or one of the destinations more difficult to reach, it might be worth hiring a car.

North along the Vltava

One of the quickest and most rewarding trips out of the capital is to follow the Vltava as it twists northwards across the plain towards the River Labe at Mělník. This is the beginning of the so-called **zahrada Čech** (Garden of Bohemia), a flat and fertile region whose cherry blossoms are always the first to herald the Bohemian spring and whose roads in summer are lined with stalls overflowing with fruit and vegetables. But the real reason to venture into this relatively flat landscape is to visit the **chateaux** that lie along the banks of the river, all easily reached by train from Prague's Masarykovo nádraží.

Beyond Kralupy

The Nobel prize-winning poet Jaroslav Seifert didn't beat around the bush when he wrote that **KRALUPY NAD VLTAVOU** (ⓦwww.kralupy.cz) "is not a beautiful town and never was". Seifert had happy childhood memories of the place, but it was heavily bombed in World War II, and postwar industrial development left it with "smokestacks like phantom trees, without branches, without leaves, without blossoms, without bees". Now, Kralupy's oil refineries and chemical plants have spread across both sides of the river, but it's still worth making the thirty-minute train journey from Prague, as just a few kilometres to the north, on either side of the Vltava, are two fine chateaux: Nelahozeves on the left bank and Veltrusy on the right – again, both accessible by train.

Nelahozeves

Shortly after pulling out of Kralupy, the train passes through a short tunnel and comes to rest at Nelahozeves zámek, the first of two stations in the village of **NELAHOZEVES** and the one to get off at. Above the railway sits the village's monumentally large **zámek** (Tues–Sun 9am–5pm; Ⓦ www.lobkowicz.org), built in the 1550s by Italian builders for one of the lackeys of the Habsburg Ferdinand I, and totally smothered in sgraffito. Unfortunately, the original owner backed the wrong side in the Thirty Years' War, and in 1623 the chateau was snapped up by the incredibly wealthy Polyxena Lobkowicz. After the fall of Communism, the chateau was returned to the Lobkowicz family, and it's now enjoying a wonderful renaissance as the family's museum showpiece.

The interior is well worth a visit, having been restored and replenished with paintings from the family's vast art collection. There's a choice of tours, though since the **art collection** is the highlight, there seems little point in opting for the half-hour tour (*okruh II*), which skips the European masters, rather than the hour-long tour (*okruh I*). You have to pay 70Kč to borrow the English guidebook, and 330Kč to have an English-speaking guide. The main problem is that you have to go on a guided tour, and therefore have to spend as much time on the Spanish portraits by Coello as you do on the handful of master-pieces. The most exceptional works on display are Pieter Brueghel the Elder's sublime *Haymaking* from the artist's famous cycle of seasons, a view of the City of London, and one of Westminster, from across the Thames, by Canaletto, and a portrait of the Infanta Margarita Teresa (possibly by Velázquez), niece and first wife of Emperor Leopold I, who was betrothed from the age of three and died at twenty-two. The family also has a long history of musical patronage (most notably Beethoven, who dedicated two of his symphonies to the seventh prince) and the original working manuscripts on show are pretty impressive, while the family library's prize possession is a Gutenberg Bible.

The other reason for stopping at Nelahozeves is that **Antonín Dvořák** (1841–1904) was born and bred under the shadow of the chateau, at the house (no. 12) next door to the post office, now his **Rodný dům** (Sat & Sun: April–Sept 10am–noon & 2–5pm; Oct–March 9am–noon & 1–4pm; Tues–Fri phone ☎315 785 099; closed first weekend of month). Dvořák was originally apprenticed to a butcher but, on the recommendation of his schoolmaster, was sent to the Prague Organ School instead. He went on to become director of the Prague conservatoire and by far the country's most famous composer. If there's someone around at the house, you can have a quick look at the great man's rocking chair and various other personal effects.

Veltrusy

The industrial suburbs of Kralupy stop just short of the village of **VELTRUSY**, which has its own **zámek** (May–Sept Tues–Sun 9am–noon & 1–5pm) set in beautiful grounds to the north. The classic Baroque symmetry of the chateau is more hospitable than the one at Nelahozeves, its green shutters and four hennaed wings pivoting round a bulbous, domed building that recalls earlier country houses in France or Italy. It was built in the early eighteenth century as a plaything for the upwardly mobile Chotek family, its 290 acres of surrounding woodland perfect for a little light hunting. It was also the unlikely venue for the world's first trade fair, which took place in 1754 under the title "The Veltrusy Large Trade Fair of Products of the Czech Kingdom", and drew a distinguished audience including Empress Maria Theresa.

Unfortunately, the floods of 2002 caused untold damage to Veltrusy and it looks like the chateau will be closed for some time to come. You can, however, visit the **Zámecký park**, which are liberally dotted with fallow deer, follies, peacocks and woodpeckers. To get to the chateau from the train station at Nelahozeves (one stop on from Nelahozeves zámek), it's a 1.5km walk across the busy road bridge, or the smaller bridge further south. There are also regular buses to Veltrusy from Prague's Florenc bus station.

Practicalities

If you fancy staying, there are several houses offering inexpensive **private rooms** on the road to Veltrusy, and just outside its chateau grounds there's a very good **campsite**, *ATC Obora* (Feb–Dec). It's a great spot for watching the barges on the Vltava, but, given the pollutants that seep into the river further upstream, no place for a dip. There are a couple of pubs in Nelahozeves, but the nicest place to **eat** is the *Zámecká restaurace* in the courtyard of Nelahozeves zámek, where you can quaff Lobkowicz wine or beer with your meal. Look out, too, for the concerts of **Dvořák's music** performed in the zámek (ⓦwww .bdiscovery.org), every year, from April to October.

Říp

Czech legend holds that the founding father of the nation, called Praotec Čech (Forefather Czech), led a group of his Slavic followers to the top of **Říp** (461m), some 20km north of Kralupy, sometime around the sixth century AD, and proclaimed all the land around as Čechy. The name has certainly stuck – Čechy translates as "the Czech lands" or Bohemia – and the legend itself renders the hill a fairly important point of pilgrimage. Říp is an upside-down bowl of a hill that forms an intriguing lump in this otherwise monotonous landscape, and is quite a popular summertime hike. At the top, the twelfth-century Romanesque **rotunda** of sv Jiří a Vojtěch (April & Oct Wed–Sun 9am–4pm; May–Sept Tues–Sun 9am–5pm) commemorates the legend. The walk up is not difficult, and judging from the splendid views of flat fields spreading for miles around, it's not hard to recognize the peaceful agrarian roots of the Czech nation. Getting to Říp is easiest from Ctiněves train station (change at Vraňany), 2km east of the hill, although there are more (and faster) trains to Roudnice, 5km north along the red-marked path.

Mělník

Occupying a spectacular, commanding site at the confluence of the Vltava and Labe rivers, **MĚLNÍK**, 33km north of Prague on route 9, lies at the heart of Bohemia's tiny wine-growing region. The town's history goes back to the ninth century, when it was handed over to the Přemyslids as part of Ludmilla's dowry on her marriage to Prince Bořivoj (see p.592). And it was here, too, that she introduced her heathen grandson, Václav (later to become St Wenceslas, aka Good King; see p.88), to the joys of Christianity. Viticulture became the town's economic mainstay only after Charles IV, aching for a little of the French wine of his youth, introduced grapes from Burgundy (over which he also ruled).

The old town

Mělník's greatest monument is its Renaissance **zámek** (daily 10am–5pm; ⓦwww .lobkowicz-melnik.cz), perched high above the flat plains and visible for miles around. The present building, its courtyard covered in familiar sgraffito patterns, is now back in the hands of its last aristocratic owners, the Lobkowicz family, who have restored the chateau's magnificently proportioned rooms, which also provide great views out over the plain. Visits are by guided tour only, and allow you to see a handful of the castle rooms, which are filled with porcelain, old maps and Old Masters returned to the family since 1989. You can also visit the castle **wine cellars** (daily 10am–6pm), finishing up with samples of plonk (extra charge).

Below the chateau, vines cling to the south-facing terraces, as the land plunges into the river below. From beneath the great tower of Mělník's onion-domed church of **sv Petr and Pavel**, next door to the chateau, there's an even better view of the rivers' confluence (to the left) and the subsidiary canal (straight ahead), once so congested with vessels that traffic lights had to be introduced to avoid accidents. The church itself contains a compellingly macabre **ossuary** or *kostnice* (Tues–Sun 10am–12.30pm & 1.15–4pm), filled with more than 10,000 bones of medieval plague victims, fashioned into weird and wonderful skeletal shapes by students in the early part of the last century.

The rest of the old town is pleasant enough for a casual stroll. One half of the main square, **náměstí Míru**, is lined with Baroque arcades typical of the region, and there's an old medieval gateway nearby, the **Pražská brána**, which has been converted into an art gallery.

Practicalities

The main line from Prague veers northwest beyond Nelahozeves, so it's easiest to take a fast **train** from Prague's Hlavní nádraží to Všetaty, and change, which gets you to Mělník in around an hour. There's a regular **bus** service from Prague, too, which takes around fifty minutes. To reach the older part of town from the **bus station**, simply head up Krombholcova in the direction of the big church tower. If your next destination is Liběchov or Litoměřice, you have the choice of either the bus or the train; the **train station** is further still from the old town, a couple of blocks northeast of the bus station, down Jiřího z Poděbrad.

The **tourist office** (May–Sept 9am–5pm; Oct–April Mon–Fri 9am–5pm) is on náměstí Míru, and can help with **accommodation**, if you're hoping to stay over. There are private rooms available on Legionářů, to the north of the old town, and on Palackého náměstí, off the main square. In the shadow of the chateau to the south you'll find the relatively plush *Hotel Jaro*, 17 listopadu 174 (☎315 626 852; ⓕ315 626 851; ❹), and diagonally opposite, the spotless *Penzion V podzámčí*, J. Seiferta 167 (☎ & ⓕ315 622 889 ⓔhrzi@post.cz; ❸). The nearest **campsite** (closed Christmas & New Year) is around 750m north of the old town, on Klášterní (a continuation of Fügnerova).

For **food and drink**, the *Zámecká restaurace* (closed Mon) is as good (and cheap) a place as any to sample some of the local wine (and enjoy the view): the Ludmila rosé is the most sought after Mělník wine, though the vineyards produce red and white, too. Equally good views can be had from the *Stará škola* restaurant, behind the church; otherwise, you could try *Na hradbách*, on náměstí Míru, which serves up big portions of rabbit and game with local wines, in a cosy brick and wood-panelled interior and a little courtyard. For some serious wine-tasting, head for *U Holečku*, a wine bar and shop at Palackého 5, just south of the main square.

Kokořínsko

Northeast of Mělník, you leave the low plains of the Labe for a plateau region known as **Kokořínsko**, a hidden pocket of wooded hills which takes its name from the Gothic castle rising through the treetops at its centre. The sandstone plateau has weathered over the millennia to form sunken valleys and bizarre rocky outcrops, providing great scope for some gentle hiking. With picturesque valleys, such as the Kokořínský důl, dotted with well-preserved, half-timbered villages and riddled with marked paths, it comes as a surprise that the whole area isn't buzzing all summer.

At the centre of the region is the village of **KOKOŘÍN** (Ⓦ www.kokorin .cz), whose dramatic setting and spectacular fourteenth-century **hrad** (April & Oct Sat & Sun 9am–4pm; May–Sept Tues–Sun 9am–5pm) greatly inspired the Czech nineteenth-century Romantics. The castle is a perfect hideaway, ideal for the robbers who used it as a base after it fell into disrepair in the sixteenth century. Not until the end of the nineteenth century did it get a new lease of life, from a jumped-up local landowner, Václav Špaček, who bought himself a title and refurbished the place as a family memorial. There's precious little inside and no incentive to endure the guided tour, as you can explore the ramparts and climb the tallest tower on your own.

If you've got your own transport, Kokořínsko makes a pleasant day-trip from Prague. For those using public transport, take a bus or train to Mělník and change there. Alternatively, you could catch the local train from Mělník to Mšeno, from where it's a three-kilometre walk west to Kokořín on the green-marked path. Finding **accommodation** shouldn't be too much of a problem, with plenty of private rooms available in Kokořín, and Kanina 2km further east. There are also some lovely new pensions: try *Milča* (Ⓣ 603 461 723, Ⓔ milca@kokorin.cz; ❸), in the southern bit of Kokořínský důl, with rooms decked out with antique wooden furniture, or *Penzion v údolí* (Ⓣ 605 775 612, Ⓔ penzion.v.udoli@seznam.cz; ❸), a farmhouse near Vojtěchov, 5km north of the hrad, with three modern, wood-panelled attic rooms. There's also a **campsite** (May–Oct) near the hrad, about 1km east of the main river valley.

East of Prague

The scenery **east of Prague** is as flat as it is around Mělník, a rich blanket of fields spreading over the plain as far as the eye can see. Two places you might consider heading for are **Mladá Boleslav**, where Škoda cars are produced, and **Přerov nad Labem**, an open-air museum of the kind of folk architecture that was common in Bohemia less than a century ago. The towns of **Poděbrady** and **Kolín** are not likely to be high on most people's itineraries, but make convenient stopoff points when heading east.

Mladá Boleslav

Fast trains from Praha hlavní nádraží take over an hour to reach **MLADÁ BOLESLAV** (Jungblunzau), 50km or so northeast of Prague on the E65, where Václav Laurin and Václav Klement set up a bicycle factory in the mid-nineteenth century. They went on to produce the country's first car in 1905, and in the 1920s merged with the Škoda industrial empire. Škoda Auto, as the company is now known, is one of the largest employers in the republic, and is entirely separate from the heavy engineering arm of the Škoda empire, which is based in Plzeň (see p.235).

The main reason for coming here is to visit the **Škoda Auto Muzeum** (daily 9am–5pm; Ⓦ www.skoda-auto.cz), which exhibits over twenty-five old Škodas and Laurin & Klements in its showroom. The exhibition starts off, as the factory itself did, with an L & K bicycle and a couple of motorbikes. There are also several vintage vehicles and a 1917 fire engine, but the vast majority of the cars date from the 1920s and 1930s – big, mostly black, gangster-style motors. You can even admire the new fleet of Škoda cars produced since the company was acquired by Volkswagen (see box opposite) – Czechs are very proud of their new international-quality Octavias and Fabias. The museum is in the modern Škoda building at třída Václava Klementa 294, 1km northeast of the town centre near the edge of the massive car plant, and very badly signposted (bus #50, #51, #60 or #61 from the staré město). Diagonally opposite the museum, and handy for orientation, is a park with a palatial neo-Baroque *Gymnasium* at the far end. Close by, there's a wonderfully provincial Art Nouveau theatre from 1912, brightly painted in white, gold and blue.

The **staré město** lies to the east of the River Jizera, in a tight bend of one of its tributaries, the Klenice. It has only a little of interest: its sgraffitoed former **radnice** has a lookout tower (May–Aug Tues–Fri 1–5pm, Sat & Sun 10–11.30am & 12.30–5pm; Sept Sat & Sun only), and the Gothic **hrad**, tucked into the southernmost part of town, used as a barracks by the Habsburgs, and now home to the recently revamped local museum, **Muzeum Mladoboleslavska** (May–Oct Tues–Sun 9am–noon & 1–5pm; Nov–April closes 4pm; Ⓦ www.muzeum-mb.cz).

Practicalities

Trains from Prague arrive at Mladá Boleslav hlavní nádraží, at least 1km southwest of the stare město (bus #10 or #11); local trains heading for Dolní Bousov and Stará Paka stop at Mladá Boleslav město, just round the corner from the Škoda museum. **Accommodation** in town is on the pricey side, no doubt as it caters to the occasional foreign executive visiting Škoda. *Hotel Trumf* (Ⓣ 326 722 813, Ⓦ www.hoteltrumf.cz; ⑤), on Českobratské náměstí, just northeast of the main square, is the top pick, followed by *Hotel U hradu* (Ⓣ 326 721 049, Ⓔ hotel -mlada-boleslav-u-hradu@quick.cz; ④) by the zámek, with the smaller pension *Zlatý kohout* (Ⓣ 326 721 937, zlaty.kohout@volny.cz; ④) opposite the radnice. The nearest **campsite**, *Škoda* (May–Sept), is 2km north of town in the suburb of Kosmonosy. If you're just looking for somewhere to **eat**, it's best to head into the stare město. The *Jihočeská hostěnice* (closed Sun), beside the castle entrance, has a big fish restaurant adjacent to it, called the *Rybářská restaurace*, with an amazing menu that includes pike, eel and plaice. *Stardust*, opposite *Hotel U hradu*, offers a free kilo steak if you can eat the lot in under half an hour.

Přerov nad Labem and Ostrá

The **open-air museum** or **skansen** (April–Oct Tues–Sun 9am–5pm; Dec Fri–Sun 10am–4pm) of folk architecture at the village of **PŘEROV NAD LABEM** was the first of its kind in central Europe when it was founded in 1895 (it is called a *skansen*, after the first such museum founded in a Stockholm suburb in 1891). Later, in the 1950s and 1960s, *skansens* became quite a fad, as collectivization and urbanization wiped out traditional rural communities, along with their distinctive folk culture and wooden architecture. During the summer, Přerov's *skansen* is busy with tour groups from Prague, wandering through the various half-timbered and stone buildings, some brought here plank by plank from nearby villages, some from Přerov itself. Particularly evocative is the reconstructed eighteenth-century village school, with a portrait of the Austrian emperor taking pride of place amid the Catholic icons, and a delicate paper theatre that was used in drama lessons.

The story of Škoda

For Czechs, the **Škoda industrial empire** is a great Czech achievement and a source of national pride. It's therefore doubly ironic that the word *škoda* means "shame" or "pity" in Czech – a marketing own-goal were it not the name of the founding father of the Czech car industry, **Emil Škoda**. The last Škoda model produced under the Communists was very favourably received, even in the West (whence a large proportion of its components derived). In 1989, there was a three-year waiting list for the car, despite a retail price equivalent to over twice the average yearly salary. Then in 1991, in one of the many controversial deals in the country's privatization programme, the German company Volkswagen bought a majority stake in Škoda for a song. Volkswagen invested heavily in the company, and set its design teams aggressively to work, bringing forth new models such as the Felicia, Octavia and Fabia. VW ultimately acquired all the remaining shares of Škoda in 2000, so that the Czech "family silver" is now completely in the hands of a foreign entity, and while the Czechs may not feel quite the same way about the company, the new models brought out under VW guidance have vastly improved the international image of Škoda Auto. In addition, observers of the Czech economy may note that this VW-Škoda joint venture/privatization programme has turned out the most successful of all major Czech company privatization efforts.

On the other side of the River Labe, 13km away by road, is the village of **OSTRÁ**, where Dr Stuart's Botanicus (Ⓦwww.botanicus.cz), one of the Czech Republic's most successful cosmetics businesses, has established a **historická vesnice**, a kind of late-medieval settlement complete with timber-framed houses and extensive organic herb and vegetable gardens. You can get a **guided tour** of the complex at any time (April–Oct Tues–Sun 10am–5pm), but it's better to time your visit with one of the many special events that take place throughout the season. Costumed festivities range from Roman Saturnalia to a tea festival, accompanied by jesters, fencers and performers, with food and drink aplenty. If you want to stay over, there's a lakeside **campsite**, *U vody* (mid-April to mid-Sept), nearby.

To get to Přerov, take one of the infrequent daily **buses** from Prague (Černý Most metro) to Poděbrady, which drop you off right in front of the *skansen*; the nearest train station is Mochov, some 4km to the southwest. Getting to Ostrá is a bit easier as Stratov train station is just one kilometre northeast of the village along a blue-marked path through the woods; **trains** from Prague's Masarykovo nádraží to Kolín (via Praha–Vysočany) call at Stratov and take around forty minutes.

Poděbrady

If spa towns evoke nineteenth-century hotels for you, then **PODĚBRADY** will come as something of a disappointment. The spa waters were actually only discovered this century, with the town's previous existence simply due to its strategic position on the east–west trade routes. However, the **spa** itself is pleasant enough, attracting thousands of patients every year, most of whom can be seen promenading through the town's park around teatime, admiring the fully functioning floral clock. For a glimpse of the town's halcyon days in the last years of the Empire, check out the local **Polabské muzeum** at Palackého 68 (May–Oct Tues–Sun 9am–5pm; Dec Tues–Sun 10am–4pm; Ⓦwww.polabske-muzeum.cz).

Facing onto the main square, **Jiřího náměstí**, is the **zámek** (May–Oct Tues–Sun 9am–5pm), birthplace of the town's most famous son, **George of Poděbrady** (Jiří z Poděbrad to the Czechs), the only Hussite (and last Czech) king of Bohemia. The present structure was actually built a hundred years after his death and houses only the minutest of historical exhibitions. The only other trace of George is the green copper equestrian statue in the main square.

Poděbrady is a convenient stop on the road heading east from Prague, and less than an hour by train or bus from the capital. To get to the main square and castle from the **train and bus stations**, simply walk south through the park of náměstí T.G. Masaryka. Poděbrady also has a wide choice of **hotels**. The *Belle-vue-Tlapák* (☎325 623 111, ⓦwww.bellevue.cz; ❻), overlooking the floral clock on náměstí T.G. Masaryka, is a spa hotel with all manner of treatments available, from massage to floating therapy. You can even stay in the *Penzion na zámku* (☎325 626 331, ⓦwww.nazamku.info; ❷), in the zámek itself, where one wing has been tastefully converted into en-suite rooms. Another option is the nicely redone *Soudek*, east of the main square at Palackého 174 (☎ & ⒻF325 613 191; ❷); try to get a room in the back to avoid the noisy street below. Alternatively, there's a **campsite**, *Golf* (April–Oct), a little further upstream from the castle.

For a daytime **café**, head for the *Lázeňská italská kavárna*, one of the 1930s pavilions near the floral clock – inside it's a 1970s period piece with beige bolstered seats, crazy light fittings and a triple towered ceramic fountain. There's a fair selection of films and classical concerts on offer all year round at the town's cinema and theatre in the zámek, along with a decent *hostinec*. **Eating** options include *Galerie*, at Palackého 239 (closed Mon & Sun), which has a pleasant café upstairs, and a evening-only restaurant downstairs serving classic Czech dishes. For something different, try a floating dinner aboard the *Král Jiří*, moored by the chateau.

Kolín

In addition to its railway sidings and industrial plants, **KOLÍN** (ⓦwww.kolin .cz) – 15km southeast of Poděbrady along the Labe – has actually managed to preserve its central medieval core. One of numerous towns in Bohemia founded by German colonists in the thirteenth century, its streets are laid out in chessboard fashion. The central, cobbled **Karlovo náměstí**, is a picture-perfect main square, with a wonderfully imposing Renaissance **radnice**, covered in sgraffito and decorated with four rose-coloured panels from the nineteenth century, and four unusual Baroque gables on the west side.

Kolín's most ancient monument is tucked away in the southeast corner of the old town. On raised ground at the end of Karlova, on a rather cramped site, stands the Gothic church of **sv Bartoloměj** (St Bartholomew), begun in 1261. The church's fairly gloomy nave is suffused with an unusually intense blue light from the modern stained-glass windows, which disturbs the otherwise resolutely medieval ambience. But it's the choir, rebuilt and extended in the fourteenth century by Peter Parler, which provides the highlight, taking up almost half the church with its seven chapels, intricate tracery and spectacular ribbed vaulting. On the weekend, you can climb the church's adjacent belfry or **zvonice** (Sat 10am–4pm & Sun 1–4pm) for a view over the stare město.

Like many towns in Bohemia and Moravia, Kolín once had a significant **Jewish community**, which was all but wiped out in the Holocaust. The ghetto was situated in the southwest corner of the old town, in what is now Na Hradbach and Karoliny Světlé, and after descending into dereliction over the course of six decades, it is now largely cleaned up. There's a plaque commemorating the 2200 Jews deported during the Holocaust at Na Hradbach 157; inside is the **tourist office** (Mon 9am–noon & 1–5pm, Tues–Fri 9am–5pm, Sat 10am–3pm; ☎321 712 021), which gives guided tours of the marvellously renovated seventeenth-century **synagogue** (Tues–Fri 9.15am & 1.30pm, Sat & Sun 9am & 12.30pm), hidden in the rear courtyard. Though much was damaged or has disappeared in the intervening years, the bright, stuccoed interior still contains portions of Hebrew writings lovingly restored on the walls, amid flourishing floral designs. This mini-complex once contained a Jewish school and residence hall for the rabbis, though these have long since been turned into offices. The synagogue is no longer active, but because of the building's fine acoustics, concerts are held here on occasion; ask at the tourist office. A few streets away on Sluneční, outside the former city walls, is an overgrown Jewish cemetery – a faint image of the famous one in Prague.

Fans of the turn-of-the-twentieth-century sculpture of František Bílek should check out his **statue of Jan Hus**, which is hidden behind the Hussite church in the Komenského park. Though slightly weathered, it's an impressive, and typically expressive, piece of work, rising a good three metres off the ground. To get there, head east down Kutnohorská, turn right into Smetanova, then right again for the park.

If you need **to stay** overnight, there's the *Hotel Theresia*, Na Petříně (☎321 711 117; ❹), on a busy road west of the old town, or two excellent pensions in the old town itself, both with equally commendable restaurants: *Pension pod věží*, Parléřova 40 (☎321 723 877; ❸), or *U rabína*, near the synagogue on Karoliny Světlé (☎ & ⒻF321 724 463; ❸). In addition to the hotel **restaurants**, there's *Café Mozart*, a smart new place in the northeast corner of the square, with tables overlooking the square, or *Oliver*, another new place, serving big salads and pasta dishes, opposite. Kolín is closely associated with **František Kmoch** (1848–1912), king of Bohemian oompah music, and every year, during a weekend in June, a brass band festival, **Kmochův Kolín**, is held. A wide range of music from Kmoch to Dvořák and a huge parade of bands from all over the country perform on the town's main square and at other indoor venues around the town.

Kutná Hora and around

For 250 years or so, **KUTNÁ HORA** (Kuttenberg) was one of the most important towns in Bohemia, second only to Prague. At the end of the fourteenth century its population was equal to that of London, its shantytown suburbs straggled across what are now green fields, and its ambitious building projects set out to rival those of the capital itself. Today, Kutná Hora is a small provincial town with a population of just over 20,000, but the monuments dotted around it, the superb Gothic cathedral, and the remarkable monastery and ossuary in the suburb of **Sedlec**, make it one of the most enjoyable of all possible day-trips from Prague. In addition to the new influx of tourists, Kutná Hora has also benefited from a large injection of cash from the American tobacco giants Phillip Morris, who now run the local tobacco factory as a joint venture.

Some history

Kutná Hora's road to prosperity began in the late thirteenth century with the discovery of copper and **silver deposits** in the surrounding area. German miners were invited to settle and work the seams, and around 1300 Václav II founded the royal mint here, importing Italian craftsmen to run it. Much of the town's wealth was used to fund the beautification of Prague, but it also allowed for the construction of one of the most magnificent churches in central Europe and a number of other prestigious Gothic monuments in Kutná Hora itself.

At the time of the Hussite Wars, the town was mostly German-speaking and staunchly Catholic; local miners used to throw captured Hussites into the deep mineshafts and leave them to die of starvation. Word got out, and the town was besieged and eventually taken by Žižka's fanatical Táborites in 1421, only to be recaptured by Emperor Sigismund and his papal forces shortly afterwards, and again by Žižka the following year.

While the silver stocks remained high, the town was able to recover some of its former prosperity, but cheap Spanish imports of silver from South America caused a collapse in the price of silver during the sixteenth century. By the end of the century the mines had dried up, and Kutná Hora's wealth and importance came to an abrupt end – when the Swedes marched on the town during the Thirty Years' War, they had to be bought off with beer rather than silver. The town never fully recovered, shrivelling to less than a third of its former size, its fate emphatically sealed by a devastating fire in 1770.

The Town

The small, unassuming houses that line the town's medieval lanes and main square, **Palackého náměstí**, give little idea of its former glories. A narrow alleyway on

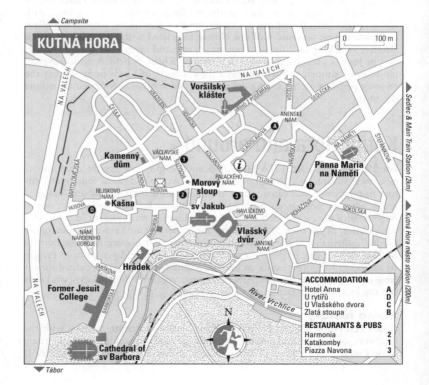

the south side of the square, however, leads to the leafy Havlíčkovo náměstí, on which lies the **Vlašský dvůr** (Italian Court), originally conceived as a palace by Václav II, and for three centuries the town's bottomless purse. It was here that Florentine minters produced the Prague Groschen (*pražské groše*), a silver coin widely used throughout central Europe until the nineteenth century. The building itself has been mucked about with over the years, most recently – and most brutally – by nineteenth-century restorers, who left only the fourteenth-century oriel window (capped by an unlikely looking wooden onion dome) and the miner's fountain unmolested. The original workshops of the minters' have been bricked in, but the outlines of their little doors and windows are still visible in the courtyard. On the thirty-minute **guided tour** (daily: March & Oct 10am–5pm; April–Sept 9am–6pm; July & Aug 10am–4pm; ⓦwww.guide.kutnohorsko.cz) – available in English – you get to see some silver Groschen, learn about the minters hard life and admire the medieval royal chapel, which shelters a superb full-relief fifteenth-century altarpiece depicting the *Death of Mary*, and which was spectacularly redecorated in 1904 with Art Nouveau murals.

Outside the court is a statue of the country's founder and first president, **T.G. Masaryk**; twice removed – once by the Nazis and once by the Communists – it has now been returned to its pride of place for the third time. Before you leave, take a quick look in the court gardens, which descend in steps to the Vrchlice valley. This is undoubtedly Kutná Hora's best profile, with a splendid view over to the Cathedral of sv Barbora (see below).

Behind the Vlašský dvůr is **sv Jakub** (St James), the town's oldest church, begun a generation or so after the discovery of the silver deposits. Its grand scale is a clear indication of the town's quite considerable wealth by the time of the fourteenth century, though in terms of artistry it pales in comparison with Kutná Hora's other ecclesiastical buildings. The leaning tower is a reminder of the precarious position of the town, the church's foundations prone to subsidence from the disused mines below.

If you want to see some of these, head for the **Hrádek** (Tues–Sun: April & Oct 9am–5pm; May, June, Sept 9am–6pm; July & Aug 10am–6pm), an old fort which was used as a second mint and now houses a **Silver Museum**. You can don period miner's garb of white coat, helmet and torch, and follow a guide through narrow sections of the medieval mines that were discovered beneath the fort in the 1960s – some of which tunnel over 100 metres below the surface. Be warned, that the mine tour is very popular, so advance booking is advisable (☎327 512 159).

Cathedral of sv Barbora

Kutná Hora's **Cathedral of sv Barbora** (Tues–Sun: April & Oct 9–11.30am & 1–3.30pm; May–Sept 9am–5.30pm; Nov–March 9–11.30am & 2–3.30pm) is arguably the most spectacular and moving ecclesiastical building in central Europe. Not to be outdone by the great monastery at Sedlec (see p.173) or the St Vitus Cathedral in Prague, the miners of Kutná Hora began financing the construction of a great Gothic cathedral of their own, dedicated to St Barbara, the patron saint of miners and gunners. The foundations were probably laid by Parler in the 1380s, but work was interrupted by the Hussite wars, and the church remained unfinished until the late nineteenth century, despite being worked on in the intervening centuries by numerous architects, including Master Hanuš, Matouš Rejsek and Benedikt Ried.

The approach road to the cathedral, Barborská, is lined with a parade of gesticulating Baroque saints and cherubs that rival the sculptures on the Charles Bridge; and on the right-hand side is the palatial seventeenth-century former

Jesuit College. The cathedral bristles with pinnacles, finials and flying buttresses which support its most striking feature, a **roof** of three tent-like towers added in the sixteenth century, culminating in unequal, needle-sharp spires.

Inside, cold light streams through the numerous plain glass windows, illuminating the lofty **nave** and Ried's playful ribbed vaulting, which forms branches and petals stamped with coats of arms belonging to Václav II and the local miners' guilds. The wide spread of the five-aisled nave is remarkably uncluttered: the multi-tiered tester of the Gothic pulpit – half-wood, half-stone – creeps tastefully up a central pillar, matching black and gold Renaissance confessionals lie discreetly in the north aisle, while nearby the filigree work on the original Gothic choirstalls echoes the cathedral's exterior. Look up, and you'll see virtually an entire chamber orchestra of gilded putti disporting themselves over the Baroque organ case.

The **ambulatory** boasts an array of early twentieth-century stained glass, but it's the medieval frescoes preserved in the southernmost chapels that really stand out. In the Smíšek chapel, there's a wonderful orchestra of angels in the vaulting and a depiction of the Queen of Sheba on one of the walls. Two chapels further along is the Minters' chapel, its walls decorated with fifteenth-century frescoes showing the Florentines at work.

The rest of the town

There are a few minor sights worth seeking out in the rest of the town. On Rejskovo náměstí, the squat, polygonal **Kašna** (fountain), built by Rejsek in 1495, strikes a very odd pose: peppered with finials and replete with blind arcading, it's actually the decorative casing for a reservoir. With so much mining going on, the town had problems with its water supply and had to pipe in water. At the bottom of the sloping Šultyskovo náměstí is a particularly fine **Morový sloup** (Plague Column), giving thanks for the end of the plague of 1713; while just around the corner from the top of the square is one of the few Gothic buildings to survive the 1770 fire, the **Kamenný dům**, built around 1480, with an oriel window and a steep gable, covered in an ornate sculptural icing. This now contains an unexceptional local museum (Tues–Sun: April & Oct 9am–5pm; May, June & Sept 9am–6pm; July & Aug 10am–6pm; Nov 10am–4pm). A couple of blocks down Poděbradova stands Kilian Ignaz Dientzenhofer's unfinished Ursuline convent or **Voršilský klášter** (April & Oct Sat & Sun 9am–4pm; May–Sept Tues–Sun 9am–5.30pm). Only three sides of the convent's ambitious pentagonal plan were actually finished, its neo-Baroque church being added in the late nineteenth century while sv Barbora was being restored.

Practicalities

The simplest way to get to Kutná Hora is to take a **bus** from Prague's Florenc bus station (1hr 15min). Fast **trains** from Prague's hlavní nádraží take around an hour (some involve a change at Kolín – not to be confused with Kolín zastávka). The main **train station** (Kutná Hora hlavní nádraží) is a long way out of town, near Sedlec; bus #1 or #4 will take you into town, or there's usually a shuttle train service ready to leave for Kutná Hora město train station, near the centre of town.

The town has a highly efficient system of orientation signs and, at almost every street corner, a pictorial list of the chief places of interest (beware, though, that the train station signposted is not the main one). The town's **tourist office** is on Palackého náměstí (April–Oct Mon–Fri 9am–6.30pm, Sat & Sun 9am–5pm;

Nov–March Mon–Fri 9am–5pm; ☎327 512 378, Ⓦwww.kutnahora.info); it has a pretty dull exhibition on alchemy in its Gothic cellars and can help with **accommodation**. *U rytířů*, on Rejskovo náměstí (☎ & Ⓕ327 512 256; ❷) is a simple inexpensive pension, while *Hotel Anna*, Vladislavova (☎ & Ⓕ327 516 315; ❹) is a bit more upmarket. Continuing on up the price scale, *U vlašského dvora*, on Havlíčkovo náměstí (☎327 514 618, Ⓦwww.ekh-hotels@iol.cz; ❸), is quite comfortable and has a decent restaurant and a sauna, while *Zlatá stoupa*, on Tylova (☎327 511 540, Ⓦwww.web.telecom.cz/zlatastoupa; ❹), is the top of the ladder here, with mahogany furnishings and its own vinárna. The nearest **campsite** is the unlikely sounding *Santa Barbara*, northwest of the town centre on Česká (April–Oct).

On the **eating and drinking** front, you're spoilt for choice: try *Harmonia* on Husova, which serves up traditional fare and has an outdoor terrace, *Katakomby,* on Václavské náměstí, a deep Gothic cellar, with slightly more upmarket Czech cuisine, or *Piazza Navona*, an excellent pizzeria on Palackého náměstí, run by an Italian.

Sedlec

Buses #1 and #4 run from the inner ringroad, 3km northeast to **SEDLEC**, once a separate village but now a suburb of Kutná Hora. Adjoining Sedlec's defunct eighteenth-century Cistercian monastery (now the largest tobacco factory in Europe, owned by Phillip Morris) is the fourteenth-century church of **Nanebevzetí Panny Marie** (Tues–Sat 9am–noon & 1–5pm) imaginatively redesigned in the eighteenth century by Giovanni Santini, who specialized in melding Gothic with Baroque. Here, given a plain French Gothic church gutted by the Hussites, Santini set to work on the vaulting, adding his characteristic sweeping stucco rib patterns, relieved only by the occasional Baroque splash of colour above the chancel steps.

Cross the main road, following the signs, and you'll come to the monks' graveyard, where an ancient Gothic chapel – again redesigned by Santini, leans heavily over the entrance to the macabre subterranean **kostnice** (daily: April–Sept 8am–6pm; Oct 9am–noon & 1–5pm; Nov–March 9am–noon & 1–4pm; Ⓦwww.kostnice.cz), the mother of all ossuaries, full to overflowing with human bones. When holy earth from Golgotha was scattered over the graveyard in the twelfth century, all of Bohemia's nobility wanted to be buried here, and the bones mounted up until there were over 40,000 complete sets. In 1870, worried about the ever-growing piles, the authorities commissioned František Rint to do something creative with them. He rose to the challenge and moulded out of bones four giant bells, one in each corner of the crypt, designed wall-to-ceiling skeletal decorations, including the Schwarzenberg coat of arms, and, as the centrepiece, put together a chandelier made out of every bone in the human body. Rint's signature (in bones) is at the bottom of the steps.

Kačina and Žleby

Nothing quite so ghoulish confronts you at the early-nineteenth-century zámek of **Kačina**, 4km northeast of Kutná Hora hlavní nádraží along route 2 to Přelouč (or a much shorter walk if you catch one of the buses heading out to the satellite village of Nové Dvory or Vrdy). It's a colossal Neoclassical summer residence, the semicircular wings of the building stretching for over 200m across the lawn. For the owners, the up-and-coming Chotek family (who also owned Veltrusy), the chateau grounds came first, with planting begun a full fifteen years before a stone was laid. The Choteks forfeited their properties after collaborating with the

Nazis, and the chateau now houses the **Muzeum českého venkova** (April–Oct daily 8am–5pm; Ⓦ www.kacina.cz), the national agricultural museum. To visit the museum (*okruh 1*), you don't need to join a guided tour; not so the period interior tour (*okruh 2*) nor the, pick of the lot, the tour of the chateau's beautiful domed and coffered library, art collection and orangerie (*okruh 3*); however, it's really the wide informal expanse of the English Park that draws carloads of Czechs here throughout the summer.

For those who prefer more exotic castles, there's a flamboyant aristocratic haunt at **Žleby** (Schleb), 20km southeast of Kutná Hora, beyond Čáslav. Here, in the mid-nineteenth century, Vinzenz Karl Auersperg created a pseudo-Gothic **zámek** (April, Oct & Nov Sat & Sun 9am–noon & 1–4pm; May–Sept Tues–Sun 9am–noon & 1–5pm; June–Aug 8am–noon & 1–5pm) out of the original medieval hrad. For once, the family failed to take the necessary precautions at the end of the war, and were forced to leave behind virtually all the castle's contents. The result is a full-blown neo-Gothic interior filled with lots of weaponry and heavy Baroque and quasi-medieval furnishings. There are two **guided tours** to choose from: *trasa 1* (35min) includes pretty much everything except the Velká věž, the castle's lookout tower, which you only get to see on *trasa 2* (1hr). Buses from Kutná Hora are direct but infrequent; by train, you must change in Čáslav and walk 500m east to get to the zámek.

Průhonice and the Sázava valley

A short train ride **southeast** of Prague is enough to transport you from the urban sprawl of the capital into one of the prettiest regions of central Bohemia, starting with the park at **Průhonice**. Until the motorway to Brno and Bratislava ripped through the area in the 1970s, the roads and railways linking the three big cities followed the longer, flatter option, further north along the Labe valley. As a result, commerce and tourism passed the **Sázava valley** (Ⓦ www.posazavi .com) by, and, with the notable exception of **Konopiště**, it remains relatively undeveloped, unspoilt and out of the way.

Průhonice

Barely outside Prague's city limits, and just off the country's chief motorway, **PRŮHONICE** (Ⓦ www.pruhonice-obec.cz) is a popular weekend destination in the summer. A whole series of new buildings, including a large conference centre, have been erected over the last decade, and have somewhat spoilt the character of the original village – now stuffed with villas full of expatriates and well-to-do Czechs and known locally as Beverly Hills. Nevertheless, it's still worth a visit, not for the newly restored neo-Renaissance **zámek**, which as a botanical and horticultural research centre (Ⓦ www.ibot.cas.cz) is out of bounds, but for the 625-acre **park** (daily: April–Oct 7am–7pm; Nov–March 8am–5pm), founded by Count Emanuel Sylva Taroucca, which boasts an unusually fine array of flora and several picturesque lakes.

Another good reason for coming to Průhonice is to have a **beer** at the family-run *U Bezoušků* at Květnové náměstí 5 (☎ 267 750 551, Ⓦ www.ubezousku .cz; ❷), one of the republic's finest micro-breweries, which serves up its very own unfiltered beers, and where you can even stay the night. Alternatively, tuck into a slap-up **fish** lunch in front of the fire or on the terrace of *Hliněná bašta* at Újezdská 619, or wade through plates of **pancakes** just off the main square at *U slepiček*, Říčanská 89. To get to Průhonice from Prague, you can either catch the **bus**, which leaves three times an hour from metro Opatov, or else you can walk the 4km along the red-marked route, via the Hostivař lake (a good place for a dip in summer), starting from the penultimate tram stop on the #22 or #26 routes.

Sázava

Rising majestically above the slow-moving Sázava river, is the **Sázavský klášter** and **zámek** (April & Oct Sat & Sun 9am–4pm; May–Aug Tues–Sun 9am–6pm; Sept Tues–Sun 9am–5pm). The monastery was founded by the eleventh-century Prince Oldřich, on the instigation of a passing hermit called **Prokop** (St Procopius), whom he met by chance in the Sázava forest. Prokop became the first abbot of what was initially a Slavonic Basilian monastery, and, for a while, Sázava became an important centre for the dissemination of Slavonic texts. Later, a large Gothic church was planned, and this now bares its red sandstone nave to the world, incomplete but intact. The chancel was converted into a Baroque church, later bought by the Tiegel family, who started to build themselves a modest chateau. Of this architectural miscellany, only the surviving Gothic frescoes – in the popular Beautiful Style, but of a sophistication unmatched in Bohemian art at the time – are truly memorable. The village itself thrived on the glass trade, and the rest of the monastery's hour-long guided tour concentrates on the local glassware.

Without your own transport, it'll take a good hour and a half by bus or train to cover the 55km from Prague to Sázava. Of the two, the **train** ride (change at Čerčany) is the more visually absorbing, at least by the time you join the branch line that meanders down the Sázava valley; the train station is a fifteen-minute walk across the river from the monastery. Try the *Hostinec za vodou*, on your right as you walk from the monastery to the village, for huge portions and a summer terrace.

Český Šternberk

Several bends later in the Sázava river, the village of **ČESKÝ ŠTERNBERK** is overlooked by the great castellated mass of its **hrad** (April & Oct Sat & Sun 9am–5pm; May & Sept Tues–Sun 9am–5pm; June–Aug Tues–Sun 9am–6pm; Ⓦ www.hradceskysternberk.cz), strung out along a knife's edge above the river. It's a breathtaking sight, rising out of thick woods, though not much remains of the original Gothic castle, headquarters of the powerful Šternberk family (who still own it now and have renovated it beautifully). The highlight of the 45-minute guided tour is the Italian stuccowork that survives from the seventeenth century. Even if you don't take the tour, it's worth popping your head into the main courtyard, where there's usually a display of birds of prey, one of Count Šternberk's chief interests, and fifteen minutes' walk through the woods behind the castle, there's a lookout tower (*rozhledna*) with great views over the hrad and valley. If you're coming by train, you'll need to change trains at Čerčany and get out at Český Šternberk zastávka, one stop past Český Šternberk's main station. If you need to stay, ask for a room at the vast *Parkhotel* (Ⓣ 317 855 168; ❸), with a view overlooking the castle and, if you're hungry, the fur-strewn castle restaurant provides cheap, hot Czech nosh.

Konopiště

The popularity of **Konopiště** (April & Oct Tues–Fri 9am–3pm, Sat & Sun 9am–4pm; May–Aug Tues–Sun 9am–5pm; Sept Tues–Fri 9am–4pm, Sat & Sun 9am–5pm; Nov Sat & Sun 9am–3pm; Ⓣ 317 721 366, Ⓦ www.zamek-konopiste

.cz), with a quarter of a million visitors passing through its portcullis every year, is surpassed only by the likes of Karlštejn (see p.178). Of the two, Konopiště is the more interesting, though Karlštejn looks more dramatic from the outside. Coach parties from all over the world home in on this Gothic castle, which is stuffed with dead animals, weaponry and hunting trophies. Most interesting are its historical associations: King Václav IV was imprisoned for a while by his own nobles in the castle's distinctive round tower, and the **Archduke Franz Ferdinand**, heir to the Habsburg throne, lived here with his wife, Sophie Chotek until their assassination in Sarajevo in 1914. The couple hid themselves away here as they were shunned by the Habsburg court in Vienna, due to the fact that Sophie was a mere countess, and not an archduchess. In addition to remodelling the chateau into its current appearance, the archduke shared his generation's voracious appetite for hunting, eliminating all living creatures foolish enough to venture into the grounds. However, he surpassed all his contemporaries by recording, stuffing and displaying a significant number of the 171,537 birds and animals he shot between the years 1880 and 1906, the details of which are recorded in his *Schuss Liste* displayed inside.

There's a choice of **guided tours**. The *I okruh* explores several salons, which contain some splendid Renaissance cabinets and lots of Meissen porcelain, while the *II okruh* takes you through the chapel, past the stuffed bears and deer teeth, to the assorted lethal weapons of one of the finest armouries in Europe. Both the above tours take roughly 45 minutes, and, you'll be relieved to know, include the hunting trophies. The *III okruh* takes an hour, is restricted to just eight people per tour, and concentrates on the personal apartments of the archduke and his wife. Occasionally there are tours in English, French and German, too, so ask at the box office before you sign up, or give them a call and book one in advance.

Even if you don't fancy a guided tour, there are plenty of other things to do in Konopiště. In the main courtyard of the chateau, you can pop into the purpose-built **Střelnice** (Shooting Range), where the archduke used to hone his skills as a marksman against moving mechanical targets, all of which have been lovingly restored. Tucked underneath the south terrace is the **Galerie sv Jiří**, which is stuffed to the gunwales with artefacts from Franz Ferdinand's collection – from paintings to statuettes and trinkets relating to St George, the fictional father of medieval chivalry, with whom the archduke was obsessed. Much the best reason to come to Konopiště, though, is to explore its 555-acre **park**, which boasts a marked red path around the largest lake, sundry statuary, an unrivalled rose garden (with café by the greenhouses) and a deer park. There are also regular one-hour displays of **falconry** in the chateau's grounds (April & Oct Sat & Sun 10am–noon & 2–4pm, May–Sept Tues–Sun same times) in English and Czech.

Practicalities

To get to Konopiště take a fast (50min) or slow (1hr 5min) **train** from Praha hlavní nádraží to **Benešov** u Prahy, 45km southeast of Prague, on the main line to České Budějovice; the castle is a pleasant two-kilometre walk west of the railway station along the red- or yellow-marked path (buses are relatively infrequent). If the weather's fine, though, you might as well come equipped with a picnic; otherwise, there are numerous **food** stalls by the main car park, and decent Czech fare available in the nineteenth-century *Stará Myslivna*, on the path to the castle, and in the bistro in the main courtyard. Back in Benešov, it's perfectly possible to while away some time before your train departs at the *Galerijní čajovna* on Malé náměstí.

Since train connections are good from Prague, you don't need **to stay** the night, but if you do, the *Nová Myslivna* (☎317 722 496; ❸) is a modern hotel right by the main car park (with cart rides offered up to the castle). If that's full, there's a **campsite** (May–Sept) a kilometre to the southeast of the castle, near the ugly *Motel Konopiště* (☎317 722 732; ❺), which has a good restaurant. If you've a car, you might want to consider staying at the *Hotel Pecínov* (☎317 763 111, ⓦwww.hotelpecinov.cz; ❾), a converted **fortress**, with French restaurant, pool, riding school and wine cellar, 5km southeast of Benešov, off route 112. Another 3km down the road, fifteen minutes' walk from Postupice train station, you can stay in *Zámek Jemniště* (☎603 819 651, ⓦwww.jemniste.cz; ❼), a simple Baroque **chateau** with beautifully appointed apartments and extensive grounds; you'll need to book ahead, though, as the place is a very popular wedding venue. At the other end of the scale, you can stay nearby at *Kršňův dvůr* (☎603 215 380, ⓦwww.krsnuvdvur.cz), the organic farm run by the Czech **Hare Krishna** movement; you don't have to be a devotee to stay there, though you must help out with the farm from 4am to 9pm. The nearest train station, Městečko u Benešova, is just 100m away.

Příbram

PŘÍBRAM (ⓦwww.pribram.cz), like Kutná Hora (see p.169), was once a royal silver-mining town, though it contains nothing like the same treasures. Among older Czechs, however, the town is better known for its notorious uranium mines, where thousands of political prisoners worked and died in appalling conditions in the 1950s. In 1991, the uranium ran out and all mining operations ceased, and there's now an extensive and smartly laid-out **Hornické muzeum** (Mining museum; hourly guided tours April–Oct Tues–Sun 9am–5pm; Nov–March Tues–Fri 9am–4pm; ⓦwww.muzeum-pribram.cz), in the southwestern suburb of Březové Hory (Birkenberg) accessible via bus #1 or #14 from the train station. The museum is divided between five separate buildings, and you'll need to buzz the doorbell in building 1 for tickets.

Architecturally, the most impressive section is the splendidly ornate pithead of the **Ševčínský šachta** (Ševčín Shaft), which was built in 1879. The other buildings contain displays on mineralogy, palaeontology, the history of mining and on the forced labour of the Communist period. There's also a traditional miner's cottage from the turn of the nineteenth century, an exhibition on toy and puppet making and at least 180m of mining railway stuffed full of old equipment. If you walk ten minutes back along the main road to the second section of the museum, you can also take a short train trip down one of the old mineshafts, the **Prokop Adit**, in the company of a retired miner, after which you're encouraged to pay a visit to the nearby miners' pub *Na vršícku* (closed off season).

The real reason most people trek out to Příbram, however, is to see the beautiful Marian shrine of **Svatá hora** (Mon–Sat 5.45am–6pm, Sun 5.45am–4.45pm; ⓦwww.svata-hora.cz), whose pepperpot domes rise up above the town on a wooded hill to the east of the main square. According to legend, the first shrine was built here in the thirteenth century, but was transformed out of all recognition by the Jesuits, who in 1658 employed Carlo Lurago to produce the striking set-piece of Italianate Baroque you see now. The best way to reach the shrine is via the Svatohorské schody or covered stairway off Dlouhá, built by Kilian Ignaz Dientzenhofer in 1728. From the stairs, you enter the arcaded ambulatory which surrounds the main church, whose restored frescoes, dating from the late nineteenth century, recount the history of Svatá hora. Thick stucco work surrounds the hell, fire and damnation ceiling paintings, with cherubs fighting and hugging, skulls surrounded by swags made from bones, and egg timers on more skulls. At the centre of the complex is the pilgrim church or basilica, its balustrade dotted with saintly statuary; inside, pride of place goes to a kitsch Gothic statue of the Madonna and Child, whose clothes are regularly changed.

The photographer, **František Drtikol** (1883–1961) was born in Příbram and there's now a permanent display of his works in the **Zámeček** (Tues–Sun 9am–5pm), just north of the main square, behind the town council building. Thanks to Prague's UPM, the exhibition has some great prints from Drtikol's career, ranging from his early Art Nouveau works to his later Art Deco nudes and avant-garde pieces. Drtikol was deeply drawn to eastern philosophy and in 1935 he sold his studio and abandoned photography to devote himself to theosophy.

Since 1997, Příbram has also been the home town of the old army football team, **Dukla Praha** – immortalized in the pop song *All I Want for Christmas is a Dukla Prague Away-Kit* by British punk band Half Man Half Biscuit (Ⓦwww .phespirit.info/music/dukla_prague.htm) – after they were forced to leave the capital due to financial difficulties, and merge with the town's local team to become Marila Příbram (Ⓦwww.fkmarila.cz). The team has since bounced back into the first division, and now play in Příbram's Na Litavce stadium, which is situated a couple of kilometres south of the town centre.

Practicalities

Příbram itself is around 50km southwest of Prague along motorway route 4. The easiest way to get there on **public transport** is by bus (a 60min trip) from Prague's Na Knížecí bus station, next to metro Anděl; the train from Prague's Smíchovské nádraží takes longer and often involves a change at Zdice, on the main line to Plzeň. Příbram is not a great place to stay the night, though the *Modrý hrozen* (Ⓣ318 628 007, Ⓦwww.modryhrozen.cz; ⑨), on the main square, is a pleasant and comfortable enough **hotel**, and boasts a restaurant with an original seventeenth-century ceiling. For cheaper food and drink, undoubtedly the best **pub** around is the *Březohorka*, on náměstí J.A. Alise 235, just above the main part of the mining museum; back in the town centre, there's *U havlínů* pub, on Václavské náměstí.

Along the Berounka river

The green belt area to the **west of Prague** is easily the most varied of the regions around the city, and consequently one of the most popular escapes for citizens of the Czech capital. The **River Berounka** carves itself an enticingly craggy valley up to Charles IV's magnificent country castle at **Karlštejn**, the busiest destination of all, and further upstream is the more isolated stronghold of **Křivoklát**.

Karlštejn and around

KARLŠTEJN (Karlstein) is a small ribbon of a village, strung out along one of the tributaries of the Berounka – no doubt once pretty, it now boasts a pricey golf course and is jam-packed with tacky souvenir stands and tourists visiting its **hrad** (Tues–Sun: March, Nov, Christmas & New Year 9am–noon & 1–3pm; April & Oct 9am–noon & 1–4pm; May, June & Sept 9am–noon & 1–5pm; July & August 9am–noon & 1–6pm; ☎274 008 154, ⓦwww.hradkarlstejn.cz), which occupies a spectacular, defiantly unassailable position above the village. Designed in the fourteenth century by Matthias of Arras for Emperor Charles IV as a giant safe-box for the imperial crown jewels and his large personal collection of precious relics, it quickly became Charles' favourite retreat from the vast city he himself had masterminded. Women were strictly forbidden to enter the castle, and the story of his third wife Anna's successful break-in (in drag) became one of the most popular Czech comedies of the nineteenth century.

Ruthlessly returned to a replica of its original Gothic style in the late nineteenth century by Josef Mocker, the castle now looks much better from a distance, with its giant wedge towers rising above a series of castellated walls. Most of the rooms visited on the fifty-minute guided tour (*trasa I*; 120Kč) contain only the barest of furnishings, the empty spaces taken up by uninspiring displays on the history of the castle. Theoretically, the top two chambers would make the whole trip worthwhile: unfortunately, on *trasa I* you can only look into (but not enter) the emperor's residential **Mariánská věž**, where Charles shut himself off from the rest of the world, with any urgent business passed to him through a hole in the wall of the tiny ornate chapel of **sv Kateřina**.

The castle's finest treasure, the **Holy Rood Chapel** (Kaple svatého kříže), connected by a wooden bridge that leads onto the highest point of the castle, the **Velká věž**, is only open to those who book the seventy-minute tour *trasa II* in advance (300Kč). Traditionally, only the emperor, the archbishop and the electoral princes could enter this gilded treasure-house, whose six-metre-thick walls contain 2200 semi-precious stones and 128 breathtakingly beautiful painted panels, the work of Master Theodoric, Bohemia's greatest fourteenth-century painter (a small selection of his panels is exhibited in Prague's Anežský klášter; see p.113). The imperial crown jewels, once secured here behind nineteen separate locks, were removed to Hungary after an abortive attack by the Hussites, while the Bohemian jewels are now stashed away in the cathedral in Prague.

Elsewhere in the village – transformed over the last decade, with every other house offering rooms to rent or selling souvenirs – most of what you see, including the decidedly iffy **Wax Museum** at no. 173 (daily 9am–6pm; ⓦwww.waxmuseumprague.cz), is eminently missable, with the exception of the **Muzeum Betlémů** (Tues–Sun 10am–5pm), which occupies a fourteenth-century house towards the top of the village at no. 11. You can admire an impressive array of nativity scenes dating back to the early nineteenth century. They range in size from complex mechanical setups to miniature affairs that can fit into small sea shells – there are even some made out of gingerbread.

Practicalities

Trains for Karlštejn leave Prague's Smíchovské nádraží roughly every hour, and take about 35 minutes to cover the 28km. The village is ten minutes' walk across the river from the station, and it's a further fifteen- to twenty-minute climb up to the castle entrance. If you're looking for somewhere to grab a beer and a fairly bog-standard bite to **eat**, try hunting-lodge-style *U Janů*, which has an outdoor terrace, or the slightly posher *Koruna*, both on the main street. Alternatively, bring a picnic with you and eat by the banks of the river.

There are loads of **accommodation** options in Karlštejn, but since prices are something like fifty percent higher than most places in the country, only a masochist would choose to stay here. If you are stuck here for some reason, your best bet is the *Hotel Mlyn* (☎311 744 411, ⓦwww.hotelmlynkarlstejn.cz; ⑤), a well-run converted fishing lodge, on the same side of the river as the train station, ten minutes' walk downstream. Karlštejn's **campsite** (open all year) is on the opposite bank, upstream from the village, and allows fires, but there's a nicer site at **Řevnice** (April–Sept), two stops on the train before Karlštejn (and, incidentally, the village in which Martina Navrátilová spent her tennis-playing childhood), with a small pool, restaurant, draught beer, and good train links with Prague.

Around Karlštejn and the Český kras

There are some great possibilities for **hiking** in the countryside around Karlštejn. Several marked paths cover the stiff climb through the forests of the Hřebeny ridge. If you're armed with a *Praha okolí* map, these are easy enough to follow; you can pick up a bus back to Prague from Mníšek on the other side of the hills.

If you're feeling energetic, you could go for a swim at the popular flooded quarry, **Malá Amerika**, a couple of kilometres from the castle. Getting there is tricky: either take the red-marked path from near the castle at Karlštejn, and head off northwest through the woods at *Čajovna U dubu* (you may need to ask a local to point you in the right direction), or head west down the track, which comes off the road between Mořina and Bubovice.

From **SRBSKO** (one stop on from Karlštejn), a red-marked path winds its way through the woods to **sv Jan pod Skalou** (St John Under the Rock), a strikingly situated monastery, as the name suggests, underneath a steep bluff in a landscape full of dramatic craggy flourishes. Designed by Christoph Dientzenhofer, the monastery was used as a training camp for the Communist secret police, but is now an ecological research centre. This is also the place where the country's remaining aristocrats were imprisoned following the 1948 coup. Again, you can catch a bus back to Prague easily enough from Vráž, a kilometre or so to the north.

Another option from Srbsko is to take the yellow-marked path west into the **Český kras** (Bohemian Karst). The geology of this region has fascinated scientists since the early nineteenth century, but the one set of caves open to the public, the **Koněpruské jeskyně** (daily: April–June & Sept 8am–4pm; July & Aug 8am–5pm; Oct 8.30am–3pm, ⓦwww.caves.cz), 3km west of Srbsko, lay undiscovered until 1950. Nowadays it's not so easy to miss, thanks to the Hollywood-style giant white lettering on the hillside above. Much more fascinating than the dripstone decorations, however, was the simultaneous discovery of an illegal mint in the upper level of the caves. A full set of weights, miners' lamps and even the remains of food were found here, dating back to the second half of the fifteenth century. To reach the caves other than by foot, you'll need to catch one of the infrequent **buses** from the nearby soap-producing town of **Beroun** (50min by train from Praha hlavní nádraží). Finally, just for the record, Czech film buffs may like to know that the station at **Loděnice**, two stops up the line from Beroun, was used as the location for Jiří Menzel's classic, Oscar-winning, 1966 film, *Closely Observed Trains*, based on the novel by Bohumil Hrabal.

Křivoklátsko

Further up the Berounka is the beautiful, mixed woodland of a UNESCO nature reserve, **Křivoklátsko** (ⓦwww.krivoklatsko.cz). Just out of reach of day-trippers, it's an altogether sleepier place than the area around Karlštejn.

The agonized twists (*křivky*) of the Berounka river cast up the highest crags of the region, which cluster round the lofty castle of **Křivoklát** (Pürglitz), first mentioned in the twelfth century and heavily renovated by the Fürstenbergs at the end of the nineteenth century (March Tues–Sun 9am–noon & 1–3pm; April & Oct Tues–Sun 9am–noon & 1–3pm; May & Sept Tues–Sun 9am–noon & 1–4pm; June–Aug Tues–Sun 9am–noon & 1–5pm; Nov & Dec Sat, Sun 9am–noon & 1–3pm Ⓦwww.krivoklat.cz). With such a perfect location in the heart of the best hunting ground in Bohemia, and a refuge from the deprivations of the plague, Křivoklát naturally enjoyed the royal patronage of the Přemyslids, whose hunting parties were legendary. Charles IV also spent the early part of his childhood here before being sent off to Burgundy. From the outside, it's a scruffy but impressive stronghold, dominated by the round tower in which English alchemist Edward Kelley was incarcerated for two and a half years for failing to reveal the secret of the philosopher's stone to Rudolf II. Kelley was, by all accounts, a slippery character, a swindler and a seducer, with a hooked nose and no ears (they were cut off by the Lancastrians as a punishment for forgery). In an attempt to escape, he jumped out of the window, only to break his leg so badly it had to be amputated.

There are now two tours round this ancient castle to choose between, with the seventy-minute guided tour (*trasa 1*) round the interior taking in most of the castle's good points, including the dungeon and pit, and the Royal Hall and the Chapel. The last two, dating back to the thirteenth century, have kept their original late-Gothic vaulting, studded with corbels carved with colourful figureheads, and retain an austere beauty quite at odds with the castle's reputation as a venue for bacchanalian goings-on. An appealing alternative for those with kids (or an aversion to guided tours) is the 35-minute scramble around the fortifications (*trasa 2*) and viewing of the hunting exhibition in the *velká věž* (great tower). During high season, you can watch traditional woodcarving demonstrations and visit the hunting exhibition in the castle's outbuildings, too. Look out for the summer festival in the first week of August, plus one-off concerts, theatrical performances and Easter and Advent fairs.

Practicalities

Virtually all journeys by **train** from Prague to Křivoklát require a change at Beroun. If you've time to kill, pop into the family-run *Pivovarský Berounský medvěd*, Tyršova 135, next to Beroun railway station, a three-tun, in-house brewery pub and restaurant, serving its own Brown Bear beer in a former sugar factory. **Buses** from the Praha-Dejvice terminal run frequently only at weekends, less regularly during the week, and take around an hour and a half. Křivoklát is just one of several castles in the region, and you could happily spend days exploring the surrounding countryside on a network of well-marked footpaths. There's an **information centre** (June & Sept Sat & Sun 10am–6pm; July & Aug Tues–Sun 10am–6pm; Ⓦwww.pvtnet.cz/www/is.krivoklat) right in the centre of the village, which can advise on walks, and also book private **accommodation**. If the office is closed, try the nearby *Sýkora* (☎313 558 114; ❸), which is a friendly family-run place, or *U Dvořáků* (☎313 558 355; ❸), a hotel in Roztoky, 1km south of Křivoklát, which serves traditional Czech fare. There are also plenty of **campsites** in the vicinity, such as *Višňová II* (June–Aug) by the river.

Around Kladno

No Czech would seriously suggest you should visit **KLADNO**, just under 30km west of Prague, but if you're heading for Lány by bus, you may need to change here. As you approach the town, it's difficult to miss the low, blue barracks of the giant Poldi Kladno steelworks, insensitively built on a section of the old town in the heyday of central planning in 1975. The first steelworks were founded way back in 1854, followed 35 years later by the Poldi works, named after the wife of the founder Karl Wittgenstein. It was here, in 1921, that the Czech Communist Party was founded, and Kladno's workers were rewarded with some of the best wages in the country after the 1948 coup. Its most famous worker was Bohumil Hrabal, who wrote about his experiences at Kladno in *Larks on a String* and *Beautiful Poldi*.

The factory, which once employed 20,000 of the town's inhabitants, was forced to shut down in 1992 due to a lack of orders. Then, two years later, it was sold to the fiery entrepreneur Vladimír Stehlík, who was known to shoot his pistol in the air on the shop floor in order to gain the attention of his employees. During the 1996 elections, he gave his entire workforce the day off so that they could march in Prague against Václav Klaus's government. The following year, having failed to pay their workers for several months, Stehlík and his son Marko were behind bars, awaiting trial for defaulting on bank loans. They were released, after four months inside, only on condition that they sell the steelworks, which they duly did to a Liechtenstein-based company. Nowadays, the factory employs just 700, and the citizens of Kladno have more or less got used to commuting to Prague for their work.

Lidice

The small mining village of **LIDICE**, 18km northwest of Prague, hit the world headlines on June 10, 1942, at the moment when it ceased to exist. On the flimsiest pretext, it was chosen as the scapegoat for the assassination of the Nazi leader Reinhard Heydrich (see p.133). All 173 men from the village were rounded up and shot by the SS, the 198 women were sent off to Ravensbrück concentration camp, and the 89 children either went to the camps or, if they were considered Aryan enough, were packed off to "good" German homes, while the village itself was burnt to the ground.

Knowing all this as you approach Lidice makes the modern village seem almost perversely unexceptional. At the end of the straight, tree-lined main street, 10 června 1942 (June 10, 1942), there's a dour concrete memorial with a small but horrific **museum** (daily: April–Sept 9am–6pm; Oct–March 9am–4pm) where you can watch a short film about Lidice, including footage shot by the SS themselves as the village was burning. The spot where the old village used to lie is just south of the memorial, now merely smooth green pasture punctuated with a few simple symbolic reminders and a new bronze memorial to the 82 local children who were gassed in the camps.

After the massacre, the "Lidice shall live" campaign was launched and villages all over the world began to change their name to Lidice. The first was Stern Park Gardens, Illinois, soon followed by villages in Mexico and other Latin American countries. From Coventry to Montevideo, towns twinned themselves with Lidice, so that rather than "wiping a Czech village off the face of the earth", as Hitler had hoped, the Nazis inadvertently created a symbol of anti-fascist resistance.

There's no place nor reason to stay, and most people come here as a day-trip from Prague on one of the regular buses from Praha Dejvická, getting off at the turn-off to the village on the main road.

Lány

On summer weekends, Škoda-loads of Czech families, pensioners and assorted pilgrims make their way to **LÁNY**, a plain, grey village on a hill by the edge of the Křivoklát forest, 12km beyond Kladno. They congregate in the town's pristine cemetery to pay their respects to one of the country's most important historical figures, Tomáš Garrigue Masaryk, the founding father and president of Czechoslovakia from 1918 to 1935.

The Masaryk plot is separated from the rest of the cemetery (*hřbitov*) by a little wooden fence and flanked by two bushy trees. Tomáš is buried alongside his American wife, Charlotte Garrigue Masaryková, who died some fifteen years earlier, and their son Jan, who became foreign minister in the post-1945 government, only to die in mysterious circumstances shortly after the Communist coup (see p.606). The Masaryks have since been joined by their daughter, Alice, who founded the Czechoslovak Red Cross and died in exile in 1966.

After laying their wreaths, the crowds generally wander over to the presidential summer **zámek** (Ⓦ www.hrad.cz), with its blue-liveried guards, on the other side of the village. The chateau still serves as the president's out-of-town retreat, and its rooms are strictly out of bounds, but the large English gardens, orangerie and deer park, which were landscaped by Josip Plečnik, are open to the public (April–Oct Wed & Thurs 2–6pm, Sat & Sun 10am–6pm). To get to Lány, either change buses at Kladno, or take the slow train to Chomutov from Prague's Masarykovo nádraží, getting out at Stochov – the nearest station to Lány, 3km away to the southwest – which boasts a presidential waiting room.

TGM

Tomáš Garrigue Masaryk – known affectionately as TGM – was born in 1850 in Hodonín, a town in a part of Moravia where Slovaks and Czechs lived harmoniously together. His father was an illiterate Slovak peasant who worked for the local bigwig, his mother a German. Tomáš himself trained as a blacksmith. From such humble beginnings, he rose to become professor of philosophy at the Charles University, a Social Democrat MP in the Viennese Reichsrat, and finally the country's first, and longest-serving, president. A liberal humanist through and through, Masaryk created what was, at the time, probably the most progressive democracy in central Europe, featuring universal suffrage, an enviable social security system and a strong social democratic thrust. The whole country went into mourning when he died in 1937, leaving Czechoslovakia one of the few remaining democracies in central Europe, "a lighthouse high on a cliff with the waves crashing on it on all sides", as Masaryk's less fortunate successor, Edvard Beneš, put it. A year later the Nazis marched into Sudetenland.

After the 1948 coup, the Communists began to dismantle the myth of Masaryk, whose name was synonymous with the "bourgeois" First Republic. All mention of him was removed from textbooks, street names were changed, and his statue was taken down from almost every town and village in the country. However, during liberalization in 1968, his bespectacled face and goatee beard popped up again in shop windows, and his image returned once more in 1989 to haunt the beleaguered Communists.

Travel details

Trains

Benešov u Prahy to: Městečko u Benešova (hourly; 20min); Postupice (hourly; 15min).
Beroun to: Křivoklát (10–13 daily; 30–45min).
Čerčany to: Český Šternberk (7–8 daily; 1 hr); Sázava (7–8 daily; 30min).
Mělník to: Litoměřice město (every 1–2hr; 35min); Mladá Boleslav (5 daily; 1hr 30min); Mšeno (6 daily; 40min); Ústí nad Labem (every 1–2hr; 1hr).
Prague Hlavní nádraží to: Benešov (hourly; 40min–1hr 5min); Beroun (hourly; 40min); Čerčany (hourly; 55min); Kolín (1–2 hourly; 45min); Kutná Hora (4 daily; 55min–1hr); Mladá Boleslav (every 2hr; 1hr 15min–1hr 50min); Poděbrady (hourly; 50min–1hr).
Prague Masarykovo nádraží to: Kladno (hourly; 40–55min); Kolín (hourly; 1hr 10min); Nelahozeves (every 1–2hr; 40min–50min); Roudnice nad Labem (every 2hr; 45min); Stochov (hourly; 1hr–1hr 15min); Stratov (hourly; 40min).

Prague Holešovice to: Kolín (5 daily; 40min).
Prague Smíchov to: Beroun (5–9 daily; 50min–1hr); Karlštejn (1–2 hourly; 30min); Příbram (2–4 daily; 1hr 15min); Řevnice (1–2 hourly; 25min).

Buses

Prague (Černý Most) to: Přerov nad Labem and Poděbrady (up to 3 daily, 30min/50min).
Prague (Dejvická) to: Kladno (1–2 hourly; 45–50min); Lidice (1–2 hourly; 25–35min).
Prague (Florenc) to: Konopiště (up to every 45min; 1hr); Kutná Hora (Mon–Fri 1 daily; 1hr 15min); Mělník (up to 10 daily; 50min); Mladá Boleslav (frequently; 1hr 15min).
Prague (Na Knížecí) to: Příbram (hourly; 45min–1hr).
Prague (Opatov) to: Průhonice (every 30min–1hr; 15min).
Prague (Želivského) to: Kutná Hora (up to 5 daily; 1hr 15min); Sázava (5–12 daily; 1hr 10min).

2

South Bohemia

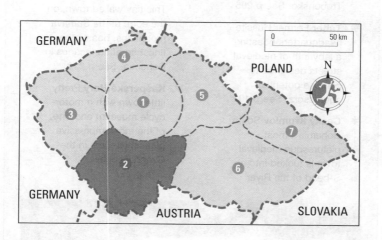

Highlights

CHAPTER 2

* **Zámek, Jindrichuv Hradec** Despite its forbidding exterior, this chateau boasts one of the finest Italianate Renaissance interiors in the country. See p.201

* **Třeboň** Perfectly preserved walled town and spa set amidst the medieval carp ponds of Třeboňsko. See p.205

* **Tábor** Former Hussite headquarters boasting a labyrinth of medieval streets designed to confuse potential aggressors. See p.192

* **Český Krumlov** South Bohemia's most picturesque medieval town is tucked into an S-bend of the River Vltava and overlooked by a Renaissance castle. See p.212

* **Hiking through the Šumava** The most unspoilt mountain range in the Czech Republic is the perfect place to do some summer hiking. See p.217

* **Sgraffito in Prachatice** This tiny walled town, on the edge of the Šumava mountains, boasts the finest sgraffito facades in Bohemia. See p.222

* **Kašperské Hory** Pretty little town with a motorcycle museum and one of the most impressive glass museums in the Czech Republic. See p.227

△ Pisek Bridge

South Bohemia

South Bohemia (Jižní Čechy), more than any other region, conforms to the popular myth of Bohemia as a bucolic backwater of rolling hills and endless forests. A century of conspicuous industrialization and destruction from two world wars have pretty much passed it by. The only city to speak of is the regional capital, **České Budějovice**, which makes up for its urban sprawl with a good-looking old town and a beer of no less standing. The rest of the countryside is dotted with a series of exceptionally beautiful medieval walled towns, known collectively as the **Rose Towns** after the emblems of the two most powerful families: the red rose of the Rožmberks and the black rose of the lords of Hradec. Both dynasties died out at the beginning of the seventeenth century, and many of their prize possessions, which have been in almost terminal decline ever since, ended up in the hands of the Bavarian-based Schwarzenberg family.

Český Krumlov is by far the most popular of the Rose Towns; others, like **Pelhřimov** and **Třeboň**, are equally well preserved, if not quite as picturesquely located. The latter lies in an uncharacteristically flat part of the country, known as **Třeboňsko**, a unique ecosystem of medieval fish ponds that still supply much of the country's Christmas carp. Bohemia's chief river, the **Vltava**, runs through South Bohemia and provides the setting for the region's most popular **castles**, some, like **Zvíkov**, almost monastic in their simplicity, and others, such as **Orlík**, **Hluboká** and **Rožmberk**, marvels of aristocratic decadence.

To the south, the **Šumava**, which forms the natural border with Austria and Germany, is one of the most unspoiled mountain ranges in the country. The German-speaking foresters and traders who settled on the northern slopes have left their mark on the architecture of the Bohemian towns and villages in that area. Following the postwar expulsions, however, the local population is now greatly reduced, their number augmented only by a seasonal influx of walkers, fishermen, canoeists and inland beachniks, drawn by the natural beauty of the region, which is probably the least affected by acid rain in the Czech Republic.

Regional **transport** in South Bohemia isn't as bad as might be expected, given the overwhelmingly hilly, rural nature of the terrain. Travelling by train allows you to experience more of the countryside, and even parts of the Šumava are served by a scenic single-track railway that winds its way from České Budějovice to Český Krumlov, along the shores of Lake Lipno and then north to Prachatice. While they can be less frequent than trains, buses go virtually everywhere and are almost invariably faster.

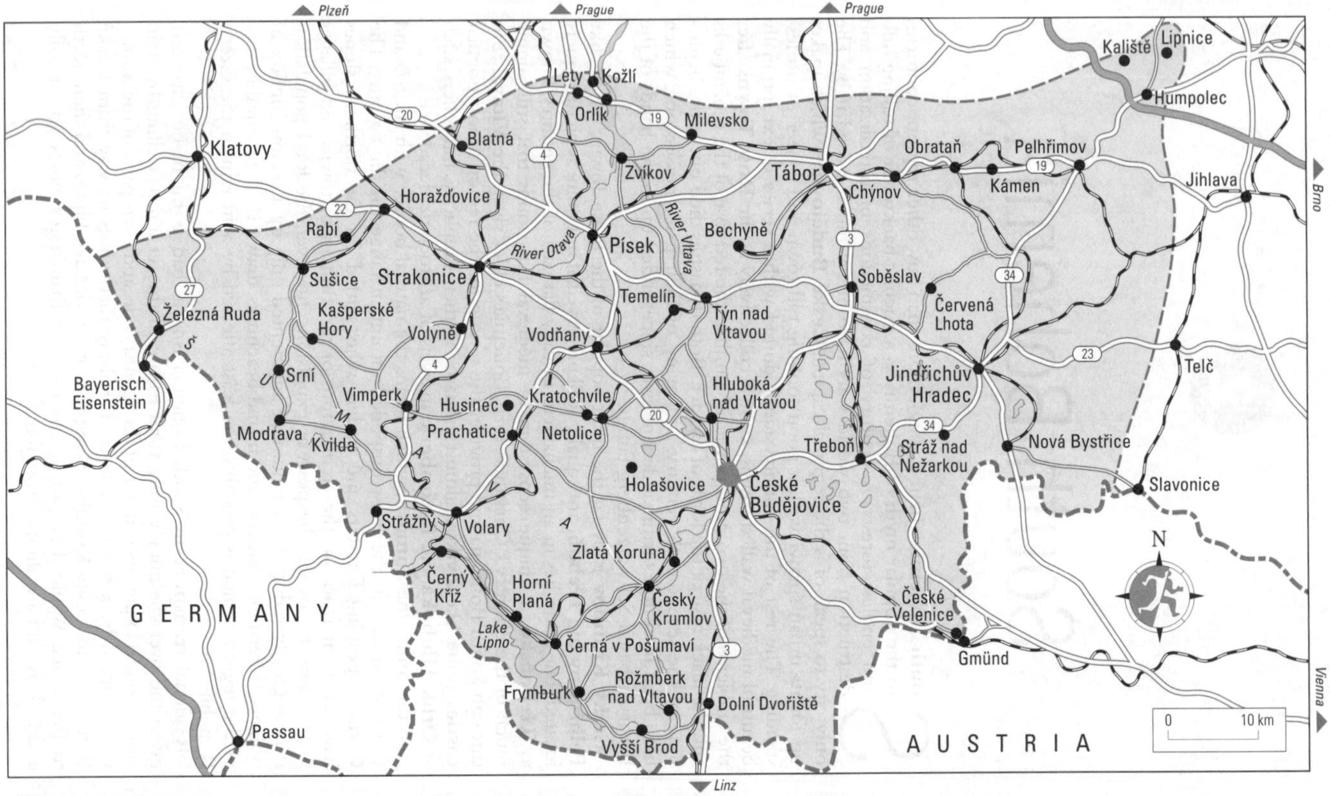
Plzeň
Prague
Prague
Brno
Vienna
Linz
Lipnice
Kaliště
Humpolec
Jihlava
Pelhřimov
Kámen
Obrataň
Chýnov
Tábor
Milevsko
Lety
Kožlí
Orlík
Zvíkov
Bechyně
River Vltava
Písek
River Otava
Blatná
Klatovy
Horažďovice
Rabí
Sušice
Strakonice
Temelín
Týn nad Vltavou
Soběslav
Červená Lhota
Jindřichův Hradec
Telč
Nová Bystřice
Slavonice
Železná Ruda
Kašperské Hory
Volyně
Vodňany
Bayerisch Eisenstein
Srní
Vimperk
Husinec
Kratochvíle
Hluboká nad Vltavou
Modrava
Kvilda
Prachatice
Netolice
Třeboň
Stráž nad Nežarkou
Holašovice
České Budějovice
Strážný
Volary
Zlatá Koruna
Černý Kříž
Horní Planá
Český Krumlov
České Velenice
Gmünd
GERMANY
Lake Lipno
Černá v Pošumaví
Frymburk
Rožmberk nad Vltavou
Dolní Dvořiště
Vyšší Brod
Passau
AUSTRIA
N
0
10 km
20
4
19
22
27
3
34
23
Š
U
M
A
V
A

There are **boat services** from Orlík to Zvíkov (early April–late June & early Sept to mid-Oct Sat & Sun; 3 daily; July & Aug Tues–Sun 5 daily; 50min; 80Kč one-way), which also head north to the Orlík dam, via the Velký Vír, Radava, Podskalí and Trhovky campsites (same price). Another less frequent service plies between Orlík and Týn nad Vltavou (July & Aug Tues, Thurs & Sat; 1 daily; 3hr 30min, departs from Týn 8am, from Orlík 4pm; 180Kč one-way), close to the nuclear power station of Temelín. For a boat tour of the area, there are irregular round-trip excursions from the pier below Orlík castle (45min; 100Kč). For more information on the timetable, call ☎382 275 333 or check out ⓦwww.lodnidopravaquarter.cz.

Up the Vltava

South of Prague and the Slapy dam, the **River Vltava** has been transformed into a series of long, winding lakes, which remain a favourite destination for Czechs in the summer. The campsites, many of them fairly ad hoc affairs, are full to capacity, and campfires burn into the night every night. There are also two **castles** worth visiting: **Orlík** and **Zvíkov**, both of which overlook the Vltava and are difficult to reach without your own transport. A possible base from which to see them is the nearby town of **Písek**, which has recently been prettily spruced up, and is easily accessible by bus or train.

Orlík nad Vltavou

With its vanilla-coloured rendering and mock castellations, you're unlikely to be disappointed by your first impressions of **Orlík** (which means "little eagle"), a creamy nineteenth-century castle which juts out into this wide stretch of the Vltava. No doubt the view was a great deal more spectacular before the valley was dammed in the 1960s; nowadays the water laps rather tamely at the foot of the castle, and concrete has been injected into its foundations to prevent it from being swept away.

As some of the region's greatest self-propagandists, the Schwarzenbergs turned this old Gothic **hrad** (Tues–Sun: April & Oct 9am–4pm; May & Sept 9am–5pm; June–Aug 9am–6pm; 130Kč; ⓦwww.schwarzenberg.cz) into a pseudo-Gothic money-waster in the second half of the nineteenth century. There's nothing among the faience, weaponry and Schwarzenberg military memorabilia on the hour-long guided tour to hint at its seven-hundred-year history, and even the gardens were only laid out in the last century, but if you're interested in the Schwarzenbergs, this is one of the best places to find out about them. Alternatively, a modest **aquarium** (Tues–Fri 11am–5pm, Sat & Sun 10.30am–5.30pm) has recently opened close to the pier below the chateau, housing a small display of fishes living in the Czech rivers and (usually artificial) lakes.

For moderately priced **food**, head for the restaurant *U Toryka* (named after the current count's pet fox terrier; closed Mon & Nov–March), located just below the castle; for cheaper fare, try the café in the orangery, or head off into the castle grounds for a picnic. There are also a handful of cheap restaurants in the village of Orlík, a kilometre or so south of the castle. Of the many **campsites** in the area, the nearest to the castle is 2km downriver (but a 7km drive) at Velký Vír (May–Sept; ☎382 275 192), which has bungalows for rent. En route, there's a nice **pension**, *U Nováků* (☎383 321 300; ❷), with a friendly pub downstairs serving cheap food and Gambrinus and Purkmistr beers.

Romany memorial at Lety

It took fifty years, but in 1995 a memorial at **Lety** was finally erected, 7km west of Orlík, to the Czech Romanies who died here during World War II. Between 1942 and 1943, some 1300 Romanies passed through the transit camp in Lety, amidst what is now a rather insensitively placed pig farm ("which is still a source of great contention and unhappiness for Roma"), en route to Auschwitz. Thousands more were imprisoned in Hodonín, Moravia. About a quarter of those interned at Lety died in the camp – in the end around ninety percent of the prewar Czech Romany population was killed. Touching the raw nerve of Czech-Gypsy relations, it is inevitable that the memorial has provoked controversy, not least because of the accusation that the camp was staffed not by Germans, nor even Sudeten Germans, but by Czechs. The small-scale memorial is made up of a series of slabs of rock, already overgrown, with an information panel in Czech, Roma and English. To get there, take the road from Lety to Kožlí u Orlíka, and follow the inconspicuous sign *památník* into the woods, a fifteen-minute walk.

Zvíkov

Fourteen kilometres upstream, hidden amid the woods of an isolated rocky promontory at the confluence of the Vltava and the Otava, is the bare medieval husk of **Zvíkov** (April & Oct Sat & Sun 9.30am–noon & 12.30–3.30pm; May & Sept Tues–Sun 9.30am–noon & 1–4pm; June–Aug Tues–Sun 9am–5pm; tours in English; @www.pamatky-jc.cz), its simplicity a welcome relief after the "romantic interiors" of Orlík. You can wander at will among the light honey-coloured stone buildings, left to rack and ruin by the Rožmberks as long ago as the fifteenth century, then further destroyed by imperial troops during the Thirty Years' War. A small dusty track passes under three gatehouses before leading to the central courtyard, which boasts a simple, early Gothic, two-storey arcade, reconstructed in the nineteenth century from the few bays that still stood. Even the meagre offerings in the museum are more than compensated for by the absence of tour groups, the cool stone floors and the wonderful views over the water. A further incentive to visit are the chapel's faded fifteenth-century frescoes, featuring a particularly memorable scene "where nimbed souls in underpants float uncomfortably through a forest", as one critic aptly described it.

Buses from Písek (weekdays only) generally only go as far as the village of **ZVÍKOVSKÉ PODHRADÍ**, 1km south of the castle, from where the castle is signposted. Here you'll find private **rooms**, as well as plusher accommodation at the friendly *Hotel Zvíkov* (☎382 285 659, @www.hotelzvikov.cz; ❹), which also rents cheaper (and often full) bungalows (April–Oct; ❷).

Písek

Twenty kilometres south of Zvíkov is the pretty little town of **PÍSEK**, which takes its name from the gold-producing sand (*písek*) of the Otava. Gold fever has waxed and waned in the town over the centuries (an annual gold-panning championship is now held every August on the river around Kestřany). At present, commercial exploration, mostly around the village of Mokrsko, has been suspended, and the likelihood of any company getting the go-ahead to mine looks very slim indeed. The problem is that the gold is dispersed in microscopic particles, which means for every tonne of gold, the mining companies would have to shift half a million tonnes of rock, crush it into powder and then leach the gold out in pools of cyanide. Obviously, the environmental consequences would be disastrous, and so far the locals (and even the government) are against any mining.

Arrival, information and accommodation

The main **bus** and **train stations** are both a kilometre or so south of town, at the end of Nádražní (buses #1, #3, #11 from Budovcova, a five-minute walk from Velké náměstí). Incidentally, in the novel by Jaroslav Hašek, the Good Soldier Švejk of the title makes his fictional appearance at Písek train station in a blizzard, handcuffed to a lance-corporal in the Austrian constabulary "for comfort", before moving on to Tábor. Pisek has a useful **information centre** (Mon–Fri 10am–5pm; July & Aug daily 9am–6pm, ☎382 213 592, ⓦwww. icpisek.cz) at Hejduková 97, just off the main square, which offers **Internet** services (30Kč for 30min), organizes accommodation and has a computerized information screen outside (in Czech, English and German) for when it's closed.

Accommodation

The *City Hotel* (☎382 215 192, ⓦwww.cityhotel.cz; ❸) is a smart Gothic **hotel** with a vaulted restaurant, in the old town at Alšovo náměstí 35; a cheaper alternative is *U Kloudů* (☎382 210 802, ⓦwww.ukloudu.infohelp.cz; ❷), a **pension** on Nerudova 66 with a café-bar and bustling restaurant downstairs – follow Heyduková through Havlíčkovo náměstí. A conveniently central option is the hotel *Bílá růže* (☎382 214 931; ❸) with a decent, spacious restaurant, which occupies the Communist-era edifice on Fráni Šrámka 169, several steps above the church of Povýšení sv Kříže. The two **campsites** nearest Písek are a long way out of town and a couple of kilometres from the nearest train stations: *Soutok* (May–Oct) is to the south, nearest Putim station, while the *Vrcovice* site (open all year) is north of town, nearest Vrcovice station.

The Town

Písek experienced its last gold rush in the thirteenth century, but its prosperity was later demolished by the Thirty Years' War. The chief reminder of those days is the town's wonderful, 111-metre-long, **medieval stone bridge** (Kamenný most), which predates even the Charles Bridge in Prague and which likewise

Temelín

The cooling towers of **Temelín**, which rise up beside the main road from Písek to České Budějovice, are a chastening sight. Built to a Soviet design technically similar to the one used at Chernobyl, Temelín was designed to be the largest nuclear power station in the world – reason enough to give the place a wide berth. A long campaign of protest by local and international (mostly Austrian) groups persuaded the first post-Communist government to postpone the opening of the power station, which is situated on a tectonic fault line. However, in 1992, the US energy giant Westinghouse was commissioned to complete at least two of the four reactor units. Eight years later the establishment was officially opened. Temelín now provides twenty percent of the nation's electricity, as does the republic's only other (much older) nuclear reactor in the south Moravian town of Dukovany. You can visit the information centre (daily 9am–4pm; July–Aug 9am–5.30pm; free ; ☎385 782 639) which has moving models of machines and a small cinema, where you can see a 3-D movie on the building of the reactors. The staff eagerly distribute propaganda brochures and posters with the cooling towers at sunset.

accrued a fine selection of beatific Baroque statuary during the Counter-Reformation. Located in the westernmost edge of the staré město, it is now closed to traffic, and has recently been restored.

From the bridge, it's a short hop to the main square, **Velké náměstí**, overlooked by the magnificent golden yellow Baroque **radnice**. Behind the town hall, at the far end of the courtyard, you'll find the entrance to the **Prácheňské muzeum** (Tues–Sun: March–Sept 9am–6pm; Oct–Dec 9am–5pm), which occupies the only surviving wing of the medieval riverside castle, built by Přemysl King Otakar II in the thirteenth century and destroyed by fire in 1532. The highlight of this recently refurbished and vast museum is the Gothic Knights' Hall, which has retained its original black floor tiles, and contains a model of how the castle once looked. The rest of the museum is also worth a quick canter for its unusually frank account of the area's history, including a section on the Gypsy concentration camp of Lety (see p.190), and the more recent events of 1968 and 1989; and before you leave, don't miss the gold exhibits in the basement.

A few doors down the main square from the radnice is the pretty little former monastery church of **Povýšení sv Kříže**, with its gabled sgraffitoed facade. It has a superbly kitsch Baroque main altar, sporting a golden sunburst in the shape of a love heart and a backdrop of blue, ruched curtains dotted with gold stars. There are several other buildings around the town which boast more recent sgraffito decoration, mostly the work of the late-nineteenth-century artist (and local student) Mikuláš Aleš. A short walk up Fráni Šrámka brings you to the **Putimská brána**, the only remaining bastion, adjoined by a number of quiet backstreets heading east. These lead to a small market which takes place under the aegis of the 74-metre-high, onion-domed *hláska* (watchtower) of the Dominican church.

Finally, the technically turned-on might consider paying a visit to Písek's latest attraction, the **Městská elektrárna** (power station; April–Sept Tues–Sun 9am–noon & 1–4pm), a short walk upstream from the Kamenný most. It became operational in 1887, thus making Písek the first Czech town to have electric lighting supplied by its very own power station.

Eating and drinking

For a fairly quaint Bohemian meal, book a table under the stone vaults at *U Přemysla Otakara II* (closed Sun; ☎382 212 132), at Velké námĕsti 114, in the courtyard of the museum, or try *Na Ostrovĕ*, on a leafy island in the river just downstream of the bridge, complete with kids' playground and minigolf. Typical Czech food is also served at *U Kamenného mostu*, which has a pleasant atmosphere and views onto the river and the old bridge from its summer garden. For Indian food, try the simple *Tandoor* (closed Sat), located next door to the information centre, whilst a good place for a beer is the nearby *Bar Monika*.

Tábor

Founded in 1420 by religious exiles from Prague, 88km away to the north, **TÁBOR** – named after the mountain where the transfiguration of Christ took place – was the spiritual and strategic centre of the social and religious revolution which swept through Bohemia in the first half of the fifteenth century. It gave its name to the radical wing of the reformist Hussite movement, the

△ Tábor

Táborites, whose philosophy – that all people should be equal on earth as in heaven – found few friends among the church hierarchy and feudal-minded nobility of the time, Hussite or Catholic. Under constant threat of physical attack, they developed into a formidable fighting force, declaring war on the established Church and remaining undefeated until 1452, when the town was taken by a force led by the moderate Hussite King Jiří of Poděbrady.

Anti-authoritarianism persists here, and despite the efforts of the Jesuits and others over the centuries, Tábor still boasts the smallest percentage of Catholics in the country. Considering its pugnacious history, though, and despite being a major bus and rail junction, Tábor is a relatively quiet little town nowadays, especially in the beautifully preserved old quarter, which is virtually devoid of traffic and has kept its labyrinthine street plan. In the staré město's back alleys, many houses have retained their rich sgraffito decoration and pretty Renaissance gables, while the main square boasts the country's premier museum devoted to the Hussite movement.

Arrival, information and accommodation

Fast trains from Prague take under two hours to reach Tábor. The train and bus stations are a twenty-minute walk or short bus ride (buses #11 and #13) east of the old town. You can leave luggage at the baggage office in the train station, or if you wish to stay the night, you can arrange **private rooms** through the friendly and efficient **information centre** at Žižkovo náměstí 2 (May–Sept Mon–Fri 8.30am–7pm, Sat & Sun 10am–4pm; Oct–April Mon–Fri 9am–4pm; ☎381 486 230, Ⓦwww.tabor.cz).

Accommodation

All the **campsites** are well out of the centre. The best of the bunch is *Autokemp Malý Jordán*, with basic chalets (June–Sept, ☎381 235 103, Ⓦwww.web.quick. cz/atc-mj; buses #20 & #21; ❶), situated north of the town in the woods between Lake Jordán – formed by the oldest dam in Europe (built in 1492) and

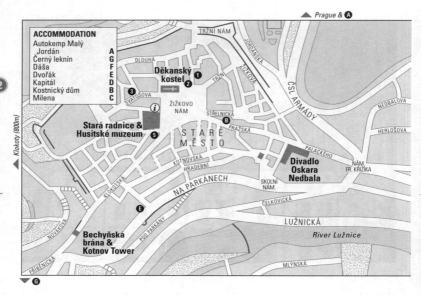

once a favourite spot for baptizing children – and its smaller sister lake, after which it's a pleasant kilometre's walk along the lakeside.

Hotels and pensions

Černý leknín Příběnická 695 ☎ 381 256 405, ☏ 381 252 574, ⓦ www.edb.cz/cernyleknin. One of the best accommodation options, located in the grandiose neo-Gothic villa beyond the Bechyňská brána. Offers comfortable en-suite rooms at moderate prices and has a sauna and swimming pool on site. ❹

Dáša Bílková 735 ☎ 381 256 253, ⓦ www .travelguide.cz/pensiondasa. Pleasant pension off the Husův park close to the station, with a sauna attached. ❷

Dvořák Hradební 3037 ☎ 381 251 290, ⓦ www .geneahotels.cz. The newest hotel in town, situated in an old brewery, south of the main square.

Comfortable rooms with satellite TV and Internet access. Swimming pool and sauna on site. ❻

Kapitál Třída 9 května 617 ☎ 381 256 096, ⓦ www.hotel-kapital.cz. Big hotel with convenient rooms and a decent restaurant. ❸

Kostnický dům Střelnická 220 ☎ 603 516 188, ⓦ www.tabor.cz/kostnickydum. Small (just nine beds) central pension, located in a Renaissance house, off the southeastern corner of the main square. ❷

Milena Husovo náměstí 529 ☎ 381 254 755, ⓦ www.tabor.cz/milena/index.html. Cheap, simple rooms with or without en-suite facilities, near the train station. ❷

The Town

To reach the staré město from the new town or **nové město**, walk west from the train or bus station through the Husův park, making sure you take note of the unusual and passionate **statue of Jan Hus** by local sculptor František Bílek (you can see more of his work at the nearby village of Chýnov; see p.198). Continue past the statue down třída 9 května until you reach the busy square, náměstí Fr. Křižíka, which straddles the ridge between the new and old towns, then head up Palackého into the old town.

The street plan of the **staré město**, with its vast maze of narrow medieval streets designed to confuse the enemy, has changed very little since its foundation back in the fifteenth century. No fewer than twelve streets lead onto the

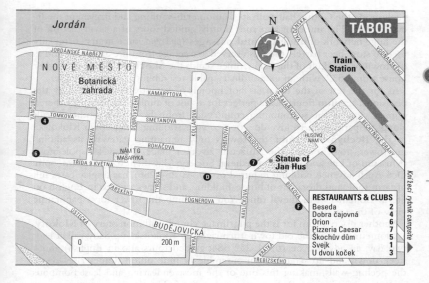

Křižecí rybník campsite

RESTAURANTS & CLUBS

Beseda	2
Dobrá čajovná	4
Orion	6
Pizzeria Caesar	7
Škochův dům	5
Svejk	1
U dvou koček	3

central square, **Žižkovo náměstí**, with its brightly coloured houses and stunning variety of gables and gargoyles, all of which had to be rebuilt after fires in the fifteenth and sixteenth centuries. The square is dominated by the **Děkanský kostel**, with its unusual triple gable; for a bird's-eye view of Tábor's weblike street layout, climb the 199 steps of the church's extremely tall **belltower** (May–Aug daily 10am–5pm; Sept & Oct Sat & Sun same hours if weather allows), and try to time your climb between the hourly tolling, since you have to pass within inches of the bell to reach the top.

It was on Tábor's main square in 1420 that the Táborites threw theological caution to the wind and set up a religious commune under the principle of *není nic mé a nic tvé, než všecko v obec rovně mají* ("nothing is mine, nothing is yours, everything is common to all"). Large urns were set up in the square and anyone – male or female – wishing to live in the commune had first to place all their possessions in them, after which they were given work on a daily rota. Men and women were granted equal rights, there was a complete ban on alcohol, and from the stone table which still stands outside the stará radnice, communion was given to the people "in both kinds" – as opposed to the established practice of reserving the wine (the blood of Christ) for the priesthood. The Hussites had this last symbolic act emblazoned on their flag – a red chalice on a black background – which, like the rousing religious war songs they sang before going into battle, struck fear into the crusaders from thirty nations who came against them.

Matching the church's triple gable on the west side of the square are the three steeply stepped neo-Gothic gables of the **stará radnice**, which now houses the **Husitské muzeum** (Hussite Museum; April–Oct daily 8.30am–5pm; rest of the year Tues–Fri same hours; ⓦ www.husmuzeum.cz). Inside, in amongst the nasty-looking pikes, there's a model of medieval Tábor, and several versions of Myslbek's late-nineteenth-century statue of **Jan Žižka**, the Táborites' brilliant, blind military leader (traditionally depicted with one eye still functioning), which stands on the square in front of the church. You also get the chance to

195

peek inside the Gothic hall, with its diamond rib-vaulting and irreverent medieval corbels. The museum also runs hourly guided tours of a small section of the huge network of **underground passages** (*podzemí*; same hours); originally used to store beer barrels, they also served as a refuge from fire and siege, and as the town prison. Left of the stará radnice stands the **Škochův dům** – a burgher house from 1532, with an extraordinary gable resembling a donkey's spine.

As for the rest of the town, its hotchpotch of backstreets, enlivened by the occasional sgraffito flourish, are perfect for a spot of aimless wandering – there's a great view of the surrounding countryside from the town's southern walls along Na parkánech. To give direction to your strolling, head down Klokotská to the **Bechyňská brána**, the town's only remaining gateway; its adjoining tower, now housing the Muzeum života a práce středověké společnosti (Museum of Life and Work in Medieval Society; May–Sept daily 8.30am–5pm; Oct–April advance booking required on ☏381 254 286), has display cases full of farm tools and dioramas of house-building, and shows a video in English on life in Bohemia in medieval times. You can climb the tower for a panoramic view of the town.

Another place to aim for is the pilgrimage church and monastery of **Klokoty**, a kilometre west of the old town (turn right off Klokotská up Sady, call at least two days in advance on ☏381 232 584; guided tours also in English) and a steep down-and-up scramble. An ensemble of nine onion domes rises above the peeling walls, making this one of the most endearing and least pompous of Bohemia's Counter-Reformation monasteries. The domes form the corner towers of a set of cloisters with a lovely rose garden as its centrepiece. The church, surprisingly, has a flat and unadorned ceiling, but the putti-strewn pulpit and main altar don't disappoint.

Eating, drinking and entertainment

There's traditional Czech fare and Budvar and Bernard beers at *Beseda* (closed Sun), the popular, old-fashioned restaurant at no. 5 at the top of the main square in the old town, whose patio spills out onto the square itself. *U dvou koček*, Svatošova 310, to the west of the Děkanský kostel, is a bit of a tourist trap but offers dark Purkmistr beer and light Pilsner to go with good solid cooking, or there's the *Dobra čajovná* (tea house) at Tomkova 2. It's also worth trying the reasonably priced Czech food in the small new restaurant in the Škochův dům, while a good place to meet the locals is the *Švejk*, a lively pub-cum-restaurant hidden behind the building that houses *Beseda*, and adorned with the Good Soldier's portraits. For pizza, try *Pizzeria Caesar*, on Husovo náměstí, near the bus and train stations.

As for **nightlife**, Tábor has its very own theatre, Divadlo Oskara Nedbala, on Palackého, though the plays are all in Czech, and a rock club, *Orion*, on náměstí Fr. Křižíka, featuring the occasional live band. If you're in town around the middle of September, be prepared for a lot of medieval fooling around as part of Tábor's annual **festival**, Táborská setkání (Tábor Meetings).

West of Tábor

Tábor's old town will keep you occupied for the best part of a day. However, if you've an afternoon to spare, a couple of side-trips are possible west of Tábor, both of them just a short train journey from the town.

Milevsko

Halfway along the branch line from Tábor to Písek, **MILEVSKO** has a couple of interesting sights besides its impressive array of late-nineteenth-century buildings. The most unusual is the former **synagogue**, on Sokolovská, designed by Oldřich Tyl and completed in 1919, which has been used by the local Hussite congregation since 1965. Its Neoclassical facade is disrupted by a double staircase that leads to the women's gallery, and by the distinctive Cubist prisms in the tympanum. There's a memorial to the town's hundred-strong Jewish community, which was wiped out in the Holocaust. The town's sturdy, twelfth-century **Basilica of sv Jiljí**, just off the main Tábor–Plzeň road, used to attract a stream of royal and ecclesiastical admirers until the Hussites wrecked it; despite repairs and later additions, it's currently in a desperate state. The nearby Premonstratensian monastery houses the small **Milevské muzeum** (March–June & Sept–Dec Tues–Sun 9am–noon & 1–5pm; July–Aug closes 6pm) charting the history of the town, with details as fascinating as the price of a fifteenth-century chicken.

Bechyně

Roughly every hour, a dinky electric train covers the 24-kilometre journey from Tábor to the small soporific spa and pottery-producing town of **BECHYNĚ**. The line from Tábor to Bechyně was the empire's first electrified line when it was opened in 1903, and on Saturdays in July and August, you can travel there and back on the original train (departure from Tábor at 10am, return from Bechyně at 2.10pm). As you enter the town, both rail and road cross a spectacular viaduct over the Lužnice gorge, known locally as the "Rainbow". The old town teeters on the edge of the gorge, ten minutes' walk southwest of the station down Libušina.

At the far side of the uninspiring main square, which has long since lost its function as a marketplace, is the **Alšova jihočeská galerie** (May–Sept daily 9am–noon & 12.30–5pm), housed in the old town castle brewery, which has an impressive collection of locally produced ceramics and hosts regular international exhibitions. Opposite is the medieval granary, now home to the **Muzeum Vladimíra Preclíka** (mid-May to Sept Tues–Sun 10am–5pm), containing over a hundred of Preclík's work, including paintings, drawings and sculptures. Just beyond lies the Rožmberks' Renaissance **zámek** (June–Aug Tues–Sun 10am–5pm; out of season ☎381 212 550, ⊛www.zamek-bechyne.cz; tour in English 150Kč), whose interiors are adorned with Renaissance frescoes and Baroque stuccowork. A guided tour also takes you through the apartments of Petr Vok, the last of the Rožmberks. The chief attraction, however, is the room with sixteenth-century vaulting supported by a single, tree-like column. The Franciscan **monastery** nearby is now a school, but the church, boasting a fine crystal vaulting, is open on Sundays for mass, and the gardens host summer concerts and afford excellent views of the gorge. Also worth exploring before you leave town is the **Hasičské muzeum** (Firefighting Museum; May–June & Sept Thurs–Sun 9am–noon & 1–5pm; July–Aug Tues–Sun same hours) on the main square, interesting less for its old fire engines than for the fact that it occupies the town's former **synagogue**. There's also a well-kept **Jewish cemetery** just beyond the old town walls on Michalská; ask at the museum. Lastly, for a **view** over the square, you can climb the belfry of the church of sv Matěj (summer daily 9am–7pm).

The last **train** back to Tábor leaves at around 7.10pm; the last **bus** some two hours later (weekdays). If you wish to **stay the night**, head for the pension *U*

Pichlů (☎77 50 74245; ❷), a lovely little Baroque cottage on the main square, with a bar and ceramics shop downstairs; alternatively, there's the rather pricey *Hotel Panská* (☎381 212 550, ⓦwww.hotel-bechyne.cz; ❹) at the upper end of the square, where you can also book the tickets to the castle. A good option is the *Hotel Jupiter*, a newly renovated late-nineteenth-century villa on Libůšina (☎381 212 631, ⓦwww.jupiter-felicitas.cz; ❸), which has a decent restaurant and also offers spa treatment. Cheaper and far less pleasant is the nearby *Hotel U draka* (☎381 211 053; ❷). For **pizza**, try the *Pizzeria Protivínka* on the main square. A few doors to the right there's the **tourist office** (☎381 213 822; ⓦwww.avantitravel.cz), that can arrange private accommodation.

East of Tábor

East of Tábor, there are several more possible day-trips: to the village of **Chýnov**, where the turn-of-the-twentieth-century sculptor František Bílek built his own house, now a museum to his exceptional talents; and, for those with an interest in the country's motorcycling history, to **Kámen**. Even **Pelhřimov** is possible as a day-trip by train or bus, though you're more likely to pass through en route to Moravia. Only devotees of Jaroslav Hašek will journey even further east beyond Humpolec to the village of **Lipnice**, to pay their respects to the last resting place of the author of *The Good Soldier Švejk*. Likewise, admirers of Gustav Mahler might want to make the trip to **Kaliště**, northwest of Humpolec, to visit his birthplace, though unfortunately there's no dedicated museum there.

Chýnov

The little village of **CHÝNOV**, three stations east of Tábor, is the birthplace of the sculptor **František Bílek** (1872–1941), whose former home (though not his birthplace), the **Bílkův dům** at Údolní 133 (mid-May to mid-Oct Tues–Sun 10am–noon & 1–5pm), has recently been restored, and is an absolute must if you're in the area. Far from being a simple house-museum, this is a remarkable piece of architecture, designed by Bílek himself in 1897. Built in red brick, with a large overhanging wooden roof and balcony, it stands out, above all, thanks to Bílek's biblical plaster relief on the south facade, and the miniature wooden chapel on the north side of the house. A large part of the interior is taken up with Bílek's studio, which is suffused with natural light and filled with studies for his large-scale works, but there is no attempt to re-create Bílek's home as it would have been in his day; instead, the building simply serves as a gallery for his works. Trained in Paris, Bílek was clearly influenced stylistically by Art Nouveau, though the tortured gestures and expressions of his subjects are derived more from the religious fervour that imbues all his work, which he himself described as "a sacrifice for the recovery of the brethren".

The Bílkův dům is situated on the south side of the river, across from the main part of town, signposted off the road to Tábor, and is a good 1.5km from Chýnov train station. While you're in the vicinity, you might consider paying a visit to the **Chýnovská jeskyně** (April–June & Sept Tues–Sun 9am–3.30pm; July & Aug Tues–Sun 9am–4.30pm; Oct Mon–Fri advance booking required, ☎381 299 034), a three-kilometre walk northeast across the fields from the train station on the blue-marked path (the entrance is also accessible by car). Amid gentle meadows and orchards, the entrance to the caves consists of a fifty-metre plunge down narrow, precipitous steps, to the sounds of Bach's *Toccata and Fugue in D minor*. What's fun about the forty-minute guided tour is that it's a lot more like real potholing than the larger caves in Moravia or Slovakia, and there are even some stalactites and stalagmites to admire when you reach the bottom.

Kámen

There's a sporadic branch-line service between Tábor and Pelhřimov, but you'll have to take the bus along route 19 to reach the one-street village of **KÁMEN** (meaning "Rock"), whose castle was once a fortified staging post between these two strongly pro-Hussite walled towns. It's worth a detour, since in 1974, after centuries of neglect, the castle was reopened – somewhat incongruously – as a **Motorcycle Museum** (April & Oct Sat & Sun 9am–noon & 1–4pm; May–Sept Tues–Sun 9am–noon & 1–5pm). Some wonderful old Czech bikes are on display, from the very first Laurin & Klement Model TB from 1899 – not much more than a bicycle with a petrol tank tacked on – to stylish examples from the heyday of Czech biking between the wars. Other machines include ČZs and Jawas, which may have cut some ice back in the 1940s when they were designed, but now only exacerbate the country's environmental problems. To trace the sad demise of the Czech motorcycle industry, you have to join the short guided tour (in Czech) of the castle before reaching the machines.

Pelhřimov

If you're heading east into Moravia and need a place to stay, make for the tiny, sleepy medieval town of **PELHŘIMOV**, only 16km further east along route 19. Barely 200m across, the walled town still retains two sixteenth-century tower gates, on one of which, the **Rynárecká brána**, two rams tirelessly butt each other on the hour. In one corner of the pretty, cobbled main square stands the beautiful Renaissance **Šrejnarovsky dům**, and the Venetian-red sixteenth-century **zámek Říčanskych**, both now part of the local **museum** (May–Oct Tues–Sun 9am–noon & 1–5pm; Nov–April Tues–Fri 9am–noon & 1–4pm). The nearby church of sv Bartoloměje has a splendid, sixty-one-metre **belfry** (May–Sept Mon–Fri 9am–noon & 12.30–5pm, Sat & Sun 10am–noon & 12.30–5pm), which you can climb for a bird's-eye panorama of the náměstí and surrounding streets. On the main square itself, just opposite the museum, it's surprisingly easy to miss a minor work of Cubist architecture by Pavel Janák, who in 1913 adapted the Baroque **Fárův dům** at no. 13 into a slightly bizarre combination of pale pink Baroque and Cubism. You can get a good feel for the angled interior by stopping for a drink at the *Vinárna U brány* upstairs. If you're on the Cubist trail, head through the chateau's archway and a short distance north up Na Hradišti and Strachovská to check out Janák's **Drechselův dům** at no. 331, right by the town brewery. The maroon and mustard colour scheme looks snazzy, especially on the stripey columns of the garden canopy, but it's not on the quietest of roads.

On the second weekend of June the rather unlikely spectacle of Pelhřimov's **Festival of Records and Curious Performances** takes place, during which Czech eccentrics attempt to enter the *Guinness Book of World Records* by whatever means necessary: recent new records include a church built with 50,000 matches, 157 people on one tractor, and a man with 82 socks on one foot, while "Železný Zekon" ("Iron Zekon") allowed seven cars to roll over him whilst lying on a bed of 970 nails. A museum cataloguing these great feats, the **Muzeum rekordů a kuriozit** (April–Sept daily 9am–5pm; Oct–March Mon–Fri 1–4.30pm; ⓦ www.dobryden.cz) is in the Dolní (Jihlavská) brána, to the east of the main square. Inside, you can see the world's longest paper chain, the longest shawl (just over 158km long) and a bicycle made entirely of wood.

There's also photographic evidence of one-off achievements, and various rather tedious displays of strength.

The **train** station is, unfortunately, a good 2km south of the town centre, and the **bus** station is about halfway along the road into town. Pelhřimov still brews its own **beer**, which you can sup to your heart's content at *U Vlasáků*, right next to the brewery, beyond the chateau; they also do passable Czech **food**, though the atmosphere is decidedly grungy. In addition to housing a simple and cheap restaurant, the Secessionist-era *Hotel Slávie* (T565 321 540, Wwww.hotelslavie. web.tiscali.cz; ❷), at no. 29 on the main square, is also one of the nicest **places to stay**. Another option is the unlovely Communist-era *Rekrea* (T565 350 111; ❷), a five-minute walk east of the historical centre, though its rooms are fine, with en-suite facilities and TVs. The *Penzion Lucerna* (T565 333 333, Wwww. penzionlucerna.cz; ❷), just behind the chateau has an arcaded patio and offers decent, clean, if somewhat unatmospheric, rooms. There's also a restaurant serving Czech food.

Kaliště

Devotees of composer Gustav Mahler might want to make a detour to his birthplace in **KALIŠTĚ**, a tiny village 24km northeast of Pelhřimov and 10km northwest of Humpolec. Several years of fundraising have finally resulted in the renovation of the building in which the great symphonist was born, in an apartment above the former town pub. The pub is now operating again (although the thoroughly modern decor lends little character), and there are plans to open the pension upstairs. If you want to make the trip, you can catch the rare bus from Humpolec, 16km northeast of Pelhřimov and linked to it by regular buses, and look for the white house opposite the church with "Mahler" painted across one side. While you're in **Humpolec**, you might want to visit the **Muzeum Dr Alše Hrdličký** (April–Oct Tues & Thurs 9–11am & 1–4pm, Wed 9–11am & 1–5pm, Fri 8–11am & 1–4pm, Sat 9–11am & 2–4pm, Sun 9–11am), which has permanent anthropological and ethnographic collections and a room full of photos and newspaper clippings of Mahler, with extensive captions in Czech only.

Lipnice nad Sázavou

Around 20km northeast of Pelhřimov, just beyond Humpolec and the Prague–Brno motorway, in the midst of some glorious Bohemian countryside, is the village of **LIPNICE NAD SÁZAVOU**. Here, Bohemia's ultimate bohemian, the writer **Jaroslav Hašek**, died on January 3, 1923, his most famous work still unfinished. The village has changed little over the intervening years; the pub he lived and drank in is still going strong, and the **hrad** (April & Sept–Oct Sat & Sun 10am–4pm; May–June Tues–Sun 10am–4pm; July–Aug Tues–Sun 9am–6pm) ruined even in Hašek's day, is still partly rubble. A flattering bust of the author has been erected on the way up to the castle, and his gravestone is a little less ignominious these days (see box opposite). Beside the castle, in the house where he died, the **Memorial to Jaroslav Hašek** (June–Sept Tues–Sun 9am–noon & 1–4pm; guided tours in Czech only) is respectfully vague about the many contradictions in Hašek's life, not least the alcoholism which eventually cost him his life. The pub is now run by his grandson, as is the *Penzion U České koruny*, where the writer also had an apartment, (T569 486 126, Wwww. hasektour.cz; rooms ❷, Hašek's apartment ❸). If you want to pay homage to Hašek at Lipnice, roughly six buses a day (weekdays only) make the fourteen-kilometre trip from Havlíčkův Brod.

> **Jaroslav Hašek**
>
> Stories about Hašek's life – many propagated by the author himself – have always been a mixture of fact and fiction, but at one time or another he was an anarchist, dog-breeder, lab assistant, bigamist, cabaret artist and people's commissar in the Red Army. He alternately shocked and delighted both close friends and the public at large with his drunken antics and occasional acts of political extremism. When, towards the end of his life, he made his home in the *Česká koruna* pub in Lipnice, he wrote happily, "Now I live bang in the middle of a *pivnice*. Nothing better could have happened to me." Few friends attended his funeral, and none of his family, with the exception of his eleven-year-old son, who had met his father only two or three times. In a final act of contempt, the local priest would only allow his body to be buried alongside the cemetery wall, among the unbaptized and suicide victims. Before long, however, the protagonist in Hašek's *The Good Soldier Švejk* had become the most famous (fictional) Czech of all time, culminating in Hašek's "canonization" by the Communist regime – his works even being published by the military publishing house.

Třeboňsko

The **Třeboňsko** region, with the picturesque town of **Třeboň** at its heart, is unlike the rest of South Bohemia – characterized not by rolling hills but by peat bogs, flatlands and fish ponds. This monotonous marshland, broken only by the occasional Gothic fortress, was moulded into an intricate system of canal-linked **ponds** (totalling over 6000) as early as the fifteenth century, ushering in profitable times for the nobles who owned the land. The fish industry still dominates the region, and around September the ponds are drained to allow the fish to be "harvested". Larger ponds, like the Rožmberk, are drained only every other year, and for several days people from the surrounding district gather to feast, sing and participate in a great local event that's worth seeking out if you're in the vicinity. Wildlife also thrives on the soggy plains – as do mosquitoes in the summer – and in 1977 UNESCO declared a large area, from Soběslav south as far as the Austrian border, a **nature reserve**.

Jindřichův Hradec

JINDŘICHŮV HRADEC (Neuhaus) is the largest of the towns set amongst Třeboňsko's fish ponds. Hemmed in by walls and water, it's typical of the region – blessed with a glorious medieval past and, structurally at least, untouched by modern conflicts. Although the staré město was robbed of much of its rich medieval dressing by a fire in 1801, the main square, **náměstí Míru**, still displays an attractive array of wealthy merchants' houses, sporting brightly coloured early-nineteenth-century facades, and an exceptionally fine Baroque Trinity column. Only one house, the **Langrův dům** from 1579, hints at the Renaissance riches that were once the norm here. The diamond vaulting in the arcaded ground floor, and the sgraffito biblical scenes that cover the facade bear closer inspection, especially the depiction of Jonah being swallowed by what looks like a giant crocodile, on the side of the oriel window.

Rybniční leads down from the main square to a bridge that bisects the Vajgar fish pond, creating a small harbour. From here, the town's thirteenth-century **zámek** (Tues–Sun: April & Oct 10am–noon & 1–4pm; May & Sept 10am–

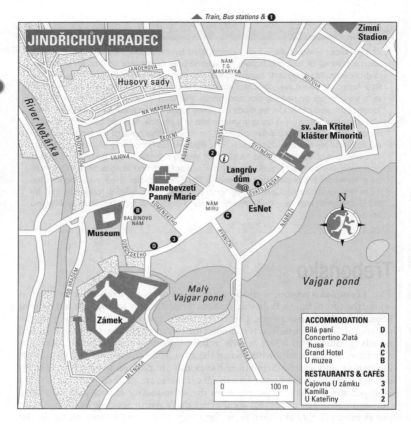

noon & 1–5pm; June–Aug 9am–5pm) – chief residence of the lords of Hradec, and later the Černíns – is picturesquely mirrored in the water, its forbidding exterior giving no hint of the exuberant interior renovations by Italian architects in the sixteenth century, which make a visit here an absolute must.

To get to the chateau's main entrance, head down Dobrovského. You currently have a choice of three different forty-five-minute **guided tours** (in English – occasionally only – 140Kč each; 360Kč for all three), which set off from the second courtyard. *Trasa A* (the *Adamovo stavení*) leads you through the Neoclassical and Baroque "Green Rooms", and past Petr Brandel's painting of St Joseph curing the lepers; *trasa B* (May Sat & Sun 10am–4pm; June–Sept Tues–Sun 10am–5pm), the *Gotický hrad*, explores the Gothic interiors, and features the starkly beautiful thirteenth-century chapel, fourteenth-century frescoes and the black kitchen; *trasa C* (July & Aug Tues–Sun 9am–5pm), the *Procházka staletími*, takes you round the slender, triple-tiered, Renaissance loggia (which you can view without a guide) and the Černíns' bizarre collection of dog portraits, as well as gaining you entrance to the chateau's pride and joy, the striking bubble-gum pink garden rotunda, known as the Rondel, with its incredible gilded stuccowork. The Spanish Wing, which was designed as a Communist conference centre, complete with lift and cinema, is under lengthy restoration. The chateau's Černá věž (Black Tower), accessible from the second courtyard, is open to the public without a guided tour (May Sat & Sun 9am–3pm; June–Sept Tues–Sun 9am–3pm, depending on the weather), and you can peek through the windows into the Rondel anytime.

With most tour groups visiting only the chateau, there's hardly anyone exploring the cobbled alleyways northwest of the main square at the top of Komenského. You can climb the tall **tower** (April–June & Sept–Dec Sat & Sun 10am–noon & 1–4pm; July–Aug daily 10am–noon & 1–4pm) of the Gothic church of Nanebevzetí Panny Marie, which is situated exactly on the fifteenth meridian east of Greenwich, and pay a visit to the former Jesuit seminary on Balbínovo náměstí, founded by Adam II of Hradec and Catherine de Montfort in 1604, and now home to the local **museum** (April–Dec Tues–Sun 8.30am–noon & 12.30–5pm; June–Sept daily same hours). Its chief exhibit is a 3-D Bethlehem Nativity scene – the world's largest – created over the course of sixty years by Tomáš Krýza (1838–1918), with fully mechanized figures. Other highlights include a seventeenth-century pharmacy and the reconstructed parlour of opera singer Ema Destinnová, who lived nearby in Stráž nad Nežárkou (see box, p.204).

Practicalities

To get to the staré město from the **bus and train stations** to the north, it's a fifteen-minute walk along Nádražní, then left down Klášterská. This brings you to the edge of the old town, where the walls have long since been replaced by a park, the Husovy sady; the old town lies beyond. A less fatiguing option is catching a bus #1 or #4 which drops you just on the main square. There's a **tourist office** on Panská (Mon–Fri 8am–5pm, Sat 8am–noon; ☎384 363 546, ⓦwww .jh.cz), just off the main square, who should be able to help with accommodation and to give information about the state-owned **narrow-gauge railway** (*úzkorozchodná železnice*) run by JHMD (ⓦwww.jhmd.cz), that winds its way north to Obrataň, and south to Nová Bystřice, with occasional steam trains on both the branch lines.

On the main square, the best of the **hotels** are the *Concertino Zlatá husa* (☎384 362 320, ⓦwww.concertino.cz; ④) and the *Grand Hotel* (☎384 361 252,

The White Lady

If you're in the castle in Jindřichův Hradec and you hear a clinking of keys or a door unexpectedly slamming, or notice a figure in white floating about in the evening, it could be the *Bílá paní* or **White Lady**, the most famous ghost in the Czech Republic, whose favourite haunt is the castle. According to legend, she is the spirit of Perchta Rožmberková, born in 1430, who fell in love with the young Count Šternberk but was married against her wishes to Count Liechtenstein of Styria. On her wedding night, she secretly met Šternberk to bid him farewell, but was caught *in flagrante* by her husband, who thenceforth mistreated his wife. Many years later, Perchta returned to Jindřichův Hradec as a widow and used to hand out porridge, warm beer and honey to the poor. Since her husband never pardoned her, she was condemned to roam the castle as a ghost, though a benevolent one, prophesying births and deaths in the Rožmberk family by wearing white gloves for the former and black for the latter, and pointing out hidden treasure in the various family properties throughout Bohemia. Evenings in August are her favourite spooking time, when she is regularly spotted handing out porridge along the approach to the castle, outside the restaurant that bears her name.

Ema Destinnová

Halfway between Jindřichův Hradec and Třeboň lies the town of Stráž nad Nežárkou, whose chateau was once the estate of Czech diva **Ema Destinnová** (1878–1930) – her initials "ED" are emblazoned on the gates – one of the world's premier sopranos of the early twentieth century. Born Ema Kittlová, she took her stage name as a tribute to her first singing teacher. She won huge critical acclaim in Berlin at the age of just nineteen as Santuzza in *Cavalleria rusticana*. As Donna Anna in Mozart's *Don Giovanni* at Covent Garden, she sang so well that they had her back for every performance of it for the next ten years. She sang opposite Enrico Caruso in the London premiere of *Madame Butterfly*, was chosen by Richard Strauss for the Berlin premiere of *Salome*, and enjoyed eight seasons as the *prima donna* at New York's Metropolitan Opera. However, she also had strong ties to the Czech independence movement, and in 1916, during the height of World War I, she decided to return to Stráž for a visit, where she was arrested for smuggling revolutionary plans over the border. She was sentenced to confinement at her estate – though given that the penalty for espionage was, in fact, death without trial, Destinnová got off relatively lightly. When the war ended, Destinnová threw herself into promoting Czech opera and went on a European tour with an exclusively Czech repertoire. Her great days as a diva were over, however, and she spent her last twelve years writing plays, novels and poetry and living off the fish she caught from the Nežárka river. After her death from a stroke at the age of 52, Destinnová was given a lavish burial at Prague's Vyšehrad cemetery, and in 1996, the Czech treasury placed Ema Destinnová on its new 2000Kč note. Her chateau, however, is closed to the public.

Ⓦ www.grand-jh.cz; ❸), which has a sauna on site. Much better value, though, is the *Bílá paní* (☎ 384 363 329, Ⓦ www.hotelbilapani.cz; ❸), in a lovely old house right by the chateau at Dobrovského 5, with a stylish restaurant on the ground floor, and real character to the rooms. Another option is *U muzea* (☎ 384 361 698, Ⓦ www.umuzea.jhweb.cz; ❷), a pension in an apricot-coloured building directly opposite the museum; its restaurant has a summer terrace.

The **restaurant** in the *Bílá paní* is a reasonable place for typical Czech dishes, and *U Kateřiny*, roughly opposite the tourist office on Panská, is very popular with the locals. There's a pleasant *Čajovna U zámku* (tea house; closed Mon) near *Bílá paní*, and an **Internet café** *EsNet* in the Langrův dům on the square. The *Kamilla*, on Pražská, ten minutes' walk north of the main square along Panská and Klášterská, is a lively **pub** with Regent on tap.

Červená Lhota

In the middle of nowhere, off the main road between Jindřichův Hradec and Soběslav, the red sugar-lump castle of **Červená Lhota** (April & Oct Sat & Sun 9am–4pm; May & Sept Tues–Sun 9am–4pm; June–Aug 9.30am–5.15pm; tour in English 120Kč; Ⓦ www.cervenalhota.com) is reflected perfectly in the still waters that surround it. This breathtaking sight – a Gothic waterfort converted into a Renaissance retreat for the rich in 1551 – appears on almost every regional tourist handout, but its isolated location makes it a nightmare to reach on public transport. Given this, and the unremarkable nature of the chateau's interior, it's really only for dedicated fans of Karl Ditters von Dittersdorf, Mozart's composing chum who died here in 1799. That said, the lakeside grounds around the chateau are perfect for a picnic, and in high season there are boats for hire, and a horse and carriage available in which to take a turn. You can also stay in the **rooms** at *U zámku Červená Lhota* (☎ 384 384 305; ❷), in some of the chateau's outbuildings.

Třeboň

Right in the midst of some of the region's largest fish ponds, the spa town of TŘEBOŇ (Wittingau) is as medieval and minute as they come. The houses lining the long, thin main square, Masarykovo náměstí, make an attractive parade, but the *Bílý koníček* (*White Horse*) – now a hotel – built in 1544, steals the show with a stepped gable of miniature turrets. The entire **staré město** is made up of just three more streets, a fourteenth-century monastery and a chateau. Three gateways (including the impressive double south gate, next to the local brewery) and the entire ring of walls have survived from the sixteenth century, though many houses suffered badly during the last great fire in 1781. For a bird's-eye view of the square climb the town hall's white **tower** from 1566 (in summer daily 9.30am–4.30pm) opposite the *Bílý koníček*.

Out of all proportion to the rest of the town is the huge Renaissance **zámek** (April–Oct Tues–Sun 9am–noon & 1–4pm; June–Aug closes 5.15pm; out of season call ☏ 384 721 193), built by Petr Vok, a colourful character, notoriously fond of sex, drugs and alchemy, friend of the mad Emperor Rudolf II, legend-ary thrower of parties, and the last heir of the Rožmberk family. The chateau, daubed in blinding white sgraffito and taking up almost a fifth of the town, is a pretty clumsy affair, but the interior is definitely worth visiting. There's a choice of three guided tours: *trasa A* is the one to go for as it concentrates on Petr Vok and the chateau's Renaissance legacy; the Baroque and nineteenth-century period furniture imported by the later owners, the Schwarzenbergs, forms the bedrock of *trasa B*, while *trasa C* focuses on the stables, dungeons and the unusual dogs' kitchen. Adjacent to the chateau and equal in size to the old town is a very pleasant "English park", where the town's spa patients can take a stroll (daily dawn–dusk). Here you'll find the entrance to the castle's new exhibition Třeboňsko – krajina a lidé (Třeboňsko – Man and the Landscape; April–Oct Tues–Sun 9am–noon & 1–5pm), featuring well-designed displays and video presentations on the region's history and nature.

South of the town is the Svět pond, beside which stands the local **fishery** on Novohradská, which handles the region's huge fish harvest and, most importantly, its *kapr* (carp) culling. **Carp**, not turkey, is the centrepiece of the Christmas meal in the Czech Lands, traditionally sold live and wriggling from town squares across the country, then transferred to the family bathtub until the big day.

The Schwarzenberg mausoleum

Head south out of Třeboň in the direction of Borovany along the lake, and you'll pick up signs to the **Schwarzenberg mausoleum** (Schwarzenberská hrobka; April–May & Sept–Oct Tues–Sun 9am–4pm; June–Aug Tues–Sun 9am–5pm), twenty minutes' walk from the town centre. Hidden among the silver birch trees south of the Svět pond, it's a rather subdued, out-of-the-way site for a family so fond of ostentatious displays of wealth. The building itself is equally strange: a seemingly brand-new neo-Gothic building, with a bare chapel above and a dark crypt below (guided tours only). Třeboň was the first Bohemi-an town to be bought up by the Bavarian-based Schwarzenberg family in 1660 who, having sided with the Habsburgs in the Counter-Reformation, became the unofficial heirs of ousted or defunct Czech aristocrats like the Vítkovci and Rožmberks. By 1875, the family owned more estates in Bohemia than anyone else and decided to "honour" Třeboň by establishing the family mausoleum in the town. After 1945, the family's possessions were expropriated and, along with all their fellow German-speakers, they were thrown out of the country.

Today, the most famous descendant is probably Count Karl von Schwarzenberg, a former emigré and one of the republic's leading businessmen.

Practicalities

The local **tourist office** (Mon–Fri 9am–4pm; ☏ 384 721 169, ⓦ www.trebon-mesto.cz, ⓦ www.regiontrebonsko.cz), on the main square in the old town, can book **private rooms**. There are also two **hotels** on the main square: the aforementioned *Bílý koníček* (☏ 384 721 213, ⓦ www.hotelbilykonicek.cz; ❸) is, in fact, not as pretty inside, but offers quite cheap en-suite rooms; the *Zlatá hvězda* (☏ 384 757 111, ⓦ www.zhvezda.cz; ❹), on the opposite side, has much more comfortable rooms with TV for roughly twice the price. Another option is *U míšků* (☏ 384 721 698, ⓦ www.misek.cz; ❹), a pension and café-gallery, with a tiny indoor pool, in a prettily gabled building just north of the main square at Husova 11. For **camping** (and swimming), head for the *Třeboňský ráj* campsite, which also has bungalows (ⓦ www.auto-camp-trebon.cz; May–Sept), situated south of the fish pond, near the mausoleum.

For a taste of the local beer, there's no better place to go than the Regent brewery's own **pub**, to the south of the main square, a simple *pivnice* just on the right inside the brewery archway. The very popular local fish **restaurant** *Supina Supinka*, lies opposite, in the twin buildings; if it's full, try the *Malá bašta*, on the main square, which offers plenty of similar dishes. If you're camping and cooking your own food, the *rybárna* (fishmonger) has fresh produce, right by the carp pools, to the south of town. For **Internet** (available daily from 6pm), head for *Torpedo Club* in the passageway that leads from the main square, through the chateau to the park.

Třeboň's main **train station** is 2km north of the old town, off the road to Tábor; Třeboň lázně station is only ten minutes' walk east of the old town. A couple of express trains stop at the latter station en route to Vienna, via Gmünd. However, there are no direct trains to or from České Budějovice or Jindřichův Hradec; for transport connections with them, you're best off heading for the **bus station**, a ten-minute walk northwest of the old town, along Jiráskova.

České Budějovice and around

The flat, urban sprawl of **ČESKÉ BUDĚJOVICE** (Budweis) comes as something of a surprise after the small-town mentality of the rest of South Bohemia. But first impressions are deceptive, for at its heart it's a laid-back city, no more cosmopolitan than anywhere else in the region, with a perfectly preserved staré město that attracts a good number of Bavarian and Austrian tourists. Founded by King Otakar II in 1265 as a German merchants' colony, the town's wealth was based on medieval silver mines and its position on the old salt route from Linz to Prague. All this was wiped out in the seventeenth century by the twin ravages of war and fire. But, perhaps because it remained a loyal Catholic town in a hotbed of Hussitism, the Habsburgs lavishly reconstructed most of České Budějovice in the eighteenth century. Miraculously, in the face of two centuries of rapid industrial growth, the city's staré město has been carefully preserved. Besides, its renown nowadays is due to its local brew Budvar, better known abroad under its original German name, Budweiser (see box p.209).

Arrival, information and accommodation

The train station has a **left-luggage** office (*úschovna zavazadel*) and lockers. Ten minutes' walk from the **train and bus stations** down Lannova třída will bring you to Na sadech, the busy ring road flanked by small parks that encloses the staré město in place of the greater part of the old town walls.

The **tourist office** in the town hall on the main square (May–Sept Mon–Fri 8.30am–6pm, Sat 8.30am–5pm, Sun 10am–noon & 12.30–4pm; Oct–April Mon–Fri 9am–4pm, Sat 9am–noon & 1–3pm; ☎386 801 413, ⓦwww .c-budejovice.cz) can help book accommodation. Its other branch (Mon–Fri 9am–4pm, Sat 9am–noon & 12.30–3pm) is situated at the train station. České Budějovice's popularity with neighbouring Austrians and Germans means that **hotels and pensions** tend to charge over the odds. From July to September rooms are available in **student halls** (*Koleje VŠ*), located west of the Vltava at Studentská 15 (☎387 774 201; ❷); take bus #1 or #3 from Na Sadech. An even cheaper option is the *Ubytovna Stavounion* (it's better to book in the tourist office; ☎387 240 758; ❶), a bunkhouse at Novohradská 3, southeast of the centre (bus #11 from the train station), offering clean, simple rooms with shared facilities and a lunchtime eatery. Another guaranteed cheap sleep is to **camp** or rent a **bungalow** at the *Dlouhá louka* site (☎387 210 601; open all year), southwest of the centre on Litvínovská silnice; (bus #16; stops running around 7pm) from Lidická třída near the Jihočeské muzeum. The *Stromovka* site (☎387 203 597; April–Oct), just opposite *Dlouhá louka*, is even cheaper and also has bungalows. The best **Internet café** in town is *Na půdě*, at Krajinská 28 (ⓦwww.napude.cz).

Hotels

Bohemia Hradební 20 ☎386 354 500, ⓦwww .hotel-bohemia-cb.cz. A comfortably modernized hotel on the northern edge of the old town, with its own little courtyard and vaulted cellar restaurant. ❹

Grand Hotel Zvon náměstí Přemysla Otakara II 28 ☎387 311 383, ⓦwww.hotel-zvon.cz. Luxurious hotel, occupying one of the former burgher palaces right on the spectacular main square, and a great best place to head for if you're feeling flush or are on business expenses. ❸

Klika Hroznová 25 ☎387 318 171, ⓦwww .hotelklika.cz. Modern, tastefully furnished rooms in a hotel-restaurant, nicely situated by an arm of the Malše, on the western edge of the old town. The restaurant has a summer terrace and a winter garden, both overlooking the river. ❹

Malý pivovar Karla IV 8–10 ☎386 360 471, ⓦwww.budva r.cz. Slick, Budvar-run hotel, located in an arcaded burgher house just off the main square, with tasteful modern en-suite rooms. ❻

U solné brány Radniční 11 ☎386 354 121, ⓦwww.hotelusolnebrany.cz. Small hotel tucked into the old town walls, with pleasant, relaxed service and tasteful, plain rooms with satellite TV. ❹

The Town

České Budějovice's medieval grid plan leads inevitably to the town's showpiece, the magnificent **náměstí Přemysla Otakara II**, one of Europe's largest squares. The buildings are supremely elegant, testifying to the last three centuries of German burgher power (it wasn't until the 1890s that the first Czech was able to buy one of the houses here), but it's the square's arcades, its magnificent Baroque radnice, whose clock tinkles out tunes, and the octagonal **Samson's Fountain** – once the only tap in town – that make the greatest impression. It was German merchants, too, who paid in silver and salt for the seventy-two-metre status symbol, the **černá věž** (Black Tower), one of the few survivors of the 1641 fire, which leans gently to one side of the square; its roof gallery (April–June, Sept & Oct Tues–Sun 10am–6pm; July & Aug Mon–Sat 10am–6pm) provides a superb view of the staré město. Next to the tower is the

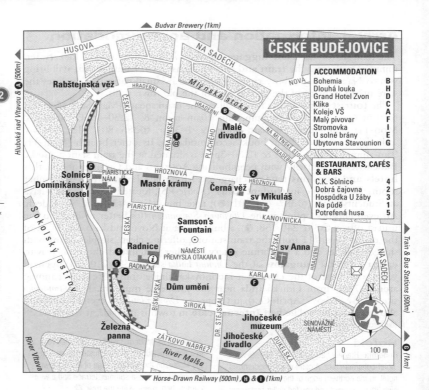

▲ Budvar Brewery (1km)

ČESKÉ BUDĚJOVICE

ACCOMMODATION
Bohemia	B
Dlouhá louka	H
Grand Hotel Zvon	D
Klika	C
Koleje VŠ	A
Malý pivovar	F
Stromovka	I
U solné brány	E
Ubytovna Stavounion	G

RESTAURANTS, CAFÉS & BARS
C.K. Solnice	4
Dobrá čajovna	2
Hospůdka U žáby	3
Na půdě	1
Potrefená husa	5

◀ Hluboká nad Vltavou & Ⓐ (500m)

Train & Bus Stations (500m) ▶

Ⓖ (1km) ▶

▼ Horse-Drawn Railway (500m), Ⓗ & Ⓘ (1km)

cathedral of **sv Mikuláš**, a church of Gothic proportions heavily overlaid with eighteenth-century plasterwork and furnishings, including a spectacular white marble pulpit with gold trimmings and cherubs.

The streets immediately off the square – Krajinská, Česká and Kněžská – are worth wandering down, and if the weather's fine, folk promenade by the banks of the Malše, where parts of the original town walls have survived along with some of České Budějovice's oldest buildings, such as the fifteenth-century prison tower, named after its most infamous torture instrument, **Železná panna** (literally "Iron Maiden"). All that is left of the bishop's palace is his serene **garden**, occasionally accessible in summer through a small gateway in the walls a little further on. At the second bridge, a right turn down Hroznová will lead you round into Piaristické náměstí, where the rough-looking, thoroughly medieval **solnice** (salt store) stands, its stepped gables proof of its former importance; later it was used as the town's arsenal and the building now houses a **Motocyklové muzeum** (Motorcycle Museum; Tues–Sun 10am–1.30pm & 2–6pm). Incidentally, the nearby church is worth a peek as it retains some of its Gothic cloisters, and patches of medieval fresco, too.

An interest in all the usual thrills of a regional museum (stuffed birds, mushrooms, armoury, coins, etc) will be needed for a visit to the grandiose **Jihočeské muzeum** (Tues–Sun 9am–12.30pm & 1–5.30pm; ☎387 929 311, ⓦwww .muzeumcb.cz), southeast of the old town on Dukelská, although it occasionally puts on an interesting exhibition. Further south, on Mánesova 10, beyond

Budvar v Budweiser

As far as taste goes, Czech **Budvar** bears little resemblance to the bland American Budweiser or Bud as it's universally known – it wins hands-down. However, the fact that two of the world's beers are sold under the same name has caused over a century of problems.

The story begins in 1857 when a German brewer named Adolphus Busch moved to the US. German beer names sold well in the States, so in 1876, Busch adopted the name Budweiser. At that time, the only beer brewed in what is now České Budějovice (but at the time was better known as Budweis) was Samson – another excellent brand which is still brewed today. It was only in 1882, that local Czech brewers registered the name Budweiser for one of their beers. As early as 1911, the Czechs and the American brewers, now known as **Anheuser-Busch**, came to an agreement, allowing the Czechs to call their beer Original Budweiser; in return, the Americans could market their Budweiser anywhere in the world, except Europe. The Czech brewery registered its trademark in the US in 1937, but two years later, under Nazi occupation, the brewery agreed to limit the use of its name outside Czechoslovakia in return for some small financial return.

After the war, the issue was forgotten behind the Iron Curtain. Then in the 1990s, the two breweries came together for talks once more, with the scales tipped even more heavily in Anheuser-Busch's favour. Not only were the American brewers now the largest brewing company in the world, the Czechs were desperate for cash to try and modernize their operation. A takeover seemed the most obvious solution. However, thanks to Britain's Campaign for Real Ale (CAMRA), worried that Czech Budvar would not be safe in Anheuser-Busch's hands, the issue became widely publicized. For the moment České Budějovice's Budvar brewery is safely protected, as it remains the only one in the country still to be state-owned, and as of 2000, the beer was finally available in the US under the name Czechvar. However, litigious skirmishes in over fifty countries look set to continue well into the future.

the pencil factory, there's a meagre museum dedicated to the **Horse-Drawn Train Station** (Nádraží koněspřežská; May–Sept Tues–Sun 9am–12.30pm & 1–5pm), which tells the history of continental Europe's first horse-drawn railway link, constructed between Linz and České Budějovice in 1827. With only a few photos and maps to accompany the video presentation, it's really only for aficionados. En route to the museum, you pass a vacant lot where the city's main **synagogue** stood until it was destroyed by the Nazis in July 1942, a few months after the city's 909 Jews had been deported to Terezín – thirty returned after the war.

The **Budvar brewery** is 2.5km up the road to Prague, on Karolíny Světlé, and has a modern *pivnice* (daily 10am–10pm) inside the nasty titanium-blue headquarters; despite appearances, the beer and food are both inexpensive. Those who wish to make a pilgrimage should join up with one of the guided tours (daily 8am–5pm by prior arrangement; ☎387 705 341, ⓦwww.budweiser .cz; ask for the *anglický tekst*; 100Kč). To reach the brewery, take bus #2 from the old town or a slow-stopping train to Tábor, and get off at the first stop (České Budějovice severní zastávka).

Eating, drinking and entertainment

Drinking is obviously an important activity in České Budějovice. As the famous *Masné krámy* are under lengthy restoration, the most atmospheric place to quaff Budvar is at *Malý pivovar*, run by the brewery itself. Typical Czech pub food is served in the cheap *Hospůdka U žáby* (closed Sun), opposite the Motorcycle Museum, but tourists seem to prefer the *Potrefená husa*, at Česká 66, behind the town hall, which has a big terrace on the roof, overlooking the river.

For chilling out, there's no better place than the *Dobrá čajovna*, on Hroznová 16, right behind the Černá věž, a typically relaxing branch of the teashop chain. The city's largest **theatre**, the Jihočeské divadlo (ⓦwww.jihoceskedivadlo.cz), mostly puts on plays, so for non-Czech speakers your best bet is to go and listen to the local **chamber orchestra** at the Koncertní síň Otakara Jeremiáše (ⓣ386 353 561), next to the church of sv Anna on Kněžská. More raucous **nightlife** is still thin on the ground, though *C.K. Solnice*, on Česká, has occasional live jazz and rock, enlivening its rather rough interior.

Across the Českobudějovická pánev

To the northwest of České Budějovice lies the flat basin of soggy land known as the **Českobudějovická pánev**. Most people head for **Hluboká**, whose chateau receives over a quarter of a million tourists each year. Its neo-Gothic pastiche is not to everyone's taste – in many ways you'd be better off seeking out the more elusive gems of **Holašovice's** folk-Baroque architecture or **Kratochvíle's** simple Renaissance beauty.

Hluboká nad Vltavou
HLUBOKÁ NAD VLTAVOU (Frauenberg), 8km northwest of České Budějovice, is a modest little village which sits below possibly the republic's most famous **zámek** (April, Sept & Oct Tues–Sun 9am–5.30pm; May & June Tues–Sun 9am–6pm; July & Aug daily 9am–6pm, last tour group enters 90min before closing; compulsory guided tours 160Kč). Originally founded as a Přemyslid stronghold as early as the thirteenth century, the royal family sold the property to the Lords of Hradec in 1562, only to confiscate it in 1622 after the Hradec clan backed the Protestant side in the Thirty Years' War. Eventually, it was given to the arriviste Schwarzenberg family, who, during the course of the nineteenth century, made Hluboká their chief seat, and spent some of their considerable fortune turning it into its present crenellated, mock-Gothic incarnation. In 1945, when all the German estates were nationalized, the Schwarzenbergs decamped with most of the loot, but they've since returned and filled the interior with the odds and ends they left behind at their numerous other castles. The results are impressive, both inside and out, and pull in a quarter of a million visitors every year, with regular guided tours in English during high season.

If Hluboká's reproduction interiors fail to move you, it's possible to seek sanctuary in the former riding school, which now houses the **Alšova jihočeské galerie** (daily: May–Sept 9–11.30am & 12.30–6pm; Oct–April 9–11.30am & 12.30–4pm), a permanent collection of Gothic religious art, Dutch and Flemish sixteenth- to eighteenth-century masters and a large hall filled with a superb collection of twentieth-century Czech art, including Art Nouveau works by Bílek and Jan Preisler, a smattering of Cubist canvases by Čapek, Kubišta and Filla, a good selection of Surrealist paintings by the likes of Toyen and Štyrský, through to 1960s Pop Art. Alternatively, you can head off into the chateau's very beautiful English-style grounds, where South Bohemia's wild boars are reputed to roam.

There are plenty of **places to stay** in Hluboká, but prices are no cheaper than in České Budějovice; ask at the **tourist office** (ⓣ387 966 164, ⓦwww .hluboka.cz) opposite the church in the village, about private rooms. Alternatively, hotel *Apartment Hluboká* (ⓣ387 967 777, ⓦwww.kamille.cz; ➍), at

Masarykova 972, has ten modern apartments (each with kitchen and two bedrooms), while in the nearby *Bakalář* (☎387 965 516, ⓦwww.hotelbakalar .cz; ❸) you can rent bicycles. There's also the lakeside *Křivonoska* **campsite** (late May to Sept), 3km to the northwest up route 105. Regular **buses** run from České Budějovice, dropping passengers off in the main square. If you're arriving by **train**, two out-of-the-way stations (nominally) serve the village: Hluboká nad Vltavou station, 3km to the southwest on the Plzeň line; and Hluboká nad Vltavou-Zámostí station, 2km to the east on the main line to Prague. There's also a **cycling path** from České Budějovice to Hluboká along the Vltava; ask the tourist office for a leaflet.

Holašovice

If you have the time (and preferably your own car or bike), it's worth making a quick detour to the UNESCO-protected village of **HOLAŠOVICE**, 15km west of České Budějovice off the road to Lhenice, where you can see some of the finest examples of **Baroque folk architecture** unique to this part of Bohemia. The stone farmhouses (including the two pubs *U Vojty* and *Jihočeská hospoda*) date from the first six decades of the nineteenth century, and face onto the original green. Every house on the square follows the same basic design, though the decorative details on barn doors and gables are unique to each. There are other nearby villages displaying similar architectural treats – like Záboří, 2km north, and Dobčice, another 2km west – but none can compete with the consummate effect of Holašovice. Ask about private **rooms** at the **tourist centre** (open in season only Tues–Sun 9am–5pm), at the corner of the square.

Kratochvíle

Further west along route 145, and 2km beyond Netolice, lies **Kratochvíle** (Kurzweil), without doubt the most charming Renaissance chateau in Bohemia. It stands unaltered since its rapid six-year construction by Italian architects between 1583 and 1589, commissioned by the last generation of Rožmberks to while away the time – the literal meaning of *kratochvíle*. The attention to detail is still clearly visible in the exquisite stuccowork and painted vaults, but the rest of the place is now given over to the **Museum of Animated Film** (April & Oct Sat & Sun 9am–noon & 1–4pm; May & Sept Tues–Sun 9am–noon & 1–4.15pm; June–Aug Tues–Sun 9am–noon & 1–5.15pm), which is aimed primarily at a young, domestic audience, with original puppet "actors" and drawings from well-known Czech kids' cartoons like *Boris* and *Mach a Šebestová*. However, the thoughtfully laid out exhibition, demonstrating all the painstaking processes involved in animation, should interest anyone, particularly with Josef Lada's amusing drawings of the Good Soldier Švejk and two typically disturbing new sculptures by Jan Švankmajer: a weird bird skeleton with butterfly wings and crab claws, and a human face formed of seashells. Kratochvíle is served by several daily **buses** plying the České Budějovice–Prachatice route, though as usual service is cut short at weekends.

The foothills of the Šumava

An alternative to heading up the Českobudějovická pánev is to aim for the large bulge of forest, known as the **Blanský les**, to the southwest of České Budějovice. Its highest point is **Mount Kleť** (1083m), which stands slightly apart from the rest of the Šumava range and looks all the more impressive for it, towering above the Vltava basin to the north. From the summit on a clear day, you can see the undulating forested peaks of the Šumava laid out before you. As well as the obligatory TV tower, the hill boasts the astronomical **Observatoř Kleť** (July & Aug Tues–Sun 10.30am–3.30pm; Oct–June Sat & Sun 10.30am–3.30pm; ☎380 711 242). To reach the top, either hop into one of the single-seat chairlifts (Wed–Sun 10am–5pm hourly) or opt for the stiff but enchanting four-kilometre hike through the woods. To reach the chairlift from České Budějovice or Český Krumlov, catch a train to the idyllic rural station at Holubov and walk the last 4km via Krasetín.

There's little **accommodation** in this neck of the woods, aside from a few private rooms and a basic **campsite** (May–Sept) in **ZLATÁ KORUNA** (Goldenkron), a tiny village on the Vltava, 6km along the line from Holubov. Here you can visit the strongly fortified **Cistercian monastery** (Tues–Sun: April, May, Sept & Oct 9am–noon & 1–4pm; June–Aug 8am–noon & 1–5pm; tour in English 170Kč), founded in 1263 by Přemysl King Otakar II. As a wealthy bastion of Catholicism, it suffered badly at the hands of the Hussites, but parts of the original medieval structures survive. In one building there's a worthy museum on Czech literature, but the main focus of interest is the vaulted chapterhouse dating from 1280 and the Gothic church, built in part by Peter Parler's masons and one of the first to employ ribbed vaulting without any accompanying capitals.

Český Krumlov

Squeezed into a tight S-bend of the Vltava, in the foothills of the Šumava, **ČESKÝ KRUMLOV** (Krumau) is undoubtedly one of the most exquisite towns in the Czech Republic. Rose-brown houses tumble down steep slopes to the blue-green river below, creating a magical effect whose beauty has barely changed in the last three hundred years. Under the Communists, few foreign visitors made it here, but nowadays the huge rise in tourism has made this the one place outside Prague where the warren of narrow streets can get uncomfortably crowded with day-trippers, including a steady parade of young backpackers. The whole town is a UNESCO-designated site, but with rich pickings now on offer, many of its residents are renovating their properties, causing great concern among conservationists, who foresee overdevelopment and insensitive restoration – not to mention the loss of character that occurs when virtually every building is turned over to pensions and restaurants. For all that, it's a place that never fails to impress.

Arrival, information and accommodation

The old town is divided into two separate quarters by the twisting snake of the River Vltava: the circular staré město on the right bank and the Latrán quarter on the hillier left bank. The best method of exploring Český Krumlov is on foot. The **train station** is twenty minutes' walk north of the old town up a precipitous set of steps, while the main **bus station** is closer to the heart of town, on the right bank. The main **tourist office**, on náměstí Svornosti (daily: April, May & Oct 9am–6pm; June & Sept 9am–7pm; July–Aug 9am–8pm; Nov–March 9am–5pm; ☎380 704 622, ⓦwww.ckrumlov.cz), has **Internet** access and helps with accommodation, as does the office UNIOS (daily 9am–noon & 1–6pm; ⓦwww.unios.cz), situated at the castle's entrance, which also provides information about the castle and sells bus tickets for Prague. It's also worth knowing about the town's useful laundry, *Lobo*, Latrán 73, which is open daily.

Accommodation

Accommodation is not in short supply, but there's an awful lot of people in town in high season. As well as the places listed below, there are also numerous small pensions and **private rooms** in town: Parkán is literally heaving with them, as is Rooseveltova. There's a huge number of lively **hostels**: the HI *Travellers Hostel* at Soukenická 43 (℡ 380 711 345, ⓦ www.travellers.cz; ❷) has bike rental, a barbecue and other amenities, and is very popular; a better bet is *Hostel Ryba* (℡ 380 711 801; ❷), which has a nice river terrace and pub attached. There's also a primitive **campsite** (June–Sept; ⓦ www.pavelec.cz), 2km south on route 160 to Nové Spolí, primarily aimed at summer canoeists (rental available). More and better campsites lie several kilometres further south along the road to Rožmberk nad Vltavou.

Barbakán Kaplická 26 ℡ 380 717 017, ⓦ www .barbakan.cz. A wonderfully refurbished pension with tastefully decorated rooms and a terraced dining area that overlooks the stone viaduct and old town. ❸

Dvořák Radniční 101 ℡ 380 711 020, ⓦ www .genea2000.cz. Smart, efficient hotel in an uncharacteristically grand late-nineteenth-century building right by the river, overlooking the castle tower and the crowded bridge connecting the staré město with Latrán. Sauna on site. ❼

Na louži Kájovská 66 ℡ 380 711 280, ⓦ www .nalouzi.cz. An excellent hotel, kitted out with antique furniture, and situated above a great pub near the Schiele Centrum. ❸

Růže Horní 154 ℡ 380 772 100, ⓦ www.hotelruze .cz. Originally built by the Rožmberks to house their guests, the Růže is right in the heart of the staré město, and is the hotel of choice, with pool, sauna, casino and the odd original Renaissance feature. ❾

U města Vídně Latrán 77 ℡ 380 720 113, ⓦ www.hmv.cz. Another recently opened upscale hotel, offering refurbished rooms in the sixteenth-century bakery at the edge of the old town. Facilities include Internet access and a relaxation centre. ❼

Ve věži Pivovarská 28 ℡ 380 711 742. Several bargain rooms hidden inside one of the town's medieval bastions, right by the Eggenberg brewery. ❸

Zlatý andel Nám. Svornosti 10 ℡ 380 712 310, ⓦ www.hotelzlatyandel.cz. Tall, thin hotel in one of the Renaissance houses on the old town square, with no lift, but pleasant stylish decor – ask for a room overlooking the square.

The Town

Český Krumlov's **history** is dominated by those great seigneurs of the region, the Rožmberks and the Schwarzenbergs. Thanks to special privileges won after the Battle of Leipzig in 1813, the Schwarzenbergs were permitted to keep a private army of twelve soldiers dressed in Napoleonic uniform (who also doubled as the castle's private orchestra), one of whom would sound the bugle at 9am every morning from the thirteenth-century round tower. In 1945, Krumau awoke abruptly from this semi-feudal coma when the Schwarzenbergs and the majority of the town's inhabitants, who were also German-speaking, were booted out; three years later, repopulated by Czech-speakers, the town went back into aspic as the Iron Curtain descended. Now the economy relies increasingly heavily on the ebb and flow of foreign tourists, a dependency that has thrown up the dubious delights of a waxworks and a torture museum, neither of which is worth visiting.

Krumlovský zámek

For centuries, the focal point of the town has been its chateau, **Krumlovský zámek** in the **Latrán quarter**, as good a place as any to begin. Once you've passed through the first gateway, you enter the sprawling first courtyard, which belongs to the older, lower castle. Cross the medvědí příkop (bear moat), where the latest batch of unfortunate bears is incarcerated, and head for the beautifully restored castle tower, the **Zámecká věž** (daily: April–May & Sept–Oct

▲ Grafitový důl (500m)   ▲ Train Station (1km)

ACCOMMODATION
Barbakán   H
Dvořák   C
Hostel Ryba   I
Na louži   E
Růže   G
Travellers Hostel D
U města Vídně   A
Ve věží   B
Zlatý anděl   F

0   100 m

CHVALŠINSKÁ SILNICE

Budějovická brána

Jelení zahrada

Convent of Poor Clares

Zámecké divadlo

PLÁŠTOVÝ MOST

Krumlovský zámek

LATRÁN

Zámecká zahrada

Former arsenal

LATRÁN

Brewery

PIVOVARSKÁ

DLOUHÁ

SODĚVSKÁ

ŠIROKÁ

STARÉ MĚSTO

Pohádkový dům

Muzeum marionet

Schiele Centrum

Radnice

MASNÁ

River Vltava

PARKÁN

NÁMĚSTÍ SVORNOSTI

HORNÍ

Museum

RYBÁŘSKÁ

KOSTELNÍ

Church of sv Vít

KAPLICKÁ

Bus station

RESTAURANTS, PUBS & TEAHOUSES
Cikánská jizba   4
Dobrá čjovna   1
Eggenberg   2
Laibon   5
Maštal   6
Na louži   9
Papa's Living   3
Rybářská bašta   7
U písaře Jana   8

Městské sady

LINECKÁ

ROOSEVELTOVA

N

HORSKÁ

ČESKÝ KRUMLOV

9am–5pm; June–Aug 9am–6pm), for a superb view over the town. Nearby there's the ticket office. There are currently two hour-long **guided tours** (Tues–Sun: April–May & Sept–Oct 9am–5pm; June–Aug 9am–6pm) to choose between, occasionally in English: *trasa 1* (160Kč) is the one to go for as it takes you through the surviving Renaissance rooms, the Rococo excesses of the blue and pink marble chapel, and the Maškarní sál, a ballroom exquisitely decorated with trompe l'oeil murals of *commedia dell'arte* scenes; *trasa 2* (140Kč) concentrates on portraits of the Schwarzenbergs and doles out rich helpings of nineteenth-century opulence. The entrances to both the tours are located on one of the two smaller prettily painted courtyards of the upper castle, added in the fifteenth century.

The castle's unique gem, however, is its ornate eighteenth-century Rococo Zámecké divadlo (May–Oct Tues–Sun tours at 10am, 11am, 1pm, 2pm & 3pm; 180Kč), on the other side of the covered Plášť'ový most, a many-tiered viaduct with a superb view over the town. This is one of the few Rococo theatres in the world to retain so much of its original scenery and wardrobe. An ingenious system of flies and flats meant that a typical comic opera of the kind the theatre specialized in could have more than forty scene changes without interrupting the action. Visits to the theatre are by forty-five minute guided tour only and it's worth booking tickets at the ticket office at least one day in advance.

Another covered walkway takes you high above the town into the unexpectedly expansive and formal terraced Zámecká zahrada (daily: April & Oct

7am–5pm; May–Sept 7am–7pm), whose tranquillity is disturbed only by the operas and ballets performed in the gardens' modern, revolving, open-air theatre (otáčivé hlediště) during July and August; details from the tourist office.

The staré město and around

Latrán, lined with shabby, overhanging houses, leads to a wooden, ramp-like bridge that connects with the **staré město**. There's a compelling beauty in the old town, whose precarious existence is best viewed from the circling River Vltava. Turning right down Dlouhá, where the houses glow red at dusk, will bring you to the site of the town's former arsenal. From here, if the river's not swollen, you can walk across the gangplanks of the footbridge to Rybářská, which then follows the left bank to the southernmost bridge, taking you back into the old town.

Heading straight up the soft incline of Radniční brings you to the main square, **náměstí Svornosti** – look back for a great view of the castle. Occupying one side of the cobbled square is the former **radnice**, which was created out of two and a half Gothic houses, and sports a strikingly long, white, Renaissance entablature of blind arcading. To the southeast, the high lancet windows of the church of **sv Vít** rise vertically above the ramshackle rooftops. Inside, the church retains its Gothic lierne vaulting, patches of medieval fresco and the remarkable tomb of Vílem of Rožmberk. One or two of the later furnishings are notable, too, particularly the Rococo organ case and the fabulously gilded pulpit.

If you continue east off the square, down Horní, you'll meet the beautiful sgraffitoed sixteenth-century Jesuit college, which now houses the *Hotel Růže*, among other things. Opposite the *Růže*, the local **museum** (Regionalní muzeum; March–April & Oct–Dec Tues–Fri 9am–4pm, Sat & Sun 1–4pm; May, June & Sept daily 10am–5pm; July & Aug daily 10am–6pm; Ⓦwww.muzeum.ckrumlov. cz) puts on small, temporary exhibitions relating to the history of the town. Also

Schiele in Krumau

In 1911, the Austrian painter **Egon Schiele** decided to leave Vienna and spend some time in Krumau, his mother's home town. During his brief sojourn here, Schiele painted a number of intense townscapes of Krumau, like *Houses and Roofs near Krumau* and *Dead City*, in which he managed to make even the buildings look sexually anguished. At the time, he was not making much money from his art, and was forced to shuffle from rooming house to rooming house with his 17-year-old lover, Wally Neuzil, a model handed down to him by Gustav Klimt. Finally he succeeded in buying a studio, a crumbling Baroque cottage by the river in Plešivec, south of the old town. Schiele and his bohemian companions, Erwin Osen and Moa Mandu, caused more than a little controversy in this resolutely petit-bourgeois town – hiring young local girls for nude modelling and painting Wally naked in the orchard were among his more famous faux pas. Forced to leave before the year was out, he vowed never to return.

Under the Communists, the town made no attempt to advertise Schiele's brief but productive stay; now, however, Schiele is for Krumlov what Kafka is for Prague. Fans of the artist should head for the Schiele Centrum (daily 10am–6pm; Ⓦwww .schieleartcentrum.cz; 180Kč), a vast, rambling art complex housed in a fifteenth-century former brewery on Široká, where a smattering of the artist's lithographs, watercolours and pencil sketches – including one of Český Krumlov – are on permanent display. In addition, there's some furniture designed by the artist for his studio, a small exhibition on Schiele's life, and regular shows by contemporary artists.

on display is the model of the town and the two-thousand-seater theatre at nearby Hořice, where elaborate Passion Plays have been staged on and off since 1816.

To the northwest of the centre up Chvalšinská lies Krumlov's active **graphite mine** (Grafitový důl; July & Aug daily 9am–3pm; 200Kč guided tour in English; May–June & Sept–Oct call ☎380 711 199, ⓦwww.grafitovydul.cz), where a tour involves exploring the tunnels wearing protective clothing and a short trip on the underground carriages.

Kids will appreciate a couple of museums located on either side of the Vltava; the **Marionette Museum** (Muzeum marionet; March–Oct daily 10am–7pm; out of season Sat & Sun only), in the former church of sv Jošt at Latrán 6, where old and new puppets from the National Marionette Theatre hang rather gruesomely from the wooden ceiling; and the **Fairytale House** (Pohádkový dům; Jan–March Sat & Sun 10am–6pm; April–Dec daily 10am–6pm), at Radniční 29, where Czech puppets, mainly from the eighteenth and nineteenth centuries, are displayed alongside an original mechanical theatre from 1815.

Eating, drinking and entertainment

As far as **eating** goes, there's certainly plenty of choice – the same goes for pubs. If you need to check email, there's an **Internet café** just inside the zámek gates; for **teas** from around the world, slip into the *Dobrá čajovna* opposite.

Restaurants

Cikánská jizba Dlouhá 31. Nifty, cheap little place with a country theme and lots of Czech, Slovak and gypsy specialities including goulash and *halušky*. Closed Sun.
Laibon Parkán. Has a surprisingly long, all-vegetarian menu with specialities from twelve countries and great riverside seating.
Maštal Nám. Svornosti 2. A smoky Gothic cellar restaurant on the main square serving typical

Czech pub food and local beers.
Papa's Living Restaurant Latrán 13. Despite the naff name, this cosy, vaulted restaurant offers funky Mexican, Italian and veggie dishes.
Rybářská bašta Na louži. Excellent, reasonably priced fish restaurant in the Krčínův dům off Široká.
U písaře Jana Horní 151. Elegant, tasteful restaurant with stucco decoration on the ceiling and a vast menu, including fish dishes from 235Kč.

Nightlife and entertainment

Na louži, at Kájovská 66, is the town's most historic **pub**, with fine food to boot, or else there's the Eggenberg brewery tap, *Eggenberg*, which also puts on occasional live events and gigs (ⓦwww.eggenberg.cz). Theatre performances take place in the **open-air revolving theatre** (otáčivé hlediště), in the castle gardens (early June to early Sept; ⓦwww.jihoceskedivadlo.cz), and there's an **open-air cinema** 500m or so west of the main road junction, off route 39 to Volary. In summer, you can **rent canoes** in the pension *Myší díra* (☎380 712 508) and float downstream (with a shuttle minibus bringing you back). They also run the hour-long cruises along the Vltava (360Kč).

Sensitive to the huge high season audience of tourists, there are now more and more cultural events throughout the summer. If you arrive in town at the weekend nearest the summer solstice, you'll witness the **Five-Petalled Rose Festival** (Slavnosti pětilisté růže), an excuse for the townsfolk to don medieval dress worn in the days of the Rožmberks, as well as let off fireworks, sing, dance and generally make merry. The town also hosts several **music festivals** (ⓦwww.czechmusicfestival.com): a chamber music festival in June or early July, one dedicated to early music, held in mid-July, an international one which takes place over three weeks in August, plus a pop (*bigbít*) festival in mid-July and a jazz festival in late August (ⓦwww.jazz-krumlov.cz).

The Šumava

The dense pine forests and peat bogs of the **Šumava** region (Ⓦ www.sumava-info
.cz, www.sumava.net) stretch for miles along the Austrian and German borders
southwest of Český Krumlov, part of the much larger Böhmerwald which
spreads across into Bavaria forming one of the last remaining wildernesses in
central Europe. The original inhabitants of this sparsely populated region were
German-speaking foresters, who scraped a living from its meagre soil – their
Austrian lilt and agricultural poverty separating them from their "civilized"
Sudetenland brothers in western and northern Bohemia. Up to the declaration of the First Republic in 1918, the economic armlock of the all-powerful
Schwarzenberg and Buquoy dynasties kept the region in a permanent semi-
feudal state. Even in the nineteenth century, peasants had to have permission
from their landlords to marry, and their customary greeting to the local squire
was *Brotvater* (literally "Breadfather").

Following the expulsion of the German-speakers in 1945, all links with the
past were severed, and despite financial incentives for Czechs to move here
the Šumava has remained underpopulated. Poor, provincial and out of the way
compared to the rest of the former Sudetenland, it had the added misfortune
of lying alongside one of the most sensitive stretches of the East–West border
during the Cold War – in the 1970s, large areas of forest along the south shore
of Lake Lipno were closed off by the military. Much of this land has now been
relinquished, the border dismantled, and contact between the two areas re-
established, all of which has revived the area considerably. Ironically, while the
Iron Curtain was there, the area was safely protected from overdevelopment,
and local campaigners are now fighting hard to try and keep it that way. As a
consequence, most of the roads to the south of Lake Lipno are still closed to
vehicles except bicycles.

Aside from the region's one truly medieval town, **Prachatice**, the majority
of visitors come here for the scenery, which is among the most unspoilt in the
country, thanks to the lack of heavy industry and minimal acid rain damage.
Most tourists crowd round the northern shore of the artificial **Lake Lipno**, creating their own peculiar brand of beach culture, while others head for the hills,
which rise up more gently than those on the Austrian and German side. The
deepest part of the forest, hugging the German and Austrian borders between
Lake Lipno and Železná Ruda, is preserved as the **Šumava National Park**
(Národní park Šumava), where tiny villages blend into the silent hills, meadows
and peat bogs. The most scenic way of **getting around**, apart from walking, is
the single-track České Budějovice–Volary train line. Local buses are much more
convenient, though at weekends services begin to peter out. Look out, too, for
the special **summer bus** services, which run up to five times daily through
the heart of the national park. Due to its gently hilly landscape, the park is also
great **cycling** territory, and in summer, Czechs often float down the Vltava in
canoes, which can be rented from towns along the river.

Rožmberk nad Vltavou

Buses from Český Krumlov follow the Vltava valley to the pretty village of
ROŽMBERK NAD VLTAVOU (Rosenberg), which is tucked into a U-bend
of the river, and overlooked by a spectacular, sgraffitoed **fortress** which teeters
on a knife's edge high above it. As the name suggests, its *raison d'être* was as the
headquarters of the powerful and single-minded Rožmberk family, regional
supremos from the thirteenth century until their extinction in 1611. Only

one round tower remains from the Rožmberk era, though the highlight of the guided tour, the castle's banquet hall with its sixteenth-century Italian frescoes, is also a Rožmberk legacy. The rest of the interior speaks little of that family, but volumes of its later French owners, the Buquoys, who stuffed the dull, mannerless rooms with heavy neo-Gothic furnishings and instruments of torture, the latter being displayed in the Katovna, separate from the tour. In summer, Czech tour groups fall over one another for a place on the forty-five minute **guided tours** (April & Oct Sat & Sun 9am–4pm; May & Sept Tues–Sun 9am–4pm; June–Aug Tues–Sun 9am–5.15pm; 140Kč; ⓦ www.pamatky-jc.cz): *trasa 1* is the main tour; *trasa 2* is specifically aimed at (Czech) kids.

Finding **accommodation** down in the village is relatively easy at any of the many private rooms on offer. Otherwise, the *Hotel Růže* (☏ 380 749 715, www .hotelruze.rozmberk.cz; ③) has well-appointed rooms and a restaurant, while the *Hotel Studenec* (☏ 380 749 818, ⓦ www.hotel-studenec.com; ③), up a hill north of the village, off route 160 to Český Krumlov, rents out canoes and bikes and has a **restaurant** with a wonderful view over the valley.

Vyšší Brod

Upriver from Rožmberk, just fifteen minutes south by bus, is **VYŠŠÍ BROD** (Hohenfurth), notable for its white Cistercian monastery on the western edge of town, founded in the thirteenth century in response to the Přemyslids' founding of nearby Zlatá Koruna (see p.212). Its proximity to the border and its extreme wealth gave rise to a set of immodest fortifications that withstood two sieges by the Hussites. Despite its pews, the essentially Gothic klášterní kostel was for the exclusive use of the monks, who sat in the fancy gilded stalls that take up almost half the church – only on religious holidays were the locals allowed in at the back. In the blue side chapel rests Petr Vok, the last of the

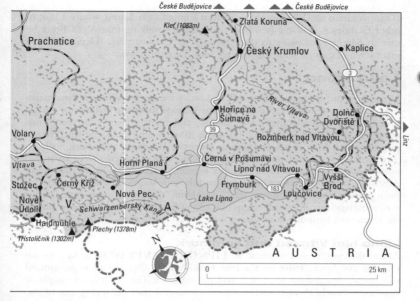

Rožmberks, who died of drink and drugs but was nonetheless given pride of place as the monastery's rich patron. Suppressed during the Communist period, Vyšší Brod is once more inhabited by monks.

The only way to see the church's interior is by fifty minute-long **guided tour** (May–Sept Tues–Sun 9–11.30am & 1.15–4.15pm; Oct–April booking necessary ☎380 746 674; 120Kč), which also takes you through the beautiful Gothic chapterhouse and ends with the star attraction, a be-frescoed Rococo library decorated with 24-carat gold, accessible only via a secret door in one of the bookcases. The monastery's outer buildings house a mildly diverting **Poštovní muzeum** (April–Oct Tues–Sun 9am–noon & 1–5pm), charting the history of the republic's postal system since the late medieval period, with displays of period uniforms, old phones and typewriters, new stamps and old stage and post coaches.

If you need a **place to stay**, try the *Hotel Šumava* (☎380 746 574, ⓦwww .hotel-sumava.cz; ❸), at Náměstí 47, in a lovely old building on the main square, with a plain, pleasant restaurant. At the opposite corner of the square stands the renovated *Hotel Panský dům* (☎380 746 669, ⓦwww.hotelpanskydum.cz; ❸) with simple, clean en-suite rooms and restaurant on the ground floor. There are also several private rooms and pensions, including *Pension Inge* (☎380 746 482, ⓦwww.pensioninge.cz; ❷), right under the monastery, which also rents out boats and canoes; you can even stay in cheap, hostel-type accommodation in the monastery itself (☎380 746 457; ❶). The *Pod hrází* **campsite** (June to mid-Sept) is a basic riverside site with cold showers only, a short walk along route 163 towards Lipno nad Vltavou.

There are **buses** from Rožmberk to Vyšší Brod, or else you can catch a **train** from Rybník, 10km east on the Prague–Linz main line (get out at Vyšší Brod klášter, not Vyšší Brod, for the monastery). Local buses and trains continue

10km to Lipno nad Vltavou, at the eastern edge of Lake Lipno, where a host of other facilities is available (see below). If you are walking from Vyšší Brod, be sure to take the red route to the viewpoint at Čertova stěna (Devil's Walls), a giant scree of granite slabs that tumble into the river below.

Lake Lipno

Upstream from the giant paper mill at Loučovice on the Vltava, a dam marks the southeastern end of **Lake Lipno**. The barrage turns the turbines of a huge underground hydroelectric power station, and on the face of it, there's not much to get excited about. The northern shore is punctuated by small beach resorts, which have developed rapidly over the last thirty years, originally to give workers some well-needed fresh air, now with more of an eye to attract euros from across the border. The area is popular with Czechs, Germans and Austrians, so the **hotels** are often full in July and August, but you're rarely far from **private rooms** – look for the "Unterkunft/ubytování" signs dotted about – or a **campsite**, often with cheap bungalows for rent. **Buses** link most places, supplemented by trains from Černá v Pošumaví westwards.

Lipno nad Vltavou and Frymburk

About the only reason to come to **LIPNO NAD VLTAVOU** is to take the one- or two-hour **cruise** on the lake. From May to October there are around two boats leaving daily from the small pier in town. The town has a couple of run-down hotels, though you're almost certainly better off trying any of the numerous pensions signposted off the road to Frymburk, or one of the campsites by the lake. Note that the train station at Lipno is situated below the dam, a couple of kilometres east of the town itself. Beyond Lipno, you can hardly miss the largest new development on the lake, **Lipno Marina** (Ⓦwww.lipno .info), with its swimming pool complex Aquaworld, yacht rental and the nearby **campsite** *Autocamp Modřín* (May–Sept; Ⓔcamp@lipno.info). A local **tourist office** (Mon–Fri 10am–noon & 1–5pm) is situated on the main road.

Some 9km along the shore from Lipno is **FRYMBURK** (Friedberg), probably the most attractive village on the lake, with its delicate white, octagonal spire and leafy, oval main square. **Accommodation** is plentiful, and first choice on the square is the family-run *Hotel Maxant* (Ⓣ380 735 229, Ⓦwww .lipnonet.cz/maxant; ❹), which has a sauna and pool, or else there's the *Hotel Vltava* (Ⓣ380 735 605; ❻), opposite, the newest and flashiest accommodation in the village. *Camping Frymburk* (May–Sept) is a well-run lakeside site, just 500m from the village back along route 163 to Lipno, with cycle and boat rental, and bungalows available. A car ferry to Frýdava runs roughly every one to two hours (10Kč per person, 50Kč with a car).

Border crossings

Before 1989, the main road from Horní Planá northwest to Volary was punctuated at regular intervals by little red signs warning about the impending Iron Curtain; all villages on the right bank of the Vltava were closed to road vehicles, with trains the only legal means of transport. The military have now given up their patch, and today there are numerous **border crossings** into Austria and Germany, with varying restrictions. The only 24-hour checkpoints open to all vehicles are Přední Výtoň/ Guglwald and Strážný/Philippsreuth, 50km to the west. In between there are six more crossing points, open only to cyclists and/or pedestrians, all with more limited opening hours – check with the local tourist office for the current restrictions.

Hiking in the Šumava

One of the most interesting Šumava hikes sets off from Ovesná station, the next one along from Nová Pec (and occasionally request only). Follow the yellow-marked route northwest through gigantic boulders and thick forest to Perník (1049m), before dropping down to Jelení, where the **Schwarzenberský kanál** emerges from a tunnel. Built at the turn of the eighteenth century, to transport the Šumava's valuable timber straight to the Danube (less than 40km due south), the canal was abandoned as a waterway in 1962. A little further on you reach the **Medvědí kámen** (Bären Stein), marking the spot where the last bear in the Šumava was shot in 1856. The only threat to hikers now is the lynx, which was reintroduced hereabouts in 1985. Moving on, you should reach the village station at Černý Kříž in around six hours (14km) from Ovesná.

From Nové Údolí (only accessible by train, bike or foot), hard by the German border, you can take the red-marked trail south, 5km to the peak of **Třístoličník** or Dreisesselberg (1302m) right on the border. From here, it's another 5km to Trojmezí, the meeting-point of the German, Austrian and Czech borders, and 1km further to the summit of the Czech Šumava's highest peak, **Plechý** or Plöckenstein (1378m), on the Austrian border. From Plechý you could make the steep descent to Plešné jezero, a glacial lake that sits in the shadow of the sheer northeast face of the mountain, from which it's another 8km via the green-marked path to Nová Pec train station.

Černá v Pošumaví

There are plenty more accommodation options 10km down the road in **ČERNÁ V POŠUMAVÍ** (Schwarzbach), a village divided into two by the lake: on the eastern shore is the village proper and the road junction; on the western shore, across the road bridge, is the train station. In addition to the regular service between České Budějovice and Volary, an **historic steam train** plies the rails at weekends (July to mid-Sept) from here to Nové Údoli, right next to the German border to the west. There's a windsurfing school in Černá (Ⓦwww.lipno-windsurfing.cz), but if you're just looking for a dip, head off to nearby **DOLNÍ VLTAVICE**, 6km south on a secluded thumb of land, where a small crowd enjoys the grassy "beach" with a view over to (and a ferry link with) the opposite shore, which is hard against the Austrian border.

Horní Planá

HORNÍ PLANÁ (Oberplan), 7km west of Černá, is the lake's chief resort, and has a useful **tourist office** (July–Aug daily 8am–6pm; out of season Mon–Fri 7.30–11.15am & noon–4pm; Ⓦwww.horniplana.cz) in the Česká spořitelna building on the leafy main square, which can help you fix up some accommodation, has computers linked to the **Internet** and also rents out **mountain bikes**. A little cultural distraction can be experienced at the birthplace (*rodný domek*) of the German-speaking writer and painter **Adalbert Stifter**, who cut short his life in 1868 by slashing his throat to escape cancer of the liver. The house (April–June & Sept Tues–Sun 10am–noon & 1–6pm; July & Aug daily 10am–noon & 1–6pm; Oct to mid-Dec Tues–Sat 9am–noon & 1–4pm), on the road into town from the east (Palackého 22), is now a small memorial to his life and work; his statue stands behind the church, and there's another memorial to him overlooking the waters of the Plešné jezero, which sits below Plechý (Plockenstein) close to the meeting of the German, Austrian and Czech borders, the Trojmezí.

There's no shortage of campsites and **accommodation** in Horní Planá. The smart *Pension Šejko* (☎380 738 830; ❸), a short way along the road to the lake shore, with decent en-suite rooms, is a good choice. Or there's the large *Hotel Na pláží* (☎380 738 374, ⓦwww.hotel-plaz.cz; ❸), with its own restaurant and kids' playground, situated, as the name suggests, opposite the beach – ask for a room overlooking the lake. For those seeking tranquillity, a good option is to stay in the waterfront village of **JENIŠOV**, a couple of kilometres south of Horní Planá, which consists of just several hotels and pensions, such as the *Hotel Na jezeře* (☎380 738 338; ❸). The local **campsite** (May–Oct; also with bungalows) is more pleasant than the sites in Horní Planá.

Prachatice and around

The slopes of Libín (1096m) merge into the Otava and Vltava plain by the amiable little market town of **PRACHATICE** (Prachatitz), dubbed by the tourist authorities as the "Gateway to the Šumava". Most people do indeed come here en route to the Šumava, but it's a beautiful medieval town in its own right, as well as being a useful base for visiting **Husinec**, birthplace of Jan Hus (see p.224). Founded in 1325, Prachatice flourished in the following century, when it controlled the all-important salt trade route into Bohemia. A fire in 1507 is responsible for the uniformly sixteenth-century appearance of the town and its famous collection of sgraffito facades.

The Town

A short walk uphill from the bus and train stations brings you to Malé náměstí, the main square-cum-crossroads of the nondescript new part of town. Everything of interest is contained within the walls of the tiny circular **staré město**, reached through the bulky fifteenth-century **Písecká brána**, a gateway with a faded mural showing Vílem of Rožmberk on horseback and, above it, in among the battlements, the red rose symbol of his family, who acquired the town briefly in 1501.

The gate's double arches open out on the small Kostelní náměstí, where old women sell spices and vegetables in the shade of the trees. The Gothic church of **sv Jakub**, with its steeply pitched, rather peculiar red-ribbed roof, is the oldest building and most obvious landmark in town. Inside, the short, tall nave is decorated with delicate lierne vaulting; the Baroque main altar, meanwhile, is much more in-your-face, with four gilded barley-sugar columns wreathed in vines dividing gold and silver relief scenes of the Nativity. Prachatice is best known, however, for the exquisitely decorative **Heydlův dům** to the left, which sports bizarre depictions of men clubbing each other to death, unintentionally apposite given its present incumbents, a family butcher's. Next door is the Latin school or **Literátská škola**, also crowned with miniature Renaissance battlements, and which local heroes Hus and Žižka are said to have attended in their youth.

At this point the cobbles open out into the old town square, **Velké náměstí**, which has a thoroughly Germanic air. Its most striking aspect is the riot of **sgraffito** on the facades of many of the buildings; if you haven't already come across the style, Prachatice is as good a place as any to get to grips with it. The technique – extremely popular in the sixteenth century and revived in the nineteenth – involves scraping away painted plaster to form geometric, monochrome patterns or even whole pictorial friezes, producing a distinctive lacework effect. The most lavish example of this style is the arcaded **Rumpálův dům**, at no. 41 on the east side of the square, which depicts a ferociously confused battle scene. At no. 45 is another arcaded building, the former **solnice** or salt house (also known as the Bozovského dům), through which the town accrued its enormous wealth in the Middle Ages and which features Vílem of Rožmberk once more on horseback.

On the west side of the square, the sixteenth-century **stará radnice** is decorated with copies of Hans Holbein's disturbing, apocalyptic parables, employing a much more sophisticated use of perspective; just a few doors down stands the **nová radnice**, whose sgraffito dates from the late nineteenth century. One of the fanciest houses on the square is the **Sittrův dům**, on the north side, now the local museum (March–June & Sept–Dec Tues–Fri 9am–4pm, Sat & Sun 10am–4pm; July & Aug Tues–Sun 9am–5pm), distinguished not by its sgraffito, but by its colourful painted facade and ornate Renaissance gable. Four doors down at no. 9 is the **Knížecí dům**, which hides its sgraffito round the side, on which you'll find, among other things, a stag hunt, several devils and an elephant, a mermaid with two tails and Joseph being put into the pit by his brothers. On Poštovní, just off the diagonally opposite corner of the square, you can find the new **Muzeum krajky** (Lace Museum; April–Dec Tues–Sun 9am–5pm), with a permanent display of lace from the republic and other European countries.

Practicalities

The **tourist office** (mid-June to mid-Sept Mon–Fri 8am–6pm, Sat & Sun 10am–noon & 1–4pm; rest of the year Mon–Fri 8am–4.30pm; Ⓦ www.prachatice .cz) in the old town hall, can help find private rooms in the town. *Hotel Parkán* (Ⓣ 388 311 868, Ⓦ www.hotelparkan.cz; ❸), on Věžní, is probably the nicest **place to stay**, with en-suite facilities and TVs in all its rooms, and a solid Czech restaurant; to get there head up Křišťanova by sv Jakub and take the first left. Alternatively, head for the *Hotel Koruna* (Ⓣ 388 310 177; ❷), tucked away just down an alleyway in the southwestern corner of the main square; the en-suite rooms are spartan, but the wood-beamed restaurant on the ground floor is cosy. Infrequent buses will drop you close to the riverside *Blanický Mlýn* **campsite** (open all year), situated 12km south, with bungalows and rooms in the main building.

Prachatice's Indian **restaurant**, *Tandoor*, Horní 165 (closed Sun & daily 3–5pm), in the backstreets, is a remarkable find; a real Indian chef cooks up tandoori dishes, masalas, kormas and thalis. For more traditional Czech food, head for the simple, cheap pub *Národní dům*, to the left of the local museum. On Poštovní, near the lace museum, there's the friendly *Čajovná U hrušky* (tea house). To check your email, head for the **Internet café** upstairs at Club 111 on Křišťanova. The town's big summer bash is the *Slavností solné Zlaté stezky*, a medieval knees-up held at a weekend towards the end of June.

Husinec

You may burn the goose [hus],
but one day there will come a swan,
and him you will not burn.

Martin Luther

Six kilometres north of Prachatice is the unassuming village of **HUSINEC**, birthplace of **Jan Hus** (see box p.224), the man whose death in 1415 triggered off the Hussite revolution. In the nineteenth century, when interest in Hus began to emerge after the dark years of the Counter-Reformation, the poet Jan Neruda visited Husinec and was horrified to find Hus' former home shabby and neglected. No expense has been spared since, with the family house at nos.

Jan Hus

The legendary preacher – and Czech national hero – **Jan Hus** (often anglicized to John Huss) was born in the small village of Husinec around 1372. From a childhood of poverty, he enjoyed a steady rise through the Czech education system, taking his degree at Prague's Karolinum in the 1390s, and eventually being ordained as a deacon and priest around 1400. Although without doubt an admirer of the English religious reformer, John Wycliffe, Hus was by no means as radical as many of his colleagues who preached at the Betlémská kaple. Nor did he actually advocate many of the more famous tenets of the heretical religious movement that took his name: Hussitism. In particular, he never advocated giving communion "in both kinds" (bread and wine) to the general congregation.

In the end, it wasn't the disputes over Wycliffe, whose books were burned on the orders of the archbishop in 1414, that proved Hus' downfall, but an argument over the sale of indulgences to fund the papal wars that prompted his unofficial trial at the Council of Constance in 1415. Having been guaranteed safe conduct by Emperor Sigismund himself, Hus naively went to Constance to defend his views, and was burnt at the stake as a heretic. The Czechs were outraged, and Hus became a national hero overnight, inspiring thousands to rebel against the authorities of the day. In 1965, the Vatican finally overturned the sentence, and the anniversary of his death (July 6) is now a national holiday.

36 & 37 converted into a **museum** (Památník M.J. Husa; May–Sept Tues–Sun 9am–noon & 1–4pm) and many of Hus' old haunts in the surrounding region turned into points of pilgrimage over the nineteenth century. That said, there are few visitors nowadays to the museum's small exhibition and only one original room, a tiny garret on the top floor. To give you an idea of Hus' place in the Czech nationalist canon, take a look at the stirring multicoloured sgraffito illustration on no. 42. Getting to Husinec is easiest on one of the regular **buses** from Prachatice; the train station is 3km east of the village.

Lake Lipno to Vimperk

The scenic train ride from Lake Lipno to Vimperk takes you deep into the Šumava forest, and it's worth breaking the journey at some point to delve further into the woods, particularly northwest of Volary, which lies 18km south of Prachatice. At **LENORA**, there's a glass factory (and the shops), several old, wooden, Šumava cottages and a picturesque covered wooden bridge over the river. You can stay in *Zámeček Lenora* (☏388 438 861; ❷), a hotel situated in an old country house, with its own restaurant and a spacious courtyard. There are some great walks possible from the next station along, Zátoň, 1.5km northeast of which, in the hamlet of Kaplice, is the primitive *Boubínský prales* campsite (open all year).

From Zátoň station, a green-marked path skirts the ancient **Boubínský prales** (Boubín Virgin Forest) that occupies the slopes of Boubín (1362m). It's forbidden to walk among the pines and firs of the forest, some of which are over 400 years old, but the green markers take you 4km around the perimeter past a small deer park and on to the summit; from here you can get back to the rail line without retracing your steps by following the blue-marked path 4km to the station at the ski resort of **KUBOVÁ HUŤ**, where there are several hotels and pensions to choose from, including the vast *Ingo Hotel Arnika* (☏338 436 326, ⓦwww.hotel-arnika.cz; ❸), with sauna, pool and bike rental, and the modern mega ski-chalet, *Amber Hotel Kuba* (☏338 436 321; ❹), which also does bike rental in the summer.

Vimperk and Volyně

From Horní Vltavice, a few local buses cover the 13km to the 24-hour Strážný–Philippsreuth German border crossing; trains continue for 13km to **VIMPERK** (Winterberg), where the first printing press in Bohemia was established in 1484 – a few decades after Gutenberg's invention. The business of the day goes on in the lower part of town, leaving the steep narrow streets of the **staré město** virtually deserted. The leafy main square, náměstí Svobody, is overlooked by the town's **hrad**, originally built in the thirteenth century by Otakar II, and last owned by the Schwarzenbergs. The castle, a stiff fifteen-minute hike up from the centre, has been knocked about a bit over the centuries, and now houses the local **museum** (May–Oct Tues–Sun 9am–noon & 1–4pm), with little of interest beyond a selective display of local glassware, though you're rewarded with great views over the old town.

Despite its relative lack of local attractions, Vimperk is another possible base for exploring this part of the Šumava. There are a couple of **hotels** by the train station, but that leaves you a good 1.5km from the town centre down Nádražní. A better idea is to head for the *Amber Hotel Anna*, Kaplířova 168 (☏ 388 412 050, ⓦ www.legner.cz; ❹), a lovely old building right in the centre that's been rather brutally modernized, but a very comfortable place to stay all the same. A good option for families is the quiet *Penzion Róza* (☏ 732 703 825, ⓦ www.penzionroza.cz; ❷), at náměstí Svobody 10, which has three comfortable apartments. The nearest **campsite** is *Vodník* (May–Oct), at Hájná Hora, a kilometre or so up the hill to the west of town. For a cheap Platán **beer** and some traditional **food**, head for the *Hospoda na náměstí* on náměstí Svobody. The **tourist office** (Mon–Fri 9am–5pm, Sat & Sun 9am–noon & 12.30–4pm; out of season Mon–Fri 9am–4pm) is situated at náměstí Svobody 8.

A train line from Vimperk to Strakonice runs along the winding River Volyňka. It's worth stopping briefly in **VOLYNĚ** to catch a glimpse of its extremely pretty **radnice**, which features typical "Czech style", arcades, sgraffitoed walls, and – rather surprisingly – an onion-shaped cupola.

Strakonice

The remaining, mountainous part of the Šumava is only accessible from the east by an infrequent bus service. The railway meanwhile veers northwards to **STRAKONICE** (Strakonitz), which qualifies as a large industrial town in these parts. It grew up as a textile town in the nineteenth century, and its factories now produce an unusual trio of products: Turkish fez hats, ČZ motorcycles, and *dudy*, the Bohemian equivalent of bagpipes.

There's a museum on these very subjects in the town's extremely large thirteenth-century **hrad** (Tues–Sun: May, June, Sept & Oct 8am–4pm; July–Aug 9am–5pm; ⓦ www.muzeum.strakonice.cz), at the confluence of the Volyňka and the Otava, on the south bank of the latter. It's a fun place to explore: there are plenty of old motorbikes to admire, an international selection of *dudy* in everything from velvet to sheepskin, and a fez-making machine. Ironically enough, the fez-making venture was established back in the nineteenth century by some enterprising local Jewish textile merchants. You also get to climb the castle watchtower, Rumpál. If you're really into *dudy*, there's an **International Bagpipe Festival** held in the castle courtyard every other year in August, which attracts a regular contingent from Scotland and elsewhere.

The rest of the town, on the other side of the river, can't quite match the eclectic attractions of the castle, though **Velké náměstí** boasts two very attractive late-nineteenth-century buildings – one a savings bank, the other the old radnice – facing each other across the square. Both are designed in florid neo-Renaissance style, and decorated with pretty floral and folk-inspired murals and friezes. East along Lidická, on the south side of the street, there's also a former butchers' stalls worth inspecting, a lovely little Baroque building with a brightly coloured naïve relief in the gable showing a butcher about to slaughter a bull.

From the **train** and **bus stations**, it's a five-minute walk to the castle – west down Alfonse Šťástného, then right down Bezděkovská. If you're staying the night, head for the excellent **information centre** (Mon–Fri 8am–6pm) in the mapové centrum, located in the main gateway of the castle, where you can book private rooms. The main tourist office (May–Sept Mon–Fri 8am–7pm, Sat 9am–1pm; Oct–April Mon, Tues, Thurs & Fri 8am–noon & 1–4pm, Wed till 6pm; ☎383 700 700, ⓦ www.strakonice.net) is on Velké náměstí. As for **hotels**, try the *Fontána* (☎383 321 440; ❷), northeast of the main square on Lidická – it doesn't look much from the outside, but it's smart enough inside. Also worth checking out is the *Hotel Bílá růže* (☎383 321 946, ⓦ www.hotelruzest.cz; ❷), at Palackého náměstí 80, two blocks down off the main square, which has a Chinese restaurant. Strakonice's cheapie is the *Hotel Bílý vlk* (☎383 323 009; ❶), at Komenského 29, near the castle, which has basic rooms with or without en-suite showers. There's a **campsite**, *Podskalí* (June to mid-Sept), by the banks of the Otava, fifteen minutes' walk west along Pod Hradem, which runs south of the castle. Strakonice brews its own **beer**, across the river from the castle, and you can sup the local Nektar (and Dudák) nearby at *U zborova*, a rough-and-ready pub at Bavorova 20, which heads off north from the western end of the main square; more civilized is the wood-panelled **restaurant** serving Budvar in the *Fontána*, or the twin, tastefully appointed restaurants *Kalich* and *U Madly* (both closed Sun), opposite the tourist office on Velké náměstí.

Rabí and Sušice

There are several ruined castles along the banks of the River Otava beyond Strakonice, but by far the most impressive – and the largest in Bohemia – are the vast and crumbling fortifications of **RABÍ**, 25km away by train (change at Horažd'ovice). A key fortress in the Hussite Wars, and allegedly the place where the Hussite general Jan Žižka lost his second eye, it was deliberately allowed to fall into rack and ruin in the eighteenth century for fear of its strategic value should it fall into the wrong hands. The village sold the castle to the state for one crown in 1920, and recent renovation work, aimed at stabilizing some of the more dangerously disintegrating bits, has now allowed the public access to most of the site (April & Oct Sat & Sun 9am–noon & 1–3pm; May & Sept Tues–Sun 9am–noon & 1–4pm; June–Aug Tues–Sun 9am–noon & 1–5pm) – however, you must endure a forty-five minute-long guided tour in English to explore it. Other attractions at Rabí include the Gothic church with recently opened cellars (June–Sept Tues–Sun 10am–5pm), the well-signposted Jewish cemetery and several examples of Baroque folk architecture on the main square (some of which have been converted into pensions).

A few stops on from Rabí is **SUŠICE** (Schüttenhofen), which means just one thing to the Czechs – matches. The local SOLO match factory is one of the largest in Europe, and dominates the domestic market. Aside from that, there's little evidence of the town's wealthy medieval past, which, like Prachatice's, was based on the salt trade. The exception is the main square, náměstí Svobody, which boasts a handful of striking Renaissance houses; the most arresting are the **Rozacínovský dům** at no. 48, with a fantastic sgraffitoed gable sporting several tiers of mini-pilasters, and the **Voprchovský dům** at no. 40, featuring a similarly eye-catching gable with a triple tier of blind arcading. The latter now houses the **muzeum Šumavy** (May–Oct Tues–Sat 9am–noon & 12.45–5pm, Sun 9am–noon), established as far back as 1880, with exhibits ranging from local glassware to fifteenth-century woodcarvings and, of course, the match-making industry, though it's the carefully restored interior that makes it worth a visit.

Sušice's **train station** is a regrettable 2.5km northeast of the town centre, with only infrequent bus connections; if you arrive by bus, make sure to get off at the town centre and not at the train and bus station, if you have the option. Sušice has a couple of decent inexpensive **hotels**: the excellent *Sport Hotel Pekárna* (T 376 526 869; ❷), painted up like a multi-flavoured ice-cream gateau, with the added attraction of a bowling alley, is located at T. G. Masaryka 129, on the road in from the train station. Closer to the square is the *Hotel Svatobor* (T 376 526 490, W www.hotel-svatobor.cz; ❶), at T. G. Masaryka 116, slightly better than it looks from the outside. In addition, there's a nice little upbeat pension, *Milli* (T 376 526 598, W www.sweb.cz/pension.milli; ❷), down Kostelní. Both hotels have their own restaurants, and there's a pizzeria at the *Pekárna*. If you're looking to camp, you're best off heading up the Otava to one of the riverside **campsites** like *Annín* (May–Oct), 7.5km south of Sušice, and a favourite spot for canoeists. The **tourist office** (Mon–Fri 9am–noon & 12.30–4.30pm; W www.sumava.net/icsusice) is located in the town hall, on the square.

Kašperské Hory and around

One bus a day from Vimperk (more frequently from Sušice) heads for **KAŠPERSKÉ HORY** (Bergreichenstein), an old German mining village on the River Otava, positioned below the semi-ruined castle of Kašperk that was built by Charles IV to guard over the local gold mines. The town's smartest building is its pristine Renaissance **radnice** with its three perfect eighteenth-century gables, featuring – from left to right – a Czech lion, a clock and the town's mining emblem.

In addition, the town's **muzeum Šumavy** (May–Oct Tues–Sat 9am–noon & 12.45–5pm, Sun 9am–noon), on the main square, below the church, displays some wonderful local glassware on its top floor, ranging from fourteenth-century to turn-of-the-twentieth-century gear, with pieces by local firms such as Lötz, Schmid and Kralik, from the neighbouring town of Klášterský Mlýn (Klöstermühle). In the late nineteenth century, Lötz in particular won many prizes in Brussels and Paris for its Tiffany-style iridescent glass vases and weird vegetal shapes, many of which inexplicably escaped the auctioneer's hammer and ended up here. There's yet more glassware on display in the next-door building (and sometimes on the ground floor), where the museum stages temporary exhibitions (times as above).

Also on the main square is the **Moto muzeum** (May–Sept daily 9am–noon & 12.30–5.30pm; Oct–April till 4pm), containing one of the finest collections of old motorbikes in the country, displayed rather surprisingly in the building's attic. More than forty bikes line the eaves, all in pristine condition, and ranging from interwar BMW boxers to domestic trials bikes; pride of place, though, goes to a beautiful red 1928 Indian. The exhibition of Czech toys (*České hračky*; May–Sept only, same hours) in an adjacent attic, is more of a blatant money-maker than a labour of love, and only really worth visiting if you want to buy something.

At the western edge of the town there's the Šumava National Park's main **information centre** (June & Sept Mon–Fri 8am–3.30pm, Sat 9.30am–

3.30pm; July–Aug daily 9.30am–3.30pm; Oct–May Mon–Fri 8am–3.30pm; ☎376 582 734, ⓦwww.npsumava.cz), a good place to go if you plan to explore the mountains.

Top **accommodation** is available at the high-class *Park Hotel Tösch* (☎376 582 592, ⓦwww.tosch-parkhotel.cz; ❺), converted from the town's brewery into a luxury hotel with German capital to cater for the German tourists who pass through, and also at a host of pensions and private rooms in the outskirts of the town. *Tösch's* rival is the new *Aparthotel Šumava 2000* (☎376 546 910, ⓦwww.sumava2000.cz; ❺), a Best Western chain hotel on the square, with an **Internet café**. At the other end of the scale is the *Turistická ubytovňa* (☎724 265 683; ❶), located behind the church; theoretically, it's open all year, but it's advisable to come early or to book in advance. You can get a decent bite to **eat** and a Gambrinus and Radegast beer at the *Pod věží* restaurant (closed Sun), at the upper end of the square.

Srní and around

The most remote part of the Šumava National Park lies south and west of Kašperské Hory, and while there are few attractions in the way of museums or churches, it's the unblemished mountains that people come to see. The first stop of note south of Kašperské Hory is **ČEŇKOVA PILA**, a spot made up of little more than the *Pension Bystřina* (☎376 599 221; ❶; usually reserved for the whole season), and a bridge across the Vydra stream, where composer Bedřich Smetana is said to have been inspired to write the swirling flute introduction to his symphonic poem "Vltava" from *Má vlast*.

A few kilometres further on, the cute village of **SRNÍ** has a wooden-shingled church and a few hotels and pensions, such as the Communist-era twin hotels *Srní* (☎376 599 222; ❷) and *Šumava* (☎376 599 212; ❷), with indoor pool, sauna, weight room, bowling and restaurant. A few kilometres deeper into the forest, **ANTÝGL** is nothing more than a few wooden houses that make up a picturesquely situated and very popular **campsite** and basic lodging (early May to early Oct; ☎376 599 331; ❶). Very nearby the campsite is *Hotel Antýgl*, a cheap but clean place with a very good, if smoky, restaurant. Srní and Antýgl both make fine bases for **hikes** in the area. One popular walk from Antýgl is to take the red-marked path 6km along the boulder-strewn Vydra stream (which was the setting for a scene in the film *Kolya*) back down to Čeňkova Pila, and you can make a longer day of it by returning via roundabout paths such as the blue-marked trail to Srní and eventually, via another red-marked path, to Modrava, or the yellow-marked trail that descends from Srní back down to the Vydra.

Pushing on, the quiet settlements of **MODRAVA**, 3km south of Antýgl, and **KVILDA**, another 4km further east, are both surrounded by peat bogs. The latter boasts the highest altitude in the whole republic (1049m) and the neo-Gothic church of sv Štěpán. These were restricted areas when the Iron Curtain was draped just a few kilometres beyond; because of this, the landscape is refreshingly underdeveloped, but there are just enough pensions and simple restaurants today to keep visitors happy. Buses from Sušice wind their way up here at fairly regular intervals.

Železná Ruda and Špičák

The northwestern tip of the Šumava centres on the town of **ŽELEZNÁ RUDA** (Eisenstein), 2km from the German border and best approached on the scenic railway line or bus from Klatovy (see p.241). In its triple role as a border town, ski resort and summer hiking base, the place has certainly lost much of its original charm. Souvenir shops, filled with "traditional" Czech art and garden gnomes, plus the odd strip club, attempt to coax every last euro out of the Germans who come here. In many ways, you're better off using quieter neighbouring resorts like Špičák as a base. Local sights are confined to the ludicrously oversized wooden onion dome over the nave of the village church, and the small **muzeum Šumavy** (Tues–Sat 9–11.45am & 12.45–5pm, Sun 9–11.45am), local repository for glassware and folk art, which is connected to the small **tourist office** (daily 8am–12.30pm & 1.30–6pm; Ⓦwww.sumava .net/itcruda).

Still, if you need to stock up on provisions or draw some cash, then Železná Ruda is a good place to come. The *Šumava* restaurant, opposite the Spar supermarket, is reasonably priced, and, as far as **accommodation** goes, you're spoilt for choice: try the *Bultas* (Ⓣ376 397 123; ❷), which has its own restaurant. An electronic board on the main road at the centre of town shows availability of many hotels and pensions, and provides a free phone from which you can call them. Finally, the town's **campsite**, *U mlýna* (June–Sept), lies a kilometre or so out of town up route 27. The nearest **train station** to the town centre is Železná Ruda město, 500m north up the road to Špičák; meanwhile, the **rail link with Germany**, which was severed during the Cold War, has been re-established, with the two countries sharing the Železná Ruda/Bayerisch Eisenstein station on the border itself, 3km southwest of the town centre; hourly trains terminate 70km away at Plattling, with connections on to Regensburg.

From **ŠPIČÁK**, one stop back along the railway from Železná Ruda, a two-stage chairlift can take you to the top of **Pancíř** (1214m) all year round (60Kč return ticket). The first stage takes you as far as Hofmanky, and the comfortable *Hotel Horizont* (Ⓣ376 397 119, Ⓦwww.sumavanet.cz/horizont; ❸); similarly convenient is the *Hotel Bohemia* (Ⓣ376 397 514; ❸), located near the main road in Špičák. Towards the German border, there are two idyllically situated glacial lakes – Černé jezero and Čertovo jezero – surrounded by forests, which you can reach via the yellow-marked path from Špičák station.

Travel details

Trains

Prague to: České Budějovice (up to 14 daily; 2hr 15min–3hr); Písek (2 daily; 2hr 30min); Strakonice (2 daily; 2hr 55min); Sušice (1 daily; 3hr 40min); Tábor (10–14 daily; 1hr 35min–2hr 20min).
České Budějokvice to: Brno (4–5 daily; 4hr 20min); Černý Kříž (up to 6 daily; 2hr 20min–2hr 45min); Český Krumlov (8 daily; 1hr); Horní Planá (6 daily; 1hr 55min–2hr 15min); Linz (2–3 daily; 2hr 10min–2hr 35min); Písek (3–5 daily; 50min–1hr 35min); Plzeň (12–13 daily; 2hr–3hr 25min); Strakonice (13–15 daily; 50min–1hr 30min); Tábor (14–19 daily; 50min–2hr 10min); Volary (up to 5 daily; 2hr 35 min–3hr).
Plzeň to: Špičák (3–4 daily; 2hr 5min–2hr 15min); Železná Ruda (3–4 daily; 2hr 10min–2hr 20min).

Tábor to: Bechyně (7–9 daily; 50min); České Budějovice (14–19 daily; 50min–2hr 10min); Jihlava (1–2 daily; 2hr 40min–3hr); Milevsko/Písek (8–9 daily; 40min/1hr 30min); Pelhřimov (5–9 daily; 55min–1hr 25min).
Volary to: Prachatice (5–7 daily; 40–45min); Vimperk/Strakonice (5–6 daily; 1hr/2hr 30min).

Buses

Prague to: České Budějovice (up to 8 daily; 2hr 30min–3hr 25min); Český Krumlov (2–6 daily; 2hr 40min–3hr 25min); Orlík/Písek (up to 15 daily; 1hr 30min/2hr); Pelhřimov (up to 15 daily; 1hr 35min–2hr 30min); Rabí/Sušice (up to 4 daily; 2hr 30min/2hr 45min); Strakonice/Prachatice (up to 15/7 daily; 2hr/2hr 30min); Tábor (up to 20 daily;

1hr 15min–1hr 55min); Volary (1 daily; 3hr 5min).
České Budějovice to: Český Krumlov (36 daily; 25–50min); Hluboká nad Vltavou (hourly; 15–40min); Holašovice (up to 7 daily; 30–35min); Jindřichův Hradec (up to 22 daily; 1hr 5min); Prachatice (up to 15 daily; 50min–1hr 15min); Tábor (5–17 daily; 1hr–1hr 35min); Třeboň (up to 14 daily; 30–40min).
Český Krumlov to: Rožmberk/Vyšší Brod (6 daily; 40/55min); Lipno nad Vltavou (up to 4 daily; 1hr 5min–1hr 15min); Horní Planá (2–8 daily; 55min–1hr); Zlatá Koruna (up to hourly; 15min).

Jindřichův Hradec to: České Budějovice (up to 20 daily; 1hr–1hr 15min); Pelhřimov (up to 4 daily; 50 min–1hr 10min); Slavonice (up to 3 daily; 1hr 15min).
Pelhřimov to: Humpolec (up to 20 daily; 30min); Jihlava (up to 15 daily; 35min–1hr); Kámen (up to 15 daily; 20–35min).
Tábor to: Bechyně (up to 17 daily; 35–55min); Kámen (up to 8 daily; 25min–1hr).
Sušice to: Srní/Modrava (up to 4 daily; 55min/1hr 20min).

West Bohemia

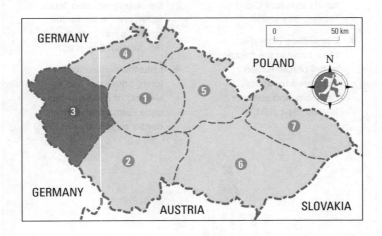

CHAPTER THREE **Highlights**

✴ **Brewery at Plzeň** Take a guided tour of the Pilsner Urquell brewery, home of the original lager – complete with a tasting session. See p.238

✴ **Kladruby monastery** A Baroque-Gothic masterpiece by Czech-Italian architect Giovanni Santini. See p.240

✴ **Domážlice** Bohemian town bang in the middle of the border region renowned for its folk traditions and summer festival. See p.243

✴ **Mariánské Lázně** Elegant fin-de-siècle spa, once the favourite watering hole of European royalty, set amidst gentle wooded hills. See p.245

✴ **Karlovy Vary** Grandiose late nineteenth-century spa, stretched out along the steeply wooded Teplá valley, and venue for the country's most prestigious film festival. See p.257

✴ **Loket** Miniature walled town, squeezed into a U-bend of a river, in this once German-speaking border region. See p.263

△ Kladruby monastery

West Bohemia

For centuries, the rolling hills of **West Bohemia** (Západní Čechy) have been a buffer zone between the Slav world and the German-speaking lands. Encouraged by the Czech Přemyslid rulers, the border regions were heavily colonized by neighbouring Germans from the twelfth century onwards. The German settlers provided urgently needed skilled craftsmen and miners for the Bohemian economy, and for much of their history vast swathes of the region were almost exclusively German-speaking.

With the emergence of nationalism, and the subsequent rise of the pro-Nazi Sudeten German Party in the 1930s, the region became deeply divided along ethnic lines. The violent expulsions of the entire German-speaking population after World War II left vast areas of the countryside and several large towns virtually empty of people. Czechs and Slovaks were encouraged to resettle the area after the war; many Czechs used empty rural homes as country cottages, yet the countryside, particularly close to the border, remains eerily underpopulated even today.

The economic mainstay of the region for the last century has been the sprawling industrial city of **Plzeň**, home of the Škoda engineering works, centre of the country's beer industry, and capital of the region. It's by no means the most picturesque of cities, but it does have a certain nineteenth-century grandeur, and remains a magnet for anyone who admires Czech beer. Within easy reach of Plzeň are the monasteries of **Kladruby** and **Plasy**, monuments to the outstanding architectural genius of Giovanni Santini, the master of "Baroque-Gothic". Further south, the historic border town of **Domažlice** is one of the best-preserved towns in the region, and a jumping-off point to the neighbouring Šumava.

West Bohemia's busiest tourist region, however, is the famous triangle of spas: **Mariánské Lázně**, **Františkovy Lázně** and **Karlovy Vary**. Conveniently scattered along the German border, these three Bohemian spa resorts were the Côte d'Azur of Habsburg Europe, attracting the European elite of the nineteenth century. Following the wholesale nationalization of the spa industry, under Communism every factory and trade union received an annual three weeks' holiday at a *lázně dům* (spa pension): a perk aimed at proving the success of socialism. Taking "the cure" remains very popular not only with Czechs, not so much as a holiday but as the serious treatment of a multitude of ills, but also with Russia's nouveaux riches, and, of course, with the neighbouring Germans. All three spa towns are very attractive visually, but they do tend to be full of the plethoric and elderly, so if you need a break from cure-seekers, head for **Cheb** or **Loket**, both beautifully preserved towns and largely crowd-free.

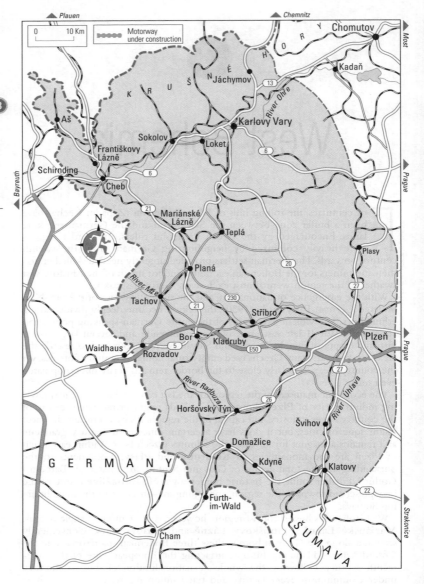

This being one of the most sparsely populated regions in the country, **public transport** is somewhat patchy. However, excellent rail and bus links exist between the major towns, so unless you're heading for the back of beyond, getting around should present few problems.

Plzeň and around

PLZEŇ (Pilsen) was built on beer and bombs. Founded in 1295 and now with a population of around 165,000, it's by far the largest city in Bohemia after Prague, but as recently as 1850 it was a small town of just 14,000, most of whom were German-speakers. Then in 1859, an ironworks was founded and quickly snapped up by the Czech capitalist **Emil Škoda**, under whose control it drew an ever-increasing number of Czechs from the countryside. Within thirty years, the overall population of the town had trebled, while the number of Germans had decreased. Although initially simply an engineering plant, the Habsburgs transformed the ironworks into a huge armaments factory (second only to Krupps in Germany), which, inevitably, was a key acquisition for the Germans when they annexed Czechoslovakia, soon attracting the attention of Allied bombers during World War II. Under the Communists, Plzeň diversified even further, producing trams, trains and buses, not to mention dodgy Soviet-designed nuclear reactors. Sadly, unlike Škoda's car-producing arm, based in Mladá Boleslav (see p.165), Škoda Plzeň is currently struggling economically, although Plzeň itself has attracted large-level foreign investment and is undergoing something of a minor renaissance. Despite the city's overwhelmingly industrial character, Plzeň has plenty of compensations: a large student population, eclectic late-nineteenth-century architecture, and an unending supply of (probably) the best **beer** in the world – all of which make Plzeň a justifiably popular stopoff on the main railway line between Prague and the West.

Arrival, orientation and accommodation

Fast trains from Prague take around one and a half hours to reach Plzeň, making it just about possible to visit on a day-trip from the capital. The town's **train stations** are works of art in themselves: there are numerous minor ones within the city boundaries, but your most likely point of arrival is Plzeň hlavní nádraží, the ornate main station east of the city centre. It has a **left-luggage** office (*úschovňa zavazadel*) and coin-operated luggage boxes. The irredeemably ugly **bus terminal**, for all national and international arrivals, is on the west side of town. From both the bus or main train stations, the city centre is just a short walk away – or a few stops on tram #2 from the bus station; trams #1 and #2 from the train station.

Accommodation

Finding a vacancy in one of Plzeň's **hotels** presents few problems, though rooms don't come cheap. **Private rooms** can be arranged through the **tourist office** at no. 41 on the main square, náměstí Republiky (April–Sept daily 9am–6pm; Oct–March Mon–Fri 10am–5pm, Sat–Sun 10am–3.30pm; ☏378 035 330, ⓦwww.plzen-city.cz), where you can also use the **Internet**. The city's university has cheap dorm accommodation available in the summer holidays at its **student hostels** (Bolevecká 34, ☏377 259 384; ❶; tram #4 north along Karlovarská; if in doubt ask at CKM on Dominikánská Mon–Fri 8am–6pm). Even cheaper and open year-round, although very basic, is the *Ubytovna Zahradní* (☏377 443 262; ❶), at Zahradní 21 (tram #1 from the train station towards Slovany, alight at Jedlová). There are two **campsites** with bungalows – *Bílá hora* (April–Sept), on 28 října, and *Ostende* (May–Sept), to the west, on Malý Bolevec – both just under 5km north of the centre on the far side of the Velký rybník, where Plzeňites go to swim on summer days. To get to *Bílá hora*, take bus #20 from náměstí Republiky, or #39 from Sady Pětatřicátníků and get off at the last stop; for *Ostende*, do the same but alight at Bílá Hora train station (the slow trains from Plzeň to Žatec, 3/4 daily, also stop here) and catch bus #30 for the remaining stops.

Hotel Central Nám. Republiky 33 ⓣ 377 226 757, ⓕ 377 226 064, ⓦ www.central-hotel.cz. Communist-era eyesore, but very well positioned, with en-suite rooms looking out onto náměstí Republiky; a 1970s-style restaurant, a sauna and a gym comprise the other facilities. ❺
Pension City Sady 5 května 52 ⓣ 377 326 069. Small, very central pension on the northeastern edge of the old town, with plainly furnished rooms with TV, and optional en-suite bathroom. ❸
Hotel Continental Zbrojnická 8 ⓣ 377 236 477, ⓦ www.hotelcontinental.cz. Painstakingly restored to something like its former glory by its original First Republic owners. The rooms have phones and satellite TV, plus there are a café and restaurant. ❺
Hotel Gondola Pallova 12 ⓣ 377 327 253, ⓦ www.hotelgondola.cz. Small hotel on the tranquil edge of the old town, with well-appointed, fully en-suite singles and doubles with satellite TV. There's a laundry service and free Internet access too. ❹

Pension K Bezručova 13 ⓣ & ⓕ 377 329 683. Pleasant rooms with satellite TV in the backstreets south of the main square. ❸
Hotel Roudná Na Roudné 13 ⓣ 377 259 926, ⓦ www.hotelroudna.cz. Small, fairly simple and only 300m from the centre; Gambrinus and Pilsner on tap plus guarded parking. ❹
Hotel Slovan Smetanovy sady 1 ⓣ 377 227 256, ⓦ hotelslovan.pilsen.cz. Hotel in a peaceful park, once splendid, with a wonderfully ornate stairwell; partially reconstructed but otherwise Communist-style. Rooms come with or without en-suite facilities and laundry service is available. ❷–❻
Pension U Salzmannů Pražská 8 ⓣ 377 235 855, ⓦ www.usalzmannu.cz. Cosy, double rooms are available at Plzeň's oldest brewery. ❹
Pension V Solní Solní 8 ⓣ 377 236 652, ⓦ www .volny.cz/pensolni. Best-value rooms in town are the three at this small pension within a sixteenth-century house just off the main square. ❸

The City

Stepping out of the main station onto Americká, you're confronted with a variety of bad-taste Communist-era buildings. Close by, the river Radbuza – one of four rivers running through Plzeň – doesn't bear close inspection, but the historical core of the city beyond it certainly does.

Laid out in chessboard fashion by Václav II in 1295, the old town is still dominated by the exalted heights of the Gothic cathedral of **sv Bartoloměj** (St Bartholomew; April–Sept Wed–Sat 10am–4pm; Oct–Dec Wed–Fri same hours), stranded awkwardly in the middle of the main square, **náměstí Republiky**. Inside, the late-Gothic vaulting of the Šternberská kaple, with its delicate pendant boss, is worth checking out, but the cathedral's prize possession is its thirteenth-century wooden statue of the Plzeň Madonna in the Beautiful Style, on the high altar. The church used to boast two towers, but one was struck by lightning in 1525 and was never rebuilt. The cathedral's remaining bile-green **spire** reaches a height of more than a hundred metres, making it the tallest in the country; you can climb up to the viewing platform (*vyhlídková věž*; daily 10am–6pm) – which doubled as the town's lookout post – for a bird's-eye view of the local industrial complexes.

The rest of the main square, presents a full range of architectural styles: some buildings, like the squat, grey *Hotel Central*, as recent as the 1960s; others, like the Italianate **stará radnice** (old town hall; daily 8am–6pm; free entrance), smothered in sgraffito in the early twentieth century, but dating from the sixteenth century. The latter houses a model of the medieval city centre. Plzeň became an unlikely imperial capital in 1599, when the Emperor Rudolf II based himself next door at no. 41 for the best part of a year, in an effort to avoid the ravages of the Prague plague. The vast majority of Plzeň's buildings, however, hail from the city's heyday during the industrial expansion around the turn of the twentieth century. In the old town, this resulted in some wonderful variations on histori-

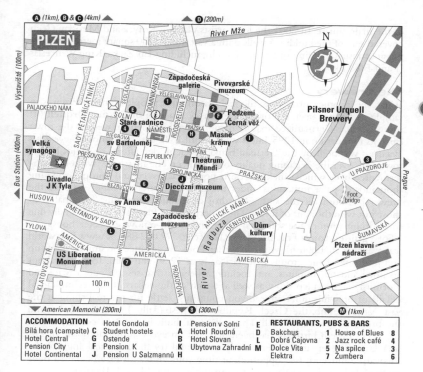

cal themes and Art Nouveau motifs, particularly to the north and west of the main square. West of Sady Pětatřicátníků, and south of Husova, there are still more blocks of late-nineteenth-century residential apartments, boasting vestiges of ornate mosaics and sculpturing, now barely visible beneath the black layer of pollution that's eating away at their fanciful facades.

On Sady Pětatřicátníků itself stands the flamboyant late-nineteenth-century **Divadlo J.K. Tyla** (Tyl Theatre; July–Aug daily 9am–4pm; obligatory guided tours hourly), named after Josef Kajétan Tyl, composer of the Czech national anthem, who died in Plzeň in 1856. Diagonally opposite the theatre is the city's imposing red-brick **Velká synagóga** (Great Synagogue; April–Sept daily except Sat 10am–6pm; Oct daily except Sat 10am–5pm; Nov Mon–Fri 10am–4pm, Sun 10am–5pm; ☎377 235 749), reopened in 1998, and looking resplendent with its brightly coloured chevroned roof, and twin onion domes topped by gilded Stars of David. The largest surviving synagogue in the whole country, and claiming to be Europe's second-largest, it was built in 1888 and could just about have seated Plzeň's entire Jewish population of nearly 3500. The city's few remaining Jews use the winter synagogue at the back of the building, while the partially restored main hall now serves as a concert venue and exhibition space. The ornate interior, which boasts an organ at the east end, also contains a permanent exhibition on the history of the local Jewish community.

If you want to get a glimpse of a dozen or so well-known Czech personalities gathered in one place, head for the **Theatrum Mundi**, on Křižíkovy sady, east of the main square. In 2001 the local artists Vladivoj Kotyza and Miroslav Čech covered one of the building's walls with a vast mural (200 square metres), featuring an unusual meeting of famous Czechs, including Jan Žižka, King Wenceslas II and Emil Škoda.

The brewery

Whatever its other attractions, the real reason most people come to Plzeň is to sample its famous beer, the original Plzeňský Prazdroj or **Pilsner Urquell** (its more familiar Germanized export name). Beer has been brewed in the town since its foundation in 1295, but it wasn't until 1842 that the famous *Bürgerliches Brauhaus* was built by the German banker Bleichröder, after a near-riot by the townsfolk over the declining quality of their beer. The new brew was a bottom-fermented beer, which quickly became popular across central Europe, spawning thousands of paler imitations under the generic name of Pilsner – hence the brewers' addition of the suffix Prazdroj or Urquell (meaning "original"), to show just who thought of it first. The superiority of Plzeň's beer is allegedly due to a combination of the soft local water and world-renowned Žatec hops.

For a **guided tour** of the **brewery** (120Kč; ☎ 377 062 888, ⓦ www.beerworld .cz; available in English), you can either book in advance or simply show up and join one of the groups that start daily at 12.30 and 2pm. Tours last about an hour and ten minutes, and include a beer tasting session and a brief and gloriously tacky video show, as well as a tour of the cellars. If the technological details of brewing don't appeal, you could just settle for the real thing at the vast *Na spilce* pub, the Czech Republic's largest (daily 11am–10pm), beyond the brewery's triumphal arch. The arch itself, built in 1892 to commemorate the beer's fiftieth birthday, has been depicted on every authentic bottle of Pilsner Urquell ever since. Alternatively, you could try the historical angle at the Pivovarské muzeum (see opposite), or time your visit with Plzeň's annual **beer festival**, held early in October, as a preamble to the Munich Bierfest.

Plzeň's museums

Plzeň has a fair few museums, the biggest being the copper-topped **Západočeské muzeum** (West Bohemian Museum; Tues–Sun 9am–5pm; ⓦ www

---

The American liberation of Plzeň

By May 6, 1945, General Patton's **US Third Army** had liberated much of West Bohemia, including Plzeň. Less than 100km of virtually open road lay between the Americans and Prague, by then into the second day of its costly uprising against the Nazis. However, the agreement between the big three Allies at Yalta was that Prague should be liberated by the Soviets, who at the time were still 200km from Prague, en route from Berlin. Patton offered to march on Prague, and in fact, on May 7, three US armoured cars reached the outskirts of the city, but the order was to stay put.

Following the 1948 coup, the Communists took down all the monuments and deleted all references in history books to the American liberation of Plzeň. They even went so far as to say that the Americans had deliberately hung back from Prague, allowing thousands to die in the uprising. However, in May 1990, the city was able once again to celebrate the liberation, and in the presence of large numbers of US army veterans, a new memorial was erected on Chodské náměstí, just off Klatovská třída. In 1995, the granite memorial planned after the war but never built was finally erected at the top of Americká, saying simply "Thank You America". Since the fall of Communism, West Bohemia has held an annual **celebration** of Plzeň's liberation in early May, with parades of army vehicles both modern and veteran through the city.

.zcm.cz), a neo-Baroque extravaganza, built in the nineteenth century to help educate the peasants who were flocking to the city. It's recently reopened, after more than a decade of restoration, and is worth a visit, if only for its ornate interior. The museum stages temporary exhibitions on the upper floor, and houses the impressive town armoury (*Plzeňská městská zbrojnice*) – established by Charles IV – on the ground floor.

More interesting than the city's big museum is the **Západočeská galerie** (Tues–Sun 10am–6pm; Ⓦ www.zpc-galerie.cz), which puts on temporary exhibitions of modern Czech art in a newly renovated Gothic building at Pražská 13, and is due to house its impressive permanent collection of Czech art (its Baroque paintings by Brandl and Škreta and sculptures by Braun are especially worthwhile), in the distinctive elongated vaults of the town's Gothic butchers' stalls or **Masné krámy** (times as above), which stand opposite the city's sixteenth-century water tower or *Černá věž* (now a commercial art gallery).

At the end of Veleslavínova is the most popular of Plzeň's museums, the **Pivovarské muzeum** (Brewery Museum; daily: April–Dec 10am–6pm; Jan–March 10am–5pm; 120Kč, or 60Kč without a guide). Housed in what was originally a Gothic malthouse and later a pub, this is a more-than-sufficient consolation for those who fail to get into the brewery itself; ask the curator to get the old Würlitzer organ going while you check out the numerous exhibits on the long tradition of brewing in Plzeň, including the smallest beer barrel in the world (a mere one-centimetre cubed) and case after case of kitsch Baroque beer mugs.

Also worth a quick once-over is the little-visited **Diecézní muzeum** (April–Oct Tues–Sun 10am–6pm), housed in the cloisters of the former Franciscan monastery on Františkánská. The highlight of the museum is the Gothic chapel of sv Barbora (Saint Barbara) in the presbytery, on whose walls beautiful rose-coloured frescoes survive from the 1460s. The frescoes depict Barbara's martyrdom, which was gruesome even by biblical standards. Condemned to death by her father for converting to Christianity, she was racked, birched, carded with a metal comb, forced to lie on a bed of shards, slashed with red-hot blades, paraded naked, dragged up a mountain and finally beheaded, upon which her father was struck down by lightning.

Of minor interest only are the **Plzeňské historické podzemí** or underground tunnels (April, May, Oct & Nov Wed–Sun 9am–5pm; June–Sept Tues–Sun 9am–5pm), accessible from Perlová 4, built as a defensive ploy in the fourteenth century, but also very useful for storing beer. The forty-minute guided tours are in Czech only, but there's a fairly lucid written commentary in English, available on request.

Eating, drinking and entertainment

All the hotels in town have **restaurants** attached to them, but most Czechs prefer to head for the city's pubs or pizzerias. Apart from the aforementioned *Na spílc* **pub** (see opposite), you can get Pilsner Urquell (and cheap grub) at *U Salzmannů*, the town's famous wood-panelled pub at Pražská 8. Gambrinus and the dark Purkmistr, Plzeň's other beers, are best drunk at the restaurant *Žumbera*, Bezručova 14, which also has a music club upstairs. Traditional Czech food is available at *Bakchus*, Veleslavínova 15, which has friendly staff and an interior with "Roman" frescoes. The city boasts several decent **Italian** joints: try the *Dolce Vita*, Prešovská 5, with a geranium-filled courtyard and occasional live music. Those aiming for the healthy life should drop by the *Dobrá čajovna* (tea house) at Perlová 10.

Plzeň's wonderful Beaux-Arts Divadlo J.K. Tyla (Tyl Theatre) is the city's main venue for opera and ballet. Most other concerts and cultural events take place at the Dům kultury on Americká, though the **Festival of Folk Songs** (known as Porta and held over the first weekend in July) is held in the Vystaviště, on Radčická, off Palackého náměstí (reconstructed at the time of research). Vystaviště is also home to the city's summer-only open-air cinema (*letní kino*), and there's an art-house cinema complex called Elektra, at Americká 24, which also has a restaurant and occasional live music. Live concerts are held every Wednesday in the Jazz rock café, Sedláčkova 18, and in the *House of Blues*, Černická 10.

Around Plzeň

Within easy reach of Plzeň are two monasteries that bear the hallmark of Giovanni Santini, arguably the most original Baroque architect to work in the Czech Lands. Of the two, **Plasy** – 18km north of Plzeň – is the easiest to get to (by train or bus), though **Kladruby** – over 30km west – is without doubt a more rewarding day-trip.

Plasy

The Cistercian monastery at **PLASY** (Plass) is submerged in a green valley around 25km north of Plzeň. Originally founded in 1144 by Vladislav II, the present muddle of partially renovated Baroque outbuildings is the work of two of Prague's leading architects, Jean-Baptiste Mathey and Giovanni Santini (also known as Jan Blažej Santini). Of the two, **Santini** (1667–1723), the Prague-born son of north Italian immigrants, is the more interesting: a popular architect, builder and stonemason whose personal, slightly ironic Baroque-Gothic style produced some of the most original works in the country. The brilliant white cloisters harbour palatial side chapels, while the rest of the monastery (April & Oct Sat & Sun 9am–noon & 1–4pm; May & Sept Tues–Sun 9am–noon & 1–4pm; June–Aug Tues–Sun 9am–5pm) is now an art gallery; the highlight of the fifty-minute guided tour is a look at the tall side chapels off the cloisters, whose frescoes create an incredible splash of colour on the ceiling. The best time to visit the monastery is during the annual **Hermit Festival** of contemporary art and music in late June/early July, which draws avant-garde artists from all over Europe.

Shortly after its Baroque redevelopment, the monastery was dissolved and in 1826 fell into the hands of **Prince Clemenz von Metternich**, the arch-conservative Habsburg chancellor and political architect of the post-Napoleonic European order. Over the road, obscured by willow trees, the cemetery church was transformed by the prince into the family mausoleum (same hours). In tune with his politics, its oppressively Neoclassical forms dwarf the commoners' graveyard behind it.

Kladruby

If Plasy fails to move you, the **Benedictine monastery** (April & Oct Sat & Sun 9am–4pm; May & Sept Tues–Sun 9am–4pm; June–Aug Tues–Sun 9am–5pm; tour in English 90Kč, tour with English text 60Kč, two tours correspondently 180Kč/120Kč; ⓦkladruby.euweb.cz) at **KLADRUBY** (Kladrau), 35km west of Plzeň, should do the trick, particularly if you manage to catch a Christmas concert or join the August music festival. An altogether less gloomy affair, the monastery was founded by Vladislav I in 1114 (he's buried here, too) and was once the largest and richest monastery in Bohemia. Gutted by the Hussites and again during the Thirty Years' War, the whole place was trans-

formed when the Counter-Reformation had set in – the monastery according
to blueprints by Kilian Ignaz Dientzenhofer, and the monastery church under
Santini's supervision. The huge monastery church, now restored, is the main
attraction, where the original Romanesque and Gothic elements blend imperceptibly with Santini's idiosyncratic additions. The original lantern tower has
been converted into an extravagant Baroque cupola, which filters a faded pink
light into the transepts, themselves covered in stars and zigzags mirrored on the
cold stone paving below.

The easiest way to get from Plzeň to Kladruby on public transport is to go as
far as **Stříbro** (Mies) by train, and then change onto one of the fairly frequent
local buses, which leave from the bus station in the town centre and cover the
last 6km to Kladruby. Dramatically poised over the Mže (Mies) river, Stříbro
itself was previously the vague frontier post between the German- and Czech-
speaking districts, its tidy square sporting arguably the most beautiful Renaissance **radnice** in Bohemia, paid for by the town's long-extinct silver mines
(*stříbro* means silver).

Klatovy and around

Tightly walled in and nervously perched on high ground, **KLATOVY** (Klattau)
warns of the approaching border with Germany. Founded by Přemyslid King
Otakar II in 1260, the town's great prosperity in the middle ages is still visible
in the main square, but it can't compete with the Rose Towns further east. Still,
there's enough to keep you occupied for at least a couple of hours, and with Plzeň
only an hour away by train it's another possible day-trip; or a potential base for
exploring the northwest tip of the nearby Šumava region (see p.217).

The town

Klatovy's best feature is undoubtedly the cluster of tall buildings jostling for
position in the southwest corner of the cramped town square, **náměstí Míru**.
The facade of the Renaissance radnice is decorated with 1920s sgraffito and
features two liberation plaques: one to the Russians (who liberated the country), and one to the Americans (who liberated the town). Tucked in beside the
town hall is the seventy-six-metre, sixteenth-century **Černá věž** (Black Tower;
April & Oct Sat & Sun 9am–noon & 1–4pm; May–Sept Tues–Sun 9am–noon
& 1–5pm), the clearest evidence of the town's bygone prosperity. Its pinnacled
parapet, once a lookout post to protect the town, offers views of the forests at
the Bavarian border and, closer at hand, across the rooftops to the smaller and
later **Bílá věž** (see p.242).

Next to the Černá věž, Dientzenhofer's white **Jezuitský kostel** exudes
incense and cooled air from its curvaceous interior emblazoned with frescoes,
including a spectacularly theatrical trompe l'oeil main altar and backdrop. More
fascinating, though, are the church's musty **katakomby** (catacombs; times as for
the Černá věž), where Jesuits and other wealthy locals are preserved in varying
stages of decomposition underneath the radnice; the entrance is round the side
of the church. Next door is **U bílého jednorožce** (At the White Unicorn),
a seventeenth-century Baroque *lékárna* or apothecary (May–Oct Tues–Sun
9am–noon & 1–5pm), which functioned until 1964 and has since become a
UNESCO registered monument. The bottles and pots are all labelled in Latin,
with swirling wooden pillars flanking the shelves, and a unicorn's horn (strictly
speaking, it's a tusk from an arctic narwhal), the pharmacists' mascot, jutting out

into the centre. The back room, where the drugs were mixed, comes complete with horror-movie flasks of dried goat's blood and pickled children's intestines. Adjacent to the pharmacy is the town's **art gallery**, Galerie U bílého jednoro-žce (Tues–Sun 10am–noon & 1–5pm; ℡376 312 049), a pristine vaulted white room used for temporary exhibitions.

Before you give up on sightseeing, it's worth strolling over to the **Bílá věž** (White Tower), built during the Renaissance period, but later Baroquified. Next door to the tower stands the Gothic church, **Arciděkanský chrám**, whose spires sport charming gilded crowns slipped on like rings on fingers. Inside, the church retains its medieval stellar vaulting, and features a fetching shell-shaped baldachin, held up by barley-sugar columns. Beyond the church and Bílá věž are the impressive remains of the town's medieval walls, which, if followed south, will bring you to the **local museum** (Okresní muzeum; May–Sept & Dec Tues–Sun 9am–noon & 1–5pm; Jan–April, Oct & Nov Tues–Fri 9am–noon & 1–5pm), on Hostašova, more interesting for its salmon-pink Austro-Hungarian architecture than for its humdrum exhibits.

Practicalities

Klatovy's main **train and bus stations** are situated over a kilometre northwest of the old town (bus #1 or #2 to the main square); Klatovy-město station, just under a kilometre south of the old town, is only served by slow trains to and from Sušice. **Accommodation**, including private rooms, can be organized through the new, efficient **tourist office** by the Černá věž on the main square (Mon–Fri 9am–5pm; ℡376 347 240, ⓦwww.klatovy.cz/icklatovy).

There are a few decent pensions in the old town, such as *U Hejtmana* on ulice kpt. Jaroše (℡376 317 918; ❷), just off the main square, plus the more expensive Renaissance *Hotel Ennius*, Randova 111 (℡376 320 567, ⓦwww .sweb.cz/ennius; ❸), also in the old town, with a thriving restaurant, and owned by the same outfit who run the *Hotel Centrál*, at Masarykova 300 (℡376 314 571, ⓦwww.centralkt.cz; ❸), which isn't really that central, but is at least conveniently situated between the old town and the train and bus stations. Another option is the *Klatovský dvůr* (℡376 316 517; ❷), out on the road to Domažlice, or the *Rozvoj*, Procházkova 110 (℡376 311 609; ❷), an unusual circular building with a restaurant and disco. Alternatively, there's an excellent **campsite**, *Sluneční mlýn* (May–Sept) by an old water mill on the River Úhlava; it's signposted a couple of kilometres along the road to Domažlice, has a swimming pool, bungalows and tent space.

Back in Klatovy, you can best admire the main square from the tables outside the *Beseda* **restaurant**. Better value is the *Těp*, at the corner of the square, which serves a wide range of dishes (even Argentinian). The *Stará rychta*, on Denisova, west of the main square, is the town's liveliest **pub**, and serves Gambrinus. By far the nicest place is the Čajovna U naší milé Paní, located in a turret behind the Arciděkanský chrám – a mixture of tea-house and ceramic shop.

Švihov

Ruined castles are ten-a-penny in these border regions; the virtue of the one at **ŠVIHOV**, 11km north of Klatovy, is that it still looks like a proper castle – and it's easy to reach by train, from either Plzeň or Klatovy. It was begun in 1480 by the Rožmberks as a vast concentric structure, with traditional double fortifications creating an inner and outer castle surrounded by a moat. Suspicious of such an unusually well-fortified stronghold, the Habsburgs ordered the owners to tear down the eastern section, and what remains today is a kind of cross-section of a castle, partially surrounded by its original moat. The highlights of the fifty-minute guided tour (April & Oct Sat & Sun 9.30am–noon & 1–3pm; May & Sept Tues–Sun 9.30am–noon & 1–4pm; June–Aug closes 5pm; Ⓦwww .pruvodce.com/svihov) are the late-Gothic chapel by Benedikt Ried, and a very fine Renaissance strapwork ceiling. It also frequently hosts concerts of classical music and theatrical performances (ask at the tourist office in Plzeň for details).

Domažlice

Fifteen kilometres from the German border, **DOMAŽLICE** (Taus) is an attractive little town, situated in one of the few border areas that has always been predominantly Czech-speaking. For centuries the town was the local customs house, and the Chodové (see box p.244), as the folk round here are known, were given the task of guarding the border with Bavaria, but in 1707 the town lost much of its former importance when the border was fixed. The town's biggest bash is the annual Chod folk festival, **Chodské slavnosti**, held in the middle of August.

The town

Like many small Bohemian towns, Domažlice starts and ends at its main square, **náměstí Míru**, a long, thin affair, positioned along an exact east–west axis. Flanked by uninterrupted arcades under every possible style of colourful gable, the pretty, elongated cobbled square seems like a perfect setting for a Bohemian-Bavarian skirmish. Halfway down one side, the thirteenth-century **church tower** or *věž* (April–Sept daily 9am–noon & 1–5pm), now leaning to one side quite noticeably, used to double as a lookout post for the vulnerable town, and ascending its 196 steps provides a bird's-eye view of the whole area. The **Děkanský kostel** itself, whose entrance is round the corner in Kostelní, has a wonderful series of Baroque frescoes, colourful furnishings and a particularly fine trompe l'oeil scenic backdrop for the gilded main altar.

The town's other remaining thirteenth-century round tower lies to the southwest, down Chodská, and belongs to the **Chodský hrad**, seat of the Chodové self-government until it fell into the hands of Wilhelm Lamminger von Albreneuth. The castle has recently been renovated and now houses the **Muzeum Chodska** (mid-April to mid-Oct Tues–Sun 9am–noon & 1–5pm; rest of the year Mon–Fri 10am–noon & 1–3pm), which worthily traces the town's colourful history.

More fascinating by half, though, is the **Muzeum Jindřicha Jindřicha**, east of the old town just beyond the medieval gateway (mid-April to mid-Oct Tues–Sun 9am–noon & 1–4pm; rest of the year Mon–Fri 9am–noon), and founded by local composer Jindřich Jindřich. His extensive collection of Chod folk costumes, ceramics and other regional items, all displayed in a mock-up cottage interior, are ample compensation if you fail to catch the annual festival.

Practicalities

The town's **main train station**, called simply Domažlice, is 1km east of town; the Domažlice město station, five minutes' walk south of the old town down Jiráskova, is served only by slow trains to Bor and Tachov. The main **bus terminal** lies just north of the main square, on Poděbradova. The town's **tourist office** (June–Sept Mon–Fri 7.30am–5pm, Sat 9am–noon; Oct–May Mon–Fri 7.30am–4pm) is situated near the nineteenth-century radnice on the main square.

The Chodové

"The spearhead of the Slavic march into central Europe", as writer Josef Škvorecký described them, the **Chodové** are one of the few Czech peoples to have kept their identity. Very little is certain about their origin, but their name comes from *choditi* (to walk about), and undoubtedly refers to their traditional occupation as guardians of the frontier. Since the earliest times, their proud independence was exploited by a succession of Bohemian kings, who employed them as border guards in return for granting them freedom from serfdom, plus various other feudal privileges.

However, after the **Battle of Bílá hora**, the Habsburgs were keen to curb the power of the Chodové, and the whole region was handed over lock, stock and barrel to one of the victorious generals, Wilhelm Lamminger von Albenreuth (also known as Lomikar). At first the Chodové tried to reaffirm their ancient privileges by legal means, but when this proved fruitless, with the encouragement of one **Jan Sladký** – better known as **Kozina** – they simply refused to acknowledge their new despot. Seventy of the rebels were thrown into the prison in Prague, while Kozina was singled out to be publicly hanged in Plzeň on November 28, 1695, as an example to the rest of the Chodové. From the gallows, Kozina prophesied the death of Lomikar "within a year and a day" – the general died as Kozina foresaw, from a stroke following a banquet held to celebrate Kozina's demise.

Although the empire prevailed, the Chodové never allowed the loss of their freedom to quash their ebullience or their peculiar local dialect, which still survives in the villages. Stubbornly resistant to Germanization, they carried the banner of Czech national defiance through the Dark Ages. Even now, of all the regions of Bohemia, Chodsko is closest to its cultural roots, known above all for its local dialect and rich local costumes, still worn on Sundays and religious holidays, and for its *dudy* (bagpipes), now played only in folk ensembles and at festivals. If you're interested in seeing a typical Chodové village, it's worth visiting Klenči pod Čerchovem, close to Domažlice.

As for **accommodation**, there are plenty of simple family-run pensions in the old town: try *Café-Pension Tiffany* (☎379 725 591, ⊛www.tiffany.wz.cz; ➋), beside the church at Kostelní 102. Alternatively, check for vacancies at *Hotel Sokolský dům* (☎379 720 084, ✉info@sokolskydum.cz; ➌), on the west side of the main square, which has tastefully furnished rooms and a restaurant. Cheaper accommodation is available at the *Hotel Koruna* (☎379 722 279; ➋), west of the square at M.B. Staška 69, which has plain rooms and a restaurant serving up Czech fare. One of the nicest places is the snug *Penzion Konšelský šenk* (☎379 720 200; ⊛www.konselskysenk.cz; ➋), at Vodní 33, in the quiet back-streets just south off the square, with pleasant en-suite rooms and an excellent pizzeria. Otherwise, there's the riverside *Babylon* **campsite** (mid-May to Sept), 6km south by bus or train. As for **food**, the *Ural* (closed Sun), on the north side of the main square, is a regular Czech pub-restaurant serving the local, dark beer, Purkmistr 11; *Dalibor Kubů*, south off the main square on Branská, is slightly pricier and more used to tourists, or else there's *Chodská rychta*, a pleasant restaurant on M.B. Staška, opposite the town's art gallery. Domažlice has its own **brewery** by the bus station, though no brewery tap; instead, head for the *Štika*, a real drinkers' pub serving the local brew, on the road out to Plzeň.

If you're heading for Germany, you can catch one of the seven trains a day from Domažlice to the Bavarian town of **Furth-im-Wald**, whose Drachen-stich festival – during which the townsfolk fight a gory battle with a giant dragon – takes place in August (⊛www.drachenstich.de).

Horšovský Tyn

A lazy afternoon could happily be spent at **HORŠOVSKÝ TYN** (Bischoftein-itz), just 10km north of Domažlice. Its main square, **náměstí Republiky**, is a picturesque grassy, sloping affair centred on the church of sv Petr and Pavel, and lined with Gothic houses sporting brightly coloured Baroque facades. At the top end, surrounded by a goat-inhabited moat, is the quadrilateral sgraffitoed **zámek** (April & Oct Sat & Sun 9am–noon & 1–4pm; May & Sept Tues–Sun 9am–noon & 1–4pm; June–Aug closes 5pm; ☎379 423 111), one of the most popular in West Bohemia and transformed by the Lobkowicz family into a rich Renaissance pile. There's a rather complicated choice of **guided tours**: the Hrad tour (*trasa 1*; 50min) takes you through the renovated Bishop's Palace, including the reconstructed interior of the Early Gothic bishop's chapel. The Zámek tour (*trasa 2*; 1hr) covers living quarters from the sixteenth to twentieth centuries, plus a gallery lined with portraits of Czech rulers; the Kuchyně tour (*trasa 3*; 40min) features a trawl round the kitchens, tacky china chandeliers equipped with their original Edison bulbs and other delights; the Burgrave's Palace (*trasa 4*; 50min) leads visitors around the reconstructed Riding School; the Erbovní sál (*trasa 5*; 30min) takes you through the rooms with sixteenth-century heraldry paintings; and Mitsuko (*trasa 6*; 40min) presents the legacy of Japanese-origin countess Mitsuko Coudenhove-Kalergi, who lived in the country at the turn of the twentieth century. Behind the chateau, the vast **Zámecký park** stretches northwards, complete with hidden chapels, a large lake and hosts of peacocks. It's a ten-minute walk to the centre from the train station: head east up Nádražní to the main crossroads, then north over the river, and the main square will appear on your right. If you want **to stay** the night, there are two good hotels on the square to choose between: the *Hotel Šumava* (☎379 422 800; ❷) with simple rooms, and the more sophisticated *Hotel Gurman* (☎379 410 020; ❹), right by the castle.

Mariánské Lázně

At the end of the eighteenth century, what is now **MARIÁNSKÉ LÁZNĚ** (Marienbad) was unadulterated woodland. It was not until the 1790s that the local abbot, Karel Reitenberger, and a German doctor, Josef Nehr, took the initiative and established a spa here. Within a hundred years, Marienbad (as it was known in its heyday) had joined the clique of world-famous European spas, boasting a clientele that ranged from writers to royalty. The inveterate spa-man Goethe was among the earliest of the VIPs to popularize the place, and a few generations later it became the favourite holiday spot of King Edward VII (who visited it nine times), a passion he shared with his pal, the Emperor Franz-Josef I. During World War I, even the incorrigibly infirm Franz Kafka spent a brief, happy spell here with Felice Bauer, writing "things are different now and good, we are engaged to be married right after the war", though in fact they never were.

Today, Mariánské Lázně is much less exclusive, though no less attractive – what was a fat-farm for the rich and famous only two generations ago is now eminently accessible to all and sundry. Over the last decade, the riotous, late-nineteenth-century architecture has been restored to its former flamboy-ance, and the whole place has been successfully brought back to life. Above all, though, it's the spa's beautiful setting, amidst thickly forested hills, that remains its most beguiling asset. The air around town is cool and refreshing and the centre of the spa is more or less free of cars (parking is a fineable offence), all of which comes as something of a relief after the usual traffic-choked streets; it's even forbidden to smoke in the centre.

Arrival and information

Passengers arriving by train or bus are unloaded at a suitably discreet distance from the spa, some 3km south of the centre; trolleybus #5 covers the 3km up the former Kaiserstrasse, now Hlavní třída. The **tourist office** (daily 10am–noon & 1–6pm, ☏ 354 622 474; Ⓦ www.marienbad.cz, www.marianskelazne .cz,), is in the dům Chopin at Hlavní 47. Although none too friendly, it does have maps and basic information, should help with accommodation (see below) and features its own **Internet café**.

Accommodation

The tourist office can book **private rooms**, or, if you have your own transport, you can search for pensions and rooms for yourself in the suburbs of Úšovice and on Palackého street, where they predominate. There's also a vast choice of spa **hotels**, all run by Hungarian-owned *Danubius Hotels* (☏ 354 655 550, Ⓦ www.marienbad.cz), based at Lečebné Lázně, Masaryková 22, which can be reserved one day in advance and are all fairly pricey (up to ❾). Be warned that, in high season, prices rise to a minimum of €100 for a double room in a central hotel, and those undergoing spa treatments will always get first refusal.

There are also two **campsites** to choose from: *Autokemping Luxor* (May–Sept), which is awkwardly located several kilometres to the west of the train station in Velká Hled'sebe, along the road to Cheb (bus #6 to Velká Hled'sebe, then walk 1km south down the Plzeň road; ☏ 354 623 504); and *Stanowitz* (April–Oct; ☏ 354 624 673, Ⓦ www.stanowitz.com), in the village of Stanoviště, 5km south of Mariánské Lázně.

Hotel Bohemia Hlavní třída 100 ☏ 354 610 111, Ⓔ hotel.bohemia@orea.cz. Late-nineteenth-century establishment, somewhat brutally modernized, but still fairly classy and very comfortable: all rooms come with en-suite facilities and satellite TV. ❼

Hotel Esplanade Karlovarská 438 ☏ 354 676 111, Ⓦ www.esplanade-marienbad.cz. Probably the snazziest of the bunch, with comfortable, air-conditioned rooms with all conceivable amenities and a sauna on site. ❾

Hvězda Goethovo nám. 7 ☏ 354 631 111, Ⓔ hvezda@marienbad.cz. Part of the spa hotel group, yet another comfortable, opulent pile in the centre of town, offering spa treatments. ❹

Hotel Kossuth/Suvorov Ruská 77 ☏ 354 627 005, Ⓔ kossuth@iol.cz. Two cheap hotels, a few doors down from each other, that have joined forces. Quiet location, good views but absolutely no frills. ❸

Nové Lázně Reitenbergerova 53 ☏ 354 644 111

or 354 644 051, Ⓔ novelazne@marienbad.cz. With its full-blown 1890s opulence, if you're here for the cure, this is the place to stay. ❽

Pension Oradour Hlavní třída 43 ☏ 354 624 304, Ⓦ www.penzionoradour.wz.cz. Best budget accommodation in the centre, with large rooms (no en-suite facilities) and its own car park. ❷

Hotel Paris Goethovo nám. 15 ☏ 354 628 894, Ⓕ 354 628 893. This white-yellow, comfortable hotel stands directly above the Kolonáda, providing delightful views over the spa park. ❺

Hotel Polonia Hlavní třída 50 ☏ 354 622 451, Ⓔ recepce@polonia.oreahotels.cz. Simply modernized, but dripping with original fin-de-siècle features in the foyer and café. Cheaper rooms with shared facilities are also available. ❸

Zlatý zámek Klíčová 167 ☏ 354 623 924, Ⓔ manaskova@seznam.cz. Clean to the point of sterility, but exceptional value for its central locale. ❷

▲ Lázně Kynžvart (7km)

MARIÁNSKÉ LÁZNĚ

RESTAURANTS, CAFÉS & BARS

Churchill's	2
Excelsior	3
Helvetia	5
Irish Pub	6
Café Polonia	D
Villa Romana	4
U zlaté koule	1

ACCOMMODATION

Autokemping Luxor	J
Hotel Bohemia	F
Hotel Esplanade	H
Hotel Hvězda	B
Hotel Kossuth/ Suvorov	E
Nové Lázně	G
Hotel Paris	A
Pension Oradour	C
Hotel Polonia	D
Stanowitz	K
Zlatý zámek	I

Mestské divadlo · Křížový pramen · Městské muzeum · Kolonáda · Hotel Weimar · Zpívající fontána · Nanebevzetí Panny Marie · Spa Gardens · dům Chopin · Anglikánský kostel · Karolinin & Rudolfův pramen · Ambrožův pramen · Nové lázně · Casino · Hotel Excelsior · Pravoslavný kostel · Kaiserturm

0   100 m

Train & Bus Stations, ❺, K (5km) & J (6km) ▼   ▼ ❻

▶ H & Chair Lift

The Spa

Mariánské Lázně was the last of Bohemia's famous triangle of spas to be built, and as such is the most consistently flamboyant in its architecture. As far as the eye can see, sumptuously regal buildings rise up from the pine-clad surrounds, most dating from the second half of the nineteenth century. For all their sculptural theatricality and invention, there's an intriguing homogeneity in the fin-de-siècle opulence, with each building dressed up, almost without exception, in buttery Kaisergelb (imperial yellow) and white plasterwork.

Hlavní třída

Hlavní třída, the spa's main thoroughfare, is several kilometres long, and forms an almost uninterrupted parade of luxury, four-storey mansions (most of which are hotels), glass shops or granny-filled cafés. The vast majority are thoroughly in keeping with the fin-de-siècle ambience of the place. There are, however, one or two hideous modern hotels built over the last decade, though even these have failed to impinge on the most impressive final section of the street, where layer upon layer of shapely balconies overlook the spa gardens. Several of the

The spa tradition

Following the Habsburg tradition, **spa treatments** remain extremely popular in the Czech and Slovak republics, which boast over a hundred spa resorts (*lázně* in Czech, *kúpele* in Slovak) between them. One of the chief perks of the Communist system, they were a form of healthcare open to all and usually paid for by one's employers (ie the state). Children, the elderly and the generally ill and infirm are still prescribed spa treatments by their doctors – it is often very difficult to book a cure, with huge waiting lists. Nowadays, the spas also attract an increasing number of Germans, Austrians and wealthy Russians, for whom stays are still relatively inexpensive compared to Western prices. At a few resorts, such as Mariánské Lázně, you can book in for half- or full-day "treatments", but most are intended for longer stays (three weeks is the norm for those sent by their doctors). If you're paying "foreign rates" for your visit, you don't actually have to be ill to be treated. Some people find spa resorts rather like open hospitals, but many are beautifully situated deep in the countryside, with fresh air and constitutionals very much part of the cure.

The basic treatment involves drinking the mineral waters from the spa's natural springs, for which many guests use their own ornate drinking vessels called *becher*. These curious miniature teapots each have a spout through which you sip the waters, thus preventing discolouration of the teeth. The waters come in an amazing variety: alkaline, chlorinated, carbogaseous and even radioactive, though they usually share one common characteristic: they are all pretty foul, or at least an acquired taste. In addition – and this is the more appealing bit – you can bathe in hot springs or sapropelic muds, breathe in pungent fumes or indulge in a new generation of complementary therapies, such as ultrasound and aerosol treatment, ultraviolet light baths, acupuncture and electrotherapy. Each spa resort tends to specialize in "curing" a particular ailment. For example, Františkovy Lázně is the best place for gynaecological problems; Luhačovice for respiratory diseases; Karlovy Vary for digestive complaints; and Trenčianske Teplice for motor problems. The most famous (and most oversubscribed) of the spa resorts are Karlovy Vary, Třeboň and Mariánské Lázně in Bohemia, Luhačovice in Moravia and Piešťany in Slovakia. The official website, ⓦwww.spas.cz, contains full information on all treatments going, and where they're on offer in the Czech Republic.

shops here sell tins of *oplatky*, the ubiquitous sugar- or chocolate-filled wafers which make the waters you are about to taste infinitely more palatable. At no. 47 is the Bílá labut' (The White Swan), a modest three-storey building where Frédéric Chopin stayed in 1836 on his way from Paris to Warsaw. Known as the **dům Chopin**, it serves as the spa's tourist office (see p.246), and has a tiny museum to the composer (mid-April to mid-Oct Tues, Thurs & Sun 2–5pm) on the first floor.

The spa's **synagogue**, which stood on Hlavní třída itself, was burnt down in 1938 on *Kristallnacht*, and no trace now remains. By contrast, the spa's small, red-brick **Anglikánský kostel** (Anglican church; Tues–Sun 9am–noon & 12.30–4pm) survives, hidden in the trees behind the *Hotel Bohemia*. Abandoned by its royal patrons and neglected under the Communists, the church has recently been restored, and is now used as an exhibition space. All that remains of the interior, however, is the pulpit, a rose window and a plaque to its most famous patron, King Edward VII. Better preserved is the nearby neo-Byzantine **Pravo-slavský kostel** (Russian Orthodox church; May–Oct Mon–Fri 8.30am–noon & 1–5pm, Sat & Sun 8.30am–5pm; Nov–April daily 9.30–11.30am & 2–4pm) on Ruská, the road running parallel to Hlavní třída. Dating from 1902, the rather plain interior is made remarkable by the spectacular iconostasis that won the Grand Prix de France at the 1900 Paris World Exhibition. Designed in the shape of a miniature Orthodox church, and made from enamel and porcelain, it is coated in over nine kilograms of gold and cobalt, and is reputedly the largest piece of porcelain in the world. Mass is still held in the church every Sunday.

The Kolonáda and around

The focal point of the spa, overlooking the town, is the gently curving **Kolonáda**. Easily the most beautiful wrought-iron colonnade in Bohemia, it's rather like a whale-ribbed nineteenth-century railway station without the trains, and despite the lurid 1970s ceiling frescoes, the atmosphere is genteel and sober. In summer, there are daily concerts by Bohemian bands, occasional performances by the local symphony orchestra, and overpriced carriage rides (*drožky*) around the spa (200Kč for 10min). Adjoining the northern tip of the colonnade is the spa's first and foremost spring, the **Křížový pramen**, housed, along with two other springs, in its very own Neoclassical colonnade (daily 6am–6pm) and reputed to be good for one's kidneys. There are two more springs in Ušovice (see p.250).

Beyond the southern end of the Kolonáda stands the **zpívající fontána**, a computer-controlled dancing fountain, no great beauty, which does its thing to a popular piece of classical music roughly every two hours from 7am (the last two shows, at 9pm and 10pm, are accompanied by a light display – see the nearby poster for the latest programme). Beyond and, more importantly, out of earshot of the fountain, is the elegant Neoclassical colonnade of the **Karolinin and Rudolfův pramen**, whose springs spurt forth water round the clock.

Behind and above the colonnades lies **Goethovo náměstí**, which boasts a new aluminium, seated statue of Goethe; the original was carried off by the retreating Nazis, leaving just the granite plinth, to which the Czechs added a commemorative postwar plaque in Czech, Latin and French (but, significantly, not German). On his last visit in 1823, Goethe stayed at the house on the corner that now houses the **Městské muzeum** (Tues–Sun 9.30am–12.30pm & 1–5pm). On the ground floor, the displays trace the history of the spa's development; upstairs, along with period furnishings from Goethe's time, there are new historical sections that are more frank about the spa's German roots (and about the American liberation), but still silent on the postwar expulsions that more or less cleared the spa of its remaining inhabitants.

The square is overlooked by yet more giant, ochre spa buildings, including the former **Hotel Weimar**, at no. 9, in which King Edward VII preferred to stay (above the central portico there's a well-concealed German Gothic plaque commemorating his visit). Below, at the centre of the square, is the unusual octagonal church of **Nanebevzetí Panny Marie** (Assumption of the Virgin Mary), built in 1844–1848 and decorated inside in rich neo-Byzantine style. Still further down the hill are two buildings definitely worth checking out. The first is the old **Casino** building, now the spa's main social centre, with an old faded dance hall (discos on most nights) of fin-de-siècle marbled elegance; the other is the equally ornate **Nové lázně** (☎354 644 111, ✉novelazne@marienbad.cz; ❽). Recently restored and over a century old, it accepts "outpatients" for nude wallows in the colonnaded Roman baths, massages, mud baths and peat packs (Mon–Fri 2–8pm, Sat 9am–8pm; booking recommended at least two weeks in advance; all heftily priced in euros); you can also stay here, although treatments are not available on Saturday afternoons and Sundays. Ask for a carbon dioxide bath in *kabina 1*, which was fitted out for Edward VII and large enough to encompass his considerable bulk.

Walks around the spa

Even if you're not booked in for treatment, you should participate in the other spa rituals – drinking the water, wolfing down the wafers and taking the obligatory constitutional. Mariánské Lázně's altitude lends an almost subalpine freshness to the air, even at the height of summer, and **walking** is as important to "the cure" as are the various specialized treatments. To this end, the expert nineteenth-century landscape gardener Václav Skalník was employed to transform the valley into an open park, providing an intricate network of paths leading to the many springs dotted around the surrounding countryside.

There are several maps posted up nearby the Kolonáda which show the various marked walks around the spa; armed with a *plán města* (available from most hotels, bookshops and newsagents), you can head off on your own. Goethe's favourite walk, up to the *Miramonte* for morning coffee, is retraced by most visitors, though the café has since been converted into a *lázně dům* (spa home) for kids; head north to the *Café Panoráma* for refreshment instead. The energetic can continue to the lower town of **Úšovice** whence you can return to town via the Rudolfův and Ferdinandův springs, where, according to one tourist brochure, you can experience "hypotonic calcareous magnesium hydrogen carbonate ferrugineous acidulous waters".

There are several vantage points to head for in order to enjoy a **panoramic view** of the spa: Na Polomu (805m) or the Podhorn (847m), north along the strenuous red-marked paths; or, with considerably less exertion, the old **Kaiserturm** or *rozhledna* (723m), on the hillside southeast of the spa. Another option is to take the **chairlift** (*lánová draha*; daily: May–Sept 9.30am–5pm; Oct–April 9.30am–4.30pm; 50Kč return) from the *Koliba* up Dusíkova, which will transport you to the *Hotel Krakonoš*. Those with small kids might want to take a peek at the nearby **Minipark Střed Evropy** (Mon–Fri 1–6pm, Sat & Sun 10am–6pm), a low-key, fairly risible stab at a miniature world.

Eating, drinking and entertainment

Café Polonia, at Hlavní třída 50, is probably Mariánské Lázně's most opulent surviving **café** offering stucco decoration as rich as its cakes. The choice of **restaurants** has improved over the last decade, with the moderately expensive *Villa Romana* on Anglická, a pretty stylish number, and romantic *U zlaté koule*, just east of Mírové náměstí at Nehrova 26, starring live violin and piano in the evenings (its menu includes a 56-gramme portion of Russian caviar for as cheap as 3950Kč). *Churchill's* pub and restaurant, near the *Excelsior* on Hlavní třída, serves Czech food, pizzas and a good range of salads, which you can wash down with Guinness or local beers. *Hotel Helvetia's* basement features a typical Czech pub that's popular with the locals, and there's a young, lively *Irish Pub* at Poštovní 96.

There's usually a fair bit of highbrow **entertainment** on offer, including an international music festival in early summer, operetta three times a week in the theatre, once-weekly concerts by the Marienbad Symphony Orchestra, an annual week-long Chopin festival in mid-August, plus a Chopin music competition for young pianists every odd-numbered year in the first week in July. For **late-night spots**, you can try your hand in the splendid surroundings of the old casino. Mariánské Lázně also boasts the best **golf course** (daily 7am–9pm) in the former Eastern bloc. Originally built for Edward VII, it was the first to hold a PGA Tour event in the 1990s; to get there, take the bus heading for the *Hotel Golf* or the village of Mnichov (a bus stop is opposite the distinctive *Excelsior* hotel or simply walk for thirty-odd minutes east from the town centre.

Lázně Kynžvart and Teplá

If you're looking for a longer excursion out of Mariánské Lázně, you could spend the afternoon walking over to **LÁZNĚ KYNŽVART** (Königswart), 10km northwest of town. Now an untypically designed, Swiss wooden chalet-style children's spa (ⓦwww.spas.cz/kynzvart), it was founded in the 1820s by the Metternich family as their own private spa, where they entertained Goethe, Beethoven and Dumas (among others) at their originally Baroque **zámek** (April & Oct Sat & Sun 9am–4pm; May–June & Sept Tues–Sun 9am–4pm; July–Aug 9am–5pm; ⓦwww.kynzvart.cz), rebuilt as a Neoclassical, Empire-style mansion in the following decade by Pietro Nobile. Recently opened after more than a decade of renovation work, the chateau contains a valuable library stuffed with incunabula, rare prints and manuscripts and a museum full of lots of period furniture and Metternich mementoes; it's surrounded by a large English park. If your legs aren't up to the return journey, the nearest train station is 2km southeast of the chateau.

A longer day-trip is to the monastery at **TEPLÁ** (Tepl), 15km to the east off route 24, whose abbots used to own the springs at Mariánské Lázně. The **Klášter premonstrátů** (May–Sept Mon–Sat 9am–5pm, Sun 11am–5pm; Feb–April, Oct–Dec Mon–Sat 9am–3.30pm, Sun 11am–3.30pm; ⓦwww.klastertepla.cz) – used as an army barracks until the 1960s, then renovated after 1989 – is 1km east of the village along the Toužim road. It's easy enough to spot, thanks to the plain stone towers of the original twelfth-century monastery church, though the rest of the monastery carries the universal stamp of the Baroque Counter-Reformation, courtesy of the Dientzenhofer duo. However, the real reason for coming here is to see the neo-Baroque library (*nová knihovna*); built in the 1900s, it boasts almost edible stucco decoration, triple-decker bookshelves and swirling black iron balconies framed by white pilasters. Many visitors choose to **stay** at the *Hotel Klášter Teplá* (☎353 392 264, ⓦwww.pmgastro.cz; ❹), listen to the frequently held summer organ concerts, or simply tuck into hearty meals at the excellent **restaurant**.

If your next stop is Karlovy Vary, be sure to take the train, which winds its way painstakingly slowly but picturesquely for 50km, via Teplá, through the **Slavkovský les**, the thick forest that lies between the two spas.

Cheb

CHEB (Eger), 10km from the German border, is a typical Czech frontier town, with prostitutes lining the main roads, and Vietnamese stallholders occupying the centre of town. For many Western visitors it's their first taste of the Czech Republic, and for most, it's a slightly bewildering introduction. Cheb is a beautiful historic town, but it is also primarily a German one, and postwar expulsion of the German-speaking population left it with less than a third of its prewar population, and an identity crisis of mammoth proportions (see box p.253). Money was poured into the town, but Czechs were reluctant to move here (not so Romanies, Hungarians and Slovaks who were financially encouraged here to work). The root of the malaise lay in the authorities' ambivalence to Cheb, simultaneously encouraging its future and denying its past. Nevertheless, the town's historic centre is worth an afternoon stopoff – even if it is overrun by German day-trippers for much of the summer.

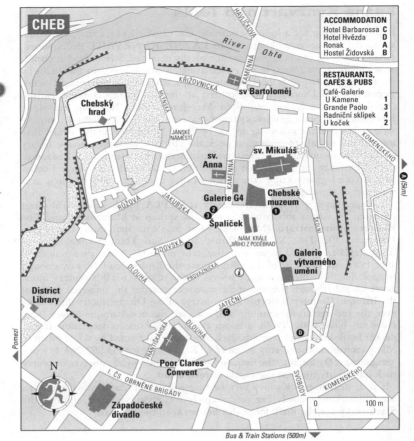

The town

Cheb's showpiece main square, **náměstí krále Jiřího z Poděbrad**, is named after one of the few Czech leaders the Egerländer ever willingly supported. Established in the twelfth century, but today lined with handsome, mostly seventeenth-century houses, with steeply pitched red roofs, this was the old Marktplatz, the commercial and political heart of Egerland for eight centuries. After four decades of neglect, commercial life has returned once more, with numerous cafés and restaurants breathing life into the square. The batch of half-timbered buildings huddled together at the bottom of the square, known as **Špalíček** (*Stöckl* in German), forms a picturesque ensemble; originally medieval German-Jewish merchant houses, they now house a café and several shops.

In the backstreets to the west of the main square, the parade of seventeenth-century German merchants' houses continues unabated. Cheb's first medieval **Jewish ghetto** is recalled in the street name, Židovská (Jewish Street), though the community was wiped out in a bloody pogrom in 1350; Jews were later expelled on another two occasions, in 1430 and 1502. Nothing remains of the

500-strong Jewish community that came under sustained attack during the 1930s as the Sudeten German Party rose to prominence in the region. Fascist thugs butchered a pig in the local synagogue shortly before its official opening, and *Kristallnacht* demolished what was left.

Chebské muzeum and art gallery

Behind Špaliček, on náměstí Krále Jiřího z Poděbrad 3, lurks the **Chebské muzeum**, which first opened to the public in 1874 (April–Sept Tues–Sun 9am–12.30pm & 1–5pm; Oct–March Wed–Sun same hours; Ⓦ www .muzeumcheb.cz). The building in which it's housed was once the Stadthaus where **Albrecht von Waldstein** (better known as Wallenstein from the trilogy by Schiller, written during the author's stay here in 1791), generalissimo of the Thirty Years' War, was murdered in 1634 following a decree by Emperor Ferdinand II. The museum pays great attention to this event, and the heavy Gothic woodwork of his reconstructed bedroom provides an evocative setting for Waldstein's murder, graphically illustrated on the walls; however, Cheb's more recent history is studiously avoided. (For more on Waldstein, see p.311.)

The **Galerie výtvarného umění** (Gallery of Fine Arts; daily 9am–noon & 12.30–5pm; ☎ 354 422 450), in the Baroque nová radnice at no. 16 on the square, seems strangely out of context in a town with such rich traditions of its own, focusing as it does on Czech modern art. Few of the town's predominantly

Egerland

Most Germans still refer to Cheb as **Eger**, the name given to the town by the German colonists who settled here from the eleventh century onwards. The settlers were typically hard-working and proud of their folk traditions and peculiar dialect. Aided by its status as a Free Imperial City of the Holy Roman Empire, the town soon came to dominate trade between Bavaria and Bohemia. Shunted around between Babenbergs, Swabians and Přemyslids, Egerland finally accepted the suzerainty of King John of Luxembourg in 1322, in return for certain privileges, and in fact the Egerländer remained self-governing until well into the nineteenth century.

Hardly surprising, then, that the town was at the centre of the (anti-Semitic) **Pan-German Schönerer movement** of the late nineteenth century, which fought desperately against the advance of Czech nationalism, aided and abetted (as they saw it) by the weak and liberal Habsburg state. Here, too, was the most vociferous protest against the 1897 Badeni Decrees, which granted the Czech language equal status with German throughout the Czech Lands. The establishment of Czechoslovakia in 1918 was seen as a serious setback by most Egerländer, who made no bones about where their real sympathies lay; Eger remained the only town to successfully rebuff all attempts at putting up street names in Czech as well as German.

Thus, in the 1930s, the pro-Nazi **Sudeten German Party** (SdP) found Egerland receptive to its anti-Semitism as much as to its irredentism. Although it's estimated that a quarter of the German-speaking voters stubbornly refused to vote for the SdP, the majority of Egerländer welcomed their incorporation into the Third Reich, completed in 1938. At the end of World War II, only those Germans who could prove themselves to have been actively anti-fascist (Czechs were luckily exempted from this acid test) were permitted to remain on Czechoslovak soil; the others were bodily kicked out, reducing the population of Cheb to twenty-seven percent of its prewar level. The mass expulsions were accompanied by numerous acts of vengeance, and the issue remains a delicate one. Havel's suggestion in his first presidential address that an apology to the Germans was in order remained one of the most unpopular statements of his entire presidency.

German tourists pay a visit to the temporary exhibitions, the superb collection of fourteenth- and fifteenth-century Bohemian sculpture, or to the wide-ranging permanent collection of modern Czech art. Kicking off with the 1890 generation, led by Jan Preisler and Antonín Procházka, there are several memorable paintings depicting Prague cityscapes, including the Belvedere, St Vitus Cathedral, and a red-and-cream city tram. More surprising is the large contingent of Cubist and Fauvist canvases, including a vivid blue *River Otava* by Václav Špála. In place of the usual Socialist Realism, a thought-provoking postwar collection rounds off the gallery.

Another private gallery worth visiting is **Galerie G4** (Tues–Fri 10am–6pm, Sat 10am–5pm; ☎354 422 838), at Kamenná 2, which regularly puts on excellent temporary photographic exhibitions.

Beyond the main square

Cheb's two largest buildings, dating from the town's early history, are out of keeping with the red-roofed uniformity of the seventeenth-century *Altstadt*. The church of **sv Mikuláš** has a bizarre multifaceted roof, like the scales of a dinosaur, though since the renowned local-born architect Balthasar Neumann restored the interior in the eighteenth century, only the bulky towers remain from the original thirteenth-century building, conceived as a monumental Romanesque basilica. Very few of the original furnishings survive, and most of what you see is neo-Gothic infill, but there are two very fine Renaissance tombs worth inspecting inside the porch of the south door.

In the northwestern corner of the town walls, by the River Ohře (Eger), is the **Chebský hrad** (April & Oct Tues–Sun 9am–noon & 1–4pm; May & Sept Tues–Sun 9am–noon & 1–5pm; June–Aug daily 9am–noon & 1–6pm; ☎354 422 942, ⓦwww.chebskyhrad.cz), or Kaiserburg as it used to be known; the sprawl of ruins built on and with volcanic rock is all that remains of the twelfth-century castle bequeathed by that obsessive crusader, the Holy Roman emperor Frederick Barbarossa, in 1179 on the foundations of a Slavic hill fort. In among the Baroque fortifications, the Gothic Černá věž (Black Tower) presents an impressive front and offers peeks at Cheb's chimneys and roof-tiles through its tiny windows. In the northeastern corner, the lower storey of the ruined chapel with its beautifully carved Romanesque capitals will give you an idea of the castle of Barbarossa's time. You may also want to catch some of the summer plays put on in the castle, if your Czech or German is up to it.

Practicalities

Had you arrived at Cheb's **train station** before 1945, you'd have had the impression of never having left Germany: by a quirk of railway history, the Deutsche Bundesbahn built and ran all the lines heading west out of Eger. It's a none too pleasant ten-minute walk from the ugly postwar station, north along **Svobody**, to the old town.

The **tourist office** is at no. 33 on the main square (Mon–Fri 9am–5pm, Sat 10am–2pm, plus Sun May–Sept 10am–1pm; ☎354 440 302, ⓦwww.mestocheb .cz), has information about the annual festivals, such as the autumn Jazz Jamm and the summer organ concerts, and can also help with private **accommodation**. There's the decent *Hotel Hvězda*, on the main square (☎354 422 549; ❸), but you'd be better off at the new *Hotel Barbarossa* (☎354 423 446, ❹), on Jateční, just off the square. A cheaper alternative is the *Hostel Židovská* at Židovská 7 (☎354 423 401; ❷; reception desk open 8am–noon & 4–8pm). Otherwise, there are **campsites** by the artificial lake

Jesenice, 5km east of Cheb, off the road to Karlovy Wary. The best is *Ronak* (☎354 435 913, ⓦwww.ronak.dosta.cz), with bungalows and basic lodging year round.

There are several **places to eat** on the main square, which basically cater for German tourists – they're not bad for a drink and to soak in the surroundings, but for something more traditional try *U koček* (closed Sat & Sun eve) for old Bohemian cuisine, at Kamenná 1, or *Radniční sklípek*, a cosy wine cellar on the main square. *Grande Paolo*, next door to *U koček*, has good pizzas and an interior filled with images and posters of the Juventus Turin stars. *Café-Galerie U Kamene* is a friendly source of **coffee** on the main square, and you can download your **emails** at the district library, Obrněné brigády 1, or *Net Café* in the Economics Faculty building on Hradební 22. Kino Art, Kamenná 5, puts on some interesting art-house **films**.

Františkovy Lázně

"The present Františkovy Lázně has nothing of historic interest", wrote Nagel's Guide in the 1960s, casually dismissing a town hailed by Goethe as "paradise on earth". Yet while **FRANTIŠKOVY LÁZNĚ** (Franzensbad), 5km north of Cheb and linked by regular trains, may not boast any individual architectural gems, it is, in many ways, the archetypal spa town. Originally known as Egerbrunnen, the spa was founded in 1793 and named Franzensbad after the then Habsburg emperor Franz I. Laid out in the early nineteenth century, the Neoclassical architecture of the period finds its way into every building – even the cinema has Doric pillars – and virtually every conceivable building has been daubed in the soft ochre colour of Kaisergelb. The centre of the spa is barely five

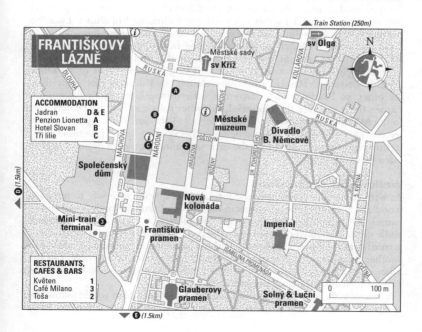

255

streets across, and surrounded on all sides by a backdrop of luscious greenery. The virtual absence of vehicles and rowdy nightlife makes it the most peaceful of the spas, though as patients stagger about and people in white coats run between buildings, it can resemble a large, open-plan hospital.

The Town

From the ochre-coloured train station, the road opens out onto the former *Kurpark* or **Městské sady**, whose principal path leads diagonally to a white, wooden bandstand at the head of pedestrianized **Národní**, the spa's modestly elegant main boulevard, lined with potted palms and diminutive lime trees. Beethoven stayed at no. 7 in 1812, as the German plaque by the entrance recalls; while *U tří lilie*, the eponymous garden café further down, features in a poem by the Czech surrealist Vítězslav Nezval. You can sit and take in the scene from an al fresco table at one of the street's cafes.

At the bottom of Národní, a plain Neoclassical rotunda shelters the **Františkův pramen** (Franzensquelle; in season daily 9–11.30am & 12.30–4.30pm). While the faithful queue to have their receptacles filled from the dazzling brass pipes, the real spa snobs retire to drink from their beakers by the fruit-encrusted sphinxes or under the nearby modern colonnade. Don't worry if you've come unprepared, as you can buy a plastic cupful, though, like most spa water, it's pretty unpalatable, on this occasion due to its high sulphur content. A different kind of faith drives women to touch the feet (and particularly another more specific part which is in danger of getting rubbed off) of a repulsive bronze cherub who sits holding a phallic fish, not far from the spring: in addition to treating diseases of the motor system and heart, Frantižkovy Lázně specializes in the treatment of gynaecological problems, and popular myth has it that doing so will ensure fertility. You've an even greater choice of tipple at the **Glauberovy pramen** (daily 7–11.30am & noon–4pm; if closed, head for the tap outside), to the south: you can get your spa water salty or not; hot or cold. Further east stands the **Kolonáda Solného a Lučního pramene** (daily 7am–4pm), where occasional exhibitions are put on.

The Neoclassical church of **sv Kříž**, dating from 1820, strikes an appropriately imperial pose at one end of Jiráskova, another riot of princely mansions with wrought-iron balconies. A more intriguing church is that of **sv Olga**, a richly decorated Russian Orthodox church on Kollárova. Set apart from the other spa buildings, and a favourite with visiting Germans, is Františkovy Lázně's finest spa villa, the **Imperial**, its corner balconies held up by caryatids. In the **Městské muzeum**, dr. Pohoreckého 8 (Tues–Sun 10am–5pm), you can see previous generations of Teutonic guests being subjected to gruesome nineteenth-century cures; don't miss the man with a leech on each buttock, held in place by two jam jars.

Walks and excursions

As with all the Bohemian spas, the formal parks quickly give way to untamed woodland, the difference being that in Františkovy Lázně the landscape is almost entirely flat, which is easier on the legs but shorter on views. A two-kilometre **walk** through the silver birches will take you to Lake Amerika (in dry weather a **mini-train**, or *mikrovláček*, runs without schedule; in summer, *Frantovláček*, another mini-train, runs hourly), though swimming is not advisable. On the other side of town, a path marked by red hearts leads to the popular *Zámeček Café*, hidden away romantically amidst the acacia.

A longer walk will bring you to Cheb itself, just over 5km south; follow the red markers down Klostermannova. Alternatively, it's 7km northeast to **Soos** (usually open till 6–7pm; ☎354 542 033), a small area of peatland pockmarked with **hot gaseous springs**. As you approach the place in summer, the smell of salt emanating from the mini-geysers wafts across from the marsh. A nature trail raised above the bogland allows closer inspection of the springs that gurgle and bubble just above the surface, staining the land with a brown-yellow crust. A unique phenomenon in mainland Europe, the area attracts rare species of flora and fauna – not to mention insects, which make it no place to linger in the height of summer. Some of the prettier species are to be seen at the **Motýlí dům** (Butterfly House; Tues–Fri 1–5pm, in summer also Sat & Sun 10am–5pm), in Žirovice, en route from Františkovy Lázně to the hot springs. Soos is also accessible by train from Cheb: three stops to Nový Drahov on the Luby u Chebu line.

Practicalities

The **train station** is a ten-minute walk north of the centre. Františkovy Lázně may not be the busiest spot in Bohemia, but with large numbers of Czech patients plus some tourists vying for **beds**, it can sometimes be difficult to find a place. It's occasionally possible to stay in spa hotels for one night, but spa guests always have priority. Probably the nicest place to stay is the *Tři lilie*, Národní třída 3 (☎354 208 900, ✉trililie@franzensbad.cz; ❻), which has been sensitively modernized and also houses the local **spa and tourist information office** (Mon–Fri 8am–5pm, Sat 8am–noon; ☎354 208 990, ✉ck3lilie@franzensbad.cz). Additional information offices exist at FL-Tour, Americká 2, by the bus stop (Mon–Fri 6am–6pm, Sat & Sun 8am–2pm; ☎354 543 162, ☻www.frantiskolazensko.cz) and at the Spa Directory Information, Jiráskova 3 (Mon–Fri 10am–4pm). Other options include the *Hotel Slovan* (☎354 542 841, ☻www.slovan-hotel.cz; ❹), at Národní 5, with a stylish, two-storey café, and the small, cheaper *Penzion Lionetta* (☎354 544 065; ❸), behind the houses roughly opposite *Slovan*, with massages on offer. The *Jadran* **campsite** (Jezerní 84, April–Oct, ☎354 542 412, ☻web.quick.cz/atc.jadran) with wooden **bungalows** and half-timbered hotel with simple rooms (❷) is 1.5km southwest of the town by the lake; you can get there on the mini-train, and can hire boats once you're there. Almost all spa hotels have reasonable **restaurants**, with the *Tři lilie* far and away the best (and most expensive), with a pleasant café, and the *Květen*, on Národní, locally renowned for its French cuisine. The *Café Milano*, next to the departure point of the *mikrovláček* on Máchova, is a popular outdoor place and *Toša* on Jirasková ulice serves decent coffee and cakes.

Karlovy Vary

KARLOVY VARY (Karlsbad) is the undisputed king of the famous triangle of Bohemian spas, with by far the most illustrious guest list of European notables. What makes it so special is its wonderful hilly setting – *Belle époque* mansions pile on top of one another along the steeply wooded banks of the endlessly twisting River Teplá. It is best known throughout the world by its German name, **Karlsbad** (Carlsbad in its anglicized form), and it was German-speakers who made up the vast majority of the town's population until their forced expulsion in 1945. Despite this violent uprooting, the spa has survived and continues to attract an international clientele – largely Russians – which annually doubles the local population, further supplemented in the summer by thousands of able-bodied day visitors, the greatest number of whom are, naturally, German.

Tradition credits the Emperor Charles IV (or rather one of his hunting dogs) with discovery of the springs (hence Karlsbad); in actual fact, the village of Vary (which means "boiling" in Czech) had existed for centuries before Charles' trip, though he did found a German town here in around 1350 and set a precedent for subsequent Bohemian rulers by granting Karlsbad various privileges. By the nineteenth century its position at the meeting point of two great German-speaking empires, and the much heralded efficacy of its waters, ensured the most impressive visitors' book in Europe. In addition, a lot of money has been spent over the last decade to ensure that Karlovy Vary returns to something like its former glory.

Arrival, information and accommodation

The main train station or **horní nádraží** is to the north of the River Ohře, while the **dolní nádraží** (where trains from Mariánské Lázně arrive), off Západní, and the **bus station**, on Varšavská, are next to each other, south of the river. The dolní nádraží has a **left-luggage** office (6.30–11.10am & 11.40am–5.55pm) and a branch of the **information** centre (Mon–Fri 8am–noon & 12.30–4pm). Don't leave hopping off the Prague bus to the bus station; along with everyone else, get off at Tržnice, one stop before, which is rather more central. Wherever you arrive, you're basically in the unattractive, northern part of town, where the otherwise invisible local residents live and shop. The spa proper stretches south along the winding Teplá Valley and, in fact, the best way to approach Karlovy Vary is from the south. However, to do that you need your own transport, in which case you'll have the devil of a job finding somewhere safe to park it, as parking and traffic in the centre of the spa are strictly controlled.

For general information, advice on **spa treatments** and for help with accommodation, go to the **information centre** (Mon–Fri 8am–5pm, Sat & Sun 10am–4pm; ☎353 224 097, ⓦwww.karlovyvary.cz), at Lázeňská 1, near the Mlýnská kolonáda. They sell a useful, monthly published guide *Promenáda*. In addition, there's a small kiosk called City-Info, opposite the post office on T.G. Masaryka (daily 10am–6pm).

Accommodation

Karlovy Vary can get pretty busy in the summer, especially in July during the film festival (see p.263), so it's best to start looking for **accommodation** early in the day. W Privat, an office on náměstí Republiky (Mon–Fri 8.30am–5pm, Sat 9am–1pm), can organize **private rooms**. If you're **camping**, head for the site with bungalows (❷) near the *Hotel Gejzír* (April–Oct; ⓦwww.hotelgejzir .cz) on Slovenská, south and upstream from the *Grand Hotel Pupp*; take bus #20 from the Divadelní náměstí. Further south, in the village of **Březová**, lies the popular campsite *Březový* háj (April–Oct; ⓦwww.brezovy-haj.cz), also with bungalows (buses from Tržnice run every 1–2hr Mon–Fri).

Astoria Vřídelní 92 ☎353 335 111, ⓔreservation@astoria-spa.cz. Central, quiet spa hotel, bang opposite the Kolonáda. ❹
Čajkovskij Sadová 44 ☎353 237 520, ⓦwww .cajkovskij.com. Once a cheap pension, now a luxury four-star hotel, located in a quiet backstreet below the Orthodox church. ❾
Clara Na kopečku 23 ☎353 449 983, ⓦwww .volny.cz/pensionclara. Very comfortable pension out of town beyond the railway station, at rock-bot-

tom prices for this spa. ❸
Grand Hotel Pupp Mírové náměstí 2 ☎353 109 111, ⓦwww.pupp.cz. They don't come better (nor more expensive) than this outside Prague – 6000Kč a double and upwards – but though the decor is pretty stunning, the service is not as good as it should be for the price. ❾
Heluan Tržiště 41 ☎353 225 756, ⓔheluan@plz .pvtnet.cz. Peaceful hotel, with spacious, tastefully uncluttered en-suite rooms. ❺

Kavalerie T.G. Masaryka 43 ☎353 229 613, ✉kavalerie@volny.cz. Relatively cheap, but at the wrong end of town, near the bus station and not in the spa proper. ❸

Kolonáda I.P. Pavlova 8 ☎353 345 555, ✉reservation@kolonada.cz. Very plush and efficient place; rooms have all mod cons, and there's even a sauna, and an acceptable cellar restaurant. ❾

Romance Puškin Tržiště 37 ☎353 222 646, ✉info@hotelromance.cz. Decent doubles with breakfast, in the central section of the spa. ❻

Vila Basileia Mariánskolázeňská 2 ☎353 224 132, ⒻAX353 227 804. Secluded late-nineteenth-century villa at the quiet, southern end of the spa, close to the *Pupp*, with just six large en-suite rooms on offer. ❹

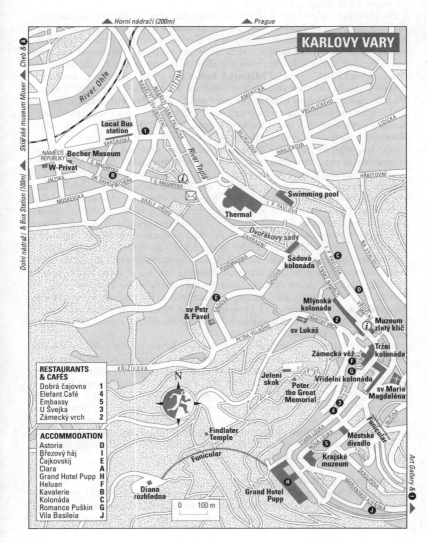

KARLOVY VARY

RESTAURANTS & CAFÉS
Dobrá čajovna   1
Elefant Café   4
Embassy   5
U Švejka   3
Zámecký vrch   2

ACCOMMODATION
Astoria   D
Březový háj   I
Čajkovskij   E
Clara   A
Grand Hotel Pupp   F
Heluan   H
Kavalerie   B
Kolonáda   C
Romance Puškin   G
Vila Basileia   J

0   100 m

The Spa

Unfortunately, many visitors' first impressions of Karlovy Vary are marred by the unavoidable sight of the **Thermal** sanatorium, an inexcusable concrete scab built in the 1970s, for whose sake a large slice of the old town bit the dust. It serves as home base for the annual film festival, and there's a certain perverse appeal to the faded 1970s kitsch interior decor, but the most useful aspect of the Thermal is its open-air *bazén*, a spring-water **swimming pool** set high up above the river (Mon–Sat 8am–9.30pm, Sun 9am–9.30pm; 50Kč per hour). The poolside view over the town is wonderful, but don't be taken in by the clouds of steam – the water is only tepid.

On the other side of the River Teplá from the *Thermal*, the late-nineteenth-century grandeur of Karlovy Vary begins to unfold along the river banks. The first of a series of colonnades designed by the Viennese duo Helmer and Fellner is the **Sadová kolonáda**, a delicate white-and-grey colonnade made of wrought iron. As the valley narrows, the river disappears under a wide terrace in front of Josef Zítek's graceful **Mlýnská kolonáda** (Mühlbrunnen Colonnade), whose forest of columns shelters four separate springs, each one more scalding than the last. At the next bend in the river stands the **Tržní kolonáda**, designed by Helmer and Fellner as a temporary structure, but one whose intricate white-washed woodwork has lasted for over a century. Directly opposite is the **dům Zawojski** (now the Živnostenska banka), one of the best Art Nouveau houses in the spa, with its green wrought-iron and gilded detailing. Rising above the colonnade is the **Zámecká věž** (Schlossberg), the only link with the spa's founder, Charles IV, built on the site of his original hunting lodge.

Most powerful of the twelve springs is the **Vřídlo** or Sprudel, which belches out over 2500 gallons of water every hour. The old wrought-iron **Vřídelní kolonáda** (daily 6am–7pm) was melted down for armaments by the Nazis, and only finally replaced in the 1970s by a rather uninspiring modern building, which the Communists liked to call the Yuri Gagarin Colonnade (his statue once stood outside, but now resides at the local airport). The smooth marble floor allows patients to shuffle up and down contentedly, while inside the glass rotunda the geyser pops and splutters, shooting hot water forty feet upwards. Ensuing clouds of steam obscure what would otherwise be a perfect view of Kilian Ignaz Dientzenhofer's Baroque masterpiece, the church of **sv Maria Magdaléna**, pitched nearby on a precipitous site. The light, pink interior, full of playful oval shapes, is a striking contrast with the relentlessly nineteenth-century air of the rest of the town.

If you've forgotten your cure cup, you can buy the faintly ridiculous *becher* vessels from one of the many souvenir shops. The purpose behind these is to avoid colouring your teeth with the water, though plenty of people cut costs and buy a plastic cup. Popular wisdom has it that "when the disorder becomes a disease, doctors prescribe the hot waters of Carlsbad" – in other words, it's strong stuff. In the eighteenth century, the poor were advised to drink up to five hundred cups of the salty waters to cure the disease of poverty. The German playwright Schiller (who came here on his honeymoon in 1791) drank eighteen cups and lived to tell the tale, but generally no more than five to seven cups a day are recommended.

Stará and Nová louka

South of the Sprudel is Karlovy Vary's most famous shopping street, the **Stará louka** (Alte Wiese), described rather mystifyingly by Le Corbusier as "a set of *Torten* (cakes) all the same style and the same elegance". Its shops, which once rivalled Vienna's Kärntnerstrasse, are beginning once more to exude the snobbery of former days – there's even a branch of Versace at the far end of the street. Don't miss the Moser shop (everyone who's anyone, from Stalin to the Shah, has had a Moser glass made for them), where you can buy some of the local glassware, made in the factory in the suburb of Dvory, just off the Cheb road.

At the end of Stará louka is the **Grand Hotel Pupp**, named after its founder, the eighteenth-century confectioner Johann Georg Pupp. Rebuilt in the late-nineteenth-century by the ubiquitous Helmer and Fellner, *Pupp's* was *the* place to be seen, a meeting place for Europe's elite. Despite the odd spot of careless modernization and rather snotty service, it boasts an interior that can't fail to impress, and the cakes are allegedly still made to Mr Pupp's own recipe. On the opposite bank, the former Kaiserbad – now known rather more prosaically as Lázně I – is another sumptuous edifice, designed like a theatre by Helmer and Fellner, with a luscious velvet and marble interior.

Back round the corner in Nová louka, the spa's richly decorated, creamy white **Městské divadlo** is another Helmer and Fellner construction, where Dvořák gave the premiere of his *New World Symphony* in 1893. What makes this place special, though, is that the frescoes and main curtain were executed by a group of painters that included a young **Gustav Klimt**, later to become one of the most famous figures in the Viennese Secession. If you ask at the box office, you should be able to get a glimpse of the auditorium, though the curtain – by far the most interesting work – is rarely fully exposed to the audience. Nevertheless, you can spot Klimt's self-portrait in the bottom right-hand corner, playing the flute and looking at the audience.

A short distance beyond the casino is the spa's main **Galerie umění** (Tues–Sun 9.30am–noon & 1–5pm), on Goethova stezka, which contains a small but interesting cross-section of twentieth-century Czech canvases, and a disappointingly limited selection of glassware. Neither of Karlovy Vary's two main museums are really worth bothering with: the **Krajské muzeum** (Wed–Sun 9am–noon & 1–5pm), on Nová louka, plods through the spa's history, glossing over the controversial (and interesting) bits, while the **Muzeum zlatý klíč**, Lázeňská 3 (same times), contains a fairly mediocre series of soft-focus oil paintings of the spa at its pre-World War I zenith, by Wilhelm Gause. More interesting is the **Sklářské muzeum Moser** (Mon–Fri 8am–5.30pm, Sat 9am–3pm; free entrance; ⊛www.moser-glass.com), Kpt. Jaroše 19, out of the centre (bus #1, #9 and #10 from the local bus station), which presents the history of glass-making, complete with some fine examples. You can also pay a visit to the famous glassworks (Mon–Fri 9am–1pm; guided tours with reservation, ☎353 449 455), established in 1857 by Ludwig Moser, that the museum refers to.

Walking in the hills

Of all the spas, Karlovy Vary's constitutional **walks** are the most physically taxing and visually rewarding. You can let the **funicular** (*lanová draha*) take the strain by hopping aboard one of the trains (daily: Feb–May & Sept–Dec 9am–6pm; June–Aug till 7pm; every 15min; 50Kč return) from behind the *Grand Hotel Pupp* up to a café and viewpoint. Alternatively, you can climb up through the beech and oak trees to the wooden crucifix above Stará louka, and then on to the spectacular panorama where the **Peter the Great Memorial** commemorates the visiting Russian tsar and his dozen or so royal hangers-on. In season you can enjoy the (not so perfect) view northwards from the **Jelení skok** restaurant (Tues–Sun 10am–6pm).

The road below *Jelení skok* slopes down to **Zámecký vrch**, where Turgenev stayed at no. 22 in 1874–75 and which the English aristocracy used to ascend

> ### Marx in Karlsbad
>
> A certain **Mr Charles Marx** from London (as he signed himself in the visitors' book) visited the spa several times towards the end of his life, staying at the former *Hotel Germania*, at Zámecký vrch 41, above the Mühlbrunnen Colonnade. He was under police surveillance each time, but neither his daughter Eleanor's letters (she was with him on both trips) nor the police reports have much to say about the old revolutionary, except that he took the waters at 6am (as was the custom) and went on long walks. The Communists couldn't resist the excuse to set up a Karl Marx Museum, just down from the Mühlbrunnen Colonnade, at the house where Marx used to visit his doctor. Somewhat unbelievably, it was the only one of its kind in the entire Communist world, Lenin being the orthodox choice. Needless to say, it has long since been dismantled, and is now the even duller Muzeum zlatý klíč.

in order to absolve their sins at the red-brick Anglican church of **sv Lukáš** (Evangelical and Methodist services are still held here, although not in English). Clearly visible from here, high on the opposite bank, is the *Imperial* sanatorium, a huge fortress hotel built in 1912 to rival *Pupp*'s and flying in the face of the popular Art Nouveau architecture of the spa; it was converted into a hospital during World War II, handed over to the Soviets during the Communist period, and has only recently been turned back into a hotel (it even has its own funicular to transport guests to and from the spa below).

An alternative route back down to the Sadová kolonáda is the street of **Sadová** itself, which is lined with some of the most gloriously flamboyant mansions in the whole spa. Topping the lot, though, is the fabulous white Russian Orthodox church of **sv Petr and Pavel** (daily 10am–5pm), built to serve the visiting Russian aristocracy and now equally popular with the spa's current crop of Russian visitors. It's the church's stunning exterior, crowned by a series of gilded onion domes, that steals the show, so don't worry if the janitor is out to lunch, thus preventing you from visiting the icon-filled interior.

Eating, drinking and entertainment

What I indulged in, what I enjoyed
What I conceived there
What joy, what knowledge
But it would be too long a confession
I hope all will enjoy it that way
Those with experience and the uninitiated.

Needless to say, Goethe had a good time here. His coy innuendoes are a reference to the enduring reputation of spas like Karlovy Vary for providing extramarital romance. Dancing, after all, was encouraged by the spa doctors as a means of losing weight. These days, it's all a bit less racy. Nevertheless, if you're looking for a spot of opulence, you might as well head for the *Grand Hotel Pupp*, whose bar and restaurant boast unrivalled Neoclassical decor. Otherwise, there's the *Zámecký vrch*, a more intimate restaurant up at no. 14 on the street of the same name; *U Švejka*, Stará louka 10, which boasts a typical Czech pub atmosphere and the Good Soldier himself sitting by the entrance; or *Embassy*, Nová louka 21, one of the oldest Baroque houses in the spa, with superlative cuisine.

Karlovy Vary is, of course, the home of one of the country's most peculiar and popular drinks, **becherovka**, a liqueur made from a secret recipe of nineteen different herbs, which really does ease digestion and is fondly referred to as Karlovy

Vary's "thirteenth spring". It was actually invented by the unlikely sounding Scot, Dr Frobig, in 1805, but only launched commercially two years later by the enterprising Dr Jan Becher. It's available in bars and restaurants all over town (and just about anywhere else in the country), though the company's factory shop is on T. G. Masaryka, near náměstí Republiky, as is the **Jan Becher Museum** (daily 9am–5pm; 100Kč; ☏353 170 156, ⊛www.janbecher.cz), where you can tour the old cellars and experience the delights of a liquer tasting as part of your visit. Be warned: it's an acquired taste – a little like cough mixture – and perhaps best drunk with tonic, ice and a slice (ask for a *beton*). Not so good for you, but all part of the spa ritual, are coffee and cakes: the *Elefant café* on Stará louka is the nearest Karlovy Vary comes to an elegant Habsburg-style café, and as a result is very popular. You can also enjoy a marginally healthier cup of tea at *Dobrá čajovna*, by the market at Varšavská 13.

Karlovy Vary's **cultural life** is pretty varied, from classical concerts at the former *Kurhaus* (Lázně III) and occasionally at *Pupp's*, to the rock club *Rotes Berlin*, Jaltská 7, which also serves as a gallery. The town also plays host to an **International Film Festival** in July, which attracts at least a handful of big names. All showings are open to the public. For details on these and the town's other events, ask at the information centre (see p.258).

Loket

The tiny hilltop town of **LOKET** (Elbogan) is an exquisite, virtually undiscovered, miniature gem, just 12km west of the crowds of Karlovy Vary. It takes its name from the sharp bend in the River Ohře – *loket* means elbow – that provides the town with its dramatic setting. The fourteenth-century **hrad** (daily: April–Oct 9am–4.30pm; Nov–March 9am–3.30pm; ⊛www.loket.cz), which slots into the precipitous fortifications, displays porcelain manufactured in the town over the last couple of centuries; you can also explore the castle's former prison, climb the lookout tower, explore the ruined Romanesque rotunda, and enjoy the pretty tacky permanent exhibition on ghosts, plus the occasional concert, medieval market, and fencing match. Loket's beautifully picturesque streets form a garland around the base of the castle, sheltering half-timbered houses and secluded courtyards like Sklenařská, where the redundant German sign *Glaser Gasse* remains unmolested since the forced expulsions of 1945 stripped the town of its German-speaking inhabitants.

Accommodation is available at various hotels and pensions, including the friendly *Hotel Goethe* (☏352 684 184, ⊛www.hotelgoethe.loket.cz; ❸) or the *Hotel Bílý kůň* (☏352 685 002, ⊛www.hotel-horse.cz; ❸), both on the main square and both with restaurants. It was at the latter, that Goethe met his last love, Ulrike von Lewetzow, he in his seventies, she a mere seventeen. Hardly surprisingly, she refused his marriage proposal – his *Marienbader Elegie* describes the event – though she remained unmarried throughout her long life.

Cheaper options include the **hostel** *Lazy River* (☏352 685 204, ✉hostelloket@yahoo .com; ❶–❷), at Kostelní 72, conveniently located between the square and the castle, and many private rooms – ask at Goethe Tour (daily 10am–noon & 1–5pm; ☏352 685 109), on the northwestern side of the square, near the bridge.

Loket is easily accessible by bus from Karlovy Vary, but by far the most inspiring way of getting there is to walk the seventeen-kilometre-long, blue-marked track from Karlovy Vary, which crosses over to the left bank of the River Ohře at the halfway point and passes the giant pillar-like rocks of the **Svatošské skály** (Hans Heiling Felsen), which have inspired writers from Goethe to the Brothers Grimm.

Travel details

Trains

Connections with Prague: Domážlice (2 daily; 2hr 30min); Frantiskovy Lázne (4 daily; 3hr 40min); Karlovy Vary (3 daily; 4hr 5min–5hr 10min); Mariánské Lázně/Cheb (10 daily; 2hr 55min/3hr 25min); Plzeň (hourly; 1hr 40min).

Cheb to: Frantiskovy Lázne (19–22 daily; 15min); Karlovy Vary (20–24 daily; 50min–1hr 5min); Mariánské Lázně (17–19 daily; 25–35min); Nürnberg (1 daily; 2hr); Plzeň (15–17 daily; 1hr 35min– 2hr 10min).

Domážlice to: Klatovy (5–6 daily; 1hr).

Karlovy Vary to: Kadaň (17–19 daily; 55min–1hr 10min).

Klatovy to: Železná Ruda (6–8 daily; 1hr 20min).

Mariánské Lázně to: Karlovy Vary (6–7 daily; 1hr 40min–2hr 20min); Teplá (7–9 daily; 30–35min).

Plzeň to: Domážlice (11–16 daily; 50min–1hr 50min); Furth-im-Wald (2 daily; 1hr 20min); Klatovy (9–16 daily; 45min–1hr); Munich (3 daily; 4hr 20min–7hr); Plasy (10–13 daily; 35–55min); Stříbro (14–17 daily; 25–50min); Železná Ruda (3–4 daily; 2hr 20min–2hr 30min).

Buses

Connections with Prague: Jáchymov (1–4 daily; 2hr 30min–3hr); Karlovy Vary (hourly; 2hr 10min– 2hr 20min); Plzeň (hourly; 1hr 25min–1hr 50min).

Karlovy Vary to: Frantiskovy Lázne (1–3 daily; 1hr); Jáchymov (3–30 daily; 30–50min); Loket (2–25 daily; 25–30min).

Plzeň to: Horsovsky Tyn (3–17 daily; 1hr); Karlovy Vary (2–12 daily; 1hr 30min–1hr 55min).

North Bohemia

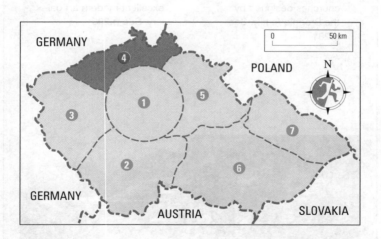

CHAPTER FOUR **Highlights**

✳ **Terezín** Habsburg-era fortress, used as a transit camp and "model ghetto" by the Nazis, which now stands as a chilling memorial to the Holocaust. See p.278

✳ **Litoměřice** Ecclesiastical town with a remarkable collection of Baroque churches designed by the Broggio family. See p.281

✳ **České Švýcarsko** Hilly, wooded border region with bizarre sandstone rock formations and boat trips along the Kamenice River. See p.287

✳ **Liberec** North Bohemia's busiest town boasts a splendid neo-Renaissance town hall and an excellent modern art gallery. See p.295

△ České Švýcarsko

North Bohemia

N**orth Bohemia** (Severní Čechy) became a byword for the ecological
cal disaster facing the country in the Communist era. Its forests all
but disappeared, weakened by acid rain and finished off by parasites,
its villages were bulldozed to make way for opencast mines, and its
citizens literally choked to death – all due to the brown-coal-burning power
stations that have provided the region with employment for the last hundred
years. As in other parts of the country though, laborious environmental
clean-up efforts have finally turned the tide as green landscapes again pre-
vail in summertime, and the air, even in winter, is remarkably cleaner than
a decade ago. Parts of North Bohemia are popular with Czech and German
tourists, in particular the eastern half of the region, where the industrial
landscape gives way to areas of outstanding natural beauty like **České Švč-
carsko** and the **České středohoří**, and towns of architectural finesse, like
Litoměřice.

Geographically, the region is divided by the River Labe (Elbe) into two
roughly equal halves. To the east, where the frontier mountains are slightly
less pronounced, two rich German-speaking cities developed: **Liberec**
(Reichenberg), built on the cloth industry, and **Jablonec** (Gablonz), famed
for its jewellery. In addition, much of Bohemia's world-famous crystal and
glass is still based in the smaller settlements located in the very north of the
region. To the west of the Labe lie the **Krušné hory** (Erzegebirge or Ore
Mountains), which, as their name suggests, were once a valuable source of
iron ore and other minerals. Nowadays, however, the mountains are better
known for their depleted forests (albeit slowly coming back to life), and for
their brown coal deposits which have permanently altered landscapes and
cityscapes alike.

Historically, the region has been part of Bohemia since the first Přemyslid
princes, but from very early on, large numbers of Germans from neighbouring Saxony drifted over the ill-defined border, some taking up their traditional
wood-based crafts, others working in the mines that sprang up along the base of
the mountains. By the end of the nineteenth century, **factories** and **mines** had
become as much a part of the landscape of North Bohemia as mountains and
chateaux. Then, with the collapse of the empire, the new-born Czechoslovak
state inherited three-quarters of the Habsburg Empire's industry, and at a stroke
became the world's tenth most industrialized country.

German and Czech miners remained loyal to the Left until the disastrous
slump of the 1930s, when the majority of North Bohemia's German-speakers
put their trust in the Sudeten German Party or SdP (see p.253), with disastrous consequences for the country – and for Europe. Allied bombings took

their toll during the war, and with the backing of the Big Three (Churchill, Roosevelt and Stalin) at Potsdam, the German-speaking population was forcibly (and bloodily) expelled in 1945. Economic necessity ensured that North Bohemia was quickly rebuilt and resettled, but its land and lives were irrevocably marred by forty years of unbridled industrialization under the Communists.

While the rest of Europe was belatedly tempering sulphur emissions and increasing fuel efficiency, the Czechs were steadily sinking to fortieth place in the world league of industrial powers and rising to first place for male mortality rates, cancer and stillbirths. It's easy to blame all these calamities on the factory fetishism of the Communists, but damage to the forests of the Krušné hory was noted well before 1948, and smog levels irritated the citizens of North Bohemia for the best part of the twentieth century. Yet the brown-coal industry that caused much of the havoc is gradually being wound down, as power generation is shifting to the newly completed nuclear plant at Temelín, and the presence of filters on the remaining smokestacks has brought forth dramatic improvements. The downside is that these measures are likely to leave the region with one of the highest unemployment rates in the Czech Republic, something that can only exacerbate the smouldering tensions between the Czechs and Romanies who have shared this polluted home since 1945.

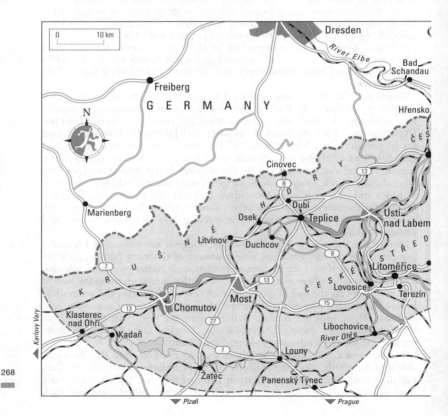

Up the River Ohře

There are five historic towns along the **River Ohře** (Eger), overlooked by most travellers eager to reach Karlovy Vary and the spas of West Bohemia. With your own car, they can all be easily covered in a day; by public transport (preferably bus), it's best to concentrate on just one or two. If you are driving, be sure to take in one of the best **views** in the entire region, from the ridge shortly after Panenský Týnec on route 7: in the foreground, bizarre hillocks rise up like giant molehills, while behind, the entire range of the Krušné hory is stretched out in all its distant glory (close up it's not so pretty).

Libochovice

The first place of interest along the Ohře is **LIBOCHOVICE** (Libokowitz), a sleepy village nestling in the shadow of the Rožmberks' mighty ruined fortress of Házmburk, whose Dracula-like profile is a prominent landmark. Libochovice has a **zámek** (April & Oct Sat & Sun 9am–noon & 1–4pm; May–June & Sept Tues–Sun 9am–noon & 1–5pm; July–Aug Tues–Sun 9am–noon & 1–6pm; tour in English 100Kč) of its own, given a Baroque cladding by the Lobkowicz family when they took it over in the seventeenth century, but with many of its

Hradec Králové

Prague

original Gothic features intact. The entrance is presided over by a brooding bust of one of the heroes of the Czech national revival movement, Jan Evangelista Purkyně, father of Czech medicine, who was born in the chateau in 1787. Two lasting Lobkowicz additions provide the highlight of the chateau tour: the rather splendid *sala terrena* featuring trompe l'oeil frescoes by Italian artists, and the grandiose Saturn Hall. You could picnic with the noisy peacocks that stalk the carefully manicured French gardens (open till 7pm), have a snack at the café in the courtyard of the chateau, enjoy good Czech food at the *Zámecký šenk* next door, or go for a cheap pizza at *Il Vulcano* nearby.

Louny

LOUNY (Laun) is the first of the medieval fortified towns on route 7 (the road from Prague to Chomutov), its perfect Gothic appearance all but entirely destroyed by fire in 1517 – all, that is, except the strikingly beautiful church of **sv Mikuláš** (May–Sept Tues–Sun 10am–5pm; Oct–April Tues–Fri 2–4pm, Sat & Sun 1–4pm), whose spiky, tent-like triple roof, the town's most famous landmark, is thought to have been rebuilt by the German mason Benedikt Ried (he used a similar design to great effect on the cathedral in Kutná Hora; see p.169), who died here in 1534. Even if the church is closed, you can peek in at his skilful ribbed vaulting through the glass in the entrance lobby. If you do get inside, be sure to check out the intricately carved limewood altars, barleysugar pillars and remarkable knobbly filigree work; when the church is open you can also climb the tower.

A couple of other isolated buildings in Louny are worth inspecting: round the back of the church in Pivovarská, the local museum occupies the **Dům rytířů sokolů z Mor** (Tues–Fri 10am–5pm, Sat & Sun 1–5pm), with its distinctive Gothic stone oriel window and wedge-shaped roof. Roughly opposite is the **Galerie Benedikta Rejta** (Benedikt Ried Gallery; Tues–Sun 10am–5pm), located in a huge former brewery, whose interiors seem too large for the modest exhibition of modern Czech art within. The town's nineteenth-century synagogue, on Hilbertova, has now been restored and houses the district archives. The **Žatecká brána**, Louny's only remaining medieval gateway, is extremely impressive and marks the beginning of a pleasant walk along the town's surviving ramparts by the river on the northern edge of the old town.

Louny is less than an hour's drive from Prague airport. There are a few direct **trains** from Prague's Masarykovo nádraží, but for most you have to change at Kralupy nad Vltavou; the main train station is a kilometre or so east of the old town, while Louny předměstí, a short walk south of the old town, is only good for trains to Rakovník, and the once daily České Budějovice–Most express. If you need a place **to stay**, the **tourist office** (Mon, Tues & Thurs 6am–5pm, Wed till 6pm, Fri till 4pm; ☎415 621 102, ⓦwww.mulouny.cz), at Mírové náměstí 35, can help with accommodation. Or try the *Hotel Union* (☎415 653 330, ⓦwww.hotel-union.cz; ❷), literally in the shadow of sv Mikuláš on Beneše z Loun, with its own half-decent restaurant serving the local **beer**. Next door is the cheap *Hotel Černý kůň* (☎415 655 096, Ⓕ415 652 044; ❷), with an Irish pub on the ground floor.

There are good pizzas and grilled meats (and great views over the ramparts) to be had at the outdoor terrace at *Vivaldi*, or the usual Czech staples (plus the odd surprise, like eel in mustard sauce) at *U Daliborky*, both east of the main square on Hilbertova.

Žatec

ŽATEC (Saaz), 24km up the Ohře from Louny, is the centre of the hop-grow-ing region that supports the famous Czech beer industry. In summer, from here as far south as Rakovník (Rakonitz), the roads are hemmed in by endless tall, green groves of hop vines. No one quite knows why Czech hops are the best in the world for brewing beer, but everyone accepts the fact, and even Belgian beer giants like Stella Artois import them in preference to their own. Since as long ago as the twelfth century, Bohemia's Red Saaz hops have been sent down the Elbe to the Hamburg hop market, and Žatec's biggest annual binge is still the September hop festival held in the town square.

The **old town** itself, on the hilltop opposite the train station, is a substantial, though scruffy, medieval affair, with two of its fifteenth-century western gates still intact. In those days the town was predominantly Czech, but during the following three centuries, wave upon wave of German immigrants gradually reversed the balance. These days, the central area contains a large Romany population. The central square, headed by the plain, grey Renaissance **radnice**, is pleasant enough, with arcades down one side and a very busy plague column in the middle. The radnice has a high (47m) **tower** (Mon & Wed 8–11.45am & 12.45–5pm, Tues & Thurs 8–11am & noon–3pm, Fri 8–11am & noon–2.30pm), which you can climb for a great panorama of the old town's red roofs. To the right there's a small garden of hops – the perfect advertisement for the town's wares – beyond which lies the town's ruined synagogue, once second largest in the republic. Behind the radnice, the town's Jesuitized church is guarded by a wonderful gallery of beatific sculptures, while the town **brewery** (not open to the public) occupies pride of place in the thirteenth-century castle.

The main square and the backstreets around are rather lonely and unpleas-ant places to hang around, though you can sit outside and have a coffee beside the Baroque statuary, or browse among the market stalls that have begun to appear in between the arcades. **Hotels** are inexplicably overpriced, and you'd probably be more comfortable spending the night in either Louny (see oppo-site) or Kadaň (see below). The *Motes* (☎415 711 169, ✉ikadnar@iol.cz; ❸), on Chelčického náměstí, is hidden in the grubby backstreets east of the main square, though it does offer good views. The more upscale *U hada* on the main square (☎415 711 000, ⓦwww.uhada-zatec.cz; ❸) is a much better bet, with pleasant rooms with satellite TV, its own decent **restaurant** and *vinárna*. Beyond this, there aren't too many other eateries you'd want to try, though *Na baště*, near the theatre on Dvořákova, has a reasonable offering of Czech dishes and its terrace overlooks the medieval Husitská bašta (Hussite Tower).

Kadaň

Very much in the same mould as Louny and Žatec, **KADAŇ** (Kaaden), 22km west, is an altogether more picturesque halt on the Ohře. From the train sta-tion, you enter the old town through the round, whitewashed barbican of the **Žatecká brána**. The town suffered badly during the Thirty Years' War, the population was driven out in 1945, and the whole place lived under a dusty air of neglect for the following fifty years. Now the town's handsome eighteenth-century buildings have all been more or less restored to their former glory, and the place has really come alive once more. The most striking sights on the partially arcaded town square are the prickly white conical octagonal spire of the **radnice** (tours in summer Sat & Sun tours at 10am, noon & 3pm), which looks like a minaret of a West African mosque, and the twin red onion domes of the imposing **Děkanský kostel**, which contains some good Baroque furnishings. Roughly opposite the radnice, you'll find **Katová ulička** (Hangman's Lane), Bohemia's narrowest street, which is barely more than a passage, the light straining to make its way past the maze of buttresses. The hangman himself used to live in the small white house below the gate at the end of the lane, which has since been converted into a cute little tea and spice shop. From the end of Katová ulička, you can gain access to the best-preserved part of the town walls or **hradby** (April–Oct 6am–8pm, Nov–March 8am–2pm), which lead round to the southern tip of town, where Kadaň's recently renovated **hrad**, a modest provincial seat, sits overlooking the Ohře. Out of the centre, along the road to Klášterec nad Ohří, a former Franciscan monastery houses the **Městské Muzeum** (May, June & Sept Sat & Sun 10am–4pm; July–Aug daily same hours), with an exhibition devoted to the town's history, though more interesting are the sixteenth-century tombs of the Lobkowicz family (including Václav Lobkowicz featured in his panoply) in the monastery church and the fifteenth-century chapterhouse – one of the oldest in Bohemia and with fine vaulting.

The **tourist office** (Mon & Wed 9am–5pm, Tues, Thurs & Fri 9am–4pm, Sat 9am–noon; ⓦwww.mesto-kadan.cz) is in the radnice, although **accommodation** shouldn't be a problem, with the lovely pension *Horoskop* (☎474 342 684, ⓔhoroskop@pension-kadan.cz; ➌), across from the hrad, easily the best of several good central places to stay. An alternative is the small *Hotel Tercier* (☎ & ⓕ474 345 234; ➋), Žatecká 566, standing directly on top of the town walls; its **restaurant** is a bizarre cave-like place, with kitsch prehistoric monsters sticking out of the walls. There are several **campsites** in the vicinity as well, with the *Hradec* site (mid-April to Sept) 3km southeast of the town, enjoying the most pleasant position of the bunch, on the banks of the Ohře, not far from Hradec train station.

Klášterec nad Ohří

Also worth a visit is **KLÁŠTEREC NAD OHŘÍ** (Klösterle-an-der-Eger), 5km west of Kadaň, the pretty quadrilateral seat of one of the many branches of the Thun family. Although, as the name suggests, the town was originally centred on a Benedictine monastery, it was the Thuns who really determined its present appearance, commissioning the two colourful Baroque churches and establishing the porcelain factory and spa facilities that made the town wealthy in the previous two centuries.

The Thuns' **zámek**, built up the hill from the village in 1646, today houses a **Muzeum porcelánu** (April–Oct Tues–Sun 9am–noon & 1–5pm), containing over 6000 pieces of local and imported china from the vast collection belonging to Prague's UPM (Decorative Arts Museum); visits are by guided tour only and leave on the hour; replicas can be purchased in the museum shop. More accessible are the wonderful **gardens** (*zámecká zahrada*) sloping down to the river, filled with 46 varieties of rare trees – there's a map to show where each one stands – dotted with Baroque sculptures by Brokoff and boasting a *sala terrena*, whose gaudy red and cream colour scheme matches the church across the road. To get inside the family vault or **Thunská hrobka**, you need to ask at the museum, though it offers little of interest besides the odd quadruple-barrelled name – viz. Josef Oswald II Thun-Hohenstein-Salm-Reifferscheid, who has barely enough room on his coffin to fit his aristocratic credentials. The guide disappointedly concedes that all that remains of the first Thun of Klášterec is "a skull and a few bones" – rather impressive, considering that he died some 300 years ago and when all that's left of another, eighteenth-century, Thun is a shoe.

The chateau is a 1.5km trek from the main bus or train station. There are a few places to **stay** in Klášterec, including the *Hotel Slavie* (☎747 375 211; ❷), opposite the gardens; although rather ugly from the outside its has a surprisingly pleasant **restaurant** with friendly staff who serve up various local dishes. Otherwise, head for the **tourist office** (Mon–Fri 8.30–11.30am & noon–5pm; June–Aug also Sat & Sun 10am–4pm), left of the church, for more information.

The North Bohemian brown-coal basin

The **North Bohemian brown-coal basin** contrives to be even less enticing than it sounds. Stretching the sixty kilometres from Kadaň to Ústí nad Labem, it comprises an almost continuous rash of opencast mines, factories and prefabricated towns, earning it the nickname *Černý trojhelník* (black triangle). The majority of the country's brown coal (lignite) is mined here, most of it from just ten metres below the surface. As a result, huge tracts of land at the foot of the **Krušné hory** have been transformed by giant diggers that crawl across fields of brown sludge like the last surviving cockroaches in a post-nuclear desert. Around one hundred villages have been bulldozed, rail and road links shifted, and the entire town of Most flattened to make way for the ever-expanding mines.

Not only is the stuff extracted here, but much of it is burnt locally, and brown coal is by far the filthiest and most harmful of all fossil fuels. To the credit of the Czech government (and not a little pushing from the EU), filters have been installed in the two main power stations at Tušimice and Prunéřov, situated less than 5km to the north and east of Kadaň, and the smoky yellow clouds that used to billow through the valley are now much less lethal. On certain winter days, when the nearby mountains cause thermal inversions, the smog can still be intense and authorities resort to distributing filter masks to local schoolchildren; but in the summer the pollution levels drop dramatically, and you'll hardly notice the effect. Nonetheless, the character of the region has been forever altered, and aside from a few engaging stops – or indeed to view the spectacle itself – there is little reason to visit.

Chomutov

CHOMUTOV (Komotau), a major road and rail junction that's difficult to avoid if you're passing through the area, has a history more notable for its repeated destruction than for anything else. Three devastating fires, sackings by the Hussites and Swedes, outbreaks of the plague, World War II bombs, the violent postwar expulsion of most of the German-speaking townsfolk, and finally the legacy of the Communist period – an ironworks, a meat-processing

---

Statistics from the black triangle

- A total of 240 square kilometres of countryside have been destroyed since 1950.
- Four square metres of earth have to be removed to extract one tonne of coal.
- The region's annual coal output peaked at 75 million tonnes in 1984.
- Every year four percent of the country's coal deposits are mined.
- Life expectancy in the region is seven years lower than the European average.
- Twenty percent of the power generated by coal is consumed by the mining industry.

factory and vast swathes of high-rise *paneláky* – have all taken a heavy toll on the town. For all this, the central square area is actually quite pretty, and if, by some unfortunate set of circumstances, you should find yourself here, you can survey the entire scene best from the top of the Renaissance **tower** (May–Oct Tues–Sun 9am–5pm), which dominates the main square; the landings on the way up trace the town's history. You can fritter still more time away at the local **museum** in the town's radnice/zámek (Tues–Fri 10am–5pm, Sat 9am–2pm, Sun 2–5pm), opposite, or the renovated Baroque church of sv Ignác, designed by the Italian Carlo Lurago. If you need to **stay the night**, make tracks to the new *Hotel Royal* (☎474 650 359, ⊛www.hotelroyal.cz; ❸), on the main square, which has cosy rooms and its own **restaurant**; the square is where you'll also find a passable pizzeria and a **pub**.

Most

MOST (Brüx) is like a sort of architectural paean to the *panelák*, the pre-fabricated high-rise blocks that are perhaps the Communists' most obvious visual legacy. The only historic building to survive the town's demolition in the 1960s was the late-Gothic church of **Nanebevzetí Panna Maria** (April & Oct Wed–Sun 9am–4pm; May–Sept Tues–Sun 9am–6pm; follow the signs "přesunutý kostel"), which was transported in one piece on a specially built railway to the edge of the mine, 841 metres away (the move took 28 days). Designed by Jakob Heilmann of Schweinfurt, a pupil of Benedikt Ried, in the early sixteenth century, it's now something of a lonesome sight, stranded between a motorway and the edge of the mining area, a short walk upriver from the train station. The original altar and numerous statues were preserved and reinstalled after the move, lending an odd juxtaposition to the otherwise clean, modern setup of the interior. Ask to see the video in the crypt which lauds the state's wonderful achievement in shifting the church – a hollow feat given that they relocated it above a polluted underground lake, whose sulphurous liquid has to be drained off to prevent the site from flooding. If your morbid fascination is captured, head for the vast **local museum** (Tues–Fri 9am–5pm, Sat & Sun 1–5pm), visible to the west beneath the hilltop castle of Hněvín; outside the museum is a new memorial to František Niedermertl, who was shot in 1952 for insubordination in one of the local forced labour camps.

Duchcov

At first, **DUCHCOV** (Dux), 20km northeast of Most, appears no different to the other brown-coal basin towns, encircled as it is by coal mines. But in this unlikely town there's a grandly conceived Baroque **zámek** (April & Oct Wed–Sun 9am–4pm; May–Sept Tues–Sun 9am–6pm; 100Kč), designed by Jean-Baptiste Mathey, which once hosted emperors and kings, as well as artistic luminaries such as Schiller, Goethe and Beethoven. The chateau's former librarian was none other than **Giacomo Casanova** (1725–98), who took refuge here at the invitation of Count Waldstein. Broke, almost impotent and painfully aware of his age, Casanova whiled away his final, fairly miserable thirteen years writing his steamy memoirs, the twelve-volume *Histoire de ma vie*. He took a vow of celibacy on entering Duchcov, though rumours continued to link him with various women, including the leading lady at the premiere of Mozart's *Don Giovanni* in Prague. The Venetians would like Casanova's remains, but no one is sure where they lie now, and the likelihood is that they have disappeared under the opencast mines.

The tour guides are well aware that today's trickle of visitors is more concerned with Casanova than with the chateau's period furniture, and so save the exhibition dedicated to the world's most famous bounder till last. Duchcov also boasts a vast collection of Czech Baroque art, including sculptures by Brokoff and Braun, and a series of obsequious portraits of the Waldstein family, mostly by Václav Vavřinec Reiner, who is also responsible for the fresco in the Great Hall. Much of the chateau park, along with the Baroque hospital designed by Octavio Broggio, was bulldozed in the 1950s by the Communists, who (wrongly) suspected that large coal deposits lay beneath the gardens. The priceless frescoes were shifted to a purpose-built concrete pavilion, where – forlorn, badly lit and brutally restored – they remain today; to see the frescoes, you must endure a thirty-minute guided tour (same hours as the chateau).

If you need a bite **to eat**, the *Valdštejn* on Masarykova, just by the chateau, serves up the usual dishes, like dumplings with goulash.

Osek

Another monument worth visiting, just out of earshot of the region's mines, is **OSEK** (Ossegg), 5km northwest of Duchcov, whose twelfth-century **Cistercian abbey** (April, Sept & Oct Tues–Sat 10am–noon & 1–4pm, Sun 1–4pm; May–Aug closes 5pm) is a reminder of the wealth of the area before the dawn of industrialization. After the destruction of the Thirty Years' War, some of the country's leading Baroque artists – painter Václav Vavřinec Reiner, architects Broggio and Santini, and the sculptor Corbellini, whose vigorous stucco drapery upstages the lot – set to work restoring the place. The abbey's real artistic treasure, however, is the thirteenth-century chapel off the cloisters, where light filters through to illuminate a central altar and an elegant stone pulpit with a rotating lectern. Under the Communists, the abbey was used as an internment camp for monks and nuns who refused to abandon their religious calling; now, happily, the Cistercians are back, preparing the place to use as a refuge for the homeless and a religious education centre for a new generation of Czech monks. There's a **campsite** (May–Sept) with bungalows just west of the monastery, by the lake.

Teplice

In the midst of this polluted region lies the traumatized town of **TEPLICE-ŠANOV** (Teplitz-Schönau), the forgotten fourth spa of the once celebrated quartet of Bohemian resorts that included Mariánské Lázně, Františkovy Lázně and Karlovy Vary (see Chapter 3). In the early nineteenth century it became "the drawing room of Europe", prompting the likes of Beethoven, Liszt and Wagner to appear on its *Kurliste*. By the 1880s, however, the adjacent mining industry had already inflicted its first blow on Teplice's idyllic way of life: the nearby Döllinger mine breached an underwater lake, flooding the natural springs, which subsequently had to be artificially pumped to the surface. The lingering smell of lignite was a characteristic of the town even then, and is now complemented by several additional chemical vapours.

The accumulative cost of this assault on the environment is extremely serious, but it has been compounded by the fact that, following the expulsion of the spa's German-speaking inhabitants, the communists proceeded to wreck the place aesthetically too, dismembering much of the old town and erecting tasteless edifices. In addition, Teplice now has more than its fair share of social

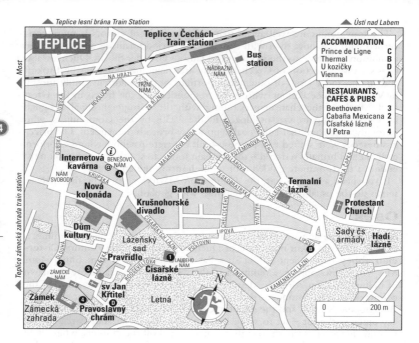

problems: there's a large and vocal skinhead movement here, which has come to blows with the town's Vietnamese and Romany communities on several occasions over the last couple of years, and until recently prostitution was endemic along route 8 to Dresden. All this doesn't make for a great introduction to the town, but elements of the old spa have survived, and if you're in the area, Teplice merits at least an afternoon's halt.

The Town

Arriving at the main train station, **Teplice v Čechách**, with its rich neo-Renaissance frescoes adorning the vaulted ceiling, injects a sense of hope in innocent minds, though this is soon dispelled by block after block of silent and peeling late-nineteenth-century houses as you head for the centre via 28 října or the main street, Masarykova třída, one block south.

At the end of Masarykova, behind the rather brutal Krušnohorské divadlo (an uncharacteristic, late work by Helmer and Fellner), the spa proper begins. Even the old *Kur Garten* – now the **Lázeňský sad** – has a somewhat diseased air about it, despite the lively sounds of birdlife. Nowadays, the communist-era white concrete **Dům kultury** is the dominant feature of the park, fronted by the **Nová kolonáda**, a glorified greenhouse made from some of Bohemia's great glass surplus.

Only when you cross the valley to the brightly coloured Neoclassical houses on **Lázeňská** is it possible to make the imaginative leap into Teplice's arcadian past. Beethoven once stayed in a house on Lázeňská, and it was in Teplice that he wrote his famous love letter to a woman he called his "Immortal Beloved", but whose identity still remains a mystery. Beyond Lázeňská lies the town's monumental **zámek**, seat of the Clary-Aldringen family until 1945, when they and most other *Teplitzer* took flight from the approaching Red Army. It was here, in 1813, that Tsar Alexander I, the Emperor Franz I and Kaiser Friedrich Wilhelm of Prussia concluded the "Holy Alliance" against Napoleon. The countless rooms of the chateau are now part of the local museum (Tues–Sun 10–11am & 1–4pm; tours on the hour), with memorials to Beethoven, Pushkin, and (of course) Goethe, wall-to-wall Biedermeyer, displays of historical clocks, old coins, ceramics and spa porcelain, and much else besides. The obligatory guided tour takes you also through the castle's courtyard, where there are remains of the medieval basilica, with a well-preserved Romanesque crypt.

Outside the main gates of the chateau is the cobbled expanse of **Zámecké náměstí** centred on Matthias Bernhard Braun's flamboyant charcoaled plague column. To the east, there are two churches: the first is the **Pravoslavný chrám**, a neo-Gothic Orthodox church; the second is the more handsome Baroque church of **sv Jan Křtitel**, whose richly painted interior is worth a quick peek. Hot water dribbles through a sculpted boar's mouth into the occasional tourist's palms from the original spring, known as the **Pravřídlo** (Urquelle), which is set into the wall opposite the southeast corner of the church on Lázeňská. Further east still, a splendid staircase, the Ptačí schody (Birds' Staircase), takes you past the twin turrets of the *U Petra* restaurant to the blissful **zámecká zahrada**, which spreads itself around two lakes still "enlivened with swans", just as Baedeker noted approvingly back in 1905.

Šanov

The rest of the spa lies in the eastern part of town, once the separate village of **Šanov** (Schönau) linked to Teplice by Lipová (Lindenstrasse), which clings to its lime trees. Like the bark on the trees, the paint is slowly dropping off many of the grandiose private villas and spa pensions that characterize this part of the spa, though at least some effort has been made to restore images of their former glory. Lipová culminates in the sady Československé armády, overlooked by a large, run-down, red-brick Protestant church and peppered with yellowing Neoclassical spa buildings. Unfortunately, the sky-blue Art Nouveau Termalní lázně, just off Lipová on Hálkova, once the city's public spa house, is completely broken down and disappearing behind exuberant arboreal growth. However, you could improve your health by climbing the 230 steps to the summit of Letná (accessible from Laubeho náměstí, at the eastern corner of the Lázeňský sad) for a great **view** over the spa.

Practicalities

The efficient **tourist office** (Mon–Fri 8am–5pm; Ⓦ www.teplice.cz), in the middle of Benešovo náměstí, should be able to help find **accommodation**. By far Teplice's nicest (and most expensive) place to stay is the *Hotel Prince de Ligne* (Ⓣ 417 537 733, Ⓦ www.princedeligne.cz; ❺), a pristinely renovated late-nineteenth-century hotel overlooking Zámecké náměstí. Another good option is the pretty comfortable *Hotel Vienna* (Ⓣ 417 534 105, Ⓦ www.hotel-vienna.cz; ❹–❺), occupying an extremely narrow building on Benešovo náměstí (though the rooms are spacious enough), while cheaper is the pension *U Kozičky* (Ⓣ 417 816 411, Ⓦ www.ukozicky.cz; ❹), Rooseveltova 262, positioned between the wooded hill of Letná and a busy road (ask for a room overlooking the former), which has a restaurant with a summer terrace overlooking the zámek. Alternatively, head for the small *Hotel Thermal* at U kamenných lázní 344 (Ⓣ 417 533 700, Ⓦ www.gasttour.cz/thermal; ❹), pleasantly located in a quiet area. One of the best **restaurants** in town is *U Petra*, on the zámecká zahrada staircase, which serves up Chateaubriand for around 200Kč. Try also the *Beethoven*, a nearby daytime-only eatery (you can also buy warm *oplatký* here), or the quite cheap *Cabaña Mexicana* (open Tues–Sat from 4pm), next door to *Prince de Ligne*, with burritos, tacos and quesadillas on offer. There's a pleasant **café** on the first floor of the smart nineteenth-century Císařské lázně, while you can check your **emails** at the simple *Internetová kavárna* on Benešovo náměstí, near *Vienna*.

Moving on from Teplice, the main **bus terminal** and **train station** (Teplice v Čechách) are next to one another just off Masarykova; Teplice zámecká zahrada train station, to the west of the chateau garden, is served only by slow trains to Lovosice. Slow, scenic trains to Děčín leave from Teplice lesní brána, 1km northwest of the centre – a fifteen-minute walk down Dubská from the town hall and across the motorway, or bus #24 from the main train station, or buses #20 and #23 from Benešovo náměstí.

Terezín

The old road from Prague to Berlin passes through the fortress town of **TEREZÍN** (Theresienstadt), just over 60km northwest of the capital. Purpose-built in the 1780s by the Habsburgs to defend the northern border against Prussia, it was capable of accommodating 14,500 soldiers and hundreds of prisoners. In 1941 the population was ejected and the whole town turned into a **Jewish ghetto**, and used as a transit camp for Jews whose final destination was Auschwitz.

Hlavná pevnost (Main Fortress)

Although the **Hlavná pevnost** (Main Fortress) has never been put to the test in battle, Terezín remains intact as a garrison town. Today, it's an eerie, soulless place, built to a dour eighteenth-century grid plan, its bare streets empty apart

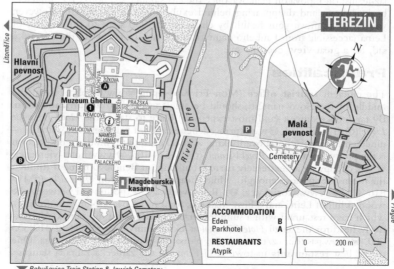

Bohušovice Train Station & Jewish Cemetery

from the residual civilian population and visitors making their way between the various museums and memorials. As you enter, the red-brick zigzag fortifications are still an awesome sight, though the huge moat has been put to good use by local gardening enthusiasts.

The first place to head for is the **Muzeum Ghetta** (Ghetto Museum; daily: April–Oct 9am–6pm; Nov–March 9am–5.30pm; 160Kč, or 180Kč for ticket including Malá pevnost), which was finally opened in 1991, on the fiftieth anniversary of the arrival of the first transports to Terezín. After the war, the Communists had followed the consistent Soviet line by deliberately underplaying the

A brief history of the ghetto

In October 1941 Reinhard Heydrich and the Nazi high command decided to turn the whole of Terezín into a **Jewish ghetto**. It was an obvious choice: fully fortified, close to the main Prague–Dresden railway line, and with an SS prison already established in the Malá pevnost (Small Fortress) nearby. The original inhabitants of the town – less than 3500 people – were moved out, and transports began arriving at Terezín from many parts of central Europe. Within a year, nearly 60,000 Jews were interned here in appallingly overcrowded conditions; the monthly death rate rose to 4000. In October 1942, the first transport left for Auschwitz. By the end of the war, 140,000 Jews had passed through Terezín; fewer than 17,500 remained when the ghetto was finally liberated on May 8, 1945. Most of those in the camp when the Red Army arrived had been brought to Terezín on forced marches from other concentration camps. Even after liberation, typhus killed many who had survived this far.

One of the perverse ironies of Terezín is that it was used by the Nazis as a cover for the real purpose of the *Endlösung* or "Final Solution", formalized at the Wannsee conference in January 1942 (at which Heydrich was present). The ghetto was made to appear self-governing, with its own council or **Judenrat**, its own bank printing (worthless) ghetto money, its own shops selling goods confiscated from the internees on arrival, and even a café on the main square. For a while, a special "Terezín family camp" was even set up in Auschwitz, to continue the deception. The deportees were kept in mixed barracks, allowed to wear civilian clothes and – the main purpose of the whole thing – send letters back to their loved ones in Terezín telling them they were OK. After six months' "quarantine", they were sent to the gas chambers.

Despite the fact that Terezín was being used by the Nazis as cynical propaganda, the ghetto population turned their unprecedented freedom to their own advantage. Since almost the entire Jewish population of the Protectorate (and Jews from many other parts of Europe) passed through Terezín, the ghetto had an enormous number of outstanding Jewish artists, musicians, scholars and writers (most of whom subsequently perished in the camps). Thus, in addition to the officially sponsored activities, countless clandestine cultural events were organized in the cellars and attics of the barracks: teachers gave lessons to children, puppet-theatre productions were held, and literary evenings were put on.

Towards the end of 1943, the so-called **Verschönerung** or "beautification" of the ghetto was implemented, in preparation for the arrival of the International Red Cross inspectors. Streets were given names instead of numbers, and the whole place was decked out as if it were a spa town. When the International Red Cross asked to inspect one of the Nazi camps, they were brought here and treated to a week of Jewish cultural events. A circus tent was set up in the main square; a children's pavilion erected in the park; numerous performances of Hans Krása's children's opera, *Brundibár* (Bumble Bee), staged; and a jazz band, called the Ghetto Swingers, performed in the bandstand on the main square. The Red Cross visited Terezín twice, once in June 1944, and again in April 1945; both times the delegates filed positive reports.

Jewish perspective on Terezín. Instead, the emphasis was on the Malá pevnost (see below), where the majority of victims were not Jewish, and on the war as an anti-fascist struggle, in which good (Communism and the Soviet Union) had triumphed over evil (fascism and Nazi Germany). It wasn't until the Prague Spring of 1968 that the idea of a museum dedicated specifically to the history of the Jewish ghetto first emerged. In the 1970s, however, the intended building was turned into a Museum of the Ministry of the Interior instead. Now that it's finally open, this extremely informative and well-laid-out exhibition at last attempts to do some justice to the extraordinary and tragic events which took place here between 1941 and 1945, including background displays on the measures which led inexorably to the *Endlösung* (Final Solution). There's also a fascinating video (with English subtitles) showing clips of the Nazi propaganda film shot in Terezín – *Hitler Gives the Jews a Town* – intercut with harrowing interviews with survivors.

The **Magdeburská kasárna** (Magdeburg Barracks), former seat of the *Freizeitgestaltung* – part of the *Judenrat*, the Jewish self-governing council – in the south of the ghetto, has recently been turned into a fascinating museum concentrating on the remarkable artistic life of Terezín. First off, however, there's a reconstructed women's dormitory, with three-tier bunks and all the luggage and belongings in place to give some kind of idea as to the cramped living conditions endured by the ghetto inhabitants. The first exhibition room has displays on the various Jewish musicians who passed through Terezín, including Pavel Haas, a pupil of Janáček, Hans Krása, a pupil of Zemlinsky, who wrote the score for *Brundibár*, and Karel Ančerl, who survived the Holocaust to become conductor of the Czech Philharmonic. The final exhibition room concentrates on the writers who contributed to the ghetto's underground magazines, but the greatest space is given over to the work of Terezín's numerous artists. Many were put to work by the SS, who set up a graphics department headed by cartoonist Bedřich Fritta, producing visual propaganda to proclaim how smoothly the ghetto ran. In addition, there are many clandestine works, ranging from portraits of inmates, to harrowing depictions of the cramped dormitories, the effects of starvation, and the transports. These provide some of the most vivid and deeply affecting insights into the reality of ghetto life in the whole of Terezín, and it was for this "propaganda of horror" that several artists, including Fritta, were eventually deported to Auschwitz.

Malá pevnost (Small Fortress)

On the other side of the River Ohře, east down Pražská, lies the **Malá pevnost** (Small Fortress; same hours as the Muzeum Ghetta), built as a military prison in the 1780s, at the same time as the main fortress. The prison's most famous inmate was the young Bosnian Serb, Gavrilo Princip, who succeeded in assassinating Archduke Ferdinand in Sarajevo in 1914, and was interned and died here during World War I. In 1940 it was turned into an SS prison by Heydrich, and after the war it became the official memorial and museum of Terezín. The majority of the 32,000 inmates who passed through the prison were active in the resistance (and, more often than not, Communists). Some 2500 inmates perished in the prison, while another 8000 subsequently died in the concentration camps. The vast cemetery laid out by the entrance contains the graves of over 2300 individuals, plus numerous other corpses, and is perhaps rather insensitively dominated by a large Christian cross, plus a smaller Star of David.

There are guides available (occasionally survivors of Terezín), or else you can simply use the brief guide to the prison in English, and walk around yourself.

The infamous Nazi refrain *Arbeit Macht Frei* (Work Brings Freedom) is daubed across the entrance on the left, which leads to the exemplary washrooms, still as they were when built for the Red Cross tour of inspection. The rest of the camp has been left empty but intact, and graphically evokes the cramped conditions under which the prisoners were kept half-starved and badly clothed, subject to indiscriminate cruelty and execution. The prison's main **exhibition** is housed in the SS barracks opposite the luxurious home of the camp Kommandant and his family. A short documentary, intelligible in any language, is regularly shown in the cinema that was set up in 1942 to entertain the SS guards.

Practicalities

Terezín is about an hour's **bus** ride from Prague's Florenc bus terminal, or a short hop from Litoměřice, just 3km to the north; the bus drops you off in front of the tourist office around the corner from the museum. The nearest **train station** to Terezín (from which the transports used to leave) is at Bohušovice nad Ohří, on the main Prague–Děčín line; occasional buses run to and from Terezín, or else it's a two-kilometre walk southwest of the main fortress. The only acceptable **restaurant** in the centre is the simple but clean *Atypík*, on Máchova, a block west of the museum. It's difficult to imagine a less appealing place **to stay**, but stay you may, at the badly run-down *Parkhotel*, on Máchova (☎416 782 260; ❶), or at the **campsite** *Eden* (April–Oct) just west of town. Alternatively, the **tourist office** (Mon–Thurs 8am–5pm, Fri 8am–1.30pm, Sun 9am–3pm) on the main square can advise you on the many accommodation possibilities in Litoměřice (see below).

Litoměřice and around

LITOMĚŘICE (Leitmeritz), 3km north of Terezín, at the confluence of the Ohře and the Labe rivers, is arguably the most appealing town in North Bohemia. It has been an ecclesiastical centre since the Přemyslid Spytihněv II founded a collegiate chapter here in 1057. From the eleventh century onwards, German craftsmen flooded into Litoměřice, thanks to its strategic trading position on the Labe, and it soon became the third or fourth city of Bohemia. Having survived the Hussite Wars by the skin of its teeth, it was devastated in the Thirty Years' War, but its most recent upheaval came in 1945, when virtually the entire population (which was predominantly German-speaking) was forcibly expelled. Since 1989 the town has begun to pick up the pieces after forty years of neglect. Restoration work is continuing apace, and the re-establishment here of a Catholic seminary has brought some pride back to the town.

Present-day Litoměřice is of more than passing interest (even if the main reason people come here is to pay their respects at Terezín), since the entire town is a virtual museum to **Octavio Broggio**. Broggio was born here in 1668 and, along with his father Giulio, redesigned the town's many churches following the arrival of the Jesuits and the establishment of a Catholic bishopric here in the mid-seventeenth century. The reason for this zealous re-Catholicization was Litoměřice's rather too eager conversion to the heretical beliefs of the Hussites and its disastrous allegiance to the Protestants in the Thirty Years' War.

The Town

Stepping out of the train station, you're greeted by the last remaining bastion of the old town walls across the road; behind it lies the historical quarter, entered

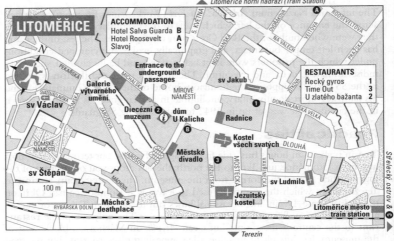

LITOMĚŘICE

ACCOMMODATION
Hotel Salva Guarda **B**
Hotel Roosevelt **A**
Slavoj **C**

Entrance to the underground passages

Galerie výtvarného umění

sv Václav

sv Jakub

Diecézní muzeum **2**

dům U Kalicha

Radnice

RESTAURANTS
Řecký gyros **1**
Time Out **3**
U zlatého bažanta **2**

Kostel všech svatých DLOUHÁ

Městské divadlo

sv Štěpán

sv Ludmila

Mácha's deathplace

Jezuitský kostel

Litoměřice město train station

0   100 m

via the wide boulevard of Dlouhá. The first church you come to is the hybrid church of **Kostel všech svatých** (All Saints) at the top of the street, which started life as a Romanesque church, and now boasts the only Gothic spires left on the skyline, a beautiful wedge-shaped affair reminiscent of Prague's right bank, plus three smaller spikier ones behind. Its present Baroque facade was designed by Broggio, but the oppressively low ceiling and dusty furnishings are disappointing, with the notable exception of the fifteenth-century panel painting by the Master of Litoměřice. More impressive is the light-infused interior of the nearby **Jezuitský kostel** (Jesuit Church), another work by Broggio, whose ceiling is adorned with colourful frescoes. While you're in the vicinity, check out the bizarre modern driftwood installation occupying the nearby flight of steps.

The town's vast cobbled marketplace, **Mírové náměstí**, once one of the most important in Bohemia, now boasts only a couple of buildings from before the Thirty Years' War. The best known is the **Mrázovský dům**, at no. 15 on the south side of the square, whose owner at the time, a devout Hussite, had a huge wooden *kalich* (chalice) – the symbol of all Hussites – plonked on the roof in 1537. Recently it's been opened to the public – ask at the tourist office (in the same building) for a guided tour (April–Oct Mon–Sat 10am–5pm, Sun 10am–3.30pm). The other building that stands out is the arcaded fourteenth-century **radnice**, at the eastern end of the square, topped by a shapely Renaissance gable. It now serves as the town museum (Tues–Sun 10am–5pm), worth a quick spin round, if only for the coffered sixteenth-century ceiling of the council hall; however, there's still precious little mention in the exhibition of the 1945 expulsions. On hot summer days you can cool off in the **underground tunnels and cellars** (*historické sklepy*; May–Sept 10am–5pm; the entrance is in the restaurant *Radniční sklípek*, Mírové nám. 21) that stretch right under the square and surrounding buildings. In medieval times the three-storey tunnels and cellars were used for storage and as a refuge during sieges; the guided tour lasts some twenty minutes.

The town's art galleries

In the western corner of the square is the town's excellent **Diecézní muzeum** (Tues–Sun: April–Sept 9am–noon & 1–6pm; Oct–March 9am–noon & 1–5pm).

As befits a rich ecclesiastical region, there are a lot of very fine religious paintings here, beginning with the serene *Madonna with Child in an Enclosed Garden*, an early oil painting from 1494. In the gruesome *Donor, Christ and Death*, Christ's flesh appears almost translucent, while Death appears as a skeleton tightly wrapped in skin. Among the museum's most valuable paintings is Lucas Cranach the Elder's *St Anthony the Hermit*, which depicts the saint being tempted heavenwards by a grisly collection of devilish animals. The most remarkable and unusual section of the gallery, however, is the timber-built building at the back of the museum, which contains a vast collection of "naive art": works from the last century by local amateur artists on a variety of themes from the religious to the political, from landscapes to portraits.

A few doors up nearby Michalská, the town's **Galerie výtvarného umění** (Gallery of Fine Art; Tues–Sun: April–Sept 9am–noon & 1–6pm; Oct–March closes 5pm) occupies a wonderfully rambling sixteenth-century building, whose inner courtyard is draped in ivy and echoes to the trickle of a modern fountain. Exhibitions doing the Bohemian circuit stop off here, supplementing the small permanent collection of late-nineteenth- and early-twentieth-century Czech canvases, including Impressionist work by Jan Preisler, Antonín Hudeček and Antonín Slavíček, plus a few pieces of Baroque art, and a bizarre Gothic statue of Mary Magdalene, depicted with her hair covering her entire body, except her knees. There's more Gothic art on the ground floor, in particular the surviving panels of the early-sixteenth-century winged altar by the Master of Litoměřice, whose paintings are peopled by folk with expressive, almost grotesque faces, their poses and gestures remarkably sophisticated for the period. Baroque dwarfs and other more modern sculptures pepper the gallery's terrace overlooking the ramparts.

Around sv Štěpán

On a promontory 500m southwest of the town centre, the **Dómský pahorek** (Cathedral Hill), where the bishop and his entourage once held residence, was originally entirely separate from the town, with its own fortifications. The small Orthodox chapel of **sv Václav** (St Wenceslas) on the northern slope is perhaps the younger Broggio's finest work, grand despite its cramped proportions and location, though suffering a little from a rather gaudy salmon-pink and silver-grey facelift. But the real reason to come out here is to wonder at the former cathedral of **sv Štěpán** (St Stephen), which looks out onto the quiet, grassy enclosure of Dómské náměstí. Redesigned by Giulio Broggio (among others) in the seventeenth century, sv Štěpán marked the start of the extensive rebuilding of Litoměřice. The cathedral's ceiling is disappointing, but the dark wood and the gloomy altar paintings from the school of Cranach the Elder add a bit of atmosphere. Outside, the freestanding Italianate campanile, designed by the Viennese architect Heinrich Ferstel in the 1880s, adds a peculiarly Tuscan touch.

A path along the north side of sv Štěpán leads down the cobbled lane of Máchova, where the Czech poet **Karel Hynek Mácha** died in 1836; there's a commemoration plaque at no. 3. In true Romantic style, Mácha died of consumption at the age of 26. His most famous poem, *Máj* (May), was hijacked by the Communists as their May Day anthem, but remains a popular love poem. He used to be buried in the local cemetery, but when the Nazis drew up the Sudetenland borders, Litoměřice lay inside the Greater German Reich, so the Czechs dug up the poet and reinterred him in the Vyšehrad cemetery in Prague (see p.137). Once you've reached the bottom of the cathedral hill, the stairway of the Máchovy schody will take you back up into town.

Practicalities

All **buses** terminate at the Litoměřice město **train station**, at the southeast corner of the old town, terminus for trains to Mělník and Ústí nad Labem; trains to Lovosice, Úštěk and Česká Lípa depart from Litoměřice horní nádraží, to the north of the old town. The town's **tourist office** (May–Sept Mon–Fri 8am–6pm, Sat 8am–5.30pm, Sun 9.30am–4pm; Oct–April Mon & Wed 8am–5pm, Tues & Thurs 8am–4.15pm, Fri 8am–4pm, Sat 8–11am; ☎416 732 440, ⒲www.litomerice.cz) is in the dům U Kalicha on Mírové náměstí, and can arrange **private rooms** or point you to the **Internet café** in the regional library opposite. If you want to treat yourself, stay at the friendly *Hotel Salva Guarda* (☎416 732 506, ⒲www.salva-guarda.cz; ❸), located in a lovely sgraffitoed building on Mírové náměstí and named after the house's sixteenth-century owner, who was an imperial bodyguard. Otherwise, the *Roosevelt*, on Rooseveltova (☎416 733 595, ⒲www.pruvodce.com/roosevelt; ❸) is perfectly comfortable. There's also the *Slavoj* **campsite** (May–Sept) with bungalows, near the open-air cinema (*letní kino*) on Střelecký ostrov, the woody island on the river, just south of the Litoměřice město train station. The **restaurant** in the *Salva Guarda* is probably the best choice in town, though the *Time Out*, near the Kostel všech svatých, offers generous salads and is a favourite spot for young locals; *U zlatého bažanta*, a couple of doors west from the tourist office, is a mixture of a typical Czech restaurant, a shop selling old furniture and the like, and a pleasant **café**; while *Řecký gyros* (closed Sat & Sun), just east of the square, is a simple eatery serving Greek-style fast food.

Ploskovice and Úštěk

An easy day-trip from Litoměřice, the village of **PLOSKOVICE**, 6km to the northeast off route 15, hides one of Octavio Broggio's few secular works, a crisp, light summer **zámek** (April–Oct Tues–Sat 9am–5pm, Sun 10am–3pm; tour in English 100Kč, with English text 60Kč; ⒲www.ploskovice.cz). After his abdication in 1848, this became a favourite summer watering hole for the Habsburg emperor Ferdinand I, who commissioned the exuberant Rococo plasterwork – sometimes frivolous, sometimes tasteless, always fun. The whole place has recently undergone a lengthy restoration: the beautiful walled grounds (daily dawn–dusk) are beginning to flourish and the fountains are issuing forth once more. To reach the chateau from the **train station**, follow the little stream north for 1km; the main **bus stop** is directly by the chateau. Simple Czech food is available at the **restaurant** *U zámku*, opposite the bus stop.

Bypassed by the main road – and, it seems, by the entire last three centuries – **ÚŠTĚK** (Auscha) originally grew up around a now-ruined medieval fortress. On one side of the main square there's a line of fourteenth-century burgher houses, which, unusually for Bohemia, still retain their original triangular gables of wood or slate. The **Jezuitský kostel**, built after the devastating fire of 1765, occupies centre stage in the square, and features a trompe l'oeil main altar, a Karel Škréta altarpiece and several fine wooden sculptures. Some 200m from the church, down Kamenná, in among the geese and hens, there are some fascinating wooden shacks known as **ptačí domky** (birds' houses). Perched on top of each other on the highest ledge of the steeply terraced banks, they provided ad hoc accommodation for Jewish families who were forced to live in ghettos until at least 1848, and for the Italian workers who built the town's railway link in the late nineteenth century. The inconspicuous, apricot-coloured synagogue nearby has recently been renovated and is open to the public (☎606 460 912).

It's fifty minutes by train from Litoměřice and about another half a kilometre's walk from the train station east to the old town. If you're **camping**, head for the *Chmelař* site (May–Sept) by the pleasant sandy shores of Chmelař lake (boat rental available in season), behind the train station, or try the *Zátiší* site (April–Oct), at 1. máje 4. You'll find alternative accommodation in the form of several modest pensions, and there are a couple of good restaurants: *Restaurace na růžku*, in a pink building off the square, and *Restaurace pod podloubím*, behind the church on the main square. In the nearby library there's a **tourist office** (9am–5pm: July & Aug daily; rest of the year Mon–Fri) with **Internet** access.

Ústí nad Labem

Twenty kilometres north, on the other side of the beautiful České středohoří (Central Bohemian Hills), which part only to allow the River Labe to slither through, lies the vast metropolis of **ÚSTÍ NAD LABEM** (Aussig). From a small town, Aussig grew very rapidly into the second largest port on the Labe (Elbe) after Hamburg, and the busiest in the Habsburg Empire. Solidly German-speaking and heavily industrialized, Aussig suffered terrible bomb damage during World War II. Worse was to follow. On July 30, 1945, a devastating terrorist attack took place when Ústí's sugar refinery, being used to store ammunition confiscated from the Germans, was blown up, killing fourteen Czechs and triggering a riot. The attack was blamed on die-hard Nazis, and enraged Czechs stormed through the town, dragging off any German they could find, and lynching hundreds before throwing them into the Labe. The incident is thought to have been instrumental in persuading President Beneš to declare the three million ethnic Germans living in Czechoslovakia enemies of the state and call for their forceful expulsion from the country.

Ústí was resettled after the war, its industries further expanded, and it now has a population of just under 100,000, making it the third largest city in Bohemia. However, the city has lost almost all of its charm – even the tram system (once second only to Prague's) was wound up in 1970. More recently, it has hit the headlines across the world as the place where the local council tried to build a wall to divide some of the city's Romany residents from their white Czech neighbours (see box p.286). Given the city's aesthetic limitations, and its almost unbearable historical baggage, most people give the place a wide berth. If, however, for whatever reason, you find yourself here, there are a couple of sights of minor interest, where you can while away an hour or so.

The Town

Trains usually stop at Ústí for only four or five minutes, which is long enough for most people – one whiff of the air and a glance at the discoloured river, tells you that this is yet another chemical town. For those venturing into town, it's just a couple of blocks west from the main train station to Ústí's chief sights, the Dominican church of **sv Vojtěch**, given a Baroque facelift by Octavio Broggio in the 1730s, and the fourteenth-century cathedral of **Nanebevzetí Panny Marie**. Destroyed by the Hussites during their bloody occupation of the town in 1426, the cathedral was rebuilt in late-Gothic style, and has recently been nicely restored. The building's outrageously leaning steeple is the result of bomb damage in World War II. From behind the churches you can view the 1930s road bridge over the Labe, opened in 1936 by President Beneš and somewhat optimistically named the Bridge of Brotherhood (between the Czech- and German-speakers).

The main square, **Mírové náměstí**, has had its entire northern side ripped out, and is now only really remarkable for the surviving Socialist Realist mosaic, depicting the inevitable road from the workers' revolution to world peace, which adorns the headquarters of the local council. One final building worthy of mention is the town's theatre or **Městské divadlo**, built in 1909 in the style of the Viennese Secession, and situated to the west of the main square, overlooking the concrete paving stones of Lidické náměstí.

On the opposite side of the Labe from the city centre is the suburb of **Střekov** (Schreckenstein), dominated by its ruined **hrad** (Tues–Sun: April & Sept–Dec 9am–4pm; May–Aug 9am–5pm; bus #1 from both the train and bus stations), a dramatic nightmare fairy-tale pile built into a bleak, black rocky outcrop high above the river. Like the Lorelei on the Rhine, it was much loved by the nineteenth-century Romantics, and provided inspiration for one of Wagner's operas (in this case, *Tannhäuser*). Set amid the tantalizing hills of the České středohoří, it's easy to see why – and to forget for a moment that this lovely landscape was pockmarked with industrial zones. Now the ruins are back in the hands of the Lobkowicz family, you're free to explore, and revel in the utterly incredible views up the hilly Labe valley and over to Ústí's grim smokestacks and awesome *paneláky*. The castle kitchen is now the *Wágnerka* **café** and **restaurant**, with a shady terrace from which you can watch the barges negotiating the lock below.

Practicalities

Ústí's **bus station** is just south of Lidické náměstí, a couple of blocks west of the main square. Travelling by fast train from Prague, Dresden or Berlin, you're most likely to arrive at Ústí's main **train station**, hlavní nádraží, at the southeast corner of the old town by the river (its left-luggage office is open 24hr); trains from Litoměřice and Mělník pass through Střekov station, on the other side of the river, and terminate at Ústí nad Labem západ, which is another couple of blocks west of the bus station, down Revoluční.

The **tourist office** (Mon–Fri 8am–5pm, Sat 8am–noon; ☎ 475 220 233, ⓦ www. usti-nl.cz) is at Hradiště 9, between the train station and the main square, and can

The wall in Ústí

Ústí nad Labem leapt into the media spotlight in 1998 when the municipal authorities decided to erect a 2.65m-high **"sound barrier"** in Matiční, a street in the city's industrial eastern suburb of Krásné Březno. White Czech residents on one side of the street had complained about "antisocial and unhygienic behaviour" by the Romanies who lived in the housing block across the street. Ultimately, however, the plan was to subject the Romanies to a 10pm curfew, by locking them inside the compound. The decision was criticized by the EU, and by the Czech parliament, though few people actually believed the city council in Ústí – where fifteen percent of the population are Romany – would go ahead with the project. Then early one morning in October 1999, the council suddenly began construction. Human rights groups protested, the Romanies attempted to tear the wall down, and the Czech parliament declared the wall illegal. After several weeks of bad international publicity, and stalemate between the central government and the municipal authorities, the council was finally forced to back down. However, the gesture was not one of peace and reconciliation. The state has offered to buy up the houses of the non-Romany residents and pay for them to be rehoused. As one Czech government minister put it, "there are many streets like Matiční in our country" – in other words, this is not an issue that's going to go away overnight.

help with accommodation. If you do need to **stay the night** in Ústí, you might as well enjoy the Communist-era luxury of the *Hotel Bohemia*, the high-rise monstrosity on the main square, Mírové náměstí (☎475 311 111, ⓦwww.ihbohemia.com; ❹). Less pricey is the *Hotel Palace* (☎475 220 953; ❶–❷), Malá Hradební 57, near the train station, where rooms overlooking the noisy street are cheaper.

České Švýcarsko

The area of sandstone rocks around Děčín is popularly known as **České Švýcarsko** (Bohemian Switzerland), a nickname coined by artists of the Romantic movement, though the landscape is in fact far from alpine. The River Labe drives a deep wedge into the geographical defences of Bohemia, forging a grand valley through the dense forests, interrupted by outcrops of sandstone rock welded into truly fantastic shapes. While it has always been a popular spot for weekend recreation, it was only in January 2000 that a portion of České Švýcarsko was officially designated a national park, the **Národní Park České Švýcarsko**, and while the park certainly contains some of the most precious natural treasures of the region, the entire area surrounding Děčín is greatly appealing.

Like the other *skalní města*, (rock "cities"), in the Český ráj (see p.305) and the Broumov region (see p.321), the whole area was formed when volcanic rock thrust its way to the surface, causing fissures and cracks that later widened. The result is probably the most impressive geological amusement park in the country, a dense network of mini-canyons and bluffs all covered in a blanket of woodland – spectacular stuff, and a favourite with rock climbers, but also fairly easy **hiking** country.

Transport throughout the region is not great – just infrequent rural bus services to most places – though the distances are small enough to make hiking an attractive proposition. In season, there's plenty of inexpensive **private accommodation** throughout the region, making it possible for non-campers to spend more than just a day in the countryside.

Děčín

Despite being German-speaking for most of the last thousand years, **DĚČÍN** has long been the geographical gateway to Bohemia, its castle rising up to the east as you enter the country from Dresden. Modern Děčín is really two towns – **Děčín** (Tetschen) itself on the east bank and **Podmokly** (Bodenbach) on the west – amalgamated in 1942 but still divided by the River Labe, which has always been the driving force behind the town's economy. As a busy industrial port, its attractions are limited, but its position on the river is quite dramatic, and, lying at the heart of České Švýcarsko, it serves as a convenient base for exploring the region.

Podmokly

The main point of arrival is Děčín's grubby **hlavní nádraží** in **Podmokly**, which looks out onto a mass of grey concrete and an unsightly supermarket. It's not a great start, but then Podmokly was a late developer, only coming into existence in 1850 through the amalgamation of three villages on the left bank. Sixty years of furious building followed, funded by the town's flourishing shipping industry, the results of which are still visible in the four or five blocks west of the station, where the locals go shopping and wolf down ice cream.

With time to kill and an interest in stuffed birds, medieval Madonnas or seamanship and navigation, you can spend a happy hour in the **Oblastní muzeum** (Tues–Sun 9am–noon & 1–5pm), situated in a former hunting lodge on třída České Mládeže. There's even a hands-on knots section, and a bit of the chain from the 720m-long cable that was cooked up in the nineteenth century

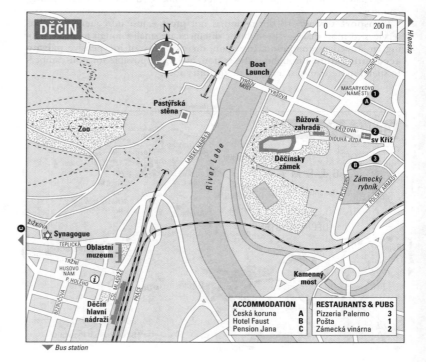

to help ships get upstream. A more miraculous sight is the Moorish Art Nouveau **synagogue**, round the corner on Žižkova, dating from 1907, which was saved from being torched on *Kristallnacht* by a local German, and is one of the few to survive in what was Sudetenland. Recently given a slightly injudicious lick of garish yellow and blue paint, it is now back in use by the local Jewish community for exhibitions (Mon–Fri 8am–3pm) and services.

Afterwards, head for the meringue-coloured mansion (with ultraviolet lighting at night) atop the precipitous **Pastýřská stěna** (Hirtenfelswände or Shepherd's Wall); follow signs for the zoo up the hill past the synagogue. At the top there's a small **café** and restaurant with an incredible view over Děčín, and, a little further back from the cliff, a small **zoo** (daily: April–Sept 8am–7pm; Oct–March 8am–4pm), with llamas, capybaras, lynxes and a grizzly bear.

Děčín

To cross the river to **Děčín** from Podmokly, follow the crowds onto the buses from outside the station (buy your ticket from a newsagent), or continue downstream from the above-mentioned Oblastní muzeum until you reach the Tyršův most. Děčín itself is much older than Podmokly, as witnessed by the austerely impressive **Děčínský zámek** (Schloss Tetschen-Bodenbach) at its centre, elevated above the town and river on an isolated lump of rock. The chateau's mostly Baroque appearance dates from the time of the Thun-Hohensteins, but it has been much abused since the family sold it to the state in the 1930s. Used as a barracks by the Germans, Czechs and lastly Russians, there's not much left of the original interior, though the exterior is finally getting a thorough make-over. Part of the newly restored interior has now been given over to the **Oblastní museum** (Tues–Sun 9am–noon & 1–5pm), with the castle's arsenal and a selection of local Baroque art on display.

The chief attraction of the chateau, however, is the **Růžová zahrada** (daily: April & Sept–Oct 10am–6pm; May–Aug 10am–8pm), a truly wonderful Baroque rose garden, laid out on a terrace cut into the north face of the rock high above the town. At one end is a befrescoed *sala terrena*, while at the far end is an ornate Baroque belvedere peppered with statuary. To gain access to the garden (and the chateau), you must walk up the sloping **Dlouhá jízda**, a gloomy three-hundred-metre-long drive cut into the rock. Directly below the garden are the distinctive black dome and twin tower lanterns of the salmon-pink Baroque church of **sv Kříž**, which has a richly painted and furnished interior. Two other sights worth noting are the striking 1906 Art Nouveau **fountain** on Děčín's main square, Masarykovo náměstí, and to the south of the castle, the slowly disintegrating stone bridge or **Kamenný most**, over the River Ploučnice, punctuated by Brokoff's Baroque statuary.

Practicalities

Most **trains** end up at Děčín hlavní nádraží in Podmokly, which has a left-luggage office; the town's **tourist office** (Mon–Fri 9am–5pm, Sat 9am–noon; ☎412 531 333, ⓦwww.mudecin.cz) is opposite on ulice Prokopa Holého. Děčín is located near the border and all international trains to and from Germany stop here. The **bus** station is a few blocks south of the train station. A much more fun way to travel is on the German-run **boat** to Hřensko, which sets off from the dock under Tyršův most (in summer from Děčín at 3.15pm; €10 one-way; ⓦwww.saechsische-dampfschiffahrt.de).

For **accommodation**, walk over or catch any bus to Děčín proper, where your best bets are probably the comfortable *Česká koruna* (☎412 516 104, ⓦwww.hotelceskakoruna.cz; ❸), on Masarykovo náměstí, or the renovated

Hotel Faust, on U plovárny (☎412 518 859, ✉faust@telecom.cz; ❷), just south of the zámek. If you have your own transport, you might also consider the pleasant *Pension Jana* (☎412 544 571, ⓦwww.penzionjana.cz; ❸), a couple of kilometres out of town on route 13 to Teplice. The **restaurant** at the *Česká koruna* features fish from Třeboň, while the nearby smoky *Pošta* is good for a beer. Moderately priced Czech food is served in the *Zámecká vinárna*, in the shadow of the church of sv Kříž, and the *Palermo* (closed Sun), just south of the church, dishes out great, thin-base pizzas.

Exploring České Švýcarsko

Loosely defined, České Švýcarsko splits neatly in half, with Děčín as the meeting point. The small **České Švýcarsko National Park** (ⓦwww.npcs.cz) occupies a stretch of land along the German border east of Hřensko. Whichever part you're heading for, it's a good idea to get hold of a proper walking **map**; those available from local tourist offices and bookshops mark all campsites and footpaths in the area, including those on the German side. The popular **Jetřichovické stěny**, mostly within national park boundaries to the northeast of Děčín, is topographically more interesting and covers a much greater area than its western counterparts. At its base runs the Kamenice river, accessible in parts only by boat (for boat trips, see opposite). The smaller range to the west, the **Děčínské stěny**, is less spectacular but doesn't suffer the same human congestion and can easily be reached on a day's hike from Děčín itself.

Děčínské stěny

If your sole aim is to see the sandstone rocks, it's simplest to catch one of the few buses a day from Děčín to Tisá, or to take the train to Libouchec station and walk the 2.5km north (and up) to Tisá. If, however, you're intent on a day's walking, follow the red-marked path from the Tyršův most in Děčín for 10km to **Děčínský Sněžník** (723m), a giant table mountain thrust up above the decaying tree line, on top of which stands a handsome sandstone look-out tower (*rozhledna*; April–Oct Mon–Fri 10am–5pm, Sat & Sun 9am–5pm; Nov–March when the weather allows), erected in 1864 by Count Thun-Hohenstein. The red-marked path eschews the direct route to Tisá and instead heads north to Ostrov, the last village before the border, where there's the luxury *Hotel Ostrov* (☎475 222 428, ⓦwww.hotelostrov.com; ❹), and a simple **campsite** with bungalows (April to mid-Nov) by a pretty lake, overlooked by the cliffs of the Ostrovské skály. (The nearest border crossing is the 24-hour one at Petrovice, northwest of Tisá.)

From the village of **TISÁ** itself, the **Tiské stěny** appear like a gloomy black wall – climb the hill and the whole sandstone "city" opens up before you. Sandy trails crisscross this secret gully, and it's fairly simple to get to the top of one or two of the gigantic boulders without any specialist equipment (the best viewpoint is to the left of the ticket office). You could spend hours here, exploring, picnicking and taking in the panoramic views. Via **Děčínský Sněžník**, it's a full day's walk from Děčín, but it's easy enough to hole up for the night, as there's plenty of private **accommodation** in the village, including the nice pension *Zlatá koruna* (☎475 222 526; ❷), en route to the ticket office; as well as a **campsite** (mid-April to mid-Oct).

Hřensko

Despite its dramatic mountainous setting, **HŘENSKO** (Herrnskretchen), at 116m above sea level, is in fact the lowest point in Bohemia. It was once a pretty village on the right bank of the Labe, dotted with half-timbered houses and redolent of Saxony on the opposite bank. However, Hřensko currently makes its living out of the German day-trippers flocking to the nearby rocks, and with their former East German neighbours now flush with euros, business is booming. Nightclubs line the road coming into Hřensko, and the village itself is barely visible under the sheer number of shops and garden-gnome stalls, the majority run by the republic's Vietnamese minority. It's unlikely you'll want to **stay** here, though there are several hotels to choose from; try the decent, four-storey *Hotel Labe* (☎412 554 088; ❷), right by the river front, which has pastel-coloured rooms with TV, or the luxury *Hotel Praha* (☎412 554 006, ⓦwww .hotel-hrensko.cz; ❺), with comfortable rooms and sauna, located in the stylish edifice at the eastern end of the village. Both hotels have **restaurants**.

Jetřichovické stěny

The only way to get to the **Jetřichovické stěny** and the Kamenice gorge is by **bus**, with three or four a day making the roundabout journey to Jetřichovice, via Hřensko, Tři prameny, Mezní Louka and Mezná; those travelling by car should note that there is no parking between Hřensko and Mezní Louka, but there are additional daily buses between the two.

By far the most popular destination is the **Pravčická brána** (ⓦwww.pbrana .cz), at 30m long and 21m high, the largest natural stone bridge in Europe. It's a truly breathtaking sight, though not one you're likely to enjoy alone unless you get there very early or out of season. Hop off the bus at Tři prameny, a clearing 3km up the road from Hřensko, and walk the remaining 2km along the trail marked in red. To get close to the bridge (as opposed to walking across it, which is forbidden), you'll have to pay an admission fee. The German border is less than 1km away, but the red-marked path that appears to head towards it actually rejoins the road 4.5km further east at **MEZNÍ LOUKA**, where you can take your pick from the **hotel** (☎412 554 084; ❸) of the same name, or the **campsite** opposite, with bungalows for rent (April–Oct; ☎412 554 084).

From Mezní Louka, the red-marked path continues another 14km to Jetřichovice, meandering through the southern part of the complex of mini-canyons, taking in the **Malá Pravčická brána**, a smaller version of the bridge, and a couple of very ruined border castles. **JETŘICHOVICE** itself is a lovely old Saxon hamlet made up of huge wooden farmsteads typical of the region. Several serve as pensions, of which *Dřevák* (☎412 555 015, 🖷412 555 222; ❸), an idyllic woodframe home with an impeccable restaurant in the centre of the village, stands out as one of the best places to stay in the entire region. There is also a **campsite**, *U Ferdinanda*, 1.5km to the south, across a ford, with bungalows and its own swimming pool (May–Sept).

The Kamenice gorge

Another option from Mezní Louka is to walk the 2km southwest to **MEZNÁ**, an unassuming little village that basks in a sunny meadow above the River Kamenice. Several basic pensions offer affordable rooms: *Pension Na vyhlídce* (☎412 554 065, ⓦwww.volny.cz/pension.mezna; ❷) has its own **restaurant**, as does *Pension Čedos* (☎412 554 064; ❶–❷), which offers cheap, simple (and clean) rooms without en-suite facilities. The latter enjoys a better location, with its summer terrace providing great views of the surrounding wooded hills.

From the village green, a green-marked path plunges a hundred feet into the cool, dank shade of the river, traversed by the wooden bridge Mezní můstek. Here you have a choice of heading up or down the **Kamenice gorge** to landing stages, where boatmen punt you along a short but dramatic boat trip down (or up) the river. The trips are justifiably popular, but boats run every ten to twenty minutes, so you shouldn't have to wait long. The downstream trip, along the **Tichá soutěska** (quiet gorge; Easter–early Nov daily 9am–6pm), drops you at the edge of Hřensko (see p.290) – you can alternatively pick it up via the yellow-marked path in Hřensko; this is perhaps the more dramatic of the two, and certainly the longer. The upstream one unloads its passengers just 500m further up the **Divoká soutěska** (wild gorge; Easter–early Nov daily 9am–5pm). With the latter trip, you can either return to Mezní Louka via the blue-marked path, or continue along first the blue- then the yellow-marked path up a shallower gorge to Jetřichovice, about 5km east.

Česká Kamenice and Benešov nad Ploučnicí

With your own transport, **ČESKÁ KAMENICE** (Böhmisch Kamnitz), 18km east of Děčín on route 13 (or forty minutes by train), makes a great alternative base for exploring České Švýcarsko. For a start, it's a lot more pleasant to rest up in than Děčín, with its interesting blend of nineteenth-century Habsburg edifices, the odd wooden folk building and a splendid Baroque pilgrimage chapel. **Accommodation** is rather limited until the hotel on the main square reopens; meanwhile *Pension Kamenice* (☎412 584 290, ✉jveidenthaler@seznam.cz; ❷), on náměstí 28 ijna east of centre, is a good choice, with clean en-suite rooms, satellite TV and a secure car park. The **tourist office** (May–Sept Mon–Fri 9am–5pm, Sat 9am–1pm; Oct–April Mon–Fri 9am–4pm, Sat 9–11am; ☎412 582 600, ⓦwww.ceskakamenice.cz) is on the main square, náměstí Míru, and you'll also find plenty of **restaurants and pubs** around here.

Five kilometres east of Česká Kamenice, on the other side of Kamenický Šenov, is another, much rarer geological phenomenon: the **Panská skála** (Herrnhausfelsen), a series of polygonal basalt columns that look like a miniature Giant's Causeway minus the sea. These are the result of a massive subterranean explosion millions of years ago, during which molten basalt was spewed out onto the surface and cooled into what are, essentially, crystals. They make a strange, supernatural sight in this unassuming rolling countryside, but are too small to be really awe-inspiring. Unlike Northern Ireland's major tourist attraction, the Panská skála are easily missed, even though they're only 500m south of route 13; look for the village of Prachen and ask the bus driver to tell you when to get out.

Halfway between Děčín and Česká Kamenice, and easily reached from either by train, is **BENEŠOV NAD PLOUČNICÍ**, a pretty little town characterized by its two connected **zámky** (April & Oct Wed–Sun 9am–4pm; May–Sept Tues–Sun 9am–6pm; 120Kč). The lower one is a neo-Gothic hunting lodge with meticulously restored interiors (restored after a fire in 1968); the upper one boasts Renaissance ceilings and an offbeat collection of Japanese and Chinese art. There is ample **accommodation**, though scout around before resorting to the rather dour *Jelen* (☎412 586 223; ❶ ❷), on the attractive main square; a safer bet, particularly for a longer stay, is one of the two basic self-service apartments at no. 6 on the square (☎412 586 262; ❷) – look for the "Apartma" sign. The nearest **campsite**, *Slunce* (mid-May to mid-Sept), is in the village of Žandov, 10km southeast of Benešov, on the road to Česká Lípa (and 2km north of the train station Police-Žandov on the Benešov–Česká Lípa railway line).

The Česká Lípa region

The eastern border of České Švýcarsko marks the beginning of Bohemia's vast glass-making industry, stretching far into the east of the region. Bohemian glass and crystal has always been considered among the world's finest, though the industry suffered badly as a consequence of the postwar expulsions of the majority German-speaking population. If you're heading east towards Liberec (see p.295) or the Krkonoše (see p.313), there are several sights worth checking out for those interested in Bohemian glass, as well as a handful of chateaux en route.

Česká Lípa, Nový Bor and Sloup v Čechách

ČESKÁ LÍPA (Böhmisch Leipa) gets its name from the Czech national tree, the linden (*lípa*). The town itself has precious few trees now, thanks to the uranium boom of the 1970s that trebled the town's population, most of whom now live in endless high-rise estates around the town. There are, however, a few minor distractions: the prettified main square, a small sgraffitoed Renaissance hunting lodge, known as the **Červený dům**, the **Vodní hrad**, or water castle, an extraordinary tent-roofed chapel of **sv Kříž** and a former Augustinian monastery. However, the town's main virtue is its location at the meeting point of five railway lines, making it a good base for exploring the area; the main **train station** is around 2km south of the old town. For central **accommodation**, try the small, peaceful *Penzión Monika* (☎487 824 997; ❶), at Jiráskova 636; the modest *Hotel Aldek* (☎487 521 523; ❷), at Jiráskova 718, some 200m from the main square; or the more upmarket *Hotel Olympia*, located in a building at Bulharská 853, which has a fine restaurant and bar (☎ & ☏487 823 800; ❸). Otherwise, the **tourist office** (Mon & Wed 9am–5pm, Tues & Thurs–Fri 9am–4pm; ☎487 881 105, ⓦwww.mucl.cz) is on the main square.

NOVÝ BOR (Haida) is 8km north of Česká Lípa, on route 9, and best approached by train. Its **Sklářské muzeum** (Glass Museum; Tues–Sun 9am–noon & 1–4pm; ⓦwww.novy-bor.cz/sklarske_muzeum) was founded over one hundred years ago and boasts a particularly rich collection of glassware, including a functionalist tea set by Adolf Loos and a great Art Deco *vitraille*. The museum is on the main square (the ticket is also valid for a small exhibition of glassworks above the **tourist office**, just off the square), itself a typical mixture of folk cottages and late nineteenth-century industrial wealth. Nearby stands the *Parkhotel* (☎487 723 157; ⓦwww.parkhotel.clnet.cz; ❺), a newly converted, very comfortable place to stay.

Three kilometres southeast of Nový Bor lies the village of **SLOUP V ČECHÁCH**, named after the thirty-three-metre-high sandstone outcrop (*sloup*) that towers over the neighbouring fish pond. First settled around four thousand years ago, in the fourteenth century rooms were dug out of its soft rock and it became a fortress. Badly damaged during the Thirty Years' War, in the last decade of the seventeenth century it became a hermitage; the little church, at the top of the rock dates from that time. Nowadays the rock is open to the public and you can either join the guided tour or explore it on your own, armed with an *anglický text* (April & Oct Sat & Sun 9am–4pm; May–Sept Tues–Sun 9am–5pm; ⓦwww.hradsloup.cz).

East of Česká Lípa

Fifteen minutes by train east of Česká Lípa is the village of **ZÁKUPY** (Reichstadt), which boasts a rather fancy **radnice** and two spiky church towers – signs of the wealth that the Habsburg Emperor Ferdinand I brought when he chose it as one of his retirement homes after his abdication in 1848. The local **zámek** (April & Oct Sat & Sun 9am–4pm; May–Sept Tues–Sun 9am–5pm) was also lavishly renovated for him in neo-Renaissance style and furnished with a giant snooker table and Rococo paintings by, among others, Josef Navrátil. Outside in the moat, the shaggy brown bears pace up and down, but there's little life in the crumbling aviary or the formal terraced gardens with their fountains, adorned with carved mermaids.

To the southeast of Zákupy is the strangely uninhabited tract of land known as **Ralsko**, after its highest peak. When the region's German-speaking population was expelled after the war, the Soviets took the opportunity to create a vast army base for their war games. When the troops finally withdrew in 1990, they left an estimated 3000 tonnes of pollutants, antitank mines and countless unexploded bombs. A clean-up operation is under way, as planners argue whether to build a giant international cargo airport here or turn the place into a safari park for the white rhino, which has been successfully bred at Dvůr Králové zoo (see p.335) for a number of years.

Fourteen kilometres northeast of Zákupy, the village of **JABLONNÉ V PODJEŠTĚDÍ** (Gabel) is dwarfed by the huge dome of the local Dominican **church** (April & Oct Sat & Sun tours at 1pm, 2pm, 3pm & 4pm; May–Sept Tues–Fri 9–11am & 1–4pm, Sat & Sun 1–4pm), an early work by the great Austrian Baroque architect Johann Lukas von Hildebrandt, dating from 1699. The inspiration for the church was the thirteenth-century wonder-worker Zdislava, wife of the lord of Lemberk (see below), who was beatified in 1907 and canonized in 1995, and whose remains (along with several mummified cadavers) lie in the crypt. For the best **view** of the church, climb the white Vyhlídková věž (Tues–Sun 9am–noon & 1–4pm), on Klášterní. Well-appointed en-suite **rooms** are available at the *Penzion U Salvátora* (℡487 754 333, Ⓦsalvator.webz.cz; ❷), on the main square; it has its own **restaurant**, which serves traditional Czech fare, as does the nearby *Český lev* restaurant.

Just over 2km northeast of Jablonné v Podještědí is the military stronghold of **Lemberk** (April & Oct Sat & Sun 9am–5pm; May–Sept Tues–Sun 9am–5pm), a thirteenth-century **zámek** which owes its Baroque outer coating to one of Waldstein's Dutch generals, who held on to the place after Waldstein's murder (see box on p.311). The overly long guided tour (*trasa 1*) is probably worth skipping in favour of a stroll round the castle's displays about Zdislava (*trasa 2*) and a look at the permanent exhibition of glassware produced in Nový Bor's Crystalex (*trasa 3*).

Doksy, Máchovo jezero and Bezděz

Trains from Česká Lípa take under 30min to reach **DOKSY** on the southernmost sandy shores of the **Máchovo jezero**, 15km southeast on route 9. The lake, created in medieval times, has been a popular recreational spot since nineteenth-century Romantics such as Karel Hynek Mácha (after whom the lake is named) used to trek out here. Nowadays it's surrounded by hotels, bungalows and campsites: the lakeside *Klůček* **campsite** (May–Sept) is the nearest to Doksy train station. There's a mercifully small museum dedicated to Mácha in Doksy itself, though you're infinitely better off going on the poet's favourite walk: the eight-kilometre hike southeast along the red-marked Máchova cesta up to the ruined hilltop **hrad** of **Bezděz** (Bösig; April & Oct Sat & Sun 9am–3pm; May–Sept Tues–Sun 9am–4pm; tour in English 100Kč), its ruins clearly visible for miles around. It was one of the most important castles in Bohemia until its destruction in the Thirty Years' War, but there's not much to see now aside from a Gothic chapel and, of course, the unbeatable view from the top of the hill (604m) – still, at least you get to explore it without taking a guided tour.

You can take the train another two stops to Bezděz to cut the walking distance down to just 2km.

Liberec and around

Lying comfortably in the broad east–west sweep of the Nisa Valley, framed by the Jizera Mountains to the north and the isolated peak of Ještěd to the south, **LIBEREC** (Reichenberg) couldn't hope for a grander location. The city itself, made prosperous and enormous by its famous textile industry, can't quite live up to its setting, but it's lively and bustling, with a smattering of interesting buildings and a couple of fairly good museums, all of which could keep you happily amused for the best part of a day. For further entertainment, you can while away a few hours in the glass and jewellery museum in the neighbouring town of Jablonec nad Nisou.

Arrival, information and accommodation

The **train station** has a **left-luggage** office (4am–11.30pm) and luggage lockers. From here (and the adjacent **bus station**), walk, or jump on tram #2 heading down 1 máje, to Soukenné náměstí, which is overlooked on one side by the city's eyesore Tesco superstore, and on the other by one of the functionalist Baťa shops designed by Vladimír Karfík in the 1930s. From here, it's a short steep walk up Pražská to the main square, Benešovo náměstí, where – in the town hall – you'll find the efficient **tourist office** (Mon–Fri 8.30am–6pm, Sat 9.30am–12.30pm; ☎ 485 101 709, ⓦ www.infolbc.cz), which can arrange very reasonable private **accommodation**. If you're scouting about yourself, you'll find that Liberec's hotels tend to be rather pricey, relying as they do on German tourists and business travellers. The nearest **campsite** is on a well-equipped site with a swimming pool, at the *Stadión Pavlovice*, Letná (May–Sept; ⓦ www .autocamp-liberec.cz), in the midst of a housing estate (bus #12 from the town hall, or #24 & #26 from behind the Divadlo F.X. Šaldy). The Krajská vědecká knihovna (State Research Library) has **Internet** access (Mon, Wed & Thurs 10am–7pm, Fri 10am–8pm, Sat 10am–2pm) and an adjoining café to provide needed booster shots of coffee.

Accommodation

Grandhotel Zlatý lev Gutenbergova 3 ☎ 485 526 700, ⓦ www.zlatylev.cz. Vast, turn-of-the-twentieth-century building with luxurious rooms and all conceivable amenities, conveniently located behind the chateau. ❺

Hotel Imperial 1. máje 29 ☎ 482 710 020, ⓦ www.hotel.cz/imperial. Giant Communist-era hotel on the way into town from the stations that undercuts the city's other big hotels. ❸

Ještěd Horní Hanychov ☎ 485 104 291, ⓦ www .hotel.jested.cz. Unbeatable location, view and kitsch 1960s decor in the TV tower on top of the mountain of the same name. ❸

Hotel Praha Železná 2 ☎ 485 102 655, ⓦ www .volny.cz/hotelpraha. Very comfortable hotel on the edge of the main square, which has preserved its original Art Nouveau entrance foyer, and a few other period fittings. ❹

Hotel Radnice Moskevská 11 ☎ 485 100 562, ⓦ www.hotelradnice.cz. Luxurious four-star hotel, on the edge of the main square, that's good value by international standards. ❺

Pension U muzea Vítězná 713/24 ☎ 485 102 693, ⓦ www.penzionumuzea.cz. Large nineteenth-century villa located in the leafy district near the Severočeské muzeum. ❷

Ubytovna Košická Košická 471/2 ☎ 486 131 470, ⓦ www.top50.cz/ubytovna. Basic, smoky and very cheap workers' dormitory a ten-minute walk east of the train station. ❶

Unihotel Voroněžská 1329/13 ☎ 485 352 211, ⓦ unihotel.vslib.cz. A real cheapie, just north of the main square, in a high-rise university complex. ❷

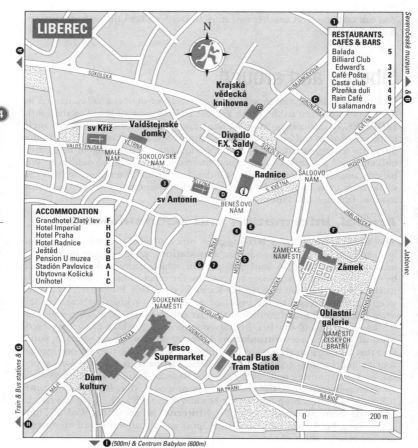

LIBEREC

N

RESTAURANTS, CAFÉS & BARS
Balada	5
Billiard Club	
Edward's	3
Café Pošta	2
Casta club	1
Plzeňka duli	4
Rain Café	6
U salamandra	7

SOKOLSKÁ

Krajská
vědecká
knihovna
@

sv Kříž
Valdštejnské
domky
VALDŠTEJNSKÁ
MALÉ
NÁM.
VĚTRNA
SOKOLOVSKÉ
NÁM.

Divadlo
F.X. Šaldy
❷

SOKOLSKÁ

ŠALDOVO
NÁM.

RUMJANCEVOVA

VORONĚŽSKÁ

❸
ŽELEZNÁ
sv Antonín

Radnice
ⓘ
S. KVĚTNA
BENEŠOVO
NÁM.

❶

Ⓒ

S. KVĚTNA

HUSOVA

JABLONECKÁ

Ⓓ

ACCOMMODATION
Grandhotel Zlatý lev	F
Hotel Imperial	H
Hotel Praha	D
Hotel Radnice	E
Ještěd	G
Pension U muzea	B
Stadión Pavlovice	A
Ubytovna Košická	I
Unihotel	C

❹ Ⓔ

PRAŽSKÁ

MOSKEVSKÁ

❺

ZÁMECKÉ
NÁMĚSTÍ

Ⓕ

Zámek

❻ ❼

RUMUNSKÁ

8. BŘEZNA

KOMENSKÉHO

Oblastní
galerie

SOUKENNÉ
NÁMĚSTÍ
REVOLUČNÍ

FUGNEROVA

JÁNSKÁ

NÁMĚSTÍ
ČESKÝCH
BRATŘÍ

Tesco
Supermarket

Local Bus &
Tram Station

Dům
kultury
1. MÁJE

NA PŘÍKNI

NA BIDĚ

0   200 m

Ⓗ

❶ (500m) & Centrum Babylon (600m)

The City

Totally dominating the attractive main square of **Benešovo náměstí**, Liberec's magnificent, cathedral-like **radnice** (guided tours April & May Sat 10am–noon; June–Sept Mon–Fri 9am–4pm, Sat 10am–noon) is probably the most telling monument the chauvinistic Reichenberger could have bestowed on the city. Purposely designed to recall Vienna's own Rathaus, its lofty trio of neo-Renaissance copper cupolas completes the effect with an impressive Flemish flourish. Several cafés now spread their tables out onto the square, from which you can contemplate this great Germanic edifice. Liberec has the distinction of being one of the few places outside Prague where there was any real fighting following the Warsaw Pact invasion of 1968; a small memorial to the right of the town hall steps commemorates those who died.

Behind the radnice is the city's theatre, **Divadlo F.X. Šaldy** (ⓦwww .saldovo-divadlo.cz), a typically solid, showy affair designed by the Viennese architects Helmer and Fellner in the 1880s. While you're admiring the theatre, you can also check the atmospheric pressure on the nineteenth-century weather machine opposite the main façade. At the beginning of Rumjancevova, behind the theatre, the brand new **Krajská vědecká knihovna** (State Research Library; Ⓦwww.kvkli.cz) has been built on the former site of the city's main synagogue, which was burnt down on *Kristallnacht* in 1938. As a gesture of reconciliation, the new building also houses a new synagogue, and

△ Liberec radnice

the library's huge collection of German documents is now open to the public. The building itself is contemporary, with a large open entrance hall and plenty of glass throughout to let in light; the structure design, which uses exposed steel, is similar to that employed at the Myslbek centre in Prague.

A couple of blocks west of the main square, on the far side of Sokolovské náměstí, the narrow side street of Větrná hides the town's most unusual treasure, the **Valdštejnské domky**, a terrace of three crisscross timber-framed houses dating from the late seventeenth century. To the east of the main square is the town's rouge-and-cream sixteenth-century **zámek**, previously owned by the Clam-Gallas family. It has recently been converted into a vast exhibition centre for the local glass giants, Glassexport, and has been remarketed as the Skleněný zámeček (temporarily closed). There's another, more historical, exhibition of glassmaking at the Severočeské muzeum (see opposite).

Oblastní galerie

Across the newly replanted formal gardens from the chateau is the **Oblastní galerie** (Tues–Sun 10am–6pm; ⓦ www.ogl.cz), a white nineteenth-century building off 8. března that has been an art gallery since 1873. Its unusually large collection includes a series of nineteenth-century French landscapes and some much earlier Dutch and Flemish masters, all of which were bequeathed to the gallery by the local German textile king, Johann Liebig.

The excellent collection of modern Czech paintings and sculptures includes two striking female portraits by the Impressionists Jiránek and Hudeček, a char-

Konrad Henlein in Reichenberg

Sited just the wrong side of the historical borders of Germany, the Reichenberger made up for this geographical oversight with their ardent pan-Germanism. Appropriately enough, it was the home town of **Konrad Henlein**, born in the nearby village of Reichenau (Rychnov) in 1898 and destined to become the leader of the Sudeten German Party (SdP). Henlein played an unheroic role in World War I, and after a spell as a bank clerk in Reichenau he became a gym teacher in the German-speaking town of Asch (Aš) in West Bohemia. The combined effects of the slump and the events in neighbouring Nazi Germany and fascist Austria, excited the Sudeten Germans, who proclaimed Henlein their Führer at a huge rally outside Saaz (Žatec) in 1933. Under Henlein, the SdP began to demand autonomy and self-determination for the German-speaking border districts of Bohemia and Moravia, and in the 1935 elections they won roughly two-thirds of the Sudeten German vote (thus becoming the largest single party in the country).

Yet despite his nationalist credentials, and the fact that the Nazis subsidized the SdP, Henlein was disliked in Nazi circles, due to his links with the **Kamaradschaftbund**, a secretive organisation inspired by Austrian clerical fascism rather than German National Socialism. The Nazis preferred the leader of the SdP's radical wing, **Karl Hermann Frank**, a one-eyed bookseller from Karlsbad, who wanted Sudetenland to be ceded to Germany. During the course of 1938, impressed by the Nazi takeover in Austria, Henlein foolishly agreed to push for the secession of Sudetenland. When the Nazis took over Sudetenland later that year, Henlein's closest associates, particularly those in the Kamaradschaftbund, were arrested and sent off to the camps. Henlein himself was too prominent a public figure to be interned; instead, he was appointed Gauleiter of Sudetenland, a position of little power, while Frank was eventually elevated to State Secretary, the second most powerful man in the Nazi Protectorate. In 1945 Henlein committed suicide after being captured by the Americans, while Frank was tried and hanged for war crimes in Prague in 1946.

acteristic canvas by super-weird Symbolist JosefVáchal, and a lovely swaggering sculpture of a woman by Šaloun. The room of Cubist and Fauvist canvases includes Josef Čapek's much reproduced *Woman Over the City*, Kubišta's grim *Kiss of Death*, and one of the few extant sculptures by Otakar Švec, the man who gave Prague the Stalin Monument. In the new postwar section there's a bevy of Surrealist paintings, Abstract Expressionist works by the likes of Mikuláš Medek, and even a smattering of pieces from the 1980s.

Severočeské muzeum and around

Liberec's grandest museum is without doubt the **Severočeské muzeum** (Tues–Sun 9am–5pm), a wonderful period piece from the 1890s built in a theatrical neo-Renaissance style. The museum is a couple of tram stops (tram #2) up 5. května, which turns into Masarykova, a long, leafy avenue flanked by decadent turn-of-the-twentieth-century mansions, once the property of a wealthy Reichenberger, now converted into pensions, flats, clinics and the like. Inside the museum, the old Communist-era displays on local and natural history are eminently skippable, but the glassware, jewellery and bronzework upstairs make a visit worthwhile. In addition to the locally produced stuff, there's an Art Nouveau lamp and vase by Lötz and another by Gallé, plus a Cubist tea set by Janák, some Wiener Werkstätte silverwork and some wacky shaggy tapestries from the 1970s.

At the top of the road is the city's chief park, and the popular **Botanical Gardens** (Botanická zahrada; daily: April–Oct 8am–6pm; Nov–March until 4pm), famous for their orchids. Here, too, you'll find the oldest **zoo** (zoologická zahrada; daily: April–Oct 8am–6pm; Nov–March until 5pm) in Bohemia, which boasts Europe's largest collection of birds of prey and two white tigers, as well as the usual array of elephants, pumas, chimpanzees and the like.

Ještěd

Liberec's top hotel – in every sense – sits on the summit of **Ještěd** (1012m) or Jeschken, from which you can look over into Poland and Germany on a clear day. Even if you don't stay the night, be sure to check out the bar-cum-diner and the restaurant with its crazy mirrors, neither of which would look out of place in a 1960s sci-fi series. To get there from the centre of town, take tram #2 to the end of the line (Dolní Hanychov), then bus #33 to the **cable car** (*lanovka*), which runs to the summit and hotel at least hourly (Mon 9am & 2–7pm, Tues–Sun 9am–7pm, out of season till 6pm; 80Kč return).

Eating, drinking and entertainment

In the centre of town there's a good choice of places to eat and drink. The simple **restaurant** *Plzeňka duli*, on Moskevská, offers typical Czech meals, pizzas and Pilsner Urquell beer, while *Balada*, also on Moskevská, is a cosy place with good pasta and Svijany beer. *U salamandra* (closed Sun), the big modern **pub** halfway down Pražská, doles out heaps of Czech food and mugs of Gambrinus.

Whatever you do, you must check out the *Pošta* **café**, across the road from the theatre, on the corner of Mariánská. Decorated inside in white and gold Neoclassical style, with dazzling chandeliers, it conjures up late-nineteenth-century Reichenberg beautifully. Also popular among locals is the *Rain Cafe*, opposite *U salamandra*, with vivid, modern decor. Late-night drinking can be happily continued until the early hours at the *Casta club*, at Tržní náměstí 11, which has live bands most nights. Alternatively, you can combine drinking with playing pool at *Billiard Club Edward's* on Sokolovské náměstí.

Liberec boasts the largest covered **amusement park** in the country, the Centrum Babylon (☏485 251 311, ⓦwww.centrumbabylon.cz), with a set of swimming pools (daily 10am–10pm), a funfair (daily 10am–8pm), a casino, and kitschy sphinxes to accompany your every step. The complex is located at Nitranská 1, a ten-minute walk southeast of the train station.

Football fans may be interested to know that the local team, Slovan Liberec, surprised the entire country by winning the league in 2002. Their stadium is south of the centre – take tram #2 to three stops beyond the railway station.

Jablonec nad Nisou

JABLONEC NAD NISOU (Gablonz) starts where the southwestern suburbs of Liberec end. It began life as a small Czech village, but was cut short in its prime by the Hussite Wars, when the whole area was laid waste by the neighbouring Catholic Lusatians. Apocryphally, the only survivor was the large apple tree (*jabloň*) that stood on the village green and gave the subsequent town its name. From the sixteenth century onwards, it was better known as Gablonz, the name used by the Saxon glassmakers who began to settle in the area, but it wasn't until the late nineteenth century that the town's **jewellery trade** really took off.

By the turn of the twentieth century Gablonz was exporting its produce to all corners of the globe, and its burghers grew very rich indeed, erecting private mansions fit for millionaires and lavish public buildings. Everything changed in 1945, when almost the entire German-speaking population of 100,000 was expelled, throwing the local glass industry into crisis (the Communists solved the problem by using forced labour in the factories). Meanwhile, uniquely for German refugees from eastern Europe, nearly a fifth of the exiled townsfolk stayed together and resettled in a suburb of Kaufbeuren, in Bavarian Swabia, which they named Neugablonz after their Bohemian home town.

The Town

The main reason for venturing into Jablonec is to visit the engaging **Muzeum skla a bižuterie** (Glass and Jewellery Museum; Tues–Sun 9am–5pm, Wed 9am–6pm), downhill from the town hall, in the palatial Zimmer & Schmidt building on U muzea, east off Dolní náměstí. The museum boasts a 3m tower of bangles set against a backdrop of hundreds of earrings, and – on the stairs – the longest necklace in the world, 220m long and made in just four hours by local art students (it shows). Among the best items are the Lötz and Moser glass, the works by Adolf Loos, the Secession and Art Deco hatpins and the incredible collection of early twentieth-century jet jewellery. Another branch of the museum is situated in the **Galerie Belveder** (Tues–Sun 9am–noon & 12.30–5pm), at Mlýnská 27, a ten-minute walk along Smetanova and Nad Mlýnem from behind the Nová radnice, boasting an eclectic array of objects, including coins, medals, hairslides and cuff links from various historical periods.

The rest of the town centre boasts a number of dour, though impressive, 1930s structures, most notably the **Nová radnice**, whose slimline clock tower dominates the skyline. Up the hill from the town hall, the gargantuan brick-built church, **Nejsvětější Srdce Páně** (Most Sacred Heart of Our Lord), towers over Horní náměstí; local boy Josef Zasche was the architect responsible. The former wealth of the town is obvious from the leafy suburbs, though many of the buildings have not been well looked after. One that has recently been beautifully restored is the town theatre or **Městské divadlo**, designed by the ubiquitous Helmer and Fellner in 1907 and located west down Generála

Mrázka; another is the graceful **Starokatolický kostel** (open for services only), a minimalist Art Nouveau church designed by Josef Zasche in 1900, situated 500m or so east of the centre, just off route 4 to Tanvald.

Practicalities

You can reach Jablonec on **tram** #16 from Liberec, which winds its way scenically and slowly up the Nisa Valley and deposits you close to the main **train station** to the southwest of the town centre. The choice of accommodation in Jablonec is more limited, though the town's **tourist office** (Mon–Fri 8am–5pm, Sat 8am–noon; ⓦwww.mestojablonec.cz), on the main square, should be able to help. The best **hotel** is the fairly brutally modernized late-nineteenth-century *Rehavital* on Jugoslavská (☏483 317 591, ⓦwww.rehavital. cz; ❹), which boasts a sauna, a gym and an excellent restaurant; alternatively, there's the white, high-rise *Hotel Merkur* (☏483 312 741, ⓦwww.hotelmerkur. cz; ❸), on Anenské náměstí, at the southwestern corner of the centre, which offers simply furnished rooms and its own restaurant and bar. For decent pizzas, head for *Pizzeria Franco*, just down from the radnice at Lidická 15; close by at no. 1 is *Balada*, a funky place (with a twin in Liberec) that has a stab at some unusual dishes. Cheap Czech food is available at the timber-decorated bistro *Adam + Eva* (closed Sun), on Mírové náměstí, while the *Internet Caffe Great Gem* (closed Sat & Sun), on A. Chvojky, a block down of the square, has **Internet** access and is often crowded with young locals.

On warm summer days, locals head out to the nearby **Mšeno lake**, north of the town centre, for a spot of sunbathing and swimming; to join them, take bus #1 or #10 from the centre.

Jizerské hory

Northeast of Liberec, the **Jizerské hory** (Isergebirge) form the western edge of the Krkonoše mountain range, which, in turn, makes up the northern border of Bohemia. Like their eastern neighbours, they have been very badly affected by acid rain, though extensive replanting has softened the impact visually. In fact, on first sight the mountains are undeniably dramatic, rising suddenly from Liberec's northern suburbs to heights of over 1000m. Large numbers of Czech and German tourists flock here in summer and winter – and you can follow suit by taking tram #3 from Liberec, or bus #1 from Jablonec to Janov or Bedřichov.

Frýdlant

It was neither an old stronghold nor a new mansion, but a rambling pile consisting of innumerable small buildings closely packed together and of one or two storeys; if K had not known that it was a castle he might have taken it for a little town.

Franz Kafka, *The Castle*

No one is quite sure which castle Kafka had in mind when he wrote his novel, but a strong candidate is surely the hybrid sprawling castle at **FRÝDLANT** (Friedland), a town on the north side of the frontier mountains, forty minutes by train from Liberec. Like his fictional character K, Kafka himself came here on business, though not as a land surveyor but as an accident insurance clerk, a job he did for most of his brief life. In Kafka's time the **hrad** and **zámek** (Tues–Sun: April & Oct 9am–3.30pm; May, June & Sept 9am–4pm; July & Aug 9am–4.30pm; 140Kč for both) were still owned by the Clam-Gallas clan, but its most famous proprietor was Albrecht von Waldstein, Duke of Friedland, whose statue stands within the castle precincts. Such was the fame of Waldstein that the Clam-Gallas family opened the castle to the public as early as 1801. The guided tour (up to 2hrs) might be a bit too much for some people, but the interior is, for once, richly furnished with period pieces and in good condition, having been a museum now for two hundred years. The complex is on a wooded basalt hill over the river, a short walk southeast of the train station and town centre along a pretty, tree-lined avenue.

If you want to stay in the area, try the large, friendly *Frýdlant* **campsite** (May–Sept) by a bend in the river beyond the castle, or the campsite (May–Sept) in **HEJNICE**, 10km southeast (30min by train; change at Raspenava), a village dominated by its towering pilgrimage church, with an attractive frescoed interior. Hejnice also has a good choice of hotels and **pensions**; try the rooms offered by the *Lázně Libverda* (☎482 368 111, ⓦwww.lazne-libverda.cz; ❷), a small spa complex that offers various treatments. You can cross the border into Poland just 13km north of Frýdlant at Habartice-Zawidów, on the road to Zgorzelec/Görlitz.

Travel details

Trains

Prague Masarykovo nádraží to: Bohušovice (up to 1 daily; 1hr); Chomutov (5 daily; 2hr 20min–2hr 50min); Děčín (3–4 daily; 1hr 40min); Kadaň (1 daily; 2hr 50min); Louny (1 daily; 1hr 50min); Most (3 daily; 2hr 30min); Ústí nad Labem (5–6 daily; 1hr 20min); Žatec (2 daily; 2hr).

Prague Hlavní nádraží to: Bohušovice (1 daily; 1hr); Chomutov (4 daily; 2hr 25min–2hr 45min); Děčín (4–5 daily; 1hr 35min–1hr 50min); Kadaň (2 daily; 3hr); Louny (1 daily; 1hr 50min); Most (3 daily; 2hr 30min); Ústí nad Labem (6 daily; 1hr 15min–1hr 25min); Žatec (1 daily; 2hr).

Prague Holešovice to: Děčín (2–3 daily; 1hr 20min); Ústí nad Labem (3–4 daily; 1hr 5min–1hr 15min).

Česká Lípa to: Benešov nad Ploučnicí (14–17 daily; 20–30min); Děčín (14 daily; 35–55min); Liberec (14–15 daily; 1hr 10min–1hr 30min); Litoměřice (8–9 daily; 1hr 10min); Jablonné v Podještědí (14–16 daily; 30–50min); Mimoň (14–16 daily; 20–30min); Zákupy (10–12 daily; 12min).

Chomutov to: Karlovy Vary (17–19 daily; 1hr 20min); Kadaň (hourly; 10–15min); Klášterec nad Ohří (16–20 daily; 20min); Most (29–31 daily; 20–25min); Plzeň (3 daily; 2hr 25min); Ústí nad Labem (hourly; 1hr 10min–1hr 25min); Žatec (10–14 daily; 20–30min).

Děčín to: Benešov nad Ploučnicí (every 1–2hr; 15–20min); Česká Kamenice (9–11 daily; 35–50min); Liberec (6 daily; 2hr–2hr 50min); Ústí nad Labem (every 1–2hr; 20–30min).

Liberec to: Frýdlant (11–14 daily; 35–40min); Jablonec nad Nisou (every 1–2hr; 25–30min); Turnov (13–18 daily; 40–55min).

Litoměřice to: Mělník (18–19 daily; 30–40min); Ploskovice (every 2–3hr; 12min); Úštěk (8–9 daily; 30min); Ústí nad Labem (15–22 daily; 25–30min).

Louny to: Libochovice (6–9 daily; 35–45min); Most (12–16 daily; 30–45min); Žatec (6–7 daily; 35min).

Most to: Děčín (3 daily; 1hr 10min); Duchcov (every 30min–1hr; 15–25min); Ústí nad Labem (hourly; 45min–1hr).

Buses

Prague to: Chomutov (6–16 daily; 2hr); Liberec (hourly; 1hr 10min–1hr 40min); Litoměřice (hourly Mon–Fri; 1hr–1hr 50min); Louny (hourly; 1hr 15min); Terezín (15 daily Mon–Fri, 2 daily Sat & Sun; 1hr).

Česká Kamenice to: Jetřichovice (Mon–Fri 4 daily; 25min).

Děčín to: Hřensko (4 daily Mon–Fri; 20min); Mezná (3 daily Mon–Fri; 35min).

Jablonec to: Harrachov (6–10 daily; 1hr 5min–1hr 15min).

5

East Bohemia

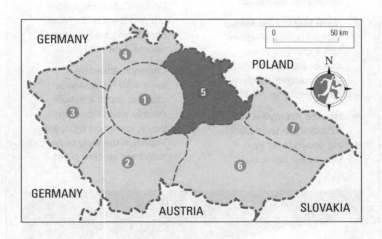

GERMANY

POLAND

GERMANY

AUSTRIA

SLOVAKIA

0   50 km

N

CHAPTER FIVE **Highlights**

* **Český ráj** Great rambling countryside, dotted with ruined castles, sandstone protrusions, chateaux and folk architecture. See p.305

* **Adršpach rocks** A bizarre rock "city" that rises out of the woods to the east of the Krknoše mountains. See p.321

* **Nové Město nad Metují** Picture-postcard square and a chateau whose interior includes work by early twentieth-century architects. See p.325

* **Hradec Králové** A picturesque old town standing opposite an innovative new town, built between the wars by Rondo-Cubist architects. See p.328

* **Kuks** Long defunct spa with the finest array of Baroque statues outside of Prague. See p.334

* **Pardubice** As well as its old town and chateau, Pardubice boasts a Rondo-Cubist crematorium and the world's most challenging steeplechase course. See p.337

* **Litomyšl** Attractive town with Renaissance chateau and the extraordinarily weird Portmonbeum, designed by Josef Váchal in the early twentieth century. See p.341

△ Kuks

5

East Bohemia

East Bohemia (Východní Čechy) is probably the most difficult Czech region to categorize. It has none of the polluting industry of its immediate neighbours, though it has suffered indirectly from their excesses; it contains some of the flattest landscape in Bohemia, but also its highest peaks; historically it has been predominantly Czech, though pockets of German settlement have left their mark in the culture and architecture. Lastly, the region has never really enjoyed fixed boundaries, a confusion compounded by the administrative borders currently in operation, which have arbitrarily added on parts of Moravia.

For variety of scenery, however, East Bohemia is hard to beat. Along the northern border with Poland, the peaks of the **Krkonoše** and the **Orlické hory** form an almost continuous mountain range, with excellent opportunities for hiking and skiing. The lower-lying **Český ráj**, to the south, and the area around **Broumov** to the east are wonderfully pastoral, and typically Bohemian, landscapes of rocky sandstone covered in thick forest. Further south still, the terrain on either side of the River Labe – the Polabí, as it is known – is flat, fertile and, for the most part, fairly dull. But the towns of the river basin do much to make up for it – **Hradec Králové**, the regional capital, and its historic rival, **Pardubice**, both boast handsomely preserved historic centres.

Český ráj

Less than 100km from Prague, the sandstone rocks and densely wooded hills of the **Český ráj** (Bohemian Paradise) have been a popular spot for weekending Praguers for over a century. Although the Český ráj is officially limited to a small nature reserve southeast of Turnov, the term is loosely applied to the entire swathe of hills from Mnichovo Hradiště to Jičín. **Turnov** is the most convenient base for exploring the region, though **Jičín** is infinitely more appealing, with its seventeenth-century old town preserved intact. But more interesting than either of the towns is the surrounding **countryside**: ruined fortresses, bizarre rock formations and traditional folk architecture, all smothered in a blanket of pine forests.

From Turnov, local **trains** run roughly every two hours to Jičín, and local **buses** from both towns infrequently wind their way through the otherwise inaccessible villages nearby. Generally, though, the distances are so small – Turnov to Jičín, for example, is just 24km – that you'd be better off buying a map and **walking** along the network of marked footpaths.

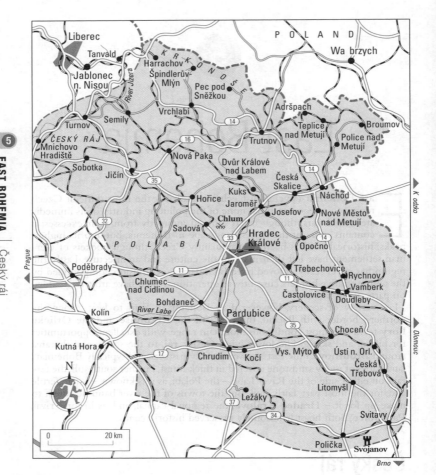

Brno ▼

Turnov and around

TURNOV (Turnau), as the name suggests, can be less than stimulating, though its main square has recently been perked up, and the town has done a good job promoting itself as the logistical and accommodation centre for the region. Its chief attraction is the **Český ráj museum**, on Skálova (May–Sept Tues–Sun 9am–6pm; Oct–April Tues–Sun 9am–4pm; ⓦwww.muzeum-turnov.cz), containing an interminable collection of semiprecious stones dug out of a nearby hillside, and temporary exhibitions of nature photography and the like. None of this matters, of course, if you're spending your days walking. The town's **tourist office** (July–Aug Mon–Fri 8am–6pm, Sat 9am–4pm, Sun 9am–2pm; Sept–June Mon–Fri 8am–5pm, Sat 9am–noon; ☎481 366 255, ⓦwww.turnov .cz, www.bohemian-paradise.info), on the main square, can help find **accommodation**, including private rooms, as can Čechotour, located on Nádražní near the train station, a ten-minute walk away west of the old town on the other side of the river. The best **hotel** in town is the late-nineteenth-century *Korunní Princ* on the main square (☎481 313 520, ⓦwww.korunniprinc.cz; ❸), which has pleasantly furnished en-suite rooms with satellite TV and a good, spacious restaurant, where they serve up Czech specialities alongside a few fish dishes; similarly modelled is the smaller and quieter *Cleopatra* (☎481 322 417, ⓔh.cleopatra@worldonline.cz; ❸), just up from the main square on 5 května, which also has a good restaurant. Cheap rooms can be had at the clean and simple *Karel IV* at Žižkova 501 (☎481 323 855, ⓦwww.hotelkareliv.cz; ❶); to get there, head left up Husova from 5 května, which then becomes Žižkova. There's also the simple **pension** *U svatého Jana* (☎481 323 325, ⓕ481 540 830; ❷), behind the *Korunní Princ*, down Hluboká. As for **restaurants**, the *U belgického dvora* (closed Sat eve), left of the *Korunní Princ*, has acceptable, cheap Czech dishes and runs an even cheaper eatery, of the same name (closed Sat afternoon & Sun), round the corner, on Hluboká.

One place worth visiting, on the outskirts of Turnov, is the chateau of **Hrubý Rohozec** (April & Oct Sat & Sun 9am–4pm; May–Sept Tues–Sun 9am–4.30pm; ⓦwww.hruby-rohozec.cz), high up on the left bank of the Jizera river, on the side of route 10 to Jelezný Brod. A Gothic castle redesigned in the Renaissance, it's a welcome contrast to the rest of the town, and its hour-long guided tour gives you access to some great views and a series of handsome Renaissance chambers.

Valdštejn and Hruboskalské skalní město

A beautiful two-kilometre walk through the woods along either the red- or green-marked path from the Turnov-město train station (one stop down the Jičín line) brings you to the former Gothic stronghold of **Valdštejn** (April & Oct Sat & Sun 9am–4pm; May–Sept daily 9am–4.30pm), ancestral seat of the Waldsteins for many years. Already in ruins by the late sixteenth century, it was occupied by vagrants, and later attempts to restore it never came to fruition, though its position remains impressive – as does the eighteenth-century stone bridge, flanked by Baroque statues.

Another 2km southeast, the first (and arguably the best) of Český ráj's skalné města (sandstone cities), **Hruboskalské skalní město**, unfolds amidst the trees. It's easy to spend hours clambering up and down the bluffs and dodging the crevices, whose names – Myší díra (Mouse Hole), Dračí věž (Dragon's Tower) and Sahara – give some idea of the variety of rock formations. Various viewpoints, like Zamecká vyhlídka or Mariánská vyhlídka, range high above the tree line, with the protruding stone slabs emerging from the pine trees like ossified giants.

The nearby castle of **Hrubá skála** is a colossal nineteenth-century reconstruction of the original Gothic castle. It's very popular with Czech film crews, and is now a wonderful and very reasonably priced **hotel**, *Zámek Hrubá Skála* (☎481 389 681, ⓔhrskala@iol.cz; ❸), with a baronial **restaurant** open to non-residents. From here, a green-marked path descends through the Myší díra and the Dračí skály, zigzagging down to the large lakeside **campsite**, *Sedmihorky* (open all year; ⓦwww.campsedmihorky.cz), near the Karlovice-Sedmihorky station on the Turnov–Jičín line. Also down here is a well-sited spa hotel, *Lázně Sedmihorky* (☎481 389 170, ⓦwww.sedmihorky.cz; ❸).

Trosky

The spectacular ruined castle of **Trosky** (April & Oct Sat & Sun 8.30am–4pm; May–Aug Tues–Sun 8.30am–6pm; Sept Tues–Sun 8.30am–4pm; ⓦwww.trosky .cz), which literally means "rubble", 5km southeast of Hrubá skála, is the Český

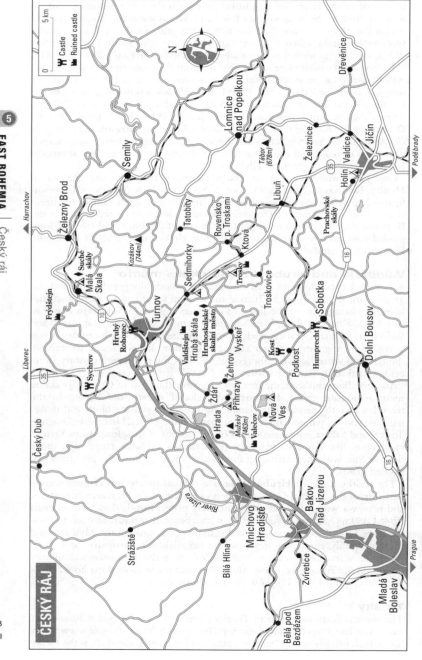

ČESKÝ RÁJ

Trutnov

N

0   5 km

☒ Castle
▲ Ruined castle

Dřevěnice

Lomnice nad Popelkou

Železnice

Jičín
Valdice

Poděbrady

Semily

Tábor (678m)

Holín

Libuň

Prachovské skály

Železný Brod

Harrachov

Tatobity

Rovensko p. Troskami

Ktová

Sobotka

Dolní Bousov

Suché skály

Kozákov (744m)

Sedmihorky

Troskovice

Frýdštejn

Malá Skála

Trosky

Kost

Humprecht

Turnov

Hrubý Rohozec

Valdštejn
Hrubá skála
Hruboskalské skalní město

Vyskeř

Podkost

Liberec

Sychrov

Žďár

Žehrov

Příhrazy

Hrada

Mužský (463m)

Nová Ves

Valečov

Český Dub

River Jizera

Strážiště

Bílá Hlína

Mnichovo Hradiště

Bakov nad Jizerou

Prague

Zvířetice

Bělá pod Bezdězem

Mladá Boleslav

ráj's number-one landmark. Its twin Gothic towers, Bába (Grandmother) and Panna (Virgin), were built on volcanic basalt rocks which burst through the sandstone strata millions of years ago. You can climb the ridge between Bába and Panna (the higher of the two) for a far-reaching view of the Jizera basin. The flash new **hotel** and restaurant complex, *Trosky* (T & F 481 382 290; ❷), by the castle car park, offers cheap and decent doubles, and there are two very basic **campsites**, the *Svitačka* site (May–Sept), a short distance to the south, and the *Vidlák* site (June–Aug), 2km northwest along the red-marked path, by the lake of the same name, with a cheap but passable hospoda across the road. Three or four **buses** a day run to Trosky from Turnov; trains are slower but more frequent and deliver you at Ktová station on the Jičín line, from where it's a two-kilometre walk uphill.

Sobotka and around

Compared to Turnov or Jičín, **SOBOTKA** is off the beaten track: 13km from either place, with limited accommodation, and only accessible by train from Jičín (50min; change at Libuň). Unless you're camping (and hiking) or staying in one of the handful of pensions, it's no good as a base for exploring the region, though it does harbour some good examples of the local brightly painted half-timbered architecture and – just northwest of the town, on a strange conical hill – the striking seventeenth-century **Humprecht** hunting lodge (April & Oct Sat & Sun 9–11.30am & 1–3.30pm; May–June & Sept Tues–Sun 9–11.30am & 1–4.30pm; July–Aug Tues–Sun 9am–5pm), named after its eccentric aristocratic instigator, Jan Humprecht Černín. It's a bizarre building, worth a peek inside if only for the central trompe l'oeil dining room, a windowless sixteen-metre-high oval cylinder with the acoustics of a cathedral. On the other side of the hill from Sobotka is a rudimentary **campsite** (mid-June to Sept) and a swimming pool. The best **hotel** in the immediate vicinity is the *Ort* (T & F 493 571 137, W www.ceskyraj.cz/hotelort; ❸), 2km to the north in Nepřívěc, which offers decent (if smallish) two- to four-bed rooms, as well as bike rental and a sauna.

Podkost

Up to 5 buses daily (weekdays only) cover the 3km northwest from Sobotka to **PODKOST**, a small settlement by a pond at the edge of the Žehrov forest. The village is dominated in every way by **Kost** castle (April & Oct Sat & Sun 9–11.30am & 1–3.30pm; May–June & Sept Tues–Sun 9–11.30am & 1–4.30pm; July–Aug daily 8am–6pm; 140Kč; W www.kinskycastles.info), which sits on top of a gigantic sandstone pedestal and sports a characteristic rectangular keep. Thanks to a fire in 1635, after which it was used as a granary, Kost was spared the attentions of later architectural trends and retains the full flavour of its fourteenth-century origins, making it the best-preserved castle in the Český ráj. The late-Gothic art exhibition is well worth seeing, too, though it's only open to tours, which can be very popular at the height of summer. Down in the village, there's one cheap **hotel**, the *Helikar* (T 493 571 127; ❷), which also has hostel beds (❶).

Mužský and around

You're more likely to find suitable accommodation at **NOVÁ VES**, another 4km northwest along the scenic red-marked path through the woods of the Žehrovský les. This tiny village by the **Komárovský lake** has three campsites and plenty of pensions along its shore. North of the lake lies a matrix of paths that crisscross the complex rock systems within the forest, emerging 3km later at a campsite (May–Sept) in Příhrazy. Paths spread out west from here and back into the woods until they reach Mužský (463m), from where it's another 2km uphill to the prehistoric burial ground of Hrada and the rocky viewpoint at Drábské světničky. The truly amazing sight of **Valečov** (April & Oct Sat & Sun 9am–5pm; May–June Tues–Sun 9am–6pm; July–Aug daily 9am–6pm; Sept Tues–Sun 9am–5pm; Nov–March Sat & Sun 10am–4.30pm), a ruined fort cut into the rock, lies another 2km to the south at the southwestern edge of the woodland. On a day's hike, you could easily do a round trip from Nová Ves or Příhrazy by heading east from Valečov, or else continuing another 3km west on the red-marked path to the station at Mnichovo Hradiště (see below), on the main railway line to Prague.

Mnichovo Hradiště

If you're thinking of exploring the area around Mužský, you could use the small industrial town of **MNICHOVO HRADIŠTĚ** (Münchengrätz), at the southwest corner of the Český ráj, as a base. The main square has a very hand-some neo-Renaissance radnice smothered in sgraffito, as well as one of the region's better **hotels**, U hroznu (☎326 771 617, ℗326 771 246; ❸), with its own *vinárna*. If you arrive by bus, you'll be deposited right on the main square; the **train station** is about five blocks to the southeast.

The town itself has an attractive Renaissance **zámek** (April & Oct Sat & Sun 8.45am–noon & 1–3pm; May–Sept Tues–Sun 8.45am–noon & 1–4pm; 120Kč), 1km north of the main square, that was owned by the Waldstein family right up to 1945. Interesting enough in itself, with lots of period furniture, a fine library, Chinese porcelain and attractive English-style grounds, the chateau is also the final resting place of **Albrecht von Waldstein**, who was murdered in Cheb (Eger) in 1634 (see opposite). Initially buried in Valdice, outside Jičín, the general's body wasn't brought to Mnichovo Hradiště until the eighteenth century, by which time the family couldn't afford the lavish mausoleum Albrecht himself had hoped for – instead, all you see is a modest plaque, which wasn't erected until 1934. Despite this, the Baroque chapel of **sv Anna**, in which Waldstein is buried, still merits a visit if only for its impressive stucco ceilings and lapidarium; the chapel is northeast of the chateau, accessible from the road to Podolí.

Jičín and around

At the southeastern tip of the Český ráj, where the fertile plain of the River Labe touches the foothills of the Krkonoše, **JIČÍN** (Gitschin), an hour by train from Turnov, is easily the most rewarding stop in the region. Its location, close to some of the Český ráj's most dramatic scenery, makes it a convenient base for some easy hiking, while its Renaissance zámek and arcaded main square make it by far the most attractive town in which to stay. Jičín is also easy to reach, with comprehensive bus connections throughout the region.

The Town

The town is closely associated with the infamous **Albrecht von Waldstein**, who, during his brief and meteoric rise to eminence (see opposite), owned almost every chateau in the region. Waldstein confiscated Jičín early on in the Thirty Years' War, and chose this rather unlikely town as the capital of his new personal empire, the Duchy of Friedland. He established a hospital to ensure his workers were not incapacitated for long, insisted everyone attend the Jesuit college he founded, and established a mint here; but for his murder, he would no doubt have fulfilled his plans for a bishopric and a university.

Albrecht von Waldstein (known to the Czechs as Albrecht z Valdštejna, and to the English as Wallenstein – the name given to him by the German playwright Schiller in his tragic trilogy) was the most notorious warlord of the Thirty Years' War. If the imperial astrologer Johannes Kepler is to be believed, this is all because he was born at four in the afternoon on September 14, 1583. According to Kepler's horoscope, Waldstein was destined to be greedy, deceitful, unloved and unloving. Sure enough, at an early age he tried to kill a servant, for which he was expelled from his Lutheran school. Recuperating in Italy, he converted to Catholicism (an astute career move) and married a wealthy widow who conveniently died shortly after the marriage. Waldstein used his new fortune to cultivate a friendship with Prince Ferdinand, heir to the Habsburg Empire, who in turn thought that a tame Bohemian noble could come in handy.

Within five years of the **Battle of Bílá hora** in 1620, Waldstein owned a quarter of Bohemia, either by compulsory purchase or in return for money or troops loaned to Ferdinand. It was a good time to go into property: Ferdinand's imperial armies, who were busy restoring Catholicism throughout Europe, provided a ready-made market for agricultural produce. And as a rising general, Waldstein could get away with a certain amount of insider trading, marching armies with as many as 125,000 men over enemy territory or land owned by rivals, laying waste to fields and then selling his troops supplies from his own pristine Bohemian estates.

As Waldstein ranged further afield in Germany, conquering **Jutland**, **Pomerania**, **Alsace** and most of **Brandenburg** on Ferdinand's behalf, his demands for reward grew ever more outrageous. Already duke of Friedland and governor of Prague, Waldstein was appointed duke of Mecklenburg in 1628. This upset not only the existing duke, who had backed Ferdinand's opponents, but even the emperor's loyalist supporters. If Ferdinand thought fit to hand one of the greatest German titles to this Czech upstart, was any family's inheritance secure? By 1630 Waldstein had earned himself the right to keep his hat on in the imperial presence, as well as the dubious honour of handing the emperor a napkin after he had used his fingerbowl. However, at this point Waldstein's services became too expensive for Ferdinand, so the duke was relieved of his command.

The following year the Saxons occupied Prague, and the emperor was forced to reinstate Waldstein. Ferdinand couldn't afford to do without the supplies from Waldstein's estates, but knew he was mortgaging large chunks of the empire to pay for his services. More alarmingly, there were persistent rumours that Waldstein was about to declare himself king of Bohemia and defect to the French enemy. In 1634 Waldstein openly rebelled against Ferdinand, who immediately hatched a plot to **murder** Waldstein, sending a motley posse including English, Irish and Scottish mercenaries to the border town of Cheb, where they cut the general down in his nightshirt as he tried to rise from his sickbed. Some see Waldstein as the first man to unify Germany since Charlemagne, others see him as a wily Czech hero. In reality, he was probably just an ambitious, violent man, as his stars had predicted.

In the 1620s he rebuilt the main square – now named **Valdštejnovo náměstí** after him – in stone, in a late-Renaissance style, full of light touches. Waldstein even lent the local burghers money to adapt their houses to suit his plans for the square. One side is still dominated by Waldstein's **zámek** (Tues–Fri 9am–5pm, Sat & Sun 9am–noon & 12.30–5pm), which now contains a dull local museum and, in the converted riding school, an art gallery, as well as the great conference hall in which the leaders of the three great European powers, Russia, Austria and Prussia, formed the Holy Alliance against Napoleon in 1813. A covered passage connects the chateau's eastern wing with the **Jesuit church** next door, allowing the nobility to avoid their unsavoury subjects while en route to Mass. But this steeple-less Baroque church is eclipsed by the mighty sixteenth-century **Valdická bréna** (April, May & Sept Tues–Sun 2–5pm; June–Aug daily 9am–5pm) close by, whose newly restored tower gallery offers a panoramic view over the town.

One of Waldstein's more endearing additions to the town is the **lipová alej** (now known as Revoluční), an avenue of 1200 lime trees, planted simultaneously in two dead straight lines, 2km long, by Waldstein's soldiers. At the far end is the once princely garden of **Libosad**, now an overgrown spinney but still worth a wander. The melancholy of its Renaissance loggia, last repaired at the end of the First Republic, is matched by the nearby Jewish cemetery, which boasts some finely carved tombstones and is overshadowed by the horror of one of the country's most brutal Communist prisons in nearby **VALDICE**. Originally a seventeenth-century Carthusian monastery, it was converted into a prison by the Habsburgs, and used after 1948 to keep the regime's political prisoners in a suitably medieval state of deprivation. It still functions as a prison today, housing some of the country's most hardened criminals.

Practicalities

The **tourist office** (late May to mid-Sept Mon–Sat 9am–5pm, Sun 9am–noon & 4–6pm; rest of the year Mon–Fri 9am–5pm, Sat 9–11.30am; ℡493 534 390, Ⓦwww.jicin.org), in the zámek, can find **accommodation**, including private rooms in and around town. Two central pensions provide simple rooms: *U České koruny* (May to mid-Sept; ℡493 531 241; ❷), on the main square, and *Na rynečku* (℡493 534 857; ❷) just off the square behind the run-down church of sv Ignác down Chelčického. There is also the friendly pension *Albrecht* (℡493 532 544; ❷), with just a pair of rooms in a family home 1km down the lime-tree avenue that leads to Valdice at Revoluční 712. Despite its prominent position just outside the Valdická brana on Žižkovo náměstí, *Hotel Paříž* (℡ & Ⓕ493 532 750; ❷) is better avoided. Two kilometres down route 16 to Mladá Boleslav the *Rumcajs* **campsite** (May–Sept) has wooden chalets.

While accommodation is fairly run-of-the-mill, there are plenty of unusual **restaurants** to choose from in the old town: *U piráta*, outside the Valdická brana at Husova 127, comes as an unexpected new addition, with trout, tuna and even shark in addition to standard Czech main dishes, to back up its off-beat buccaneer theme. Highly imaginative and filling pizzas, as well as what the menu describes as "food for those who say meat is meat", can be had in the pleasing little patio at *Pizzerie U Henryho*, just behind U České koruny on the main square. Good salads and a wide range of goulashes, steaks and dumplings are available in the cellar restaurant *Valdštejn* (closed Sun), on Chelčického, just off the southwest corner of the square.

Prachovské skály

Despite the very real attractions of the town, the reason most people come to Jičín is to see the **Prachovské skály**, a series of sandstone and basalt towers hidden in woods 8km to the northwest. To get there, it's a gentle walk along the yellow-marked path, via the *Rumcajs* campsite, though there are local buses too. The rocks lack the subtlety of the Hruboskalské skalní, but make up for it in sheer size and area; their name derives from the dust (*prach*) that covers the forest floor, forming a carpet of sand. In high season, swarms of climbers cling to the silent, grey rocks like a plague of locusts, but out of season it's possible to find a tranquil spot; try the green- or yellow-marked path. It's worth knowing that the viewpoints on the south side of the skalní město (eg Vyhlídka míru or Vyhlídka Českého ráje) are better than those opposite. There are dorm beds available in the primitive *ubytovna* right by the rocks, but these are usually booked solid in summer; try instead a private room, or the *Parkhotel Skalní město* (☎493 525 011, ⓦwww.skalnimesto.cz; ❸), a fine place back down the road to Jičín.

Železný Brod, Malá Skála and Sychrov

Heading northeast from Turnov, the railway follows the course of the Jizera river to **ŽELEZNÝ BROD** (Eisenbrod), one of the many centres of Bohemia's world-famous glass-making industry. It's a town of contradictions, its factories and high-rises spread along the banks of the river, while half-timbered cottages in the traditional Český ráj colours cover the hillside. The tiny main square is a typical mix of styles: one side is taken up by two wholly uninspiring 1950s buildings – the glass and crystal factory and the now-abandoned *Hotel Cristal* – while the other side shelters the nineteenth-century town hall and the timber-framed **museum** (May–Sept Tues–Sun 8.30am–noon & 1–4pm; Oct–April Sat & Sun only) of local arts and crafts. Up the hillside by the town church, which sports a nifty little wooden belfry, are some outstanding examples of **folk architecture**, usually confined to more inaccessible villages.

Železný Brod is really not an appealing town in which to stay, so you're much better off heading to the wonderful little village of **MALÁ SKÁLA**, 5km back down the valley towards Turnov (and also accessible by train and bus). Nothing much ever really happens here, but it's a supremely pretty place to be based for hikes into the surrounding hills. A steep red-marked path leads from behind the train station to the **Suché skály** (Dry Rocks) and a number of rock caves, used during the Counter-Reformation as safe houses for persecuted Protestants. A green-marked path then leads to the hamlet of Prosíčka, after which the blue-marked path heads back to Malá Skála; the whole route can easily be covered in a half day. Another red-marked path from Malá Skála follows a ridge on the other side of the river, from where the view across the valley to the ruined castle of **Frýdštejn** (May–Sept Tues–Sun 9am–4pm; Oct Sat & Sun only; ⓦwww.frydstejn .cz) is the reward for your pains. You could extend the day by dropping into the castle, then continuing on, up the blue-marked path, to the viewpoint atop Kopanina, and returning to Malá Skála via the green-marked path. As for accommodation, there's a **campsite** (May–Sept) on the right bank of the river, and a delightful little pension with a very good restaurant, *Teta Marta* (☎483 392 140, ⓦwww.tetamarta .net; ❷), 1km up the road to Frýdštejn. Right near the train station is the larger *Hotel Skála* (☎483 342 299, ⓦwww.hotelskala.cz; ❷), a reasonable enough place that also serves up steaks and chops from its outdoor grill.

Six kilometres northwest of Turnov, off route 35, **Sychrov** (daily: April, Sept & Oct 9am–noon & 1–3.30pm; May–Aug 9am–noon & 1–4.30pm; Nov–March 10am–2pm; 150–200Kč; ⓦwww.zamek-sychrov.cz) is a relatively recent aristocratic pile, romantically remodelled in neo-Gothic style by the Rohans, who bought the estate in 1820 having been forced into exile by the French Revolution. Apart from the pseudo-medieval craftsmanship of its interior, the castle is famed for its long-standing connections with Dvořák, who enjoyed the family's patronage and visited often. This partly explains the excellent season of concerts that take place here each year. The castle is only about ten minutes by train from Turnov on the railway line to Liberec.

The Krkonoše

The **Krkonoše** (Giant Mountains) are the highest mountains in Bohemia and formed part of the historical northeastern border of its ancient kingdom. They

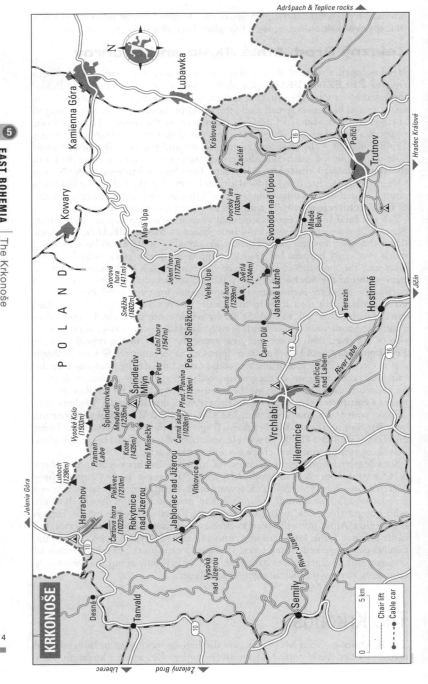

KRKONOŠE

Lubawka

Kamienna Góra

Kowary

P O L A N D

Královec

Žacléř

Trutnov

Svoboda nad Úpou

Mladé Buky

Hostinné

Malá Úpa

Dvorský les (1033m)

Jeleni hora (1172m)

Velká Úpa

Světlá (1244m)

Janské Lázně

Svorová hora (1411m)

Sněžka (1602m)

Černá hora (1299m)

Pec pod Sněžkou

Černý Důl

Terezín

Lučni hora (1547m)

Špindlerův Mlýn

sv Petr

Kunčice nad Labem

Vrchlabí

Vysoké Kolo (1503m)

Špindlerovka

Medvědin (1235m)

Pred. Planina (1196m)

Černá skála (1038m)

Luboch (1296m)

Pramen Labe

Kotel (1435m)

Horní Mísečky

Jilemnice

Harrachov

Plešivec (1210m)

Čertova hora (1022m)

Rokytnice nad Jizerou

Jablonec nad Jizerou

Vítkovice

Vysoké nad Jizerou

Semily

River Labe

River Jizera

Desná

Tanvald

Jelenia Góra ▲

Železný Brod ▼

Liberec ▼

Hradec Králové ▼

Jičín ▼

N

0   5 km

⚬ Chair lift

● Cable car

were uninhabited until the sixteenth and seventeenth centuries, when glass-making and ore-mining brought the first German and Italian settlers to the Riesengebirge, as they were then known. The mountains' undoubted beauty ensured an early tourist following, and, for resorts like Špindlerův Mlýn and Pec pod Sněžkou, it's now the sole industry. Despite being one of the few protected national parks in the country, the Krkonoše suffered considerably from **acid rain** in the decades up to the 1990s – much of which was caused by heavy industries over the borders in East Germany and Poland. Once the trees were badly affected, insects did the rest, transforming them into grey husks, devoid of foliage. Extensive felling took place, aimed at stopping the spread of the destructive insects, but it was a bit like a smoker removing their lungs to prevent cancer. For many, the fate of Bohemia's ancient forests was the most damning indictment of the Communists' forty years of mismanagement, and as if to rub it in, the focus during the 1980s was on new hotels and chairlifts rather than environmental measures.

Since 1989, however, the condition of the mountains has improved remarkably, with plenty of new tree planting and rebirth on the heels of much stricter emissions controls in both Poland and the Czech Republic. Czechs will reassure you that things here were never as bad as in the Krušné hory (see p.273) anyway, and it's true: if you stay in the largely unspoiled valley, or come here in winter when the snow obscures much of the damage, it's possible to remain oblivious. In summer, though, when walking is the main pastime, you can still see the relics of barren hillsides and ashen tree trunks amid the general greenness.

Practicalities

The Krkonoše has long been the country's top outdoor resort area, which means **accommodation** should be booked in advance at the height of the winter ski season, and in July and August. That said, the entire mountain range is teeming with cheap **private rooms**, which can be booked through the numerous accommodation agencies in the resorts. Špindlerův Mlýn and Jánské Lázně are undoubtedly the prettiest towns in which to stay; theoretically, you can also sleep at one of the **bouda** (chalet) dotted across the mountains, originally hideouts for the fleeing Protestants in the seventeenth century, but even these often require advance planning. Armed with a map, you could head for *Josefova bouda* (T & F 499 523 422, W www.josefovabouda.cz; ❷), near the end of the bus line from Špindlerův Mlýn to Špindlerova bouda, or to *Bradlerovy boudy* (T 499 422 056; ❷), along the green-marked trail east of the source of the Labe (*pramen Labe;* see p.318). The former is conveniently situated near the Slezské sedlo (pass), the meeting point of several very attractive walking trails; the latter boasts a pleasantly quiet location and can serve as a base for exploring the western part of the main ridge. Positioned in a beautiful location, although not so pretty itself, is *Labská bouda* (T & F 499 421 755, W www.labskabouda .cz; ❷), at the edge of the Labe valley. An hour's walk west of Sněžka, along a blue-marked path, stands the area's largest, newly restored, wooden *Luční bouda* (T 499 736 144; ❷), where during World War II Luftwaffe pilots were trained. **Camping** is one way of ensuring a place for the night, although facilities are somewhat restricted. Within the strict boundaries of the national park are just two sites, though plenty more lie along the fringes.

As for transport, **buses** are the best way to get around, with plenty of fast connections to Prague and throughout east Bohemia. **Trains** can get you as far as Harrachov, Vrchlabí and Trutnov, though these connections can be awkward. There are also numerous **chairlifts** that operate even in summer. However, **hiking** is undoubtedly the best way of getting around, since each valley is basically a long, winding dead end for motor vehicles, with pretty hefty car-parking fees (and sometimes queues) aimed at dissuading drivers from bringing their vehicles into the park. There are now three 24-hour **border crossings into Poland**: Harrachov–Jakuszyce, Královec–Lubawka and Pomezní Boudy–Przełęcz Okraj. More convenient for walkers are four additional tourist border crossings on the ridge itself (daily: April–Sept 8am–8pm; Oct–March 9am–4pm), only accessible on foot.

For those intent on serious hiking, a detailed **map** of the mountains, showing the network of colour-coded marked paths, is essential. **Warm clothing** is also important, no matter what the season – the summits are battered by wind almost every day, and have an average annual temperature of around freezing. Persistent mist – around for about 300 days in the year – makes sticking to the marked paths a must. In winter, most of the high-level paths are closed, and recently, even in summer, several have been closed to give the mountains a rest. To find out the latest details, head for the tourist information offices in any of the resorts. Keep in mind, too, that you will hardly be alone on the trails, as the mountains are immensely popular among Czechs, Poles and Germans.

The Krkonoše is also the most popular region in the Czech Republic for **skiing**, since it receives by far the longest and most reliable snowfall in the country. Pec pod Sněžkou is the largest resort, followed by Špindlerův Mlýn and Harrachov. Queues for lifts everywhere can be long and slow, but are more than compensated for by the cheapness of the ski passes and accommodation – although these have risen to levels formidable to the average Czech. Lift tickets cost upwards of 600Kč per day, and ski rental is easily had for around 250Kč per day. In summer, numerous outlets in each resort offer mountain bike rental – ask at the tourist office for the cycling map.

Vrchlabí

VRCHLABÍ (Hohenelbe) is the hub of the Krkonoše for transport and supplies, and not as well situated for skiing or hiking as the other main towns. Reservations are recommended for the direct **buses** from Prague, some of which continue on to Špindlerův Mlýn (see opposite); if you're travelling by **train**, you'll need to change at Kunčice nad Labem, 4km south. Hotel **accommodation** boils down to the good-quality *Labuť* (℡ 499 421 964, ⓦwww.hotellabut .cz; ➋–➌) on the main street, Krkonošská, and the similarly recommendable *U Svatého Vavřince* (℡499 421 044, ⓦwww.usvatehovavrince.cz; ➌), located in a sizeable yellow building on náměstí Míru. There are also many small, centrally located **pensions** to choose from, such as the self-service apartments above the *Klasika* pizzeria and steakhouse just beyond *Labuť* (℡ & ⓕ499 421 260; ➋). Of the three local **campsites**, the *Vejsplachy* (mid-June to Sept), just south of route 14, has the best locale, alongside a lake. For **food**, the aforementioned *Klasika* has become a local favourite for pizzas and steaks, or you can stretch out in the outdoor grill of the *Krušovická restaurace* on the main square. This place also has an **Internet café** upstairs.

Vrchlabí's official **tourist office** (Mon–Fri 9am–12.30pm & 1.30–5pm; ℡499 422 136, ⓦwww.vrchlabi.cz) is in the radnice on the main square, náměstí T.G. Masaryka. For comprehensive room booking and tour services right across the Krkonoše, check out the ING Tours travel agency (Mon–Fri 8am–6pm, Sat 8am–noon; ℡499 453 623, ⓦwww.ingtours.cz) in the IT Centrum near the square. This complex also contains the best **supermarket** in town.

Vrchlabí's long main street stretches for 3km along the banks of the Labe, taking you past the pleasing gardens and zoo of the sixteenth-century chateau and a number of traditional wooden, arcaded folk buildings around the centre. A trio of folk houses at the far end of the street (náměstí Míru) – one in stone, flanked by two timber-framed neighbours – have been converted into the small **Krkonošské muzeum** (June–Oct Mon–Sat 9am–noon & 1–4.30pm; Nov–May Mon–Fri 9am–noon & 1–4pm), containing, among other things, folk art, glassware and sundry stones. Displays on regional life through the ages (*Člověk a hory*; Tues–Sun 8am–5.30pm) and the local environment (*Kámen a život*; Tues–Sun 8am–3.30pm) feature at the museum's other branch, located in the former Augustan monastery, on Husova, a five-minute walk to the west. Attached to the museum (on náměstí Míru) is an office of the Krkonošský národní park (KRNAP; June–Oct Mon–Sat 9am–noon & 1–4.30pm; Nov–May Mon–Fri 9am–noon & 1–4pm), good for maps and information on weather conditions.

Špindlerův Mlýn and around

No doubt **ŠPINDLERŮV MLÝN** (Spindlermühle), 15km north up the Labe Valley, was once an idyllic, isolated mountain hamlet. Successive generations, however, have found it difficult to resist exploiting a town where seven valleys meet, and countless private pensions and hotels lie scattered across the hillsides. Still, the place retains a cosy feel, and makes a fine base for a few days of outdoor activity. The river Labe, here still a stream, flows through its tiny centre, which is just a convergence of a few roads.

It's important to book **accommodation** in advance during summer and winter high seasons. The booking office of the Info Pavilon (☎499 523 364, Ⓦwww.spindleruvmlyninfo.cz), right in the centre, can help, as well as provide ski rental. This is a private agency with ties to particular local hotels; if you prefer impartial advice, make for the official **tourist office** (daily 9–11.30am & 12.30–5pm; Ⓦwww.mestospindleruvmlyn.cz), hidden beyond the post office on the other side of the stream, which posts a complete list of accommodation possibilities in the vicinity. Recommendable hotels include the lovely wood-panelled mountain lodge *Start Hotel* (☎499 433 305, Ⓦwww.hotelstart.cz; ❹), Horská 17, which stands on a slope just west of the central area. Equally well-appointed is the new *Hotel Praha* (☎499 523 516, Ⓦwww.hotelprahaspindl.cz; ❸), Okružní 118, to the north of centre, with a slight Art Nouveau theme, and a nice restaurant with a terrace overlooking the town. Lower-end rooms can be found in the very pretty *Pension U Čeňků* (☎499 523 700, Ⓦwww.ucenku .cz; ❷), near the tourist office. Up the hill to the east in Svatý Petr is the modernized *Hotel Esprit* (☎499 433 468, Ⓦwww.esprithotel.cz;). There are two fairly pricey **campsites** a couple of kilometres north of the central area, both open all year.

A good place to grab a bite **to eat** is the terrace pizzeria in the Pavilon, by the edge of the stream. The aforementioned hotels both have good restaurants, and the *Pension U Čeňků* has a cute patio from which to sip a beer or have a meal. Finally, the *Špindlerovská hospoda* right bang in town is a decent pub with good food. If you're driving, keep in mind that **parking** is severely restricted in town, and unless your hotel has reserved space you'll have to leave your vehicle at the car park just to the south, and pay an exorbitant fee for the privilege.

Other than hanging around alongside the pretty riverbanks or poking into shops, there's little else to do in town other than ride the year-round Medvědín **chairlift** (*lánová dráha*; daily 8am–6pm) up the mountain of the same name (1235m), to the north of the central area (follow the signs from the left bank of the river; chairlift runs every half-hour), or try out the year-round **bobsleigh track** (*bobová dráha*; snowless days only 10am–6pm; Ⓦwww.bobovka.cz) nearby.

The **River Labe**, which flows into the North Sea (as the Elbe) near Hamburg, has its source in the Krkonoše. It takes about three hours to reach the source (*pramen Labe*): a long, boulder-strewn walk along the valley, followed by a short, sharp climb out of the forest. Characteristically for the Krkonoše, the upper plateau is disappointingly flat and boggy, and the source itself (500m from the Polish border) no great sight. If you're carrying your pack with you, continue for three hours along the blue-marked track to Harrachov (see below). Otherwise, it's around two hours back to Špindlerův Mlýn, via Horní Misečky and Medvědín. Another worthwhile trek is along the red-marked path to *Luční bouda*, a huge chalet at the edge of Krkonoše's largest (and potentially dangerous) marsh. It takes two hours from Svatý Petr and includes an extremely steep climb up the Kozí hřbety. From the bouda you can descend to Špindlerův Mlýn along the beautiful, perfectly V-shaped Bílé Labe valley (blue markers; 2hr).

Harrachov

Five buses and three trains a day (change at nearby Tanvald or Turnov) make the journey from Prague to the westernmost resort in the Krkonoše, **HARRACHOV** (Harrachsdorf), whose cottages are scattered about the Mumlava Valley. There's been a **glassworks** in action here since 1712, and the adjacent **Muzeum skla** (Glass Museum; Mon–Fri 9am–5pm, Sat & Sun 9am–1pm; ☎481 528 141, Ⓦwww.sklarnaharrachov.cz) has a small sample of glassware throughout the ages, as well as a shop; you can take a tour of the factory (Mon–Fri 8am–2pm; 130Kč, combined admission to glassworks and the museum 160Kč; book a day or two in advance) that includes a one-hundred-year-old cutting room with original equipment. There's also a **Lyžařské muzeum** (Ski Museum; Tues–Sun 9–11.30am & noon–4pm), further up the road, which traces the history of skiing, and celebrates Harrachov's occasional hosting of a round of the world ski-jump championships (most recently in December 2004). The **Hornické muzeum** (Mining Museum; Tues–Sun 10am–6pm; Ⓦwww .ados-harrachov.cz), opened in 2003 near the main car park, features a collection of minerals as well as the leftovers of a mineral mine, which functioned here until as recently as 1992. In addition, you can take an hour-long guided tour down into the extensive system of tunnels, whose total length exceeds twenty kilometres. Otherwise, you could aim for the rather pretty waterfall known as Mumlavský vodopád, up a trail north of the bus station. Harrachov is basically a ski resort though, so unless you're aiming for the slopes, your time is best spent hiking the surrounding mountains. The official national park tourist office, KRNAP (daily 8am–noon & 1–4.30pm) is close to the bus station, and can help with maps and walking suggestions.

 Accommodation in Harrachov can be significantly cheaper than in the neighbouring resorts, but it can still take some effort to secure a room in high season. The official **tourist office**, MIC (Mon–Fri 9am–5pm, Sat & Sun 10am–4pm; out of season only Mon–Fri 9am–3pm; Ⓦwww.harrachov.cz), can book hotels, pensions and private rooms in the area; there's even a free phone outside the office so you can ring round yourself after hours. The office is on the main road at the western edge of town. There are dozens of pensions all over the valley, and in Harrachov itself these include the pleasing *Pension Ploc* (☎ & Ⓕ481 528 194, Ⓦwww.pensionploc.euroregin.cz; ❷), owned by a former Czech ski-jumping champion, located near the MIC office. Also near the MIC office is the basic dorm-style *Chata Kamenice* (☎ & Ⓕ481 529 287, Ⓦwww .harrachovka.kamenice.euroregin.cz; ❷), and the partly wooden *Hotel Šedý vlk* (☎481 528 159, Ⓦwww.hotelsedyvlk.cz; ❸), with a gym, pool and sauna. These facilities are also available at the large *Sporthotel Rýžovište* (☎481 528

102, Ⓦ www.harrachov.cz/sporthotel; ❷), located in the hamlet of Rýžovište, southeast of the centre. Alternatively, there's a **campsite** (open all year; Ⓦ www .camp.cz/harrachov) up the road towards the Polish border. The hotels generally have good **restaurants**, otherwise you can try the *Restaurant Novosad* with its own brewery, recently opened at the glassworks. Those seeking a view with their meal would do well at the *Myslivna*, halfway up the **chairlift** to Čertova hora. For cheap thrills, continue on up above the dry tobogganing course to the top of the mountain, which at 1022m is high enough to view the barren hilltops around.

Pec pod Sněžkou and Janské Lázně

The sole attribute of **PEC POD SNĚŽKOU** (Petzer) is its proximity to the mountains. In winter this becomes the Czech Republic's chief ski centre, strung along an endless winding road. In summer it is the main hiking base for climbing **Sněžka** (Schneekoppe or Snow Peak), at 1602m the highest mountain in Bohemia and the most impressive in the entire range. Its bleak, grey summit rises above the tree line, relieving walkers of the painful sight of gently expiring pines, and making for a fine panorama – which you'll likely share with literally hundreds of others. If you don't fancy the six-kilometre ascent, take the **chairlift** (daily 8am–6pm; May–Sept also at 7pm; 300Kč return; Ⓦ www .snezkalanovka.cz) from the village, which will take you in two stages right to the top (departing on the hour). The border, signified by discreet white-and-red stone markers, divides the rounded summit; the seventeenth-century wooden chapel of sv Vavřinec (St Lawrence), an unappealing restaurant and a couple of snack stands are at the top.

Many Czechs use the chairlift as a launching pad for further **hiking**. To the east of the summit, a path follows the narrow mountain ridge (which also marks the border) for 2.5km to another peak, Svorová hora (Czarna Kopa to the Poles). To the west, there's a steep drop, again along the ridge, to *Slezská bouda*, a decent restaurant on the Polish side. To reach Špindlerův Mlýn from here (3hr 30min), follow the blue markers (via *Luční bouda*) forking off to the left, and not the red and blue ones that veer into Polish territory. Anyone wishing to cross the border should carry their passport, just in case the border guards want something to do.

Practicalities

There are regular **buses from Prague** to Pec pod Sněžkou, plus the occasional two or three to Janské Lázně (see p.320) and many to Trutnov. The Krkonoše National Park **information centre** (daily 7.30am–noon & 12.30–6pm; out of season Mon–Fri 7.30am–noon & 12.30–4pm), on the main road up from the bus station, has good maps and can provide hiking and skiing information. There is a second national park visitors' centre (same hours) with mundane exhibits on local flora and fauna, 2km up Obří důl, a valley to the north of town that provides an alternate hiking route to Sněžka. Ski rental is available from dozens of shops around town. As for **accommodation**, Pec has no campsite and its hotels are generally overpriced and booked-up, though the concentration of private rooms strewn across the hills is even denser here than in other Krkonoše resorts. The Turista information and travel agency (daily in winter 9am–6pm, shorter hours out of ski season; ☏ 499 736 280, Ⓦ www.turistapec .cz) in the centre of town handles the whole range of accommodation, including cheap rooms and chalets (*boudy*) that can make a nice escape from the crowds. There is also an information stand down the road from the bus station with an electronic board posting hotel and pension vacancies, and you can call from the free telephone provided. One well-priced option is the *Penzion Veronika* (☎ 499 736 135, ⓦ www.veronikapec.wz.cz; ❸), a comfortable, recently built place with its own restaurant, a short drive or steep ten-minute walk uphill to the west of the centre, beyond the *Hotel Horizont*. A bit up the price scale though still not expensive, is the *Pension Nikola* (☎ & ⓕ 499 736 251, ⓦ www. nikolapec.cz; ❸), near the park information centre. If you're travelling on a business-level budget, you'll find the plush and very central *Hotel Hořec* (☎ 499 736 422, ⓕ 499 736 424; ❸) to be a good deal. It's hard not to notice the eyesore (and expensive) *Hotel Horizont* (☎ 499 861 222, ⓦ www.hotelhorizont.cz; ❹), Pec's most complete hotel with all conceivable amenities, though the rooms themselves are undistinguished. Many hotels and pensions have their own **restaurants**, and the *Hospoda na Peci* across from the Turista office provides a smoky mountain-lodge atmosphere to go with your cheap beer and goulash. Up the road toward the Pension Nikola, *Enzian Gril* is a tasty little pub and grill with outside tables round the back.

Janské Lázně

JANSKÉ LÁZNĚ (Johannisbad), hidden away in a sheltered, fertile valley on the southern edge of the national park, has a different atmosphere from the other resorts, and as such is probably the nicest and cheapest place to base yourself in the entire Krkonoše. Visitors tend to come here to take the cure rather than climb the surrounding peaks, although even the lazy can reach the top of Černá hora by the hourly cable car (8am–6pm). On a hot summer's day all the classic images of spa life converge on the central stretch of lawn in front of the modest Kolonáda: a brass band plays oompah tunes in slightly lackadaisical fashion, while the elderly and disabled spill from the tearoom on to the benches outside. The best **place to stay** is the friendly, cosy *Villa Ludmila* (☎ & ⓕ 499 875 260, ⓦ www.volweb.cz/villa.ludmila; ❷), followed by the more rustic *Lesní dům* (☎ 499 875 385, ⓦ www.lesnidum.cz; ❷), which has a sauna and hot tub and its own country-themed **restaurant**. Another option is the large, stylish pension *Brigáda* (☎ 499 875 293; www.pensionbrigada.cz; ❷), at Černohorská 57, less than 200m from the Kolonáda, which provides ski rental and also has its own restaurant.

Trutnov

The modern factories and housing complexes that ring Bohemia's easternmost textile town, **TRUTNOV** (Trautenau), signal the end of the national park, though the town is easily within striking distance of the Krkonoše and an equally good base for exploring the Adršpach and Teplice rocks (see opposite).

The busy arcaded main square, **Krakonošovo náměstí**, downstream and uphill from the railway station, has been beautifully restored. Alongside its plague column stands a fountain depicting Krakonoš (*Rübezahl* to the Germans), the sylvan spirit who guards the Giant Mountains and gave them their Czech name, both best appreciated from one of the cafés under the arcades of the main square. If you have time to kill, there's the odd exhibition at the **museum** (Tues–Sun 9am–noon & 1–5pm) in the former *stará škola*, behind the church, just off the old town square. Trutnov's most recent claim to fame is that in the early 1970s, **Václav Havel** used to work in the local brewery, which produces a very good beer called, predictably enough, Krakonoš. His experiences later provided material for *Audience*, one of three plays centred around the character Vaněk (a lightly disguised version of himself).

The brewery lies roughly halfway between the train station and the main square. The **tourist office** (Mon–Fri 9am–6pm, Sat 9am–noon; ☏ 499 818 245, ⓦ www.trutnov.cz/infocentrum) in the radnice can point you towards some **private rooms**, or else you could try one of Trutnov's **hotels**: the *Grand* (☏ 499 819 144, Ⓕ 499 815 427; ❷), which has seen better days but is conveniently located on the main square, or the pleasanter *Adam* (☏ 499 811 955, ⓦ www .hotel-adam.cz; ❹), with spacious, simply furnished rooms in an arcaded house near the square on Havlíčkova. Each of these hotels has its own **restaurant**, while the *No. 1*, on Horská between the bus station and the square, is recommended for good, cheap pub grub. Even cheaper is the smoky *U draka*, at the corner of the main square. The *Dolce Vita* **campsite** (open all year; ⓦ www .dolce.cz) is by a small lake, 4km southwest of Trutnov – take the blue-marked path from the centre of town. The town's mid-August annual **open–air music festival** (ⓦ trutnov.openair.cz) – also known as the "Czech Woodstock" – is the largest rock festival in the country, featuring mostly Czech bands, plus the odd headline Western band.

East to Broumov

Between Trutnov and Broumov, some 30km east, lie two seemingly innocuous hilly strips smothered in trees, which only on much closer inspection reveal themselves to be riddled with sandstone protrusions and weird rock formations on the same lines as those in the Český ráj (see p.305). Distances here are small and the gradients gentle, making it ideal for a bit of none-too-strenuous – but no less spectacular – **hiking**. If you're thinking of exploring the rocks, get hold of the extremely detailed *Teplicko-Adršpašské skály / Broumovské stěny* **map** before you get there, which shows all the colour-coded footpaths and campsites. The local **buses** do serve the more out-of-the-way places like Broumov, but it's worth taking advantage of the slow but scenic **train** service from Trutnov to Teplice nad Metují, via Adršpach.

The Adršpach and Teplice rocks

The **Adršpach and Teplice rocks** (Teplicko-Adršpašské skály), 15km east of Trutnov, rise up out of the pine forest like petrified phalluses. Some even take trees with them as they launch themselves hundreds of feet into the air. German tourists have flocked here since the nineteenth century, though nowadays they are outnumbered by Czech rock climbers and ramblers. The rocks are concentrated in two separate *skalní města*, (rock "cities"): the Adršpach rocks, just south of the village of the same name, and the Teplice rocks, 2km south through the woods. The latter can also be approached from the villages of Janovice or Teplice.

Adršpach

ADRŠPACH (Adersbach) train station (one stop on from Horní Adršpach) lies at the northern extremity of the rock system, though you can't really miss it, since some of the rocks have crept right up to the station itself. There are two entrances close to each other (open roughly till dusk), and a nearby kiosk with the **tourist office** (Mon–Fri 7–11.30am & noon–3pm; ⓦ www.skalyadrspach .cz). Once through the perimeter fence, the outside world recedes and you're surrounded by new sensations – sand underfoot, the scent of pine, boulders and shady trees. Most of the sandstone rocks are dangerous to climb without the correct equipment and experience, so you'll probably have to content yourself with strolling and gawping at the formations best described by their nicknames: Babiččina lenoška (Grandmother's Armchair), Španělská stěna (Spanish Wall) and the ironic Trpaslík (Dwarf).

The green-marked path winds its way along and over a stream, through narrow clefts between the rocks, eventually bringing you to a couple of waterfalls (*vodopády*). From here, steps hewn out of the rock lead up to the Adršpašské jezírko, a lake trapped above ground level between the rocks, where jovial boatmen pole you along in rafts a short distance to the other side. From here, the yellow-marked path continues through the woods for 2km to the entrance to the Teplice rocks (see below). If you fancy a swim or a spot of nude bathing, head for the Pískovna lake to the east of the Adršpach entrance, with its dramatic backdrop of craggy rocks and pine trees. The *Hotel Lesní zátiší* (☎491 586 202; ❸), right by the entrance to the rocks, offers decent **rooms** and **food**. More comfortable is the new *Pension Adršpach* (☎491 586 102, ⓦwww .adrspach-skaly.cz; ❸), located on the road to Teplice nad Metují, which also has a restaurant.

Teplice nad Metují

The easiest approach for the **Teplické skalní město** is from Teplice nad Metují-skály station, just across the river from the entrance (usually open until 6pm, June–Aug till 8pm; ⓦwww.teplickeskaly.cz) to the rocks. A blue-marked path heads west for 2km, after which you reach the Anenské údolí, the main valley of the *skalní město* – another theatrical burst of geological abnormalities that form a narrow valley of rocks. Right by the woods' edge you can also explore the rock fortress of **Střmen**, which once served as a Hussite hide-out (accessible by a system of ladders and steps). The *Hotel Orlík* (☎491 581 025, ⓦorlik.hotel-cz.com; ❸) is situated right by the entrance to the rocks, though you'd be better off heading for the well-run and friendly *Penzion U Skalního potoka* (☎491 581 317, ⓦwww.penzion.adrspach.cz; ❸), which has six pleasant rooms in a building located behind the ticket office (reservation is advised at least several days in advance).

Alternatively, **TEPLICE NAD METUJÍ** (Wekelsdorf) itself, 2km east, is a functional base, with a supermarket, a cinema, several pensions and a couple of hotels. There's also the *Bučnice* **campsite** (May–Sept), 1km up the road from Teplice nad Metují-skály station. If you're a keen rock climber, then the annual **festival of mountaineering films** (Medzinárodní horolezecký filmový festival; ⓦwww.teplicenadmetuji.cz), held here on the last weekend of August, may be of interest. It's basically an excuse for a lot of boozing and boasting, though it attracts people from all over Europe, who come to share their experiences, many demonstrating their skills on the local formations.

The Broumov walls

The **Broumov walls** (Broumovské stěny) make up a thin sandstone ridge that almost cuts Broumov off from the rest of the country. From the west, there's no indication of the approaching precipice, from which a wonderful vista sweeps out over to Broumov and beyond into Poland, but from the east, the ridge is clearly spread out before you. The best place to appreciate the view is from Dientzenhofer's chapel of **Panna Maria Sněžná**, situated in among the boulders at the edge of the big drop. The best rock formations are 9km south of here, close to the highest point of the wall, **Božanovský Špičák** (733m), only a few hundred metres from the Polish border. You can approach the Dientzenhofer chapel from either Police nad Metují, 5km to the southwest, or Broumov (see below), 6km to the east. To get to the rocks around Božanovský Špičák, take the bus from Police to Machov, or the train from Broumov to Božanov, and walk the final 3.5km.

Broumov

BROUMOV (Braunau), a predominantly German-speaking town before the war, 30km due east of Trutnov, is probably the best place to base yourself if you're thinking of exploring the Broumov walls. The town is particularly impressive from a distance, with its colossal Baroque **Benediktinský klášter**, perched on a sandstone pedestal above the River Stěnava. The monastery was used by the Communists to incarcerate much of the country's Benedictine priesthood after 1948, most of whom were old and passed their remaining days here. During the 1960s numerous nuns were also imprisoned here – up to 300 at one point – and forced to labour in local factories and fields, until they too eventually died. This sad recent past seems to echo throughout the monastery, which, apart from the nicely repainted entrance gates, stands mostly unused and lonely. Guided tours (April–Oct Tues–Sat 9–11am & 1–4pm, Sun 10–11am & 1–4pm on the hour) lead through the stunning Baroque chapel, designed by Dientzenhofer, who lived here from 1727 to 1738, and featuring paintings by his contemporary Vratislav Vavřinec Reiner. Upstairs, the musty library contains what is said to be the only copy of the Shroud of Turin in central Europe. The complex also houses the town museum, with an exhibition on local history plus a display of old weaponry and several eighteenth-century Benedictine manuscripts (May–Sept Tues–Sun 8am–noon & 1–5pm). The rest of Broumov's compact old town is mildly interesting, with a handsome cobbled main square, Mírové náměstí, lined with lime trees and pastel-coloured houses, and centred on a fine barleysugar Marian column.

One attraction you shouldn't overlook is the Silesian fourteenth-century **wooden church** (the oldest in the country) on the Křinice road out of the centre. With a car and a passion for Baroque churches, you could also happily spend a morning exploring the local Stěnava valley. In the eighteenth century, Kilian Ignaz Dientzenhofer, Bohemia's foremost ecclesiastical architect, was chosen by the local abbot to redesign the Broumov monastery. He was also commissioned to build numerous **Baroque churches** in the area (and in the Klodzko region, over the border in Poland), in an attempt to Catholicize the staunchly Protestant Silesian Germans who used to live here. For each church, he experimented with a different design – a simple oval plan at Verneřovice (Wernersdorf), an elongated octagon at Ruprechtice (Rupperdorf), and a crushed oval at Vižňov (Wiesen). Most are now down to their bricks and mortar and firmly closed, but the key is usually traceable, and the effort well rewarded.

Practicalities

The **train** and **bus stations** are both close to one another, five to ten minutes' walk southeast of the old town. As for **accommodation**, the *Hotel Veba* (☎491 580 211, ⓦwww.hotel.veba.cz; ❸) is the town's finest, set in its own grounds and with an excellent restaurant, to the southwest of the centre off Šalounova. A more central option is the Communist-era *Hotel Praha* (☎491 523 786, ⓦwww.hotel-praha.cz; ❸) on the main square. In the radnice, a couple of doors to the left, is the **tourist office** (May & Sept Mon–Fri 8am–4pm, June–Aug Mon-Sat 8am–noon, Oct–April Mon–Thurs 8am–4pm, Fri 8am–3pm; ⓦwww.broumov.net), which can help with private rooms.

Try to sample the local beer, Opat, if the **restaurants** at *Veba* and *Praha* still offer it – the larger national brands are doing a good job of taking over pub menus. If you follow the red-marked trail heading southwest to the chapel of Panna Maria Sněžná (2hr) you'll find a nearby nineteenth-century mountain hut that houses an atmospheric restaurant (closed Mon & Tues) serving simple, hearty food.

Náchod and around

Cowering at the base of its large, lordly seat, built to guard the gateway to Bohemia from Silesia, **NÁCHOD** is one of the few Czech border towns that has been predominantly Czech for most of its life. Even the Nazis stopped short of annexing it when they marched into the Sudetenland in 1938, since at the time there were only four German-speaking families in the whole town. Nowadays, most people just stop off in order to break the journey and spend their last remaining crowns en route to Poland. Although the Polish border is a couple of kilometres east of the town centre, Náchod actually makes a useful base for exploring the surrounding area, including the two exceptional **chateaux** at Nové Město nad Metují and Opočno.

The Town

Náchod is a lot better looking than your average border town: the main square, **náměstí T.G. Masaryka**, in particular, has had a new lease of life following its recent restoration. Its two most winsome buildings are the fourteenth-century church of **sv Vavřinec** (St Lawrence) at the centre of the square, its entrance flanked by two fat square towers sporting comically large wooden onion domes, and the Art Nouveau *Hotel U beránka*, with sinewy lines and marvellously detailed mosaic lettering and interior light fittings. At one corner of the square is the town **museum** (Tues–Sun 9am–noon & 1–5pm), with a quite good display on local history that includes folk dress and dioramas describing the 1866 Austro-Prussian wars waged in the area.

Peeking out of the foliage, high above the town, and a very stiff climb from the main square, is Náchod's sprawling, unassailable, sgraffitoed **zámek** (April & Oct Sat & Sun 10am–noon & 1–4pm; May & Sept Tues–Sun 9am–noon & 1–4pm; June–Aug Tues–Sun 9am–noon & 1–5pm). The original Gothic structure survives only in the pretty little round tower in the centre of the complex; everything else is the result of successive building projects spanning the Renaissance and Baroque periods. There's a choice of two tours: the *malý okruh* (short tour; without a guide), which allows access to the tower, the dungeons and the viewing terrace, and the *velký okruh* (long tour; with a guide), which guides you through the interior. Inside, you get to see the castle art collection courtesy of the exiled Duke of Kurland, and an interesting hotchpotch of furnishings and exhibits accrued over the centuries by descendants of the Italian Ottavio Piccolomini-Pieri, Waldstein's bodyguard, who was given the castle by Ferdinand II after informing the emperor of Waldstein's secret plans (see p.311).

The former riding school, or **jízdárna** (Tues–Sun 9am–noon & 1–5pm), situated beyond the bear-inhabited moat by the car park, houses a surprisingly healthy permanent collection of **Russian paintings**. The highlights include two finely studied female portraits by Ilya Repin, the most famous of the "Wanderers" who broke away from the official Russian academy of art, better known for his epic works filled with fiery bearded figures like the *Trial of Christ*. The

The Cowards in Náchod

The exiled writer **Josef Škvorecký** was born and bred in Náchod – a "narrow cleavage between the mountains", as he characteristically dubbed it. During his wartime adolescence he was joined by film-director-to-be **Miloš Forman**, then only a young boy, who came to stay with his uncle when his parents were sent to a concentration camp from which they never returned. Later, in the cultural thaw of the 1960s, before they were both forced to emigrate, the two men planned (unsuccessfully) to make a film based on *The Cowards*, Škvorecký's most famous novel. Set in "a small Bohemian town" (ie Náchod) in the last few days of the war, the book caused a sensation when it was published (briefly) in 1958 because of its bawdy treatment of Czech resistance to the Nazis. Škvorecký also set the action of a later novel, *The Miracle Game*, in the nearby village of Hronov. In both novels, and in *The Engineer of Human Souls*, the name of the main character is Danny Smiřický, after Náchod's local aristo family.

leader of the Wanderers, Ivan Kramskoy, is responsible for the superbly aloof portrait of an aristocratic lady in a carriage, with a St Petersburg palace as a backdrop. Also on display are works by Serov and Makovsky, but best of all by far are the wildly colourful depictions of peasant women by turn-of-the-twentieth-century artist Filip Malyavin, who was a lay brother on Mount Athos in Greece before he took up painting full-time.

Practicalities

The town's **train** and **bus stations** are both five minutes' walk east of the centre, at the end of Kamenice. The **tourist office** (Mon–Fri 8am–5pm, Sat 8.30–11.30am; ☏ 491 420 420, ⓦ www.icnachod.cz), in a travel agency near the square at Kamenice 144, should be able to help with **accommodation**. The aforementioned *U beránka* (☏ 491 433 118, ⓦ www.beraneknachod.cz; ❸) is a comfortable option and probably the town's greatest institution: a hotel, café, theatre and restaurant (serving the local Primátor beer as well as traditional Czech food) in one. The nearby *U města Prahy* (☏ & ⓕ 491 421 817; ⓦ web .quick.cz/hotpraha/; ❷) is a simple, reasonably priced hotel, also with a restaurant and *vinárna*. Náchod's pretty riverside **campsite** (mid-May to mid-Sept) is by the woods 1.5km east of the centre, signposted down Běloveská. Another cheap option (although extremely basic) is the *Ubytovňa KČT* (April–Oct; ☏ 491 431 547; ❶), located in a yellow barrack on Železniční, off the road to Broumov.

Nové Město nad Metují

NOVÉ MĚSTO NAD METUJÍ, 9km south of Náchod, boasts a stunningly beautiful old town square, with one of the country's most interesting chateaux crouched in one corner. While the town's modern quarter sprawls unattractively over the lower ground, the staré město sits quietly (and extremely prettily) on a high spur hemmed in by the River Metuje, a tributary of the River Labe. Restored sixteenth-century houses line each side of the rectangular arcaded main square, **Husovo náměstí**, though the most photographed set of gables are the identical cream-coloured ones that parade along the north side.

What makes Nové Město's old town extra special is its remarkable seventeenth-century **zámek** (April & Oct Sat & Sun 9am–4pm; May, June & Sept Tues–Sun 9am–4pm; July & Aug daily 9am–5p), which looks out across the

Labe basin (known as the Polabí) from the northeast corner of the square. After piecemeal alterations, it fell into disrepair in the nineteenth century, until the industrialist Josef Bartoň bought the place in 1908 and commissioned the quirky Slovak architect **Dušan Jurkovič** to entirely redesign it – which he did, most notably with the timber-framed structures, redolent of his native land, in the terraced gardens (May–Sept), and the bizarre wall-to-wall leather vaulting of the Žebrový sál (Ribbed Hall). The other rooms are lavishly furnished in every period from the original Renaissance to Cubism, including highly unusual works by Czech Cubists like **Pavel Janák**. Bartoň eventually died here in 1951, at the ripe old age of 98. In an uncharacteristically magnanimous gesture, the Communists had allowed him and his wife (and their cook) to live out their last days in three rooms at the top of the chateau. The place is now back in the hands of the Bartoň family, who actually live here and run it with great efficiency. Before you buy your ticket, be sure to check out the set of dwarves by the Baroque sculptor Braun, which stand along the terrace and bridge across the moat. For a great view over the square and gardens, climb the castle's tower, which can be done without a guide.

An extra treat is on hand in the outlying village of **Slavoňov** in the form of a precious little wooden church dating from 1533. The wood-panelled interior is exquisite, with virtually all surfaces painted in simple, yet rich designs. The flat ceiling panels are each distinct, while the almost cartoon-like paintings on the choir depict local scenes and nobility. Be sure to ask the tourist office in Nové Město to call ahead to the friar's office next door, so that someone will be on hand to let you in. To get to Slavoňov, follow the yellow-marked path 4km through the woods from Nové Město's main square, or catch the occasional bus which leaves from there too.

Nové Město nad Metují itself is a beautiful eight-kilometre **walk** from Náchod down the winding River Metuje (yellow-marked path, followed by red). If you arrive here by **train**, you'll end up 2km northwest of the chateau, in Nové Město's new town; infrequent local buses link the old town square with the station or you can follow the blue markers. If you arrive by **bus** from Náchod or Hradec Králové, you can get off at Husovo náměstí itself. If you want to **stay the night**, the *Hotel U Broučka*, on Husovo náměstí (☏491 472 571; ❷), offers simple rooms with en-suite facilities, as well as a very pleasant **restaurant** (Oct–April closed Mon). Even simpler is the Communist-era *Hotel Metuj* (☏491 814 615, ⓦwww.hotel-metuj.cz; ❶), on Klosova, 500m off the square, where facilities are shared. The **tourist office** (May–Sept Mon–Fri 8am–5pm, Sat & Sun 9am–noon & 1–5pm; Oct–April Tues–Fri 8am–5pm, Sat & Sun 1–4pm), diagonally opposite the zámek, can set you up in a private room or nearby pension. Another branch is located in the modern art gallery Zázvorka, just off the square.

Opočno

Ten kilometres south of Nové Město nad Metují is the town of **OPOČNO**, whose **zámek** (April & Oct Sat & Sun 9–11.30am & 12.30–4pm; May–June & Sept Tues–Sun 9–11.30am & 12.30–5pm; July–Aug closes 6pm) is spectacularly poised on a knife's edge above the Polabí plain. The main attraction here is the triple-decker loggia, built in the sixteenth-century by Italian architects around the chateau's three-sided courtyard. Clinging to the chateau's foundations are the lovely wooded grounds (daily: April–Sept 7am–8pm; Oct–March 8am–3pm; free) with a summer palace or *letohrádek*, now used for temporary exhibitions (mainly of local modern art). All these treats, and the view, can be appreciated without having to sign up for either of the two guided tours, though these are something of a must if you've made it here. You may go for the full load as well, as this includes the armoury for which Opočno is famous: a priceless collection of rifles, swords, a Roman helmet, and even a well-worn chastity belt. The rest of the chateau consists of beautifully-restored rooms in which are contained sundry possessions of the Colloredo family, who owned the place until 1945; the last remaining family member is in the process of reacquiring it. Highlights include hunting trophies, ivory-inlaid furniture, thirteenth-century crystal and numerous portraits, many of which hang underneath extravagant stucco ceilings that practically sag with the extra weight.

Buses are the most direct means of getting to Opočno; several connect with Hradec Králové daily. The **train** station (Opočno pod Orlickými horami) is a good 2km below the town to the west. Of the town's **places to stay**, *Hotel Jordánek* (☎494 667 555, ⓦwww.jordanek.cz; ❶–❷), quietly located at Nádražní 447, on the road to the train station, offers decent en-suite rooms with TV for very reasonable prices; it also has a pleasant (and popular in the evenings) **restaurant** serving traditional fare.

The Babiččino údolí

Ten kilometres west of Náchod by train, the town of **ČESKÁ SKALICE** marks the beginning of the Úpa Valley, better known as the **Babiččino údolí** after the novel that has made it famous, *Babička* (Grandmother) by **Božena Němcová** (1820–62). A very precise and realistic portrait of Czech peasant life in the mid-nineteenth century, dominated by the kindly wisdom of the story's grandmother figure, the tale is still required reading for Czechs of all ages. Němcová's tragic life is almost as well known as the tale itself: forced to marry at seventeen to a man more than twice her age, Němcová wrote, "The years of my childhood were the most beautiful of my life. When I married I wept over my lost liberty, over the dreams and ideals forever ruined." Moving in Czech republican and literary circles in the 1840s, she caused considerable outrage with her numerous passionate and very public affairs. Her independent spirit, her championing of women's education, and her involvement in the 1848 revolution have endeared her to many Czech women. Nowadays, she is still very much a household name, and one of the few Czech women to have entered the country's literary canon; Němcová is featured on the 500Kč note.

There are now several **museums** dedicated to Němcová in the area, two in Česká Skalice itself. The first is in her old schoolhouse, the timber-framed Barunčina škola (May–June Tues–Sun 8am–5pm; July–Aug daily 9am–5pm; Sept Tues–Sun 9am–4pm), northwest off the main square up B. Němcové; the second is in the former pub, *U bílého českého lva*, in which she got married, now part of the town's Textilní muzeum (Textile Museum; same hours plus Oct–April Mon–Fri 8am–3pm; ⓦwww.bozenanemcova.cz), further up B. Němcové and across the river. Her birthplace in Červený Kostelec, 8km north of Česká Skalice, is also now a museum (times as for the škola). Perhaps the most rewarding of the lot, though, for the non-Czech-speaker is **Ratibořice**, 2.5km north of Česká Skalice, (April & Oct Sat & Sun 10am–3pm; May & Sept Tues–Sun 9am–4pm; June–Aug Tues–Sun 9am–5pm; guided tours only), the pretty little pink chateau with green shutters where Němcová's father was equerry, and her mother laundress.

An alternative to visiting one of the above is to explore the gentle valley, which was her childhood haunt and the main inspiration for the book – a very beautiful place in its own right. Be sure not to miss the modern statue group by

Otto Gutfreund, north of the chateau; walk through the chateau's lovely English gardens (daily: May–Sept 8am–8pm; Oct–April 9am–5pm) and upstream through the fields.

Hradec Králové

Capital of East Bohemia and the largest city on the fertile plain known as the Polabí, **HRADEC KRÁLOVÉ** (Königgrätz) has a typically handsome historical quarter, paid for by the rich trade that used to pass through en route to Silesia. But there's another side to the town, too. To the west of the medieval centre is one of the great urban projects of the interwar Republic, built by the leading modern Czech architects of the day. The two towns don't really blend in with one another – in fact, they barely communicate – and these days the staré město is more like a museum piece. Even if you don't particularly take to the new town, it's a fascinating testimony to the early optimism of the First Republic, and gives the whole of Hradec Králové a unique, expansive and prosperous atmosphere.

Hradec Králové spreads itself out on both banks of the Labe: on the left bank, the **staré město** (old town) sits on an oval rock between the Labe and the Orlice rivers; the **nové město** (new town) begins as soon as you leave the old town, straddling the river and then composing itself in fairly logical fashion between the river and the station to the west.

The Staré Město

In the eighteenth century, the **staré město** was entirely surrounded by zigzag red-brick fortifications (those at nearby Josefov can still be seen), though they've now been replaced by a modern ring road that keeps most of the traffic out of the old quarter. With nearly all daily business conducted over in the new town, a few shops and restaurants are all that remain to disturb Hradec Králové's two adjoining medieval squares, **Velké náměstí** and the much smaller **Malé náměstí**. At the western end of Velké náměstí, the skyline is punctuated by five towers. Two of them belong to the church of **sv Duch** (Holy Ghost), one of Bohemia's few great brick-built churches, a style more commonly associated with neighbouring Silesia. Jan Žižka, the blind Hussite warrior, died of the plague here in 1424, and was for a while buried in this church. Given its grand Gothic scale, though, the whitewashed interior, filled for the most part with neo-Gothic furnishings, is a letdown, despite Petr Brandl's *St Anthony* in the north aisle, and a superb stone tabernacle dating from 1497.

The church's twin towers are outreached by the once-white **Bílá věž** (White Tower; April–Sept daily 9am–noon & 1–5pm), built in the sixteenth century from the profits of Bohemian–Silesian trade, and *the* place to get a bird's-eye view of the town. Also in this corner of the square is the town **brewery**, invisible but for the terrace of Baroque former canons' houses that leads to its gate. To the east, where the two sides of the square begin to converge, the older Renaissance houses on the north side have kept their arcades. Opposite stands the distinctive pink **Dům U Špuláka**, with its projecting oriel and copper dome, and, close by, the Jesuits' Baroque "barracks" and church of **Nanebevzetí Panny Marie**, the latter beautifully maintained, its trompe l'oeil altarpiece providing a suitable repository for Brandl's work.

HRADEC KRÁLOVÉ

Train Station

Bus Station

Blažíčkovo Náměstí
KABILA ČAPKA
HOŘICKÁ
DUKELSKÁ
RESSLOVA
WONKOVA
ŠKROUPOVA
PRŮMYSLOVA
TŘÍDA KARLA IV
STŘELECKA
BAAROVA
HOROVA
V LIPKÁCH
V LIPKÁCH

NÁMĚSTÍ 28. ŘÍJNA
GOČAROVA
NERUDOVA
HOROVA

N O V É M Ě S T O

MÁNESOVA
JIŘÍCHOVO NÁM.
GOČAROVA

Masarykovo Náměstí

NÁM. SVOBODY

Nerudova
Ambrožův sbor

Gymnázium

SMETANOVO NÁBŘEŽÍ
ELIŠČINO NÁBŘEŽÍ

S T A R É M Ě S T O

Swimming Baths **B**

Filharmonie

Muzeum Východních Čech

Hotel Bystrica

PALACKÉHO
DIVIŠOVA
PRAŽSKÝ MOST

River Labe
TŘÍDOV NÁBŘEŽÍ

Aquarium

Jiráskovy sady
Wooden Church

River Orlice

Stadión **I**

sv Duch U Špuláků **5**
Bílá věž **F**
2 3
V KOPEČKU
ČESKOSLOVENSKÉ ARMÁDY

VELKÉ NÁMĚSTÍ **G**
ŠPITÁLSKÁ
DLOUHA
TOMKOVA
KLICPEROVA
ÚZKA **E**
Galerie moderního umění **4**
Nanebevzetí Panny Marie
MALÉ NÁMĚSTÍ
DLOUHA
C D

ČESKOSLOVENSKÉ ARMÁDY
ŠIMKOVA

Former Synagogue

Šimkovy sady

HERMANNA
JANA KOŽINY
HRADEBNÍ
KOMENSKÉHO

N

H

0 — 100 m

RESTAURANTS, CAFÉS & PUBS

Buvol pub	3
C.K. Restaurant	2
Ferdinanda D'Este	4
Kavárna U knihomola	1
Old England pub	5
U Čáryfuka	6
U svatého Lukáše	E

ACCOMMODATION

Amátka	D
Amber Černigov	A
Nové Adalbertinum	G
Pod věží	F
Stadión	I
Stříbrný rybník	H
U královny Elišky	C
U svatého Lukáše	E
Ubytovna Městské lázně	B

The Galerie moderního umění

Hradec Králové's **Galerie moderního umění** (Tues–Sun 9am–noon & 1–6pm), opposite the Jesuit church, houses one of the country's finest permanent collections of twentieth-century Czech art. The building itself – designed by Osvald Polívka in 1910–12, the genius behind much of Prague's finest Art Nouveau structures – is also a treat: five storeys high, with a large, oval glass-roofed atrium at the centre that sheds light onto the corridors and ground-level foyer.

The ground floor is given over to temporary exhibitions, while on the first floor, the collection of works by fin-de-siècle artists is entirely in keeping with its surroundings. Among the highlights are a couple of lesser-known **Mucha** drawings, an early **Kupka**, and a whole series by **Jan Preisler**, including a study for the mural which now adorns the former *Hotel Bystrica* (see opposite). The unexpected pleasure is **Josef Váchal**'s work, in particular the mysterious *Satanic Invocation* (*Vzývaci d'abla*), which spills over onto its carved wooden frame. Several wood sculptures by **Bílek** and three bronze reliefs by **Sucharda** make for a fairly comprehensive overview of Czech Secessionist art. The floor ends with the beginnings of the Czech obsession with Cubism, most famously **Emil Filla**'s own version of *Les Demoiselles d'Avignon* and *Salome's Dance*.

The second floor is almost wholly devoted to Czech Cubist and Fauvist painters, interspersed with a few from the Realist and Surrealist schools, prominent in the 1920s. **Josef Šíma**'s semi-surreal work is probably the most original (he was a member of the avant-garde group *Devětsil*), though only two canvases and a pen-and-ink sketch are displayed here. Postwar art up to 1968 is the subject of the third floor, interesting if only for the fact that many of the artists, like **Mikuláš Medek**, have only recently been exhibited in public galleries. The views from the top floor should be sufficient incentive to get you up there, and again there's plenty of previously censored post-1968 material to feast your eyes on, like the psychedelic *Přátelé*, though patently political works like *Red Wall* (*Červená zeď*) are the exception. Surrealism was always frowned upon, hence artists like **Jiří Kolář**, two of whose classic collages are shown here, are much better known in the West.

The Nové Město

Most of what you now see outside the old town is the result of an architectural master plan outlined between 1909 and 1911, though much of the work wasn't carried out until the 1920s. Building began on a grand scale with the **Muzeum východních Čech** (Tues–Sun 9am–noon & 1–5pm; ⓦ www.muzeumhk.cz) on the leafy waterfront, designed by the father of the Czech modern movement, **Jan Kotěra**. With the rest of central Europe still under the hold of the Viennese Secession, Kotěra's museum, crowned with one of his characteristic domes, represents a shot across the bows of contemporary taste, finished in what was at the time an unconventional mixture of red brick and concrete rendering. The entrance is guarded by two colossal sphynx-like janitors, but otherwise the ornamentation is low-key – as is the exhibition inside, a straightforward though attractive display of nineteenth- and twentieth-century arts and crafts, books and posters, plus a model of the town from 1865, showing the fortifications intact.

Further down the Labe embankment is the Hradec Králové Filharmonie building, a stern structure that nonetheless hosts a good year-round orchestral concert series. Just beyond is an excellent **swimming pool** open to the public, designed in the 1920s, equipped with an artificial wave machine, a sauna, massage parlour, and, of course, a pub.

Close by, on the inner ring road, is another work by Kotěra, the **Hotel Bystrica** (originally called, simply, the *Grand Hotel*), built immediately after the museum. It's currently in such a desperate state it's difficult to see beyond the pollutant-caked rendering to appreciate the subtleties of the facade. If and when it is ever renovated, head for the Art Nouveau restaurant – the fruit of an earlier work by Kotěra – adorned with murals by Jan Preisler and František Kysela's graceful stained-glass cranes. Kotěra is also responsible for the distinctive **Pražský most** (Prague Bridge), with its squat kiosks at either end and wrought-iron arch decorated with fairy lights.

Before crossing the river into Gočár's new town, there are a couple of minor attractions around the inner ring road. To the northeast is the town's **former synagogue** (now a library), a very handsome Art Nouveau edifice with an oddly oriental flavour to the lantern above the dome and the adjacent pagoda-style tower. To the southwest, the **Jiráskovy sady** occupy the slip of land at the confluence of the rivers Labe and Orlice and boast a colourful rose garden and a sixteenth-century **wooden Greek-Catholic church** (invariably closed) in the Lemk style, transported here from Sub-Carpathian Ruthenia in 1935.

Gočár's new town

Kotěra died shortly after World War I, and it was left to one of his pupils, **Josef Gočár**, to complete the construction of the new town. Gočár had been among the foremost exponents of Czech Cubist architecture before the war, but, along with Pavel Janák, he changed tack in the 1920s and attempted to establish a specifically Czechoslovak style of architecture, which incorporated prewar Cubism. It was dubbed "Rondo-Cubism" because of its recurrent semicircular motifs, and though few projects got off the ground, elements of the style are reflected in the appealing homogeneity of the new town. On a sunny day, the light pastel shades of the buildings provide a cool and refreshing backdrop; bad weather brings out the brutalism that underlies much of Gočár's work.

This brutalism is most evident in his largest commission, the **Státní gymnázium** on the right bank, a sprawling series of buildings with an L-shaped, four-storey, red-brick structure, fronted by an atypically slender bronze nude by Jan Štursa. Up the side of the school, on V lipkách, is a later, still more uncompromising work, the Protestant **Ambrožův sbor**, built in functionalist style on a striking angular site. But by far Gočár's most successful set-piece is **Masarykovo náměstí**, two blocks north, which basks in the sun at the heart of the new town, shaped like a big slice of lemon sponge, with a pivotal statue of Masaryk back in its rightful place after a forty-year absence. Lastly, if you're travelling by train, be sure to admire the **train station**'s splendidly modernist design, again by Gočár, in particular the wonderfully slimline 1930s clock tower.

Hradec Králové's newest attraction is its mini **aquarium** (Obří akvárium; Tues–Sun 9am–6pm; July–Aug also Mon 11am–4pm; Ⓦ www.obriakvarium.cz) at Baarova 10, a ten-minute walk south of the new town in an otherwise faceless neighbourhood. Though it's hardly "giant" as it claims to be, its centrepiece is a glass tunnel large enough to walk through and view Amazonian fish, while a small construction of a rainforest helps you forget briefly that you're still in central Europe.

Practicalities

The **train** and **bus** stations are located in the nové město. To reach the staré město, either take bus #5, #6, #11, #15 or #17, all of which plough down Gočárova, or take trolleybus #2, #3 or #7 and get off by the Krajské muzeum.

Hradec Králové's **tourist office** (Mon–Fri 8am–5.30pm; ☏495 534 482, ⓦwww.ic-hk.cz) is located near the stations at Gočarova 1225; its recently opened branch (June–Sept daily 10am–4pm; Oct–May Mon–Fri 8am–noon & 12.30–4.30pm) is to be found at Velké náměstí 165.

A good number of **restaurants** in town dish up the usual plain but filling fare. Apart from those in the pensions below, of which the tasteful *U svatého Lukáše* is the best, there are plenty of other restaurants and cafés in the old town. For a Habsburg Empire atmosphere try the *C.K. Restaurant Ferdinanda D'Este*, on V Kopečku, with additional tables on a little patio. Another pleasant option is the *U čáryfuka* (closed Sun), an elegant restaurant with a vast menu in the shadow of the church of sv Duch. *Kavárna U knihomola* (At the Bookworm) is an appropriate complement to the modern art gallery opposite, a soothingly hip spot for coffee or a light lunch, while you can get online at the **Internet café** next door. **Nightlife** is rather slow in Hradec Králové, but the *Buvol* on V Kopečku is a lively Czech-Irish pub open until 2am and the *Old England* pub, also on V Kopečku, is open nonstop.

Accommodation

Accommodation should not be a problem, as several hotels and pensions have opened up in recent years – happily driving prices down with them. The *Stříbrný rybník* **campsite** (mid-May to mid-Sept), with cabins, and adjacent to a lake, is very popular in the height of summer; you can even rent **bicycles**. To get there, take bus #11 or #17.

Amátka Kavčí Plácek 120 ☏603 331 991, ⓦwww.sweb.cz/amatka. A simple, cheap pension at the corner of the Malé náměstí, the quieter of the two main squares in the old town. ❷

Amber Hotel Černigov Riegrovo náměstí 1494 ☏495 814 111. A comfortable Communist-era high-rise hotel opposite the train station. Lower prices for Czechs. ❺

Nové Adalbertinum Velké náměstí 32 ☏495 063 111, ⓦwww.adalbertinum.diecezehk.cz. Tastefully refurbished doubles and four-bed rooms in the former Jesuit college. ❸

Pod věži Velké náměstí ☏495 514 932, ⓦwww.pod-vezi.cz. Little pension right under the tower (as its name states), offering comfortable, airy rooms overlooking the square. ❸

Stadión Komenského 1214 ☏495 514 664. A basic hotel just outside the staré město by the ice hockey stadium. ❷

U královny Elišky Malé náměstí 117 ☏495 518 052. An excellent four-star hotel with sauna aboard, next door to *Amátka*. ❻

U svatého Lukáše Úzká 208 ☏495 518 616, ⓦwww.usvateholukase.com. Another nice place with rooms situated around a quiet courtyard, just off the main square. ❸

Ubytovna Městské lázne Eliščino nábřeží 842 ☏495 211 998, ⓦwww.sportovistehk.cz. Hostel-type accommodation (small rooms) in the grounds next to the swimming baths. ❶

Around Hradec Králové

The flat expanse around Hradec Králové, known as the **Polabí**, is a fertile region whose hedgeless cornfields stretch for miles on end. It's pretty dreary to look at, baking hot in summer and covered in a misty drizzle most of the winter, but there are several places worth a day-trip or overnight stop within easy reach of Hradec Králové by bus or train.

Třebechovice, Častolovice and Doudleby

TŘEBECHOVICE POD OREBEM, 11km east of Hradec Králové along route 11, is a nondescript town, famous only for its wood-carved Nativity scene or *Betlém*, housed in a purpose-built **museum** (Tues–Sun: May–Sept

9am–noon & 1–5pm; Oct–April closes 4pm; ⓦwww.betlem.cz). It all began in 1871, when local joiner Josef Probošt and his wood-carving friend, Josef Kapucián, set out to create the largest Nativity scene in the world. Only the death of Kapucián forty years later brought the project to an end, by which time the two men had carved 400 moving figures, many of them modelled on their friends and neighbours. And if you think that's kitsch, take a look at the museum's other room, which displays *Betlém* scenes in glass, pottery and paper.

Eighteen kilometres on is the Renaissance chateau of **Častolovice** (April & Oct Sat & Sun 9am–6pm; May–Sept Tues–Sun 9am–6pm; ⓦwww.zamek-castolovice .cz), recently returned to the Šternberk family, who acquired it back in 1694. It's a pretty hybrid pile, right by route 11, with a huge English-style park stretching away to the north. The inner courtyard is particularly beautiful, and the tour takes you through the glorious Rytířský sál (Knights' Hall), with a Renaissance painted panel ceiling and portraits of various regional noblemen. If you're heading in this direction, you could continue another 6km to **Doudleby** (April–Sept Tues–Fri 8am–5pm, Sat & Sun 9am–5pm), a lovely little chateau, again right by route 11, but this time covered in intricate swirling sgraffito, not unlike the locally made lace displayed inside. Tours lead through predictably elaborate Baroque rooms, many with frescoes and paintings, including a satirical *Devil's Wedding*.

Jaroměř and Josefov

JAROMĚŘ, 36km northeast of Hradec Králové and accessible by train, is a pleasant enough town with a curving cobbled square, arcaded on one side and with one of its medieval gateways intact. The main attraction, though, is one of Gočár's early works, the **Wenke department store**, situated on route 33, the busy main road from Hradec Králové to the Polish border. In this exceedingly unpromising street (now called Husova), Gočár undertook one of the first self-conscious experiments in Cubist architecture in 1911. It's an imaginative, eclectic work, quite unlike the much plainer Cubism of Prague's Vyšehrad villas or the nearby spa of Bohdaneč, the plate-glass facade topped by a Neoclassical upper floor and the monochrome, geometric interior still intact. Instead of selling goods, it now serves as the **Městské muzeum a galerie** (April–Nov Tues–Fri 9am–5pm, Sat & Sun 1–5pm), its tiny art gallery upstairs displaying works by all three of Jaroměř's home-grown artists: the sculptors Otakar Španiel and Josef Wagner, and the *Devětsil* painter Josef Šíma, whose wilfully optimistic painting of Jaroměř is just one of a number of his works on show. If you want to **stay** the night, you can choose between the two hotels on the main square: the *Hotel 28* (☎491 815 311; ❷), with decent, clean rooms and pizzeria; or the very basic *U dvou jelenů* (☎491 815 230; ❶), with a smoky pub, a couple of doors to the left.

One kilometre south of Jaroměř, where the Labe and the Metuje rivers converge, is the fortress town of **JOSEFOV** (Josefstadt). In the 1780s the Habsburgs created three fortified towns along the northern border with their new enemy, Prussia: Hradec Králové (which has since lost its walls), Terezín and Josefov – the last two purpose-built from scratch and preserved as they were. Terezín was put to terrible use by the Nazis during World War II (see p.278), but Josefov remains the great white elephant of the empire, never having witnessed a single battle. Their mutual designs are unerringly similar: two fortresses (one large, one small), identikit eighteenth-century streets, and a grid plan whose monotony is broken only by the imposing **Empire Church** on the main square. Again like Terezín, Josefov is still a garrison town, though there aren't many soldiers left; the empty buildings have mostly been taken over by Romany families. Though not a great day out, it's worth taking a stroll along the thick zigzag trail of red-brick fortifications, now topped by beautiful tree-lined paths, with views across the wheat fields of the Polabí. If you're really keen, you can even visit the town's **underground tunnel system**, where costumed soldiers lead you through claustrophobic candle-lit passageways; follow the signs to the Podzemí (April & Oct Sat & Sun 9am–noon & 1–4pm; May–Sept Tues–Sun 9am–noon & 1–5pm).

Kuks and around

Magnificently poised above a rustic village of timber-framed cottages, the great complex of Baroque spa buildings at **KUKS**, just 5km north of Jaroměř, on the banks of the Labe, was the creation of the enlightened Bohemian dilettante Count Franz Anton Graf von Sporck (Špork in Czech). Work began, largely according to Sporck's own designs, in the 1690s, after the discovery of a nearby mineral spring with healing properties – by 1730 he had created his own private **spa resort**, with a garden maze, a hospital, a concert hall (complete with its own orchestra) and a racecourse (surrounded by statues of dwarves). For a while, Kuks' social life was on a par with the likes of Karlsbad; then, in 1738, the impresario died, and two years later, on December 22, 1740, disaster struck when the river broke its banks, destroying all the buildings on the left bank and, worse still, the springs themselves.

All that remains of the original spa is an overgrown monumental stairway leading nowhere, and, on the right bank, the hospital building fronted by **Matthias Bernhard Braun**'s famous terrace, now the chief reason for visiting Kuks. Sporck became the Tyrolean sculptor's chief patron in Bohemia, commissioning from him a series of **allegorical statues** intended to elevate the minds of his spa guests: to the west, the twelve *Vices* culminate in the grim *Angel of Grievous Death*; to the east, the twelve *Virtues* end with the *Angel of Blessed Death*. Over the years the elements have not been too kind to Braun's work, whose originals, including a few surviving dwarves, have retreated inside the hospital building and now provide the highlight of the forty-five-minute guided tour (April & Oct Sat & Sun 9am–noon & 1–3pm; May–Aug Tues–Sun until 5pm; Sept Tues–Sun until 4pm). Also in the tour is the beautifully restored eighteenth-century pharmacy (arguably second oldest in Europe to the one in Dubrovnik) and Baroque chapel, though Sporck's subterranean mausoleum is no longer on show.

There's a good **restaurant** *Zámecká vinárna* next to the zámek, ladling out big portions of meat and gravy. Buses will either drop you at the main road, a short walk north of the village, or in the village itself; the **train station** lies to the south, behind the hospital building and formal gardens (follow the blue-marked path).

Betlém

One stop along the tracks, or a steep 5km walk along the blue-marked path, upriver from Kuks, is **Betlém** (Bethlehem), Braun's outdoor Nativity sculpture park, again sponsored by Sporck. It's an unlikely, ingenious location, deep in the midst of a silver birch wood, and used to include several working springs, including one that shot water high up into the foliage. However, centuries of neglect, pilfering and weathering have taken their toll (many of the sculptures have been covered with cheap wooden roof shelters in a much-belated attempt to prevent any further damage) and what you see now are the few survivors of what would once have been a remarkable open-air *atelier* – exclusively the ones that Braun hacked out of various boulders he found strewn about the wood. In contrast to Kuks, the theme here is more explicitly religious, with the best-preserved sculptural groups depicting *The Journey of the Magi* and the *Nativity*. The dishevelled man crawling out of his cave, and looking very much like a 3-D representation of William Blake's *Fall of Man*, is in fact an obscure Egyptian hermit called Garinus.

Dvůr Králové nad Labem

DVŮR KRÁLOVÉ NAD LABEM, 8km northwest of Kuks, is familiar to postwar generations of Czech kids as the site of the country's largest **zoo** (daily 9am–6pm or dusk; 100Kč; ⓦ www.zoodk.cz). As underfunded eastern European zoos go, Dvůr Králové has tried harder than most to make the animals' lives bearable, but a safari park it is not. The section of the zoo nearest the entrance is full of caged animals like any other zoo; all the usual beasts are here – lions, elephants, monkeys and so on. In addition, the zoo specializes in breeding African hoofed animals, including the rare white rhino. There's a *dětský koutek* (kids' corner), where children can stroke the more domesticated animals. The "safari" bit consists of a free bus ride through a series of open enclosures, where there's a serious surfeit of antelopes. The safari bus sets off from the far side of the zoo – a long way to walk for smaller kids, so it's best to take the horse and cart or mini-train there.

Dvůr Králové **bus station** is on 17 listopadu; to get to the main square, walk north two blocks, then left down Švehlova. The **train station** is 2km southwest of the centre; a bus meets all trains and drops passengers in the centre, or you can walk down 5 května, which becomes 28 října before crossing the river, after which it's due north up Riegrova and Revoluční to the main square. The zoo is 1km west of the town, on Štefánikova, and is well signposted. The town itself has an arcaded main square, with a **tourist office** (Mon–Fri 8am–5pm, Sat 9am–1pm). Just off the square, on Revoluční, is the small, peaceful *Pension Labe* (ⓣ & ⓕ 499 329 128; ➋), run by a private travel agency.

Hořice

Just about every Czech sculptor over the last hundred years was trained at the School of Masonry and Sculpture founded in 1884 at **HOŘICE V PODKRKONOŠÍ**, 23km northwest of Hradec Králové. As a result, the town now boasts one of the country's richest collections of sculpture and plays host to an annual **international symposium of contemporary sculpture** in July and August.

There are sculptures all over town and exhibitions of contemporary works in the town museum (Tues–Fri 9am–noon & 1–5pm) on the main square, but the largest collection is in the **Galerie plastik** (Tues–Sun 9am–noon & 1–5pm), halfway up the sv Gothard hill to the east of town (five minutes' walk down Janderova). Half the gallery is given over to temporary exhibitions, but the permanent collection is still impressive. All the leading lights of Czech sculpture are represented here, even Šaloun, famous for his Jan Hus Monument in Prague, and Bílek, neither of whom actually studied here, as well as one of the few extant works by Otakar Švec, the man responsible for Prague's since-dynamited Stalin Monument. In the meadows and orchards to the north of the gallery is the **symposium area**, with previous years' exhibits out on show. To the east is the local **cemetery** (*hřbitov*), which has a wonderful triumphal arch over the entrance and a scattering of well-sculpted headstones. To the west, the **Smetanovy sady** are dotted with mostly nineteenth-century sculptures of leading figures of the Czech national revival.

Despite the town's enormous artistic treasures, it sees very few visitors. The helpful **tourist office** (Mon–Fri 7.30am–5pm, Sat & Sun 8am–noon; ⓦwww .horice.org) is located in the pretty town hall on the main square. Decent **accommodation** is available at the nearby *Hotel Královský Dvůr* (☎493 624 527, ⓦwww.kralovskydvur.com; ❷).There are also no fewer than three **campsites** in the area, the nearest being the *U věže* site (March–Nov), 1km north of town on the road to Dvůr Králové.The **train station** (Hořice v Podkrkonoší) is 1km south of town down Husova (there's an occasional connecting bus).

Chlum

A short 9km northwest of Hradec Králové, the flat fields around **CHLUM** make an ideal **battleground**. And in 1866, the forces of the Prussian and Austro-Hungarian armies clashed here as part of a long-running disagreement over how to divide central Europe. Following the 1848 revolts against the Habsburgs, the Austro-Hungarian Empire found itself in a precarious position, with the Prussians gaining increasing power over German matters. Both sides flexed their muscles in the spring and summer of 1866, with several skirmishes taking place across what is now eastern Bohemia. By late June, the Austrians had established a tenuous position around the tiny village of Chlum, but early in the morning of July 3, the Prussians attacked on the northern and western flanks, and by early afternoon had clearly gained the upper hand. At day's end, over 5500 Austrian soldiers and some 2100 Prussians lay dead, and what remained of the Habsburg army had begun its retreat.This marked a decisive defeat for Austria, as it lost yet more control over its German-speaking constituency. Its weakened status had no benefits for the Czechs either, as they remained second-class citizens to the Germans in an increasingly unstable Habsburg Empire.

Despite its rather important role in the downfall of the Habsburgs, Chlum is really only appealing for war buffs. The site of the battle is marked with a monument, a mass grave, a viewing tower over the fields (April–Oct Tues–Sun 9am–noon & 1–5pm) and a small **museum** (same hours as tower), which displays uniforms worn by some of the fallen as well as a thorough description, with dioramas, of the battle, but only in Czech and German.Two or three mid-day buses run to Chlum from Hradec Králové (the stop is marked Všestary, Chlum), but service is curtailed at weekends.

Chlumec nad Cidlinou

CHLUMEC NAD CIDLINOU, 29km west of Hradec Králové, in the middle of the featureless, dusty Polabí, was the scene of one of the largest peasant uprisings in the country in 1775, after which 3000 of those who had taken part were burned to death in a nearby farm. Just over fifty years before that bloody incident, Count Kinský built himself one of Bohemia's most exquisite provincial chateaux, **Karlova Koruna** (April & Oct Sat & Sun 9am–noon & 1–4pm; May–June Tues–Sun 8am–noon & 1–5pm; July–Aug Tues–Sun 8am–5pm; Sept Tues–Sun 9am–noon & 1–5pm). Begun in 1721 by Giovanni Santini, it stands on a rare patch of raised ground to the northwest of the town, south of the train station. Santini's ground plan is a simple but intriguing triple-winged affair, dominated by a central circular hall, with a two-storey pink-and-grey marble dome and a grand staircase leading to the upper balcony.The building's exterior and grounds are both in need of some tidying up, however. In the grounds, the modest Baroque pleasure house displays copies of Braun's statuary.

Pardubice

There's always been a certain amount of rivalry between the two big cities of the Polabí, Hradec Králové and **PARDUBICE**, just under 20km to the south. On balance, Pardubice's historical core is probably more immediately appealing than Hradec Králové's, and it has a lovely newly renovated chateau, but its new town lacks the logic and cohesion of its neighbour, which makes the whole place feel a lot smaller. Throughout the horse-racing world, Pardubice is best known for its **steeplechase course** (second only to Liverpool's Aintree course for difficulty), where the *Velká Pardubická* (first run in 1874) takes place in early October, usually accompanied by protests by Czech animal rights activists.

The Town

The section of the walk from the bus and train stations along **Míru** contains an arresting threesome of late Secession buildings on the left-hand side, with *U lva* at the centre, distinguished by the two tiny lion heads on its gable. Míru comes to an end at **náměstí Republiky**, which marks the transition from the new town to the old. At one end, the seriously striking Art Nouveau **Městské divadlo** (town theatre) is a deliberately Czech structure, designed by Antonín Balšánek (who collaborated with Polívka on Prague's Obecní dům), its magnificent facade flanked by multicoloured mosaics: Libuše founding Prague on one side and a blind Žižka leading the Hussites into battle on the other. The other truly arresting building on the square is the church of **sv Bartoloměj**, originally Gothic but more memorable for the Renaissance additions to its exterior – courtesy of local bigwigs, the Pernštejns – which makes up for its lack of a tower with a syringe-like central spike. Josef Gočár worked in Pardubice, as well as in Hradec Králové: the squat, grey Komerční banka, and the recently restored *Hotel Grand* opposite, are both his.

The soaring Gothic gateway, **Zelená brána** (May–Sept Tues–Sun 9am–noon & 1–5pm; Oct Sat & Sun only), with its twisted uppermost tower and wonderful baubled spikes, makes for a memorable entrance to the old town, and a good place from which to survey it. The main square, **Pernštýnovo náměstí**, is an intimate affair, an effect made all the more pronounced by the tall three-storey buildings on each side, handsome gabled sixteenth- and eighteenth-century houses for the most part, with the exception of the flamboyant neo-Renaissance **radnice**. The sculptural decoration throughout the old town is remarkable and at its most striking on **U Jonáše**, whose plasterwork includes an

Semtex

Pardubice is the home of the most famous Czech export, Semtex. This plastic explosive became a firm favourite with the world's terrorists during the 1980s because of its ability to avoid electronic detection in customs halls and withstand rough handling. Approximately 1000 tonnes of the explosive is reckoned to have gone to Libya alone (and from there – it seems – into the hands of the IRA). It's still produced at the huge chemical complex in the village of Semtín (from which it gets its name), a few kilometres northwest of Pardubice – until recently the village was etched out of all maps due to the sensitive nature of its operations. Selling arms and explosives is not at all new to the Czechs, but it sits ill with the republic's new squeaky-clean image, and the company has pledged to tag all future exports of the explosive so that it can be easily spotted by airport X-ray machines. A local firm has since cashed in on the name by producing a high-energy soft drink.

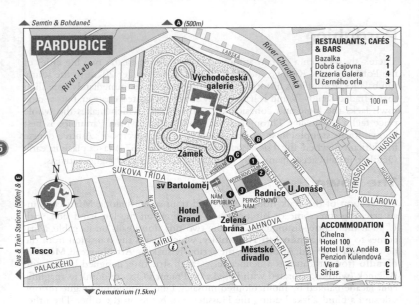

PARDUBICE

LABSKÁ
River *Chrudimka*
River *Labe*

Východočeská galerie

Zámek

N

SUKOVA TŘÍDA

ZÁMECKÁ

sv Bartoloměj

WERNEROVO NÁBŘ.
PERNŠTÝNSKÁ

NA TŘÍSTLE

STROSSOVA

HUSOVA

NÁM.
REPUBLIKY

PERNŠTÝNOVO
NÁM.

Radnice

U Jonáše

KOLLÁROVA

**Hotel
Grand**

**Zelená
brána**

JAHNOVA

NA HRÁDKU

KARLA IV.

JIRÁSKOVA

LINDNERKA

Tesco

MÍRU

SLADKOVSKÉHO

ⓘ

**Městské
divadlo**

PALACKÉHO

▼ *Crematorium (1.5km)*

**RESTAURANTS, CAFÉS
& BARS**

Bazalka	2
Dobrá čajovna	1
Pizzeria Galera	4
U černého orla	3

0   100 m

ACCOMMODATION

Cihelna	A
Hotel 100	D
Hotel U sv. Anděla	B
Penzion Kulendová	
Věra	C
Sirius	E

exuberant depiction of Jonah at the moment of digestion by the whale. Inside there's a branch of the Východočeská galerie (Tues–Fri noon–6pm, Sat & Sun 10am–6pm) with a permanent exhibition of Czech nineteenth- and twentieth-century art, including works by the locally born artist Jaroslav Grus, and temporary exhibitions of modern art. A handful of picturesque backstreets spread north from here, with the buttressed beauty of Bartolomějská or the crumbling facades of Pernštýnská, both leading eventually to the romantic embankment, Wernerovo nábřeší, whose drooping willow trees provide a perfect spot of shade in summer.

At this point, you should head up Zámecká, and cross the vast dry moat to the newly restored **zámek** (Tues–Sun 10am–6pm), which is protected by an impressive series of walls, gates and barbicans, and occupies more space than the entire staré město. The chateau's sgraffitoed appearance, and its beautiful loggia in the main courtyard, amongst which a happy congregation of peacocks and turkeys struts its stuff, date from the sixteenth century when it became the chief seat of the powerful Pernštejn family. The latter were also responsible for the chateau's precious Renaissance wall paintings, which have been partially preserved in the **Rytířské sály** on the first floor. There are trompe l'oeil door-frames and decorative motifs, plus two very large pictures: the first is of Moses being given the ten commandments, while the second (and best preserved) one features Delilah cutting the hair of the sleeping Samson, while a phalanx of Philistines arrives hotfoot. You can see the frescoes – and the tiny arms collection and the local museum, which are also housed in the chateau – without a guided tour; just make sure you buy the useful English information leaflets when you purchase your ticket.

On the other side of the outer courtyard is the **Východočeská galerie** (Tues–Fri noon–6pm, Sat & Sun 10am–6pm), which puts on temporary exhibitions on the ground floor, and contains a small collection of modern Czech art on the first floor. The gallery owns works by all the major Czech artists

△ Pardubice old town

Janák's crematorium and Gočár's spa

Pardubice boasts two fine buildings from a unique period in Czech architectural history. The first is the town's crematorium on Pod břízkami (trolley bus #1 from náměstí Republiky), designed by **Pavel Janák** in the 1920s, and, with its feast of semicircular motifs and garish colours, one of the finest extant Rondo-Cubist buildings in the country. The other architectural gem is **Josef Gočár**'s sanatorium at the nearby spa of Bohdaneč, accessible on trolley bus #3 (via Semtín). Built in 1909, it was, in all probability, the first Cubist structure ever built.

of the last century, from Čapek to Medek, but only a few pieces stick out: in particular Kamil Lhoták's realist canvases from the 1940s and 1950s, the giant (cracked) *Human Egg* by Eva Kmentová, and a great little pair of papier-mâché wellingtons called *Homage to Jules Verne* by Jiří Kolář.

Practicalities

You could easily come to Pardubice on a day-trip from Hradec Králové (it's only 30min away by train); the **train** and **bus stations** lie at the end of Palackého in the new town, a busy thoroughfare and the beginning of Pardubice's long parade of shops. It's a good ten-minute walk from here (or a short ride on trolley bus #2) northeast to the old town, much of it along Míru, a busy commercial street.

There are a few reasonable **hotels** in the old town should you choose to stay longer. *Hotel 100* (☎466 511 179; ③) has a fine location and clean rooms on Kostelní, matched in appearance and price by *Penzion Kulendová Věra* right next door (☎ & ℱ466 511 153; ③). *Hotel U sv. Anděla* (☎466 511 575, Ⓦwww .hotelzlandel.pardubicko.com; ③), down the street on Zámecká, is a tad larger and dearer, but similarly well-kept. At the other end, both geographically and aesthetically, the *Sirius* (☎466 511 548, Ⓦwww.hotel-sirius.wz.cz; ①) rises above the train station and is only recommended if you're pinching pennies. Otherwise, the town's *Cihelna* **campsite** (June to mid-Oct) is just north of the river up K cihelně.

There's a very pleasant chilled-out *Dobrá Čajovna* on Wernerovo nábřeží, and a great little *vinárna* named *Bazalka* across the way, which serves good salads at its wicker tables. You'll also find several **restaurants** on the old town square, most of which also have outdoor seating: *U černého orla* is a typical Czech goulash-and-dumplings kind of place, while *Pizzeria Galera* (whose entrance is actually on Bartolomějská) serves up decent fish and Italian entrées.

Note that accommodation is impossible to find over the weekend of the *Velká Pardubická* in early October. Less prestigious **horse races** take place every other weekend at Pardubice's **steeplechase course** (*závodiště*), which is 2km out of town; take bus #8. Pardubice's **tourist office** (daily 9am–6pm; Ⓦwww .ipardubice.cz) is located at Míru 60.

Chrudim, Kočí and Ležáky

Twelve kilometres south of Pardubice, the pretty little town of **CHRUDIM** springs into life in early July for its annual **Puppet Festival**. At other times of the year, it's still worth the short train ride to visit the marvellous **Puppet Museum** (Muzeum loutkářských kultur; April–Sept daily 9am–noon & 1–5pm; Oct–March Tues–Fri 9am–noon & 1–5pm, Sat & Sun 1–5pm), housed in the splendid sixteenth-century Mydlářovský dům on Břetislavova, just off the main square. The Czech Lands have a long tradition of puppetry, going back to the country's peasant roots, and the museum acts as a repository for marionettes and puppets donated from all over the world. If you're looking for cheap **accommodation**, head for the *Sporthotel* (☎469 621 028; ❶), situated on Tyršovo náměstí, 200m from the main square, which has spacious rooms without en-suite facilities.

The village of **KOČÍ**, 4km due east of Chrudim, on route 17, boasts the unusual Gothic church of **sv Bartoloměj**, founded in 1397 by Queen Žofiá, wife of Václav IV. At first glance it appears to be made of timber, but its brick body is simply enveloped by a wooden cover. This effect is intensified by the Baroque, wooden, arcaded bridge (18m long) that connects the church with the road. To see the interior, which has Gothic cross vaulting, you need to find the custodian (ask at house no. 40).

Southeast of Chrudim off route 37, in a quiet, shady glen, is a memorial to the village of **LEŽÁKY**, which suffered an even worse fate than Lidice (see p.182). On June 24, 1942, the SS rounded up the village's entire adult population and shot all 56 of them; two children were deemed fit for Germanization and the rest were sent off to the camps. The motive for Ležáky's destruction was the same as for Lidice's: Hitler wanted revenge for the assassination of Reinhard Heydrich, Reichsprotektor of Bohemia and Moravia. Exactly two weeks after Lidice was wiped out, Ležáky suffered the same fate for concealing a resistance transmitter. Today the foundation stones of the houses, which were all burned down, are all that remain of the village, and these have been carefully rearranged and topped with memorial stones. The main difference between Ležáky and Lidice, though, is that no new town was built here: the road simply passes through, with signs to mark the boundaries. A **museum** (May–Sept Tues–Sun 9am–5pm) displays photographs of the town after the destruction, as well as of each of the victims. There are no buses to Ležáky, only a few daily ones from Chrudim to Miřetice, 2km to the west.

Litomyšl and around

For a small town in the northern reaches of the Bohemian-Moravian Uplands, **LITOMYŠL** (Leitomischl) has big ideas. In 1992 a School for Restoration and Conservation was founded here and immediately set to work restoring the Portmoneum, a house decorated with fantastical murals and furniture by Josef Váchal, which opened the following year. Soon after the town pulled off an even more amazing coup by getting seven presidents of central Europe – including Václav Havel, Lech Walesa and Richard von Weizsäcker – to meet here for a summit.

The Town

The town's picturesque main square, **Smetanovo náměstí**, is strung out like a juicy fat Czech sausage and lined with almost uninterrupted arcades, a pastel parade of Baroque and Neoclassical facades, all pristinely repainted in preparation for the presidents' visit. The sixteenth-century **U rytířů**, at no. 110 (Tues–Sun 10am–noon & 1–5pm; out of season closes 4pm), is the finest of the lot, decorated with medieval knights and merchants holding bags of money, clinging mischievously to their carved columns; the building now hosts art exhibitions, worth checking out if only to admire the coffered Renaissance

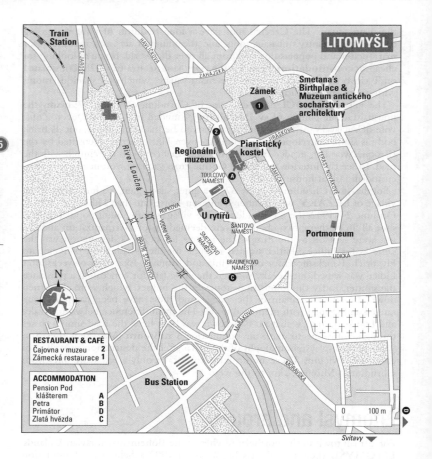

LITOMYŠL

Train Station

Zámek ❶

Smetana's Birthplace & Muzeum antického sochařství a architektury

Piaristický kostel

Regionální muzeum ❷

River Loučná

TOULCOVO NÁMĚSTÍ Ⓐ

Ⓑ

U rytířů

ŠANTOVO NÁMĚSTÍ

Portmoneum

LIDICKÁ

ⓘ

SMETANOVO NÁMĚSTÍ

BRAUNEROVO NÁMĚSTÍ Ⓒ

N

RESTAURANT & CAFÉ
Čajovna v muzeu   2
Zámecká restaurace   1

ACCOMMODATION
Pension Pod
  klášterem   A
Petra   B
Primátor   D
Zlatá hvězda   C

Bus Station

0   100 m

Svitavy ▼

ceiling inside. The town's most famous son is the composer **Bedřich Smetana**, who was born here in 1824, hence Jan Štursa's effete statue of the composer at the northwest corner of the main square. Every year in his honour, the town puts on a ten-day **international opera festival**, *Smetanova Litomyšl*, towards the end of June. Smetana was not the only Czech aesthete to stroll the streets of Litomyšl, though; nationalist writers Božena Němcová and Alois Jirásek also lived here for short periods, as plaques on their homes on the square recall.

To the northeast of the main square, a knot of ramshackle backstreets, punctuated by churches, leads up to the town's most celebrated monument, the Pernštejns' **zámek** (April & Oct Sat & Sun 9am–noon & 1–4pm; Sept Tues–Sun same hours; May–Aug Tues–Sun 9am–noon & 1–5pm), a smart, sgraffitoed affair that bursts into frivolous gables and finials on its roof and which boasts one of Bohemia's finest triple-decker loggias inside. You'll have to join a guided tour to view the interior, and you have a choice. *Trasa 1* leads you through state and banquet rooms richly decorated in porcelain and period furniture. The highlight, though, is the remarkable late eighteenth-century theatre where the young Smetana made his debut as a pianist, accompanied by much of the original scenery painted by Josef Platzer. *Trasa 2* extends the trip through a rather unanticipated collection of torture instruments, as well as a small gallery featuring local artists. If you don't fancy either tour, head instead for the former riding school, which now houses the **Muzeum antického sochařství a architektury** (May–Oct Tues–Sun 9am–noon & 1–5pm), a bizarre collection of plaster and bronze casts of Greek and Roman classical statues from museums around the world. Also worth a visit is the **Regionální muzeum** (May–Oct Tues–Fri 9am–noon & 1–4pm, Sat & Sun 9am–noon & 1–5pm; Dec Tues–Sun 8am–4pm), located in the former Piaristic gymnasium, opposite the giant Piaristic church, where, among other things, painted shooting targets are on display.

Smetana himself was born in the former town brewery, opposite the castle, one of eighteen children to an upwardly mobile beer maker. The building now houses the **Rodný byt Smetany** (April & Oct Sat & Sun 9am–noon & 1–4pm; May–Aug Tues–Sun 9am–noon & 1–5pm; Sept until 4pm), a modest memorial museum to the composer. Smetana was a veritable *Wunderkind*, playing in a string quartet at the age of five and composing his first symphony at eight, but a year before that, the family moved to Jindřichův Hradec. Catalyzed by the events of 1848, Smetana became a leading figure in the Czech national revival (despite German being his mother tongue), helping to found Prague's Národní divadlo. In 1874 he had to resign as the theatre's chief conductor after becoming deaf through a syphilitic infection. He went on to promote the nationalist cause through works like *Má vlast* ("My Country"), a symphonic poem inspired by Czech legends, but sadly ended his days in a mental asylum.

A short walk southeast of the chateau, at Terézy Novákové 75, is without doubt Litomyšl's most extraordinary and unique artistic treasure, the **Portmoneum** (May–Oct Tues–Sun 9am–noon & 1–5pm), painstakingly restored and opened in 1993. From the outside, it looks like any other provincial town house, but inside, the walls, ceilings and furniture of two rooms are decorated with the strange and wonderful work of the self-taught artist **Josef Váchal** (1884–1969), from the early 1920s. Váchal's ghoulish art is difficult to categorize (though "weird" would be the simplest shorthand): the ceiling in one room is a whirlwind of devils, spirits and sinful creatures; elsewhere there are cherubs, Kupkaesque celestial orbs of light, quotations from Hindu religious poems and a Crucifixion, while Váchal himself appears at one point as a rat-catcher. The man who wanted his house decorated with such disturbing murals was **Josef Portman** (after whom the house is named), a civil servant, amateur printer and lifelong collector of Váchal's art, who died here in 1968.

Practicalities

Buses are probably the easiest way to get to Litomyšl, since the town lies on a little-used branch line from Choceň. The **bus station** is on Mařákova, five minutes' walk southeast of the centre, a pleasant stroll along (and across) the River Loučná; the **train station** is five minutes' walk west of the old town, again along (and across) the river. As befits a town with ambition, there's an efficient **tourist office** (April–Sept Mon–Fri 9am–7pm, Sat & Sun 9am–3pm; Oct–March Mon–Fri 8.30am–6pm, Sat 9am–2pm; ☎461 612 161, ⓦwww .litomysl.cz/ic) on the west side of the main square at no. 72, which can help with **accommodation**. The upmarket *Zlatá hvězda* on the main square (☎461 615 338, ⓦwww.zlatahvezda.com; ❸), where Havel stayed, is the town's finest

Schindler's Svitavy

When Spielberg's Holocaust film, *Schindler's List,* reached the Czech Republic in 1994, it was premiered in **Svitavy** (Zwittau), a small Moravian town (currently in East Bohemia) 20km southeast of Litomyšl. The simple reason for this was that the "hero" of the film, Nazi industrialist **Oskar Schindler**, was born here in 1908, son of an insurance salesman, at Iglauerstrasse (now Poličská) 24. In Svitavy, he was known as a hard-drinking womanizer who was expelled from school for falsifying his school report and some years later arrested in the *Hotel Ungar,* on the town's main square, for supplying the German Abwehr with information.

Schindler became a member of the Nazi Party early on and, during the war, he used his Party contacts to establish a kitchenware factory in Kraków, using Jewish slave labour. It was here that Schindler began to shelter Jews, hiring them even though they were too sick or weak to work, in order to save them from certain death in the nearby camps. In 1943 he took 900 Jewish workers with him and set up an armaments factory in Brněnec, a town 15km south of Svitavy. In fact, Schindler made sure that not a single weapon was actually produced at the factory and by the end of the war he had saved 1200 Jews from deportation. He died in 1974 in Hildesheim in Germany, though his remains were transferred to Israel as a mark of gratitude.

The majority of Svitavy's population (most of whom were German-speaking) were expelled after the war, and only a few of the older inhabitants can remember Schindler from his Svitavy days. The film therefore came as something of a revelation to many of Svitavy's residents, who had previously been told only the Communists' postwar version of events: that Schindler was simply the Nazi chief of the local concentration camp. Despite the release of the film, the town council still had to overcome fierce local opposition in order to erect a memorial plaque – in Czech and German – in the park opposite Schindler's birthplace. The plaque was eventually unveiled by the republic's Chief Rabbi shortly after the film's premiere.

hotel, or there's the clean, modern pension *Petra* on B. Němcové (T461 613 061, Wwww.pension-petra.cz; ❸). Comfortable enough is also the little *Pension Pod klášterem* (T461 615 901, Wwww.podklasterem.cz; ❷), crouched on B. Němcové, in the shadow of the Piaristic church. The *Primátor* **campsite** (May–Sept) with bungalows is 2km southeast of the town centre, off route 35/E442 to Moravská Třebová. If it's **food** you want, the *Hotel Zlatá hvězda* has an excellent restaurant and surprisingly good prices, or you can lunch at the fine *Zámecká restaurace,* in the chateau grounds. The best place for a cup of tea is the quiet, Indian-style *Čajovna v muzeu,* located in the regional museum's building.

Polička

The Bohemian-Moravian Uplands are clearly a musically fertile region: Mahler spent his childhood in Jihlava (see p.391), while the town of **POLIČKA**, 18km south of Litomyšl, produced **Bohuslav Martinů**, who was born in 1890 at the top of the 75-metre tall fairy-tale neo-Gothic tower of the church of sv Jakub, just west of the main square. The composer's father – a cobbler by trade – was also the local watchman, and the single room in which the family of five lived until 1902, has to be one of the most memorable memorials to any composer. To climb the tower, you must first buy a ticket from the local **museum** (May–Aug Tues–Sun 9am–5pm; Sept–April Tues–Sun 9am–noon & 12.30–4pm), on Tylova, north off the main square, where you can see an exhibition and watch a video on Martinů's life. Despite spending much of his life in exile, Martinů always carried a postcard of the view from the tower, and twenty years after his death in a Swiss hospital in 1959, he was finally buried in the town cemetery, within sight of the tower.

Apart from the composer, there's little other reason for coming to Polička, which had its aesthetic charms altered in a devastating fire in 1845. The main square was nicely rebuilt, however, and it boasts the highest plague column (22m) in Bohemia. You can explore the town's beautifully preserved and pretty impressive **fortifications** (April & Oct Mon–Fri 9am–4pm; May & Sept Mon–Fri 9am–4pm, Sat 1–4pm; June Mon–Fri 9am–5pm, Sat & Sun 1–4pm; July–Aug Mon–Fri 9am–5pm, Sat 9am–4pm) with a guide from the **tourist office** (Mon–Fri 8.30am–6pm, Sat 9am–2pm; Ⓦwww.policka-mesto.cz) on the main square. The **train station** is north of the town, off route 359 to Litomyšl, but only connects with Svitavy and Česká Třebová, not Litomyšl. The best place to stay in town is the pretty blue *Penzion U purkmistra* (Ⓣ461 722 310; ❷), on Riegrova near the church of sv Jakub; otherwise you can try the cheaper and less civilized *Hotel Pivovar* (Ⓣ461 725 269; ❶), also on Riegrova, just below the church, or the Communist-era *Hotel Opus* (Ⓣ461 722 103, Ⓦwww.hotelopus.cz; ❷) at Družstevní 893, just off the centre. Alternatively there's a **campsite** (May–Sept), 1.5km south of the town off route 360 to Nové Město na Moravě.

Svojanov

In addition to being one of the prettiest castles in the charming Bohemian-Moravian Uplands, **Svojanov** (April & Oct Sat & Sun 9am–noon & 1–4pm; May & Sept Tues–Sun 9am–5pm; June–Aug Tues–Sun 8.30am–5pm), 15km southeast of Polička, commands admiration for its impressive stance atop a granite protuberance. It's a small place, and each stage of its many constructions is clearly visible, from a thirteenth-century guard tower through to the Empire-style ornamentation of the interior halls. The guided tour takes you through the usual collection of paintings and glassware, along with an exceptional array of old clocks. If you're here in mid-July, you can also go to the annual **puppet festival**, where some of the country's leading artisans put on displays and shows of the craft particular to this region. You can **sleep** in the castle's dormitory (Ⓣ461 741 124; ❶) and eat at the simple **restaurant** *Na hradě*. Svojanov is served by fairly regular buses from Polička on weekdays, though at the weekend there are only two a day, which continue on to Brno.

Travel details

Trains

Prague to: Hradec Králové (12–16 daily; 1hr 25 min–1hr 45 min); Pardubice (30 daily; 1hr 10min–1hr 30min); Trutnov (1–2 daily; 3hr–3hr 20 min); Turnov (8–12 daily; 2hr–3hr).
Hradec Králové to: Častolovice/Doudleby nad Orlicí (5 daily; 40min/1hr); Chlumec nad Cidlinou (every 1–2hr; 20–40min); Dvůr Králové (7 daily; 40min); Hořice (11–17 daily; 30–50min); Jaroměř (hourly; 20–30min); Jičín (11–15 daily; 1hr 15min–1hr 25 min); Kuks (1 daily; 30min); Pardubice (1–2 hourly; 25–30min); Třebechovice pod Orebem (15–20 daily; 15min).
Náchod to: Nové Město nad Metují/Opočno (9–18 daily; 15–25min/25–35min); Teplice nad Metují (11–18 daily; 30–40min).

Pardubice to: Chrudim (hourly; 20–30min); Liberec (7 daily; 3hr–3hr 30 min).
Trutnov to: Adršpach/Teplice nad Metují (7–9 daily; 1hr/1hr 15min); Česká Skalice/Jaroměř (13–17 daily; 1hr/1hr 15min); Chlumec nad Cidlinou (9 daily; 2hr–2hr 30min); Kunčice nad Labem (11–15 daily; 30min).
Turnov to: Hradec Králové (13–14 daily; 2hr–2hr 30 min); Jičín (9–10 daily; 50min–1hr); Železný Brod (16–23 daily; 20min).

Buses

Connections with Prague: Harrachov (up to 5 daily; 3hr); Hradec Králové (hourly; 1hr 30min–2hr); Jičín (7–15 daily; 1hr 10 min–2hr); Litomyšl

(4–7daily; 3hr–3hr 30min); Náchod (5–18 daily; 2hr 30 min–3hr); Pec pod Sněžkou (2–7 daily; 3hr–3hr 30 min); Špindlerův Mlýn (up to 6 daily; 2hr 30min–3hr); Trutnov (5–12 daily; 2hr 45min); Vrchlabí (7–11 daily; 2–3hr).

Hradec Králové to: Jaroměř (6 daily; Mon–Fri over 30; 25min–1hr); Kuks (13 daily Mon–Fri; 30–45 min); Litomyšl (hourly; 1hr 10min–1hr 30 min); Náchod (25 daily Mon–Fri, 5 daily Sat & Sun; 1hr); Nové Město nad Metují (3–10 daily; 45 min–1hr 10 min); Pec pod Sněžkou (1–2 daily; 1hr 35

min–2hr); Trutnov (up to 7 daily; 1hr–1hr 30min); Vrchlabí (3–8 daily; 1hr 30min).

Jičín to: Turnov (2–15 daily; 30min–1hr).

Náchod to: Broumov (7–20 daily; 45min–1hr); Nové Město nad Metují (1–2 per hour Mon–Fri; 15–30min).

Trutnov to: Janské Lázně (hourly; 30min); Pec pod Sněžkou (hourly; 35–50mins); Vrchlabí (up to 10 daily; 35–50min).

Vrchlabí to: Špindlerův Mlýn (16–22 daily; 20min).

6

South Moravia

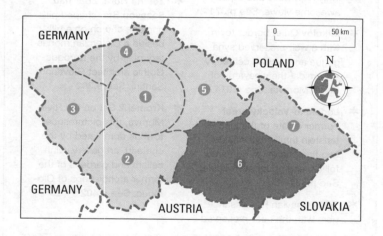

CHAPTER SIX **Highlights**

✳ **Moravský kras** Limestone karst region of caves, underground rivers and gorges within easy reach of the Moravian capital, Brno. See p.368

✳ **Pernštejn** Classic hilltop medieval castle with dizzyingly high walls and equally awesome views. See p.371

✳ **Mikulov** Quiet border town with a well-preserved synagogue and Jewish cemetery set amidst the vineyards of South Moravia. See p.374

✳ **Lednicko-Valtický areál** Former estate of the Liechtenstein family that boasts two fine chateaux, numerous follies, and abundant wildlife. See p.377

✳ **Telč** Moravian Renaissance gem with the best-preserved sixteenth-century square in the country, and a chateau to match it. See p.386

✳ **Slavonice** Border town with two remarkably well-preserved squares featuring apocalyptic sgraffito facades. See p.387

✳ **Zelená Hora, Žďár nad Sázavou** Star-shaped pilgrimage church on a hill beside a Cistercian monastery built by the Baroque-Gothic architect Giovanni Santini. See p.392

✳ **Kroměříž** Set on the River Morava, this picturesque town is dominated by the chateau, art gallery, wine cellars and gardens of the former archbishops of Olomouc. See p.402

△ Telč

South Moravia

A t first sight, the landscape of **South Moravia** (Jižní Morava) appears little different from that of much of Bohemia, a mixture of rolling hills and dense forests. Only as you move south towards Vienna does the land become noticeably more plump and fertile, with the orchards and vineyards continuing into Austria itself. **Brno** is the most obvious starting point: an engaging city, whose attractions are often underrated due to its heavy industrial base and conspicuous peripheral housing estates. Brno is also within easy reaching distance of a host of sights, most notably Moravia's karst region, the Moravský kras, which boasts the country's most spectacular **limestone caves**, and the atmospheric medieval castle of **Pernštejn**.

South of Brno a whole string of pretty villages, towns and chateaux punctuate the **River Dyje** (Thaya) as it meanders along the Austrian border. Historically, the land on either side of the Dyje was for centuries German-speaking, its buildings designed by Austrian architects and its sights set firmly on Vienna, just 60km to the south. However, as in the rest of the country, the ethnic German population was forcibly removed from South Moravia after 1945. The region's viticulture kept going on private plots even after nationalization in 1948, but in every other way the last half century has driven a great wedge between two previously identical regions on either side of the river. **Mikulov**, on the main road from Vienna, is a great introduction to the region; close by, at the chateaux of **Lednice** and **Valtice**, the Liechtensteins had their base for many centuries. Further west, another border town, **Znojmo**, harbours the country's most precious medieval frescoes, and is a great jumping-off point for the **Podyjí** national park, formed by the damming of the Dyje and dotted with castles and chateaux.

Further west still, on the Bohemian border, **Telč** and **Slavonice** are two of the most beautiful Renaissance towns anywhere in Europe. Yet while Telč is a popular stopoff on whirlwind tours of the country, Slavonice – every bit as perfect – sees far fewer visitors. Telč and Slavonice sit at the southern end of the **Bohemian–Moravian Uplands** or Vysočina, a poor and sparsely populated area which separates Bohemia and Moravia, and which is viewed by most travellers only from the window of their bus, train or car en route to Brno. **Jihlava** is the area's most convenient starting point, but it won't hold you long. More compelling is the pilgrimage church at **Žďár nad Sázavou**, another of Santini's Baroque-Gothic confections.

To the east of Brno, the landscape around the River Morava is visually pretty uninspiring, but the wine and rich folk heritage are good reasons for stopping here. To the south, the area known as **Slovácko** hosts the country's two largest **folk festivals**, in Vlčnov and Strážnice. Further north, the provincial treasure house and graceful gardens of **Kroměříž** provide a fascinating contrast with the modernist

aesthetics of **Zlín**, where the multinational Baťa shoe empire has its roots.

Transport is fairly good throughout Moravia, though the train system is not quite as comprehensive as that of Bohemia, petering out in the Vysočina and degenerating into a series of overcomplex branch lines along the more industrialized River Morava. In such instances, buses are invariably quicker and more direct.

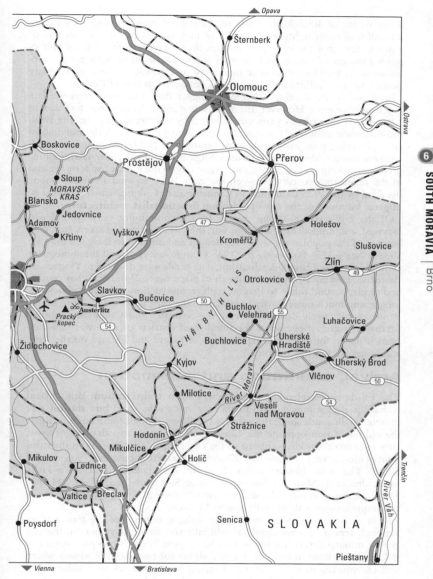

Brno

BRNO (Brünn) "welcomes the visitor with new constructions", as one Communist-era tourist brochure euphemistically put it. In fact, the high-rise *paneláky* that surround the Moravian capital play a major part in discouraging travellers from stopping here. But as the second-largest city in the Czech Republic, with a population of 400,000, a couple of really good museums and art galleries, a handful of other sights and a fair bit of nightlife, it's worth a day or two of anyone's time. For the most part, though, the city receives few foreign visitors outside the annual trade fairs, though of course this has its advantages too: tourists are welcomed here with genuine interest, and the pace of life is endearingly (some might say infuriatingly) provincial, compared to that of Prague.

Brno was a late developer, being no bigger than Olomouc until the late eighteenth century. However, the town's first cloth factory was founded in 1766, and within fifteen years was followed by another twenty, earning Brno the nickname *rakouský Manchestr* (Austrian Manchester). With the building of an engineering plant early in the next century, the city began to attract Czech workers, along with Austrian, German, English and, in particular, Jewish entrepreneurs, making it easily the second largest city in the Czech Lands by the end of the nineteenth century. Between the wars, Brno enjoyed a cultural boom, heralded by the 1928 Exhibition of Contemporary Culture, which provided an impetus for much of the city's pioneering **functionalist architecture**.

Of the city's 10,000-strong prewar Jewish community, only around 670 survived, and immediately after the war, the city's German-speakers (some 25 percent of the population) were rounded up and ordered to leave, on foot, for Vienna (see p.375). Following the 1948 Communist coup and the subsequent centralization (and later federalization), state funds were diverted to Prague and Bratislava, pushing Brno firmly into third place. Since 1989, Brno has continued to play second fiddle to Prague, with reconstruction and restoration work progressing much more slowly here than in the capital. To add insult to injury, Brno was effectively demoted during the country's post-Communist administrative reorganization, when the number of districts or *kraje* was increased from seven to fourteen, putting the likes of Jihlava and Ostrava on the same administrative footing as Brno.

Arrival, orientation and information

The fin-de-siècle splendour of the city's main **train station**, Brno hlavní nádraží, is a great introduction to the city; not so the main **bus station**, five minutes' walk south along the overhead walkway, though some buses arrive at the old bus station opposite the *Grand Hotel*. Brno's Tuřany **airport** (Ⓦwww. airport-brno.cz) is 6km southeast of the city centre: bus #76 runs to the main train station (every 30min–1hr; 22min) and a taxi should cost you around 300Kč. The main **tourist office** is in the stará radnice (Old Town Hall), on Radnická 8 (Mon–Fri 8am–6pm, Sat & Sun 9am–5pm; ℡542 211 090, Ⓦwww.kultura-brno.cz); the staff are friendly enough, though the office is not as comprehensive as those in Prague or Bratislava.

Most of Brno's sights are within easy walking distance of the train station, although **trams** (Ⓦwww.dpmb.cz) will take you almost anywhere in the city within minutes. Brno has, unfortunately, adopted Prague's complex system of ticketing: you need to buy either a 8Kč **ticket** for two zones (2 *pásma*), which will last you ten minutes without changing trams or buses, or a 13Kč ticket, again for two zones (2 *pásma*), which is valid for forty minutes and allows changes between trams or buses. Tickets must be bought beforehand from news kiosks or yellow ticket machines and punched on board; if you're going to be whizzing about on the trams all day, you might want to buy a 24-hour *celodenní jízdenka*, currently 50Kč, or a three-day ticket for 100Kč. A couple of trams run all night, but many have been replaced by night buses which run along the old tram routes – all gather together in front of the station on the hour, every hour. The same tickets are valid for the city's **buses** and **trolleybuses**, which congregate at Moravské náměstí and Mendlovo náměstí, though you're unlikely to need to use them unless you're staying right out in suburbia.

Accommodation

Finding **accommodation** in Brno is relatively easy, though prices are fairly high, thanks to the expense-account business people who come here for the various trade fairs (when prices can double or even triple). The tourist office in Radnická (see opposite) can arrange cheap **private rooms**, though many of the ones on their books are out of the centre. The most centrally located **hostel** is the *Travellers Hostel* at Jánská 22 (☎542 213 573), but it's only open in July and August. The rest of the year, you'll have to head for the *Student Pension Palacký* (☎541 641 111), a high-rise block on the far northern edge of the city at the end of Kolejní; take tram #12 or #13 to their terminus and then trolleybus #53 to the end of the line.

There are several **campsites** along the shores of the Brněnská přehrada (Brno Dam), 10km northwest of the city centre; the nearest one is *Radka* (June–Aug), on the east bank beyond the hostel-style *Hotel Přehrada* (☎546 210 167) and the Sokolské swimming pool; to reach the dam, take tram #1, #3 or #11.

Hotels and pensions

Amphone Třída kpt. Jaroše 29 ☎545 428 310, ⓦwww.amphone.cz. A really good choice: clean, plain and positioned on a lovely tree-lined boulevard, just ten minutes' walk from the city centre. ❸

Grand Hotel Benešova 18–20 ☎542 518 111, ⓦwww.grandhotelbrno.cz. The Art Nouveau mural on the facade is sadly no indication of the interior, which retains no original features whatsoever. Still, it's Austrian-run and efficient enough, if somewhat overpriced. ❾

Pegas Jakubská 4 ☎542 210 104. Small, basic rooms located right in the old town above the micro-brewery/pub of the same name (although this doesn't make it especially noisy). ❹

Pyramida Zahradnická 19 ☎543 427 310. Perfectly comfortable and pleasant, Communist-era high-rise hotel a couple of tram stops southwest of the old town, near Výstaviště. ❸

Royal Ricc Starobrněnská 10 ☎542 219 262, ⓦwww.romantichotels.cz. Lovely position in the backstreets of the old town, and the odd original Renaissance feature and tasteful repro furnishings make this Brno's luxury hotel of choice. ❼

Slavia Solniční 15–17 ☎542 321 249, ⓦwww.slavia.hotel.cz. Communist-era hotel that's actually pretty comfortable, very central and competitively priced. ❻

Slovan Lidická 23 ☎541 321 207, ⓦwww.hotelslovan.cz. Another comfortable and unpretentious Communist-era hotel, just a step away from the Janáčkovo divadlo. ❹

The City

One of the nicest things about Brno is that its historical centre is compact and almost entirely traffic-free. The city's main action goes on within the small, egg-shaped old town, pedestrianized for the most part and encircled by a swathe of parks and the inner ring road. Around **Zelný trh** and **náměstí Svobody** you'll find most of the city's shops and markets. In the southwestern corner raised above the old town are the quieter streets around **Petrov**, the lesser of Brno's two hills, topped by the cathedral. Further west, the squat fortress of **Špilberk** looks down on the old town to the east and Staré Brno to the south, site of the original early medieval settlement. Worth a visit, but still further from the centre, are Brno's new **Technické muzeum** and the city's two modernist architectural landmarks: the exhibition grounds of **Výstaviště** and – on the opposite side of town – Mies van der Rohe's **Vila Tugendhat**.

BRNO

Bílý dům

Červený kostel ✝

Masaryk University

KOMENSKÉHO NÁM.

Masaryk University

Špilberk

PELLICHOVA

15

Augustinian Monastery

PEKAŘSKÁ

7 6 5

ANENSKÁ

18

Mendel Museum

Brewery

MENDLOVO NÁMĚSTÍ

LEITNEROVA

19

1 2 HYBEŠOVA

HYBEŠOVA

Výstaviště (300m) ◄

354

GORKÉHO

VEVEŘÍ

3
3 11 12 13

KOUNICOVA

JASELSKÁ

ÚVOZ

4 ◄

ÚDOLNÍ

ÚDOLNÍ

TVRDÉHO

ÚVOZ

PIVOVARSKÁ

ÚVOZ

PUBS	
Charlie's Hat	**11**
Elektra	**9**
Kabinet múz	**10**
Pegas	**D**
Pivovarská pivnice	**18**
Potrefená husa	**4**
Skleněná louka	**3**
Špalíček	**16**
U dvou kozlů	**5**

CAFÉS	
Adria	**17**
Avatár	**19**
Blau	**7**
Fischer	**14**
Rendezvous	**6**
Spolek	**13**
Švanda	**12**

RESTAURANTS	
Aura	**2**
Haribol	**1**
Taj	**8**
U královny Elišky	**15**

▼ **G**

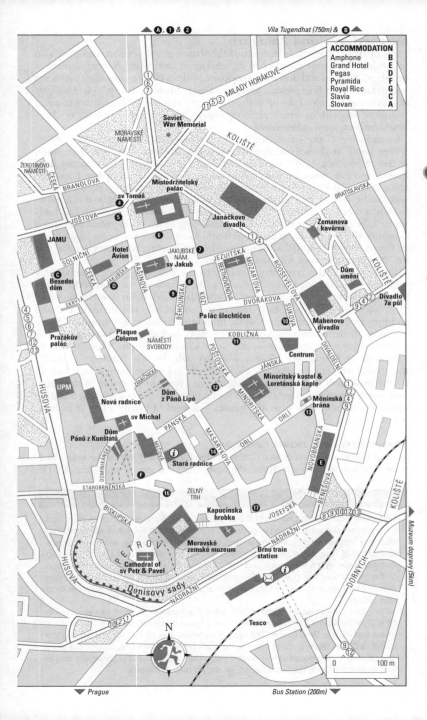

▲ Ⓐ, ❶ & ❷   Vila Tugendhat (750m) & Ⓑ ▲

ACCOMMODATION
Amphone	B
Grand Hotel	E
Pegas	D
Pyramida	F
Royal Ricc	G
Slavia	C
Slovan	A

MILADY HORÁKOVÉ

Soviet War Memorial

MORAVSKÉ NÁMĚSTÍ

KOLIŠTĚ

ŽEROTÍNOVO NÁMĚSTÍ

ČESKÁ

BRANOLOVA

BRATISLAVSKÁ

Místodržitelský palác

sv Tomáš ❹

JOŠTOVA ❺

Janáčkovo divadlo

Zemanova kavárna

KOLIŠTĚ

JAMU

SOLNIČNÍ

Hotel Avion

❻

JAKUBSKÉ NÁM. ❼

sv Jakub

JEZUITSKÁ

MOZARTOVA

ROOSEVELTOVA

Dům umění

Ⓒ Besední dům

ČESKÁ

JAKUBSKÁ

Ⓓ

BEETHOVENOVA

Divadlo 7a půl ❾❹❷

SKRYTÁ

RAŠINOVA

❾ ❽

KOZÍ

DVOŘÁKOVA

SUKOVA

DIVADELNÍ

❾ Mahenovo divadlo

Pražákův palác

④⑤⑥⑦⑫⑬

Palác šlechtičen

KOBLIŽNÁ

❿

HUSOVA

UPM

Plaque Column

NÁMĚSTÍ SVOBODY

⓫

Centrum

JÁNSKÁ

Minoritský kostel & Loretánská kaple

②④

Nová radnice

ZÁMEČNICKÁ

Dům z Pánů Lípé

⓬

POŠTOVSKÁ

MINORITSKÁ

Měnínská brána ⓭

sv Michal

PANSKÁ

MASARYKOVA

ORLÍ

NOVOBRANSKÁ

Dům Pánů z Kunštátů

MEČOVÁ

ⓘ

⓮ Stará radnice

Ⓔ

DOMINIKÁNSKÁ

Ⓕ

STAROBRNĚNSKÁ

⓰

ZELNÝ TRH

⓱

JOSEFSKÁ

BENEŠOVA

⑧⑨❿⑫⑬

BISKUPSKÁ

Kapucínská hrobka

NÁDRAŽNÍ

KOLIŠTĚ

P E T R O V

Moravské zemské muzeum

Brno train station

ⓘ

Muzeum dopravy (5km) ▶

Cathedral of sv Petr & Pavel

Denisovy sady

NÁDRAŽNÍ

HUSOVA

❿②⑦

DORNYCH

Tesco

⑨ ⑫

N

0   100 m

▼ Prague   Bus Station (200m) ▼

Masarykova and Zelný trh

Most of Brno's trams pass in front of the station at some point, and there's an infectious buzz about the place in the afternoon, after work. A steady stream of people ploughs up and down **Masarykova**, with its cobbles, steaming manholes and defunct tram lines, which leads to náměstí Svobody (see p.358). Don't let that stop you from looking up at the five-storey mansions, laden with a fantastic mantle of decorations which perfectly express the confidence of the city's late-nineteenth-century industrialists.

Immediately to the left as you head up Masarykova is Kapucínské náměstí, where you'll find the macabre **Kapucínská hrobka** (Tues–Sat 9am–noon & 2–4.30pm, Sun 11–11.45am & 2–4.30pm), a gruesome collection of dead monks and top nobs, mummified by chance in the crypt of the Capuchin church. Until the eighteenth century, Brno's moneyed classes forked out large sums to be buried here in the monks' simple common grave, in the hope of finding a short cut to heaven – righteousness by association, perhaps. The bodies lie fully clothed, some with the hollow expressions of skeletons, others still frozen in the last painful grimace of death. Just to drive the point home, signs in Czech chime in with "What we are, they once were; what they are, we will be." Not an experience for the faint-hearted.

To the west of the crypt steps lead up to the Biskupský dvůr, which, along with the neighbouring Dietrichsteinský palác, is home to the **Moravské zemské muzeum** (Tues–Sat 9am–5pm; ⓦwww.mzm.cz). Brno is at the centre of quite an extensive area of early human settlement, and the museum contains an impressive collection of prehistoric finds from the surrounding region (there are more in the Anthropos annexe, see p.364), including the famous *Venus of Věstonice*, plus a large section on the Great Moravian Empire. Opening out to the north of Kapucínské náměstí is **Zelný trh** (literally "cabbage market"), the chaotic vegetable market on a sloping cobbled square, somewhat ill-served by the mishmash of buildings which line its edges. At its centre is the petrified diarrhoea of the huge *Parnassus* fountain by Fischer von Erlach, featuring mythological beasts and Hercules himself – it worked briefly a few years back, but is currently dry.

The stará and nová radnice

Tucked down a side street, but clearly visible from Zelný trh, is the **stará radnice**, whose best feature is Anton Pilgram's Gothic doorway on Radnická. The

---

The Brno mascots

Countless local legends surround the **Brněnský drak** (Brno dragon, though in fact it's a stuffed alligator), which hangs from the ceiling of the town hall entrance. The standard version is that the marauding beast was tricked into eating a carcass stuffed full of lime, upon which it rushed down to the River Svratka and quenched its thirst, causing the lime to expand and its stomach to burst. The most likely origin of the creature is that it was a gift from the Turkish sultan to Archduke Matthias, who in turn bequeathed it to Brno in an attempt to ingratiate himself with the local aristocrats.

The other town mascot displayed here is the **Brněnské kolo** (Brno wheel), made in 1636 by a cartwright from Lednice, who bet a friend that he could fell a tree, make a wheel and roll it to Brno (some 50km away), all before sunset. He won the bet and the wheel has been given pride of place in the stará radnice ever since, though the story goes that following his great feat people began to suspect that the cartwright was in league with the devil: his business fell off and he died in poverty.

tallest of the five thistly pinnacles above the statue of Blind Justice is deliberately twisted as if it's about to fall on your head – Pilgram's testament to the corrupt town aldermen who shortchanged him for his work (he went on to help furnish Vienna's Stephansdom). Inside, the town hall's courtyards and passageways are home to the **Brněnský drak** (Brno dragon), the **Brněnské kolo** (Brno wheel) – for more on which see the box opposite – the town's main tourist office, an exhibition space, a café and an observation tower (*vyhlídková věž*; April–Sept daily 9am–5pm), worth a climb for the panorama across the city's red-tiled rooftops. Next door to the town hall at no. 6 is a small **akvárium** (Tues–Fri 9.30am–5.30pm, Sat & Sun 9.30am–4pm).

Round the back of the stará radnice, to the north, the cobbled square below the Dominican church of **sv Michal** serves as a car park for the functionaries of the present city council who hold office at the adjacent **nová radnice**, founded in 1935 in the former Dominican monastery. It's a passable effort by Mořic Grimm, the city's chief Baroque architect, "a provincial talent but a sound craftsman", as one critic described him. There are a couple of pretty sundials in the echoing first courtyard, and a modern fountain from the 1928 Exhibition in the second courtyard, but otherwise nothing much to get too excited about unless someone's getting married. The handful of cobbled streets that lead south from here to Petrov hill are the nearest Brno gets to a secluded, intimate spot: walk up Dominikanská from the cobbled square, and take a quick look inside the **Dům pánů z Kunštátu** (Tues–Sun 10am–6pm), one of Brno's few surviving Renaissance buildings, with a lovely arcaded courtyard and, inside, a café, temporary exhibitions put on by the city museum, and a small display on Janáček in Brno (for more on Janáček, see p.360).

Petrov

Continue up Biskupská to **Petrov**, the smaller of the city's two central hills and one of the best places in which to make a quick escape from the choked streets below. At the top of the hill stands the **Cathedral of sv Petr and Pavel**, whose needle-sharp neo-Gothic spires from 1901 dominate the skyline for miles around. The cathedral holds a special place in Brno's history for having been instrumental in saving the town from the Swedes during the Thirty Years' War. After months besieging the town during the course of 1645, the Swedish general Tortennson decided to make one last attempt at taking the place, declaring he would give up at midday if the town hadn't surrendered. In a fit of inspiration, the bell-ringer, seeing that the town was on the brink of defeat, decided to ring the midday bells an hour early. The Swedes gave up their attack, the city was saved, and as a reward the Habsburg emperor switched the Moravian capital from Olomouc to Brno (well, so the story goes). The clock strikes twelve at 11am to this day. Inside the lofty nave, there's a valuable fourteenth-century *Madonna and Child*, but the most intriguing art treasures are the aluminium *Stations of the Cross*, by Jiří Marek. Constructed in the early 1960s, these get progressively more outrageous and abstract as the story unfolds, until the final relief is no more than flailing limbs and anguished metal.

The cathedral is not the only reason to climb Petrov: from the nearby **Denisovy sady**, tucked into the city ramparts, there's a far-reaching view over the great plain south to Vienna, and an interesting angle on the cathedral itself. In among the trees and courting couples, a slender obelisk, resting on several squashed lions, commemorates the end of the Napoleonic Wars (the Battle of Austerlitz took place just outside Brno – see p.373), lining up perfectly with the avenue of Husova which leads to the red-brick Protestant church, known as the **Červený kostel** (Red Church), and, beyond it, the bright white former

Party headquarters, known affectionately as the **Bílý dům** (White House). When this was at the planning stages in the 1950s, the more committed cadres wanted to remove the offending Protestant church, which blocked the view up Husova. Fortunately, aestheticism triumphed over atheism and the plan was somehow foiled.

Náměstí Svobody

Back down on Masarykova, follow the flow north and you'll end up at **náměstí Svobody**, the city's main square since the early thirteenth century. The medieval church, which once stood at the centre of the square, was torn down in 1870, leaving only a Baroque plague column (see box below). Still, in summer, you can sit out, drink coffee and admire the square's finer buildings, which together span almost four centuries. The earliest is the **Dům z panů Lipé** (House of the Lords of Lipá), with an ornate Renaissance facade decorated with sgraffito, added as late as 1938. The building has recently been restored and its arcaded courtyard rather brutally converted into a "muzak"-filled shopping mall. However, it's worth venturing inside and taking the lift to the fifth floor, from which there's access to a rooftop **viewing platform** (*vyhlídková terasa*), which gives out great views over the old town, the cathedral and Špilberk. A few doors along, at no. 15, the **Kleinův palác** was designed around 1848 in neo-Renaissance style by Theophil Hansen, the Danish architect responsible for some of the finest buildings on Vienna's Ringstrasse; the Klein family owned a nearby ironworks, hence the elegant wrought-iron oriel windows held up with miniature Atlantes. Opposite, and totally lacking in such subtlety, is **Dům u čtyř mamlasů** (House of the Four Idiots), belonging to another of Brno's richest nineteenth-century Jewish industrialists, whose four muscle-bound employees struggle to hold up both his building and their loincloths. And in the 1930s, the functionalist **Moravská banka** (now the Komerční banka), designed by Arnošt Wiesner and Bohuslav Fuchs, was erected in the northwest corner of the square.

Heading north from náměstí Svobody, a steady stream of people flows past the concentration of book and record shops, pubs and cafés on **Česká**, wolfing down takeaways and *zmrzlina* on the way and, at the top, waiting for the trams and buses that congregate on Joštova, which marks the end of the old town. On the northeast corner of the square is the wonderfully named, tonsil-twisting **Palác šlechtičen** (Noblewomen's Palace), which was founded in the 1670s as a school for twelve orphaned girls; four from poor families, four from burgher

---

Plague columns

The **plague column** (morový sloup) is a frequent feature of Catholic towns and cities across Central Europe. When the plague struck a city, as it did frequently right up until the eighteenth century, the locals would gather at the column and pray for deliverance. The plague columns you see today date from the Baroque period, when they took on an extra religious and political significance, as the image of the Virgin Mary praying for the sins of the world, surrounded by twelve stars, became a popular and distinctively Catholic image. Many columns, like the one in Brno, were in fact erected in 1648, in thanks for the town's liberation from the Protestant "plague", in this case the unsuccessful Swedish (Protestant) siege of the city. In the Czech Lands, the columns came to be regarded by Czech nationalists as symbols of the Austro-Hungarian hegemony, and a number were torn down during the celebrations following the foundation of Czechoslovakia in 1918, including the one which used to grace Prague's Old Town Square.

△ Church of sv Jakub, Brno

families and four from noble families. The building currently hosts temporary ethnographic exhibitions (Tues–Sat 9am–5pm).

North and east of náměstí Svobody

Clearly visible, to the north of náměstí Svobody, up Rašínova, is the late Gothic church of **sv Jakub** (St James), with its distinctive onion dome and needle spire. Erected and paid for by the local burghers, it took two centuries to complete, and is perhaps best known for the sixteenth-century copulating couple on the south side of the tower. The whole church has recently been beautifully restored and the pulpit in particular is worth a look: the stone base dates from 1526 and features three exquisite relief scenes – the Nativity, Jesus in the Temple and the Mount of Olives – and a lovely lion beneath the pedestal; above is a much later multi-tiered wooden tester packed with saints.

The finest architectural work of the Grimm brothers (there really were two of them) was the **Minoritský kostel** on the corner of Minoritská and Jánská, whose vivacious frontage makes the most of its cramped site. The right-hand portal leads to the main gilded nave, whose interior represents much the best slice of Baroque in town, high to the point of giddiness, an effect that's intensified by the illusionistic frescoes. Linked to the church next door by double doors in the north aisle is an equally stunning chapel, with a steep altar staircase that must be ascended on bended knee, and full-size colour terracotta statues of Jesus and the two robbers looking down from the gallery above. The greater part of the church is taken up with a **Loretanská kaple** (Loreto Chapel), its outer walls smothered in grisaille depictions of the miracle; the atmospheric

---

Janáček in Brno

Although he was born in Hukvaldy (see p.436), in northern Moravia, **Leoš Janáček** (1854–1928) moved to Brno at the age of eleven and spent most of his life here, first as a chorister and then teacher and choirmaster at the local Augustinian monastery. Battling against the prejudices of the German-speaking town administration, he managed to drag Czech music out of the pub and into the concert hall, eventually founding the Brno Conservatoire and Organ School in 1882. All but one of his operas were premiered in Brno, and as a composer he remained virtually unknown outside Moravia until well into his sixties, when he began the last and most prolific creative period of his life. For much of the twentieth century, Janáček was overshadowed by his compatriots, Smetana (whom the Communists were particularly keen on) and Dvořák (whom the West has always revered), but in the last couple of decades his music has become increasingly popular, with works such as *Jenůfa* enjoying international acclaim.

Across the park from the opera house named after him, at the junction of Kounicova and Smetanova, is the **Památník Leoše Janáčka** (Mon–Fri 9am–noon & 1–4pm), in the cottage where the composer lived, at the back of the Organ School. One part of one room has some period furniture, the rest displays Janáček's metronome, baton, train pass, passport, portable icon and several original manuscripts. Look out for Čapek's original designs for the première of the *Makropulos Case*, and ask to watch some of the BBC cartoon version of *The Cunning Little Vixen*. Unlike his predecessors, Smetana and Dvořák, Janáček chose not to be buried in Prague's illustrious Vyšehrad cemetery, opting instead for Brno's municipal one. If you're on the Janáček trail, bus #62 from outside Tesco, behind the train station, terminates at the main entrance off Jihlavská; or else tram #5, #7 or #8 will take you to within walking distance – the cemetery is easy enough to spot, thanks to the bright white pinnacles of Arnošt Wiesner's strikingly modern crematorium, designed in 1930.

red-brick interior holds the standard *Black Madonna and Child* set against a rich marble backdrop.

At the bottom of Jánská, the department store **Centrum**, built in 1928 by the shoe magnate Tomáš Baťa, still cuts a bold figure. It was originally intended to be 28 storeys high (rather than its current seven), which would have made it the tallest building in Europe at the time, but not surprisingly the local council refused planning permission. Beyond lies one of Brno's finest late-nineteenth-century buildings, the **Mahenovo divadlo**, a forthright structure designed by Helmer and Fellner, exuding the municipal confidence of its original German patrons with its Corinthian columns and pediment. Its insides are smothered in gold sculpturing and glittering chandeliers, and it had the distinction of being the first theatre in the Austro-Hungarian Empire to be fitted with electric light bulbs. In total contrast to the flamboyant Mahenovo is Bohuslav Fuchs' squat functionalist **Dům umění** (Tues–Sun 10am–6pm; ⓦwww.dumb.cz), which puts on some of the city's most innovative art exhibitions, theatre performances, and even the occasional gig. A little further up Rooseveltova from the Mahenovo is the grey and scruffy looking **Janáčkovo divadlo**, built in the 1960s as the city's – indeed the country's – largest opera house.

Moravská galerie: UPM, Pražákův palác and Místodržitelský palác

Brno's **Moravská galerie** (Wed–Sun 10am–6pm, Thurs until 7pm; ⓦwww .moravska-galerie.cz) has one of the best art collections in the country, spread out over three premises. Probably the most universally appealing is the applied art collection in the recently renovated Uměleckoprůmyslové muzeum or **UPM**, on Husova, which forms the western limit of the old town. The building itself is a neo-Renaissance pile built as a museum in the 1880s by one of Brno's many wealthy Jewish industrialists. The richly decorated ground floor plays host to wacky installations and temporary exhibitions of anything from avant-garde photomontages to the work of the local art school. The gallery's imaginatively designed permanent applied arts collection starts on the first floor, and continues on the top floor, with captions in Czech and English throughout.

The museum begins with a room devoted to medieval craftsmanship, the centrepiece of which is a wonderful silver-gilt crozier from the 1330s belonging to the abbots of Rajhrad. The highlight of the Renaissance room is an incredible seventeenth-century Swiss ceramic stove with matching seta, all smothered in pictorial depictions of the months of the year. After a room of Baroque and Rococo glassware, snuff boxes, fans and pocket watches, and the simple, almost modernist lines of the Biedermeier or Empire period, you reach a whole selection of Thonet furniture. Thonet, whose factories were mostly located in Moravia, fitted out the fin-de-siècle cafés of the Habsburg Empire with their bentwood chairs and tables. The Art Nouveau or Secession section is particularly rewarding, with a vast, curvaceous Gaillard sideboard, some beautiful iridescent Lötz glassware from Klašterský Mlýn and a Klimt clay *jardinière*, which was bought in 1987 from an antique shop in Brno by a canny local collector.

Further up Husova is the Moravská galerie's **Pražákův palác**, another sturdy nineteenth-century edifice, designed by Theophil Hansen and now housing an excellent permanent collection of twentieth-century Czech art on its first and second floors. The pictures are re-hung every year or so, but you're bound to get to see at least some of the gallery's best works, which include sculptures by Bílek, Štursa and Gutfreund; some early Cubist works by Kubišta and Procházka, plus later pieces by Josef Čapek and Šíma; black-and-white photographs by Sudek and others; political works by Nepraš; and abstracts by Mikuláš Medek.

The third building belonging to the Moravská galerie is the **Místodržitelský palác**, the former residence of the governor of Moravia, originally built as an Augustinian monastery at the eastern end of Joštova. Under the Communists it served as a museum of the working class, but it now hosts temporary exhibitions, plus a small permanent collection that includes a smattering of Gothic works, a few minor Baroque works by fresco specialists Kremser Schmidt, Maultbertsch and Daniel Gran, and some sentimental Biedermeier paintings. The final room contains the palace's only truly memorable works: a portrait of a woman by Hans Makart, painted with his characteristically dark, chocolate-brown palette, and Max Švabinský's striking *Red Sunshade*.

Špilberk

Skulking on a thickly wooded hill to the west of Husova and barely visible through the trees, the ugly, squat fortress of **Špilberk** (⊛www.spilberk.cz) acquired a reputation as one of the most god-awful prisons in the Habsburg Empire. As you walk up through the castle grounds, a monument featuring a wolf suckling Romulus and Remus commemorates the many Italians who died here, having been incarcerated fighting for their country's freedom in the northern regions – then under Austrian rule – of what is now Italy. The testimony of one Italian inmate, the poet Count Silvio Pellico, so shocked the empire's middle classes that the prison was closed down in 1855. In 1880 it was opened up to the public as a tourist attraction by the local military commander, Costa-Rosetti, who installed a model torture chamber and wrote the guide himself, recounting and embellishing myths and legends associated with the place. Sixty years later, it was put back into use by the Nazis who confined, tortured and killed countless prisoners here during the war.

There are now two entrances to the fortress, the first of which, on the east side, leads to the atmospheric **kasematy** (dungeons; Tues–Sun: May–Sept 9am–6pm; Oct–April 9am–5pm). The most chilling section is the reconstruction of the so-called "dark cells" in the north wing, installed by the great reforming Emperor Josef II, who first turned the barracks into a prison. In these, prisoners were chained by the neck and hands in complete darkness and given only bread and water – a practice eventually stopped by Josef II's successor, Leopold II. Silvio Pellico and his contemporaries were actually incarcerated in the upper storey of the fortress, in – as it were – the best cells. Before you set off round the dungeons, make sure you pick up a leaflet with a plan, since the place is a veritable labyrinth. For the best view over Brno, head for the **rozhledna** (April & Oct Sat & Sun 9am–5pm; May–June & Sept Tues–Sun 9am–6pm; July & Aug daily 9am–6pm), the fortress's observation tower.

The entrance on the far, west side of the fortress leads to the exhibition rooms of the **Muzeum města Brna** (Museum of the City of Brno; April & Oct Tues–Sun 9am–5pm; May–Sept Tues–Sun 9am–6pm; Nov–March Wed–Sun 10am–5pm), which is best taken at a canter. Temporary exhibitions take place on the ground floor, along with a permanent display on the history of the prison (plus a few torture instruments and diagrams for good luck), and an *anglický text* in each room to help you decipher the exhibits. On the second floor, Baroque statues and sixteenth-century votive paintings from the church of sv Jakub, paid for by rich local burghers and painted by Dutch masters, hang alongside a decent collection of eighteenth- and nineteenth-century portraits of rich local townsfolk. There's also a modest selection of works from the first half of the last century, including a good spread by Antonín Procházka, from his Cubist *Girl with Garland* to the loose brushwork of *Bathing Horses* from the 1940s. Also worthy of note are Jaroslav Král's Cubist paintings, such as his portrait of Cubist architect Emil Králík; František Foltýn's pastel-shaded abstract works; and the minimalist egg cups and glasses designed by Bohuslav Fuchs.

But by far the most interesting part of the museum is the section on Brno's **interwar architecture**, a long overdue tribute to the city's modern golden age. The work of Bohuslav Fuchs occupies centre stage, and rightly so, as he was without doubt the most successful of the city's functionalist architects (see p.364). There's a good section on the Nový dům colony (see p.364) and the original plans for the (unrealized) Centrum skyscraper. For the most part, it's an exhibition of photos and architectural drawings, but there are a couple of pieces of original furniture by the likes of Adolf Loos, Alvar Aalto and Mies van der Rohe.

Gregor Mendel and the Augustinian monastery

The area south of the Špilberk hill, where the first settlements sprang up in the early Middle Ages, is known as **Staré Brno**. Few traces of these survive and nowadays there's nothing particularly old or interesting about this part of town, with the exception of the fourteenth-century **Augustinian monastery** on Mendlovo náměstí. Despite its unpromising locale – the square is little more than a glorified bus terminal – the monastery's **Bazilika** is one of Brno's finest Gothic buildings, its interior walls and pillars smothered in delicate geometric patterning dating from 1905. Be sure to take a look at the church's *Black Madonna* icon set beneath a silver crown at the high altar, which dates from the thirteenth century and which, it was believed, protected the city from foreign troops. The best time to get here is just before a service (Tues, Thurs, Fri & Sun 5.45–7.15pm); alternatively tours can be arranged from the Mendel Museum (see below).

The monastery is best known for one of its monks, **Gregor Mendel** (1822–84), whose experiments in the abbey gardens with cultivating and hybridizing peas and bees eventually led to the discovery of the principles of heredity and, subsequently, genetics. Despite the publication of several seminal papers outlining his discoveries, his work was ignored by the scientific establishment of the day, and in 1868 he gave up his research to become the monastery's abbot. Only after his death was he acknowledged as one of the greats of modern biology, and only very recently have the city authorities woken up to Mendel's world stature.

As a result there is now a new **Mendel Museum** (April–Oct daily 10am–6pm; Nov–March Wed–Sun 10am–6pm; Ⓦ www.mendel-museum.org) in the west wing of the monastery. Apart from his glasses and the tools of his trade, there's not much of Mendel the man in the museum. Instead, interactive computers explain the basics of genetics, while modern art installations provoke visitors into thinking about the ethical minefield of genetics. There are plans to rebuild Mendel's greenhouse, the foundations of which are visible just outside the museum entrance. You can also ask to go and see Mendel's **beehives**, which are still going strong and are hidden round the back of the monastery church. Before you leave, don't miss the monks' eighteenth-century **refectory**, opposite the ticket office, with its florid Art Nouveau stuccowork and vast relief depicting the abbot ascending into heaven.

Výstaviště and around

To the southwest of the city centre, where the River Svratka opens up to the plain (tram #1 from the station), is the **Výstaviště** (Ⓦ www.bvv.cz) or exhibition grounds. The main buildings were laid out in 1928 for the city's Exhibition of Contemporary Culture, and most of the leading Czech architects of the day were involved in the scheme, which prompted a flurry of functionalist building projects across the city's burgeoning suburbs.

Although Brno produced two great modern architects in Adolf Loos and Jan Kotěra, they spent most of their time in Vienna and Prague respectively, and it was left to another Moravian, **Bohuslav Fuchs**, who began working here in 1923, to shape the face of modern Brno. Fuchs and his functionalist cohorts turned their hand to everything from the town's crematorium to the Protestant church on Botanická, its interior decoration as "low-church" and prosaic as you can get. Fuchs' own hand is everywhere in the city, in the low-slung post office extension to the main train station, in the Alfa *pasáž* off Jánská, in the slimline *Hotel Avion*, on Česká, and in Výstaviště itself. His most famous works are the open-plan boarding school and Vesna girls' school (on Lipová, just north of Výstaviště), two simple four-storey functionalist buildings, way ahead of their time. Perhaps the best way to appreciate Fuchs' work, though, is to head out to the outdoor swimming pool he built in the city's eastern suburbs, just off Zábrdovická (tram #2 or #3; stop Vojenská nemocnice), where you can laze by the pool and take in the culture at the same time.

As you approach the concave entrance to the trade fair grounds, you're greeted by *Atomový věk* (Atomic Age), a classic Social Realist sculpture on a towering plinth. Inside the grounds, the first building you come to is **Pavilón A**, a vast exhibition hall built in 1928, with distinctive concrete parabolic arches; two constructivist red-brick buildings, to the south, also date from the original 1928 exhibition. At the end of the main avenue, you'll find the two postwar additions which have kept closest to the spirit of the original concept: **Pavilón G**, with its glass encased tower, a 1990s reconstruction of an original 1928 building, and the circular crystal-and-concrete **Pavilón Z**, the largest building on the site. The only building which predates the exhibition is the eighteenth-century **zámek**, which features a marble hall on the ground floor designed in 1924 by Brno-born arch-minimalist Adolf Loos.

The part of the 1928 exhibition that really caused a sensation was the **Nový dům** settlement, worth a look if you're keen on Bauhaus-style architecture. Inspired by the Weissenhofsiedlung built a year earlier in Stuttgart, Bohuslav Fuchs and various others designed a series of boxy, white, concrete villas by the woods of the Wilsonův les, north of Výstaviště, up Žabovřeská (tram #1 from Výstaviště), in the streets of Drnovická and Petřvaldská. The brief for each architect was to create modest two-storey houses for middle-income families, using standard fittings and ordinary materials to keep the unit cost down. Many are now grey, peeling and overrun by vegetation, and it takes a leap of imagination to appreciate the shock of the new that these buildings must have aroused at the time.

There are two other sights worth visiting, close, but entirely unrelated, to Výstaviště. The first, visible from the main trade-ground entrance, is a Louis XIV summer palace, **Letohrádek Mitrovských**, an unusual sight in this part of the world. Napoleon stayed here the night before the Battle of Austerlitz (see p.373), while his opposite number, the Russian general Kutuzov, stayed in the Dietrichsteinský palác on Zelný trh. On the opposite side of Výstaviště, over the River Svitava, is **Pavilon Anthropos** (due to re-open in 2005), an annexe of the Moravian Museum, which concentrates on Ice Age geology and fauna, including remains of mammoths, Neanderthals and early *Homo sapiens*. As well as fossil bones and replicas of prehistoric cave paintings, the museum contains numerous paintings by Zdeněk Burian, a Czech painter who specializes in scientifically authentic illustrations of Stone Age life.

Vila Tugendhat

On the opposite side of town, in the northeastern suburb of Černá Pole, modernist guru Mies van der Rohe built the **Vila Tugendhat** (hourly guided tours Wed–Sun 10am–6pm; ☎545 212 118, ⓦwww.tugendhat-villa.cz) in the same functionalist style as the above-mentioned Nový dům settlement, but to a very different brief: the Tugendhats, an exceptionally rich Jewish family who ran a number of the city's textile factories, wanted a state-of-the-art house kitted out in the most expensive gear money could buy. It was completed in 1930, but the family had barely eight years to enjoy the luxury of the place before fleeing to South America (with most of the period furniture) in the wake of the Nazi invasion. For the next fifty years it was put to many uses – both the Nazis and Communists were particularly partial to it for exclusive social functions. From the street, you enter through the top floor, but the main living space is actually downstairs, open-plan for the most part and originally decked out in minimalist monochrome furnishings offset by colourful Persian carpets. The Communists' "modernization" after the war was depressingly thorough, and the huge unbroken front window, which looked out over the garden and the whole cityscape beyond it, has been replaced by a series of much smaller panes, being all the Communists' glassworks could muster. However, plans are afoot to restore the house and gardens to their original state. The house is situated at Černopolní 45, off Merhautova, itself a continuation of M. Horákové (tram #3, #5 or #11; stop Dětská nemocnice). The house is very popular, so it's a good idea to book ahead.

Technické muzeum

Brno's latest attraction is its brand new **Technické muzeum** (Tues–Fri 9am–5pm, Sat & Sun 10am–6pm; ⓦwww.technicalmuseum.cz), located in the far northern suburb of Královo Pole, by the terminus of tram #13. The ticket office is on the first floor from which you should head straight for the museum's **Panoptikon** (April–Oct daily 9am–5pm; Nov–March Mon–Fri 9am–5pm), a large wooden stereoscope built in 1890 and designed to allow several viewers to see its three-dimensional slides simultaneously (the slides are changed every fortnight or so). The permanent exhibition kicks off with a whole host of beautiful **vintage and veteran cars** from a lovely 1910 Austro-Daimler to a postwar Praga limo – look out, too, for the Z4, made by Brno's own Zbrojovka car factory. On the ground floor, there's some pretty technical stuff on steam engines and turbines, with a special section on Viktor Kaplan, who invented his turbine whilst working in Brno. With labelling mostly in Czech, though, it's probably best to head for the more visually engaging exhibits on the second floor, where there are lots of dioramas and mechanical music boxes, model planes, old radios, TVs and telephones plus a wonderful cobbled street of old shops. Finally, on the top floor is the **Experimentárium**, the museum's excellent hands-on section where you can learn some basic scientific principles by playing with plasma balls, gyroscopes, mirrors, magnets and so forth. Anyone with a special interest in trams should visit the museum's transport annexe, **areál MHD** or **Muzeum dopravy** (April & Oct Sat & Sun 9am–5pm; May–Sept Tues–Sun 9am–5pm), Holzova 4, in the eastern suburb of Líseň (tram #8 to terminus, then bus #78).

Eating, drinking and entertainment

There's no shortage of good **places to eat and drink** in Brno, but equally, there's nothing like the choice of cuisines available now in Prague. Brno also has nowhere near the same volume of expats, so prices are uniformly low, and the clientele predominantly Czech. As for **nightlife**, lovers of classical music and opera are well catered for, with two big opera houses/theatres, a philharmonic orchestra, and numerous smaller venues. And with a large contingent of students, the city usually has something a bit less formal going on, particularly during term time. One word of warning, however: Brno (including most of its shops, and even some of its pubs and restaurants) tends to close down for the weekend at around noon Saturday, so if you want to experience city life to the full, come on a weekday.

Eating and drinking

For **Vietnamese fast food** head for one of the branches of the *Asijské bistro*, such as the one on Zelný trh, whose **vegetable market** is also worth a visit if you need provisions. *Paneria*, Česká 32, north of Joštova, is a great **bakery** offering a wide range of sandwiches and pastries. For tasty fresh takeaway Bosnian **burek**, head for the outlet on Minoritská. Also worth knowing about is the useful 24-hour bakery/**deli** called *Jasa*, upstairs at the bottom of Masarykova, opposite the train station.

For simple, traditional **Czech food**, the pubs listed overleaf are likely to be the cheapest; the restaurants, while offering much the same food, are likely to be a bit pricier and a lot more formal.

Restaurants

Aura Kabátníkova 2 ⓦ www.aura.cz. Clean, bright and pleasant veggie restaurant up Lidická just beyond Lužánky, that serves some very unusual and interesting dishes (take a dictionary). Daily 11am–11pm.

Haribol Lužánecká 4. Self-service Hare Krishna restaurant, off Lidická, with a cheap fixed menu of veggie slop. Mon–Fri 10.30am–5pm.

Hotel Slavia Solniční 15–17. Experience Czech cuisine as it was at its best under the Communists in the excellent hotel restaurant. Daily noon–11pm.

Taj Běhounská 12/14. Large, first-floor Indian restaurant with a vast menu that includes lots of veggie options – if you want spice, go for the hottest dishes. Mon–Sat 11am–11pm, Sun noon–10pm.

U královny Elišky Mendlovo náměstí 1a ⓦ vinarna.ukralovnyelisky.cz. Atmospheric cellar *vinárna* tucked into the hillside behind the Augustinian monastery, offering the whole Moravian caboodle, including live folk music. Tues–Sat 7pm–3am.

Cafés

Brno is better for pubs than **cafés**, though of course you can get a coffee in either. During the summer, outdoor tables abound at the various cafés around náměstí Svobody and Zelný trh.

Adria Josefská. A wood-panelled, high-ceilinged café with coffee, cakes and pizzas, run by Yugoslavs but very much in the Viennese tradition. Daily 7am–midnight.

Blau Jakubské nám. Designer café, decked out in (you guessed it) blue, and something of a media hang-out, due to it being located in the same building as Czech TV's Brno studios. Mon–Fri 8am–10pm, Sat 11am–10pm, Sun 2–10pm.

Fischer Masarykova. Continuing the city's tradition for minimalism, this is a stylish designer café in a prime location. Mon–Fri 8am–10pm, Sat 9am–10pm, Sun 10am–10pm.

Rendezvous Moravské nám. Small café next to the Scala cinema, opposite the Místodržitelský palác, serving sweet and savoury *palačinky*.

Mon–Sat 8am–10pm, Sun 10am–10pm.

Spolek Orlí 22. Very pleasant bookshop café with an imaginative veggie-friendly menu featuring soups, risotto, pasta and *palačinky* dishes. Mon–Sat 10am–10pm, Sun 1–10pm.

Švanda Poštovská 8d (Alfa pasáž). Smoky modernist café in the functionalist Alfa pasáž, next door to HaDivadlo. Mon–Fri 9.30am–midnight, Sat & Sun 3pm–midnight.

Zemanova kavárna off Jezuitská ⓦ www .zemanka.cz. An exact replica of Fuchs' functionalist café of 1923, which was torn down by the Communists in order to build the Janáčkovo divadlo; it stands in the park to the southeast of the theatre. Mon–Fri 10am–10pm, Sat & Sun 11am–10pm.

Pubs and bars

Starobrno is the local brew, though according to many the best pubs are those that don't serve it. Brno has its fair share of traditional old boozers, now joined by numerous trendy pubs for the city's young urban professionals.

Charlie's Hat Kobližná 12. Unpretentious pub down a passageway off Kobližná, with a nice shady courtyard and a louder cellar bar with occasional DJs. Mon–Thurs 11am–4am, Fri 11am–5am, Sat noon–5am, Sun 3pm–4am.

Elektra Běhounská ⓦ www.elektra.cz. Cellar pub with modernist decor, serving decent pub grub and Starobrno to a youngish, unpretentious crowd. Mon–Fri 11am–2am, Sat & Sun 5pm–late.

Kabinet múz, Sukova 4–6 ⓦ www.7apul.cz. Lively arty café attached to Divadlo 7 a půl, which puts on films, gigs and events. Mon–Fri 7.30am–1am, Sat 9am–1am, Sun 10am–1am.

Pegas Jakubská 4. If there are any foreigners in town, it's guaranteed they'll be drinking here – and fair enough, for this is a large and very pleasant pub that brews its own light and dark beers on the premises. Daily 9am–midnight.

Pivovarská pivnice Mendlovo nám. The true Starobrno experience: a rough-and-ready drinkers' pub right by the brewery itself, perfectly served 12-degree Starobrno and the rarer 14-degree Baron Trenck. Daily 10am–midnight.

Potrefená husa Joštova 2. Upwardly mobile drinkers head for this modern, designer pub, which shows sports on TV screens and serves the popular Staropramen's ale and stout, Velvet and Kelt. Daily 11am–1am.

Skleněná louka Kounicova 23 ⓦ www .sklenenalouka.cz. Great barrel-vaulted cellar bar by Brno's *Moulin Rouge*, that has occasional live music, and, above it, the city's best Internet café and *čajovna*. Mon–Fri 11am–1am, Sat & Sun 4pm–1am.

Špalíček Zelný trh 12. A Starobrno pub with tables outside in summer overlooking the vegetable market. Daily 11am–11pm.

U dvou kozlů Joštova 1. Old-style big, smoky, beery pub in the pea-green building opposite the church of sv Tomáš, with a youngish crowd supping Velkopopovický *kozel*. Mon–Thurs 9am–1am, Fri 9am–3am, Sat 9am–2am, Sun 10am–midnight.

Entertainment and nightlife

To find out what's on, get hold of the monthly **listings** pamphlet *Kam v Brně* (ⓦ www.kultura-brno.cz) or the more populist weekly *Metropolis*. The Mahenovo divadlo, which boasts the most ornate interior, mostly puts on plays in Czech; the Janáčkovo divadlo stages **opera and ballet**, while the Besední dům, home to the Státní filharmonie Brno (ⓦ www.sfb.cz), hosts regular **classical concerts**. Tickets for the above can be bought in advance from the box office at Dvořákova 11 (Mon–Fri 8am–5.30pm, Sat 9am–noon; ⓦ www.ndbrno.cz), or from the venue itself, half an hour before the performance starts. For chamber music, check out the concert hall of the local music academy, JAMU, on Komenského náměstí.

The same few DJs tend do the rounds of Brno's **clubs**: look out for the flyposters or try *Fléda*, Štefánikova 24 (ⓦ www.fleda.cz), *Remix*, Brandlova 4 (ⓦ www.remixclub.cz) or *Zelená kočka*, Masarykova 25–27 (ⓦ www .zelenakocka.cz). One of the best places to catch **jazz and world music** is at the *Jazzová Kavárna Podobrazy* in the Místodržitelský palác; more traditional jazz enthusiasts flock to Šelepova 1 to the club of the same name (tram #12 or #13 from Joštova, stop Klusáčkova; ⓦ www.selepova.cz). The local **folk music** club meets at the *Klub Leitnerova*, Leitnerova 2 (Tues–Thurs 7.30pm; tram #1 or #2 two stops west from the train station; ⓦ www.volny.cz/leitnerka).

There's an excellent **art-house cinema**, Kino Art, at Cihlářská 19 (ⓦ www .kinoartbrno.cz), a short distance up Lidická from Moravské náměstí. The city hosts its own week-long European film festival, Dny evropského filmu (ⓦ www .eurofilmfest.cz) in February; a festival of spiritual music at Petrov around Easter, Velikonoční festival duchovní hudby; a summer music festival and occasional open-air opera in the Špilberk courtyard; while in late September/early October, there's a three-week-long **international classical music festival**, known as Moravský podzim (ⓦ www.mhfb.cz).

Listings

Books Barvič & Novotný, Česká 13. Brno's best-stocked bookshop, with lots of maps, guides, CDs and posters. Daily until 7pm.

Currency exchange Komerční banka, nám. Svobody 21. 24hr exchange at the main train station.

Hospital Bratislavská 2; emergency medical attention ☎155.

Internet Skleněná louka, Kounicova 23 ⓦwww.sklenenalouka.cz; Čítárna, the municipal reading room on the corner of Kobližná and Poštovská; closed Sun.

Laundrette Self-service laundrette, Údolní 37 (tram #4); Mon–Wed noon–8pm, Thurs & Fri phone ☎604 347 537 to book an appointment.

Left luggage The main train station has 24hr left luggage and lockers.

Motorcycle Grand Prix Brno hosts a world championship motorcycle grand prix at the end of August at the Masarykův okruh (ⓦwww.brnograndprix.com). Special buses are laid on during the competition; otherwise take bus #52 or #54 and walk westwards for five minutes.

Newspapers The newsagents in the train station and the kiosk opposite the main train station has the best selection of foreign newspapers.

Pharmacy All-night service at Kobližna 7 ☎542 210 222.

Police The main police station is at Kounicova 46.

Post office The most convenient post office is next door to the train station. It runs a 24hr telephone exchange.

Taxis The main taxi ranks are outside the station and on Solniční, or dial ☎542 321 321 for City Taxi.

Around Brno

Brno has plenty to keep you occupied, but if you're staying any amount of time, follow the advice of the health authorities (and the example of most of its citizens) and get out of the city at the weekend. One of the few good things about living in Brno's drab concrete suburbs is that you can walk straight out into the woods and bump into a deer or chamois. If that doesn't take your fancy, the most popular day-trip is to the limestone caves of the **Moravský kras**, closely followed by the castle of **Pernštejn** and the battlefield at **Slavkov** (Austerlitz). Potentially more interesting than any of those, however, is the Renaissance chateau at **Moravský Krumlov**, which houses a museum dedicated to the work of the Art Nouveau painter Alfons Mucha.

Moravský kras

Well worth a visit is Moravia's number-one tourist attraction: the limestone **karst region** of the **Moravský kras** (ⓦwww.smk.cz), just over 25km northeast of Brno. There is a whole series of caves to visit, the most popular (and rewarding) being the Punkevní jeskyně, which is the most extensive cave system, and includes an underground river, a giant chasm and the possibility of a cable-car ride. The other caves also feature spectacular stalactites and stalagmites and suffer much less from overcrowding. Quite apart from the caves, the whole karst region boasts some dramatic and varied scenery, all smothered in a thick coating of coniferous forest and riddled with marked paths, providing great **walking** country. If you're not in a hurry, the three churches in Křtiny, Jedovnice and Senetářov and the town of Boskovice deserve a visit, providing a more relaxed alternative to the crush of tourists along the Punkva river.

The caves

The most popular tour target is the **Punkevní jeskyně**, at the deepest part of the gorge – get there early, or get the tourist office to book in advance for you, as tickets can sell out for the whole day in high season. In the summer, tours run every fifteen minutes (April–June & Sept Mon 10am–3.50pm, Tues–Sun 8.20am–3.50pm; July & Aug Mon 10am–3.50pm, Tues–Sun 8.20am–5pm; Oct Tues–Fri 8.40am–2pm, Sat & Sun 8.20am–3.40pm; Nov–March Tues–Sun 8.40am–2pm; ☎516 418 602, ⓦ www.cavemk.cz) and take around an hour. The fantastic array of stalactites and stalagmites justifies the hassle of getting here. After a series of five chambers, you come to the bottom of the **Propast Maco-cha** (Macocha Abyss), a gigantic 138-metre mossy chasm created when the roof of one of the caves collapsed. The first man to descend into the abyss and return alive was Father "Lazarus" Erker in 1728, almost two hundred years before the caves themselves were properly explored. From the abyss, you're punted 500m along the slimy underground Punkva river, which gives the cave its name. Just beyond the entrance to the caves, there's a very steep **cable car** (*lanová dráha*), which can whisk you swiftly to the top of the abyss, so you can look down on where you've just been. If you're going to take the Eko-Train (*vláček*) and the cable car, be sure to buy a *Kombi-Karte* when you first set out.

The two other caves open to the public are only slightly less spectacular, with the added advantage that the queues are correspondingly smaller. The **Kateřin-ská jeskyně** (30min tour: Feb & March Tues–Sun 10am, noon & 2pm; April & Oct Tues–Sun 8.20am–4pm; May–Sept daily 8.20am–4pm), 1.5km before the Punkevní jeskyně at the point where the Punkva river re-emerges, is the largest single cave in the karst region, one huge "cathedral" of rock formations, 100m long and 20m high. The smallest of the lot is the **Balcarka jeskyně** (50min tour: Feb & March Tues–Sun 9am, 11am & 1pm; April Tues–Sun 8am–4pm; May–Sept Mon–Fri 8am–4pm, Sat & Sun 8.30am–4pm; Oct Tues–Sun 9am, 11am, noon, 1pm & 2pm), which lies 2km east of the Propast Macocha. A fourth cave system called **Sloupsko-Šošůvské jeskyně** (60–100min tour: Feb & March Tues–Sun 10am, noon & 1pm; April Tues–Sun 8am–3.30pm; May–Sept Mon 8am, 10am, noon, 2pm & 3pm, Tues–Sun 8am–3.30pm; Oct Tues–Sun 9am, 10am, noon & 1.30pm) sits on the southern edge of the village of Sloup, and has the country's largest underground chasm.

Karst topography

Named after the Karst, the barren limestone plateau around Trieste, **karst** landscapes are formed by the action of rainwater on limestone. Rain picks up small amounts of carbon dioxide from the atmosphere, which, when it falls on limestone rock, slowly dissolves it. Gradually, over millions of years, the action of rain attacking the rock causes hairline cracks in the limestone, which are steadily enlarged by running water. In its early stages, karst scenery is characterized by narrow ridges and fissures; as these grow and deepen, the dry limestone is raked into wild, sharp-edged fragments – practically bare of vegetation since any topsoil is blown away – and bleached bright white, like shards of bone. Karst scenery is found throughout the Czech and Slovak republics, particularly in southern **Moravia** and central and eastern **Slovakia**.

Rivers do odd things in karst landscapes: they disappear down holes where the limestone is weakest, and flow for miles underground, suddenly bursting from rocks when the geology changes. When an underground river widens and forms a cavern, the drips of rainwater percolating through the soil deposit minuscule amounts of the calcium bicarbonate that it has dissolved from the limestone above. Over millions of years these deposits form stalactites hanging from the roof of the cavern; the drips on the floor form columns called stalagmites. Traces of other minerals such as iron and copper colour the stalactites and stalagmites, and the whole process forms cave systems like the **Punkevní jeskyně**.

Practicalities

To get to the caves by public transport, catch a morning **train** from Brno to Blansko station (not Blansko město), and walk 200m southwards to the bus station. From here, **buses** depart for **Skalní Mlýn**, location of the main ticket office and information centre for the **Punkevní jeskyně** caves. Ask at Brno tourist office (see p.352) before setting out, to check that trains and buses connect. All visitors to the caves must either walk the 1.5km from Skalní Mlýn or catch the regular **Eko-Train** service; there are also bikes for hire. Alternatively, it's a very nice five-kilometre walk through the woods all the way from Blansko station along the green-marked path. Make sure you take some warm clothing, as the temperature in the caves is a constant 8.7 degrees Celsius.

The **hotel** *Skálni Mlýn* (☎516 418 113; ❸), in Skálni Mlýn itself, is busy with tourists, but the perfect place to stay if you're keen to visit several of the caves. The nicest **campsite** in the region is *Relaxa* (May–Sept; ☎516 435 237) in Sloup, to the north of the caves, though you'll have to walk or cycle the 5km to the caves, if you've no transport of your own.

Křtiny, Jedovnice and Senetářov

Although buses run to Křtiny, the most rewarding way to reach the village is to take the train from Brno to Adamov zastávka (not Adamov itself) and walk east up the **Josefovské údolí** (the blue-marked path follows the road), a steep, craggy valley with remnants of the original primeval forest cover and open-air stalagmites. After 3km, at the top of the valley, there's a special nature trail round a mini-karst region of around five caves, none of which is actually accessible. Another 3km further east along the blue path, and out of the woods, leaps the enormous dome and tower of the pilgrimage church of **KŘTINY**, designed by the Baroque genius Giovanni Santini. One door is usually open to let you inside, where the nave has been handed over to a series of interlinking frescoed domes that fuse into one, giving the church a Byzantine feel. The interior decor is gaudy High Baroque, especially the main altar, sheltering under its marble baldachin, with technicolour cherubs and saints strewn about the place, but the overall effect is satisfyingly impressive and unified. Only one set of curvaceous cloisters was completed, now filled with the gifts of paintings from previous pilgrims.

Taking the yellow-marked path, skirt the edge of the woods to the northeast, which rise gently past the understated summit of Proklest (574m). Six kilometres on from Křtiny, you emerge from the trees at the small lake by the village of **JEDOVNICE**, no beauty itself, thanks to a fire in 1822, which also torched the late-eighteenth-century village church. From the outside the latter looks hurriedly restored; the interior, however, redesigned in the 1960s, contains symbolic art, stained glass and, as the centrepiece, a striking **altar** painting by Mikuláš Medek, *persona non grata* in Czechoslovakia in the 1950s for his penchant for abstract art, surrealism and social comment. His choice of colours is didactic: a blue cross for hope, and red for the chaos of the world. Unless it's a Sunday, you'll have to get the key from the *kaplan* who lives opposite the church and who can also furnish you with an *anglický text*.

There's no escaping the modernity of Ludvík Kolek's concrete church at **SENETÁŘOV**, completed in 1971, 4km down the road to Výskov; it's built in the shape of a ship, its "mast" visible as you approach from the plateau – though as a concept, its symbolism is reminiscent of the work of Santini. It's an uncompromising building, with huge plate-glass panels at the west end, through which you can clearly see the main altarpiece, an abstract version of the *Last Supper* against a vivid blue background. But it's Medek's *Stations of the Cross*, on the north wall and difficult to see without getting inside, that are the church's masterpiece. Starting with a deep red crown of thorns, the pictures progress in bold, simple colours and symbols, fusing into one long fourteen-piece canvas and signalling an original working of an otherwise hackneyed theme.

On a completely different note, there's a minute folk museum, the **Expozice tradičního bydlení a perlěvářství** (April–Oct Sat & Sun 8am–6pm) in a thatched house opposite the church, with displays on the region's mother-of-pearl button cottage industry, introduced in the 1880s, that flourished until World War I. It was all over by the 1930s, though there is still a button-making factory in the area; ask for an *anglický text* to find out more.

Buses from Brno and Blansko run regularly to Jedovnice, passing through Křtiny and occasionally continuing to Senetářov. Křtiny makes for a good base, with several new pensions such as the *Santini* (☎516 439 432; ❷) and there's the *Olšovec* **campsite** (April–Oct; ⓦwww.olsovec.cz) on the southeastern corner of the lake in Jedovnice.

Boskovice

BOSKOVICE, 17km north of Blansko, guards the Svitava valley. On the whole, it's a sleepy little place, with a modest chateau and a ruined hilltop castle, though it does have one of the best-preserved Jewish quarters in Moravia. Jews began to settle in Boskovice from the fifteenth century onwards, and from 1727 they were incarcerated in a ghetto, with five gates, one of which remains to this day. By the mid-nineteenth century, Jews made up a third of the town's population of around six thousand. To find out more about the town's Jewish history, head for the town's seventeenth-century **synagogue** (April & Oct Sat & Sun 1–5pm; May–Sept Tues–Fri 9am–5pm, Sat & Sun 1–5pm), south of the main square on Antonína Trapla, whose walls and vaults feature beautifully preserved frescoes of flora and fauna. The exhibition inside has photos of the community at its prime and of the transport in March 1942, which sent the town's 458 Jews to Terezín.

To the south of the old town, down Hradní, stands the town's Neoclassical **zámek** (May–Sept Tues–Sun 9am–5pm), built in the 1820s, and with very little of any great interest inside. It was handed back to its former owners, the Mensdorff-Pouilly family, in the 1990s, along with the ruined **hrad** (April & Oct Sat & Sun 10am–4pm; May & Sept Tues–Sun 10am–5pm; June–Aug daily 9am–6pm), which is a five-minute walk further south through the woods.

For something much more mind-blowing, however, you should head out to the **Westernové městečko Boskovice** (from 10am: May & June Sat & Sun; July & Aug Tues–Sun; ⓦwww.wildwest.cz), a wild west theme park about 2km northeast of the town along the blue-marked path. Saloons, rodeos and open-air extravaganzas are just some of the attractions, and you can even stay there on set or in a wagon round the campfire.

Boskovice is a perfectly feasible base for exploring the whole of the Moravský kras, if you have your own transport. To get there by **train** from Brno or Blansko, you need to change at Skalice nad Svitavou. If you want **to stay** somewhere other than the theme park, go to the *Hotel Slavia* (☎501 454 126, ⓦwww.bosnet.cz/hotel-slavia; ❸), by the train station; its restaurant will serve up the usual Czech fare, plus the local Černá hora beer. For a snack, pop into the *Literární čajovna*, a nice little teahouse and bookshop on U císařské, just up from the synagogue.

Pernštejn and Tišnov

The Gothic stronghold of **Pernštejn** is many people's idea of what a medieval castle should look like, and is consequently one of the most popular targets around Brno. The nearest station to Pernštejn is at the village of **NEDVĚDICE** – from the platform, the castle is immediately visible to the west; to get there follow the yellow-marked track. After a series of outer defences, the **hrad** (April & Oct Sat & Sun 9am–noon & 1–4pm; May, June & Sept Tues–Sun 9am–noon & 1–5pm; July & Aug Tues–Sun closes 6pm; Ⓦwww.pamatkybrno.cz) proper is a truly dramatic sight, with kestrels circling the dizzying sheer walls. It was originally built in the thirteenth century, and various reconstructions have left it a jumble of unpredictable angles and extras, including a death-defying covered wooden bridge that spans the castle's main keeps. There's a choice of four different guided tours: *trasa A* is the standard hour-long tour; *trasa B* is twenty minutes longer as it takes in the nineteenth-century period interiors; *trasa C* is also twenty minutes longer, but concentrates on the dungeons and the attics; *trasa D* is a half-hour canter through the chapel, sacristy and clock tower.

The picturesque **train** journey up the Svratka Valley to Nedvědice takes just over an hour from Brno, making this one of the easiest and most rewarding day-trips. If you have to change at **TIŠNOV**, be sure to check out the former Cistercian nunnery, **Porta coeli** (Tues–Sun: May–Sept 9am–noon & 1–5pm; Oct–April 8am–noon & 1–4pm; Ⓦwwwmuzeumbrnenska.cz), named after the church's remarkable Romanesque portal; to get there, take the blue-marked path from the train station for 2km to the neighbouring settlement of Před-klášteří.

Moravský Krumlov

Squeezed into a tight bend of the Rokytná river, southwest of Brno, is **MORAVSKÝ KRUMLOV**, whose **zámek**, to the west of town, boasts a delicate arcaded loggia from 1557, and an **art gallery** (Tues–Sun: April–June, Sept & Oct 9am–noon & 1–4pm; July & Aug closes 5pm), housed in one of the outbuildings, containing paintings and drawings by one of the better-known Czech artists, **Alfons Mucha** (1860–1939). Mucha was actually born in the mining town of Ivančice, a few kilometres to the north, an odd starting point for an artist who is best known for his graceful Art Nouveau posters. The Mucha Museum in Prague (see p.131) has the country's best selection of works from Mucha's most popular period, when he was living in Paris. What you get to see here is the one major work missing from that collection, the *Slovanská epopej* (Slav Epic), a cycle of twenty monumental canvases, commissioned by an American millionaire. In Czech terms they're well-worn themes – Komenský fleeing the "fatherland", the Battle of Vítkov and so on – but they were obviously heartfelt for Mucha, who saw the project as his life's work. In the end he paid for his nationalism with his life: dragged in for questioning by the Gestapo after the 1939 Nazi invasion, he died shortly after being released. In this slightly forlorn chateau, Mucha's gloomy, melodramatic paintings take on a fascination all of their own.

Trains from Brno are fairly frequent and direct (those from Znojmo or Mikulov require you to change at Hrušovany nad Jevišovkou), but the station is a good 2km east of the town; **buses** from Brno and Znojmo will drop you in the centre, but timings are only really any good from Znojmo.

Slavkov and the Battle of Austerlitz

Twenty kilometres by train across the flat plain east of Brno, **SLAVKOV** (Austerlitz) would be just another humble ribbon village were it not for the great mass of Martinelli's late Baroque **zámek** (Tues–Sun: April, Oct & Nov 9am–noon & 1–4pm; May–Sept 9am–noon & 1–5pm; Ⓦwww.zamek-slavkov

.cz). Like so many chateaux close to the Austrian border, its contents were quickly and judiciously removed by their owners before the arrival of the Red Army in 1945; in their place are changing exhibitions, usually on a military theme. The highlight of the 45-minute guided tour is the central concave hall, **Sál předků**, which has the most incredible acoustics. Every whisper of sound in the giant dome echoes for a full ten seconds, while outside not one word can be heard. Martinelli also designed the village's imposing Neoclassical church, with its massive Corinthian portico; inside there are some great high-relief sculptures along the walls and above the high altar.

On December 2, 1805, in the fields between Slavkov and Brno, the Austrians and Russians received a decisive drubbing at the hands of the numerically inferior Napoleonic troops in the **Battle of Austerlitz** (also known as the "Battle of the Three Emperors"). The Austrians and Russians committed themselves early, charging into the morning fog to attack the French on both flanks. From his vantage point on the Žuráň hill to the north, Napoleon, confident of victory, held back until the enemy had established its position, and then attacked at their weakest point, the central commanding heights of the Pratzen hill (Pracký kopec), splitting their forces and throwing them into disarray. It was all over by lunchtime, with over 24,000 troops dead. After the battle, all three emperors signed a peace treaty, marking an end to Napoleon's eastern campaign until the fateful march on Moscow in 1812. There's a graphic description of the battle in Tolstoy's epic novel *War and Peace*.

Just over one hundred years later, on the strategic Pratzen hill, 8km southwest of Slavkov, the **Mohyla míru** (Monument of Peace) was erected on the instigation of a local pacifist priest, and paid for by the governments of France, Austria and Russia, who within three years of pledging the money were once again at war with one another. There's a superb view of the surrounding killing fields, now just a series of ploughed fields peppered with crosses and dotted with the odd little Calvary. The tent-like stone monument, designed by the Art Nouveau architect Josef Fanta, contains a small chapel, and nearby there's a **museum** (April Tues–Sun 9am–5pm; May, June & Sept daily 9am–5pm; July & Aug daily 9am–6pm; Oct–March Tues–Sun 9am–3.30pm; ⓦ www.muzeumbrnenska.cz), including the obligatory toy soldier mock-up of the battle. Military enthusiasts without their own transport have a choice of uphill walks: 2km to the southeast from Ponětovice train station, 3km to the northeast from Sokolnice train station, or 1.5km to the south from the bus stop in Prace. If you happen to be here on the anniversary of the battle, the Friends of the French Revolution treat onlookers to a chilly re-enactment.

There's a **tourist office** next door to the zámek (April, May & Sept–Nov Tues–Sun 9am–4pm; June–Aug Mon–Sat 9am–noon & 12.30–5pm, Sun 11am–5pm; Dec–March Mon–Fri 9am–4pm). For **food**, head for the *Hotel Sokolský dům* (☎544 221 103; ❷), which also offers **rooms** for the night. Another good option is the *Stará pošta* (☎517 375 985, ⓦ www.staraposta.cz; ❻), 4km northwest of Slavkov, on the north side of the motorway, where Napoleon stayed before the battle; it serves decent food, has very nicely furnished rooms, has a small **museum** of militaria and offers horse-drawn tours of the battlefield in the summer.

Bučovice

Ten kilometres further east, and accessible by train from Brno, the **zámek** (April & Oct Sat & Sun 9am–noon & 1–4pm; May–Aug Tues–Sun 9am–noon & 1–4.30pm; Sept Tues–Sun 9am–noon & 1–4pm) at **BUČOVICE**, circled by kestrels, gets a fraction of the visitors of Slavkov, partly perhaps because of its unpromising exterior: a dull grey fortress with four ugly squat towers. None of it prepares you for the subtle, slender Italianate arcading of the courtyard's three-sided loggia, with each set of supporting columns topped by a different carved motif. At the centre of the courtyard a stone fountain was added a few generations later – "a little too robust", as the guide puts it, and out of keeping with the rest of the masonry. The towers, the gardens and countless rooms once matched the charm and elegance of the courtyard, but the Liechtensteins, who obtained the chateau through marriage in 1597, soon turned it into little more than a storage house for the family records, scattering its original furnishings among their many other Moravian residences.

The only things they couldn't remove were the original sixteenth-century **ceiling decorations**, a fantastical mantle of sculpture and paint, coating just five or so rooms, none more than twenty feet across. The first few are just a warm-up for the thick stucco of the **císařský sál**, with the bejewelled relief figures of Mars, Diana, a half-naked Europa and, most magnificent of all, the emperor Charles V trampling a turbaned Turk into the paintwork. But the decoration of the **zaječí sál** (The Hall of Hares) is the real star turn, an anthropomorphic work reckoned to be one of the few of that period still in existence. It's a comical scene, with the hares exacting their revenge on the world of man and his closest ally, the dog. The aftermath of the hares' revolution sees them sitting in judgement (wigs and all) over their defeated enemies, as well as indulging in more highbrow activities – hare as Rembrandt, hare as scholar and so on.

Mikulov and around

Clinging on to the southern tip of the **Pavlovské vrchy**, the last hills before the Austrian plain, **MIKULOV** (Nikolsburg) is one of South Moravia's minor gems. Slap bang in the middle of the wine-producing region, it's been a border post for centuries – hence the narrow streets and siege mentality of much of the architecture. The town still functions as a busy crossing point between the two countries; if you're driving from Vienna, it's a great introduction to the country and, given its strategic locale, surprisingly tourist-free except after the **grape harvest** in late September, when the first bouquet of the year is being tried and tested in vast quantities at the local *sklepy* (wine caves) on the edge of town.

Raised above the jumble of red rooftops is the **zámek** (April & Oct Sat & Sun 9am–4pm; May–Sept Tues–Sun 9am–5pm; Ⓦwww.rmm.cz), an imposing complex built right into the rocky hill on the west side of town. Used by the Gestapo to hoard confiscated art objects, it was blown to smithereens by them in the last days of the war in a final nihilistic gesture. Rebuilt in the 1950s, it now houses the local museum and a large portrait collection, mostly Habsburg royalty, Dietrichsteins and cardinals, though the future George III makes a surprising appearance.

From 1575 onwards, the castle and town were in the hands of the fervently Catholic Dietrichsteins, who established various religious edifices and institutions here. They're also responsible for the hint of Renaissance in the town and the main square itself, which is called simply **Náměstí**, appealingly misshapen and centred on a vast, ornate Trinity column. **U rytířů**, on the corner of the square, has a sixteenth-century sgraffito facade, depicting, among other things, Noah's flood, with the ark in a sea of drowning sinners. The local church of **sv Václav**, to the north of the square, boasts a galleried Renaissance tower – its interior is worth a quick peek for its heavy stuccoed vaulting and the ubiquitous Dietrichstein coat of arms.

Later, behind the square's vast, ornate Trinity column, the family built the church of sv Anna, with a Loreto chapel within – this popular pilgrimage church burned down in the town fire of 1784. The imposing Neoclassical facade that you now see, with its stumpy square towers, dates from the mid-nineteenth century, when the Dietrichsteins decided to turn the church into the family mausoleum or **Dietrichštejnská hrobka** (guided tours every 30min; April–Oct Tues–Sun 9am–5pm). The whole place has recently been thoroughly restored, though the main reason to have a wander inside is for the view from amidst the angels on the church's roof. The family was also responsible for the series of chapels visible to the east of the town on the bleak, exposed limestone hill of **Svatý kopeček**, well worth the climb for the view across the vineyards towards Vienna.

Mikulov boasted one of the most important Jewish communities in central Europe until the advent of the Nazis: in the mid-nineteenth century it was the second largest in the Czech Lands, with twelve synagogues, and was the seat of the chief rabbi (Landesrabbiner) of Moravia from the sixteenth century until 1851. The old **Jewish ghetto** lies to the west of the castle, where the town's sixteenth-century **synagogue** (mid-May to Sept Tues–Sun 10am–5pm), on Husova, has been renovated. Uniquely for a Czech synagogue, the Baroque interior is in the Lvov style, with a four-columned pink marble pillar over the bimah; the main body of the building is used for temporary exhibitions while the women's gallery houses an exhibition on Jewish religious practices. Round the corner in Brněnská, a rugged path leads to the overgrown medieval **Jewish cemetery** (Židovský hřbitov), with over four thousand graves and some finely carved marble tombstones dating back to 1605; to get into it, you'll need to pick up the key from Husova 4 or the tourist office, though it's closed on Saturdays.

The town is rarely busy, except during the September wine festival, the majority of visitors pausing for a couple of hours at the most before moving on. The town centre is ten minutes' walk northeast of the **train station**: take the footbridge over the main road and continue up the hill. There's a **tourist office** on the main square (daily: May–Sept 8am–6pm; Oct–April Mon–Fri 8.30am–noon & 1–5pm, Sat & Sun 9am–4pm; Ⓦwww.mikulov.cz), which can help with **accommodation** and any other queries. The best of the hotels is the *Rohatý krokodýl*, in the former Jewish quarter at Husova 8 (☎519 510

The Brno Death March

On May 30, 1945 an estimated 23,000 German-speaking Czechs from Brno and its environs were rounded up and forced to walk the 60km from Brno into Austria. Deportees were allowed to take only what they could carry (and no money or jewels). The following night, the refugees reached the village of **Pohořelice**, just over halfway from Brno to the border. Those who were too weak or ill with dysentery to continue were housed in a local brick factory. The Czechs maintain that their doctors treated the sick and that all those who died were victims of dysentery. Sudeten Germans argue that acts of brutality and mass murder were committed, while others died of starvation. No one knows quite how many Germans were buried in Pohořelice, but after years of official silence on the matter during the Communist period, a memorial to 890 known victims was finally erected in 1992 by the farm field in which the victims were buried, on route 52, just south of Pohořelice.

692, Ⓦwww.rohatykrokodyl.cz; ❸), with the *Pension Moravia* (☎777 634 560, Ⓦwww.moravia.penzion.com; ❷), at Poštovní 1, off Česká, a useful fall-back. Good quality **bike rental** is available from *Topbicycle*, on Kostelní náměstí, just north of the main square.

The *Rohatý krokodýl's* **restaurant**, and the *Alfa* restaurant on the main square, both serve the usual Czech pub fare, while *Petit Café*, next door to the *Alfa*, specializes in *palačinky*. But the home cooking at *U nás doma*, at the far end of 1 května, ten minutes' walk northeast of the town centre, is better than any of the above.

Pálava

Mikulov is the starting point for hiking and exploring the **Pavlovské vrchy**, a big, bulging ridge of rugged and treeless limestone hills, and the surrounding region, known as the **Pálava**. Since the damming of the Dyje and the creation of the artificial Nový mlýn lake, the rare plant life on the Pavlovské vrchy has suffered badly. On the plus side, the lake has attracted much greater numbers of waterfowl, as well as eagles, falcons and black and red kites, and the whole area is now a protected region. It's also good, gentle **hiking country**, with wide-angle views on both sides and a couple of picturesque ruined castles along the ten-kilometre red-marked path to Dolní Věstonice.

Archeological research has been going on here since 1924, when an early Stone Age settlement was discovered. Brno's Moravské zemské muzeum (see p.356) displays the best findings, which include wolves' teeth jewellery and clay figurines such as the voluptuous *Venus of Věstonice*, a tiny female fertility figure with swollen belly and breasts. However, there is a small **Archaeologická expozice** (Tues–Sun 8am–noon & 1–5pm) in Dolní Věstonice, which, despite the lack of information in English, exhibits some interesting finds: skulls, a woolly mammoth's tooth, several animal and fertility statues, including, inevitably, a copy of the aforementioned Venus. From Dolní Věstonice you can either walk another 4km to the station on the main Brno-Břeclav line at Popice or catch one of the hourly buses back to Mikulov.

If you want to stay in the area, *Vinařský dům* (☎519 515 395, Ⓦwww.silinek.nakupujeme.cz; ❷) is a lovely small seventeenth-century **pension** in Pavlov. 3km east of Dolní Věstonice. Alternatively, there are several **campsites** along the shores of the Nový mlýn lake – *Merkur* (mid-April to Oct; Ⓦwww.pasohlavky.cz), near Pasohlávky, 10km north of Mikulov, has its own lagoons, bungalows for hire, windsurfing and bike rental.

Lednicko-Valtický areál

To the southeast of Mikulov, nose to nose with the Austrian border, is the UNESCO-protected **Lednicko-Valtický areál**, a landscape dominated by the twin residences of the Liechtensteins, one of the most powerful landowning families in the country until 1945 (see box opposite). The chateaux lie 7km apart at either end of a dead-straight lime-tree avenue, in a vast, magnificent stately park, dotted with follies (including a sixty-metre minaret) and fish ponds and surrounded by acres of woodland – in many ways, it's this delightful setting that is the best feature of the whole area. However, being in a low-lying area prone to flooding, mosquitoes can be something of a problem in summer – worth bearing in mind if you're camping.

The Liechtensteins

The **Liechtensteins** (of Grand Duchy fame) were for many centuries one of the most powerful families in the Czech Lands, particularly in Moravia. At their peak in the seventeenth century they owned no fewer than 99 estates – one more and they would have had to maintain a standing army in the service of the emperor. The one who made the most of all this wealth was Prince-Bishop Karl Eusebius von Liechtenstein-Kastelcorn, who came into the family fortune in 1627, and whose motto – "Money exists only that one may leave beautiful monuments to eternal and undying remembrance" – can be seen in practice all over Moravia.

Like nearly all the ethnic Germans who lived in Czechoslovakia, the Liechtensteins were forced to leave in 1945 and retreat to their minuscule alpine country. For the next 45 years it looked like the long history of the Liechtensteins in the Czech Lands had come to an end. Then, in 1990, the new government passed a law of *restituce* (restitution), which meant that all property confiscated by the Communists from 1948 onwards was to be handed back to its original owners. Despite having had their property taken from them in the earlier appropriations of 1918 and 1945, the Liechtensteins continue to request compensation from the Czech government for the seizure of their former residences, which comprise something like 1600 square kilometres of land – ten times the area of present-day Liechtenstein.

Lednice

The most popular of the two chateaux is undoubtedly the family's summer residence at **LEDNICE** (Eisgrub). Part of the Liechtenstein estate since 1243, the **zámek** (April & Oct Sat & Sun 9am–noon & 1–4pm; May–Aug Tues–Sun 9am–noon & 1–6pm; Sept closes 5pm; ⓦ www.lednice.cz) was subjected to a lavish rebuild job in the 1840s, which turned it into a neo-Gothic extravaganza. Part of the chateau is occupied by an exhibition devoted to agriculture, but there's plenty to look at on the main guided tour, with vivid, over-the-top Romantic interiors crowding each of its wood-panelled rooms. If fake medievalism doesn't turn you on, however, head instead for the chateau's vast wrought-iron and glass palm house or **palmový skleník** (April & Oct Tues–Sun 9am–noon & 1–3.30pm; May–Sept Tues–Sun 9am–noon & 1–5.30pm; Nov, Dec, Feb & March Sat & Sun 9am–noon & 1–3.30pm). Those with kids in tow might want to seek out the new **Akvárium Malawi** (April–Oct daily 9am–5pm; Nov–March Sat & Sun 9am–4pm), in a wing of the Baroque stables. It's something of an ad-hoc installation, and there's very little information on offer, but you're guaranteed to see piranhas, alligators, terrapins and countless colourful tropical fish.

Zámecký park

Best of all in Lednice is the expansive, watery **Zámecký park**, home to numerous herons, grebes and storks, as well as regular falconry displays in summer. You can either explore the park on foot, or catch one of the **boats** (ⓦ www.1plavebni.cz) that head off from the first bridge you come to for the minaret (every 20–30min; 25min) and the Janův hrad (hourly; 45min). Piqued by local objections to their plan for a colossal church, the Liechtensteins decided in 1797 to further alienate the village by building the largest **minaret** (April & Oct Sat & Sun 10am–4pm; May–Aug Tues–Sun 10am–6pm; Sept Tues–Sun 10am–5pm) outside the Islamic world, which dominates the view of the park from the chateau; it's equally impressive close to, smothered in Arabic script, golden baubles and crescent moons, and you can climb to the top (60m) for a great view over the park. Further east is the Janův hrad or **Janohrad** (April & Oct Sat & Sun 9am–4,45pm; May–Sept Tues–Sun 9am–4,45pm), a ruined "Gothick" castle, round which there are guided tours every 45 minutes.

Valtice

VALTICE (Feldsberg), 7km southwest of Lednice, was ceded to the Czechs by the Austrians during a minor border adjustment dictated by the 1920 Treaty of St Germain, and from the end of the English-style gardens of the town's enormous Baroque **zámek** (Tues–Sun: April, Sept & Oct 9am–noon & 1–4pm; May–Aug 8am–noon & 1–5pm; Ⓦwww.valtice.cz) you used to be able to see the watchtowers of the Iron Curtain in amongst the chateau's vineyards (which incidentally produce a good Moravian red). Once the family's foremost residence – over and above Liechtenstein itself – Valtice looks great from the outside, but was cleaned out just before the end of World War II, leaving its beautifully restored interior relentlessly bare. However, the east wing has been converted into a budget hotel and restaurant that does a brisk trade with holidaying Austrians.

The follies

Apart from the minaret and the ruined Janův hrad in Lednice's chateau grounds, numerous other **follies** were erected on a grand scale for the Liechtensteins in the early nineteenth century by Josef Kornhäusel and Josef Hardtmuth amidst the woods of the **Boří les** and the ponds that lie between Lednice and Valtice. The easiest to reach from Valtice, however, is the **Kolonáda na Rajstně**, a vast Neoclassical colonnade about 1km southwest of the town along the red-marked path or just off the road to Schrattenberg in Austria. To reach the Boří les, take the scenic red-marked path from Valtice train station, 2km through the woods, part of the way along a tree-lined avenue, to the triumphal arch called **Rendezvous**, which contains a concert hall and ballroom on the top floor. Another 1.5km deeper into the woods brings you to the Neo-Gothic chapel of **sv Hubert**, a popular picnic spot, and then for a similar distance north to the **Chrám tří grácií**, a curving colonnade sheltering a copy of the *Three Graces*; on the opposite bank of the nearby pond stands another Kornhäusel folly, the **Rybniční zámeček**.

A short distance east of the Tří Grácií, by the railway line, stands the **Nový dvůr**, an ornate structure with a central rotunda-cum-cowshed, which featured glass partitions, built by the Liechtensteins for rearing sheep, rare-breed cattle and more latterly horses. Beyond, on the other side of the railway, is the **Apollonův chrám**, a Neoclassical pavilion overlooking one of the two fifteenth-century fish ponds, now a popular summer swimming spot. A couple of kilometres west of the Tří Grácií, on the other side of the village of **HLOHOVEC** (Bischofswarth), is the **Hraniční zámeček**, which used to stand on the historic border between Austria and Moravia (hence its name – *hranice* meaning "border"), and now houses a very smart hotel and restaurant (see opposite).

Practicalities

Valtice is just twenty minutes by **train** from Mikulov and twenty-five from Břeclav. Between Valtice and Lednice, there are just a couple of buses a day. If you're here at the weekend, it's worth taking the lovely red 1955 Tatra diesel train to Lednice from Břeclav (April–Sept Sat & Sun; mid-May to mid-June Tues–Sun); you can even go by **boat** up the Dyje from Břeclav (July & Aug Sat & Sun; Ⓦwww.lodnidoprava.com). The most convenient place to stay if you're travelling by train might well be the rather drab town of Břeclav (Lundenberg), 8km east of the two chateaux, on the main line from Prague to Bratislava or Vienna, but you'll have a much better time in either Lednice or Valtice.

The best **accommodation in Lednice** is *My Hotel* (℡519 340 130, Ⓦwww.myhotel.cz; ❹), a large modern hotel up the road to Podivín, with good disabled access; alternatively, there's the by no means small *Pension Jordán* (℡519 340 285; ❷), which has clean, brightly painted en-suite rooms. The *Zámecká restaurace*, just inside the chateau gates, will furnish you with inexpensive Czech **food** and beer.

The **accommodation in Valtice** tends to be better value, particularly the plain rooms of the *Hubertus* (℡519 352 537; ❸) in the chateau itself, and the *Apollon* (℡519 352 625; ❷), set in its own gardens up the *lipovej alej* at P. Bezruče 720. The best place to **eat and drink** the local wine in Valtice is the *Vinářský dům*, opposite the church. An even better restaurant, with views across one of the lakes, can be found in the *Hraniční zámeček* (℡519 354 353, Ⓦwww.hranicnizamecek.cz; ❹), in Hlohovec, which also offers excellent rooms, some with facilities for the disabled. Note, however, that all accommodation in the area tends to be fully booked in the middle of August when there's a Baroque Music Festival in Valtice.

Znojmo

Like Mikulov, 45km to the east, **ZNOJMO** (Znaim) enjoys a spectacular hilltop location, this time high above the Dyje, along with an old town blessed with an unrivalled set of Romanesque frescoes. What puts many first-time visitors off is that, unlike Mikulov, Znojmo's industry and suburbs have spread out in an unsightly fashion to the north and east over the last hundred years. It's also something of a classic Czech border town, long blighted by the Iron Curtain, and now plagued by brothels and other institutions making a quick euro or two out of day-tripping Austrians.

The Town

Znojmo's main square, **Masarykovo náměstí**, was badly damaged in World War II, and the former Capuchin monastery at the bottom of the square is as uninspiring as the concrete supermarket that squats at the opposite end. The central Marian column survives, however, with its striking pink sandstone plinth and four accompanying saints. A couple of attractive surviving buildings on the east side of the square also deserve attention: the **Měšťanský dům**, which has a very fine sixteenth-century stone portal and matching pilasters, and the **Dům umění** (Tues–Sat 9am–5pm; ℡515 282 211), a beautiful Renaissance building, two doors down. The latter has an arcaded courtyard out back, and diamond vaulting on the first floor, where temporary exhibitions are held. On the second floor there's a room devoted to local artist, Jan Tomáš Fisher, a pupil of Otakar Španiel, who, like his master, specialized in designing reliefs on medals. There's also a small collection of Gothic and Baroque art, particularly strong on sculpture, and a genial English-speaking curator to show you round.

Hope rears up at the top of the square, in the shape of the late-Gothic pinnacled and baubled **radniční věž** (May–Sept Mon–Fri 9am–6pm, Sat & Sun 9am–5pm; Oct–April Mon–Fri 9am–6pm, Sat 9am–noon), all that's left of the old town hall, burnt down by the Nazis in the closing stages of the war. From this soaring romantic affair, its uppermost gallery twisting at an angle to the

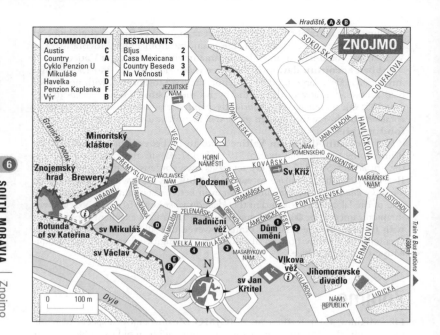

main body, the view through its wooden hatches is little short of spectacular – a good way to get your bearings and a feel for the old town. One block east on Slepičí trh (Chicken Market) is the entrance to the town's underground tunnels or **podzemí** (April Mon–Sat 10am–4pm; May–June & Sept daily 9am–4pm; July–Aug daily 9am–5pm; Oct Sat 10am–4pm) that run for miles under the old town; originally built for defensive purposes, they were later used for storing wine.

At this point you can head off in a number of directions, but the most interesting is the narrow lane of Velká Mikulášská, which leads to the oldest part of Znojmo – a tight web of alleyways woven round the cathedral of **sv Mikuláš**, a plain Gothic hall church sporting an unusual gable embellished with blind arcading. Inside, it has retained its elegant Gothic net vaulting and slender round pillars, but the most amazing thing about the church is its Baroque pulpit: a giant globe, with its top sliced off, crowned by a sounding board of free-flying clouds, sunbursts, cherubs and saints. Also worth inspecting is the glass coffin underneath the organ loft, containing the macabre clothed skeleton of a Christian martyr.

Set at a right angle to the cathedral is the much smaller **chapel of sv Václav**, tucked into the town walls, from which you get a commanding view up and down the Dyje valley as it blends into the Austrian plain. The chapel itself is a curious building, built literally on top of its Gothic predecessor in the sixteenth century, when the town's fortifications against the Turks were erected (and smothered the old building). The church now belongs to the local Orthodox community, and the priest will happily show you round the chapel and the bare Gothic original.

"Better a living brewery than a dead castle", goes one of the more obscure Czech proverbs, and as far as **Znojemský hrad** (May–Sept Tues–Sun

9am–5pm; ⓦwww.znojmuz.cz) goes it's hard to disagree. The parts that didn't become a brewery have since been turned into a deceptively large local **museum** distinguished, for the most part, by its trompe l'oeil Baroque fresco in the oval entrance hall, glorifying the Deblín family, who rebuilt the chateau in 1720 only to run out of male heirs in 1784. To reach the museum, take the special path (daily: May–Sept 9am–9pm; Oct–April 9.30am–8pm) that runs along the perimeter of the brewery. The castle's most precious relic is the **Rotunda** (times as above), home to the best-preserved twelfth-century frescoes in the country, including contemporary portraits of the Přemyslid princes. Note that access is sometimes restricted in bad weather in order to protect the paintings.

In fine weather the local museum in the former **Minoritský klášter** (Mon–Fri 9am–5pm; plus May–Aug Sat & Sun same hours), opposite the brewery, is worth skipping in favour of a scramble in the thickly wooded deep gorge of the Podyjí national park, that begins as soon as you leave the town walls at the end of Přemyslovců. It's a gentle wander round the foot of the castle to the chapel of sv Václav, but for a longer **walk** and an unbeatable vista of Znojmo and the Dyje, take the blue-marked path down to the stream and then the green-marked path past the Stations of the Cross, up to the village and nunnery of Hradiště; bus #1 will run you back into town.

Practicalities

Trains run fairly frequently from Mikulov to Znojmo, taking around an hour; trains from Brno take around two hours, often with a change (but no wait) at Hrušovany nad Jevišovkou. The old town is a stiff hike from the station: up 17 listopadu to Marianské náměstí, then west along Pontassievská and Zámečnická. If you're heading into Austria, there's a 24-hour **border crossing** at Hatě, 12km southeast on route 38 (the occasional bus goes there), and a railway border crossing at nearby Šatov.

The **tourist office** (April–Sept Mon–Fri 8am–6pm, Sat 9am–5pm; Oct–March Mon–Fri 8am–6pm, Sat 8am–12.30pm; ⓦwww.znojmocity.cz), at Obroková 12, can help with **accommodation**. It has two branches: in the Vlkova věž, on the southeast corner of the main square (same hours), and near the castle (Tues–Sun 9.30am–4.30pm). Your best bet is to try one of the town's small pensions, such as the excellent *Havelka* (☎515 220 138; ❷), right by the church of sv Mikuláš, or the *Austis*, Václavské náměstí 5 (☎515 241 949; ❸). Another good choice is the *Cyklo Penzion U Mikuláše*, Mikulášské náměstí 8 (☎515 220 856; ❷), a Dutch pub run by a couple of sculptor brothers keen on cycling. Directly behind it is the *Penzion Kaplanka* (☎515 224 093, ⓦwww .kaplanka.cz; ❷), wonderfully located at the edge of the Dyje valley. There are two good **campsites** to the north of Znojmo: the family-run *Country* **campsite** (May–Oct; ⓦwww.camping-country.com,), in Hluboké Mašůvky, 7km up route 361, and the lakeside *Výr* (June–Sept) site near Výrovice, 10km away off route 399 to Plaveč.

There are plenty of **restaurants** to choose from, but *Na Věčnosti*, Velká Mikulášská 11, is a real find: a pleasant, mostly veggie restaurant-gallery, which offers *bryndzové halušky*, a whole range of *smažený sýr*, pasta and even fish dishes; they have **Internet** access and even put on the occasional bit of live music. Another interesting option is *Bljus*, Dolní Česká 21 (closed Sat & Sun), which serves Russian staples like borscht and dumplings washed down with the local Hostan beer. Opposite, *Casa Mexicana* is good for tortillas and *pescado empanado*, while the *Country Beseda*, Masarykovo náměstí 22, offers an interesting mix of Czech and American food, like *Kuřecí prsa Bronko Billy*. Znojmo stages its own **wine** festival, *Znojemské vinobraní*, in the middle of September. Aside from booze, **pickled gherkins** (*kyselá okurka*) flavoured with paprika are another Znojmo speciality to look out for.

Podyjí

The meandering River Dyje and the artificial Vranov lake to the west of Znojmo are now part of the heavily forested and very pretty **Podyjí** national park, which provides a summer playground for large numbers of holidaying Czechs. There are plenty of opportunities for swimming and lazing around, plus a couple of interesting chateaux and lots of hiking possibilities. Without your own transport, getting about can be time-consuming, so you might want to plan to spend at least two or three days in the area.

Vranov

The village of **VRANOV NAD DYJÍ** (Frain), 20km west of Znojmo, is a scruffy place, but it sits below an incredible cliff-top **zámek** (April & Oct Sat & Sun 9am–noon & 1–4pm; May, June & Sept Tues–Sun 9am–noon & 1–5pm; July & Aug 9am–noon & 1–6pm; 130Kč; ⓦwww.pamatkybrno.cz), magnificently poised on a knife's edge above the Dyje. Originally a medieval stronghold, it was converted into a beautiful Baroque chateau by the Viennese genius Johann Bernhard Fischer von Erlach after a fire in 1665. Nothing else on the guided tour of the sprawling complex (not even the medieval sauna) can quite compare to Fischer's trump card at the far end – the cavernous dome of the **Sál předků** (Ancestors' Hall), whose truly awesome overall effect is as much due to Rottmayr's wild frescoes as to Fischer's great oval skylights: its frenzied, over-the-top paintings depict the (fictitious) achievements of the Althan family who commissioned the work. One other piece of Fischer von Erlach genius worth inspecting is the palace's tiny **chapel** (June & Sept Sat & Sun 9am–5pm; July & Aug Tues–Sun 9am–6pm), a visit to which is not included in the chateau tour. Again, it's the frescoes, executed by a pupil of Rottmayr, that make the place so special: the main fresco features the Archangel Michael smiting Satan's followers who tumble over the cornice itself, while in the side chapels skeletons frolic and angels pray.

One of the most interesting **walks** in the area is to take the red-marked path from Vranov village along the Dyje, then up into the woods and hills until you reach the road which runs from Čížov to the Austrian border (6km). From here, it's just 2km by either the blue-marked path by the road, or the green-marked path through the woods via the Hardeggská vyhlídka, a lookout post from which you can view the picturesque Austrian border village of Hardegg with its own castle (April to mid-Nov 9am–5pm; July–Aug till 6pm; €6.50), accessible via a small footbridge. The round trip is about 16km and will take all day, so carry a picnic, or some euros, in order to grab a bite to eat in Hardegg (and, of course, your passport).

Practicalities

At the weekend **buses** run regularly from Znojmo to Vranov, less often during the week. Alternatively, you could take the more frequent **train** to Sumná station and walk the 4km along the green-marked path to Vranov. In the centre of Vranov, you can **stay** above the friendly, family-run *Country Saloon* courtyard pub (☏515 296 238, ⓦwww.country.saloon.web.wo.cz; ➋) or in the newly refurbished en-suite rooms of the grandiose *Zámecký hotel* (☎515 296 101, ⓦwww.zameckyhotel.cz; ❸), some of which have views of the chateau. From the village, it's a fifteen-minute walk to the dam (*přehrada*) and the sandy **beach** known as Vranovská pláž, accessible via the new footbridge across the lake. From May to September there's a fair bit of life here: a couple of **campsites** (May–Sept), chalets, boat rental, a couple of shops and an occasional **boat service** up the lake to Bítov and beyond. The sun-worshippers are shoulder to shoulder on the beach in the high season, but it's easy to lose the crowd by picking a rocky spot further upstream.

Bítov

The village of **BÍTOV**, 8km west up the lake, and high above the shore, is nowhere near as dramatically situated as Vranov. It does, however, have at least one decent **place to stay**: the popular café/pension *U Tesařů* on the main square (☎ & ⓕ515 294 616, ⓦutesaru.hyperlinx.cz; ❷), which offers modern, comfortable rooms and decent Czech food. The nearby *Bítov-Horka* **campsite** (May–Sept; ⓦwww.volny.cz/mucha_karel) is ideally situated down by the lakeside. The only way to get from Vranov to Bítov – apart from hitching or walking – is to take the aforementioned **boat** from the Vranovská pláž. There are just one or two buses from Znojmo to Bítov; connections with Jihlava (see p.388) are much the same.

The ruined castle that can be seen from the lake is the fourteenth-century fort of **Cornštejn** (July–Aug daily 9am–5pm), which unfortunately can be explored only with a guide. Bítov's own **hrad** (April & Oct Sat & Sun 9am–noon & 1–4pm; May, June–Sept Tues–Sun 9am–noon & 1–5pm, July & Aug closes 6pm) has weathered slightly better and is located 2.5km to the west of the village, along the red-marked path. Like Vranov, it boasts a classic defensive location on a spit of grey rock high above the river, which the flooding of the valley has diminished only slightly, and for this reason alone it's worth clambering up to enjoy the view. In the castle's courtyard there's a lovely, cool thirteenth-century **wine cellar** where you can taste and purchase the local wine, and an *občerstvení* where you can get a snack and a glass of beer, but inside, lacking Fischer's ingenious touch, the castle's not a patch on Vranov. The hour-long **guided tour** (*trasa 1*; 130Kč) through the contrived neo-Gothic decor and soulless, unlived-in rooms is enlivened only by a pack of stuffed dogs. The castle's second floor is occupied by the **armoury** (*trasa 2*; 170Kč), with a wide-ranging collection of seventeenth-century weapons.

Třebíč and around

TŘEBÍČ, 70km due west of Brno, is best known for its Romanesque basilica and its newly restored Jewish ghetto – both protected by UNESCO since 2003. In most other respects, it's a fairly nondescript town, though it does serve as a useful jumping-off point for the tongue-twisting Baroque chateaux of Jaroměřice nad Rokytnou and Náměšť nad Oslavou.

The Town

Apart from a couple of sgraffito facades, the main square, **Karlovo náměstí**, is pretty undistinguished, though its grandiose scale gives some hint of the town's medieval importance. Třebíč's former glory is almost entirely down to the Benedictine monastery, which was founded in 1101 on a hill on the north bank of the River Jihlava, to the west of the town centre. The monastery was closed down as early as the fifteenth century, and transformed into a chateau, which now houses the local **museum** (April–June & Sept–Oct Tues–Sun 8am–noon & 1–5pm; July–Aug daily 8am–5pm; Nov–March Tues–Sun 8am–noon & 1–4pm; ⓦwww.zamek-trebic.cz), whose displays include an unusually large selection of nativity scenes. However, it's the former monastery church, the big grey **Basilica of sv Prokop** (Tues–Thurs 9am–noon & 1–5pm, Fri 9am–noon & 1–4.30pm, Sat–Mon 1–5pm), that's the real draw here. Although heavily restored in the Baroque period, and again between the wars, the church nevertheless retains much of its original mid-thirteenth-century architecture, a transitional style between Romanesque and Gothic, particularly in the vast north portal, the chancel, the galleried apse and the crypt.

Back down in the town, squeezed up against a hill, the northern bank of the river was for centuries the town's **Jewish ghetto** known as Zámostí. Třebíč's Jewish population peaked at the end of the eighteenth century, at over 1700 (nearly 60 percent of the total population of the town), but by the 1930s had dwindled to just 300, most of whom subsequently perished in the Holocaust. The ghetto was already a shadow of its former self by the outbreak of the war, but it's ironic that only now, with virtually no Jews left in Třebíč, is the Jewish quarter finally being restored. Architecturally, the ghetto remains remarkably intact – it's currently home to many of the town's local Romanies, though with renovation (and gentrification) continuing apace, probably not for long.

Now linked by a new pedestrian bridge to a passageway on the north side of the main square, the ghetto originally had to be approached from what is now Žerotinovo náměstí, by the road bridge to the west of the main square. Here, the narrow ghetto entrance by no. 114 was sealed off by a chain on the Sabbath, beyond which the quarter's two main cobbled streets run parallel with each other. At the western end of the ghetto, on Tiché náměstí, is the former **Přední synagoga** (Front Synagogue), which had to be reduced in height in the Baroque period after complaints by the Countess of Valdštejn; it was handed over to the Czechoslovak Hussite Church in the 1950s. At the eastern end of the two streets you can visit the **Zadní synagoga** (Rear Synagogue; daily 10am–noon & 1–5pm), whose walls are painted in Hebrew script and decorated with vegetal and floral motives. In the women's gallery there's an exhibition on the Jewish life of Třebíč, and, in the main body of the synagogue, a memorial to the 290 Jews who died in the Holocaust. To reach the **Jewish cemetery** (Židovský hřbitov; daily: March–April & Oct 8am–6pm, May–Sept 8am–8pm; Nov–Feb 9am–4pm; free), which contains some three thousand graves dating from the seventeenth century to the 1930s, follow the signs up the hill and down Hrádek.

You can gain a good overview of the town from the **Městská věž** (May–Sept daily 10am–5pm), which belongs to the church of sv Martin, to the south of the main square.

Practicalities

Třebíč is on the main line from Brno to Jihlava, and the **train station** is fifteen minutes' walk south of the main square; the **bus station** is a block or so west of the main square on Komenského náměstí, while the **tourist office** (April–May & Oct Mon–Fri 8am–6pm, Sat 9am–1pm; June & Sept Mon–Fri 8am–6pm, Sat 9am–noon & 1–5pm; July–Aug Mon–Fri 8am–6pm, Sat & Sun 9am–noon & 1–5pm; Nov–March Mon–Fri 8am–5pm, Sat 9am–1pm; ⓦwww.kviztrebic.cz)

is in the town hall, at the western end of the main square. **Accommodation** is thin on the ground, with the *Hotel Slavia*, Karlovo náměstí 5 (☎568 848 560, ⓦwww.hotel-trebic.cz; ❸), leading the charge; it's supremely ugly on the outside but inside is not so bad. A better bet is the *Penzion U synagogy* (☎568 823 005; ❷), next door to the Žádní synagoga. For **food** and **beer**, try the smart *V černem domě*, with outdoor seating, in the sgraffito house at no. 16, on the north side of the main square. Alternatively, there's the fish restaurant *Neptun* near the Přední synagoga.

Jaroměřice nad Rokytnou

The small town of **JAROMĚŘICE NAD ROKYTNOU**, 14km south of Třebíč, is completely overwhelmed by its gargantuan russet-and-cream Baroque **zámek** (April & Oct Sat & Sun 9am–noon & 1–4pm; May–June & Sept Tues– Sun 9am–noon & 1–5pm, July & Aug closes 6pm), built over the course of 37 years by the wealthy and extravagant Johann Adam von Questenberg. For the most part it's the work of Dominico d'Angeli, but the two Austrian architects Jakob Prandtauer and Johann Lukas von Hildebrandt also appear to have been involved at various stages. The highlights of the chateau are the elegant Rococo halls, the Hlavní sál and the Táneční sál, where Questenberg used to put on lavish classical concerts. To see these you must join the forty-five-minute *1. trasa*; the twenty-five-minute *2. trasa* only takes you round the later interiors and the porcelain collection. Alternatively, you could skip both tours and spend the morning exploring the great domed and frescoed chapel (now the local parish church) or pottering around the formal gardens. Even better, come during July and August, when the chateau stages a festival of classical music. Jaroměřice is on the train line from Znojmo to Jihlava, but from Třebíč you have to change trains, which means you'd be better off travelling by bus. Note that the train station is 2km west of the town in the village of Popovice. If you're stuck in town, you'll have the chance to check out the kitsch decor in the Communist-era *Hotel Opera* (☎568 440 230, ⓕ568 440 232; ❷).

Náměšť nad Oslavou

Tucked into one of the many twists and turns of the River Oslava, the town of **NÁMĚŠŤ NAD OSLAVOU**, 18km east of Třebíč, sits below its big white Renaissance **zámek** (April & Oct Sat & Sun 9am–4pm; May, June & Sept Tues–Sun 9am–5pm; July & Aug closes 6pm; 100Kč), built by the Žerotín family in the sixteenth century. The grandiose double staircase leading to the main entrance, and the arcaded inner courtyard, give some indication of the chateau's former glories but belie the rather dull interior. What makes the chateau worth visiting are the large collection of remarkably well-preserved sixteenth- to eighteenth-century French tapestries and the Baroque library, whose barrel-vaulted ceiling is decorated with colourful frescoes. The gardens give out the most wonderful views, and are perfect for a picnic, but it's worth venturing down into the town to admire the **medieval bridge**, the country's third oldest, after Písek and Prague's Charles Bridge, and, like those two, lined with Baroque statues of saints and guarded by angels.

The **train** and **bus** stations are 1km or so to the west of the main square, Masarykovo náměstí, where there's a **tourist office** (9am–noon & 1–4pm: June & Aug daily; Sept–May Mon–Fri) in the stará radnice. You can enjoy **food** and **drink** in the chateau's courtyard at the *Zámecká restaurace*, and you can even **stay** in the *Zámecký penzion* (☎ & ⓕ568 620 425; ❷). There are several lovely **walks** to be had in the woods to the south of Náměšť, along the meandering

Oslava: follow the red-marked path down to the river as far as the neo-Gothic hunting lodge of **Lovecký zámeček**, 5km to the south, and return via the green-marked path.

Telč

It's hardly an exaggeration to say that the last momentous event in **TELČ** (Telt-sch) was the great fire of 1530, which wiped out all the town's wooden Gothic houses and forced it to start afresh. It is this fortuitous disaster that has made Telč what it is: a perfect museum-piece sixteenth-century provincial town. Squeezed between two fish ponds, the Štěpnický to the east and the Ulický to the west, the **staré město** is little more than two medieval gate towers, one huge wedge-shaped square and a chateau. Renaissance arcades extend the length of the main square, **náměstí Zachariáše z Hradce**, lined with pastel-coloured houses (including the town's fire station) that display a breathtaking variety of gables and pediments, none less than two hundred and fifty years old. At the eastern end of the square, you can climb the **věž sv Ducha** (June–Sept Mon–Sat 10am–noon & 1–5pm) for an overview of the ensemble.

At the narrow western end of the square, the **zámek** (Tues–Sun: April & Oct 9am–noon & 1–4pm; May–Sept until 5pm; 140Kč; @ www.zamek-telc.cz) in no way disturbs the sixteenth-century atmosphere of the town; it too was badly damaged in the fire and had to be rebuilt in similar fashion. Like the chateau at the nearby Bohemian town of Jindřichův Hradec (see p.201), it was the inspiration of Zachariáš of Hradec, whose passion for all things Italian is again strongly in evidence. Of the two guided tours on offer, the hour-long *trasa A* is the one to go for, as it concentrates on the Renaissance-era rooms, which boast a truly exceptional array of period ceilings. The shorter *trasa B* features living spaces from later periods, but even this can be fun as the whole place is refreshingly intimate and low-key after the intimidating pomposity of the Baroque chateaux of the region.

Even if you don't fancy going on a guided tour, you should take a look inside the chateau's exquisite All Saints' **chapel**, opposite the ticket office. The chapel was built in 1580 as the last resting place of Zachariáš of Hradec and his wife Kateřina of Valdštejn, who lie, arms outstretched in prayer, surrounded by a beautiful, multicoloured wrought-iron grille. For a funereal chapel, the decor is surprisingly bright and upbeat, and the stuccowork is absolutely outstand-ing, with gilded trumpets erupting from a farrago of figs, olives, pomegranates and other fruit. In the central relief on the ceiling of the nave, a whole host of skeletons is being restored to life on the Day of Judgement, as prophesized by Ezekiel: "there was a noise, and behold a shaking, and the bones came together, bone to his bone".

You can also stroll through the cloistered formal garden at leisure, and pay a visit to the **Galerie Jana Zrzavého** (April & Sept–Oct Tues–Sun 9am–noon & 1–4pm; May–Aug closes 5pm; Nov–March Tues–Fri 9am–noon & 1–4pm, Sat 9am–1pm) in the east wing, dedicated to the Surrealist painter Jan Zrzavý (1890–1977), whose career spanned the first three quarters of the twentieth century. Born in nearby Havlíčkův Brod, Zrzavý's early works were Post-Impressionist, but he quickly adopted his own peculiar dreamlike, slightly surreal style. His paintings are definitely an acquired taste, though they are by no means monotonous; particularly striking are his pallid, grey, virtually unin-habited Breton landscapes painted between the wars.

The local branch of the **muzeum Vysočiny** (times as for the zámek) is housed in the chateau, too, with a model of the town, a miniature Bethlehem scene and displays on local history. More intriguing, though, is the exquisite ceramic World War I memorial, at the end of the covered passageway that leads to the town's church. Although the adjacent World War II memorial doesn't explicitly say so, it's clear that the majority of the town's victims in the last war were from the local Jewish community.

Practicalities

The **train station** is a ten-minute walk east of the old town along Masarykova, but with direct trains only connecting with Jihlava, you're more likely to find yourself arriving at the nearby **bus station**. The **tourist office** (May–June & Sept Mon–Fri 8am–5pm, Sat & Sun 10am–5pm; July–Aug closes at 6pm; Oct Mon–Fri 8am–5pm, Sat & Sun 10am–4pm; Nov–April Mon & Wed 8am–5pm, Tues & Thurs 8am–4pm, Fri 8am–3pm; ⓦwww.telc-etc.cz), at no. 10 on the main square, is helpful and friendly and can book **private rooms**. Most tour groups come here only for a couple of hours, so **accommodation** shouldn't be too much of a problem and there's plenty of choice.

The *Hotel Celerin* (☎567 243 477, ⓦwww.hotelcelerin.cz; ❹) enjoys a great location, at no. 43, at the wide end of the main square, as does the *Černý orel* (☎567 243 222, ⓦwww.cernyorel.cz; ❹), at no. 7, though neither has much character inside. The *Na hrázi* (☎567 213 150, ⓦwww.nahrazi.cz; ❹) is a pleasant pub-hotel overlooking the fish ponds to the south of the old town on Na hrázi, and there are numerous other pensions to choose from in the old town. The nearest **campsite** is the *Velkopařezitý* lakeside site (open all year), 7km northwest of Telč.

U Zachariáše is a very popular **pub**, as is *Na kopečku*, a short walk north of the old town up Jihlavská. Another good choice is *U Marušky*, in a quiet spot at the opposite end of the square from the chateau, or the *Šenk pod věží* restaurant, next door; both offer reasonably priced Czech specialities. Telč can get busy in the summer, but it gets even busier for two weeks at the turn of July and August when the town hosts a non-traditional folk music **festival**.

Slavonice

SLAVONICE (Zlabings), 25km south of Telč and a stone's throw from the Austrian border, is in many ways even more remarkable. It's a monument to a prosperity that lasted for just one hundred years, shattered by the Thirty Years' War, which halved the population, then dealt its deathblow in the 1730s when the post road from Prague to Vienna was rerouted via Jihlava. In 1945 the forced removal of the local German-speaking inhabitants emptied Slavonice, and matters deteriorated even further when the Iron Curtain wrapped itself around the village, severing road and rail links with the West.

Even now, the **staré město** – not much larger than the one at Telč – still has a strange and haunting beauty. The impression is further enhanced by the bizarre biblical and apocalyptic sixteenth-century "strip cartoons" played out on the houses in monochrome sgraffito. The best way to start a tour of the town is to visit the tourist office (see p.388), on **náměstí Míru**, the larger of the town's two squares, located in a building with stunning diamond vaulting in the entrance hall. From here, the steep staircase descends to the thirteenth-century **Podzemní chodby** (underground tunnels; July–Aug daily 9am–6pm) running under a line of houses and the square itself. Next, you should pay a visit to the former **Lutheran prayer room** (Protestantská modlitebna; May–Sept daily 10am–noon & 1–5pm; ☎384 493 048) at house no. 517 on Horní náměstí, known locally as *U itala*, as the friendly owner is Italian. Here, on the first floor, they will show you the exceptional wall paintings of the Apocalypse, which miraculously survived the Counter-Reformation: look out, in particular, for the mischievous depiction of the Devil as a crocodile wearing the papal crown, not to mention the horse-riding Whore of Babylon. Last of all, you can now climb the **Městská věž** (May & Sept Sat & Sun 10am–noon & 1–5pm; June–Aug daily 9am–noon & 1–6pm), which is attached to the town's central church.

Practicalities

Trains from Telč take fifty minutes, but from Jihlava they take an incredible two hours (with a change at Kostelec u Jihlavy); the train station is five minutes' walk south of the town centre, and a short walk from the **Austrian border** (daily 6am–10pm) and town of Fratres. Slavonice is also connected by the occasional **bus** to Jindřichův Hradec and points to the west. Most people come to Slavonice on a day-trip, but the **tourist office** on náměstí Míru (April & Oct Mon–Fri 10am–4pm; May daily 10am–noon & 1–5pm; June–Sept daily 9am–noon & 1–5pm; Nov–March Mon–Fri 10am–noon & 1–4pm; ⓦwww .i.slavonice-mesto.cz) provides information if you wish to **stay the night**. You can stay on náměstí Míru, at the *Hotel Alfa* (☎384 493 261; ❶), which is basically a pub with simple rooms upstairs, or at the more comfortable *U růže* (☎384 493 004, ⓦwww.dumuruze.cz; ❸) or the *Hotel Arkáda* (☎384 408 408, ⓦwww.hotelarkada.cz; ❷), which has pleasant one- to four-bed en-suite rooms in the arcaded house opposite *Alfa*. On Horní náměstí, there are rooms behind the Lutheran prayer room at no. 517 (☎384 493 159; ❷). For **food**, you can also try *Appetito*, on the main square, with its own courtyard out back, which serves traditional Czech fare.

Landštejn

Nestled in the idyllic, wooded hills west of Slavonice is a bizarre structure that could almost be a huge bunker from the Iron Curtain era, or perhaps yet another nuclear power station. In actual fact, it's the ruined castle of **Landštejn** (April & Oct Sat & Sun 9am–noon & 1–4pm; May & Sept Tues–Sun 9am–noon & 1–4pm; June–Aug Tues–Sun 9am–noon & 1–5pm), built back in the thirteenth century close to where the Bohemian, Moravian and Austrian borders meet. Nowadays, Landštejn constitutes the largest and finest remains of a Romanesque stronghold in the republic. Unusually, you can explore it without a guide; don't miss the solid tower, which provides views over the surrounding hills good enough to reward the stiff ascent (though the rest of the castle is hidden from sight behind the thick walls).

Up to six **buses** a day link Landštejn with Slavonice; the bus stop is under the castle, as is the **hotel** *Landštejnský dvůr* (☎384 498 726, ⓦwww.landstejn.cz; ❸), with a pleasant restaurant (closed Mon).

Jihlava

When silver deposits were discovered in the nearby hills in the 1240s, **JIH-LAVA** (Iglau) was transformed overnight from a tiny Moravian village into one of the biggest mining towns in central Europe. Scores of German miners came and settled here, and by the end of the century Jihlava boasted two hospitals, two monasteries and, most importantly, the royal mint. The veins of silver ran out in the fourteenth century, but the town continued to flourish thanks to the cloth trade, reaching its zenith around the latter half of the sixteenth century when over 700 master spinners worked in the town.

Jihlava retains a surprisingly attractive **staré město**, which has been painstakingly renovated over the last decade. That the town isn't quite as lovely as it should be is partly down to a fire in 1523 and the ravages of the Thirty Years' War, which drastically reduced Jihlava's population. Most of all, however, it was the expulsion of ethnic Germans from this *Sprachinsel* (language-island) after 1945 that changed the face of the town forever, or, as the Communist guidebooks euphemistically put it, "marked the beginning of a new stage in the development of Jihlava". In reality, the town immediately went into decline, plagued by an ignorant Communist council which, in its comparatively brief forty-year rule, left the most indelible mark on the town: the mud-brown, multi-storey car park/supermarket complex plonked in the middle of Jihlava's huge main square in place of a block of medieval houses.

Arrival, information and accommodation

The **main train station** – simply called Jihlava – is a good 2km northeast of the town centre, so hop on trolleybus #A or #B; slow trains to or from Tábor, Jindřichův Hradec or České Budějovice also stop at **Jihlava–město**, 1km north of the old town – there are no trolleybuses, but it's an easy walk to the staré město along třída Legionářů. From the **bus station**, northwest of the old town, it's a five-minute walk to the main square or a short hop on trolleybus #C. Jihlava's **tourist office** (Mon–Fri 8am–noon & 1–5pm, Sat 8am–noon; July–Aug also Sun 1–5pm) is at no. 19 on the main square and can organize **private rooms**.

Jihlava sees relatively few tourists, other than passing business folk, Austrians and homesick Sudeten Germans, so **accommodation** is limited to a few medium-priced choices. Perhaps the most reliable place to stay is the *Hotel Gustav Mahler*, Křížová 4 (☎567 320 501, ⓦwww.hotelgmahler.cz; ❹), which has taken over the former Dominican monastery north of the main square; the hotel is wonderfully spacious, though there's little original decor left – ask for a room with shared facilities (❷) if you want to save money. The sgraffitoed *Hotel Zlatá Hvězda* (☎567 309 421, ⓦwww.zlatahvezda.cz; ❷) is cheaper and enjoys a good position on the main square, though it has a seedy non-stop bar in the basement. Other fall-backs include the Art Nouveau *Grand Hotel* (☎567 303 541, ⓦwww.grandjihlava.cz; ❹), which has a few cheap rooms (❷) with shared facilities, and is at the junction of Komenského and Husova. If you're camping, take a local bus to the lakeside *Pávov* **campsite** (May–Sept) situated 4km north of Jihlava, not far from the motorway.

The Town

If you can look beyond Jihlava's most glaring addition, the cobbled main square, **Masarykovo náměstí**, is actually a wonderfully expansive space. Sloping steeply to the south and lined with restrained Baroque and Rococo houses, it sports two fountains, and a Marian column, beside which is a plaque to Evžen Plocek, the 41-year-old who set himself alight on April 4, 1969, in protest against the Soviet invasion. At the top of the square, in no. 58, is the **muzeum Vysočiny** (Tues–Sun 9am–noon & 12.30–5pm; ⓦmuzeum.ji.cz), worth a visit

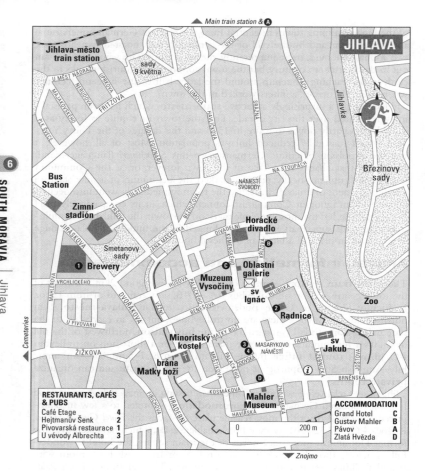

Jihlava-město train station

U MĚST NÁDRAŽÍ

NERUDOVA

MAJAKOVSKÉHO

P.K. SPĚCE

UPÁKOVA

TŘITOVA

sady 9 května

CHLUMOVA

TŘÍDA LEGIONÁŘŮ

HAVLÍČKOVA

LIVOV

SRÁZNA

NA STOUPACH

Jihlavka

N

Březinovy sady

Bus Station

TOLSTÉHO

TYRŠOVA

NÁMĚSTÍ SVOBODY

NA STOUPACH

Zimní stadión

JIRÁSKOVA

JANA MASARYKA

BŘEZINOVA

DIVADELNÍ

KOMENSKÉHO

Horácké divadlo

Ⓑ

KŘIŽÍKA

Smetanovy sady

Ⓒ

Oblastní galerie

MAHLEROVA

VRCHLICKÉHO

Ⓞ Brewery

HUSOVA

PALACKÉHO

Muzeum Vysočiny

✉

sv Ignác

HLUBOKÁ

Zoo

DVOŘÁKOVA

VĚŽNÍ

BENEŠOVA

Ⓞ Radnice

U PIVOVARU

FARNÍ

✝ sv Jakub

ŽIŽKOVA

Minoritský kostel

MATKY BOŽÍ

Ⓞ

MASARYKOVO NÁMĚSTÍ

Ⓞ

LAZEBNICKÁ

JOŠTOVA

◀ Cemeteries

brána Matky boží

MRŠTÍKOVA

PALACKÉHO

JODOVSKÁ

ⓘ

BRNĚNSKÁ

HRADEBNÍ

TŘEBÍZSKÉHO

KOSMÁKOVA

Ⓞ

Mahler Museum

ZNOJEMSKÁ

HAVÍŘSKÁ

▼ Znojmo

for the interior alone, being one of the few Renaissance houses to survive the 1523 fire. Its covered inner courtyard, with an arcaded gallery, patchy murals and diamond vaulting, is perfectly preserved. The museum's collections of stuffed animals and mushrooms are less remarkable, though there is a well-preserved eighteenth-century pharmacy from nearby Polná.

You can see different kinds of interior design in the **oblastní galerie Vysočiny** (Tues–Sun 9am–12.30pm & 1–5pm), round the corner at Komenského 10, north off the main square, which houses a small but excellent permanent collection of nineteenth- and twentieth-century Czech art. You can also take a trip down into the town's extensive catacombs, known as **katakomby** (daily: April 10am–4pm; May & Sept 9am–4pm; June–Aug 9am–5pm, tours on the hour) or *historické podzemí*. The entrance to the tunnels is beside the imposing early Baroque facade of the Jesuit church of **sv Ignác**, built at the top of the square in the 1680s. Unfortunately, the church is usually closed, so to see the ceiling fresco and the stupendous trompe l'oeil main altar, you'll need to get there before or after one of the services.

Apart from the Jesuit church, all the town's other churches comply with medieval requirements and are set back from the square. The most obvious of these is the church of **sv Jakub** (St James), east of the square down Farní, whose two plain stone towers and steeply pitched, chevroned roof rise majestically above the surrounding burgher houses. The church is best admired from afar, though it's also possible to climb the church's northern **tower** (10am–1pm & 2–6pm: May & Sept Sat & Sun; June–Aug Tues–Sun) for a panoramic view over the town. You

Mahler in Iglau

"I am thrice homeless, as a native of Bohemia in Austria, as an Austrian among Germans and as a Jew throughout the world. Everywhere an intruder, never welcomed." **Gustav Mahler's** predicament was typical of the Jews of Mitteleuropa, and it only exacerbated his already highly strung personality. Prone to Wagnerian excesses and bouts of extreme pessimism, he would frequently work himself into a state of nervous collapse when composing or conducting. It was this Teutonic temperament as much as his German-speaking background that separated him from his more laid-back Czech musical contemporaries.

Mahler was born in 1860 in the nearby village of **Kaliště** (Kalischt) on the Bohemian side of the border, the second son of Bernhard Mahler, an ambitious Jewish businessman. The very same year, the Mahlers, who were the only non-Czechs in the entire village, moved to **Iglau** (Jihlava), where there had been a strong Jewish community since the mid-fourteenth century. The family moved to **Wienerstrasse** (now Znojemská) 4, where there is now a plaque recording this fact. Mahler's father opened a pub here, a drunken dive by all accounts, and it proved a big success, allowing Bernhard eventually to open his own distillery, but at home there was little to rejoice about. Judging by his frequent court appearances, Bernhard was a bad-tempered, violent man, while his wife, Marie, was a frail woman, whose minor heart condition was only exacerbated by her fourteen pregnancies (only six children survived to adulthood).

Mahler went to school at the German Gymnasium on Hluboká (some fifty years after Smetana), but showed more musical, than academic, promise. At the age of just ten, he made his first public appearance as a pianist at the town's municipal theatre, then in a converted church on **Komenského**. A local farmer persuaded Bernhard to send his boy to **Prague** to study music, but Mahler returned homesick after less than a year. After completing his studies in **Jihlava**, where he later claimed "I didn't learn anything", he was accepted as a student at the Vienna conservatoire. Mahler then enjoyed a fairly stormy career as a conductor that included stints at, among other places, Olomouc and Prague, before finally settling in **Vienna**, the place with which he is most closely associated. His links with Jihlava were permanently severed in 1889, when both his parents died, the family property was sold, and his remaining siblings moved away.

Under the Communists there was little mention of the town's greatest son – now, predictably enough, all that has changed. The house in which Mahler grew up has recently been restored and turned into a gallery, while round the corner a branch of the muzeum Vysočiny (see p.392) contains a permanent exhibition on him – and of course, there's the *Gustav Mahler* hotel. Mahler's parents' grave still stands in the Jewish cemetery, 1km west of the town centre on U cvičiště, off Žižkova, close to the municipal cemetery. Dedicated fans who wish to track down the village of Mahler's birth should be aware that there are several villages called Kaliště in Bohemia: the right one is listed in map indexes as Kaliště (Pelhřimov), roughly 7km northwest of Humpolec, and confusingly not Kaliště (Jihlava). The house in which Mahler was born (which burned down in 1937 and had to be rebuilt) has recently been restored (see p.200).

can peek at the spectacular gilded Baroque altarpieces, but if you want a closer look you'll have to ask round for the key or wait for one of the church services. The town walls run round the back of the church, and in the leafy gorge below are the woods of the Březinovy sady and the town's **zoo** (daily: April & Oct 9am–5pm; May–Sept 8am–6pm; Nov–March 9am–4pm), where tigers, zebras, kangaroos, monkeys, hippos and snakes share cramped quarters.

For a town originally built on silver, Jihlava lacks the vestiges of prosperity that grace, for example, Kutná Hora. A few finely carved portals and the remnants of fifteenth-century frescoes survive here and there, but just one gateway, **brána Matky boží** (Tues–Fri 9am–noon & 1–4pm, Sat 1–4pm, Sun 2–5pm), guarding the road from the west, is all that's left of the town's five gates. Near the gateway is the beautifully restored **Minoritský kostel**, a remarkable little church that dates back to around 1250. The building's antiquity – it's the oldest stone building in the town – is evident in the thick Romanesque pillars and fragments of medieval frescoes in the nave. However, the Baroque fittings are no less interesting, particularly the technicolour Crucifixion scene opposite the pulpit, which is played out in front of a ruched silver drape. Make sure you venture into the choir to admire the mural depicting the medieval town, located above the sedilia, which harbours three finely sculpted female saints.

Another branch of the **muzeum Vysočiny** (May–Sept Tues–Fri 9am–noon & 1–5pm, Sat & Sun 1–5pm), at Kosmákova 9, off the southwest corner of the square, houses a permanent exhibition on **Gustav Mahler**'s childhood in Jihlava (expozice mladý Gustav Mahler a Jihlava); for more on Mahler's time here, see the box on p.391. The captions for the black-and-white photos are in Czech and German only, so you'll need to buy the English catalogue to get anything out of the museum. Even so, there's not a lot to get excited about: no original artefacts and little imagination to the displays.

Eating, drinking and entertainment

All the hotels mentioned on p.389 will happily serve you food and drink, but Jihlava's most aesthetically pleasing **restaurant** is U vévody Albrechta, which occupies a banquet room decorated with Renaissance frescoes, on the first floor at no. 41 on the west side of the main square. It offers a wide range of Czech dishes, as does Hejtmanův Šenk, located in the radnice, on the opposite side of the square. If you want to sample Jihlava's local Ježek (hedgehog or Iglau in German) **beer**, head for the brewery's own cavernous Pivovarská restaurace on Vrchlického, which offers the entire range of Ježek beers including the 18-degree Grand, and the usual pub grub. A more mellow place to spend the evening is Café Etage, a trendy hangout on the first floor of no. 39 on the main square. As for high culture, Jihlava's Horácké divadlo boasts a brand new **theatre** building, and though it usually puts on plays, it does stage the occasional classical or jazz **concert**.

Žďár nad Sázavou

The highest point in the Bohemian-Moravian Uplands, or Vysočina, is around 40km northeast of Jihlava, though the whole range is actually more like a high rolling plateau. This has always been a poor region, but one really good reason for venturing into the hinterland is to visit **ŽĎÁR NAD SÁZAVOU** (Ⓦ www.zdarns.cz), established in the thirteenth century as a small settlement pitched near its Cistercian monastery. Since World War II the population has increased tenfold, making it one of the largest towns in the region, producing, among other things, ice skates. The only thing worth seeing, however, is the **monastery** complex, a three-kilometre walk (or short bus #2 ride) north through the grey new town of Žďár – instructive if nothing else. As you approach the woods and fish ponds, there's a small bridge decorated with the familiar figures of eighteenth-century saints, on the other side of which is the monastery, now back in the hands of the Kinský family.

The whole complex is the work of **Giovanni Santini** (who also had a hand in the monasteries of Plasy and Kladruby, near Plzeň), perhaps the most gifted architect of the Czech Counter-Reformation. His two great talents were marrying Gothic and Baroque forms in a new and creative way, and producing buildings with a humour and irony often lacking in eighteenth-century architecture. The monastery church isn't a particularly good example, but the wooded hill to the south of the complex conceals the one that is: the UNESCO-protected **Zelená hora** (Green Hill) pilgrimage church (May–Oct Tues–Sun 9am–5pm). It's a unique and intriguing structure, with zigzag cemetery walls forming a decagon of cloisters around the central star-shaped church, a giant mushroom sprouting a half-formed, almost Byzantine dome, dedicated to sv Jan Nepomucký (St John of Nepomuk). The interior is filled with details of his martyrdom, along with symbolic and numerical references to the saint and the Cistercians. On the pulpit, a gilded relief depicts his being thrown off the Charles Bridge in Prague by the king's men, while everywhere in macabre repetition are the saint's severed tongue and the stars that appeared above his head: above the pulpit, on the ceiling, in the shapes of the windows, and in the five side chapels.

Back in the main part of the monastery there's a **Muzeum knihy** (Book Museum; April & Oct Sat & Sun 8am–noon & 12.30–4pm; May, June & Sept Tues–Sun same hours; July–Aug Tues–Sun 9am–noon & 12.30–5pm), housed in the stables designed by Santini, with swirling zigzag patterning on the ceiling. The exhibition on Santini himself and other personalities of the local Baroque (daily 9am–5pm) is located in the former convent, to the right of the monastery church, along with a display of old pianos. Near the entrance gate there's a ticket office, able to give information on the whole complex.

Santini in the Žďár region

A number of Santini's lighthearted minor buildings are dotted about the Žďár region. The first, a couple of hundred yards further north of the Cistercian monastery in Žďár, is the eerie **dolní hřbitov** (lower cemetery), whose three simple chapels symbolize the Trinity. Built to accommodate plague victims who never materialized, the graveless space is empty but for a lonesome angel calling the tune for Judgement Day, and is enclosed by the gentle ripples of the cemetery walls.

Down the road at **Ostrov nad Oslavou** (7min by train), using a similar design to the one he employed in the chateau at Chlumec nad Cidlinou, Santini built a *hostinec* in the shape of a "W" in memory of his local patron, the Abbot of Žďár, Václav Vejmluva (the initials W.W. in German). It has seen a lot of use and abuse over the years, but is still the local boozer: buy a pint and appreciate the architecture at leisure.

Just 2km northeast of Ostrov and within easy walking distance, the local church at **Obyčtov** is another Santini design, built in the shape of a turtle, one of the Virgin Mary's more obscure symbols. Four chapels mark each leg, a presbytery the neck, and the west onion-domed tower the distorted head. Ask around for the key to the whitewashed interior, which features more turtle symbolism.

Practicalities

Žďár is only an hour's fast train ride from Brno; the town centre is 1km north of the train station, and it's another 2km to the monastery (both sections are covered by the bus #2). It's easy to get a room in the town, whose **hotels** include the characterful *U labutě* (℡566 622 949, ⓦwww.oxygen.cz/u-labute; ❷), on the main square, and the less prepossessing high-rise *Hotelový dům Morava* (℡566 625 826, ⓦwww.cerum.cz; ❶), just below the square. **Hostel**-type accommodation is also available at the *Hotel Jehla* (℡566 624 147, ⓦwww.hoteljehla.cz; ❶), a Communist-era building on Kovářova, en route from the square to the monastery. There's a decent *hostinec* called *Teferna*, serving Starobrno, by the monastery, and, a little further up the road, the *Pilská nádrž* lakeside **campsite** (May–Sept).

The Slovácko region

What the Labe basin is to the Bohemians, the **Slovácko region**, around the plains of the River Morava 50km east of Brno, is to the Moravians. They settled in this fertile land around the late eighth century, taking their name from the river and eventually lending it to the short-lived Great Moravian Empire, the first coherent political unit in the region to be ruled by Slavs and the subject of intense archeological research (and controversy) over the last forty years. Geographically, the River Morava (along with the River Odra further north) forms a natural corridor between east and west, difficult to defend against intruders and consequently trashed by numerous armies marching their way across Europe, from the Turks to the Tatars. Nowadays, at various different points, the Morava forms the border between Slovakia and Austria, then, moving north, Moravia and Slovakia.

Ethnically, it's a grey area where Moravians and Slovaks happily coexist – the local dialect and customs virtually indistinguishable from West Slovakia – despite the new cross-border restrictions now in place. Tomáš Garrigue Masaryk, the country's founder and first president, hailed from here, and his mixed parentage – his mother was German-speaking, his father a Slovak peasant – was typical of the region in the nineteenth century. For the visitor, though, it's a dour, mostly undistinguished landscape – flat, low farming country, with just the occasional

---

Velká Morava - the Great Moravian Empire

The Moravians took their name from the **River Morava** when they settled here around the late eighth century; their Great Moravian Empire was the first coherent political unit in the region to be ruled by Slavs. At its peak under the Slav prince Svätopluk (870–94), the territories of **Velká Morava** (the Great Moravian Empire) extended well into Slovakia, Bohemia, and parts of western Hungary and southern Poland, and arguments over the whereabouts of its legendary capital, Veligrad, have been puzzling scholars for many years. At first, the most obvious choice seemed to be Velehrad in Moravia, but excavations there have proved fruitless. Opinion is nowadays divided among Nitra, in West Slovakia, Mikulčice, right on the Slovak border southeast of Hodonín, and Staré Město, now part of Uherské Hradiště. Whatever the truth, the whole lot had been laid waste by the Magyar hordes by 906, not long after the death of Svätopluk, and Slovakia remained under Hungarian rule for the following millennium.

The apostles of the Slavs

The significance of saints **Cyril** (827–69) and **Methodius** (815–85) goes far beyond their mere canonization. Brothers from a wealthy family in Constantinople, they were sent as missionaries to the Great Moravian Empire in 863 at the invitation of its ruler, Rastislav, less for reasons of piety than to assert his independence from his German neighbours. Thrust headlong into a political minefield, they were given a hard time by the local German clergy, and had to retreat to Rome, where Cyril became a monk and died. Methodius, meanwhile, insisted on returning to Moravia, only to be imprisoned for two years at the instigation of the German bishops. The pope eventually got him released, but dragged him back to Rome to answer charges of heterodoxy. He was cleared of all charges, consecrated bishop of Pannonia and Moravia, and continued to teach in the vernacular until his death in 885.

More important than their achievements in converting the local populace was the fact that they preached in the tongue of the common people. Cyril in particular is regarded as the founder of Slavonic literature, having been accredited with single-handedly inventing the Glagolitic script, still used in the Eastern Church and the basis of the modern Cyrillic alphabet that takes his name, while Methodius is venerated by both Western and Eastern Christians as a pioneer of the vernacular liturgy and a man dedicated to ecumenism. After Methodius' death, his followers were duly chased out and forced to take refuge in Bulgaria. The Czech Lands and most of Slovakia came under Rome's sway once and for all, and had to wait until the end of the fourteenth century before they once more heard their own language used to preach the gospel.

---

factory or ribbon village to break the monotony – and most people pass through en route to more established sights. In summer this can be a great mistake, for almost every village in the area has its own folk festival, and in early autumn the local wine caves are bursting with life and ready to demonstrate the region's legendary and lavish hospitality.

Uherské Hradiště and around

The industrial town of **UHERSKÉ HRADIŠTĚ** (Ungarisch-Hradisch), like many towns on the Morava, has made a remarkable recovery after the devastating floods of 1997. The town sees few visitors at the best of times, and the only reason travellers stray into its shapeless centre is in their search for the **Památník Velké Moravy** (daily 9am–noon & 12.30–5pm), suspected site of the capital of the Great Moravian Empire, which is actually north of the centre, across the Morava, on Jezuitská in a part of town known confusingly as Staré Město (10min by foot, follow the white signs *památník*). The archeological remains, housed in what looks like a concrete bunker from the last war, include the foundations of a ninth-century church, discovered in 1949, and a lot of bones and broken crockery – a specialist's paradise, but less gripping for the rest of us.

A more accessible load of old rocks, along with a good selection of folk costumes and suchlike, is on display at the **Slovácké muzeum** (daily 9am–noon & 12.30–5pm) in the Smetanovy sady, to the east of town. The obligatory Jesuit church aside, the town's only other sight as such is the late Baroque **apothecary U zlaté koruny** on the main square; it's still functioning as a *lékárna* (pharmacy), and you can peep through into the frescoed back room.

Arriving at Uherské Hradiště by **bus**, simply walk west along Velehradská třída to the centre; arriving by train is more complicated – **trains** travelling north or south tend to arrive at Staré Město u Uherského Hradiště on the north bank of the river, while trains from the east arrive in the southern suburb of Kunovice. The more central Uherské Hradiště station, southwest of the main square, is only served by the occasional shuttle service between the two. The best place to **stay** is the *Hotel Slunce* (℡572 432 640, Ⓦwww.synothotels.com; ❺), on the main square, opposite the church; it's an efficient, modern, air-conditioned place, with a few surviving features from its Renaissance days. If the *Slunce* is full, try the *Grand* (℡572 551 511, Ⓦwww.grand-uh.cz; ❸) on Palackého náměstí, which has clean, simply furnished rooms. For something cheaper in the town's vicinity, ask at the **tourist office** (daily 8am–6pm; Ⓦwww.mic.uh.cz), also on the main square, to the right of the church.

Velehrad

The **Cistercian monastery** at **VELEHRAD**, just 9km across the fields from Uherské Hradiště, is one of the most important pilgrimage sites in the Czech Republic. It's an impressive sight, too, with the twin ochre towers of its **church** (daily 7am–7pm) set against the backdrop of the Chřiby hills, a low beech-covered ridge that separates Brno from the Morava basin.

The monastery's importance as an object of pilgrimage derives from the belief (now proved to be false) that it was the seat of St Methodius' archbishopric, the first in the Slav Lands, and the place where he died on July 5, 885 (see box p.224). The 1100th anniversary of this last fact attracted over 150,000 pilgrims from across Czechoslovakia in 1985, the largest single, unofficial gathering in the country since the first anniversary of the Soviet invasion in August 1969 (July 5 is now a national holiday). Five years later, Velehrad entertained Pope John Paul II, and half a million people turned up.

There's certainly something about the place that sets it apart, whether it's the historical associations, the sheer magnificence of its High Baroque, or its strange limitless emptiness outside of the annual pilgrimage. The church owes its gigantic scale to the foundations of the original Romanesque church on which it's built. This burned down in 1681 after being sacked several times by marauding Protestants, but you can visit its remains in the crypt's **lapidárium** (9am–noon & 1–5pm: April–May & Sept–Oct Tues–Sun; June–Aug daily). Inside the church itself, the finer points of the artistry may be lacking in finesse, but the faded glory of the frescoed nave, suffused with a pink-grey light and empty but for the bent old women who come here for their daily prayers, is bewilderingly powerful.

At the edge of the village, en route to Uherské Hradiště, is the **Archeoskanzen** (May–Sept daily 9am–5pm; Oct–April Tues–Sun 9am–4pm; Ⓦwww.archeoskanzen.cz), a reconstructed Great Moravian settlement. Surrounded by a tall palisade, the skanzen contains various wooden structures, including a sheep run and church; the best time to visit is during one of the numerous festivals held here, such as the Day of Great Moravian Cuisine held here between April and mid-September. Ask at the tourist office in Uherské Hradiště for further details.

For accommodation there's the **hotel** *Mlýn* (℡572 571 460, Ⓦwww.mlyn .genea2000.cz; ❸), located in the pleasantly refurbished former monastery mill; the new, less appealing hotel *U Velehradu* (℡572 571 475, Ⓕ572 571 309; ❷); and a **campsite** (March–Oct), 1.5km up the road to Salaš. The village is served by regular **buses** from Uherské Hradiště.

Buchlovice and Buchlov

Four kilometres west of Velehrad, still just out of reach of the Chřiby hills, is the village of **BUCHLOVICE** (Buchlowitz), easily accessible by bus from

Uherské Hradiště. The reason for coming here is to see the Berchtolds' pretty little eighteenth-century **zámek** (April & Oct Tues–Sun 9am–noon & 1–3pm; May, June & Sept Tues–Sun 9am–noon & 1–4pm; July & Aug daily 9am–noon & 1–5pm; Ⓦ www.zamek-buchlovice.cz), a warm and hospitable country house with a lovely arboretum bursting with rhododendrons, fuschias and peacocks. The house, composed of two symmetrically opposed semicircles around a central octagon, has been recently renovated, and the smallish suite of rooms still contains most of its original Rococo furniture, left behind by the family when they fled to Austria in 1945. Another prize exhibit abandoned in haste was a leaf from the tree beneath which Mary Queen of Scots was executed.

A stiff three-and-a-half-kilometre climb up into the forest of the Chřiby hills will take you to the Gothic hrad of **Buchlov** (April & Oct Sat & Sun 9am–3pm; May–June & Sept Tues–Sun 8am–4pm; July & Aug daily 9am–5pm), which couldn't be more dissimilar. In bad weather, as the mist whips round the bastions, it's hard to imagine a more forbidding place, but in summer the view over the treetops is terrific and the whole place has a cool, breezy feel to it. Founded as a royal seat by the Přemyslids in the thirteenth century, it has suffered none of the painful neo-Gothicizing of other medieval castles – in fact the Berchtolds had turned it into a museum as early as the late nineteenth century. Heavy, rusty keys open up a series of sparsely furnished rooms lit only by thin slit windows, and dungeons in which the Habsburgs used to confine the odd rebellious Hungarian. If you're on for a bit of hiking, the stillness and extraordinary beauty of the surrounding beech forests are difficult to match, but make sure you stock up with provisions as there are few shops in the area. There's a restaurant in the castle, and the *Smraďavka* **campsite** (April–Oct) is 2km southeast of Buchlovice.

Strážnice and around

For most of the year **STRÁŽNICE** (Strassnitz), 20km or so southwest of Uherské Hradiště, sees perhaps a handful of visitors, but on the last weekend of June thousands converge on this unexceptional town for the annual **International Folk Festival** (Ⓦ www.straznice-mesto.cz) – the largest in the country – held in three purpose-built stadiums in the grounds of the local chateau. During the festival, hotels are booked solid for miles around, and the only thing to do is to bring your own tent and try to squeeze onto the castle **campsite** (May–Oct) or just crash out somewhere in your sleeping bag.

If you're here at any other time of the year, there's only enough to keep you occupied for an hour or two. Though no work of art itself, the **zámek**, ten minutes' walk north of the centre, off the road to Bzeneč, contains an exceptionally good **folk museum** (May–Oct Tues–Sun 8am–5pm), part of the Institute of Folk Art. En route to the chateau, you'll pass the town's excellent **skanzen** (May–June & Sept–Oct Tues–Fri 9am–4pm; Sat & Sun 9am–5pm; July–Aug daily 9am–5pm), with numerous restored thatched, timber-built cottages and peasant gear from the outlying villages.

The **train station** is five minutes' walk south of the town centre. Outside of the festival, it should be easy enough **to stay** at the *Flag Hotel* (☎ 518 332 059, Ⓦ www.hotelflag.cz; ❷), or the opposite *Hotel Černý orel* (☎ & Ⓕ 518 333 330; ❷); both are simple, but perfectly acceptable. If they're full, you can try the basic *Turistická ubytovna TJ Strážnice* (☎ 518 334 501; ❶), situated east of town, behind the skanzen. A good **place to eat** Czech food and meet the locals is the popular (and smoky) restaurant *Na rynku*, on náměstí Svobody, which turns into a **pub** in the evening. For local **wine**, head for the *Vinárna Botur*, pleasantly adorned with local floral motives; it's situated near the Černý orel.

Wine caves and festivals around Strážnice

Strážnice makes a good base for visiting the private *sklepy* or **wine caves** that provide the focus of village life in the summer months before and after the grape harvest. Perhaps the easiest *sklepy* to visit for those without their own transport are the Plže caves at **PETROV**, a thin settlement strung out along the main road from Hodonín, one stop down the railway line from Strážnice. Hidden from sight, on the other side of the railway track, are around eighty whitewashed stone caves over two hundred years old, some beautifully decorated with intricate floral designs, others with just a simple deep-blue stripe. Around late September there are usually one or two locals overseeing their new harvest who'll be happy to show you around and no doubt invite you to sample (and of course buy) some of their wine. During the rest of the summer, merry-making goes on in the evenings at weekends. Those with their own transport and a taste for the stuff could check out Polesovice, 12km north, or Mutěnice, 15km west, or better still the thatched *sklepy* at Prušánky.

There are countless other festivals in the area, such as the Dolmácké slavnosti, held every three years in Hluk (next one is in 2005), and pilgrimages to places like Blatnice, held in September. The most famous festival of the lot after Strážnice is the annual *Jízda králů* (Ride of the Kings) held over the weekend of Whitsuntide (the last Sunday in May) in **VLČNOV**, which lies south of route 50 between Uherské Hradiště and the pistol-producing town of Uherský Brod. Young villagers in traditional folk costumes ride through the town on horseback, and folk concerts and dances are staged all weekend.

Luhačovice

Twenty-seven kilometres east of Uherské Hradiště is the genteel spa town of **LUHAČOVICE**, decidedly lush after the rather demure Morava valley but without the pomp and majesty of the west Bohemian spas. Although its springs are mentioned as far back as the twelfth century, nothing much was done about developing the place until it was bought up in 1902 and building began on the first of Slovak Dušan Jurkovič's quirky, folksy, half-timbered villas, which have become the spa's hallmark.

The largest of these buildings, the **Dům Dušana Jurkoviče** (recently converted into a hotel for spa guests), dominates the central spa gardens spreading northeast from the train station. The beams are purely decorative, occasionally breaking out into a swirling flourish, and the roof is a playful pagoda-type affair, creating a uniquely Slovak folk version of Art Nouveau. The blot on Luhačovice's copybook is the new **Kolonáda**, a graceless curving concrete colonnade that's nevertheless a good place to sit and watch the patients pass by as they sip the waters from their grotesquely decorated mugs. The rest of the spa forms a snake-like promenade boxed in by shrubs and trees, with folksy bridges spanning the gently trickling river. Soon enough you hit another cluster of Jurkovič buildings, one of which is the open-air natural spring **swimming pool**, good for a cheap, unchlorinated dip. The villas continue into the leafy suburbs, but unless you fancy a hike into the surrounding woods or are staying at the lakeside **campsite** (May–Oct) 1km up the main road, there's no reason to continue walking. If you're interested in finding out more about the folk traditions of the area, and the history of the spa, hop across to the west bank of the stream to the museum in the **Vila Lipová** (April–Oct Tues–Sun 9am–noon & 1–5pm, Nov & March Thurs only 9am–noon & 1–4pm).

To get to Luhačovice by train from Uherské Hradiště, you need to change at Uherský Brod; buses run direct, but less frequently. The **bus** and **train stations** are at the southwestern end of the spa, ten minutes' walk form the centre, where, at Masarykova 950, there's an efficient **tourist office** (Mon–Fri: March–May & Oct 8am–5pm; June–Sept 8am–6pm; Nov–Feb 8am–4pm; Ⓦwww.mesto.luhacovice.cz). Reasonable **accommodation** can be found all over the spa, but call ahead at least a day in advance as Luhačovice is a popular regional getaway. The pension-style *Hotel Lužná* (Ⓣ & Ⓕ577 131 112; ❸) is very central, just south of the spa proper on Solné. Between the centre and the spa, on pedestrianized Dr. Veselého, is the simple but tidy *Hotel Vltava* (Ⓣ & Ⓕ577 131 376; ❷). If you're planning to continue into Slovakia, the scenic train journey from Uherský Brod through the White Carpathians to Trenčianska Teplá is as good a way as any to get there.

Zlín

Hidden in a gentle green valley east of the Morava, **ZLÍN** is one of the most fascinating Moravian towns. Despite appearances, it's not just another factory town, it is *the* factory town – a museum of functionalist architecture and the inspiration of one man, **Tomáš Baťa** (pronounced "Batya"). When Baťa founded his company in 1894 with his brother and sister, Zlín's population was less than 3000. Now, with suburbs trailing for miles along the River Dřevnice, it's approaching 90,000. The town's heyday was during the First Republic, when Baťa planned and started to build the ultimate production-line city, a place where workers would be provided with good housing, schooling, leisure facilities and a fair wage. "Work collectively, live individually" was one of Baťa's favourite aphorisms, and all along the approach roads to the town centre you can see the red-brick shoe-box houses that Baťa constructed for his workers as "temporary accommodation" – houses which have lasted better than anything built after 1948. The combined effects of Allied bombing, nationalization and economic stagnation have left only a hint of the model garden city Baťa had in mind. Zlín can't hope to appeal to everyone's aesthetic tastes, but it does present an entirely different side of the country from the usual provincial medieval staré město.

Some history

Son of a local cobbler, Tomáš Baťa worked his way up from nothing to become the First Republic's most famous millionaire. He grew rich supplying the Austro-Hungarian army with its boots during World War I, and between the wars quickly became the largest **manufacturer of shoes** in the world, producing over 50 million pairs annually. Baťa became the town's mayor in 1923, but died in a plane crash in 1932 at the peak of his power, and although his work was continued by his son (also called Tomáš), the firm and most of the family were forced to leave the country in 1938. Tomáš junior elected to go to Canada, taking his own management team (100 families) and shoemaking machinery with him. There, he quickly set about building another model factory town, known as Bataville, just outside Ottawa, and the company continued to expand into the vast multinational it is today; much of its production now takes place in low-cost Asia.

Nationalization in 1945 robbed Baťa of the company's spiritual home, and in 1949 zealous Party hacks added insult to injury by renaming the town

Gottwaldov after the country's notorious first Communist president, Klement Gottwald, also known as the "Stalinist butcher". It was no doubt seen as a just revenge on Baťa, who rid his shop floor of Communists by decree in the 1920s. When the Communists fell from power in November 1989, Tomáš junior paid his first visit to Zlín for over forty years, and the whole town turned out to greet him, draping banners out of their windows proclaiming "ať žije Zlín" (Long live Zlín). In 1990 the town once more became officially known as Zlín, but due to alleged Nazi collaboration by members of his family, Baťa was unable to reclaim the factory through restitution. Nevertheless, Baťa now has a significant stake in the shoe market, with numerous outlets across the country, including the flagship modernist store on Wenceslas Square in Prague.

Arrival, information and accommodation

Arriving at Zlín's **train station** (Zlín-střed) or **bus terminal**, you're just a few minutes' walk from the centre and everything there is to see. The **tourist office** (June–Sept Mon–Thurs 6am–6pm, Fri 6am–5pm, Sat 9am–noon; Oct–May weekdays only; Ⓦ www.mestozlin.cz), in the radnice on náměstí Míru, should be able to help with any enquiries. **Accommodation** is uniformly overpriced, catering mostly for business clientele. At one time, *the* hotel to stay at was Gahura's high-rise *Hotel Moskva* (☏ 577 561 111, Ⓦ www.moskva-zlin.cz; ❸), on náměstí Práce, though it's become something of an all-purpose building with offices, pseudo-glitzy shops and the centre of the town's fairly dubious nightlife. Next door, you can enjoy the gleaming white decor – and less fuss – of the *Hotel Garni* (☏ 577 212 074, Ⓦ www.hotelgarnizlin.cz; ❸) for the same price.

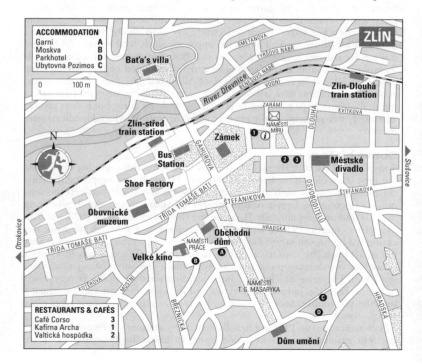

Perhaps better than the two, however, is the new *Parkhotel* (☎577 056 111, Ⓦwww.parkhotelzlin.cz; ❹), with decent, small rooms and a simply furnished restaurant; it's in a quiet location at Růmy 1393, almost at the edge of the forest. A cheap option is the nearby *Ubytovna Pozimos* (☎577 210 614; ❶), Růmy 1741, offering rooms with or without en-suite facilities.

The Town

Baťa was a long-standing patron of modern art that he felt would reflect the thrust and modernity of his own business. In 1911 he had his own **villa** built on the north side of the river by the leading Czech architect of the time, Jan Kotěra; it's a very understated affair, virtually devoid of ornamentation, and now institutionalized. In the late 1920s Le Corbusier was called in to design the town, but after an abortive sketch of the place, this chance of a lifetime fell to local-born architect **František Gahura**, who had studied under Kotěra.

Unlike any other town in the country, Zlín does not revolve around the local chateau or marketplace but around the **shoe factory** itself. Its sixteen-storey office building, called *mrakodrap* (skyscraper), was designed by one of Gahura's assistants, the Slovene Vladimír Karfík, and nowadays serves as the city's administration office. The style – concrete frame, red-brick infill and plate-glass windows – was intended to be "the leitmotif of Zlín's architecture", as Gahura put it, and is indeed typical of all the town's original 1930s buildings, later copied and barbarized by undistinguished postwar architects. Baťa's own office was a huge, air-conditioned, glass-encased lift, capable of visiting every floor. Near the mrakodrap is Zlín's main "sight", **Obuvnické muzeum** (Shoe Museum; April–Oct Tues–Sun 10am–noon & 1–5pm, Nov–Dec & Feb–March Tues–Fri only). Even if you're not a foot fetishist, it's a wonderful 1930s-style museum, with shoes from all over the world from medieval *boty* to the sad attempts of the Communist Svit factory in Zlín, plus a final section on Baťa himself, and, tucked away in one corner, the old man's fantastic lift/office. It's also worth asking if you can see the museum's video on the architectural development of the town. The rest of the complex nowadays serves as the seat of numerous wholesale houses and stores (the shoe production has been transferred to the east), and has nothing in common with the shoes, except for the shop at no. 24.

Directly opposite the main entrance, across třída Tomáše Bati, is Karfík's plate-glass department store, **Obchodní dům**, which naturally includes a shoe shop (the country still led the world in one respect in 1989 – in shoe consumption, which stood at an annual rate of 4.2 pairs per capita). Beyond here, on náměstí Práce (Work Square), lies Gahura's 1931 **Velké kino**, which holds 2000 moviegoers – now unfortunately redone with new white vinyl siding, it's undistinguished – and the eleven-storey Společenský dům, built by Karfík and Lorenz in 1932–33 and now occupied by the **Hotel Moskva**.

Gahura's master plan was never fully realized, and much of the town is accidental and ill-conceived. Only the sloping green of **náměstí T.G. Masaryka**, flanked by more boxy buildings, gives some idea of the trajectory of Gahura's ideas. The first block on the left is Gahura's Masarykovy Školy, where Baťa pursued his revolutionary teaching methods still admired today. At the top of this leafy space is the **Dům umění** (Mon–Fri 9am–5pm, Sat & Sun 9am–noon & 1–5pm), designed by Gahura in 1932 as a memorial to Baťa, where his (recently re-erected) statue, some memorabilia, and the wreckage of the biplane in which he crashed, used to stand. It now serves as the concert hall for the town's orchestra and for exhibitions of contemporary art – appropriate enough, given Baťa's tireless patronage of the **avant-garde**, which he not only utilized in his photographic advertising but also produced in the film studios that were built here between the wars, where many of the country's renowned animation films are still made.

The only other place of interest is the modest country **zámek** (Tues–Sun 9am–noon & 1–5pm) in the park opposite the factory, which houses the town's **Muzeum jihovýchodní Moravy** (South Moravian Museum) boasting a small, but excellent, collection of **twentieth-century Czech art**, ranging from the Cubists Kubišta, Filla, Čapek and Procházka, to wacky Pop Art sculptures from the 1960s and more contemporary works.

Lastly, Zlín is the birthplace of two unlikely bedfellows: the not so avant-garde playwright **Tom Stoppard** and New York magnate, Donald Trump's ex-wife, Ivana. Stoppard's father was a Czech doctor by the name of Eugene Straussler, who fled with his wife and two-year-old son to Singapore to escape the Nazis. After his father's death, Tom's mother married a major in the British army (named Stoppard) and settled in England. These two snippets explain two otherwise puzzling points: why Stoppard has a slight foreign accent and why the Tom Stoppard Prize is given to Czech or Slovak authors in translation. **Ivana Trump** (Trumpová to the Czechs) was born here as Ivana Zelníčková, and rose to fame in her home country in the 1972 Olympic ski team. Her shocking blonde hair and formidable physique allowed her to pursue a modelling career in Canada before making the headlines as wife (and now ex-wife) of New York tycoon Donald Trump.

Eating, drinking and entertainment

Zlín has a decent selection of **restaurants** and cafés. *Valtická hospůdka*, by náměstí Míru on třída Tomáše Bati, is a pleasant place for steak and potatoes, beer and Moravian wine. *Café Corso* (closed Sun), down the street and above the Česká spořitelna, has a good vegetarian selection and the usual Czech staples. Right by the tourist office, *Kafírna Archa* (closed Sun) is a cool little coffee spot with Internet access. Avoiding the casino and disco in the *Moskva*, and the tacky *Flip* disco in the Dům kultury, your choices for **nightlife** boil down to listening to the local philharmonic orchestra in the Dům uměni, and catching a band or playing ten-pin bowling at the *Golem* on náměstí Práce.

Otrokovice

An alternative Baťa experience can be had in neighbouring **OTROKOVICE**, 11km west of Zlín, by the River Morava. As is evident from the architecture, this is another Baťa town, built as an extension of Zlín in the 1930s – in fact the town was originally named Baťov, and was only renamed Otrokovice (after *otrok*, meaning "slave") by the Communists. Despite the overwhelming presence of the local factory (in this case Barum), Otrokovice works better than Zlín as a planned "garden city". At its centre is the Constructivist *Společenský dům*, Karfík's three-winged radial building in reinforced concrete, shaped rather like the sails of a windmill.

The nearest **campsite** to Zlín is the *Pahrbek* site (open all year), 7km south of (and one stop down the line from) Otrokovice in **NAPAJEDLA**, on the River Morava.

Kroměříž and around

KROMĚŘÍŽ (Kremsier), 30km or so up the Morava from Uherské Hradiště and seat of the bishops of Olomouc from the Middle Ages to the nineteenth century, is one of Moravia's most graceful towns. Its once-powerful German-speaking population has long since gone, and nowadays the town feels pleasantly provincial, famous only for its Moravian male-voice choir and folk music tradition. Though quiet, Kroměříž is definitely worth a day-trip, if only for the chateau's rich collections and the town's very beautiful and extensive gardens.

Savagely set upon by the Swedish army in the Thirty Years' War, Kroměříž was rebuilt by order of **Prince–Bishop Karl Eusebius von Liechtenstein-Kastelcorn**, a pathological builder (see p.377) and a member of the richest dynasty in Moravia at the time. Vast sums of money were spent not only on hiring Italian architects, but also on enriching the chateau's art collection and establishing a musical life to rival Vienna. Liechtenstein founded a college for choristers, maintained a thirty-piece court orchestra and employed a series of prestigious *Kapellmeister*, though nowadays, aside from the chateau's extensive archives, there's little evidence of the courtly life.

The staré město

Set back from the banks of the River Morava, the centre of the staré město is the former marketplace of **Velké náměstí**. A broad, gracious square, its sea of cobblestones is interrupted only by the lime trees that surround a gilded plague column and fountain (there's an even better column and fountain ensemble on Riegrovo náměstí). Arcades have survived here and there round the square, the radnice has a fine white Renaissance tower, and the houses themselves, though they have suffered over the years, are now prettily painted up. Jánská, just off the square, hides the town's finest ensemble: a flourish of terraced canons' houses with bright Empire frontages in primary colours.

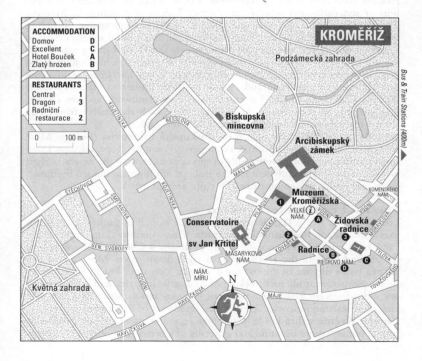

Arcibiskupský zámek

The houses at the northern corner of Velké náměstí part to reveal the UNESCO-protected **Arcibiskupský zámek** (Archbishop's Palace; April & Oct Sat & Sun 9am–4pm; May–June & Sept Tues–Sun 9am–5pm, July & Aug until 6pm; tour in English 180Kč; ⓦ www.azz.cz), a vast Baroque fortress whose severity is relieved only by the fifteenth-century lanterned tower, sole survivor of the Swedes' rampage in the Thirty Years' War. Inside, the chateau is a more gentle Rococo than its uncompromising exterior might suggest. The dark wood and marble decor of the small **Manský sál**, where the bishops held court, is overwhelmed by Maulbertsch's celebratory frescoes, which bear down on guests from the unusually low ceiling. The archbishop's bedroom rather alarmingly contains a double bed – the official story being that it was for his parents when they came to visit.

The showpiece of the palace is the fiddly white-and-gold excess of the **Sněmovní sál**, as high and mighty as anything in Prague, and featured in Miloš Forman's film *Amadeus*. In the first three months of 1849, Reichstag delegates from all parts of the Habsburg Empire met to thrash out a new liberal constitution in the face of the revolutionary events of the previous year. In the end, though, the Kremsier Constitution that came out of these brainstorming sessions and acknowledged "equality of national rights", was unceremoniously ditched by the new imperial government, who drew up their own version. Police were sent to Kremsier to close down the Reichstag, with orders to arrest the most radical delegates. The Habsburgs' final bout of absolutism had begun.

After – or instead of – the main guided tour (*trasa 1 – historické sály*) you can visit the **Zámecká obrazárna** (Chateau Gallery; same hours), which contains what's left of the Liechtensteins' vast art collection, still the best selection of sixteenth- and seventeenth-century European paintings in Moravia. There's plenty of bucolic frolicking supplied by the Flemish masters, including an earthy Breughel, a trompe l'oeil Hoogstraten, and a more sober portrait of Charles I of England and his wife Henrietta by Van Dyck. Others worth noting are Veronese's awestruck bearded *Apostles*, Cranach's richly coloured and exquisitely executed, but gruesome, *Beheading of St John the Baptist* (with a cute dog lapping up the spillage), and the gallery's prize possession, *Apollo Punishing Marsyas*, a late Titian, with characteristically loose brushwork, and yet another dog slurping up the remains. At last, you may climb the castle's **tower** and admire the panorama of neighbouring streets and gardens.

Another minor episcopal sight is the **Biskupská mincovna** (Bishop's Mint; May–Sept Tues–Sun 9–11.30am & noon–5pm), down Na Kopečku, now a well laid-out museum, though really only of specialist interest. At the height of their powers in the seventeenth century, the Bishops of Olomouc minted their own coins, and to this day, commemorative coins are still struck.

The rest of the staré město

Like Olomouc (see p.411), Kroměříž is a place as rich in gardens as in buildings. The watery **Podzámecká zahrada** (daily: summer 7am–7pm; winter 7am–4pm) established by one of the green-fingered Chotek family who held the archbishopric in the 1830s, stretches right down to the Morava, covering an area twice the size of the old town. Having long since lost its formality, it's now a pleasantly unruly park, reeking of wild garlic in spring and hiding an aviary and menagerie, harbouring raccoons, baboons and parrots, plus a deer park and a few stalking peacocks. Ten minutes' walk west of the chateau is the early Baroque **Květná zahrada** (daily: summer 7am–7pm; winter 7am–4pm), more formal but also more beautiful and generally in a better state of repair. The garden was laid out by the Liechtensteins in the 1670s, "ten years and no expense spared" as the Latin inscription reminds you. Its finest vista is the Neoclassical colonnade along the garden's north side, with each of the 46 columns topped by a Roman bust. There are chestnut and lime hedges and tall avenues of trees, plus two waist-high mazes and a wonderful greenhouse filled with orchids, palm and cacti. At the centre stands a huge domed **rotunda**, thickly stuccoed and gaudily frescoed by Italian artists, and featuring mini-grottoes stuffed with satyrs and strange wild creatures. Equally remarkable is the **Foucault pendulum**, suspended from the ceiling, which, as the guide proudly tells you, is one of only four in the world.

The **Muzeum Kroměřížska** (Tues–Sun 9am–noon & 1–5pm), on the main square, puts on temporary art exhibitions, and contains a large collection of work by Max Švabinský, a late-nineteenth-century artist and graphicist who was born at Panská 11 in 1872. There's no denying his skill nor his prolific output, but he's a mite too gushy and Romantic for some people's tastes, and the drawings of nudes and tigers, not to mention his collection of exotic butterflies and stuffed birds, displayed here are unlikely to make many new converts. Of the town's churches, the Gothic sv Mořič is the oldest, but its innards were ripped out by fire in 1836 and rebuilt without much feeling. A better bet is the Baroque church of **sv Jan Křtitel** at the top of Jánská, whose sensuous lines and frescoed oval dome combine to form one of the showpieces of Moravian Baroque.

Lastly, it's worth wandering round to Moravcova in the easternmost corner of the old town, which was formerly the Jewish ghetto. Jewish communities in places like Kroměříž, Uherské Hradiště and Prostějov were among the largest in the Czech Lands before World War II, and since they provided many essential services the local bigwigs left them alone. The **Židovská radnice** (Jewish Town Hall) in Moravcova – one of the few outside Prague – is remarkable not for its architectural beauty but for its mere existence, the result of a magnanimous gesture by the prince-bishop for services rendered in the Thirty Years' War; today it serves as a local cultural centre and gives little hint of its previous life.

Practicalities

The **train station** and the **bus station** are on the opposite bank of the River Morava from the chateau gardens; head down Vejvanovského to reach the old town. The local **tourist office** (Mon–Fri 8.30am–5pm, Sat & Sun 9am–1pm; ⓦ www.mesto-kromeriz.cz) is on Velké náměstí and can arrange private rooms (but note that they charge 20Kč for each single call). The **accommodation** scene has improved over the last few years, with the *Hotel Bouček* (☏573 342 777, ⓦ www.hotelboucek.cz; ❸), on the main square, and three pensions on Riegrovo náměstí, a block southeast of the square: the tasteful *Domov* (☏573 344 744, ⓦ www.penziondomov.cz; ❷), the simple *Zlatý hrozen* (☏573 331 070, ⓦ www.zlatyhrozen.cz; ❷) with its own *vinárna* (closed Mon), and the well-run *Excellent* (☏573 333 023, ⓦ www.excellent.tunker.com; ❷) with free Internet access for guests. A good place to eat is the *Radniční restaurace*, Kovářská 20, a wine **restaurant** in the cellars of the town hall, serving delicious food and a good range of wines from Valtice. The *Central* on the main square contains a very pleasant restaurant on the ground floor and weekend dances in the café upstairs (closed Sun). The cheap *Dragon*, Farní 97, with a long Asian menu (each dish featured on its own picture), also enjoys a well-deserved popularity. To email, head for the **Internet café** *U m@xe*, near the museum. You can buy the local **wine** and have a tour of the cellars at the *Arcibiskupské zámecké sklepy*, behind the archway beside the chateau.

Holešov

HOLEŠOV (Holleschau), 15km northeast on route 432 (and just 15min by train), makes an interesting day-trip from Kroměříž. The town had one of the largest Jewish communities in Moravia, peaking at around 1700 in the mid-nineteenth century. It also has the dubious distinction of being a victim of the last Jewish pogrom on Czech soil in December 1918, during which two Jews were killed. The old ghetto lies to the northwest of the town square, náměstí dr. E. Beneše, centred on the unique, Polish-style **Šachova synagoga** (9am–noon & 1–5pm: April–June & Sept–Oct Wed–Sun; July–Aug Tues–Sun; Nov–March Fri–Sun), on Příční. Built in 1560, the synagogue retains its remarkably ornate eighteenth-century interior, with scallop shells and floral stucco on the ceiling, and ornate wrought-iron filigree work around the bimah. On the second floor there's an exhibition on, and a few relics from, the town's Jewish history, a model of the old ghetto gateway which was demolished in 1906, and of the new synagogue which was burned down in World War II by Czech collaborators. Further north, in a kink of the River Rusava, lies the **Jewish cemetery** (Židovský hřbitov), with graves dating back to 1647, including – enclosed within a protective glass case – the tomb of Rabbi Shabtai ben Meir Kohen, known as Shakh (after whom the synagogue is named). The town's seventeenth-century, dry-moated **zámek**, off the main square, is closed to the public, but its neglected formal French gardens are accessible (daily 8am–5.30pm).

The **train** and **bus stations** lie ten minutes' walk west of the square, where there's a friendly **tourist office** (Mon–Fri 8.30am–8pm, Sat & Sun closes 4pm; Ⓦ www.holesov.mic.cz).

Travel details

Trains

Connections with Prague: Brno (every 1–2hr; 2hr 40min–3hr 40min); Žďár nad Sázavou (7 daily; 2hr 10min–2hr 20min).

Brno to: Blansko (hourly; 20–30min); Bratislava (8 daily; 1hr 30min–2hr); Bučovice (hourly; 35–50min); České Budějovice (4 daily; 4hr 25min); Jihlava (every 1–2hr; 1hr 55min–3hr 20min); Kroměříž (1–2 daily; 1hr 20min); Moravský Krumlov (hourly; 45–50min); Náměšť nad Oslavou (hourly; 45min–1hr; 45min); Olomouc (up to 7 daily; 1hr 25min); Pardubice (every 2hr; 1hr 35min–1hr 50min); Slavkov (hourly; 25–35min); Třebíč (every 1–2hr; 1hr 10min–1hr 45min); Vienna (5 daily; 1hr 45min); Žďár nad Sázavou (hourly; 1hr 5min–1hr 35min); Znojmo (1 daily; 1hr 55min).

Telč to: Slavonice (2–8 daily; 50min–1hr).

Znojmo to: Jaroměřice nad Rokytnou (every 2hr; 50min–1hr 45min); Jihlava (2 daily; 2hr–2hr 20min); Mikulov (every 1–2hr; 1hr–1hr 45min);

Retz (4–8 daily; 22min); Šatov (up to 8 daily; 12min); Valtice (every 1–2hr; 1hr 20min).

Buses

Connections with Prague: Brno (every 30min–1hr; 2hr 20min–3hr 30min); Znojmo (2 daily; 3hr 10min–3hr 25min).

Brno to: Buchlovice (up to hourly; 55min–1hr 25min); Jaroměřice nad Rokytnou (2–7 daily; 1hr 30min–1hr 55min); Jedovnice (24 daily Mon–Fri; 45min); Kroměříž (hourly Mon–Fri, 2–4 daily Sat & Sun; 1hr 10min–1hr 40min); Křtiny (hourly Mon–Fri; 35min); Luhačovice (1–6 daily; 2hr 15min–2hr 55min); Mikulov (19–20 daily Mon–Fri; 45min–1hr 40min); Moravský Krumlov (2–13 daily; 50min–1hr 10min); Telč (2–6 daily; 1hr 55min); Uherské Hradiště (hourly Mon–Fri, up to 7 Sat & Sun; 1hr 50min–1hr 30min); Zlín (hourly Mon–Fri, 4 daily Sat & Sun; 1 hr 50min–2hr 25min); Znojmo (up to 8 daily; 1hr–1hr 15min).

Jihlava to: Telč (hourly Mon–Fri; 40min–1hr).

Uherské Hradiště to: Buchlovice (up to hourly; 10–30min); Kroměříž (1 daily; 1hr 20min); Luhačovice (3 daily Mon–Fri; 40min–1hr 25min); Strážnice (8 daily Mon–Fri; 45min–1hr 10min); Trenčín (7–10 daily; 1hr 10min–1hr 40min); Velehrad (3–11 daily; 10–25min); Zlín (every 30min Mon–Fri, 2 daily Sat & Sun; 35min–1hr 10min).

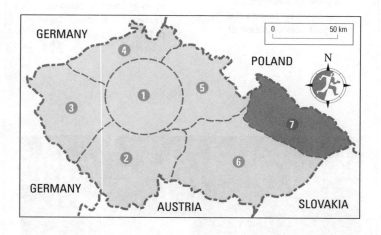

North Moravia

GERMANY

0   50 km

POLAND

N

GERMANY

AUSTRIA

SLOVAKIA

CHAPTER SEVEN Highlights

＊ **Olomouc** Moravia's most handsome city is replete with cobbled squares, fountains and Baroque churches, and worth a day of anyone's time. See p.411

＊ **Wooden churches in the Beskydy** The densely wooded countryside of the Beskydy boasts the largest concentration of wooden churches in the Czech Republic. See p.433

＊ **Štramberk** Hilly Beskydy village with a remarkable array of wooden architecture in situ. See p.434

＊ **Rožnov pod Radhoštěm** The country's largest and most impressive open-air museum or skansen. See p.437

△ Beehives, Rožnov pod Radhoštěn

7

North Moravia

N orth Moravia (Severní Morava) is not the never-ending conglomeration of factories that its critics would have you believe, though it
certainly has more than its fair share of ecological disaster zones, in particular the industrial belt in the Odra (Oder) basin, now in the grip of
an economic depression. At the same time, the north also boasts some of Moravia's wildest and most varied countryside, including the **Jeseníky**, the region's
highest peaks, which form part of what is still – nominally at least – known
as Czech Silesia. As with the Sudetenland regions of Bohemia, Silesia's long-
standing German community was forcibly expelled after World War II, leaving
many villages and towns visibly underpopulated even today.

To the east, near the border with Slovakia, the traditional communities in the
nether reaches of the **Beskydy** hills have fared much better. Wooden houses
and churches are dotted along the valley, and a whole range of folk buildings has
been gathered together and restored in the republic's largest open-air museum
in **Rožnov pod Radhoštěm**. In addition to its folk culture and hiking potential, the Beskydy is endowed with some intriguing museums: a large car collection at the technical museum in **Kopřivnice**, a hat museum in **Nový Jičín**,
and two memorials to famous local boys – Sigmund Freud, who was born in
Příbor, and Leoš Janáček, who lived and composed in **Hukvaldy**.

The region's two largest cities typify North Moravia's contradictions: **Ostrava**,
the country's largest mining and steel town, is a place no Moravian would
ever recommend you visit (with some justification); **Olomouc**, on the other
hand, the old medieval capital on the banks of the River Morava, is arguably
Moravia's most attractive and vibrant city along with Brno, and a must on
anyone's itinerary.

Olomouc

OLOMOUC (pronounced "Olla-moats" and known to the city's sizeable prewar German-speaking community as Olmütz) is easily the most immediately
satisfying of Moravia's three big cities, thanks to its well-preserved staré město,
sloping cobbled squares, Baroque fountains, and healthy quota of university
students. Occupying the crucial Morava crossing point on the road to Kraków,
Olomouc was actually the capital of Moravia from 1187 to 1641 and the seat of
a bishopric (later archbishopric) for even longer. All this attracted the destruc-

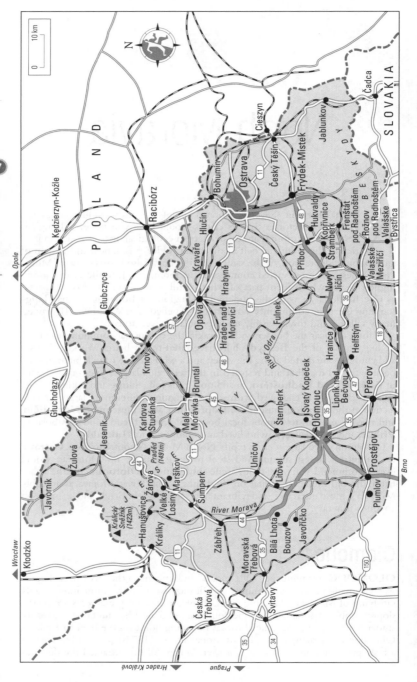

tive attention of Swedish troops in the Thirty Years' War, and their occupation in the 1640s left the town for dead. During this period, Brno took over as capital, in reward for its heroic stand against the Swedes; only the wealth of the church and its strategic trading position kept Olomouc alive. Meanwhile, the military threat from Prussia confined the town to within its eighteenth-century red-brick fortifications, and only after these were finally torn down in 1888 did the city begin to evolve into the industrial centre it is today.

Arrival, information and accommodation

The **train station**, with a rather useless branch of the tourist office (daily 6am–6pm) is 1.5km east of the old town, and the **bus terminal** is a good half-kilometre beyond this. On arrival, walk or take any **tram** from the train station heading west up Masarykova and get off after three or four stops; from the bus station take tram #4, which then proceeds down Masarykova, or tram #5, which runs along třída Svobody south of the old town. The city is divided into two zones: to go to the centre of town you need only an inner zone ticket (*vnitřní jízdenka*). Tickets should be bought beforehand from machines or news kiosks, and there is also a one-day ticket (*jednodenní lístek*), available from the main bus station. The **tourist office** in the arcades on the north side of the radnice (daily 9am–7pm; ☎585 513 385, ⊛www.olomoucko.cz, www.olomouc-tourism .cz) provides information as well as booking **private rooms**.

Accommodation

Hotel **accommodation** is uniformly pricey as the city receives mostly tour groups and flush business folk. The **hostel**-style *Ubytovna Zora* (☎585 234 709; ❶) provides very cheap, clean rooms with shared facilities, at U stadionu 2, ten minutes' walk north from the centre. If you want to **camp**, head to the site in Šternberk (see p.423). A word of warning: rooms can be hard to come by in May when the Spring Music Festival (Olomoucké hudební jaro) follows the Flower Festival (Flora Olomouc).

Arigone Univerzitní 20 ☎585 232 351, ⊛arigone .web.worldonline.cz. Wonderful new hotel, with original wood ceilings and parquet floors. Small, so book in advance. ❹

Gemo Pavelčákova 22 ☎585 222 115, ⊛www .hotel-gemo.cz. Something of a modern eyesore from the outside, but an efficiently run, centrally located place nevertheless, with all mod cons. ❼

Lafayette Alšova 8 ☎585 436 600, ⊛www .lafayette.cz. Late-nineteenth-century hotel that's been fairly tastefully renovated, but is a good ten minutes' walk south of the old town. ❺

Na hradbách Hrnčířská 14 ☎585 233 243, ⊚aquaveri@iol.cz. Small, inexpensive, eight-bed pension hidden away in one of the city's prettiest, quietest backstreets. ❷

Národní dům 8 května 21 ☎585 224 806, ℻585 223 284. No doubt this late-nineteenth-century hotel was once a glorious place to stay, but, despite vestiges of its original decor, it's fallen well below standard. ❷

Palác 1 máje 27 ☎585 223 284. A Communist-era hotel that needs a thorough going over, and is overpriced for what you get. ❸

U dómu Dómská 4 ☎585 220 502, ℻585 220 501. Small, centrally located twenty-beds hotel near the cathedral. ❸

U Jakuba 8 května 9 ☎585 209 995, ⊛www .pensionujakuba.com. Spacious apartments in a newly reconstructed fifteenth-century house, par-ticularly good for families. ❷

The City

Despite being a quarter the size of Brno, Olomouc has the same exciting buzz, with its main arteries clogged with shoppers in the afternoon rush. The **staré město** is a strange contorted shape, squeezed in the middle by an arm of the Morava.

△ Olomouc radnice

Horní and Dolní náměstí

In the western half of the staré město, all roads lead to the city's two central cobbled main squares, which are hinged to one another at right angles. The lower of the two, Dolní náměstí, is more or less triangular, but the upper one, **Horní náměstí**, is thoroughly irregular. At its centre is the **radnice**, a cream-coloured amalgamation of buildings and styles with the occasional late-Gothic or Renaissance gesture – a freestanding flight of steps, the handsome lanterned tower soaring up to its conclusion of baubles and pinnacles, and, tucked round the back, a lonely oriel window above a self-portrait of the mason holding out his hand for more money from the miserly town council. But it's the north side that draws the crowds, with its crude arcade of shops and **astronomical clock**, which was originally built by Master Hanuš, like its more famous successor in Prague, but destroyed in World War II. The rather soulless workerist remake chimes all right, but the hourly mechanical show of proletarians is disappointing.

Far more action-packed is the monumental, polygonal **Holy Trinity Column** (Sousoší nejsvětější Trojice), erected in the first half of the eighteenth century to the west of the radnice, its ornamental urns sprouting dramatic gilded flames. The largest plague column in either republic, it's big enough to be a chapel and in some ways acts like one: inside you'll find a nun telling the stories of the saints featured on the outside (daily 9am–noon). Set into the west facade of the square is the **Moravské divadlo**, a Neoclassical theatre designed by Josef Kornhäusel in 1830, and previously known as the *Olmützer Stadttheater*, where the young Gustav Mahler arrived as the newly appointed *Kapellmeister* in 1883. The local press took an instant dislike to him: according to his own words, "from the moment I crossed the threshold . . . I felt like a man who is awaiting the judgement of God". No doubt there was a strong element of kneejerk anti-Semitism in his hostile reception, but this was not helped by Mahler's autocratic style, which caused a number of the local prima donnas to live up to their name. He lasted just three months.

Olomouc makes a big fuss of its sculpture, like that adorning the Edelmannův palác, at no. 28, and even more of its **fountains** (*kašna*), which grace each one of Olomouc's six ancient market squares. Horní náměstí boasts three of them: Hercules, looking unusually athletic for his years; a vigorous depiction of Julius Caesar to the east of the radnice; and, added in 2002, one dedicated to the ancient Greek poet Arion, featuring several turtles and a woman holding a dolphin. Jupiter and Neptune can be found in **Dolní náměstí**, which has a dustier feel to it, sloping down to the characteristically low-key Capuchin church. Of all the square's subdued Baroque facades, it's the **Haunschildův palác**, on the corner with Lafayettova, which stands out, its single Renaissance oriel decorated with scenes from Ovid.

The central side streets

From the bile-green late-Secession bank (now the main post office) on Horní náměstí, it's worth taking a quick turn northwest up Riegrova to see a cluster of fine **Art Nouveau** buildings: the first, at no. 10, has a ceramic facade and a delicate wrought-iron canopy, while the second, at no. 18, is decorated with low-relief figures, and the third, at no. 24, sports sapphire ovals. North of Horní náměstí, off Opletalova, is the church of **sv Mořic**, an oddly mutant building from the west at least, and defensive like a Norman fort, but inside overcome by a thick coat of pink paint that makes the original Gothic interior difficult to stomach. It does, however, boast the Engler organ, the largest in either republic; an ugly, dark, wooden affair with over 10,000 dirty grey pipes and a fair few

OLOMOUC

Bus Station (1.5km) & ▲ Train Station (1km)

Football Stadium (150m) ▲

Flora Exhibition Grounds (300m) ▶

ACCOMMODATION

Arigone	F
Gemo	G
Lafayette	I
Na hradbách	E
Národní dům	C
Palác	B
U dómu	D
U Jakuba	H
Ubytovna Zora	A

RESTAURANTS, CAFES & BARS

Caesar	6
Café Mahler	5
Captain Morgan's	13
Hanácká hospoda	11
Jazz Tibet Club	1
Konvikt	2
Maruška	3
Moravská restaurace	7
Shanghai	4
U bakaláře	8
U červeného volka	10
U kapucínů	9
U-Klub	12
Botanická zahrada	

Map labels

Dóm
Přemyslovský hrad
Arcibiskupský palác
Palacký University
Vlastivědné muzeum
Panna Maria Sněžná
Muzeum umění
Vila Primavesi
Bezručovy sady
Šarkandrova kaple
sv Michal
Kapucínský kostel
Radnice
sv Mořic
Former Edison Cinema
Holy Trinity Column
Moravské divadlo
Haunschildův palác
Puppet Theatre
Zimní stadión

Streets

KOMENSKÉHO
VÁCLAVSKÉ NÁMĚSTÍ
DÓMSKÁ
WURMOVA
1 MÁJE
BISKUPSKÉ NÁMĚSTÍ
NÁM. REPUBLIKY
MARIÁNSKÁ
DENISOVA
KŘÍŽKOVSKÉHO
UNIVERZITNÍ
ŽEROTÍNOVO NÁM.
MICHALSKÁ
ŽIŽKOVA
ZÁMEČNICKÁ
SOKOLSKÁ
OSTRUŽNICKÁ
OPLETALOVA
HORNÍ NÁMĚSTÍ
28. ŘÍJNA
8. KVĚTNA
DOBROVSKÉHO
KOŽELUŽSKÁ
STUDENTSKÁ
RIEGROVA
MLÝNSKÁ
TŘÍDA SVOBODY
PAVELČÁKOVA
PANSKÁ
HRNČÍŘSKÁ
DOLNÍ NÁMĚSTÍ
MALÉ NÁMĚSTÍ
KATEŘINSKÁ
JAVOŘÍČSKÁ
UHELNÁ
ALEŠTOVA
VÍDEŇSKÁ
PALACHOVO NÁMĚSTÍ
JAVOŘÍČSKÁ
HAVLÍČKOVA
ČECHOVY SADY
ŠKARAPOVA
SPOJENCŮ
VANČUROVA
TYLOVA
SVĚROVA
KOLLÁROVO NÁM.
PALACKÉHO
LEGIONÁŘSKÁ
17. LISTOPADU

N

0   100 m

cherubs, it sounds better than it looks (there's an organ festival held here in early September). You can also climb the church **tower** (May–Sept Mon–Fri 9.15–11.45am & 12.30–4pm, Sat 9.15–11.45am & 12.45–4pm, Sun 1–4pm) for an overview of the staré město. Opposite its west door is a typical 1970s supermarket building, which muscled its way into the historic part of town with the connivance of the philistine Communist council.

Two of the city's best-looking backstreets, Školní and Michalská, lead southeast from Horní náměstí up to the long slope of Žerotínovo náměstí, which features an appealing ensemble of lime trees, streetlamps and Baroque statuary at its upper end. Overlooking them all is the Italianate church of **sv Michal**, whose rather plain facade hides a cool, spacious interior clad in the masterly excess of High Baroque. Three octagonal saucer domes rise up in Byzantine fashion atop Roman pilasters with gilded Corinthian capitals so large their acanthus leaves bear fruit. There's a very high cherub count on the side altars and a wonderful silver relief of sheep on the gilded pulpit; before you leave, look up at the equally exuberant late-nineteenth-century organ loft. Close to sv Michal, on the corner of Univerzitní, is the late-nineteenth-century **vila Primavesi**, designed in the Viennese Secession style by, among others, the local sculptor Anton Hanak and the Viennese architect Josef Hofmann for the Primavesi family who went on to finance the Wiener Werkstätte in the 1920s. Recently restored, it now houses the **Galerie Primavesi** (Tues–Fri 8.30am–12.30pm & 1–5pm, Sat 8.30am–12.30pm), which puts on temporary exhibitions of modern art, worth seeing if only for the sophisticated mosaics by the entrance.

Also worth checking out is the mini-dome of the neo-Baroque **Sarkandrova kaple**, which replaced the old prison on Mahlerova at the beginning of the twentieth century. It's hardly big enough to kneel in, though this is perhaps its main charm. The chapel takes its name from a Catholic priest of Silesian origin, **Jan Sarkander** (1576–1620), who was incarcerated in the aforementioned prison and died after being tortured by local Protestants. In 1995 Pope John Paul II visited Olomouc and officially canonized Sarkander, whose relics now rest in the gilded casket opposite the pulpit in the local cathedral (see p.418). His canonization angered the local non-Catholic community, who claimed that Sarkander was extremely anti-evangelical and a willing instrument of the Counter-Reformation, taking over the parish of Holešov after the local Protestants had been kicked out by the Jesuits, and that he was implicated in a very unsaintly treason plot involving Polish Cossacks.

Muzeum umění to the Dóm

Firmly wedged between the two sections of the staré město is the obligatory Jesuit church of **Panna Maria Sněžná**, deemed to be particularly necessary in a city where Protestantism spread like wildfire among the German community during the sixteenth century. Jutting out into the road, the church marks the former gateway from the old town to the archbishop's territory to the east, where the great mass of the former Jesuit College, now the **Palacký University**, dominates the neighbouring square, náměstí Republiky.

Above the Divadlo hudby, on the opposite side of the square, is the **Muzeum umění** (Tues–Sun 10am–6pm; ⓦwww.olmuart.cz), which has a nice café (open until 10pm) and a permanent collection of fourteenth- to eighteenth-century Italian paintings, including one or two excellent sixteenth-century Venetian works. Best of all, though, is the **gallery** in the attic, which features a model of the town from 1895 with the zigzag fortifications still intact, 1930s photos of the city by, among others, the outstanding Otakar Lenhart (from a local-born family of fine artists), plus models of the city's modernist Konstandt Haus by Adolf Loos and Paul Engelmann and the Vila Primavesi. From the latter have been salvaged an Art Nouveau stained-glass window, table and chair by Anton Hanak, and a model of his strange *Child over an Ordinary Day* (a cherub standing over a four-headed plinth around which four snakes have wrapped themselves), originally positioned under the pergola in the villa's garden. There are lots of other great exhibits here, not least a model of the famous statue of Stalin and Lenin that once graced the city (see opposite), or a new display dedicated to the turn-of-the-twentieth-century Czech art. You can also gain access to the gallery's *vyhlídkova věž* for a rooftop view over Olomouc. Next door is the town's **Vlastivědné muzeum** (April–Sept Tues–Sun 9am–6pm; Oct–March Wed–Sun 10am–5pm; Ⓦwww .vmo.cz), housed in the former Poor Clares' convent and cloisters, with a pretty dull permanent display on the region's natural history.

The trams and cars hurtling across the cobbles make this one of Olomouc's least accommodating squares, so, after admiring the Bernini-esque Triton fountain, you'd be as well to slip down Mariánská to leafy **Biskupské náměstí**, one of the most peaceful spots in town. Among its fine Baroque buildings, erected after the destructive occupation of the Swedes, is the **Arcibiskupský palác** (Archbishop's Palace; closed to the public), financed by the multimillionaire Bishop Liechtenstein in the 1660s; it was here, at a safe distance from Vienna, that the eighteen-year-old Franz Josef I was proclaimed emperor in 1848. On the south side of the square is the former armoury, placed there by Maria Theresa after a disagreement with the archbishop. A popular spot nearby is the **student centre** (and British Council reading room) in the main university building, up Wurmova, which has a sunny terrace café.

On the other side of the tramlines, the Cathedral of sv Václav, or **Dóm**, started life as a twelfth-century Romanesque basilica, but, as with Brno and Prague, the current structure is mostly the result of nineteenth-century neo-Gothic restoration, which included the addition of the 100-metre-high eastern spire. However, the nave is bright and airy, its walls and pillars prettily painted in imitation of the great Romanesque churches of the West; the modern, high-relief Stations of the Cross are quite striking, and the **krypta** (Tues & Thurs–Sat 9am–5pm, Wed 9am–4pm, Sun 11am–5pm) has a wonderful display of gory reliquaries and priestly sartorial wealth.

Next door in the chapterhouse, you can view the fascinating remains of the original twelfth-century Románský biskupský palác or **Přemyslovský palác** (April–Sept Tues–Sun 10am–6pm), now believed to have been built as a bishop's (and not a royal) palace. The common name refers to the Olomouc princes of the Přemysl dynasty, Czech rulers from the 9th century to the early 14th century, though recent archeological and historical research suggests it is more likely that the royal family lived in a part of the Přemyslid castle that used to stand at what is now the deanery, across the square. The bishop's palace was built in the early 12th century in the Romanesque style, but it was revised through several subsequent architectural styles over the centuries. A late Gothic cloister lies between the palace and the Dóm, while Renaissance frescoed corridors lead down to the restored chapel of sv Jan Křtitel (St John the Baptist), in which are exhibited fine statuary and fragments of the original palace. Upstairs the palace's origins are much more clearly on display, and you can peer down into what is now believed to be the bishop's living quarters from at least the year 1141, lined with Romanesque columns unrivalled in the Czech lands. Right by the entrance is the Baroque chapel of sv Anna (open for morning and evening services only) and, set back from it, the university deanery where the teenage King Václav III, the last of the Přemyslids, was murdered in mysterious circumstances in 1306, throwing the country into a blood-letting war of succession.

Beyond the staré město

The Habsburg defences to the west of the staré město were completely torn down in the late nineteenth century to make way for what is now a long, busy thoroughfare known as **třída Svobody**. Starting in the north with the former **Edison cinema**, a late-Secession building from 1913 decorated with caryatids worshipping light bulbs, it continues with the familiar trail of Habsburg bureaucratic architecture. Halfway down on the right, a leftover water tower is the only survivor on Palachovo náměstí, a square that contained a synagogue until the Nazis burnt it down in 1939, and where a double statue of Stalin and Lenin subsequently stood. The former (and only the former) was defaced badly towards the end of the 1980s, apparently by an outraged Gorbachev-supporting Soviet soldier; neither survived the iconoclasm of November 1989, and the square is now named after the 1969 martyr Jan Palach (see p.127).

If you're tired of Olomouc's uneven cobbles, the best places to head for are the **parks**, which practically encircle the town. A couple of blocks of *fin-de-siècle* houses stand between Svobody and the long, well-maintained patchwork strip of crisscross paths, flowerbeds and manicured lawns. It's just a small sample of what goes on show at the annual **Flower Festival** (Flora Olomouc), a minor international gathering of florists, held at the end of April or beginning of May in the Flora Výstaviště (exhibition grounds). The grounds also contain the city's **botanical gardens** (*botanická zahrada*; daily: March–April 9.30am–5pm; May–Sept 9.30am–6pm), which are worth visiting at any time of the year. Another pleasant walk is out of the southern end of Dolní náměstí and left into the tiny Malé náměstí, which has a flight of steps leading down to the Bezručovy sady, once the city moat, where the local youth likes to hang out.

Eating, drinking and nightlife

For a big city, most of Olomouc goes to bed pretty early. As far as **nightlife** goes, there's always a good turnout at the Moravské divadlo (ⓦwww.moravskedivadlo .cz), on Horní náměstí, which puts on a good selection of opera as well as regular concerts by the city's philharmonic orchestra. In late May, Olomouc has its own Spring Music Festival (Olomoucké hudební jaro), when concerts are spread evenly around the city's churches, monasteries and other venues. The Divadlo hudby, below the Muzeum umění at Denisova 47, puts on a more adventurous programme of **gigs**, films and videos. Olomouc has its own jazz club, the *Jazz Tibet Club*, Sokolská 48, which mostly features trad and swing bands, with the music kicking off at 8pm. It's also worth checking out what's on at the student *U-Klub*, which hosts gigs east of the city centre at the student union, Šmeralova 12. Art-house **films** can be seen on Tuesdays at the Metropol, Sokolská 25, but for a full rundown of the month's events, buy the **listings** magazine *Kdy-Kde-Co v Olomouci* at the tourist office or newsagents around town. And before you leave town be sure to try out the city's famously pungent local cheese, *Olomoucký sýr*, known also as *tvarůžky*.

Caesar Horní nám. An excellent, popular pizzeria in the cobbled vaults of the radnice, from which the smell of garlic wafts enticingly across the main square. Daily 9am–1am.

Café Mahler Horní nám. 11. Popular place to go for coffee and cake, with tables outside looking over to the radnice. Mon–Sat 8am–10pm, Sun 10am–9pm.

Captain Morgan's Mlynská 2. Hip dark café/bar/ pizzeria situated in the old fortifications, with an outside patio and beer from nearby Litovel. Daily 10am–2am.

Hanácká hospoda Dolní nám. 38. A large, crowded restaurant in the Haunschildův palác, with a wide choice of Czech dishes and moderate prices. Mon–Sat 10am–midnight, Sun 10am–8pm.

Konvikt A very pleasant two-storey, modern café in the grounds of the Palacký University. Mon–Fri 9am–midnight, Sat & Sun 10am–11pm.

Maruška 28 října 2. More functional than the Mahler, but a decent coffee-and-cake dispenser, with seating upstairs. Mon–Sat 8am–10pm, Sun 10am–10pm.

Moravská restaurace Horní nám. 23. Slap bang next to the main theatre on the main square, with traditional Moravian ambience; a good place for pre- or post-theatre food and drink. Daily 11.30am–11pm.

Shanghai Horní nám. 8. New, spacious Chinese restaurant, located upstairs opposite the radnice, with large windows offering an unbeatable view over the main square. Daily 11am–11pm.

U bakaláře Žerotínovo náměstí 2. Nice modern take on the traditional pub, with wooden benches and tables. Daily 10am–11pm.

U červeného volka Dolní nám. 39. Wide choice of pasta and veggie dishes as well as the usual Czech pub-restaurant food and cheap Pilsner Urquell. Mon–Sat 10am–11pm, Sun 11am–11pm.

U kapucínů Dolní nám. 23. Odd combination of gothic and modern styles that works; a different menu from most, that includes pastas and fish. Mon–Thurs 10am–10pm, Fri–Sat 10am–11pm, Sun 11am–8pm.

Around Olomouc

Olomouc sits happily in the wide plain of the **Haná region**, famous for its multifarious folk costumes and for its songs reflecting the fertility of the land. Naturally enough in a strongly agricultural area, the harvest festivals (*Hanácké dožínky* or *dožínkový slavnost*) are the highlight of the year, advertised on posters everywhere in the second half of September. All the places covered below are situated in the Morava plain, and easily reached by bus or train on day-trips from Olomouc, with the exception of Helfštýn and the area round Bouzov, which are really only accessible to those who have their own transport.

Přerov and around

Twenty-three kilometres southeast of Olomouc, and twenty minutes by train, **PŘEROV** (Prerau; ⓦ www.prerov.cz) is an important rail junction and ungainly town dedicated to the chemical and engineering industries. Apart from a brief jazz festival in late September, its chief redeeming feature is the endearing old town square, **Horní náměstí**, a tight semicircle of colourful houses elevated above the rest of the town. At its centre is a typically anguished statue by František Bílek, depicting the sixteenth-century religious reformer Jan Blahoslav brandishing his Czech translation of the New Testament. The straight side of the square is taken up by the sixteenth-century chateau, whose **Muzeum Komenského** (March & Nov Wed, Sat & Sun 9am–noon & 1–5pm; April–Oct Tues–Sun 9am–noon & 1–5pm; ☏ 581 797 093) commemorates Blahoslav's more famous successor in the Protestant Unity of Brethren, Jan Ámos Komenský (aka Comenius; see box opposite). The **bus** and **train stations** are about 1km southwest of the town centre.

If you're heading east into the Beskydy by rail or road, it's difficult to miss the spectacular ruined castle of **Helfštýn** (March & Nov Sat & Sun 9am–4pm; April, Sept & Oct Tues–Sun 9am–5pm; May–Aug closes 6pm), which looks down from the wooded hills to the south of River Bečva, 15km east of Přerov. Founded sometime in the fourteenth century, it's one of the largest medieval castles in the Czech Republic, and was used by the Hussites as a base from which to attack Olomouc, before being deliberately laid to waste by the Habsburgs following the Thirty Years' War. Sections of the complex have since been restored, but the place is still, for the most part, a ruin and you can wander at will. Concerts, mock battles and various other attractions are staged here over the summer (check out ⓦ www.helfstyn.cz, or ask at the Muzeum

Comenius

Jan Ámos Komenský (John Amos Comenius) was born in 1592 in a village close to Uherský Brod, but his Latin schooling took place at the Unity of Brethren's school in Přerov. He served as a Protestant minister in Fulnek from 1616 to 1621, before being forced to flee the Czech Lands after the victory of the papal forces at the Battle of Bílá hora. Komenský and the Brethren set up an academy in the Polish city of Leszno, until forced to move on once more by the Swedish Wars of the 1650s. Of his many writings, Komenský's graded and pictorial Latin textbooks (the first of their kind) have proved more influential than his religious treatises, and he was called to put his educational theories into practice in Sweden, Hungary, Holland and England. He even received invitations from the Protestant-loathing Cardinal Richelieu in France, and from Harvard University, which wanted him as its president. He is buried in Naarden, Holland. Throughout the eastern part of Moravia, the Brethren rode out the Counter-Reformation to emerge in significant numbers once Austrian liberalism began to take effect in the late eighteenth century. They were later transformed into the Moravian Church, a body which continues to have an influence out of all proportion to its size, particularly in the Czech Lands and the USA.

Komenského) and there's a permanent display of modern **blacksmith** artistry in one of the castle wings (*expozice kovářství*; May–Sept Tues–Sun 9am–5pm), plus an annual blacksmiths' convention in late August. To get to the castle, you can either walk the 5km along the red-marked path from the train station at Lipník nad Bečvou, or catch one of the infrequent buses to Týn nad Bečvou, 1.5km below the castle.

Prostějov and around

Twenty kilometres and half an hour by train from Olomouc, the big textile town of **PROSTĚJOV** (Prossnitz) has a more grand and spacious old centre based around a large, well-laid-out main square, Masarykovo náměstí. Dominating this is the **nová radnice**, with its ludicrously large landmark tower built just before World War I and an asymmetrical appearance caused by the council's failure to purchase one of the neighbouring houses. The Renaissance **stará radnice**, in the opposite corner of the square, now houses the local **museum** (Tues–Sun 9.30am–noon & 1–5pm), with folk artefacts from the Haná region, including old clocks and watches, but very little on the town's brightest star, **Edmund Husserl** (1859–1938), the founder of phenomenology. A better bet is to pop into the nearby **church**, which has some terrific Baroque furnishings, a technicolour pulpit covered with carved figures and an extravagant crown-shaped baldachin, as well as a set of Stations of the Cross carved by František Bílek.

Just off the main square is the town's prettily sgraffitoed Renaissance **zámek** (times as at museum), which puts on art exhibitions and contains a permanent collection of graphics by Jan Köhler. The town's real architectural highlight, however, is Jan Kotěra's 1908 **Národní dům** (ⓦ www.narodni-dum.info), northeast of the main square near the last remaining bastion of the old town walls and now housing a theatre and restaurant. As in his museum at Hradec Králové (see p.330), Kotěra was moving rapidly away from the "swirl and blob" of the Secession, but here and there the old elements persist in the sweep of the brass door handles and the pattern on the poster frames. Apart from its furniture, the restaurant has been left unmolested, and the bold Klimt-like ceramic relief of the *Three Graces* above the mantelpiece is still as striking as ever.

To reach the old town from the main **bus** and **train stations**, head west down Svatoplukova. The **tourist office** (Mon–Fri 8am–5pm), on the main square, can help with accommodation. Prostějov doesn't get too many visitors, but there are a couple of **hotels**, ranging from the expensive *Grand Hotel* (☎582 332 311, ⓦwww.grandhotel.cz; ❺), on Palackého, a couple of blocks south of the main square, to the old stalwart *Hotel Avion* (☎582 344 561, ⓦwww.avion .prostejov.cz; ❷), east of the main square on náměstí Husserla. Five kilometres west of Prostějov are two good **campsites**, *Přehrada* (mid-May to mid-Sept) and *Žralok* (May–Sept), whose lakeside locations provide plenty of opportunities for swimming. The latter sits below a high mound above the westernmost reservoir, on top of which stands the imposing slab of the chateau at **PLUMLOV** (Plumenau), another of the Liechtensteins' fancies. Designed by Prince-Bishop Karl Eusebius von Liechtenstein-Kastelcorn himself, only one wing of the four planned got off the drawing board. Reconstruction work continues slowly, but you can now wander round the courtyards, and visit a small exhibition on the **zámek** (10am–noon & 2–6pm: April–June & Sept Sat & Sun; July & Aug Tues–Sun), which makes a scenic backdrop if you're swimming.

Bouzov and around

The northernmost tip of the Drahanská vrchovina around **BOUZOV** (Busau) – an extension of the hills of the Moravský kras – has enough to keep you occupied on a lazy weekend. The village itself is nothing but its **hrad** (April & Oct Sat & Sun 9am–3pm; May–Sept Tues–Sun 9am–4pm; ⓦwww.hrad-bouzov .cz), a Romantic neo-Gothic fortress right on the high point of the vrchovina, and perfectly suited as a base for its former proprietors, the Teutonic Knights. Predictably enough, it also took the fancy of the Nazi SS, who used it as a base during World War II. The pompous pseudo-medievalism of the interior decor is not to everyone's taste, and the place is absolutely huge, so there's a choice of guided tours: *trasa 1* (klasická; 80Kč) is the regular one that gives you an hour-long whirl around the place; *trasa 2* (velká; 120Kč) lasts an extra fifty minutes and is for real enthusiasts, as is *trasa 3*, called Mix Speciál (150Kč). Tours are in Czech only, so ask for an *anglický text*. On the village's square there's the **hotel** *U Cimbury* (☎585 346 491, ⓦwww.cimbura.hotel-cz.com; ❷), though you'd be better off staying at the *Váláškův grunt* (☎585 346 312, ⓦwww.valaskuvgrunt. cz; ❷), in the nearby village of Kozov, which has a peaceful courtyard (both hotels have restaurants).

Four kilometres south at **JAVOŘÍČKO**, the local SS burnt the village to the ground and shot 38 of the inhabitants in the last days of the war. This futile and tragic act aside, the reason for coming here is to visit the **Javoříčské jeskyně** (Tues–Sun: April & Oct 9am–3pm; May–Sept 8am–4pm), limestone karst caves on a par with those near Brno but without the crowds. On weekdays up to ten buses a day link Bouzov with **BÍLÁ LHOTA**, five kilometres east, which has an eighteenth-century chateau worth visiting for its beautiful **arboretum** (April & Oct Sat & Sun 9am–4pm; May–Sept Tues–Sun 8am–6pm). The **Mladečské jeskyně** (hours as for the Javoříčské), a less extensive and popular limestone cave system another couple of kilometres on, is just off the main Olomouc–Prague road, at the end of the most twig-like of branch lines from Litovel.

Svatý Kopeček and Šternberk

If you're heading north from Olomouc on route 46, you can't fail to spot the twin clock towers of the gleaming yellow-and-white Baroque pilgrimage church on the nearby hill of **Svatý Kopeček** (Heiligberg), just 8km northeast of the city. Perched 200m above the plain and flanked by its vast convent wings, the site and scale are truly spectacular. Close up, though, it doesn't live up to expectations, and is really only worth visiting for its adjoining **zoo** (daily 8am–7pm or dusk); bus #11 from Olomouc train station will take you there.

Further north on route 46, you hit the ridge of the Jeseníky foothills at **ŠTERNBERK** (Sternberg), where the annual *Ecce Homo* motor race is held in mid-September over the lethal switchbacks on the road to Opava. The town itself, a long two-kilometre haul north of the train and bus stations, is dominated by its giant Baroque church and **hrad** (April & Oct Sat & Sun 9am–3pm; May–Sept Tues–Sun 9am–4pm), the latter rebuilt in Romantic style in the late nineteenth century and worth a visit for its chapel with a Gothic statue of the Šternberk Madonna, carved in the Beautiful Style. The famous castle's **Muzeum hodin** (Clock Museum) will be reopened in 2006 near the **tourist office** (Mon–Fri 9am–noon & 1–5pm; Ⓦwww.sternberk.cz), which is located at ČS Armády 30 and can help with **accommodation** – though the neighbouring *Hotel Šternberský dvůr* (☎585 012 990, Ⓦmujweb.cz/www /sterndvur; ❷) is a good place to start. Šternberk's two **campsites** (both mid-May to mid-Sept) are the nearest you'll get to Olomouc: the *Šternberk* site is slightly closer to the town than *U zlatého muflona*, in Dolní Žleb, 3km north of Šternberk.

The Jeseníky

Extending east from the Bohemian Krkonoše are the **Jeseníky** (Altvaterge-birge), the highest peaks in what is now Moravia. Sparsely populated, the region is worlds apart from the dense network of industrial centres in the north and east of the province, or even the vine-clad hills of the south. The highest reaches, to the northwest between Šumperk and Jeseník, have been damaged by acid rain, but the mountains as a whole are peaceful and green. One of the nicest areas to head for is the foothills on either side of the big peaks, which harbour some low-key spa resorts like Lázně Jeseník, Karlova Studánka, and the histori-cal remains of Czech Silesia in Krnov and Opava.

Šumperk

ŠUMPERK (Schönberg) is the gateway to the upper Jeseníky, and has the feel of a mountain town, despite the fact that the shift from plain to hills is much less dramatic here than at Šternberk. Unusually for a provincial town, there's no obvious centre to Šumperk. The main drag is **Hlavní třída**, beyond the park to the north of the train station, and, at the far western end of Hlavní, the tiny old town is easy to miss, its neo-Renaissance radnice standing on the pretty little square of **náměstí Míru**. For the panorama of the town and surrounding hills you can climb its **tower** (Mon–Fri & Sun: June & Sept 9am–3pm; July–Aug 9am–noon & 1–5pm), though far better **views**, including the whole range of the Jeseníky, are from the hilltop Rozhledna na Háji (March–April & Oct Sat & Sun 10am–4pm; May–June & Sept Sat & Sun 10am–5pm; July–Aug Tues–Sun 10am–5pm; Nov–Feb Sat & Sun 10am–3pm), just west of the town (the blue markers followed by the green).

Unreconstructed street names were a feature of most towns under the Com-munist regime, but Šumperk topped the lot with a Stalin Square, a Stalingrad Street and a statue of the man himself in a car park by the old town walls – all intact right up to November 1989.

Nowadays, there's not much to see here, but if you end up staying, details of current entertainments – such as at the beautifully restored theatre – are available from the **tourist office** in the local museum by the park (Mon 8am–noon & 12.30–5pm, Tues–Fri 8am–5pm; ☎583 214 000, ⓦwww.infosumperk.cz). **Rooms** are available at the utterly basic *Grand* (☎ & Ⓕ583 212 141; ❶), by the park, or the more comfortable *Pension U Jiráska* (☎ & Ⓕ583 213 849; ❸), on the road heading northeast to the suburb of Vikýřovice.

Velké Losiny

One good reason for staying in Šumperk is to visit the tiny Moravian spa of **VELKÉ LOSINY** (Gross-Ullersdorf), 9km northeast of Šumperk and one of the last oases of civilization before you hit the deserted heights of the Jeseníky. The town's Renaissance **zámek** (April & Oct Sat & Sun 9–11am & 1–3pm; May–Aug Tues–Sun 9–11am & 1–4pm; Sept Tues–Sun 9–11am & 1–3pm; ⓦwww.losiny.cz) is set in particularly lush grounds beside a tributary of the River Desná. It's a three-winged, triple-decker structure, part Renaissance and part Baroque, opening out into a beautifully restored sixteenth-century arcaded loggia, and for once the guided tour is really worthwhile. The chateau was the northernmost property of the extremely wealthy Žerotín family, but was inhabited for less than a hundred years; its grandest chamber is the Knights' Hall, which has retained its original parquet floor and leather wall hangings. Strong supporters of the Unity of Brethren, the Žerotíns were stripped of their wealth after the Battle of Bílá hora and the chateau was left empty – except as a venue for the region's notorious witch trials (56 sentenced to death) during the Counter-Reformation.

Velké Losiny is also home to the country's one remaining **paper mill** or *papírna* (April–June & Sept Tues–Fri 9am–5pm, Sat & Sun 9am–noon & 12.30–5pm; July–Aug also Mon 10am–2pm; Oct–March Tues–Fri 9am–3pm, Sat & Sun 9am–noon & 12.30–4pm), which still produces handmade paper. Built in the 1590s by the Žerotín family, and still bearing the family's coat of arms on its watermark, the mill is situated between the chateau and the spa and houses a small museum on the history of paper. The **train** and **bus stations** are in the spa itself, from which the chateau is a pleasant one-kilometre walk south through the verdant garden buildings. Those especially interested in **wooden churches** might consider visiting the nearby villages of **ŽÁROVÁ**, 3km northwest of Velké Losiny, and **MARŠÍKOV**, 2km to the east. Both churches were built at the beginning of the seventeenth century, in the Renaissance style, using wood from the demolished church in Velké Losiny. Ask round for the keys.

Hrubý Jeseník

The River Desná peters out before the real climb into the central mountain range of **Hrubý Jeseník**. A bus from Šumperk runs roughly every two hours via the last train station, Kouty nad Desnou, to the saddle of Červenohorské sedlo (1013m) and beyond. The ascent by route 44 from Kouty is a dramatic series of hairpin bends, but the top of the pass is a disappointment. The tourist board may talk of "mountain meadows and pastures", but the reality is low-lying scrub and moorland: any spruce or pine trees that dare to rise above this are new growth, only recently conquering the effects of acid rain. There's a restaurant by the roadside for beer and food, and an impromptu and very basic **campsite**, 500m away to the northwest, along with plenty of private rooms. For a better view, it's a forty-five-minute walk northwest to **Červená hora** (1333m) and another hour and a half to **Šerák** (1351m), which looks down onto the Ramzovské sedlo, the much lower pass to the west that the railway from Šumperk to Jeseník wisely opts for. A chairlift from Šerák will take you down to the campsite and train station at Ramzová, in the valley bottom. Alternatively, you could walk two hours east from Červenohorské sedlo to **Praděd** (The Great Grandfather), at 1491m the highest and most barren peak in the range.

Below and to the east of Praděd is the picturesque Silesian spa resort of **KAR-LOVA STUDÁNKA**, strung out along the valley of the bubbling River Bílá Opava. The spa has a useful **information centre** (daily 9am–5pm; out of season closes 4pm; ⓦ www.jeseniky-praded.cz), and is dotted with cold fizzy springs (with an extraordinarily high iron content) and attractive dark-brown weatherboarded spa buildings, many with cream shutters and balconies for enjoying the fresh mountain air. Most of the **accommodation** in the spa is for patients, but you could try the *Hotel Džbán* (ⓣ554 772 014, ⓔ hoteldzban@seznam.cz; ❸), in the centre of town, which has pleasant rooms (some overlooking the spa park) and a restaurant downstairs. There's also the *Dolina* **campsite** (mid-May to Sept), 7km northeast of the spa near Vrbno pod Pradědem (Würbenthal).

Another option is to stay in **MALÁ MORÁVKA**, 8km to the south down route 445, which has the advantage of being at the end of an idyllic little branch line from Bruntál (trains don't always run daily on this line so check it's running; more reliable are the frequent bus connections with Bruntál). M Servis acts as a sort of **tourist office** (in season daily 8am–6pm; ⓦ www.malamoravka.cz) and can help with accommodation in the area; you can rent bikes and skis there, too. There are numerous inexpensive pensions and rooms along the valley between here and Karlova Studánka, so **accommodation** shouldn't be a problem.

BRUNTÁL (Freudenthal) is 14km east of Malá Morávka on the scenic railway line between Olomouc and Krnov, and has the dubious distinction of having one of the highest rates of unemployment in the country. It's worth a mention, though, for its Baroque **zámek** (Tues–Sun: April & Oct 9am–noon & 1–4pm; May–Sept 9am–noon & 1–5pm; 100Kč), another hangout of the Teutonic Knights. After the chateau's solid Baroque exterior, the beautiful six-teenth-century arcaded courtyard with loggia comes as something of a surprise; inside, amidst the lush furnishings, is a series of vast Baroque landscape frescoes. Between the castle and the newly refurbished main square, on Dukelská, is the ugly **hotel** *Hvězda* (ⓣ554 717 249; ❷) with a cheap restaurant (closed Sat & Sun). The **tourist office** (Mon–Fri 8am–4.30pm; in summer also Sat 8.30am–noon) is on the square itself and can help in finding other options.

Jeseník and around

On the other side of the pass, the road plunges down with equal ferocity to **JESENÍK** (Freiwaldau), a fairly nondescript town busy in summer with Polish day-trippers. Over the stream, north of the main square in the Smetanovy sady, there's a wonderful Art Nouveau monument to local farmer Vincent Priess-nitz, founder of the nearby spa (see below), presiding godlike over the skinny and ill on his right and the "cured" (or at least plump) on his left. Otherwise, Jeseník is mainly useful as a base for exploring the surrounding area; there are several reasonably priced hotels and pensions, and a **campsite** (open all year; ⓔ camp-bobrovnik@iol.cz) with a swimming pool less than 2km west along the valley en route to another spa resort, Lipová Lázně.

Two kilometres above the town, with fantastic views south to the Jeseníky and north into Poland, is **LÁZNĚ JESENÍK** (Gräfenberg). Here Priessnitz established one of the most famous Silesian spas in the nineteenth century, where the likes of Russian writer Gogol and King Carol I of Romania took the cure. Nowadays, the only grandish spa building is the grey rendered **Priessnitz Sanatorium**, built in 1910. Scattered about the surrounding countryside, and interspersed with numerous monuments erected by grateful patients, are the **natural springs**, which provide hot and sulphuric refreshment on the obligatory constitutionals (you can buy a map from the Priessnitz Sanatorium). If you'd prefer to get clean away from people, and particularly sickly spa patients, make your way to the viewpoint from the summit of Zlatý chlum, 2km east of Jeseník.

From Lipová Lázně, a tiny, picturesque branch line heads northeast, eventually terminating at Javorník (see below), in the northernmost Silesian salient. The first stop, though, is Lipová Lázně jeskyně, just over the ridge from the entrance to the **Jeskyně na pomezí** (currently closed for renovation), a mini-karst cave system with colourful stalactites and stalagmites in the shape of fruit, vegetables and fungi. Another two stops along the line is **ŽULOVÁ**, whose local fortress, precipitously situated on a moated island of rock, was converted into a church in the nineteenth century. Beyond Žulová, the countryside flattens out as it slips into Poland, and the train continues to **JAVORNÍK** (Jauernig), where the local chateau, **Janský vrch** (April & Oct Sat & Sun 9am–noon & 1–3pm; May–Aug Tues–Sun 8am–noon & 1–4pm; Sept Tues–Sun 9am–noon & 1–3pm), perches high above the village. There's a choice of guided tours: the 45-minute tour (*trasa 1*) takes you round the period interior which features a collection of historical pipes and ornate smoking devices, as well as a small theatre, where the composer **Karl Ditters von Dittersdorf** used to stage operas (when he wasn't being the local forest warden); the half-hour tour (*trasa 2*) whisks you round the servants' quarters, the chapel and the lookout tower. If you need a place to stay, head for the small, quiet *Hotel pod zámkem* (☎584 440 154, ⓦpodzamkem.hotel-cz.com; ❶), down in the village.

Krnov

As if to underline the arbitrary nature of the region's current borders, the railway line from Jeseník passes in and out of Polish territory en route to **KRNOV** (Jägerndorf), famous for its Rieger-Kloss organ factory – the largest in Europe – established here in 1873. The town was flattened in World War II and the current population of 26,000 is only two-thirds of the town's prewar level – but it's still worth a brief stopover if you're heading for Opava or into Poland just 3km away.

From the town's otherwise nondescript main square, **Hlavní náměstí**, two buildings stand out: the salmon-pink-and-white **radnice** from 1902, topped by an excitable clock tower, modelled on the one in the Viennese suburb of Währing and decorated with patterned tiling; and the late-nineteenth-century **spořitelna**, a savings bank, in two shades of green. Beyond the Atlantes who guard the entrance to the latter, you can see the beautifully restored foyer and staircase, its stained glass, ironwork and plastering smothered in Art Nouveau floral motifs. On the ground floor is the *Dynasty* café and restaurant, restored and slightly modernized, but with enough of its original fittings – brass chandeliers, wooden panelling and so forth – to give some idea of its glory days. To the west on Zámecké náměstí, one side of the street features an unusual arcade held up by round, squat pillars, while beyond, to the north, lies the so-called **Švedská zed'** (Swedish Wall), a short, surviving stretch of the town's fortifications with decorative Renaissance battlements, later used in the unsuccessful defence of the town against the Swedes during the Thirty Years' War.

Krnov's main **train station** is 1km west of the centre along Mikulášská, though most trains heading to or from Opava and Ostrava also stop at Krnov-Cvilín, about half the distance northeast of the centre down Hlubčická. The **tourist office**, at Hlavní náměstí 25 (Mon–Fri 9am–5pm, Sat 9am–1pm), can help with private rooms. Other **accommodation** is in rather short supply, with the only two real options being the overpriced *Hotel Pepa* (☎554 611 005, Ⓦwww.pepa.hotel-cz.com, Ⓔpepa@hotel-cz.com; ❸), on Zámecké náměstí, or the kitsch but cheap Communist-era *Hotel Praha* (☎554 610 741, Ⓦwww.praha.hotel-cz.com; ❷), west of the historical core at Revoluční 10.

Opava and around

Right by the Polish border, 24km southeast of Krnov, **OPAVA** (Troppau) is one of the oldest towns in the country, an important trading centre on the Amber Road from the Adriatic to the Baltic Sea, but perhaps better known as **Troppau**, capital of Austrian (and later Czech) Silesia (see box p.428). Badly damaged in the last few weeks of World War II, it nevertheless retains enough grandiose nineteenth-century buildings to give some idea of how it looked in its heyday. Much has been rebuilt since 1945, and while Opava may not merit a detour, it's a good place to break a journey or do a bit of chateau-seeing.

The most spectacular reminder of the town's former days, the huge church of **Nanebevzetí Panny Marie**, lies in the west of the old town, built in Silesian Gothic style in the late fourteenth century, and sheltering a lovely crown-shaped high altar. East of this giant red-brick church is the town's main square, **Horní náměstí**, above which rises the tall tower of the old *Schmetterhaus*, or **Hláska**, symbol of the town's forgotten prosperity, where foreign merchants were permitted to sell their wares. Opposite this stands another object of civic pride, the neo-Baroque **Slezské divadlo**. Opava's best-looking street is Masarykova třída, lined with noble Baroque palaces that once belonged to the likes of General Blücher and one of Beethoven's chief patrons, Count Razumovský. The **Silesian Diet** used to meet in the Jesuit college at the northern end of the street, while the Minorite monastery, further south, was the venue for the 1820 Troppau Conference, when the "Holy Alliance" of Austria, Russia and Prussia met to thrash out a common policy towards the revolutionary stirrings of post-Napoleonic Europe.

Set in the town's pretty semicircle of parks to the east is the grandiose **Slezské zemské muzeum** (Tues–Sat 9am–noon & 1–4pm, Sun 9am–noon & 2–4pm; Ⓦwww.szmo.cz), built in neo-Renaissance style in 1893. It has been painstakingly restored since the war and houses a large but uninspiring exhibition that manages to avoid all the most controversial aspects of Silesian history. Opava does have one superb piece of twentieth-century architecture worth seeking out, the **church of sv Hedvik**, about 500m up Krnovská, one block to the south. The western facade is truly striking, made from big slabs of rusticated stone with concrete infill, plastered with giant Latin lettering and rising vertically in steps to form a strictly geometric tower. Begun in 1933 by local architect Leopold Bauer, it was used as a storehouse by the Nazis and Communists, and was only finished and opened for religious services in 1992.

Opava has two **train stations**; the main one – and the most central – is Opava východ, at the southeastern corner of the old town. Opava suffers from a dearth of accommodation, which makes the regional **tourist office** (Mon–Fri 8am–6pm, Sat 8–11am; ☎553 756 143, Ⓦwww.infocentrum.opava.cz), on the main square behind the radnice, especially useful. There are just two central **hotels** to speak of at present, the none-too-cheap, dark-red, modern monstrosity known as the *Koruna*, náměstí Republiky 17 (☎553 621 132, ⓦwww.hotelkoruna.cz; ④), and the new, pleasant *Hotel Iberia* (☎553 776 700, ⓦwww.hoteliberia.cz; ③), at Pekařská 11, just north of the main square. As for **food**, *U bílého koníčka*, on Dolní náměstí, is a vaulted beer hall, serving mugs of Gambrinus and all the usual Czech dishes, or else there's *Pizzeria Veneto* (closed Sun), opposite the tourist office. It only remains to say that lion-lovers all over the world might be interested to know that **Joy Adamson** (of *Born Free* fame) was born Friderika Viktoria Gessner at Na rybníčku 48 in 1910 – and there's a plaque on the house to prove it.

Hradec nad Moravicí

The castle high above the town of **HRADEC NAD MORAVICÍ**, 8km south on route 57, is a Hammer-horror neo-Gothic castle – or so it appears at first sight. In fact, the red-brick castle's magnificent gateway opens up to reveal another, earlier, Neoclassical zámek covered in smooth white plaster. The **Červený zámek**, or *Rotes Schloss* as the red-brick castle was known, is now occupied by the hotel of the same name, while the **Bílý zámek** or *Weisses Schloss* (April, Oct & Dec Sat & Sun 10am–noon & 1–4pm; May–Sept Tues–Sun 9am–noon & 1–5pm; 120Kč) contains a collection of porcelain and paintings. The latter used to belong to the Lichnovský family, who invited performances from the likes of Beethoven, Liszt and Paganini – in early June there's a Beethoven music festival, *Beethovenův Hradec*, held here. On a clear day it's well worth exploring the lovely grounds that stretch out along the ridge beyond the white castle.

Lying at the end of its very own branch line, and offering a wide range of **accommodation**, Hradec is a suitable base for visiting Opava and even Ostrava. First choice for a bed has to be the aforementioned *Hotel Červený zámek* (☎553 783 021, ⓦwww.cervenyzamek.hotel-cz.com; ②), with a restau-rant open to non-guests. There's also the *Hradec* **campsite** (May–Sept) a short distance to the south of the town and castles, along route 57.

Hrabyně

No one driving between Ostrava and Opava on route 11 can fail to notice the ugly great slab of concrete which crowns the strategic heights around the village of Hrabyně. In the final few weeks of World War II, the Red Army was forced to engage in a costly pitched battle for the area. As recently as the 1980s, the sycophantic Communist regime decided to erect this bombastic **tribute** to the fallen, at a cost of millions of crowns, thereby proving the indissoluble friendship between Czechoslovakia and the Soviet Union – "Together with the Soviet Union for ever and ever and never any other way", as the slogans used to say. The army vehicles that used to be scattered across the hilltop now line the alley behind the structure, and the monument gives out superb views north into Poland. Inside, there's a typically lavish but dull permanent display on the military operation, and rather more enlightening temporary **exhibitions** (also on a military theme) upstairs (April–June & Sept–Oct Thurs–Fri 9am–3.30pm, Sat & Sun 11am–5pm; July–Aug Tues–Fri 9am–5pm, Sat & Sun 11am–5pm).

Ostrava

If you told a Czech you were going to **OSTRAVA** (Ostrau), they'd probably think you were mad. Although the situation has improved in recent years, the city used to be regularly shrouded in a pall of pungent sulphurous smog. Ostrava's coalmines were closed down in 1994 and since then huge efforts have been made to clean up the centre; however, it's hard to hide the fact that it's coal and steel that made the town, and pollution from nearby mining towns can still have an unfortunate effect on the city's air quality. From a village of less than 2000 inhabitants at the beginning of the nineteenth century, Ostrava has grown into the Czech Republic's third largest city with a population of 315,000, a significant number of whom are Polish due to its position as the main gateway into Poland. Ostrava does, however, have plenty of high culture and a packed sporting calendar, so if you should end up having to stay in the North Moravian coal basin, this is as good a place as any.

Arrival, information and accommodation

Ostrava's main **train station**, Ostrava hlavní nádraží, is 2km north of the city centre (tram #1, #2 or #8). Trains from Krnov and Opava terminate at Ostrava-Svinov (most fast trains also call here), 5km west of the centre (tram #4, #8 or #9). One or two trains an hour from the main train station (including trains to and from Frýdek-Místek and Kroměříž) will take you to the most central of the city terminals, Ostrava střed, next door to the main **bus station** and just ten minutes' walk west of the centre (tram #1, #2 or #6). The **tourist office** (Mon–Fri 8am–6pm, Sat 9am–2pm; ☎596 123 913, ⓦ www.ostravainfo.cz), on Nádražní, is helpful. Anyone needing a Polish visa can get one quickly and easily at the **Polish consulate** (Mon–Fri 8.30am–noon; ☎596 118 074), at Blahoslavova 4, just north of the Nová radnice.

Accommodation

Despite the lack of tourists, Ostrava's **hotels** can get booked up by people on business, so it's worth ringing in advance or starting your search early in the day.

City Hotel Macharova 16 ☎596 134 090, Ⓦwww.hotelsavoy.cz. Inexpensive, but comfortable, modernized hotel situated within walking distance of the main train station. ❸
Dom Polski Poděbradova 53 ☎596 122 001, Ⓦwww.polskydum.cz. A striking Art Nouveau villa dating from 1899, that has been modernized inside, but is probably the place with most character in Ostrava. ❸
Imperial Tyršova 6 ☎596 112 065, Ⓦwww.imperial.cz. A luxury, four-star hotel that has all the mod cons, but is expensive at nearly 4000Kč

a double. ❼
Jindřich Nádražní 66 ☎596 112 979, Ⓕ596 112 776. Smart, modern, red-brick hotel with a sauna, situated right by the disused nineteenth-century pithead of the same name. ❸
Maria Přívozská 23 ☎596 110 676, Ⓦwww.hotel-maria.cz. A decent, medium-range hotel, a short walk from the city centre. ❷–❸
Palace 28 října 59 ☎596 158 111, Ⓔpalace@applet.cz. An old Communist-era luxury hotel that can't quite pass muster in that category any more, hence the bargain prices. ❸

The City

Ostrava divides into three distinct districts: **Slezská Ostrava**, on the east bank of the River Ostravice, where the first black-coal deposits were discovered back in the 1760s, **Vítkovice**, south of the centre on the opposite side of the river, where the first foundry was set up in 1828, and **Moravská Ostrava**, the largely pedestrianized downtown district.

It's in Moravská Ostrava that you'll find most of the town's shops and department stores, bunched up around the old marketplace and main square, **Masarykovo náměstí**. Under the Communists the square was known as náměstí Lidových milicí (People's Militia Square) – a once-proud reference to the city's strong working-class traditions and staunch postwar support for the Party (the Communists still capture a high percentage of the vote here). This largely unspoken alliance ensured high wages and well-stocked shops, and for the two decades after 1968, the commercial district was always crowded with Poles and Soviet soldiers gaping in awe at what to them was an unbelievably wide range of products. Hard times have now hit the local heavy industries, with steel production at less than half its 1989 level and thousands of workers being laid off. Similarly, the coal industry has drastically cut its workforce and closed down mines, owing to the decrease in demand for Czech coal stemming from greater environmental awareness, competition from other Eastern and Western European countries, and since the Temelín nuclear plant began functioning (see p.191).

Though hardly an architectural masterpiece, the square still vaunts a handful of swanky late-nineteenth-century facades erected by the rich German and Austrian capitalists who owned the mines here until nationalization in 1945. The sixteenth-century **stará radnice**, in the southeastern corner of the square, is one of the oldest buildings in the city and now houses the less than thrilling **Ostravské muzeum** (Mon–Fri 9am–5pm, Sat & Sun 9am–1pm; July–Aug closed Sun). Ostrava's most lavish museum, at Nádražní 10, was the one dedicated to the working-class movement, though it has now reverted to its original function as the **Investiční banka**, the muscular proletarians above the portico now simply employees. The city's purpose-built **Dům umění** (Tues–Sat 10am–1pm & 1.30–6pm), a red-brick Functionalist building from the 1920s, on Jurečkova, one block west of Nádražní, displays an unexceptional collection of nineteenth- and twentieth-century Czech art on the ground floor, with temporary exhibitions upstairs.

With so much money sloshing around in the late nineteenth and early twentieth centuries, it comes as no surprise that Ostrava boasts one or two grandiose reminders of those golden years. The gargantuan salmon-pink-and-cream-coloured **Bazilika**, northwest of the main square, built in a heavy neo-Renaissance style in the 1880s, is the second largest church in Moravia, capable of seating a congregation of four thousand. One of the finest Art Nouveau buildings in the city stands to the north at the top of Milíčova, its facade decorated with delicate floral stuccowork – just don't look at the modern extension round the back. Directly opposite is Ostrava's imposing brick-built **Evangelický kostel** (Protestant Church), designed in Dutch Renaissance style in 1907. However, by far the most awesome monument to Ostrava's former municipal pride is the **nová radnice**, at the end of 30 dubna. Erected in the 1920s, it is the largest town hall in the country, and its slender, 72-metre-high, copper-clad clock tower has a viewing platform open to the public (daily: May–Oct 9am–7pm; Nov–April 9am–5pm).

When the coal industry took off in the nineteenth century, the city just grew up around the pitheads – a convenient, but ecologically disastrous, piece of town planning. The **Karolina coking plant**, right in the city centre and pulled down only in the 1980s, spewed out lethal carcinogenic filth over the city's main shopping district for over a century, and you can still see the red-brick **Jindřich pithead** (těžní věž), just past 30 dubna on Nádražní. Elsewhere, antiquated derricks, silver snaking pipes and red-and-white-striped chimneys

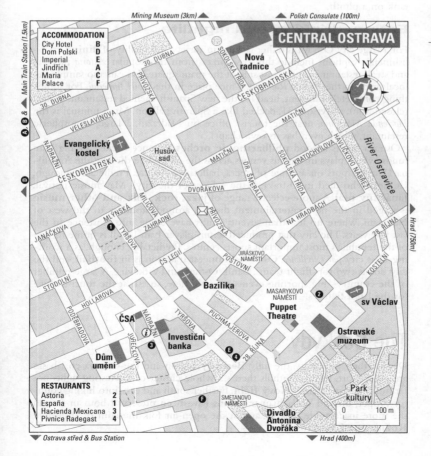

CENTRAL OSTRAVA

Mining Museum (3km) ▲

▲ Polish Consulate (100m)

▲ Main Train Station (1.5km)

ACCOMMODATION
City Hotel — **B**
Dom Polski — **D**
Imperial — **E**
Jindřich — **A**
Maria — **C**
Palace — **F**

Nová radnice

30. DUBNA

PŘÍVOZSKÁ

SOKOLSKÁ TŘÍDA

ČESKOBRATRSKÁ

Ⓒ

VELESLAVÍNOVA

MATIČNÍ

Evangelický kostel ✚

Husův sad

MATIČNÍ

DR. ŠMERALA

SOKOLSKÁ TŘÍDA

KRATOCHVÍLOVA

HAVLÍČKOVO NÁBŘEŽÍ

River Ostravice

NÁDRAŽNÍ

ČESKOBRATRSKÁ

DVOŘÁKOVA

NA HRADBÁCH

28. ŘÍJNA

Hrad (750m) ▶

JANÁČKOVA

MLÝNSKÁ

TYRŠOVA

ZAHRADNÍ

MILÍČOVA

PŘÍVOZSKÁ

✉

Ⓐ, Ⓑ & Main Station (1.5km) ◀

Ⓓ ◀

①

ČS LEGIÍ

JIRÁSKOVO NÁMĚSTÍ

POŠTOVNÍ

STODOLNÍ

HOLLAROVA

PODĚBRADOVA

Bazilika ✚

MASARYKOVO NÁMĚSTÍ

②

sv Václav ✚

KOSTELNÍ

ČSA

NÁDRAŽNÍ

TYRŠOVA

PUCHMAJEROVA

Puppet Theatre

Ⓘ

③

Investiční banka

Ⓔ

④

28. ŘÍJNA

Ostravské muzeum

JUŘÍČKOVA

Dům umění

SMETANOVO NÁMĚSTÍ

Ⓕ

Park kultury

RESTAURANTS
Astoria — **2**
España — **1**
Hacienda Mexicana — **3**
Pivnice Radegast — **4**

Divadlo Antonína Dvořáka

0 — 100 m

N

▼ Ostrava střed & Bus Station

▼ Hrad (400m)

are very much a part of the cityscape: an awesome sight, lit up at night like proverbial satanic mills. Those with a passionate interest in the local mining industry should hop on bus #34, #52 or #56 at the top of Sokolská třída, east of the main train station, which provide a regular service north across the River Odra to the suburb of Petřkovice (get off at the U Jana stop). Here, at the now defunct Anselm mine (once owned by the Rothschilds), there's a **Hornický skanzen** or open-air mining museum (Tues–Sun 9am–6pm guided tours on the hour), where you can descend into the pit, inspect the seams and take a look at the exhibition in the manager's villa.

The city continues to pay a high price for the mining exploitation of the last two centuries, especially when it comes to subsidence. The local **hrad**, originally built in the thirteenth century to guard the border between Moravia and Silesia, has already sunk fourteen metres and, according to city officials, is now beyond redemption. You can still visit it at any time by crossing one of the bridges over the Ostravice and negotiating the motorway (alternatively, take tram #9 and get off at the first stop across the river). If you're walking, as you cross the bridge, Sýkorův most, you'll pass by one of the few surviving monuments celebrating the city's liberation by the Soviets, which features a tank on a plinth.

Eating, drinking and nightlife

For a large city Ostrava is rather lacking in variety and quality of **dining** establishments. Options include thin-base pizzas from the popular *Astoria* pizzeria and steak restaurant, on the east side of the main square. You can also sample the local pride in the *Pivnice Radegast*, a nice place in the *Hotel Imperial*. For something completely different, head for the new Spanish-themed restaurant, *España* (closed Sun), at Tyršova 31, decked like a Spanish galleon. More unusual is the *Hacienda Mexicana*, near the tourist office on Nádražní, a large, atmospheric restaurant, which even has its own chapel.

Ostrava boasts a good **philharmonic orchestra**, once backed by big state funds, which plays in various venues across the city, while the Divadlo Antonína Dvořáka puts on a range of opera, ballet and theatre. Predictably enough, Janáček, who died in Ostrava, is the subject of the city's May music festival, **Janáčkův máj**. A more eclectic range of **jazz, rock, folk and other music** is staged in the new entertainment district, around Stodolní, to the west of Nádražní, where no less than seventy clubs have come into existence in the last few years. The city that produced tennis player Ivan Lendl is home to one of the republic's most important sports centres. Predictably enough, as a working-class city *par excellence*, Ostrava's strongest tradition is in **football**, and the city boasts two top-flight teams, Baník Ostrava and Vítkovice. A large number of the country's big sporting events are held here, so ask at the tourist office for the latest fixtures.

The Beskydy

Despite their proximity, the hilly **Beskydy** region and the Ostrava coal basin are poles apart. In the foothills there's a whole cluster of interesting sights not far from (and including) **Nový Jičín**. Further south and east, into hiking country proper, the old Wallachian traditions have been preserved both in situ, in the more inaccessible villages, and at the open-air folk museum or *skansen* at **Rožnov pod Radhoštěm**.

Nový Jičín

NOVÝ JIČÍN (Neu-Titschein) is a typical one-square town on the main road from Olomouc to Ostrava. That said, Masarykovo náměstí is a particularly fine square, with wide, whitewashed arcades tunnelling their way under a host of restrained, late-Baroque facades in pastel colours. The **radnice** is an unusual white, boxy affair rebuilt in the 1930s, its wonderfully jagged gable a reminder of its seventeenth-century origins. However, the one building that stands out (literally) from the rest is the **stará pošta**, where Tsar Alexander I and General Suvorov have both stayed the night; its pretty two-storey loggia dates from the town's boom time in the sixteenth century when it bought its independence from the Žerotín family.

Nowadays, the town's chief attraction is its **Kloboučnické muzeum** (Hat Museum; April–Oct Tues–Fri 8am–noon & 1–4pm, Sat & Sun 9am–3pm; Nov–March closed Sat), laid out in the Žerotíns' old chateau, accessed through the covered passageway of Lidická underneath the radnice. Thankfully, the present exploits of the old state hat enterprise, Tonak (based in the town), are only lightly touched on, leaving most of the museum to a wonderful variety of hats produced in Nový Jičín since 1799 by the original firms of Hückel, Peschel and Böhm. The bit that gets the Czechs going is the array of hats worn by famous national personages – a bit esoteric for non-Czechs, though some might be stirred by the sight of Masaryk's topper.

Wooden churches in the Beskydy

If you can't make it out to the Greek-Catholic churches of East Slovakia (see p.576), the next best place for visiting **wooden churches** is the Beskydy region. Although numerous timber-framed houses were torn down during the course of the nineteenth century, churches appear to have fared a little better. Below is a selection of the region's best examples.

Bílá 25km east of Rožnov pod Radhoštěm. A mountain hamlet near the Slovak border boasts an untypical, slender Scandinavian church, brought here from Sweden by Cardinal Fürstenberg and built here in 1875.

Bystřice nad Olší 12km southeast of Český Těšín. Polish/Czech town in the Olše valley, with a wooden neo-Gothic Catholic church, built in 1896 to replace the sixteenth-century stone one.

Guty 11km south of Český Těšín. Probably the most striking of all the Beskydy's wooden churches, with its bulky Lemk-style western tower erected in 1781 above the narthex (entrance porch).

Hodslavice 8km south of Nový Jičín. Birthplace of Czech nationalist and historian František Palacký, one of the chief political figures of the nineteenth-century Czech national revival. Hodslavice also boasts the sixteenth-century wooden church of sv Ondřej.

Kunčice pod Ondřejníkem 4km east of Frenštát pod Radhoštěm. This mountain village was a favourite summer resort of the wealthy steel and coal magnates of Ostrava, one of whom, in 1931, brought an entire Greek-Catholic church over from what is now the Ukraine for his wedding.

Radhošť 6km south of Frenštát pod Radhoštěm. You have to climb a mountain to see the wooden chapel of sv Cyril a Metoděj, built in neo-Byzantine style in 1905, from which there's an unbeatable view across the Beskydy.

Rybí 4km northwest of Štramberk. Fifteenth-century Gothic church with shingled roof, tower and onion dome steeple, plus a dinky little sundial in its main gable.

Nový Jičín has two **train stations**, both located at the end of obscure and inconvenient branch lines, making the **bus** by far the easiest way to come and go. The **tourist office** (Mon–Fri 8am–5pm, Sat & Sun 9am–noon; ⓦwww .novyjicin.cz), on Úzká near the chateau, can help find **accommodation** in the area. Otherwise, try the newly refurbished *Hotel Praha* (☎556 701 229, ⓦwww.prahahotel.cz; ➋), at Lidická 6, in a late-nineteenth-century building opposite the chateau, or the decent *Rusty's Hotel* (☎556 707 722; ➋), at Tolstého 13, near the train and bus stations.

Štramberk

Eight kilometres east of Nový Jičín, accessible by the occasional bus or an easy two-hour walk, the smokestack settlement of **ŠTRAMBERK** (Strallenburg; ⓦwww.stramberk.cz) is one of the best places to take your first dip into Wallachian culture. Clumped under the conic Bílá hora (not to be confused with *the* Bílá hora in Prague) like an ancient funeral pyre, Štramberk feels very old indeed, yet many of its wooden cottages were built as recently as the first half of the nineteenth century. Its virtue is in displaying Wallachian architecture in situ, the cottages simply constructed out of whole tree trunks, unpainted and free of tourists rather than cooped and mummified in a sanitized *skansen*.

Despite being no more than a hillside village, Štramberk does have a nominal main square. At one end are several stone buildings in folk Baroque style, behind which rises up the galleried wooden *klopačka* (belfry) of the original church. At the other end is an old Jesuit church painted in sherbet orange, next door to a small **Muzeum Štramberk** (April–Oct Tues–Sun 9am–noon & 1–5pm; Nov–March until 4pm & closed Sat) displaying archeological finds from the nearby Šipka cave (see below). The castle, laid waste by the Tatars and never rebuilt, has just one remaining round tower, **Trúba** (April & Oct daily 9am–5pm; May–Sept daily 9am–7pm; Nov–March Fri–Sun 10am–4pm), which translates as "The Tube" and is now a lookout post, with a restaurant nearby.

Just below the main square is the **Zdeněk Burian Museum** (May–Sept Tues–Sun 9am–noon & 12.30–5pm, Oct–April until 4pm), dedicated to the work of this prolific painter, who was born in nearby Kopřivnice and spent his childhood in Štramberk. Burian (1905–81) was a book illustrator and palaeontologist, but is perhaps best known (to Czechs, at any rate) for his painstaking representations of the world of prehistoric humans. His inspiration came from the nearby **Šipka cave**, beneath the limestone hill of Kotouč (532m), where remains of Neanderthal man were discovered in the late nineteenth century. The caves are a short walk through the woods of the Národní sad, signposted off the road to Kopřivnice. You may also reach Kopřivnice by taking the path climbing Bílá Hora, which is topped with an ugly (but high) **lookout tower**

Wallachian culture

As far as anybody can make out, the **Wallachs** or **Vlachs** were semi-nomadic sheep and goat farmers who settled the mountainous areas of eastern Moravia and western Slovakia in the fifteenth century. Although their name clearly derives from the Romanian Vlachs, it is believed that they arrived from eastern Poland and the Ukraine, and the name Vlach is simply a generic term for sheep farmer. Whatever their true origins, they were certainly considered a race apart by the surrounding Slav peasants. Successive Habsburg military campaigns against the Vlachs in the seventeenth century destroyed their separate identity, and nowadays Wallachian culture lives on only in the folk customs and distinctive wooden architecture of the region.

(*rozhledna*; May–Oct Tues–Sun 8am–6pm), offering an unbeatable view across the mountains.

Štramberk is a fine place to spend a night, and *Hotel Šipka* (☎556 852 181, Ⓦwww.hotelsipka.cz; ❷), on the main square, has simple **rooms** and serves good Czech food and beer. A more comfortable option is the tastefully timber-clad *Hotel Roubenka* (☎556 852 566, Ⓦwww.roubenkahotel.cz; ❸), which enjoys great views up to the Trúba; to get there follow the signs off the road from Nový Jičín, or head down Dolní from the post office. Another, more expensive option is *Hotel Gong* (☎556 721 036, Ⓦwww.hotel-gong.cz; ❹), a slightly unsightly modern edifice next door to the post office, with a restaurant which once hosted Václav Havel. At the bakery on the corner of the main square, you can sample the local speciality, *Štramberské uši* (Štramberk Ears), honeyed gingerbread (often filled with cream), which commemorates a particularly gruesome legend: during the Tatar invasion, the local people were saved by a judiciously timed flood which kept the marauders at bay – when the waters subsided, so the story goes, sacks full of the ears of Tatar victims were found.

Kopřivnice

On the other side of Bílá hora from Štramberk (and an easy half-hour walk), **KOPŘIVNICE** (Nesselsdorf) is an ugly, sprawling factory town, but nevertheless worth a quick visit for its **Technické muzeum** (May–Sept Tues–Sun 9am–5pm; Oct–April until 4pm), in a new blue-and-white pavilion in the centre of town. The main draw here is the collection of Tatra cars, and even if spark plugs don't usually fire your imagination, there are some wonderful old cars here. Unlike the popular and ubiquitous Škoda, Tatra cars have always aimed to be exclusive: the first model, which came out in 1897, was called the President, and from 1948 onwards that's exactly who rode in them. The silent and powerful black Tatra, looking like something out of a gangster B-movie, became the ultimate symbol of Party privilege. Ordinary mortals could buy any colour they liked except black – the colour reserved for Party functionaries. When you've seen the Tatra 87 and the 603, it's a slightly hysterical and somewhat frightening thought to imagine the country's top Stalinists cruising around in these cars, which were succeeded in the 1970s by the Tatra 613. The post-Communist leadership has decided to do away with the stigma of the Tatra, and with the Party no longer in a position to pay for its usual bulk order, the firm has had a hard time trying to modernize its Tonka-tough trucks and continue production of its super-luxury cars.

Příbor

Five kilometres and one train station north of Kopřivnice, **PŘÍBOR** (Freiberg) appears at first to be a rerun of Nový Jičín, with a similarly pleasant, arcaded main square. However, as the birthplace of **Sigmund Freud**, Příbor has a much greater claim to fame. Although the family's financial problems forced them to leave for Vienna when Sigmund was only four, it's difficult to resist the chance to visit the place where Freud went through his oral and anal phases: the ten-metre-square room at Freudova 117 (then belonging to Zajík the blacksmith; now, appropriately enough, a therapy centre offering reflexology and herbal remedies), which is now marked by a plaque. The local **Muzeum v Příboře** (Tues & Thurs 8am–noon & 1–4pm, Sun 9am–noon), situated in the former monastery on Lidická, has devoted only one of its four rooms to the man, and sadly there are no pictures of baby Sigi, only dull official photos of learned and bearded men (including Jung) at conferences on psychoanalysis. In the rest of the town, few associations present themselves, apart from Freud's bust, which stands just outside the pretty main square, náměstí S. Freuda.

Freud in Freiburg

Born in 1856 to a hard-up Jewish wool merchant and his third wife, **Freud** had no hesitation in ascribing significance to events that took place during the family's brief sojourn here. "Of one thing I am certain," Freud wrote later, "deep within me, although overlaid, there continues to live the happy child from Freiberg [Příbor], the first-born child of a young mother who received from this air, from this soil, the first indelible impressions." Things were not always so idyllic, and Freud later used a number of events from his early childhood to prove psychoanalytical theories. The family maidservant, "my instructress in sexual matters" in Freud's own words, was a local Czech woman who used to drag him off to the nearby Catholic church and in Freud's eyes was responsible for his "Rome neurosis." She was eventually sacked for alleged theft (and for encouraging baby Sigmund to thieve, too) and sent to prison. Things weren't too bad on the Oedipal front either, Freud suspecting his half-brother of being the father of his younger sister, Anna.

Hukvaldy

Moravians hold Janáček much dearer to their hearts than Freud, and the village of **HUKVALDY**, 6km east of Příbor, has become a modest shrine to the composer. Born just two years before Freud, **Leoš Janáček** was the fifth of nine children, too many for his impecunious father who taught at the local school. Thus, at the age of eleven, Janáček was sent to Brno to be a chorister, and from then on he made his home in the city, battling against the prejudices of the powerful German elite who ruled over the Moravian classical music scene. When at last he achieved recognition outside Moravia, through the success of the opera *Jenůfa*, he was already in his sixties. Having bought a cottage in Hukvaldy, he spent his last, most fruitful years based here and in Brno, composing such works as *The Glagolitic Mass*, *The Cunning Little Vixen* and *From the House of the Dead*. The music of this period was fired by his obsessive love for a woman called Kamila Strösslová, wife of a Jewish antique dealer in Písek, who had sent him food parcels throughout World War I. Although he never left his wife, Janáček wrote over 700 letters to Kamila, the most passionate ones written almost daily in the last sixteen months of his life. In August 1928 he caught a chill searching for her son in the nearby woods, and died in a hospital in Ostrava.

Even if you've no interest whatsoever in Janáček, Hukvaldy is a homely little village nestling into a wooded hill on top of which sits a ruined **hrad** (April & Oct Sat & Sun 9am–4pm; May–Aug Tues–Sun 9am–6pm; Sept Tues–Sun 9am–5pm), complete with deer park – there's a statue of the Cunning Little Vixen in the woods. The composer's **museum**, housed in his sandy-yellow cottage, is pleasantly low-key (April & Oct Sat & Sun 10am–noon & 1–4.30pm; May & Sept Tues–Sun 10am–noon & 1–5pm; June–Aug Tues–Sun till 6pm), containing just a little modest furniture and his lectern (he always composed standing up). However, it's the gentle pastoral setting, an element underlying all Janáček's music, that provides the most instructive impression of the place. If you come here in July, you'll coincide with the **Janáčkovy Hukvaldy** (ⓦwww .janackovy-hukvaldy.cz), an international music festival which includes concerts in the castle and open-air opera performances. Should you wish **to stay**, there's the *Hukvaldský dvůr* (ⓣ558 699 241, ⓦwww.volny.cz/hukvaldsky.dvur; ❷), in the village, or the **tourist office** (April–Oct Mon & Wed 7–11am & noon–5pm, Tues 7–11am & noon–3pm, Fri 7–11am; ⓣ & ⓕ558 699 221) opposite, can help to find accommodation. Eight buses a day link Hukvaldy with Ostrava, and a few more run irregularly to Kopřivnice and Příbor.

Into the hills of the Beskydy

Between the sparsely wooded pastureland around Nový Jičín and the Rožnovská Bečva valley to the south are the **hills of the Beskydy**. Starting off in North Moravia and entering Poland, they actually extend right over into the Ukraine, shadowing the much higher Carpathian range to the south. Spruce has gradually given way to pine, which, though damaged by acid rain, is not too badly affected by pollutants, and in the westernmost reaches patches of beech forest still exist.

Around Radhošt'

During the Cold War, **FRENŠTÁT POD RADHOŠTĚM** (Frankstadt) was dominated by its Red Army barracks, but over the last decade the town has been spruced up, and the main square, which is peppered with Baroque statuary, is now looking very pretty indeed. Though not exactly in the thick of the Beskydy, it's easily the chief starting point for people heading off into the hills. There's a **tourist office** (Mon–Fri 8.30am–noon & 12.30–5pm, Sat 8.30–11.30am; July–Aug also Sun 8.30–11.30am; ☎556 836 916, ⓦwww.frenstat .info) in the town hall, and a couple of decent **hotels** in town. The *Přerov* (☎556 835 991, ⓦwww.frenstat.cz/prerov; ❷), on the main square, is cheap, friendly and has a restaurant on the ground floor, and a cellar **pub** a few doors down, named after Oliver Hardy. A touch nicer is the *Radhošt'* (☎ & ⓕ556 831 340; ❷), also on the square. There's also the *Frenštát* **campsite** (May to mid-Oct), on the north bank of the river, 1km northwest of the town centre.

Radhošt' (1129m), which Rožnov (see below) and Frenštát both dub themselves under (*pod*), is the most famous peak – thanks to its legends – though not the tallest. The view from the summit is still pretty good, and there's a fanciful wooden chapel, done out in neo-Byzantine style. Two kilometres east, there's a statue of Radegast, the mountain's legendary pagan god (who lends his name to the famous local beer). Another kilometre east is **Pustevny** – a series of late-nineteenth-century timber-slat buildings designed by Dušan Jurkovič, including the fantastical hotel, the *Tanečnica* (☎556 835 341, ⓦwww.tanecnica. cz; ❸), named after the nearby mountain, as well as the newly opened, equally comfortable *Maměnka* (☎556 836 207; ❸). With the help of a **chairlift** (*lanovka*; Mon–Fri 8am–4pm, Sat & Sun 7am–6pm on the hour, in winter every other hour) from Trojanovice-Ráztoka, 6km southeast of Frenštát, the less athletic can reach Pustevny; the yellow- and/or green-marked path will take you down to the *Kněhyně* **campsite** (open all year) with bungalows in Prostřední Bečva. You can also reach Pustevny by **bus** from Rožnov pod Radhoštěm (3–4 daily).

Rožnov pod Radhoštěm

Halfway up the Rožnovská Bečva valley, on the south side of Radhošt', lies the former spa town of **ROŽNOV POD RADHOŠTĚM**, now home of the biggest and most popular **skansen** of folk architecture in the Czech Republic, the main entrance to which lies on the other side of the river from the train station. The open-air museum – officially entitled **Valašské muzeum v přírodě** (admission to each of the three is 50–60Kč; combined admission to all three is 120Kč and a family pass is also available for 240Kč; ⓦwww.vmp.cz) – is divided into three parts, each with a different opening time; in the Mlýnská dolina, guided tours (usually in Czech) are compulsory, so ask for the *anglický text*.

The moving force behind the first part, the Wooden Town or **Dřevěné městečko** (Jan–March & Oct Tues–Sun 9am–4pm; April & Sept daily 9am–5pm; May–Aug daily 8am–6pm; Christmas season daily 9am–4pm), was local artist

Bohumír Jaromek, who was inspired by the outdoor folk museum in Stockholm (from which the word *skansen* derives). In 1925 Rožnov's eighteenth-century wooden radnice was moved from the main square to its present site, followed by a number of other superb timber buildings from the town and neighbouring villages like Větřkovice u Příbora, which supplied the beautiful seventeenth-century wooden church (where services are still held). There are Wallachian beehives decorated with grimacing faces, a smithy and even a couple of *hospoda* selling food and warm *slivovice*.

The second part of the museum, the Wallachian Village or **Valašská dědina** (April Sat & Sun 10am–5pm exteriors only; May–Aug daily 9am–6pm; Sept daily 10am–5pm) was built in the 1970s on a hillside across the road from the Dřevěné městečko. It takes a more erudite approach, attempting to recreate a typical highland sheep-farming settlement – the traditional Wallachian community – complete with a variety of farm animals and organic crops, plus a schoolhouse, dairy and blacksmith. Enthusiastic guides take you round the third and newest section, **Mlýnská dolina** (Mill Valley; May–Aug daily 9am–6pm; Sept daily 9am–5pm), which is centred around an old flour mill and includes a water-powered blacksmith's and sawmill, peopled by period-dressed artisans.

Rožnov attracts a lot of coach parties who tend to book out the cheaper hotels, so head for the efficient **tourist office** (May–Sept daily 8am–noon & 1–6pm; Oct–April Mon–Fri 8.30am–noon & 1–4pm; ⓦ www.valasske-kralovstvi .cz, www.roznov.cz), on Palackého, near the *skansen*, which can help with **accommodation**. One of the best hotels in town is the flashy *Eroplán* (☎571 648 014, ⓦ www.eroplan.cz; ❸), with sauna, weight room and its own restaurant, and situated, like the nearby *Hotel Energetik* (☎571 648 377; ❷), up the hill across from the *skansen*. The new *Hotel AGH* (☎571 625 666, ⓦ www .hotel-agh.cz; ❹), at Čechova 142, with very tasteful rooms and a good restaurant downstairs, is also worthwhile. **Campsites** are thick on the ground to the east of the open-air museum in Rožnov, with one on either side of the road to Prostřední Bečva – the *Rožnov* (open all year) and the *Sport* (mid-June to mid-Sept) – and a third, *Pod lipami* (July & Aug), 3km up the road in Dolní Bečva. On Rožnov's main square, there's an atmospheric **restaurant** *Rožnovský rynek*, with tables in the Společenský dům.

Frýdek-Místek

Lying halfway between the Beskydy and Ostrava, and accessible by train from either, **FRÝDEK-MÍSTEK** (Friedeck-Friedburg) is a rather rude re-entry into the Ostrava coal basin. Its charms are few – the tourist authorities call it "a city of possibilities" – and its soulless industrial quarter has assumed a much greater importance than its twin old towns straddling the River Ostravice: **Místek**, on the flat left bank, where the business of the town now goes on, and **Frýdek**, the prettiest and quietest part of town on the hill opposite. Frýdek's main square has now been beautifully restored, with a statue of St Florian, patron saint of firefighters, superintending the central fountain, and the town's landmark **zámek** (Tues, Wed & Fri 8am–noon & 12.30–4pm, Thurs closes 5pm, Sat & Sun 1–5pm) in one corner. Once the property of the lords of Těšín, it now contains an art gallery, and a small museum with tributes to Janáček, Óndra Ľysohorsky (see box opposite) and the Silesian poet Petr Bezruč, who stayed in Místek for a while, championing the grievances of the poverty-stricken local miners. Also worth noting is the newly renovated Knights' Hall (Rytířský sál), with its collection of Silesian coats of arms.

The ninth child of a Frýdek miner, the poet **Óndra Łysohorsky** (whose real name was Erwin Goy) took his pen name from the local Robin Hood rebel, Ondráš, who was imprisoned in, and escaped from, Frýdek castle back in the seventeenth century, when it was owned by the wicked Duke Pragma. His surname comes from the highest peak in the Beskydy, Lysá hora (Bare Mountain). Łysohorsky was brought up speaking German and the local Slav dialect, but, after writing his first verses in German, decided to change to Lachian, a written form of the local dialect that he himself invented, but which never really caught on. The dialect (or language, depending on your point of view), somewhere between Czech and Polish, survives in the towns and villages along the Polish border and was spoken by around a million people (mostly miners) at its peak between the two world wars. Łysohorsky's obstinacy on this linguistic point eventually brought him into conflict with the postwar Communist authorities, who accused him of supporting the region's Polish irredentists. Apart from a brief reprise in 1958, his verse remained unpublished in Czechoslovakia, despite his being one of the country's better-known poets abroad. Łysohorsky died shortly after the upheavals of 1989 in Bratislava, and the poet's vast archives are now safely deposited in Frýdek castle.

Český Těšín

If you fancy a quick jaunt into **Poland**, the easiest place is probably **ČESKÝ TĚŠÍN** (Cieszyn), 20km east of Frýdek-Místek, which found itself arbitrarily divided when the borders were drawn up following the collapse of the Habsburg Empire after World War I. The town was claimed by both Poland and Czechoslovakia, and it was finally decided in 1920 to use the fairly insignificant River Olše (Olza) as the frontier. In this instance, the Poles got the best deal, ending up with most of the town, including the staré město and the castle on the right bank. The Czech part is made up of grim, grey housing blocks built between the wars, and the only reason for coming here is to cross over to see the more interesting sights of the Polish side (see *The Rough Guide to Poland* for details).

When **crossing the border** into Poland, you have to use the Střelniční most (Most Wolności), 400m due east of the train station; when returning to the Czech side, use Hlavní most (Most Przyjaźni), 700m downstream, at the end of Hlavní třída; both bridges are for pedestrians and cyclists only. Visa regulations and price disparities between the two countries have fluctuated over the years. At the height of Solidarity, during the 1980s, it was almost as difficult for Czechs to get into Poland as to travel to the West. Then the tables were turned and, with the Polish economy in free fall, the Czechs clamped down on Poles entering the country. Nowadays, people on either side of the border can cross using just their ID cards.

Travel details

Trains

Connections with Prague: Olomouc (1–2 hourly; 3hr 10min–3hr 30min); Ostrava (every 2–3hr; 3hr 50min–5hr 30min).

Jeseník to: Javorník (3 daily; 1hr 5min–1hr 15min); Žulová (4 daily; 30–40min).
Lipová Lázně to: Javorník (3 daily; 1hr–1hr 15min); Žulová (3 daily; 30–40min).
Olomouc to: Bruntál (every 1–2hr; 1hr 20min–1hr

45min); Jeseník (3 daily; 2hr 15min–3hr 45min); Krnov (every 1–2hr; 1hr 45min–2hr 15min); Lipová Lázně (3 daily; 2hr 5min–3hr 30min); Opava (up to 9 daily; 2hr 20min–3hr 20min); Ostrava (every 1–2hr; 1hr 15min–2hr); Přerov (1–2 hourly; 25min); Prostějov (every 1–2hr; 15–25min); Šumperk (10 daily; 1hr 10min–1hr 35min).

Opava to: Hradec nad Moravicí (every 1–2hr; 12min); Jeseník (4 daily; 2hr–2hr 10min); Krnov (hourly; 30–45min); Ostrava (hourly; 30–30min).

Ostrava to: Český Těšín (1–2 hourly; 40–55min); Frýdek-Místek (1–2 hourly; 30–40min).

Šumperk to: Jeseník (9 daily; 1hr 45min–2hr 15min); Lipová Lázně (8–9 daily; 1hr 25min–1hr 45min).

Buses

Connections with Prague: Nový Jičín (2 daily; 5hr); Olomouc (up to 8 daily; 3hr 50min–5hr); Ostrava (6–7 daily; 5hr 20min–7hr 30min).

Olomouc to: Nový Jičín (up to 9 daily; 50min–1hr 15min); Opava (4 daily Mon–Fri; 1hr 50min–2hr); Ostrava (up to 15 daily; 1hr 30min–2hr 10min); Příbor (up to 5 daily Mon–Fri; 1hr 20min–1hr 30min); Rožnov pod Radhoštěm (1–2 daily; 1hr 25min–1hr 55min).

Nový Jičín to: Frenštát pod Radhoštěm (hourly; 40min); Frýdek-Místek (3–18 daily; 25–45min); Kopřivnice (hourly; 30–45min); Příbor (hourly; 25min); Štramberk (1–2 hourly; 15–35 min).

Rožnov pod Radhoštěm to: Frenštát pod Radhoštěm (1–2 hourly; 15–30min); Valašská Bystřice (1–2 hourly; 20–25min).

The Slovak Republic

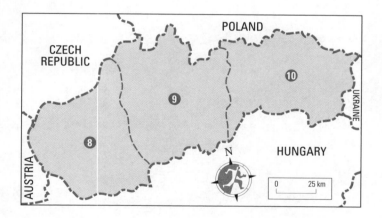

The Slovak Republic

Basics

After centuries of cultural repression by the Hungarians, followed by 75 years of playing second fiddle to the Czechs within Czechoslovakia, the Slovaks finally gained their independence on January 1, 1993. After those heady celebratory days, however, life proved much harder for the Slovaks than for the Czechs. With no internationally popular figurehead to act as a public relations officer, the new Slovakia found it difficult jockeying for a position in the new Europe. Political instability, corruption and slow-moving reforms initially deterred overseas investors and drew criticism from abroad, though the country has since recovered and recently joined both NATO and the EU.

For the first-time visitor, however, perhaps the most striking difference between the Czechs and the Slovaks is their attitude to religion. **Catholicism** is much stronger in Slovakia and the country's churches are visibly fuller on a Sunday; indeed, it is not uncommon to see people crowded outside the entrance of an overflowing church with a service in progress. The republic also has a much more diverse population, with over half a million **Hungarian-speakers** in the area bordering Hungary, one of the largest **Romany** minorities in Europe and thousands of **Rusyns** in the east of the country bordering Ukraine. Geographically, Slovakia lies between two extremes: the flat, parched plains of the Danube basin in the west, and the limestone and granite peaks of the central mountains – including some of Europe's highest mountains outside the Alps – to the east. These have long formed barriers to industrialization and modernization, preserving and strengthening regional differences in the face of centralization from Vienna, Budapest, Prague and now Bratislava.

Getting around

Geographical considerations mean that Slovakia has nothing like the same density of **railways** as the Czech Republic. Some of the lines, however, are breathtakingly beautiful and serve most places along the chief valleys – after that you'll have to rely on the patchy **bus** network and, in some places (particularly in the far east of the country), you really need your own transport. Bus and train frequencies can be found in the "Travel details" section at the end of each chapter.

Trains

With two-thirds of the Slovak train network made up of single-track lines, services are predictably slow. However, some **scenic journeys** are worth making for the views alone: try the Banská Bystrica–Diviaky line, the Brezno–Margecany trip in the Low Tatras, or any of the electric trains in the High Tatras. Ticket prices are still remarkably low at around 3Sk per kilometre.

The state railways are **Železnice Slovenskej Republiky** or **ŽSR** (ⓦ www.zsr.sk or ⓦ www.slovakrail.sk, though the best online timetable in English is ⓦ www.busy.sk). They run two main types of service: *rýchlik* trains are the faster, stopping only at major towns; the *osobný vlak*, or local train, stops everywhere and averages about 30km an hour. Fast trains are further divided into Euro-city (EC), Inter-city (IC), *expresný* (Ex) and *zrýchlený* (Zr). For EC trains, and occasionally for IC and Ex trains, you need to pay a supplement which you should purchase before boarding the train (it costs more otherwise).

Tickets and fares

Once you've worked out when your train leaves (for which, see p.444), the best thing to do when buying a **ticket** (*lístok*) is to write down all the relevant information (date/time/destination) on a piece of paper and hand it to the ticket clerk.

Fares are cheap, with a second-class single from Bratislava to Košice currently costing around £10/$18. First-class carriages (*prvá trieda*) exist on all fast trains, and though tickets are fifty percent more expensive, they should guarantee you a seat on a busy train. There are half-price discounts (*zľavy*) for chil-

B

dren (*deti*) aged 6 to 15, and you can take two under-6s for free. Sleepers (*lôžkový vozeň*) and couchettes (*ležadlový vozeň*) should be booked as far in advance as possible and certainly no later than six hours before departure.

For all international services (and any other trains marked with an "R" on the timetable), you can buy a **seat reservation** (*miestenka*). It's advisable to get one if you're travelling at the weekend on one of the main routes and want to be sure of a seat. The *miestenka* costs very little, but you must get it at least an hour before your train leaves, and either after or at the same time as you purchase your ticket.

Information and timetables

Obtaining **train information** can be problematic unless you have some knowledge of the language. Most stations have poster-style displays of arrivals (*príchod*) and departures (*odchod*), the former on white paper, the latter on yellow, with fast trains printed in red; **timetables** in the smaller stations are displayed on simple boards (*smer*). Rollers (timetables fixed on large revolving rolls) are an alternative source of information available in most stations. See the box below for advice on how to read them.

Buses

Trains will take you most places, but if you have to change a lot, it might be easier to take one of the regional **buses** (*autobus*), run by numerous private operators. Bus stations (*autobusová stanica*) are usually next to the train station, and where there's no office (or it's closed) you'll have to buy your ticket from the driver. It's a good idea to book your ticket

in advance if you're travelling at the weekend or early in the morning on one of the main routes.

Tickets can be bought at the station before or on the day of departure; for more minor routes, tickets are on sale from the driver. Large items of luggage (*batožina*) have to go in the boot, for which the driver will charge you an extra 10–15Sk. Minor bus stops are signposted *zastávka*. To get off, say *ja chcem vystúpiť*; "the next stop" is *ďalšia zastávka*. For help with the symbols commonly used on bus timetables, see the Czech section on p.50; for online timetables visit ⓦwww.busy .sk or ⓦwww.eurolines.sk.

City transport

Buses (*autobus*) and trolleybuses (*trolejbus*) – plus trams (*električka*) in Košice and Bratislava – combine to provide a generally excellent urban **public transport** system that operates from dawn until around 11pm in most major towns (and all night in Bratislava). Ticket prices currently start at 14Sk in Bratislava for an adult (less elsewhere); with reduced rates for those aged 6–15 and free travel for those under 6. Though costs can vary, they are universally cheap.

In most cases, you have to buy your ticket before travelling; these are available from newsagents, tobacconists and the yellow machines at major stops, and must be validated in the punching machine on board; plain-clothes inspectors will impose an on-the-spot fine of 1400Sk on anyone caught without a ticket. You should also buy a reduced rate ticket for any large items of baggage, though the fine for failing to do so is only 35Sk.

Reading Slovak train timetables

Select your route on the diagrammatic map and make a note of the number printed beside it, then find the appropriate number on the timetable rollers. Crucial notes and explanations are in Slovak: arrivals are often abbreviated to *pr.* or *prích.* and departures to *od.* or *odch.*; a platform or *nástupište* is usually divided into two *koľaj* on either side. At the side of the timetable you'll often find the notes *chodí v* (running on), or *nechodí v* (not running on), followed by a date or a number/symbol: 1–6 for Monday–Saturday, two hammers for a weekday and a cross for a Sunday. The main station in larger towns is known as *hlavná stanica*, while minor stations often have the suffix *mesto* or *zástavka* after the name. If you're planning on using the trains a lot, you could invest in a ŽSR timetable (*cestovný poriadok*), which comes out every May and is available from most bookshops and tobacconists.

Driving

Driving under your own steam is a viable alternative to public transport in Slovakia. Traffic is light and road conditions usually good. Only in Bratislava might you encounter difficulties, due to the confusing lane system, tramlines and lack of parking facilities. Although there are only a few short stretches of motorway to speak of, to use them, you'll need a **motorway sticker** (*úhrada* in Slovak) currently costing 60Sk for fifteen days, or 400Sk for a year, and available from border crossings, post offices and some petrol stations. Note that many border crossings have special restrictions attached to them, with some operating only during hours of daylight, and others for use only by the nationals of the two countries who share the border.

Most foreign driving licences are valid – including all EU, US and Canadian ones – but getting an **International Driver's Licence** can set your mind at rest. If you're driving your own car, you are legally required to carry its registration document; if it's not in your name, you must have a letter of permission signed by the owner and authorized by an official motoring organization (not applicable to a rented car). Other legally required items are a red warning triangle, a first-aid kit, a set of replacement bulbs, and a national identification sticker. Your insurance company at home will advise you as to whether you need a green card; without one you may only be able to get third-party insurance.

Rules of the road

The **rules of the road** are pretty strict and on-the-spot fines are common with speeding fines starting at 1000Sk. Basic rules are: drive on the right, always wear your seatbelt, never take the wheel with any alcohol in your bloodstream, and give way to pedestrians on zebra crossings, and those crossing the road at traffic lights if you're turning right or left. Road markings at junctions are sparse, so look out for the yellow diamond sign, which means you have right of way; a black line through it means you haven't.

Speed limits are 130kmh on motorways and 90kmh on other roads, except in cities, towns and villages where the maximum is 50kmh. There's a special speed limit of 30kmh at level crossings, where instead of a barrier you'll often find simply the sign *pozor* and a series of lights: a single flashing light means the line is live; two red flashing lights mean a train is approaching. *Odčhadžka* is a diversion; *prújezd zákazany* or *zákaz vjazdu* means no entry.

Fuel and car rental

Petrol (*benzín*) is sold as *natural* (unleaded 95 or 98 octane) or *UNI* (91 or 95 octane), which can be used in leaded or unleaded engines; diesel (*nafta*) is also available. Bear in mind that petrol stations are few and far between in the more remote areas and that some close at lunchtimes and after 6pm (though the number of 24-hour ones is increasing steadily). The price of petrol is cheaper than in much of the EU, currently costing around 35Sk a litre (£0.60/$1). If you have car trouble, dial ☎154 and wait for assistance. You might consider an insurance policy that covers on-the-spot repairs, car rental and travel home for you and your passengers in case of an emergency.

Car rental is easy to arrange. To rent a car, you have to be at least 21 years of age (sometimes 25) and have a clean licence. Booking from abroad will cost you an incredible £280/$420 a week for a small car. Some of the multinationals have offices in Bratislava, but local agents offer far better deals. For details of international car rental agencies, see p.52.

Cycling and hiking

Cycling (*cyklistika*) is now fairly popular as a leisure pursuit in Slovakia – less so as a means of getting to work – and in the more touristy areas such as the High Tatras, you'll find plenty of bike rental outlets. Spare parts are more difficult to obtain, so if you're cycling your own machine, bring as many with you as you can. On the faster trains you can take your bike (*bicykel*) for a small supplement, and it's easy enough to persuade the guard on the slower trains to let you on, for a small fee. Special cyclists' maps (*cykloturistická mapa*), produced by both VNÚ and Freytag & Berndt, are also now available in the shops.

Walking is a popular pastime, with a dense network of trails covering the entire countryside; each path is colour-coded with clear markers every 100m or so and signs indicate how long it'll take you to reach your destina-

Useful hiking terms

cesta	path
chata	mountain refuge
dolina	valley
hranica	border
jaskyňa	cave
lanovka	chairlift/cable car
les	forest
lyžiarsky vlek	ski lift
prameň	spring
rozhladňa/prehliadka	viewpoint
skala	rock
vodopád	waterfall

tion. The walks are usually fairly easy-going, but if you venture into the mountains proper, you'll need some sturdy boots. In the High Tatras, you must stick to the paths indicated and should really have some serious walking experience before attempting any ascent; this mountain range is one of the few areas on which hiking guides have been published in English, so you might consider investing in one before you leave home. Wherever you're going, it's a good idea to get hold of a 1:50,000 (or even better 1:25,000) *turistická* map, which details all the marked paths in the area (see p.40).

Accommodation

On the whole, **accommodation** in Slovakia is still relatively inexpensive. However, improvement in hotel standards is slow, and, in terms of quality of service, you'll often be better off staying in the privately owned pensions, or private rooms, than in the old Communist-era hotels – even those that have been nominally "modernized". The further east you go, the more difficult it becomes to find accommodation, and service can be quite poor. For a rundown on the price codes used in this book, see the inside front cover.

Hotels, pensions and private rooms

The modernization of Slovakia's **hotels** is proving a piecemeal process, resulting in the temporary closure of large numbers while looking for new investors. In some areas, you'll still come across the old state-owned behemoths, whose standards are stuck in the Communist era. Prices vary enormously – they're at their highest in Bratislava and the High Tatras – but are generally lower than in the Czech Republic. Most hotels now operate some kind of star system, though it gives only a very vague indication of what to expect.

In many areas, the gap in the market has been filled by newly established **pensions** (often written as *penzión*), which are frequently excellent value, though not necessarily any less expensive than hotels. **Private rooms** are also available along many of the main roads and in the more tourist-frequented regions. You can be sure that these will be pristine, though how much privacy you'll have and to what extent you'll have to share facilities with the family will vary. Outside the bigger cities and more popular mountain areas, accommodation can be hard to come by and standards low, particularly in the eastern part of the country, so flexibility and an open mind can be valuable assets.

Hostels and campsites

There is no real network of **hostels** in Slovakia; a few are affiliated to Hostelling International (ⓦ www.iyhf.org), but you're better off visiting a website like ⓦ www.cheap-hostels-in.com. Slovak hostels range from places run much like hotels to dormitories primarily used by domestic tour groups or local workers, but which may have a spare bed if you're lucky.

More useful are the **mountain huts** (*chaty*) on the hillsides of the High Tatras; though few are accessible by road, most are just a few kilometres' walk from civilization. Some cost as much as £10/$18 per person, while the more isolated and basic ones can cost as little as £6/$11 per person. These can really only be booked through local agencies or tourist offices within the republic, though you're unlikely to be turned away if you turn up before 6pm at the more isolated ones.

There are a large number of **campsites** (usually known as *autokemping*) scattered throughout Slovakia, varying enormously in standards and facilities. Many have "**bungalows**" (*chaty*), which are simple and very cheap to rent, but are often block-booked by groups. Most sites are open from April or May until September or October, with a handful open all year round. The more basic campsites (*táborisko*) are marked on hiking maps; open only in the height of summer, they provide just ad hoc toilets and a little running water. Prices are very reasonable; two people plus car and tent weigh in at around £5/$9.

Communications

The Slovaks are currently in the middle of radically overhauling their telecommunications network. The phone system, in particular, is being dragged kicking and screaming into the twenty-first century, with the result that a lot of the country's phone numbers and codes have recently been changed. The Slovaks are keen Internet users, and access is possible in most towns and cities across the country.

Post

Post offices (*pošta*) are usually open between 8am and 5pm Monday to Friday. Letters or postcards take around five working days to reach the UK, and a week to ten days to North America. Stamps (*známky*) are available from newsagents and kiosks as well as post offices, though often only for domestic mail. See p.632 for a list of countries in Slovak.

Poste restante (pronounced as five syllables in Slovak) is available in major towns. The sender should write Pošta 1 (the main office), followed by the name of the town, and their name and address on the back. It might be safer to have mail sent to your embassy in Bratislava, though you should inform them of this beforehand.

Phones

Slovak **public phones** (*telefón*) are pretty reliable, with instructions in English – despite the graphic description you may still encounter problems. The **dialling tone** is a short pulse followed by a long one; the **ringing tone** is long and regular; **engaged** is short and rapid, but shouldn't be confused with the very rapid tone which indicates the line is being connected. The standard Slovak response is *prosím*; and the word for extension is *linka*. If you have any problems, dial ☏149 and ask for an English-speaking operator.

Fortunately, most phones are now cardonly, which makes **international calls** much easier. Phone cards (*telefonní karty*), currently available in 75 and 150 units (prices vary), can be bought at post offices and most tobacconists and kiosks. Insert the card into the telephone, and the number of units remaining on the card appears on the phone's display. Alternatively, you can buy **pre-paid phone cards**, which will give you much longer call time from any public or private phone; simply phone the toll-free access number and then punch in the PIN given on the card. As well as the aforementioned pre-paid phone cards, you can also get a **telephone charge card** from your phone company back home (see p.56 for more details).

Useful telephone numbers

The Slovak phone system is gradually being digitalized, which means all numbers are slowly getting longer or changing completely.

Phoning Slovakia from abroad
From Britain & Ireland: ☏00 + 421 (Slovakia) + area code minus first 0 + number.
From USA and Canada: ☏011 + 421 (Slovakia) + area code minus first 0 + number.
From Australia and New Zealand: ☏0011 + 421 (Slovakia) + area code minus first 0 + number.

Phoning abroad from Slovakia
To the UK: ☏0044 + area code minus 0 + number.
To the Republic of Ireland: ☏00353 + area code minus 0 + number.
To the USA & Canada: ☏001 + area code + number.
To Australia: ☏0061 + area code minus 0 + number.
To New Zealand: ☏0064 + area code minus 0 + number.

You may still find it simpler to make international calls from one of the **telephone exchanges** found in the major towns. Write down the town and telephone number, leave a deposit of around 200Sk, then wait for your name to be called out; bear in mind that international calls are extremely expensive at any time. Calls can be made from most hotels, but the surcharge is usually quite heavy. An easier option is a collect call, which will cost the recipient less than it would cost you. Dial ☏0131 and ask for an English speaker.

If you want to use your **mobile** in Slovakia, you'll need to check with your phone provider whether it will work abroad, and what the call charges are. Unless you have a tri-band phone, it is unlikely that a mobile bought for use in the US will work in Europe. By contrast most mobiles in Australia and New Zealand use GSM, which works well in Europe.

Email

One of the best (and cheapest) ways to keep in touch while travelling is to sign up for a **free Internet email address** – if you haven't already done so – that can be accessed from anywhere, for example Yahoo! (🖥mail.yahoo .com) or Hotmail (🖥www.hotmail.com). Once you've set up your account, you'll be able to pick up and send mail from any Internet café, web kiosk or hostel or hotel with Internet access.

You can usually get online somewhere in most Slovak towns and cities, though there aren't many specialist cybercafés. The easiest way to find out how to get online is to ask the local tourist office. For details of how to plug your laptop in when abroad, plus information on country codes around the world, and electrical systems in different countries, check out the useful website 🖥www.kropla.com.

Media

In Bratislava, it's possible to get day-old copies of most of the broadsheet **English papers**, though one that you can buy on the day of issue is the European edition of *The Guardian*, printed in Frankfurt (it arrives around noon). Similarly, the *International Herald Tribune* is widely available the same day, and contains a useful distilled English version of the *Frankfurter Allgemeine Zeitung*. Other papers tend to be a day or so old.

In addition, there's the weekly *Slovak Spectator* (🖥 www.slovakspectator.sk), a thin, broadsheet newspaper that concentrates on current affairs and finance, but carries a useful listings section on Bratislava. Unfortunately, it is hard to find anywhere but in Bratislava. Outside the capital, English-language newspapers are rare; your best bet is the more expensive hotels. If all you want are the soccer or ice hockey results, then the Slovak sports daily *Šport* will do the job.

The **Slovak press** were under constant pressure when Mečiar and his allies were in power. Shortly after independence in 1993, Mečiar sacked the editor of the government-backed daily, *Smena*, for publishing critical articles. Eighty percent of the staff then left in protest and formed *Sme*, a paper whose readership quickly overtook that of *Smena*. As a further humiliation, *Sme* later took over *Smena* – it has a one-page English-language section covering the main news on Tuesdays and Thursdays.

The only good thing to be said about Czechoslovak state **television** under the Communists was that after federalization in 1969 it consistently broadcast in Czech and Slovak. This commitment to bilingual broadcasting was strictly adhered to, so that in the course of an ice hockey match, the first half would be commentated on in Czech and the second in Slovak. For twenty years, this helped nurture a generation for whom the differences between the two nations, at least linguistically, were irrelevant. Now the Slovaks and Czechs have gone their different ways, and both have their own commercial channels. The main Slovak commercial station, Markíza, now attracts by far the largest slice of the country's audience, pushing the more interesting state-run channels, STV1 and STV2, into second place.

As far as **radio** goes, most cafés and bars tune in to one of the FM pop/muzak stations. You can pick up the BBC World Service (🖥 www.bbc.co.uk/worldservice) fairly easily now from the two big cities, around the 100MHz mark, and on shortwave; most FM stations give out pretty weak signals, so don't expect much once you leave the suburbs.

Eating and drinking

Seventy-five years of close contact with the Czechs and forty years of Communist rule have left **Slovak cuisine** with many of the same predilections as the Czechs. The secret ingredient, however, is the Hungarian influence, which left a legacy of marginally spicier cooking.

For a fuller list of Slovak food and drink terms, see the "Language" section in Contexts, p.635.

Food

The similarities between Slovak and Czech cuisine mean that much of the information contained in the section on Czech food starting on p.57 is relevant here. The few differences are outlined below.

There are several types of **eating establishments**: the *řěšťařáčia* is the most common and varies in formality; a *viňářěň* (wine cellar), which often stays open later, will also guarantee a full meal; a *pivňiča* or *pivářěň* (pub) is based on the Czech version but less commonplace, usually serving filling food at a good price; and, at the budget end of the scale, you can stoke up with the local workers at very cheap self-service *bůfěť*.

Slovak cuisine

The usual mid-morning Slovak snack at the *bufet* (stand-up canteen) is *párek*, perhaps the most ubiquitous **takeaway food** in Central Europe: a hot frankfurter, dipped in mustard or horseradish and served inside a white roll. *Langoše* – deep-fried dough smothered in a variety of toppings, most commonly garlic butter – are very popular, too.

Most Slovak menus start with **soup** (*poľěvký*), followed by a main course of meat (*mäšo*) – usually pork or beef – with potatoes, pickled cabbage and/or dumplings (*kňědľě*). **Goulash** (*gůľáš*) is popular, often *Šžěgědiň-ský* (pork with sauerkraut) though it's usually more of a stew than a spicy soup. The Slovak **national dish**, *brýňdžové haľůšký*, is potato gnocchi with a heavy sheep's cheese sauce, usually topped with specks of fried pork fat or bacon (veggies beware).

Main courses are overwhelmingly based on pork or beef, but trout and carp are usually featured somewhere on the menu and you may find catfish or pike-perch if you're lucky, and occasionally lamb. Most main courses are served with delicious potatoes (*žěmiaký*) – but fresh salads or green vegetables are still a rarity in local restaurants. In addition to *paľačiňký* (pancakes) filled with chocolate, fruit and cream, Slovak desserts invariably feature apple or cottage-cheese strudel and ice cream.

Drinking

The Slovaks make some medium-quality white **wine**, though exports are low compared to neighbouring Hungary. Wine consumption is highest along the hot southern edge of the republic; from the vineyards of the Small Carpathians, which touch the suburbs of Bratislava, to the tiny Slovak Tokaj, which border the main Hungarian wine-producing region of the same name, and produce sweet Muscat wines and a good dry white known as Furmint.

The most famous of the **spirits** available in Slovakia is the plum brandy *šlívovičě*, which originated in the western border hills but is now available just about everywhere. You'll probably come across *bořovička* at some point, a

Vegetarian food

Though the Slovaks are a nation of carnivores, the outlook is not all bleak for **vegetarians**. Many menus have a section called *bezmäsité jedlá*; beware, however, that although this translates literally as "without meat", this can simply mean that meat is included to a lesser degree than usual. The most popular non-meat dish is *vyprážený syr*, a slab of melted cheese fried in breadcrumbs served with potatoes and a large dose of tartare sauce, though watch out – if it's *plnený* or *se šunkou*, then it will certainly include ham. The phrases to remember are *som vegeterián/vegeteriánka*, and for emphasis add *nejem ani mäso ani rybu* (I don't eat meat or fish), at which point your server may shake his or her head in disbelief.

popular firewater from the Slovak Spiš region, made from juniper berries; *myslivec* is another rough brandy with an ardent following.

Unlike the Czechs, the Slovaks have no great tradition of **beer** drinking, but union with the Czech Lands in 1918 gradually changed things, and since 1945, their beer consumption has increased tenfold. The Slovaks do, of course, brew their own, though Zlatý bažant (Golden Pheasant) currently has over forty percent of the market. The central Slovak town of Martin also produces a distinctive porter, a dark, heady brew which is notoriously difficult to get hold of – try looking out for Cassovar instead. Other ubiquitous Slovak beers include Šariš and Smädný Mních. Czech beers are also widely available, with the Bohemian Pilsner Urquell, Gambrinus and Budvar leading the field.

Castles, churches and museums

The Slovak countryside is dotted with **chateaux** (*zámok*) and **castles** (*hrad*), many of them reduced to rubble, others converted for modern use, into old people's homes, trade-union holiday retreats and even training centres for the secret police. Some have been returned to their former owners, and plenty more have been restored and opened to the public. The country's **churches** (*kostol*) and monasteries (*kláštor*) have generally been better looked after than those in the Czech Republic, though many lock their doors outside worshipping hours. **Museums** (*múzeum*) and **galleries** (*galéria*) thrived under the Communists, and those that have survived the subsequent ideological purging have little money to bring themselves up to date.

Castles and guided tours

Basic **opening hours** for castles and other historical buildings are usually May to September Tuesday to Sunday 9am to noon, then 1pm to 5pm; in April and October, opening times are usually restricted to weekends and holidays; the rest of the year the buildings are often closed. Access to the interior is usually only possible with a **guided tour** (*sprievodza*), which usually sets off on the hour, the last one

leaving an hour before closing time. Tours are usually conducted in Slovak, occasionally in German or Hungarian, rarely in English, but it's always worth asking for a written **English resumé** (*anglický text*). Entrance tickets cost very little – rarely more than 50–100Sk – hence only prices over 100Sk are quoted in the text.

Churches, monasteries and synagogues

A few of the most popular **churches** operate in much the same way as museums, occasionally even charging an entrance fee. Other churches are usually closed except for services, for which times are often posted outside the main doors, but it is worth asking around for the local *kňaz* (priest) or *kaplan* (caretaker), who will usually be only too happy to oblige with the key (*kľúč*).

In the north and east of the country, there are a small number of **Orthodox** (*Pravoslavny*) believers and a much larger contingent who belong to the **Greek-Catholic Church** (*Grécko-katolický*), an obscure branch of Roman Catholicism whose small wooden churches, packed with icons and Byzantine paraphernalia, appear just like Orthodox churches to the uninitiated. You'll find a much more thorough account of the Greek-Catholics and their churches in the section on Carpatho-Ruthenia in Chapter Ten. Suffice to say that the buildings are fascinating, especially their dark and poky interiors, but they are kept firmly locked with little indication of what time the next service will be held.

Slovakia once boasted a considerable **Jewish** population, but most fell victim to the Nazi Holocaust, helped on their way by certain members of the Slovak wartime government. Today, an estimated 2000 still live in the republic, but Bratislava is one of the few places where regular worship still takes place. Most of the country's **synagogues** still stand, but many need considerable repairs – notable exceptions are those at Trenčín, Liptovský Mikuláš and Prešov.

Museums and galleries

Outside of Bratislava, Slovak **museums** have changed little since the days of Communism, mostly, it has to be said, due to lack of funding. Nevertheless, you do still come across the odd gem, and most local museums boast decent collections of folk art. It's worth asking for an **English commentary** or *anglický text*, or else you'll normally have to make do with Slovak-only labelling. The **art galleries** of Bratislava and Košice will disappoint those hoping to find masterpieces by either Slovak or non-Slovak painters. In fact, some of the country's best indigenous art – Rusyn icons and the work of Pavol of Levoča – can only be found in the small-town galleries and churches of East Slovakia.

Opening hours for museums and galleries tend to be from 9am to 4pm or 5pm, usually without a break at lunch. Many stay open all year round or switch from a Tuesday–Sunday summer routine to a Monday–Friday one during the winter. Full opening hours are detailed in the guide, but ticket prices are not, since they are rarely more than 50–100Sk.

Public holidays, festivals and entertainment

Aside from **religious celebrations** and pilgrimages, the cultural calendar is dominated by **arts-** and **music-based festivals** unique to individual towns. In addition, summer is the season for village folkloric events, of which

the most famous is the Východná folk festival, which takes place near Poprad. As for the arts and sport, both have had a bumpy ride whilst learning to live without massive state subsidies.

Festivals and other annual events

Slovakia may not have a bevy of international composers to its name, but it boasts an even stronger folk tradition than the Czech Republic. The Východná Folk Festival, in late June/early July, is the biggest and most prestigious of the many annual **folk festivals**, with groups from all over Europe performing. Others worth looking out for are the one in Detva in early July, a Rusyn-based one in Svidník in mid- to late-June, and a festival with a Hungarian flavour in Gombasek every August.

The 1980s witnessed a revival of **pilgrimages** (*púť*), usually centred around the cult of the Virgin Mary. The biggest gathering is on the first weekend in July at Levoča in the Spiš region of East Slovakia, when up to 250,000 people descend on the small pilgrimage church above the town. Lesser celebrations go on in the region for the following two months.

For the Orthodox rites churches, which predominate in the east of the country, **Easter** (*Veľká noc*) is much more important than Christmas (*Vánoce*), and the often elaborate and lengthy processions and services can be

Public holidays

January 1 Independence Day/Deň vzniku Slovenskej republiky
January 6 Epiphany/Zjavenie Pána
Good Friday Veľkonočný piatok
Easter Monday Veľkonočný pondelok
May 1 Sviatok práce
May 8 VE Day/Deň víťazstva nad fašizmom
July 5 Introduction of Christianity by ss Cyril and Methodius/Sviatok svätého Cyrila a Metoda
August 29 Slovak National Uprising 1944/Výročie SNP
September 1 Constitution Day/Deň ústavy Slovenskej republiky
September 15 Assumption of the Virgin Mary/Sviatok Panny Márie Sedembolestnej
November 1 All Saints' Day/Sviatok všetkých svätch
November 17 Struggle for Freedom and Democracy Day/Deň boja za slobodu a democraciu
December 24 Štedrý deň
December 25 První sviatok vianočný
December 26 Druhý sviatok vianočný

well worth catching.

The arts

As in the Czech Republic, the **theatre** (*divadlo*) industry in Slovakia played an important part in the events of 1989, leading the way in the strikes that eventually toppled the Communist regime. In 1997, the country's theatre community found itself once more thrown into the political arena, staging what was ultimately an unsuccessful strike against the government, after they replaced several key figures in the industry with people who supported the governing HZDS party. The problem is that theatres throughout the country are still heavily subsidized by the authorities, and this allows a certain amount of political leverage over appointments.

For those with no knowledge of Slovak, it's best to stick to productions with less of a linguistic problem, such as opera or ballet. That said, **ticket prices** are cheap, and the venue and the event itself are often interesting enough to sustain you. The other genre for which language is not always a barrier is **puppetry** or *bábkové divadlo* as it's known in Slovak. Unfortunately, few traditional marionette shows are put on nowadays, with live actors taking centre stage in more and more productions, making the shows less accessible if you don't speak the language.

The **cinema** (*kino*) is cheap and generally rudimentary in Slovakia. Most foreign films tend to be shown with Slovak subtitles (*titulky*), with only the big Hollywood blockbusters getting dubbed. Beware, however, that film titles are usually translated into Slovak, so you'll need a dictionary to identify films like *Pekelná Hora* as *Dante's Peak*.

Sport

If there's one thing that makes Slovak sports fans really angry, it's the way that everyone assumes all the best players in the old Czechoslovak teams were Czech. In fact, many of Czechoslovakia's finest sporting moments were Slovak-inspired, most notably the European Championship-winning soccer team of 1976. The Swiss tennis star Martina Hingis, frequently referred to in the Western press as Czech, has her roots in Slovakia. As a result, nothing makes Slovak sports fans happier than when they beat their former compatriots, as they have done since the split, in the country's two top sports, ice hockey and soccer. Getting tickets to watch either sport is easy (and cheap) enough on the day as matches rarely sell out. Taking part is much more difficult as there are still relatively few facilities for the general public – your best bet is likely to be to go to the plusher hotels, whose sports facilities are often open to non-guests.

Ice hockey is probably the country's most popular sport right now. The Slovaks surprised everyone in 2002 by winning the World Championships for the first time ever, beating the Russians in the final. Domestic games, which can take anything up to three hours, are held in the local *zimný stadión* (winter stadium) on Sunday afternoons. The season starts at the end of September and culminates in a series of play-offs to decide the league's winner. Slovan Bratislava, Trenčín and Zvolen are usually among the favourites. In the annual World Championships, the fortunes of the national side are also subject to close scrutiny, especially if pitched against the Czechs.

The Slovak national **football** team has yet to qualify for either of the two major international soccer finals. Slovak club football also looks a long way off repeating Slovan Bratislava's famous victory over Barcelona in 1969 to lift the European Cup Winners' Cup (the only European title won by either a Czech or Slovak club). Slovan won the first three Slovak league titles on the trot and achieved the double in 1994 and 1999, but have since disappeared into the second division. FC Košice reached the group stage of the Champions League in the late 1990s, but were then relegated from Slovakia's Super Liga and, due to financial meltdown, now no longer exist. Žilina have recently won two consecutive Super Liga titles, while humble Petržalka are currently the capital's in-form team. The season runs from August to late November and from March to late June, with most matches held on Saturday afternoons.

8

Bratislava and west Slovakia

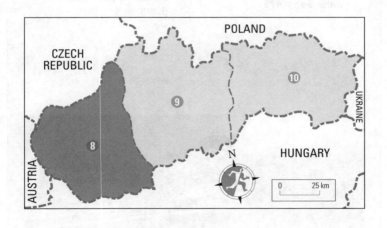

* **Bratislava** The much maligned Slovak capital has a small but beautifully restored old town, its Baroque palaces interspersed with leafy squares. See p.455

* **Trnava** Slovak ecclesiastical capital boasting a whole host of ornate churches, and a virtually complete circuit of town walls. See p.479

* **Čachtice** Hilltop ruined castle with chilling associations with the "Blood Countess". See p.492

* **Trenčín** Attractive town on the Váh river, overlooked by an impressive ruined castle. See p.494

* **Třenčianske Teplice** Relaxing spa town with a functionalist thermal swimming pool. See p.495

△ Primaciálny palác, Bratislava

Bratislava and
west Slovakia

I

n many ways, the western third of Slovakia is the least typically Slovak part of the country. For a start, it's flat, fertile and fairly treeless, its only mountain range, the Small Carpathians, tame in comparison with the central mountains further east. Even the Slovak capital **Bratislava** was for centuries an Austro-Hungarian city in which the Slovaks, like the Romanies and Jews, were a distinct minority, and far removed from the true heart of the country in the central mountain regions. The great flat plain of the **Danube**, to the east of Bratislava, is inhabited largely by ethnic Hungarians, well over half a million at the last count. The two major cities on the plain – **Trnava** and **Nitra** – although now mostly Slovak, contain some of the most important religious institutions of the old Hungarian Kingdom; and in the Váh valley, the spa town of **Piešťany** was, in its heyday, one of the favourite watering holes of the Hungarian nobility. Further up the Váh, however, begins the Slovak mountain region and the real heartland of Slovakia, heralded by the stronghold of **Trenčín**.

Bratislava and around

Caught between the westernmost tip of the Carpathians and the flat plain of the Danube, with both Austria and Hungary tantalizingly close, **BRATISLAVA** has two distinct sides to it. On the one hand, there's the old town or staré mesto, a manageable, attractive, mostly pedestrianized quarter lined with renovated baroque palaces; on the other hand, there's the rest of the city or nové mesto, a mixture of interwar tenements and postwar high-rises typical of the former Eastern bloc. More buildings have been destroyed here since the war than were bombed out during it, not least the Jewish quarter, bulldozed to make way for the colossal new suspension bridge, most SNP, symbol of the city's upwardly mobile thrust under Communism.

For centuries, Bratislava was known as *Pressburg* to the German-speaking world, which supplied around half its inhabitants until the 1945 expulsions, and as *Pozsony* to the Hungarians, who were forced to use it as their capital for several centuries during the Turkish occupation of much of Hungary, crowning

8

BRATISLAVA AND WEST SLOVAKIA | Bratislava and around

455

8

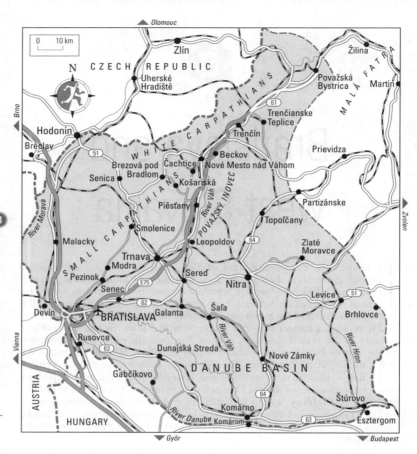

their kings and queens in the cathedral and holding their Diet here until the Turks were finally beaten back from the Hungarian plain. At the turn of the twentieth century, the city had barely 60,000 inhabitants, most of whom were German, Hungarian and/or Jewish, with a smattering of Romanies and Slovaks. The balance shifted with the establishment of Czechoslovakia in 1918, which gave a leg-up to the Slovaks, who took over the cultural and political institutions and renamed the place Bratislava after Bratislav, the last Slav leader of the Great Moravian Empire.

Over the last eighty years, the population has increased more than sevenfold to 450,000, making it by far the country's largest city, occupied by roughly eight percent of the Slovak population. However, the historical centre is surprisingly small, with most of the population living in the city's mushrooming high-rise estates. Whatever Bratislava's previous identity, it's now Slovak through and through, its youthful centre packed out with students and the new Westernized generation of Slovakia's burgeoning population. The multicultural atmosphere of the prewar days is only vaguely echoed in the city's smattering of Magyars, Romanies and day-tripping Austrians, but there's still a ring of truth to Metter-nich's much-quoted aphorism, "East of Vienna, the Orient begins".

You'll need a couple of days at least to soak the city in; and with none of the sightseeing crowds of Prague, the relaxed feel of the old town, and some of the best weather in the country, you may want to stay longer.

Arrival

The geography of Bratislava is easy to get to grips with: the **staré mesto** – where you'll spend most of your time – lies on the north side of the Danube; on the rocky hill to the west is the city's most enduring landmark, the **Hrad** (castle). Equally difficult to miss is the spectacular suspension bridge over the Danube, **most SNP** (also called Nový most), leading to the vast **Petržalka** housing development that continues as far as the eye can see on the south bank. Northeast of the staré mesto are the late-nineteenth-century and early-twentieth-century residential blocks of **nové mesto**, which gradually give way to the postwar housing of the city's sprawling suburbs.

Points of arrival are less straightforward. A kilometre or so north of the staré mesto is the city's scruffy **main train station**, Bratislava-Hlavná stanica, where most international and long-distance trains pull in. The station **tourist information** office (June–Sept Mon–Fri 8am–7.30pm, Sat & Sun 8am–4.30pm; Oct–May Mon–Fri 8.30am–2pm & 2.30–5pm) arranges accommodation and provides maps and city guides (℡02/5249 5906). To get into town, go 200m down to the tram terminus below the station and – having bought your ticket from one of the machines on the platform (see below) or from one of the many kiosks – hop on tram #1, which will deposit you on Obchodná, behind the *Hotel Fórum*. Buses (take #81 or #93) and trolleybuses leave from directly outside the station steps.

For trains to and from destinations within West Slovakia, you're most likely to use **Bratislava-Nové Mesto** train station, situated on Bajkalská, 4km northeast of the centre; tram #6 will take you into town. The **main bus station**, Bratislava autobusová stanica (often written as Bratislava, AS on timetables) is a twenty-minute walk east of the centre on Mlynské nivy; trolleybus #210 will take you across town to the main train station (a less convenient option is bus #21), while #206 and #208 will drop you on Hodžovo námestie near the *Hotel Fórum*. The regional bus station is next door to the Bratislava-Nové Mesto train station (directions as above).

Low budget airlines have begun to use **Bratislava's M. R. Štefánik airport** (Letisko Bratislava; ℡02/4857 3353, ⓦwww.airportbratislava.sk), some 9km northeast of the city centre; from there bus #61 goes to the main train station (every 10–20min; 25min). Plenty of folk still use **Vienna's Schwechat Airport**, 45km away to the west, linked by the Eurolines buses running hourly to the main bus station in Bratislava (℡02/5542 4870). Another possible arrival point from Vienna or Budapest is the **hydrofoil terminal** on Fajnorovo nábrežie, opposite the Slovenské národné múzeum, a very brief walk from the old town.

Transport and information

The best way to see Bratislava is to **walk** – in fact it's the only way to see the mostly pedestrianized staré mesto and the Hrad where the city's sights are concentrated. However, if you're staying outside the city centre or visiting the suburbs, you'll need to use the city's cheap and comprehensive **transport system** (ⓦwww.dpb.sk) of buses, trolleybuses and trams (*električky* in Slovak). Tickets (14Sk for 10min, 18Sk for 30min, 22Sk for an hour's journey) are standard for all

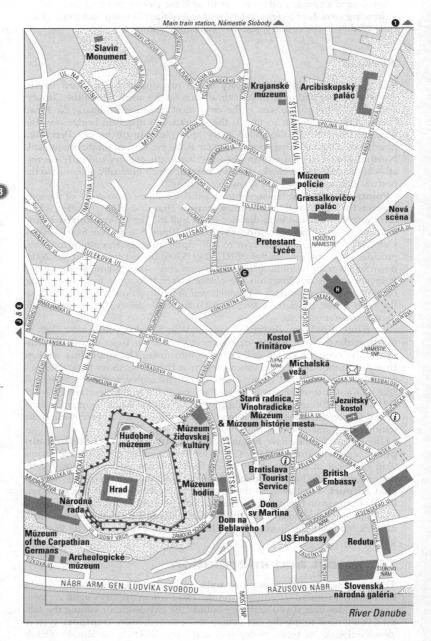

Slavín
Monument

Krajanské
múzeum

Arcibiskupský
palác

SPOJNÁ UL

Múzeum
polície

Grassalkovičov
palác

Nová
scéna

HODŽOVO
NÁMESTIE

Protestant
Lycée

Kostol
Trinitárov

ŽUPNÉ
NÁM.

Michalská
veža

Stará radnica,
Vinohradické
Múzeum
& Múzeum história mesta

Jezuitský
kostol

Hudobné
múzeum

Múzeum
židovskej
kultúry

Bratislava
Tourist
Service

British
Embassy

Hrad

Múzeum
hodín

Národná
rada

Dom
sv Martina

Dom na
Beblavého 1

US Embassy

Reduta

Múzeum
of the Carpathian
Germans

Archeologické
múzeum

STÚROVO
NÁM.

NÁBR. ARM. GEN. LUDVÍKA SVOBODU

RÁZUSOVO NÁBR.

Slovenská
národná galéria

River Danube

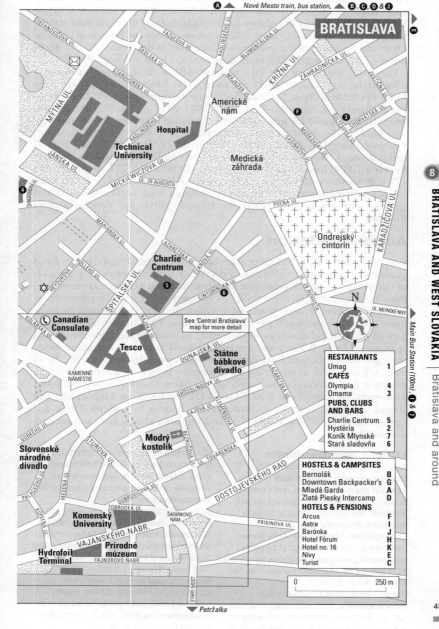

ŠTEFANOVIČOVA UL.
FAZUĽOVA UL.
RADLINSKÉHO UL.
BLUMENTÁLSKA UL.
KRÍŽNA UL.
ZÁHRADNÍCKA UL.
JUSTIČNÁ UL.
ŠKOLSKÁ UL.
STAROHORSKÁ UL.
MAJAKOVA UL.
MÝTNA UL.
RADLINSKÉHO UL.

Americké
nám
🅕
MOSKOVSKÁ UL.
CHORVÁTSKA UL.
❸
SOĽLÉSOVSKÁ UL.

Hospital
Technical
University
JÁNSKA UL.
MICKIEWICZOVA UL.
Medická
záhrada
SASINKOVA UL.
UL. 29 AUGUSTA
POČNÁ UL.
KARADŽIČOVA UL.

🅐
DRONGBERSKA

MARIÁNSKA UL.
HOLLÉHO UL.
Ondrejský
cintorín

Charlie
Centrum
LAZARETSKÁ UL.
ČIKKOVA UL.
❺
UL. 29 AUGUSTA
UL. MLYNSKÉ NIVY

CINTORÍNSKA UL.
❻
N

HEYDUKOVA UL.
SPITÁLSKA UL.
RAJSKÁ UL.

KOLÁRSKA UL.
ⓒ Canadian
Consulate
See 'Central Bratislava'
map for more detail
Main Bus Station (100m) ❶ & ❼

Tesco
KAMENNÉ
NÁMESTIE
DUNAJSKÁ UL.
Štátne
bábkové
divadlo
LAZARETSKÁ UL.

GRÖSSLINGOVA UL.
KEMENSKÁ UL.

RESTAURANTS   1
Umag
CAFÉS
Olympia   4
Omama   3
PUBS, CLUBS
AND BARS
Charlie Centrum   5
Hystéria   2
Koník Mlynské   7
Stará sladovňa   6

GAJOVA UL.
BEZRUČOVA UL.
Modrý
kostolík
UL. TOVÁRENSKÁ

Slovenské
národné
divadlo
ŠTÚROVA UL.
MEDENÁ UL.
DOSTOJEVSKÉHO RAD

SORKÉHO UL.
PALÁCKEHO UL.

DOBROVIČOVA UL.
HOSTELS & CAMPSITES
Bernolák   B
Downtown Backpacker's G
Mladá Garda
Zlaté Piesky Intercamp D
HOTELS & PENSIONS
Arcus   F
Astra   I
Barónka   J
Hotel Fórum   H
Hotel no. 16   K
Nivy   E
Turist   C

KÚPEĽNÁ UL.
Komenský
University
TOBRUCKÁ UL.
ŠAFÁRIKOVO
NÁM.
PRIBINOVA UL.

Hydrofoil
Terminal
Prírodné
múzeum
VAJANSKÉHO NÁBR.
FAJNOROVO NÁBR.

STARÝ MOST

0   250 m

▼ Petržalka

types of transport: buy your ticket beforehand (from newsagents, kiosks or ticket machines), and validate it as soon as you get on. To avoid the hassle of buying single tickets, it might be worth buying a 90Sk one-day (*24 hodinový lístok*) or 170Sk two-day ticket (*48 hodinový lístok*), available from the main train station, and from some street-side yellow ticket machines. Trams and buses stop between 11pm and midnight (some even earlier, especially at the weekend), and **night buses** take over, congregating every quarter to the hour at námestie SNP.

The main branch of the city **tourist office**, Bratislavské kultúrne a informačne stredisko or BKIS for short, is at Klobučnická 2 (June–Sept Mon–Fri 8.30am–7pm, Sat 9am–5pm, Sun 9.30am–4pm; Oct–May Mon–Fri 8.30am–6pm, Sat 9am–2pm; ℡02/5443 3715 or 02/16 186, ⓦwww .bratislava.sk), good for general queries (English is spoken there) and getting hold of the monthly listings magazine, *Kam do mesta* (in Slovak but easily decipherable). They can also help with accommodation (see below) and sell you a detailed *orientačná mapa*. The excellent **Bratislava Tourist Service** (BTS; usually daily 10am–5pm; ℡0900/211 221 or ℡02/5464 1794; ⓦwww.bratislava-info.sk), Ventúrska 9, in action since 2004, is an equally reliable source of information, helping with accommodation and running city tours (April–Oct) for around 350Sk per person (also in English).

Accommodation

Bratislava has none of the logistical problems that plague Prague, but its status as capital, its proximity to Vienna, and the fact that it receives only a trickle of independent tourists, mean that **accommodation** is more expensive here than anywhere else in the country – inexpensive, or even medium-range hotels and pensions are few and far between, and for an old-town location, more often than not you'll pay through the nose. The cheaper hotels tend to lurk to the east and northeast of the centre, in amongst the high-rise *panelák* apartment blocks. While these are not the most appealing neighbourhoods, they are within easy striking distance of the centre by bus or tram. In all cases, try to reserve at least a day in advance to be sure of a room. There are relatively few accommodation agencies, but Satur, Jesenského 5–9 (Mon–Fri 9am–6pm, Sat 9am–noon; ℡02/5441 0133), and BKIS, on Klobučnícká (see above), can book centrally located **private rooms** for around 750Sk and upwards per person (for a 50Sk fee), and the latter should have information on hostels too.

Hotels and pensions

Arcus Moskovská 5 ℡ & ℡02/5557 2522. Small pension within walking distance of the old town, just east of Americké nám., and a rarity in Bratislava: clean, quiet, comfortable and relatively affordable. Take any tram heading up Špitalská from Kamenné námestie. ❺

Astra Prievozská 14a ℡02/5341 4183, ⓦwww .hotelastra.sk. Just over 2km east of the centre, with pleasantly refurbished rooms; take trolleybus #218 from the main train station or walk from the main bus station. ❸

Barónka Murdorchova 2 ℡02/4488 2089, ⓦwww.baronka.sk. Comfortable, refurbished hotel with swimming pool, fitness centre and restaurant, outside the city centre on tram #3, with parking. ❹

Botel Grácia Rázusovo nábrežie ℡02/5443 2132, ⓦwww.botel-gracia.sk. Floating hotel moored on the main embankment. Overpriced and not everyone's cup of tea, especially in summer when the mosquitoes arrive. ❹

Carlton Hviezdoslavovo nám. 3 ℡02/5939 0000, ⓦwww.radissonsas.com. Vast, imposing 1920s hotel, recently refurbished by the Radisson chain, with every conceivable creature comfort and a great position on one of Bratislava's finest squares. ❾

Chez David Zámocká 13 ℡02/5441 3824, ⓦwww.chezdavid.sk. Plush kosher pension with excellent kosher restaurant attached, superbly located in the old Jewish quarter behind the castle. Less expensive and better value than many other places in this price range. ❼

Danube Rybné námestie 1 ☎02/5934 0000,
🌐www.hoteldanube.com. This deluxe Austrian-run
hotel, built in blue and grey titanium, has views of
the castle, most SNP and the river, and charges for
the privilege. ❾

Devín Riečna 4 ☎02/5998 5111, 🌐www
.hoteldevin.sk. Businessperson's hotel on the
waterfront; not quite as flash as the others in town,
but pricey nevertheless. ❾

Gremium Gorkého 11 ☎02/5413 10 26, 🌐www
.gremium.sk. This is really the only halfway decent,
relatively inexpensive option in the whole of the
old town. Centrally located, clean with extremely
basic en-suite bathrooms, plus a great café on the
ground floor. ❸

Hotel no. 16 Partizánska 16a ☎02/5441 1672,
🌐www.internet.sk/hotelno16. Opulent, wood-
panelled villa, ten minutes' walk from the staré
mesto. It's not cheap, but it's better value and more
charming than the big hotels. ❼

Kyjev Rajská 2 ☎02/5964 1111, 🌐www
.kyjev-hotel.sk. Sky-rise Communist-style 1960s
hotel near Kamenné nám., with great views from
the top floor. ❺–❻

Nivy Líščie Nivy 3 ☎02/5541 0390, 🌐www
.hotelnivy.sk. A splash of blue amid the grey nové
mesto high-rises, this hotel is good value and has
a swimming pool and weight room; take tram #8
from the main train station, #9 from Obchodná or
#12 from Kamenné nám. ❸

Perugia Zelená 5 ☎02/5443 1818, 🌐www
.perugia.sk. Probably the best of the old town's
plush and pricey hotels, located right in the centre
of the old town in a former palace. ❾

Turist Ondavská 5 ☎02/5557 2789, 🌐www.turist

.sk. Bargain Communist-era high-rise hotel verging
on the grotty; it's located 2.5km northeast of the
centre, off Trnavská cesta, bus #22 or #34 from the
main train station. ❸

Hostels and camping

Downtown Backpacker's Panenská 31
☎02/5464 1191, 🌐www.backpackers.sk. Pleasant and convenient (though not cheap) hostel,
located five minutes' walk north of Michalská
veža. Dorms from 600Sk per person plus doubles
available. ❷

J.Hronca Bernolákova ☎02/5249 7723,
📠02/5249 7724. The liveliest hostel in the city,
only a short tram ride northeast of the centre; tram
#11 from Kamenné námestie or trolleybus #210
from both the bus or train station. Breakfast is
included, and there's a bar and regular discos and
gigs. Open June–Aug. ❷

Mladá Garda Račianska 103 ☎02/4425 3065,
🌐www.mladagarda.info. Student dorm that
becomes a tourist hostel in summer. Low prices
make up for its distance from the centre. Tram
#3 from the train station or #11 from Kamenné
námestie. Open July & Aug. ❷

Svoradov Svoradova 13 ☎02/5441 1908. Another
bustling, youthful hostel, centrally located just two
blocks north of the castle. Open July & Aug. ❷

Zlaté Piesky Intercamp Senecká cesta 2 ☎ &
📠02/4425 7373, 🌐www.intercamp.sk. Two fairly
grim campsites, 8km northeast of the city centre,
near the swimming lake of the same name; tram
#2 from the main train station or #4 from town.
Bungalows (❶–❷) on offer all year round; tent
camping May to mid-Oct only.

The Staré Mesto

Bratislava's mostly pedestrianized **staré mesto** is, without a doubt, the nicest
part of the city to explore. It's been massively overhauled over the last decade,
and now looks really quite stunning. The best way to approach the old town is
from Obchodná – literally Shop Street – where trams #1, #5, #6, #7 and #9 all
off-load their passengers to walk down to Hurbanovo námestie, a busy whizzing
junction on the northernmost edge of the staré mesto.

Hurbanovo námestie and Michalská veža

On **Hurbanovo námestie** you'll find the city's biggest (albeit now rather dismal)
shoe store **Dom obuvi** and, unmoved by the vulgar clamour of it all, the hefty
mass of Galli da Bibiena's **kostel Trinitárov**. Inside, the single-domed nave is
filled with red and grey stuccoed marble, lending the place a faded musty ambience, while the exuberant trompe l'oeil frescoes create a magnificent false cupola
on the ceiling, typical of the Bibiena family who excelled in theatrical design.

Across the road and past the functionalist shoe shop, originally built for Bat'a
by the architect Vladimír Krafík and known locally as Vel'ký Bat'a, a footbridge
passes under the first tower of the city's last remaining double gateway. Below,

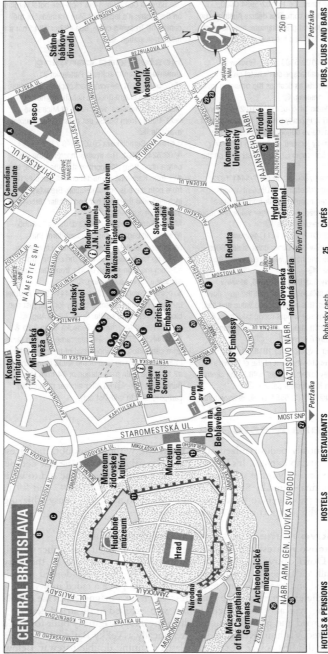

CENTRAL BRATISLAVA

HOTELS & PENSIONS		
Botel Grácia	G	
Carlton	F	Devín	I
Chez David	C	Gremium	F
Danube	G	Kyjev	C
		Perugia	G

HOSTELS	
Svoradov	B

RESTAURANTS		
Apetit	B	
Chez David	H	
El Diablo	D	
Modrá hviezda	A	
Passage Rybárska brána	E	
Prašná bašta		

Rybársky cech	25	
Slovenská reštaurácia	20	
Tempus Fugit	7	
Tokyo	21	
U Filipa	4	
Vegetarian	15	
Woch	5	

CAFÉS		
Bystrica	25	
Café Français	7	
Gremium	21	
Kaffé Mayer	4	
Krym	15	
London Café	5	
Múzeum	27	
Parnas	6	
Piano Bar	D	
Radnička	14	
Roland	23	
U anjelov	18	

PUBS, CLUBS AND BARS		
Dubliner	24	12
Hradná Vináreň	17	11
Smirnoff Klub	10	22
U-Club	8	26
	13	
	3	

in what used to be the city moat, is a tiny, neglected garden, which belongs to the **Baroque apothecary** or Lekáreň U Červeného raka (At the Red Lobster), immediately on your left between the towers (currently under reconstruction).

The second and taller of the two gateways is the **Michalská veža** (April–Sept Tues–Fri 10am–5pm, Sat & Sun 11am–6pm; Oct–March Tues–Fri 9.30am–4.30pm, Sat & Sun 11am–6pm), an evocative and impressive entrance to the staré mesto whose outer limits are elsewhere hard to distinguish. Climb the tower for a great rooftop view of the old town, pausing en route for a glance round to the vertical **expozícia zbraní a mestského opevnenia** (exhibition of weaponry and town fortifications).

Michalská and Ventúrska

Pedestrianized **Michalská** and **Ventúrska**, which run into each other, have both been beautifully restored and are lined with some of Bratislava's finest Baroque palaces. There are usually plenty of students milling about amongst the shoppers, as the main university library is on the right, in the building that once held the Palace of the Royal Hungarian Court Chamber, later the seat of the **Hungarian Parliament**. From here a passageway leads west to the **convent of sv Klara**, whose chapel spire is one of the city's most beautiful pieces of Gothic architecture. Sadly, the convent now houses another university library and, except for the occasional concert, the chapel can only be admired from its southern wall. The backstreets around sv Klara are among the most deserted (and evocative) in the staré mesto, and, at the time of writing, were still awaiting the forces of restoration. Back on Venturská 10, a few doors down on the corner of Zelená street, is the **Mozartov dom** (legend has it that Mozart once performed here at the age of six in December 1762), one of three Baroque palaces owned by the Pálffy family and rebuilt by Marshal Leopold Pálffy in 1747. Here, Verejnost' proti násiliu (People Against Violence), the Slovak sister of the Czech Civic Forum, seconded what was then the Institute for Political Education into their headquarters during the student strike of 1989 (it's now the Austrian embassy). Opposite the Mozartov dom is the **Academia Istropolitana**, the first Hungarian (or, if you prefer, Slovak) humanist university. Founded in 1465 as the Universita Istropolitana by King Matthew Corvinus, it continually lost out to the more established nearby universities of Vienna, Prague and Kraków, and was eventually forced to close down in 1490. The buildings and inner courtyard were modernized in the 1960s for the faculty of performing arts, who put on some interesting shows and exhibitions in the chapel and crypt.

Pálffyho palác

The palaces of the Austro-Hungarian aristocracy continue right round into Panská, starting with the **Pálffyho palác**, which now serves as part of the Galéria mesta Bratislavy (Tues–Sun 11am–6pm). Temporary exhibitions are held on the ground floor, basement and third floor, and occasionally on the first floor, too; the gallery's permanent collection seems to get shifted round a bit, but usually occupies the middle two floors. As well as a smattering of Gothic paintings and sculptures, there's a selection of pretty dreadful early nineteenth-century landscapes and portraits, plus a few languid late-nineteenth-century works by Hungarian and Slovak artists.

The most interesting works, though, are by the founding generation of **twentieth-century Slovak artists**, such as Gustáv Mally and Martin Benka, whose depictions of Slovak peasantry from the 1930s gently portray a way of life that forms the backbone of Slovak national identity, but has now more or less disappeared. Peasant life is also the subject of Ľudovít Fulla's paintings which deliberately recall folk tapestries. Other eye-catching canvases include Janko Alexy's wonderfully exaggerated rendering of Košice's hoary Gothic cathedral, and Miloš Bazovský's *Devil Reading a Book*.

Hlavné námestie and Františkánske námestie

Slightly further east are the tranquil twin main squares of the staré mesto: the shady **Františkánske námestie** and **Hlavné námestie**, a delightful patch of cobbled granite focused on a Roland column, with a few acacia trees and a fountain sporting the usual cherubs seemingly peeing out of fishes' mouths; the dramatically renovated surrounding buildings indicate this was once the city's main marketplace. In summer craft stalls aimed at the tourist trade line the periphery, while in December the square heaves with locals enjoying roast sausages, pork and trout, mulled wine and hot meat at the traditional Christmas market.

On the east side of the square is the **stará radnica**, or Old Town Hall, a two-storey building in a lively hotchpotch of styles with a splash of beautifully patterned roof tiles. With a Gothic core, Renaissance innards and nineteenth-century detailing, it surpasses itself in the fanciful Baroque tower and serene half-moon crenellations and fragile arcading of the inner courtyard. The building itself, with its fine Gothic vaulting and superb Baroque ceilings, is the star of any visit, but the town hall also hosts the **Múzeum histórie mesta** (Tues–Fri 10am–5pm, Sat & Sun 11am–6pm; Ⓦ www.muzeumbratislava.sk), a less-than-fascinating collection of historical odds and sods, saved by some winsome Art Nouveau metalwork and a torture chamber (part of the feudal justice exhibition) in the basement. Sports fans will be thrilled to see the silver sequinned suit which belonged to 1970s Slovak ice-skating champion Ondrej Nepela, and, of course, pictures from Slovan Bratislava's famous victory over Barcelona in the 1969 Cup Winners' Cup. In the adjacent Apponyiho palác there's the **Vinohradnícke múzeum** (May–Sept Tues–Fri 10am–5pm, Sat & Sun 11am–6pm; Oct–April Tues–Sun 9.30am–4.30pm; entrance at Radničná 1), a scholarly tribute to Bratislava's position at the centre of the country's wine industry.

The Counter-Reformation, which gripped the parts of Hungary not under Turkish occupation, exudes from the **Jezuitský kostol**, just off the main square. This was nicked from the local German Protestant community – hence its lack of tower and its relatively plain facade (the gilded relief and the ornate main doors were added by the Jesuits during the Counter-Reformation). Inside, the nave seems to stop rather short, its best feature undoubtedly the richly decorated black and gold pulpit which is dripping with gilded tassles. Nearby, opposite the gaudy yellow Františkánov kostol, is the **Mirbachov palác** (Tues–Sun 11am–6pm), arguably the finest of Bratislava's Rococo buildings, still sporting much of its original stucco decor. The Galéria mesta Bratislavy puts on some interesting temporary exhibitions here, but the permanent collection of Rococo and Baroque art and sculpture isn't up to much, save for the room of wall-to-wall miniatures set into the wood panelling and busts by František Xaver Messerschmidt and canvases by František Xaver Palko. The recent addition of a few paintings by early-twentieth-century Slovak artists such as Miloš Bazovský and Mikuláš Galanda adds spice to the proceedings.

Primaciálny palác and around

Round the back of the old town hall, with the stillness of a provincial Italian piazza during siesta, is **Primaciálne námestie**, dominated by the pastel-pink

Neoclassical **Primaciálny palác** (Tues–Sun 10am–5pm), built in 1778–81 for Cardinal Jozef Batthyány, head of the Hungarian Church. The palace's uninspiring pediment frieze, which dates from the 1950s, is topped by a 300-pound cast-iron archbishop's hat, for it was originally designed as the winter residence of the Archbishop of Esztergom. The palace's main claim to fame, however, is as the place where Napoleon and the Holy Roman emperor Francis I signed the Treaty of Pressburg in 1805, following the Battle of Austerlitz (see p.373). Fully renovated, it now houses yet more of the city's art collection, primarily portraits of the Habsburgs, but also minor works by seventeenth-century Dutch and Italian masters.

What also makes the palace worth visiting, though, is the dramatic **Zrkadlová sieň** (Mirror Hall), actually several interconnecting rooms, each lined with different-coloured damask, and, of course, with mirrors. The other highlight is the set of excellently preserved **seventeenth-century Bratislava tapestries**, discovered by chance during the building's restoration in 1903. Woven in Mortlake, London, how they ended up in Bratislava remains a mystery. The tapestries depict the tragedy of Hero, a priestess of Venus, and Leander, the lover who swam across the Bosphorus to be with her, until one night he drowned in a storm. The gallery terminates at a small balcony from which you can view the late-Baroque chapel of sv Ladislav, completed in less than a year in 1781, and sporting a lovely oval ceiling fresco by Maulpertsch or one of his followers.

All over the staré mesto, commemorative plaques make much of Bratislava's musical connections. But, apart from the reflected glory of its proximity to Vienna and Budapest – not to mention the prewar presence of a large German-speaking population who ensured a regular supply of Europe's best artistes – the city only produced a handful of composers, including **Johann Nepomuk Hummel** (1778–1837). Hummel's birthplace, **Rodny dom J.N. Hummela** (Tues–Fri 10–11.45am & 12.30–6pm, Sat 10–11.45am & 12.30–2pm), an apricot-coloured cottage swamped by its neighbours and hidden behind a row of fashionable shops at Klobučnícka 2 (Hat Street), is now a museum documenting his life and work and the musical history of Bratislava. Like Mozart, who was sufficiently impressed to give him free lessons and even put him up for a while in Vienna, Hummel was a *Wunderkind*, who began performing at the tender age of ten and was touted round Europe by his ambitious father. As a pianist in the 1820s, Hummel was one of the most celebrated performers in Europe, yet although he wrote many fine classical works, his music has been largely ignored since his death.

From the Dóm to the Hrad

On the side of the staré mesto nearest the castle, the most insensitive of Bratislava's postwar developments took place. As if the Nazis' annihilation of the city's large and visible Jewish population wasn't enough, the Communist authorities tore down virtually the whole of the **Jewish quarter** in order to build the brutal showpiece bridge, most SNP, in 1972 (see p.469). At the same time they sliced Rybné námestie in two, leaving its central plague column looking forlorn right by the motorway bridge. And finally, the best-preserved section of the old town walls now serves simply as a kind of sound barrier, protecting the rest of the staré mesto from the noise of the traffic. At least a memorial to Bratislava's Jews has finally been set up near the underpass to most SNP, a dense iron concoction of handprints and barbed wire, with a sign commanding *Zachor!* (Remember!).

Dóm sv Martina

Quite apart from the devastation of the ghetto, the traffic that tears along the busy thoroughfare of Staromestská has seriously undermined the foundations of the Gothic **Dóm sv Martina** (Rudnayovo námestie; Mon–Fri 10–11.30am & 2–4.30pm, Sat 10–11.30am, Sun 2–4.30pm), coronation church of the kings and queens of Hungary for over 250 years, whose ill-proportioned steeple is topped by a tiny gilded Hungarian crown. The new road misses the west facade by a matter of metres, engulfing the exterior in noise and fumes. The interior is disappointing, decorated mostly with neo-Gothic furnishings, the best of which are the carved animals and figures on the pews in the choir, but there are one or two outstanding Baroque features which survived the re-Gothicization. Perhaps the most striking piece is the dramatic **equestrian statue of St Martin**, executed in lead by the Baroque sculptor Georg Raphael Donner, which formed the centrepiece of the overblown main altar, erected in 1735 but removed in the nineteenth century. Far from being about to run the naked beggar through with his sword, St Martin, dressed in fashionable aristocratic garb and modelled on the donor, Count Esterházy, is depicted cutting his coat in two to share it with the supplicant. The only other slice of Baroque to have survived is the spectacular side chapel of **sv Ján Almužník** in the north aisle, once again the work of Donner, its red marble portal draped with stucco curtains and cherubs; unfortunately, you can only peer through the wrought-iron gates at the sarcophagus, baldachin and frescoed cupola within.

The Jewish quarter

Passing under the approach road for the new bridge, an old, thin yellow Rococo fancy called U dobrého pastiera (The Good Shepherd) houses the **Múzeum hodín** (Clock Museum; Židovská 1; May–Sept Tues–Fri 10am–5pm, Sat & Sun 11am–6pm; Oct–April Tues–Sun 9.30am–4.30pm) with a display of – depending on your tastes – nauseatingly vulgar or brilliantly kitsch Baroque and Empire clocks.

Further north along Židovská, in the former heart of the city's **Jewish quarter**, you'll find the **Múzeum židovskej kultúry** (no. 17; 11am–5pm; closed Sat; 200Sk), a fairly straightforward museum tracing the history of the Jewish community in Bratislava and Slovakia and explaining the basic religious practices of Judaism. There's also a memorial to the rabbis who perished in the camps, and to the Slovaks who helped save Jews from deportation.

Close by the Múzeum hodín, at the bottom end of Beblavého, the **Dom na Beblavého 1** (Museum of Arts and Crafts; May–Sept Tues–Fri 10am–5pm, Sat & Sun 11am–6pm; Oct–April Tues–Sun 9.30am–4.30pm) contains a few period dining rooms and a smallish collection of national folk art objects.

Beblavého then begins the steep climb up to the castle. For many years this was one of the city's more infamous red-light districts, serving both town and barracks from its strategic point between the two, and described evocatively by **Patrick Leigh Fermor**, who passed through Bratislava en route to Constantinople in 1934:

During the day, except for the polyglot murmur of invitation, it was a rather silent place. But it grew noisier after dark when shadows brought confidence and the plum brandy began to bite home. It was only lit by cigarette ends and by an indoor glow that silhouetted the girls on their thresholds. Pink lights revealed the detail of each small interior: a hastily tidied bed, a tin basin and a jug, some lustral gear and a shelf displaying a bottle of solution, pox-foiling and gentian-hued; a couple of dresses hung on a nail.

Jews probably settled in **Bratislava** during the thirteenth century, after which they were forced to move around the city, and expelled several times, before finally finding refuge in Podhradie (literally "under the castle"), just outside the city walls, in the sixteenth century. Before World War II, Jews made up ten percent of the city's population (the vast majority Orthodox), maintaining no fewer than nineteen synagogues and prayer rooms. Bratislava was also a significant centre of Jewish **education**; the yeshivah was founded here, in 1806, which became one of the most famous Orthodox institutions in Europe, a tradition carried on today by the Pressburger Yeshivah in Jerusalem. Its founder, Rabbi Hatam Sofer, died here in 1839, and his grave continues to attract Orthodox pilgrims from all over the world; it is situated in a grim mausoleum by the western exit of the tram tunnel under the castle, built by the Nazis over the original cemetery. Today, Bratislava's Jewish community is very small, with only one working synagogue escaping the attentions of both communism and fascism, at Heydukova 11–13, and a large cemetery, west of the city centre on Žižkova.

Of **Slovakia**'s considerable prewar Jewish population of 95,000, only an estimated 3000 remain. Slovak Jews were deported to Auschwitz from where two, Rudolf Vrba and Alfred Wetzler, were practically the only people to successfully escape. Their aim was to warn the last remaining Jewish community in occupied Europe – that of Hungary – about its forthcoming fate, and to get the Allies to bomb Auschwitz or the rail links leading to it. Their reports were dismissed as untenable and impractical. The fate of Slovak Jewry under the wartime Tiso regime is still a potent political issue – the suggestion made by the Czech ambassador to the USA that anti-Semitism was, and still is, "endemic" in Slovakia caused anger among many Slovaks, who argue that several leading members of Tiso's government did their best to prevent the Jews from being deported. Yet since 1989, there have been several disturbing developments: a plaque commemorating Tiso has been unveiled and several Jewish cemeteries have been vandalized across the country. These incidents do not necessarily confirm the widely held Czech view of Slovakia as a hotbed of anti-Semitism, but it is particularly distasteful that anti-Semitism should continue to be a useful political tool in a place where so few Jews remain.

Like the Jewish cafés Leigh Fermor also hung out in (along with, though not necessarily at the same table as, the young Orthodox Jew Ludvík Hoch – better known as Robert Maxwell), all this has long since gone, but there's only a vague hint of the bohemian about the ramshackle houses now slowly being turned into swish galleries, chic bars and restaurants.

Bratislavský hrad

Bratislava's castle or **Hrad** (grounds open daily: April–Sept 9am–8pm; Oct–March 9am–6pm), often likened to an "inverted bedstead", is an unwelcoming giant box, built in the fifteenth century by Emperor Sigismund in expectation of a Hussite attack, a one-time seat of the Habsburg empire, burned down by its own drunken Austrian soldiers in 1811, and restored under the Communists. Your first port of call should be the **Klenoty dávnej minulosti Slovenska** (Tues–Sun 10am–noon & 1.30–4pm), a dimly lit treasury on the left as you enter the main gate, whose most precious exhibit is in the ticket office: the *Venus of Moravany*, a tiny fertility figure said to be made from a mammoth's tusk around 22,800 BC.

The rest of the castle, housing around half of the vast collections of the **Slovenské historické múzeum** (Tues–Sun 9am–5pm; 60Sk; guided tour in English 200Sk; ⑩www.snm-hm.sk), is made up of two main parts. The second floor includes a long-winded exhibition of farm implements and wood- and metalworking tools; pass on through and up to the third floor until you get to the period furniture section, which ranges from heavy Renaissance wardrobes to Biedermayer dining-room sets to twentieth-century gear. The most interesting section, by far, begins with iridescent Art Nouveau glassware and bronze chandeliers, and features a whole set of bedroom furniture decorated with a peacock feather motif by Dušan Jurkovič, finishing up with a wild, Oriental-style Art Deco bed in golden-yellow. The castle's small collection of old clocks is also worth viewing, just in case you missed the museum on Židovská, and you also get the chance to climb to the top of the Korunná veža, one of the castle's four corner towers. The castle's top floor also houses the **Hudobné múzeum** (Music Museum; same hours), which includes a few scores, recordings and folk instruments.

Even if you don't make it up the Korunná veža, you can get a pretty good view south across the Danube plain from outside the castle gates. From either vantage point, the panorama is nothing short of mind-blowing. Although you can gaze out over the meeting point of three countries, most of the immediate foreground is taken up with the infamous **Petržalka** estate, symbol of the new Slovak nation, dragged forcibly into the twentieth century at great social cost. A third of the city's population – an incredible 150,000 people – live in Petržalka, whose estates retain cruelly ironic names like Háje (Woods) and Lúky (Meadows), though barely a tree remains amid this expanse of mud and high-rises; until 1989 it had the added bonus of being surrounded by the barbed wire and watchtowers of the Iron Curtain. In many respects, most notably crime and drugs, it can't compete with the worst housing estates in the West, but with the highest suicide rate in the country and a dearth of amenities, it's not a place anyone would choose to live.

Around the castle

From the Hrad it's possible to take an alternative route back down to the staré mesto by following the path that winds down the hillside from west of the Leopoldova brána. This will bring you to a neglected couple of streets – the old fishing quarter, squeezed between the waterfront motorway and the castle hill, which harbours several little-visited minor branches of the Slovenské národné múzeum. The first is the **Archeologické múzeum** (Tues–Sun 9am–5pm), Žižkova 12, whose few notable Roman exhibits include a winsome stone lion, a sleeping marble cherub, a votive relief and a stone altar to Jupiter. The **Muzeum kultúry karpatských Nemcov** (Tues–Sun 10am–4pm) at Žižkova 14, examines the history of ethnic Germans living in the territory of current Slovakia, while the **Muzeum kultúry Maďarov na Slovensku** (May–Oct Tues–Sat 10am–5pm; Nov–April Mon–Fri 8am–3pm), at Žižkova 18, concentrates on the country's Hungarian minority.

Hviezdoslavovo námestie and the waterfront

Between the staré mesto and the waterfront lies the graceful, tree-lined boulevard of **Hviezdoslavovo námestie**, with restaurants and cafés along one side and, on the other, the mammoth *Hotel Carlton*, an amalgamation of three hotels originally built in the 1920s and recently restored to its former glory by the Radisson chain. Pride of place in the square, and a prime spot for casual loitering, is the larger-than-life statue of Pavol Országh Hviezdoslav, "father of Slovak poetry" a minor government official in the Orava region whose poetry is still a source of great national pride.

At the square's eastern end are two magnificent late-nineteenth-century edifices: the first, fronted by the elaborate bronze **Ganymedova fontána** depicting the Trojan youth being kidnapped by Zeus disguised as an eagle, and featuring some wonderful frogs, tortoises, pike and crayfish, is now the **Slovenské národné divadlo** (Slovak National Theatre), built as a top-quality German-speaking opera house; the second, diagonally opposite, is the later, more Secessionist **Reduta**, a casino and restaurant as well as home to the Slovenská filharmónia (Slovak Philharmonic) and the site of the Bratislava Music Festival every autumn.

In between the two is a surprisingly playful **Soviet war memorial**, a complete contrast to the Slavín (see p.471), depicting a woman doing gymnastics with a laurel leaf. At the end of Mostova, which runs south along the side of Reduta, is **Štúrovo námestie**, its modern statue of **Ľudovít Štúr** (see p.477) and his followers – appearing to levitate – a replacement for the grandiose statue of Maria Theresa blown up by Slovak nationalists in 1919 and erected in 1972.

The Danube and the Nový most (most SNP)
Beyond Štúrovo námestie and the fast dual carriageway of Rázusov nábrežie, you can stroll along the banks of the (far from blue) **River Danube** – Dunaj in Slovak. At this point the Danube is terrifyingly fast – witness the speed to which the massive double-barges are reduced when going against the current and, by contrast, the velocity of those hurtling downstream. There's a regular (and hazardous) summer-only ferry service across the river, an alternative to crossing by either of the two bridges. The larger of these is the infamous **Nový most or most SNP** (Bridge of the Slovak National Uprising), for which the old Jewish Quarter was ripped up. However destructive its construction, it's difficult not to be impressed by the sheer size and audacity of this single open suspension bridge. Its one support column leans at an alarming angle, topped by a saucer-like penthouse café reminiscent of the *Starship Enterprise*. The view from the café is superlative (except after dark due to the reflection of the interior lights on the windows), but the cost of the lift and a drink puts many locals off: there's a cheaper and equally good view from the toilet.

The best place from which to view the structure is the rather forlorn funfair in the **Sad Janka Kráľa** on the opposite bank – all that's left of what Baedeker described in 1904 as "a favourite evening-promenade . . . with café and pleasant grounds" – its statue of the nineteenth-century poet Sándor Petöfi a reminder of the city's Hungarian heritage.

The Slovenská národná galéria
When the Slovaks took control of Bratislava in 1918, a town in which they had previously made little impression, they set about establishing their own cultural monuments to rival those of their predecessors, the Austrians and Hungarians. Three such buildings were put up in the waterfront district, of which the most rewarding is the **Slovenská národná galéria** (entrance on Rázusovo nábrežie 2; Tues–Sun 10am–5.30pm; ⓦwww.sng.sk), housed in a converted naval barracks (*vodné kasárne*) and in the neighbouring Esterházyho palác (nám. Ľ. Štúra 4, currently under reconstruction).

The main building now contains a collection of **sixteenth- to eighteenth-century European art** on its first floor, which repays merely selective viewing. Only the bizarre seventeenth-century Dutch painting of *A Frog Trial*, and two very fine portraits by the Scottish artists Henry Raeburn and David Wilkie really stand out.

On the second floor you'll usually find a couple of temporary exhibitions, as well as the gallery's collection of **Gothic art**, much of it from the German-speaking Spiš region in eastern Slovakia. The most compelling works in the **Baroque art** section are the hyperrealist "character heads", carved by the eccentric sculptor Franz Xaver Messerschmidt, each depicting a different grimace, and the icons, particularly the seventeenth-century *Last Judgement*, in which the sinful tumble into the mouth of a fish-devil. The nineteenth-century works, back on the first floor, are less than inspiring, with the exception of the dark, expressionist works by Ladislav Medňanský (aka Mednyánszky) from the 1890s. For an overview of Slovak artists of the twentieth century, you need to go to the section of the Bratislava gallery based in Pállfyho palác at Panská 19 (see p.463).

The Slovenské národné múzeum and the Modrý kostolík

Further along the quayside, past the hydrofoil terminal, is the **Prírodovedné múzeum** (Tues–Sun 9am–5pm; ⓦwww.snm.sk), the unremarkable natural history section of the Slovenské národné múzeum, housed in a dark and dingy 1930s building, and only really worth visiting for its excellent temporary exhibitions and its café round the back of the building. Further east along Vajanského nábrežie stands the equally dour **Komenský University**, founded along with the Republic in 1918, whose students spill out into the nearby bars and cafés and mingle with the crowds awaiting buses in Šafárikovo námestie.

The only specific sight around here is Ödön Lechner's sky-blue Art Nouveau **Modrý kostolík** (Little Blue Church) of St Alžbeta on Bezručova – a delicious, almost edible, concrete monument by one of Hungary's leading early twentieth-century architects. Decorated, inside and out, with the richness of a central European cream cake, it's dedicated to St Elizabeth, the city's one and only famous saint, who was born in Bratislava in 1207. The most reliable way to get inside is to come just before the service (daily at 6pm). Lechner quite clearly also designed the Gymnasium, one block north of the church, which shares the same shabby blue paint.

Námestie SNP and the suburbs

At the northern end of Štúrova, under the shadow of the high-rise *Hotel Kyjev* and the city's gargantuan Tesco department store, is **Kamenné námestie**. It's not exactly picturesque, but this is where the whole city seems to wind up after work, to shop, grab a beer or takeaway from one of the many stand-up stalls, gossip away the early evening and, above all, catch the bus or tram home.

To the northwest, Kamenné námestie melds imperceptibly into the slightly more accommodating **námestie SNP**, with a few trees and a host of sit-down cafés with outdoor terraces. In 1989 the Slovaks gathered here in their thousands for their part in the Velvet Revolution; nowadays it's a favourite spot for political activists. At its centre is the Monument to the Slovak National Uprising, the unsuccessful antifascist coup against the Nazis in the summer of 1944 which cost the country so dear. A macho bronze partisan guards the eternal flame, while two Slovak women (heads suitably covered) maintain a respectful distance. The one building worth noting on the square is the main **post office**, on the west side, whose Art Deco atrium of coloured glass has been lovingly restored.

Hodžovo námestie and beyond

Behind námestie SNP is the brown marble and onyx abomination of the *Hotel Fórum* (currently under reconstruction), which looks out onto **Hodžovo námestie**, nowadays one of the city's busiest intersections, though no doubt once a princely foil for the **Grassalkovičov palác** cowering in the top corner. Seat of the president under the clerico-fascist Jozef Tiso during World War II, and later home to the Communist youth organization, the palace is now once more the official residence of the Slovak president, though its gardens, which excel in ugly modern fountains, are open to the public in daylight hours. One block north of the park up Banskobystrická there's another grandiose Baroque palace, once the former summer residence of the archbishop of Esztergom and, until recently, home to the Slovak Parliament, which now occupies the ugly bunker to the west of the castle.

Devotees of totalitarian architecture might also visit **Námestie slobody**, a grandiose space designed by the local Party as a monumental setting for a giant statue of Klement Gottwald, the first Communist president. Gottwald has gone, thankfully, leaving only the wickedly unappealing Fountain of Friendship and the severe concrete mass of the General Post Office building, which takes up the entire length of the east side of the square and claims to be the largest in the world – although only a minute hall is actually open to the public. A more successful modern addition to the city is the striking inverted pyramid of the Slovak radio building, up Mýtna, northeast of the square. If you're on for a wander, head southeast two blocks or so to the **Medická záhrada** (summer 8am–9.30pm; winter 8am–6pm), a dog-free, peaceful garden marred only by the dodgy 1970s park benches and lights. Further southeast still, on the other side of Poľná, lies the city's oldest cemetery, the **Ondrejský cintorín** (daily 7am–dusk), established in 1784. More park than graveyard now, the predominantly Hungarian and German graves are rarely tended these days.

To the west of Hodžovo námestie, block after block of late-nineteenth-century buildings in faded colours squat under Slavín hill. The only sight as such is the pale-blue and exceedingly plain **Protestant Lycée** on Palisády (closed to the public), outside which a tall granite column commemorates the many leading Slovak men of letters who were educated here in the nineteenth century. Surprisingly for a fervently Catholic peasant country, the Protestants produced Slovak leaders far in excess of their numerical strength, including the entire 1848 triumvirate of Štúr, Hodža and Hurban. The city's Lenin Museum used to reside in a nineteenth-century neo-Baroque palace three-quarters of the way up Štefánikova at no. 25; to make up for this irrevocable loss, there's a **Múzeum polície SR** (Tues–Sat 10am–5pm; free) on the corner of Gunduličova itself, at no. 2, with a rather comical exhibition on the heroics of the Slovak police. It features a mock-up murder scene, detailed displays of feats such as nabbing bank robbers and drug smugglers, and a machine that recognizes counterfeit notes. The highlight is a model of the Communist-era border crossing at Petržalka, with a double row of electrified razor-wire fences and lookout towers for the armed guards. The old Lenin Museum itself is now the Dom zahranizanych Slovákov (House of Slovaks Abroad) with a little-visited **Krajanské múzeum** (Compatriot's Museum; Tues–Sun 10am–6pm), at Štefánikova 25, run by the Matica slovenská (see p.515) and focusing on Slovaks who have made it big abroad and temporary exhibitions.

The Slavín Monument

Slavín hill, to the northwest of Hodžovo námestie, is crowned by the gargantuan **Slavín Monument** to the 7000 Soviet soldiers who lost their lives in the battle for Bratislava. Ceremoniously completed in 1960 to mark the fifteenth anniversary of the city's liberation, this is now one of the largest Soviet monuments still standing in the entire country, and visible from virtually every street corner in Bratislava. It's predictably militaristic, not to say phallic, a giant ribbed obelisk thrusting into the sky, topped by an anguished Soviet soldier holding the victory banner outstretched.

Dubček

The mild-mannered **Alexander Dubček** used to live at Mišikova 46 (Mouse Street), close to the Slavín Monument. In 1968 he became probably the only Slovak ever to achieve world fame, a feat he accomplished by becoming the somewhat unlikely leader of a deeply divided Communist Party as it attempted to bring about *perestroika* twenty years ahead of its time. Crushed by the subsequent Soviet invasion, he spent his twenty years of internal exile here, under constant surveillance, working for the Slovak equivalent of the local forestry commission. He lived long enough to witness the happy events of 1989, appearing alongside Václav Havel to cheering crowds on Wenceslas Square and later becoming the parliamentary speaker. The circumstances of his death, in a car crash in 1992, are shrouded in controversy; his demise was a tragedy for Slovakia, which sorely lacks a politician of his international standing.

Eating

The choice of places **to eat** in Bratislava has improved enormously over the last few years, as have standards, though you're still unlikely to have the meal of a lifetime here. The most memorable aspect of the whole experience is often the ambience, and exploring the atmospheric streets of the old town by night is all part of the fun. In addition, you can also be fairly sure that, away from the places catering for those on expenses, prices remain uniformly low. Phone numbers are provided where reservations are advised.

Apetit Dunajská 18. A traditional Slovak beer hall in an unlikely setting just off noisy Kamenné nám., but its prices are low and the atmosphere (and Budweiser) is good. Mon–Sat 11am–11pm.

Chez David Zamocká 13 ☏02/5441 3824. Strictly kosher restaurant serving fresh, beautifully prepared Jewish cuisine, but pricey for Bratislava. Daily 11.30am–10pm.

El Diablo Sedlárska 6. Mexican restaurant opposite *Tempus Fugit* (see below). Hearty but none-too-cheap US-style steaks. DJs occasionally play in the evening. Daily 2.30pm–midnight.

Modrá hviezda Beblavého 14. Restaurant en route to the castle serving decent Slovak and Hungarian specialities washed down with local wines. Daily 11.30am–11pm.

Passage Rybárska brána Gorkého 1. Small complex of inexpensive restaurants, including *Spaghetti & Co*, a Balkan grill, a Chinese takeaway and a pseudo-English pub.

Prašná bašta Zámočnícka 11. Soothing interior and a lovely courtyard, perfect for the tasteful cross-cultural cuisines on offer, with Mediterranean-influenced salads and creative main dishes. Live music. Daily 11am–10pm.

Rybársky cech Žižkova 1a ☏02/5441 3049. Popular, reliably good but pricey fish restaurant on the ground floor of a former fisherman's house down by the waterfront below the castle (there's a posher, more expensive version upstairs). Reservations recommended. Daily 11am–11pm.

Slovenská reštaurácia Hviezdoslavovo nám. 20. Traditional Slovak specialities served by staff dressed in folk costumes. The atmosphere is pleasant but prices are fairly high. Daily 11am–11pm.

Tempus Fugit Sedlárska 5. Fifteenth-century burgher house converted into a three-storey restaurant, with a row of stone columns and covered courtyard. Long menu with Slovak and international dishes. Daily 10am–1am.

Tokyo Straková ulica. Small, simple bar serving Japanese and Thai specialities at moderate prices. Daily 11am–midnight.

U Filipa Hlavne nám. Renaissance house nicely converted into a café and restaurant, with triangular, arcaded patio and a museum devoted to local sculptor Arthur Fleischmann. Live piano in the evenings. Daily 11am–midnight.

Umag Žilinská 2. Small Croat-run pizzeria on the corner of Štefanovičova near the train station, with excellent thin-base pizzas. Mon–Fri 8am–10pm, Sat 9am–10pm, Sun 11am–10pm.

Vegetarian Laurinská 8. Plain and simple vegetarian lunch spot, with a short list of salads and soya-based main dishes. Mon–Fri 11am–3pm.

Woch Františkánske nám. 7 ☏02/5443 2928. Yet another tastefully refurbished vaulted cellar, located diagonally opposite the Stará radnica. Live music in the evenings (usually jazz). Daily 11am–midnight.

Cafés

For a relatively small city, Bratislava has an incredible number of **cafés**, ranging from coffee-and-cake pit stops for the older generation to smoky student dives. Many have tables outside in the summer, and warm snugs to sink into in the winter.

Bystrica Most SNP. Recently reconstructed sky-high café (prices as well as location) at the top of the city's main suspension bridge. Daily 10am–10pm.

Café Français Sedlárska 7. Decent croissants and other French snacks in the Institut Français. Mon–Fri 9am–9pm.

Gremium Gorkého 11. Wonderful, smoky café/gallery in the centre, with a high ceiling and a nice balcony where you can play pool. Daily 8.30am–midnight.

Kaffé Mayer Hlavné nám. 4. A resurrected late-nineteenth-century café that tries very hard to emulate its Viennese-style ancestor – very popular with the city's older coffee-and-cake fans. Daily 9m–midnight.

Krym Šafaríkovo nám. Cheap pub/café with a short menu, and without atmosphere. Mon–Fri 7.30am–11.pm, Sat 9am–11pm, Sun 11.30am–11pm.

Kút Zámočnická 11. Light Mediterranean salads served in this café with burgundy walls, attached to the *Prašná bašta* restaurant. Techno in the evenings. Daily 11am–10pm.

London Café Panská 17. Tiny British Council tearoom that's famous for its quiche and salad, popular with expats and a good place to catch up on the English press. Mon–Fri 10am–7pm, Sat 10am–3pm.

Múzeum Vajanského nábr. 2. Appealingly gloomy mustard-yellow faux-marble foyer café round the back of the Prírodné múzeum, with an Internet off-shoot, *Klub Internet*, in the same building. Mon–Fri 9am–7pm.

Olympia Kollárovo nám. 20. Wonderfully tacky Communist-era decor in this café above the Nová scéna theatre. Daily 11am–midnight.

Omama Sasinkovo 19. Fun, off-beat café decorated with classic old advertisements from the interwar period. Decent menu selection too. Mon–Fri 9am–10pm.

Parnas Panská 12. Nice café in the old town that's a favourite coffee and cigarette pit stop for students and arty types. Mon–Fri 9am–midnight, Sat & Sun 4pm–midnight.

Piano Bar Laurinská 11. Popular little bar run by one of the stars of Slovak commercial TV, who occasionally treats his guests to an impromptu jam session. Daily 10am–midnight.

Radnička Hlavné nám. 1. Cosy café tucked into the Old Town Hall. Daily 9.30am–9pm.

Roland Hlavné nám. Pricey but splendid fin-de-siècle café overlooking the main square and spilling outdoors in summer. Open daily 8.30am–midnight.

U anjelov Laurinská 19. Cosy café/bar that attracts a discerning, black-clad crowd. Mon–Sat 9am–midnight, Sun 5pm–midnight.

Entertainment and nightlife

Bratislava's nightlife is still heavily biased towards high culture, with few out-and-out dance music venues or **nightclubs** to choose from. On the other hand, there are a number of bars and pubs that play loud music and stay open late, where dancing has been known to break out. For more mainstream fare, and cinema listings, pick up the monthly Slovak-language magazine, *Kam do mesta* from BKIS or check the listings in the weekly English-language *Slovak Spectator* (Ⓦ www.slovakspectator.sk). In season, there are **opera and ballet** performances at the Slovenské národné divadlo (Ⓦ www.snd.sk) and **classical concerts** at Reduta, both on Hviedoslavovo námestie, as well as a more varied programme at the modern Istropolis complex on Trnavské mýto (tram #2 from the station; tram #4 or #6 from the centre).

Bratislava hosts a couple of annual large-scale **festivals**, the most prestigious being the classical music festival in October – without the big names of Prague's, but a lot easier to get tickets for. There's also a biennial international festival of children's illustrations held in September and October in odd-numbered years, as much of interest to adults as to kids. While on the subject, if you've **kids** in tow, it's worth finding out what's on at the Bibiana children's cultural centre (Tues–Sun 10am–6pm) on Panská, which stages events, shows and exhibitions aimed at kids.

Pubs, clubs and bars

Charlie Centrum Špitálska 4. Arts cinema complex that has a café upstairs and a spacious, loud, reasonably priced nightclub/pub downstairs. Situated behind the *Hotel Kyjev*, with its entrance on Rajská. Daily until 4am.

Dubliner Sedlárska 6. Very popular over-the-top Irish-themed pub, complete with mock cobbled street. Mon–Sat 11–3am, Sun 11–1am.

Hradná Vináreň Námestie A. Dubčeka 1. Stunning restaurant, serving excellent wine, Slovak vodkas *slivovica* and *borovička*, and local specialities with breathtaking views from its summer terrace. Daily 9am–11pm.

Hystéria Odbojárov 9 🕸 www.hysteria-pub.sk. Worth the trek out to the Zimný štadión (tram #4 or #6 from Kamenné námestie) for this lively Tex-Mex pub, with regular pool and live music. Mon–Thurs 10–1am, Fri 10–5am, Sat 11–5am, Sun 11–1am.

Koník Mlynské nivy 8. Lively pub near the main bus station, which attracts a young crowd. Mon–Thurs & Sat 10am–1am, Fri until 2am, Sun until midnight.

Smirnoff Klub Štúrova (at the Šafárikovo nám. end). Lots of neon lights, bad DJs and dubious punters, but it can be fun if you're out late and still steaming. Mon–Fri 10.30–3.30am, Sat 6pm–4am.

Stará sladovňa Cintorínska 32. The city's malthouse until 1976, *Mamut*, as it's also known, is Bratislava's most famous (and largest) pub. Czech Budvar on tap, big band and country & western music Thurs–Sat, and a bingo hall and casino on site as well. Daily 11am–11pm.

U-Club nábrežie arm. gen. L. Svobodu. Cheap, loud and slightly weird club located in an old nuclear bunker underneath the Hrad. Draws the best of the city's DJs. Fri & Sat from 7pm.

Listings

Airlines Aeroflot, Grösslingova 43 (☏ 02/5263 4337-9); Air France, Razusovo nabrezie 6 (☏ 02/5443 4108, 🕸 www.airfrance.com); Air Slovakia, Bratislava airport (☏ 02/4342 2742, 🕸 www .airslovakia.sk); Austrian Airlines, Rybné nám. 1 (☏ 02/5910 2600, 🕸 www.austrian.sk); British Airways, Štefánikova 22 (☏ 02/5710 2030, 🕸 www .british-airways.com); ČSA, Štúrova 13 (☏ 02/5296 1325, 🕸 www.csa.cz); Delta, Hotel Kyjev, Rajská 2 (☏ 02/52 92 09 40, 🕸 www.delta-air.com); LOT, Špitálská 51 (☏ 02/5263 4775, 🕸 www.lot .com); Lufthansa, Dunajská 3 (☏ 02/5292 0422, 🕸 www.lufthansa.sk); Sky Europe, Ivanská cesta 26 (☏ 02/4850 4850, 🕸 www.skyeurope.com); Slovak Airlines, Bratislava airport (☏ 02/4870 4870, 🕸 www.slovakairlines.sk).

Car rental Two good local firms are Auto Danubius, Trnavská 39 (☏ 02/4437 3566), and Auto Rotos, Račianska 184/B (☏ 02/4487 2666, 🕸 www .autorotos.sk).

Cultural centres Austrian Cultural Centre, Zelená 7; British Council, Panská 17; Canadian Bilingual Institute, Mostová 2; České centrum, Hviezdoslavovo nám. 8; European Information Centre, Palisády 29; Goethe Institute, Panenská 33; Institut Français, Sedlárska 7; Hungarian Cultural Institute, Palisády 54; Italian Cultural Institute, Kapucínska 7; Poľský institút, nám. SNP 27; Pro Helvetia, Tolstého 9; Russian Centre for Science and Culture, Fraňa Kráľa 2; United States Information Service, Hviezdoslavovo nám. 4.

Embassies and consulates Austria, Ventúrska 10 (☏ 02/5443 2985); Britain, Panská 16 (☏ 02/5441 9632); Canada, Mostová 2 (☏ 02/5920 4031); Czech Republic, Hviezdoslavovo nám. 8 (☏ 02/5920 3303); Hungary, Sedlárska 3 (☏ 02/5443 0541-4); Poland, Hummelova 4 (☏ 02/5441 3174); Russia, Godrova 4 (☏ 02/5441 5823); Ukraine, Radvanská 35 (☏ 02/5920 2810); USA, Hviezdoslavovo nám. 4 (☏ 02/5443 0861).

Football Bratislava's premier team has always been Slovan Bratislava, the only Slovak club to have won a European competition. However, Slovan have recently been relegated to the second division, and the capital's in-form team are currently Petržalka, who prefer to be known as Artmedia Bratislava, and whose stadium is on the east side of Sad Janka Kráľa, a short walk from the south end of the Starý most. Slovan's ground is the Tehelné Pole stadium, built during World War II and also used for international games. For details of how to get there, see "Sports facilities" opposite.

Internet Internet cafés should cost between 1–2Sk per minute. Central cafés include: *Klub Internet*, in the *Múzeum* café at Vajanského nábr. 2 (Mon–Fri 9am–9pm, Sat & Sun noon–9pm); *Internet Centrum Nextra* at Michalská 2 (open Mon–Sat 9am–midnight, Sun noon–midnight); *C@fe online*, Obchodná 48 (Mon–Thurs 9.30am–midnight, Fri 9.30–1am, Sat 10–1am, Sun 11am–11pm; or *Internet Te@*, Námestie SNP 25 (Mon–Fri 8am–10pm, Sat 10am–10pm).

Left luggage Offices at either train station (daily 5.30am–midnight) and bus station (Mon–Fri 6am–10pm, Sat & Sun 6am–6pm).

Libraries British Council Teaching Resource Centre, Panská 17 (Mon–Fri 10am–7pm, Sat 10am–3pm).

From mid-April to mid-October, Slovenská plavba dunajská run a variety of hydrofoil services from Bratislava: boats go as far as Vienna (1hr 30min–1hr 45min; 480Sk one-way) and Budapest (4hr–4hr 30min; €68 one-way). There are also shorter domestic services to Devín (see p.476), sightseeing around Bratislava itself and down to the Gabčíkovo dam (see p.487). All boats leave from the jetty on Fajnorovo nábrežie, near the Prírodovedné múzeum. For the current timetable, ask at the BKIS.

Markets The best fruit-and-vegetable market in town takes place Mon–Sat in the Tržnica covered market hall on Trnavské mýto (tram #4 or #6 from Kamenné námestie). Early Saturday morning is the busiest and best time to go. Another option is the atmospheric stará tržnica, at nám. SNP 25, which has an internet café (see opposite) and a cheap self-service restaurant upstairs.

Medical emergency Go to Limbová 3, Bezručova 5 or Ružinovská 10, or call ☎155. The 24hr pharmacies are at Námestie SNP 20 and at Račianska 1.

Newspapers Interpress Slovakia, Sedlárska 2 (Mon–Sat 7am–10pm, Sun 10am–10pm), Hviezdoslavovo nám. 3, *Carlton Hotel*, Panská 31 or one of the many kiosks dotted all over town.

Post office Main post office (Hlavná pošta), nám. SNP 35 (Mon–Fri 7am–8pm, Sat 7am–6pm, Sun 9am–2pm). There are also branches on the train and bus stations.

Sports facilities There are two main sports complexes, Tehelné pole and Pasienky, next to one another in the nové mesto (tram #2 from the station; tram #4 or #6 from the centre); facilities include an outdoor pool, ice-hockey stadium, cycle track, a new tennis centre and the big Slovan football stadium.

Taxis Not as bad a reputation as in Prague; try VIP Taxi (☎02/160 00), BP Taxi (☎163 33) or Fun Taxi (☎02/167 77).

Telephones International calls are best made at the 24-hour exchange at Kolárska 12.

Around Bratislava

Most people find enough in the city centre to occupy them for the average two- or three-day stay, but if you're staying around for longer, or would prefer to be among the vine-clad hills which encroach on the city's northern suburbs, there are several places where you could happily spend a lazy afternoon, all within easy reach of the city centre.

Zlaté Piesky

Out on the motorway to Piešťany, just past the city's huge chemical works, **Zlaté Piesky** (the last stop on tram #2 from the train station and tram #4 from town) is a popular destination for weekending Bratislavans. Despite its name, meaning "Golden Sands", it's a far cry from the Côte d'Azur, though on a baking hot day in August not even the stench from the nearby chemical factory can deter large numbers of sweltering Slovaks from stripping off and throwing themselves into the lake's lukewarm waters.

Kamzík

North of the main train station the city immediately gives way to the vineyards and beechwood slopes of the suburb of Vinohrady (a world apart from its almost vine-less namesake in Prague), perfect for a quick escape from the city. From the station you can walk for 2.5km along a yellow-marked path through the woods to the summit of **Kamzík** (439m), topped by a two-hundred-metre TV tower with a revolving restaurant from where you can see the Austrian alps if the weather's on your side. If you don't fancy the walk, take bus #33 to the chairlift on the north side of the hill, or simply trolleybus #203 from námestie Slobody to the last stop and walk along the red-marked path for 1km.

Devín

Bus #29 from beneath most SNP or trolleybus #502 from the train station (at
night only) will get you to the village of **DEVÍN** (Theben), 9km northwest of
Bratislava, whose ruined **hrad** (May–Oct Tues–Fri 10am–5pm, Sat & Sun 11am–
6pm), first established in the fifth century BC, perches impressively on a rocky
promontory at the confluence of the Morava and the Danube. With the West just
a stone's throw away across the river, border precautions used to be particularly
excessive on the road to Devín – a continuous twenty-foot barbed-wire fence,
punctuated at regular intervals by fifty-foot watchtowers and hidden cameras that
monitored all passing vehicles. Today, though, such Cold War images seem as far
removed from reality as the traditional Slovak legends that surround Devín.

In 864 and again in 871, the Slavs of the Great Moravian Empire gave the
Germans two serious drubbings at Devín, the last of which is said to have left
the Germans with so few prisoners with which to barter that they could only
succeed in retrieving one half-dead hero named Ratbod. In the nineteenth century, Ľudovít Štúr and his fellow Slovak nationalists made Devín a potent symbol
of their lost nationhood, organizing a series of publicity stunts in and around
the castle in the run-up to 1848. Because of its importance in the national lore,
Devín remains a symbol of Slovak strength and independence for its people, and
its defining architectural feature, a lonesome round tower perched atop a spindle
of rock, appears in many advertisements and political placards.

There's a good view over into Austria from the craggy ruins, as well as an
archeological museum with objects from as far back as 1800 BC (hours as
above). A favourite place for weekend picnics, the castle also hosts nationalist events in July and sometimes performances in the open-air amphitheatre
amongst its ruins; for details ask at BKIS. If you fancy a walk, follow the red
markers from just above the last stop on tram #4 or #9 for a pleasant two-hour
trail through the woods to Devín. At the castle itself you can also pick up the
naučný chodník, a quiet, twelve-kilometre-long educational walking trail along
the Morava river floodplain to Vysoká pri Morave.

Rusovce

In 1945, to shore up its exposed western flank, Czechoslovakia was handed a
small stretch of forested marshland on the previously Hungarian right bank of the
Danube. Much of this land is now taken up with the unavoidable Petržalka housing estate (see p.468), but there are at least a couple more villages along the road
to Györ, shortly before the Hungarian border; one of these is **RUSOVCE**, 17km
south of Bratislava, a possible half-day trip by bus #91 or #191 which runs regularly from most SNP. Originally the Roman camp of Gerulata, it now harbours a
small **Múzeum antická Gerulata** (May–Oct Tues–Sun 10am–5pm), signposted
off the main road to the north, containing the results of extensive archeological
excavations that have uncovered two large Roman burial sites. Nearby, a neo-
Gothic **zámok**, or manor house, houses the SĽUK Folk Ensemble (ⓦ www.sluk
.sk), although the English-style park is open at all times for picnicking under the
oaks and plane trees and there's a series of reservoirs popular with naturists.

The Small Carpathians

From the Bratislavan suburbs to the gateway into the Váh valley, the **Small
Carpathians** (Malé Karpaty) form a thin, abrasive strip of limestone hills altogether different from the soft, pine-clad hills of the Czech Lands. These are the

modest beginnings of the great Carpathian range that sweeps round through the back door into Romania. Throughout much of the year, a thoroughly Balkan heat bounces off the sun-stroked plains of the Danube and permeates even these first foothills, whose south-facing slopes are excellent for vine-growing. There's also a smattering of castles and a whole host of hiking opportunities, all making for a welcome release from the Bratislavan smog. Keen walkers might consider getting hold of the *Turistická mapa Malé Karpaty – Bratislava* (1:50,000) hiking map, published by VKÚ.

The Small Carpathians force their way right into the city boundaries, making Bratislava a good starting point for **hiking** in the hills. Kamzík (440m) is the first peak (see p.475), and on a clear day the view from its television tower is difficult to beat, but if you want to do some serious trekking in unmolested countryside, continue along the red-marked path (previously known as the cesta Hrdinov SNP) that wiggles its way along the ridge of the hills all the way to Brezová, 75km away at the end of the range. There are campsites and hotels peppered along the route, and it's easy enough to drop down off the hills and grab a bed for the night. Unfortunately, **biking** is still not brilliant as biking lanes are yet to be introduced in and around the capital; however, if you're interested, it may be worth investing in the Slovak-language *Okolo Bratislavy* (Pedál Publishing, 1998) for details of more than 700km of suggested tours around the region.

Modra and around

If you're going in search of víno, **MODRA** (Modern; ⓦ www.modra.sk), just under 30km from Bratislava and entirely surrounded by the stuff, is the most convenient place to head for, particularly in September when fresh fermented grape juice known as *burčiak* is glugged at Vinobranie festivals (held in every even-numbered year). Modra is a typical ribbon-village with one long street lined with barn-door cottages growing fancier the nearer you get to the centre. There's an excellent little wine shop at no. 92 (closed Sun), or you can imbibe the **local wines** at the *Vinotéka Vincúr*, behind the tourist office, or tuck in at the *Vinohradický dvor Modra* at Štúrova 108. Gracing the square at its widest point is a light stone statue of Slovak nationalist **Ľudovít Štúr**, who is buried in the local cemetery. The nearby **Štúr Museum** (April–Oct Tues–Fri 8am–4pm, Sat 9am–3pm; Nov–March Tues–Fri only, same hours), in the Renaissance former town hall, is predictable enough and makes a classic Slovak school trip, though kids are generally more interested in the ice cream outlet judiciously placed next door.

Ľudovít Štúr

Son of a Protestant pastor, **Ľudovít Štúr** (1815–56) rose to become the only Slovak deputy in the Hungarian Diet prior to 1848. In the turmoil of 1848 itself, Štúr sided with the Habsburgs against the Magyar revolutionaries, in the hope of gaining concessions from the regime. In the end, despite aiding the Habsburgs in their modest victory, the Slovaks were offered nothing. Disappointed and disillusioned, Štúr retreated to Modra, where he lived until his premature death in 1856, the result of a gun accident. In his later years, he became convinced that Slovakia's only hope lay with Russia – now a distinctly unpopular viewpoint. Perhaps his most lasting achievement – and the reason why Slovak nationalists adore him – was the formation of what is now the official Slovak written language, based on the Central Slovak dialect he himself spoke, although even this was only achieved in the face of vehement opposition from the more Czechophile scholars who advocated either Czech or its nearest equivalent, West Slovak.

Modra is also famous for its **folk majolica**. There are shops around the town and a workshop at its southeastern outskirts, Slovenská ľudová majolika (Ⓦwww.majolika.sk), where you can join the occasional guided tour of the workshop or pay a visit to the factory's own shop (Mon–Fri 8am–4pm).

The *Modra*, at no. 111 on the main street (Ⓣ033/647 22 65, Ⓦwww .hotelmodra.sk; ❷), is the village's chief **hotel**, though the *Pension Club MKM* (Ⓣ033/647 20 09; ❸) at Štúrova 25 is much better and has a decent restaurant and swimming pool. Alternatively, head 1km north towards the Harmónia suburb, where you've a choice of pensions such as *Zita* (Ⓣ033/647 36 64, Ⓦwww .penzionzita.sk; ❷), just along the road to Trnava. The **tourist office** (Mon–Fri 9.30am–4.30pm; June–Sept also Sat & Sun 8.30am–12.30pm; Ⓣ033/647 43 02, Ⓦwww.tik.sk), Štúrova 84, can help book accommodation and should have hiking maps of Malé Karpaty.

If you follow the road north from Harmónia for another 5km into the hills, you'll come to **PIESOK**, a good base for exploring the surrounding area. Piesok itself is just a five-kilometre walk from **Vysoká** (754m), quite the most rewarding peak in terms of views. For a more gentle stroll, you could head 5km east to the hulking chateau of **Červený Kameň** (March–April & Sept–Oct Mon–Fri 9am–4pm, Sat & Sun till 5pm; May–Aug Mon–Fri 9am–5pm, Sat & Sun till 6pm; Nov–Feb daily 9.30am–3.30pm; 100Sk). Designed to put fear into enemies approaching from the plain, its defensive position and big fat bastions were created by the painter Albrecht Dürer for the unlikely sounding Fugger family. However, it was the powerful Pálffy dynasty who later transformed it into a more luxurious family residence, adding formal gardens and various other creature comforts. The castle now houses an impressive collection of period furniture, a medieval torture chamber and a seventeenth-century apothecary.

Brezová pod Bradlom and Košariská

Tucked away into a peaceful swathe of the northern Small Carpathians, the region around **BREZOVÁ POD BRADLOM** is the home of Slovak national hero Milan Rastislav Štefánik (see box below). Štefánik was born in

Milan Rastislav Štefánik

Like so many nineteenth-century Slovak nationalists, **Milan Rastislav Štefánik** was the son of a Lutheran pastor. He got into trouble with the Hungarian authorities while still only a teenager, and later left for France to study astronomy at the Paris Observatoire. He took part in astronomical expeditions to the Sahara and the Pacific islands, and in 1914 volunteered as a pilot for the French Air Force. Along with Masaryk and Beneš, Štefánik formed the famous triumvirate which campaigned tirelessly for an independent Czechoslovak state during the war. On May 4, 1919, Štefánik died when his plane crashed just outside Bratislava, within sight of the airport. As he was the only true Slovak in the triumvirate, it was a devastating blow for Slovak aspirations, and rumours quickly spread that the plane had been deliberately shot down by the Czechs.

Under the Communists, Štefánik suffered the same posthumous fate as Masaryk: his name was expunged from the history books and his statues taken down. Again, like Masaryk, he has returned with a vengeance – many squares and streets have been renamed and his statue is now a common sight throughout Slovakia, though his pro-Czechoslovak views are not popular with all Slovaks. In addition to the new museum in Košariská and mausoleum atop Bradlo, there's a small stone pyramid commemorating his death to the east of Bratislava's M.R. Štefánik Airport.

the village of **KOŠARISKÁ**, 3km east of Brezová, in 1880, and his birthplace is now an engaging **museum** (mid-April to mid-Oct Tues–Sun 8.30am–4.30pm; mid-Oct to Nov & March to mid-April Mon–Fri 8am–3.30pm; Dec–Feb closed) tracing his adventurous life and untimely death. If you've any interest in Štefánik, you'll get a kick out of his personal photos, boyhood folk outfit, pipes, flying uniforms and personal letters from T.G. Masaryk. Much is made of his travels and diplomatic exploits, and the model and photos of the plane in which he was killed really bring to light how important his role was to the Slovak national cause.

Even more acclaim is bestowed upon Štefánik at his colossal **mausoleum** atop nearby Bradlo (543m), a short drive or steep one-hour hike up the red-marked path from Brezová. The imposing white stone really is overdone, as if you're standing at a temple, but at least the views from the hilltop are splendid. Košariská is connected by a few daily buses to Piešťany, though there are more connections in Brezová to Bratislava and Trnava. If you wish to **spend the night**, head for the *Mladosť* (☎034/624 24 82; ❷), in Brezová pod Bradlom, with a restaurant, sauna and tennis courts.

Trnava

Forty-five kilometres northeast of Bratislava, and just 35 minutes by fast train, **TRNAVA** (Nagyszombat) is one of the few towns on the plain to have survived with its walled-in medieval character intact. The town's rich ecclesiastical history took off in 1543, when the archbishop of Esztergom and primate of Hungary moved his seat here, and reached its zenith during the Counter-Reformation, with the founding of a Jesuit university in 1635. When the Turkish threat receded, these institutions moved out, and, despite the re-establishment of Trnava's archbishopric in 1990, and the frequent references in tourist literature of the town as a "Slovak Rome", its golden days are clearly over. Nowadays, it's a sleepy place, with a pleasant old town, a couple of very fine churches and a fairly good museum – enough for an afternoon or so, but by no means an essential overnight stop.

Information and accommodation

The local **tourist office** (May–Sept Mon–Sat 8am–6pm, Sun 2–6pm; Oct–April Mon–Fri 9am–5pm; ☎033/551 10 22, ⓦwww.trnava.sk), is located in the mestská veža at Trojičné námestie 1, and can help with **accommodation**. There should, in any case, be few problems finding a room at the swanky *Apollo*, Štefánikova 23 (☎033/551 19 39, ⓦwww.hotelapollo.sk; ❺); other central options include the comfortable *Barbakan* on Štefánikova 11 (☎033/551 40 22, ⓦwww.barbakan-trnava.sk; ❺) which features its own in-house brewery, and three new, excellent hotels between the Dóm and the Západoslovenské museum; try the large *Phoenix* (☎033/551 32 47, ⓦwww.hotelphoenix.sk; ❹), opposite the museum, with spacious rooms overlooking the quiet patio, or the sterile *London* (☎033/534 05 86, ⓦwww.hotellondon.sk; ❺), decorated with a stucco frieze and located in a shady place closer to the Dóm.

Staré Mesto

From the bus and railway **stations**, cross the new footbridge over the main ring road, Hospodárska, and head north along the leafy banks of the River

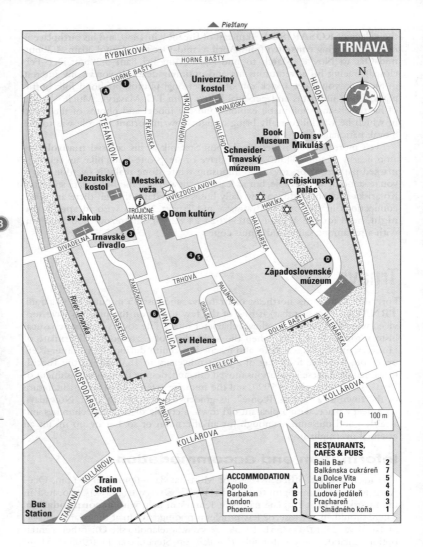

Piešťany

TRNAVA

N

RYBNÍKOVÁ

HORNÉ BAŠTY

HORNÉ BAŠTY

Univerzitný kostol

INVALIDSKÁ

HORNOPOTOČNÁ

HOLLÉHO

HĹBOKÁ

Book Museum

Dóm sv Mikuláš

Schneider-Trnavský múzeum

ŠTEFÁNIKOVA

PEKÁRSKA

Arcibiskupský palác

Jezuitský kostol

Mestská veža

HVIEZDOSLAVOVA

HAVLÍKA

KAPITULSKÁ

TROJIČNÉ NÁMESTIE

Dom kultúry

sv Jakub

Trnavské divadlo

DIVADELNÁ

HALENÁRSKA

Západoslovenské múzeum

TRHOVÁ

ZÁMOČNÍCKA

VALJANSKÉHO

HLAVNÁ ULICA

ORBSKÁ

PAULÍNSKA

DOLNÉ BAŠTY

HALENÁRSKA

sv Helena

River Trnávka

STRELECKÁ

KOLLÁROVA

HOSPODÁRSKA

A ŽARNOVA

KOLLÁROVA

0   100 m

Train Station

Bus Station

STANIČNÁ

KOLLÁROVA

ACCOMMODATION
Apollo	A
Barbakan	B
London	C
Phoenix	D

RESTAURANTS, CAFÉS & PUBS
Baila Bar	2
Balkánska cukráreň	7
La Dolce Vita	5
Dubliner Pub	4
Ludová jedáleň	6
Prachareň	3
U Smädného koňa	1

Trnavka. Parallel to this runs the most impressive section of the old **town walls**, reinforced in the sixteenth century (and up to six metres thick in places) in anticipation of the marauding Turks; the only surviving gateway is the red-brick Bernolákova brána, popularly known as the Franciscan gate after the nearby church of **sv Jakub**.

Soon after the church, you come to **Trojičné námestie**, the spacious main square centred on a lively plague column, pristinely restored and dramatically lit at night. Here, Trnava's institutions old and new congregate: the **mestská veža**, dating from the beginning of the town's golden age in the sixteenth century; the Neoclassical **radnica**; the salmon-pink, Empire-style **Trnavské divadlo**, the oldest theatre building in Slovakia, dating from 1831; and last, but in no way least, the **Dom kultúry**, just one of a number of modern eyesores in Trnava that have risen up from the rubble in the old quarter.

A short walk up Štefánikova from the square is the surprisingly interesting **Jesuitský kostol**. The typically High Baroque nave is suffused with a pink light emanating from the marble pilasters; more startling though is the deliciously decorative north chapel, with bounteous vegetative motifs and floral stucco. On the east side of the chapel is a bizarre watery grotto, with a statue of Mary lit only by a dramatic shaft of light, the grotto's grille entirely surrounded by plaques and graffiti in Hungarian, Slovak and even Latin, thanking the Virgin for her various intercessions in answer to prayers.

The modern-day focus of Trnava is the paved main boulevard, **Hlavná ulica**, which leads south from Trojičné námestie: a pleasant window-shopping stroll. Its southern end is marked by the church of **sv Helena**, the town's oldest and most beguiling church, whose bare and miniature Gothic style is untouched by the suffocating hand of the Counter-Reformation. Next door is the town's former hospital, a Neoclassical building in an inappropriately sickly version of imperial yellow. South of sv Helena, a swathe of parkland has replaced the old fortifications, and boasts a working fountain and a relatively new statue of Štefáník (see p.478).

The Dóm and Katedrálny chrám

East off Trojičné námestie, the **Dóm sv Mikuláš** beckons with two rather clumsy but eye-catching Baroque steeples. Its Gothic origins are most obvious in the chancel, which boasts slender stained-glass windows and a fine set of choir stalls. It was promoted from a mere parish church following the Battle of Mohács in 1526, which caused the Hungarians to retreat behind the Danube; the royalty moved to Bratislava and the archbishop transferred his see to Trnava, setting up next door to sv Mikuláš. A century later, Trnava's position as a haven for Magyar cultural institutions seeking refuge from the Turks was further bolstered by the establishment of a university. In common with all Habsburg institutions of the time, it was under the iron grip of the Jesuits, and Trnava soon became the bastion of the Counter-Reformation east of Vienna.

The importance of religious over purely scholarly matters is most clearly illustrated by the sheer size of the **Univerzitný kostol**, down Hollého, one of the largest and most beautiful in Slovakia. The decor is mostly Italianate Rococo, with the apricot and peach pastels of the nave offset by darker stucco vegetation. The oval frescoes appear like giant lacquered miniatures, but the whole lot is upstaged by the vast wooden altarpiece, decked out in black and gold, peppered with saints, and looking more like an Orthodox iconostasis than a Catholic altar. These glory days were short-lived: with the expulsion of the Jesuit order from the Habsburg Empire and the defeat of the Turks, Trnava lost its university to Budapest, its archbishop's see to Esztergom, and consequently both its political and religious influence.

Trnava's museums

Kapitulská, the broad, leafy street that sets off south from the archbishop's palace, is probably the prettiest street in town, with a cathedral-close feel about it. At its end, the plain cream mass of the seventeenth-century convent of sv Klara, now the **Západoslovenské múzeum** (Tues–Fri 8am–5pm, Sat & Sun 11am–5pm), offers a variety of exhibitions including eight rooms of folk ceramics by local potter Štefan Cyril Parrák; best of all, though, is the glimpse of the convent's former chapel, and the bits and bobs salvaged from the town's now-defunct **Jewish community**.

Trnava's Jews were actually expelled from the city in the sixteenth century, when, on the usual trumped-up charge of ritual murder, Emperor Ferdinand sent them packing through the Sered' gate, walling it up with ripped-up Jewish gravestones to bar their return. For three hundred years, Trnava was *Judenfrei*, then in 1862 the gate was removed, and the Jews began to filter back to the unofficial ghetto, located about where the main supermarket car park lies today. The disused and weed-ridden orthodox **synagogue** on Havlíka is on the brink of collapse, but the more prominent Moorish onion-domed **synagogue** (Tues–Fri 9am–noon & 1–5pm, Sat & Sun 1–6pm) on the other side of the street has been at least structurally restored and is used as temporary exhibition space. The reason to visit, though, is to wander about the gloomy interior, damaged by fire in the 1980s, but still retaining fragments of gorgeous frescoes and stonework. Out front there's a large, black, tomb-like memorial to more than 2000 local Jews who were victims of the Holocaust.

The **Schneider-Trnavský museum** (Tues–Fri 9am–4.30pm, Sun 1–5pm), at no. 5 ulica M. Schneidra-Trnavského, is devoted to the Slovak composer who was choirmaster at sv Mikuláš from 1909 until his death in 1958, and who clearly had very good taste in 1920s furniture. The little-visited **Book Museum** (Múzeum knižnej kultúry; same hours), further up the street opposite sv Mikuláš, focuses on the many printing presses set up in Trnava by the Hungarians in the seventeenth century, and on the Slovak intellectual society here in the mid-nineteenth century.

Eating and drinking

The cheap *Prachareň*, next door to the Trnavské divadlo, has a few vegetarian dishes on the menu, and the *La Dolce Vita*, Paulínska, does big pizzas. Another cheap option, *Ľudová jedáleň* (Mon–Fri lunchtime only), is in the southern part of Hlavná, while the *Balkánska cukráreň*, diagonally opposite, serves good cakes and 24 kinds of ice creams. For beer pop into the *U Smädného koňa* (At the

△ Univerzitný Kostol, Trnava

Thirsty Horse) on Horné bašty or head for the ubiquitous *Dubliner Pub*, next
door to the *La Dolce Vita*. The dubious *Baila Bar* on the corner of Trojičné
námestie continues to be the only vaguely happening late-night place.

Nitra

While Trnava is stuck in the past, **NITRA** (Nyitra), 40km further east across
the plain, has effectively shed its old skin and rushed headlong into the modern
world. The result is a clearly divided town: on the one hand, the peaceful old
quarter wrapped around the foot of the castle rock; on the other, the ungainly
sprawl of modern Nitra, third largest city in the country with a population of
90,000, agricultural capital of the nation and a bustling market town with that
symbol of development, a Tesco hypermarket. Sadly, to get to the former you
must pass through the latter, since the sights are all situated in the old town,
which has a certain national kudos attached to it as a centre of Slovak Catholicism, ancient and modern.

Arrival, information and accommodation

If you're coming to Nitra from Bratislava, you're best off coming by **bus**, as
there are no direct trains. Both the stations are situated fifteen minutes' walk
south of the centre (all local buses except #5 and #20 cover the distance). Staff
at Nitra's **tourist office**, NISYS, at Štefánikova 1 (Mon–Fri 8am–6pm; July &
Aug also Sat 9am–6pm, Sun 2–6pm; ☎037/161 86 or 741 09 07, ⓦwww.nitra
.sk), can help out with **accommodation**, the choice of which has improved
over the last few years. The most central is, as the name suggests, the *Hotel
Centrum* (☎037/655 43 97, ⓦwww.hotelcentrumnitra.sk; ❹), on the main
square, which has comfortable, if smallish, rooms. Also near the square are the
decent *Penzión Atrium* (☎037/652 37 90, ⓦwww.penzionatriumnitra.sk; ❹),
on Štefánikova 8, and the excellent *Hotel Alexander's* (☎037/792 04 01, ⓦwww
.alexanders.sk; ❻), Mostná 68, located in a new building which itself is a work
of art. Otherwise try the new, equally good *Hotel Capital* (☎037/692 52 01,
ⓦwww.hotelcapital.sk; ❹), at Farská 16. The only time you may have problems
finding a room is during the agricultural fair and the music festival, which take
place in August and September respectively. The nearest **campsite,** with bungalows, *Thermal Emília* (mid-June to mid-Sept; ☎037/778 71 44), lies some 20km
south of Nitra, near the thermal swimming pool in Poľný Kesov.

To check your **emails** head for the *Internetová kaviareň Orange*, opposite the
Izba starej matere.

The City

The central axis of the nové mesto is the busy crossroads by the city's main
market (*tržnica*) where the region's rich produce is sold daily. The staré mesto
and the main sights are all north of here, except for the **Kalvária**, a kitsch
mock-up of the Crucifixion, which crowns the summit of a small limestone
hill southeast of the train station. The brutality of Nitra's modern development
serves as the apocalyptic backdrop for three ugly concrete crosses, the two robbers grey and unpainted on either side of a technicolour Jesus.

Visible to the east of the market as you cross over Štúrova is the country's
main **College of Agriculture**, a flying-saucer-shaped building, whose research
department famously invented a strain of tree that could withstand acid rain

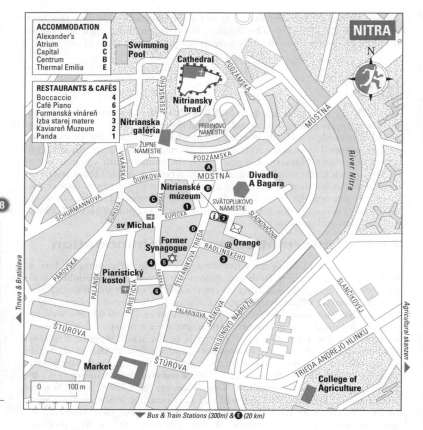

◀ Trnava & Bratislava

Agricultural skanzen ▶

ACCOMMODATION
Alexander's	A
Atrium	D
Capital	C
Centrum	B
Thermal Emília	E

RESTAURANTS & CAFÉS
Boccaccio	4
Café Piano	6
Furmanská vináreň	5
Izba starej matere	3
Kaviareň Muzeum	2
Panda	1

Swimming Pool

Cathedral

Nitriansky hrad

PODZÁMSKA

River Nitra

MOSTNÁ

JESENSKÉHO

Nitrianska galéria

PRIBINOVO NÁMESTIE

ŽUPNÉ NÁMESTIE

PODZÁMSKA

VIKÁRSKA

MOSTNÁ

ĎURKOVA

Divadlo A Bagara

Nitrianské múzeum

SVÄTOPLUKOVO NÁMESTIE

FARSKÁ

KUPECKA

SLADKOVIČOVA

SCHURMANNOVA

ĎURKOVA

sv Michal

Former Synagogue

@ Orange

RADLINSKÉHO

ŠTEFÁNIKOVA TRIEDA

PÁROVSKÁ

PALÁNOK

Piaristický kostol

PARISTICKÁ

FARSKÁ

PALÁRIKOVA

JASÍKOVA

WILSONOVO NÁBREŽIE

SLANČÍKOVEJ

ŠTÚROVA

ŠTÚROVA

Market

TRIEDA ANDREJA HLINKU

College of Agriculture

N

0   100 m

▼ Bus & Train Stations (300m) & ⑤ (20 km)

⑧

– progress indeed. Beyond the college lies the Agrokomplex exhibition grounds, which also contain the marvellous **Slovenské poľnohospodárske múzeum** (Slovak Agricultural Museum or *skansen*; May–Sept Tues–Sun 9am–5pm; Oct–April closes 4pm; Ⓦwww.agrokomplex.sk). Though you wouldn't know it from the name or the setting – it's located at the rear of the Agrokomplex behind banks of ugly apartment blocks – this is a real gem, one of the very best museums of its kind in central Europe. In one large, barrack-like building there's a display on the history of farming and commerce in Slovakia up to the Middle Ages, with an impressive array of artefacts such as 3000-year-old wheat kernels and relics from the medieval amber trade route, which passed from the Baltic Sea to Italy through Slovakia. Another concrete structure holds a fun collection of interwar tractors, including a massive red Russian combine and a wooden thresher, claimed to be the only one of its kind in the world. In the vicinity are several smaller houses with a variety of folk displays inside; an early-twentieth-century bakery, a distillery, a mill, a honeycomb pressing shop and a one-room schoolhouse with original furnishings all vie for attention. In August, at the time of the National Agrocomplex Exhibition, the whole complex comes alive as costumed guides demonstrate how the old shops work (many are still operational), and an 1885 narrow-gauge railway toots around the grounds, much to the delight of visiting children. To get to the museum, you'll need to take bus #8, #12, #15, #19 or #31 to the last stop at the end of Dlhá.

North of Štúrova, the main street of Štefánikova trieda has been pedestrianized and leads north past the giant neo-Renaissance **Nitrianské múzeum** (Tues–Fri 8–11.30am & noon–5pm, Sat & Sun 10am–5pm), which puts on riveting exhibitions such as "Stones today and yesterday", to the town's octagonal, Communist-designed theatre, **Divadlo A. Bagara**, on the dusty expanse of Svätoplukovo námestie. On ulica pri synagóge, west off Štefánikova, the sheer size of Nitra's Moorish **synagogue** is an indication of the strength of the town's prewar Jewish community and is now restored. Currently used as an exhibition and concert hall, it is due to become a Holocaust museum at some point in the future. Farská, which leads you away from the chaos of the new town to the sights around the castle, is one of the most pleasant streets in the nové mesto, dotted with churches, grocery stores and snack bars.

The staré mesto

Nitra's **staré mesto** is actually very small, consisting of just a handful of streets huddled under the castle. The entrance is formed by the former Župný dom on Župné námestie, a handsome Art Nouveau building, now the **Nitrianska galéria** (Tues–Sun 10am–5pm), which is used for temporary exhibitions. The right-hand arch of the building leads to the steeply sloping old town square, **Pribinovo námestie**, a very modest affair but quite pretty and totally peaceful after the frenetic activity of the lower town. At its centre stands a recent (and fairly ugly) statue of **Prince Pribina**, the ninth-century ruler of Nitra, who erected the first church in what is now Slovakia here in 828. Though no great believer himself, he shrewdly realized such a gesture would keep him on good terms with his German neighbours. There's also a fair amount of evidence to suggest that St Methodius, the first bishop of (Great) Moravia, was stationed at Nitra and not at Velehrad in the Morava Valley, as was once claimed by the Czechs.

Nitriansky hrad is a scruffy little hybrid, saved only by its lofty position above the river, which allows a great view north over to Mount Zobor (588m), the southwesternmost tip of the Tribeč mountain range. A fortress since the time of the Great Moravian Empire (of which it may have been the capital), it provided refuge for various Hungarian kings over the centuries until its destruction by the Turks in the seventeenth century. Crusty saints, a very fine plague column, a stone bread covered with glagolitic inscriptions (now a favourite meeting place for local dope fiends) and two massive gateways mark the route to the remains, most of which have been turned over to the Archeological Institute and are closed to the public.

The one sight left in the complex is the **Katedrála sv Emeráma** (April–Oct Mon–Fri 9am–noon & 1–5pm, Sat 9am–noon & 2–5pm, Sun 10am–noon & 2–5pm; Nov–March closes 4pm), an old structure which adjoins the bishop of Nitra's cosy Baroque residence. Confusingly, you enter the south door and pass through two antechambers – the first, the Pribinova kaplnka, is a Romanesque rotunda, the second is late-Gothic – before going up some more steps to the compact main church, its Baroquized marble interior in muted greys and reds. Frescoes adorn every possible space, and the modern blue stained glass in the chancel lends the whole place a magical quality. The cathedral is associated with two tenth-century Slovak saints, **Ondrej Svorad** and **Benedikt Junior**, both religious hermits who lived in the hills near Trenčín and spent most of their lives tending their gardens and vineyards. The locals, who had little time for able-bodied young men devoting their lives to spiritual contemplation, gave both of them a hard time; Ondrej Svorad escaped their wrath by diplomatically giving away a portion of his harvest, but Benedikt Junior failed to appease his enemies, who threw him off a nearby cliff and then drowned him in the River Váh.

Eating and drinking

Nitra has a fair range of **eating** establishments, including the Chinese restaurant *Panda* on Kupecká, at the corner of the main square, and the semi-rustic *Furmanská vináreň* at Pri synagóge 6, specializing in live music and fresh fish. Another good eatery is the *Izba starej matere*, at Radlinského 8, which has a nice garden and offers Slovak specialities plus Nitria, the local sweet white wine. *Boccaccio*, Farská 36, is a comfortable Italian-Slovak restaurant-pizzeria with a pleasant summer courtyard, and *Café Piano* at Farská 46 and *Kaviareň Muzeum* on Štefánikova 1 are both laid-back **cafés**.

The Danube basin

To the east of Bratislava lies the rich agricultural region of the **Danube basin** Podunajsko to the Slovaks; Felvidék to the Hungarians), a flat, fertile expanse of land that benefits from some of the warmest temperatures in the country and is riddled with meandering rivers, ponds and steaming thermal springs. One of the few places in Slovakia where you can go for miles without spotting a hill, its chocolatey soil sprouts vast melons, plus apricots, grapes and peppers, all of which are sold road-side throughout the summer. Although originally Hungarian for about a millennium, and once an outpost of the Roman Empire with the remains of military camps by the Danube, the region has formed the border between Slovakia and Hungary since being handed over from Hungary to Czechoslovakia in 1918. However, it remains the traditional haunt of most of Slovakia's ethnic Hungarian minority. Sadly, this was one of the regions that suffered badly during World War II, and the subsequent rebuilding has made one place very much like another. The chief exception is **Komárno**, which, while not worth a detour in itself, has enough to make you pause en route to Hungary.

Senec

The towns of the Danube basin are probably the nearest either republic comes to seaside resorts, and in the summer the "beaches" are packed with windsurfers, canoeists and sun-seekers slobbing out along reservoirs, lakes, swimming pools and any stretch of water they can find. If you're staying in Bratislava, **SENEC** (Szenc), 26km east and just over thirty minutes by train, is the warmest part of the country, the easiest place to get to and fairly indicative of the region. The Turks left one of their few monuments here, the creamy, crenellated **Turecký dom** (built in 1556 and now the town's poshest restaurant), which, along with the large, crumbling synagogue topped by a rusting Star of David, relieves the town's otherwise unprepossessing main street.

The real crowd puller is the **Slnečné jazerá** (Sunny Lakes), a couple of reasonably warm former gravel pits southeast of town, within sight of the train station, which simply heave with visitors during the hot months, especially August. By the larger lake you'll find water sports equipment for hire, two **campsites** (May–Sept and mid-June to mid-Sept), bungalows and rudimentary

The Gabčíkovo-Nagymaros dam

The **Gabčíkovo-Nagymaros Hydroelectric Barrage** project was a megalomaniac idea dreamed up in 1977 by the Communist old guard of Hungary and Czechoslovakia, with the cynical collusion and capital of the Austrians, who were on the lookout for cheap electricity at someone else's environmental expense. However, following intense protest by the green lobby, the Hungarians unilaterally withdrew from the project in 1989 and called for an international enquiry into the environmental effects of the dam. The Czechoslovak government, however, having invested huge sums of money and desperate for an alternative source of energy to brown coal – the pollution from which continues to kill off the country's forests – pressed on and completed a scaled-down version of the scheme, diverting part of the Danube in 1993.

In 1997, after several years of verbal and legal sparring, the International Court in the Hague finally made a decision over the whole unhappy mess. It declared that Hungary had violated international law by reneging on the 1977 agreement. Most Slovaks rejoiced that, for once, their country had been found in the right, and that Hungarian propaganda had finally been unmasked. Unfortunately, however, the dispute is far from over. While deciding overall in Slovakia's favour, the court also ruled that the Slovaks had been wrong in diverting the Danube, which means that both sides can legitimately claim damages. Somewhat hopefully, the court ordered the two sides to come up with a joint proposal for the project (and for the damages), but this too has been stalled and generally the issue has slipped out of the limelight over the past five years. Sadly, in environmental terms, the damage has already been done, according to the WWF and ecologists on both sides of the border. You can visit the Danube barrage for yourself by boat (see p.475) or, better still, cycle along the new channel from Bratislava.

---

hotels, such as the *Amúr* (☎02/4592 4081; ❶), with bungalows and campsite. Alternatively, you can stay at the rather snazzy new *Penzión Labuť* on the banks of the northern lake (☎02/4565 0041, ⓦwww.labut.sk; ❸). The **tourist office** at Mierové nám 19 (☎ & Ⓕ02/4592 8224, ⓦwww.senec.sk) can also book accommodation. One place that doesn't draw the crowds (but should) is the extraordinary open-air **Museum of Bee-keeping** (Včelárska paseka; June–Sept Mon–Fri 9am–5pm, Sat & Sun 9am–1pm), signposted off route 62, close to the hamlet of Lučny dvor, and representative of a thriving local cottage industry. There's honey for sale and hives of all shapes and sizes spread out in a shady glade by the bee-keeping school.

Komárno

Situated right on the confluence of the Váh and the Danube, **KOMÁRNO** (Komárom) is a Hungarian town through and through, albeit divided by the Danube, which forms the Slovak-Hungarian border. Bilingual street and shop signs abound, and in shops you'll be greeted with *tessék* ("what would you like?") rather than the usual *prosím*. Ethnic niceties aside, however, Komárno is not going to win over many people's hearts; this Danube port town is only worth a stopoff if you're passing through on the way to Budapest.

Arrival, information and accommodation

To get to the town centre from the **train** and **bus stations** to the northwest, take Petöfiho and you'll hit the main street, Záhradníčka, which heads south to the bridge over the river and into Hungary. The town **tourist office** (Mon–Fri 7.30am–3.30pm; ☎ & Ⓕ035/773 00 63, ⓦwww.komarno.sk) at Župná 5, can help with **accommodation**. The *Európa*, on the main street (☎035/773 13 49, ⓦwww.hoteleuropa.sk; ❸), looks unprepossessing on the outside, but the rooms have been splendidly modernized and feature en-suite facilities and TVs. A better bet, however, is the new, equally central (but quieter) *Pension Banderium* (☎035/773 01 56, ⓦwww.banderium.sk; ❸), Námestie M.R. Štefánika 11, which offers plain rooms adorned with old images of Komárno. *Ring Bar Penzión*, just off the main square at Letná 4 (☎035/771 31 58; ❸), has fairly cosy rooms above a bar, while the *Hotel Panoráma*, on Športova ulica (☎035/771 31 13; ❷) is a Socialist-style eggbox where you can also **camp** (mid-June to mid-Sept) and park your caravan. However, the riverside site 11km west (and just 15min by train) in Zlatná (May–Oct) is preferable. Another option is the *Oáza camp* (June to mid-Sept), in Komoča, on the River Váh, 26km northwest of Komárno.

The Town

When the Czechoslovak border was dreamed up in 1919, the Hungarians of Komárom found their town split in two, with by far the most significant part – and what few sights there are – on the Slovak side. Both sides now annually reunite in late April/early May for a week of joint cultural events, known as the *Komárňanské dni/Komáromi napok* (Komárno Days), which include sports events, markets and open days in the fortress.

The pedestrianized section of town, and the cobbled main square, **námestie gen. Klapku**, lies to the east. The latter is named after the general who fought against the Austrians in the Hungarian uprising of 1848, and whose statue is overlooked by several solid late-nineteenth-century buildings. The **Podunajské múzeum** (April–Oct Tues–Sat 9am–5pm; Nov–March closes 4pm), with two subsidiary branches, one at Palatínova 13, and the other at námestie gen. Klapku 9, covers the town's history and the latter branch additionally pays tribute to the town's two most illustrious and somewhat controversial sons. The first is the composer **Franz Lehár**, whose father was military bandmaster with the local garrison. Lehár enjoyed the dubious privilege of having written one of Hitler's favourite works, the operetta *Die lustige Witwe* (*The Merry Widow*), and despite the fact that his native tongue was Hungarian and his own wife Jewish, he found himself much in demand during the Third Reich. The nineteenth-century Hungarian writer **Mór Jókai**, on the other hand, was an extremely patriotic Hungarian, who wrote a glowing account of the Hungarian aristocracy and would have had nothing good to say about Komárno's modern-day split nationality.

More fascinating than either of the above is the disorientating sight of a small **Orthodox church** (Pravoslávny kostol), also on Palatínova, behind Záhradníčka, testifying to the Serbian colonists who settled around Komárno in the early eighteenth century in a desperate attempt to escape the vengeful Turks. Small pockets of Orthodox believers still exist in the region, and the seventeenth- and eighteenth-century Greek and Serbian icons on display here constitute one of the best collections outside Serbia. Opposite the museum at Palatínova 13 stands the stunning twin-spired Baroque **church of sv Ondreje**, which has a cool, peach-coloured interior.

The town is also notable for its vast zigzag **fortifications** that seem much too big for the town, and its **fortress**, east of the town centre at the confluence of the Váh and the Danube, which has served as a strategic base for everyone from the Romans to the Russians, and is still in the hands of the military today (though tours are occasionally organized – ask at the tourist office). One of the town's bastions, **Bašta VI** (May to mid-Oct Tues–Sun

The creation of separate Czech and Slovak republics has brought into much sharper relief the rather more volatile relationship between the Slovaks and the 600,000 **Hungarians** who live along the southern border regions of Slovakia, and make up eleven percent of the country's total population. Like so many ethnic disputes in central Europe, it's an age-old conflict, one that remained fairly dormant during the Communist period, but which has now returned with a vengeance.

For almost a millennium, Slovakia – known as the Upper Lands – was an integral part of Hungary where Slovaks were very much the peasants, and Germans and Hungarians the merchants and ruling classes. Both Slovak language and culture were severely **suppressed** right up until the foundation of the First Republic in 1918, when 750,000 Hungarians were left on the Slovak side of the Danube after the borders for the new republic were drawn up. Like the Germans who lived in the border regions of the Czech Lands for several centuries, Slovakia's Hungarians were not assimilated in the interwar period and were only too happy to unite with the fascist Magyar state during World War II, when Hungary was handed most of the Hungarian-speaking regions of Slovakia and Slovakia itself became an independent, albeit fascist, state for the duration (for the first time in its history). Unlike their Germanic counterparts, the attempt by Beneš to expel the Hungarians in 1945 was successfully blocked by the government in Budapest, although Slovakization of ethnic Hungarians was nonetheless enforced fairly brutally and many were forcibly moved to other regions of Czechoslovakia such as North Bohemia.

In 1989 the enforced fraternal friendship of the Communist period finally came to an abrupt end with the dispute over the **Gabčíkovo-Nagymaros dam** (see p.487). The rise of Slovak nationalism that took place after the Velvet Revolution understandably worried the Hungarian community, which itself was wooed by increasingly chauvinistic politicians, keen to score cheap political points at home. On the Slovak side, former premier Vladimír Mečiar did little to calm the fears of the Hungarian community, rejecting an EU-backed ethnic-minority law, forbidding the public use of foreign languages and even suggesting the community should be expelled. Fortunately, the June 1999 election of **Rudolf Schuster** – a Hungarian-speaker from Košice and an advocate of governing "for all citizens" – to the presidency, combined with Prime Minister Dzurinda's EU-friendly **multi-party government**, paved the way to more productive dialogue and a considerable relaxing of tension. And now, when both countries have successfully entered the big European family, ethnic conflicts should recede into the background (in theory at least).

10am–5pm), on Okružná cesta, to the north of the town centre, beyond the railway lines, has been turned into a small Roman lapidarium. Summer visitors should also give the local thermal pools a whirl, such as the Komárno thermal swimming pool (mid-June to mid-Sept daily 9am–7pm) on the main Bratislava–Komárno road.

Eating

Basic **food** can be had at the decent *Bistro Gyros* (closed Sun), situated on Nádvorie Európy, a new square surrounded by buildings designed (rather unsuccessfully) to imitate the burgher houses found all over Europe. More upscale is the *Platán* on Alžbetin island, en route to the border crossing. For pizza and pasta, head to the simple *Pasta Grosso* at Valchovnícka, while Slovak, Czech and Hungarian food is served at the atmospheric *U čierného psa* (At the Black Dog), on Námestie Štefánika. Next door, the *Jadran Café* is good for **coffee** and cakes, as is the elegant *Art Café* on Nádvorie Európy. For those who know the language, there's a Hungarian theatre, Jókaiho divadlo, halfway down Petöfiho.

"The Danube threads towns together like a string of pearls", wrote Claudio Magris, but it's doubtful he had **ŠTÚROVO** (Párkány) in mind at the time. Its major saving grace is the unbeatable view of the great domed basilica of Esztergom (Ostrihom to the Slovaks), on the Hungarian side of the river, to which it's been linked by a ferry service ever since the bridge was blown up by the retreating German army in 1944. The new (partly EU-funded) bridge, symbolically linking the two, was finally opened in autumn 2001; a hugely positive step in Hungarian–Slovak relations. However, the town's name remains a bone of contention, with the current Slovak government insisting on keeping Štúrovo, the name given to the town by the Communists in 1948 after the Slovak nationalist (and virulent anti-Magyar) Ľudovít Štúr (see p.477), despite a local referendum which voted in favour of reverting to Párkány.

As the last town on the Slovak Danube, it's not a bad place to break your journey. Ferries over to Esztergom are frequent and you can take your car across, or you can hop on one of the international express trains that pause here en route to Budapest. The **train** and **bus stations** are actually an inconvenient 2.5km west of the town, though several local buses cover the distance. In the summer the focus of life is the town's outdoor swimming pool, fed by thermal springs, Termálne kúpalisko Vadaš, by the local **campsite** (☎036/751 14 10, with chalets and a mind-boggling range of water sports; mid-May to Sept; ❶), just north of the town.

Brhlovce

The tiny village of **BRHLOVCE** (ⓦwww.brhlovce.sk) nestles into the hills some 60km northeast of Štúrovo. Many of its 400-odd residents live in caves dug into the hills' soft rock faces, an oddity dating back to the sixteenth century when fears of Turkish attacks drove their ancestors into hiding. Simple holes in the short cliffs were expanded into habitable homes, and this inexpensive form of housing soon caught on. More cave homes were built in the late nineteenth and early twentieth centuries, and the troglodytes even made money by selling the rock they had hewn to local quarries. Once the living space was dug out, the walls were matted with straw and painted, and windows were carved out; in more recent years modern comforts, such as electricity and running water, have also been introduced. Although most of the cave homes are private residences, a pair of adjoining caves have been turned into a **museum** (Skalné obydlia; April–Oct Mon, Thurs, Sat & Sun 9am–noon & 1–4pm), where you can wander through the few tiny rooms. To get to Brhlovce, you'll have to rely on the infrequent **buses** from Levice (up to 8 daily), 10km west of Brhlovce, a fairly major bus and train stop in the region, which also has a **campsite** (mid-May to mid-Sept) and yet another set of thermal swimming pools.

Piešťany and the Váh valley

Finding its source in the Tatras and carving a southwesterly course right the way to the Danube at Komárno, the **Váh** is one of the great rivers of Slovakia. Tourist office circles like to talk of the "Slovak Rhine", but despite the appearance of ruined cliff-top castles at every turn of the river, it lacks the magic of the Rhine valley. Heading north up the Váh from Piešťany to Trenčín, the mountains on either side keep their distance and the whole area still has the feel of the Danube basin. Beyond Trenčín, the industry, river dams and lorry-congested highway all dampen the effect of brigand hide-outs such as Vrsatec and Považský hrad. The best way to weigh up the relative merits of the region is on one of the fast and frequent **trains** from Bratislava that twist their way up the Váh valley en route to the Tatras.

Piešťany

The most convincing claim the local tourist board makes about **PIEŠŤANY**, just over an hour by train from Bratislava, is that it's the largest spa town in Slovakia. But, although the place is overrun with the unhealthily rich from different parts of the German- and Russian-speaking world, the town itself is slowly catching up with the rather grander late-nineteenth-century West Bohemian spas. Millions of crowns have been injected into the spa facilities, which include freshly painted Art Nouveau spa accommodation on the spa island, well-planted green spaces, clean swimming pools, and a host of other resources to which the public has access, making it a pleasant alternative to most of the "beachy" resorts further south.

The town divides conveniently into two parts: the spa island cut off from the mainland by a thin arm of the River Váh, and the rest of the town on the right bank between the main arm of the river and the **bus** and **train stations** to the west. It's a fifteen-minute walk into town down A. Hlinku and Štúrova (bus #1, #2, #4, #11, #12 or #14) to **Winterova**, the main drag through the centre of town, a patchwork of muted fin-de-siècle and Secession buildings decorated with balconies and lined with cafés and trinkety shops. The main spa building at no. 29 is a typical example of Piešťany's understated architecture. Behind the bandstand in the Mestský park, there's a **Balneologické múzeum** (Spa Museum; Tues–Sun: April–Sept 9am–noon & 1–5pm; Oct–March closes 4pm) devoted to the local spa industry, but also displaying everything from a woolly mammoth's tusk to a mock-up of a Slovak folk cottage. The rest of the spa is on the opposite bank, a short stroll past **Barlolamač**, the town's famous, optimistic statue of a man breaking his crutches in two, and connected by the partially covered **Kolonádový most**, a graceful 1930s modernist structure, rebuilt under the Communists "for the benefit of the working class", in the words of the 1950s commemorative plaque.

One place that definitely wasn't built with the latter in mind is the vaguely Art Nouveau *Thermia Palace* hotel, which has regained its bygone opulence and – if the flash cars parked outside are anything to go by – now serves the new European aristocracy. The woods and park on the **Kúpeľný ostrov** (spa island) are decidedly verdant, with sculptures peeping out of every conceivable shrub and bush – part of the spa's annual international open-air sculpture

Bohunice and Mochovce

As you approach Piešťany from Bratislava, the cooling towers of the country's first nuclear power station at **Bohunice** are clearly visible on the western horizon. Built in the 1960s, but temporarily closed down in 1979 after two hushed-up accidents and only seven years of operation, Bohunice is due to be closed down by 2008, as part of Slovakia's EU accession deal. However, since Bohunice alone provides nearly 25% of Slovakia's electricity, the country is heading for something of an energy crisis. All of which makes the Slovaks even keener to finish the second of two equally controversial Soviet-designed nuclear reactors at **Mochovce**, some 50km further east. Anti-nuclear protestors – and, in particular, the Austrians – would rather Mochovce was shut down too.

symposium. The nearby low-lying annexes are still used for "mud wrapping and electro-treatment" to cure rheumatic illnesses (spa patients only). If you fancy a dip, the old-fashioned Eva swimming pool, 200m further north, is open to the public. From here, the sleek, ultramodern Balnea sanatorium spreads its luxurious wings the full length of the island.

Practicalities

Even if you haven't come here for treatment, you should have few problems finding **accommodation** on the left bank. The centrally located *Pension Villa Veres* (☎033/776 31 10, ℱ033/776 31 26; ❹), Winterova 21, has comfortable en-suite rooms and a quiet patio. Other options include splashing out at the opulent spa hotel *Thermia Palace* on the spa island (☎033/775 61 11, ℮reservations.thr@healthspa.sk; ❾), or playing it safe at the boxy but comfortable *Magnolia* with pool and spa facilities at Nálepkova 1 (☎033/762 62 51, ⓦwww.hotelmagnolia.sk; ❺), and the *Eden*, Winterova 60 (☎033/762 47 09; ❷), which has rooms with en-suite bath and satellite TV. If these don't suffice, the staff at the efficient IVCO **tourist office** (Mon–Fri 9am–5.30pm, Sat 8am–noon; ☎033/774 33 55, ⓦwww.ivco.sk), Nalepkova 2, opposite the *Magnolia*, are only too pleased to help arrange accommodation. **Camping** is possible (May–Sept) on either side of the mouth of the action-packed Sĺňava lake (bus #12 or walk 1km to either the *Sĺňava* or *Lodenica* sites, ☎033/762 35 63 or 033/762 60 93), south of town; simple bungalows are also available and Sĺňava boasts a thermal pool and water skiing.

Restaurant prices are a little inflated, but you can get fairly cheap Chinese food at the simple *Kanton*, on Winterova, and the usual Slovak specialities at the next-door *Central*. *Čajovna Pyramída* (A. Dubčeka 27) serves up a range of teas, while *Kantina* is a café wonderfully located at the Neoclassical Napoleon Baths, near Thermia. The obligatory bandstand and gleaming **Dom umenia** (which puts on plenty of free concerts of Bach, Mozart and oompah for the foreign guests in high season) are laid out in the nearby Sad Andreja Kmeťa.

Čachtice and Beckov

Halfway between Piešťany and Trenčín to the north is the industrial town of Nové Mesto nad Váhom, not a place to hang about in if you can help it, but a necessary halt if you're changing trains or buses to get to the ruined castles of Čachtice and Beckov (see below).

Of the two lofty piles of rubble perched on opposing sides of the Váh, the one at **ČACHTICE**, 8km southwest of Nové Mesto, has the edge on atmosphere, for it was here that the "Blood Countess" **Elizabeth Báthory** was walled in for almost four years to pay for her crimes, before her death in 1612 (see opposite). Thirteenth-century **Čachticky hrad** was her favourite castle; "she loved it for its wildness", wrote one of her posthumous biographers, "for the thick walls which muffled every sound, for its low halls, and for the fact of its gloomy aspect on the bare hillside". The prize exhibit of the village **museum** (May–Oct Wed–Sun 9am–5pm), an impassive portrait of Elizabeth herself, was stolen in 1990 and has yet to be recovered. The quickest way up to the castle is actually the stiff climb from Višňové train station (15min from Nové Mesto), rather than the two-kilometre haul from Čachtice village itself (though if you've got a car, the road from Čachtice can take you to the car park just five minutes' walk from the castle).

There's substantially more of a **hrad** (March–April & Sept–Oct Mon–Fri 9am–4pm, Sat & Sun 9am–5pm; May–Aug closes one hour later) above the village of **BECKOV**, 5km northeast of Nové Mesto and accessible only by

Born in 1560, **Countess Elizabeth Báthory** was the offspring of two branches of the Hungarian noble Báthory family, whose constant intermarriage may have accounted for her periodic fainting spells and fits of uncontrollable rage: other Báthorys, such as Prince "Crazy" Gábor, were similarly afflicted. As a child she was intelligent and well educated, being fluent in Latin, Hungarian and German at a time when many nobles, including the ruling prince of Transylvania, were barely literate. Brought up in the family castle at Nagyecsed, a humble town near what is now the Hungarian-Romanian border, she absorbed from her relatives the notion that peasants were little more than cattle – to be harshly punished for any act of insubordination.

As was customary in the sixteenth century, her marriage was arranged for dynastic reasons, and an illegitimate pregnancy hushed up. Betrothed in 1571 – the same year that her cousin István became Prince of Transylvania – she was married at 15 to 21-year-old **Ferenc Nádasdy**. Over the next decade Ferenc was usually away fighting Turks, earning his reputation as the "Black Knight", and Elizabeth grew bored at their home in Sárvár Castle. There she began to **torture** serving women, an "entertainment" that gradually became an obsession. With the assistance of her maids **Dorothea Szentes** and **Anna Darvulia** (who was also her lover), Elizabeth cudgelled and stuck pins into servants to "discipline" them; even worse, she forced them to lie naked in the snowy courtyard and then doused them with cold water until they froze to death. On his return, Ferenc baulked at this (although he too enjoyed brutalizing servants), and it wasn't until after his demise in 1604 that Elizabeth started torturing and **murdering** without restraint. Her victims were invariably women or girls, and – most importantly – always peasants, as killing peasants could be done with impunity. Poor women could always be enticed into service at Beckov and Čachtice – Elizabeth's residences after she quit Sárvár, both then located within the borders of Transylvania – and, should word of their deaths leak out, the authorities could hardly believe the accusations of the victims' parents against the Countess Báthory. With the assistance of Szentes, Darvulia, her son's former wet-nurse **Helena Jo**, and one man, the diminutive **Fizcko**, Elizabeth allowed her sadistic fantasies full rein. On occasion she bit chunks of flesh from servants' breasts and necks – probably the origin of the legend that she bathed in the blood of virgins to keep her own skin white and translucent.

In this fashion Elizabeth murdered over six hundred women and would probably have continued undetected had Darvulia not died. Grief-stricken, the countess formed an attachment to a local widow, **Erzsi Majorová**, who encouraged her to seek aristocratic girls for her victims. Enquiries by their parents could not be so easily ignored by the authorities, who in any case by now had their own motives for investigating *Die Blutgräfin*. Ferenc Nádasdy had loaned the Habsburg crown 17,000 gulden, which Elizabeth had persistently – and vainly – demanded back. Should she be found guilty of serious crimes this debt would be forfeited. Among Elizabeth's other adversaries were her son **Paul**, who had grown up apart from her at Sárvár, and one **Count Thurzo**, both of whom were anxious to prevent the confiscation of the Báthory estates and gathered evidence against her throughout 1610.

On December 29, Thurzo's men raided Čachtice castle, and on entry almost tripped over the corpse of a servant whom Elizabeth had just bludgeoned for stealing a pear. Thurzo secretly imprisoned the "damned woman" in her own castle immediately, so that (in his words) "the families which have won such high honours on the battlefield shall not be disgraced . . . by the murky shadow of this bestial female". Due to his cover-up the scandal was mainly confined to court circles, although when Elizabeth died in 1612 the locals protested at her burial in Čachtice cemetery. She was later reburied at Nagyecsed in the precincts of the family vault. Due to her sex (then considered incapable of such deeds) and rank, records of her trial were hidden and mention of her name subsequently prohibited by royal command.

bus. Erected in the mid-twelfth century, this was another of Báthory's torture chambers, ruined by a fire that ripped through its apartments in 1729. The ruins are fun to explore and there's a Jewish cemetery at the base of the castle and a small **folk museum** (May–Oct Tues–Sun 9am–4pm) in the village at the foot of the 245m cliff below the hrad.

Trenčín and around

Despite the usual high-rise accompaniments, **TRENČÍN**, 42km north of Pieš-ťany, is the most naturally appealing of the towns on the Váh. Its central histori-cal core sits below by far the most impressive castle in the valley, best known as the centre of **Matúš Čák**'s (aka Csák Máté in Hungarian) short-lived inde-pendent kingdom, which even had its own currency. Čák was little more than a rebellious feudal despot who set up a mock royal court, crowning himself "King of the Váh and the Tatras". He supported the young Přemyslid Václav III in his unsuccessful quest for the Hungarian crown, and had John of Luxembourg and the Hungarian King Charles Robert on the run for a number of years. Defeated only once, near Košice, he remained in control of his fief until his death in 1321, and is now happily lauded as one of the first great Slovak heroes.

The Town

Trenčiansky hrad (daily: May–Oct 8am–6pm; Nov–April 9am–3.30pm; 100Sk) itself – part ruins, part reconstruction – is a fiercely defensive sprawl of vaguely connected walls and ramparts on a steeply pitched and craggy site, spec-tacularly lit at night and hosting music, fencing, and folk displays in the summer months. Even in its present state, it's a great place to explore, though to visit the recently restored fifteenth-century palace complex, which contains a fairly dull gallery of rather dodgy oil paintings of nobility from the region, seals and coats-of-arms, you must sign up for a 45-minute guided tour (available also in English). Slovakia's one and only **Roman inscription** of any worth was carved into the rock face below the castle (you can see it from the first floor of the *Hotel Tatra* – just ask the reception desk), commemorating Marcus Aurelius' victory over the German hordes in 179 AD, when the Romans had a fortified winter camp here known as Laugaritio.

Back down the cobbled lane which leads to the castle, in the elbow of the first sharp bend, is a radiant white-and-yellow **Farský kostol** (parish church) on its own paved plateau – packed on Sundays, closed the rest of the week. A covered walkway leads down Hradná to the main square, **Mierové námestie**, whose young plane trees give it a Mediterranean feel. Straight ahead is the **Piaristicky kostol**, ablaze with the fury of the Counter-Reformation and definitely worth checking out if it's open. Close by, at Palackého 27 (opposite the passage Zlatá Fatima, that leads from the square) is the **Galéria M.A. Bazovského** (Tues–Sun 9am–5pm), named after the Slovak sculptor and painter who died here in 1968 and whose statues stand inside. It also contains a permanent display of works by local artists, dominated by Bazovský's beguilingly simple depictions of peasant life from the 1930s.

One side of the square is closed by Trenčín's only remaining gateway, the **Dolná brána** – talk while you're walking beneath it and you'll never get mar-ried, according to locals. Once through it, take a sharp right and you'll discover the former **synagogue**, a grey hulk of a building – Moorism meets Modernism – completely ransacked during the war, but one of the few in Slovakia to have been fully restored. Now used as an exhibition hall, only the arcaded women's gallery and the vivid-blue painted dome give any hint of its former role.

Practicalities

The **bus** and **train stations** are located next to each other, five minutes' walk east of the old town, which can be reached by crossing the park adjacent to the stations. The **tourist office** (mid-April to mid-Oct Mon–Fri 8am–6pm, Sat 8am–1pm; mid-Oct to mid-April Mon–Fri 8am–5pm; ℡032/16186, ⓦwww .trencin.sk), on Sládkovičova, near the Dolná brána, can fix balloon rides above the town, night-time guided tours of the castle and boat trips on the river, and generally helps with most problems, including **accommodation**, which is rather limited.

Trenčín's finest **hotel** is the grandiose late-nineteenth-century *Tatra* (℡032/650 61 11, ⓦwww.hotel-tatra.sk; ❸), a pricey and plush Canadian-Slovak joint venture, built at the very northeastern tip of the main square at ulica Gen. M.R. Štefánika 2, and which is also the home of an inscription carved into the rock by the second Roman legion in 179 AD (see opposite). Otherwise, try the *Penzión Artur* (℡032/748 10 26, ⓦwww.arturtn.sk; ❸), at Palackého 23, which has comfortable rooms but a smoky restaurant, or – on the other hand – the non-smoking *Penzión Svorad* (℡ & ℻032/743 03 32, ⓦwww .svorad-trencin.sk; ❷), located 50m on, in the former Piaristic gymnasium. On the main square itself is the *Penzion Scarlet* (Mierové námestie 27; ℡032/743 28 40, ⓔsk-scarlet@post.sk; ❹), which has just eight beds. The *Autokemping na ostrove* **campsite** (May to mid-Sept; ℡032/743 40 13) offers bungalows and tent spaces; pass under the railway lines and look for signposts pointing off to the right.

The *Tatra* has undoubtedly the best (and most expensive) **restaurant** in town, with a long menu containing mostly Slovak dishes, or else you could try passable pizza at the *Pizza Giuseppe* on Štúrovo námestie or at the *Venezia*, Hviezdoslavova 4, where there's a shady patio. Simple, cheap food is served at the *Gastrocentrum* (open weekdays for a lunchtime only), opposite the latter. For **beer**, the *Piváreň U byka*, near the Giuseppe, is good, while in the *Dublin's Pub*, next door to the *Scarlet*, you may imbibe at least six kinds of whisky.

Trenčianske Teplice

While Trenčín bakes down in the valley, **TRENČIANSKE TEPLICE**, 12km northeast, marinates in the green glades of the Teplička valley. The nicest way to get there is on the narrow-gauge train-cum-tram that trundles up the valley from Trenčianska Teplá, less than ten minutes by train from Trenčín. Alternatively, you could follow the red-marked path 9km across the hills from Trenčín and end your walk with a dip in Bohuslav Fuchs' pool (see below).

The spa itself is little more than a collection of sanatoria, ranging from the typical nineteenth-century ochre mansion of the *Sina* to the concrete *Krym*. The town's most unusual building is the stripey *Hammam* bathhouse, whose Moorish interior is officially open only to male spa guests, though the attendants sometimes let visitors peek into this delightful Turkish bath. If they don't, you can join the tour (each Monday at 3pm at the time of writing), occasionally organized by the tourist office (see p.496), opposite the *Hammam*. Architecture buffs should check out the *Mahnáč* sanatorium, a top-notch Bauhaus-style building by Jaromír Krejcar. From the same period, Brno-born Bohuslav Fuchs' swimming pool complex, **Zelená Žaba** (Green Frog; currently under reconstruction), has a much wider appeal; concealed in some woods to the north of the town and cut into the curve of the hillside, it looks as good as new seventy years on, and swimming in its spring water gives the weird sensation of bathing in warm lemonade. Like all spas, the strenuous stroll is an all-important part of the cure here; so continue up the valley from the Zelená Žaba, then, at the *Baračka* restaurant head up to **Heinrich's spring**, and thence on to Krájovec (557m) for the definitive view over the Teplička valley. The whole trip should take around two hours.

To complement its resort function, Trenčianske Teplice hosts two significant cultural **events** every summer. Art Film is a small international film festival held in mid-June, which draws the occasional big-name star; in addition, *Hudobne léto* (Musical summer), spanning mid-June to mid-August, is a series of solo and chamber music performances. The **tourist office** at Kúpeľna 15 (Mon–Fri 10am–12.30pm & 1–4pm; ℡032/655 91 28) is happy to help and can also organize spa visits and accommodation.

Travel details

Trains
Bratislava hlavná stanica to: Brno (8 daily; 1 hr 30min–2hr); Budapest (7 daily; 2 hr 20min–3 hr); Piešťany/Trenčín (1–2 hourly; 1hr 15min–2 hr 30min); Prague (7 daily; 4hr 15min–6 hr); Štúrovo (8 daily; 1hr 20min–2hr 20min); Trnava (24–30 daily; 35–55min); Vienna Südbahnhof (up to 14 daily; 1hr 15min).
Bratislava-Nové Mesto to: Trnava (up to 4 daily; 35–55min); Komárno (6 daily; 1hr 45min–2hr 30min).

Buses
Bratislava to: Brezová pod Bradlom (1–6 daily; 1hr 50min–2hr 10min); Komárno (1–2 hourly; 1hr 30min); Modra (every 15–30min; 35min–1hr); Nitra (every 15–30min; 1hr 30min); Piešťany (every 30min; 1hr); Senec (every 15–30min; 30min); Trnava (every 20–30min; 1hr); Vienna Schwechat Airport/city centre (hourly; 1hr 10min/1hr 30min).
Trenčín to: Beckov (every 1–2hr; 30–45 min); Trenčianske Teplice (every 15–30min; 15–25 min).
Trnava to: Nitra (hourly; 1hr–1hr 30min).

The mountain regions

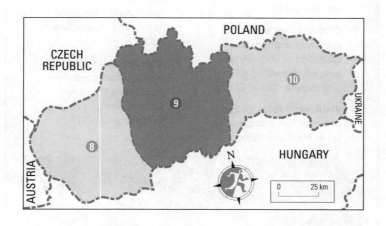

CHAPTER NINE

Highlights

＊ **Banská Štiavnica**
Former mining town filled
with magnificent monu-
ments to a bygone era
and situated on a splen-
did sloping site. See
p.508

＊ **Vratná dolina, Malá
Fatra** The finest hiking
outside of the High Tat-
ras. See p.521

＊ **Čičmany** This village
preserves a remarkable
collection of uniquely and
ornately decorated folk
architecture. See p.522

＊ **Vlkolínec** Hillside village
of timber folk cottages
set in blissful isolation

near Ružomberok. See
p.530

＊ **Demänovská dolina** The
chief northerly approach
to the Low Tatras is also
home to several world-
famous underground
caves. See p.534

＊ **Hron valley railway**
Spectacular scenic train
ride that includes a 360-
degree switchback. See
p.536

＊ **High Tatras** Jagged
granite peaks of alpine
proportions that offer
the best hiking in either
republic. See p.537

△ High Tatras

The mountain regions

T
he great virtue of Slovakia is its mountains, particularly the High Tatras, which, in their short span, reach alpine heights and have a bleak, stunning beauty. By far the republic's most popular destination, they are, in fact, the least typical of Slovakia's **mountains**, which tend on the whole to be densely forested and round-topped limestone ranges. The Low Tatras and Malá Fatra, for example, are less monumental but also much less crowded and developed and much more typical of the country.

Geographically speaking, the region splits into two huge corridors, with the Váh valley to the north and the Hron valley to the south. **Banská Bystrica**, in the Hron valley, is one of the many towns in the region originally settled by German miners, and its old quarter is still redolent of those times. Two other medieval mining towns worth visiting are **Banská Štiavnica**, best known for its silver, and **Kremnica**, a gold-mining town set in the nearby hills. For the Slovaks, by far the most important towns historically and culturally are **Martin** and **Liptovský Mikuláš**, both situated in and around the Váh valley, centres of the nineteenth-century Slovak national revival and bastions of Slovak nationalism to this day.

In general, though, the towns in the valley have been fairly solidly industrialized and are often best used as bases for exploring the surrounding **countryside**, most easily done by a combination of hiking, cycling and taking the bus. That said, **railways**, where they do exist, make for some of the most scenic train journeys in either country. As for the region's innumerable **villages**, from which many urbanized Slovaks are but one or two generations removed, they're mostly one-street affairs seemingly unchanged since the last century.

Banská Bystrica

Lying at the very heart of Slovakia's mountain ranges, **BANSKÁ BYSTRICA** (Neusohl) is a useful introduction to the area. Connected to the outlying districts by some of the country's most precipitous railways, it's a handsome historic town in its own right, once you've made it through the tangled suburbs of the burgeoning cement and logging industry. A prosperous royal free town in the Middle Ages, Banská Bystrica was the capital of seven Hungarian mining towns colonized by German miners who, in this case, extracted copper from the nearby hills until the seams ran dry in the eighteenth century. Since then, the town has shaken off its Teutonic past, and is perhaps best remembered today as the centre of the 1944 Slovak National Uprising, whose history, lav-

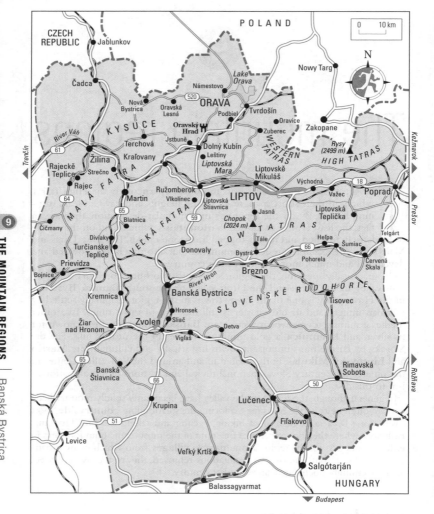

ishly embellished and glorified by the Communists, is now undergoing a more critical reassessment.

Arrival, information and accommodation

Banská Bystrica's main **bus** and **train stations** are in the modern part of town, ten minutes' walk east of the centre; if you're on a slow train, you can alight at Banská Bystrica mesto train station, just five minutes' walk south of the main square. The main train station has a **left-luggage** office. There's a **tourist office** inside the barbakan (mid-May to mid-Sept Mon–Fri 8am–7pm, Sat 9am–1pm; out of season Mon–Fri 9am–5pm; ☎048/16186 or 415 50 85, ⊛www.kisbb.sk) which can help you arrange **accommodation**. The finest of the hotels is the luxurious *Arcade* (☎048/430 21 11, ⓦwww.arcade.sk; ➎), a converted Renaissance building hidden away down a passageway beside the town's museum. The fourteen-storey Communist-era *Lux*, on Námestie slobody (☎048/414 41 41, ⓔhotellux@pcb.sk; ➍), enjoys great views over the town, but is overpriced; the other central option is the late-nineteenth-century *Národný dom* (☎048/412 37 37 or 415 45 37; ➋), at Národná 11, which has a casino, a restaurant and a wonderful café but is a little dated in decor and facilities. If you're on a tight budget, head for the *Turistická ubytovňa Milvar* (☎048/413 87 73; ➊), that occupies a grubby high-rise estate at Školská 9, 2km west of the main square – walk along Tajovského, turn right behind the viaduct, then left onto Školská. There's also a **campsite** (open all year; ☎048/419 73 20) in Tajov, 5km west of the town.

The Town

On arrival, you'll find yourself in the monumental part of town, built up after the war and planned as a showpiece of Communist architecture. It's a thoroughly alienating space with few redeeming features, designed to culminate in a statue of Lenin (now removed), and, behind where he once stood, the high-rise cornflake-packet *Hotel Lux* (symbol of the town's inexorable progress and sophistication).

Beyond is the **Múzeum SNP** (Tues–Sun: May–Sept 9am–6pm; Oct–April 9am–4pm; ⓦwww.muzeumsnp.sk) at Kapitulská 23, resembling a giant mushroom chopped in half. Originally dedicated to a lavish though insubstantial display on the triumphant march of Communism from the Slovak National Uprising (Slovenské národné povstanie, or SNP, for more on which see box on p.504) to the present day, nowadays the museum also deals with aspects of World War II, such as the deportation and extermination of Slovak Jews, through special exhibitions on the ground floor. The main collection of militaria on the top floor remains relatively unchanged, but the two multiprojector film and slide shows (also in English) have been remade. The current stance is anti-Tiso, with the Communists' huge contribution to the wartime resistance currently entirely ignored (though this may change). Whatever the outcome, the impressive facilities create a very powerful exhibition. Outside, between the town's last two surviving medieval bastions, there's a collection of hefty tanks and guns from the uprising.

From the giddy monumental heights of the Múzeum SNP, it's just a short step up Kapitulská to the town's restored centrepiece, **námestie SNP**, the old medieval marketplace and still the hub of life in Banská Bystrica. There are lots of cafés in which to soak up the local scene and admire the brutal fountain, the Marian column and the charcoal-black obelisk of the Soviet war memorial (although there is still talk of replacing this with the square's plague column that was moved in 1964 in preparation for a visit by Khrushchev). A plaque at the corner of the square and Lazovná commemorates the citizens of Banská Bystrica who were imprisoned under the Communists for their active religious beliefs. One or two of the Renaissance burgher houses bear closer inspection, particularly the so-called **Benického dom** (Venetian House), at no. 16, with a slender first-floor arcaded loggia. The sgraffitoed building opposite is now an art gallery, a few doors down from which is the most imposing building on the square, at no. 4, the honey-coloured Thurzo Palace, decorated like a piece of embroidery and sporting cute oval portholes on the top floor. This now houses the **Stredoslovenské múzeum** (Mon–Fri 8am–noon & 1–4pm, Sun 10am–5pm; ⓦwww.stredoslovenske.muzeum.sk), which contains an interesting selection of folk and "high" art.

At the top end of the square, beyond the leaning Baroquified **clock tower** (Mon–Fri 11am–6pm), on námestie Š. Moyzesa, is all that's left of the old castle. The first building in this interesting ensemble is the last remaining **barbakan**,

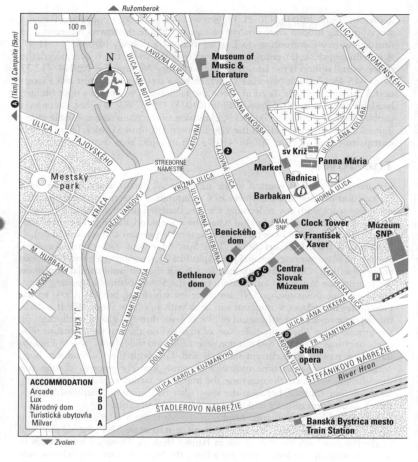

Ružomberok

0   100 m

N

Museum of
Music &
Literature

ULICA JÁNA BOTTU

LAVOZNÁ ULICA

ULICA J. G. TAJOVSKÉHO

ULICA JANA BAKOSSA

ULICA J. A. KOMENSKÉHO

STRIEBORNÉ
NÁMESTIE

KATOVNÁ

LAZOVNÁ ULICA

ULICA JÁNA KOLLÁRA

Mestský
park

J. KRÁĽA

TERÉZIE VANSOVEJ

KRÍŽNA ULICA

ULICA HORNÁ STRIEBORNÁ

sv Kríž

Panna Mária

Market

Radnica

HORNÁ ULICA

Barbakan

M. HURBANA

M. HODŽU

J. KRÁĽA

ULICA MARTINA RÁZUSA

Benického
dom

NÁM
SNP

Clock Tower

sv František
Xaver

Múzeum
SNP

KAPITULSKÁ ULICA

Bethlenov
dom

Central
Slovak
Múzeum

DOLNÁ ULICA

ULICA JÁNA CIKKERA

FR. ŠVANTNERA

Štátna
opera

NÁRODNÁ ULICA

ŠTEFÁNIKOVO NÁBREŽIE

River Hron

ULICA KAROLA KUZMÁNYHO

ŠTADLEROVO NÁBREŽIE

Banská Bystrica mesto
Train Station

Zvolen

ACCOMMODATION
Arcade   C
Lux   B
Národný dom   D
Turistická ubytovňa
Milvar   A

(1km) & Campsite (5km)

curving snugly round a Baroque tower. Next door, the boxy Renaissance **radnica** (Tues–Fri 10am–5pm, Sat & Sun 10am–4pm; ☏048/412 41 67) is now the town's main art gallery, which puts on temporary exhibitions from its extensive catalogue of twentieth-century Slovak art, including works by the Slovak Jewish artist Dominik Skutecky, who spent much of his life in Banská Bystrica. Another branch, which focuses on the modern Slovak and European art, (same hours and tel) is located in the pretty, fourteenth-century **Bethlenov dom**, at Dolná 8, just below the square.

Behind the *radnica* is the most important building of the lot, the rouge-red church of **Panna Mária**, which dates back to the thirteenth century and contains the town's greatest art treasure, a carved late-Gothic **altarpiece** by Master Pavol of Levoča, in the north side chapel. At its centre stands the figure of St Barbara, the patron saint of miners, though more interesting are the side-panel reliefs, including one of St Ursula and her posse of shipwrecked virgins. Unfortunately, the church is only open for services, but if you do get inside, be prepared also for Schmidt and Kracker's fiery German frescoes, the result of

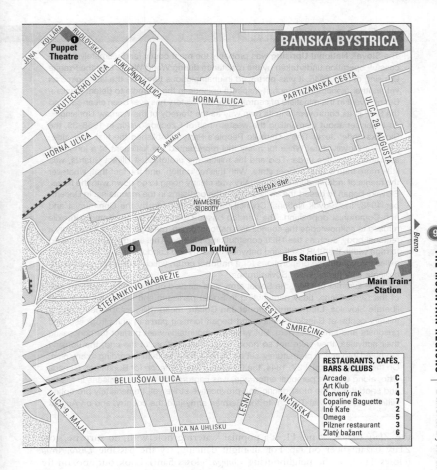

Puppet Theatre ①

KUKUČÍNOVA ULICA

RUDLOVSKÁ

JANA

KOLLÁRA

SKUTECKÉHO ULICA

HORNÁ ULICA

PARTIZÁNSKA CESTA

ULICA 29. AUGUSTA

HORNÁ ULICA

UL. ČS. ARMÁDY

TRIEDA SNP

NÁMESTIE SLOBODY

Dom kultúry ⑧

Bus Station

STEFÁNIKOVO NÁBREŽIE

Main Train Station

CESTA K SMREČINE

BELLUŠOVA ULICA

ULICA 9. MÁJA

MIČINSKÁ

LESNÁ

ULICA NA UHLISKU

▲ Brezno

⑨

THE MOUNTAIN REGIONS | Banská Bystrica

RESTAURANTS, CAFÉS, BARS & CLUBS	
Arcade	C
Art Klub	1
Červený rak	4
Copaline Baguette	7
Iné Kafe	2
Omega	5
Pilzner restaurant	3
Zlatý bažant	6

heavy Baroquification in the eighteenth century. To the left of the main door, on the exterior of the church, is another Baroque addition, a wonderful 3D tableau of the Mount of Olives, surrounded by snakes and creepy crawlies, with a premonition of Judas's betrayal in relief above the main scene.

Eating, drinking and entertainment

Eating options in Banská Bystrica have improved greatly over the last decade. You can grab a freshly baked baguette sandwich at the self-service *Copaline Baguette*, námestie SNP 12, or try the local fare washed down with Pilsner Urquell at the *Pilzner restaurant*, on the northern side of the square. Alternatively, the *Červený rak* (closed Sun), on the southwestern end of the square, offers pizzas and Slovak dishes in a pleasant interior and, in summer, on a shady patio with wicker tables and chairs. For a coffee, try the atmospheric, two-storey *Iné Kafe*, at Lazovná 16, some 200m north of the main square.

Surprisingly for provincial Slovakia, the **nightlife** scene here is fairly active. Most of the cafés on the main square stay open until midnight or beyond, and

503

The **Slovak National Uprising** was probably the most costly (and ultimately unsuccessful) operation undertaken by the resistance during World War II. Like the Prague Uprising of May 1945, it was portrayed in unambiguous terms by the last regime as yet another glorious (Communist-inspired) episode in the struggle to defeat fascism. But no event in the minefield of central European history has ever been clear-cut, and the SNP is as controversial in its own way as the tragedy of the Warsaw Uprising.

As Hitler set about dismantling the western half of Czechoslovakia in 1938–39, the Slovaks under Jozef Tiso's Catholic People's Party established the first ever independent Slovak state. While for many this represented the fulfilment of a long-held aspiration, Slovakia under Tiso and his militia, the protofascist Hlinka Guards, was little more than a Nazi puppet state. With this realization, and the fact that, whatever the merits of independence, the country was clearly going to go down with the Nazis, Slovaks began to desert the army and join the partisans in the mountains. In December 1943, the Slovak National Council (SNR) was formed by the Communist and non-Communist opposition. The London-based Czechoslovak government-in-exile refused to acknowledge the council as a national organ, maintaining that it was only a regional body, such as the 1920 constitution permitted. These arguments continued to rage within the SNR itself, and between the SNR and London- and Moscow-based exiles throughout the preparations for a **national coup**, which Moscow hoped to coordinate with the arrival of Soviet troops.

By the summer of 1944, the Soviet army was massed on the Polish-Ukrainian side of the Carpathians, busy parachuting in Soviet partisans and seemingly poised to liberate Slovakia. **Lieutenant-Colonel Ján Golián**, meanwhile, established a secret military centre at Banská Bystrica and began forming partisan units from escaped prisoners and army deserters. But while the mountains were perfect for concealing their activities, they were not so good for communication. In the end, the uprising stumbled into action prematurely, set off by default rather than according to any plan. On the night of August 27, 1944, the German military attaché for Bucharest, General Otto, along with his personal entourage, was captured by Slovak partisans in Martin and shot. It was the most daring and provocative strike yet, immediately prompting Hitler to demand that Tiso invite the German army into the country, and on August

the *Zlatý bažant*, at no. 11, is a popular watering hole with, no surprise, good Zlatý bažant beer on tap. For all-night dancing, try the passable *Disco Arcade* (closes 4am), or the neighbouring *Omega* (closes 5am). Look out, too, on fly-posters for any gigs and events at the *Art Club* on Rudlovská, northeast of the town centre just before the railway bridge. The **Štátna opera** is the town's bastion of high culture, while the local **puppet theatre** (Bábkové divadlo), on Jána Kollára, has regular shows for adults and kids and occasional performances by foreign touring companies.

From Banská Bystrica to Zvolen

The wide valley that stretches between Zvolen and Banská Bystrica provides a perfect site for the largest air-force base in the country, used by the Soviets until recently. Zvolen itself is worth visiting for its chateau, which contains one of the finest collections of European Masters in Slovakia. If you're travelling there by train, you could also take in Hronsek en route, and given that Banská Bystrica's attractions are fairly limited, both destinations make for pleasant day-trips.

29, five SS and two Wehrmacht divisions plus sundry other troops entered Slovakia. Events could not be delayed any longer, and the uprising was officially declared by partisan radio from Banská Bystrica.

In the eyes of the Czechs at home and abroad, the Slovaks, by starting the uprising, were at last making amends for their treacherous declaration of independence in 1939, which had helped Hitler to annex the Czech Lands. Yet the majority of Slovaks who took part in the uprising (there were fewer than 500 Czechs involved) were not fighting to restore Czechoslovakia, but to help liberate Slovakia from Tiso and the Nazis. For them the SNR was the new postwar Slovak government in waiting, and when the London-based Czechoslovak government sent a delegate, the Slovaks would only recognize him as a liaison officer, and not as a superior government official. The SNR were fighting to have an equal say in negotiations after the war was over, with a view to perhaps gaining a much greater degree of autonomy, if not independence, in the new postwar arrangement with the Czechs.

Ultimately, however, the uprising failed. The Soviets flew in 2500 paratroopers, along with hundreds of tonnes of weaponry and supplies, Russian advisers, and even a dozen American OSS and British officers. Yet it was not enough, and many blamed the Soviets for not launching a full-scale offensive to relieve the uprising. To be fair, though, their supply lines were already stretched, and breaching the Carpathians was no easy task. In the end, it took the 4th Ukrainian Army over two months and some 80,000 lives to capture the Dukla Pass and reach Svidník, the first major town to be liberated. More disheartening was the Soviet refusal to allow the Allies to use Soviet air bases to drop essential equipment into Slovakia. The Slovaks kept going for almost two months before the Nazis succeeded in entering Banská Bystrica on October 28, but apart from tying down a number of German divisions, it was a costly sacrifice to make. The reprisals went on for months: whole villages were given the "Lidice treatment" (see p.182), and women and children were no longer considered sacrosanct. All in all, well over 30,000 Slovaks lost their lives as a result of the uprising, even though by the end of the uprising, the Soviets had already begun to liberate the country.

Hronsek

Two stops further up the track towards Banská Bystrica is the small village of **HRONSEK**, by the banks of the River Hron. Here, on Hronsecká cesta, west off the road to Sliač, is one of Slovakia's more unusual wooden churches, erected in 1726 on what was originally an island in the river (the two giant lime trees were planted at the same time). With the Counter-Reformation still in full swing, as a Protestant church, it had to be built within a year according to strict guidelines: wood was the only material allowed, which is why there are no metal nails or plaster in the Scandinavian-style timber frame, and the belfry had to be separate. The interior, capable of squeezing in over 1000 worshippers, features seating rather like a theatre in the round. The church is normally kept locked; ask at the nearest house for a key. If you'd rather **stay** out in the countryside, the local hunting lodge 2km north of Hronsek, *Kaštieľ Bocian* (☎048/418 83 92, ⓦwww.hotelkastielbocian.sk; ❸), has been nicely converted into a hotel, or else the *Kongres Hotel Gala* (☎048/418 85 50, ⓦwww.kongreshotel.sk; ❹), halfway between the church and the *Kaštieľ Bocian*, has comfortable, spacious rooms. Apart from trains, **buses** #52 and #55 link Banská Bystrica with Hronsek (both depart from the Banská Bystrica mesto train station).

Zvolen

Once the effective capital of a Hungarian *župa* (regional district) stretching as far as the Orava and Liptov regions, **ZVOLEN** (Altsohl), 20km and a forty-minute train ride south of Banská Bystrica, has come a long way since those halcyon days. Today, Zvolen lives off its logging industry and its key position in the country's road and rail system, and, thanks to the new bypass, its wide main thoroughfare, námestie SNP, is now a much more pleasant place to stroll. The **Lesnícke a drevárske múzeum** (Forestry and Wood Museum; Tues–Fri & Sun 9am–5pm), on the west side of the square at no. 31, has a good selection of folk art that includes decorated crosses from nearby Detva, as well as a series of photographs portraying forests damaged by acid rain.

The main reason for coming here, however, is to see the town's four-cornered **zámok** (May–Sept Tues–Sun 10am–5.30pm; Oct–April Wed–Sun same hours; ☎045/532 19 03), which squats on a big mound of earth at the southern end of the square, with a makeshift armoured train – built in Zvolen's railway workshops to protect the Slovak National Uprising – situated beneath it. Built in the fourteenth century, the chateau fell to the exiled Czech Hussite leader, Jiskra of Brandys, who for nearly twenty years ruled over much of what is now Slovakia. Later, it became the property of the powerful Hungarian Esterházy family, and, as the Turks got too close for comfort, it was transformed into the stern fighting fortress it now resembles. Nowadays, few rooms contain any of their original decor beyond some fine Renaissance portals, though one room boasts a splendid wooden ceiling decorated with no fewer than 78 portraits of successive Holy Roman and Habsburg emperors. The rest of the apartments have been turned into an **art gallery** displaying a decent range of mostly sixteenth- to nineteenth-century European masters belonging to the Slovenská národná galéria, including works by Hogarth, Brueghel, Caravaggio and Veronese. Yet another section concentrates on Master Pavol of Levoča, easily the most original sculptor of the fifteenth century – a good opportunity to catch his work if you're going no further east – while the top floor hosts temporary exhibitions of Slovak art.

Practicalities

Zvolen is an easy day-trip from Banská Bystrica, but there are several places to stay, should you wish to, and a **tourist office** (in summer Mon–Fri 8am–5pm, Sat 8–11.30am; out of season Mon–Fri 8am–4.30pm; ☎045/16186, Ⓔicko@zv.psg.sk) to help you, east off the main square at Trhová 4. Zvolen boasts several reasonable **hotels** worth trying, including the modern *Penzión Quatro* (☎045/532 32 56; ❸) on the main square at no. 32, and opposite, the *Mestský hotel* (same tel; ❸) run by the same owner. Another option is the *Hotel Poľana* (☎045/532 01 24, Ⓦwww.hotelpolana.sk; ❹) in the southeastern corner of the square; it's ugly from the outside but the rooms are decent and have satellite TV. A short distance along route 66 to Krupina there's the *Neresnica* **campsite** (open all year; ☎045/533 26 51) at Neresnica cesta 19. For **food**, there's a branch of the ever-popular *Copaline Baguette*, on the east side of the main square, with a pizzeria out the back; the nearby *Jadran* is good for coffee, cakes and ice cream, while the *Victoria*, north of the main square by the main crossroads, has decent Zubr beer and pub food.

From Zvolen to Lučenec

Heading south or east from Zvolen by train takes you through the wilds of southern Slovakia to the Hungarian border. The southbound route 66 to Šahy is the more direct if you're heading for Budapest, but the eastbound route 50 via Lučenec is more interesting. For a start, it takes you past the imposing ruined castle of **Vígšášsky zámok**, 15km east of Zvolen, just beyond Zvolenská Slatina. Originally a Gothic castle, later an anti-Turk fortress, and finally an aristocratic manor house, the whole place burnt down during fighting in World War II. The ruins are a stiff but straightforward climb up from the train station. Another 8km down the tracks is the village of **DETVA**, only really worth visiting in early July when the **folk festival** is on, reputedly one of the best in Slovakia. The traditional skills of the community lie in woodcarving, particularly the *fujara*, a cross between a flute and a bassoon, and an instrument commonly used in folk music right across central Europe. You can **stay** at the *Hotel Detva* (Záhradná 22, ☎045/545 64 80, Ⓦwww.hotel.detva.biz; ❷) or contact the **tourist office** located in the same building (Mon–Fri 9am–5pm; ☎045/545 76 92) which can arrange accommodation.

Lučenec and around

Some 60km southeast of Zvolen, **LUČENEC** (Losonc) is, for the most part, a scruffy, ramshackle place typical of the border regions, with a population of Slovaks, Magyars and Romanies in roughly equal proportions. It gets few visitors, but if you're passing through it's worth checking out the two churches on the old town square, **Kubínyiho námestie**. Also worth a quick look is the **Novohradské múzeum** (Tues–Fri 9am–5pm, Sun 1–4pm), on the east side of the square, which puts on interesting temporary exhibitions on local history and crafts. You might also take a closer look at the enormous disused Art Nouveau **synagogue**, a few blocks south of the square beyond the *Hotel Pelikán*, one of the three that used to serve the town's large prewar Jewish population, and in line for reconstruction.

It's a good fifteen-minute walk south along Železničná from the **bus** and **train stations** to the town centre, but once you've hit T.G. Masaryka, the main drag through town, there are a few places to break your journey. Due to its location right near the border, Lučenec has its fair share of **accommodation**, starting with the *Reduta* (☎047/433 12 37, Ⓕ047/433 12 40; ❺), a Best Western chain hotel dating back to 1810, just round the back of the wonderful neo-Gothic shopping precinct on the south side of Kubínyiho námestie at Vajanského 2. The recently opened, gaudily green *Pelikán* (☎047/433 08 72, Ⓔpelikan@wft.sk; ❸) has clean rooms, but lacks atmosphere. If you're minding your pennies, try the *Novohrad*, Novohradská 27 (☎047/433 12 11; ❷), or the even cheaper *P-7*, north of the main square at Kármána 22/A (☎047/432 12 55; ❷), which is kitsch but acceptable. For **food** and **drink**, try the *Restaurant Vináren*, in the cellars below the aforementioned mall. For local and regional information, head for the **tourist office** (Mon–Fri 8am–noon & 12.30–5pm, Sat 8am–noon; ☎047/451 20 22, Ⓦwww.lucenec.sk) at T.G. Masaryka 14.

Fiľakovo and the Hungarian border

FIĽAKOVO (Fülek), a small Hungarian-speaking town just 13km southeast of Lučenec, is worth a brief stopoff, if only for the extremely photogenic ruins of **Fiľakovsky hrad** (April–Oct Tues–Sun 10am–6pm), perched on a craggy hilltop in the Romany part of town and destroyed during the Turkish invasion in 1554, or the museum below (open Tues–Fri 8am–noon & 12.30–4pm; April–Oct also Sat 8am–noon), stuffed with local memorabilia. If you're heading south for Salgótarján in Hungary, you could also happily spend an afternoon exploring the **Dolina Bukovinkového potoka**, a gently wooded valley that starts 1km from the Hungarian border. Some 3km along the valley, you come to **Šomošský hrad**, another picturesque Gothic castle in ruins, right on the border, squatting upon vast blocks of eroded volcanic stone. Founded during the fifteenth century, its five towers survey impressive basalt formations, resembling giant organ pipes, some of which form part of a waterfall known as the *kammený vodopad*. Below the castle lies the Hungarian village of Somoskö, to which there is no access.

Banská Štiavnica

High above the Štiavnica river, on the terraced slopes of the Štiavnické vrchy, **BANSKÁ ŠTIAVNICA** (Schemitz), 25km southwest of Zvolen, couldn't wish for a more picturesque setting. An old German-speaking silver- (and gold-) mining town, its historic core has suffered from centuries of sheer neglect. The development of a modern lower town has saved the place in terms of its architecture, but turned the old town into little more than an ancient monument, as lifeless and isolated as it is beautiful. In 1993, however, the town gained UNESCO-protected status, and a concerted restoration effort is slowly taking effect.

Arrival, information and accommodation

Bus connections to and from Zvolen and Banská Bystrica are fairly good, but the scenic **railway**, built by "voluntary brigades" of Communist youth workers back in the 1950s, is easily the most rewarding way of getting to Banská Štiavnica (3 trains daily; 1hr from Zvolen – change at Hronská Dúbrava). The station is south of the new town, with the old town a long, steep hike away; there are occasional buses linking the two. Drivers must buy a *celodenná karta* from one of the shops, restaurants or hotels in order to park. Any queries should be taken to the **tourist office** (Námestie sv Trojice 3; May–Sept daily 8am–5.30pm; Oct–April Mon–Fri 8am–4pm, Sat 8am–2pm; ☎045/161 86 or 691 18 59, ⊛www.banskastiavnica.sk), opposite the Berggericht, which also offers **guided tours** in a multitude of languages. For **Internet** access, drop by *Rebel u Jašteričiek*, to the west of the Protestant church (weekdays open 24hr).

Banská Štiavnica is justifiably popular with German and Austrian tourists, but there should be little problem getting a **room** for the night at either of the town's two best hotels, the excellent *Salamander*, J. Palárika 1 (☎045/691 39 92, ⊛www.hotelsalamander.sk; ❹), which has comfortable rooms with satellite TV above a restaurant and café, and the equally good *Grand-Matej* at Kammerhofská 5 (☎045/691 37 82, ⊛www.grandmatej.sk; ❹). The *Penzión Kachelman*, Kammerhofská 18 (☎045/692 23 19, ⊛www.kachelman.sk; ❷), housed in a Renaissance building, offers cosy, comfortable rooms, while *Penzión Tomino*, at Akademická 9 (☎045/692 13 07, ⊛www.penziontomino.host.sk; ❷), has shared facilities but is perfectly clean and a bargain for budget travellers. There are numerous other pensions and private rooms further out and in neighbouring villages. Campers can choose between **campsites** southwest of the town, in amongst the many artificial lakes; originally built in the eighteenth century as part of the town's ambitious water-pumping project, they're now popular summer bathing spots. The *Autocamp* at the Počúvadlo lake (☎045/699 41 12; mid-June to mid-Sept) is recommended for both camping and basic bungalows.

The Staré Mesto

Banská Štiavnica earned its medieval wealth from the silver deposits discovered here in the thirteenth century. As at Banská Bystrica, skilled German miners were brought in to work the seams, the town was granted special privileges by the Hungarian crown, and the good times rolled – as testified by the handsome burgher houses and the wonderful red marble Trinity column erected on the main square, **Námestie sv Trojice**. Recently restored to their former glory, their names recall their German heritage: Baumgartner, Rubigall and Hellenbach. One, the **Berggericht** (May–Sept daily 9am–5pm; Oct–April Mon–Fri 8am–4pm), at no. 6, features a collection of minerals from all over the world as well as the eighty-metre-long, sixteenth-century štolňa Michal (Michal Mine Gallery), which can be explored without a guide. Of more universal interest, further up the square in a beautiful sgraffitoed building, is the **Galéria Jozefa Kollára** (May–Oct daily 9am–5pm; Nov–April Mon–Fri 8am–4pm), which puts on interesting temporary exhibitions of modern Slovak art as well as permanent displays of paintings and sculpture from the thirteenth- to twentieth-centuries, including works by local interwar artists Jozef Kollár, Edmund Gwerek and Jaroslav August. The headquarters of the town's **Banské múzeum** (Mining Museum; same hours as Galéria Jozefa Kollára; ⓦ www.muzeumbs.sk), Kammerhofská 2, occupies a huge edifice called Kammerhof, which served as the mining court from the fifteenth-century, and now contains a display on mining in Slovakia, focusing on miners' clothing, equipment and the like. A few steps to the east there's an entrance to the recently

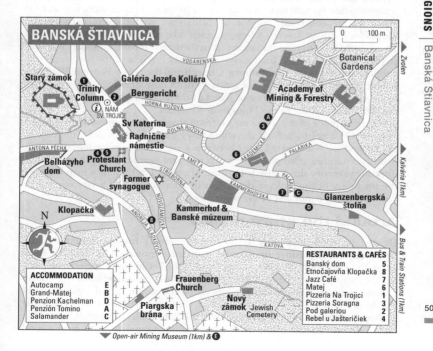

opened **Glanzenbergská štolňa** (Glanzenberg Mine Gallery; 100Sk; ☎045/692 05 35), which spreads exactly under the town centre. It's famous for being one of the oldest galleries in the region; its claustrophobic tunnels were inspected by, among others, the eighteenth-century Habsburg emperors and present-day personalities, such as the former Slovak president Rudolf Schuster and Prince Albert of Monaco (in 2002). Currently it can be visited only with a guide and only on Saturday at 2pm.

It's worth asking around for the key to the Gothic church of **sv Katerína**, at the bottom of the main square alongside the old **radnica**; the hands of its Baroque clock are set back-to-front and the clock itself runs backwards. Lutheranism caught on fast in Slovakia during the Reformation, especially among the German communities, and opposite the radnica is one of the most impressive Lutheran churches in the country, the black-roofed bulk of the **Protestant Church**, gilded urns atop its tympanum, built shortly after the 1781 Edict of Tolerance.

Up the steps from the radnica is the thirteenth-to-eighteenth century walled **starý zámok** (old castle; May–Oct daily 9am–5pm; Nov–April Mon–Fri 8am–4pm; ⊛ www.hrady.sk/stary_zamok/english.html), once the town's most important building. It was built on the same lines as Kremnica's castle (see opposite) – as the town's strongbox as well as a fortified residence for the local bigwigs – and the central church-turned-fortress testifies to the panic that beset the Hungarian Kingdom during the peak of Ottoman expansion in the sixteenth century. Currently undergoing slow but extensive restoration, it houses an exhibit of Baroque sculptures, Štiavnica tobacco pipes, religious art and medieval blacksmiths' works.

Below the castle, Sládkovičova leads past the **Belházyho dom**, a beautifully restored white Renaissance chateau, now a hospital, with an attractive arcaded loggia in the courtyard. Further up Sládkoviča is the seventeenth-century **klopačka** (Clapper Tower), whose wooden "clapper" (something like a public alarm clock) used to raise the miners from their beds at 5am; nowadays it "claps" at 10am and 2pm during the tourist season only. From here the road continues uphill to the red-brick **Frauenberg Church** and the portly Baroque **Piargska brána**, one of the town's former gateways that's now stranded out on the road to Levice, giving an indication of Banská Štiavnica's original size when it was the third-largest town in the Hungarian Kingdom.

As further proof of this, there are no fewer than twelve cemeteries in this part of town. On a nearby hillock, the white **nový zámok** (times as for the Galéria Jozefa Kollára) – a turreted cross between a sugar lump and a lookout tower – was yet another attempt by the town to guard against a Turkish attack. The Turkish weaponry on display is far from gripping, but there is a map showing the proximity of the Turks at the height of their power, and a viewing gallery with a fantastic panorama of the town.

Around the staré mesto

By far the most interesting section of the town's mining museum is the **open-air mining museum** (Banské múzeum v prírode; J.K. Hella 12; April Mon–Fri 8am–4pm; May–Oct daily 9am–5pm), set in some disused medieval mines, another 1.5km beyond the nový zámok, along the road to Levice. Above ground, a cluster of technical exhibits charts the technological innovations of the local mining school (information in German and Slovak only), but the highlight of the museum is the trip down the Bartolomej mine shaft in hard hat and overcoat. The tour of the narrow labyrinthine tunnel network gives a good impression of the appalling conditions medieval miners must have endured, and is not recommended for claustrophobes.

For the best view of Banská Štiavnica, though, head northeast, past the imposing nineteenth-century building of the **Academy of Mining and Forestry**, whose botanical gardens (daily dawn–dusk) boast one of the finest arboretums in Slovakia, replete with Californian redwoods, woodpeckers and tree creepers, to the copper-coloured hilltop church of **Štiavnicka kalvária**. The green-marked path zigzags past a succession of Baroque chapels up the hill to the lower church, then on to the summit where the climactic uppermost chapel contains a gruesome, fantastical tableau of the Crucifixion.

Eating and drinking

For **food**, you can't beat the fine soups and great Slovak specialities prepared by the *Matej*, Akademická 4. The usual range of pizzas and pastas is offered at the *Pizzeria Soragna* (closed Sun), a couple of doors up, and at the pleasant *Pizzeria Na Trojici*, at the upper end of Námestie sv Trojice. Alternatively, you can choose from a range of Slovak dishes at the *Pod galeriou*, set in a Renaissance building between the Berggericht and the Galéria Jozefa Kollára.

The *Banský dom* is a stylish **café**, near the Protestant church, complete with chandeliers; other good options include the tasteful *Jazz Café* on Kammerhofská 12, or the *Etnočajovňa Klopačka* tea-house on Sládkoviča.

Kremnica

KREMNICA (Kremnitz) isn't really what you'd expect from a wealthy gold-mining town. Perched on a semi-plateau midway up the Rudnica Valley, it's a surprisingly modest place, little more than its duo of castle and square, and certainly no match for the wealth and beauty of Banská Štiavnica, though it attracts a few more visitors thanks to its gold mint. Accommodation can be something of a problem, particularly during the Festival of Satire and Humour (Kremnické gagy; ⓦwww.gagy.sk) in late August/early September, so it's worth considering coming on a day-trip.

Founded by the Hungarian King Charles Robert in 1320, Kremnica's gold seams were once the richest in medieval Europe, keeping the Hungarian economy buoyant and booming throughout the Middle Ages. The thick walls and bastions that still surround the town and castle were built to protect what was effectively the Bank of Hungary – the royal mint. Yet **Štefánikovo námestie**, the steeply pitched main square on which the mint stands, is now little more than a provincial village green, dotted with pollarded ornamental trees, park benches and a particularly ornate **plague column** which, topped with a flash of gold, is the only obvious reference to the town's wealth. The heavily fortified **Mestský hrad** (May–Sept Tues–Sun 8.30am–noon & 1–5.30pm; Oct–April Tues–Sat 8.30am–noon & 1–4.30pm) sits amid fruit orchards above the square, and has been restored to sparkling cleanliness. To see it, though, you're supposed to join the two-hour tour – more than enough time to view every room, painting, and statue in the small lower living quarters, plus the richly decorated church of sv Katerína, which takes up most of the upper courtyard. The atypical Gothic nave is broader than it is long, and holds five altars, all bathed in local gold, plus a stupendous 3500-pipe organ. To cap off the tour, you can climb the adjoining tower for superlative views of the grassy square below and lolling hills around. If you don't want to go on the tour, you can come and hear the organ in action during Sunday Mass (9.15am). The ossuary, adorned with faded Gothic frescoes, is accessible without a guide.

Back on Štefánikovo námestie, at no.10/19, there's a **Museum of Coins and Medals** (Múzeum mincí a medailí; May–Sept Tues–Sun 9am–1pm & 2–5.30pm; Oct–April Tues–Sat 8.30am–1pm & 2–4.30pm) that's been attracting visitors from all around the world since 1890. From Stalin to Churchill, they've all had anniversary Kremnitzerducats minted for them in their time. As well as some exceptionally beautiful Renaissance coins, there's a whole room of paper money, which, during the First Republic, became an art in itself, with designs by top Czech artists like Alfons Mucha and Max Švabinský. More Slovak and Hungarian medals are sometimes displayed in the gallery (Mon–Fri 8am–1pm & 1.30–4pm) on the southwestern corner of the square, while the next-door branch of the museum (May–Sept Mon–Fri 8am–12.30pm & 1–5pm, Sat & Sun from 9am; Oct–April Mon–Fri 8am–12.30pm & 1–3pm) features a collection of historical arms. The mines still produce a small amount of gold, and the odd commemorative coin is sporadically struck at the **Štátna mincovňa** (State Mint; no admission) on the northwestern corner of the square.

Practicalities

From Banská Štiavnica, it's simplest to catch a **bus** to Kremnica, but from Zvolen you also have the choice of the **train** with its wonderful views as the track switches back and forth through the hills, climbing over 460m in just 14km before depositing you above Kremnica itself, about a kilometre southeast of the centre. The **tourist office** (Námestie gen. M.R. Štefánika 35; Mon–Fri 8am–5pm, Sat 9am–2pm; July–Aug also Sun 9am–2pm; ⊛www.kremnica.sk), in between the double gateway on the south side of the main square, can help with booking **accommodation**. Above, there's a small collection of antique skis and a miniature model of Kremnica. The best hotel in town is the well-renovated *Centrál* at Dolná 40/3, just outside the double gateway (☎045/674 42 10; ❸), with a sauna and a bright restaurant. Alternatively, there's the *Veterník* (☎045/674 27 09; ❷), a few hundred metres south of the centre on Veternická 19 with a popular restaurant, or the small, quiet pension *Dajana* (☎045/674 37 11, ⊛www.dajan.sk; ❷), just behind the castle. The *Vofri* Gothic wine bar (closed Sun) on Štefaníkovo námestie 34 offers good Slovak and Hungarian grub and wine, and the new restaurant *Silvanus*, with its own patio, behind the gallery, is popular with the locals. For coffee and pastries, head for the *Espresso Permoník*, on the northeastern corner of the square, below the castle.

The Turiec valley

From Kremnica, the railway climbs another 18km or so before hitting the mill-pond flatness of the **Turiec valley**. Having climbed this far up a valley which gets progressively narrower and more dramatic, it comes as something of a surprise to find yourself in such a wide plateau: but for the cool mountain air and the Veľká and Malá Fatra in the distance, you could be back down in the Danube basin.

Turčianske Teplice

TURČIANSKE TEPLICE is the first stop on the railway as it romps across the valley floor to Martin (see opposite). A modern spa town (for the treatment of facial diseases and urinary tract problems), despite its fourteenth-century origins, it boasts very hot natural springs and a striking Bedouin-blue domed nine-teenth-century **bathhouse**, the Modrý kúpeľ (call ☏043/491 31 11 to reserve spa treatments if you are not staying as a spa guest), with an ornate Moorish treatment. You can wander through the peaceful wooded spa park towards the **Dom Mikuláša Galanda** (Tues–Sun 10am–1pm & 2–5pm), southwest of the centre at Kollárova 74, where the influential Slovak painter Mikuláš Galanda was born in 1895. The home has been converted into a museum, with photos and personal effects of the artist to complement a small but vibrant collection of his works. Galanda studied in Budapest, where his early pen-and-ink sketches included cartoons published in the Hungarian magazine *Hárman* between the wars. In the 1920s and 1930s, he fell under the spell of Picasso, adopting the Spanish painter's styles in most of his subsequent works. Particularly striking among these are the gloomy Cubist *Pijani* (*Drinkers*), and the touching *Mother with Child and Poppy Flower*. Galanda won a silver medal at the Paris Exhibition in 1937, a year before he died prematurely, in Bratislava, of a stomach ailment.

The town also makes a good base for exploring the Veľká Fatra (the yellow-marked path from the station heads off into the hills), though, unfortunately, most of the town's **hotels** are filled with guests here for the spa (contact Slovenské liečebné kúpele Turčianske Teplice for further **information** about spa accom-modation and treatments, ☏043/491 31 11, ⓦwww.turcslk.sk). You could, how-ever, try the simple, cheap *Hotel Relax* (☏043/492 37 17, ⓦwww.hotelrelax.sk; ❷), on Partizánska, across the park from the Modrý kúpeľ, or the *Penzión Milka* (☏043/492 26 31, ⓦwww.penzion-milka.sk; ❷), a bright pink house behind the *Relax*, with comfortable rooms, sauna and a **restaurant** serving Slovak fare. The nearest **campsite** (open all year) is a two-kilometre train journey north at Divi-aky, across the river and the highway from the white seventeenth-century country house (closed to the public), but if you've got your own wheels, you'll find more appealing opportunities further north up the valley.

Martin

A town of considerable historic importance for the Slovaks, **MARTIN** and its industrial baggage occupy the last seven kilometres of the banks of the River

---

Hiking in the Veľká Fatra

To the east of the Turiec valley lie the **Veľká Fatra**, a line of craggy mountain tops surrounded by a sea of uninhabited, undulating forest. The ridge of brittle limestone peaks from Krížna (1574m) to Ploská (1532m), via the highest of the lot, Ostredok (1592m), is the most obvious area to aim for, but the thin craggy valleys leading up to the mountains are actually much more enthralling to walk along: the two most acces-sible and geologically exciting are the **Gaderská dolina** and the **Blatnická dolina**. The return trip along either, including ascending at least one of the big peaks, is a full day's hike (6–7hr); it's a good idea to get hold of the green *Veľká Fatra* hiking map, published by VKÚ Harmanec and available from the local tourist offices and book-shops around the country. Both valleys begin at **BLATNICA**, one of the most idyllic villages in the Turiec valley, with half-timbered cottages spread along both banks of the village stream. The local manor house, which features a lovely circular Neoclassi-cal portico, is now a **museum** (May–Oct Tues–Sun 9am–5pm) dedicated to the great grandfather of Slovak photography, **Karol Plicka**, whose images of the Slovak coun-tryside are reproduced in countless coffee-table books. There are several pensions at the northern edge of the village, a *chata* colony at the entrance to the Gaderská dolina, and a **campsite** 1km south of Blatnica (though the latter is currently closed).

Turiec before it joins forces with the mighty Váh. Perhaps unfairly, it's best known nowadays for its ZTS engineering works, but while this once had a monopoly on Warsaw Pact tank production, it's struggling to cope in the post-Cold War era and has had to halve its 16,000 workforce. Yet there's more to Martin than a five-minute drive through the town's confusing one-way system might suggest: for example, the country's most encyclopedic folk museum, a better-than-average Slovak art gallery and an open-air folk museum on the outskirts of the town. There's also the possibility of a day's hiking in the less visited southern range of the Malá Fatra, the Lúčanská Fatra (see box p.516).

Some history

Established back in the fourteenth century, Martin remained the extremely unexceptional town of Turčiansky Svätý Martin until well into the nineteenth century. Then, in 1861, a group of Slovak intellectuals and clergy gathered under the linden tree in front of the Protestant Church and proclaimed the **Martin Memorandum**, which declared boldly that the Slovaks "were as much a nation as the Magyars" and asked the Viennese Parliament to establish a North Hungarian Slovak District (which would remain an integral part of Hungary) with Slovak as the official language.

Their demands caused outrage among the Magyars and were studiously ignored by the Austrians. Nevertheless, a number of important Slovak institu-

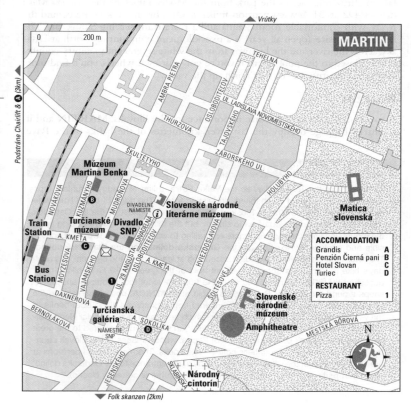

tions were founded in the town, of which by far the most important was the **Matica slovenská**, set up to promote the embryonic national culture through education, literature and the arts. It was short-lived. The infamous Ausgleich of 1867, which effectively gave the Hungarians a free hand in their half of the empire, ensured that all Slovak institutions of higher education were closed by the mid-1870s.

During the next forty years of heavy-handed Magyarization, Martin remained the spiritual centre of the Slovak nation, and on May 24, 1918, Slovak nationalists of all hues gathered for the last time at Martin to sign the **Martin Declaration**, throwing in their lot with the Czechs and scuppering the Hungarians' various proposals for a "Greater Hungary". At this point Martin was still seriously under consideration as the potential Slovak capital: it was centrally located, less exposed to attack and infinitely more Slav than the Austro-Hungarian town of Pressburg (Bratislava), the other main contender, to which it eventually lost out. Since 1989, however, the Matica slovenská has re-established itself in the town and is earning Martin a reputation as a hotbed of Slovak nationalism, not to say chauvinism.

The Town

There's not much to choose aesthetically between what might nominally be called the old town in the south and the industrial estates to the north, but the sights are all located in the south. From the train station, Martin's modern chessboard street-plan becomes quickly apparent as you hit the first major crossroads, on which stands the **Turčianské múzeum** (April–Oct Tues–Sun 9am–5pm; Nov–March Mon–Fri 9am–5pm), named after Andrej Kmeť – paradise for your average botanist, geologist or zoologist, but of limited appeal to anyone else. Of more general interest is the **Turčianská galéria** (Tues–Sun 10am–4.30pm; Ⓦwww.turiecgallery.sk), one block south on Daxnerova, which houses a good range of Slovak artists in its permanent collection on the first floor. Works by Miloš Alexander Bazovský, Ľudovít Fulla and Mikuláš Galanda are all featured, while the seminal Martin Benko, who lived and worked in Martin, has a whole room devoted to him – his simple form of Expressionism became a hallmark of much of Slovak art between the world wars. The plain interwar house at Kuzmányho 34, where Benko lived from 1958 until his death in 1971, is now the **Múzeum Martina Benka** (May–Oct Tues–Fri 9am–4pm, Sat & Sun 9am–5pm; Nov–April closed Sun), containing his archive, much of the original furniture and plenty more of his paintings.

Straight ahead, two or three blocks up tree-lined Andreja Kmeťa (which then becomes Muzeálna), is the barracks-like mass of the **Slovenské národné múzeum** (Slovak National Museum; Tues–Sun 9am–5.30pm), which commands a great view of the Malá Fatra from its steps. The museum houses the country's Institute of Ethnography and one of the best and most extensive and exhaustive folk collections in the country. Richly decorated costumes and folk artefacts from every region of Slovakia are on display, with Slovak and English captions explaining the exhibits.

On the other side of the open-air amphitheatre, to the south, is the **Národný cintorín**, which, like the Slavín cemetery in Prague, contains the graves of most of the leading Slovaks of the národné obrodenie. It's nothing like as impressive as the Slavín, not least because of the subdued artistry of the headstones, as demanded by Lutheranism, the religion of many of those buried here. Using the master plan near the entrance, you can find the graves of Andrej Kmeť, Janko Kráľ, Janko Jesenský, Martin Benko, Andrej Švehla, Karol Kuzmány and Svet Hurban-Vajanovský, all leading figures in the Slovak society of the nineteenth century.

The southern ridge of the Malá Fatra (see opposite), the **Lúčanská Fatra**, rises swiftly and dramatically from Martin's westernmost suburbs, making the town a suitable base for ascending the five big, bare peaks of the southern Malá Fatra. If you're staying in town, you can take a chairlift (*lanovka*) from Podstráne, 3km west of town (bus #40 or #41), which deposits you just over 1km below the highest peak, **Veľká lúka** (1476m); on foot, it'll take nearly four hours. Ten kilometres north along the ridge are the ruins at Strečno (see p.521), about a two-hour walk. If you're camping at Vrútky, Martin's northernmost suburb, the nearest peak is the northernmost summit of **Minčol** (1364m).

Neither the old nor the new buildings of the **Matica slovenská**, founded in 1863, are anything to get excited about. The older of the two, on Oslobodi-teľov, has been nicely restored, and now serves as the **Slovenské národné literárne múzeum** (Slovak National Literary Museum; Tues–Sat 8am–4pm). The Matica's current home, which looks rather like a giant domestic radiator, is easily spotted to the north of the Slovak National Museum.

Perhaps the most rewarding place to visit, though, is the **folk skanzen** (Múzeum slovenskej dediny; May–Aug Tues–Sun 9am–6pm; Sept–Oct clos-es 5pm; Nov–April 10am–2pm with prior arrangement; ☎043/413 26 86), 2km south of town near the Jahodnícky háj (bus #11 or #41, then follow the signs through the apartment blocks and into the woods), which gives some idea of what Martin was like during the nineteenth century. It's also the biggest open-air museum in the country and contains buildings from all over Slovakia, even retaining a feeling of some authenticity with a section of shops and homes laid along a road, rather than randomly strewn about.

Practicalities

Only one or two daily trains from Bratislava pass through Martin's small sta-tion; most use the train station at **Vrútky**, in a working-class suburb 7km north (numerous buses go from here to the centre of Martin), while local trains to Žilina and Zvolen use both stations. The helpful **tourist office** (Mon–Fri 9am–5pm; ☎043/423 87 76 ⊛www.turiecinfo.sk) occupies the new, purpose-built glass edifice in the middle of Divadelné námestie. **Accommodation** is not a problem, with at least a couple of cheaper options to challenge the comfortable *Turiec* (☎043/422 10 17–9, ⊛www.hotel-turiec .sk; ❹), near the town's Catholic church at A. Sokolíka 2, and the pyramidical *Grandis* (☎043/422 00 15–6, ⊛www.grandis.sk; ❼), 3km west of the centre (bus #40 or #41), which boasts a wealth of mod cons and is situated near the chairlift to Martinské hole, at the foot of Veľká lúka. The *Penzión Čierná pani*, Kuzmányho 24 (☎043/413 15 23, ⊛www.penzion-cierna-pani.sk; ❷), has modestly priced rooms and a popular restaurant, while the most central *Hotel Slovan* (☎043/413 55 32; ❷), on A. Kmeťa, occupies an ugly, dirty grey building, but has en-suite rooms with TV. The nearest **campsite** (open all year) is in the woods west of Vrútky. As for **food**, options are surprisingly limited and, apart from the restaurants in the above hotels, and the simply named *Pizza* restaurant, serving Slovak pizzas, on 29 augusta, there's virtually no choice in the centre.

The Malá Fatra

The **Malá Fatra** are the first real mountains on the road from Bratislava and are one of the most popular and accessible of the Slovak ranges. They are split in two by the sweeping meanderings of the Váh; the northern ridge is by far the more popular, boasting the highest peaks and the most spectacular valley, Vrátna dolina. The southern ridge, including the Lúčanská Fatra, is less geographically pronounced and drifts more gently southwestwards, but contains a couple of non-hiking attractions. Most people use **Žilina** as a base simply because it's on the main line from Bratislava, though in fact it's too far from the mountains to be really convenient. Accommodation in the area is now much easier to come by, but if you're serious about hiking, you'll solve a lot of problems by bringing your own tent.

Žilina

Throughout the summer season **ŽILINA** (Sillein/Zsolna) is awash with coach parties, school kids and backpackers, all heading for the mountains. Few bother to venture far from the bus and train stations, though the town itself has a pleasant, compact old quarter, originating from the fourteenth century when the town was colonized by German settlers. The whole place suffered badly during the Thirty Years' War and only really began to recover with the industrial development of last century. In October 1938, following the Munich Agreement ceding the Sudetenland to Hitler, the first Slovak government was formed in what became known as the Žilina Accord. It remains a bastion of

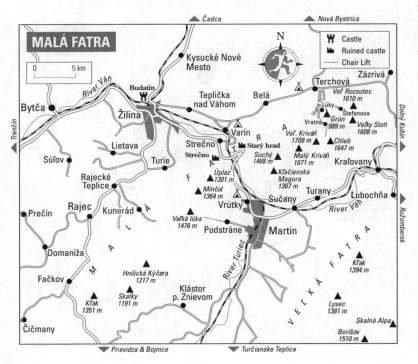

Slovak nationalism, with the chief of the Slovak National Party, Ján Slota, as its mayor and with the nation's highest percentage of votes for local-boy Vladimír Mečiar's HZDS party.

Arrival, accommodation and information

The **train station** is conveniently located ten minutes' walk northeast of the centre, along the pedestrianized Národná; the **bus station** is within an equal distance to the east of the centre (and only a five-minute walk south of the train station). Few people come to Žilina to sightsee in town, but a lot of people end up using it as an initial base – so many in fact that it may not be easy to get a bed in high season. The local **tourist office** (Mon–Fri 8.30am–5pm; ☎041/562 07 89, ⓦwww.selinan.sk), hidden off Mariánske námestie at Burianova medzierka 4, can organize private accommodation in town or in the mountains themselves (they charge 30Sk). For **Internet** access, there's the basement Internet café on Kálov, just off námestie Andreja Hlinku, behind Tesco.

The nicest **place to stay** is the plush *Astoria* (☎041/562 47 11, ⓦwww .astoria-zilina.sk; ❻), at the top of Národná by námestie Andreja Hlinku, followed by the *Hotel Grand*, (☎041/564 32 65, ⓦwww.hotelgrand.sk; ❹), just off Mariánske námestie at Sladkovičova 1, which has pleasant modern rooms, some

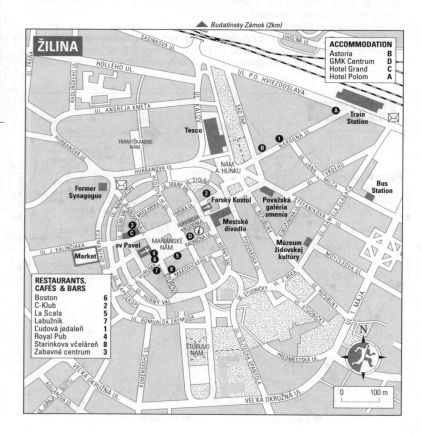

▲ Budatínsky Zámok (2km)

ŽILINA

ACCOMMODATION
Astoria   B
GMK Centrum   D
Hotel Grand   C
Hotel Polom   A

Train Station

Tesco

Bus Station

Former Synagogue

Farský Kostol

Považská galéria umenia

Mestské divadlo

sv Pavel

Market

Múzeum židovskej kultúry

RESTAURANTS, CAFÉS & BARS
Boston   6
C-Klub   2
La Scala   5
Labužník   7
Ľudová jedaleň   1
Royal Pub   4
Starinkova včeláreň   8
Zabavné centrum   3

N

0   100 m

with views of the square (if you crane your neck). The best budget option is *GMK Centrum* (☏041/562 21 36; ❷), an office/restaurant/pension through a passage at Mariánske námestie 3; it's worth booking ahead as there are only three rooms. Otherwise, try the Art Nouveau *Hotel Polom* (☏041/562 11 52; ❷–❸), opposite the train station, which has rooms with a choice of en-suite or shared facilities.

The Town

Between the stations and the old town to the west is the pedestrianized street of **Národná**, the town's main shopping drag, which ends at the amorphous expanse of **námestie Andreja Hlinku**, featuring a larger-than-life statue of the cleric, known affectionately as *otec národa* (father of the nation). Statues of saints Cyril and Methodius look down from the Farské schody, the steps that lead up to the back end of the **Farský kostol** (parish church), with its freestanding belfry. Beside the Farské schody, and contemporary with them, is the **Mestské divadlo**, with its unusually tall Moorish arches, built during World War II.

A couple of minor sights lie just off the square to the southeast. First off, on Štefánikova, there's the main branch of the **Považská galéria umenia** (Tues–Fri 9am–5pm, Sat & Sun 10am–5pm), which puts on temporary art exhibitions; in addition, there's a small display on Žilina's Jewish community in the **Múzeum židovskej kultúry** (Fri 3.30–5.30pm, Sun 2.30–5.30pm) on ulica Daniela Dlabača. Žilina had a large Jewish community of around 3500 before the war – as attested by the imposing 1930s functionalist synagogue (now a cinema) at the far end of Sladkovičova – though of the 700 who survived the Holocaust only a handful remain.

Beyond the Farský kostol is the staré mesto (old town), centred on **Mariánske námestie**, a very pleasant, partly arcaded square overlooked by the big ochre frontage of the Jesuit church of sv Pavel. There are several good cafés from which to admire the square's very Germanic, neat proportions and its fountain fringed by lofty lime trees. The backstreets are also great to wander round, but the staré mesto won't detain you long.

Žilina's most impressive sight, the attractive **Budatínsky zámok** (Tues–Sun 8am–4pm; June–Aug Mon 8am–4pm, Tues–Sun 8am–5pm; ⓦ www.povazske .muzeum.sk), is actually 2km north of the town centre, in the suburbs on the right bank of the Váh (bus #21, #22, #25 or #30). A characteristically hybrid Slovak affair, whitewashed over in the 1960s and now crumbling around the edges, the zámok now houses several exhibitions – a faintly hysterical Communist-era English commentary will guide you around the display of carved wooden furniture, and you can also climb the original thirteenth-century tower, but the most interesting section is the exhibition of *Slovenské drotárstvo* (wire sculptures and utensils) once sold by the region's tinkers (who made up an estimated two-thirds of the local population at the beginning of the nineteenth century).

Eating, drinking and nightlife

For **eating out**, there are a handful of outdoor cafés and cellar wine bars on Mariánske námestie, of which *La Scala*, a designer wine cellar on the south side is probably the most likeable. For Turkish (and Slovak) specialities, head for the *Labužník*, on Vuruma, just off the southern corner of the square. Other, cheaper options include the *C-Klub* (closed Sun), a *palačinkáreň* (pancake house) by the Farský kostol, serving sweet and savoury crepes, or the decent self-service *Ľudová jedáleň*, located upstairs on Národná, en route to the train station.

If you're here for the **nightlife** and want to drink with the locals, cut a path to the *Royal Pub*, by the Jesuit church, which throbs until late, play billiards at the *Zabavné centrum* on Sladkovičova, or head for the *Boston*, to the left of the *Royal*, with live music in the evening. There's a chilled-out *Čajovna* called *Starinkova včeláreň* on the first floor of Štúrova 1.

Terchová and the Vrátna dolina

Twenty-five kilometres east of Žilina, at the mouth of the Vrátna dolina, **TERCHOVÁ** is a vast, straggling village, famous for being the birthplace of the Slovak folk hero **Juraj Jánošík** (see below). A small **museum** (May–Aug daily 8.30am–6pm; out of season Tues–Thurs 9am–3.30pm, Fri–Sun 9am–4pm) draws links between Jánošík and the partisans who took part in the 1944 Slovak National Uprising, and though all the texts are in Slovak, there's enough local folk art to keep you going, not to mention Jánošík's celebrated brass-studded belt (thought to bring good luck) and jaunty hat. On the low hill overlooking the town stands a giant futuristic aluminium statue of the man himself, one of the many mass-produced in the region. Late July and early August are good times to visit the village, during the international **folk festival** of music and dance – the valley is said to produce a higher than normal concentration of musicians. The **tourist office** (Mon–Fri 8am–4pm, Sat 9am–1pm; Ⓦwww .terchova.sk, www.ztt.sk) is next door to the museum. There are several **hotels** and pensions, including the central *Penzión Covera* (Ⓣ041/569 52 63; ❷) above a bar; the new, more upscale *Hotel Gavurky* (Ⓣ041/500 35 02, Ⓦwww .hotelgavurky.sk; ❸), with a restaurant and sauna, at the eastern end of Terchová; and the *Hotel Gold* (Ⓣ041/599 31 09, Ⓦwww.hotel-terchova.sk; ❸), which sits overlooking the Jánošík statue, a short distance up the Vratna dolina road. There's also a good, small, riverside **campsite** (May to mid-Oct), just 3km west

---

Juraj Jánošík

Juraj Jánošík (1688–1713) is the most famous of the many Robin Hood figures who form an integral part of the songs and folklore of the Slovak mountain regions. Most originate from the turn of the seventeenth century when the central authority of the Habsburgs was at a weak point, worn down by the threat of Turkish invasion. Like many of the rural youth of his generation, Jánošík joined up with the anti-Habsburg army of the Hungarian rebel Ferenc Rákóczi II in 1703. When they were finally defeated by the imperial forces at Trenčín in 1711, large numbers fled into the hills to continue the fight from there. Jánošík, however, opted for the priesthood and left for Kežmarok to complete his religious training. While he was away, his mother fell ill and died, and his father – who had absconded from work in order to build a coffin for her burial – was given a hundred lashes, which proved fatal for the old man. With both parents dead, Jánošík finally took to the hills and gathered round him the obligatory band of merry men, indulging in the usual deeds of wealth redistribution.

Sadly – though this, too, is typical of Slovak folklore – the crucial difference between Robin Hood and characters like Jánošík is that the latter nearly always come to a sticky end. In March 1713 Jánošík was captured after the landlord of the pub he was drinking in betrayed him, and an old woman threw peas under his feet to make him fall over. The lords of Liptov cruelly tortured Jánošík in an attempt to extract a confession, and sentenced him to death in the central square of Liptovský Svätý Mikuláš, where he was hung by the ribcage. It's impossible to overestimate the importance of Jánošík to both the oral and written Slovak literary tradition, and more poems, novels and plays have been inspired by his exploits than by any other episode in Slovak history – except perhaps the Slovak National Uprising (see p.504).

Most people head for the **chairlift** at Vrátna (out of action at time of writing), which takes you to Snilovské sedlo, a high saddle between **Veľký Kriváň** (1709m), the highest peak, and **Chleb** (1647m). The views are fantastic from either of the summits, but head away from the chairlift to lose the overwhelming coachloads of day-trippers; you can walk in either direction along the ridge and then head back down to Vrátna. If you're out for the whole day from Žilina, you could descend Chleb's southern face, tracking the blue-marked path that runs via the Šútovský vodopád (waterfall) to Šútovo, fifty minutes by train from Žilina. Otherwise it's over six hours across the peaks to Strečno (see below).

A pleasant alternative to the above is to turn left at the Vrátna dolina fork for Štefanová (2km), in the shadow of **Veľký Rozsutec** (1610m), whose sharply pointed rocky summit is arguably the most satisfying to climb. Follow the yellow-marked path to Podžiar, where you should change to the blue path up **Horné Diery**, an idyllic wet ravine that has to be traversed using ladders and steps. The ravine ends at sedlo Medzirozsutec, the saddle between Malý and Veľký Rozsutec. The ascent takes around four hours, and the descent via sedlo Medziholie about half that. The telephone number for the local mountain **rescue service** (Horská služba) is: ☎041/569 52 32, or ☎18 300 (from a mobile).

of the village in Nižné Kamence. For **food**, try the *Pizzeria U Adama*, just west of the centre of Terchová, a typical Slovak cottage with a wood-burning oven. Another good option, worth considering if you have your own transport, is the *Chata pod Malým Rozsutcom* (☎0908/785 092; ❸), a wooden chalet with a lovely restaurant and simple rooms upstairs, situated 3km east of Terchová, on the road to Dolný Kubín.

The Vrátna dolina

The Vrátna dolina itself actually owes its winsome reputation to the gritty cliffs of **Tiesňavy**, the sharp-edged defile that acts as the gateway to the valley. A fair few buses go this way from Terchová, as well as several daily from Žilina, or you can take the Kofola Expres – a tourist **mini-train** plying between the *Hotel Gold* and the southern end of the valley (early July to mid-Sept daily 8am–8pm on the every other hour). Alternatively, it's a gentle twenty-minute walk. After such a dramatic overture, the valley itself is surprisingly sheltered and calm. The road continues a short way south through Lúky, a fairly major ski resort in winter, set against a scenic backdrop of thickly forested hilltops, and on to a smaller resort at Vratná. You can rent skis and bikes at a rental office along this road, some 2km short of Vratná.

There's a wide choice of **accommodation** throughout the valley, cheapest of which is the hostel-style *Chata Vrátna* (☎041/569 57 39, ⓦwww.vratna. sk; ❶) by the inactive chairlift in Vratná, but you may do better in Štefanová, a small village at the end of a spur road heading east just before Lúky. Two good-value pensions here are the *Starek* (☎041/569 53 59, ⓦwww.vratna.com /penzionstarek; ❷) and the *Chata pod Skalným mestom* (☎041/569 53 63; ❷), both clean and cosy, and both with **restaurants**.

Strečno and Starý hrad

Impressive in scale and setting, the fourteenth-century ruins of **Hrad Strečno** (May–Sept Mon 8am–3pm; Tues–Sun 9am–5pm; Oct Mon–Fri 7.30am–2.30pm, Sat & Sun 9am–4pm; Nov–April daily 7am–2pm) crown the summit of a two-hundred-foot cliff 11km east of Žilina, commanding the entrance to the Váh valley as it squeezes through the Malá Fatra to Martin. You can climb up to the castle from the nearby train station, but the 45-minute guided tour round the cleaned-up insides and dull exhibition is worth skipping. More interesting is the nearby monument to the **French partisans**, escaped POWs from a camp in Hungary, who took part in the 1944 Slovak National Uprising.

There's a fairly basic **campsite** (May to mid-Oct), with its own swimming pool, in Varín, on the other side of the river, near the road to Terchová: if you don't have your own transport, it's actually a more convenient base for ascending the northern peaks of the Malá Fatra than Vrátna dolina. Alternatively, you could try the decent *Penzión Irenka* (☏041/569 76 73; ❷), with its own restaurant, in the village of Strečno below the hrad, or the *Chata pod Suchým* hostel (☏041/569 73 94; ❶), a two-kilometre walk from Strečno along the red-marked path via the Váh gorge's other ruined castle, **Starý hrad** – it's over 1000m above sea level, so expect a chilly night.

South of Žilina

Just south of Žilina, along route 64 or the railway, the cement works of Lietavská Lúčka coat the valley with a grey-white dust, before a bend in the River Rajčanka brings you into the verdant wooded spa town of **RAJECKÉ TEPLICE** (Ⓦwww.spa.sk). The town centre revolves around a small artificial lake, where you can hire boats, or tuck into some fish dishes at the *Rybárska bašta*, and the monstrous *Veľká Fatra* hotel (☏041/549 37 27; ❹) on Osloboditeľov, which has a multicoloured overhead walkway connecting it to the thermal **swimming pools** (38°C; open to the public Tues–Sat 1–9pm, Sun 10am–9pm) across the main road. For **accommodation**, however, you should plump for the *Hotel Talisman* (☏041/549 32 94, Ⓦwww.talisman.miesto.sk; ❸), a chalet-style wine bar, restaurant and pension in a quieter part of the spa on ulica R. Suľovského. Otherwise, there's a small **tourist office** (daily 9.30–11.30am & 12.30–6.30pm; Ⓦwww. rajecketeplice.info) at Osloboditeľov 90, which helps with accommodation. The nearest **campsite** is the primitive but beautifully situated *Slnečné skály* campsite (May–Sept), 3km back down the valley (alight at Poluvsie station).

Rajecké Teplice is a convenient base for a series of day **hikes** in the surrounding hills. The most obvious is across the valley via **Zámok Kunerad**, an early twentieth-century chateau, and up Veľká lúka (1476m), which overlooks Martin and the Turiec valley. The blue-marked path is an alternative route back to the spa, and the whole trip is a full day's walk. A more leisurely afternoon's hike north along the green-marked path from the station takes you to the ruined castle of **Lietava**, a shade less spectacular than Strečno but still an impressive pile, some 100m above the village of the same name. The most popular destination, though, is across the hills to the **Súľovské skály** (3hr on the yellow-marked path via Zbyňov), a rock "city" made up of contorted slabs of limestone, with the ruined castle of Súľov at its centre. For a wet-weather destination, pay a visit to the **Slovenský betlehem** (daily 9am–noon & 1–6pm; free), a vast nativity scene carved out of wood and dotted with automated figures, housed in a purpose-built building next door to the church in the village of Rajecká Lesná, 10km or so south of Rajecké Teplice.

Čičmany

ČIČMANY is probably one of the most hyped villages in the whole of Slovakia, and with good reason. Lying in a wide, gently undulating valley, it's a Slovak village *par excellence*: a cluster of typical wooden cottages-cum-farms haphazardly strewn about the banks of the River Rajčanka, which at this point is little more than a mountain stream. What makes Čičmany special, though, is the unique local tradition of **house-painting**, based on the patterns of the locally produced lacework. Each cottage is smothered in a simple, largely abstract, decorative mantle of white snowflakes, flowers and crisscrosses, and the only signs of modernity are electricity, telephone cables and the odd tractor. Only occasional tour groups break the spell, but even they don't stay longer than it takes

△ Čičmany

to visit the branch of the **Považské múzeum** (Tues–Sun 8am–4pm), located at no. 42 and in the opposite Radenov dom. The disadvantage of Čičmany's isolated position is its inaccessibility; only infrequent **buses** cover the 38km from Žilina, and though you could try hitching, the traffic is light, especially on the last 7km from route 64. Somewhat remarkably, should you make it out here, there are a few **places to stay** – try the shady, arcaded *Kaštieľ* (℡041/549 21 19, Ⓦwww.kastiel.cicmany.szm.sk; ➋), or the new, wooden *Penzión Javorina* (℡041/549 21 09, Ⓕ041/542 21 92; ➋), 50m up the road; both have their own simple restaurants that are open to non-guests.

Prievidza and Bojnice

Continuing south for another 30km along route 64 will eventually bring you to **PRIEVIDZA**, an unlovely town after the joys of Čičmany, but an essential stop for those travelling by public transport. The only reason to pause at all in the town itself is to visit the eighteenth-century Piarist church situated between the bus and train stations and the town centre, which contains a spectacular array of trompe l'oeil Baroque ceiling paintings.

Most people, though, are simply passing through en route to the very photogenic **Bojnický zámok** (May–Sept Tues–Sun 9am–5pm; July–Aug also Mon; Oct–April 10am–3pm; 130Sk), which stands on the slopes of a woody hill to the west of Prievidza, in neighbouring **BOJNICE**. From afar, it is indeed an arresting sight, a slice of French pastiche straight out of the Loire Valley, with its conical Gothic turrets and crenellations. In actual fact, what you see now is the result of Romantic reconstructions wrought by the last aristocratic owner, Count Ján Pálffy, who inherited the family pile in 1852. Such pseudo-Gothic splendour may not be everyone's cup of tea, but it sure pulls in the crowds; with some 350,000 visitors a year, this is by far the most popular castle in Slovakia. Ghost sightings are frequent, according to the chateau's efficient PR department, but not half as exciting as the unidentified goo that's been oozing out of Count Pálffy's neo-Romanesque sarcophagus in the castle chapel's crypt over the last few years. Those with children may like to know that Slovakia's largest and oldest **zoo** (daily: March–April & Sept–Oct 7am–5pm; May 7am–6pm; June–Aug 7am–7pm; Nov–Feb 7am–3.30pm) is situated beside the chateau.

To get to the chateau from Prievidza bus and train stations, take bus #3 or walk the 2.5km. Since Bojnice is not really a viable day-trip from Žilina, you may find yourself spending the night here. If so, your best bet is to head for the **tourist office** (Mon–Sat 8am–noon & 12.30–4pm; Ⓦwww.bojnice.net), on the oblong Hurbanovo námestie, under the castle. Of the local places to **stay** the best is the *Hotel Pod Zámkom* (℡046/518 51 00, Ⓔrecephotel@stonline .sk; ➍), at the end of the square, opposite the castle, which has modern rooms, sauna and gym. Other options include the *Penzión Pod Zámkom* (℡046/541 29 63; ➋), Hurbanovo námestie 13, and the *Hotel Lipa* (℡046/543 03 08, Ⓦwww .hotel-lipa-bojnice.sk; ➋), Sládkovičova 14, both with restaurants. There's also a **campsite** (mid-May to Sept), with nearby swimming pool, in the woods behind the chateau; take the road to Nitrianske Rudno.

The Kysuce region

Thirty kilometres north of Terchová, the little-known and little-visited **Kysuce region**, rubbing up against the Polish border and wedged in between the Malá Fatra and Orava regions to its south and east, respectively, is a tranquil area of rolling hills and small farming and logging towns. To maintain its withering folk traditions, the local authorities have established the open-air **Múzeum kysuckej dediny** (Kysuce folk museum; May–Oct Tues–Sun 9.15am–3.45pm every 45min, Sun also 4.30pm; Ⓦ www.kysucke.muzeum.sk) in the hamlet of Vychylovka, near Nová Bystrica, which is well worth a visit if you're in the area. Timbered homes, barns, a functioning mill and a whitewashed church, most dating from the nineteenth and early twentieth centuries, were all rescued from imminent submergence when the nearby dam was built, and have been carefully relocated in a shady green glen. A **narrow-gauge forest railway** (May–Oct Tues–Fri 9.15am–3.30pm about every hour, Sat & Sun till 5pm; minimum 10 persons), originally built in the early twentieth century to carry logs out of the hills, now runs through the *skanzen* and a few kilometres into the hills around. Try to visit at the weekend when the original steam engine pulls the single open carriage.

Transport to the region is very difficult – only the occasional bus makes it here from Čadca, 25km northwest (alight at Vychylovka-Riečky) – and there is no accommodation anywhere in the vicinity. You can, however, get simple *bryndzové halušky* and cabbage soup at the *Krčma z Korne*, one of the folk structures. If you're driving, you can continue on to the Orava region by taking the tiny, unsealed mountain road behind the *skanzen*, skirting within 1km of Poland, before linking up with route 520 at Oravská Lesná. Route 520 is permanently closed between Nová Bystrica and Oravská Lesná, even though maps show it goes through.

The Orava region

Despite its wonderful mountainous backdrop and winding river valley, the **Orava region** (Ⓦ www.orava.sk), northeast of the Malá Fatra and flush with the Polish border, is generally fairly bleak. For centuries it remained an impoverished rural backwater on the main road to Poland, so poor that when the Lithuanian army marched through in 1683 en route to Vienna, they burned most of the villages to the ground (including the former capital of Veličná) in disgust at the lack of provisions. Emigration to America was widespread during the late nineteenth and early twentieth centuries, and after World War II, industry was hastily foisted onto the region in an attempt to save it from extinction. As a consequence, the towns are short on excitement and long on eyesores, but the artificial **Lake Orava** to the north is recommended for relatively clean swimming, and the **Western Tatras** provide a uniquely unspoilt alpine experience.

Accommodation can be a problem, so it's worth booking ahead at least a couple of days in advance from Dolný Kubín, the largest town in the region. **Transport** relies heavily on the branch line that stretches the length of the Orava valley from Kraľovany on the Váh to Trstená by the Polish border; elsewhere you're dependent on local buses or hitching.

Dolný Kubín and around

The Orava's administrative capital, **DOLNÝ KUBÍN**, is typical of the region, its faultlessly pretty, hilly locale lending a kind of surreal beauty to the gleaming white high-rise *paneláky* that house most of the town's residents. Despite its unattractive suburbs, the town makes for a convenient base and stopover, and its main square, **Hviezdoslavovo námestie**, is moderately pretty. Here, behind a statue of the square's eponymous poet, you'll find the town's **Oravské múzeum** (April–Sept Tues–Sat 8am–4pm, Sun 10am–5pm; Oct–March Mon–Fri 8am–4pm), dedicated to the mild-mannered "father of Slovak poetry", Pavol Országh Hviezdoslav (1849–1921), who was born in neighbouring Vyšný Kubín. Next door to the museum is the town's blue-and-white Art Deco former **synagogue**, converted to the Choč cinema during the 1970s, with a plaque dedicated to the town's Holocaust victims.

A few doors down, the **Oravská galéria** (Tues–Sun 10am–5pm; Ⓦwww .oravskagaleria.sk) is a surprisingly large gallery of art from the Orava region, located in a spiffed-up Baroque palace and well worth a visit. Chronologically, the gallery starts on the second floor, with several rooms of medieval icons, statuary and some very basic portraits of local noblemen. The focus then leaps to the twentieth century, with mostly local scenes of farmers, shepherds and the Orava hills painted by, among others, Miloš Alexander Bazovský and Mikuláš Galanda. The back rooms of the gallery contain some cutting-edge sculpture – look for Jozef Jankovič's gruesome *Red Wedge* – while the avant-garde theme continues upstairs, with 1980s and 1990s Slovak Pop Art predominating. Back down on the ground floor are some more gentle landscape paintings by Maria Medvecká, who hailed from nearby Tvrdošín (see p.528) and had a hand in the establishment of this gallery in 1965. Also down here are some beautiful examples of painted glass and Romantic-era folk sculpture.

Dolný Kubín is probably the best place to stay in the region, though you can book **accommodation** for here or for further up the valley, through the local **tourist office** (Mon–Fri 9am–5pm; ℡043/586 75 82 or 043/16186), just off the southwest corner of Hviezdoslavovo námestie. The *Marína* (℡043/586 43 51, Ⓦwww.marina.sk; ❸), a fine little pension across from the Oravská galéria, is without doubt the best option, as it offers cosy en-suite doubles with cable TV, a guarded car park and a good location on the main square. Otherwise, you've a choice between the Communist-era *Severan* (℡043/586 46 66; ❷), just off the main square, or the nearby *Hotel Park* (℡043/586 41 10; ❹), a reliably comfortable option, with satellite TV and indoor swimming. There's also a **campsite**, the *Gäceľ* (open all year), with bungalows, 1km or so west beside the Orava river. For food, the excellent **restaurant** underneath the *Marína* (open till midnight) serves hearty Slovak dishes and has a summer terrace on the square.

Istebné and Leštiny

The giant alloy plant and its attendant quarry at **ISTEBNÉ**, 6km west of Dolný Kubín, appear to offer little respite from the valley's depressing industry. Until a few years ago, the level of dust in the atmosphere was intolerable, regularly blackening the skies over the valley at midday. Only in the mid-1980s, when the local population threatened to move out en masse, were dust separators finally fitted onto the factory chimneys.

Miraculously, the pre-industrial settlement still exists, tucked into the hills to the north, fifteen minutes' walk from the bus and train stations. Among its few remaining wooden buildings, it boasts one of the country's four surviving **wooden Lutheran churches**, built in 1686 on slightly raised ground above the village, with the support of the Swedish king; a separate belfry was added in 1731. Inside, it's richly and prettily decorated with folk painting, especially around the pulpit and on the gallery parapet, which features naive eighteenth-century paintings of the apostles.

In the other direction in **LEŠTINY**, some 8km southeast of Dolný Kubín, there's another wooden Lutheran church, dating back to the late seventeenth century. It's a simple, barn-like structure from the outside, but the interior walls and ceiling are covered in eighteenth-century folk paintings; once again, the gallery, and even the staircase leading to the pulpit, feature naive religious paintings from this period.

Oravský hrad

Eleven kilometres upstream from Dolný Kubín and accessible by train, **Oravský hrad** (May & Sept daily 8.30am–5pm; June daily 8.30am–5.30pm; July–Aug daily 8.30am–6pm; Oct daily 8.30am–4pm; Nov–April Tues–Sun 10am–3pm; 100Sk; ⓦwww.oravamuzeum.sk) is one of Slovakia's truly spectacular clifftop sights. Perched like an eyrie more than 100m above the village of **Oravský Podzámok** (literally "Below Orava Castle"), it's an impressive testament to the region's feudal past. Whoever occupied Orava Castle held sway over the entire region and made a fortune taxing the peasants and milking the trade into Poland. You may want to ask about the availability of English-speaking guides before signing up for a tour – it may take over an hour to get one. Inside, you'll be treated to hearty dollops of folk art, natural history, instruments of feudal justice and Romantic wood-panelled interiors courtesy of the last owners, the ubiquitous Pálffy family.

The village offers a few **accommodation** options, including the *Hotel Oravan* (☎043/589 31 15, ⓦwww.hoteloravan.sk; ❷) with a large, decent restaurant, on the main road.

Podbiel and Zuberec

PODBIEL, thirty minutes by train up the valley from Oravský Podzámok, marks the entrance to the Studená dolina, the valley leading eastwards into the Western Tatras impressively arrayed on the horizon. Many of the village's collection of traditional wooden cottages have been converted into tourist **accommodation**. Ask at no. 71, on the road to Zuberec, during office hours on the off chance, but it's better to try and book in advance through the tourist office in Dolný Kubín or Zuberec; another alternative is the *Tatria penzion* (☎0903/555 212, ⓦwww.tatria.com; ❷), which also rents out *chaty*. In any case, the only reason to stop at Podbiel is to hitch, walk or catch one of the very few local buses going east up Studená dolina.

Fifteen kilometres east up the Studená dolina, **ZUBEREC** is only worth pausing in if you want to book accommodation through its **tourist office** (Mon–Fri 7.30–10.30am & 11.30am–4pm, Sat 8am–noon; ☎043/532 07 77; ⓦwww.zuberec.sk). Three kilometres or so beyond lies the **Múzeum oravskej dediny** (June & Sept daily 8am–5pm; July–Aug daily 8am–6pm; Oct–May Tues–Sun 10am–3.30pm), a *skanzen* of about twenty traditional wooden buildings from the surrounding area, including a fifteenth-century **wooden Catholic church** from Zábrež, one of the few to escape the pillaging of the local Protestants. Originally built in the fifteenth century, its simple exterior gives no indication of the intricate seventeenth-century folk panel paintings inside, at their best around the main altar. There's an English-language commentary if you want to go round on your own, but you'll get to see more of the interior with a guide.

The Western Tatras (Západné Tatry)

With the High Tatras reaching saturation point during most of the climbing season, the **Western Tatras** (Západné Tatry) are a refreshingly undeveloped alternative. They boast the same dog-tooth peaks and hand-mirror lakes, but with half the number of visitors. The best base is 3km beyond the folk *skanzen*, where you'll find the *Primula* **hotel** (☎043/539 50 01, ⓦwww.primula.sk; ❷), which also functions as a hostel, and the chalet-style *Chata Zverovka* (☎043/539 51 06, ⓦwww.chatazverovka.sk; ❷).

Unless you've pre-booked from Dolný Kubín, however, you may have problems finding a room, though there is some private accommodation and plenty of discreet spots in which to pitch your tent. Alternatively, you could make your base further north, at Oravice, the only official **campsite** (open all year; ⓦwww.oravice.sk) on this side of the mountains, with an adjacent swimming pool. The main problem is getting to Oravice, which either means catching one of the few buses from Trstená (the last station on the Orava rail line) or walking 7km from the Orava folk skanzen. Whatever you do, don't let the logistics get you down – you'll encounter similar problems in the other parts of the Tatras. More importantly, get hold of a good VKÚ Harmanec hiking map from the tourist office in Zuberec, plus the requisite camping gear, and you'll have a smooth trip. Don't, however, undertake any mountain hiking if you've no experience, and always get a weather check before you start on a long walk that goes above 1500m. For more **information** on hiking and climbing, and important **safety tips**, see p.542.

Around Lake Orava

Back at Podbiel, the rail line continues to the village of **TVRDOŠÍN**, which boasts a **wooden church** (July–Sept daily 9am–3pm) containing some fantastic primitive altar paintings, all dating from the fifteenth century. The last stop on the line is **TRSTENÁ**, 6km from the Polish border, which has several **accommodation** options: the *Skalka* (☎043/539 27 58, ℱ043/539 27 86; ❸) is on the main square, as is the elegant, Art Nouveau *Roháč* (☎043/532 49 61, ⓦwww.hotelrohac.sk; ❸). If you're moving on to Poland, there's enough traffic to make hitching feasible.

Hiking in the Western Tatras

From **Oravice**, two main trails head south 6km to the Polish border, of which the blue-marked one is the gentler. Once you reach the border, at the Bobrovecké sedlo, the blue-marked path will take you onto the ridge between the two countries and up to **Volovec** (2063m) and **Ostrý Roháč** (2084m), 1km from the border. It could easily take four hours to reach the more spectacular scenery around Volovec, making a return trip a full day's hike. If you're carrying a pack, it's possible to drop down onto the blue-marked path to the twin lakes of the Jamnicke plesá and then continue for 8km to the beautifully peaceful Račková dolina **campsite** (May–Oct) or a little further to the *Esperanto* **hotel** in Pribylina (☎044/528 06 40; ❷); this is probably the quickest way to approach the High Tatras from the Orava region. If you do make it to Pribylina, take a turn around the *skanzen* behind the hotel (May–June daily 9am–4.30pm; July to mid-Sept daily 9am–6.30pm; mid-Sept to Oct daily 9am–4pm; Nov–April Mon–Fri 9am–3.30pm; 80Sk).

From the **Roháčska dolina**, everything happens much more quickly. As you head down the valley the brooding grey peaks begin to gather round and by the end of the road (8km from the *skanzen*; 3km from the final car park) it's only a steep 1.5-kilometre walk on the green path to the still, glacial waters of the **Roháčske plesá**, hemmed in by the Tatras' steep, scree-ridden slopes. A punishing 2.5km (reckon on about 2hr) along the blue path leads to the Smutne sedlo (Sad saddle – sad because it's the mountain's cold north face), which lies on the main Roháč ridge. Ostrý Roháč is less than an hour to the east and **Baníkov** (2178m) the same distance west, but the king of the lot is **Baranec** (2184m), a good two hours' ridge walk to the south.

What was once the Orava plain became **Lake Orava** in 1954 when five villages were submerged by the damming of the river. The wooded western shore has a fair smattering of *chata* settlements and two **campsites**: *Jami* (May to mid-Sept) and *Slanická osada* (mid-June to mid-Sept). One of the lost villages, **SLANICA**, was the birthplace of an early pioneer of the Slovak language, the Catholic priest Anton Bernolák (1762–1813). Hidden in the trees, on Slanícky ostrov, is the village's only surviving building, a twin-domed **church of sv Kríž** (June–Sept 9am–5pm) with an attractive Neoclassical loggia set into its facade, now a museum of folk art and ceramics as well as a memorial to Bernolák. To reach the island, take the hourly **boat** from the pier next to the *Hotel Goral* (☎ & ℱ043/552 22 69; ➊), at Oravská priehrada 308, or from **NÁMESTOVO**, the big new town to the far west of the lake (and thankfully out of sight from the main recreational area). Standard Slovak food can be had at the *Šalaš*, a typical **pub** right near the Slanická osada campsite.

The Liptov region

The **Liptov region** (ⓦwww.liptov.sk), to the south of the Orava region and the Western Tatras, offers a similar cocktail of traditional Slovak villages and depressed industrial towns against a backdrop of spectacular mountains. **Ružomberok**, the first town you come to, at another T-junction on the River Váh, has very little to offer except easy access to the surrounding peaks. East of Ružomberok, the Váh valley widens into a vast, partially flooded plain, whose main town, **Liptovský Mikuláš**, is similarly uninspiring, but the best placed for exploring the Low Tatras.

As in the Orava, the traditional way of life in these parts has disappeared over the last two generations. But while few mourn the demise of subsistence farming, more lament the fact that it was destroyed by forced collectivization and industrialization. Some things survive – the patchwork fields and terraces and the long timbered cottages – but give it a few more decades and the songs, dances and costumes will be of historical and folkloristic interest only.

Ružomberok and around

RUŽOMBEROK (Rosenberg), like so many big towns on the Váh, has more than its fair share of industrial suburbs and ungainly high-rise estates, not to mention a persistent smell of synthetic fabrics that's enough to put most people off. The place to head for is the church of **sv Ondrej**, pleasantly aloof from the rest of town up the covered stairway, the Tmavé schody (Dark steps). Before the war, the local priest was **Andrej Hlinka** (see p.531), spiritual leader of Slovak separatism, *persona non grata* under the Communists but now fully rehabilitated. The church, on raised ground in the centre of town, stands on a square now named after him and sporting a statue of the cleric; on the south side of the church is his mausoleum. On one corner of the square is another curiosity – a monument in honour of the "Scotus Viator", Scottish academic **R.W. Seton–Watson** (1879–1951), "for defending the Slovak nation", erected in 1937 and miraculously still standing.

To the west of the church, the square stretches along a lovely avenue of lime trees, to the north of which (and below) lies námestie Š. N. Hýroša, home to the **Liptovské múzeum** (Mon–Fri 8am–4pm, Sat & Sun 10am–4pm; ⓦwww .liptovskemuzeum.sk). It's a substantial museum, with Jánošík's jaunty hat hidden amidst the usual stuffed animals on the first floor, and a whole section on Hlinka on the top floor, which is at pains to refute the charges of anti-Semitism regularly made against him. Behind the museum, you'll also find the **Galéria Ľudovíta Fullu** (Tues–Sun 9am–4pm), devoted to Ružomberok's talented painter of the same name.

Practicalities

The **train station** is east of the town centre, on the other side of the River Váh (bus #1, #3 or #4). The **tourist office** (April–Sept Mon–Fri 8am–5pm, Sat & Sun 9am–noon; Oct–March Mon–Fri 8am–5pm; ☎044/432 10 96, ⓦwww .kic-rk.sk), at Madačova 3, can assist with finding **accommodation**, most of which is way out of the centre (no bad thing). The most central place is the new, spacious *Hotel Kultúra* (☎044/431 31 11, ⓦwww.hotelkultura.sk; ❺), Bernoláka 1, with a gym and sauna, followed by the decent *Penzión Blesk* (☎044/432 17 50, ⓦwww.liptov.sk/penzionblesk; ❸), fifteen minutes' walk west of the centre at Vajanského 9, which has a pleasant restaurant. Another option is *Hotel Hrabovo* (☎044/432 87 44, ⓦwww.hotelhrabovo.sk; ❸), which has a grassy banked lake in which you can swim, but is only accessible via the infrequent bus #4. A cheap alternative is the *Ikar* (Bystrická cesta 21; ☎044/432 42 41; ❶), a good-value student hostel (open all year), situated half a kilometre from the main junction in town, towards Banská Bystrica.

For **food**, the best bet in the centre is probably the *Koruna*, Mostová 13, which has a courtyard and cellar dining. Another pleasant place is the small pizzeria *Bella*, near the tourist office.

Vlkolínec and Liptovská Štiavnica

One of the few redeeming features of Ružomberok is its proximity to the surrounding hills and villages. It's only a three-kilometre walk to the conic peak of **Sidorovo** (1099m) or 5km to **Malinné Brdo** (1209m) both of which are accessible via the cable car behind *Hotel Hrabovo* and guarantee extensive panoramas over the Váh and Revúca valleys.

Dropping down off the fell on the south side, head for the ribbon village of **VLKOLÍNEC**, on a windy hillside to the south (and thankfully out of view) of Ružomberok. The village is accessible by bus #4 from Ružomberok to Biely Potok, but the final two-kilometre walk from the bus stop is hard work and you might be better off approaching from Sidorovo or Malinné. This is one of the best environments in which to see Liptov wooden folk architecture, though as ever there's a note of melancholy about the place. It was badly damaged by the Nazis in September 1944 in the reprisals that followed the Slovak National Uprising, but those cottages that remain now form a protected natural *skanzen* of timber structures. One house, the Roľnícky dom, at no. 17, serves as a **museum** (mid-June to mid-Sept daily 9am–5pm; mid-Sept to mid-Oct Tues–Fri 9am–2.30pm, Sat & Sun 9am–4pm; mid-Oct to mid-June Tues–Fri 10am–2.30pm, Sat & Sun 10am–4pm), while another, by the car park, provides **information** (summer 9am–5pm; winter 10am–3pm) and offers guided **tours**.

With your own transport you could also explore nearby **LIPTOVSKÁ ŠTIAVNICA**, east of Ružomberok, whose whitewashed manor house or *kaštieľ* was converted into the local church in 1973 and is worth a look for its shingled onion dome and conical turrets. Before you leave, be sure to appreciate the rare surviving socialist mural entitled *The Battle for Love and Truth*.

Liptovský Mikuláš and around

As in Orava, the broad sweep of the main Liptov plain east of Ružomberok has been turned, for the most part, into a vast lake, whose beautiful sandy shoreline is set against the distant backdrop of the Western Tatras. On its easternmost edge

Born in the neighbouring village of Černová in 1864, **Andrej Hlinka** served most of his life as a Catholic pastor of Ružomberok. He became a national martyr in 1906 when he was arrested by the Hungarian authorities and sentenced to two years' imprisonment for "incitement against the Magyar nationality", topped up by another eighteen months for "further incitement" in his inflammatory farewell address to the local parishioners.

Although at the time still in prison, he was also viewed by the authorities as the prime mover behind the demonstration of October 27, 1907, popularly known as the **Černová Massacre**, the Bloody Sunday of Hungarian rule in Slovakia. When the local Slovaks protested against the consecration of their church by a strongly pro-Magyar priest, the Hungarian police opened fire on the crowd, killing fifteen people and wounding countless others.

Although Hlinka was among those Slovaks who approved of the establishment of Czechoslovakia, it wasn't long before Hlinka began campaigning for Slovak autonomy, and travelled to Paris on a false Polish passport to press the point at the Versailles Peace Conference. This earned him a spell in a Czechoslovak prison, from which he was only released (without charge) after being elected leader of the newly founded **Ľudová strana** (People's Party, or HSĽS), strongly Catholic, vehemently nationalistic and the largest single party in Slovakia between the wars. From 1925 to 1928, the HSĽS's electoral clout ensured it a place in the Czechoslovak coalition government. However, the party's nationalist policies were constantly at odds with its collaboration in the Prague-based government, and eventually, in 1928, when the editor of the HSĽS newspaper was convicted of treason for publishing a seditious article, Hlinka withdrew from the coalition, never to return.

Hlinka's death in August 1938 was the only thing that saved him from suffering the fate of his successor in the People's Party, Jozef Tiso, who went on to become the Slovak Quisling, as leader of the Nazi puppet government, and was eventually executed as a war criminal in 1947. Nevertheless, his name lived on posthumously in the regime's elite **Hlinka Guards**, the wartime Slovak equivalent of the SS. Under the Communists, Hlinka was deemed a clerico-fascist pure and simple, but since 1989, Slovak nationalists have conducted a concerted campaign to rehabilitate Hlinka, Tiso and company. Most Slovaks are very much in sympathy with such moves, and town councils across the republic have successfully renamed streets and squares after Hlinka, although when a plaque in honour of Tiso was unveiled in his home town of Bánovce nad Bebravou, above the Catholic teacher-training college he founded, it provoked outrage in many quarters and was eventually removed. Undeterred, the Slovak government went ahead and chose Hlinka as one of the national figures to grace the country's new currency.

9

THE MOUNTAIN REGIONS | The Liptov region

sits **LIPTOVSKÝ MIKULÁŠ**, which, like Martin and Ružomberok, played a major part in the Slovak national revival or *národné obrozenie*. Nowadays, it's really only worth coming here if you're intending to explore the Low Tatras.

The Town

You can get a taste of the literary milieu of nineteenth-century Mikuláš from the **Múzeum Janka Kráľa** (July & Aug daily 10am–5pm; Sept–June Tues–Fri 9am–4pm, Sat 10am–5pm), housed in a striking peach-coloured Baroque building on the town's large, pedestrianized main square, **Námestie osloboditeľov**. Local boy Kráľ was the foremost Slovak poet of the Romantic movement, "a lawyer who preferred the company of shepherds", or the Slovak Lord Byron as some would have it. Needless to say, he was a fervent nationalist, and only just escaped being executed for his beliefs in 1848. The museum also contains a reconstructed chamber, where Jánošík was tortured; his trial is thought to have taken place here, and he was sentenced to death in 1713 on the square outside, which currently sports a statue of the local artist Gašpar Belopotocký.

The first rumblings of the Slovak national revival in Liptovský Mikuláš occurred in the late 1820s when a Slovak reading room was founded, followed much later by the Tatrín literary society established by the Lutheran pastor Michael Miloslav Hodža, one of the leading lights of 1848. Hodža's house, by the Lutheran church east of the square, off ul. l. mája, at Tranovského 8, now hosts **Exhibition Tatrín** (Tues–Fri 8am–2pm), which touches on the events of May 10, 1848, when some of Mikuláš's leading Slovaks published the "Demands of the Slovak Nation" in response to the Hungarian uprising against the Habsburgs, then quickly fled the country to avoid arrest.

Opposite the Hodža's house, in a drab grey concrete building, is the much more palatable **Galéria P.M. Bohúňa** (daily 10am–5pm), whose spacious interior houses an impressive array of Slovak art. Baroque, Gothic and pre-nineteenth-century works fill the ground floor, but it's the nineteenth- and twentieth-century collection on the top floor that justifies a visit here. In addition to depictions of peasant life by the likes of Martin Benka and Gustáv Mallý, there's a whole room devoted to Bohuň's own portrait of wealthy local burghers. Bazovský and Janko Alexy weigh in with a couple of mystical, almost ghostly canvases, and there are even works by contemporary artists like Rudolf Fila.

In addition, nearby there's a rather uninspiring **Múzeum ochrany prírody a jaskyniarstva** (Museum of Nature Protection and Speleology; April–Oct Mon–Fri 8am–noon & 12.30–5pm, Sat & Sun 10am–5pm; Nov–March Mon–Fri 8am–noon & 12.30–4pm), which has a permanent display on caves and local nature (1.mája 38), as well as a collection of minerals (Školská 4).

Like many Slovak towns, Liptovský Mikuláš had a large Jewish community before World War II, established back in the early eighteenth century when Jews moved here from Holešov in Moravia. The vast majority of the 885 Jews who were transported to the camps never returned, and there is now a plaque – a hand scraping its nails down a Jewish gravestone – outside the town's huge Neoclassical **synagogue** (mid-June to mid-Sept daily 10am–5pm), which has been restored and stands west of the main square on Hollého. When there's no exhibition on, you'll need to get hold of the key from the Múzeum Janka Kráľa to inspect the starkly beautiful, empty interior.

In the suburb of **Palúdza**, a kilometre west of Mikuláš town centre (bus #2 or #7 from Štúrova), is the *kaštieľ*, in whose dungeon Jánošík was tortured before his public execution on Mikuláš's main square. The largest **wooden Protestant church** in Slovakia (daily: June–Sept 9am–5pm; Oct–May 9am–3pm) used to stand opposite, but was transferred in the 1970s to the edge of **LAZISKO**, 5km to the southwest, beyond the village of Svätý Kríž. Built in 1774 for the local Lutheran community without a single nail being used, it's a remarkable building, with a vaguely cruciform groundplan and a weatherboarded exterior. Inside, it seats over two thousand and looks almost new, with decoration only around the pulpit, gallery and organ gallery. There are up to ten buses a day from Mikuláš to Svätý Kríž.

Practicalities

The **bus** and **train stations** are next door to each other, a ten-minute walk north of the town centre. The efficient **tourist office** (mid-June to mid-Sept & mid-Dec to March Mon–Fri 8am–7pm, Sat 8am–2pm, Sun noon–6pm; April to mid-June & mid-Sept to mid-Dec Mon–Fri 9am–6pm, Sat 8am–noon;

044/552 24 18, ⓦwww.lmikulas.sk), on Námestie mieru, can help with
information and accommodation in the Low Tatras.

For a **place to stay**, the plain, newly furnished rooms at the *Kriváň*, Štúrova 5
(☎044/552 24 14; ❷), opposite the tourist office, are the cheapest in town, while
the swankiest of the central hotels are the *Elan*, 1.mája 35 (☎044/551 44 14; ❻),
located east off Námestie osloboditeľov, and the new *Steve* (☎044/552 89 99,
ⓦwww.hotelsteve.sk; ❹), on the same street, but closer to the square. In between,
you have the *Janošík* (☎044/552 27 21, ⓕ044/552 27 26; ❷), a Communist-era
high-rise at the busy road junction of Janošíkovo nábrežie and Jilemnického.

The nearest **campsite** (May–Oct) is by the lake at Liptovský Trnovec (20min
by bus) on the northern shores of the Liptovská Mara, with another, smaller, more
secluded lakeside site, another 5km further on by *Villa Betula* (ⓦwww.villabetula
.sk) in Liptovská Sielnica. If you're aiming to hike in the Low Tatras, you'd be better
off at the *Borová Sihoť* site just 1km west of Liptovský Hrádok train station, 8km
east (10min by train), or the *Bystrina* site up the Demänovská dolina (both open all
year). If you're staying in the area, it's worth knowing about the very popular and
very hot outdoor **thermal swimming pool** complex (daily 10am–9pm; 150Sk;
ⓦwww.tkb.sk) in Bešeňová; the nearest train station is 1.5km west of the pool in
Liptovská Teplá. Its latest rival is the **Aquapark Tatralandia** (daily: mid-April to
June & Oct–Dec 10am–9pm; July–Sept 9am–9pm; 250Sk; ⓦwww.tatralandia.sk),
a set of swimming pools, helter-skelters, saunas and suchlike, located in the middle
of nowhere, on the road to Zuberec, 2km of Mikuláš.

There's a very good **restaurant**, *Liptovská izba*, on Námestie osloboditeľov,
serving *guláš* and Slovak specialities, along with an equally good pizzeria, the
Taverna, upstairs. For **Internet** access, head for the next-door *Z@vináč*.

Vychodná and Vazec

The annual **Slovak folk festival** held around late June to early July in
VÝCHODNÁ, 15km east of Liptovský Mikuláš and thirty minutes by train,
is in every way equal to Strážnice's international affair (see p.397), attracting
groups from every region of Slovakia. There's no accommodation in the village
(a pleasant 2km hike north from the station), but during the festival there's a
makeshift campsite, with many more people crashing out in the haylofts and
barns of the local farmers (ask first). At any other time of the year, Východná is
a modest little village, whose nondescript facades hide an array of interesting
wooden buildings.

VAŽEC, one stop further on, was renowned for being one of the most beautiful villages in Slovakia and built almost entirely from wood, until it was destroyed
by a catastrophic fire in 1931. However, its former reputation as a photographer's
dream means that it is immortalized in many prints on display in the village
folk museum. The purpose of most visits, though, is the **Važecká jaskyňa**
(Tues–Sun: Feb–May & Sept–Nov tours at 10am, noon, 2 & 3pm; June–Aug
hourly tours 9am–4pm), a limestone cave system discovered back in the 1920s
but only recently opened to the public. To get there from the train station, walk
to the other side of the village.

The Low Tatras (Nízke Tatry)

The rounded peaks of the **Low Tatras** (Nízke Tatry) may have less of an immediate impact than the sharp craggy outline of the High Tatras on the northern
horizon, but they do constitute a more extensive range, in parts much wilder and

Most people start walking from **Chopok** (2024m), the second highest peak in the range, situated only an hour's hike from Luková, a meadow reached by a chairlift from Jasná (daily 8.30am–4pm). It's about two hours across the bare fell to the top of **Ďumbier** (2043m), king of the Low Tatras and the easternmost limit of this central ridge. From Ďumbier, it's six or more hours for each of the following routes: via Krupova hoľa, back down the yellow-marked path to the campsite at the bottom of Demänovská dolina; down Jánska dolina on the blue-marked path to the campsite in Podtureň, or further east to the campsite at Malužiná (turn right either at sedlo Javorie or Pred Bystrou). Westwards, it's about five hours along the ridge to the isolated hamlet of Magurka, which has a *chata* but no official campsite; otherwise it's a good ten hours' walk to the campsite and hotel at Donovaly, at the top of the pass from Banská Bystrica over to Ružomberok.

Accommodation high in the mountains is in extremely short supply, with the only real mountain refuge, *Chata gen. M.R. Štefánika* (☎048/619 51 20; ❶), on Ďumbier's hillside, supported by the small, crowded *Kamenná chata pod Chopkom* (☎048/617 00 39; ❶), just under the top of Chopok, three primitive shelters (two of whom with no service) and several campsites without facilities.

less explored, still home to the odd lynx and bear. The crudest development is on either side of the two tallest central mountains, **Chopok** and **Ďumbier**, but particularly to the east, the crowds are thin and, with the aid of a hiking map, the countryside is yours for the taking. If you're not planning anything as strenuous as hiking, you could happily spend a day or two visiting some of the **caves** in Demänovská dolina, swimming at the foot of the mountains at Tále or simply riding the chairlift from Jasná or Srdiečko and effortlessly soaking up the view.

On the practical front, **accommodation** is now no longer a problem, with plenty of private rooms available and several campsites, though still very few hotels outside the main resorts. **Transport** is also fairly good, with two rail lines serving the Váh and Hron valleys and buses taking you the rest of the way into the mountains: of course, to get the most out of the region, you'll need to walk – preferably armed with the map mentioned above and a stout pair of walking boots. **Ski rental** is possible both in Demänovská dolina and in Jasná.

Demänovská dolina and the caves

Extremely overloaded buses wend their way hourly up **Demänovská dolina**, by far the most popular valley on the north side of the mountains. As soon as you enter the narrow, forested part of the valley, signs point off to the left to the **Demänovská ľadová jaskyňa** (Tues–Sun: mid-May & Sept tours at 9.30 & 11am, 12.30 & 2pm; June–Aug hourly tours 9am–4pm; 130Sk), one of Slovakia's two ice caves. After a sweaty fifteen-minute walk up through the woods to the entrance, there's a chilly forty-minute guided tour through the cave, starting in a vast hall-like chamber of mini-stalactites and stalagmites, its walls covered in eighteenth-century graffiti testifying to the early discovery of the caves. For the final section you descend into the claustrophobic **ice chamber**, where the temperature even in summer is well below zero. The best time to visit, though, is in the spring, when the ice formations are at their best, creating huge stalactites of frozen water that drip down onto a massive frozen lake. Two kilometres further on, signs indicate the **Demänovská jaskyňa slobody** (Cave of Freedom; Tues–Sun: mid-Dec to May & Sept to mid-Nov tours at 9.30 & 11am, 12.30 & 2pm; June–Aug hourly tours 9am–4pm; 130Sk), used for storage by frostbitten partisans during World War II – hence its name. It's an iceless cave (though no less freezing), with a much larger and more impressive variety of rock formations than Demänovská ľadová jaskyňa.

A little further on, the road swings violently to the right and begins to climb steeply for about 1.5km until it reaches **JASNÁ** (Ⓦwww.chopok-jasna .sk), a major ski resort for this part of the world, with sundry chair and ski lifts, as well as a smattering of **hotels** wedged into the hillsides. The nicest of the bunch is the brand-new *Grand* (Ⓣ044/559 14 41; ❻), complete with indoor pool, weight-training room and billiards. The *Liptov* (Ⓣ044/559 15 06; ❸), conveniently situated near the chairlift, is a cheaper, Communist-era resort hotel offering many of the same features, while the smaller and nicely renovated *Mikulášská chata* (Ⓣ044/559 16 76, Ⓦwww.mikulasskachata.sk; ❹) by the lakeside is another good option. It's worth enquiring about vacancies for all the above places beforehand at the helpful **tourist office** Slovakotour (7.30am–7pm; Ⓣ044/554 81 07, Ⓦwww.slovakotour.sk) located at the mouth of Demänovská dolina.

If you're trying to save money, it's reassuring to know that there are plenty of **pensions** and private **rooms** back down in the bit of Demänovská dolina, just before the caves, such as the good value *Kamenná chata* (Ⓣ044/554 82 31; ❷), which offers clean doubles as well as more basic, even cheaper dorm accommodation. In fact, Demänovská dolina is generally a more congenial place to be, and the hourly bus up to Jasná makes getting to the slopes a cinch.

As for **food**, practically all the hotels in Jasná have restaurants, and the one at *Mikulášská chata* stands out. In Demänovská dolina, the *Koliba* is a typically rustic Slovak pub with a fireplace in front of which to enjoy your mulled wine or a full meal.

The Hron valley

If you're coming from Banská Bystrica and the Hron valley, you'll approach the Low Tatras from the south. The Hron valley as far as **BREZNO** has been marred by industry, and the latter only has one cheap hotel to recommend it, the *Ďumbier* (Ⓣ048/611 26 61; ❷), on námestie gen. M.R. Štefánika 31, the leafy main square. There's also a **tourist office** (mid-June to mid-Sept Mon–Fri 9am–5pm, Sat & Sun 10am–2pm; mid-Sept to mid-June Mon–Fri 8am–5pm; Ⓦwww.brezno.sk – in Slovak only) at námestie gen. M. R. Štefánika 3, which can help with **accommodation** in and around the area.

The main approach to Chopok from this side is via **Bystrá dolina**, the flip-side valley of Demänovská dolina. At its southern base is **BYSTRÁ** (bus from Podbrezová station or 5km walk over the hills along the green-marked path from Brezno), a neat village riddled with private accommodation. Close by is the **Bystrianska jaskyňa** (Tues–Sun: Jan–May & Sept–Oct tours at 9.30 & 11am, 12.30 & 2pm; June–Aug hourly tours 9am–4pm), the only underground cave system on offer on this side.

If you haven't booked **accommodation** in advance, scour the private rooms and pensions in Bystrá, or head 2.5km up the road to the clutter of hotels known as **TÁLE**. At the main junction signs point to the ageing *Hotel Partizán* (Ⓣ048/617 00 31, Ⓦwww.partizan.sk; ❸) which nonetheless enjoys every facility under the sun. However the nearby *Stupka* (Ⓣ048/671 23 01; ❸) is slightly better value, with its own swimming pool and sauna, and it can organize bike rental and other outdoor activities.

Buses can take you (and a whole load of others) to the very northern reaches of the valley, past the *Trangoška* (Ⓣ & Ⓕ048/617 00 20; ❷), to the beginning of

Railways around Brezno

The Brezno area pulls in a fair few railway enthusiasts, not least because the line from **Brezno to Margecany** is one of the country's most scenic, including a 360-degree switchback around Telgárt. In addition, though, the line to Tisovec, to the southeast, includes what is probably the only state-owned **rack-and-pinion** railway in the world, originally built to help trains, heavily laden with iron ore, make the ascent from Pohronská Polhora to Zbojská. Last, but by no means least, there's the Čiernohronská Železnica **forest railway**, built in 1896 between Hronec, 8km west of Brezno, to Čierny Balog. This last seventeen-km-long narrow-gauge railway runs only in summer (May to mid-Sept; ⊛www.chz.sk), occasionally pulled by steam locomotives; for details enquire at the Brezno tourist office.

the chairlift, which rises to the *Chata Kosodrevina* (☎048/617 00 15; ❸), halfway up the path to Chopok. To avoid disappointment you should **book in advance** for these hotels through the tourist office in Brezno. If you're walking from Tále to the main ridge, it'll take you three to four hours along the yellow–marked path to the top of **Dereše** (2003m).

The eastern Low Tatras

East of the central Chopok ridge, the real wilderness begins. The peaks are even less pronounced and rarely raise their heads above the turbulent sea of forest where some of Slovakia's last remaining wild bears, wolves, lynx and chamois hide out. Meanwhile, the villages in the **Hron valley** are still a world of shepherds and horses and carts, with wooden houses surviving here and there among the stone, brick and cement; naturally, there's virtually nothing in the way of conventional tourist facilities. If this has whetted your appetite, the best thing to do is book your accommodation through the tourist office in Brezno – or pack a tent and provisions and start walking.

The **railway** that climbs the Hron valley is one of the most scenic in the whole country (see box above), and if you pick the right train you can travel from Banská Bystrica through the Slovenský raj, finally coming to a halt at Košice, in three to four hours. The slower trains take significantly longer, stopping at even the most obscure villages, such as **HEĽPA** (1hr by slow train from Brezno), which has just one cheap hotel, *Hotel Heľpa* (☎048/618 62 35–6; ❷), at Hlavná 65. To get the magnificent view from the top of **Veľká Vápenica** (1691m), follow either the yellow- or the blue-marked tracks from the station (2–3hr), making sure the stream is on your right-hand side. One stop further on, **POHORELÁ** lies on the footpath to the next peak along, **Andrejcová** (1519m). The only campsite in the region, *Gindura* (open all year), is close by the next station along, Pohorelská Masa.

A lot of the slower trains pause for breath at Červená Skala, not a bad place to start one of the **best hikes** of the eastern range. Take the road to the village of **ŠUMIAC**, which sits on the broad sweep of the mountainside with a panoramic view west and south over the valley; then follow the blue-marked path up to **Kráľova hoľa** (1948m), the biggest bare-topped mountain east of Ďumbier. It's another three hours to **LIPTOVSKÁ TEPLIČKA**, once one of the most isolated communities in the Slovak mountains. If you want to remain in the Hron Valley, there's the pretty mountain hotel *Pusté Pole* (☎048/611 18 80; ❷) in **TELGÁRT**, 4km from Kráľova hoľa (get out at Švermovo-penzión zástavka), where the railway doubles back on itself before climbing to its highest point (999m) shortly before Vernár station, on the edge of the Slovenský raj (see p.561).

The High Tatras (Vysoké Tatry)

Rising like a giant granite reef above the patchwork Poprad plain, the **High Tatras** (🌐www.tatry.net, www.tatry.sk) are for many people the main reason for venturing this far into Slovakia. Even after all the tourist-board hype, they are still an incredible, inspirational sight – sublime, spectacular, saw-toothed and brooding. A wilderness, however, they are not. At the height of summer, visitors are shoulder to shoulder in the necklace of resorts at the foot of the mountains, and things don't necessarily improve when you take to the hills. The crux of the problem lies in the scale of the range, a mere 25km from east to west, some of which is shared with the equally eager Poles, and a lot of it out of reach to all but the most experienced climber. This is not helped by the saturation tactics of the tour operators, a logical extension of the region's overdevelopment. Yet when all's said and done, once you're above the tree line, surrounded by bare primeval scree slopes and icy blue tarns, nothing can take away the exhilarating feeling of being on top of the world.

Visiting the Tatras: practicalities

Most fast trains to the Tatras arrive at the **main train station** in Poprad (known as Poprad-Tatry), which is adjacent to the **bus station**. If your budget is tight, it might be worth staying in Poprad (for which see p.539); otherwise, you may as well get straight onto one of the little red electric trains that connect all the main resorts and leave from a separate platform above the main line. There are only a few flights a day from Poprad's tiny **airport**, west of the town (take a taxi), which means you need to book in advance to be sure of a place in summer and winter high seasons; make your reservation in Poprad at the ČSA office (Mon–Fri 8.30am–4.30pm) next door to *Hotel Garni*.

In view of the region's popularity, sorting out **accommodation** should be your priority, though with so many places to stay now available, you should have few problems getting something. Whatever your budget, you should book at least a day in advance, or be prepared to take whatever's on offer (within reason); with your own transport, towns like Kežmarok are possible bases (see p.552). Be aware that prices fluctuate wildly depending on the season, with winter (excluding Christmas week) the most expensive time, followed by high summer. The PIA in Poprad (☎052/161 86), as well as the Tatranská informačná kancelária or TIK (☎052/442 34 40), T-Ski (☎052/442 32 65), SATUR and Slovakoturist in Starý Smokovec, can all book **pensions** and **private rooms** for around 300–500Sk per person.

One option worth considering is the **mountain chaty** dotted across the range, aimed primarily at walkers and therefore often only accessible on foot; prices are around 300–400Sk per person, and some also serve a limited selection of food in the evening. PIA in Poprad or Slovakoturist in Starý Smokovec have the latest on availability, although to take advantage of anything they offer you'll have to be flexible about your itinerary and plan your hiking around your accommodation.

The cheapest and most reliable option (providing the weather is warm enough) is **camping**, though having said that, the big swanky international sites are among the most expensive in either republic. The best of the dear ones are the *Eurocamp FICC*, *Tatranec* (both open all year) and *Športcamp* (May–Sept), all three just south of Tatranská Lomnica (get off at Tatranská Lomnica-Eurocamp FICC station). The cheapest and most basic is the *Jupela* site (June to mid-Sept), 1km south of Stará Lesná. Two other options that you'll need your own transport to reach include the *Šarpanec* site (mid-June to mid-Sept), on route

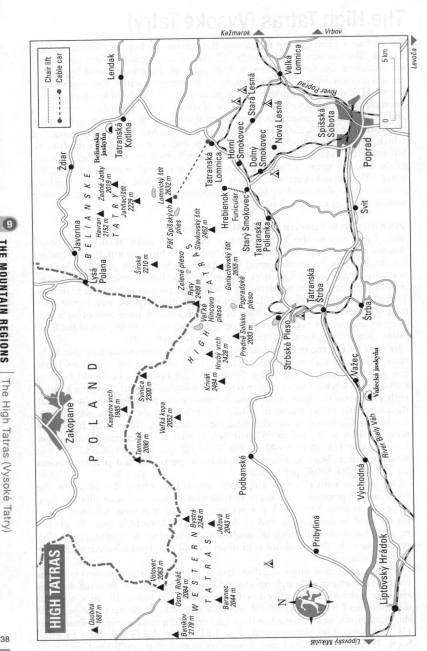

HIGH TATRAS

Chair lift
Cable car

0   5 km

Kežmarok   Vrbov

Levoča

River Poprad

Velká Lomnica

Poprad

Lendak

Tatranská Kotlina

Belianska jaskyňa

Stará Lesná

Nová Lesná

Spišská Sobota

Ždiar

Zadné Jatky 2019 m

Havran 2152 m

Jahňací štít 2229 m

Lomnický štít 2632 m

B E L I A N S K E   T A T R Y

Horní Smokovec

Dolný Smokovec

Svit

Javorina

Tatranská Lomnica

Pät Spišských plies

Slavkovský štít 2452 m

Hrebienok

Funicular

Starý Smokovec

Tatranská Polianka

Lysá Polana

Široká 2210 m

Zelené pleso

Rysy 2499 m

H I G H   T A T R Y

Gerlachovský štit 2655 m

Popradské pleso

Kasprov vrch 1985 m

Velké Hincovo pleso

Hrubý vrch 2428 m

Tatranská Štrba

Strba

Štrba

P O L A N D

Zakopane

Svinica 2300 m

Kriváň 2494 m

Veľká kopa 2052 m

Predné Solisko 2093 m

Strbské Pleso

Važec

Važecká jaskyňa

Temniak 2090 m

Banikov 2178 m

Ostrý Roháč 2084 m

Volovec 2063 m

Bystrá 2248 m

Ježová 2043 m

W E S T E R N   T A T R A S

Baranec 2044 m

Osobitá 1687 m

Podbanské

River Biely Váh

Vychodná

Pribylina

Liptovský Hrádok

Liptovský Mikuláš

N

67 between Spišská Bela and Tatranská Kotlina, which is relatively secluded, and the *Vrbov* site (late June to Aug), to the east, is located near the thermal swimming pool complex.

Poprad and around

It would be difficult to dream up a more unprepossessing town than **POPRAD** (Deutschendorf) to accompany the Tatras' effortless natural beauty, with a great swathe of off-white high-rise housing encircling the town. A tiny old town centre, a museum and a couple of art galleries go some way to counterbalance initial bad impressions. And while it's no great joy to hang around, Poprad is refreshingly free of tour groups and a lot less pretentious than the higher resorts. It's also not a bad place to organize **accommodation** for the rest of your stay in the Tatras.

The Town

Poprad was originally one of the twenty or so Spiš towns (see p.550), though the only clue to this is the long, village-like main square, **námestie Svätého Egídia**, a ten-minute walk southeast of the train station. Here you'll find the typical Spiš burgher houses, whose two storeys are distinguished by their stone facades and wooden gables, with eaves overhanging by six feet or so. If you're planning any hiking, you can stock up on provisions at the bakery and small vegetable market on the north side of the square, while the south side is taken up with a host of new shops, including a bookshop where you might be able to pick up relevant **maps** – look out for the invaluable *Tatranské strediská* one, which contains street plans of all the major resorts (excluding Poprad, which has its own map).

If you have some time to spare, you could pop into one of the town's museums. The long-established **Podtatranské múzeum** (Tatra Region Museum; Tues–Sun 9–11.30am & noon–4pm) on Vajanského, near the tourist office, traces the history of human settlement in the Tatras from the time of the earliest Neanderthal inhabitants. If this doesn't grab you, you could inspect either of the two branches of the **Tatranská Galéria**: the Výstavná sieň (Mon–Fri 9am–5pm, Sat 9am–2pm) at Alžbetina 30 contains nineteenth- and twentieth-century landscape paintings of the Tatra and Spiš regions, while the Elektráreň (May–Sept Tues–Sun 10am–5pm), in a former electric plant at Hviezdoslavova 12, focuses on the area's tradition of weaving and folk dress. Otherwise, you can swim, or bake in the sauna, at the new complex of swimming pools, **Aquacity** (daily 9am–10pm; ⓦ www.aquacity.sk), located a kilometre or so northeast of the centre.

Spišská Sobota

If you do end up staying in Poprad, the village of **SPIŠSKÁ SOBOTA** (Georgenberg), just 2km northeast (bus #2 or #4), makes for an enjoyable outing on a cloudy afternoon. Only a handful of the thousands of visitors who pass through Poprad make it here, yet it couldn't be more different from its ugly, oversized neighbour. Except during Mass on Sundays, there are few signs of life in its leafy square, and only the burgher houses hint at the fact that this was once a thriving Spiš town. At the eastern end of the square, an entire row has been recently renovated and smartly whitewashed, while in the centre huddle the old radnica, the obligatory Renaissance belfry, and the church of **sv Juraj** (St George; May–Oct Mon–Sat 9am–5pm), whose origins go back even further than its present late-Gothic appearance. Its vaulting is incredibly sophisticated

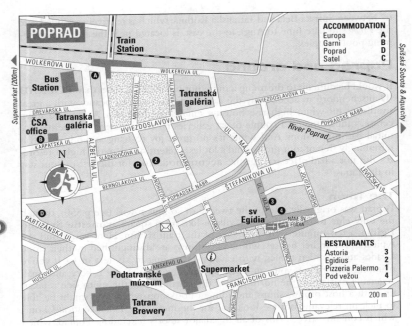

for this part of the world, as are the font and a couple of the smaller chapels, but the real treat is the main **altar** carved by Pavol of Levoča in 1516, which features a gilded George vanquishing the dragon, with a reworking of the famous *Last Supper* predella from the main church in Levoča, below. The **museum** (April–Oct Tues–Fri 10.30am–4pm, Sat 11am–3pm) at no. 33, on the south side of the square, is worth a look if only to see the inside of a typical town house.

Practicalities

Poprad's train station has a **left-luggage** office. The **tourist office**, PIA (Mon–Fri 9am–12.30pm & 1–5pm, Sat 9am–noon; July–Aug Mon–Fri 8am–6pm, Sat 9am–1pm, Sun 1–4pm; ☎052/161 86 or 052/772 13 94, ⓦ www.poprad.sk), at the western end of námestie sv Egídia, can organize private rooms in town and all types of **accommodation** elsewhere in the Tatras. The high-rise *Satel*, on Mnoheľova (☎052/716 11 11, ⓦ www.satel-slovakia.sk; ➍), has lots of excellent facilities, as does the slightly smaller *Poprad* on Partizánská (☎052/787 08 11, ⓦ www.hotel-poprad.sk; ➍). However, if you've got your own transport or don't mind taking the bus (#2 or #4), you'll get much better value for money and a friendlier welcome at the pub *Sv. Juraj* (☎052/776 95 58, ⓦ www .penzion-sv-juraj.sk; ➌), one of at least eight pensions on the main square in Spišská Sobota. Cheaper rooms with shared facilities are available at the less appealing *Hotel Europa* (☎052/772 18 97; ➋), opposite Poprad's train station.

Eating and **drinking** in Poprad has improved a little of late. You can grab a baguette sandwich or a salad at the *Astoria*, on ulica 1. mája just off the main square, or wolf down one of the many excellent pizzas or desserts at *Pizzeria Palermo*, Štefáníkova 4. For a more formal meal, the best place to head for is the *Egidius*, behind the *Satel* on Mnoheľova, a popular folksy restaurant specializing in traditional Slovak fare, with occasional live music. Less fancy is the smaller *Pod vežou* on the main square which also serves up local specialities. If dancing's your thing, the *Surprise* **disco**, in the same building as the *Pizzeria Palermo*, has an animated bar as well as billiard tables.

The Tatra National Park (TANAP)

Cute, red, tram–like trains trundle between Poprad and the necklace of resorts and spas that nestle at the foot of the Tatras and lie within the **Tatra National Park** or **TANAP** (Ⓦ www.tanap.sk). To be honest, the resorts are all much of a muchness, a mixture of half–timbered lodges from the nineteenth century, interwar villas and tasteless new hotels, all set in eminently civilized spa gardens and pine woods – it's the mountains to which they give access that make them worth visiting.

Štrbské Pleso

Founded in 1873 by the local Hungarian lord József Szentiványi, **ŠTRBSKÉ PLESO**'s life as a mountain resort began in earnest some twenty years later, with the building of the rack railway that climbs 430m in just 5km from Štrba on the main line below. At 1351m, it's the highest Tatran resort. It's also the brashest, with reams of takeaway kiosks and tatty, eyesore hotel hoardings, though this has more to do with its having hosted the 1970 World Ski Championships than anything else. The ski resort part of town is north of the *pleso*, the second largest of the Tatran glacial lakes from which the spa gets its name; swimming in the lake is forbidden. There's a useful **tourist office** (Mon–Fri 8.30–11.30am & noon–4pm, Sat & Sun 9am–4pm; ☎052/449 23 91) opposite the train station, which has a **left-luggage** office.

In summer, the only working lift is the chairlift to Solisko, from where the climb to the top of **Predné Solisko** (2093m) takes well under an hour. As with all such lifts in the Tatras, book your ride well in advance to avoid the snake-like ticket queues that have usually formed by mid-morning. If you want to explore a whole ring of mystical glacial lakes – in folk legends known as "the eyes and windows of another sea" – make the trek over **Bystré sedlo** (2314m), which skirts the jagged Solisko range; it's a round trip of around eight hours, and best done anticlockwise, heading from east to west.

A gentle one-hour walk through the forest along the red-marked path to **Popradské pleso** is all many people manage on a lightning Tatra tour. It's a beautiful spot to have a picnic, although given its popularity, by no means tranquil. Those with sufficient stamina can try the punishing hour-long climb to the **sedlo pod Ostrvou** (1959m), which gives a fantastic bird's-eye view of the lake. This red-marked path, known as the Magistrála, skirts the tree line all the way to **Zelené pleso**, 20km away in the far east of the range. If you don't have boundless enthusiasm for walking, stroll along the yellow-marked track to the **symbolický cintorín** of wooden crosses set up to commemorate the considerable number of people who've lost their lives in the mountains.

One of the most popular climbs in the Tatras is **Rysy** (2499m), on the Slovak-Polish border, which Lenin himself once climbed (from the Polish side). If you're planning on conquering Rysy, you won't have time to picnic by the lake, since it's a good six hours' return trip from Popradské pleso. Just below the first peak of Váha (2343m) is the *Chata pod Rysmi* (☎052/442 23 14; mid-June to Oct), at 2250m the highest (and coldest) of the mountain chalets. If you can find a place to sit down on the often crowded summit of Rysy, it has to be one of the best views in Europe (some one hundred peaks and twelve mountain

It is as well to remember that the High Tatras are an alpine range and as such demand a little more respect and preparation than other Slovak mountains. Most of the trails described in the text are far from easy, and many involve the use of chains to traverse rock screes. The whole area is part of the **Tatra National Park (TANAP)**, whose often quite strict rules and regulations are designed to protect what is a valuable, fragile ecosystem – you may find that you have to pay a small fee to use some of the trails, so take some money with you. The most important rule is to stick to the marked paths; before setting out, get hold of a green *Vysoké Tatry* **map**, which is available from most tourist offices and bookshops and shows all the marked paths in the TANAP.

In the summer months, the most popular trails and summits are literally chock-a-block with Czech, German and Slovak walkers. One of the reasons for the summer stampede is that all treks above the mountain *chaty* are only open from June 16 to October 30. This is primarily due to the **weather**, probably the single most important consideration when planning your trek. Rainfall is actually heaviest in June, July and August; thunderstorms and even the occasional summer snowstorm are also features of the unpredictable alpine climate, and it may be scorching hot down in the valley yet below freezing on top of Rysy. Note also that the Tatras are frequently affected by hurricanes, known here as *halny*; one of them, on November 19, 2004, badly damaged the forests in the whole range between Podbanské and Tatranská Kotlina, making many of the hiking paths temporarily inaccessible – ask at the tourist office before you set off.

Hiking: the golden rules

- Watch the **weather forecast** (☏052/776 55 51, ⓦwww.shmu.sk).
- Set out **early** (the weather is always better in the morning), and tell someone when and where you're going.
- Don't leave the **tree line** (about 2000m) unless visibility is good, and when the clouds close in, start descending immediately.
- Bring with you: a pair of **sturdy boots** to combat the relentless boulders in the higher reaches; a **whistle** (for blowing six times every minute if you need help); a **flashlight** (for the same reason at night); and a **flask of water**.

---

lakes can be seen). Another possible climb from Popradské pleso is the eight-hour sweep over **Vysoké Kôprovské sedlo** (2180m) via the largest lake of the lot, **Veľké Hincovo pleso**; while you're there, it's worth making the effort to take in the summit of Kôprovský štít (2367m) itself, less than an hour's climb.

Kriváň (2494m), the westernmost High Tatran peak (and, in comparison, relatively easy to climb), is an eight-hour return journey from Štrbské Pleso via Jamské pleso. In 1841, Slovak nationalists Štúr and Hurban staged a patriotic march up the mountain, a tradition that is continued to this day at the end of August. Like Rysy, it's a popular route, swarming with walkers at the height of summer. If that sounds like your idea of hell, try some of the trails around Podbanské or even further afield in the Western Tatras (see p.527).

Starý Smokovec

The old Saxon settlement of **STARÝ SMOKOVEC** (Altschmecks) is the most established and most central of all the spas. Along with neighbouring settlements of Nový, Horni and Dolný Smokovec, it makes up the conglomeration known as **Smokovce**. The spa's old nucleus is the stretch of lawn between the half-timbered supermarket and the sandy-yellow *Grand Hotel*, a sight in its own right. It was built in 1904 in a vaguely alpine neo-Baroque style, and though

Skiing

The High Tatras are as popular for **skiing** in winter as they are for hiking in summer. The first snows arrive as early as November, but the season doesn't really get going for another month. By the end of March, you can only really ski on the higher slopes reached by chair (as opposed to ski) lifts. The main ski resort is Štrbské Pleso (ⓦ www.parksnow.sk), which hosts the occasional international as well as national event; Hrebienok (near Starý Smokovec) and Skalnaté pleso (near Tatranská Lomnica) are the other two main ski areas. Lifts generally run from sunrise to sunset, and while lift operators keep things flowing as smoothly as they can, queues for the lifts can be pretty horrendous at the busiest times – if so, head out to the quieter pistes around Ždiar or even Jezersko in the **Spišská Magura** hills.

Ski hire facilities have improved enormously over the last few years, so if you haven't brought your own equipment, gear can be rented from the likes of T-Ski in Starý Smokovec. If you've cash to spare and want to have it all planned out before you go, contact the specialist agents who organize skiing holidays to the High and Low Tatras (see pp. 28, 32 & 34).

Climbing

To go **climbing** (as opposed to hiking) in the High Tatras you need to be a member of a recognized mountain-climbing club and be able to produce a membership card. Otherwise, you are required by law to hire a guide from the Spolok horských vodcov (daily noon–6pm; ☎052/442 20 66; ⓦ www.tatraguide.sk), Stary Smokovec 66, which costs 3000–4000Sk a day, though up to four people can share the cost of one guide. It's possible to climb throughout the year, but as with skiing, beware of avalanches. Note that *Cesta uzavretá – nebezpečenstvo lavín* means "Path Closed – Beware of Avalanches". The most popular climbs are in the vicinity of Lomnický štít, but **Gerlachovský štít**, the highest peak in the Tatras, is also high on the hit list.

For **advice** on where to and where not to climb, tips on the weather and emergency help, contact Horská služba, the **24-hour mountain rescue service** next door to the Spolok horských vodcov in Starý Smokovec (☎052/442 28 20, or ☎18 300, ⓦ www .hzs.sk).

THE MOUNTAIN REGIONS | The High Tatras (Vysoké Tatry)

the staff can be a bit snooty it's worth having a drink in the hotel café, if only to check out the wonderful 1920s decor. There are also two **wooden churches** worth seeking out in Smokovce: the red neo-Gothic parish church behind the *Grand Hotel*, and, in Dolný Smokovec, the turn-of-the-twentieth-century chapel perching on arcaded stilts.

The best place to head for help with **accommodation** is the **TIK office** (Mon–Fri 9am–4pm; in summer Mon–Fri 8am–5pm, Sat & Sun 8am–2pm; ☎052/442 34 40) across from *Hotel Smokovec*, northwest of the train station, followed by SATUR (Mon–Fri 8am–4.30pm), on the main street, or nearby Fun Travel, (daily 9.30am–12.45pm & 1.30–6pm; ☎052/442 20 93). You can rent **bikes** (for around 200Sk per day) at Unijunior Šport (daily 9am–6pm), just by the train station. The *Grand Hotel* (☎052/478 00 00, ⓦ www.grandhotel.sk; ❼), with all conceivable amenities, is without doubt the finest guesthouse around; the large *Hotel Smokovec* (☎052/442 51 91–3, ⓦ www.hotelsmokovec.sk; ❺) has none of the atmosphere, but is still convenient and boasts the most central location of the lot. To the west in Nový Smokovec, the distinctive neo-Gothic *Villa Dr. Szontagh* (☎052/442 20 61–3, ✉szontagh@isternet.sk; ❹) is a decent, cheaper alternative, though, rather surprisingly, the cheapest rooms are offered on the top floor of the giant *Palace Royal* (☎052/442 20 41, ⓦ www.tatrasan.sk; ❷), also in Nový

If the weather's good, the most straightforward and rewarding climb is along the blue-marked path from behind the *Grand Hotel* to the summit of **Slavkovský štít** (2452m), a return journey of nine hours. Again from behind the *Grand Hotel*, a narrow-gauge **funicular** (daily 7.30am–7pm; 110Sk return; closed for maintenance late April & Nov) climbs 250m to Hrebienok (45min by foot), one of the lesser ski resorts on the edge of the pine forest proper. The smart wooden *Bilíkova chata* (℡052/442 24 39, ℮bilik@nextra.sk; ❸) is a five-minute walk from the top of the funicular. Just past the *chata*, the path continues through the wood, joining up with two others, from Tatranská Lesná and Tatranská Lomnica respectively, before passing the gushing waterfalls of the **Studenovodské vodopády**.

At the fork just past the waterfall, a whole variety of trekking possibilities open up. The right-hand fork takes you up the **Malá Studená dolina** and then zigzags above the tree line to the *Téryho chata* (℡052/442 52 45; ❷), set in a lunar landscape by the shores of the **Päť Spišských plies**. Following the spectacular, hair-raising trail over the Priečne sedlo to the more atmospheric *Zbojnicka chata* (℡0903/619 000; ❷), you can return via the Veľká studená dolina – an eight-hour round trip from Hrebienok. This is a one-way hiking path, so you have to do it this way round; note that it involves a 100-foot rock climb on a fixed chain, and is not recommended for the fainthearted. Alternatively, you could continue from the *Téryho chata* to Tatranská Javorina, nine hours away near the Polish border, and return by bus.

Another possibility is to take the left-hand fork to the *Zbojnicka chata* and continue to Zamrznuté pleso, in the shadow of **Východná Vysoká** (2428m); only a thirty-minute hike from the lake, this dishes out the best view there is for the non-climber of **Gerlachovský štít** (2655m), the highest mountain in Slovakia. To get back down to the valley, either descend the Poľský hrebeň and return to Starý Smokovec via the *Sliezsky dom* (9hr round trip without the Východná Vysoká ascent), or continue north and track the Polish border to Lysá Poľana, the Slovak border post (10hr one-way), returning by bus to Starý Smokovec.

Smokovec, which otherwise is much more expensive. You can book yourself into a **mountain chata** through Slovakoturist (Mon–Fri 8am–4pm), a couple of minutes' walk east of the main train station in Horný Smokovec (the closest station is Pekná vyhliadka). The self-service **restaurant** in the Central supermarket, and the nearby *Tatra* restaurant, are both okay, and situated just a short step from the train station, though for a proper evening meal, you're better off heading for the *Taverna restaurant*, en route to the *Grand* or for the *Grand* itself.

Tatranská Lomnica

TATRANSKÁ LOMNICA, 5km northeast of Starý Smokovec, is a smaller version of the latter. It's a pleasant place to sit out bad weather, and of course gives access to **Lomnický štít** (2632m), the second highest mountain in the Tatras, accessible by cable car (*lanová dráha*). It's difficult to fault the view from Lomnický štít, but purists may disapprove of the concrete steps and handrails built to prevent the crowds from pushing each other off the rocky summit. The cable car (closed for maintenance late May/early June & Nov) goes up in three stages: first, to Štart, then to Skalnaté Pleso (daily: July–Aug 8.30am–6.30pm; out of season 8.30–4.30pm; 380Sk return), the lake that sits below the mountain, from which you can either head for the summit (daily: July–Aug 8.50am–5.50pm; out of season 8.50–3.50pm; 500Sk return; book a couple of days in advance), or opt for the chairlift (daily: July–Aug 8.30am–5pm; out of season 8.30–4pm; 160Sk return) to **Lomnické sedlo**, the craggy saddle 500m below Lomnický štít.

Hiking options are not as good from Tatranská Lomnica, and most treks are best started from other resorts. Otherwise, cloudy days can be filled with horseracing (Sun only), the new, twisting **bobsleigh-track** (Tatrabob; open all year daily 9am–8pm; 50Sk; ⓦwww.tatrabob.szm.sk) and the **TANAP museum** (Mon–Fri 8am–noon & 1–4.30pm, Sat & Sun 8am–noon), whose smart displays of stuffed Tatran animals and plants accompany a brief history of the region. It was only explored for the first time in the late eighteenth century when a Scotsman, Robert Townson (see p.568), who was botanizing his way round Hungary, ascended Kežmarský štít and a number of other peaks, against the advice of the local guides. There's also a garden where you can mug up on your Tatran flowers (mid-May to mid-Sept), a couple of hundred metres away, near the hotel *Odborar*.

If you're looking for **accommodation**, head for the efficient **tourist office** (summer daily 7.30am–6pm; out of season Tues–Fri 10am–6pm, Sat 9am–1pm; ⓣ052/446 81 18), located on the main street, opposite the hotel *Slovakia*. Otherwise, there's a free phone by the train station, with an information panel detailing your options. Tatranská Lomnica's finest hotel is the *Grandhotel Praha* (ⓣ052/446 79 41, ⓦwww.grandhotelpraha.sk; ⓻), a vast hotel in the forest right by the inactive branch of cable car, built in 1905 by the Wagons-Lits-Cook company; another top-class option is the newly built *Vila Beatrice* (ⓣ052/446 71 20, ⓦwww.beatrice.sk; ⓺), to the south of the train station, between the tracks; each room has its own small kitchenette. Cheaper are the *Hotel Slovakia* (ⓣ052/446 72 61, ⓦwww.hotel-slovakia.sk; ⓸), right in the centre, which has a pool, sauna and gym, and the more characterful *Penzión Encián* (ⓣ052/446 75 20, ⓔpenzion-encian@sinet.sk; ⓷). For **food**, the *Slovenská restaurácia*, right under the cable car, offers traditional Slovak fare in carriage-shaped booths. To check your **emails** head for Townson Travel (daily 9am–6pm), between the train and bus stations.

Tatranská Kotlina, Ždiar and on to Poland

The overkill in the central part of the TANAP makes trekking from the relative obscurity of **TATRANSKÁ KOTLINA** an attractive alternative. Most people, however, come here not to walk, but to visit the **Belianska jaskyňa** (Tues–Sun: mid-Dec to May & Sept to mid-Nov tours at 9.30 & 11am, 12.30 & 2pm; June–Aug hourly tours 9am–4pm; 130Sk), fifteen minutes from the main road, whose pleasures include rock formations whimsically named the Leaning Tower of Pisa and White Pagoda, and an underground lake; another bad-weather time-filler. You can **stay** at the new, wooden *Penzión Koliba* (ⓣ052/446 82 74, ⓦwww.penzion-koliba.host.sk; ⓷), on the main road, which has a decent restaurant (closed Mon).

The **Zelené pleso** makes a good hiking target, surrounded by a vast rocky amphitheatre of granite walled peaks including the mean-looking north face of Lomnický štít. To get there, take the blue-marked path from the southwest end of Tatranská Kotlina, and turn right onto the green trail which ends at the ruined *chata* by Biele pleso (2–3hr). From here it's half an hour to the fully functioning *Chata pri Zelenom plese* (ⓣ052/446 74 20; ⓶), which is wonderfully located by the green tarn itself. If you've still got time and energy on your hands, traverse the ridge to the north and mount the summit of Jahňací štít (3–4hr round trip).

The mountains of the **Belianske Tatry**, which form the final alpine ridge in the north of the TANAP and are home to chamois and offer an alternative to skirting their southern slopes via the Kopské sedlo (30min on the blue trail from Biele pleso) and then on to Javorina (2–3hr).

On the other side of the Belianske Tatry, on the main road to Tatranská Javorina (and to Zakopane in Poland), is **ŽDIAR**, a traditional Góral community founded in the seventeenth century. The Górale are fiercely independent mountain farmers, speaking a Polish dialect, the majority of whom live on the Polish side of the border. The village has numerous wooden cottages in varying stages of modernization, a half-timbered cinema and an unremarkable brick church. One of the houses has been converted into a modest Góral folk museum, the **Ždiarska izba** (May–Oct Mon–Fri 9am–5pm, Sat & Sun 9am–2pm; Nov–April Mon–Fri 9am–4pm), while *Penzión Diana* (☎052/449 81 27, ⓦwww.zdiar.sk/diana; ❸), and numerous smaller houses, offer pine-clad rooms for the night.

If you're continuing your journey **into Poland**, a daily bus service will take you as far as Lysá Poľana, 12km west of Ždiar. From there you can walk across the border into Poland and catch a bus or one of the many minibuses to the main Polish Tatra resort of Zakopane (see *The Rough Guide to Poland* for details).

Travel details

Trains

Bratislava to: Banská Bystrica (2 daily; 3hr 10 min–3 hr 45min); Liptovský Mikuláš (up to 10 daily; 3–7hr); Martin (1 daily; 3hr 15 min); Ružomberok (6 daily; 3hr 40min–6 hr); Poprad (every 2hr; 3hr 40min–7hr 40min); Žilina (up to 15 daily; 2hr 10min–4hr 30 min); Zvolen (up to 6 daily; 2hr 40min–3hr 15min).

Banská Bystrica to: Brezno (up to 13 daily; 45min–1hr 15min); Červená Skala (2 daily; 1hr 35min–2hr 5min); Košice (1 daily; 3hr 50min); Martin (6–7 daily; 1 hr–1hr 30min); Žilina (up to 5 daily; 1hr 20min–1hr 40min); Zvolen (hourly; 30–40min).

Kralovany to: Dolný Kubín (every 2hr; 30min); Istebné (every 2hr; 20min); Oravský Podzámok (every 2hr; 1hr); Podbiel (every 2hr; 1hr 25min); Trstená (every 2hr; 1hr 50min).

Poprad (Poprad-Tatry) to: Starý Smokovec (hourly; 35min); Štrbské Pleso (hourly; 1hr 10min).

Stary Smokovec to: Tatranská Lomnica (hourly; 15min).

Žilina to: Kraľovany (every 1–2hr; 30–40min); Liptovský Mikuláš (every 2hr; 1hr 10min–2 hr); Martin (6 daily; 30min); Poprad (every 1–2hr; 1hr 55min–2 hr 50min); Rajecké Teplice (8 daily; 25–45min);

Ružomberok (every 2hr; 50min); Strečno (12–14 daily; 15min); Vrútky (every 1–2hr; 20–25min).

Zvolen to: Budapest (1 daily; 4hr 40min); Detva (up to 13 daily; 20–30min); Fiľakovo (up to 11 daily; 1hr–1hr 40min); Kremnica (6 daily; 1hr); Lučenec (every 2hr; 50min–1hr 20min); Martin (up to 10 daily; 1hr 30min–2hr 15min); Turčianske Teplice (up to 11 daily; 1hr 10min–1hr 40min).

Buses

Banská Bystrica to: Banská Štiavnica (up to 6 daily; 1hr 30min); Martin (7–20 daily; 1hr 15min); Ružomberok (every 30min; 1hr 20min); Žilina (every 1–2hr; 2hr).

Liptovský Mikuláš to: Demänovská dolina/Jasná (hourly; 25–40min).

Martin to: Turčianske Teplice (1–2 hourly; 30min).

Poprad to: Lysá Poľana (9 daily; 1hr 25min); Ždiar (hourly; 1hr).

Žilina to: Banská Bystrica (7–20 daily; 1hr 45min); Čičmany (up to 4 daily; 1hr 20min); Strečno/Martin (1–5daily; 30min/45min); Terchová/Vrátna dolina (hourly; 45min/1hr).

Zvolen to: Banská Štiavnica (hourly; 45min); Kremnica (3 daily Mon–Fri; 1hr 5min); Lučenec (every 1–2hr; 1hr 20min).

Highlights

East Slovakia

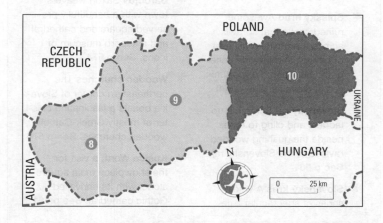

⑩

CHAPTER TEN # Highlights

* **Rafting in the Pieniny** Take a ride down the rapids of the River Dunajec, which forms the border between Slovakia and Poland. See p.554

* **Levoča** Perfectly preserved medieval town originally settled by Germans, now home to some of the finest Gothic altarpieces in the country. See p.556

* **Spišský hrad** Awesome ruined castle that sprawls across a prominent hill east of Levoča and provides one of the best photo opportunities in Slovakia. See p.560

* **Slovenský raj** Scramble up ladders and cling to ropes beside the gushing wooded ravines of the Slovenský raj. See p.561

* **Slovenský kras** A whole series of spectacular lime-stone caves is dotted about the Slovak karst region, by the border with Hungary. See p.565

* **Andrássy mausoleum, Krásnohorské Podhradie** This Art Nouveau memorial is the most remarkable single monument in the country. See p.566

* **Bardejov** Saxon weavers' town with a beautifully preserved square and cathedral and a superb museum of icons. See p.574

* **Wooden churches** The northeastern corner of Slovakia boasts a fascinating cluster of mostly Greek-Catholic wooden churches. See p.576

* **Košice** Worth a visit for the showpiece main square alone, with its unrivalled Gothic cathedral. See p.581

△ Spišský hrad

East Slovakia

S tretching from the High Tatras east to the Ukrainian border, the countryside of **East Slovakia** (Vychodné Slovensko) is decidedly different
from the rest of the country. The Carpathian mountains, which build
up to a crescendo around the High Tatras, revert to gentle rolling hills,
while the obligatory forests of pine and spruce give way gradually to acres of
beech forests, at their best in September and October, when the hills turn into
a fanfare of burnt reds and browns.

Ethnically, East Slovakia has always been the most diverse region in the country,
with different groups coexisting even within a single valley. In medieval times, the
towns were settled predominantly by Germans and Hungarians, who were later
joined by Jews and Romanies. Even today, the Polish-speaking **Górale** minority
continue to inhabit the northern border regions, as do the hill-dwelling **Rusyns**,
whose chief homeland became part of the Soviet Union after 1945 and is now in
Ukraine. Ethnic Hungarians survive in large numbers in the south of the region,
but only a minority of the **Germans** or Karpathendeutschen survived the expulsions that followed World War II. The region's once-large Jewish population was
decimated in the Nazi Holocaust, but the **Romanies**, for the most part, escaped
the genocide, and now form a large minority, mostly residing on the edge of
Slovak villages, in ghettos of almost medieval squalor. Even the **East Slovaks**
themselves are thought of as some kind of separate race by other Slovaks; indeed,
before 1918 there was a movement to create a separate state for them.

A short train ride east of the High Tatras, the intriguing medieval towns of
the **Spiš region** constitute East Slovakia's architectural high point, while to the
south, the **Slovenský raj** offers some highly unorthodox hiking possibilities.
Further south still, along the Hungarian border, the karst region of the **Slovenský kras** boasts one of the longest underground cave systems in the world.
Along the northern border with Poland, **Carpatho-Ruthenia** – home of the
country's remaining Rusyn population – is a fascinating, isolated landscape.
Rich medieval towns, like Bardejov and Prešov, originally built by German
colonists, still stand today, while the countryside is replete with wooden churches. Many towns were badly damaged in the last war – in fact, the further east
you go, the more densely concentrated are the Soviet monuments of former
times: retired tanks still line the highways along which they liberated Slovakia
at the end of World War II, and the plaques and statues that were ripped down
after the revolution in other parts of the two republics still stand proudly. After
spending time in the rural backwaters, **Košice**, the East Slovak capital, provides
a welcome, though somewhat startling, return to city life, containing enough of
interest for a stopover at least before heading east towards the Ukrainian border
and the deserted beech forests of the **Vihorlat**.

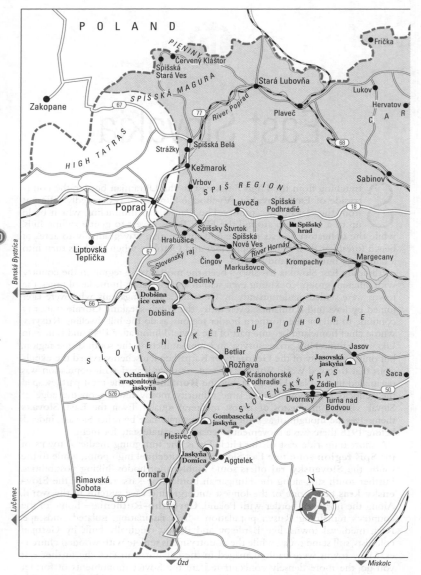

The map shows the following labelled places and features:

POLAND

Frička

Zakopane

PIENINY
Červený Kláštor
Spišská
Stará Ves

SPIŠSKÁ MAGURA
Stará Ľubovňa
Lukov
Hervatov
River Poprad
Plaveč
C A R
77
67
68
HIGH TATRAS
Strážky
Spišská Belá
Kežmarok
Vrbov
SPIŠ REGION
Sabinov
Poprad
Levoča
Spišská
Podhradie
18
Spišský
hrad
Liptovská
Teplička
Hrabušice
Spišský Štvrtok
Spišská
Nová Ves
River Hornád
Margecany
67
Slovenský raj
Čingov
Markušovce
Krompachy
Dedinky
66
Dobšina
ice cave
Dobšiná
SLOVENSKÉ RUDOHORIE
SLOVENSKÝ KRAS
Betliar
Rožňava
Jasov
Jasovská
jaskyňa
Šaca
Ochtinská
aragonitová
jaskyňa
Krásnohorské
Podhradie
Zádiel
Dvorníky
Turňa nad
Bodvou
50
526
Gombasecká
jaskyňa
Plešivec
Jaskyňa
Domica
Aggtelek
Rimavská
Sobota
Tornaľa
50
67
N

▼ Ózd

▼ Miskolc

The Spiš region

The land that stretches northeast up the Poprad valley to the Polish border and east along the River Hornád towards Prešov is known as the **Spiš region**, for centuries a semi-autonomous province within the Hungarian kingdom. After a series of particularly devastating Tatar raids in the thirteenth century

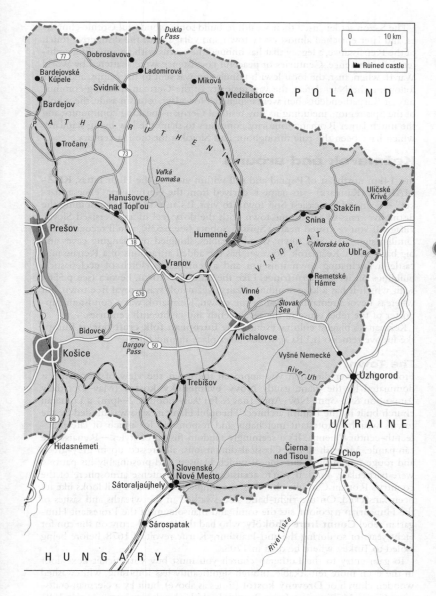

practically wiped out the local population, the Hungarian kings began to encourage German craftsmen to colonize the area. With the whiff of valuable ore deposits in the air, families from Saxony (to whom the area was known as Zips) came in ever greater numbers, eventually establishing a federation of twenty-four Zips towns that were quickly granted special trading privileges and began to thrive.

The Saxon settlers used their wealth to build some wonderful Gothic churches, and later enriched almost every town and village with the distinctive touch of the Renaissance, a legacy that has imbued the towns with an appealing architectural coherence. Centuries of peaceful coexistence were shattered by World War II, when, first, the local Jewish population was sent to the camps, and then, following the Nazi defeat, the vast majority of the German-speaking community or Karpathendeutschen were expelled. Nowadays, tourism aside, the whole of the Spiš region, including its tiny residual German-speaking community, and the much larger Romany minority, continues to share the low living standards which have been the rule throughout East Slovakia for the last century.

Kežmarok and around

Just 14km northeast of Poprad and still within view of the High Tatras, **KEŽMAROK** (Käsmark) – its name is derived from the German for "cheese market" – is one of the easiest Spiš towns to visit. It's an odd place, combining the distinctive traits of a Teutonic town with the dozy feel of an oversized Slovak village. If you've visited nearby Spišská Sobota (see p.539), you'll recognize the familiar signs of a Spiš town: wooden gables, shingled overhanging eaves and big barn doors. Kežmarok, however, has the added attractions of a Renaissance castle, a fascinating town museum and a remarkable clutch of ecclesiastical buildings on its southern fringe. Like the chief Spiš town, Levoča (see p.556), with which it has a long-standing rivalry, Kežmarok was a royal free town, but whereas Levoča remained loyal to the crown, Kežmarok was a consistent supporter of the rebel cause in the seventeenth and eighteenth centuries.

Kežmarok's biggest cultural event is the **European folk craft fair** or Európské ľudové remeslo (EĽRO), which takes place in mid-July.

The Town

From whichever direction you approach the town, the view of Kežmarok is dominated by the giant, gaudy **Nový evanjelický kostol** (May–Oct daily 9am–noon & 2–5pm; Nov–April Tues & Fri 9am–noon & 2–4pm), a Lutheran church built by the Danish architect Theophil Hansen, who was funded by the town's wealthy Protestant merchants and responsible for much of late-nineteenth-century Vienna. It's a seemingly random fusion of styles – Renaissance campanile, Moorish dome, Classical dimensions, all dressed up in grey-green and rouge rendering – but one of which Hansen, and presumably his patrons, were particularly fond. If you're accustomed to the intense atmosphere of the country's Roman Catholic churches, the simple whitewashed hall looks like it's been ransacked. On the right-hand side, swathed in the wreaths and sashes of the Hungarian tricolour, sits the tomb and mausoleum of the Protestant Hungarian rebel **Count Imre Thököly**, who had the Imperial army on the run for eight years or so during the anti-Habsburg Kuruc revolt of 1678, before being exiled to Turkey, where he died in 1705.

To gain entry to the Lutheran church you must buy your ticket next door in the even more remarkable, though significantly less imposing, whitewashed wooden church or **Drevený kostol** (times as above), built by a German craftsman, Georg Müttermann from Poprad. It abides by the strictures of the 1681 edict, which stipulated that Protestant churches could only be erected outside the town walls. Constructed entirely of wood, it couldn't be further from the Viennese cosmopolitanism of its neighbour. The interior, capable of seating almost 1500 people, is surprisingly ornate for a Protestant church, with florid Baroque furnishings: font, pulpit, organ and a limewood main altar flanked by barley-sugar columns, and full of curving flourishes and sunflowers. The ceiling is painted to look like the sky on a summer's day, while the balcony features wonderful wooden panel paintings of the Old and New Testaments.

One more building here deserves mention: the pink Lutheran Lycée library or **Lyceálna knižnica** (Mon–Fri 8am–3pm), architecturally fairly nondescript but historically and culturally significant. Lutheranism, which was rife in the nether regions of the Hungarian Empire, especially those parts colonized by Germans, was also the religion of many of Slovakia's leading nineteenth-century nationalists. The Czechophile Pavol Šafárik, the poet Martin Rázus and the writer Martin Kukučín all studied here before the Hungarians closed it down in the 1860s.

The old town itself is little more than two long, leafy streets punctuated by a mixture of plane and fir trees radiating out in a V-shaped fork from the big, boxy, Neoclassical radnica at the centre. The town's fifteenth-century Catholic basilica of **sv Kríž** is tucked away in the dusty back alleys between the two prongs; once surrounded by its own line of fortifications, it's now protected by an appealing Renaissance belfry, whose uppermost battlements burst into sgraffito life in the best Spiš tradition. The church itself has been recently restored, and is well worth a look inside, not least to admire the exquisite net vaulting, and the sixteenth-century main altar, which comes from the workshop of Pavol of Levoča.

The **hrad** (May–Sept Tues–Sun hourly 9am–4pm; Oct–April Mon–Fri 8am–3pm), at the end of the right-hand fork, is the main reason for the occasional Tatran tour group. For many years the property of the Thököly family, it was confiscated by the Habsburgs as punishment for their support of the aforementioned Kuruc revolt. It's impressively fortified with round towers, bulwarks, bastions and decorative Renaissance crenellations, but the museum of historical artefacts that now occupies its bare rooms doesn't really justify the hour-long guided tour. A much more interesting half hour can be spent in the **Meštiansky dom** (May–Sept Tues–Sun 9am–noon & 1–5pm; Oct–April Mon–Fri 8am–4pm), a late-seventeenth-century timber-framed house at Hradné námestie 55 (ask for the *anglický text*). It contains, among other things, the personal effects of Countess Hedviga Mária Szirmayova-Badányiova (1895–1973), last survivor of the aristocratic Badányi family. In among the beautiful gowns and period furniture, there's a brass samovar from Tula, and lots of luxury goods imported to the town to satisfy the tastes of the local wealthy German and Hungarian burgher families.

Finally, if you've time to spare, you could do worse than take a quick turn under the sycamore trees of the vast local **cemetery**, just off the ring road (at this point called Toporcerova, and the main road from Poprad), which gives out great views of the Tatras on a clear day. It's a fascinating testament to the diverse nationalities – Polish, Hungarian, German and Slovak – that have inhabited the region over the last century. The remaining Slovak peasantry continue to honour their dead with simple wooden crosses, while the vestigial Karpathendeutschen stubbornly stick to their own language; *Ruhe Sanft!* (Rest in Peace) is to be seen on the more recent headstones, not just on the ornate, rusting, turn-of-the-twentieth-century graves belonging to the now displaced German and Hungarian elite.

Practicalities

Arriving in Kežmarok by **train** is by far the most pleasant introduction to the town, thanks to the yellowing late-nineteenth-century station (there's also a regular **bus** service from Poprad). Kežmarok is near enough to the High Tatras to figure as a possible base for exploring the mountains, providing you have your own transport. Few people bother to do this, though, so **accommodation**, while limited, is fairly easy to find. The **tourist office** (Mon–Fri 8.30am–noon & 1–5pm; June–Sept also Sat & Sun 9am–2pm; ⓦwww.kezmarok .net), on the main square at Hlavné námestie 46, can book cheap private rooms; otherwise the best option is the excellent *Hotel Club*, on ulica MUDr. Alexandra (ⓣ052/452 40 51, ⓔhotelclub@sinet.sk; ❹), an efficiently run, tastefully modernized place right in the old town, with an excellent **restaurant** on the ground floor. Cheaper options include the *Štart* (ⓣ052/452 29 16; ❷), Pod lesom 24, which lies in the woods to the north of the castle, a good twenty-minute walk from the train station.

Strážky

Just 4km northeast of Kežmarok on route 67, on the outskirts of the village of **STRÁŽKY** (Nehre), is the Slovenská národná galéria's furthest-flung outpost, the pretty little Renaissance chateau of **Kaštieľ Strážky** (mid-June to mid-Sept daily 9am–7pm; mid-Sept to mid-June Tues–Sun 10am–5pm; ask for the *anglický text*). Unfortunately you have to go on a guided tour in order to visit the chateau, which was rather brutally converted following the death of the last inhabitant, the countess Margita Czóbel. The large gallery of nineteenth-century portraits by the likes of Peter Bohúň and Dominik Skutecký is less interesting than the collection of works by **Ladislav Medyánszky** (1852–1919) – aka Medmanský – the wayward son of the local baron, who spent his youth in the bohemian Paris of the 1870s. His landscapes are reminiscent of early Impressionists like Corot, but his depictions of local peasants, gypsies and beggars are much more severe, and full of insight. The **Countess Margita Czóbel** was herself something of an amateur artist, producing some winsome pen and ink drawings and watercolours in the 1920s. She was also clearly quite a character, enjoying daily swims in the local river until her death aged 81, and entertaining Alain Robbe-Grillet during the filming of *L'Homme qui ment* in the 1960s (there are photos in the chateau to prove it).

Spišský Štvrtok

Fourteen kilometres south of Kežmarok, just off the main road from Poprad and Levoča, is **SPIŠSKÝ ŠTVRTOK** (Donnersmark), whose splendid thirteenth-century church sits atop the village hill, its masonry tower topped by an impressive wooden spire with four corner pinnacles. The perfect French late-Gothic side chapel, built by Master Puchsbaum and tacked onto the south wall of the church, was commissioned by the Zápoľskýs in 1473 as the family mausoleum, and is, without doubt, one of the most surprising architectural sights in East Slovakia.

The Pieniny

The **Pieniny** (ⓦwww.pieniny.sk) is characterized by a small eruption of fissured limestone rocks that straddles the Dunajec river, which briefly forms the border between Poland and Slovakia. As early as the 1930s, the Polish and Czechoslovak governments declared this area a national park, the PIENAP, and today, despite the continuing isolation of the Zamagurie region (Zamagurie means literally "behind the Spišská Magura hills"), tourism in the Pieniny is flourishing for the Góral folk on both sides of the border, particularly the ever-popular **raft trips** (ⓦwww.pltnictvo.sk, www.pltnici.sk) down the Dunajec. Weather permitting, the rafting season runs from mid-April to late October, operating roughly between 9am and 5pm from mid-April to August, but finishing earlier in the last two months. In addition to the regular raft trips there's a canoe slalom competition on the river held over the first weekend in September, and a folk festival in mid-June.

Trips set off from various points along the seven-kilometre stretch of the river that starts just north of Spišská Stará Ves, and finishes at the main base of **ČERVENÝ KLÁŠTOR** (Unterschwaben). At each of the embarkation points (*prístav pltí*) along the river, tour operators will relieve you of your money (around 250Sk per person) and give you a departure time and ticket (the earlier you get here, the less likely it is you'll have to queue). Each *plt'* (raft) is made up of five log pontoons lashed together with rope and capable of carrying around ten passengers, plus two navigators, who are dressed up in the traditional Góral rafters' costume. Though the waters are not particularly rapid, the river winds through beautiful rocky scenery, and the guides can be a barrel of laughs. River meanderings make the whole excursion take about an hour and half, but if you'd prefer to do your own thing, the trip can be made on foot by following the red-marked path 10km along the tree-lined river bank.

At the end of the gorge you can catch an hourly bus (50Sk), organize a minibus (90Sk) or rent a bike (120Sk per day) or else walk the 3km along the road to Lesnica, then 5km across the hills back to Červený Kláštor. The town gets its name from the **Kartuziánsky kláštor** (monastery; April–Oct daily 9am–5pm), founded in the fourteenth century and occupied by first the Carthusians and then the Camaldolensians. In the nineteenth century, the monks here compiled the first Slovak grammar and the first complete Slovak translation of the Bible, and there are also valuable sixteenth-century murals to see. The nearest **hotel** is the *Pltník* (℡052/482 26 56, Ⓦwww.hotelpltnik.sk; ❷), just by the pier, about 1km upriver from Červený Kláštor. Alternatively, there's the *Dunajec* (℡052/482 20 27, Ⓦwww.dunajec.sk; ❷), a wood-clad *chaty* complex with its own restaurant and simple rooms above (❶), 1km southeast of Červený Kláštor along route 543. In addition, there are plenty of very small family-run pensions, and two riverside **campsites**: *Pltníca* (mid-May to Sept) by the hotel *Pltník* and *Červený Kláštor* (June–Sept), just outside the monastery walls.

Stará Ľubovňa

The slightly forlorn town of **STARÁ ĽUBOVŇA** (Altlublau), 25km northeast of Kežmarok and linked by road and rail, is another possible jump-off point for the Pieniny. The town itself has little to detain you, though if you've time to spare, head in the direction of the mostly ruined castle, **Ľubovniansky hrad** (May–Sept daily 9am–6pm; Oct daily 10am–3pm; Nov–April Mon–Sat 10am–3pm), which occupies a dramatic, high spur overlooking the town, 2km north of the centre. From the fifteenth to the eighteenth century, it was the main residence of the local Polish despot, who lorded it over the thirteen Zips towns pawned to the Polish crown by the Hungarians in the fifteenth century. Certain sections have remained intact and now contain local folk art, crafts and costumes, as well as a memorial commemorating those who were tortured in the castle by the Nazis.

Far more interesting than the above, however, is the **Múzeum zamagurskej dediny** (daily: May–Sept 9am–6pm; Oct 10am–3pm; 40Sk, or 80Sk for combined ticket with the castle), an open-air folk museum, or *skanzen*, set up in the grassy meadow below the castle in the late 1970s to preserve the precious wooden architecture of the Zamagurie region, to the west of Stará Ľubovňa. In the late nineteenth century, malnutrition was the norm in rural parts of

East Slovakia, and people emigrated in droves to other parts of Europe and the United States. Many of the cottages brought here from the surrounding villages were simply abandoned, and some of them now contain mementoes and personal details of the last owners (occasionally in English). It's a well-thought-out museum, and includes an early-nineteenth-century wooden Greek-Catholic church originally from Matysová, whose richly decorated interior, including an eighteenth-century iconostasis, can be viewed on request for the key.

The most basic **accommodation** option is the *Peters* (℡052/432 48 91, Ⓦwww.peters.sk; ❶), right by the castle. You can also try the more upscale pensions *Gurmen* (℡052/428 18 11, Ⓦwww.gurmen.sk; ❸) and *U jeleňa* (℡052/432 16 80, Ⓦwww.ujelena.itourshop.sk; ❷), both on the town's pleasant main square. If you're continuing **north into Poland**, six trains a day cross the border to the Polish spa town of Muszyna (change at Plaveč on the Slovak side), two of them continuing on to Kraków; the nearest border checkpoint on the roads is 15km north of Stará Ľubovňa, on route 68 at Mníšek nad Popradom.

Levoča

Twenty-seven kilometres southeast of Kežmarok across the broad sweep of the Spiš countryside, the walled town of **LEVOČA** (Leutschau), positioned on a slight incline, makes a wonderfully medieval impression. Capital of one of the richest regions of Slovakia for more than four centuries, its present-day population of around 11,000 is, if anything, less than it was during its halcyon days. The town's showpiece main square is hit by the occasional tour group from the Tatras, but otherwise its dusty backstreets are yours to explore.

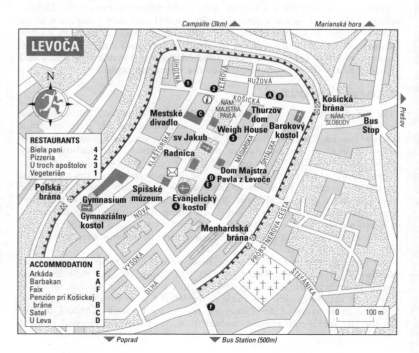

LEVOČA

Campsite (3km) ▲   Marianská hora ▲

RUŽOVÁ

KOŠICKÁ

Ⓐ Ⓑ   Košická brána

NÁM. SLOBODY   Bus Stop

▶ Prešov

NÁM. MAJSTRA PAVLA

Mestské divadlo   Ⓒ

Thurzov dom

sv Jakub   Weigh House ❸   Barokový kostol

Radnica

Dom Majstra Ⓓ Pavla z Levoče
Ⓔ

Poľská brána

Gymnasium   Spišské múzeum   Evanjelický ❹ kostol

Gymnaziálny kostol

Menhardská brána

RESTAURANTS
Biela pani   4
Pizzeria   2
U troch apoštolov   3
Vegeterián   1

ACCOMMODATION
Arkáda   E
Barbakan   A
Faix   F
Penzión pri Košickej   B
  bráne
Satel   C
U Leva   D

STEFÁNIKA

PROBSTNEROVA CESTA

0   100 m

▼ Poprad   ▼ Bus Station (500m)

The first attempts at founding a town here were completely trashed by the Tatars. Then, in the thirteenth-century wave of Saxon immigration that followed, Levoča became the capital of the Spiš towns, a position it maintained until its slow but steady decline in the eighteenth and nineteenth centuries. This led to a kind of architectural mummification, and it's the fifteenth and sixteenth centuries – the golden age of Levoča – that still dominate the town today.

The old town

The Euclidian efficiency with which the old town is laid out, chessboard-style, means that wherever you breach the walls, you'll inevitably end up at the main square, **námestie Majstra Pavla**, itself a long, regular rectangle. Most of Levoča's treasures are located here, and a foursome of free-standing buildings occupies the central space: the Protestant church, the old town hall, the Catholic church and the new town hall. The latter, by the small park and bandstand, is possibly the least distinguished, but, in its former incarnation as the *Waaghaus* or municipal **weigh-house**, by far the most important building on the square, and the focus of the town's financial might during its trading heyday. In 1321 King Charles Robert granted the town the Law of Storage, an unusual medieval edict that obliged every merchant passing through the region to remain in Levoča for at least fourteen days, pay various taxes and allow the locals first refusal on all their goods. In addition, Levoča merchants were later exempted from such laws when passing through other towns. Small wonder then that the town burghers were exceptionally wealthy.

Of the freestanding buildings on the main square that were paid for with these riches, it's the Roman Catholic church of **sv Jakub** (Easter to June & Sept–Oct Mon tours at 11.30am & 1–4pm hourly, Tues–Sat hourly tours 8.30–11.30am & 1–4pm, Sun hourly tours 1–4pm; July–Aug every 30min Mon 11am–5pm, Tues–Sat 9am–5pm, Sun 1–5pm; Nov to Easter Tues–Sat hourly tours 8.30–11.30am & 1–4pm) that contains the most valuable booty. Every nook and cranny of the building is crammed with medieval religious art, the star attraction being the early sixteenth-century wooden altarpiece by **Master Pavol of Levoča**, topped by a forest of finials and pinnacles, which, at 18.6m in height, makes it reputedly the tallest of its kind in the world. At the time, the clarity and characterization of the figures in the predella's *Last Supper* must have seemed incredible: they were modelled on the local merchants who commissioned the work (Pavol and his apprentices can also be seen behind the figure of St James in the central panel). The disciples are depicted in various animated poses – eating, caught in conversation or, in the case of St John, fast asleep across Christ's lap. Only Judas, with thirty pieces of silver over his shoulder, has a look of anguish, while Christ presides with serene poise. The work took over ten years to complete, and is only one of the many Gothic altars in the church that deserve attention. The church can be visited only with a guide, and tours leave from the *kassa* opposite the main entrance.

To the south of the church is the most attractive of the central buildings, the former **radnica** (daily: May–Oct 9am–5pm; Nov–April 8am–4pm), built in a sturdy Renaissance style. Downstairs, the local administration still holds sway, along with a few tables and chairs for ice-cream eaters; upstairs (where you get your ticket) there's a museum on the Spiš region, and some fairly dubious contemporary art exhibitions on the top floor. Close by the southeastern corner of the town hall stands the **Klietka hanby** (Cage of Disgrace), a rather beautiful wrought-iron contraption erected by Protestants in around 1600 as a pillory for women. The third building in the centre of the square is the oddly squat domed **Evanjelický kostol** (Lutheran church), which replaced its wooden predecessor in the early nineteenth century in an uncompromisingly Neoclassical style, its bare pudding-basin interior not worth the search around for the key.

The square is otherwise lined with some fine sixteenth-century burgher houses, at their most eye-catching in the **Thurzov dom** at no. 7 – at first glance a flamboyant Renaissance structure, though in fact its most striking feature, the sgraffito decoration around the windows, dates from restoration work in 1824. Further down on the east side of the square at no. 20 is a simple two-storey building, **Dom majstra Pavla z Levoče** (daily: May–Oct 9am–5pm; Nov–April 8am–4pm), which was the house of Master Pavol. All that's known about him is what little can be gleaned from the town-hall records: he was born around 1460; sat briefly on the town council; died in 1537; and his son accidentally murdered a young man from Kraków and then escaped from Levoča. Even this much is missing from the house's exhibition, which concentrates more on the Kotrba brothers who made good the woodworm of the centuries in the 1950s. Unless you're a real fan of Master Pavol's work it hardly seems worth the effort, since it contains only copies of the same work displayed in the church; however, it does allow you to get a closer look at some of the carving. If you've come this far in search of art, the **Spišské múzeum** (daily: May–Oct 9am–5pm; Nov–April 8am–4pm) at no. 40 by the post office, is also worth a peek for its icons, paintings and furniture culled from the Spiš region, dating as far back as the fourteenth century. Among the most important works is a beautiful Renaissance portal and accompanying frescoes, carved out from a local church.

The rest of the town's grid plan is made up of modest one-storey houses, once the exclusive abodes of Saxon craftsmen, now crumbling homes to the town's Slovaks and Romanies. You could spend an enjoyable hour wandering the streets and doing the circuit of the run-down walls: the late nineteenth-century German Gymnasium in the southwest of the town has a certain curiosity value, and the sandy-coloured **Barokový kostol**, the former Franciscan monastery church next to the Košická brána, has a glorious Baroque interior complete with frescoes.

Practicalities

If you arrive by **bus** (as trains no longer ply to Levoča), you'll find yourself a short walk southeast of the old town; there is also a bus stop close to the Košická brána in the northeast corner of town. A useful **tourist office** on the northwest corner of the main square (May–Sept Mon–Fri 10am–4.30pm, Sat

---

The Marian Pilgrimage

Once a year, Levoča goes wild. As the first weekend of July approaches, up to 250,000 Catholics have been known to descend on the town to attend the biggest of Slovakia's **Marian pilgrimages**, which takes place in (and inevitably around) the church on Marianska hora, the sacred hill 2km north of the town. Families travel – in some cases on foot – for miles to arrive in time for the first Mass, which takes place around 6pm on the Saturday evening. The party goes on throughout the night, with hourly Masses in the church and singing and dancing (and drinking) outside in the fields until the grand finale of High Mass at 10am Sunday morning, generally presided over by someone fairly high up in the Church hierarchy. If you've never witnessed a Marian festival, this is the place to do it, though it only marks the beginning of a whole host of festivals which take place over the next two months in villages all over the republic. The main Greek-Catholic pilgrimage takes place some 40km northeast of Levoča, near the village of Ľutina, on the third weekend in August.

& Sun 9.30am–1.30pm; Oct–April Mon–Fri 9am–4.30pm, Sat 9am–noon; ⓣ053/451 37 63, ⓦwww.levoca.sk) can help with any enquiries. Levoča has a sufficient range of **accommodation** options and outside the annual pilgrimage (see box opposites) rooms shouldn't be hard to find. The most luxurious hotel is the *Satel* (ⓣ053/451 29 43, ⓦwww.satel-slovakia.sk; ❼), Námestie Majstra Pavla 55, with a beautiful arcaded Renaissance courtyard, while good for families is the *Penzión U Leva* (ⓣ053/450 23 11, ⓦwww.uleva.szm.sk; ❺), Námestie Majstra Pavla 24, which has several very spacious apartments in one of the burgher houses. The *Arkáda* (ⓣ053/451 23 72; ❸), also on the main square, is cheaper and also comfortable inside. The *Barbakan* (ⓣ053/451 43 10, ⓦwww.barbakan.sk; ❹), at Košická 15, is less attractive but still very good value (though they charge less for Slovaks), while the *Faix* (ⓣ & ⓕ053/451 11 11; ❷), Probsnerova 22, five-minutes' walk south of the square, is pretty spartan. In addition, there are a couple of inexpensive pensions, the best of which is the *Penzión pri Košickej bráne* (ⓣ053/451 28 79; ❸), right next door to the *Barbakan*. There's also a **campsite**, *Kováčova vila* (open all year), 3km north of Levoča, in the woods by Levočská dolina.

Eating options are pretty good. Authentic Slovak pub food can be had at *Biela pani*, which occupies two cellars at the southern end of the main square, and at *U troch apoštolov*, above a butcher's at no. 11 on the eastern side of the square. There's also a lunchtime-only veggie restaurant, *Vegeterián* (closed Sat & Sun) at Uhoľná 3, and a pizzeria at Vetrová 4, both off the northwestern corner of the main square.

Spišská Nová Ves and around

Thirteen kilometres south of Levoča, **SPIŠSKÁ NOVÁ VES** (Neudorf) is the modern-day capital of the Spiš region, a relatively industrious town with a population of around 40,000, whose origins are as old as Levoča's, but which has borne the brunt of the changes wreaked on the region over the twentieth century. Pawned to the Poles at the height of the Hussite Wars, along with twelve other Spiš towns, it fell to the Habsburgs when Poland was partitioned in 1772, and was immediately made the Spiš capital, a fact that played a significant part in the demise of its old rival, Levoča. As a mining town, it was virtually guaranteed to get itself on the main Košice–Bohumín railway line, built in the nineteenth century. Today, therefore, it's a good place from which to visit both the Slovenský raj and Levoča, but otherwise has only a few residual pleasures.

The main square, **Radničné námestie**, is a very long, leafy spindle-shaped avenue in the style of Prešov and Košice, with **Zimná ulica** (Winter Street) to the south, and **Letná ulica** (Summer Street), which gets the sun, to the north. The central space between the two is dotted with important-looking buildings, not least the municipal theatre, **Spišské divadlo**, a grand turn-of-the-twentieth-century building topped by a gilded swan, and worth a peek inside if only to gape at the awesome light fittings. The massive Gothic **Rímsko-katolícky kostol** boasts the tallest church tower in Slovakia and contains a couple of minor works by Master Pavol of Levoča, and there's a small **Múzeum Spiša** (Mon–Fri 8am–noon & 12.30–4.30pm, Sat 9am–1pm, Sun 1–5pm), housed in the best-looking building in town, Letná 50, which laboriously documents the mining history of the town.

The **train station** (with a left-luggage office) lies ten minutes' walk northwest of the main square, where there's a useful **tourist office** (summer Mon–Fri 8am–5pm, Sat 9.30am–1.30pm; winter Mon–Fri 8am–4.30pm), a couple of doors down from the museum, which can help you find **accommodation**. Of

the town's hotels, the monstrous high-rise *Metropol* (☎053/442 22 41, ⓦwww
.hotel-metropol.sk; ❹), west of the main square on Štefánikovo námestie, has
recently been refurbished, and now offers "luxury sweets" (sic), while the *Šport*
(☎053/442 67 53; ❷), in a large Communist-era building ten minutes' walk
south of the main square down Gorkého and across the river, is cheap and has
decent en-suite doubles and three-bed rooms. Slightly cheaper is the *Limba*
(open all year; ☎053/441 42 03; ❶), Markušovska cesta 2, a large hostel ten
minutes' walk east of the square. Decent local **food** can be had from the *Spiš*
restaurant, a couple of doors from the tourist office, which also has a self-service
section (the latter closed Sat eve & Sun).

Markušovce

A possible day-trip from Spišská Nová Ves, or from the Slovenský raj, is
MARKUŠOVCE, 5km to the southeast on the River Hornád and on the main
railway line to Košice (trains every 2–3hr; buses more frequently). Here, in this
raggle-taggle village, are the **Kaštieľ and Letohrádok Dardanely** (May–Sept
Tues–Sun 9am–5pm; Oct–April Tues–Fri & Sun 8am–4pm), originally built for
the Hungarian Mariássy family in 1643. The main kaštieľ is a wonderful yellow
chateau, built four-square with big corner drum towers topped with wooden
shingled onion domes. Inside, two floors of rooms contain the best period furniture and costumes that survive from the Spiš region, including a great room
of hunting-themed furnishings. Behind the main chateau stands the smaller,
matching summer house or Letohrádok Dardenely, built by Wolfgang Mariássy
in order to entertain Joseph II, though in the end the emperor never turned
up. It's an unusual building: named after the Dardanelles simply because Wolfgang liked Turkey, and not completed until the 1970s when the Communists
decided to add the two wings. It now houses a collection of musical keyboard
instruments, from organs to clavichords and grand pianos; concerts take place in
the fine acoustics of the Great Hall, which is lavishly decorated in amateurish
mythological trompe l'oeil frescoes.

East to Spišský hrad

The road east from Levoča takes you to the edge of the Spiš territory, clearly
defined by the Branisko ridge, which blocks the way to Prešov, and through
which the new motorway is currently being tunnelled. Even if you're not planning on going any further east, you should at least go as far as Spišské Podhradie
for arguably the most spectacular sight in the whole country.

En route, you might spot the palatial neo-Baroque chateau at **Spišský Hrhov**
peeping through its half-tamed grounds (only the latter are open to the public as the chateau is now an orphanage). Don't miss the nearby church with
a Renaissance belfry topped with an unusually sophisticated white-and-pink
pinnacle. There's no point in stopping off, at least until just past the village of
Klčov, at which point you get your first glimpse of the **Spišský hrad** (May–Oct
daily 9am–6pm), its chalk-white ruins strung out on a bleak, green hill in the
distance – an irresistibly photogenic shot, and one that finds its way into almost
every tourist brochure in the country. As a supremely strategic spot, the place
was occupied from Neolithic times onwards, but the majority of what you see
now dates from the thirteenth to the fifteenth century, when it served as the seat
of the lords of Spiš; burnt to the ground in 1781, it has been ruined ever since.
It's difficult to resist the impulse to get nearer but the ruins are less impressive
from close up; the view from the top is undeniably good, however.

If you do wish to wander round the castle, stay on the bus until **SPIŠSKÉ
PODHRADIE** (literally "below the castle") and then follow the signs to the

hrad; Spišské Podhradie also has a **train station**, linked to Spišské Vlachy by a small branch line. For **accommodation**, the *Penzión Podzámok* at Podzámková 28 (☎ & ℱ053/454 17 55, ⓦwww.penzionpodzamok.sk; ❷) has rooms and a garden with superb views up to the castle and can organize horseriding. If you've time to spare, and energy to expend, take the path from Spišský hrad towards Dreveník, the limestone hill 2km southeast of the ruins, and continue another kilometre as far as the village of **ŽEHRA**. The lure here is the UNESCO-protected thirteenth-century church of **sv Duch** (Mon–Fri 10am–4pm, Sat 2–5pm; otherwise get key at house no. 80), which sports a delicately balanced shingled onion dome and matching white perimeter walls. Inside this compact little church are faded frescoes painted around 1400, and a wonderful set of richly decorative black-and-gold early-Baroque altarpieces.

Spišská Kapitula

One kilometre west of Spišské Podhradie, and more rewarding than a wander round Spišský hrad, is the walled, one-street city of **SPIŠSKÁ KAPITULA** (Zipser Kapitel), once the ecclesiastical capital of the Spiš region, whose plain monastic towers are often featured in the foreground of the aforementioned photographs. From the front, the **Katedrála of sv Martin** is clearly a Romanesque church, built as a defiant outpost of Christianity shortly after the Tatar invasions. To get inside, you must buy a ticket from the **tourist office** (Mon–Sat 10am–noon & 1–4.30pm, Sun open from 11am) in the belfry, opposite the north door of the cathedral. The interior was originally decorated with colourful fourteenth-century frescoes celebrating the coronation of the Hungarian king Charles Robert. Here and there these have been restored after their whitewashing by Protestants during the Reformation. The furnishings are, for the most part, neo-Gothic, but there is one altarpiece worth noting in the Zápoľský chapel south of the main nave, where a fifteenth-century depiction of the Virgin Mary clearly shows the influence of Pavol of Levoča's workshop. Outside, a couple of graceful cypress trees stand at the top of the town's single street, which is lined with canons' houses, all of which are currently being restored since the re-establishment of the local Catholic seminary, where the likes of Andrej Hlinka once studied.

The Slovenský raj

After the upfront post-glacial splendour of the High Tatras, the low-key pine forests of the **Slovenský raj** (pronounced "rye" – meaning paradise, ⓦwww.slovenskyraj.sk), 20km or so to the southeast of Poprad, might seem more than a little anticlimactic at first glance. No hard-slog hiking or top-of-the-world views here, but, if your inclination is towards more frivolous outdoor pursuits, such as scrambling up rocky gorges and clinging onto chains and ladders beside shooting waterfalls, then the Slovenský raj may not be far from nirvana after all.

Covered in a thick coat of pine forest, the terrain – covering just twenty square kilometres – is typically karstic, with gentle limestone hills whittled away in places to form deep, hairline ravines and providing a dank, almost tropical escape from the dry summer heat of the Poprad plain. To the north, the Hornád river has made the deepest incision into the rock, forming a fast-flowing, snaking canyon flanked by towering jagged bluffs that attract some of the country's dedicated rock-climbers. The most dramatic ravines climb up to the grassy plateau of the Veľká poľana at the centre of the region. To the south, the geography becomes more conventional in the hills around Dedinky, and in winter the whole area turns into a popular ski resort.

Slovenský raj practicalities

It's perfectly possible to explore the area from Poprad (see p.539) by taking the **local train** to Vydrník, Letanovce or Spišské Tomášovce. However, as Poprad is not particularly conducive to lingering, it might be more pleasant to hole up at **Čingov**, where you can **stay** at the friendly, family-run *Flóra* (℡053/449 11 29, ⓦwww.hotelfloraslovenskyraj.sk; ❸), which also rents out bikes, or the *Čingov*, which has en-suite doubles with satellite TV and its own restaurant and sauna (℡053/443 36 33, ⓦwww.hotelcingov.sk; ❸). Both hotels are in quiet locations at the edge of the forest. You could also use the village of **Hrabušice** as a base, as it sports a number of cheap private rooms; less appealing Smižany, 3km northeast of Čingov, on the edge of Spišská Nová Ves, also contains a good handful of pensions. Another good option is the modern hotel *Slovenský raj* (℡ & ⓕ053/449 04 94; ❸), near Podlesok, to the west of Hrabušice, which has a swimming pool. Dedinky (see opposite) offers up a large number of private rooms, or you could even stay in Spišská Nová Ves (see p.559). If you've got a

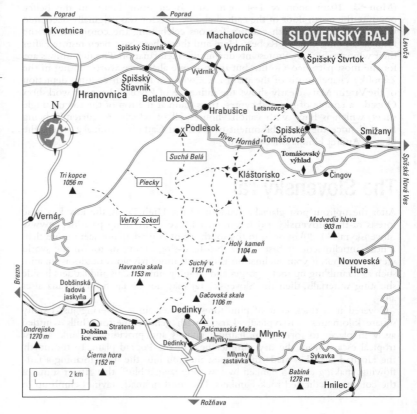

tent or caravan, the ATC Podlesok **campsite** (☎053/429 91 65) is the most convenient and open all year round, as is the more basic and less crowded ATC Tatran at Čingov (☎053/429 71 05, ⓦwww.durkovec.sk). Both have bungalow (*chaty*) accommodation (❶–❷).

Transport from the north to the south of the region is difficult, though there are buses from Poprad; otherwise you're best approaching from the picturesque Hron valley railway from Brezno (see p.536). Better still is to rely on your own two feet if the weather's good – it's not much more than 10km cross-country from Podlesok to Dedinky, but take adequate provisions with you. **Walking** is also the only way of seeing the canyons, and it's not a bad idea to try to get hold of the detailed walking map published by VKÚ Harmanec and available from local tourist offices and bookshops, which marks all the one-way paths, before you arrive in the area. The most exhilarating tracks are those designated one-way – a strange concept to get your head round until you've been up one – and it's important to stick to the direction indicated. However much you're walking, it's best to bring a pair of sturdy boots, preferably with a good grip and at the very least splash-proof – it's extremely wet and slippery underfoot all year round. Bear in mind, too, that if you're at all scared of heights, you might encounter a few problems with some of the deeper canyons. Note that occasionally some of the one-way paths are closed off to walkers, either for repairs or to give the ravine a rest. Note also that on entering the Slovenský raj you'll be charged a small fee (around 20Sk per day).

Dedinky lies on the wonderful Červená Skala–Margecany branch line, one of the prettiest **train journeys** in Slovakia. It's a slow run if you're going all the way to Košice (2hr 30min), considerably less on the midday *Horehronec* express. If you're heading south to the Slovenský kras, you may have to walk the 9km to the unprepossessing old German mining town of Dobšiná, since there's only a couple of buses a day – if you do make it, it's a spectacular thousand-foot drop from the Palcmanská Maša. Most buses continue from Dobšiná to Rožňava, or you could take one of the seven trains a day which also cover the route.

Dedinky and the Dobšiná ice cave

Since the creation of the nearby reservoir, Palcmanská Maša, **DEDINKY** has become a thriving little tourist spot all year round, and with good reason. Nestling below Gačovská skala (1106m), whose spruce trees spill down to the grassy banks of the reservoir, it's the ideal recreational centre, with plenty of opportunities for swimming, rowing, cycling, hiking and, of course, visiting the great Dobšiná ice cave. The best place **to stay** is the new pension *Anežka* (☎907/531 616; ❸), which has good views. Its rooms are also more comfortable than in the simply furnished *Hotel Priehrada* (☎058/798 12 12; ❷), by the reservoir and the Dedinky–Geravy chairlift, which also has wooden chalets and **camping** facilities (mid-June to mid-Sept). There are also some options in Mlynky, 3km east of the lake, including the stylish *Pension Salamander* on Palcmanská Maša 293 (☎053/449 35 45, ⓦwww.penzionsalamander.sk; ❸), close to the Palcmanská Maša dam, plus the pensions *Šafrán* (☎ & ⓕ058/798 11 18; ❷) and *Stratená* (☎058/798 11 32; ❷), both with restaurants, in Stratená, 4km west of Dedinky in the beautiful Stratenská valley.

Dobšiná ice cave

The most obvious day-trip from Dedinky is the **Dobšiná ice cave** (Dobšinská ľadová jaskyňa; Tues–Sun: mid-May to late May & Sept guided tours at 9.30am, 11am, 12.30pm & 2pm; June–Aug guided tours hourly 9am–4pm; 140Sk), by

With the 1:50,000 *Slovenský raj* green hiking map, published by VKÚ Harmanec (and available from many tourist offices and bookshops), you can plan your own routes. If you're staying at Podlesok and follow the green markers, you immediately enter the **Suchá Belá**, one of the most exciting river beds to explore, but also one of the most accessible and therefore extremely popular at the height of the season, causing the occasional queue at crucial ladders. With so many obstacles en route, it takes nearly everyone a full two hours to stumble up this one-way ravine to the top. Similarly breathtaking stuff can be experienced up the gladed ravine of **Piecky**, which starts from 3km along the green-marked track to the Dobšinská ľadová jaskyňa.

Should you need a rest after the morning's exertions, head down to **Kláštorisko**, whose sunny, sloping meadow is perfect for picnicking. If you've forgotten your packed lunch, the small *reštaurácia* at the top of the field might oblige. At the bottom of the clearing is an ongoing archeological dig where local Slavs built a monastery to give thanks for their safe deliverance from the Tartar invasions of the mid-thirteenth century.

If you continue for another half an hour along the green-marked path to the Dobšinská ľadová jaskyňa past the bottom of Piecky, you come to the deepest one-way gorge of the lot, **Veľký Sokol**, another succession of wooden ladders slung over rock pools and rapids, up the side of waterfalls and riverine gulleys. From the top, you can either walk north across the Veľká poľana plateau to Kláštorisko (1hr 30min) or head west to the top of the Malý Sokol, which swings round to join the last two-way quarter of the Veľký Sokol gorge.

The third main area to head for is the **Prielom Hornádu**, a sheer-sided breach (*prielom*) in the limestone rock forced by the Hornád river and Slovakia's longest river canyon. Until recently it was impossible to enter the gorge except on ice skates in winter or by kayak in summer. Now, in keeping with the vaguely vandalistic tendencies of the nation's trekkers, steel steps have been jammed into the rocks and rope bridges slung across the river, and the whole trip takes just three and a half hours from Podlesok to Čingov. If you're doing a round trip, take the yellow-marked path on the way back, which follows the limestone ridge high above the Hornád. The views are amazing, especially from the **Tomášovský výhlad**, a stick of exposed rock some 150m above the Prielom Hornádu.

far the more impressive of Slovakia's two accessible ice caves (the other is in the Low Tatras), at its best in spring or early summer although a steady 0°C year-round. Opened to the public in 1871, and the first in Europe to be electrically illuminated, in 1887, it's basically one vast underground lake frozen to a depth of over 20m and divided into two halls, the biggest of which, the Veľká sieň, is over 100m across. Although the ice formations are a long way from the subtleties of your average limestone cave, it rarely fails to impress by the brute force of its size and weight.

From Podlesok, it's a three-and-a-half-hour hike, mostly through the forest. From Dedinky, simply take the train two stops in the direction of Brezno, after which it's a twenty-minute walk into the hills. It's worth bearing in mind that the caves are very popular (so get there early) and very cold (so take something warm to put on). Should you wish to **stay** over, there's the *Hotel Ruffíny* (T & F 058/798 12 77; ②), which appears to be slipping slowly into the road, plus a clutch of pensions and private rooms.

The Slovenský kras

Like the Moravian karst region north of Brno, the **Slovenský kras** boasts some of the finest limestone caves in central Europe, the highlight of which is the Domica caves, stretching right under the border into Hungary (where they're known as the Aggtelek caves). Even now, the surrounding hills are still plundered for their ores – copper, iron and, once upon a time, gold – and the largest town in the area, Rožňava, continues to make its living from the local mines, even if the original intrepid German miners have long since gone. The towns and villages are for the most part dusty, characterless places; people are by far the dominant feature of the landscape, with large communities of Hungarians, Slovaks and Romanies living side by side.

Rožňava and around

Once the seat of a bishopric and a flourishing German mining centre, **ROŽŇAVA** (Rozsnyó) enjoys a great setting, at the meeting point of several dramatic valleys lined with rocky bluffs. Nowadays, it's a sleepy, mostly Hungarian-speaking, garrison town, though it's also an undeniably useful base when it comes to making excursions into the karst region and the nearby aristocratic haunts of Krásna Hôrka and Betliar.

The town does have a couple of redeeming features of its own: it once boasted a mint, a cathedral and an episcopal palace. Of the three, only the former **Biskupská katedrála** (now just a parish church) is worth bothering with, largely on account of its sixteenth-century altarpiece depicting the life of local miners; you'll find it just to the northwest of the expansive main square, námestie Baníkov. Also worth a look on the main square is the late-Gothic watchtower (**Strážna veža**; July–Aug Mon–Fri 10–11.30am & 1–5.30pm, Sat 10am–3.30pm, Sun noon–3.30pm; Sept–June entrances at 10am, 11am, 1pm & 2pm), which has a superb view of the town and surrounding green hills, and the statue of the much-mourned Františka Andrássy (see p.566), with Dionysus looking on adoringly as she comforts (someone else's) children. Lastly, there's the **Banícke múzeum** (Mining Museum; March–Dec Tues–Fri 8am–4pm), set in a lovely *fin-de-siècle* block, five minutes' walk along the road to Šafárikovo – it's the second museum building you want, not the first one you come to. The museum is run by a lively retired Hungarian miner who does his best to make up for the lack of information in English. Ask to see the reconstructed (and somewhat over-clean) mine shaft tucked round the back of the building (along with an iron statue of the Hungarians' hero, Kossuth), bearing the traditional, though rather ominous, inscription *Zdar Boh* (Good Luck).

All **transport** in the region has to pass through Rožňava at some point, although three train stations still seem a mite excessive. The one closest to the centre is Rožňava mesto, ten minutes' walk west along **Štítnicka**; the main one, called simply **Rožňava**, is a two-and-a-half-kilometre walk from town (bus #1 from the bus station); the bus station is just southeast of the main square. **Accommodation** is fairly limited, though the very helpful **tourist office** (mid-May to mid-Sept Mon–Fri 8am–6pm, Sat 8am–4pm, Sun noon–4pm; mid-Sept to mid-May Mon–Fri 8am–4pm, Sat 8am–noon; ☎058/732 81, ⓦwww.roznava.sk), at námestie Baníkov 32, can help if you get stuck. The ugly green *Hotel Kras* (☎058/732 42 43, ⓔhotel.kras@nextra.sk; ❸), on the corner of Štítnicka and Šafárikova, is comfortable enough inside, though you'll do much better at the *Čierný orol* (☎058/732 81 86, ⓦwww.ciernyorol.sk; ❸), a lovely place at no. 17 on the main square, with all requisite mod cons. Also recommendable is the pension *Atrium* (☎0907/589 901; ❷), just northeast of the square, while the upappealing *Úbytovňa* (☎058/732 82 00; ❷), housed in a grubby high-rise opposite the *Kras*, has the cheapest rooms in the centre. In addition to the fine **restaurant** in the *Čierny orol*, the *Atrium* does some very good Slovak dishes, or there's the *Sabi* pizzeria on the main square.

Krásnohorské Podhradie and around

Plenty of buses run the 5km to the village of **KRÁSNOHORSKÉ POD-HRADIE** (Krasznahorkaváralja), which means "below Krásna Hôrka castle". Dramatically situated on top of the nearby limestone col to protect the trade route between the Spiš region and Košice, the gaunt Gothic fortress of **Krásna Hôrka** (Tues–Sun: May–Oct 8.30am–4.30pm; Nov–April tours at 9.30am, 11am, 12.30pm & 2pm) looks utterly impregnable. The original owners, the Bebeks, fell from favour when it was discovered that they had been counter-feiting money, and the castle was subsequently confiscated and handed over to the Andrássy family. Such was the wealth of the Andrássys that they were able to turn the whole place into a family museum in 1910, having a number of other places in which they actually lived. Sadly, the compulsory guided tours are overlong (1hr 20min) and of limited general appeal.

A better bet down in the western part of the village is the original Rožňava mining museum, a fabulous Secession building from 1906, which has been recently restored and turned into the **Andrássy galéria** (mid-May to Aug Tues–Fri 9am–5pm, Sat & Sun 9am–2pm). The main glass-roofed hall now contains portraits of the Andrássy family, including the two buried in the mau-soleum described below, plus a large, dramatic canvas by the Hungarian painter, Ferenc Paczka, depicting the death of Attila the Hun. Look out, too, for the stork's nest on one of the building's chimneys.

Within sight of both castle and village, and without doubt the most beautiful Art Nouveau building in Slovakia, is the **Andrássy Mausoleum** (same hours as Krásna Hôrka), east of Krásnohorské Podhradie along route 50. It was built in 1903–04 at great expense by Count Dionysus Andrássy, in memory of his wife, the celebrated Czech opera singer Františka Hablavcová, who died in 1902. Dionysus himself was disowned by the family for marrying below his station, an action which no doubt stiffened his resolve to build an even more extrava-gant resting place for his lover. Set in its own carefully laid-out gardens with sombre wrought-iron gates and characteristic angelic janitors, the mausoleum itself is a simple dome structure of austere classicism. Inside, though, it bursts into an almost celebratory orgy of ornamentation: Venetian gold for the cupola, coloured marble from every corner of the globe, and as the centrepiece, two white Carrara marble sarcophagi in which both Františka and Dionysus (who died not long after the building was completed) are buried.

If you're looking for a **place to stay**, ignore the rather grim motel in favour of the more upmarket pension *Vila Erika* at Lípová 39 (☎058/734 61 84; ❷), with bikes for rent. There's also a **campsite**, *Pod hradom* (mid-May to mid-Sept), to the north of the village en route to the castle.

Betliar

Though owned by the same aristocratic family, the frivolous hunting chateau at **BETLIAR** (hours as for the Krásna Hôrka castle – see above), 5km northwest of Rožňava by train, couldn't be further from the brooding intensity of Krásna Hôrka. It was adapted as late as the 1880s in an "indefinite style", as the local tourist brochures put it, to accommodate the Andrássys' popular hunting parties. The guided tour takes you past a fairly surprising array of artefacts, including some exotic arms and armour from the Far East, an Egyptian mummy, a giant elephant tusk, as well as the usual period furniture, dull portraits, and (naturally enough) rows of hunting trophies. If the tour wears you down, though, the large, well-groomed English-style park easily makes up for it, with its playful, folksy rotundas, Japanese bridge, and various mock-historic edifices. If you're looking for somewhere **to stay**, the *Chatová osada* (open all year; ☎058/798 31 14; ❶–❷), near the chateau, rents out *chaty* with or without facilities.

The Gombasek, Domica and Ochtina caves

The majority of the **cave systems** in the Slovenský kras lie within 30km to the south and west of Rožňava, though without your own transport it's difficult to explore them in a day. As it is one of the prime tourist destinations in Slovakia, it's possible that you may have to queue for the more popular caves.

Gombasecká jaskyňa

The most impressive of the cave systems, featuring on the UNESCO World Heritage list since 1995 (along with the Ochtinská, Domica and Jasovská caves), the **Gombasecká jaskyňa** (Tues–Sun: April–May & Sept–Oct guided tours at 9.30am, 11am, 12.30pm & 2pm; June–Aug tours hourly 9am–4pm) is also one of the most accessible. To reach the caves, you can catch a direct bus from Rožňava, or take the train one stop south of Rožňava to Slavec Jaskyňa station, whence it's 2km further south. There's a rudimentary **campsite** (June–Sept) near the caves, and every June the nearby village of Gombasek (Gömbaszog) is the venue for the largest annual Hungarian folk bash in Slovakia.

The Jaskyňa Domica and Silická ľadnica

Ten kilometres due south of Gombasek, hard by the Hungarian border, are the **Jaskyňa Domica** (Tues–Sun: Feb–May & Sept–Dec tours at 9.30am, 11am, 12.30pm & 2pm; June–Aug tours hourly 9am–4pm): at 25km in length, this is the second longest cave system in the country. The short passage from Robert Townson (see p.568), one of the caves' earliest explorers, should give you an idea of the gushing prose they often inspire. The tours last less than an hour; theoretically, it should soon be possible to continue on a longer tour over the border into Hungary, where most of the cave system lies, but so far visiting it is possible only from the Hungarian side. Occasionally there are also longer tours including a quick boat trip (*veľký okruh s plavbou*; 130Sk) on the underground river named, rather sinisterly, Styks (Styx).

More than ten buses a day (four at weekends) ply to Plešivec, 10km away, but the most rewarding way of getting there is to follow the yellow-marked track from Gombasek. The path climbs up onto the *planina* (see p.568) and through the oak trees via the **Silická ľadnica** cave (1hr). The cave itself is closed to the public, but its ominous entrance is impressively encrusted with ice throughout the summer, melting to a dribble by late autumn, only to be replenished when the first cold spell of November arrives. Keep following the yellow markers east for 500m or so, then hang a right when you hit the red-marked path, from where it's a two-hour trek across the pockmarked tableland to Domica.

Ochtinská aragonitová jaskyňa

Of all the cave systems, the **Ochtinská aragonitová jaskyňa** (Tues–Sun: April–May & Sept–Oct guided tours at 9.30am, 11am, 12.30pm & 2pm; June–Aug tours hourly 9am–4pm) is without doubt the thinking person's cave, set apart from the others geographically and geologically. Though by no means

The following is an extract from Robert Townson's Travels in Hungary, *published in 1793. Townson, a Scottish scientist, botanized his way around the old kingdom of Hungary, staying with a lot of good-humoured Calvinists on the way, and in the passage quoted below recounts a visit to the Domica caves, long before the days of safety barriers and electric lighting.*

I descended rapidly for a short distance and then I found myself in an immense cave . . . where large stalactites, as thick as my body, hung pendant from the roof, and I was shown others where the sides were ornamented in the manner of the most curious Gothic workmanship. In some the stalactites were so thick and close together that we were in danger of losing one another if we separated but a few yards. Here aged stalactites, overloaded with their own weight, had fallen down and lay prostrate; and there an embryo stalactite was just shooting into existence.

After I had wandered about for three or four hours in this awful gloom and had reached the end of the caverns in one direction, I thought it time to come out, and I desired my guide to return. After we returned, as we thought, some way, we found no passage further; yet the guide was sure he was right. I thought I recognized the same rocks we had just left, and which had prevented our proceeding further, but the guide was positive he was in a right direction. Luckily for us I had written my name on the soft clay of the bottom of the cave, which had been the extent of our journey; on seeing this the guide was thunderstruck, and ran this way and that way and knew not where he was, nor what to do. I desired him not to be frightened, but to go calmly to work to extricate us from this labyrinth . . .

After wandering about till all our wood was nearly exhausted, we found a great stalactite from which, on account of its remarkable whiteness, I had been induced to knock off a specimen as I came by: I recollected how I stood when I struck it: this at once set us right, and after walking a little further we made ourselves heard to the other guide, from whom we got fresh torches, and we continued our route homewards without further difficulty.

So complete a labyrinth as these caverns are in some places, is not I am sure to be found in similar caverns: large open passages proved cul de sacs, whilst our road was over and under, through and amongst grotto work of the most intricate nature. I finally believe that though a man should have lights and food enough to last him a month – he would not be able to find his way out.

as spectacular in scale as the other limestone caves, it has the unique and breathtakingly beautiful feature of spiky aragonite "flowers", which form like limpets on the cave side. From Plešivec, there's an infrequent train service to Ochtiná (35min), after which the cave is a three-kilometre walk uphill southwest along the blue-marked path; from Rožňava, there are even more infrequent buses (40min). If you're travelling by car, you can reach the cave most easily from the turn-off to Hrádok on route 526 from Štítnik to Jelšava.

Zádielska dolina and the caves at Jasov

One of the more bizarre karstic features of the Slovenský kras is the forested sheets of **planina** or tableland which rise above the plains like the coastal cliffs of a lost sea. In fact, the opposite is the case, the rivers having whittled down what would otherwise be a featureless limestone plateau. Mostly, these erosions form broad sweeping valleys, but in a few cases cracks appear in the more familiar form of riverine crevices.

The most dramatic of these is the **Zádielska dolina**, a brief but breathtaking three or four kilometres of sky-scraping canyon. To get there, take the train or bus to Dvorníky, 25km east of Rožňava and 1km south of the Hungarian-speaking village Zádiel (Szádelö), at the entrance to the dolina. There's none of the Slovenský raj assault course on this hike, just a gentle yet magnificent stroll between the two bluffs. For something slightly more death-defying, return along the blue-marked track, which ascends the right-hand ridge and shadows the canyon back to Zádiel, then drops down 2.5km east of Dvorníky near the cement works of Turňa nad Bodvou. For a longer hike (15km) you could follow the blue-marked path over the hills to Jasov, or take the green- then red-marked track to Pipitka (1225m), 10km away, returning to Rožňava by bus from the Úhornianske sedlo down below.

Jasov

The Premonstratensian monastery at **JASOV** (Jászó) is visible across the fields long before you reach the town. It's actually much older than its eighteenth-century Baroque appearance would suggest. The monastery church contains some superb, recently restored frescoes by the Austrian painter J.L. Kracker, who also embellished the ceiling of the library, to which you may be able to gain access. The formal gardens behind the monastery are also worth exploring. The chief reason most locals visit Jasov, though, is to see the **Jasovská jaskyňa** (Tues–Sun: April–May & Sept–Oct guided tours at 9.30am, 11am, 12.30pm & 2pm; June–Aug tours hourly 9am–4pm), the least-hyped caves in the karst region, which specialize in forests of "virgin" stalactites and contain some amazing graffiti scrawled on the walls by fugitive Czech Hussites in 1452. The only accommodation is the village's lively **campsite** (open all year), which also rents out *chaty*, but if you're coming from Košice, Jasov can be done easily enough as a day-trip.

Carpatho-Ruthenia

Carpatho-Ruthenia* is one of those places where people hail from rather than go to. Infamous media mogul Robert Maxwell and the parents of Andy Warhol were just a few of the million or so inhabitants who left the northeastern corner of what was then the Austro-Hungarian Empire (and later Czechoslovakia) in the late nineteenth and early twentieth centuries to seek fame and fortune elsewhere, mostly in North America.

They left to escape not so much the region's unerring provinciality, but its grinding poverty and unemployment, only quite recently abated. Even in the 1950s, an estimated 41 percent of Rusyn villages were still without electricity, and by 1968 their living standards were less than half the national average. Today, the villages are still visibly poorer and more isolated than their western counterparts – until recently, few visitors had passed through since the Russians in 1945 (and again in 1968). Some things have changed, though not always for the best: parts of the region took a hammering in the

---

*Carpatho-Ruthenia or Sub-Carpatho-Ruthenia (Podkarpatská Rus in Slovak) was the name for the easternmost province of Czechoslovakia taken as war booty by the Soviet Union in 1945. Here, the term is used loosely to refer to the East Slovak districts on the border with Poland and Ukraine, where the Rusyn minority still predominate.

last war, and wooden buildings, once the norm, have gradually been replaced by concrete and brick; traditional costumes are now worn almost exclusively by the over-seventies; and the heavy industry, which was crudely implanted here by the Communists to try to stem the continuing emigration, is now struggling to survive.

From a visitor's point of view, **Prešov** and **Bardejov** are both easy to reach and immediately appealing. Further afield, transport becomes a real problem (as it is for the local inhabitants), the north–south axis of the valleys in particular hindering the generally eastbound traveller. Accommodation also peters out and declines in quality the deeper you go, so unless you have a car, you'll want to book rooms in advance. Nevertheless, it's worth persevering, if only to visit the region's most unusual sight, the Andy Warhol Museum in **Medzilaborce**.

Prešov

PREŠOV (Eperjes) has a long and chequered ethnic history. Situated on a major north–south trade route, it was a Hungarian Royal Free Town from medieval times, and one, like Levoča, where Saxons were encouraged to settle. Nowadays, with few Germans and Hungarians remaining, it serves as the capital of the Slovak Šariš region and the cultural centre of the outlying Rusyn community. With a population approaching 100,000, Prešov is a large, and – for the most part – unattractive town. However, in the centre, there are glimpses of the town's past prosperity in those buildings that survived the 1887 fire. The old town, in particular, has been treated to a wonderful facelift, and although there's not much of interest beyond its main square, Prešov is a refreshingly youthful and vibrant university town worth at least a half day's halt.

Arrival, information and accommodation

The **bus** and **train stations** are situated opposite one another about 1km south of the main square, and connected by trolleybus (take any one which stops at Na Hlavnej). There's a **tourist office** (Mon–Fri 9am–6pm, Sat 9am–1pm; ☎051/773 11 13, ⓦwww.presov.sk) at Hlavná 67, very near to the radnica. An additional information office (Mon–Fri 6am–6pm, Sat 6–11am) is located in the underground passage leading to the train station. Prešov's best **hotels** are the *Senátor* (☎051/773 11 86; ❹), a newly done-up place above the tourist office with small self-catering apartments, or the nicely refurbished Communist-era *Dukla*, south of the main square (☎051/772 27 41, ⓦwww.hoteldukla.sk; ❺). There are a few smaller **pensions** in the streets west of the square, such as the *Antonio* (☎051/772 32 25, ⓦwww.antoniopension.sk; ❸), at Jarková 22 (also accessible from the square), or the cheaper *Sen* **hostel**, Vajanského 65 (☎051/773 3170; ❷).

The Town

The lozenge-shaped main square, **Hlavná ulica**, is flanked by creamy, pastel-coloured, almost edible eighteenth-century facades, some topped by exceptionally appealing and varied gables and pediments, others, as at no. 22, embellished with frolicking cherubs, angels and even monkeys. Prešov's Catholic and Protestant churches vie with each other at the widest point of the square. Naturally enough, the fourteenth-century Roman Catholic church of **sv Mikuláš** has the edge, not least for its Gothic vaulting, its

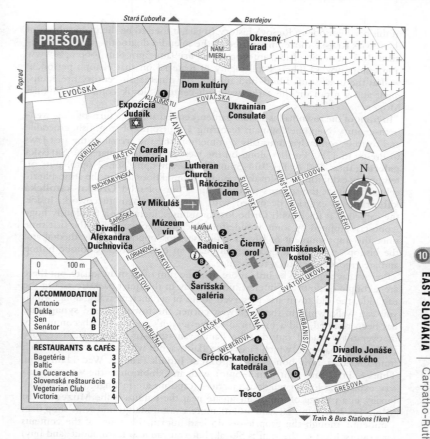

modern Moravian stained-glass windows and its highly theatrical Baroque altarpiece, flanked by barley-sugar columns and complete with matching pulpit and side altars.

Behind sv Mikuláš, the much plainer **Evanjelický chrám** (Lutheran Church), built in the mid-seventeenth century, bears witness to the strength of religious reformism in the outer reaches of Hungary at a time when the rest of the Habsburgs' lands were suffering the full force of the Counter-Reformation. In the 1670s, the tide turned, and a wave of religious persecution followed, culminating in the 1687 Blood Tribunal in which twenty-four leading Lutherans were publicly hanged in Prešov's main square. The prime mover behind the trial was **Count Caraffa**, the papal nuncio in Vienna, whose moustached figure, flanked by a hooded executioner, stands above the grim memorial (in Hungarian) on the corner of the Protestant Lycée, next door to the church.

To the south is Prešov's **radnica**, from whose unsuitably small balcony the Czechoslovak Republic was declared in October 1918. Eight months later, Béla Kun's Hungarian Red Army declared the Slovak Socialist Republic, which lasted a mere three weeks. Searching for a socialist tradition that never really existed in this part of the country, the Slovak Communists made much of this brief episode in Prešov's history. In fact, it used to be the main subject of the town's Krajské múzeum, situated in the splendid dogtooth-gabled **Rákóc-ziho dom** at no. 86 (Tues 9am–6pm, Wed–Fri 9am–5pm, Sun 1–6pm; ⓦ www .muzeumpresov.sk). There's still plenty of material on that chaotic period, as well as the usual stuffed birds and animals, the nineteenth-century fire equipment and a room on the early twentieth-century Slovak composer, Mikuláš Moyzes.

In front of the town hall is a small garden, centred around a turn-of-the-twentieth-century Neptune fountain featuring a foursome of frog, fish, crocodile and tortoise, somewhat unusually commemorating the arrival of the first Jews to Prešov in 1780. Further along on the west side of the square, the **Šarišská galéria** (Tues, Wed & Fri 9am–5pm, Thurs 9am–6pm, Sun 2–6pm) puts on temporary exhibitions of Slovak art on the ground floor and in the atmospheric cellar. Finally, at the square's southern tip, is the splendid **Grécko-katolícká katedrála**, its exterior decorated with delicate Rococo stuccowork. Inside, the cathedral is filled with Orthodox furnishings, including a fabulously huge iconostasis, topped by some wonderful gilded filigree work. For the first time since the imprisonment of Pavel Gojdič (see box opposite), the cathedral and the bishop's palace next door actually have an extant Greek-Catholic bishop and are enjoying a cultural renaissance.

Prešov may appear to be little more than the sum of its main square, but there are a couple of points of interest hidden away in the quiet backstreets. On the east side, the old town has preserved some of its ancient walls, along which you can walk, while in the northwest corner, the town's disused **synagogue** has been restored, and a memorial to the region's prewar Jewish community of over 6000 placed outside. The flamboyant turn-of-the-twentieth-century Orthodox synagogue, which faces onto Baštova, but which you must approach from Okružná, now houses an **Expozícia Judaik** (Tues & Wed 11am–4pm, Thurs & Fri 10am–1pm, Sun 1–5pm), with an exhibition in the women's gallery explaining Jewish religious practices (captions are in English and Slovak). Finally, in a passage off the main square near the radnica is the **Múzeum vín** (Mon–Fri 9am–6pm, Sat 8am–noon), more a vast underground wine shop than a museum, though the proprietors do lead informative tours of the contents for visitors. Most of the stuff is Slovak, but you can also learn about (and buy) anything from French to Ukrainian tipple as well.

Eating, drinking and entertainment

Away from the big hotels, **eating** possibilities are improving. If it's lunch you're looking for, a freshly baked Slovak baguette from *Bagetéria*, on the main square at no. 36, is probably your best bet; for coffee and cakes, Habsburg-style, head for the *Victoria*, on the corner of Svätoplukova, with its high ceiling and chandeliers. Nothing less than eleven **restaurants** are housed around the main square, including the cheap but decent *Baltic*, upstairs at no. 26. For vegetarian food, try *Vegetarian Club*, at no. 70, while more traditional fare can be had at the *Slovenská reštaurácia* (closed Sat eve & Sun), no. 11, which is pleasant and unpretentious. For pizza, try the *La Cucaracha*, on ulica Ku Kumštu, just north off the main square.

Prešov prides itself on its cultural traditions, with two large-scale **theatres** in town, and an annual *Hudobná jar* (Musical Spring), a cultural feast that takes place in April and May. The mainstream Divadlo Jonáša Záborského (DJZ) is south of the main square, while the more famous Divadlo Alexandra Duchnoviča (DAD), is based in a theatre on Jarková, west off the square, and is home to the renowned PUĽS Dukla Folk Ensemble (ⓦ www.lemko.org); though

The **Rusyns** or Ruthenians are one of the lost peoples of central Europe. Even their name is the subject of debate, since *Rusyn* is often taken to mean Little Russian or Ukrainian, though in the Hungarian kingdom it simply referred to any non-Roman Catholic Slavs. As to their political history, the picture is equally confusing. Their language is considered by scholars to be a western Lemko dialect of Ukrainian, but their homeland actually never was part of Ukraine, and the mountains in which they had settled soon became a permanent political barrier, dividing their territory between Hungary and Poland.

Meanwhile, the Rusyns' great cultural institution, the Orthodox Church, underwent a series of crises and schisms which resulted in the Act of Union of 1596; this established the Uniate Church as part of the Roman Catholic Church, and after 1772 it became known as the Byzantine-Catholic or **Greek-Catholic Church**. This unique religion, tied to Rome but with all the trappings of Eastern Orthodoxy, became (and still is) the carrier of the Rusyn national identity. In every other way – dress codes, mores and folklore – they were hardly distinguishable from their Magyar and Slovak neighbours. Throughout this period, they remained, as they still do to a great extent, hill-dwelling peasants with no political or economic influence.

The first national leaders to emerge in the nineteenth century were, predictably enough, Greek-Catholic priests, and – like many Slovaks at the time – fiercely Russophile and pro-tsar. They played little part in the downfall of the Habsburg Empire, and when Ruthenia became a province of the new Czechoslovak Republic in 1918, it was largely due to the campaigning efforts of a handful of well-connected Ruthenian immigrants in the USA. The Slovaks laid claim to most of the land west of the River Uh (Uzh in Ukrainian), an area containing around 100,000 Rusyns; the actual province of Ruthenia, to the east, which contained not only 370,000 Rusyns but large numbers of Hungarians, Jews, Romanies and even Romanians, was annexed by the Soviet Union following "liberation" in 1945, when the area around the River Uh became a permanent border.

On the surface, the Rusyns who remained in Czechoslovakia were treated better than any other minority since the war. Scratch this surface, however, and things begin to look much less rosy. Given a free choice (as they were between the wars and before 1948), the Rusyns tended to opt for either the local dialect or Russian as the language of instruction in their schools. After the 1948 coup, however, the Communist regime intervened and ruled that the term *Rusyn* was "an anti-progressive label" – all Rusyns became officially known as Ukrainians, and the language of instruction in Rusyn schools was changed to literary Ukrainian. The reaction of the Rusyns to the resulting pedagogical chaos was to opt for Slovak rather than Ukrainian schools. Secondly, collectivization, which disrupted all peasant communities in Eastern Europe, encouraged urbanization (and therefore Slovak assimilation). Lastly, and perhaps most cruelly of all, following the example of the Stalinist authorities, the Greek-Catholic Church was forcibly amalgamated into the Orthodox Church. Its priests and dissenting laity were, for the most part, rounded up and thrown in prison, including the Church's one and only Slovak bishop, **Pavel Gojdič,** who received a life sentence and died in Leopoldov prison in 1960.

Hardly surprising then that in the last three censuses, fewer than 40,000 declared themselves as Rusyn. No one knows the real numbers, but it's estimated that as many as 130,000 Rusyns still live in East Slovakia. Since the Velvet Revolution things have begun to look up. The Greek-Catholics (who include large numbers of Slovaks) have managed to get back much of the property handed over in the 1950s to the Orthodox community (reckoned to be as few as 30,000). Meanwhile, **Ján Hirka** was ordained as Prešov's Greek-Catholic bishop in 1990, and the martyr Pavel Gojdič was beatified. In 1991, the first World Congress of Rusyns was held in Medzilaborce; in 1995, literary Rusyn was officially codified and proclaimed before government, state and academic officials in Bratislava; and in 1997, a second Greek-Catholic bishopric was established in Košice.

a Rusyn/Ukrainian theatre, plays are generally performed in Rusyn. It's also worth checking out what's on at the Čierny orol **concert hall**, down the passage to the east of the square.

Bardejov and around

Over 40km north of Prešov, not far from the Polish border, **BARDEJOV** (Bartfeld) was built by Saxon weavers who colonized the area in the twelfth century. Today, it is an almost perfectly preserved walled medieval town, comfortably positioned on its own rock with the obligatory sprawl of postwar development below. However, while the buildings remain remarkably intact, the population of the town has changed immeasurably since World War II. Bardejov's Jewish community (over fifty percent of the town's total population) was devastated in the Holocaust, and the rest of its German-speaking population were kicked out after the war. Nowadays, like Prešov, Bardejov acts as a commercial and administrative centre for the outlying Rusyn villages, most obviously during the Saturday morning market.

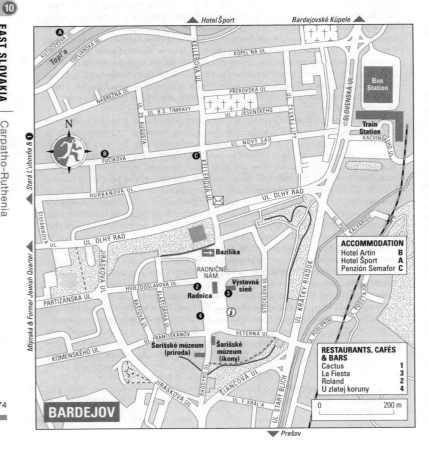

▲ Hotel Šport   Bardejovské Kúpele ▲

Stará Ľubovňa &

Mlynská & Former Jewish Quarter ◀

ACCOMMODATION

Hotel Artin	B
Hotel Šport	A
Penzión Semafor	C

Bazilika

RADNIČNÉ NÁM.

Výstavná sieň

Radnica

Šarišské múzeum (príroda)

Šarišské múzeum (ikony)

RESTAURANTS, CAFÉS & BARS

Cactus	1
La Fiesta	3
Roland	2
U zlatej koruny	4

0   200 m

BARDEJOV

▼ Prešov

The Town

The **staré mesto** (a 5min walk southwest of the bus and train stations) remains remarkably unchanged since its Saxon days, retaining most of its Gothic fortifications, including four of the original bastions along the eastern wall. The pristine cobbled main square, **Radničné námestie**, with its characteristic triangular gables (many of which are still faced with wooden slats), is straight out of the German Middle Ages. Along the north side is the **Bazilika** (Mon–Fri 9.30am–4.30pm, Sat 10am–3pm, Sun 11.30am–2pm), a suitably vast Gothic church thanks to the burghers' wealth at the time. The interior is stuffed full of fifteenth-century carved wooden side altars – eleven in all – though only two sculptures and one painting survive from the original main altar by Pavol of Levoča; the current work is neo-Gothic. The fifteenth-century stone tabernacle is also noteworthy, as are the pew ends which feature grinning half-dog, half-monkey creatures. Don't miss climbing the belltower, the top of which offers great photo opportunities over the square.

The sandy-coloured building in the centre of the square is the town's Renaissance **radnica**, whose eastern facade boasts a beautiful stone staircase and oriel window, and whose gables sport sculptures of strange animals and figures. No longer a town hall, the radnica now forms part of the **Šarišské múzeum** (May–Sept daily 8.30am–noon & 12.30–5pm; Oct–April Tues–Sun 8am–noon & 12.30–4pm), housing a number of striking fifteenth-century wooden sculptures and epitaphs, as well as the original of the rather battered statue of Roland, a copy of which adorns the apex of the gable. The finest selection of exhibits is housed in another branch of the museum on the corner of Rhodyho, at the top end of the square (same hours as above). Inside, there's an impressive collection of sixteenth- to nineteenth-century icons (many in need of serious restoration) and a fascinating series of models of the region's Greek-Catholic churches (see p.576).

A couple of blocks west of the old town is the former **Jewish quarter**, from which 3700 local Jews were rounded up and dispatched to the camps; a small plaque depicting two hands tearing through Hebrew script was erected on Mlýnská, ten minutes' walk west along Dlhý rad from the Republika, to mark the spot. There are now just two Jews in Bardejov, one of whom administers the cluster of buildings remaining along Mlýnská, which are undergoing slow restoration. The plaque itself is mounted on the walls of the former ritual baths, the domed building next door to what was the kosher butcher's, and behind them is the former eighteenth-century **synagogue**, which is currently rented out to a plumbing supply firm; they are only too happy to show visitors the building's rich ceiling decoration and its Polish-style four-pillared interior.

Practicalities

It's possible to come here on a day-trip from Prešov, though given the added attractions of the nearby spa, Bardejovské kúpele (see p.577), and the proximity of several wooden churches, you might prefer to stay overnight. That said, **accommodation** is pretty limited, with the town's chief hotel, the *Republika*, still out of action. The **tourist office** (mid-June to mid-Sept Mon–Fri 9am–6pm, Sat & Sun 10am–noon & 1.30–4pm; mid-Sept to mid-June Mon–Fri 9am–noon & 1–4.30pm; ☎054/472 62 73, Ⓦwww.bardejov.sk), on the main square at no. 21, can be valuable in helping to arrange private rooms, or you might consider heading over to Bardejovské Kúpele, where there's more choice. In Bardejov, there's just the *Penzión Semafor* (☎0905/830 984, Ⓔsemafor@stonline.sk; ❷), an excellent family pension at Kellerova 13, *Hotel Artin* (☎054/472 30 50, Ⓦwww.hotelartin .sk; ❸), which offers clean, modern rooms in a soulless edifice at Fučíkova 25, five

In the villages around Bardejov, Svidník and Humenné, a remarkable number of **wooden churches** have survived to the present day. Many (but by no means all) are Greek-Catholic churches located within Rusyn villages, and most date from around the eighteenth century, when the influence of Baroque was beginning to make itself felt even among the carpenter architects of the Carpathians. A threesome of shingled onion domes, as at Dobroslava, is the telltale sign, though the humbler churches opt for simple barn-like roofs. Below is a list of eight of the best, though there are plenty of other superb examples out there.

To visit many of the churches in situ, you really need your own transport, although there's a whole cluster within easy walking distance of the main road from Svidník to the Polish border. The tourist office in Bardejov occasionally organizes trips to four of the nearest wooden churches for around 260Sk per person, or can give contact details as you'll need to get hold of a key (*kľúč*). Most custodians will charge a small entrance fee to let you in (20–30Sk). The easiest way of having a close look, of course, is to visit one of the **skanzens** at Bardejovské kúpele, Svidník or Humenné, each of which contains a wooden church.

The dark and intimate interior of a Greek-Catholic/Orthodox church is divided into three sections (from west to east): the narthex or entrance porch, the main nave, and the naos or sanctuary. Even the smallest Greek-Catholic church boasts a rich iconostasis all but cutting off the sanctuary, with the familiar icons of (from left to right) St Nicholas, the Madonna and Child, Christ Pantocrator and, lastly, the saint to whom the church is dedicated. Above the central door of the iconostasis (through which only the priest may pass) is the Last Supper, while to the left are busy scenes from the great festivals of the church calendar – the Annunciation, the Assumption and so on. The top tier of icons features the Apostles (with St Paul taking the place of Judas). Typically, the *Last Judgement* covers the wall of the narthex, usually the most gruesome of all the depictions, with the damned being burned, boiled and decapitated with macabre abandon.

Dobroslava 7km north of Svidník. A delightful pagoda-style Orthodox (formerly Greek-Catholic) church, with a wide cruciform ground plan, distinctive triplet of shingled onion domes and an amazing Bosch-style *Last Judgement*.

Hervartov 8km southwest of Bardejov. This Roman Catholic church, erected in the 1490s, is the oldest in the country, and features some remarkable seventeenth-century murals depicting "wise and crazy virgins".

Ladomírová 4km northeast of Svidník. Greek-Catholic church on the main road to the Dukla Pass, with an eccentric mishmash of pagodas, baubles and cupolas.

Lukov 14km west of Bardejov. Orthodox, previously Greek-Catholic, church, which boasts a fantastic red-black, sixteenth-century, diagrammatical depiction of the *Last Judgement* on the iconostasis.

Miroľa 12km east of Svidník. Eighteenth-century Greek-Catholic/Orthodox church, one of the most perfect examples of the triple Baroque cupolas descending in height from west to east.

Nižný Komárnik 12km northeast of Svidník. An unusual Greek-Catholic church, built in 1938, in the unique Bojko style, with the central cupola higher than the other two.

Tročany 15km south of Bardejov. Eighteenth-century Greek-Catholic church with simple cupolas like candle extinguisher caps; renowned for its lurid, rustic icon of the *Last Judgement*.

Uličské Krivé 35km northeast of Snina. Eighteenth-century Greek-Catholic church rich in seventeenth-century icon paintings, including one depicting the archangel Michael casually pulverizing Sodom and Gomorrah.

minutes' walk northwest of the square, or the basic, hostel-style *Šport* (☎054/472 49 49; ❷), on Kutuzovova, on the north bank of the River Topľa, some ten minutes' walk from the old town. Adequate **food** and beer can be had at the *U zlatej koruny* café-restaurant and snack-bar complex on the main square, but for a proper sit-down meal, your better bet is the pizzeria *La Fiesta*, a couple of doors to the left, or *Roland*, a congenial wine bar in the cellar under no. 12 on the main square, which serves passable pizzas. For beer, head for the *Cactus*, a relax centre at Štefániková 61, a fifteen-minute walk west of the centre, along Dlhý rad and Štefániková, which has a pub, sauna and gym.

Bardejovské kúpele

Hourly buses cover the 4km north from Bardejov to the spa town of **BARDE-JOVSKÉ KÚPELE** (Bad Bartfeld; ⓦwww.kupele-bj.sk), once a favourite playground of the Austro-Hungarian and Russian nobility. A series of devastating fires in 1910–12 destroyed most of the spa's old wooden buildings, and nowadays, only a few surviving nineteenth-century mansions hint at its former glory. Still, there's lots of greenery and traffic-free streets, and you can sample the hot waters at the 1970s concrete **Kolonáda** (daily 6–8am, 10.30am–1pm & 4.30–6.30pm), in the centre of the spa.

The major attraction for non-patients, however, is the excellent *skanzen*, **Múzeum ľudovej architektúry** (May–Sept daily 8.30am–6pm; Oct–April Tues–Sun 8am–noon & 12.30–4pm), clearly signposted on the far northwestern side of the spa, which contains a whole series of timber-framed buildings, thatched cottages and two eighteenth-century wooden Greek-Catholic churches transferred from the surrounding Rusyn villages of Mikulášová and Zboj (for more on the region's wooden churches, see opposite). Tickets for the *skanzen* also give entry to the Vila Rákoczi, which has permanent displays on the history of the spa and local folk traditions, as well as interesting temporary exhibitions covering similar ground.

The spa's only other claim to fame is its seated bronze statue of the **Empress Elisabeth**, wife of the Habsburg Emperor Franz-Josef I, who was a frequent visitor to the spa until her death at the hands of an Italian anarchist in 1898. A group of Hungarian admirers erected the statue in 1903, but wisely left the empress's name off the plinth, allowing her real identity to remain hidden during the ideological vicissitudes of the last century. The statue stands in front of the *Hotel Dukla*, just east of the *skanzen*.

Accommodation choices are limited if you're not actually receiving spa treatment. The most impressive place (on the outside at least) is the *Hotel Astória* (☎054/472 412 2; ❾), a yellow and salmon-pink hotel built in 1898 and situated opposite the Kolonáda – however, it's seen better days; or else there's the gargantuan *Hotel Satel Minerál* (☎052/472 41 22, ⓦwww.satel-slovakia.sk; ❸), a Communist-era high-rise at the southern edge of the spa, that's probably improved slightly since it was first built.

Svidník and the Dukla Pass

Twenty kilometres or so due east of Bardejov and almost completely obliterated in the heavy fighting of October 1944, **SVIDNÍK** today is, not surprisingly, a characterless concrete sprawl. However, it does contain a clutch of intriguing museums and an open-air *skanzen* of Rusyn folk architecture, and hosts a Rusyn folk festival each year in the middle of June. It's also by far the most convenient base from which to explore the wooden Greek-Catholic churches in the Rusyn villages, chiefly those near the Dukla Pass.

△ Roadside chapel, East Slovakia

The town's main street is **Sovietskych hrdinov** (Soviet Heroes' Street), which heads northeast towards the Dukla Pass and boasts a statue of Ludvík Svoboda, leader of the Czechoslovak Army during World War II. The first turning on the right is Centrálna, a pedestrianized street, on which you'll find the **Múzeum ukrajinsko–rusínskej kultúry** (Tues–Fri 8.30–11am & 11.30am–4pm, Sat & Sun 10–11am & 11.30am–4pm; ⓦ www.muk.sk), containing a fine array of Rusyn folk gear and models of various Greek-Catholic churches, as well as a beautiful collection of traditional painted Easter eggs. Ten minutes' walk further east up Centrálna past the bus station, and clearly signposted round town, is the **Galéria Dezidera Millyho**, on Partizánska (same hours as above), mostly given over to contemporary Rusyn artists but with a couple of retrospective rooms devoted to Milly, one of the first Rusyn artists to win acclaim for his Expressionist paintings of local peasant life. The gallery also houses some weird and wonderful sixteenth- to nineteenth-century icon paintings, among the finest in East Slovakia.

Back at the town's main crossroads, and looking something like the Slovak answer to New York's Guggenheim Museum, is the **Dukelské múzeum** (July–Aug Tues–Fri 8am–4pm, Sat & Sun 8.30am–5pm; Sept–June Tues–Fri 8am–4pm, Sat & Sun 10am–2pm), housing a fairly standard exhibition on World War II, with plenty of military paraphernalia and a diorama of the Valley of Death (see The Dukla Pass, below). If you follow the path past the military detritus behind the museum, you'll eventually reach the town's gigantic **Soviet war memorial** (Památník sovietskej armáde), commemorating the many thousands who fell in the fighting. It's a typically overblown affair, full of reliefs of victorious soldiers and sprinkled with quotes from Czechoslovakia's postwar Communist leader, Klement Gottwald.

Crossing the main road to Bardejov, to the south of the memorial, there are signs to Svidník's open-air folk *skanzen*, **Múzeum ukrajinskej a rusínskej dediny** (May to mid-Oct Tues–Fri 8.30am–6pm, Sat & Sun 10am–6pm), on Festivalová. If you're not planning to visit any of the less-accessible villages, this is a great opportunity to get a close look at some thatched Rusyn cottages and a typical wooden Greek-Catholic church, transplanted from the nearby village of Nová Polianka.

Svidník really has few redeeming features, and the only decent **accommodation** is at the *Hotel Rubín* (☎054/752 28 78; ❷), one of the many eyesores on Centrálna, followed by the even uglier *Hotel Hubert* (☎054/752 33 88; ❷), on Sovietskych hrdínov, just southwest of the main crossroads. Otherwise, head for the **tourist office** (Mon–Fri 9am–noon & 1–4.30pm; ☎054/16186, ⓦwww. svidnik.sk), hidden in the local cultural building on the corner of the main crossroads, at Sovietskych hrdinov 38. Trains don't run to Svidník, but the **bus station** is ten minutes' walk southeast of the centre along Centrálna.

The Dukla Pass

The **Dukla Pass** (Dukliansky priesmyk), a fifteen-kilometre bus trip northeast of Svidník, was for centuries the main mountain crossing on the trade route from the Baltic to Hungary. This location has ensured a bloody history, the worst episode occurring in the last war, when some 60,000 Soviet soldiers and 6500 Czechs and Slovaks died trying to capture the valley from the Nazis. There's a giant granite memorial to the Dukla Heroes at the top of the pass, 1km from the Polish border, as well as an open-air museum of underground bunkers, tussling tanks and sundry armoured vehicles, strung out along the road from Vyšný Komárnik, the first village to be liberated in Czechoslovakia (on Oct 6, 1944), to Krajná Poľana. For a bird's-eye view over the battleground climb the massive concrete **lookout tower**, (*Vyhliadková veža na Dukli*; mid-April to mid-Oct Tues–Fri 8.30am–5pm, Sat & Sun 9.30am–6pm).

Humenné

HUMENNÉ, like Prešov and Bardejov, is another Slovak town serving as a centre for the neighbouring Rusyn villages. It is a modern and spacious place, with more charm than you'd expect from a town based on the chemical industry; the few visitors who do make it this far (mostly Slovak emigrés) head straight down the leafy main boulevard, Námestie slobody, from the train station to Humenné's one and only sight, the stately seventeenth-century **zámok** (May–Oct Mon–Fri 9am–6pm, Sat & Sun 2–6pm; Nov–April Mon–Fri 9am–4pm), which is guarded by two female and two male lead lions. However, the local museum inside is not really worth visiting unless you need to escape from the rain. Instead, head northeast across the adjacent park to the open-air folk *skanzen* (**Expozícia ľudovej architektúry a bývania**; May–Oct Tues–Sun 10am–5pm) round the back of the chateau gardens. Set in a pretty little meadow-cum-orchard, there's a whole series of thatched cottages and farmhouses, and a characteristic eighteenth-century wooden Greek-Catholic church from Nová Sedlica; ask for an *anglický text*.

To get into town from the main **bus** and **train stations**, turn right and continue along the main road, Staničná ulica, until you come to the leafy pedestrianized promenade of Námestie slobody, which leads up to the zámok. If you need to **stay**, head for the high-rise *Hotel Chemes* (☎057/776 26 09, ⓦwww.chemes.sk; ❸), behind the Hummené mesto train station on Námestie slobody, which is at least newly refurbished, or the small, violet *Penzión Albina* (☎057/775 63 03; ❹), at the opposite end of the main square (no. 61). Cheap en-suite rooms are available at the *Domov mládeže SOU služieb* (☎057/775 21 73; ❶), at Mierová 79, ten minutes' walk west of the zámok. For **food**, there's the inexpensive *Gastrocentrum* (closed in the evening) on the main square, though you'd be better off heading opposite to the friendly, unpretentious *Dukla*, which serves up hearty Slovak and international fare.

Medzilaborce

Although actually closer to Svidník, **MEDZILABORCE** is best approached by train from Humenné, 42km to the south. The main reason for making the long journey out here is to visit the town's **Múzeum moderného umenia** (Tues–Sun 10am–3.30pm; 100Sk), one of the most surreal experiences this side of the Carpathians.

The inspiration for the museum came from local Rusyn artists and relatives of **Andy Warhol**, both from the US and the area around Medzilaborce, following the death of the artist in 1987. Although Warhol was born in Pittsburgh, the steel, aluminium and glass capital of the US, his real name was Andrej Varchola and his parents hailed from the Rusyn village of Miková, 8km northwest of Medzilaborce; his father was a coal miner who, like many Rusyns, emigrated to the States shortly before World War I and was joined by the rest of the family in 1918. When fame and fortune hit in the 1960s, Warhol rarely made reference to his Slav origins, either in his work or conversation – "I come from nowhere" was his favourite enigmatic response.

Since Medzilaborce is a one-street town, it's impossible to miss the museum, a strikingly modern building, with two giant Campbell's soup cans standing guard outside the side entrance and Andy himself as a fountain by the main one. The modest collection of original screen prints, on loan from the Andy Warhol Foundation in New York, is displayed upstairs in the main hall – the psychedelic *Red Lenin* and *Hammer & Sickle* are particularly appropriate choices – along with biographical details and quotes from Warhol (in Slovak, Rusyn and English) and a smattering of works by Ultra Violet. In the upper gallery, there are some derivative prints by Andy's brother, Paul, and his nephew, James, followed by a room of family portraits.

In addition to the Warhol stuff, the museum hosts temporary exhibitions, ranging from work by other Pop artists to contemporary Rusyn art, and organizes various cultural events, gigs and talks throughout the year. The gallery shop sells Warhol souvenirs (including tins of Campbell's soup) as well as information on Rusyn culture and language.

Medzilaborce has two **train stations**: the main one, Medzilaborce, is 1km south of the museum; the minor one, Medzilaborce mesto, is 1km north of the museum; two trains a day continue across the border into Poland. **Accommodation** has improved over the last few years, with the *Penzión Andy* (☎057/732 16 40, ⓦwww .penzionandy.host.sk; ❹), opposite the museum, competing with the new, quite cheap *Eurohotel Laborec* (☎057/732 13 07, ⓦwww.eurohotel.sk; ❷), at Andyho Warhola 195/28. The third option is the primitive *Penzión Šport* (☎057/732 29 10; ❶), offering four-bed rooms, just behind the Medzilaborce mesto train station.

Košice

Rather like Bratislava, **KOŠICE** was, until relatively recently, a modest little town on the edge of the Hungarian plain. Then, in the 1950s, the Communists established a giant steelworks on the outskirts of the city. Fifty years on, Slovakia's second-largest city has a population of over 250,000, a stunningly rejuvenated main square, a number of worthwhile museums, arguably the finest cathedral in the republic, and a lively cosmopolitanism that's reassuring after a week in the Slovak back of beyond. Just 21km north of the Hungarian border, Košice also acts as a magnet for the Hungarian community – to whom the city is known as *Kassa* – and for the terminally underemployed and neglected Romanies of the surrounding region, lending it a diversity and vibrancy absent from many provincial Slovak towns.

Arrival and accommodation

The **train** and **bus stations** are opposite each other, ten minutes' walk east of the old town, which is little more than five or six blocks across from east to west. To get to the centre from the stations, head across the park to the fanciful neo-Gothic **Jakabov palác**, on Mlynská, built with stone left over from the renovation of the city's cathedral. The city **tourist office** (Mon–Fri 8am–7pm, Sat 8am–1pm; ☎055/16186, ⓦwww.mickosice.sk or www.kosice.sk) is located in the Dargov department store at Štúrova 1, at the southern end of the spectacular main square; another, equally useful information service (Mon–Fri 8am–7pm, Sat & Sun 8am–4.30pm) is in the Tesco department store, at Hlavná 111. Given the compact nature of the city's old town, you shouldn't need to use the efficient **public transport** system, unless you're staying out in the suburbs. In any case, it's easy enough to use; just buy your ticket (which is valid for trams, buses and trolleybuses) from the tourist office or machines beforehand and punch it when you get on board in the little devices to hand.

Accommodation

You might want to leave it to the city tourist office to help you book your accommodation, since they can deal with anything from hotels to small pensions and **private rooms**. With one or two exceptions, the city's hotels are overpriced Communist-era places, with little to recommend them. *Domov mládeže* (☎055/643 56 88; ❶) is a year-round **hostel** on Medická, west of the centre via bus #17 or #34, or follow Poštovna to Vojenská, which becomes Ondavská, and turn left on Považská. Cheap dorm beds are also available at the *Student Hostel* (July–Aug; ☎055/633 34 37; ❶) at Podhradová 11. The nearest **campsite**, *Salaš Barca* (open all year) is 5km south of the city centre and also rents out bungalows; take tram #1, #3 or #4, or bus #12 or #52, from the *Slovan* hotel to the flyover, then get off and walk the remaining 500m west along Alejová, the road to Rožňava.

Alessandria Jiskrova 3 ☎055/622 59 03. Košice's newly modernized top hotel, with doubles going for nearly 3000Sk, but inconveniently located ten minutes' walk northeast of the old town. ❻

Centrum Južná trieda 2 ☎055/678 31 01. A short stroll south of the old town and, from the outside, a pretty ugly high-rise. Inside, however, it's probably the best of a bad bunch. ❹

Gloria Palac Bottova 1 ☎055/625 73 27, ⓦwww.gloriapalac.sk. A modern hotel with large rooms on one of the main crossroads at the southeastern corner of the centre. You can even choose the prezidentský apartmán for 8000Sk. ❺

Krmanová Krmanová 14 ☎055/623 05 65, ⓦwww.elvservis.sk. New pension in the old town. A good alternative if the others are full, though the decor is rather sterile. ❸

Penzión pri radnici Bačíkova 18 ☎055/622 86 01. Small pension with self-catering apartments, above a good restaurant in the backstreets of the old town, that offers, without a doubt, the most welcoming stay in the city for those with the dosh. ❹

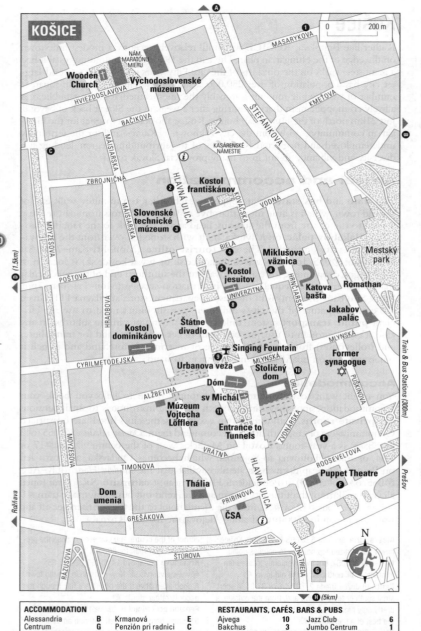

KOŠICE

◄ D (1.5km)

◄ Rožňava

B ►

Train & Bus Stations (300m) ►

Prešov ►

▼ H (5km)

NÁM. MARATÓNCA MIERU

Wooden Church

Východoslovenské múzeum

HVIEZDOSLAVOVA

BAČÍKOVA

MASARYKOVA

KMEŤOVA

ŠTEFÁNIKOVA

KÁSÁRENSKÉ NÁMESTIE

(i)

ZBROJNIČNÁ

MAISIARSKA

MAISIARSKA

MOYZESOVA

Kostol františkánov

KOVÁČSKA

VODNÁ

Slovenské technické múzeum ③

BIELA

④

⑤ Kostol jezuitov

Miklušova väznica ⑥

HRNČIARSKA

Mestský park

Katova bašta

Romathan

Jakabov palác

MLYNSKÁ

POŠTOVA

HRADBOVÁ

⑦

②

HLAVNÁ ULICA

UNIVERZITNÁ

⑧

Štátne divadlo

Kostol dominikánov

CYRILMETODEJSKÁ

⑨ Singing Fountain

Urbanova veža

MLYNSKÁ

Stoličný dom ⑩

ORLIA

Former synagogue

PUŠKINOVA

ZVONÁRSKA

Dóm

sv Michál

⑪

Múzeum Vojtecha Löfflera

ALŽBETINA

Entrance to Tunnels

E

ROOSEVELTOVA

VRÁTNA

MOYZESOVA

TIMONOVA

Puppet Theatre

F

Dom umenia

Thália

PRIBINOVA

HLAVNÁ ULICA

ČSA

(i)

GREŠÁKOVA

RAZUSOVA

ŠTÚROVA

JUŽNÁ TRIEDA

G

N

0 — 200 m

The Staré Mesto

You'll find almost everything of interest on Košice's long, pedestrianized main square, which is called **Hlavná ulica**. The whole area has been sensitively and superbly restored in the last few years, and, lined with a handsome parade of Baroque and Neoclassical palaces, it's really looking like the city's showpiece square nowadays, a favourite place for the local version of the evening *passeggiata*. Much of the credit for the square's wonderful revival is given to Rudolf Schuster, Košice's mayor until 1999, when he was elected president of Slovakia. Schuster put heavy emphasis on the idea that a physically attractive city is the keystone of urban renewal, and he mobilized his finances to assure that one of the republic's most beautiful old towns would remain as such.

At the centre, dominating the scene, is the city's unorthodox – and Europe's easternmost – Gothic **Dóm**, whose charcoal-coloured stone has been sand-blasted back to its original honeyed hue. Begun around 1390, the cathedral was paid for by the riches of the salt trade, which reached their peak in the following century. It's dedicated to St Elizabeth (sv Alžbeta), patron saint of the cathedral, despite the fact that the city had a long and bitter row with her father, Charles of Anjou, over its monopoly of the salt trade. From the outside, it's an unusual, slightly misshapen building, with striped roof tiles like those of Vienna's Stephansdom, and a great gilded copper cupola that sits like a helmet on the main clock tower. Inside, the stellar vaulting and Gothic furnishings create quite an impression, particularly the main gilded **altar** which has a total of 48 panels depicting the Passion and the life of the Virgin. Also worth a closer inspection is the tall Gothic pastophory on the north side of the presbytery. One of the best features of the church is the intricate **relief work** above the north and west doors, their tympana respectively depicting the frantic scenes of the Last Judgement, and Christ and his sleepy disciples squeezed onto the Mount of Olives. Finally, you can descend into the Rákóczi **crypt** under the northern nave or ascend the belltower's 160 steps for an expansive panorama of Košice (Mon–Fri 9.30am–4.30pm, Sat 9am–1.30pm).

South of the cathedral is the similar but much smaller Gothic chapel of **sv Michal**, converted into a storehouse for weapons and ammunition during the sixteenth century when the threat of a Turkish invasion caused a mass exodus from the region and turned the town into little more than a military barracks. Opposite sv Michal, at no. 27 on the east side of the square, is the pale, ice-blue Baroque **Stoličný dom**, where the postwar government was declared by President Edvard Beneš on April 4, 1945, in what became known as the Košice Agreement. For the first time, the Slovaks were given equal nation status with the Czechs, but this was overshadowed by the fact that, for many, Beneš had sealed the fate of the country by handing over four key ministries to the Communists, including the Ministry of the Interior. The Communists also saw this as a turning point, and chose the house as the venue for Košice's museum of the working class; it now serves as the site of the Vychodoslovenská galéria (see p.584).

Opposite the Stoličný dom is a small park in which a newly built passage leads down to a series of **tunnels** (Tues–Sun 10am–6pm; tours every 30min) underneath the city. These tunnels were only discovered in 1996 during the installation of new utility pipes as part of the square's revitalization effort, and after archeological work had been carried out on them, they were opened to the public for half-hour tours in 1998. Used during the Middle Ages for shelter and storage, the tunnels wiggle past sections of the old city walls, moat and alongside the foundation of the cathedral.

On the busy north side of the cathedral, Košice's trickle of tourists dutifully admire the fourteenth-century **Urbanova veža**, the town tower which stands on its own set of mini-arcades, lined with gravestones discovered under the building during nineteenth-century renovation. Now it serves as the rather overpriced waxworks museum (Tues–Sun 10am–2pm & 2.30–6pm; 120Sk). The public park and fountains at the centre of the main square are a favourite spot for hanging out and make an appropriately graceful foil for the city's grandiose **Štátne divadlo**, designed by the Austro-Hungarian firm of theatre-builders, Helmer & Fellner, in 1899.

Close by, on the east side of the square, are two very fine facades dating from the same period: the one at no. 63 is the Art Nouveau *Café Slavia*, which features ceramic murals of storks and a large ceramic rondel on its central gable; no. 71, beyond the **Kostol jesuitov**, sports a neo-Gothic stepped gable topped by a statue of a guy doffing his cap, and has wonderful lion brackets holding up its balcony. Further up on the same side, you might want to take a closer look at the **Kostol františkánov**, whose Baroque facade is adorned with an intricate Gothic stone relief of the Crucifixion, flanked by stucco curtains and cherubs added later on for dramatic effect; the ceiling frescoes inside the church will look great once they're restored to their former glory.

The tiny **water channel** you see running down the length of the square is another Schuster-inspired project. Centuries ago the cathedral and the small parks surrounding it stood on a small island in a stream; the stream was diverted so that Hlavná ulica could be built, but today's townsfolk wanted their stream back, so a narrow stone gulley was inlaid and the water again trickles through. This is topped by an – admittedly kitsch – "singing" fountain in the middle of the square, replete with recorded music and night-time coloured lights.

Museums and galleries

Košice's most gruesome museum is the **Miklušova väznica** (Mikluš Prison; Tues–Sat 9am–12.30pm & 1–5pm, Sun 9am–1pm), down Univerzitná, whose original dimly lit dungeons and claustrophobic cells graphically transport you into the house's murky history as the city prison. Tickets for the prison must be bought from the ticket office of the geological and zoological museum in the **Katova bašta** (Hangman's bastion), through the arches diagonally opposite. If you're interested in Ferenc Rákóczi II, the museum also contains a few personal belongings and a mock-up of the rebel's house. A couple of blocks south, on Puškinova, is another grim reminder of human cruelty, the city's former **synagogue**, a pink crenellated affair built in 1927, with a memorial to the 12,000 local Jews sent to the camps during World War II. Back on the main square at Hlavná 88, opposite the Kostol františkánov, the **Slovenské technické múzeum** (Tues–Fri 8am–5pm, Sat 9am–2pm, Sun noon–5pm) holds a large and eclectic selection of "technical" exhibits, from a giant pair of seventeenth-century bellows to a Braille map of Europe. The emphasis, though, is on the wrought ironwork for which the region is famous – everything from gates to lampposts and church bells.

The city's **Východoslovenská galéria** (June–Sept Tues–Sat 11am–7pm, Sun 11am–5pm; Oct–May Tues–Sat 10am–6pm, Sun 10am–2pm), located in the **Stoličný dom** on Hlavná, usually puts on interesting temporary exhibitions culled from its large collection of twentieth-century Slovak, Hungarian and Austrian art. The peculiar and fascinating **Múzeum Vojtecha Löfflera** (Tues–Sat 10am–6pm, Sun 1–5pm), which features the work and private collections of Košice's most prominent Communist-sanctioned sculptor, is to be found at Alžbetina 20. Löffler is the man we have to thank for many of the country's most conspicuous Socialist Realist monuments of the 1960s and 1970s (a few of which litter the back courtyard), though he himself preferred working on abstract, wooden sculptures. More intriguing, though, is Löffler's collection of Slovak artists' self-portraits, which spans the entire twentieth century, and a display of local ceramics and crucifixes.

At the northern tip of the main square is námestie Maratónu mieru, named after the city's annual marathon, whose winners' names are etched into the monument at the centre of the square. On either side are the two bulky late-nineteenth-century buildings that make up the **Vychodoslovenské múzeum** (Tues–Sat 9am–5pm, Sun 9am–1pm) on Hviezdoslavova 3. The museum building to the west is the one you want for its basement collection of extremely valuable fifteenth- to seventeenth-century **gold coins** – 2920 in all – minted at Kremnica, but stashed away by city burghers loyal to the Habsburgs when Imre Thököly's rebel force took Košice briefly in the 1670s. They were discovered by accident in 1935 by builders renovating no. 74 on the main square, appropriately enough the city's Finance Directorate. And just for good measure, if you haven't yet seen one, hidden round the back of the museum is a **wooden Greek-Catholic church**, brought here from Kožuchovce in Carpatho-Ruthenia.

Eating, drinking and entertainment

Košice's choice of places to **eat and drink** is underwhelming to say the least, though it has improved by leaps and bounds over the last few years. The best places are mostly located in the streets to the east of the main square: *Ajvega*, Orlia 10, is a popular vegetarian place with a summer terrace, and serves soya versions of standard Slovak dishes, washed down with fresh juices, while *Sedliacky dvor*, at Biela 3, is a hymn to more traditional Slovak and Czech folk culture and cuisine. Similar fare is served at *Veveríčka*, near Štátne divadlo, which has a coffered ceiling, and at the dark-red *Bakchus*, diagonally opposite the Kostol františkánov, which also dishes out Hungarian specialities.

Several **cafés** line the west side of Hlavná ulica: *Carpano*, north of the cathedral at no. 42, aspires to be Italian and offers a limited menu of salads and light fare, while *Kleopatra Pizza Bar*, south of the cathedral at no. 24, occupies one of the finest settings of all, with outdoor tables overlooking a small park. The atmosphere at the city's most attractive café, the Art Nouveau *Slávia*, Hlavná 65, is too snooty to be relaxing, but the soothing *Dobrá čajovna*, Mäsiarská 42, does the job admirably and serves a wide variety of teas. In addition, you can try the ubiquitous *Irish pub*, which buzzes at Hlavná 92.

As for **nightlife**, mainstream culture still predominates, particularly during the *Hudobná jar* (Musical Spring) festival in May. Full-scale **operas**, **ballets** and **plays** go on all year round (except summertime) at the wonderfully ornate Štátne divadlo (also known as the Divadlo Janka Borodáča) at Hlavná 58. Košice's philharmonic orchestra plays regular **concerts** at the Dom umenia on Grešákova and occasionally inside the cathedral itself. Košice has a **Hungarian theatre**, Thália, on Mojmírova, and also boasts Slovakia's one and only **Romany theatre**, Romathan (Štefánikova 4), which puts on a whole range of events from concerts to plays. You can catch **live jazz** most nights at the smoky *Jazz Club*, Kováčska 39 (daily 5pm–2am). The city's **nightclubs** are mostly worth avoiding, though if you're really keen to disco, head for the tacky *Jumbo Centrum*, at Masarykova 2, to the east of námestie Maratónu mieru. To find out what's on at any of the above venues, and on the city's cinema screens, get hold of the free **listings booklet** *Kultúrny informátor* from the tourist office.

East to Michalovce and the Vihorlat

One of the most unusual sights in East Slovakia is the spectacular **Herľany geyser**, 22km northeast of Košice in the foothills of the Slanské vrchy, which shoots a jet of tepid water over fifteen metres into the air for about twenty minutes or so every 32 to 36 hours. To get there, turn off route 50, up route 576 at Bidovce; Košice's tourist office will have the expected time of the next eruption, so you can plan your arrival to coincide with the geyser. East of Bidovce, route 50 winds its way over the **Dargov Pass** (Dargovský priesmyk), which cuts the low-lying north–south ridge of the Slanské vrchy in two – that is, until the motorway supersedes it. The pass is gentle enough to the eye, but it was captured at a cost of over 22,000 Soviet soldiers in World War II, a fact recorded by two tanks and a vast **war memorial** at the top of the pass. Coming down from the hills, you can see the hazy **Zemplín plain** below, stretching south into Hungary's Tokaj wine region and east into Ukraine.

Michalovce

Just under 60km east of Košice, and 35km west of the Ukrainian border, **MICHALOVCE** (Ⓦ www.michalovce.sk) is the main point of arrival for people heading for the Zemplínska Šírava or Slovak Sea. Frequent buses and trains run from Košice to Michalovce, though for some train services, you may have to change at Bánovce nad Ondravou. Note, too, that the train station is a good 2km west of the town centre, whereas the bus station is just east of the main square.

Other than to change buses, there's no compelling reason to hang around in Michalovce. However, if you do find yourself with an hour to spare between departures, you could head for the **Zemplínske múzeum** (June–Aug Tues–Fri 9am–noon & 1–5pm, Sun 2–5pm; Sept–May Tues–Fri 9am–noon & 1–3.30pm), housed in the chateau behind the bus station. The elongated, pedestrianized main square, **Námestie osloboditeľov**, makes for a pleasant stroll; note the great turquoise tenement from 1911, now housing the bank and *Bohéma* café, topped by a giant beehive and decorated with attractive stuccowork.

If you wish **to stay** the night, there are just two mid-range modern hotels to choose from: the *Hotel Jalta* (Ⓣ 056/642 60 86, Ⓦ www.jalta.sk; ❺), Námestie osloboditeľov 70, is the newcomer, and probably has the edge over the *Hotel Družba* (Ⓣ 056/642 04 52, Ⓦ www.hoteldruzba.sk; ❹), by the bus station, though both are pretty comfortable. For local Zemplín **cuisine**, try *Lagúna*, a block north of the main square in the Centralný mestský park, where there's also a café and wine shop.

Zemplínska šírava (Slovak Sea)

A large artificial lake created in the 1960s for industrial purposes, the **Zemplínska šírava** (Slovak Sea; Ⓦ www.sirava.com), to the east of Michalovce, is a popular summer destination for Slovaks. Brash, cheek-by-jowl *chata* colonies make up the resorts that merge into one another along the lake's northern shores; not everyone's cup of tea, to be sure, but there are compensations – it's hotter here than anywhere else in the country, with the sun continuing to shine well into October. The water is far from crystal clear, but there are plenty of opportunities for **hiking** in the hills of the Vihorlat to the north of the lake (see opposite).

VINNÉ, the first settlement you come to from Michalovce, isn't actually on the lake shore, but has its own swimming possibilities in the much cleaner mini-lake, Vinianske jazero, a short walk northeast of town, plus there's the ruined **Viniansky hrad** above the village (1hr 30min by foot). There is also a nice **campsite** (June–Sept) along the lake shore here with cheap bungalows – preferable to the sites along the Slovak Sea itself. The resorts along the sea are much of a concrete muchness, though the further east you go, the less crowded they get. In August, **accommodation** can be a problem unless you have a tent, although many campsites have cheap bungalows to rent. The *Šírava* (☎056/649 25 56, ⓦwww.hotelsirava.sk; ❷) in Kamenec is no aesthetic beauty, but it's clean and modern and has views over the sea; another option, further along the shore, is the newly built *Penzión Family* (☎056/648 20 25, ⓦwww.penzionfamily .sk; ❸), in Kaluža, with very spacious en-suite rooms above a restaurant. Of the many lakeside **campsites**, your best bet is the site just past Klokočov (mid-June to mid-Sept).

The Vihorlat

The volcanic hills of the **Vihorlat** offer some of the most rewarding **hiking** outside the main Tatra ranges, in particular the trek up to the glacial lake of **Morské oko**. The best time to come is in late September, when the beech trees turn the hills a brilliant golden brown. There are plenty of buses as far as **Remetské Hámre**, the village 7km south of (and a gentle 2hr hike from) the lake. In July and August, a daily bus from Michalovce should take you right to the car park just a twenty-minute walk from Morské oko. Unfortunately, it's not possible to swim in the lake since the whole area has been declared a nature reserve, but you can picnic wherever you please.

Alternatively, it's two hours or so from the shores of the lake to **Sninský kameň** (1005m), a slab of sheer rock rising up above the tree line and accessible only by ladder. The view from the top is outstanding – the blue-green splodge of Morské oko, the Slovak Sea and Zemplín plain beyond are all clearly visible, and on a good day you can see over into Ukraine, just 15km to the east. If you'd prefer not to backtrack, it's less than an hour's walk north to the village of Zemplínske Hámre, from where it's a further 5km to Belá nad Cirochou (a short train ride from Humenné).

Travel details

Trains

Connections with Bratislava: Čierna nad Tisou (2 daily; 8hr–10hr 50min); Humenné (2 daily; 8hr 20min); Košice (up to 14 daily; 5–9hr); Prešov (1 daily; 6hr 20min); Rožňava (2 daily; 5hr 50min–6hr 10min).

Humenné to: Łupków (1 daily; 1hr 40min); Medzilaborce (up to 10 daily; 1hr 10min–1hr 30min).

Košice to: Čierna nad Tisou (every 1–2hr; 1hr 45min); Kiev (1 daily; 22hr); Kraków (1 daily; 6hr 10min); Lučenec (up to 4 daily; 2hr 30min); Plešivec (up to 10 daily; 1hr 5min–1hr 50min); Prešov (up to 19 daily; 30–50min); Rožňava (up to 10 daily; 1hr–1hr 30min).

Poprad to: Kežmarok (every 2hr; 25min); Košice (every 2hr; 1hr 15min–2hr 10min); Markušovce (up to 8 daily; 30–40min); Prešov (1 daily; 1hr 20min); Spišská Nová Ves (every 1–2hr; 20–30min); Stará Ľubovňa (every 2hr; 1hr 10min).

Prešov to: Bardejov (up to 9 daily; 1hr 15min); Humenné (8 daily; 1hr 50min); Košice (up to 15 daily; 50min).

Buses

Košice to: Michalovce (1–2 hourly; 1hr 30min); Miskolc (1 daily; 2hr 10min); Svidník (every 2hr; 2hr 10min–2hr 20min); Uzhgorod (up to 6 daily; 4hr).

Levoča to: Kežmarok (up to 8 daily; 1hr); Poprad (every 30min; 30–50min); Spišské Podhradie (every 30min; 25min).

Poprad to: Červený Kláštor (1–2 daily; 1hr 40min); Prešov (every 1–2hr; 1hr 30min–2hr); Rožňava (2–5 daily; 2hr–2hr 15min); Spišské Podhradie (every 1–2hr; 45min–1hr 20min); Važec (13–16 daily; 25min–1hr).

Prešov to: Košice (every 20min; 40min–1hr); Levoča (hourly; 2hr 45min); Medzilaborce (up to 6 daily; 2hr); Michalovce (up to 15 daily; 1hr 45min); Stará Ľubovňa (hourly; 1hr 30min); Svidník (hourly; 1hr 15min–2hr); Uzhgorod (1 daily; 4hr).

Rožňava to: Betliar (hourly; 10min); Dobšiná (hourly; 45min); Krásnohorské Podhradie (up to 1 hourly; 10min); Ochtiná (6 daily Mon–Fri.; 30min–1hr).

Spišská Nová Ves to: Čingov (up to 13 daily; 15min); Dedinky (up to 10 daily; 1hr 30min); Levoča (every 30min; 30min).

Stará Ľubovňa to: Bardejov (up to 20 daily; 1hr 20min); Červený Kláštor (up to 9 daily; 40min); Prešov (hourly; 1hr 30min–2hr); Svidník (1–2 daily; 1hr 45min).

Svidník to: Bardejov (hourly; 1hr 5min); Dukla Pass (up to 3 daily; 35min); Medzilaborce (1 daily; 1hr 30min); Prešov (every 1–2hr; 1hr 30min).

Contexts

Contexts

History

C zechoslovakia had been in existence for a mere 74 years when it officially split on January 1, 1993. Before that period, its constituent parts – Bohemia, Moravia and Slovakia – enjoyed quite separate histories: the first two under the sway of their German and Austrian neighbours, and Slovakia under the Hungarian crown. Only in the early days of Slav history were all three loosely linked together as the Great Moravian Empire; later, Bohemia consistently played a pivotal role in European history, prompting the famous pronouncement (attributed to Bismarck) that "he who holds Bohemia holds mid-Europe".

Beginnings

According to Roman records, the area now covered by the Czech and Slovak republics was inhabited as early as 500 BC by **Celtic tribes**: the Boii, who settled in Bohemia (which bears their name), and the Cotini, who inhabited Moravia and parts of Slovakia. Very little is known about either tribe except that around 100 BC they were driven from these territories by two **Germanic tribes**: the Marcomanni, who occupied Bohemia, and the Quadi, who took over from the Cotini. These later seminomadic tribes proved awkward opponents for the Roman Empire, which wisely chose the River Danube as its natural eastern border.

The disintegration of the Roman Empire in the fifth century AD corresponded with a series of raids into central Europe by eastern tribes: firstly the **Huns**, who displaced the Marcomanni and Quadi, and later the **Avars**, who replaced the Huns around the sixth century, settling a vast area including the Hungarian plains and parts of what are now the Czech and Slovak republics. About the same time, the **Slav tribes** entered Europe from east of the Carpathian mountains, and appear to have been subjugated by the Avars, at the beginning at least. Their first successful rebellion seems not to have taken place until the seventh century, under the Frankish leadership of **Samo** (624–658 AD), though the kingdom he created died with him.

The Great Moravian Empire

The next written record of the Slavs in this region isn't until the eighth century, when East Frankish (Germanic) chroniclers reported that a people known as the **Moravians** had established themselves around the River Morava, a tributary of the Danube, which now forms part of the border between the Czech and Slovak republics. It was an alliance of Moravians and Franks (under Charlemagne) that finally expelled the Avars from central Europe in 796 AD, clearing the way for the establishment of the **Great Moravian Empire**, which at its peak included Slovakia, Bohemia and parts of Hungary and Poland. Its significance in terms of Czech-Slovak relations is that this was the first and last time (until the establishment of Czechoslovakia, for which it served as a useful precedent) that Czechs and Slovaks were united under one ruler (though both sides argue over whether the empire was more Czech or Slovak in character).

The first attested ruler of the empire, **Mojmír** (836–846 AD), found himself at the political and religious crossroads of Europe, under pressure from two sides: from the west, where the Franks and Bavarians (both Germanic tribes) were jostling for position with the Roman papacy; and from the east, where the patriarch of Byzantium was keen to extend his influence across eastern Europe. The Germans pulled off the first coup, by helping to oust Mojmír and replace him with his nephew, **Rastislav** (846–870 AD). However, Rastislav proved to be nobody's puppet and, dissatisfied with the German missionaries, he called on the Byzantine emperor to send some missionaries who knew the Slav language. SS **Cyril and Methodius** were sent and given the job of making a written language and introducing Christianity, using the Slav liturgy and Eastern rites. Rastislav, in turn, was captured and blinded by his nephew, **Svätopluk** (871–894 AD), again in cahoots with the Germans. Eventually, however, Svätopluk also managed to shake free of the Germans, defeating them at the Battle of Devín in 873. During Svätopluk's reign of nearly a quarter of a century, the empire reached its greatest extension.

Svätopluk died shortly before the **Magyar invasion** of 896, an event that heralded the end of the Great Moravian Empire and a significant break in Czech and Slovak history. The Slavs to the west of the River Morava (ie the Czechs) swore allegiance to the Frankish emperor, Arnulf; while those to the east (ie the Slovaks) found themselves under the yoke of the Magyars. This separation, which continued for the next millennium, is one of the major factors behind the distinct social, cultural and political differences between Czechs and Slovaks, which culminated in the separation of the two nations in 1993.

The Přemyslid dynasty

There is evidence that Bohemian dukes were forced in 806 to pay a yearly tribute of 500 pieces of silver and 120 oxen to the Carolingian Empire (a precedent the Nazis were keen to exploit as proof of German hegemony over Bohemia). These early Bohemian dukes "lived like animals, brutal and without knowledge", according to one chronicler. All that was to change when the earliest recorded Přemyslid duke, **Bořivoj** (852/53–888/89 AD) appeared on the scene. The first Christian ruler of Prague, Bořivoj, was baptized in the ninth century, along with his wife Ludmilla, by the Byzantine missionaries Cyril and Methodius (see above). Other than being the first to build a castle on Hradčany, nothing very certain is known about Bořivoj, nor about any of the other early Přemyslid rulers, although there are numerous legends, most famously that of **Prince Václav** (St Wenceslas), who was martyred by his pagan brother Boleslav the Cruel in 929 AD (see p.88).

Cut off from Byzantium by the Hungarian kingdom, Bohemia lived under the shadow of the **Holy Roman Empire** from the start. In 950, Emperor Otto I led an expedition against Bohemia, making the kingdom officially subject to the empire and its king one of the seven electors of the emperor. In 973 AD, under Boleslav the Pious (967–999 AD), a bishopric was founded in Prague, subordinate to the archbishopric of Mainz. Thus, by the end of the first millennium, German influence was already beginning to make itself felt in Bohemian history.

The **thirteenth century** was the high point of Přemyslid rule over Bohemia. With the emperor Frederick II preoccupied with Mediterranean affairs and dynastic problems, and the Hungarians and Poles busy trying to repulse the

Mongol invasions from 1220 onwards, the Přemyslids were able to assert their independence. In 1212, Otakar I (1198–1230) managed to extract a "**Golden Bull**" (formal edict) from the emperor, securing the royal title for himself and his descendants (who thereafter became kings of Bohemia).

The discovery of silver and gold mines throughout the Czech Lands and Slovakia heralded a big shift in the population from the countryside to the towns. Large-scale **German colonization** was generally encouraged by the Přemyslids in Bohemia and Moravia, and by the Hungarian Árpád dynasty in Slovakia. German miners and craftsmen founded whole towns in the interior of the country, where German civil rights were guaranteed them, for example Kutná Hora, Jihlava, Banská Bystrica and Levoča. At the same time, the territories of the Bohemian crown were increased to include not only Bohemia and Moravia, but also Silesia and Lusatia to the north (now divided between Germany and Poland).

The beginning of the fourteenth century saw a series of dynastic disputes – messy even by medieval standards – that started with the death of Václav II from consumption and excess in 1305. The following year, the murder of his heirless teenage son, Václav III, marked the **end of the Přemyslid dynasty** (he had four sisters, but female succession was not recognized in Bohemia). The nobles' first choice of successor, the Habsburg Albert I, was murdered by his own nephew, and when Albert's son, Rudolf I, died of dysentery not long afterwards, Bohemia was once more left without any heirs.

The Luxembourg dynasty

The crisis was finally solved when the Czech nobles offered the throne to **John of Luxembourg** (1310–46), who was married to Václav III's youngest sister. German by birth and educated in France, King John spent most of his reign participating in foreign wars, with Bohemia footing the bill, until his death on the field at Crécy in 1346. His son, **Charles IV** (1346–78), was wounded in the same battle but, thankfully for the Czechs, lived to tell the tale.

It was Charles who ushered in the Czech nation's **golden age**. Although born and bred in France, Charles was a Bohemian at heart (his mother was Czech and his real name was Václav); he was also extremely intelligent, speaking five languages fluently and even writing an autobiography. In 1346, he became not only king of Bohemia, but also, by election, Holy Roman emperor. Two years later he founded a university in Prague and began to promote the city as the cultural capital of central Europe, erecting rich Gothic monuments – many of which still survive – and numerous ecclesiastical institutions. As emperor, Charles issued many Golden Bull edicts that strengthened Bohemia's position, promoted Czech as the official language alongside Latin and German, and presided over a period of relative peace in central Europe, while western Europe was tearing itself apart in the Hundred Years' War.

Charles' son, **Václav IV** (1378–1419), who assumed the throne in 1378, was no match for such an inheritance. Stories that he roasted a cook alive on his own spit, shot a monk whilst hunting, and tried his own hand at lopping off people's heads with an axe are almost certainly myths. Nevertheless, he was a legendary drinker, prone to violent outbursts, and so unpopular with the powers that be that he was imprisoned twice – once by his own nobles, and once by his brother, Sigismund. His reign was also characterized by religious divisions within the Czech Lands and Europe as a whole, beginning with the **Great**

Schism (1378–1417), when rival popes held court in Rome and Avignon. This was a severe blow to Rome's centralizing power, which might otherwise have successfully rebuffed the assault on the Church that got under way in the Czech Lands towards the end of the fourteenth century.

The Czech Reformation

The attack was led by the peasant-born preacher **Jan Hus**, who gave sermons at Prague's Betlémská kaple. A follower of the English reformer John Wycliffe, Hus preached in the language of the masses (ie Czech) against the wealth, corruption and hierarchical tendencies within the Church at the time. Although a devout, mild-mannered man, he became embroiled in a dispute between the conservative clergy, led by the archbishop and backed by the pope in Rome, and the Wycliffian Czechs at the university. When the archbishop gave the order to burn the book of Wycliffe, Václav backed Hus and his followers, for political and personal reasons (Hus was, among other things, the confessor to his wife, Queen Sophie).

There can be little doubt that Václav used Hus and the Wycliffites to further his own political cause. He had been deposed as Holy Roman emperor in 1400 and, as a result, bore a grudge against the current emperor, Ruprecht of the Palatinate, and his chief backer, Pope Gregory XII in Rome. His chosen battleground was Prague's university, which was divided into four "nations" with equal voting rights: the Saxons, Poles and Bavarians, who supported Václav's enemies, and the Bohemians, who were mostly Wycliffites. In 1409 Václav issued the **Kutná Hora Decree**, which rigged the voting within the university giving the Bohemian "nation" three votes, and the rest a total of one. The other "nations", who made up the majority of the students and teachers, left Prague in protest.

Three years later the alliance between the king and the Wycliffites broke down. Widening his attacks on the Church, Hus began to preach against the sale of religious indulgences to fund the inter-papal wars, thus incurring the enmity of Václav, who received a percentage of the sales. In 1412, Hus and his followers were expelled from the university and excommunicated, and spent the next two years as itinerant preachers spreading their reformist gospel through-out Bohemia. Hus was then summoned to the **Council of Constance** to answer charges of heresy. Despite a guarantee of safe conduct from the emperor Sigismund, Hus was condemned to death and, having refused to renounce his beliefs, was burned at the stake on July 6, 1415.

Hus' martyrdom sparked off a **widespread rebellion** in Bohemia, initially unit-ing virtually all Bohemians – clergy and laity, peasant and noble (including many of Hus' former opponents) – against the decision of the council and, by inference, against the established Church and its conservative clergy. The Hussites imme-diately set about reforming Church practices, most famously by administering communion *sub utraque specie* ("in both kinds", ie bread and wine) to the laity, as opposed to the established practice of reserving the wine for the clergy.

The Hussite Wars: 1419–34

In 1419, Václav inadvertently provoked large-scale rioting by endorsing the readmission of anti-Hussite priests to their parishes. In the ensuing violence, several Catholic councillors were thrown to their death from the windows of Prague's Novoměstská radnice, in Prague's **first defenestration** (see p.132). Václav himself was so enraged (not to say terrified) by the mob that he suffered a heart attack and died, "roaring like a lion", according to a contemporary chronicler. The pope, meanwhile, declared an international crusade against the Czech heretics, under the leadership of Václav's brother and heir, the emperor Sigismund.

Already, though, cracks were appearing in the Hussite camp. The more radical reformers, who became known as the **Táborites**, after their south Bohemian base, Tábor, broadened their attacks on the Church hierarchy to include all figures of authority and privilege. Their message found a ready audience among the oppressed classes in Prague and the Bohemian countryside, who went round eagerly destroying Church property and massacring Catholics. Such actions were deeply disturbing to the Czech nobility and their supporters, who backed the more moderate Hussites – known as the **Utraquists** (from the Latin *sub utraque specie*) – whose criticisms were confined to religious matters.

For the moment, however, the common Catholic enemy prevented a serious split among the Hussites, and, under the inspirational military leadership of the Táborite **Jan Žižka**, the Hussites' (mostly peasant) army enjoyed some miraculous early victories over the numerically superior "crusaders", most notably at the Battle of Vítkov in Prague in 1420. The Bohemian Diet quickly drew up the **Four Articles of Prague**, which were essentially a compromise between the two Hussite camps, outlining the basic tenets on which all Hussites could agree, including communion "in both kinds". The Táborites, meanwhile, continued to burn, loot and pillage ecclesiastical institutions from Prague to the far reaches of Slovakia.

At the **Council of Basel** in 1433, Rome reached a compromise with the Utraquists over the Four Articles in return for ceasing hostilities. The peasant-based Táborites rightly saw the deal as a victory for the Bohemian nobility and the status quo, and vowed to continue the fight. However, the Utraquists, now in cahoots with the Catholic forces, easily defeated the remaining Táborites at the **Battle of Lipany**, outside Kolín, in 1434. The Táborites were forced to withdraw to the fortress town of Tábor. Poor old Sigismund, who had spent the best part of his life fighting the Hussites, died just three years later.

Compromise

Despite the agreement of the Council of Basel, the pope refused to acknowledge the Utraquist church in Bohemia. The Utraquists nevertheless consolidated their position by electing the gifted **George of Poděbrady** as first regent and then king of Bohemia (1458–71). The first and last Hussite king, George (Jiří to the Czechs), is remembered primarily for his commitment to promoting religious tolerance and his far-sighted efforts to establish some sort of "Peace Confederation" in Europe.

On George's death, the Bohemian Estates handed the crown over to the **Polish Jagiellonian dynasty**, who ruled in absentia and effectively relinquished the reins of power to the Czech nobility. In 1526, the last of the Jagiellonians, King Louis, was decisively defeated by the Turks at the Battle of Mohács and died fleeing the battlefield, leaving no heir to the throne. The Roman Catholic Habsburg Ferdinand I (1526–64) was elected king of Bohemia – and what was left of Hungary – in order to fill the power vacuum, marking the **beginning of Habsburg rule** over what are now the Czech and Slovak republics. Ferdinand adroitly secured automatic hereditary succession over the Bohemian throne for his dynasty, in return for which he accepted the agreement laid down at the Council of Basel back in 1433. With the Turks at the gates of Vienna, he had little choice but to compromise at this stage, but in 1545, the international situation eased somewhat with the establishment of an armistice with the Turks.

In 1546, the Utraquist Bohemian nobility provocatively joined the powerful Protestant Schmalkaldic League in their (ultimately unsuccessful) war against the Holy Roman emperor Charles V. When armed conflict broke out in Bohemia, however, victory fell to Ferdinand, who took the opportunity to extend the influence of Catholicism in the Czech Lands, executing several leading Protestant nobles, persecuting the reformist Unity of Czech Brethren who had figured prominently in the rebellion, and inviting Jesuit missionaries to establish churches and seminaries in the Czech Lands.

Like Václav IV, **Emperor Rudolf II** (1576–1611), Ferdinand's eventual successor, was moody and wayward, and by the end of his reign Bohemia was once more rushing headlong into a major international confrontation. But Rudolf also shared characteristics with Václav's father, Charles, in his genuine love of the arts, and in his passion for Prague, which he re-established as the royal seat of power, in preference to Vienna, which was once more under threat from the Turks. Czechs tend to regard Rudolfine Prague as a second golden age, but as far as the Catholic Church was concerned, Rudolf's religious tolerance and indecision were a disaster. In the early 1600s, Rudolf's melancholy began to veer dangerously close to insanity, a condition he had inherited from his Spanish grandmother, Joanna the Mad. And in 1611, the heirless Rudolf was forced to abdicate by his brother **Matthias**, to save the Habsburg house from ruin. Ardently Catholic, but equally heirless, Matthias proposed his cousin **Ferdinand II** as his successor in 1617. This was the last straw for Bohemia's mostly Protestant nobility, and the following year conflict erupted again.

The Thirty Years' War: 1618–1648

On May 23, 1618, two Catholic nobles were thrown out of the windows of Prague Castle – the country's **second defenestration** (see p.90) – an event that's now taken as the official beginning of the complex religious and dynastic conflicts collectively known as the **Thirty Years' War**. Following the defenestration, the Bohemian Diet expelled the Jesuits and elected the youthful Protestant "winter king", Frederick of the Palatinate, to the throne. In the first decisive set-to of the war, the Protestants were utterly defeated at the **Battle of Bílá hora** (Battle of the White Mountain), which took place on November 8, 1620, on the outskirts of Prague. In the aftermath, 27 Protestant nobles were executed on Prague's Staroměstské náměstí, and the heads of ten of them displayed on the Charles Bridge.

It wasn't until the Protestant Saxons occupied Prague in 1632 that the heads were finally taken down and given a proper burial. The Catholics eventually drove the Saxons out, but for the last ten years of the war, Bohemia and Moravia became the main battleground between the new champions of the Protestant cause – the Swedes – and the imperial Catholic forces. In 1648, the final battle of the war was fought in Prague, when the Swedes seized Malá Strana, but failed to take Staré Město, thanks to the stubborn resistance of Prague's Jewish and newly Catholicized student populations on the Charles Bridge.

Counter-Reformation to Enlightenment

The Thirty Years' War ended with the **Peace of Westphalia**, which, for the Czechs, was as disastrous as the war itself. An estimated five-sixths of the Bohemian nobility went into exile, their properties handed over to loyal Catholic families from Austria, Spain, France and Italy. The country was devastated, towns and cities laid waste, and the total population reduced by almost two-thirds. On top of all that, the Czech Lands and Slovakia were now decisively under Catholic influence, and the full force of the **Counter-Reformation** was brought to bear on its people. All forms of Protestantism were outlawed, the education system handed over to the Jesuits and, in 1651 alone, over two hundred "witches" burned at the stake in Bohemia.

The next two centuries of Habsburg rule are known to the Czechs as the **Dark Ages**. The focus of the empire shifted back to Vienna, the Habsburgs' absolutist grip catapulted the remaining nobility into intensive Germanization, while fresh waves of German immigrants reduced Czech to a despised dialect spoken by peasants, artisans and servants. The situation was so bad that Prague and most other urban centres became practically all-German cities. By the end of the eighteenth century, the Czech language was on the verge of dying out, with government, scholarship and literature carried out exclusively in German. For the newly ensconced Germanized aristocracy, of course, the good times rolled, and the country was endowed with numerous Baroque palaces and monuments.

After a century of iron-fisted Habsburg rule, the accession of Charles VI's daughter, **Maria Theresa** (1740–80), to the throne, marked the beginning of the **Enlightenment** in the empire. The empress acknowledged the need for reform and, despite her own personal attachment to the Jesuits, followed the lead of Spain, Portugal and France in expelling the order in 1773. But it was her son, **Joseph II** (1780–90), who brought about the most radical changes to the social structure of the Habsburg lands. His 1781 **Edict of Tolerance** allowed a large degree of freedom of worship for the first time in over 150 years, and went a long way towards lifting the restrictions on Jews. The following year, he ordered the dissolution of the monasteries and embarked upon the abolition of serfdom. Despite all his reforms, though, Joseph was not universally popular. Catholics – by now some ninety percent of the population – viewed him with disdain. His centralization and bureaucratization placed power in the hands of the Austrian civil service, and thus helped to entrench the **Germanization** of the Czech Lands. He also offended the Czechs by breaking with tradition and not bothering to hold an official coronation ceremony in Prague.

The Slovaks under Hungarian Rule

Following the fall of the Great Moravian Empire (see p.p.591), the Slovaks became subjects of the Hungarian crown for the next one thousand years. For most of those centuries, modern-day Slovakia was simply known as the Feldivék or **Upper**

Hungary, with the idea of Slovakia as a nation-state, or the Slovaks as a separate people, emerging only in the wake of nineteenth-century nationalism. In fact, over the centuries, the Slovaks proved themselves pretty loyal Hungarian subjects. In those days, Hungary was home to numerous minorities: Rusyns, Germans, Poles, Romanians, Jews and Roma, as well as Slovaks. Magyar nationalism as such didn't yet exist and Latin was the language of correspondence, with a bit of Hungarian at a local level – if there was oppression, it was feudal in nature, which affected all the kingdom's peasants, whether Magyar or Slav.

Once or twice, in times of civil war, Upper Hungary became a semi-independent fiefdom, most notably under **Matúš Čák** (1271–1321), who held sway from Trenčín on the River Váh, and again under the Czech **Jan Jiskra** (1420–1466), who made his base in Zvolen. However, it was Hungary's defeat at the hands of the Turks in 1526 that had the biggest impact on Upper Hungary, with the Turks then controlling most of the Hungarian plain, with Transylvania as a loyal ally. What little remained of the Hungarian kingdom – essentially Upper Hungary – was claimed for the **Habsburgs** by Ferdinand I (1526–64).

As in the Czech Lands, Hungary was by this time mostly Protestant, but although the Hussites reached parts of Slovakia during their military campaigns, the **Reformation** didn't arrive in Slovakia until a century later. The Germans in the mining towns of central Slovakia were among the first to convert to Lutheranism, followed by the Slovaks; the Magyars tended to convert to Calvinism. However, the Habsburgs were determined to re-convert the masses and pursue the **Counter-Reformation** just as they had done in the Czech Lands. Eventually, the Jesuits were brought in to lead the campaign, founding a university in Trnava in 1635.

Things didn't go as smoothly in Upper Hungary as they had in the Czech Lands, and periodically the country was caught up in religious rebellions. At the beginning of the seventeenth century, a Transylvanian nobleman of Slovak origin, **Štefan Bocskay** (1577–1606), revolted against the emperor Rudolf and succeeded in gaining religious concessions. At the outbreak of the Thirty Years' War, another Transylvanian prince, Gabor Bethlen (1580–1629) invaded Upper Hungary. Military campaigns such as these helped stave off the worst excesses of the Counter-Reformation, but they could do nothing in the face of the **Turkish invasion**. In 1663, the Turks burst into Upper Hungary, capturing towns across the south region from Nitra to Košice, forcing the Habsburgs to hand over parts of what is now southern Slovakia.

The Hungarian nobles were outraged and in 1678, the Protestant noble **Imre Thököly** (1657–1705) launched a *kuruc* (crusader) revolt. For a while Thököly had the Habsburgs on the run, and once again they made religious concessions, but when Thököly helped the Sultan besiege Vienna in 1683, he backed the wrong side, and ended his days in exile in Turkey. The last time the Slovaks, Hungarians and Rusyns united against the Habsburgs was during the 1703 *kuruc* revolt of **Ferenz Rákoczi II** (1635–1735). Ultimately, they were defeated by superior Habsburg power and the desertion of their ally, Louis XIV of France.

The Slovak national revival

In Hungary, the eighteenth-century Enlightenment boosted the **Magyar national revival**, and in 1792 Hungarian finally replaced Latin as the official state language throughout the Hungarian Kingdom. But Magyar nationalism was essentially chauvinistic, furthering the interests only of the Magyarized nobility, and the idea that non-Magyars might want to assert their own identity was regarded as highly subversive.

With a thoroughly Magyarized aristocracy, and a feudal society with virtually no Slovak middle class, the **Slovak national revival** or *národné obrodenie* was left to the tiny Slovak intelligentsia, comprising mostly Lutheran clergymen – passionately pro-Czech and anti-Magyar, but alienated from the majority of the (by now) devoutly Catholic Slovak peasantry on account of their religious beliefs. The leading Slovak figure throughout this period was **Ľudovít Štúr** (see p.477), son of a Lutheran pastor. Although a pan-Slavist, he was also, unlike many of his contemporaries, an ardent advocate of a separate Slovak language based on his own central Slovak dialect.

The Czech national revival

The Habsburgs' enlightened rule inadvertently provided the basis for the economic prosperity and social changes of the **Industrial Revolution**, which in turn fuelled the Czech national revival of the nineteenth century. The textile, glass, coal and iron industries began to grow, drawing ever more Czechs in from the countryside and swamping the hitherto mostly Germanized towns and cities. An embryonic Czech bourgeoisie emerged and, thanks to Maria Theresa's educational reforms, new educational and economic opportunities were given to the Czech lower classes.

For the first half of the century, the **Czech national revival** or *národní obrození* was confined to the new Czech intelligentsia, led by philologists like Josef Dobrovský and Josef Jungmann at Prague's Charles University or Karolinum. Language disputes (in schools, universities and public offices) remained at the forefront of Czech nationalism throughout the nineteenth century, only later developing into demands for political autonomy. The leading figure of the time was the Moravian Protestant and historian **František Palacký**, who wrote the first history of the Czech nation, rehabilitating Hus and the Czech reformists in the process. He was in many ways typical of the early Czech nationalists – pan-Slavist and virulently anti-German, but not yet entirely anti-Habsburg.

1848 and all that

The fall of the French monarchy in February 1848 prompted a crisis in the Habsburg Empire. The new bourgeoisie, of Czech-, German- and Hungarian-speakers, began to make political demands: freedom of the press, of assembly, of religious creeds and, in the nature of the empire, more rights for its constituent nationalities. In the **Czech Lands**, liberal opinion became polarized between the Czech- and German-speakers. Palacký and his followers were against the dissolution of the empire and argued instead for a kind of multinational federation. Since the empire contained a majority of Slavs, the ethnic Germans were utterly opposed to Palacký's scheme, campaigning instead for unification with Germany to secure their interests. So when Palacký was invited to the Pan-German National Assembly in Frankfurt in May, he refused to go. Instead, he convened a **Pan-Slav Congress** the following month, which met in Prague.

Meanwhile, the radicals and students (on both sides) took to the streets in protest, erecting barricades and giving the forces of reaction an excuse to declare martial law. In June, the Habsburg military commander bombarded Prague; the following morning the city capitulated – the counter-revolution in the Czech Lands had begun.

In the **Hungarian Kingdom**, the 1848 revolution successfully toppled the Habsburgs, and a liberal, constitutional government was temporarily set up in Budapest. However, Hungarian liberals like Lajos Kossuth (himself from a Magyarized Slovak family) showed themselves to be more reactionary than the Habsburgs when it came to opposing the aspirations of non-Magyars. The "Demands of the Slovak Nation", drafted by Štúr, were refused point-blank by the Hungarian Diet in May 1848. Incensed by this, Štúr and his small Slovak army went over to the Habsburgs and into battle (mostly unsuccessfully) against Kossuth's revolutionaries. Only in August 1849 was Habsburg rule reinstated, thanks to the intervention of imperial Russian troops on the streets of Budapest.

In both cases, the upheavals of 1848 left the absolutist Habsburg Empire shaken but fundamentally unchanged. The one great positive achievement in 1848 was the **emancipation of the peasants** and the emancipation of the empire's **Jewish population**. Otherwise, events only served to highlight the sharp differences between German and Czech aspirations in the Czech Lands, and between Hungarian and Slovak aspirations in the Hungarian Kingdom. The Habsburg recovery was, however, short-lived. In 1859 and again in 1866, the new emperor, Francis Joseph II, suffered humiliating defeats at the hands of the Italians and Prussians respectively. In order to buy some more time, the compromise or *Ausgleich* of 1867 was drawn up, establishing the so-called **Dual Monarchy** of Austria-Hungary – two independent states united under one ruler.

Dualism: The Czech lands

The *Ausgleich* came as a bitter disappointment for the Czechs, who remained second-class citizens while the Magyars became the Austrians' equals. The Czechs' failure to bend the emperor's ear was no doubt partly due to the absence of a Czech aristocracy that could bring its social weight to bear at the Viennese court. Nevertheless, the *Ausgleich* did mark an end to the absolutism of the immediate post-1848 period, and, compared to the Hungarians, the Austrians were positively enlightened in the wide range of civil liberties they granted, culminating in universal male suffrage in 1907.

Under Dualism, the Czech **national revival** flourished – and splintered. The liberals and conservatives known as the **Old Czechs**, backed by the new Czech industrialists, advocated working within the existing legislature to achieve their aims. By 1890, though, the more radical **Young Czechs** had gained the upper hand and instigated a policy of non-cooperation with Vienna. The most famous political figure to emerge from the ranks of the Young Czechs was the Prague university professor **Tomáš Garrigue Masaryk** (see p.183), who founded his own Realist Party in 1900 and began advocating the (then rather quirky) concept of closer cooperation between the Czechs and Slovaks.

Dualism: Slovakia

For the Slovaks, the *Ausgleich* was nothing less than a catastrophe. In the 1850s and 1860s, direct rule from Vienna had kept Magyar chauvinism at bay, allowing the Slovaks to establish various cultural and educational institutions. After 1867, the Hungarian authorities embarked on a maniacal policy of **Magyarization**, which made Hungarian (and only Hungarian) compulsory in both primary and secondary schools. Large landowners were the only ones to be given the vote (a mere six percent of the total population), while the majority of non–Magyars remained peasants. Poverty and malnutrition were commonplace throughout Upper Hungary, and by 1914, twenty percent of the Slovak population had emigrated, mostly to the USA.

Given the suffocating policies of the Magyars, it's a miracle that the Slovak national revival (and even the language itself) was able to survive. The leading Slovak political force, the **Slovenská národná strana** (Slovak National Party), was driven underground, remaining small, conservative, and for the most part Lutheran, throughout the latter part of the nineteenth century. The one notable exception was the Catholic priest **Andrej Hlinka** (see p.529), whose unflinching opposition to Magyar rule earned him increasingly wide support among the Slovak people.

World War I

At the outbreak of **World War I**, the Czechs and Slovaks showed little enthusiasm for fighting alongside their old enemies, the Austrians and Hungarians, against their Slav brothers, the Russians and Serbs. As the war progressed, large numbers defected to form the **Czechoslovak Legion**, which fought on the Eastern Front against the Austrians. Masaryk travelled to the USA to curry favour for a new Czechoslovak state, while his two deputies, the Czech Edvard Beneš and the Slovak Milan Štefánik, did the same in Britain and France.

Meanwhile, the Legion, now numbering around 100,000 men, became embroiled in the Russian revolutions of 1917 and, when the Bolsheviks made peace with Germany, found itself cut off from the homeland. The uneasy cooperation between the Reds and the Legion broke down when Trotsky demanded that they hand over their weapons before heading off on their legendary **anabasis**, or march back home, via Vladivostok. The soldiers refused and became further involved in the Civil War, for a while controlling large parts of Siberia and, most importantly, the Trans-Siberian Railway, before arriving back to a tumultuous reception in their new joint republic.

In the summer of 1918, the Allies finally recognized Masaryk's provisional government. On October 28, 1918, as the Habsburg Empire began to collapse, the first **Czechoslovak Republic** was declared in Prague. Two days later, a group of Slovaks gathered in Martin, not realizing what had taken place in Prague, but wishing to scupper any of the compromise plans put forward by the Hungarians. They issued the **Martin Declaration**, demanding self-determination and accepting in principle the union with the Czechs. Meanwhile, the German-speaking border regions of Bohemia and Moravia (later to become known as the Sudetenland) declared themselves autonomous provinces of the new republic of Deutsch-Österreich (German-Austria), which it was hoped would eventually unite with Germany itself. The new Czechoslovak government was having none of it, but it took the intervention of Czechoslovak troops before control of the border regions was wrested from the secessionists.

In Slovakia, any qualms the Slovaks may have had about accepting rule from Prague were superseded by fear of Hungarian military action. Košice (Kassa), Bratislava (Poszony) and various other Hungarian-speaking regions were only rested from Hungarian control in January 1919. Not long afterwards, Béla Kun's Hungarian Red Army reoccupied much of the country, and were only booted out by the Czechoslovak Legion in the summer of 1919. In June 1920, the **Treaty of Trianon** confirmed the controversial new Slovak-Hungarian border along the Danube, leaving some 750,000 Hungarians on Czechoslovak soil, and a correspondingly large number of Slovaks within Hungarian territory.

Last to opt in favour of the new republic was **Ruthenia** (officially known as Sub-Carpatho-Ruthenia), a rural backwater of the old Hungarian Kingdom that became officially part of Czechoslovakia in the Treaty of St Germain in September 1919. Its incorporation was largely due to the campaigning efforts of Ruthenians who had emigrated to the USA. For the new republic, the province was a strategic bonus but a huge drain on resources.

The First Republic

The new nation of Czechoslovakia began **postwar life** in an enviable economic position – tenth in the world industrial league table – having inherited seventy to eighty percent of Austria-Hungary's industry intact. Less enviable was the diverse make-up of its population – a melange of minorities that would in the end prove its downfall. Along with the six million Czechs and two million Slovaks who initially backed the republic, there were over three million Germans and 600,000 Hungarians, not to mention sundry other Ruthenians (Rusyns), Jews and Poles.

That Czechoslovakia's democracy survived as long as it did is down to the powerful political presence and skill of **Masaryk**, the country's president from 1918 to 1935, who shared executive power with the cabinet. It was his vision of social democracy that was stamped on the nation's new constitution, one of the most liberal of the time (if a little bureaucratic and centralized), aimed at ameliorating any ethnic and class tensions within the republic by means of universal suffrage, land reform and, more specifically, the Language Law, which ensured bilinguality to any area where the minority exceeded twenty percent.

The elections of 1920 reflected the mood of the time, ushering in the left-liberal alliance of the **Pětka** ("The Five"), a coalition of five parties led by the Agrarian Antonín Švehla, whose slogan "We have agreed that we will agree" became the keystone of the republic's consensus politics between the wars. Gradually, all the other parties (except the Fascists and Communists) – including even Hlinka's Slovak People's Party (HSMS) and most of the Sudeten German parties – began to participate in (or at least not disrupt) parliamentary proceedings. On the eve of the Wall Street Crash, the republic was enjoying an economic boom, a cultural renaissance and a temporary *modus vivendi* among its minorities.

The 1930s

The 1929 Wall Street Crash plunged the whole country into crisis. Economic hardship was quickly followed by **political instability**. In Slovakia, the HSMS fed off the anti-Czech resentment fuelled by Prague's manic centralization, and the appointment of Czechs to positions of power throughout the region. Taking an increasingly nationalist/separatist position, the HSMS was by far the largest party in Slovakia, consistently polling around thirty percent. In Ruthenia, the elections of 1935 gave only 37 percent of the vote to parties supporting the republic, the rest going to the Communists, pro-Magyars and other autonomist groups.

But the most intractable of the minority problems was that of the Sudeten Germans, who lived in the heavily industrialized border regions of Bohemia and Moravia. Nationalist sentiment had always run high in the Sudetenland, many of whose German-speakers resented being included in the new republic, but it was only after the Crash that the extremist parties began to make significant electoral gains. Encouraged by the rise of Nazism in Germany, and aided by rocketing Sudeten German unemployment, the far-right **Sudeten German Party** (SdP), led by a bespectacled gym teacher named Konrad Henlein, was able to win over sixty percent of the German-speaking votes in the 1935 elections.

Although constantly denying any wish to secede from the republic, the activities of Henlein and the SdP were increasingly funded and directed from Nazi Germany. To make matters worse, the Czechs suffered a severe blow to their morale with the death of Masaryk late in 1937, leaving the country in the less capable hands of his Socialist deputy, Edvard Beneš. With the Nazi annexation of Austria (the *Anschluss*) on March 11, 1938, Hitler was free to focus his attention on the Sudetenland, calling Henlein to Berlin on March 28 and instructing him to call for outright autonomy.

The Munich Crisis

On April 24, 1938, the SdP launched its final propaganda offensive in the **Karlsbad Decrees**, demanding (without defining) "complete autonomy". As this would clearly have meant surrendering the entire Czechoslovak border defences, not to mention causing economic havoc, Beneš refused to bow to the SdP's demands. Armed conflict was only narrowly avoided and, by the beginning of September, Beneš was forced to acquiesce to some sort of autonomy. On Hitler's orders, Henlein refused Beneš's offer and called openly for the secession of the Sudetenland to the German Reich.

On September 15, as Henlein fled to Germany, the British prime minister, Neville Chamberlain, flew to Berchtesgaden on his own ill-conceived initiative to "appease" the Führer. A week later, Chamberlain flew again to Germany, this time to Bad Godesburg, vowing to the British public that the country would not go to war (in his famous words) "because of a quarrel in a far-away country between people of whom we know nothing". Nevertheless, the French issued draft papers, the British Navy was mobilized, and the whole of Europe fully expected war.

Then, in the early hours of September 30, in one of the most treacherous and self-interested acts of modern European diplomacy, prime ministers Chamberlain (for Britain) and Daladier (for France) signed the **Munich Diktat** with Mussolini and Hitler, agreeing – without consulting the Czechoslovak government – to all of Hitler's demands. The British and French public were genuinely relieved, and Chamberlain flew back to cheering home crowds, waving his famous piece of paper that guaranteed "peace in our time".

Betrayed by his only Western allies and fearing bloodshed, Beneš capitulated, against the wishes of most Czechs. Had Beneš not given in, however, it's doubtful anything would have come of Czech armed resistance, surrounded as they were by vastly superior hostile powers. Beneš resigned on October 5 and left the country. In Slovakia many Slovaks viewed the Munich Diktat as a blessing in disguise, and on October 6 they declared their own autonomous government in Žilina. On October 15, **German troops occupied Sudetenland**, to the dismay of the forty percent of Sudeten Germans who hadn't voted for Henlein (not to mention the half a million Czechs and Jews).

However, the "rump" **Second Republic** (officially known as Czecho-Slovakia), was not long in existence before it too collapsed. On March 15, 1939, Hitler informed Hácha of the imminent Nazi occupation of what was left of the Czech Lands, and persuaded him to demobilize the army, again against the wishes of many Czechs. The invading German army encountered no resistance (nor any response from the Second Republic's supposed guarantors, Britain and France) and swiftly set up the Nazi **Protectorate of Bohemia and Moravia**. At the same time, with the approval of the Germans, **Slovak independence** was declared. The Hungarians, however, had other plans, crushing Ruthenia's one-day-old republic, and occupying parts of southern Slovakia, including Košice.

World War II

In the Czech Lands, during the first few months of the occupation, left-wing activists were arrested and Jews placed under the infamous Nuremburg Laws, but Nazi rule in the Protectorate at that time was not as harsh as it was to become – the economy even enjoyed a mini-boom. Then in late October and November 1939, Czech students began a series of demonstrations against the Nazis, who responded by closing down all institutions of higher education. Calm was restored until 1941, when Himmler's deputy in the SS, **Reinhard Heydrich**, was put in charge of the Protectorate. Arrests and deportations followed, reaching fever pitch after Heydrich was assassinated by the Czech resistance in June 1942 (see p.133). The reprisals were swift and brutal, culminating in the destruction of the villages of Lidice (see p.182) and Ležáky (see p.341). Meanwhile, the "final solution" was meted out on the country's remaining Jews, who were transported first to the ghetto in Terezín (see p.278), and then on to the extermination camps. The rest of the Czech population was frightened into submission, and there were very few acts of active resistance in the Czech Lands until the Prague Uprising of May 1945.

In independent Slovakia, **Jozef Tiso**'s government met with widespread support, since, for the first time ever, the Slovaks were able to establish and run their own national institutions. For many, wartime Slovak independence, which lasted from 1939 to 1944, was a genuine expression of Slovak statehood, even if, at the end of the day, the country was little more than a Nazi puppet state, whose Jews shared the fate of their brethren in the Nazi-occupied Protectorate. The Nazification of Slovak society was inevitable, however, as the extremist Hlinka Guards (the paramilitary wing of the HSMS), under Vojtech Tuka, got the upper hand. Tiso maintained his position as president, but from 1942 was known as *Vodca* (the Slovak equivalent of *Führer*). And it was at this point that the Tiso government agreed to oversee the deportation of Slovakia's Jewish population.

The resistance movement was slow to start, but, with Nazi defeat looking more and more likely, it became strong enough by August 1944 to attempt an all-out rebellion in the central mountains. The **Slovak National Uprising** (see p.504), as it was later dubbed by the Communists, was seen by many as yet another plea for sovereignty, rather than a call for the re-establishment of Czechoslovakia. However, when the hoped-for Soviet offensive failed to materialize, the uprising was brutally suppressed and any pretence at Slovak independence abandoned for full-scale Nazi occupation.

By the end of 1944, Czechoslovak and Russian troops had begun to liberate the country, starting with Ruthenia, which Stalin decided to take as war booty despite having guaranteed to maintain Czechoslovakia's pre-Munich borders. On April 4, 1945, under Beneš's leadership, the provisional **Národní fronta** government – a coalition of Social Democrats, Socialists and Communists – was set up in Košice. On May 5, the people of Prague finally rose up against the Nazis, many hoping to prompt an American offensive from Plzeň, recently captured by General Patton's Third Army. In the end, the Americans made the politically disastrous (but militarily wise) decision not to cross the previously agreed upon demarcation line. The Praguers held out against the Nazis until May 9, when the Russians finally entered the city.

The Third Republic

Violent reprisals against suspected collaborators and the German-speaking population in general began as soon as the country was liberated. All Germans were given the same food rations as the Jews had been given during the war. Starvation, summary executions and worse resulted in the deaths of thousands of ethnic Germans. With considerable popular backing and the tacit approval of the Red Army, Beneš began to organize the **forced expulsion of the German-speaking population**, referred to euphemistically by Czechs and Slovaks as the *odsun* (transfer). Only those Germans who could prove their antifascist credentials were permitted to stay – the Czechs and Slovaks were not called on to prove the same – and by the summer of 1947, nearly 2.5 million Germans had been kicked out or had fled in fear. On this occasion, Sudeten German objections were brushed aside by the Allies, who had given Beneš the go-ahead for the *odsun* at the postwar Potsdam Conference. Attempts by Beneš to expel Slovakia's Hungarian-speaking minority in similar fashion, however, proved unsuccessful.

On October 28, 1945, in accordance with the leftist programme thrashed out at Košice, sixty percent of the country's industry was nationalized. Confiscated Sudeten German property was handed out by the largely Communist-controlled police force, and in a spirit of optimism and/or opportunism, people began to join the Communist Party (KSČ) in droves, membership more than doubling in less than a year. In the **May 1946 elections**, the Party reaped the rewards of their enthusiastic support for the *odsun*, of Stalin's vocal opposition to Munich, and of the recent Soviet liberation, emerging as the strongest single party in the Czech Lands, with up to forty percent of the vote (the largest ever for a European communist party in a multiparty election). In Slovakia, however, they achieved just thirty percent, while the Democratic Party got over sixty percent. President Beneš appointed the KSČ leader, **Klement Gottwald**, prime minister of another Národní fronta coalition, with several, strategically important, cabinet portfolios going to Party members, including the ministries of the Interior, Finance, Labour and Social Affairs, Agriculture, and Information.

Gottwald assured everyone of the KSČ's commitment to parliamentary democracy and, initially at least, even agreed to participate in the Americans' Marshall Plan (the only Eastern Bloc country to do so). Stalin immediately summoned Gottwald to Moscow, and on his return the KSČ denounced the plan. By the end of 1947, the Communists were beginning to lose support as the harvest failed, the economy faltered and malpractices within the Communist-controlled Ministry of the Interior were uncovered. In response, the KSČ began to up the ante, constantly warning the nation of imminent "counter-revolutionary plots", and arguing for greater nationalization and land reform as a safeguard.

Then in February 1948 – officially known as **Victorious February** – the latest in a series of scandals hit the Ministry of the Interior, prompting the twelve non-Communist cabinet ministers to resign en masse in the hope that this would force a physically weak President Beneš to dismiss Gottwald. No attempt was made, however, to rally popular support against the Communists. Beneš received over 5000 resolutions supporting the Communists and just 150 opposing them. Stalin sent word to Gottwald to take advantage of the crisis and ask for military assistance – Soviet troops began massing on the Hungarian border. It was the one time in his life when Gottwald disobeyed Stalin; instead, by exploiting divisions within the Social Democrats, Gottwald was able to maintain his majority in parliament. The KSČ took to the streets (and the airwaves), arming "workers' militia" units to defend the country against counter-revolution, calling a general strike and finally, on February 25, organizing the country's biggest-ever demonstration in Prague. The same day, Gottwald went to an indecisive (and increasingly ill) Beneš with his new cabinet, all Party members or "fellow travellers". Beneš accepted Gottwald's nominees, and the most popular Communist coup in eastern Europe was complete, without bloodshed and without the direct intervention of the Soviets. In the aftermath of the coup, thousands of Czechs and Slovaks fled abroad.

The People's Republic

Following Victorious February, the Party began to consolidate its position, a relatively easy task given its immense popular support and control of the army, police force, workers' militia and trade unions. A **new constitution** confirming the "leading role" of the Communist Party and the "dictatorship of the proletariat" was passed by parliament on May 9, 1948. President Beneš refused to sign it, resigned in favour of Gottwald, and died (of natural causes) shortly afterwards. Those political parties that were not banned or forcibly merged with the KSČ were prescribed fixed-percentage representation and subsumed within the so-called "multiparty" Národní fronta.

With the Cold War in full swing, the **Stalinization** of Czechoslovak society was quick to follow. In the Party's first Five Year Plan, ninety percent of industry was nationalized, heavy industry (and, in particular, the country's defence industry) was given a massive boost, and compulsory collectivization forced through. Party membership reached an all-time high of 2.5 million, with "class-conscious" Party cadres rewarded with positions of power. "Class enemies" (and their children), on the other hand, suffered discrimination, and it wasn't long before the Czechoslovak mining "gulags" began to fill up with the regime's political opponents – "kulaks", priests and "bourgeois oppositionists" – who numbered over 100,000 at their peak.

Having incarcerated most of its external opponents, the KSČ, with a little prompting from Stalin, embarked upon a ruthless period of internal bloodletting. As the economy nose-dived, the press was filled with calls for intensified "class struggle", rumours of impending "counter-revolution" and reports of economic sabotage by fifth columnists. An atmosphere of fear and confusion was created to justify **large-scale arrests of Party members** with an "international" background – those with a wartime connection with the West, Spanish Civil War veterans, Jews and Slovak nationalists.

In the early 1950s, the Party organized a series of Stalinist **show trials** in Prague, the most spectacular of which was the trial of Rudolf Slánský, who had been second only to Gottwald in the KSČ before his arrest. He, Vladimír Clementis, the former KSČ foreign minister, and twelve other leading Party members (eleven of them Jewish, including Slánský) were sentenced to death as "Trotskyist-Titoist-Zionists".

After Stalin

Gottwald died in mysterious circumstances in March 1953, nine days after attending Stalin's funeral in Moscow (some say he drank himself to death). The whole nation heaved a sigh of relief, but the regime seemed as unrepentant as ever, and the arrests and show-trials continued. Then, on May 30, the new Communist leadership announced a drastic currency devaluation, effectively reducing wages by ten percent while raising prices. The result was a wave of isolated **workers' demonstrations** and rioting in Prague, Plzeň and the Ostrava mining region. Czechoslovak army units called in to suppress the demonstrations proved unreliable, and it was left to the heavily armed workers' militia and police to disperse the crowds and make the predictable arrests and summary executions.

In 1954, in the last of the show trials, Gustáv Husák, the post-1968 president, was given life imprisonment, along with other leading Slovak comrades. So complete were the Party purges of the early 1950s, so sycophantic (and scared) was the surviving leadership, that Khrushchev's 1956 thaw was virtually ignored by the KSČ. An attempted rebellion in the Writers' Union Congress was rebuffed and an enquiry into the show trials made several minor security officials scapegoats for the "malpractices". The genuine mass base of the KSČ remained blindly loyal to the Party for the most part; Prague basked under the largest statue of Stalin in the world; and in 1957, the dull, unreconstructed neo-Stalinist **Antonín Novotný** – alleged to have been a spy for the Gestapo during the war – became first secretary and president.

Reformism and Invasion

The first rumblings of protest against Czechoslovakia's hardline leadership appeared in the official press in 1963. At first, the criticisms were confined to the country's worsening economic stagnation, but soon they developed into more generalized protests against the KSČ leadership. Novotný responded by ordering the belated release and rehabilitation of victims of the 1950s purges, permitting a slight cultural thaw and easing travel restrictions to the West. In effect, he was simply buying time. The half-hearted economic reforms announced in the 1965 **New Economic Model** failed to halt the recession, and the minor political reforms instigated by the KSČ only increased the pressure for greater reforms within the Party.

In 1967, Novotný attempted a pre-emptive strike against his opponents. Several leading writers were imprisoned, Slovak Party leaders were branded as "bourgeois nationalists", and the economists were called on to produce results or else forgo their reform programme. Instead of eliminating the opposition, however, Novotný unwittingly united them. Despite Novotný's plea to the Soviets, Brezhnev refused to back a leader whom he regarded as "Khrushchev's man in Prague". On January 5, 1968, Novotný was replaced as First Secretary by the young Slovak leader **Alexander Dubček**, and on March 22 was dislodged from the presidency by the Czech war hero Ludvík Svoboda.

1968: The Prague Spring

By inclination, Dubček was a moderate, cautious reformer, the perfect compromise candidate – but he was continually swept along by the sheer force of the reform movement. The virtual **abolition of censorship** was probably the single most significant step Dubček took. It transformed what had hitherto been an internal Party debate into a popular mass movement. Civil society, for years muffled by the paranoia and strictures of Stalinism, suddenly sprang into life in the dynamic optimism of the first few months of 1968, the so-called "**Prague Spring**". In April, the KSČ published their Action Programme, proposing what became popularly known as "socialism with a human face" – federalization, freedom of assembly and expression, and democratization of parliament.

Throughout the spring and summer, the reform movement gathered momentum. The Social Democrat Party (forcibly merged with the KSČ after 1948) re-formed, anti-Soviet polemics appeared in the press and, most famously of all, the writer and lifelong Party member Ludvík Vaculík published his personal manifesto entitled "**Two Thousand Words**", calling for radical de-Stalinization within the Party. Dubček and the moderates denounced the manifesto and reaffirmed the country's support for the Warsaw Pact military alliance. Meanwhile, the Soviets and their hardline allies – Gomułka in Poland and Ulbricht in the GDR – took a very grave view of the Czechoslovak developments on their doorstep, and began to call for the suppression of "counter-revolutionary elements" and the reimposition of censorship.

As the summer wore on, it became clear that the Soviets were planning military intervention. Warsaw Pact manoeuvres were held in Czechoslovakia in late June, a Warsaw Pact conference (without Czechoslovak participation) was convened in mid-July and, at the beginning of August, the Soviets and the KSČ leadership met for **emergency bilateral talks** at Čierná nad Tisou on the Czechoslovak-Soviet border. Brezhnev's hardline deputy, Alexei Kosygin, made his less-than-subtle threat that "your border is our border", but did agree to withdraw Soviet troops (stationed in the country since the June manoeuvres) and gave the go-ahead to the KSČ's special Party Congress scheduled for September 9.

In the early hours of August 21, fearing defeat for the hardliners at the forthcoming KSČ Congress and claiming to have been invited to provide "fraternal assistance", the Soviets gave the order for the **invasion of Czechoslovakia** to be carried out by Warsaw Pact forces (only Romania refused to take part). Dubček and the KSČ reformists immediately condemned the invasion before being arrested and flown to Moscow for "negotiations". President Svoboda refused to condone the formation of a new government under the hardliner Alois Indra, and the people took to the streets in protest, employing every form of nonviolent resistance in the book. Apart from individual acts of martyrdom, like the self-immolation of **Jan Palach** on Prague's Wenceslas Square (see p.127), casualties were light compared to the Hungarian uprising of 1956 – the cost in terms of the following twenty years was much greater.

Normalization

In April 1969, StB agents provoked anti-Soviet riots during the celebrations of the country's double ice hockey victory over the USSR. On this pretext, another Slovak, **Gustáv Husák**, replaced the broken Dubček as First Secretary and instigated his infamous policy of "**normalization**". Over 150,000 fled the country before the borders closed, around 500,000 were expelled from the Party, and an estimated one million people lost their jobs or were demoted. Inexorably, the KSČ reasserted its absolute control over the state and society. The only part of the reform package to survive the invasion was **federalization**, which gave the Slovaks greater freedom from Prague (on paper at least), though even this was severely watered down in 1971. Dubček, like countless others, was forced to give up his job, working for the next twenty years as a minor official in the Slovak forestry commission.

An unwritten social contract was struck between rulers and ruled during the 1970s, whereby the country was guaranteed a tolerable standard of living (second only to that of the GDR in Eastern Europe) in return for its passive collaboration. Husák's security apparatus quashed all forms of dissent during the early 1970s, and it wasn't until the middle of the decade that an organized opposition was strong enough to show its face. In 1976, the punk rock band "The Plastic People of the Universe" was arrested and charged with the familiar "crimes against the state" clause of the penal code. The dissidents who rallied to their defence – a motley assortment of people ranging from former KSČ members to right-wing intellectuals – agreed to form **Charter 77** (*Charta 77* in Czech and Slovak), with the purpose of monitoring human rights abuses in the country (which had recently signed the Helsinki Agreement on human rights). One of the organization's prime movers and initial spokespersons was the absurdist Czech playwright **Václav Havel**. Over the next decade, Havel, along with many others, endured relentless persecution (including long prison sentences) in pursuit of its ideals. The initial gathering of 243 signatories increased to over 1000 by 1980, causing panic in the moral vacuum of the Party apparatus, but consistently failed to stir a fearful and cynical populace into action.

The 1980s

In the late 1970s and early 1980s, the inefficiencies of the economy prevented the government from fulfilling its side of the social contract. As living standards began to fall, cynicism, alcoholism, absenteeism and outright dissent became widespread, especially among the younger (post-1968) generation. The arrest and imprisonment in the mid-1980s of the **Jazz Section** of the Musicians' Union, who disseminated "subversive" pop music (like pirate copies of "Live Aid"), highlighted the ludicrously harsh nature of the regime. Pop concerts, annual religious pilgrimages and, of course, the anniversary of the Soviet invasion all caused regular confrontations between the security forces and certain sections of the population. Yet still a mass movement like Poland's Solidarity failed to emerge.

With the advent of **Mikhail Gorbachev**, the KSČ was put in an extremely awkward position, as it tried desperately to separate perestroika from comparisons with the reforms of the Prague Spring. Husák and his cronies had prided themselves on being second only to Honecker's GDR as the most stable and orthodox of the Soviet satellites – now the font of orthodoxy, the Soviet Union, was turning against them. In 1987, **Miloš Jakeš** – the hardliner who oversaw Husák's normalization purges – took over smoothly from Husák as general (first) secretary and introduced *přestavba* (restructuring), Czechoslovakia's luke-warm version of perestroika.

The Velvet Revolution

Everything appeared to be going swimmingly for the KSČ as it entered 1989. Under the surface, however, things were becoming increasingly strained, with divisions developing in the KSČ leadership as the country's economic perform-ance worsened. The protest movement, meanwhile, was gathering momentum: even the Catholic Church had begun to voice dissatisfaction, compiling a stag-gering 500,000 signatures calling for greater freedom of worship. But the 21st anniversary of the Soviet invasion produced a demonstration of only 10,000, which was swiftly and violently dispersed by the regime.

During the summer, however, more serious cracks began to appear in Czecho-slovakia's staunch hardline ally, the GDR. The trickle of East Germans fleeing to the West turned into a mass exodus, forcing Honecker to resign and, by the end of October, prompting nightly mass demonstrations on the streets of Leipzig and Dresden. The opening of the Berlin Wall on November 9 left Czechoslovakia, Romania and Albania alone on the Eastern European stage, still clinging to the old truths.

All eyes were now turned upon Czechoslovakia. Reformists within the KSČ began plotting an internal coup to overthrow Jakeš, in anticipation of a Soviet denunciation of the 1968 invasion. Their half-baked plan to foment unrest backfired, however. On Friday, **November 17**, a 50,000-strong peace-ful demonstration organized by the official Communist youth organization was viciously attacked by the riot police. Over 100 arrests, 500 injuries and one death were reported – the fatality was in fact an StB (secret police) *agent provocateur*. Ultimately, events overtook whatever plans the KSČ reformists may have had. The demonstration became known as the *masakr* (massacre), and Prague's students immediately began an occupation strike, joined soon after by the city's actors, who together called for an end to the Commu-nist Party's "leading role" and a general strike to be held for two hours on November 27.

Civic Forum and the VPN

On Sunday, November 19, on Václav Havel's initiative, the established opposi-tion groups such as Charter 77 met and agreed to form Občanské fórum or **Civic Forum**. Their demands were simple: the resignation of the present hard-line leadership, including Husák and Jakeš; an inquiry into the police actions of November 17; an amnesty for all political prisoners; and support for the general strike. In Bratislava, a parallel organization, Verejnosť proti nasiliu, or **People Against Violence** (VPN), was set up to coordinate protest in Slovakia.

On the Monday evening, the first of the really big **nationwide demon-strations** took place – the biggest since the 1968 invasion – with more than 200,000 people pouring into Prague's Wenceslas Square. This time the police held back, and rumours of troop deployments proved false. Every night for a week people poured into the main squares in towns and cities across the country, repeating the calls for democracy, freedom and the end to the Party's monopoly of power. As the week dragged on, the Communist media tentatively began to report events, and the KSČ leadership started to splinter under the strain, with the prime minister, **Ladislav Adamec**, alone in sticking his neck out and holding talks with the opposition.

The end of one-party rule

On Friday evening, Dubček, the ousted 1968 leader, appeared alongside Havel before a crowd of over 300,000 in Prague, and in a matter of hours the entire Jakeš leadership had resigned. The weekend brought the largest demonstrations the country had ever seen – over 750,000 people in Prague alone. At the invitation of Civic Forum, Adamec addressed the crowd, only to get booed off the platform. On Monday, November 27, eighty percent of the country's workforce joined the two-hour **general strike**, including many of the Party's previously stalwart allies, the miners and engineers. The following day, the Party agreed to the end of one-party rule and the formation of a new "coalition government".

A temporary halt to the nightly demonstrations was called and the country waited expectantly for the "broad coalition" cabinet promised by Prime Minister Adamec. On December 3, another Communist-dominated line-up was announced by the Party and immediately denounced by Civic Forum and VPN, who called for a fresh wave of demonstrations and another general strike for December 11. Adamec promptly resigned and was replaced by the Slovak **Marián Čalfa**. On December 10, one day before the second threatened general strike, Čalfa announced his provisional "**Government of National Understanding**", with Communists in the minority for the first time since 1948 and multiparty elections planned for June 1990. Having sworn in the new government, President Husák, architect of the post-1968 "normalization", finally threw in the towel.

By the time the new Čalfa government was announced, the students and actors had been on strike continuously for over three weeks. The pace of change had surprised everyone involved, but there was still one outstanding issue, the election of a new president. Posters shot up all round the capital urging **"HAVEL NA HRAD"** (Havel to the Castle – the seat of the presidency). The students were determined to see his election through, continuing their occupation strike until Havel was officially elected president by a unanimous vote of the Federal Assembly on December 29.

The 1990 elections

Czechoslovakia started the new decade full of optimism for what the future would bring. On the surface, the country had a lot more going for it than its immediate neighbours (with the possible exception of the GDR). The Communist Party had been swept from power without bloodshed, and, unlike the rest of Eastern Europe, Czechoslovakia had a strong, interwar democratic tradition with which to identify – Masaryk's First Republic. Despite **Communist economic mismanagement**, the country still had a relatively high standard of living, a skilled workforce and a manageable foreign debt.

In reality, however, the situation was somewhat different. Not only was the country economically in a worse state than most people had imagined, it was environmentally devastated, and its people were suffering from what Havel described as "post-prison psychosis" – an inability to think or act for themselves. The country had to go through the painful transition "from being a big fish in a small pond to being a sickly adolescent trout in a hatchery". As a result, it came increasingly to rely on its new-found saviour, the humble playwright-president Václav Havel.

In most people's eyes, "Saint Václav" could do no wrong, though he himself was not out to woo his electorate. His call for the rapid withdrawal of Soviet troops was popular enough, but his apology for the postwar expulsion of Sudeten Germans was deeply resented, as was his generous amnesty which eased the country's overcrowded prisons. The amnesty was blamed by many for the huge **rise in crime**; in the first year of freedom, every vice in the book – from racism to homicide – raised its ugly head.

In addition, there was still plenty of talk about the possibility of "counter-revolution", given the thousands of unemployed StB at large. Inevitably, accusations of previous StB involvement rocked each political party in turn in the run-up to the first free elections. The controversial **lustrace** (literally "lustration" or "cleansing") law, which barred all those on StB files from public office for the following five years, ended the career of many a politician and public figure, on the basis of often highly unreliable StB reports.

Despite all the inevitable hiccups and the increasingly vocal Slovak nationalists, Civic Forum/VPN remained high in the opinion polls. The **June 1990 elections** produced a record-breaking 99 percent turnout. With around sixty percent of the vote, Civic Forum/VPN were clear victors (the Communists got just thirteen percent), and Havel immediately set about forming a broad "Coalition of National Sacrifice", including everyone from Christian Democrats to former Communists.

The main concern of the new government was how to transform an outdated command-system economy into a **market economy** able to compete with its EU neighbours. The argument over the speed and model of economic reform caused Civic Forum to split into two separate parties: the centre-left Občanské hnutí or Civic Movement (OH), led by the foreign minister and former dissident Jiří Dienstbier, who favoured a more gradualist approach; and Občanská democratická strana or the right-wing **Civic Democratic Party** (ODS), headed by the finance minister **Václav Klaus**, whose pronouncement that the country should "walk the tightrope to Thatcherism" sent shivers up the spines of those familiar with the UK in the 1980s.

One of the first acts of the new government was to pass a **restitution law**, handing back small businesses and property to those from whom it had been expropriated after the 1948 Communist coup. This proved to be a controversial issue, since it excluded Jewish families driven out in 1938 by the Nazis, and, of course, the millions of Sudeten Germans who were forced to flee the country after the war. A law has since been passed to cover the Jewish expropriations, but the Sudeten German issue remains a tricky one.

The Slovak crisis

One of the most intractable issues facing post-Communist Czechoslovakia – to the surprise of many Czechs – turned out to be the **Slovak problem**. Having been the victim of Prague-inspired centralization from just about every Czech leader from Masaryk to Gottwald, the Slovaks were in no mood to suffer second-class citizenship any longer. In the aftermath of 1989, feelings were running high, and, more than once, the spectre of a "Slovak UDI" was threatened by Slovak politicians hoping to boost their popularity by appealing to voters' nationalism. Despite the tireless campaigning and negotiating by both sides, a compromise agreement failed to emerge.

The differences between the Czechs and Slovaks came to a head in the summer of 1990, when it came to deciding on a new name for the country. In what became known as the **great hyphen debate**, the Slovaks insisted that a hyphen be inserted in "Czechoslovakia". The demand was greeted with ridicule by most Czechs; Havel was one of the few who understood that what was just a hyphen to the Czechs meant a whole lot more to the Slovaks.

The **June 1992 elections** soon became an unofficial referendum on the future of the federation. Events moved rapidly towards the break-up of the republic after the resounding victory of the Movement for a Democratic Slovakia (HZDS), under the wily, populist politician and former boxer **Vladimír Mečiar**, popularly known as "Vladko", who, in retrospect, was quite clearly seeking Slovak independence, though he never explicitly said so during the campaign. In the Czech Lands, the right-wing ODS emerged as the largest single party, under the leadership of Václav Klaus, who – ever the economist – was clearly not going to shed tears over losing the economically backward Slovak half of the country.

Talks between the two sides got nowhere, despite the fact that opinion polls in both republics consistently showed majority support for the federation. The HZDS then blocked the re-election of Havel, who had committed himself entirely to the pro-federation cause. Havel promptly resigned, leaving the country without a president, and Klaus and Mečiar were forced to discuss the terms of what has become known as the "Velvet Divorce". On January 1, 1993, after 74 years of troubled existence, Czechoslovakia was officially divided into two countries: the Czech Republic (Česká republika) and Slovakia (Slovensko) or the Slovak Republic (Slovenská republika).

Independent Slovakia

Compared to the Czechs, the Slovaks have had a much harder time in the ten years since independence. Economically, the country has struggled, but more worrying by far has been Slovakia's **political instability**. Throughout his first term as Slovak prime minister, Vladimír Mečiar was plagued by allegations of corruption and charges of political interference in the media, and made inflammatory comments about the country's large Hungarian minority. Finally in March 1994, the Slovak president, Michal Kováč – no angel himself and once an HZDS ally of Mečiar – orchestrated his removal from office and replaced him with Jozef Moravčík, another former HZDS ally of Mečiar who had recently fallen from grace.

Moravčík's coup lasted just six months until the **September 1994 elections**, in which Mečiar's HZDS emerged once more as the largest party with 35 percent of the vote. Back at the helm, in coalition with, among others, the extreme nationalist Slovak National Party (SNS), Mečiar continued his uncompromising political style, repeating most of the gaffes of his first term of office. He conducted a relentless (but unsuccessful) campaign to remove Kováč from office – the president's son was kidnapped and later dumped, soaked in vodka, in the boot of a car abandoned in Vienna, an act he alleges was carried out by the Slovak secret service.

Perhaps the single most embarrassing episode in the country's recent history was the **national referendum**, which took place in 1997. Along with questions on NATO membership, there was a question asking whether the president should be elected by popular vote (as Kováč and the opposition wanted) rather than by members of parliament (as Mečiar preferred). So as not to lose the vote, the interior minister removed the question from most (but not all) of the ballot papers, and the voters showed their disgust with only ten percent casting ballots. When Mečiar was asked by reporters why the question had been removed, he replied "that's none of your business". The Constitutional Court ruled that the interior minister should be prosecuted, but, not for the last time, the government ignored the Court's decision.

In the **1998 elections**, the HZDS emerged once more as the largest single party with 27 percent of the vote, but Mečiar was outmanoeuvred by the Slovak Democratic Coalition or SDK (with 26.2 percent) which formed an anti-Mečiar bloc with three other smaller parties, including the Hungarian coalition bloc (SMK) and the former Communists (SDL'). Over the next four years, the new premier Mikuláš Dzurinda, managed to win back friends in the West, and got the country back on track for EU and NATO membership. However, the economy faltered and his domestic popularity plummeted. The **2002 elections** saw the further fragmentation of the Slovak political scene, with seven different parties gaining seats in parliament. The HZDS still emerged as the largest party, but its vote dropped to 19.5 percent, with the SDKÚ (as the SDK are now known) taking just 15.1 percent. This time the SDKÚ formed a mostly right-wing coalition government under Dzurinda, with the Christian Democrats (KDH) and the SMK.

Mečiar's demonisation in the West and his bellicose personality have proved consistently popular domestically, but they have left him isolated politically. Despite having attracted the support of around 40 percent of the electorate, he has failed to win two presidential bouts, and has left the HZDS with no political allies on a national level. It looks now as if he has had his day. Even without Mečiar, however, Slovakia still has more than its fair share of **problems**. As in much of the former Eastern Bloc, corruption is rife and looks set to increase with accession to the EU. An energy crisis is looming, with the forced closure of the country's Soviet-designed nuclear reactors by 2008. But probably the most shameful blot on Slovakia's copybook is the fact that the country's Roma population continue to be treated as second-class citizens.

In 2003 the Dzurinda government just managed to get the requisite 50 percent of the electorate to turn out to vote in the **EU referendum**, with 97 percent voting in favour of joining. The following year, Slovakia joined both the EU and NATO. By then, however, the Slovaks had had enough of voting, and less than 17 percent bothered to participate in the 2004 European elections – the lowest turnout in the entire EU. Nevertheless, more than a decade after independence, most Slovaks are happy to be back in the European fold, with a relatively stable pro-Western government and an economy that is growing – something which looked like a pipe dream when Mečiar was still in power.

The Czech Republic

Generally speaking, post-Communist life has been much kinder to the Czechs than to the Slovaks. Under Klaus, the country enjoyed a long period of **political stability**, jumped to the front of the queue for the EU and NATO, and was widely held up as a shining example to the rest of the former Eastern Bloc. Klaus and his party, the ODS, proved themselves the most durable of all the new political forces to emerge in the former Eastern Bloc. Nevertheless, in the **1996 elections**, although the ODS again emerged as the largest single party, it failed to gain an outright majority. They repeated the failure again in the first elections for the

Czech Senate, the upper house of the Czech parliament. The electorate was distinctly unenthusiastic about the whole idea of another chamber full of overpaid politicians, and a derisory thirty percent turned out to vote in the second round. In the end, however, it was – predictably enough – a series of corruption scandals that eventually prompted **Klaus's resignation** as prime minister in 1997.

One of the biggest problems to emerge in the 1990s was the issue of Czech racism towards the **Roma minority** within the country. A misleading documentary in 1997 showed life for the handful of Czech Roma who had emigrated to Canada as a proverbial bed of roses. At last, the documentary seemed to be suggesting, they had found a life free from the racism and unemployment that is the reality for most of the Czech Republic's estimated quarter of a million gypsies. The programme prompted a minor exodus of up to one thousand Czech Roma to Canada. Another Nova documentary, this time extolling life for Czech Roma in Britain, had a similar effect, with several hundred Czech and Slovak Roma seeking political asylum on arrival at Dover.

The **1998 elections** proved that the Czechs had grown sick and tired of Klaus's dry, rather arrogant, style of leadership. However, what really did it for Klaus was that for the first time since he took power, the economy had begun to falter. The **ČSSD** or Social Democrats, under **Miloš Zeman**, emerged as the largest single party, promising to pay more attention to social issues. Unable to form a majority government, Zeman followed the Austrian example, and decided to make an **"opposition agreement"** with the ODS. This Faustian pact was dubbed the "Toleranzpatent" by the press, after the 1781 Edict of Tolerance issued by Joseph II (see p.597). The Czech public were unimpressed, seeing the whole deal as a cosy stitch-up, and in 2000, thousands turned out in Wenceslas Square for the *Díky a odejděte* (Thank you, now leave) protest, asking for the resignation of both Zeman and Klaus.

Havel stepped down in 2003 after ten years as Czech president, to be replaced by his old sparring partner, Václav Klaus. No Czech president is ever likely to enjoy the same moral stature, though even Havel's standing is no longer what it used to be, particularly at home. His marriage to the actress Dagmar Veškrnová, seventeen years his junior, in 1997, less than a year after his first wife, Olga, died of cancer, was frowned upon by many. And his very public fall-out with his sister-in-law, Olga Havlová, over the family inheritance of the multi-million crown Lucerna complex in Prague, didn't do his reputation any favours either.

Meanwhile, Czechs have become more and more disillusioned with their politicians, with just 58 percent turning out for the **2002 elections**, and 18 percent of them voting for the Communists. In 2003, 55 percent of the population turned out to vote in the **EU referendum**, with a convincing 77 percent voting in favour of joining. Despite growing cynicism towards politics of any kind, Czechs genuinely celebrated their entry into the EU in 2004; for many, it was the culmination of everything they had fought for in 1968 and 1989, a final exorcism of the enforced isolation of the Communist period.

In a bid to boost their waning popularity, the Social Democrats replaced Špidla with the former interior minister, Stanislas Gross, who was in his thirties (and looked about twenty). He proved an unmitigated disaster, incapable of stopping the inexorable slide of the party in the polls, yet perfectly capable of committing appalling gaffs. Gross eventually resigned and was replaced by Jiří Paroubek, but there's no doubt that the future in Czech politics belongs to the ODS.

Books

A great deal of Czech fiction and poetry has been translated into English and is easily available, and the key moments in Czech twentieth-century history are also well covered in English. The same cannot be said for Slovak fiction and non-fiction, hence the rather uneven balance of Czech and Slovak books here. Those tagged with the ★ symbol are particularly recommended.

History, politics and society

Peter Demetz *Prague in Black and Gold; Scenes from the Life of a European City*. Demetz certainly knows his subject, both academically and at first hand, having been brought up here before World War II (where his account ends). His style can be a little dry, but he is determinedly unpartisan and refreshingly antinationalist in his reading of history.

Jim Downs *World War II: OSS Tragedy in Slovakia*. The story of Anglo-American involvement in the ultimately unsuccessful 1944 anti-Nazi Slovak National Uprising.

R.J.W. Evans *Rudolf II and His World*. First published in 1973, and still the best account there is of the alchemy-mad emperor, but not as salacious as one might hope given the subject matter.

Jan Kaplan & Krystyna Nosarzewska *Prague: The Turbulent Century*. This is the first real attempt to cover the twentieth-century history of Prague with all its warts. The text isn't as good as it should be, but the book is worth it just for the incredible range of photographs and images from the century.

Karel Kaplan *The Short March* is an excellent account of the electoral rise and rise of the Communists in Czechoslovakia after the war, which culminated in the bloodless coup of February 1948. *Report on the Murder of the General Secretary* is a detailed study of the most famous of the anti-Semitic Stalinist show trials, that of Rudolf Slánský, number two in the Party until his arrest.

★ **Callum MacDonald** *The Killing of SS Obergruppenführer Reinhard Heydrich*. Gripping tale of the build-up to the most successful and controversial act of wartime resistance, which took place in May 1942, and prompted horrific reprisals by the Nazis on the Czechs.

Callum MacDonald & Jan Kaplan *Prague in the Shadow of the Swastika*. Excellent account of the city under Nazi occupation, with an incisive, readable text illustrated by copious black-and-white photos.

Jiří Musil (ed) *The End of Czechoslovakia*. Academics from both the Czech and Slovak Republics attempt to explain why Czechoslovakia split into two countries just at the point when it seemed so successful.

Derek Sayer *The Coast of Bohemia*. A very readable cultural history, concentrating on Bohemia and Prague, which aims to dispel the ignorance shown by the Shakespearean quote of the title, and particularly illuminating on the subject of twentieth-century artists.

R.W. Seton-Watson *The History of the Czechs and Slovaks*. Seton-Watson's informed and balanced account, written during World War II, is hard to beat, although unfortunately out of print. The Seton-Watsons were lifelong Slavophiles but maintained a scholarly distance in their writing, rare among emigré historians.

Mark Stolarik (ed) *Slovakia: A Decade of Independence*. An uneven, but nevertheless interesting collection of essays on modern Slovak politics by the country's leading politicians (excluding Mečiar).

Kieran Williams *The Prague Spring and its Aftermath: Czechoslovak Politics, 1968-70.* This book draws on declassified archives to analyse the attempted reforms under Dubček and to take a new look at the 1968 Prague Spring.

★ **Elizabeth Wiskemann** *Czechs and Germans.* Researched and written in the build-up towards Munich, this is the most fascinating and fair treatment of the Sudeten problem. Meticulous in her detail, vast in her scope, Wiskemann manages to suffuse the weighty text with enough anecdotes to keep you gripped. Unique.

Essays, memoirs and biography

Margarete Buber-Neumann *Milena.* A moving biography of Milena Jesenská, one of interwar Prague's most beguiling characters, who befriended the author while they were both interned in Ravensbrück concentration camp.

Karel Čapek *Talks with T. G. Masaryk.* Čapek was a personal (and political) friend of Masaryk, and his diaries, journals, reminiscences and letters give great insights into the man who personified the First Republic.

Helen Epstein *Where She Came From: A Daughter's Search for her Mother's History.* Daughter of a Holocaust survivor, the author traces the effects of anti-Semitism through three generations of women.

Timothy Garton Ash *We The People: The Revolutions of 89.* A personal, anecdotal, eyewitness account of the Velvet Revolution (and the events in Poland, Berlin and Budapest) – by far the most compelling of all the post-1989 books. Published as *The Magic Lantern* in the US.

Patrick Leigh Fermor *A Time of Gifts.* The first volume of Leigh Fermor's trilogy based on his epic walk along the Rhine and Danube rivers in 1933–34. In the last quarter of the book he reaches Czechoslovakia, indulging in a quick jaunt to Prague before crossing the border into Hungary. Written forty years later in dense, luscious and highly crafted prose, it's an evocative and poignant insight into the culture of Mitteleu-

ropa between the wars.

Hugo Gryn *Chasing Shadows.* A rabbi in London later in life, this is the moving story of Gryn's childhood in a small town in Carpatho-Ruthenia, and his experiences in Auschwitz as a teenager.

Václav Havel The first essay in *Living in Truth* is "Power of the Powerless", Havel's lucid, damning indictment of the inactivity of the Czechoslovak masses in the face of "normalization". *Letters to Olga* is a collection of Havel's letters written under great duress (and heavy censorship) from prison in the early 1980s to his wife, Olga – by turns philosophizing, nagging, effusing, whingeing. *Disturbing the Peace* is probably Havel's most accessible work, a series of autobiographical questions and answers in which he talks interestingly about his childhood, the events of 1968 when he was in Liberec, and the path to Charter 77 and beyond (though not including his reactions to being thrust into the role of president). *Summer Meditations* are post-1989 essays by the playwright-president, while *The Art of the Impossible* is a collection of speeches given after becoming the country's president in 1990.

Miroslav Holub *The Dimension of the Present Moment; Shedding Life: Disease, Politics and Other Human Conditions.* Two books of short philosophical musings/essays on life and the universe by this unusual, clever scientist-poet.

Leoš Janáček, *Intimate Letters.* Selection of the countless letters written by the elderly composer Leoš Janáček to Kamila Strösslová, a young married woman with whom he fell passionately in love in his later years.

John Keane *Vaclav Havel: A Political Tragedy in Six Acts.* The first book to tell both sides of the Havel story: Havel the dissident playwright and civil rights activist who played a key role in the 1989 Velvet Revolution, and Havel the ageing and increasingly ill president, who, in many people's opinion, simply stayed on the stage too long.

★ **Heda Margolius Kovaly** *Prague Farewell.* An autobiography starting in the concentration camps of World War II, and ending with the author's flight from Czechoslovakia in 1968. Married to one of the Party officials executed in the 1952 Slánský trial, she tells her story simply, and without bitterness. The best account there is on the fear and paranoia whipped up during the Stalinist terror. Published as *Under a Cruel Star* in the US.

Milan Kundera *Testaments Betrayed.* A fascinating series of essays about a range of subjects, from the formation of historical reputation to the problems of translations.

Benjamin Kuras *Czechs and Balances, Is There Life After Marx?* are witty, light, typically Czech takes on national identity and Central European politics; *As Golems Go* is a more mystical look at Rabbi Löw's philosophy and the Kabbalah.

Ota Pavel *How I Came to Know Fish.* Pavel's childhood innocence shines through particularly when his Jewish father and two brothers are sent to a concentration camp and he and his mother have to scrape a living.

★ **Angelo Maria Ripellino** *Magic Prague.* A wide-ranging look at the bizarre array of historical and literary characters who have lived in Prague, from the mad antics of the court of Rudolf II to the escapades of Jaroslav Hašek. Scholarly, rambling, richly and densely written – unique and recommended.

Martin Šimečka *Letters from Prison.* A leading Slovak dissident, Šimečka was imprisoned in the early 1980s for smuggling his own work out of the country. Forbidden to mention politics, he nevertheless manages to convey much of his personal philosophy.

Josef Škvorecký *Talkin' Moscow Blues.* Without doubt the most user-friendly of Škvorecký's works, containing a collection of essays on his wartime childhood, Czech jazz, literature and contemporary politics, all told in his inimitable, irreverent and infuriating way. Published as *Head for the Blues* in the US.

Elizabeth Sommer-Lefkovits *Are You Here in This Hell Too?* Harrowing Holocaust experience told by a Slovak Jewish woman who worked as a pharmacist in Prešov until 1944.

Ludvík Vaculík *A Cup of Coffee With My Interrogator.* A Party member until 1968, and signatory of Charter 77, Vaculík revived the feuilleton – a short political critique once much loved in central Europe. This collection dates from 1968 onwards.

Zbyněk Zeman *The Masaryks – The Making of Czechoslovakia.* Written in the 1970s while Zeman was in exile, this is a very readable, none too sentimental biography of the country's founder Tomáš Garrigue Masaryk, and his son Jan Masaryk, the postwar Foreign Minister who died in mysterious circumstances shortly after the 1948 Communist coup.

Czech and Slovak fiction

Josef Čapek *Stories about Doggie and Pussycat*. Josef Čapek (Karel's older brother) was a Cubist artist of some renown, and also a children's writer. These simple stories about a dog and a cat are wonderfully illustrated, and seriously postmodern.

Karel Čapek *Towards a Radical Centre*. Karel Čapek was the literary and journalistic spokesperson for Masaryk's First Republic, but he's better known in the West for his plays, some of which, such as *R.U.R.*, feature in this anthology. Probably the best of his novel writing is contained in the trilogy, *Three Novels*, set in Czechoslovakia in the 1930s. His *Letters from England* had the distinction of being banned by the Nazis and the Communists for its naive admiration of England in the 1920s.

Daniela Fischerová *Fingers Pointing Somewhere Else*. Subtly nuanced, varied collection of short stories from dissident playwright Fisherová.

Ladislav Fuks *The Cremator* is about a man who works in a crematorium in occupied Prague, and is about to throw in his lot with the Nazis when he discovers that his wife is half-Jewish; *Mr Theodore Mundstock* is set in 1942 Prague, as the city's Jews wait to be transported to Terezín.

Jaroslav Hašek *The Good Soldier Švejk*. This classic, by Bohemia's most bohemian writer, is a rambling, picaresque tale of Czechoslovakia's famous fictional fifth columnist, Švejk, who wreaks havoc in the Austro-Hungarian army during World War I.

Václav Havel *Selected Plays 1963–87, Selected Plays 1984–87*. Havel's plays are not renowned for being easy to read (or watch). *The Memorandum* is one of his earliest works, a classic absurdist drama that, in many ways, sets the tone for much of his later work, of which the *Three Vaněk Plays*, featuring Ferdinand Vaněk, Havel's alter ego, are perhaps the

most successful. The 1980s collection includes *Largo Desolato, Temptation* and *Redevelopment*; freedom of thought, Faustian opportunism and town planning as metaphors of life under the Communists.

⭐ **Bohumil Hrabal** A thoroughly mischievous writer, Hrabal's slim but superb *Closely Observed Trains* is a postwar classic, set in the last days of the war and relentlessly unheroic; it was made into an equally brilliant film by Jiří Menzl. *I Served the King of England* follows the antihero Dítě, who works at the *Hotel Paříž*, through the decade after 1938. *Too Loud a Solitude*, about a waste-paper disposer under the Communists, has also been made into a film, again by Menzl.

Alois Jirásek *Old Czech Legends*. A major figure in the nineteenth-century Czech *národní obrození*, Jirásek popularized Bohemia's legendary past. This collection includes all the classic texts, including the story of the founding of the city by the prophetess Libuše.

⭐ **Franz Kafka** A German-Jewish Praguer, Kafka has drawn the darker side of central Europe – its claustrophobia, paranoia and unfathomable bureaucracy – better than anyone else, both in a rural setting, as in *The Castle*, and in an urban one, in one of the great novels of the twentieth century, *The Trial*.

Ivan Klíma A survivor of Terezín, Klíma is a writer in the Kundera mould as far as sexual politics goes, but his stories are a lot lighter. *Judge on Trial*, written in the 1970s, is one of his best, concerning the moral dilemmas of a Communist judge. *Waiting for the Dark, Waiting for the Light* is a pessimistic novel set before, during and after the Velvet Revolution of 1989. *The Spirit of Prague* is a very readable collection of biographical and more general articles and essays on subjects ranging from

Klíma's childhood experiences in Terezín to the current situation in Prague. *Ultimate Intimacy* is his latest novel, set in the cynical post-revolutionary Czech Republic.

Pavel Kohout *I am Snowing: The Confessions of a Woman of Prague* is set in the uneasy period just after the fall of Communism amid accusations of collaboration. *The Widow Killer* is a thriller about a naive Czech detective partnered with a Gestapo agent in the last months of World War II.

★ Milan Kundera Kundera is the country's most popular writer – at least with non-Czechs. His books are very obviously "political", particularly *The Book of Laughter and Forgetting*, which led the Communists to revoke Kundera's citizenship. *The Joke*, written while he was still living in Czechoslovakia and in many ways his best work, is set in the very unfunny era of the Stalinist purges. Its clear, humorous style is far removed from the carefully poised posturing of his most famous work, *The Unbearable Lightness of Being*, set in and after 1968, and successfully turned into a film some twenty years later. His two most recent novels are *No Saints and Angels*, set in bleak, contemporary Prague, but spanning three generations from World War II, and *Ignorance* which deals with the problems of exile and return.

Arnošt Lustig *Diamonds of the Night; Night and Hope; Darkness Casts No Shadow; A Prayer for Kateřina Horovitová; Lovely Green Eyes*. A Prague Jew exiled since 1968, Lustig spent World War II in Terezín, Buchenwald and Auschwitz, and his novels and short stories are consistently set in the Terezín camp.

Gustav Meyrink Another of Prague's weird and wonderful characters, Meyrink started out as a bank manager, but soon became involved in cabalism, alchemy and drug experimentation. His *Golem*, based on Rabbi Löw's monster, is one of the classic versions of the tale, set in the Jewish quarter. *The Angel of the West Window* is a historical novel about John Dee, an English alchemist invited to Prague in the late sixteenth century by Rudolf II.

Ladislav Mňačko *The Taste of Power*. Now living in Israel, Mňačko is one of the few Slovak writers to have been widely published abroad, most frequently this novel about the corruption of ideals that followed the Communist takeover.

Jan Neruda *Prague Tales*. Not to be confused with the Chilean Pablo Neruda (who took his name from the Czech writer), these are short, bitter-sweet snapshots of life in Malá Strana at the close of the last century.

Ivan Olbracht *The Sorrowful Eyes of Hannah Karajich*. A moving novel set in the vanished world of a Jewish village in Carpatho-Ruthenia which shows the effects of Zionism and the terror of Hitler, although his more famous work is *Nicola the Outlaw*, a sort of Ruthenian Robin Hood.

Iva Pekárková *Truck Stop Rainbows*. A heroine who attempts to fight, often by using sexual politics, against the grim realities of the Communist system in Czechoslovakia in the 1980s.

Peter Petro *A History of Slovak Literature*. Comprehensive overview of Slovak literature from 800 to 1990.

Karel Poláček *What Ownership's All About*. A darkly comic novel set in a Prague tenement block, dealing with the issue of fascism and appeasement, by a Jewish-Czech Praguer who died in the camps in 1944.

Robert Pynsent (ed) *Modern Slovak Prose*. Literary criticism on Slovak fiction since 1954 by Slovaks and Western Slavists; hardback only.

Rainer Maria Rilke *Two Stories of Prague*. Both tales deal with the artificiality of Prague's now defunct German-speaking community, whose claustrophobic parochialism drove the author into self-imposed exile in 1899 (for more on Rilke see Poetry, below).

Martin Šimečka *The Year of the Frog*. Largely autobiographical account of a young Slovak intellectual, whose father is a prominent dissident, living through the last years of Communism in Bratislava.

Peter Sís *The Three Golden Keys*. Short, hauntingly illustrated children's book set in Prague, by Czech-born American Sís.

Josef Škvorecký *The Cowards*; *The Miracle Game*; *The Swell Season*; *The Bass Saxophone*; *Miss Silver's Past*; *Dvořák in Love*; *The Engineer of Human Souls*; *The Republic of Whores*. A prolific writer and relentless anti-Communist, Škvorecký is typically Bohemian in his bawdy sense of humour and irreverence for all high moralizing. The *Cowards* (which briefly saw the light of day in 1958) is the tale of a group of irresponsible young men in the last days of the war, an antidote to the lofty prose from official authors at the time, but hampered by its dated Americanized translation. *The Miracle Game* enjoys a better translation and is set against the backdrop of the Prague Spring. Less well known (and understandably so) are Škvorecký's detective stories featuring a podgy, depressive Czech cop, Lieutenant Boruvka, which he wrote

in the 1960s at a time when his more serious work was banned. His latest Boruvka book, *Two Murders in My Double Life*, is a mystery story set in Canada, where he now lives, and the Czech Republic.

Božena Timrava *That Alluring Land: Slovak Stories*. Not strictly a feminist as such, Timrava tells her Slovak tales from a decidedly female perspective.

★ **Zdena Tomin** Although Czech-born, Tomin writes in English (the language of her exile since 1980); she has a style and fluency all her own. *Stalin's Shoe* is the compelling and complex story of a girl coming to terms with her Stalinist childhood, while *The Coast of Bohemia* is based on Tomin's experiences of the late 1970s dissident movement, when she was an active member of Charter 77.

Ludvík Vaculík *The Guinea Pigs*. Vaculík was expelled from the Party in the midst of the 1968 Prague Spring; this novel, set in Prague, catalogues the slow dehumanization of Czech society in the aftermath of the Soviet invasion.

Jiří Weil *Life With a Star*; *Mendelssohn is on the Roof*. Two novels written just after the war and based on Weil's experiences as a Czech Jew in hiding in Nazi-occupied Prague.

Poetry

Jaroslav Čejka, Michal Černík and Karel Sýs *The New Czech Poetry*. Slim but interesting volume by three Czech poets all in their late forties at the time, all very different. Čejka is of the Holub school, and comes across simply and strongly; Černík is similarly direct; Sýs the least convincing.

Sylva Fischerová *The Tremor of Racehorses: Selected Poems*. Poet and novelist Fischerová in many ways continues in the Holub tradition. Her poems are by turns powerful,

obtuse and personal, and were written in exile in Switzerland and Germany after fleeing in 1968.

Josef Hanzlík *Selected Poems*. Refreshingly accessible collection of poems written over the last 35 years by a poet of Havel's generation.

Miroslav Holub Holub is a scientist and scholar, and his poetry reflects this unique fusion of master poet and chief immunologist. Regularly banned in his own country, he is the Czech poet *par excellence* – classically trained, erudite, liberal and Westward-leaning. The full range of his work, including some previously unpublished poems can be found in *Intensive Care: Selected and New Poems*.

Rainer Maria Rilke *Selected Poetry*. Rilke's upbringing was unexceptional, except that his mother brought him up as a girl until the age of six. In his adult life, he became one of Prague's leading German-speaking authors of the interwar period.

Marcela Rydlová–Herlich (ed) *Treasury of Czech Love Poems*. A good way to get a taste of Czech poetry from over 33 poets represented, most of whom are twentieth-century.

Jaroslav Seifert *The Poetry of Jaroslav Seifert*. Czechoslovakia's only author to win the Nobel prize for literature, Seifert was a founder-member of the Communist Party and the avant-garde arts movement *Devětsil*, later falling from grace and signing the Charter in his old age. His longevity means that his work covers some of the most turbulent times in Czechoslovak history, but his irrepressible lasciviousness has been known to irritate.

Miroslav Válek, Miroslav Cipar, Ewald Osers *The Ground Beneath Our Feet: Selected Poems*. The first-ever Slovak poets to be published in Britain.

Literature by foreign writers

David Brierley *On Leaving a Prague Window*. A very readable thriller set in postcommunist Prague which shows that past connection with dissidents can still lead to violence.

Bruce Chatwin *Utz*. Chatwin is one of the "exotic" school of travel writers, hence this slim, intriguing and mostly true-to-life account of an avid crockery collector from Prague's Jewish quarter.

Lionel Davidson *The Night of Wenceslas*. A Cold War thriller set in pre-1968 Czechoslovakia that launched Davidson's career as a spy-writer.

Sue Gee *Letters from Prague*. The central character fell in love with a Czech student in England in 1968, but he returned home when the Russians invaded. Twenty years later, together with her ten-year old daughter, she goes in search of him.

Martha Gellhorn *A Stricken Field*. The story of an American journalist who arrives in Prague just as the Nazis march into Sudetenland. Based on the author's own experiences,

this is a fascinating, if sentimental, insight into the panic and confusion in "rump" Czecho-Slovakia after the Munich Diktat. First published in 1940.

Kathy Kacer *Clara's War*. The story of a young girl and her family who are sent from Prague to Terezín in 1943. The horror is played down as the book is aimed at children aged around ten, but nevertheless it's based on truth.

★ **Jill Paton Walsh** *A Desert in Bohemia*. A gripping story set against the aftermath of World War II and the subsequent political upheaval in Czechoslovakia.

Philip Roth *Prague Orgy*. A novella about a world-famous Jewish novelist (ie Roth) who goes to Communist Prague to recover some unpublished Jewish stories. Prague "is the city I imagined the Jews would buy when they had accumulated enough money for a homeland", according to Roth. A coda to Roth's Zuckerman trilogy.

Art, photography and film

Czech Modernism 1900–1945
Wide-ranging and superbly illustrated, this American publication records the journey of the Czech modern movement through Cubism and Surrealism to Modernism and the avant-garde. The accompanying essays by leading art and film critics cover fine art, architecture, film, photography and theatre.

Devětsil – Czech Avant-Garde Art, Architecture and Design of the 1920s and 30s Published to accompany the 1990 Devětsil exhibition at Oxford, this is the definitive account of interwar Czechoslovakia's most famous left-wing art movement, which attracted artists from every discipline.

Nature Illuminated Lee Hendrix. Exquisite paintings of flora and fauna, commissioned by Rudolf II to illuminate a master calligrapher's manuscript.

Prague – A guide to Twentieth-century Architecture Ivan Margolius. Dinky little pocket guide to all the major modern landmarks of Prague (including a black-and-white photo of each building), from the Art Nouveau Obecní dům, through functionalism and Cubism, to the Fred & Ginger building.

Language

Language

Language

The official language of the Czech Republic is **Czech** (*český*), that of the Slovak Republic, **Slovak** (*slovenský*). Both are mutually intelligible, highly complex Slav tongues. Whether they are separate languages or simply diverse dialects of a common one is still a hotly disputed issue. However, for the non-Slav, they are sufficiently distinct to cause serious problems of understanding. Unless you're here for some time, however, it's all rather academic, since you're not likely to make any great inroads into either.

That said, any attempt to speak Czech or Slovak will be heartily appreciated, though don't be discouraged if people seem not to understand, as most will be unaccustomed to hearing foreigners stumble through their language. If you know some **German** already, brush up on that, since, among the older generation in particular, German is widely spoken. Most folk will claim to know no **Russian**, though it was once the compulsory second language (and therefore is theoretically spoken by most of the middle-aged population). **English** is now the foreign language most commonly taught in schools, and the number of English-speakers has been steadily increasing.

Pronunciation

English-speakers often find Czech impossibly difficult to pronounce, Slovak less so. In fact, neither are half as daunting as they might first appear from "the traffic jams of consonants" that crop up on the page, as Patrick Leigh Fermor put it. Apart from a few special letters, each letter and syllable is pronounced as it's written, with virtually no letter unvoiced. The trick is always to **stress the first syllable** of a word, no matter what its length; otherwise you'll render it unintelligible.

Short and long vowels

Czech and Slovak have both **short** and **long vowels** (the latter being denoted by a variety of accents). The trick here is to lengthen the vowel without affecting the principal stress of the word, which is invariably on the first syllable.

There are very few **teach yourself Czech** guides available – even fewer for Slovak – and each has drawbacks. *Colloquial Czech* and *Colloquial Slovak*, both by James Naughton, are good, but a bit fast and furious for most people; *Teach Yourself Czech* is a bit dry for some. The best portable **dictionaries** are the *kapesní slovník* for Czech and the *vreckový* slovník* for Slovak, most easily purchased in the Czech and Slovak republics themselves. The Rough Guides also produces an excellent dictionary-style **Czech phrasebook**.

a like the u in c**u**p
á as in f**a**ther
ä closer to the e in l**e**t than an a
e as in p**e**t
é as in f**ai**r
ě like the y in **y**es
i or y as in p**i**t
í or ý as in s**ea**t
o as in n**o**t
ó as in d**oo**r
ô like the u in l**u**rid
u like the oo in b**oo**k
ů or ú like the oo in f**oo**l

Vowel combinations & diphthongs

There are very few diphthongs in Czech, substantially more in Slovak.
Combinations of vowels not mentioned below should be pronounced as two
separate syllables.

au like the ou in f**ou**l
ie like the ye in **ye**s
ia like the ya in **ya**k
iu like the u in fl**u**te
ou like the oe in f**oe**

Consonants and accents

There are no silent **consonants**, but it's worth remembering that r and l can
form a syllable if standing between two other consonants or at the end of a
word, as in Brno (Br–no) or Vltava (Vl–ta–va). The consonants listed below are
those that differ substantially from the English. Accents look daunting, but the
only one that causes a lot of problems is ř (Czech only), probably the most
difficult letter to say in the entire language – even Czech toddlers have to be
taught how to say it.

c like the **ts** in boats
č like the **ch** in chicken
ch like the **ch** in the Scottish loch
ď like the **d** in duped
g always as in goat, never as in general
h always as in have, but more energetic
j like the **y** in yoke
kd pronounced as **gd**
ľ like the **lli** in colliery
mě pronounced as mnye
ň like the **n** in nuance

The alphabet

In the Czech and Slovak alphabets, letters that feature a háček (as in the č of the word itself) are considered separate letters and appear in Czech and Slovak indexes immediately after their more familiar cousins. More confusingly, the consonant combination of ch is also considered as a separate letter and appears in Czech and Slovak indexes after the letter h. In the index of this book, we use the English system, so words beginning with c, č and ch all appear under c.

p   softer than the English p
r   as in rip, but often rolled
ř   like the sound of r and ž combined
š   like the **sh** in shop
ť   like the **t** in tutor
ž   like the **s** in pleasure; at the end of a word like the **sh** in shop

A Czech and Slovak language guide

In many instances the **Czech** and **Slovak words** for things are the same. Where they're different, we've separated them below, giving the Czech word first and the Slovak word second.

Basic words and phrases

Yes	ano/áno or hej	Tomorrow	zítra/zajtra
No	ne/nie	The day after tomorrow	pozítra/pozajtra
Excuse me/please/ don't mention it	prosím	Now	hnet/teraz
You're welcome	není zač/nemáte začo	Later	později/neskôr
Sorry	pardon/pardón	Leave me alone	dej mi pokoj/nechaj ma osamote
Thank you	djkuju/ďakujem	Go away	jdi pryč/choď preč
OK	dobrá/dobre	Help!	pomoc!
Bon appétit	dobrou chuť	This one	tento
Bon voyage	šťastnou cestu	A little	trochu
Hello/goodbye (informal)	ahoj	Large–small	velký–malý
Goodbye (formal)	na shledanou/do videnia	More–less	více–méně/ viac–menej
Good day	dobrý den	Good–bad	dobrý–zpatný
Good morning	dobré ráno	Hot–cold	horký–studený/ horúci–studený
Good evening	dobrý veber	With–without	s–bez
Good night (when leaving)	dobrou noc	How are you	jak se máte/ako sa máte?
Today	dnes		
Yesterday	včera		

629

Getting around

Over here	tady/tuná	Ticket	jízdenka/lístok
Over there	tam	Return ticket	zpátečá jízdenka/ spiatočný lístok
Left	nalevo/nanavo	Railway station	nádraží/železničná stanica
Right	napravo		
Straight on	rovně/priamo		
Where is . . .?	kde je . . .?	Bus station	autobusové nádraží/ autobusová stanica
How do I get to Zvolen?	jak se dostanu do Zvolena/ako sa dostanem do Zvolena?	Bus stop	autobusová zastávka
		When's the next train to Prague?	kdy jede další vlak do Prahy/kedy ide najbližší vlak do Prahy?
How do I get to the university?	jak se dostanu k univerzitě/ako sa dostanem k univerzite?		
By bus	autobusem/autobusom	Is it going to Brno?	jede to do Brna/ide to do Brna?
By train	vlakem/vlakom	Do I have to change?	musím přestupovat/ musím prestupovat?
By car	autem/autom		
By foot	pěšky/pešo	Do I have to have a reservation?	musím mit místenku?
By taxi	taxíkem/taxíkom		

Questions and answers

Do you speak English?	mluvíte anglicky/ hovoríte anglicky?	Why	proč/prečo
I don't speak German	nemluvím německy/ nehovorím nemecky	How much is it?	kolík to stojí/koľko stojí?
I don't understand	nerozumím/ nerozumiem	Are there any rooms available?	máte volné pokoje/ máte voľné izby?
I understand	rozumím/rozumiem	I want a double room	chtěl bych dvou lůžkovy pokoj/chcem dvojpostľovú izbu
Speak slowly	mluvte pomalu/ hovorte pomalzie		
How do you say that in Czech/Slovak?	jak se tohle vekne česky/ako sa to povie slovenský?	For one night	na jednu noc
		With shower	se sprchou/se sprchy
		Are these seats free?	je tu volno/sú tieto miesta vonná?
Could you write it down for me?	mužete mí to napsat/ mohli by ste mi to napísať?	May we (sit down)?	můžeme/môžme?
		The bill please	zaplatím prosím
What	co/čo	Do you have . . .?	máte . . .?
Where	kde	We don't have	nemáme
When	kdy/kedy	We do have	máme

Some signs

Entrance	vchod	Open	otevřeno/otvorené
Exit	východ	Closed	zavřeno/zavreté
Toilets	záchod	Danger!	pozor!
Men	muži	Hospital	nemocnice/nemocnica
Women	ženy	No smoking	kouření zakázáno/ zákaz fajčiť
Gentlemen	pánové		
Ladies	dámy		

No bathing	koupání zakázáno/ zákaz kúpania	Arrivals	příjezd/príchod
No entry	vstup zakázáno	Departure	odjezd/odchod
		Police	policie/polícia

Days of the week

Monday	pondělí/pondelok	Sunday	neděle/nedľa
Tuesday	úterý/utorok	Day	den/deň
Wednesday	středa/streda	Week	týden/týždeň
Thursday	čtvrtek/štvrtok	Month	měsíc/mesiac
Friday	pátek/piatok	Year	rok
Saturday	sobota		

Numbers

0	nula	21	dvacetjedna/dvadsaťjeden
1	jeden	30	třícet/tridsať
2	dva	40	čtyřícet/štyridsať
3	tří/tri	50	padesát/päťdesiat
4	čtyří/štyri	60	šedesát/šesťdesiat
5	pět/päť	70	sedmdesát/sedemdesiat
6	šest/šest	80	osumdesát/osemdesiat
7	sedm/sedem	90	devadesát/deväťdesiat
8	osum/osem	100	sto
9	devět/deväť	101	sto jedna
10	deset/desať	155	sto padesát pět/stodpäťdesiatpäť
11	jedenáct/jedenásť	200	dvěstě/dvesto
12	dvanáct/dvanásť	300	tři sta/tristo
13	třínáct/trinásť	400	čtyři sta/štyristo
14	čtrnáct/žtrnásť	500	pět set/päťsto
15	patnáct/pätnásť	600	šest set/šesto
16	šestnáct/šestnásť	700	sedm set/sedemsto
17	sedmnáct/sedemnásť	800	osum set/osemsto
18	osmnáct/osemnásť	900	devět set/deväťsto
19	devatenáct/devätnásť	1000	tisíc
20	dvacet/dvadsat		

Months of the year

Czechs and Slovaks use completely different words to denote the **months of the year**. While the Slovaks copy the Roman calendar names, Czech uses the highly individual Slav system, in which the names of the month are descriptive nouns sometimes beautifully apt for the month in question.

Czech

January	leden	ice
February	únor	renewal
March	březen	birch
April	duben	oak
May	květen	blossom
June	červen	red
July	červenec	redder

August	srpen	sickle
September	zaří	blazing
October	říjen	rutting
November	listopad	leaves falling
December	prosinec	slaughter of the pig

Slovak

January	leden	januar
February		februar
March		marec

April	apríl
May	máj
June	jún
July	júl
August	august
September	september
October	október
November	november
December	december

Some foreign countries in Czech

Australia	Austálie
Austria	Rakousko
Canada	Kanada
Ireland	Irsko
Germany	Německo

Great Britain	Velká Britanie
Hungary	Maďarsko
Netherland	Nizozemí
New Zealand	Novy Zéland
USA	Spojené státy americké

Some foreign countries in Slovak

Australia	Austrália
Austria	Rakúsko
Canada	Kanada
Czech Republic	Česká republika
Germany	Nemecko
Great Britain	Veľká Británia
Hungary	Maďarsko

Ireland	Írsko
Netherlands	Nizozemí
New Zealand	Nový Zéland
Poland	Poľsko
Ukraine	Ukrajina
USA	Spojené štáty americké

Czech food and drink glossary

Basics

chléb	bread
chlebíček	(open) sandwich
cukr	sugar
hořice	mustard
houska	round roll
jídla na	main dishes
knedlíky	dumplings
křen	horseradish
lžíce	spoon
máslo	butter
maso	meat

med	honey
mléko	milk
moučník	dessert
nápoje	drinks
nůž	knife
oběd	lunch
objednávku	to order
obloha	garnish
ocet	vinegar
ovoce	fruit
pečivo	pastry

pepř	pepper		sůl	salt
polévka	soup		talíř	plate
předkrmy	starters		tartarská omáčka	tartare sauce
přílohy	side dishes		těstoviny	noodles, pasta
rohlík	finger roll		večeře	supper/dinner
ryby	fish		vejce	eggs
rýže	rice		vidlička	fork
šálek	cup		volské oko	fried egg
sklenice	glass		zeleniny	vegetables
snídaně	breakfast			

Soups

boršč	beetroot soup		hrachová	pea soup
bramborová	potato soup		kuřecí	thin chicken soup
čočková	lentil soup		rajská	tomato soup
fazolová	bean soup		zeleninová	vegetable soup
hovězí vývar	beef broth		zelná	sauerkraut and meat soup

Fish

kapr	carp		sardinka	sardine
losos	salmon		štika	pike
makrela	mackerel		treska	cod
platýs	flounder		úhoř	eel
pstruh	trout		zavináč	herring/rollmop
rybí filé	fillet of fish			

Meat dishes

bažant	pheasant		kýta	leg
biftek	beef steak		ledvinky	kidneys
čevapčiči	spicy meatballs		řízek	steak
drštky	tripe		roštěná	sirloin
drůbež	poultry		salám	salami
guláš	goulash		sekaná	meat loaf
hovězí	beef		skopové maso	mutton
husa	goose		slanina	bacon
játra	liver		šunka	ham
jazyk	tongue		svíčková	fillet of beef
kachna	duck		telecí	veal
karbanátky	minced meat rissoles		vepřové	pork
klobásy	sausages		vepřové řízek	breaded pork cutlet or
kotleta	cutlet			schnitzel
kuře	chicken		žebírko	ribs

Vegetables

brambory	potatoes		kyselá okurka	pickled gherkin
brokolice	broccoli		kyselé	zelí sauerkraut
celer	celery		lečo	ratatouille
česnek	garlic		lilek	aubergine
chřest	asparagus		okurka	cucumber
cibule	onion		pórek	leek
čočka	lentils		rajče	tomato
fazole	beans		ředkev	radish
houby	mushrooms		řepná bulva	beetroot
hranolky	chips, French fries		špenát	spinach
hrášek	peas		žampiony	mushroom
karotka	carrot		zelí	cabbage
květák	cauliflower			

Fruit, cheese and nuts

banán	banana		niva	semi-soft, crumbly, blue cheese
borůvky	blueberries		oříšky	peanuts
broskev	peach		oštěpek	heavily smoked curd cheese
bryndza	goat's cheese in brine		ostružiny	blackberries
citrón	lemon		parenica	rolled strips of lightly smoked curd cheese
grep	grapefruit			
hermelín	Czech brie		pivní sýr	cheese flavoured with beer
hrozny	grapes		pomeranč	orange
hruška	pear		rozinky	raisins
jablko	apple		švestky	plums
jahody	strawberries		třešně	cherries
kompot	stewed fruit		tvaroh	fresh curd cheese
maliny	raspberries		urda	soft, fresh, whey cheese
mandle	almonds		uzený sýr	smoked cheese
měkký sýr	soft cheese		vlašské ořechy	walnuts
meruňka	apricot			

Common terms

čerstvý	fresh		nadívaný	stuffed
domácí	home-made		nakládaný	pickled
duzený	stew/casserole		(za)pečený	baked/roast
grilovaný	roast on the spit		plněný	stuffed
kyselý	sour		sladký	sweet
m.m. (maštěny máslem)	with melted butter		slaný	salted
			smažený	fried in bread-crumbs
na kmíně	with caraway seeds		studený	cold
na roztu	grilled		syrový	raw
na smetaně	in cream sauce		sýrový	cheesy
na zdraví	cheers!		teplý	hot

LANGUAGE | Czech food and drink glossary

| uzený | smoked | znojemský | with gherkins |
| vařený | boiled | | |

Drinks

bílé víno	white wine	led	ice
burčák	young wine	minerálka	mineral water
čaj	tea	mléko	milk
červené víno	red wine	pivo	beer
destiláty	spirits	suché víno	dry wine
káva	coffee	svařák	mulled wine
koňak	brandy	vinný střik	white wine with soda
láhev	bottle	víno	wine

Slovak food and drink glossary

Basics

chlebíček	open sandwich	pečivo	pastry
chlieb	bread	pohár	glass
chren	horseradish	polievka	soup
čierne korenie	pepper	predkrmy	starters
cukor	sugar	raňajky	breakfast
horčica	mustard	rezance	noodles/pasta
jedálny lístok	menu	rohlík	finger roll
jidla na objednávku	main dishes to order	ryba	fish
knedle	dumplings	ryža	rice
lyžica	spoon	šalát	salad
máslo	butter	šálka	cup
mäso	meat	soľ	salt
med	honey	tanier	plate
mlieko	milk	tartarská omáčka	tartare sauce
múčnik	dessert	vajcia	eggs
nôž	knife	večera	supper/dinner
obed	lunch	vidlička	fork
ocot	vinegar	zeleniny	vegetables
ovocie	fruit		

Soups

boršč	beetroot soup	kuracia	thin chicken soup
fazuľová	bean soup	paradajková	tomato soup
hovädzia	beef soup	šošovicová	lentil soup
hrachová	pea soup	zeleninová	vegetable soup
kapustnica	sauerkraut and meat soup	zemiaková	potato soup

Fish

kapor	carp	sardinka	sardine
losos	salmon	šťuka	pike
makrela	mackerel	treska	cod
pstruh	trout	zavináč	herring/rollmop

Meat dishes

baranina	mutton	kurča	chicken
bravčové	pork	obličky	kidneys
bravčové rezeň	breaded pork cutlet/l schnitzel	pečeň	liver
		rebierko	ribs
čevabčiče	spicy meatballs	saláma	salami
dršky	tripe	sekaná	meat loaf
hovädzie	beef	slanina	bacon
hydina	poultry	stehno	thigh
jazyk	tongue	šunka	ham
kačica	duck	sviečková	sirloin
klobásy	sausages	teľacie	veal
kotleta	cutlet		

Vegetables

cesnak	garlic	liečo	ratatouille (canned)
cibuľa	onion	mrkva	carrots
cukrová repa	beetroot	paradajka	tomato
fazuľa	beans	rajčina	tomato
hranolky	chips, French fries	reďkovka	radish
hrášky	peas	šošovica	lentils
huby	mushrooms	špargľa	asparagus
kapusta	cabbage	špenát	spinach
karfiol	cauliflower	uhorka	cucumber
kyslá okurka	pickled gherkin	zemiaky	potatoes
kyslá kapusta	sauerkraut		

Fruit, cheese and nuts

banán	banana	jablko	apple
borievky	blueberries	jahody	strawberries
broskyňa	peach	kompot	stewed fruit
bryndza	goat's cheese in brine	maliny	raspberries
čerešňa	cherry	mandle	almonds
černica	blackberries	marhuľa	apricot
citrón	lemon	niva	semi-soft crumbly blue cheese
hrozienky	raisins	orechy	walnuts
hrozny	grapes	oriezky	peanuts
hruška	pear	pomaranč	orange

slivky	plums
tvaroh	fresh curd cheese

údený syr	smoked cheese
urda	soft, fresh whey cheese

Common terms

čerstvý	fresh
domáci	home-made
dušený	stew/casserole
grilovaný	roast on the spit
kôpar	dill
kyslý	sour
miešaný	mixed
na rasci	with caraway seeds
na ražni	grilled
nadívaný	stuffed
nakládaný	pickled

(za)pečený	baked/roast
plnený	stuffed
sladký	sweet
slaný	salted
studený	cold
surový	raw
teplý	hot
údený	smoked
varený	boiled
vyprážený	fried in breadcrumbs
znojmský	served with gherkins

Drinks

biele víno	white wine
čaj	tea
červené víno	red wine
destiláty	spirits
fľaša	bottle
káva	coffee
koňak	brandy

led	ice
mlieko	milk
nazdravie	cheers!
pivo	beer
suché víno	dry wine
víno	wine

An A–Z of Czech and Slovak street names

After 1989, most of the streets named after erstwhile stars of the Communist Party disappeared. This was not the first (nor the last) time that the sign writers had put their brushes to use: after World War I, the old Habsburg names were replaced by Czech and Slovak ones; then under the Nazis, the streets were named after Hitler and his cronies, only for the Czech and Slovak names to be reinstated in 1945; while under the Communists, the names were changed once (or twice) more. Since independence in 1993, the Slovaks have expunged a few Czechs and supplanted them with newly rehabilitated Slovak nationalists, and so the process continues. The following names are currently the most popular in the Czech and Slovak republics; remember that street names always appear in the genitive or adjectival form, eg Palacký street as Palackého or Hus street as Husova.

5 května (May 5). The day of the Prague Uprising against the Nazis in 1945.

17 listopadu (November 17). In fact, this street name commemorates the anti-Nazi demonstration of November 17, 1939, after which the Nazis closed down all Czech institutions of higher education. The November 17, 1989 demonstration was held to commemorate the 1939 one, but, after the attack by the police, signalled the beginning of the Velvet Revolution.

28 října (October 28). Anniversary of the foundation of Czechoslovakia in 1918.

29 August. The day the unsuccessful Slovak National Uprising against the Nazis began in 1944.

Beneš, Edvard (1884–1948). Hero to some, traitor to others, Beneš was president from 1935 until 1938, when he resigned, having refused to lead the country into bloodshed over the Munich Crisis, and again from 1945 until 1948, when he acquiesced to the Communist coup.

Bernolák, Anton (1762–1813). Slovak theologian and pioneer in the Slovak written language. Author of the first Slovak dictionary.

Bezruč, Petr (1867–1958). Pen name of the Czech poet Vladimír Vayek, who wrote about the hardships of the Ostrava mining region.

Čapek, Karel (1890–1938). Czech writer, journalist and unofficial spokesperson for the First Republic. His most famous works are *The Insect Play* and *R.U.R.*, which introduced the word robot into the English language.

Čech, Svatopluk (1846–1908). Extreme Czech nationalist and poet whose best-known work is *Songs of a Slave*.

Chelčicky, Petr (born c.1390). Extreme pacifist Hussite preacher who disapproved of the violence of Žižka and his Taborite army.

Dobrovský, Josef (1753–1829). Jesuit-taught pioneer in Czech philology. Wrote the seminal text *The History of Czech Language and Literature*.

Dukelské hrdiny (The Dukla Heroes). The name given to the soldiers who died capturing the Dukla Pass in October 1944, the first decisive battle in the liberation of the country from the Nazis.

Dvořák, Antonín (1841–1904). Perhaps the most famous of all Czech composers, whose best-known work, the *New World Symphony*, was inspired by his extensive sojourn in the USA.

Fiano (1903–55). A Slovak Communist poet.

Havlíček-Borovský, Karel (1821–56). Satirical poet, journalist and nationalist, exiled to the Tyrol by the Austrian authorities after 1848.

Hlinka, Andrej (1864–1938). Leader of the Slovak People's Party, which went on to form the government of the Slovak Nazi puppet state (see p.505).

Hodža, Milan (1878–1944). Slovak politician who was in favour of the establishment of Czechoslovakia, led the Agrarian Party, and served as prime minister for a brief period in the 1930s.

Horáková, Milada (1901–1950). Socialist parliamentary deputy who was killed in the Stalinist purges.

Hurban, Jozef Miroslav (1817–88). Slovak writer and journalist who edited various pioneering Slovak-language journals.

Hus, Jan (1370–1415). Rector of Prague University and reformist preacher who was burnt at the stake as a heretic by the Council of Constance (see p.594).

Hviezdoslav, Pavol Orságh (1849–1921). The father of Slovak poetry, who lived in the Orava region working as a court official until his retirement.

Janácek, Leos (1854–1928). Moravian-born composer, based in Brno for most of his life, whose operas in particular have become quite widely performed in the West.

Jánošík (1688–1713). Fabled Slovak folk hero, modelled along the lines of Robin Hood, who operated in the Malá Fatra range (see p.520).

Jesenský, Janko (1874–1945). Slovak poet who accompanied the Czechoslovak Legion in its long trek across Russia during the Bolshevik Revolution.

Jirásek, Alois (1851–1930). Writer for both children and adults who popularized Czech legends and became a key figure in the national revival.

Jiří z Poděbrad (1458–71). The only Hussite and last Czech king of Bohemia, better known to the English as George of Poděbrady.

Jungmann, Josef (1773–1847). Prolific Czech translator and author of the seminal *History of Czech Literature* and the first Czech dictionary.

Karl IV (1346–78). Luxembourgeois king of Bohemia and Holy Roman Emperor responsible for Prague's golden age in the fourteenth century. Better known to the English as Charles IV.

Kollár, Ján (1793–1852). Professor of Slav archeology in Vienna and Slovak poet who wrote in Czech and opposed the formation of a separate Slovak written language.

Komenský, Jan Amos (1592–1670). Leader of the Protestant Unity of Czech Brethren. Forced to flee the country and settle in England during the Counter-Reformation. Better known to the English as Comenius.

Kráľ Janko (1822–76). A Slovak poet who wrote folk ballads.

Lidice. Bohemian village outside Prague which fell victim to the Nazis in June 1942 in retaliation for the murder of Reinhard Heydrich: the male inhabitants were shot, the women and children were sent to the camps and the entire place was burnt to the ground.

Mácha, Karel Hynek (1810–36). Romantic nationalist poet and great admirer of Byron and Keats, who, like them, died young. His most famous poem is *Máj*, published just months before his death.

Masaryk, Tomáš Garrigue (1850–1937). Professor of Philosophy at Prague University, President of the Republic (1918–35). His name is synonymous with the First Republic and was removed from all street signs after the 1948 coup. Now back with a vengeance.

Nálepka, Ján (1912–43). Slovak teacher and partisan in World War II who won fame through his daring antics in Nazi-occupied Ukraine, where he eventually died.

Němcová, Božena (1820–62). Highly popular writer who got involved with the nationalist movement and shocked with her unorthodox behaviour. Her most famous book is *Grandmother*.

Neruda, Jan (1834–91). Poet and journalist for the Národní listy. Wrote some famous short stories describing Prague's Malá Strana.

Opletal, Jan (1915–39). Czech student killed by Nazis in 1939 during anti-Nazi demonstration.

Palach, Jan (1947–69). Philosophy student who committed suicide by self-immolation in protest against the 1968 Soviet invasion.

Palacký, František (1798–1876). Nationalist historian, Czech MP in Vienna and leading figure in the events of 1848.

Pavlov, I.P. (1849–1936). Russian Nobel prize-winning scientist, famous for his experiments on dogs (hence, "Pavlov's dogs"), from which he developed the theory of conditioned reflexes.

Purkyně, Jan Evangelista (1787–1869). Czech doctor, natural scientist and pioneer in experimental physiology who became professor of physiology at Prague and then Wrocław universities.

Ressel, Josef (1793–1857). Fascinatingly enough, the Czech inventor of the screw-propeller.

Rieger, Ladislav (1818–1903). Nineteenth-century Czech politician and one of the leading figures in the events of 1848 and its aftermath.

Šafárik, Pavol Jozef (1795–1861). Slovak scholar and son of a Slovak Lutheran pastor whose major works were actually written in Czech and German.

Sládkovič, Andrej (1820–72). Slovak poet who lived and worked in the Detva region and whose pastoral love poem *Marína* is regarded as a classic.

Smetana, Bedřich (1824–84). Popular Czech composer and fervent nationalist whose *Má vlast* (My Homeland) traditionally opens the Prague Spring Music Festival.

SNP (Slovenské národné povstanie). The ill-fated Slovak National Uprising against the Nazis which took place in August/September 1944.

Sokol (Falcon). Physical education movement founded in 1862 and very much modelled on its German counterpart. The organization was a driving force during the Czech national revival, but was banned by the Nazis and later the Communists.

Štefánik, Milan Rastislav (died 1919). Slovak explorer and fighter pilot who fought and campaigned for Czechoslovakia during World War I.

Štúr, Ľudovít (1815–56). Slovak nationalist who led the 1848 revolt against the Hungarians and argued for a Slovak language distinct from Czech.

Svoboda, Ludvík (1895–1979). Victorious Czech general from World War II who acquiesced to the 1948 Communist coup and was Communist president during the Prague Spring in 1968 and until 1975.

Tajovský, Jozef Gregor (1874–1940). Slovak dramatist and short-story writer whose moral ethics and identification with the underdog made him a sharp social critic of the times.

Tyl, Josef Kajetán (1808–56). Czech playwright and composer of the Czech national anthem, *Where is my Home?*

Vajanský, Svetozár Hurban (1847–1916). Romantic Slovak novelist whose Russophile views were as unpopular then as now.

Wilson, Woodrow (1856–1924). US president who oversaw the peace settlement after World War I, and was therefore seen by many as one of the founders of Czechoslovakia.

Wolker, Jiří (1900–24). Czech Communist who died of TB aged 24 and whose one volume of poetry was lauded by the Communists as the first truly proletarian writing.

Žižka, Jan (died 1424). Brilliant, blind military leader of the Táborites, the radical faction of the Hussites.

A glossary of Czech and Slovak words and terms

brána gate.

čajovna tea-house.

český Bohemian.

chata chalet-type bungalow, country cottage or mountain hut.

chrám large church.

cintorín cemetery (Slovak only).

cukrárna/cukáreň pastry shop.

divadlo theatre.

dolina valley (Slovak only).

dóm cathedral.

dům/dom house.

dům kultury/dom kúltury communal arts and social centre; literally "house of culture".

hrad castle.

hranice/hranica border.

hřbitov cemetery (Czech only).

hora mountain.

hospoda pub.

hostinec pub.

jeskyně/jaskyňa cave.

jezero/jazero lake.

kámen/kameň rock.

kaple/kaplnka chapel.

kaštieľ manor house (Slovak).

katedrála cathedral.

kavárna/kavárieň coffee house.

klášter/kláštor monastery.

kostel/kostol church.

koupaliště/kúpalisko swimming pool.

kúpele spa (Slovak).

Labe River Elbe.

lanovka funicular or cable car.

lázně spa (Czech only).

les forest.

město/mesto town; staré město – old town, nové město – new town, dolní město – lower town, horní město – upper town.

moravský Moravian.

most bridge.

nábřeží/nábrežie embankment.

nádraží train station (Czech only).

náměstí/námestie square, as in náměstí svobody/námestie slobody – freedom square.

Nisa River Neisse.

Odra River Oder.

okruh route (of a guided tour).

ostrov island.

památník/pamätník memorial or monument.

paneláky prefabricated high-rise housing.

pivnice/pivnica pub.

planina valley basin (Slovak).

pleso mountain lake (Slovak).

pokladna ticket office

pramen natural spring.

prohlídka/prehliadka viewpoint.

radnice/radnica town hall.

řeka/rieka river.

restaurace/reštaurácia restaurant.

sad park.

sál room or hall (in a chateau or castle).

schody steps.

sedlo saddle (of a mountain).

skála/skala crag/rock.

skansen/skanzen an open-air folk museum, with reconstructed folk art and architecture.

slovenský Slovak.

stanica train station (Slovak).

staré město/staré mesto old town.

štít peak (Slovak).

svatý/svätý saint – often abbreviated to sv.

teplice spa.

trasa route (of a guided tour).

třída/trieda avenue.

ulice/ulica street.

věž/veža tower.

vinárna/vináreň wine bar or cellar.

Vltava River Moldau.

vrchovina uplands.

vrchy hills.

výstava exhibition.

zahrada/záhrada gardens.

zámek/zámok chateau.

An architectural glossary

Ambulatory Passage round the back of the altar, in continuation of the aisles.

Art Nouveau Sinuous and stylized form of architecture and decorative arts. Imported from Vienna and Budapest from 1900–10 and therefore known in Czechoslovakia as the Secession rather than Jugendstil, the German term.

Baroque Expansive, exuberant architectural style of the seventeenth and mid-eighteenth centuries, characterized by ornate decoration, complex spatial arrangement and grand vistas.

Beautiful Style Also known as the Soft Style of painting. Developed in Bohemia in the fourteenth century, it became very popular in Germany.

Chancel Part of the church where the altar is placed, usually at the east end.

Empire A highly decorative Neoclassical style of architecture and decorative arts practised in the first part of the nineteenth century.

Fresco Mural painting applied to wet plaster, so that the colours immediately soak into the wall.

Functionalism Plain, boxy, modernist architectural style, prevalent in the late 1920s and 1930s in Czechoslovakia, often using plate-glass curtain walls and open-plan interiors.

Gothic Architectural style prevalent from the twelfth to the sixteenth century, characterized by pointed arches and ribbed vaulting.

Loggia Covered area on the side of a building, often arcaded.

Nave Main body of a church, usually the western end.

Neoclassical Late eighteenth- and early nineteenth-century style of architecture and design returning to classical Greek and Roman models as a reaction against Baroque and Rococo excesses.

Oriel A bay window, usually projecting from an upper floor.

Predella Small panel below the main scenes of an altarpiece.

Rococo Highly florid, fiddly though (occasionally) graceful style of architecture and interior design, forming the last phase of Baroque.

Romanesque Solid architectural style of the late tenth to thirteenth centuries, characterized by round-headed arches and geometrical precision.

Secession Style of early-twentieth-century art and architecture based in Germany and Austria and a reaction against the academic establishment (see also "Art Nouveau").

Sgraffito Monochrome plaster decoration effected by means of scraping back the first white layer to reveal the black underneath.

Shingle Wooden roof tiles.

Stucco Plaster used for decorative effects.

Trompe l'oeil Painting designed to fool the onlooker into believing that it is actually three-dimensional.

Tympanum Area above doorway or within a pediment.

Historical and political terms

Czech Lands A phrase used to denote Bohemia and Moravia.

First Republic The new Czechoslovak Republic founded by Masaryk after World War II, made up of Bohemia, Moravia, Silesia, Slovakia and Ruthenia, dismantled by the Nazis in 1938–39.

Great Moravian Empire The first Slav state covering much of what is now Czechoslovakia, which ended shortly after the Magyar invasion of 896 AD.

Greek-Catholic Church Formed from various breakaways from the Eastern (Orthodox) Church in the sixteenth century, the Greek-Catholic Church retains many Orthodox practices and rituals but is affiliated to the Roman Catholic Church. Also known as the Uniate Church.

Habsburgs The most powerful royal family in central Europe, whose power base was Vienna. They held the Bohemian and Hungarian thrones from 1526 to 1918, and by marriage and diplomacy acquired territories all over Europe.

Historic Provinces Land traditionally belonging to the Bohemian crown, including Bohemia, Egerland, Moravia, Silesia and Lusatia.

Holy Roman Empire Name given to the loose confederation of German states (including for a while the Czech Lands) which lasted from 800 until 1806.

Hussites Name given to Czech religious reformers who ostensibly followed the teachings of Jan Hus (1370–1415).

Jagiellonians Polish-Lithuanian dynasty who ruled the Czech Lands from 1471 to 1526.

Magyars The people who ruled over the Hungarian Kingdom and now predominate in modern-day Hungary.

Mitteleuropa Literally German for "central Europe", but it also conveys the idea of a multilingual central European culture, lost after the break-up of the Habsburg Empire.

Národní fronta Literally the National Front, the dummy coalition of parties dominated by the Communists which ruled the country until December 1989.

Národní obrození/národné obrodenie Czech/Slovak "national revival" movements of the nineteenth century, which sought to rediscover the lost identities of the Czech and Slovak people, particularly their history and language.

Přemyslid The dynasty of Czech princes and kings who ruled over the Historic Lands of Bohemia from the ninth century to 1306.

Ruthenia Officially Sub-Carpatho-Ruthenia, the easternmost province of the First Republic, annexed by the Soviet Union at the end of World War II.

Sudetenland Name given to mostly German-speaking border regions of the Czech Lands, awarded to Nazi Germany in the Munich Diktat of September 1938.

Velvet Revolution The popular protests of November/December 1989 which brought an end to 41 years of Communist rule. Also known as the Gentle Revolution.

Abbreviations

ČD (České dráhy) Czech Railways.

CKM (Cestovní kanceláu mládeze) Youth Travel Organization.

ČSAD (Česká státní automobilová doprava) Czech state bus company.

HDĽS Andrej Hlinka's Slovak People's Party, the largest political party in Slovakia between the wars, and later the leading political force in the wartime clerico-fascist state.

HZDS (Hnutie za democratické slovensko) Movement for a Democratic Slovakia.

KSČ (Komunistická strana československá) The Czechoslovak Communist Party (now defunct).

KSČM Communist Party of Bohemia and Moravia (still functioning).

ODS (Občanská demokratická strana) Civic Democratic Party – right-wing faction of Civic Forum.

SAD (Slovenská automobilová doprava) Slovak bus company.

SdP Sudeten German Party (Sudetendeutsche Partei), the main proto-Nazi Party in Czechoslovakia in the late 1930s.

SNS (Slovenská národná strana) Slovak National Party – extremist Slovak nationalists.

StB (Státní bezpečnost) The Communist secret police (now disbanded).

ŽSR (Železnice Slovenskej republiky) Slovak Railways.

Travel store

Rough Guides travel...

UK & Ireland
Britain
Devon & Cornwall
Dublin DIRECTIONS
Edinburgh DIRECTIONS
England
Ireland
Lake District
London
London DIRECTIONS
London Mini Guide
Scotland
Scottish Highlands &
   Islands
Wales

Europe
Algarve DIRECTIONS
Amsterdam
Amsterdam
   DIRECTIONS
Andalucía
Athens DIRECTIONS
Austria
Baltic States
Barcelona
Barcelona DIRECTIONS
Belgium & Luxembourg
Berlin
Brittany & Normandy
Bruges DIRECTIONS
Brussels
Budapest
Bulgaria
Copenhagen
Corfu
Corsica
Costa Brava
   DIRECTIONS
Crete
Croatia
Cyprus
Czech & Slovak
   Republics
Dodecanese & East
   Aegean
Dordogne & The Lot
Europe
Florence & Siena
Florence DIRECTIONS
France

French Hotels & Restos
Germany
Greece
Greek Islands
Hungary
Ibiza & Formentera
   DIRECTIONS
Iceland
Ionian Islands
Italy
Italian Lakes
Languedoc &
   Roussillon
Lisbon
Lisbon DIRECTIONS
The Loire
Madeira DIRECTIONS
Madrid DIRECTIONS
Mallorca & Menorca
Mallorca DIRECTIONS
Malta & Gozo
   DIRECTIONS
Menorca
Moscow
Netherlands
Norway
Paris
Paris DIRECTIONS
Paris Mini Guide
Poland
Portugal
Prague
Prague DIRECTIONS
Provence & the Côte
   d'Azur
Pyrenees
Romania
Rome
Rome DIRECTIONS
Sardinia
Scandinavia
Sicily
Slovenia
Spain
St Petersburg
Sweden
Switzerland
Tenerife & La Gomera
   DIRECTIONS
Turkey
Tuscany & Umbria

Venice & The Veneto
Venice DIRECTIONS
Vienna

Asia
Bali & Lombok
Bangkok
Beijing
Cambodia
China
Goa
Hong Kong & Macau
India
Indonesia
Japan
Laos
Malaysia, Singapore &
   Brunei
Nepal
The Philippines
Singapore
South India
Southeast Asia
Sri Lanka
Taiwan
Thailand
Thailand's Beaches &
   Islands
Tokyo
Vietnam

Australasia
Australia
Melbourne
New Zealand
Sydney

North America
Alaska
Boston
California
Canada
Chicago
Florida
Grand Canyon
Hawaii
Honolulu
Las Vegas DIRECTIONS
Los Angeles
Maui DIRECTIONS

Miami & South Florida
Montréal
New England
New Orleans
   DIRECTIONS
New York City
New York City
   DIRECTIONS
New York City Mini
   Guide
Orlando & Walt Disney
   World DIRECTIONS
Pacific Northwest
Rocky Mountains
San Francisco
San Francisco
   DIRECTIONS
Seattle
Southwest USA
Toronto
USA
Vancouver
Washington DC
Washington DC
   DIRECTIONS
Yosemite

Caribbean
& Latin America
Antigua & Barbuda
   DIRECTIONS
Argentina
Bahamas
Barbados DIRECTIONS
Belize
Bolivia
Brazil
Cancùn & Cozumel
   DIRECTIONS
Caribbean
Central America
Chile
Costa Rica
Cuba
Dominican Republic
Dominican Republic
   DIRECTIONS
Ecuador
Guatemala
Jamaica

...music & reference

Mexico
Peru
St Lucia
South America
Trinidad & Tobago
Yúcatan

Africa & Middle East

Cape Town & the
  Garden Route
Egypt
The Gambia
Jordan
Kenya
Marrakesh
  DIRECTIONS
Morocco
South Africa, Lesotho
  & Swaziland
Syria
Tanzania
Tunisia
West Africa
Zanzibar

Travel Theme guides

First-Time Around the
  World
First-Time Asia
First-Time Europe
First-Time Latin
  America
Travel Online
Travel Health
Travel Survival
Walks in London & SE
  England
Women Travel

Maps

Algarve
Amsterdam
Andalucia & Costa
  del Sol
Argentina
Athens
Australia
Baja California
Barcelona
Berlin
Boston

Brittany
Brussels
California
Chicago
Corsica
Costa Rica & Panama
Crete
Croatia
Cuba
Cyprus
Czech Republic
Dominican Republic
Dubai & UAE
Dublin
Egypt
Florence & Siena
Florida
France
Frankfurt
Germany
Greece
Guatemala & Belize
Hong Kong
Iceland
Ireland
Kenya
Lisbon
London
Los Angeles
Madrid
Mallorca
Marrakesh
Mexico
Miami & Key West
Morocco
New England
New York City
New Zealand
Northern Spain
Paris
Peru
Portugal
Prague
Rome
San Francisco
Sicily
South Africa
South India
Sri Lanka
Tenerife
Thailand

Toronto
Trinidad & Tobago
Tuscany
Venice
Washington DC
Yucatán Peninsula

Dictionary
Phrasebooks

Croatian
Czech
Dutch
Egyptian Arabic
European Languages
  (Czech, French,
  German, Greek,
  Italian, Portuguese,
  Spanish)
French
German
Greek
Hindi & Urdu
Hungarian
Indonesian
Italian
Japanese
Latin American
  Spanish
Mandarin Chinese
Mexican Spanish
Polish
Portuguese
Russian
Spanish
Swahili
Thai
Turkish
Vietnamese

Music Guides

The Beatles
Bob Dylan
Cult Pop
Classical Music
Elvis
Frank Sinatra
Heavy Metal
Hip-Hop
Jazz
Opera
Reggae

Rock
World Music (2 vols)

Reference Guides

Babies
Books for Teenagers
Children's Books, 0–5
Children's Books, 5–11
Comedy Movies
Conspiracy Theories
Cult Fiction
Cult Football
Cult Movies
Cult TV
The Da Vinci Code
Ethical Shopping
Gangster Movies
Horror Movies
iPods, iTunes & Music
  Online
The Internet
James Bond
Kids' Movies
Lord of the Rings
Macs & OS X
Muhammad Ali
Music Playlists
PCs and Windows
Poker
Pregnancy & Birth
Sci–Fi Movies
Shakespeare
Superheroes

Unexplained
  Phenomena
The Universe
Weather
Website Directory

Football

Arsenal 11s
Celtic 11s
Chelsea 11s
Liverpool 11s
Newcastle 11s
Rangers 11s
Tottenham 11s
Man United 11s

DIRECTIONS

100s of colour photos, maps and listings

Algarve ● Amsterdam
Antigua & Barbuda ● Athens ● Barbados ● Barcelona
Bruges ● Cancún & Cozumel ● Costa Brava
Dominican Republic ● Edinburgh ● Florence
Ibiza & Formentera ● Las Vegas ● Lisbon ● London
Madeira ● Madrid ● Mallorca ● Malta & Gozo
Marrakesh & Essaouira ● Maui ● New Orleans
New York City ● Paris ● Prague ● Rome ● San Francisco
Tenerife & La Gomera ● Venice ● Washington DC

Free e-book CD
containing the full text and 100s of weblinks

US\$10.99 · CAN\$15.99 · £6.99
www.roughguides.com

Visit us online
roughguides.com

Information on over 25,000 destinations around the world

- **Read** Rough Guides' trusted travel info
- **Share** journals, photos and travel advice with other readers
- Get exclusive Rough Guide **discounts** and travel **deals**
- Earn membership points every time you contribute to the Rough Guide **community** and get **free** books, flights and trips
- Browse thousands of CD reviews and artists in our **music** area

ROUGH GUIDES

COLUMBUS DIRECT

Travel insurance

Travel Insurance

Wherever you are, wherever you are going, we've got you covered!

Visit our website at

www.roughguides.com/insurance

or call:

- UK: 0800 083 9507
- Spain: 900 997 149
- Australia: 1300 669 999
- New Zealand: 0800 55 99 11
- Worldwide: +44 870 890 2843
- USA, call toll free on: 1 800 749 4922

Please quote our ref: *Rough Guides Newsletter*

Cover for over 46 different nationalities and available in 4 different languages.

Small print and Index

A Rough Guide to Rough Guides

In the summer of 1981, Mark Ellingham, a recent graduate from Bristol University, was travelling round Greece and couldn't find a guidebook that really met his needs. On the one hand there were the student guides, insistent on saving every last cent, and on the other the heavyweight cultural tomes whose authors seemed to have spent more time in a research library than lounging away the afternoon at a taverna or on the beach.

In a bid to avoid getting a job, Mark and a small group of writers set about creating their own guidebook. It was a guide to Greece that aimed to combine a journalistic approach to description with a thoroughly practical approach to travellers' needs – a guide that would incorporate culture, history and contemporary insights with a critical edge, together with up-to-date, value-for-money listings. Back in London, Mark and the team finished their Rough Guide, as they called it, and talked Routledge into publishing the book.

That first *Rough Guide to Greece*, published in 1982, was a student scheme that became a publishing phenomenon. The immediate success of the book – with numerous reprints and a Thomas Cook prize shortlisting – spawned a series that rapidly covered dozens of destinations. Rough Guides had a ready market among low-budget backpackers, but soon also acquired a much broader and older readership that relished Rough Guides' wit and inquisitiveness as much as their enthusiastic, critical approach. Everyone wants value for money, but not at any price.

Rough Guides soon began supplementing the "rougher" information about hostels and low-budget listings with the kind of detail on restaurants and quality hotels that independent-minded visitors on any budget might expect, whether on business in New York or trekking in Thailand.

These days the guides – distributed worldwide by the Penguin Group – offer recommendations from shoestring to luxury and cover more than 200 destinations around the globe, including almost every country in the Americas and Europe, more than half of Africa and most of Asia and Australasia. Our ever-growing team of authors and photographers is spread all over the world, particularly in Europe, the USA and Australia.

In 1994, we published the *Rough Guide to World Music* and *Rough Guide to Classical Music*; and a year later the *Rough Guide to the Internet*. All three books have become benchmark titles in their fields – which encouraged us to expand into other areas of publishing, mainly around popular culture. Rough Guides now publish:

- Travel guides to more than 200 worldwide destinations
- Dictionary phrasebooks to 22 major languages
- History guides ranging from Ireland to Islam
- Maps printed on rip-proof and waterproof Polyart™ paper
- Music guides running the gamut from Opera to Elvis
- Restaurant guides to London, New York and San Francisco
- Reference books on topics as diverse as the Weather and Shakespeare
- Sports guides from Formula 1 to Man Utd
- Pop culture books from *Lord of the Rings* to Cult TV
- World Music CDs in association with World Music Network

Visit **www.roughguides.com** to see our latest publications.

Rough Guide credits

Text editors: Chloë Thomson & Geoff Howard
Layout: Dan May
Cartography: Ashutosh Bharti
Picture editor: Sarah Smithies
Production: Julia Bovis
Proofreader: Amanda Jones
Cover design: Chloë Roberts
....

Editorial: **London** Kate Berens, Claire Saunders, Ruth Blackmore, Polly Thomas, Richard Lim, Clifton Wilkinson, Alison Murchie, Sally Schafer, Karoline Densley, Andy Turner, Ella O'Donnell, Keith Drew, Edward Aves, Nikki Birrell, Helen Marsden, Alice Park, Sarah Eno, Joe Staines, Duncan Clark, Peter Buckley, Matthew Milton, Daniel Crewe; **New York** Andrew Rosenberg, Richard Koss, Steven Horak, AnneLise Sorensen, Amy Hegarty, Hunter Slaton, April Isaacs
Design & Pictures: **London** Simon Bracken, Dan May, Diana Jarvis, Mark Thomas, Jj Luck, Harriet Mills, Chloë Roberts; **Delhi** Madhulita Mohapatra, Umesh Aggarwal, Ajay Verma, Jessica Subramanian, Amit Verma, Ankur Guha
Production: Julia Bovis, Sophie Hewat,

Katherine Owers
Cartography: **London** Maxine Repath, Ed Wright, Katie Lloyd-Jones; **Delhi** Manish Chandra, Rajesh Chhibber, Jai Prakash Mishra, Ashutosh Bharti, Rajesh Mishra, Animesh Pathak, Jasbir Sandhu, Karobi Gogoi
Online: **New York** Jennifer Gold, Suzanne Welles, Kristin Mingrone; **Delhi** Manik Chauhan, Narender Kumar, Shekhar Jha, Rakesh Kumar, Chhandita Chakravarty
Marketing & Publicity: **London** Richard Trillo, Niki Hanmer, David Wearn, Demelza Dallow, Louise Maher; **New York** Geoff Colquitt, Megan Kennedy, Katy Ball; **Delhi** Reem Khokhar
Custom publishing and foreign rights: Philippa Hopkins
Manager India: Punita Singh
Series editor: Mark Ellingham
Reference Director: Andrew Lockett
PA to Managing and Publishing Directors: Megan McIntyre
Publishing Director: Martin Dunford
Managing Director: Kevin Fitzgerald

Publishing information

This seventh edition published January 2006 by
Rough Guides Ltd,
80 Strand, London WC2R 0RL
345 Hudson St, 4th Floor,
New York, NY 10014, USA
14 Local Shopping Centre, Panchsheel Park,
New Delhi 110017, India
Distributed by the Penguin Group
Penguin Books Ltd,
80 Strand, London WC2R 0RL
Penguin Putnam, Inc.
375 Hudson Street, NY 10014, USA
Penguin Group (Australia)
250 Camberwell Road, Camberwell
Victoria 3124, Australia
Penguin Books Canada Ltd,
10 Alcorn Avenue, Toronto, Ontario,
Canada M4V 1E4
Penguin Group (New Zealand)
Cnr Rosedale and Airborne Roads
Albany, Auckland, New Zealand

Typeset in Bembo and Helvetica to an original design by Henry Iles.
Printed in China
© Rob Humphreys 2006
No part of this book may be reproduced in any form without permission from the publisher except for the quotation of brief passages in reviews.
666pp includes index
A catalogue record for this book is available from the British Library
ISBN 1-84353-525-4

The publishers and authors have done their best to ensure the accuracy and currency of all the information in **The Rough Guide to the Czech and Slovak Republics**, however, they can accept no responsibility for any loss, injury, or inconvenience sustained by any traveller as a result of information or advice contained in the guide.

1 3 5 7 9 8 6 4 2

Help us update

We've gone to a lot of effort to ensure that the 7th edition of **The Rough Guide to the Czech and Slovak Republics** is accurate and up to date. However, things change – places get "discovered", opening hours are notoriously fickle, restaurants and rooms raise prices or lower standards. If you feel we've got it wrong or left something out, we'd like to know, and if you can remember the address, the price, the time, the phone number, so much the better.

We'll credit all contributions, and send a copy of the next edition (or any other Rough Guide

if you prefer) for the best letters. Everyone who writes to us and isn't already a subscriber will receive a copy of our full-colour thrice-yearly newsletter. Please mark letters: "**Rough Guide Czech and Slovak Republics Update**" and send to: Rough Guides, 80 Strand, London WC2R 0RL, or Rough Guides, 4th Floor, 345 Hudson St, New York, NY 10014. Or send an email to **mail@roughguides.com**

Have your questions answered and tell others about your trip at
www.roughguides.atinfopop.com

SMALL PRINT

Acknowledgements

Thanks to Geoff for overseeing everything. Thanks too for Gordon for drinking champagne at the appropriate moments, to Elizabeth for allowing us to enjoy her swansong in Prague, and of course for the coat and plate from Murmansk, and to Val for the biblio. This book is dedicated to Petr Brabec (1963–2005), a wonderful friend who is sorely missed.

Readers' letters

Thanks to all the readers who have taken the time to write in with comments and suggestions (and apologies if we've inadvertently omitted or misspelt anyone's name):

Rob Addlestone, Richard Alexander, Sally Amis, Louise Blair, David Burchnall, Rosemary & Colin Cheshire, Jennifer Colbert, John Fisher, Debra Fuccio, Denise Greene, Sima Gupta, Verena Haug, Bryn Haworth, Anne Jorysz, Cat Lund, Dave Marshall, James McNay, Kate Palmer, John Ponter, Sue Rhee, Thomas Roberts, Peter Sebastian, Rosamund Spinnler, Barbara & Derek Taylor, Lesley Thompson, Max Thorne, Pat & Bill Urry, Steve Vickers, Peter Walling, Diane Waudby, Mark Whittard, Michael Wiffin, and Elayne Wilks.

SMALL PRINT

Photo credits

Index

Map entries are in colour.

INDEX

L

M

N

O

INDEX

Map symbols

maps are listed in the full index using coloured text

------	International boundary	⌂	Cave
----	Chapter division boundary	⊙	Statue
▬▬▬	Motorway	⚱	Fountain
═══	Road	⚔	Battle site
::::::	Pedestrianized street/alley	✈	Airport
⊞⊞⊞	Steps	@	Information office
------	Footpath	ⓘ	Internet access
━━━	Railway	ℂ	Telephone
⋯⋯	Funicular	🅿	Parking
—Ⓜ—	Metro line & station	⊠	Post office
═══	River	✡	Synagogue
▬▬	Wall	▬	Building
⊠ ⊠	Gate	⊞	Church
⊐	Bridge	▭	Market
♦	Point of interest	▨	Park
▲	Mountain peak	▨	Forest
♜	Castle	⊞	Cemetery
Å	Campsite	▱	Jewish cemetery